The Routledge Handbook of Critical Pedagogies for Social Work

The *Routledge Handbook of Critical Pedagogies for Social Work* traverses new territory by providing a cutting-edge overview of the work of classic and contemporary theorists, in a way that expands their application and utility in social work education and practice; thus, providing a bridge between critical theory, philosophy, and social work.

Each chapter showcases the work of a specific critical educational, philosophical, and/or social theorist including: Henry Giroux, Michel Foucault, Cornelius Castoriadis, Herbert Marcuse, Paulo Freire, bell hooks, Joan Tronto, Iris Marion Young, Karl Marx, Antonio Gramsci, and many others, to elucidate the ways in which their key pedagogic concepts can be applied to specific aspects of social work education and practice. The text exhibits a range of research-based approaches to educating social work practitioners as agents of social change. It provides a robust, and much needed, alternative paradigm to the technique-driven 'conservative revolution' currently being fostered by neoliberalism in both social work education and practice.

The volume will be instructive for social work educators who aim to teach for social change, by assisting students to develop counter-hegemonic practices of resistance and agency, and reflecting on the pedagogic role of social work practice more widely. The volume holds relevance for both postgraduate and undergraduate/qualifying social work and human services courses around the world.

Christine Morley is Professor and Head of the Social Work and Human Services Discipline in the School of Public Health and Social Work at Queensland University of Technology, Brisbane, Australia, and Adjunct Professor at the University of the Sunshine Coast, Queensland, Australia.

Phillip Ablett is a Senior Lecturer in Sociology, teaching in the social work and human services programmes in the School of Social Sciences at the University of the Sunshine Coast, Queensland, Australia.

Carolyn Noble is Professor of Social Work at the Australian College of Applied Psychology (ACAP) in Sydney and Emerita Professor of Social Work at Victoria University, Melbourne, Australia.

Stephen Cowden is a Senior Lecturer in Social Work at Coventry University, UK, where he has worked since 2001.

The Routledge Handbook of Critical Pedagogies for Social Work

Edited by Christine Morley, Phillip Ablett,

Carolyn Noble, and Stephen Cowden

LONDON AND NEW YORK

First published 2020
by Routledge
2 Park Square, Milton Park, Abingdon, Oxon OX14 4RN

and by Routledge

52 Vanderbilt Avenue, New York, NY 10017

Routledge is an imprint of the Taylor & Francis Group, an informa business

© 2020 selection and editorial matter, Christine Morley, Phillip Ablett, Carolyn Noble, and Stephen Cowden; individual chapters, the contributors

The right of Christine Morley, Phillip Ablett, Carolyn Noble, and Stephen Cowden to be identified as the authors of the editorial material, and of the authors for their individual chapters, has been asserted in accordance with sections 77 and 78 of the Copyright, Designs and Patents Act 1988.

All rights reserved. No part of this book may be reprinted or reproduced or utilized in any form or by any electronic, mechanical, or other means, now known or hereafter invented, including photocopying and recording, or in any information storage or retrieval system, without permission in writing from the publishers.

Trademark notice: Product or corporate names may be trademarks or registered trademarks, and are used only for identification and explanation without intent to infringe.

British Library Cataloguing-in-Publication Data
A catalogue record for this book is available from the British Library

Library of Congress Cataloging-in-Publication Data
Names: Morley, Christine, editor.
Title: The Routledge handbook of critical social work pedagogies / edited by Christine Morley, Phillip Ablett, Carolyn Noble and Stephen Cowden.
Description: Abingdon, Oxon ; New York, NY : Routledge, 2020. | Includes bibliographical references and index.
Identifiers: LCCN 2019043524 (print) | LCCN 2019043525 (ebook) | ISBN 9781138545748 (hardback) | ISBN 9781351002042 (ebook)
Subjects: LCSH: Social work education. | Social service. | Critical theory.
Classification: LCC HV11 .R664 2020 (print) | LCC HV11 (ebook) | DDC 361.3071--dc23
LC record available at https://lccn.loc.gov/2019043524
LC ebook record available at https://lccn.loc.gov/2019043525

ISBN: 978-1-138-54574-8 (hbk)
ISBN: 978-1-351-00204-2 (ebk)

Typeset in Bembo

by Swales & Willis, Exeter, Devon, UK

To our parents, who in one way or another, all taught us the value of a good education.

Contents

List of Contributors	xii
Foreword	xxi
Henry Giroux and Ourania Filippakou	
Preface	xxv
Acknowledgements	xxviii

1 Introduction: the imperative of critical pedagogies for social work   1
   Christine Morley, Phillip Ablett, Carolyn Noble

PART I
Key foundational concepts   17

2 Karl Marx: capitalism, alienation and social work   19
   Michael Lavalette

3 Reaching back to go forward: applying the enduring philosophy of Jane Addams to modern-day social work education   32
   Carolyn Hanesworth

4 Lifting the veil of our own consciousness: W.E.B. Du Bois and transformative pedagogies for social work   45
   David Hollinsworth

5 Reaching higher ground: the importance of Lev Vygotsky's therapeutic legacy for social work   58
   Katherine Reid

6 A prophet without honor: Bertha Capen Reynolds' contribution to social work's critical practice and pedagogy   71
   Michael Reisch

7 Reflecting on Antonio Gramsci's *Prison Notebooks*: Marxism and social work   83
   Paul Michael Garrett

Contents

8 From language to art: a Marcusian approach to critical social work pedagogy 96
   Adi Barak

9 Theodor Adorno: 'education after Auschwitz': contributions toward a critical social work pedagogy 108
   John G. Fox

10 Paulo Freire's critical pedagogy for critical consciousness and practice 120
    Stephen Cowden, Nilan Yu, Wilder Robles, and Debora Mazza

11 Teaching democracy in the social work and human service classroom: inspiration from Myles Horton and the Highlander Folk School 131
    Trevor G. Gates

12 Pedagogy and power through a Foucauldian lens 143
    Julie King

13 'A social work counter-pedagogy yet-to-come': Jacques Derrida and critical social work education and practice 153
    Peter Westoby

14 From privileged irresponsibility to shared responsibility for social injustice: the contributions of Joan Tronto and Iris Marion Young to critical pedagogies of privilege 165
    Bob Pease

15 Critical social work education as democratic *paideía*: inspiration from Cornelius Castoriadis to educate for democracy and autonomy 176
    Phillip Ablett and Christine Morley

16 Sociology for the people: Dorothy Smith's sociology for social work 189
    Michelle Newcomb

17 Henry Giroux's vision of critical pedagogy: educating social work activists for a radical democracy 201
    Christine Morley and Phillip Ablett

18 Social work through the pedagogical lens of Jacques Rancière 213
    Stephen Cowden

19 Giorgio Agamben: sovereign power, bio-politics and the totalitarian tendencies within societies 223
    Goetz Ottmann and Iris Silva Brito

20 Avishai Margalit's concept of decency: potential for the Lived
    Experience Project in social work? 233
    Lorna Hallahan

21 The relevance of Nancy Fraser for transformative social work education 245
    Dorothee Hölscher, Vivienne Bozalek, and Mel Gray

22 Roberto Esposito, biopolitics and social work 260
    Stephen A. Webb

23 Gilles Deleuze: social work from the position of the encounter 271
    Heather Lynch

PART II
Specific applications: fields of practice, postcolonial and Southern voices, practice methods, and fields of practice 283

24 Donna Haraway: cyborgs, making kin and the Chthulucene in a
    posthuman world 285
    Jim Ife

25 Critical (animal) social work: insights from ecofeminist and critical animal
    studies in the context of neoliberalism 296
    Heather Fraser and Nik Taylor

26 Thomas Piketty's inequality and educational convergence concepts
    for transformative social policy practice 310
    Jenni Mays

27 The radical potential of Carl Jung's wounded healer for social
    work education 322
    Selma Macfarlane

28 Embedding the queer and embracing the crisis: Kevin Kumashiro's
    anti-oppressive pedagogies for queering social work education and practice 333
    Jen Kaighin

29 The panopticon effect: understanding gendered subjects of control
    through a reading of Judith Butler 345
    Jamilla Rosdahl

30 Disrupting ableism in social work pedagogy with Maurice Merleau-Ponty
    and critical disability theory 359
    Lisa Stafford

Contents

Postcolonial and Southern pedagogies — 373

31 No more 'Blacks in the Back': adding more than a 'splash' of black into social work education and practice by drawing on the works of Aileen Moreton-Robinson and others who contribute to Indigenous Standpoint Theory — 375
Jennie Briese and Kelly Menzel

32 Healing justice in the social work classroom: engaged Buddhism, embodiment, and the legacy of Joanna Macy — 388
Loretta Pyles

33 Frantz Fanon's revolutionary contribution: an attitude of Decoloniality as critical pedagogy for social work — 399
Linda Harms Smith

34 Samkange's theory of *Ubuntu* and its contribution to a decolonised social work pedagogy — 412
Jacob Mugumbate

35 The relevance of Gandhi for social work education and practice — 424
Lata Narayan

Practice methods — 437

36 Teaching community development with Hannah Arendt: enabling new emancipatory possibilities — 439
Uschi Bay

37 The transformation and integration of society: developing social work pedagogy through Jürgen Habermas' theory of communicative action — 450
Rúna í Baianstovu and Phillip Ablett

38 Alain Touraine: the politics of collective action — 465
Goetz Ottmann and Carolyn Noble

39 Boal and Gadamer: a complementary relationship toward critical performance pedagogy in social work education — 477
Jean Carruthers and Phillip Ablett

40 Critical transformative learning and social work education: Jack Mezirow's transformative learning theory — 489
Peter Jones

41 bell hooks trilogy: pedagogy for social work supervision   501
    Carolyn Noble

42 Navigating the politics and practice of social work research: with advice
    from Pierre Bourdieu   512
    Mark Brough, Rod Kippax and Barbara Adkins

43 Stephen Brookfield's contribution to teaching and practising critical
    reflection in social work   523
    Christine Morley

Index   *536*

Contributors

Phillip Ablett, PhD is a Senior Lecturer in Sociology, teaching in the social work and human services programmes in the School of Social Sciences at the University of the Sunshine Coast, Queensland. His research interests include critical theory, social inequality, alternatives to capitalism, and critical social work education. He is a co-author of the introductory Australian text, *Engaging with Social Work: A Critical Introduction* (2nd edn, 2019) (with Christine Morley and Selma Macfarlane).

Barbara Adkins, PhD is Adjunct Associate Professor and a social scientist in the Faculty of Creative Industries at the Queensland University of Technology. Her research focuses on relationships of power, ethics, and justice across diverse fields of social life including human services, health, design, and housing. Her research is informed by theories and philosophies of Bourdieu, Ricœur, and Lefebvre and she employs ethnomethodological and ethnographic approaches in her qualitative investigations.

Rúna í Baianstovu, has a PhD in Social Work and is a Senior Lecturer at the School of Law, Psychology and Social Work, Örebro University, Sweden. She has published on social work, migration, violence, inclusion, and normative transformation through communication. Currently, she is developing conceptual tools for understanding honour related norms and violence and explaining the mechanisms behind it. She has published the book *Honour: Honour Related Violence, Oppression and Social Work* (2017) and the report *Honour Related Violence and the Responsibility of Society* (2018).

Adi Barak, PhD is a stage director and social worker who serves on the Faculty of the School of Social Work at Bar-Ilan University in Israel. He earned his MFA in Theatre Directing and a PhD in Social Work from Tel-Aviv University, Israel. Barak is a qualitative researcher who looks at the intersections between art, politics, and therapy. In his research and practice, he explores creative arts as a means for developing a critical consciousness and negotiating ideologies in therapeutic and community settings.

Uschi Bay, PhD is Senior Lecturer in the Department of Social Work, Faculty of Medicine, Nursing and Health Sciences at Monash University, Australia. Her publications focus on social work and the environment, climate change, critical reflexivity, biopolitics, neoliberalism, and social work education. Her most recent evaluation project used a feminist participatory action research approach to a mid-term reflection for a major international women's development agency, with a major focus on women's action, voice, and empowerment in Cambodia.

Vivienne Bozalek, PhD is the Director of Teaching and Learning at the University of the Western Cape, South Africa. Prior to this she was Chairperson of the Department of Social Work, University of Western Cape. She holds a PhD from Utrecht University. Her areas of research, publications, and expertise include the use of social justice and the political ethics of care perspectives, innovative pedagogical approaches in higher education, feminist and participatory research methodologies, posthumanism, feminist new materialist, and critical family studies.

Jennie Briese is a proud First Nations Australian woman with placial connections to Giabal Country in rural Queensland. She is a mother, grandmother, social worker, student, and early career academic with a passion for unveiling and challenging social injustices. Jennie is also a life-long learner with a goal of normalizing First Nations' perspectives in higher education curricula. Jennie shares her experiences of western education to contribute to the advancement and self-determination of First Nations Australian peoples.

Mark Brough, PhD is a social scientist in the School of Public Health and Social Work, Queensland University of Technology, Brisbane, Australia. His research is concerned with the socio-political drivers of health inequality and he has published widely in relation to Aboriginal and Torres Strait Islander health, refugee health, as well as health promotion. He predominantly uses immersive qualitative methods informed by critical theory and teaches social research methods in social work within an agenda of social change.

Jean Carruthers is a Lecturer in Social Work in the School of Public Health and Social Work, Faculty of Health, at Queensland University of Technology, teaching in social work and human services. Her current research programme is focused on using the arts, particularly drama, to expose novel and innovative directions in critical social work pedagogy.

Stephen Cowden, PhD is a Senior Lecturer in Social Work at Coventry University, UK, where he has worked since 2001. He has a longstanding interest in critical pedagogy and in its application to social work teaching and practice and this has formed an important part of the work he has undertaken over the previous decade. He was a member of the *West Midlands Critical Pedagogy Group* and has co-authored *Acts of Knowing: Critical Pedagogy In, Against and Beyond the University* (2013) and *The Practice of Equality: Jacques Rancière and Critical Pedagogy* (2019).

John G. Fox, PhD is Lecturer in Social Work, Deakin University, Australia. John lectures in social work with a focus on social theory, social work theory, and social policy. He is the author of *Marx, the Body, and Human Nature* (2015), and was the 2015/2016 inaugural Scholar-in-Residence of the Jewish Holocaust Centre, Melbourne, Australia (JHC). Drawing on the works of Hegel, Marx, Adorno, and post-humanist theorists, he researches the importance of bodily experience and relational models of the self, and the harms enabled by liberalism and the devaluation of bodily experience (including the extremities of the Holocaust). He is keenly engaged in developing critical, transformative pedagogies in higher education, in partnership with organizations such as the JHC and through bodily experience.

Heather Fraser, PhD is an Associate Professor and critical social worker who teaches theory-practice units in the Social Work and Human Services programmes at the Queensland University of Technology. Heather's research focuses on violence, gender, sexuality, species, and class. Her most recent book with Nik Taylor is *Companion Animals and Domestic Violence: Rescuing You, Rescuing Me* (2019).

Paul Michael Garrett, PhD is the author of a number of books, including *Welfare Words: Critical Social Work & Social Policy* (2018) and *Social Work and Social Theory* (2018, 2nd edition). His interventions, in a range of debates on social work and social policy, have appeared in peer-reviewed journals across a range of disciplines and he has provided keynote papers at various international conferences. He is a member of the Critical Social Policy Editorial Collective. During 2018, Paul was Visiting Professor at the City University of New York (CUNY) and, in 2017, he was invited to teach in Shanghai in the People's Republic of China. Paul is based at NUI Galway in the Republic of Ireland.

Trevor G. Gates, PhD is Senior Lecturer in Social Work, School of Social Sciences, University of the Sunshine Coast. Trevor completed his PhD in Social Work (Gender and Women's Studies) at the University of Illinois-Chicago. Other postgraduate qualifications include the MSW and MS in Adult Education. Trevor's research interests include social justice issues with lesbian, gay, bisexual, transgender, and queer communities, gay-affirmative social work practice, and strengths-based practice. He is also interested in the outcomes of social work and human service education, including online/blended education and other creative pedagogies that help widen access to social work and human service education.

Mel Gray, PhD is Emeritus Professor (Social Work) at the University of Newcastle, Australia. She has a longstanding interest in social work theory having authored numerous papers and book chapters on the subject and edited *Social Work Theories and Methods* (2008 and 2013, first and second editions respectively). She also has a longstanding interest in theories of social justice with this a major focus of her PhD thesis and subsequent publications, including *Indigenous Social Work around the World: Towards Culturally Relevant Education and Practice* (2008), *Decolonizing Social Work* (2013), *The New Politics of Social Work* (2013), *Evidence-based Social Work: A Critical Stance* (2009), *Critical Supervision for the Human Services* (2016), and *The Handbook of Social Development and Social Work in Africa* (2017).

Lorna Hallahan, PhD is Head of Social Work at Flinders University and has been a significant and long-term contributor to the development and analysis of disability policy, including the development and evaluation of the Trial of The National Disability Insurance Scheme. Lorna speaks and writes regularly on ethical issues for workers in complex human services.

Carolyn Hanesworth, MSW is Director of Social Work and Assistant Professor at Mercy College in New York City. Prior to her work in academia, Carolyn provided direct services, programme administration and consultation to organizations serving homeless families in Texas and New York. Carolyn is currently a doctoral candidate in Social Welfare at the CUNY's Graduate Center. Carolyn's current scholarship examines managerialism in higher education and its consequences for social work programmes and faculty.

Linda Harms Smith, PhD is based at Robert Gordon University, Aberdeen, Scotland, and is Research Associate of the University of Johannesburg, South Africa. She was previously at Witwatersrand University, South Africa. She is a registered social worker. She researches and writes on decoloniality; ideology; social work knowledge and discourse; collective trauma; critical social work; and oppressive and radical social work histories. Her critical social work commitment developed during the oppressive, apartheid South Africa. She is on the editorial boards of *Critical and Radical Social Work* (African section editor) and *International Social Work*.

David Hollinsworth, BA (Hons) is Adjunct Professor at the University of the Sunshine Coast, Queensland. David has taught Indigenous studies, sociology, and anti-racism since 1974 at various Australian universities. He has been an elected member of the *Australian Institute of Aboriginal and Torres Strait Islanders Studies* since 1998. David won an Office of Learning and Teaching Citation for Outstanding Contributions to Student Learning: 'For inspirational teaching that challenges and supports social science students to critically examine racism, social justice and positionality, transforming their personal and professional lives'.

Dorothee Hölscher, PhD is a Lecturer at the School of Human Services and Social Work, Griffith University and research associate with the Department of Social Work, University of Johannesburg. Prior to this she was with the School of Applied Human Sciences at the University of KwaZulu Natal. Dorothee has a key interest in questions of social justice and has conducted studies in a range of settings, including social work with migrants and higher education. She currently serves as the secretary of the Association of Schools of Social Work in Africa and as a member of the Australasia-Pacific Associate Board of the journal *Ethics & Social Welfare*.

Jim Ife, PhD is Professor of Social Work at Western Sydney University. He has previously been Professor of Social Work and Social Policy at The University of Western Australia and at Curtin University, and was Head of the Centre for Human Rights Education at Curtin, where is he Emeritus Professor. He has written extensively in the areas of community development, social work and human rights, and is the author of *Community Development* (latest edition 2016), *Human Rights and Social Work* (2013, 3rd edition), *Human Rights from Below* (2010) and *Rethinking Social Work* (1997). He is co-editor of two 2020 publications, *Disrupting Whiteness in Social Work* and *Populism, Democracy and Community Development*.

Peter Jones, PhD is a Senior Lecturer in Social Work and Human Services at James Cook University, Queensland, Australia, and a Fellow of the Higher Education Research and Development Society of Australasia. Peter's research and practice interests include social work education, eco-social work, sustainable community development, international social work, and international student exchange. He has published scholarly work in all of these areas.

Jen Kaighin, MA (Justice Studies) is an academic in the School of Public Health and Social Work, Queensland University of Technology. Jen engages in teaching and research in the areas of critical social work practice and pedagogy, youth work theory and practice, queering social work, and basic income. She also has qualifications in Welfare Studies, Aboriginal Studies, and Higher Education.

Julie King, PhD is a Senior Lecturer and Deputy Director of International Engagement and Recruitment in the School of Public Health and Social Work at Queensland University of Technology. She publishes in the area of gender, disability, and refugees in both the global North and South, taking a human rights approach. She teaches human rights and global development.

Contributors

Rod Kippax, PhD is fascinated with the practical applications of social scientific discovery and this has driven a reflexively progressive bent in his youth work practice for the past 35 years. In 2013 he completed a social science doctorate conceptualizing inclusive and exclusive interactions with young people diagnosed with 'mental disorders'. His book on this topic, *Disrupting Schools: The Institutional Conditions of Disordered Behaviour*, was published in 2019. Apart from serving as an Industry Fellow at Queensland University of Technology, he is currently engaged developing organizational inclusion frameworks.

Michael Lavalette, PhD is Professor of Social Work and Head of the School of Social Sciences at Liverpool Hope University. He is the national co-ordinator of the Social Work Action Network in the UK and editor-in-chief of the journal *Critical and Radical Social Work*. His most recent books are *Global Social Work in Political Context* (2018, written with Iain Ferguson and Vassilios Ioakimidis), the edited collection *What Is the Future for Social Work?* (2019) and a book on *Palestinian Artists: Palestinian Cultures of Resistance* (2020)

Heather Lynch, PhD is a Lecturer in Social Work at Glasgow Caledonian University. She has a doctorate from the University of Dundee for an interdisciplinary study in fields of critical disability studies and fine art. Her research interests include the ecology of social order as this relates to the contemporary challenges and opportunities of emergent more than human worlds. Her published work includes a monograph entitled 'The art of collaboration' and articles published in titles relevant to social work, education, sociology, and cultural studies. She recently co-edited a special edition of the *European Journal of Social Theory* entitled 'The Politics of Life: A Biopolitical Mess'.

Selma Macfarlane, PhD has been involved in social work education for 20 years, primarily as a Lecturer at Deakin University in Geelong, Victoria. She has publications in the areas of critical social work education and practice, mental health, and older women and ageing. She is a co-author, with Christine Morley and Phillip Ablett, of *Engaging with Social Work: A Critical Introduction*.

Jenni Mays, PhD is a Senior Lecturer in the School of Public Health and Social Work, Queensland University of Technology, Australia. She is recognized as an international expert on basic income and has a long history in researching, writing, and advocating on basic income, social policy, poverty, and social justice. She has co-edited the texts: *Implementing a Basic Income in Australia* (with E. Klein, J. Mays, and T. Dunlop, 2019); and *Basic Income in Australia and New Zealand* (with J. Mays, G. Marston, and J. Tomlinson, 2016).

Debora Mazza, PhD is an Associate Professor in the Department of Social Sciences and Education at the Universidade Estadual de Campinas (Unicamp), Brazil. Dr Mazza is also an Associate Director of the Faculty of Education at Unicamp. She obtained her doctoral degree in Education at Unicamp (1997) and completed post-doctoral work at the Centre de Recherche sur le Brésil Contemporain/École des Hautes Études en Sciences Sociales/Paris (2003) and Laboratoire Genre, Travail et Mobilité/Paris (2011). Her research interests are in popular education, educational policies and practices, and Brazilian social science philosophy.

Kelly Menzel is a proud Ngadjiri woman from the Adelaide Hills in South Australia. She is the youngest and only girl in her family. She is a child of teachers and a nurse by trade.

She is a healer, teacher, and learner. She is a holder of her ancestral knowledge and still has very much to learn. She has been in adult education for 20 years and is a Senior Lecturer in an Indigenous learning space.

Christine Morley, PhD is Professor and Head of the Social Work and Human Services Discipline in the School of Public Health and Social Work at Queensland University of Technology and Adjunct Professor at the University of the Sunshine Coast. She is passionate about critical theories and their application to social work education and practice. She has published extensively in this area including books: *Practising Critical Reflection to Develop Emancipatory Change* (2014) and *Engaging with Social Work: A Critical Introduction* (with Phillip Ablett and Selma Macfarlane, 2nd edition, 2019).

Jacob Mugumbate, PhD is a Social Work Lecturer in the School of Health and Society at the University of Wollongong in Australia. Prior to this appointment, Jacob was a research and sessional academic at the University of Newcastle in the same country. Previously, he was a Social Work Lecturer at the Bindura University of Science Education in Zimbabwe and a social work practitioner at the Epilepsy Support Foundation in the same country.

Lata Narayan, PhD is a retired Professor (1984–2017) from the Tata Institute of Social Sciences, Mumbai, India. She has a Master's degree and Doctorate in Social Work from Mumbai University. Her recent publications include, *The World of Indian Parsi Youth'*, and she is co-editor of 'Field Action Projects: Parts I and II' (2017). Her current areas of interest and work include issues concerning youth, training methodology, and dance movement therapy. Dr Narayan also serves on the boards of four NGOs engaged with urban issues, social and financial empowerment of children and youth, tribal rights, and education.

Michelle Newcomb, PhD is a Lecturer and Social Work Programme Advisor at Griffith University in Queensland, Australia. She has a Bachelor of Human Services (Hons), Master of Social Work, and a PhD in the area of social work education. Her research interests include student disadvantage, social work pedagogy, feminism, and community work. Before entering academia, Michelle worked extensively in the not-for-profit sector in both Australia and the United Kingdom.

Carolyn Noble, PhD is Professor of Social Work at the Australian College of Applied Psychology (ACAP) in Sydney and Emerita Professor of Social Work at Victoria University, Melbourne. She has taught and developed undergraduate and postgraduate programmes in social work, counselling and psychotherapy, social science, mental health and professional supervision; all with a critical lens. Her research interests include social work theory, work-based learning and professional supervision, gender democracy, and equal employment opportunity for women in higher education and human services. She is editor-in-chief of *Social Dialogue*, an open access social issues magazine for IASSW (www.socialdialogue.online).

Goetz Ottmann, PhD. Following post-doctoral fellowships at New York University and La Trobe University, he has been working in the tertiary, government, private, and humanitarian sectors in various capacities. Over the least ten years, he has worked as a researcher focusing on psychosocial needs within the context of chronic/terminal illness and end of life care as well as social work issues in aged and disability care. He is currently an Associate Professor at the Australian College of Applied Psychology where he is coordinating the Social Work Bachelor's Programme.

Contributors

Bob Pease, PhD is Honorary Professor in the School of Humanities and Social Science at Deakin University and Adjunct Professor in the Centre for the Study of Social Change at the University of Tasmania. His most recent books are: *Men and Masculinities Around the World* (co-editor, 2011), *Men, Masculinities and Methodologies* (co-editor, 2013), *The Politics of Recognition and Social Justice* (co-editor, 2014), *Doing Critical Social Work* (co-editor, 2016) *Men, Masculinities and Disaster* (co-editor, 2015), *Radicals in Australian Social Work* (co-editor 2017), *Critical Ethics of Care in Social Work* (co-editor, 2019), and *Facing Patriarchy* (2019).

Loretta Pyles, PhD is Professor at the School of Social Welfare at the University at Albany, SUNY, in the USA. She holds a PhD in Social Work and an MA in Philosophy from the University of Kansas. She is also a meditation and yoga teacher, workshop leader, organizational consultant, and activist. She is the author of *Healing Justice: Holistic Self-Care for Change Makers* (2018); *Progressive Community Organizing: Reflective Practice in a Globalizing World* (2013); co-author of *Production of Disaster and Recovery in Post-Earthquake Haiti: Disaster Industrial Complex* (2018); and co-editor of *Holistic Engagement: Transformative Social Work Education in the 21st Century* (2015).

Katherine Reid, BSW Hons, Grad Dip Narrative Therapy, is a social worker who has worked with children experiencing mental health concerns in the context of childhood abuse and/or neglect. Her current research at Queensland University of Technology, Australia, investigates how discursive therapeutic interactions can support the co-production of children's knowledge. She delivers training in discursive therapeutic approaches and enjoys engaging social work students in critical pedagogical processes.

Michael Reisch, PhD is Distinguished Professor Emeritus at the University of Maryland. His publications include *Social Policy and Social Justice* (2013), *Social Work and Social Justice: Concepts, Challenges, and Strategies* (2016), *Macro Social Work Practice: Working for Change in a Multicultural Society* (2018), and *The Road Not Taken: A History of Radical Social Work in the United States* (2001). He was named 'Social Work Educator of the Year' by the Maryland Chapter of the National Association of Social Workers, 'Teacher of the Year' by the University of Maryland, Baltimore, and received the 'Significant Lifetime Achievement Award' from the Council on Social Work Education. In 2017, he became a Fellow of the American Academy of Social Work and Social Welfare.

Wilder Robles, PhD is an Associate Professor of Rural Development at Brandon University, Manitoba, Canada. Dr Robles' research focuses on global poverty, peasant movements, agrarian reform, and rural development. He published the book *The Politics of Agrarian Reform in Brazil: The Landless Rural Workers Movement* (with Dr Henry Veltmeyer from Saint Mary's University, 2015). Dr Robles has received two prestigious Teaching Excellence Awards from the University of Manitoba (2011) and the Manitoba Association of Home Economists (2010).

Jamilla Rosdahl, PhD is Senior Lecturer at the Department of Social and Psychological Studies at Karlstads University where she specialises in violence, social control and surveillance, nineteenth- and twentieth-century philosophy, gender and the body. She has worked for the Swedish Prison and Probation Service within the areas of male sexual crimes, abuse, and violence as part of her ongoing research into violent human behaviours. In 2017 she worked as Senior Research Officer for the Queensland Centre for Domestic and Family Violence

Research at Central Queensland University, Australia. She is also active in gender and identity politics, human rights, anti-war politics, and public and moral philosophy. Dr Rosdahl is the author of the book *Sculpting the Woman* (2017).

Iris Silva Brito, BSW, MBA is a Lecturer in Social Work at the Australian College of Applied Psychology (ACAP). She chairs Live and Learn Environmental Education's board and is a director of ATEC Biodigesters International. Iris has great interest in education, social policy, community development, and research. Born in Brazil, Iris draws her search for and appreciation of knowledge from both her parents who have dedicated their lives to the education of children living in poverty, and scholars such as Paulo Freire who combined education with social and political consciousness raising.

Lisa Stafford, PhD is a Senior Lecturer and ARC DECRA Fellow in the School of Public Health and Social Work at Queensland University of Technology and identifies as a disabled, chronically ill person. Lisa is a social scientist in disability policy, community planning, and disability geography. She has 20 years of experience in the field of disability and inclusion with specific focus on children and young people. Her research areas are: social-spatial injustice, inclusive communities, participation, and transition to work. She has expertise in qualitative interpretive studies, person–environment interaction studies, and participatory research methods that enable all voices, particularly children and people with complex communication needs, to be heard in research.

Nik Taylor, PhD is a critical and public sociologist whose research focuses on mechanisms of power and marginalization expressed in/through human relations with other species and is informed by critical/intersectional feminism. Nik currently teaches topics in the Human Services programme at the University of Canterbury that focus on human–animal violence links; scholar-advocacy; social change, and crime and deviance, particularly domestic violence and animal abuse.

Stephen A. Webb, PhD is Professor of Social Work and Assistant Vice Principal of Community and Public Engagement at Glasgow Caledonian University, Scotland. He is author of *Social Work in a Risk Society* (2006), and co-author of *The New Politics of Social Work* (2013); *Evidence-based Social Work: A Critical Stance* (2009); *Ethics and Value Perspectives in Social Work* (2010); *Social Work Theories and Methods* (2012, second edition, translated into Korean and Polish); *Professional Identity and Social* Work (2017); The *SAGE Handbook of Social Work* (2012); the major international reference work *International Social Work* (2010, 4 volumes); and *Information and Communication Technology in the Welfare Services* (2003). He has recently completed the *Routledge Handbook of Critical Social Work* (2019) a major international reference work. His research interests focus on social theory, biopolitics, and community engagement and he draws on Actor Network Theory, economic sociology, and agential realist theory. In 2018 he was awarded the prestigious Fellowship of the Academy of Social Sciences.

Peter Westoby, PhD is an Associate Professor of Social Science and Community Development at the School of Public Health & Social Work, Queensland University of Technology, Australia; and a Visiting Professor at the Centre for Development Support, University of Free State, South Africa. He has published widely in the community development and development studies field.

Contributors

Nilan Yu, PhD is Program Director of the Master of Social Work, School of Psychology, Social Work and Social Policy, University of South Australia. He is editor of the book *Consciousness-raising: Critical Pedagogy and Practice for Social Change* (2018) and co-editor of *Subversive Action: Extralegal Practices for Social Justice* (2015, with Deena Mandell) and *Faces of Homelessness in the Asia Pacific* (2017, with Carole Zufferey). His current research interests are in the areas of critical practice, disability, and migration.

Foreword

Critical pedagogy in an age of tyranny
Henry Armand Giroux and Ourania Filippakou
The limits of tyrants are prescribed by the endurance of those whom they oppress.
Frederick Douglass

All over the world, the forces of neoliberalism and fascism have merged, dismantling the historically guaranteed social provisions provided by the welfare state while defining profit making and market freedoms as the essence of democracy. The savagery of the market has provided the preconditions for white supremacy, ultra-nationalism, and a culture of cruelty to gain ascendency and in some countries such as the United States, Brazil, and Poland to become normalized. Secure in its dystopian vision, neoliberalism eliminates issues of contingency, struggle, and social agency by celebrating the inevitability of economic laws in which the ethical ideal of intervening in the world gives way to the idea that we 'have no choice but to adapt both our hopes and our abilities to the new global market.'[1] Coupled with the power of new digital technologies along with a culture of surveillance and fear, market freedoms seem securely grounded in attacking the welfare state, existing social provision, and those populations considered increasingly disposable. This is all the more reason to take seriously the political responsibilities and moral obligations of social work and social workers as both educative and political in terms of shaping culture and influencing social change.

Social workers as educators need a new political and pedagogical language for addressing the changing contexts and issues facing a world in which capital draws upon an unprecedented convergence of resources – financial, cultural, political, economic, scientific, military, and technological – to exercise powerful and diverse forms of domination, both material and symbolic. If social workers are to counter global capitalism's increased power to both depoliticize and disempower, it is crucial to develop educational and political approaches that reject a collapse of the distinction between market liberties and civil liberties, a market economy and a market society. This suggests developing forms of critical and public pedagogy capable of appropriating from a variety of radical theories whose progressive elements might be useful in both challenging neoliberalism on many fronts while resurrecting a militant democratic socialism that provides the basis for imagining a life beyond the "dream world" of capitalism. Redefining themselves as public intellectuals, it is imperative for social workers to locate their practice within the broader concept of public pedagogy which both politicizes their work and enables them to interrogate the ideologies that shape it.

Under such circumstances, public pedagogy becomes central to such a project. Public pedagogy in the broadest sense refers to both the educational force of the larger culture and the sites in which it takes place. Our own interest in education and the politics of social work emerges out of an ongoing project to theorize the regulatory and emancipatory relationship among culture, power, and politics as expressed through the dynamics of what can be called "public pedagogy." This project concerns, in part, the diverse ways in which culture functions as a contested sphere over the production, distribution, and regulation of power and how and where it operates both symbolically and institutionally as an educational, political, and economic force.

Drawing upon a long tradition in social theory, culture is viewed as constitutive and political not only reflecting larger forces but also constructing them; in this instance, culture not only mediates history, it shapes it. In this formulation, power is a central element of culture just as culture is a crucial element of power.[2] What is crucial to recognize in the work of social theorists such as Raymond Williams, Stuart Hall, Pierre Bourdieu, Robert McChesney, and others is that culture occupies a fundamental role in shaping the conditions for a radically refigured cultural politics, of which social work is one register. That is, it provides, to use Raymond Williams' term, a new mode of "permanent education" in which dominant sites of pedagogy engage in diverse forms of pedagogical address to put into play a limited range of identities, ideologies, and subject positions that both reinforce dominant social relations and undermine the possibility for democratic politics.[3] For instance, many theorists in the age of Trump want to roll back the twenty-first century literally by establishing the priority of market identities, values, and the tenets of white supremacy and ultra-nationalism as the organizing principles of public life. This a public discourse that wants to squeeze out ambiguity from public space, dismantle the social provisions and guarantees provided by the welfare state, and eliminate democratic politics by making the notion of the social impossible to imagine beyond the isolated individual, the individualizing of social problems, and the savage logic of neoliberalism.[4] This is the new disimagination machine of neoliberal public pedagogy.

In the age of growing authoritarianism, something sinister and horrifying is happening to liberal democracies all over the globe. Democratic institutions such as the independent media, schools, the legal system, the welfare state, unions, and higher education are under siege. The promise of democracy is receding as right-wing demagogues and reactionaries work to subvert language, values, courage, vision, and a critical consciousness. Education has increasingly become a tool of domination as the entrepreneurs of hate deploy right-wing pedagogical apparatuses to attack workers, black youth, refugees, immigrants, poverty stricken populations, and others they consider disposable. In the midst of a moment when an older social order is crumbling and a new one is struggling to define itself, there emerges a time of confusion, danger, and moments of great restlessness. We are once again at a historical juncture in which the structures of liberation and authoritarianism are fighting over the future.

It is hard to imagine a more urgent moment for social workers to develop a politics capable of awakening critical, imaginative, and historical sensibilities along with a language of critique and possibility. Such a language is necessary to enable the conditions to forge a collective international resistance among social workers in defense of public goods, the social contract, and a radical democracy. In an age of social isolation, information overflow, a culture of immediacy, consumer glut, and spectacularized violence, it is all the more crucial to take seriously the notion that a democracy cannot exist or be defended without informed and critically engaged citizens.

Social work, in both its symbolic and institutional forms, has a central role to play in fighting the resurgence of neoliberalism, the sanctioning of a politics of disposability, and the emerging ideologies of privatization and deregulation. Social work as a form of public pedagogy is crucial to challenging and resisting the rise of neoliberal pedagogical formations and their rehabilitation of corporate principles and ideas endemic to ruling class power formations.[5]

Cultural politics in the last 20 years has turned toxic as ruling elites increasingly gain control of commanding cultural apparatuses, turning them into pedagogical machines that serve the forces of ethical tranquilization by producing and legitimating endless degrading and humiliating images of the poor, welfare recipients, and others considered excess, wasted lives, doomed to terminal exclusion. The capitalist dream machine is back with huge profits for the ultra-rich, hedge fund managers, and major players in the financial service industries. In these new landscapes of wealth, fraud, and social atomization, a brutal and fanatical capitalism promotes a winner-take-all ethos, a culture of cruelty and white nationalism, aggressively undermining the welfare state while pushing millions into hardship and misfortune. The geographies of moral and political decadence have become the organizing workstations of the dream worlds of consumption, privatization, surveillance, and deregulation. Within this increasingly neoliberal landscape, public spheres are replaced by zones of social abandonment and thrive on the energies of the walking dead and avatars of cruelty and misery.

Social work within the last 40 years, especially with the elections of Ronald Reagan in the US and Margaret Thatcher in the UK, has diminished rapidly in its capacities to address important social problems. Under neoliberal regimes, the apostles of authoritarianism have deemed the utopian possibilities formerly associated with serving the public good and expanding the social contract as too dangerous to go unchecked. Increasingly social work – which could have such a radical potential to promote social equality and support democracy – is falling subject to the toxic forces of privatization, state surveillance, and political abandonment, while social workers are subjected to intolerable working conditions. The commanding visions of democracy are in exile. The struggle, however, is far from over. The good news is that there is an increasing wave of strikes by public servants, teachers, and mental health workers in the US, the UK, and abroad who are resisting the cruel machinery of exploitation, racism, austerity, and disposability unleashed by neoliberalism.

It is crucial for social workers to remember that language is not simply an instrument of fear, violence, and intimidation; it is also a vehicle for critique, civic courage, resistance, and engaged and informed agency. We live at a time when the language of democracy has been pillaged, stripped of its promises and hopes. If the social contract is to be reclaimed while expanding the meaning and substance of a radical democracy, there is a need to make education an organizing principle of politics. In part, the practice of social work can meet this challenge by first developing a language that exposes and unravels falsehoods, systems of oppression, and corrupt relations of power while making clear that an alternative future is possible. Under such circumstances, the language of public pedagogy can be a powerful tool in the search for truth and the condemnation of falsehoods and injustices at the heart of a critical and transformed practice. What must be remembered is that power and its workings must be understood before practices can be developed through which substantive change takes place. One of the most important challenges facing social workers today is to imagine a world in which critical pedagogies for social work become a mode of moral witnessing while turning militant hope into a reality in which the connection between social work and the struggle over democracy become indistinguishable from its practice. *The Routledge Handbook of Critical Pedagogies for Social Work* offers much needed new insights and perspectives for social change in an age of tyranny. This is a book that must be read and studied for all those who view the struggle over the welfare state and public good as one of the most important issues of our time.

Notes

1 Stanley Aronowitz (1998). Introduction. In Paulo Freire (ed.) *Pedagogy of Freedom*. Lanham, MD: Rowman & Littlefield, p. 7.
2 Michele Barrett (1999). *Imagination in Theory*. New York: New York University Press, p. 161.
3 For some general theoretical principles for addressing the new sites of pedagogy, see Jeffrey R. DiLeo, Walter Jacobs, and Amy Lee (2003). The Sites of Pedagogy. *Sympolke*, 10 (1–2): 7–12.
4 One interesting analysis on the contingent nature of democracy and public space can be found in Rosalyn Deutsche (1998). *Evictions: Art and Spatial Politics*. Cambridge, MA: The MIT Press.
5 See, for example, Jane Mayer, 'The Making of the Fox News White House'. *The New Yorker* (March 4, 2019). Online: www.newyorker.com/magazine/2019/03/11/the-making-of-the-fox-news-white-house

Preface

It has been a privilege to work on this book. The opportunity to immerse ourselves in the transformative ideas of critical social and educational thinkers who have informed many of social work's critical theoretical developments, along with the gathering of their revolutionizing implications for social work education and practice into one large volume, has offered much inspiration for us as editors, and hopefully for our readers too.

The idea for this book first emerged in conversations between Christine and Phillip. Christine was at the time reading Peter Jones' PhD thesis, which explored the contributions of Jack Mezirow's transformative learning to social work education, alongside working with Phillip on an article about Cornelius Castoriadis, whose work holds direct implications for a revolutionary social work practice. Tapping into the richness of the ideas of these two thinkers sparked a curiosity to learn more about what other critical thinkers, if explored more fully, might offer social work's theory base and pedagogy. Lecturing in social theory for social work students, Phillip was familiar with many of these thinkers, but acknowledged that the connections with social work education and practice were, in a number of cases, yet to be fully explored. They both wished to see a resource that did this, making accessible to a range of readers the richness of various critical philosophers', theorists', and educationalists' ideas in relation to social work practice and education. In their enthusiasm, Christine and Phillip discussed these thoughts with friend and colleague Carolyn Noble. Carolyn, too, shared similar thoughts and was keen to embark on a collaborative project that focused on the many critical thinkers who have influenced social work theory, education, and practice in a single volume. Carolyn saw this project as an opportunity to develop her longstanding interest in critical thinking in social work and to explicate how critical philosophy can and does enrich social work's standing in the social sciences.

As the project grew, we asked Stephen Cowden to join the editing team. Stephen's expertise in social theory and his previous work on critical pedagogy in social work meant he, too, could pursue his passion for social theory and further explore the many thinkers who have inspired his work. Our overlapping interests brought us together through this volume of critical thinkers and their application to social work education and practice. What united us above all else, though, was a shared vision that social work, if it is to be empowering and liberating in people's lives, must be a reflective and activist practice. As such, its educators and practitioners should have an accessible entry point to the widest range of critical theories and pedagogies. So, the point of our assembling such a diversity of thinkers and their ideas was, at the risk of cliché, not just to interpret the world but to help change it for the better. Needless to say, with the editorial team complete our enthusiasm was hard to contain!

We purposely asked our contributors to write about how they have used the ideas of a critical theorist, philosopher, and/or educationalist in their scholarship and teaching, to identify

Preface

the potential of these ideas to enhance social work's critical praxis. This was to highlight the central role critical social theory and philosophy must continue to play if social work is to remain both a robust academic discipline as well as a potentially emancipative practice. Word spread as we discussed the project with potential chapter authors. To our surprise, several colleagues approached us with proposals to focus on a particular theorist who had inspired them, offering to be involved in the project. Thankfully, we were not alone in being inspired by the works of critical social thinkers. The idea of the book had wide appeal and was taking shape.

To focus solely on one thinker was a difficult task for some colleagues because, as social workers or social work educators, we tend to think in terms of multiple ideas or theories. In so doing, there is a risk that we celebrate the eclectic nature of our work without thoroughly examining the ideas of particular thinkers in depth or of not linking them back to their original source or the problems they addressed. This tendency has sometimes resulted in the use of these ideas in quite superficial ways and without appropriate attributions or tracing of the lineage of the ideas. This impoverishes social work's development as an academic discipline, hampers a deeper engagement with other disciplines, and reinforces a narrow technicism of practice.

The volume features leading scholars throughout the world who have a strong track record of critical scholarship in the teaching and practice of social work. Each chapter showcases how their work has been inspired or informed by the work of a specific critical educational, philosophical, and/or social theorist to elucidate how their key pedagogic concepts can be applied to specific aspects of social work education and practice. All our authors were excited about the project. On completion of final drafts, many contributors remarked how they had enjoyed re-engaging deeply with their chosen social theorist or philosopher, and seriously considering their contributions to social work education and practice, and ultimately a better future. This act in itself stands counter-posed to the standardized conformity, anti-intellectualism, and technical rationality that increasingly pervade our neoliberal academy. Many contributors expressed a keen desire to read the other chapters in the volume, indicating a thirst for this kind of critical scholarship, presently marginalized in mainstream academia. We hope our book will make some contribution toward countering this trajectory.

During the editing of this volume, we were struck by the amazing diversity among the chapters, demonstrating the broad ranging, contested nature of critically informed pedagogies and practice. This type of diversity builds on the existing scholarship on critical theory and practice in social work (see for example, Allan et al., 2009; Ferguson, 2007; Fook, 2016; Garrett, 2017, 2018; Gray & Webb, 2013a, 2013b; Hick et al., 2005; Morley et al., 2019; Noble et al., 2016; Pease et al., 2016; Thorpe, 2018), and is necessary to augment/galvanize our agency in responding to some of the most vexing dilemmas created by our current contexts that pose great challenges for social work and our social world more broadly.

Beyond the teaching and learning of social work, this book also explores the neglected role of education in social work practice. In much of the Anglo-American literature, social work education is exclusively conceived as the education of student/future social work practitioners. However, this overlooks a key dimension of social work practice that is educative of its constituents. Viewed through a critical lens, education also holds vital implications for practice. The role of social workers as public or community educators has been referred to elsewhere as social pedagogy (Singh & Cowden, 2009). Understanding social work as including a social or critical pedagogy broadens our scope to work toward social justice, and potentially changes the way social workers think about and engage in practice.

Due to the finite space available in any one volume, many worthy critical thinkers are not included in this volume, and some who were to be included have not been because of the publishing deadline. The absence of particular thinkers will no doubt be a critique of the volume, but clearly it was not possible to include every thinker deserving of attention. We also acknowledge that while there are many possible readings of each theorist, it is the chapter authors' views that are privileged in these pages. We hope that the theorists that are represented provide readers with an entrée to dip into some of the ideas and consider what these might mean for their own work, and that collectively the chapters help to reinvigorate social work's engagement with social theory and critical pedagogy and the untapped potential that these ideas offer.

While managing the contributions of more than 40 chapters has been challenging and overwhelming at times, it has been a wonderful collaborative project. We thank the thinkers whose ideas have inspired this volume, and the authors who have enriched this journey of disovery.

References

Allan, J., Briskman, L., & Pease, B. (2009). *Critical Social Work: Theories and Practices for a Socially Just World* (2nd ed.). Crows Nest, NSW: Allen & Unwin.

Ferguson, I. (2007). *Reclaiming Social Work: Challenging Neo-Liberalism and Promoting Social Justice*. London: Sage.

Fook, J. (2016). *Social Work: A Critical Approach to Practice* (3rd ed.). London: SAGE Publications Ltd.

Garrett, P. (2017). *Welfare Words Critical Social Work & Social Policy*. London: SAGE Publications.

Garrett, P. (2018). *Social Work and Social Theory: Making Connections* (2nd ed.). Bristol: Policy Press.

Gray, M & Webb, S. (2013a). *Social Work Theories and Methods* (2nd ed.). London: Sage.

Gray, M. & Webb, S. (2013b). *The New Politics of Social Work*. Houndsmills: Palgrave Macmillan.

Hick, S., Fook, J., & Pozzuto, R. (2005). *Social Work: A Critical Turn*. Toronto: Thompson Educational Pub.

Morley, C., Ablett, P., & Macfarlane, S. (2019). *Engaging with Social Work: A Critical Introduction* (2nd ed.). South Melbourne: Cambridge University Press.

Noble, C., Gray, M., & Johnston, L. (2016). *Critical Supervision for the Human Services: A Social Model to Promote Learning and Value-Based Practice*. London: Jessica Kingsley Publishers.

Pease, B., Goldingay, S., Hosken, N., & Nipperess, S. (2016). *Doing Critical Social Work: Transformative Practices for Social Justice*. Crow's Nest, NSW, Australia: Allen & Unwin.

Singh, G. & Cowden, S. (2009). The Social Worker as Intellectual: Der Sozialarbeiter als Intellektueller. *European Journal of Social Work*, 12(4), 479–493. https://doi.org/10.1080/13691450902840689

Thorpe, C. (2018). *Social Theory for Social Work: Ideas and Applications*. Oxford: Routledge.

Acknowledgements

We wish to acknowledge and thank all of the authors who contributed to the chapters that comprise this volume; many of whom diligently drafted and re-drafted their submissions several times before they were accepted. Without the work of these authors, this volume would not have been possible. We also wish to acknowledge and thank our reviewers who generously gave their time and expertise to assist the authors in refining their chapters.

We also thank Claire Jarvis of Routledge for her affirmation of the original proposal, Georgia Priestly of Routledge for her assistance throughout the writing and editing process, other Routledge staff involved in the publication process, and Rachel Carter for her incredible copyediting of the entire volume.

Our thanks also go to Hugo Heikenwaelder who allowed us to use his image 'Universum' on the front cover of this book. This image was first published in 1888 in the book by Camille Flammarion on 'The Atmosphere' as a black and white wood carving. Hugo reproduced this as a coloured artwork in 1998. The image is significant to the editors because we too are seeking to reach beyond the boundaries of current thinking around social work education, just as the image captures a person piercing the veil of illusions about the state of the world to grasp the harsh realities we must understand in order to make change.

Finally, we wish to acknowledge and thank Naomi Stekelenburg of Queensland University of Technology, who copyedited and formatted a number of the submissions and attempted to source photographs for each chapter, although she found that copyright conventions and permissions were prohibitive.

Christine Morley, Queensland University of Technology
Phillip Ablett, University of the Sunshine Coast
Carolyn Noble, Australia College of Applied Psychology
Stephen Cowden, University of Coventry

1

Introduction
The imperative of critical pedagogies for social work

Christine Morley
QUEENSLAND UNIVERSITY OF TECHNOLOGY, AUSTRALIA

Phillip Ablett
UNIVERSITY OF THE SUNSHINE COAST, QUEENSLAND, AUSTRALIA

Carolyn Noble
AUSTRALIAN COLLEGE OF APPLIED PSYCHOLOGY, SYDNEY, AUSTRALIA

Introduction

This Handbook brings together the work of critical educational, philosophical and social theorists to reinvigorate social work education as an emancipatory practice. Although we are not accustomed to thinking of social work and public education together, they are products of—and responses to—social problems arising from modernity. In this context, as Walter Lorenz (2004) has insightfully observed, both social work and education have always been conceived as instruments for socialising individuals to become 'citizens'. However, citizenship is a contested and multilayered term. On the one hand, it means democratic agents capable of collective deliberation and self-determination. On the other, it is a marker for drawing boundaries, enforcing exclusion and disciplining people into being productive workers for the dominant economic system. In this collection, while favouring the former view, all contributions critically explore the nature or impact of this contestation as it is expressed in social work education and practice.

When discussing our enthusiasm for this project, some people asked us: why a book on critical pedagogies? What has that got to do with social work? We assert that critical pedagogies hold fundamental importance for social work because:

1. current contexts mean social work practitioners, now, and into the future, need to know how to think critically and engage in praxis (the linking of theory and practice) to formulate effective and ethical responses to some of the anticipated social problems facing humanity in the coming decades (we know critical pedagogies are central to this);

2   the way education is shaped by current contexts closes down spaces for critical thinking and therefore restricts social work's effectiveness to respond ethically to new and emerging social problems, thus necessitating the need to mobilise critical pedagogies as strategies for resistance;
3   the synergistic overlap between social work and education means both disciplines—with their potentials and pitfalls—have a role in either supporting or undermining a democratic public, which we believe should be activated for the former;
4   there is an urgent need for critical pedagogies in social work to counter global social problems, and mitigate restriction of social work's capacity to maintain integrity as a social justice profession; and
5   there is a current lack of critical theorising around pedagogy (beyond knowledge transfer) within social work, and a need to realise educational alternatives to contribute to a more socially just world.

Our current contexts

We inhabit a world of glaring divisions, crises and change, escalating disparities in wealth and power, human rights violations, wars and unprecedented ecological despoliation. Jim Ife (2019, p. viii), a contemporary social work commentator (and author of Chapter 24 on Donna Haraway and the Chthulucene), describes our troubled contexts as

> characterised by runaway growth regardless of social and environmental cost, neoliberal economics, global capitalism 'on steroids', managerialism pervading social work organisations, increasing inequality, individualism, consumerism, greed, intolerance of difference, and a blatantly unsustainable social, economic and political order supported by powerful media and corporate interests.

Similarly, critical educationalist Henry Giroux (co-author of the Foreword for this collection with Ourania Filippakou; see also Chapter 17 by Christine Morley and Phillip Ablett) reminds us that the contemporary rise of authoritarianism, the election of populist right-wing governments, the resurgence of fascism, and the mobilisation of xenophobic views, scapegoating ethnic and religious difference for the problems caused by global capitalism, creates the perfect conditions for what Hannah Arendt (see Chapter 36 by Uschi Bay) refers to as 'dark times' (Giroux 2015, p. 3). These crises are accompanied and often bolstered by a global technological revolution, centred on information technology, computerisation, digitisation, the enhancement of artificial intelligence and robotisation that are radically transforming education, social work and society generally. Education, including social work education, does not stand outside of these issues and trends. Consequently, those concerned with education in the social professions must find ways to resist the forces that produce oppression, and simultaneously, play a role in the formation of change makers who will work toward a more socially just, democratic, ecologically sustainable and compassionate world.

In many ways, we see social work education as one of the last bastions upholding social justice ideals within social work, even if the walls have been breached and struggle ensues within. It is therefore more important than ever that social work education is revitalised as a progressive project in influencing future practitioners, the field, and society more generally. Given the dominance of conservative, New Public Management approaches to social policy (in many Western capitalist countries), critical practices consistent with the espoused values of social work, such as 'empowerment' and 'social justice', will not necessarily emerge from, or be supported by, mainstream human service organisations within the field. Social work education, we argue, must play a leading role in preserving and advancing an emancipatory agenda through a multiplicity of strategies.

The contemporary contexts of social work practice

The contemporary contexts in which social work operates have been dominated by aggressive neoliberal governmentality for more than three decades (see for example Boryczko 2019; Ferguson & Lavalette 2006; Garrett 2018a, 2018b; Madhu 2011; Rees 1991). This has profound implications both for the populations that social workers serve and for social work itself. The people and communities with whom social workers engage are subjected to increasing economic inequalities and poverty, a greater sense of precariousness created by employment insecurity and flexibility, and dominant discourses of individual responsibility and blame for structural problems, which are used to justify punitive social reforms (Garrett 2010). In Australia, the introduction of mandatory drug testing for welfare recipients and the cashless welfare card that simultaneously stigmatises marginalised populations and controls their spending, provide pertinent examples. Such economic injustice often amplifies other forms of oppression along ethnic, ability, gender, age, sexuality and other dimensions of diversity lines.

Social work's aim, according to the Global Definition of the International Federation of Social Workers (IFSW 2014) is to promote 'social justice, human rights, collective responsibility and respect for diversities' for everyone, regardless of their social positioning. Yet social work's responses to increasingly harsh welfare regimes that orchestrate hardship, often reflect neoliberal social control agendas (Agllias et al. 2016; Marston & McDonald 2008; Parrott 2014); or at best, are ambiguous. Neoliberal, managerial and right-wing populist discourses have significantly shaped the types of practices social workers deliver, resulting in a deleterious impact on social workers' capacities to keep faith with their espoused emancipatory values and vision (see for example, Allan 2009; Fenton 2014).

By no means immune to the preceding hegemonic influences, social workers can become trained in practices of surveillance and extending the assertion of state power and authority in people's lives' that are oppressive. This leads to victim blaming discourses that construct people in need of support as 'undeserving', the diligent implementation of austerity measures and administration of punitive sanctions for 'troublesome' groups. Many practitioners are reluctant to challenge organisational injustices in the context of job insecurity and a decline in unionised workplaces, thereby mistaking organisational compliance as 'ethical' practice (Banks 2012). Hence, the neoliberal context in which human service organisations operate, promote an uncritical, passive, technique-driven, formulaic, rule-bound and competency-based style of practice. Understanding this context highlights the imperative of social work education to disrupt and, where possible, counter dominant approaches to practice.

In addition, business and market principles have colonised the sector with managerial practices focused mostly on cost containment and risk management. This means services function without adequate resourcing and are preoccupied with protecting themselves from potential litigation. This has resulted in:

- auditing, surveillance and compliance with operational standards at the expense of service quality;
- standardisation of practice at the expense of practitioner autonomy and discretion;
- risk assessment and management at the expense of people's rights and needs;

- the quest for objectivity and evidence-based practice in an attempt to eliminate uncertainty at the expense of multiple and diverse forms of knowledge; and
- the privileging of technical practices and individualised and medicalised views of the world at the expense of critical theory, critical analysis and critical self-reflection.

Such practices have, unfortunately, become commonplace in contemporary human service organisations. The consequences of these changes, which include conservatising the profession to make it more '*politically acceptable*' to government and industry employers (Dominelli 1996, p. 163, italics in original), has led commentators such as Gray and Webb (2013, p. 7), to designate neoliberalism the most 'vicious adversary' to the possibility of social work developing a more emancipatory agenda.

The impact of neoliberalism on social work education

Consistent with the trends toward managerialisation in social work practice, and in recognising education can be a powerful source of resistance to neoliberal orthodoxy, the policies of conservative governments have sought to strip universities of their critical faculties (Hil 2012). While there is considerable research evidence outlining the consequences of neoliberalism for higher education generally (see for example, Berg et al. 2016; Fraser & Taylor 2016; Giroux 2014, 2015; Hil 2012, 2015; Marginson & Considine 2000; O'Sullivan 2016; Williams 2016), an emerging body of literature has specifically critiqued the impact of neoliberalism on social work education, noting the adverse consequences for teaching, curricula development and research (Fenton 2014; Garrett 2010, 2015; Hanesworth 2017; Morley et al. 2017; Preston & Aslett 2014; Wagner & Yee 2011; Zuchowski et al. 2014).

Current policy directions within the academy seek to eradicate opportunities for critical thinking (Garrett 2009), instead valorising market-driven, technicist practices across all disciplines, including social work (Fenton 2014; Fraser & Taylor 2016; Hil 2012). With this backdrop, mainstream educational approaches to social work have been complicit in reducing learning and teaching to the most efficient and cost-effective transfer of information from educators to students. This rarely results in transformative learning, and socialises students to be technically competent practitioners who accept the status quo, even when it is against social work's defining ethical principles (Fenton 2014; Garrett 2009; Macfarlane 2016). In this way, mainstream social work education serves the goals of neoliberal governance by encouraging students to 'fit in'; to not 'make waves' or 'rock the boat' (Morley 2019, p. 440).

Increased administrative interference into teaching and curriculum by learning design specialists (who rarely have discipline-specific knowledge in the areas they advise upon), also promotes a focus on technique and technologies at the expense of substantive content. Academics subject to this managerial regime are time poor and operate in a culture of perpetual audits and reviews, mediated by templates, and have reduced discretion to develop creative or rigorous teaching practices. This results in teaching being undertaken as a technical, rather than intellectual and political activity concerned with the formation of critical professionals and citizens. In fact, as universities increasingly prioritise competitive research grant (funding) over all other educational functions and activities, teaching is often used to punish those who are assessed as not performing highly enough as researchers (Hil 2012). Alongside this devaluing of teaching is a push for rote learning, measured by multiple choice exams and on-line quizzes that generate passive learners focused on skills acquisition, rather than transformative learning (Giroux 2011). In this context, students are often more focused and 'energised' by technological glitches than the content of their courses.

By contrast, transformative learning of the sort advocated in this collection, involves deep learning that confronts and challenges taken-for-granted assumptions. This is the sort of learning that 'is essential for a democratic society and fundamental to creating the conditions for producing citizens who are critical, self-reflective, knowledgeable, and willing to make moral judgments and act in a socially responsible way' (Giroux 2011, p. 3). In view of its global definition (IFSW 2014) and the concordant value statements of most social work professional associations throughout the world, such qualities are crucial to the development of social workers.

Within the managerial revolution, there is also a strong emphasis on presenting all knowledge as if it is neutral and objective. Curriculum is therefore limited to covering knowledge considered to be 'safe'; that is—knowledge that does not fundamentally contest the interests of power elites. Safe knowledge is not, of course, neutral or objective, but masquerades as such to affirm the status quo. It legitimises neoliberal values and views, such as the idea that 'society should construct and produce self-enterprising individuals solely interested in enhancing their human [and financial] capital' (Fraser & Taylor 2016, p. 5). Hence the teaching of safe knowledge lends credibility to the asocial and atomised 'individual responsibility' doctrines that are central to neoliberalism, while depoliticising social injustices, including the aforementioned introduction of austerity measures in public provision (Baines & McBride 2014; Fenton 2014; Reisch 2013). This process of normalising neoliberal values as if they are universally desirable and accepted (Fenton 2014) can co-opt social work educators 'into being submissive operatives—afraid to question the system or to engage their students with radical ideas for fear of the consequences' (Down & Smyth 2012, p. 15). While most social work educators would still not openly identify with this position, it seems that such approaches are widespread in social work education throughout Western countries (Fenton 2014; Morley 2019; Morley et al. 2017; Reisch 2013). Recent research that examined the development of social work students' sense of professional identity during their final field education placements, for example, found that 'rather than enacting the emancipatory values prized by the social work profession,' most 'appeared to embody a rather conservative approach which is largely and unquestioningly accepting of the … status quo' (Smith, unpub., p. 61). Compounding this situation is the expectation that educators will become 'industry responsive' through various consultative mechanisms that implore the need to prepare graduates who will be 'work ready', 'flexible' and 'adaptable' employees in ways that are malleable for organisations and dominant (neoliberal) discourses dominating the sector.

Thus, social work education within the neoliberal university is being undermined, de-theorised, and redefined in terms of perfunctory professional competencies and techniques (Webb 2017). Within this construction, the imperative for students to develop a sense of conformist 'professional identity' (not necessarily a sense of purpose) is seen to be of profound importance. Again, this has a diversionary/conservatising impact. By obscuring critical analysis and social change agendas, with narrow concerns about professional expertise, accreditation bodies, standards of practice and education, and professional recognition through registration, neoliberal constructions of 'professional identity as "corporate professional" are promoted over "activist citizen"' (Morley 2019, p. 439). Essentially, this dilution of social work education through the evasion, reduction or removal of 'critical theory' (Garrett 2009; Reisch 2013) ensures social work graduates will not be adequately equipped with the critical thinking capacities that enable creative and ethical responses to the urgent, complex problems of the future, including the organisation of a democratic society (Fenton 2014; Garrett 2009; Preston & Aslett 2014).

According to Giroux (2011, 2014), among many others, fostering democracy is the ultimate purpose of public education. This echoes a longstanding tradition in educational philosophy originating with the ancient Greeks but revitalised in the Enlightenment and subsequent democratic revolutions. It is the idea that a vibrant, democratic and just society requires an educated public to flourish. However, as indicated, current mainstream approaches to education subjugate the nature and purpose of education (including social work education) to the imperatives of capitalist markets and political expedience rather than any ethical ideal. Neoliberalism compounds this by promulgating the view that 'there is no alternative' to current trends, making it difficult to think outside existing inequitable arrangements. Hence critical approaches to education, particularly those 'critical pedagogies' articulated by the diverse thinkers and educators influenced by critical theory, are absolutely fundamental for disrupting the fatalism and determinism that neoliberal regimes engender, and for imagining and enacting alternatives.

Critical theory as catalyst for change

Critical theory is a movement with its roots in the Enlightenment notion of 'critique' as something emancipatory—involving liberation from falsehoods and illusions, particularly those that support tyranny and oppression. In the work of the Enlightenment philosopher, Immanuel Kant [1784] (1996), such critique exposes contradictions in arguments and dares one to 'think for oneself' in the quest for truth. Embedded within our construction of critical theory is a Kantian critique of authority that involves rigorous reflection on dominant and received ideas about reason and morality (Kellner 2003). Georg Wilhelm Friedrich Hegel and Karl Marx (see Chapter 2 by Michael Lavalette) extended this notion of critique to include a focus on culture and political economy, respectively; criticising all static and one-dimensional positions or worldviews. This dialectical approach also informs later critical traditions that foster holistic perspectives in the search for emancipative possibilities (Kellner 2003; Morley & Macfarlane 2011). Critical theory, in this modernist sense, shared the Enlightenment belief that universal truths, based on scientific investigation were possible and desirable (Seidman 2016) in building a better society. Marx went beyond Hegel to link critical theory with political action. As he states, 'philosophers have only interpreted the world, the point however is to change it' (Marx 1888 [1845], n.p.). Notably, neither Marx nor Hegel regarded critique as a purely cognitive or contemplative endeavour but, like other Enlightenment thinkers, linked knowledge to a moral vision of human emancipation. A Marxian critique, therefore, points to 'the need for pedagogical and social transformation to free individuals from the fetters of consumer capitalism and to help make possible a free, more democratic and humane culture and society' (Kellner 2003, p. 53). While this form of emancipatory critique is not limited to the Marxian tradition, for over a century, Marxist thinkers were the most robust and explicit in developing the practice. An original Italian Marxian theorist (c. 1920s and 1930s), Antonio Gramsci for example (see Chapter 7 by Paul Michael Garrett), sought to explain the lack of revolutionary success in Western, liberal-capitalist societies, and formulated new strategies, highlighting the politico-cultural and educational basis of capitalist domination in his concept of 'hegemony' (Gramsci 1971). Consequently, he pointed toward (without using the phrase) 'counter-hegemonic' forms of organisation and education to resist the ways dominant ideas are uncritically reproduced in mainstream education (Kellner 2003).

Around the same time in Germany, The Frankfurt School, (an even more unorthodox group of Marxist thinkers) including Herbert Marcuse (see Chapter 8 by Adi Barak) and Theodore Adorno (see Chapter 9 by John G. Fox) (in particular), were similarly critical of educational institutions implicated in the reproduction of dominant ideologies of oppression. Outside the Marxist tradition, in the United States, other critical traditions, such as the radical pragmatism of John Dewey (pioneer of public education), Jane Addams (pioneer of social work) (see Chapter 3 by Carolyn Hanesworth) and later, Myles Horton (pioneer of community organising and education) travelled analogous paths in dealing with social divisions, albeit within a reformist (rather than revolutionary) tradition of extending democracy in everyday life (see Chapter 11 by Trevor G. Gates).

Both revolutionary and reformist theories of change in the early 20th century focused primarily on the 'social problem', understood 'as the extreme economic class inequalities, exploitation and poverty, produced by industrial capitalism' (Lengermann & Niebrugge 2018, p. 185). However, these were not the only sources of social oppression and suffering characterising modern societies.

Other critical thinkers (often beyond the academy) identified the issues of gender, race and colonial oppression as of crucial significance, frequently compounding the injuries of class and poverty. In regard to racialised oppression, the African-American sociologist, W.E.B. Du Bois was among the first to identify the social construction of the 'colour line' as the basis for enormous and continuing social exclusion, discrimination and harm (see Chapter 4 by David Hollinsworth). Du Bois' work was seminal in influencing educators, social workers and activists in subsequent struggles for equal rights and combatting racism.

Indigenous knowledges similarly challenge the devastating impact of colonialism and white privilege on their culture, knowledge and practices (see, for example, Chapter 31 on Aileen Moreton-Robinson by Jennie Briese and Kelly Menzel; Chapter 33 on Frantz Fanon by Linda Harms Smith; Chapter 34 on Stanlake Samkange by Jacob Mugumbate; and Chapter 35 by Lata Narayan on Mohandas Gandhi). The success of decolonisation and the self-assertion of Southern perspectives can also be seen in the way non-Western worldviews such as Buddhism can influence dominant paradigms in their homelands (see, for example, Chapter 32 on Joanna Macy by Loretta Pyles).

Additionally, activist-intellectuals such as Jane Addams and her feminist colleagues highlighted how gender inequalities were a central barrier to equality and democracy. Both Du Bois and Addams placed great faith in the power of popular education to promote progressive social change but also saw (in a comparable vein to the Marxist tradition) that this had to accompany social action, often in the form of social movements. The feminist movement exemplifies this marriage of theory and practice in producing many political, educational and social reforms for women. Feminist theory and pedagogy represents a vast family of ideas, too rich to summarise here, or identify with one thinker, but subsequent feminist thinkers such as Susan Griffin and Vandana Shiva (see Chapter 25 by Heather Fraser and Nik Taylor), Iris Marion Young and Joan Tronto (see Chapter 14 by Bob Pease), Nancy Fraser (see Chapter 21 by Dorothee Hölscher, Vivienne Bozalek and Mel Gray), Dorothy Smith (see Chapter 16 by Michelle Newcomb) and bell hooks (see Chapter 41 by Carolyn Noble), provide valuable insights into the diversity and power of this tradition in influencing social work practice and education. In this broad sense, when applied to social work education, critical theories have had (in varying degrees) a 'utopian dimension' in their presentation of alternatives to the dominant modes of education that sustain existing inequitable states of affairs (Kellner 2003, p. 53).

However, many social critics and educators highlight the universalist and subsequently oversimplified or limited conceptions of subjectivity, identity and power represented by 'modernist' versions of critical theory. These poststructural and postmodern critics point to the failure of modernism to adequately address various aspects of diversity within, and at the intersection of, identities based on class, gender, sexuality, ethnicity, ability status, age, geographic and historical location, and other dimensions of difference. Writers such as bell hooks (1994) have emphasised the significance of hearing the voices of groups historically silenced in gaining agency and expression in educational practices. Additionally, several authors in this volume have adopted the ideas of critical thinkers to create more inclusive practices with disability (see Chapter 30 by Lisa Stafford drawing upon the phenomenological writings of Maurice Merleau-Ponty on the body; and Chapter 23 on the poststructural ideas of Gilles Deleuze by Heather Lynch), and how social work education can be more inclusive of diverse communities such as those identifying as queer or transgender (see Chapter 28 on Kevin Kumashiro by Jen Kaighin).

'Critical poststructuralist' theories, which focus on the significance of diversity and marginality, are therefore an essential inclusion in critical approaches to social work education that emphasise the emancipatory potential of human agency. The nature of the agency suggested by poststructuralism is not prescriptive or programmatic but is rather characterised by constant reflexivity in regard to positionality and power. As Kellner (2003, p. 56) puts it, given that many theorists occupy a privileged positioning:

> A critical poststructuralism also radicalizes the reflexive turn found in some critical modern[ist] thinkers, requiring individuals involved in education and politics to reflect upon their own subject-position and biases, privileges, and limitations, forcing theorists to constantly criticize and rethink their own assumptions, positions, subject-positions, and practices, in a constant process of reflection and self-criticism.
>
> *(citing Best & Kellner 1997)*

Whether located at the critical modernist pole (epitomised by the Marxist tradition, including the materialist, cultural psychology of Lev Vygotsky covered in Chapter 5 by Katherine Reid); or the diverse poststructural end of the spectrum (see, for example, Chapter 12 on Michel Foucault by Julie King; Chapter 29 on Judith Butler by Jamilla Rosdahl; and Chapter 13 on Jacques Derrida by Peter Westoby); or somewhere in between, attempting to transcend the binaries (see Chapter 42 on Pierre Bourdieu by Mark Brough, Barbara Adkins and Rod Kippax; Chapter 18 on Jacques Rancière by Stephen Cowden and Chapter 19 on Giorgio Agamben by Goetz Ottmann and Iris Silva Brito); the different views represented in this collection all lay claim to the most vital task of social critique and reflection, without which the future of human societies (and life on earth as we know it) looks bleak. It is for this reason that social work educators committed to transformative learning and 'care for the world' (as Hannah Arendt puts it) can benefit from heeding these differing voices in questioning and addressing of our current situation. In our view it is only through such fundamental questioning that social workers can accompany as allies, and in some small measure assist, social work's constituents in their diverse quests to lead worthy and fulfilling lives.

Critical theory can shape both social work practice and education along more emancipatory critical lines (see, for example, Morley & Macfarlane 2014; Morley et al. 2019; Nicotera & Kang 2009; Preston & Aslett 2014). Social work education influences the types of theorising and practices future practitioners will privilege in their work and so, in turn, influence the kinds of impacts they will make on society. Specifically, social work education impacts whether social work graduates develop a critical analysis of society, privilege and oppression, a capacity for critical self-reflection, and so practices to facilitate progressive social change, or whether they become narrow, professional technicians who are not fully cognisant of the social, political and moral implications of their work. To promote the former and avoid the latter, we contend social work education must be *critical*.

However, our potential to mobilise the critical pedagogic dimensions of social work, depends on our capacity to build this understanding into social work education itself. This is becoming an increasingly difficult task, as the same systemic imperatives that undermine social work are similarly de-democratising and impoverishing higher education (Morley et al. 2017). As Rúna í Baianstovu and Phillip Ablett outline in discussing the contribution of Jürgen Habermas (see Chapter 37), the systemic features of society exemplified in the state and corporate practices, with their imposition of metrics, technical control and financialisation, are increasingly colonising the life world (i.e. everyday lived experience), and in doing so, degrade all other human interactions and values, including those related to critical social work and democratic education. However, we may perhaps draw some hope from the thought that 'the system' actually presupposes and cannot operate effectively or indefinitely without the understandings that can only be achieved in the communicative spheres of everyday life. The latter, of course, is the sphere in which social workers engage directly with service users and can play a modest but important role in fostering the dialogues across difference that are essential to mutual solidarity, equality and democracy.

At the end of the day, a 'critical view of the world provides a more humane vision of a society better than the one we currently have' (Noble et al. 2016). A critical lens focuses on the 'social space of marginality, stigma and oppression where the work of the "social" involves empowering and liberating people denied justice and rights' (Noble et al. 2016, p. 13). Critical theory critiques the ways dominant power interests and elites promote their benefits, relegating others to the margins of society. The task of critical analysis is to undermine these interests and open up spaces for freedom, justice and emancipation for all, 'where human rights and social justice is the "natural order"'(Noble et al. 2016, p. 114).

Education informed by critical theory is transformative by valorising critique and fostering democratic citizenship. However, education as 'reproduction' of dominant discourses without critical thought, risks inertia, rigidity and thoughtless complicity in systems that police rather than uplift those experiencing social marginalisation and exclusion.

A critical perspective on modern public education, dating back to Dewey (1916), views democracy and education as symbiotic: the purpose of education is to help build a democratic society; and a democratic society cannot exist without education, as people cannot fully participate in democracy unless they are informed. As Kellner (2003, p. 55) notes:

> For Dewey, education was the key to making democracy work since in order to intelligently participate in social and political life, one had to be informed and educated to be able to be a good citizen and competent actor in democratic life.

Straume (2014) argues that in our current context, democracy is broken. The impetus to replace critical thinking in education with the reproduction of dominant discourses, erodes students' capacities to become informed citizens capable of contributing to a civil society. So, a key question for progressive social work educators today is how are we supported in (and how can we support) the re-institution of the critical mission that is both educative and democratic?

Pedagogy

While every profession or social group has a body of knowledge or practices into which it inducts new members, the pedagogic purpose is typically 'reproduction' (of dominant ideas) rather than creativity or conscious transformation. This type of education does not equip learners with the capacity to question received wisdom or to imagine new ideas that respond to new situations or fundamentally challenge their own or their professions' dominant assumptions and practices.

The term 'pedagogy', as a number of the thinkers covered in this collection point out, is derived etymologically from the Ancient Greek *paideía* (παιδεία), which refers to the education or formation of a citizen fit to participate in the affairs of a democratic city or society, deliberating on the creation of a worthy life and a good society. This was in contrast to the older aristocratic education that served the interests of a wealthy elite, trained to dominate others. According to Butts (1973, p. 86) *paideía*, as conducted in ancient Athens once it became a democracy, meant that education became more 'broadly "civil" … in the sense that it attempted to form the citizen for a life of full participation in the wide range of activities worthy of the city'.

Related to this, Jack Mezirow, (see Chapter 40 by Peter Jones) saw contemporary adult education as involving transformation, including pedagogies that contest dominant discourses and create a shift in the way we make meaning of the world. In a vein analogous to Henry Giroux's work (see Chapter 17 by Christine Morley and Phillip Ablett), like many critical pedagogues in public education (see, for example, Apple 2004; Giroux 2011; McLaren 1989), we are advocating 'critical pedagogy' as a rich, theoretical and political approach to social work education; an approach that involves the critical analysis of society and critical reflection on one's-self in a way that dialogically fosters the 'unsettling common sense assumptions' (Giroux 2011, p. 3) and with the practical intent of emancipative change.

Critical pedagogy

The first person to coin the term 'critical pedagogy' in English was Henry Giroux (1983). Giroux's approach is influenced by critical theorists such as Adorno, Marcuse, Gramsci, Habermas (as in chapters of this volume previously noted) and the seminal work of Paulo Freire (see Chapter 10 by Stephen Cowden, Nilan Yu, Wilder Robles and Debora Mazza). It seeks to question ideologies and structures considered oppressive in order to undermine the practices and beliefs that enforce their domination. These critical thinkers all shared an understanding that education, as a site of knowledge production, has a social purpose—to either extend or deny social justice (Noble et al. 2016). According to Brookfield (see Chapter 43 by Christine Morley), critical theory and its contemporary educational applications, such as critical pedagogy, seek to challenge oppression and create socially just alternatives. Similarly, other critical thinkers, such as Freire, believed that emancipatory education as a dialogical, rather than 'banking' model of education, could free people from oppression. A 'pedagogy of the oppressed', according to Freire (1970), involves a process of consciousness raising that enables decolonisation from dominant discourses and values, a critique of dominant modes of education involved in reproduction, and the development of more liberatory pedagogies aimed at progressive social change.

Another key idea from critical pedagogy that holds direct relevance for social work is the notion that teaching (both formal and informal) is not just a practice that occurs in classrooms between students and teachers, but can occur anywhere, in any context, and in any circumstance. Hence, critical pedagogy is intimately connected with critical social work that is educative of its constituents, and therefore has implications for the scope of social work practice. In other words, the educative role of social work extends well beyond the classroom for social work students or even the professional learning of practitioners, to the educative impact of workers and their organisations on the social world of their service-users.

Critical pedagogy also critiques the reduction of education to 'training'. That is the reduction of education as a search for truth via critical analysis and self-reflection to the search for the most efficient techniques for knowledge transfer from teacher to students. This also means questioning the reduction of learning to a purely individualised, cognitive event, best enhanced by psychology or neuroscience. For critical pedagogy, learning always entails vital social, aesthetic and affective dimensions that are perhaps more amenable to artistic and creative performance-based pedagogies than logocentric, cognitive transfer models (see, for example, Chapter 39 on Augusto Boal and Hans Georg Gadamer by Jean Carruthers and Phillip Ablett). Arts-based pedagogies also resist the tendency of technical rationality to marginalise critical thought and can potentially open up productive educational spaces where a different sort of thinking can flourish.

Praxis is another defining feature of critical pedagogy for social work. Numerous critical scholars discuss the importance of praxis. Praxis, according to Marx's re-working of Aristotle, involves the reflective integration between theory and practice with an emancipatory intent (Critchley 1997), which is broadly echoed in the aims of critical social work education. Likewise, for critical educationalists, praxis involves human action and reflection, potentially giving rise to new knowledge and improved social conditions. Cornelius Castoriadis (see Chapter 15 by Phillip Ablett and Christine Morley), for example, contrasts praxis with technique. As he states: 'the relations of praxis to theory … are … more profound than those of any "strictly rational" technique or practice; for the latter, theory is only a code of lifeless prescriptions which can never, in its manipulations, encounter meaning' (Castoriadis 1987, p. 76). Praxis, by contrast, is a lucid, creative and critical process concerned with realising an ethical human purpose. Praxis questions about 'what' is being done in this or that practice, program or policy, and 'for what' purpose? (Castoriadis 1984, p. 235). It therefore cannot be reduced to the 'know how' of technique. Dewey's concept of 'pragmatism' is also relevant here: enjoining that theory should develop from practice, and therefore highlighting that education, even when theoretically focused, is intensely practical (Kellner 2003, p. 55).

Developing a critical consciousness is also central to critical pedagogy. This involves teaching a critical analysis of society, capable of identifying power relations between dominant groups and the oppressed, linking the personal with the political and highlighting the need for change. Michael Lavalette's chapter on Marx (see Chapter 2) highlights how a structural worldview can prepare social workers for critical practice. This speaks to social work at the level of both micro and macro practices. At the confluence of Marxism and social work, Michael Reisch's chapter on Bertha Capen Reynolds (see Chapter 6), likewise addresses social work education for critical practice at both of these levels. Jenni Mays' chapter on French economist Thomas Piketty, also speaks to the importance of contemporary structural analysis of the economy, particularly informing our teaching of social policy (see Chapter 26). Goetz Ottmann and Carolyn Noble's work on Alain Touraine (see Chapter 38) directly addresses the importance of collective action and social movements for social work if broader social changes are to be achieved. Posing and answering difficult questions encourages reflection as well as deep, sustained discussion that also disrupts speculation, stereotypes and assumptions distorted by hegemony that block critical learning (see, for example, Chapter 40 on Jack Mezirow by Peter Jones). Critically informed questions such as education for what, for whom and to what end, inform the basis of a critical pedagogy.

Critical reflection and disruption of hegemonic views is another fundamental aspect of critical pedagogy. Freire's (1970) notion of 'critical consciousness' holds that people have been silenced and their voices not heard by the dominant ideologies and power structures. Central to the process of consciousness raising is critical reflection, which is enlisted to unmask how domination and silencing work but, more importantly, to awaken the possibilities for change and transformation.

For Habermas, amongst others, critical reflection has its roots in Kantian ethics and philosophy and is a particular form of reasoning that is undertaken with the understanding that ideas are shaped by societal processes that privilege some forms of knowledge over others and these knowledges must be subject to public scrutiny and deliberation so as to expose arbitrary power structures and imbalances. Critical reflection enables social work practitioners to transcend dominant constructions of social problems and conceptualise new ways of thinking about how to address them. In exploring one's own construction of existing social conditions, and the impact of one's own biographical positioning in how this influences our interpretation of 'reality', critical reflection is facilitated by the use of critical questioning, that moves beyond our own analysis.

Critical reflection may, therefore, help interrupt what Joan Tronto has termed as 'privileged irresponsibility' and 'epistemological ignorance' (see Chapter 14 by Bob Pease).

Tronto's analysis of the ways in which privileged individuals can disregard the needs of others and preserve their own dominant positioning can assist social work students (and people generally) to recognise that inaction on issues of social justice, fuelled by ignorance of structural forms of privilege, 'makes them complicit in the reproduction of that injustice'. According to Freire (1970), ignorance brings oppression and education brings empowerment and freedom.

Critical reflection may similarly be enhanced by thinkers such as Avishai Margalit (1996), whose work highlights the ways that social work practices and organisations are implicated in perpetrating humiliation, instead of enabling self-respect and autonomy (see Chapter 20 by Lorna Hallahan). This is increasingly important as the language we use as social workers, described as 'Welfare Words' by Paul Michael Garrett (2018a), is increasingly co-opted by hegemonic assumptions, allowing us to engage in potentially restrictive, abusive, manipulative and punitive practices, while continuing to use terms such as 'empowerment' and 'participation' for camouflage. Similarly, the objectifying and stigmatising language of 'us and them', so central to neoliberal agendas, subtly pervades social work discourse in which workers/professionals and service users/clients are constructed in binary and fixed terms (see Chapter 27 on Carl Jung by Selma Macfarlane).

Stephen A. Webb, in commenting on the contribution of Roberto Esposito to critical pedagogy (Chapter 22), suggests it can provide 'tactics of resistance' against social work's co-option into neoliberal bio-politics, defined as a profoundly negative form of 'power over life' that is totally focused on the management, regulation and administration of populations. Webb argues that Esposito's ideas can assist social work educators to re-claim what is potentially lost from liberal education—'the body, the outside, the recognition of the Other' (see p. XX). Such a radical change is necessary, he argues, to imagine a critical pedagogy for social work that serves a public good.

Importantly many critical theorists argue that critical education is a practice of hope and freedom, never just about training or credentials. Critical theory and its pedagogical applications offer pathways to build more hopeful and just futures. bell hooks (1994), for example, discusses how critical pedagogy provides a sense of hope and inspires educators to work toward justice, even when injustices continue. According to hooks' vision, the classroom becomes a site for diverse students to retrieve their stories, histories, languages, social practice and sense of community. This can engender a source of hope and empowerment. Hence, critical pedagogy is intimately connected to the struggles of individuals and populations that experience marginalisation and oppression. According to Noble et al. (2016, p. 129), critical pedagogies seek to:

engage in forms of reasoning that challenge dominant ideologies and question the socio-political and political-economic order maintaining oppression;

interpret experiences of marginalisation and oppression in ways that emphasise our relational connections to others and the need for solidarity and collective organisation;

unmask the unequal operations of power in our communities and lives;

understand hegemony and our complicity in its continued existence;

contest the pervasive effect of oppressive ideologies and discourses;

recognise when an embrace of alternative views might support the status quo it appears to be challenging;

embrace freedom to change the world;

participate in democracy despite its contradictions.

The handbook

In the discussion above we have drawn together key theories from eminent scholars in the social science and philosophies to define our understanding of critical theory and a critical pedagogy. There are many more critical thinkers whose links with social work's critical approach to education are compelling. Indeed, the potential applications of critical thinkers to enhance the development of critical pedagogies in social work are limited only by our imagination. Developing a deeper knowledge of some of these thinkers' ideas and how social work educators and practitioners can use them to reinvigorate social work as an emancipatory project, is the essence of this volume.

This Handbook of critical pedagogies for social work includes contributions from leading social work academics who have a track record of critical scholarship on the teaching and practice of social work. Each writes about how their work has been informed by a critical educationalist, social theorist or philosopher, thus generating new scholarship for critical social work practitioners. This book unites social work education and practice with critical pedagogies in ways that foster the potential of each to act as catalysts for broader social change, and is, in this sense, unique.

In writing their chapters, the contributing authors have first outlined a brief biographical background of their chosen critical thinker, summarised key concepts and, crucially, applied the concepts and ideas to explicate, inform or design a critical approach to education and practice. The chapters individually and collectively demonstrate the possibilities for counter-hegemonic responses to the harmful impacts of dominant discourses and technicist pedagogies that cultivate and reproduce the normality of a power-divided and inequitable society.

The key argument underpinning each chapter is that critical pedagogy can make an important contribution to redressing and transforming the pressing challenges our times. The richness and diversity of the ideas that emerge from the chapters cover a vast literature of social science scholarship in the critical tradition. Each chapter demonstrates how critical theory, that embraces both modernist and/or critical poststructural theories, can inform transformative pedagogies in social work education and its related implications for practice. Though divergent in their views, the writers represented in this collection all maintain that a critical theory-informed social work education that involves transformative learning can still inspire antidotes to the neoliberal colonisation of social work and its role in society.

In conclusion, a critical perspective is of vital importance to social work and the human services, particularly within contemporary contexts. We believe that a comprehensive international handbook that addresses critical and transformative education strategies has direct relevance for both social work education and practice that aims to be consistent with the espoused emancipatory goals of social work. We hope you enjoy the ensuing chapters as much as we have. We are optimistic that they will enrich your teaching practices and inspire you to take up the challenge of reconstructing a radically democratic social work education. Without critical theory-informed practice, social work can be co-opted and reduced to micro-level practices that focus on redefining social problems as individual problems that require individual adaptation (e.g., treatment of presumed psychological pathologies, budget counselling, etc), rather than dismantling structural inequalities that cause disadvantage (Hanesworth 2017). Fostering the development of the critical scholarship required to counteract the 'conservative revolution' (Garrett 2010, p. 340) currently being waged in social work should be the ultimate priority for all involved in social work education.

Acknowledgements

Many thanks to Dr Selma Macfarlane (of Deakin University) for her helpful feedback on this chapter and Tania Cusack (of QUT) who assisted with compiling the reference list.

References

Agllias, K., Howard, A., Schubert, L., & Gray, M. (2016). Australian workers' narratives about emergency relief and employment service clients: Complex issues, simple solutions. *Australian Social Work*, 69(3), 297–310. 10.1080/0312407X.2015.1049627

Allan, J. (2009). Doing critical social work. In J. Allan, L. Briskman, & B. Pease, (eds.), *Critical social work; Theories and practices for a socially just world*. Crow's Nest: Allen & Unwin, 30–44.

Apple, M. (2004). *Ideology and curriculum* (25th anniversary, 3rd edn.). New York: Routledge.

Baines, D., & McBride, S. (2014). *Orchestrating austerity: Impacts & resistance*. Halifax & Winnipeg: Fernwood Publishing.

Banks, S. (2012). *Ethics and values in social work* (4th edn.). Basingstoke: Palgrave Macmillan.

Berg, L., Huijbens, E., & Larsen, G. (2016). Producing anxiety in the neoliberal university. *The Canadian Geographer*, 60(2), 10.1111/cag.12261

Best, S., & Kellner, D. (1997). *The postmodern turn*. New York: Guilford Press.

Boryczko, M. (2019). Neoliberal governmentality in social work practice. An example of polish social security system. *European Journal of Social Work*, 1(1), 1–12. 10.1080/13691457.2019.1617678

Brookfield, S. (2017). *Becoming a critically reflective teacher* (2nd ed.). San Francisco, CA: Jossey-Bass.

Butts, R. (1973). Reconstruction in foundations studies. *Educational Theory*, 23(1), 27–41. 10.1111/j.1741-5446.1973.tb00588.x

Castoriadis, C. (1984). *Crossroads in the Labyrinth* (trans. K. Soper and M. Ryle) Cambridge: MIT Press.

Castoriadis, C. (1987). *The imaginary institution of society*. Cambridge: The MIT Press.

Critchley, P. (1997). The Philosophy of Praxis. In P. Critchley, *Beyond modernity and postmodernity: Vol 2 active materialism*. [e-book] Available through http://independent.academia.Edu/PeterCritchley/Books.

Down, B., & Smyth, J. (2012). *Critical voices in teacher education: Teaching for social justice in conservative times*. Basel: Springer.

Dewey, J. (1916). *Democracy and education: An introduction to the philosophy of education*. New York: Macmillan.

Dominelli, L. (1996). Deprofessionalising social work: Anti-oppressive practice, competencies and postmodernism. *British Journal of Social Work*, 26, 153–75. https://doi-org.ezp01.library.qut.edu.au/10.1093/oxfordjournals.bjsw.a011077

Fenton, J. (2014). Can social work education meet the neoliberal challenge head on? *Critical and Radical Social Work*, 2(3), 321–35. 10.1332/204986014X14074186108718

Ferguson, I., & Lavalette, M. (2006). Globalization and global justice: Towards a social work of resistance. *International Social Work*, 49, 309–18. 10.1177/0020872806063401

Fraser, H., & Taylor, N. (2016). *Neoliberalism, universities and the public intellectual: Species, gender and class and the production of knowledge*. London: Palgrave.

Freire, P. (1970). *Pedagogy of the oppressed*. Baltimore, MD: Penguin Books.

Garrett, P. (2018a). *Welfare words critical social work & social policy*. London: SAGE Publications.

Garrett, P. (2018b). *Social work and social theory: Making connections* (2nd edn.). Bristol: Policy Press.

Garrett, P.M. (2009). *Transforming children's services: Social work, neoliberalism and the 'modern' world*. Berkshire: McGraw-Hill Education.

Garrett. P.M. (2010). Examining the 'conservative revolution': Neoliberalism and social work education. *Social Work Education*, 29(4), 340–55. 10.1080/0261540903009015

Garrett, P.M. (2015). Words matter: Deconstructing 'welfare dependency' in the UK. *Critical and Radical Social Work*, 3(3), 389–406. 10.1332/204986015X14382412317270

Giroux, H. (1983). *Theory and resistance in education: A pedagogy for the opposition*. South Hadley, MA: Bergin & Garvey.

Giroux, H. (2011). *On critical pedagogy*. New York: Continuum.

Giroux, H. (2014). *Neoliberalism's war on higher education*. Chicago, IL: Haymarket Books.

Giroux, H. (2015). *Dangerous thinking in the age of new authoritarianis*. Boulder, CO: Paradigm Publishers.

Gramsci, A. (1971). *Prison notebooks*. London: Lawrence and Wishart.

Gray, M, & Webb, S. (2013) *The new politics of social work*. Houndsmills: Palgrave Macmillan. ISBN: 9780230296787.

Hanesworth, C. (2017). Neoliberal influences on American higher education and the consequences for social work programmes. *Critical and Radical Social Work*, 5(1), 41–57. 10.1332/204986017X14835298292776

Hil, R. (2012) *Whackademia*. Sydney: New South Publishing. ISBN: 9781742245867.

Hil, R. (2015). *Selling students short*. Crows Nest: Allen and Unwin.

hooks, b. (1994). *Teaching to transgress education as the practice of freedom*. New York: Routledge.

Ife, J. (2019). Foreword. In C. Morley, S. Macfarlane, & P. Ablett, *Engaging with social work: A critical introduction*. South Melbourne: Cambridge, vii–ix.

IFSW. (2014). Global definition of social work. *International Federation of Social Workers*. www.ifsw.org/what-is-social-work/global-definition-of-social-work/

Kant, I. [1784]. (1996). An answer to the question: What is enlightenment? In M. J. Gregor (ed.), *Kant's practical philosophy*. Cambridge: Cambridge University Press, 11–22.

Kellner, D. (2003). Toward a critical theory of Education. *Democracy and Nature*, 9(1), 51–64. 10.1080/1085566032000074940

Lengermann, P., & Niebrugge, G. (2018). Settlement Sociology. In A. Treviño, (ed.), *The Cambridge handbook of social problems*. Cambridge: Cambridge University Press, 185–202. 10.1017/9781108656184.012

Lorenz, W. (2004). *Towards a European paradigm of social work – Studies in the history of modes of social work and social policy in Europe*. Dresden: PHD Fakultät Erziehungswissenschaften der Technischen Universität Dresden.

Macfarlane, S. (2016). Education for critical social work: Being true to a worthy project. In B. Pease., S. Goldingay, N. Hosken, & S. Nipperess, (ed.), *Doing critical social work: Transformative practices for social justice*. Sydney: Allen & Unwin, 326–38.

Madhu, P. (2011). *Praxis intervention: Towards a new critical social work practice*. [e-book] SSRN eLibrary. Available through *Social Science Research Network*. http://ssrn.com/paper=1765143

Margalit, A. (1996). *The decent society*. Cambridge, MA: Harvard University Press.

Marginson, S., & Considine, M. (2000). *The enterprise university: Power, governance and reinvention in Australia*. New York: Cambridge University Press.

Marston, G., & McDonald, C. (2008). Feeling motivated yet? Long-term unemployed people's perspectives on the implementation on workfare Australia. *The Australian Journal of Social Issues*, 43(2), 255–69. 10.1022/j.1839-4655.2008.tb00101.x

Marx, K. 1888 [1845] *Theses again Feuerback. The Marx/Engles Selected Works*, Vol. 1. Moscow: Progress Publishers.

McLaren, P. (1989). *Life in schools: An introduction to critical pedagogy and the foundations of education*. New York: Longman.

Morley, C. (2019). Social work education and activism. In S.A Webb, (ed.), *The Routledge handbook of critical social work*. London: Taylor & Francis, 437–49.

Morley, C., & Macfarlane, S. (2011). The nexus between feminism and postmodernism: Still a central concern for critical social work. *British Journal of Social Work*, 42(4), 687–705.

Morley, C., & Macfarlane, S. (2014). Critical social work as ethical social work: Using c ritical reflection to research students' resistance to neoliberalism. *Critical and Radical Social Work*, 2(3), 337–55. 10.1332/204986014X14096553281895

Morley, C., Macfarlane, S., & Ablett, P. (2017). The neoliberal colonisation of social work education: A critical analysis and practices for resistance. *Advances in Social Work and Welfare Education*, 19(2), 25–40. https://search-informit-com.au.ezp01.library.qut.edu.au/documentSummary;dn=295064490880318;res=IELHSS

Morley, C., Macfarlane, S., & Ablett, P. (2019). *Engaging with social work: A critical introduction* (2nd edn.). South Melbourne: Cambridge University Press.

Nicotera, N., & Kang, K. (2009). Beyond diversity courses: Strategies for integrating critical consciousness across social work curriculum. *Journal of Teaching in Social Work*, 29(2), 188–203. 10.1080/08841230802240738

Noble, C., Gray, M., & Johnston, L. (2016). *Critical supervision for the human services: A social model to promote learning and value-based practice*. London: Jessica Kingsley Publishers.

O'Sullivan, M. (2016). *Academic barbarism, universities and inequality*. New York: Palgrave Macmillan.

Parrott, L. (2014). *Social work and poverty: A critical approach*. Bristol: Policy Press.

Preston, S., & Aslett, J. (2014). Resisting neoliberalism from within the academy: Subversion through an activist pedagogy. *Social Work Education*, 33(4), 502–18.

Rees, S. (1991). *Achieving power: Practice and policy in social welfare*. Sydney: Allen & Unwin.

Reisch, M. (2013). Social work education and the neoliberal challenge: The US response to increasing global inequality. *Social Work Education*, 32(6), 715–33. 10.1080/02615479.2013.809200

Seidman, S. (2016). *Contested knowledge: Social theory today* (6th edn.). Melbourne: Blackwell.

Smith, F.L. (2018). *Identifying the key factors shaping the construction of a social work identity in mental health.* Unpublished Doctoral dissertation, Victoria: The University of Melbourne, Melbourne.

Straume, I. (2014). Education in a crumbling democracy. *Ethics and Education, 9*(2), 1–14. 10.1080/17449642.2014.921973

Wagner, A., & Yee, J. (2011). Anti-oppression in higher education: Implicating neo-liberalism. *Canadian Social Work Review, 28*(1), 89–105. https://gateway.library.qut.edu.au/login?url=https://search-proquest.com.ezp01.library.qut.edu.au/docview/1364704704?accountid=13380

Webb, S.A. (2017) *Professional identity and social work.* New York & London: Routledge. ISBN:9781138234437.

Williams, J. (2016) *Academic freedom in the age of conformity.* New York: Palgrave Macmillan. ISBN:1-137-51478-7.

Zuchowski, I., Hudson, C., Bartlett, B., & Diamandi, S. (2014). Social work field education in Australia: Sharing practice wisdom and reflection. *Advances in Social Work & Welfare Education, 16*(1), 67–79. https://search-informit-com.au.ezp01.library.qut.edu.au/documentSummary;dn=517037503078399;res=IELHSS

Part I
Key foundational concepts

2
Karl Marx
Capitalism, alienation and social work

Michael Lavalette

LIVERPOOL HOPE UNIVERSITY

Introduction

This chapter will look at the ideas of Karl Marx. Marx was one of the greatest social theorists and philosophers to have lived, despite the way he is often dismissed as someone whose ideas have 'failed'. While Marx wrote nothing about social work, I will argue in this chapter that social workers have a great deal to learn from engagement with his work. It will be suggested that, while there isn't a 'Marxist social work', Marx's work provide us with a powerful set of ideas that help us understand the contemporary world of competitive, global capitalism and the myriad problems such a system creates. It provides social workers with a set of ideas that can help orientate them to the problems and dilemmas faced by workers and service users. It can help them manage their way through the conflicts and contradictions of social work practice – navigating the conflicts inherent within a profession that claims to meet human need and pursue social justice, while often carrying out and administering state policies that can be shaped by concerns of controlling 'difficult', non-labouring, or 'problem' communities.

The chapter starts with a brief biography of Marx, and then discusses his critique of modern capitalist society. Marx starts by noting the huge potential the development of capitalism brings for human society, but he goes on to argue that the fundamental class divisions of society mean that the vast wealth created by the system is not used in the interests of the many, but, rather, to reinforce the power and wealth of the few. We will then look at one of Marx's most powerful analytic concepts, especially for social workers, that of 'alienation'. For Marx, our feelings of isolation, loneliness and despair are experiences that are essentially rooted in social processes. They are a reflection of the ways that capitalism pits us against each other and disconnects us from others and our communities. Capitalism is a system under which we have little control over our lives and this is a contributing factor to so many social problems. Finally we look at the relevance of Marx's ideas for social work.

Marx and the 'philosophy of praxis'

Karl Marx was born on 5 May 1818 in Trier in Germany. He was raised in a relatively comfortable middle-class home in the Rhineland – a region annexed by the Prussian state at the end of the Napoleonic Wars in 1815. After annexation, the region remained one of the most economically and politically advanced areas of Germany, the political culture heavily influenced by the impact of the French Revolution of 1789. But Germany as a whole, in this period, was an economically backward place, dominated by the states of Austria, Prussia and Russia and, below them, a vast number of petty princedoms each claiming absolute power and authority over their subjects.

In 1835 Marx left to study law at the University of Bonn and in 1836 he met his future life-partner Jenny von Westphalen. The same year he moved to Berlin University where he changed direction and focused on the study of philosophy. Despite its economic backwardness, German intellectual life flourished and the early decades of the nineteenth century are often regarded as the golden era of German abstract philosophy. As Marx (1843) himself noted of this period: 'In politics the Germans *thought* what other nations did'.

In Berlin Marx engaged with the ideas of the pre-eminent German philosopher of the day, Georg Wilhelm Friedrich Hegel and worked with the Young Hegelians, a group of radical philosophers who utilised Hegel's philosophical framework, but were critical of his increasingly conservative politics. The Young Hegelians, for example, decried the accommodation of some of Hegel's supporters with the Prussian state and rejected Hegel's religiosity in favour of atheism.

What Marx got from Hegel was a dialectical method that saw the world as an internally contradictory totality, in a constant process of change. But he 'turned Hegel on his head' because, unlike Hegel, he did not see these as being rooted in 'ideas' or 'thought' rather, he argued, they were rooted in the material realities of social life. For Marx, the starting point in understanding human societies is not the ideas and belief systems that may dominate at any point; rather, it is how societies are organised to produce their means of survival. As Marx (1845) put it:

> The premises from which we begin are not arbitrary ones, not dogmas, but real premises from which abstraction can only be made in the imagination. They are the real individuals, their activity and the material conditions under which they live, both those which they find already existing and those produced by their activity. These premises can thus be verified in a purely empirical way.

This focus on how societies produce the goods they need to survive and prosper, and on the relationships (often unequal and exploitative) that exist between producers in any epoch is at the heart of Marx's *materialist* method.

What was exciting about Hegel, for Marx, was his understanding of 'contradiction' and movement being at the root of all life. When applied to society (not just thought and ideas) this understanding becomes subversive. It opens up the possibility that the present world is not inevitable, or static; it confronts the notion that the world 'has always been like this', and it challenges the idea that 'there is no alternative' to our present society and its priorities (Rees, 1998).

Thus Marx's materialism is also historical, concerned with the development of societies and their internal contradictions, and so Marx's method is known as *historical materialism*.

Using the historical materialist method allowed Marx and Engels to identify various types of societies (ancient slave societies, feudalism, capitalism), which have existed across human history. These societies have been organised along different principles and the social relationships between people have varied significantly. In each society, there were relationships of exploitation that allowed a minority to live a more or less leisured existence by exploiting the labour of the vast majority. More generally, it means recognising that the 'totality of relationships' in each society is, and has been, different in different types of societies. 'The family', for example, has not always existed in the same way; the relationships between men and women, gay and straight, black and white, for example, that are often assumed to be a fixed part of 'human nature', have not always been the same. Of course, if they have not always been the same in the past then, crucially, it opens up the possibility that they will not be the same in the future. And for Marx the future was one of great possibilities. Marx believed that the present system (capitalism) had created a powerful opponent (the working class) whose collective interest is in getting rid of capitalism and replacing it with a system of collective control, run democratically in the interests of the many and opening up a new, great era of human liberation and freedom.

To conclude this section, I want to draw out the relevance of the above discussion for social workers and social work educators. Marx's method allows us to see the range of ways that human societies have organised themselves to meet their needs. Though many commentators and media outlets suggest that modern capitalism is 'natural' and has always been around, it has actually only lasted for a short period of human history. Further, the vast range of oppressions that we see in the modern world, are not inevitable, or a reflection of 'human nature', rather they are 'socially constructed' – though they were constructed within a particular context: the development of modern capitalist social relations.

Further, Marx's emphasis on totality and contradiction allows us to see the connections between apparently separate spheres of life. For example, we are often told to think about poverty, or crime, or inequality or suicide rates as separate social problems. But the emphasis on totality forces us to think about the connections between things – and once we see the connections between inequality and suicide, or between poverty and crime it helps us come to a different understanding of all these elements from when we thought of them as occupying different realms of social life.

Having developed these insights and his method of 'historical materialism', Marx turned to analysing the present world of capitalism.

Understanding capitalism

Perhaps rather surprisingly for those who read Marx for the first time, aspects of his work praise the potential that capitalism has given humanity to meet people's needs. At the start of the *Communist Manifesto*, for example, Marx and Engels note the very significant economic growth that capitalism had delivered. They write that:

> The bourgeoisie, during its rule of scarce one hundred years, has created more massive and more colossal productive forces than have all preceding generations together. Subjection of Nature's forces to man, machinery, application of chemistry to industry and agriculture, steam-navigation, railways, electric telegraphs, clearing of whole continents for cultivation, canalisation of rivers, whole populations conjured out of the ground – what earlier century had even a presentiment that such productive forces slumbered in the lap of social labour?
> *(Marx and Engels, 1848)*

As we approach the third decade of the twenty-first century the 'potential' to meet human need has never been greater. We produce enough food, for example, to ensure that no one, anywhere in the world, should go to sleep at night hungry. We have the resources to house everyone in an adequate, energy-efficient home. We could easily make sure everyone had free access to the highest quality medical care and that preventable and curable illnesses (such as malaria, for example) are eradicated. Education could be free and available to all. We have, potentially, the ability to develop green-friendly, public transport systems that would allow people to move around freely and cheaply. We could make sure that everyone had a decent well-paid job – and that working hours were significantly reduced and employment conditions improved dramatically. And we could do all this while reducing climate change gases, expanding renewable energy sources and developing alternatives to plastics and other environmentally damaging products.

We could do all this – and more – given the wealth in the system – and the modern world is today wealthier than all previous forms of human society.

But the reality is that capitalism, as a social system, is not geared to meeting people's needs. The vast wealth generated by the system is not used to benefit ordinary people. Instead it is used to make the fabulously wealthy even wealthier. For example, in 2018, the global charity Oxfam noted the latest figures on global inequality and that just:

> 42 people hold as much wealth as the 3.7 billion who make up the poorest half of the world's population … the wealth of billionaires [has] risen by 13% a year on average in the decade from 2006 to 2015, with the increase of $762bn (£550bn) in 2017 enough to end extreme poverty seven times over.
>
> *(Elliott, 2018)*

The wealth of a tiny minority at the top of society combined with the horror of desperate poverty for billions of people at the bottom, is not down to individual greed, ability or intelligence, it is the outcome of a system of exploitation that operates to the benefit of the few.

Marx spent the main part of his intellectual life studying how the capitalist system worked, exploring its contradictions and its inevitable crisis tendencies. The three volumes of *Capital* were his crowning achievement. His analysis of capitalism remains the most significant study of the dynamics of the system ever produced. Marx's work helps us understand how capitalism works. Let us look at the basic points of his argument.

First, Marx notes that capitalism is a system divided by our relationship to what he called the *means of production*. The means of production are all the things we need to produce society's wealth: offices, factories, machines, land, energy and labour. But under the present system these are not held in common. Rather, there are a minority who own (or control) the offices, factories, land, etc. but, on their own, these resources do not produce anything: empty factories and offices, or untilled land create no wealth. For wealth to be created the owners of the means of production have to hire 'labour power' from the vast majority of the population who, in turn, have no means of surviving, except by selling their ability to work. This description defines the two great social classes of capitalism: those who own and/or control the means of production he called the bourgeoisie; those who have no option but to sell their labour power to survive he called the proletariat (or, more commonly, the working class).

In capitalist society, these two great classes are 'tied together' (they need each other) but their relationship is not equal, in fact it is an 'antagonistic relationship'. The reason for this is because the relationship between the two is exploitative.

The only thing that creates wealth in society is labour; without people to work in factories, fields and offices nothing will be made and no wealth created, so the bourgeoisie need to employ workers. But in turn, there is no mechanism that forces them to pay the workers a full return for the wealth they create. For example, if you work in a car factory, you and your colleagues will be involved in making thousands of cars each week, but your wages will be tiny in comparison to the wealth you have created. The wealth needed to pay your wages will be created on the Monday morning, for the rest of the week you are creating what Marx called 'surplus value', but the work task you undertake on a Monday morning will be exactly the same as that which you do late on a Friday afternoon. In this sense, exploitation (the creation of surplus value) is hidden from view, buried within the production process. The surplus value created is used to pay power/energy costs, pay for raw materials and components, invest in new machinery, pay off bank loans or debts and is the source of all profits.

The owners of the means of production are always trying to increase the level of surplus value extraction. If they can reduce wages, or increase the speed of work, or lengthen the working day, it means that the worker will spend less time creating the wealth to pay for their wages and more time creating surplus value. By the same token, workers want higher wages, more holidays, a shorter working week, etc. In this way conflict is built into the system.

There is one further, crucially important feature to acknowledge. The reason the owners of the means of production want to increase the rate of worker exploitation is not simply because they are nasty or greedy individuals (though they may be, of course). The real reason is that capitalism is a system of competitive accumulation. It is a system of competing firms, each trying to get a bigger share of the market and each, effectively, trying to put their competitor out of business. Marx called the bourgeoisie 'a band of warring brothers': 'Capitalists are like hostile brothers who divide among themselves the loot of other people's labour' (Marx, 1863). What he meant here is that the bourgeoisie have a 'brotherly' interest in keeping their working-class opponents in place. But at the same time, they are constantly striving to outdo each other; they are in competition with each other and forever trying to force each other out of business, so they can command an ever greater share of the market and expand their profits.

This gives the system a relentless drive to expand and capitalism's insatiable drive has brought us, in the twenty-first century, to the edge of climate chaos and environmental destruction. It also means it is a system built upon regular cycles of economic booms and slumps – each following the other like night follows day. During economic downturns goods and resources are left unsold, or left to rot and workers face unemployment and are left facing a struggle to survive. But downturns also have beneficial effects for the system. During a downturn inefficient businesses will go bust (keeping the system as a whole 'leaner and fitter'), high unemployment will force workers to accept lower wages, low growth helps squeeze inflation out of the system and, together, these factors create the conditions for a new economic boom to take place. The boom/slump cycle causes periods of immense hardship to people (and emphasises that unemployment and poverty are not caused by individual failings but are a result of the workings of the system) but the cycle, by itself, does not threaten capitalism as a whole.

There is, however, one aspect of the workings of the system that is much more problematic for the system. Marx termed this the *'tendency of the rate of profit to fall'* and the impact of this tendency upon the system is to make the booms shorter and the slumps longer and deeper – intensifying the crisis-based nature of the system. The reason this happens is because the system is one of 'many competing capitals' (Rosdolsky, 1977). Because they are a 'band of warring brothers' each firm is constantly trying to put the other out of business and secure a greater share of the market for their goods. The 'best' way to do this is by making your goods cheaper than your rival's, and this happens if you can make 'your workers' take a wage cut or work longer during the day (but there are strict limits as to how far these can go), or produce more goods during the working day. This final option comes about, primarily, by investing in newer or bigger machinery, or some kind of technological advance. But there is a problem. Machines (Marx called them 'dead labour') do not create wealth, only 'living labour' does that. But the drive to new investment, the result of competition, means the costs of investment in capital (e.g. machines) gets larger than the investment costs in labour. Marx called this a rise in the 'organic composition of capital to labour'. The long-term consequence of this process is to undermine the general rate of profit, pushing slumps into depressions, from which there is no easy, or obvious, way out (see Harman, 2009; Roberts, 2016).

Marx's analysis shows capitalism to be a system of chaotic, unplanned growth, followed by economic slump and longer-term depression. It is a crisis-prone system. The regular economic crises bring immense hardship to people – people who are the victims of the anarchic nature of the system.

Capitalism has developed significantly, of course, since Marx's time. When he and Engels wrote the *Communist Manifesto* (1848) capitalism existed in Britain, France, Belgium, the Netherlands, and the Eastern Coast of the US. Today it is a truly global system. As it has grown it has become more integrated and more complex. Manufacturing and the production of goods remains at the heart of the system. Globally, there are very large numbers of people employed in manufacturing and some of them in gigantic factory complexes. For example, in China the Foxxcon Technology Group makes a range of electronic components from Intel-branded motherboards, to iPhones, to key components for all-electric cars. Their largest factory site is located in Longhua Town, Shenzhen, where it is estimated that up to 450,000 workers are employed at one of 15 factories on a 1.4 square mile site (Merchant, 2017).

But increasing numbers of people are involved in subsidiary tasks that form part of the production cycle. These people are not directly involved in productive labour – but Marx still considered them part of the working class. The Belgian Marxist Ernest Mandel argued that Marx had a 'broad definition' of the proletariat. He argued:

> The defining structural characteristic of the proletariat in Marx's analysis of capitalism is the socio-economic compulsion to sell one's labour power. Included in the proletariat, then, are not only manual industrial workers, but all unproductive wage-labourers who are subject to the same fundamental constraints … this definition of the proletariat includes the mass of … wage earners (not only commercial clerks and lower government employees, but domestic servants as well).
>
> *(Mandel, 1976: 48)*

Thus the working class is not just industrial workers such as miners, dockers or factory workers. It includes men and women, old and young working in shops, call-centre workers and health and welfare work. It includes teachers, social workers and nurses, for example. For Marx, all these people would be part of the modern working class.

Further, since Marx's time, the role of the state in the modern world has greatly expanded. The state is more than the elected government in any society. It includes institutions such as the armed forces, the police, the secret services, elements of the top civil service, and their links with networks of banks and industry. The primary role of the state is to protect the interests of the bourgeoisie and 'local capital' at home and abroad – and it does this by promoting the interests of major companies, engaging in political negotiations, establishing trading partners and – on occasion – threatening military action against perceived enemies.

But the state network also provides, or regulates for the provision of, a variety of services that help the system develop and 'reproduce itself'. This includes educational systems, health care systems and even social work activities. As the Marxist historian John Saville argued, the development of state welfare systems across the globe has reflected the interaction of three pressures on society. First, the needs of an increasingly complex socio-economic system (for better educated or healthier workers, for example). Second, the divisions at the top of society over the best way to maintain social harmony, or the best way to facilitate economic growth (for example, see the immense divisions dividing British society at present over their relationship to the EU). Finally, the pressure for social reform from political parties, or as a result of collective action, from those at the bottom of society (Saville, 1957). So, for Marxists, educational and social welfare systems have developed in contradictory ways, and to reflect contradictory pressures. This means they bring benefits to people, but also regulate their lives in various ways. In social work, for example, it means social work services can be about both 'care' and 'control' – the contradiction in the task a reflection of the contradictory nature of the social totality that is modern capitalism.

To conclude this section we can note that while the world may be more integrated and complex than in Marx's time, the importance of his analysis of capitalism is no less relevant. It is an analysis that identifies capitalism as a system that is:

1 *Divided by social classes.* The main determinant of one's class is whether one owns or controls the means of production (the bourgeoisie), or whether one has to sell one's labour power in order to survive (the working class). Today the majority of people in the world are part of the international working class.
2 *Built upon exploitation.* Only workers (living labour) create wealth, yet there is no mechanism that forces employers to pay workers the full return of the wealth they create. Instead employers extract 'surplus value' from workers – and this is where profits come from.
3 *Built upon boom/slump cycles.* The competition within the system means there are recurrent periods of economic boom and slump. But the tendency of the rate of profit to fall means that booms tend to get shallower and shorter and slumps tend to get longer and deeper. During periods of recession people's lives become harder, the struggle to survive more brutal.
4 *Destructive of people and planet.* Capitalism is a system of competitive accumulation. Unplanned competition within the system drives it forward relentlessly. This unplanned, chaotic process causes immense destruction to people's lives, our environment and to the ecological system.

For social workers these insights usefully frame our macro-understandings of the system within which we work. Social work service users are regularly blamed for the situation they find themselves in, but Marx's analysis shows that social problems such as poverty, unemployment and inequality, for example, are not caused by individual failings, they are a direct cause of the system and its priorities, these are the 'public causes of private pain' that Mills (1959) alluded to.

Within Marx's work, however, there is another very powerful concept that speaks to the impact of 'public causes' on private pain and trauma: this is his understanding of alienation. Writing alongside Iain Ferguson, I have argued that this is a powerful concept that can be applied to social work. In previous papers we suggested how it might be used to help understand aspects of domestic violence, male power and racism (Ferguson and Lavalette, 2004) and health, sexuality and changes to the social work labour process (Lavalette and Ferguson, 2018). What did Marx mean by alienation?

Alienation

The starting point for understanding Marx's concept of alienation is his view of human nature. Today when we hear the term 'human nature' it is often used to defend the most reactionary ideas. We are told that it is human nature to be greedy and selfish, when actually these are ideas that only really fit into the modern world of capitalism and when, in other types of societies, other virtues are promoted and identified as 'human'. Racism, sexism or homophobia are often defended on the grounds that it is only 'human nature' to look after 'our own' and be wary of 'the other', or for women to be carers, or for sex to be driven by the demands of procreation. And we are often told that human nature is fixed and 'can't be changed'

Let us start by making it clear that Marx had no truck with these notions of 'human nature' or the idea that it is fixed and untransmutable. He was aware of the huge variations in the ways in which people lived and worked together and rejected any notion of human nature that was unchanging. Instead, he argued that the dominant social relations of the society in which they live shape people's values, behaviours and feelings, as well as the ideas in their heads. But this does not mean that Marx did not have a concept of human nature. Rather, as Geras (1983) noted, in *Capital* Marx distinguished between what he called 'human nature in general' and 'human nature as historically modified in each epoch'.

What, then, did Marx mean by 'human nature in general'? First, Marx asserted that, in our essence, humans are socially productive animals. He believed that our human nature was expressed in a drive to spontaneously and creatively produce products in a manner that is conducive to social and individual satisfaction. In *Capital* Volume III he argued:

> Just as the savage must wrestle with Nature to satisfy his wants, to maintain and reproduce life, so must civilized man, and he must do so in all social formations and under all possible modes of production.
>
> *(Marx, 1894)*

Alongside the notion of humans as social producers, Geras (1983) argues that freedom and self-determination are key aspects of what it means to be human. As he points out:

> The need of people for a breadth and diversity of pursuit and hence of personal development, as Marx himself expresses these, 'all-round activity', 'all-round development of individuals', 'free development of individuals', 'the means of cultivating [one's] gifts in all directions', and so on.
>
> *(Geras, 1983: 72–73)*

Thus central to Marx's concept of 'human nature in general' was our open-endedness, our potential for development, for self-determination and freedom.

So while Marx's starting point was the basic needs of human beings – physical, social and psychological – beyond this, he saw human needs as fluid, dynamic and changing – our needs expand as societies develop and produce new needs. Furthermore, he located these needs and their satisfaction (or lack of satisfaction) within the conditions of class society. His theory of human needs and of human nature, therefore, provided the basis for a critique of class society and especially capitalism. As Terry Eagleton explains:

> Animals that are not capable of desire, complex labour and elaborate forms of communication tend to repeat themselves. Their lives are determined by natural cycles. They do not shape a narrative for themselves, which is what Marx knows as freedom. The irony in his view is that, though this self-determination is of the essence of humanity, the great majority of men and women throughout history have not been able to exercise it. They have not been permitted to be fully human. Instead, their lives have been determined for the most part by the dreary cycle of class society.
>
> *(Eagleton, 2011: 137–138)*

Class societies constrain human freedom and self-determination and thus restrict our ability to be fully human.

Within traditional social work literature, self-determination is usually seen in purely normative terms, as a value to which we should aspire and that we should encourage in our work with people using social work services. Marx, by contrast, rejected that distinction between 'is' and 'ought'. Self-determination, above all the ability consciously to control our labour, was a basic need and was what defined us as human. However, the satisfaction of that need was denied by a system that subordinated everything to the accumulation of capital. Under capitalism, for the first time in history, the great mass of the population – the working class – have completely lost control over both the means of production and the products of their labour: capitalism, therefore, alienates us from the essence of our human nature.

Marx identified three other dimensions of alienation. First, there was the lack of control over the work process. What distinguishes capitalism from earlier forms of production is that everything becomes a commodity, produced not primarily for use but for sale on the market. Moreover, that includes our labour power, our ability to work. When we sell that to an employer, we lose all control over how our time and our abilities are deployed. The result is that whereas in earlier types of society, individual craftsmen (and to a lesser extent, women) had a degree of control over their work and could take a pride in what they produced, under capitalism work simply becomes a chore and a burden. In Marx's own words:

> Labour is external to the worker i.e. does not belong to his essential being; that he therefore does not confirm himself in his work, but denies himself, feels miserable and not happy, does not develop free mental and physical energy, but mortifies his flesh and ruins his mind. Hence the worker feels himself only when he is not working; when he is working he does not feel himself. … His labour is therefore not voluntary but forced, it is forced labour. It is therefore not the satisfaction of a need but a mere means to satisfy needs outside itself. Its alien character is clearly demonstrated by the fact that as soon as no physical or other compulsion exists it is shunned like the plague.
>
> *(Marx, 1844)*

What the Marxist theorist Harry Braverman (1974) called 'the degradation of work in the twentieth century' has intensified in the era of neoliberalism. People are working longer, more intensively, in more regulated and controlled environments and levels of alienation are increasing.

Then there is alienation from other people. Most obviously, this concerns the relationship between worker and employer. In a capitalist society, the worker depends on the employer to provide her with work. At the same time, however, she resents and often hates that employer (or his immediate representative, the front-line manager) for exploiting, oppressing and bullying her. No less important, however, is the antagonism that capitalism creates between workers. We are made to see other workers as competitors for jobs or scarce resources. That relentless emphasis on the need to compete with others, coupled with the insecurity of the job market, are two features of life under capitalism that provide the ideological and material basis for the major divisions that characterise the world we live in, including racism, sexism and homophobia (Ferguson and Lavalette, 2004).

The third aspect of alienation identified by Marx was alienation of the worker from the product of her labour. This belongs to, and is disposed of, by the employer. In previous societies, people have used their creative abilities to produce goods that they would consume, exchange or sell. By contrast, under capitalism, the products of workers' labour confront them as alien objects. One aspect of this is that workers often cannot afford to buy the things – the iPhones, the expensive trainers, the cars – they produce.

There is a further aspect to consider here. Late capitalism has brought the spread of commodity production far deeper into areas of social life than was the case previously, almost every area of social life has become commodified. There used to be an old joke that said that capitalists would sell us the air we breathe if they could get away with it. In 2018 *The Guardian* newspaper ran a story about two businesses (one in Canada, one in Austria) selling bottles of 'mountain air' to wealthy customers in pollution-infested China and India – now even clean air has become a commodity to be bought and sold (Moshakis, 2018).

Increasingly, we are encouraged to express ourselves, to assert our individuality, through the purchase and consumption of ever greater quantities of commodities. We are told to aspire to be like any number of stars or people who are famous, simply because of their wealth. In the *Economic and Philosophical Manuscripts*, Marx (1844) described the power of money (the most fetishised of commodities) in this way:

> Money, inasmuch as it possesses the property of being able to buy everything and appropriate all objects, is the object most worth possessing … The extent of the power of money is the extent of my power. Money's properties are my – the possessor's – properties and essential powers. Thus, what I am and am capable of is by no means determined by my individuality. I am ugly, but I can buy for myself the most beautiful of women. Therefore I am not ugly, for the effect of ugliness – its deterrent power – is nullified by money. I, according to my individual characteristics, am lame, but money furnishes me with twenty-four feet. Therefore I am not lame. I am bad, dishonest, unscrupulous, stupid; but money is honoured, and hence its possessor. Money is the supreme good, therefore its possessor is good. Money, besides, saves me the trouble of being dishonest: I am therefore presumed honest. … Do not I, who thanks to money am capable of all that the human heart longs for, possess all human capacities? Does not my money, therefore, transform all my incapacities into their contrary?

Today, the fabulously wealthy express their power through money, shares and holdings, but also by the possession of commodities such as football and sports clubs, super-yachts, exclusive properties, fabulously expensive watches, cars, art, wine, coins and a range of other 'things' which assert their power and standing in society (Smith, 2016).

Modern consumerism means that we become objectified: it is the commodities that we purchase – the cheaper, paler imitations of those made for the wealthy – which come to define who we are.

For social workers, the concept of alienation is a powerful analytical tool that helps us understand the despair, isolation and lack of control people experience in their lives. These personal feelings, however, are not the result of individual biological or psychological aspects of life, rather, for Marx, they are the result of social processes, the consequence of life in modern capitalism.

Marx and social work

By way of a conclusion, in this final section I want draw upon the above discussion to suggest that Marxism can help us orientate to the world and guide our thinking and practice as social workers. It can do this, in particular, by taking cognisance of the following five themes:

1. *Understanding context – the 'public causes of private pain'*
   Marxism as a theory and a practice can guide us through the crises, conflicts and contradictions of the modern world. Marx's method allows us to analyse the dynamic of the system and to recognise that poverty, inequality, oppression and exploitation are endemic to

capitalism. Marx's analysis points to the structural roots of all manner of social and health problems – important because politicians, media commentators, policy analysts and even occasionally social workers (!), want to blame victims for the failings of the system. Marx's analysis allows us to look at the 'public causes of private pain'.

2. *Understanding the state: control and regulation*

   Marxism emphasises contradictions in the social world. State social work operates within a 'dialectic of care and control'. Some activities performed by social workers are controlling of service users, others are supportive and at times tasks can be both, at the same time. Our understanding of social work is enriched when we view it as a contradictory activity. Too often social work is promoted as a unified and uniform profession – but such an understanding hollows out the important role played by values, by judgement and by action within the social work task. It also ignores the fact that social work is divided by politics and differing conceptions of its tasks. Historically social work has been involved in a range of tasks which Ferguson et al. (2017) describe as 'horrible histories' – carrying out tasks, uncritically, on behalf of the state and at huge cost to service users. Social work in the UK, for example, was deeply implicated in the scandal of 'children of empire' when looked after children were 'exported' across the former empire and often found themselves facing abusive living circumstances (Bean and Melville, 1989). There are other examples when social work has stood alongside the oppressed and disadvantaged in their fight for a better world (Schilde, 2009).

3. *Understanding social work – as work*

   Marxism emphasises that social work is a work task in the modern world – and social workers are workers. Currently, across the globe, new models of working in social work (where social workers operate in increasingly marketised systems, within a target-driven culture) are leading to reduction in space for worker discretion. The task is increasingly controlled, by managers and by IT systems, and space for interaction with service users is being squeezed – producing a work arena that is increasingly alienating (Yuill, 2018). This is not what many social workers come into the profession for – but it emphasises that front-line social work is a contested work task and that workers need to organise together to protect and promote their conception of a social justice-driven profession fighting to support people's needs and rights.

4. *Understanding service users' lives*

   The contemporary world produces isolation and alienation. People feel powerless in the face of neo-liberal marketisation, consumerism and individualism. These impact on all our lives, but are often felt particularly acutely by service users. For many social work service users it is poverty, inequality and oppression which impact upon their lives. The actions of state and welfare agencies can exacerbate difficulties. Debates led by politicians and media commentators can fuel hostility toward service user groups. In all these areas, a social work informed by Marxism promotes a deep understanding of complex lives and motivates social work action in defence of service user rights.

5. *There is no 'Marxist social work method'*

   Finally, it is important to stress that there is no 'Marxist social work method'. Marxism provides an 'orientation' onto the world. It helps us to understand people's complex lives in the context of present unequal and oppressive societies. But it does not determine a particular social work approach or method. Of course, because social problems are overwhelmingly viewed as 'structural' in origin, then most Marxists in social work would tend to more collective approaches – and would certainly look to collectivise social problems where possible and appropriate. Nevertheless, social workers influenced by Marxism will be perfectly at ease working with individuals, with groups and with communities.

But this should not be taken to mean that Marxism is of only intellectual interest: a radical social work theory confined to the university and social work theory. Marxism can inform social work practice. Fundamentally, what Marx allows us to understand are the social and indeed the structural causes of the human misery that we see in much of our day-to-day social work practice. It is by understanding the essentially social nature of this that we can develop a social work practice committed to social action informed by social justice, to fighting for people's rights (individually and collectively) and to asserting that 'another world is possible'.

References

Bean, P. and Melville, J. (1989) *Lost Children of the Empire: The Untold Story of Britain's Child Migrants* (London: Unwin and Hyman).
Braverman, H. (1974) *Labour and Monopoly Capitalism* (New York: Monthly Review).
Eagleton, T. (2011) *Why Marx was Right* (Yale University Press).
Elliott, L. (2018) Inequality gap widens as 42 people hold same wealth as 3.7bn poorest. *The Guardian*, 22 Jan 2018. Available at: www.theguardian.com/inequality/2018/jan/22/inequality-gap-widens-as-42-people-hold-same-wealth-as-37bn-poorest
Ferguson, I. and Lavalette, M. (2004) Beyond power discourse: Alienation and social work. *British Journal of Social Work*, Vol. 34, pp. 304.
Ferguson, I. Ioakimidis, V. and Lavalette, M. (2017) *Global Social Work in a Political Context: Radical Perspectives* (Bristol: Policy Press).
Geras, N. (1983) *Marx and Human Nature: Refutation of a Legend* (London: Verso).
Harman, C. (2009) *Zombie Capitalism* (London: Bookmarks).
Lavalette, M. and Ferguson, I. (2018) Marx: Alienation, commodity fetishism and the world of contemporary social work. *Critical and Radical Social Work*, Vol 6: 2, pp. 197–213.
Mandel, E. (1976) *Introduction to Marx, K Capital*, Vol. 1 (Harmondsworth: Penguin).
Marx, K. (1843) Introduction. A contribution to the critique of Hegel's philosophy of right (originally published in Deutsch-Französische Jahrbücher, 7 & 10 February 1844, Paris). Available at Marxists Internet Archive: www.marxists.org/archive/marx/works/1843/critique-hpr/intro.htm
Marx, K. (1844) Economic and philosophical manuscripts. Available at Marxist Internet Archive: www.marxists.org/archive/marx/works/1844/epm/index.htm
Marx, K. (1845) The German ideology: Critique of modern german philosophy according to its representatives Feuerbach, B. Bauer and Stirner, and of German Socialism according to its various prophets. Available at the Marxist Internet Archive: www.marxists.org/archive/marx/works/1845/german-ideology/ch01a.htm
Marx, K. (1863) Theories of surplus-value, Vol. II. Available at Marist Internet Archive: www.marxists.org/archive/marx/works/1863/theories-surplus-value/ch08.htm
Marx, K. (1894) Capital, Vol. III. Available at Marxist Internet Library: www.marxists.org/archive/marx/works/subject/hist-mat/capital/vol3-ch48.htm
Marx, K. and Engels, F. (1848) The manifesto of the communist party. Available at Marxist Internet Archive: www.marxists.org/archive/marx/works/1848/communist-manifesto/ch01.htm
Merchant, B. (2017) Life and death in Apple's forbidden city. *The Observer*, 18 June. Available at: https://www.theguardian.com/technology/2017/jun/18/foxconn-life-death-forbidden-city-longhua-suicide-apple-iphone-brian-merchant-one-device-extract
Mills, C. W. (1959) *The Sociological Imagination* (New York: Oxford University Press).
Moshakis, A. (2018) Fresh air for sale. *The Observer*, 21 January. Available at: www.theguardian.com/global/2018/jan/21/fresh-air-for-sale
Rees, J. (1998) *The Algebra of Revolution* (London: Routledge).

Roberts, M. (2016) *The Long Depression* (Chicago, IL: Haymarket books).

Rosdolsky, R. (1977) *The Making of Marx's 'Capital'* (London: Pluto).

Saville, J. (1957) The welfare state: An historical approach. The New Reasoner No.3, Winter 1957–58, pp. 5–25. Available at: https://www.marxists.org/archive/saville/1957/xx/welfare.htm

Schilde, K. (2009) Oppressed today – The winners tomorrow. The ways and works of International Red Aid. A communist world organisation in the force field between Government oppression and social work for political prisoners. In Haus, G. and Schulte, D. (eds) *Amid Social Contradictions* (Leverkusen: Barbara Budrich Publishers).

Smith, M.N. (2016) These are the 11 things the 'ultra-rich' are spending their money on. Business Insider, 3 March. Available at: http://uk.businessinsider.com/things-rich-people-are-buying-more-of-in-last-ten-years-2016-3?r=US&IR=T/#cars--yes-wealthy-people-still-really-like-cars-knight-frank-recorded-a-490-growth-in-the-price-of-automobiles-in-the-10-years-since-its-last-luxury-index-report-supercars-which-can-cost-over-a-1-million-in-some-cases-are-popular-but-the-report-said-that-eight-of-the-25-cars-ever-to-have-sold-for-over-10-million-at-auction-went-under-the-hammer-in–2015-1

Yuill, C. (2018) Social workers and alienation: The compassionate self and the disappointed juggler. *Critical and Radical Social Work*, Vol. 6: 3, pp. 275–290.

3

Reaching back to go forward

Applying the enduring philosophy of Jane Addams to modern-day social work education

Carolyn Hanesworth

MERCY COLLEGE, NEW YORK

Introduction

This chapter will examine the life, work, and philosophy of Jane Addams as a means to re-invigorate social work education. Jane Addams emerged as a pioneer in social welfare in the years just following the Gilded Age of the late 1800s, and her work was largely in response to its consequences (Davis, 1973). According to historians, we are currently living in the "second Gilded Age" (Schlozman, Brady, & Verba, 2018). The social work profession, with its mission to enhance the wellbeing of all human beings, particularly the vulnerable, oppressed, and poor (NASW, 2019), should be well poised to address the poverty and the structures that cause it. However, due to pressures since the advent of neoliberalism in the 1970s, the field now leans heavily toward a behavioral health orientation that emphasizes altering individuals rather than the structures that promote their poverty (Morley & Ablett, 2017; Reisch, 2013; Reisch & Jani, 2012). This tension is hardly new, and Addams confronts it head on in her autobiography, *Twenty Years at Hull House* (Addams, 1912). In an attempt to cultivate valuable lessons from social work's foremost pioneer, this chapter will begin with an overview of Addams' life, followed by a review of the most salient ideas from Addams' work as they relate to modern-day social problems and their application to social work education. Specifically, these include: Addams' main philosophy and its relevance to the aforementioned trend of devaluing structural intervention, and Addams' and John Dewey's views on democracy.

Background and context

Jane Addams remains one of the most significant pioneers in the history of social welfare. At the turn of the twentieth century, Addams was famous in America for her roles as a social reformer, suffrage leader, and peace activist. She is perhaps most well known for co-founding Hull House in 1889, the Chicago settlement house where Addams began her groundbreaking work on the front lines of urban poverty. In 1931, Jane Addams became the first woman to receive the Nobel

Peace Prize, for her anti-war efforts and international peace building work. Addams served as the chair of the International Congress of Women at the Hague in 1915. She took part in the effort to form the American Civil Liberties Union and established the International League for Peace and Freedom in 1919. Addams worked to prevent the United States' entry into World War I, which caused her to be labeled a dangerous radical by the United States government (Hamington, 2009).

Addams did not have formal social work training, and her work at Hull House consisted mainly of trial and error. In her autobiographical account, *Twenty Years at Hull House*, she describes an internal grappling with the most basic and critical of social issues, many of which persist today, including labor, racism, immigration, poverty and inequality, women's rights, and child protection. Along the way, Addams developed a philosophical approach that is uncannily relevant to modern-day social workers, who find themselves, as Addams did, grappling with social problems in the context of deep cultural divisions and extreme political views. Instead of adopting the views of society, Addams allowed the poor themselves, who were neighbors of Hull House, to directly shape her ideas, as she believed that "nobody so poignantly realizes the failures of the social structure as the man [*sic*] at the bottom, who has been in direct contact with those failures and has suffered the most" (Addams, 1961, p. 122). On a fundamental level, Jane Addams was a deeply compassionate humanitarian and a pragmatist. Her work was, by nature, intensely political, although she did not set out to take sides, but rather to bring opposing sides together. She was a humble learner, an observer of human nature, and an accomplished philosopher, although not recognized as such until the 1990s (Whipps, 1998). Addams believed that improving the lives of the poor ultimately lifted our entire culture, even benefitting those who claimed not to care about them, as those people mattered to her too. This idea is critically important today, in an era when society is deeply divided and entrenched in ideologically opposing views about the causes and nature of poverty (Hunt & Bullock, 2016). During a time of polarization, similar to our current day, Jane Addams approached from the standpoint of an observer in full acknowledgment of her bias and privilege, with openness to learning, to being corrected, and to changing her view. The only strong opinion she had was that human misery should be understood and ameliorated, whatever the source, and whomever the victim. Whatever worked to achieve that outcome became her course of action.

There is an abundance of literature on Jane Addams that lists the details of her work at Hull House, and her subsequent peace work in her later years. This chapter will not attempt to repeat these, but will instead focus on the philosophy behind her work and the manner in which she arrived at her ideas, as a means to find lessons of value for the current day. There are undeniable parallels between the social problems at the turn of the twentieth century and today. Both time periods – the Progressive Era (1890s–1920s) and the current day (the time period between the advent of neoliberalism in the 1970s and 2019) – have brought increases in poverty, inequality, overt acts of racism, hostility toward immigrants and women, and political corruption (Bartels, 2018). Both time periods came after a period of rapid but concentrated economic gain for a limited few, and economic crisis for the rest. Others have suggested a resurrection of Jane Addams' philosophy, and those interested in this topic should note that there have been more extensive volumes dedicated to her life and work, with commentary on its modern-day applications (Hamington, 2009; Knight, 2010; Shields, 2011, 2016). Hamington (2009), Knight (2010), and Shields (2011, 2016) have suggested a resurrection of Jane Addams' philosophy and produced extensive volumes dedicated to her life, and the practical applications of her work in the current day.

Jane Addams did not have direct feelings or guidance for social work education because –it hardly existed in her time. The first school of social work – the Summer School in Philanthropic

Work established in New York – appeared in 1898, nine years after the founding of Hull House. However, she had significant ideas about education in general, which were developed alongside those of John Dewey, the pre-eminent educational philosopher of the same era. The life and work of Jane Addams has always been taught to social work students, but is often simplified into a historical presentation of her work as the Hull House settlement house founder, and a progressive social justice pioneer. Admittedly, the literature on Jane Addams is significant and extensive, and cannot be fully captured in the span of this chapter, much less an introductory level social work course. My purpose here is to attempt a targeted curation of her work by illuminating Addams' philosophical stance toward social and economic justice as it applies to modern-day social work education and the specific challenges we face today. This chapter will begin with an overview of Addams' life, and then attempt to (1) cultivate from Addam's expansive body of work the most salient ideas as they relate to modern-day social problems, and (2) apply these ideas to a re-invigoration of social work education, incorporating the values and philosophy of John Dewey. Much of the content here is taken directly from Addams' autobiography, *Twenty Years at Hull House*, primarily because Hull House was the environment in which her ideas about the poor emerged, but also because it is written in her own words.

Jane Addams: early years

Jane Addams was born in 1860, right on the cusp of the Civil War. Her family lived in Cedarville, Illinois and was rooted in the Protestant work ethic that permeated American life at the time. Jane lost her mother at age two, and subsequently became very close to her father, John Addams. John Addams was a staunch conservative, a devout supporter of Lincoln, and a self-made man who made his fortune in sawmills, railroad investments, and various other pursuits. The Addams family, like others of their generation, valued hard work, achievement, integrity, and commitment (Addams, 1961).

John Addams was supportive of education for women and sent Jane and her sister to the Female Seminary in Rockford, Illinois. Like most men of his era, he did not believe education for women should lead to a professional life, but that it should serve to improve their roles as wives and mothers. Davis (1973) concludes that the conflicting messages of realizing one's full intellectual potential only to maintain a submissive, domestic existence, served as a source of internal conflict for Jane. Jane Addams came of age during a time of tremendous transition in the western world. In 1860, the year of her birth, a society formerly dependent on agriculture was completing its shift to industry. The "problems of industry" came with this shift, and included immigration, poverty, and poor labor conditions. In this era, women were the first to hold professional jobs, to vote, to attend college, and to escape the confines of domestic labor. Jane Addams' young life was set in the latter part of the Gilded Age, a time of rampant economic expansion spurred by the railroad and the development of factories, and the steel and coal industries. Along with this growth came the rise of a small but very wealthy class of citizens, many of whom became rich due to the lack of government regulations on industry, as well as greed and corruption (Calhoun, 2006).

Addams' college years were extremely influential. Science and critical thought were emerging, which led her to question religion and the prescribed roles of women in society. Her work reveals a young scholar grappling with the desire to do something meaningful in a world that still viewed women as subservient and domestic. In a college debate, Jane declared that men had finally come to the realization that women had an intellect, and that women's education was a pathway for women to move beyond the confines of simply pleasing others. Her senior paper, titled *Cassandra*, revealed a leaning toward feminist views. Cassandra was a prophetess, a Trojan woman who predicted the victory of the Greeks and her father's defeat in the destruction of Troy, but nobody would listen to her. Jane concluded that this is the plight of all women – to know the truth but not to have their words or facts believed by men. She idealized a world where feminine qualities of intuition would be valued in a world quickly becoming mechanized. She believed that what women needed was the power, the authority, and the right to speak (Davis, 1973). These views, coupled with her deep abiding respect for democracy, were precursors to her philosophy and life's work.

Addams grew up in a community greatly impacted by losses during the Civil War. Although very young during its aftermath, Addams acutely perceived the pain and grief of her neighbors, whom she learned had lost sons so that slaves could be freed. She, like her father, was an admirer of Abraham Lincoln and all that he stood for. John Addams was a member of the Illinois State Senate between 1854 and 1870, and so, for the first ten years of her life, Addams was entrenched in an atmosphere of political engagement, civic duty, and patriotism: "My father always spoke of the martyred president as Mr. Lincoln, and I never heard the great name without a thrill" (Addams, 1961, p. 20). Lincoln, for Jane, epitomized the idea that ordinary people are the core, the foundation, and the future of the country. Jane felt that Lincoln gave Americans the "title" to modern democracy, and that this remained America's greatest gift to the world.

Between graduating from the Seminary, and founding Hull House, Jane spent eight years in a state of confusion and frustration about her future. She experienced a long bout of illness that left her bedridden for six months following a failed attempt at medical school. She ached with the knowledge that she wanted to "to live fully in the world, and not in the intellectual shadow of it", but despaired over how to do so. Jane's idea for a settlement house was ultimately influenced by her travels to the East End of London and the famed settlement house, Toynbee Hall. This was her first exposure to abject poverty, and she shares a disturbing recollection of people bidding at a late Saturday food auction – where spoiled and rotting food from the week's market was sold at bargain prices to the poor. She later recalls feeling as though nothing else she experienced on her travels after that was "real" except the pain and degradation she witnessed there: "In time all huge London came to seem unreal save the poverty in its East End" (Addams, 1961, p. 44).

Jane describes her despair at this time as a type of spiritual poverty experienced by being too idle and too comfortable to fully experience life. In a sense she felt that the extreme ends on the spectrum from material wealth to poverty brought a similar sort of moral deprivation. For the rich – especially for wealthy women – being sheltered from life's hardships led to a depressing moral decay. Along the same vein, the poor were also kept from developing a spiritual and cultural inner life as their entire existence was given over to the business of survival. She longed to act, to be involved, and to experience the hardness of life. She was by no means a martyr, and did not do this from a sense of guilt, but rather from the pragmatic conclusion that this was the best and most meaningful way to live.

The founding of Hull House

In 1889, Jane Addams, together with her partner Ellen Gates Starr, founded Hull House at age 29. Starr was a classmate of Addams at Rockford Seminary, and accompanied her on her trip to London and Toynbee Hall. They were both domestic partners and collaborators in the evolution of Hull House. Starr was responsible for establishing the Butler Art Gallery and a bookbindery at Hull House. She was a staunch social advocate in her own right, working alongside Addams to reform child labor laws and improve industrial working conditions in Chicago (Starr, 2019). Addams and Starr founded Hull House just as the Gilded Age was giving way to the Progressive

Era, which was characterized by its reaction to the problems caused by the Gilded Age, including immigration, urbanization, industrialization, and political corruption (Calhoun, 2006). Reform in these four areas comprised the bulk of the work at Hull House.

The reformist settlement house movement actually emerged in the 1880s in London, and persisted until the 1920s. Its purpose was to establish a residence wherein members of all different backgrounds, social, and economic classes could live and work together for the purpose of social, cultural, intellectual exchange, and the alleviation of poverty. Settlement houses provided services, such as after-school or child care and healthcare, but also education in the form of classes, clubs, lectures, and workshops on topics ranging from art and literature, to domestic and employment-based skills. Residents of settlement houses served as teachers but also students, regardless of class or ethnicity. They included the residents of the neighboring community as well as well-educated professionals – most of whom lived there as a means to learn more about social problems and reform (Reinders, 1982).

Addams and Starr chose to locate Hull House in a west Chicago community populated by immigrants and entrenched in poverty. They did not have specific plans as they set out, but rather allowed the settlement to evolve naturally, with the belief that its existence justified itself. Reflecting on development of the settlement, Jane noted,

> I think that time has also justified our early contention that the mere foothold of a house, easily accessible, ample in space, hospitable, and tolerant in spirit, situated in the large foreign colonies which so easily isolate themselves in American cities, would be a serviceable thing in Chicago.
>
> *(Addams, 1961, p. 59)*

Although it seemed peculiar to some that Addams and Starr would give up their comfortable lives to live modestly, and side by side with the poor, Addams felt this was a more natural state for people to live in, rather than being separated by wealth. She reasoned that "Hull House was soberly opened on the theory that (the) dependence of classes on each other is reciprocal", and that

> in time it came to seem natural that the settlement should be there. If it is natural to feed the hungry and care for the sick, it is certainly natural to give pleasure to the young, comfort to the aged, and to minister to the deep seated craving for social intercourse that all men feel.
>
> *(Addams, 1961, p. 72)*

Addams firmly believed that isolating the poor damages them, and that this damage is then used to justify further isolating them.

Although she is considered the "mother of social work", she did not use the term social worker to describe herself, and she did not view the settlement house as a social service center, although people were served there. Hull House was a communal living space where people of differing classes and ethnicities could intermingle naturally. At times people would be served or be helped depending on what the circumstances dictated, but to Addams this made it a proper human community – not a place where the "haves" give to the "have-nots". In that sense, it was not meant to be a place where educated, wealthy people came to serve the poor, but rather where the poor and rich came to exist among each other, to learn from one another and expand their own inner lives and cultures. However, it would always remain true that it was the privilege of the wealthy, educated residents (including Addams) to make this choice, and this was not lost on Addams. They could always walk away and resume a comfortable life, whereas the poor could not leave the reality of the west side of Chicago – a place that was characterized by poor sanitation, pollution, overcrowding, hunger, and dilapidated tenements. Addams was acutely aware of this, and did not pretend that her circumstances were equal, as they could never be (Addams, 1961).

Although many settlement houses were run by churches and infused Christian values into their activities, Hull House was mainly secular, and Addams has been identified by some as a secular humanist (Pois, 1999; Scimecca & Goodwin, 2003). Addams was a Christian, and had extensive religious training, but viewed Christianity as a belief system that should be embodied throughout a person's life and in their behavior toward others, and less so as a set of principles meant to be rigidly applied or imposed on those of other religions. Some in the literature (Redi, Linder, Shelley, Stout, & Noll, 2002; Tangenberg, 2003) have characterized her attempts to have Bible study at Hull House as evidence that its purpose was, in part, as a place to convert the residents of the neighborhood, but in her own words, Addams describes these activities as a means to simply provide a place for spiritual community. Although she attempted to institute a type of non-secular spiritual service, she ultimately abandoned the idea, feeling it was too hard to accommodate the multiple and various faiths in one activity without diluting each person's beliefs (Addams, 1961).

Addams and Starr were joined at Hull House by several other well-known social justice pioneers, including Florence Kelley, Alice Hamilton, Julia Lathrop, Sophonisba Breckinridge, and Grace and Edith Abbott. The modern-day definitions of micro, mezzo, and macro social work would have seemed odd to this group, whose days were infused by all three quite naturally. Addams and her colleagues engaged extensively in social reform efforts, including lobbying for an eight-hour work day for women, improved labor and housing tenement conditions, and the first juvenile court of law. Her efforts led to the formation of the Juvenile Protection Association (JPA), which provided the first juvenile probation officers in the United States. The JPA went on to address child labor and exploitation, child abuse, neglect, and prostitution. In 1910, Addams went on to become the first female president of the National Conference on Social Work (Hamington, 2009; Shields, 2016).

Addams' central guiding philosophy was her emphasis on the dignity and worth of all human life; a value steadfastly maintained in today's Social Work Code of Ethics (Reamer). In her recollections of Hull House, Addams consistently returns to an observation of "good" in all the various people she encounters. She marvels at the warmth, kindness, and generosity of those in the direst of life states, and remarks of her time at Hull House, that

> in the words of Canon Barnett, the things which make men alike are finer and better than the things that keep them apart, and that these basic likenesses, if they are properly accentuated, easily transcend the less essential difference of race, language, creed, and tradition.
>
> *(Addams, 1961, p. 73)*

The philosophy of Jane Addams

Addams, along with John Dewey and George Herbert Mead, developed the philosophy of Classic American pragmatism, although she was not recognized for her role in this until the 1990s (Hamington, 2009; Shields, 2011; Whipps, 1998). Pragmatism, the most significant American contribution to philosophy, has its roots in a post-Civil War response to absolutism and rigid thinking, which Menand (2001) felt was a way of thinking that ultimately led to the Civil War. William James, Oliver Wendell Homes, Jr., and Charles Pierce first conceived of pragmatism in 1872 in Cambridge, Massachusetts. The theory explains that a set of ideas hold true insofar as they can be successfully tested in actual experience. Knowledge, therefore, develops in the interface between human beings and their environment (Pfeiffer, 2003). Pierce was a mentor to John Dewey, whose work as a Progressive Era reformer and philosopher has led him to be identified as the most significant contributor to American philosophy (Hickman & Alexander, 1998). Dewey applied pragmatism to education and democracy, and whereas Pierce viewed "inquiry as a self correcting process whose procedures and norms must be evaluated and revised in the light of subsequent experience ... Dewey regarded this reworking as a social and communal process" that was based in the experiences of ordinary people (Ormerod, 2006, p. 893). For the pragmatist, truth is determined by what works given a certain environment, therefore truth shifts as the environment shifts. Dewey's belief that social action and knowledge were interdependent led him to intellectually partner with Addams and the work of Hull House. As Dewey was constructing and developing his theory, Addams was actually living and testing it, however some scholars believe that Addams has not been duly credited for her part in developing American pragmatism (Hamington, 2009; Shields, 2011, 2005; Whipps, 1998). Dewey himself credits her with helping him develop his ideas, however her noted absence in the literature on early American philosophy is evidence of the marginalization women philosophers endured throughout the twentieth century (Whipps, 1998). Dewey and Addams became very close friends and colleagues, so much so that Dewey used her books in his courses, named his daughter after her, and further credited Addams with helping him shape his views on education and democracy (Hamington, 2009; Shields, 2011).

Addams' brand of pragmatism has been identified as feminist, because she applied it to the experiences of women, but she did not set out to create this precedent and did not identify with feminism (Addams, 1961). Her approach valued social cohesion and cooperation above the value of ideas from any one group, be they socialists, feminists, labor unions, or political bosses. She was neither a capitalist nor a socialist, and in today's polarized political climate may have been viewed a moderate, or a person without party. She eschewed extremism in any form. In her presidential address to the Conference on Charity and Corrections (1910, p. 23), she remarked:

> Is it because our modern industrialization is so new that we have been slow to connect it with the poverty all around us? The socialists talk constantly of the relation of economic wrong to destitution and point out the connection between industrial maladjustment and individual poverty, but the study of social conditions, the obligation to eradicate poverty, cannot belong to one political party nor to one economic school, and after all it was not a socialist, but that ancient friend of the poor, St. Augustine, who said, "thou givest bread to the hungry, but better were it that none hungered and thou had'st no need to give him."

Addams did not seek to promote a community that adhered to one set of values, but a space that allowed for debate, cooperation, and competing ideas to result in a true collective social progress. In the spirit of pragmatism, she was not interested in who was right, she was interested in what worked in terms of alleviating human misery – both at the point of manifestation and at its roots. At all times, she combined the pursuit of theoretical understanding with practical social action in pursuit of this goal. She was fiercely non-partisan and had what Brown (as cited in Reardon, 2006) called "more 'floor space' in it than any other I have known. She could set a subject down, unprejudiced, and walk all around it, allowing fairly for everyone's point of view." This approach has remarkable applicability to today's political divisiveness, both in our communities and in our classrooms.

Hamington (2009) characterizes Addams' philosophy as critical feminist pragmatism that is centered on her notion of "sympathetic knowledge". Sympathetic knowledge is gained in the interaction between two human beings via the (openness to) disruption of previously held knowledge. Learning does not just come in the form of facts, but in one's openness to new experience, and to letting go of previously formed knowledge. This idea is at the core of the settlement house movement, which positions people of various backgrounds into one physical space, thereby removing distance that causes people to think in terms of "us" and "them". Addams demonstrated through her own experiences and observation that active and empathic caring for others had the power to disrupt previously held ideas. There are many examples of this in her chronicles of Hull House, which was a place of discovery grounded in real-life experience (Addams, 1961).

Prior to Hull House, Addams herself was somewhat naive to social injustices, other than what she had observed on her travels. She recounts first learning of the issue of child labor after encountering a group of young children who refused the offer of candy because they had worked 12-hour days in candy factories and could not bear to eat it. Addams surely abhorred the reality of child labor, but was able to set this aside in order to more deeply understand the problem from various points of view. She sought to understand what causes a parent to allow their child to work. What causes a company to pursue children as employees? She seeks the nuances, the less obvious or hidden truths in what would seem, on the surface, a case of bad policy, but in doing so she discovers how to best approach a successful effort for reform. In *Twenty Years at Hull House*, Jane reflects on her efforts to understand what caused families to send their children to work:

> We learned to know many families in which the working children contributed to the support of their parents, not only because they spoke English better than the older immigrants and were willing to take lower wages, but because their parents gradually found it easy to live upon their earnings. A South Italian peasant who has picked olives and packed oranges from his toddling babyhood cannot see at once the difference between the outdoor healthy work which he had performed in the varying seasons and the long hours of factory life which his child encounters when he goes to work in Chicago.
>
> *(Addams, 1961, p. 133)*

From this comes an understanding that reform must address the needs of the children, but encompass worries and burdens of the parent. Addams knew that simply changing the laws would not protect children if communities did not address the plight of a poor household that depended on the child's wages for survival. In this way, Addams approached each situation by viewing it in its entirety, and from a position of being open to new ideas (sympathetic knowledge) based on her experiences with the families, from the micro level suffering to the macro level laws that allowed for it.

In her writings, Addams reflects on the social interactions at Hull House as a true education, because they broke down barriers and allowed a person to experience another person's life view. This was particularly apparent in her empathy for immigrant parents, who experienced the difficulties of acculturation and the pain of losing their purpose in the old country. She recalls, "I was walking down Polk Street, perturbed in spirit, because it seemed so difficult to come into genuine relations with Italian women and because they themselves had lost their hold upon their Americanized children" (Addams, 1961, p. 156). From this, Addams, with the help of Dewey, devised to create a "bridge" between American and European experiences by creating classes and exhibits on the old crafts, as a means to draw in immigrant children and expose them to their heritage, and to the antecedents of modern factory-made clothing. This evolved into the Hull House Labor Museum. This was but one of many activities, including literature, theater, and art, that was infused with the notion that a healthy democracy depends on the ability to imagine and empathize with an "other". In this way, sympathetic knowledge is a form of education, which is essential to democracy.

The philosophy of Addams applied to modern-day social work education

Although Addams was not directly involved with social work education in colleges and universities, she was a leader in the profession as it emerged, and her opinions on the state of the profession can be extrapolated from her early speeches and writings. In the following section, I attempt to draw upon these ideas to make some suggestions about the value of her philosophy in the context of modern-day social work education. This approach could reasonably include Addams' entire breadth of work, as the issues she touched are all related to social work today, including immigration, women's issues, unemployment and labor, poverty, and child welfare, and others. I have therefore chosen to focus on two broad areas that encompass the myriad social issues she addressed, and that seem most salient to current trends in social work education. These include: the relevancy of Addams' philosophy when considering (in modern terms) macro vs. micro levels of social work, and the application of Addams' and John Dewey's views on democracy and *radical inclusion* to modern social work education.

Micro and macro

In her presidential address to the 1910 Conference on Social Work, Addams focused on the transition of the profession from one of charity and amelioration, to one of research, prevention, advocacy, and structural reform (Addams, 1910). She skillfully characterizes the front line charitable workers as perfect partners to the "radicals" whose efforts were directed not at the alleviation of immediate suffering, but rather to restructuring the society causing it. Addams made a case for the resolution of poverty as possible only when there is a marriage between the micro and the macro level (or formerly known as cause and function) approaches; a stance sorely needed in today's social work curricula (Reisch, 2016; Rothman & Mizrahi, 2014). Addams believed the blending of these two approaches was intrinsic to any real effort to eradicate poverty. As she stated:

> [B]ut is it not true that the members of this Conference who have been brought close to suffering, feebleness and wrong-doing, are but fulfilling a paramount obligation when they take up the study of social conditions? Does not the obligation to trace poverty back to its immediate or contributing sources belong foremost and professionally to those whose business it is to care for the wounded in the unequal battle of modern industry?
>
> *(Addams, 1910, p. 2)*

Social work has since skewed heavily to a direct practice, or micro-oriented focus due to market trends that reward direct practice work (particularly in behavioral health) over work in the areas of community, policy, and advocacy. Today's students are not choosing career tracks focused on structural advocacy (Reisch, 2013), despite a mandate from the Council on Social Work Education (CSWE) for programs to "advance human rights, and social, economic, and environmental justice" (CSWE, 2015, n.p.). A reintegration of micro and macro work would challenge the usefulness of their isolation, which has been driven by social work's need to engage in a market driven by health and behavioral sciences. Focusing on the problems in the individual presumes they are the source of and the solution to their problems (Reisch, 2013).

Education, democracy and Dewey

Fischer, (2013, p. 227) explains that for both Addams and Dewey, democracy is a "way of life … through which individuals' potentialities can flourish," and these extended beyond the political realm into the cultural, social, and intellectual. This was extremely progressive at the time, since the political sphere did not include women, and although Black men could vote, they were systematically marginalized and oppressed. Essentially, Dewey and Addams were attempting to bring democracy to all people through other means, which was radical and bold. The very nature of Addams' position as a woman confronting these issues was an act of political and social defiance. Quite notably, Addams did not become a socialist, but held fast to her belief in democracy (Addams, 1961). Literature on the gender wage gap (England & Gad, 2002) emphasizes the difference between *equality* of people and *equity*, with the former being a declaration of position, and the latter an accumulation of benefits and resources acquired from that (supposed) position. Whereas the articles of democracy may declare citizens equal, this does not guarantee their equity, and the wealth gap is an example of how this manifests. This was not a new concept for Addams, as she witnessed it first hand at Hull House. Democracy is a necessary but not sufficient condition for *equity*, as it is supposed to be an environment where citizens can interact and influence each other as they reach for a more unified and just society that benefits all, and yet chronic poverty prevents this participation. Addams was acutely aware that democracy did not extend to all in her Chicago neighborhood, and while she worked on their behalf to secure safe working conditions, minimum standards for sanitation, and child labor restrictions, she placed the most value on avenues available for their participation in democracy (Addams, 1961). In the chapter entitled, "The Subjective Necessity for Social Settlements", Addams argued that the purpose of a settlement was to *socialize* democracy, especially among those whose poverty kept them from understanding civil engagement, or having the time, energy, and will to engage in it (Addams, 1912). Participation in democracy depends on access to civil discourse, to information, to common spaces and dialogue with others so that an opinion can be formed and acted upon.

In essence, both Dewey and Addams felt that education meant raising the critical consciousness. Helping social work students to raise their own critical consciousness and to pass that forward to their clients is crucial for social change, particularly at a time when higher education is moving away from the liberal arts (Baker & Baldwin, 2015). Addams had a very nuanced view of politics, education, economics, law, and history and drew on her understanding of these disciplines to inform her philosophy and approach. Social work programs today rely on a liberal arts curriculum to create a foundational understanding in these disciplines, but these too are under threat as universities are pressured to vocationalize the general curriculum and emphasize science, technology, engineering, and math in response to market pressures (Hanesworth, 2017). Social work students often do not have a basic understanding of political economy, which is essential in understanding the mechanisms behind poverty and inequality (Tully, Nadel, & Lesser, 2005). In our current socially and politically divided climate, social work educators and students should take the lead in ensuring that marginalized and oppressed populations are socialized to participate in democracy. This begins with students, who are eager to promote social justice but may be disheartened by government and uninterested in civic participation; however, it is critical they understand how participation in democracy impacts their own lives and the people served by social work. As Chomsky (2014, n.p.) describes it, "in order to think outside the box, you must know the box, and know you are in it". Addams provides us a great example of what can be accomplished in the darkest, most corrupt and hopeless of circumstances. This work is valuable for all areas of social work practice, as it relates to the rights, opportunities, and entitlements for people across the spectrum of services.

Conclusion

Social work education contains much in both content and process that can be traced to Addams' influence, including a robust tradition of field-based, case-based, and lifelong learning. *Twenty Years at Hull House* is actually a series of case studies, wherein she chronicles what happens alongside her observations and conclusions. This is not unlike the processes we use today to socialize new practitioners to the work. Addams described Hull House as:

> an experimental effort to aid in the solution of the social and industrial problems which are engendered by the modern conditions of life in a great city …. From its very nature it can stand for no political or social propaganda. It must in a sense, give the warm welcome of an inn to all such propaganda, if perchance one of them be found an angel. The one thing to be dreaded in the Settlement is that it lost its flexibility, its power of quick adaptation, its readiness to change its methods as its environment may demand. It must be open to conviction and must have a deep abiding sense of tolerance. It must be hospitable and ready for experiment.
>
> *(Addams, 1910, p. 126)*

Despite the deep ideological divisions in her time, Addams was fiercely non-partisan (Knight, 2008), but rather perceived the problems and solutions of human suffering due to poverty as failure of society as a whole, not of one political party over another. Despite her critics, she worked tirelessly to educate Americans about the ways in which poverty degraded all citizens, and that its eradication would ultimately benefit all. Her solution was to take action in ways that connected people to their agency, to information, to civic engagement, which is "empowerment" as taught today in social work classrooms. She was not feeding or indoctrinating the poor (or the rich) with information, but rather, in the tradition of Dewey, trusting that the most useful knowledge would come naturally to those allowed to explore, question, and experiment in their environment. What was necessary to form a just society would reveal itself, if people from diverse backgrounds were allowed to build bridges of understanding by sharing their lives and cultures. It seems plausible that if Addams were a social work professor today, she would welcome students with views across our polarized political spectrum, so long as they shared a desire to eradicate suffering. If their reasoning did not seem to align with hers, her approach would have been to listen deeply, observe, and understand the student. Her strategy would be to trust the student's ability to develop sympathetic knowledge, or knowledge gained through experience over the course of the curriculum, and she would have likewise acquired her own and eagerly learned from them. If we are to emulate our pioneer, this demands a setting aside of our preconceived notions about what is "right" in favor of what "works", and developing our own sympathetic knowledge in the context of our radically shifting environment.

References

Addams, J. (1910). *Presidential address*. National Conference on Charities and Corrections. St. Louis, MO.
Addams, J. (1912). *Twenty years at Hull House*. New York: Macmillan Publishing.
Addams, J. (1961). *Twenty years at Hull House*. New York: Penguin Publishing.
Baker, V. L., & Baldwin, R. G. (2015). A case study of liberal arts colleges in the 21st century: Understanding organizational change and evolution in higher education. *Innovative Higher Education*, 40(3), 247–261.
Bartels, L. M. (2018). *Unequal democracy: The political economy of the new gilded age*. Princeton, NJ: Princeton University Press.
Calhoun, C. (2006). *The gilded age: Perspectives on the origins of modern America*. New York: Rowman & Littlefield Publishers.
Chomsky, N. (2014). *Pedagogy of the oppressed: Noam Chomsky, Howard Gardner, and Bruno della Chiesa*. Boston, MA: Askwith Forum. Harvard Graduate School of Education. Retrieved from: www.youtube.com/watch?v=2Ll6M0cXV54.
Council on Social Work Education. (2015). *Educational and professional standards*. Retrieved from: https://www.cswe.org/getattachment/Accreditation/Accreditation-Process/2015-EPAS/2015EPAS_Web_FINAL.pdf.aspx
Davis, A. F. (1973). *American heroine*. New York: Oxford University Press.
England, K., & Gad, G. (2002). Social policy at work? Equality and equity in women's paid employment in Canada. *GeoJournal*, 56(4), 281–294.
Fischer, M. (2013). Reading Dewey's political philosophy through Addams's political compromises. *American Catholic Philosophical Quarterly*, 87(2), 227–243.
Hamington, M. (2009). *The social philosophy of Jane Addams*. Champaign, IL: University of Illinois Press.
Hanesworth, C. (2017). Neoliberal influences on American higher education and the consequences for social work programmes. *Critical and Radical Social Work*, 5(1), 41–57.
Hickman, L. A., & Alexander, T. M. (1998). *The essential Dewey, volume 1: pragmatism, education, democracy*. Bloomington, IN: Indiana University Press.
Hunt, M. O., & Bullock, H. (2016). Ideologies and beliefs about poverty. In D. Brady & L. M. Burton (Eds.). *The Oxford handbook of the social science of poverty* (pp. 93–116). New York: Oxford University Press.
Knight, L. W. (2008). *Citizen: Jane Addams and the struggle for democracy*. Chicago, IL: University of Chicago Press.
Knight, L. W. (2010). *Jane Addams: Spirit in action*. WW Norton & Company.
Menand, L. (2001). *The metaphysical club*. New York: Macmillan Publishing.
Morley, C., & Ablett, P. (2017). Rising wealth and income inequality: A radical social work critique and response. *Aotearoa New Zealand Social Work*, 29(2), 6–18.
National Association of Social Workers. (2019). NASW code of ethics. Retrieved from: https://www.socialworkers.org/About/Ethics/Code-of-Ethics/Code-of-Ethics-English
Ormerod, R. (2006). The history and ideas of pragmatism. *Journal of the Operational Research Society*, 57(8), 892–909.
Pfeiffer, R. (2003). Introduction to classic American pragmatism. *Philosophy Now*, 43, 6–7.
Pois, A. M. (1999). Perspectives on twentieth-century women's international activism: Peace, feminism, and foreign policy. *Journal of Women's History*, 11(3), 213–222.
Reardon, P. (2006, June 11). *Why you should care about Jane Addams*. The Chicago Tribune. Retrieved from: www.chicagotribune.com/news/ct-xpm-2006-06-11-0606110193-story.html.
Reid, D. G., Linder, R. D., Shelley, B., Stout, H. S., & Noll, C. A. (Eds.). (2002). *Concise dictionary of Christianity in America*. Eugene, OR: Wipf and Stock Publishers.
Reinders, R. C. (1982). Toynbee Hall and the American settlement movement. *Social Service Review*, 56(1), 39–54.
Reisch, M. (2013). Social work education and the neo-liberal challenge: The US response to increasing global inequality. *Social Work Education*, 32(6), 715–733.
Reisch, M. (2016). Why macro practice matters. *Journal of Social Work Education*, 52(3), 258–268.
Reisch, M., & Jani, J. S. (2012). The new politics of social work practice: Understanding context to promote change. *The British Journal of Social Work*, 42(6), 1132–1150.
Rothman, J., & Mizrahi, T. (2014). Balancing micro and macro practice: A challenge for social work. *Social Work*, 59(1), 91–93.
Schlozman, K. L., Brady, H. E., & Verba, S. (2018). *Unequal and unrepresented: Political inequality and the people's voice in the new gilded age*. Princeton, NJ: Princeton University Press.

Scimecca, J. A., & Goodwin, G. A. (2003). Jane Addams: The first humanist sociologist. *Humanity & Society, 27*(2), 143–157.

Shields, P. (2011). Jane Addams's theory of democracy and social ethics: Incorporating a feminist perspective. In M. D'Agostino & H. Levine (Eds.). *Women in public administration: Theory and practice* (pp. 15–34). Burlington, MA: Jones & Bartlett Learning.

Shields, P. (2016). Building the fabric of peace: Jane Addams and peacekeeping. *Global Virtue Ethics Review, 7*(3), 21–33.

Starr, E. (2019). *On art, labor, and religion*. New York: Routledge.

Tangenberg, K. M. (2003). Linking feminist social work and feminist theology in light of faith-based service initiatives. *Affilia, 18*(4), 379–394.

Tully, G., Nadel, M., & Lesser, M. (2005). Providing economics content for the 21st century BSW student. *Journal of Teaching in Social Work, 25*(3–4), 19–34.

Whipps, J. D. (1998). *Philosophy and social activism: An exploration of the pragmatism and activism of Jane Addams, John Dewey and engaged Buddhism*. Retreived from UMI Company Microform Database. (Accession No. 9902711).

4

Lifting the veil of our own consciousness

W.E.B. Du Bois and transformative pedagogies for social work

David Hollinsworth

UNIVERSITY OF THE SUNSHINE COAST, QUEENSLAND, AUSTRALIA

[L]et the ears of the guilty people tingle with truth.

Du Bois [1989] cited in Back, 2017

It is a peculiar sensation, this double-consciousness, this sense of always looking at one's self through the eyes of others, of measuring one's soul by the tape of a world that looks on in amused contempt and pity.

(Du Bois, 2007d)

Introduction

This chapter outlines the work of black American sociologist, W.E.B. du Bois, and how his insights into racism and racial consciousness are used to engage Australian social work students in learning about their own racial identities in the context of how best to work alongside Indigenous Australians. The chapter begins with a short biography, and then describes his key intellectual contributions to sociology, in particular the twin concepts of 'the veil' and double consciousness. These ideas anticipate or prefigure concepts fundamental to the study of racism, whiteness and blackness as social constructions, privilege and domination as both personal property and global systems, intersectionality, and standpoint theory. These tools allow us to move beyond crude binaries that 'other' Indigenous people and other minorities in both our classrooms and our practice.

Biography

William Edward Burghardt (W.E.B.) Du Bois was born in Great Barrington, Massachusetts, on February 23, 1868. This was a liberal and relatively integrated community that paid for his attendance at the historically black Fisk University in Nashville, Tennessee. This was at the height of the Jim Crow segregation era, with brutal lynchings that shocked the twenty year old profoundly (Rabaka, 2007; Lewis, 2009). From Fisk, Du Bois was able to attend Harvard where he repeated a Bachelor of History degree, as Harvard did not allow credit for degrees from historically black colleges (HBC). His results were outstanding and he was awarded a scholarship to the Harvard sociology graduate program in 1891, becoming the first African American to receive a doctorate in 1895 (Lewis, 2009).

Critically for his future academic approach (Appiah, 2014), Du Bois interrupted his graduate studies to travel to Berlin on scholarship to study with some of Germany's best social scientists and philosophers in an atmosphere where his colour was not an impediment to intellectual recognition. Not so back in the USA. He only received job offers from HBCs, including the famous Tuskegee University, but went to Wilberforce University in Ohio. From there he went to the University of Pennsylvania in Philadelphia as a research assistant examining African-American communities, work that he published as *The Philadelphia Negro* in 1899. The first of such studies, his strict empiricism countered dominant deficit discourses of pathological slum dwellers while documenting the damages and exploitation caused by segregation (Jerabek, 2016).

In 1897 Du Bois went to the HBC Atlanta University of Georgia, beginning the first coordinated research centre into race relations, marked by publication of *The Philadelphia Negro* and multiple other studies. At this time he also championed international Pan-Africanist movements and was active in denouncing local lynchings as well as legal barriers to African-American freedoms. He espoused a form of black nationalism (see below) alongside education and political organization, in contrast to the assimilationist and limited ambitions of Booker T. Washington and his white supporters (Aiello, 2016). Du Bois was also very critical of black churches that he felt encouraged acceptance of a diminished existence in anticipation of salvation in the afterlife.

While this period saw great research that led to significant publications, his work was largely ignored by mainstream academia, and he spent more and more time publishing polemics on all aspects of race relations. In 1910, Du Bois joined in the creation of the *National Association for the Advancement of Colored People*, and left Atlanta to lead publicity and research for the NAACP. For the next two decades Du Bois published hundreds of articles attacking discrimination, including in the army during the First World War. His complex relationships with unions, socialism and the Communist Party saw him make enemies on all sides, while attracting surveillance from the authorities (Reed, 1997; Rabaka, 2007; Lewis, 2009).

In some tension with these class-based alliance politics was his embrace of separatist, Africanist and international movements. One consequence of his disparate and ever-evolving output is the contemporary tendency for vastly different schools of thought and activism to claim him as an antecedent (Reed, 1997).

Du Bois steadily became more internationalist in his interests, and opposed entry into the Second World War, partly as he saw Japan and China breaking free of white supremacy (Lewis, 2009). He went on to unsuccessfully push the United Nations to oppose colonialism, and was active in Pan-African movements. His associations with communists led to resignation from the NAACP and his anti-nuclear activism led to charges from the FBI of being an agent of a foreign power in 1950. While the trial collapsed, US authorities confiscated his passport for eight years (Mullen, 2016). Once his passport was restored, Du Bois travelled widely (including to China and the Soviet Union) to investigate racism and the struggles of coloured peoples. He continued to argue that capitalism was at the heart of racial oppression as a part payment, part control of the white working class (Marable, 2015). Always the contrarian, in 1961 Du Bois, aged 93, joined the Communist Party when the Supreme Court upheld McCarthyite laws requiring all communists to register with the US government. He moved to Ghana, and when the US government refused to renew his passport, took up Ghanaian citizenship. He died there on August 27, 1963 and was given a state funeral by President Nkrumah (Lewis, 2009).

Intellectual contributions to sociology and social work education

For most of his life Du Bois was regarded as an exceptional polemicist and writer, even by those who persecuted him. His academic work added to his stature but was remarkably underestimated by most of the American academy (Rabaka, 2010; Morris, 2015). This was partly because his university career was almost always in marginalized HBC institutions that were excluded from mainstream collegiality, academic honours and prestigious journals (Bulmer, 2016; Collins, 2016). His work was often denounced as partisan or unscholarly because of his advocacy and critical social constructionist position. Most influential was the hostility of key figures including Robert Park, a founder of the Chicago school of functionalist sociology and advocate of Booker T. Washington's accommodationist position so despised by Du Bois (Schwartz, 2017). This scholarly denial and efforts to rehabilitate Du Bois as a founding father of sociology have been extensively debated in recent years, vindicating the sustained efforts of Morris and especially Rabaka. This chapter aims to encourage social work educators to not just acknowledge him in some panoply of sociological forebears, but to use his theoretical insights in our teaching and his commitment to racial justice as a public intellectual as a call to an engaged professional practice. Such efforts can form part of the intellectual reparations for denial of Du Bois called for by Hunter (2016).

The veil and race as social construction

Du Bois' earliest notions of race, for example *The Philadelphia Negro* (2007a), reflected environmental understandings of geographical and political influences, including slavery and segregation, on different racial groups. By 1920 with the publication of *Darkwater: Voices from Within the Veil* (2007b), and *Dusk of Dawn: An Essay towards an Autobiography of a Race Concept* (2007c), he took an anti-essentialist stance highlighting race as a social construction, years before this became the orthodox academic position. Such an historicist understanding led him to highlight the 'colour line' or the global significance of racial segregation between the social and cultural worlds of whites and people of colour.

Social segregation between whites and non-whites was also invoked in the powerful notion of the 'veil': a concept taken up in literary works by James Baldwin and Ralph Ellison. The veil is not a wall (although in later life Du Bois was increasingly frustrated with its impermeability). Rather it demarcates and separates racial domains, rendering non-whites invisible to the dominant white world in much the same way orthodox sociology invisibilized his own work. At the same time, it acts to distort identity and self-consciousness among blacks, who are always aware of how they are seen from the other side (see double consciousness below). Howard Winant (2004) expands our understanding of the veil by emphasizing Du Bois' dialectical argument that the veil is both antagonist and interdependent, both splitting and binding. Departing from more individualized readings, Winant argues that the veil operates across scales of micro and macro, to replicate schisms and adhesions in the self with national and even global racial structures:

> The veil signifies a profound social structure that has been built up for centuries, accumulating among the infinite contradictions of race and racism as they have shaped our identities and social organization.
>
> *(Winant, 2004: 29)*

One of the pedagogical gifts Du Bois offers is this concept of forces working simultaneously at identity and broader structural levels, as instances of the same phenomenon.

Du Bois (in his early works) saw his role as 'renting the veil asunder' for both whites and non-whites, arguing that the latter were 'gifted with second sight', being able to observe and better know their 'masters' (Du Bois, 2007d). Such ideas are often espoused within feminist and subaltern studies and can support students' understandings of positionality, standpoint theory, and critical race theory in sociology and social work classes today (Swigonski, 1994; Fischetti, 2013; Collins, 2016).

Apple (2013) argues Du Bois' powerful invocations of African-American experience offered a transformative deconstruction of race as a social construction designed to suppress the white working class along with blacks. He quotes David Lewis' assessment:

> *Darkwater* was meant to be drunk deeply by whites … Du Bois has set out to lift the veil of race enough for white people to see—even to feel—through the medium of arresting language and moral signposts what it was like to be a second-class citizen in America …
>
> Obscured and distorted by the veil, the real and relative differences between people based on geography, natural resources, and history became moral and genetic manifestations of inferiority justifying dominion and debasement.
>
> *(2000: 20, cited in Apple, 2013: 38)*

While the oppressions imposed on non-whites by the veil need to be overcome, the inherent dualism of the veil meant it also fuelled the lived experience of African-Americans as a people:

> Dualism remains the essential meaning of the veil, the heart of its dialectic: racial identity establishes not only the norms of oppression and subordination but also those of self-assurance and autogestion or self-determination.
>
> *(Winant, 2004: 35)*

Thus oppression calls forth resistance, and resistance is met with accommodation and co-option, especially in our 'colour-blind' world (Bonilla-Silva, 2018).

Double consciousness

Du Bois first wrote of double consciousness in his 1897 article in *Atlantic Monthly* entitled 'Strivings of the Negro People'. It reappears almost unaltered in chapter one of the 1903 *Souls of Black Folk*.

> It is a peculiar sensation, this double-consciousness, this sense of always looking at one's self through the eyes of others, of measuring one's soul by the tape of a world that looks on in amused contempt and pity. One ever feels his two-ness, an American, a Negro; two souls, two thoughts, two unreconciled strivings; two warring ideals in one dark body, whose dogged strength alone keeps it from being torn asunder. The history of the American Negro is the history of this strife—this longing to attain self-conscious manhood, to merge his double self into a better and truer self. In this merging he wishes neither of the older selves to be lost. He does not wish to Africanize America, for America has too much to teach the world and Africa. He wouldn't bleach his Negro blood in a flood of white Americanism, for he knows that Negro blood has a message for the world. He simply wishes

to make it possible for a man to be both a Negro and an American without being cursed and spit upon by his fellows, without having the doors of opportunity closed roughly in his face.

(Du Bois, 2007d: 2–3)

This disempowering and split self-image accounts for much of the dysfunction others attributed to the inherent racial inferiority of African-Americans. As an Australian educator, I can see aspects of what Yin Paradies calls internalized racism or the 'incorporation of racist attitudes, affect and beliefs into one's own worldview' (Paradies & Cunningham, 2009: 551). One way that racist attitudes are manifested is in the deployment of essentialism. In a seminal work on diversity and anti-essentialism in Indigenous studies, Paradies cautioned against strategic essentialism of pan-Aboriginality given that:

> such a deployment of Indigeneity also results in every Indigenous Australian being interpellated, without regard to their individuality, through stereotyped images that exist in the popular imagination. The essentialized Indigeneity thus formed coalesces around specific fantasies of exclusivity, cultural alterity, marginality, physicality and morality, which leave an increasing number of Indigenous people vulnerable to accusations of inauthenticity. Only by decoupling Indigeneity from such essentialist fantasies can we acknowledge the richness of Indigenous diversity and start on the path towards true reconciliation in Australia.
>
> *(2006: 355)*

After decades of teaching Aboriginal studies to students in all the 'helping professions', I find that breaking their tendency to essentialize Indigeneity, often romantically or as victims of racism, is as much of a problem as resistance to acknowledging racism (Hollinsworth, 2013, 2016a, 2016b). This anti-essentialist position is contested especially in Indigenous and other minority identity politics (D'Cruz, 2008; but see also Appiah, 2018). Nevertheless, I remain concerned about the constraints placed by such strategic essentialism on settler recognition of diversity and especially on many Aboriginal students who fail to fit the template.

Intersectionality

Du Bois often falls into generic rhetoric about white souls, black souls, African blood, but a more careful reading shows his attentiveness to class, gender, geographical and occupational factors that today we would include within intersectionality. Here I am not claiming, as Morris (2015) does, that Du Bois is a founder of modern post-colonial, feminist or intersectionalist thought (Collins, 2016). I am arguing that in our classes we can use Du Bois (and many other women and men) to convey to our students the crucial need to problematize both the notion of a canon and the homogenizing and universalizing tendencies of knowledge production and our own experiences of hegemonic commonsense. In my feedback on assignments (apart from 'reference needed'), the most common comment is: 'Use many or some or may or often to acknowledge the diversity within Aboriginal people' (or any other social category).

Du Bois saw himself as an insider/outsider who was very familiar with dominant knowledge and ways of being but also emotionally cognisant of racial discrimination and marginalization, as argued in all three of his autobiographies. The position of reconciling his own double consciousness could be achieved by other people of colour who realized the hypocrisy of white supremacy with its rationalizations of democratic and meritocratic ideals. Like him, others could use the second sight to excoriate white domination, arrogance and hubris at home and globally.

Consequently, while fully aware of the limitations of much American schooling under segregation, Du Bois continued to argue for the transformative and liberatory potential of education (Apple, 2013).

Du Bois and sociology education

As noted previously, education for Du Bois meant a liberal arts education that encouraged criticism of existing social and economic relations as fundamental to genuine democracy in contrast to Booker T. Washington's industrial training for a black working class (Aiello, 2016). The task of enhancing current social work curricula to include the work of Du Bois and other 'minority' thinkers is equally fraught, with many Australian university courses trying to embed Indigenous, feminist, queer, and culturally and linguistically diverse knowledges and perspectives. Yet how often do we see in social science courses, week 4 being 'women', week 5 'Indigenous', week 6 'migrants', etc., or the insertion of a single reading or essay topic making such inclusion tokenistic?

This partial incorporation of previously absent or silenced voices risks fundamental errors and the perpetuation of harmful binaries. First, courses may present essentialized, generic representations of (for example) Indigenous cultures and histories that do not adequately recognize diversity among Aboriginal and Torres Strait Islander peoples, the complex and dynamic intersectionality of their complex identities, and the intercultural nature of their daily lives. Second, such curricula can 'other' Aboriginal and Torres Strait Islander students and put them in culturally unsafe classroom situations by such representations (Hollinsworth, 2016a).

The story of the exclusion and denigration of Du Bois within sociology provides students with a classic case of how disciplinary canons entrench hegemonic knowledges that support the status quo (Seltzer, 2017). It is clear from recent debates that to simply insert Du Bois alongside existing founding 'fathers' will not of itself remove the distortions and discursive powers of orthodox theorizing (Morris, 2015; Hunter, 2016; Back, 2017). At the same time, exposing students to Du Bois, and especially the concepts of the veil and double consciousness as well as his fierce global perspectives, can allow deeper understandings of notions of racism as relationships of dominance and subordination rather than caused by ignorance or personality disorders. These ideas, alongside more contemporary formulations, can be used to call for the decolonization of (Australian) social work (Walter et al., 2011) as a thoroughgoing, transformative process well beyond simple inclusion of minority voices.

Du Bois within Australian Aboriginal studies courses

Reed (1997) and Collins (2016) rightly caution against hagiographic accounts of Du Bois as an/the antecedent of contemporary social theories, but students in my classes often import learnings about Du Bois from a colleague's Social Theory course to connect with my discussions of research and standpoint epistemology from an Indigenist position (Foley, 2003). A core-learning outcome from one of my courses (compulsory within the social work program) is the intergenerational impact of racism, repressive legislation, child removals and other abuses of the Australian racial state on Aboriginal families. As Patrick Wolfe (2006: 388) declared: 'Settler colonizers come to stay: invasion is a structure not an event.'

In weekly journal writing, discussed in class, students read usually three articles and choose one of two set questions. These questions are not focussed on the details of Aboriginal history (covered in a previous compulsory course) but on the implications of colonialism for engagement between mostly settler/white social workers and Aboriginal clients and their families. In week 3, the two questions are:

a. Why is the establishment of trust between Aboriginal and non-Aboriginal people and institutions so difficult on **both** sides?

OR

b. How can the desire to help and the act of caring work to uphold colonizing relations and enable unjust practices?

Almost all of the literature explains why Aboriginal people fear or distrust non-Aboriginal people and institutions such as welfare, ignoring the anxieties and judgementalism common among non-Aboriginal social workers. Our approach foregrounds the need for cultural courage when working with those who are positioned differently to ourselves in a variety of ways, including 'race'. Cultural courage requires workers to 'acknowledge and confront fears, uncertainties, and anxieties that can arise in practice and to resist the temptation of becoming immobilized' (Bennett et al., 2011: 34).

By demanding that trust is seen as a 'two-way street', and while most workers are well intended they often commit serious abuses (for example, in the 'best interests of the child'; Long & Sephton, 2011), we develop capacity to be honest and critically self-reflective as learners and as practitioners. By teaching about white privilege rather than Indigenous disadvantage, we ensure that students recognize we are all implicated in these intercultural and structured encounters and bear some responsibility for the unearned benefits that flow so seamlessly to those who are positioned as white or settler in Australia (Young & Zubrzycki, 2011).

In line with Du Bois' increasing concerns with global colonialism and imperialism, Hammer (2018) argues for a post-colonial, critical sociology informed by Southern theory that decentres both whiteness and American/parochial approaches. In a quote that also illustrates his exquisite use of language, she cites Du Bois:

> Here for instance is a lovely British home, with green lawns, appropriate furnishings and a retinue of well-trained servants. Within is a young woman, well trained and well dressed, intelligent and high-minded. She is fingering the ivory keys of a grand piano and pondering the problem of her summer vacation. ... How far is such a person responsible for the crimes of colonialism? It will in all probability not occur to her that she has any responsibility whatsoever, and that may well be true. Equally, it may be true that her income is the result of starvation, theft, and murder; that it involves ignorance, disease, and crime on the part of thousands; that the system which sustains the security, leisure, and comfort she enjoys is based on the suppression, exploitation, and slavery of the majority of mankind.
>
> *([1946] cited in Hammer, 2018: 135)*

Such examples of global networks of resources, bodies, commodities, profit and pain provide all of us with crucial understandings of our responsibilities to other humans and non-humans, given the extreme privileges those of us in Australian universities enjoy, which is surely core curriculum for social workers.

Some students actively or passively resist these revelations, especially when they have faced serious obstacles (of class, gender, disability or sexuality) in their own lives, but the majority come to understand the intersectionality of domination and subordination, and the consequent contextual nature of their challenges (Hollinsworth, 2016b). Such work allows us to examine in a more nuanced way, notions of hybridity and a third space including the work of Paradies (2006) and Nakata (2007).

How Du Bois informs contemporary debates around identity, privilege, standpoint and critical social work

Martin et al. argue for

> a reconceptualization of current debates and positions that are currently bound up within the limitations of questionable binary divides and oppositions, for example, educational psychology/sociology, transmission/critical or decolonial pedagogies and Indigenous/Western Knowledge. Nakata's concept of the Cultural Interface is mobilized to acknowledge some of the nuances and complexities that emerge when Indigenous and Western knowledge systems come into convergence within the higher education classroom.
>
> *(2017: 1158)*

Their principal aim is to reduce the culturally unsafe and intellectually flawed pressures on Indigenous students. We have had a significant number of Indigenous students in our social work programs over the last ten years (well above the university average). I have taught most of the Indigenous studies courses and have been able to support these students, most of whom are friends of mine. Yet for some of these students, studying in these classes has been very challenging, and some have not attended or have been obviously uncomfortable, despite my best efforts. One student confided that: 'I'm so depressed. In this course, more than any other Indigenous Studies course, the binaries between Indigenous peoples and the others are more stark and more debilitating than I can deal with' (Carter & Hollinsworth, 2017: 182).

Indigenous students also regularly report being called upon to represent their 'race'/culture regardless of how their own autobiographies have placed them socially, culturally or politically (Hollinsworth, 2013). Teachers, perhaps lacking confidence in their own knowledge, often ask Indigenous students to explain or justify complex issues that they have less knowledge of (indeed they may have come to university to gain access to such awareness and understanding). This is a pedagogic form of 'dumping' described decades ago by Dominelli (1989). Other students also assume that an Indigenous peer is able and willing to stand for, and give voice to, their racialized expectations, which in social work are often heroic or exotic but, nevertheless, are predicated on a fundamental alterity and othering. Consequently, many students whose appearance allows them to do so, choose not to self-identify in class (Carter et al., 2017).

While this is fairly easy in engineering or business (programs that have virtually no Indigenous content), social work students are confronted in almost every course with references to Indigenous peoples. While all staff would not see themselves as racist, some do racialize and problematize or valorize Indigenous people and their culture/'behaviours'. Often this takes the form of culturalism where choices, values, poor health or social outcomes are seen as caused or determined by Indigeneity, rather than systemic racism, history and complex intercultural dynamics (Hollinsworth, 2013).

Again we are undermined by the prevalence and potency of rigid binaries. Most of the available literature takes for granted the statistical categories of Indigenous and non-Indigenous, homogenizing both, and denying the lived, messy, interconnections between them (Walter, 2010). Most research is done in remote or rural areas while the majority of the Indigenous population (and almost all Indigenous university students) are urban. While recruitment of

Indigenous students in higher education grows, retention remains poor (Wilks & Wilson, 2015). How much is this due to inappropriate curriculum and pedagogy, including the racialization of these students as learners within deficit discourses (Fforde et al., 2013)? Two of the journal questions that frame classroom debates about such understandings are:

Why do representations of Aboriginality as dysfunctional or pathologized continue to have such emotional and political power today?

and

Does the elimination of Aboriginal disadvantage require the minimization of social and cultural differences from the 'mainstream'?

Of note, most students say no to the second question, in contrast to both the current tone of Australian Indigenous policy and a growing number of Aboriginal commentators/leaders. Here the work of Emma Kowal (Kowal & Paradies, 2005) has been extremely valuable in exposing tensions and contradictions.

Questions of resilience among Indigenous higher education students are beyond the scope of this chapter, but Du Bois remains relevant in his determination to liberate the educational and social aspirations of people of colour. Building relationships between Indigenous Australians and social workers is inherently challenging given the role played by welfare authorities in their oppression. Communication is also often difficult, partly because of language differences but more so because of lack of trust and power imbalances (Cox, 2007). Most social work students seem confident in their motivation for 'wanting to help people' and are confused or surprised when they encounter or are warned of a hostile or skeptical reception. This is why a critical Indigenous history is mandatory for Australian social work programs (McAuliffe et al., 2015, but see Bennett, 2015).

Reference to Du Bois' concept of the veil opens up less personally threatening but still profound understandings of the extent to which racist ideologies and segregation result in distorted apprehension on both sides (Winant, 2004). Classroom discussions of how we come to see others and be seen by them through the veil as opaque, indeterminate, vague or obscure are lively and generative of other insights about gender, body shape, disability, etc. experienced by students. These allow for greater understanding of hybridity and intersectionality, and for the insight that we/they embody different identities in different contexts and in response to others' expectations and actions. See, for example, two of Hankivsky's key tenets of intersectionality (2014: 3):

> When analyzing social problems, the importance of any category or structure cannot be predetermined; the categories and their importance must be discovered in the process of investigation.
>
> People can experience privilege and oppression simultaneously. This depends on what situation or specific context they are in.

It also introduces the politics of recognition and misrecognition of racial, gender or other identities (Fraser, 2000). The idea of double consciousness similarly opens up profound learnings around hegemonic discourses and colonizing structures. These are obviously potent for many Indigenous and other racialized students (including significant numbers of international students). But they are also crucial in enabling white students to see themselves as racial beings (Todd & Abrams, 2011) through an interrogation of white privilege.

Class small-group discussions and individual journaling again allow students to discover for themselves more nuanced understandings of relative and intersectional privilege and impediments (a la Hankivsky). Questions for critical reflection include:

How do you understand the privilege of your whiteness in relation to working with Aboriginal people?

and

How would you describe your own feelings of doubt or guilt or exclusion in relation to working with Aboriginal people in the light of Ranzijn and McConnochie's (2013) paper?

In summary, Du Bois' concepts of the veil and double consciousness offer many different insights and entry points into the sociology of race and class and other intersectional identities that enable social work students to turn their concern and gaze from those who are othered toward themselves and the structures and processes that reproduce oppression and subordination.

Intellectual contributions to social work practice and the fight for social justice

Du Bois was more of a polemicist than a community organizer, more of a strategist than an activist. As such, his work supports our capacity to analyse complex problems and identify fundamental structural and intellectual causes rather than as a guide to social work practice skills. One area of practice where his ideas, especially as built upon with critical race theory, offer sound advice relates to the importance of experience, voice and story (Ladson-Billings, 1998: 13). As López argues:

> The counterstories of people of color ... are those stories that are not told, stories that are consciously and/or unconsciously ignored or downplayed because they do not fit socially acceptable notions of truth. By highlighting these subjugated accounts, CRT hopes to demystify the notion of a racially neutral society and tell another story of a highly racialized social order: a story where social institutions and practices serve the interest of White individuals.
> *(2003: 84–85)*

When my students tell me they recognize that their clients are the 'experts in their own lives', they perform non-judgementalism as they have been taught. Abandoning claims to expertise and superior insight can be more of a challenge, especially given colonial discourses of dysfunction and deficit common within the public domain and the profession.

When combined with a critical self-reflection on positionality and privilege, the crucial issues of relationship building in the absence of earned trust from a racialized minority as preconditions for effective social work become clear. Particular attention to self-disclosure, authenticity, deep listening, silence, and strength-based and place-based approaches can all be conveyed using parts of Du Bois' philosophy (Bennett et al., 2011). Many students warmed to the use of narrative approaches that are often seen as closely aligned to Aboriginal cultural 'yarning' practices (Bacon, 2013). The capacity to 'externalize' and to 're-author' stories of our own failings and inadequacies such that 'I am not the problem, the problem is the problem' can link to Du Bois' understandings of double consciousness and the veil (Akinyela, 2002).

The other major contribution of Du Bois to practice/praxis is his own story. The extraordinary mix of research, scholarship, publishing and campaigning are the epitome of the modern public intellectual (Apple, 2013). As his champion, Aldon Morris declares:

> Thus, long before sociologists called for a rigorous public sociology, Du Bois engaged in a public sociology that was both scientific and politically engaged. Du Bois, therefore, a hundred years ago, provided a challenging example of how radical scholars can act as change agents despite the clamouring voices of purists claiming science and protest do not mix.
>
> *(2017: 12)*

In a time of extreme pressures of neoliberalism on both social work policy and practice and social work education (Singh & Cowden, 2009; Pease et al., 2016), W.E.B. Du Bois provides an inspirational counterstory for orthodox sociology and for those social workers wanting to work for social justice 'within and against the state'.

References

Aiello, T. (2016). *The Battle for the Souls of Black Folk: W.E.B. Du Bois, Booker T. Washington, and the Debate that Shaped the Course of Civil Rights*. Santa Barbara, CA: Praeger.

Akinyela, M. (2002). De-colonizing our lives: divining a post-colonial therapy. *International Journal of Narrative Therapy & Community Work, 2002*(2), 32–43.

Appiah, A. (2014). *Lines of Descent: WEB Du Bois and the Emergence of Identity*. Cambridge, MA: Harvard University Press.

Appiah, K. A. (2018). *The Lies that Bind: Rethinking Identity*. London: W.W. Norton.

Apple, M. W. (2013). Can education change society? Du Bois, Woodson and the politics of social transformation. *Review of Education, 1*(1), 32–56.

Back, L. (2017). "Let the ears of the guilty people tingle with truth": W. E. B. Du Bois as an original sociologist. *The British Journal of Sociology, 68*(1), 31–36.

Bacon, V. (2013). Yarning and listening: yarning and learning through stories. In B. Bennett, S. Green, S. Gilbert & D. Bessarab (Eds.), *Our Voices: Aboriginal and Torres Strait Islander Social Work* (pp. 136–165). South Yarra: Palgrave Macmillan.

Bennett, B. (2015). "Stop deploying your white privilege on me!" Aboriginal and Torres Strait Islander engagement with the Australian Association of Social Workers. *Australian Social Work, 68*(1), 19–31.

Bennett, B., Zubrzycki, J. & Bacon, V. (2011). What do we know? The experiences of social workers working alongside Aboriginal people. *Australian Social Work, 64*(1), 20–37.

Bonilla-Silva, E. (2018). *Racism without Racists: Color-Blind Racism and the Persistence of Racial Inequality in America*. (5th ed.). New York: Rowman & Littlefield.

Bulmer, M. (2016). A singular scholar and writer in a profoundly racist world. *Ethnic and Racial Studies, 39*(8), 1385–1390.

Carter, J. & Hollinsworth, D. (2017). Teaching Indigenous geography in a neo-colonial world. *Journal of Geography in Higher Education, 41*(2), 182–197.

Carter, J., Hollinsworth, D., Raciti, M. & Gilbey, K. (2017). Academic 'place-making': fostering attachment, belonging and identity for Indigenous students in Australian universities. *Teaching in Higher Education, 23*(2), 243–260.

Collins, P. H. (2016). Du Bois's contested legacy. *Ethnic and Racial Studies, 39*(8), 1398–1406.

Cox, L. (2007). Fear, trust and aborigines: the historical experience of state institutions and current encounters in the health system. *Health and History, 9*(2), 70–92.

D'Cruz, C. (2008). *Identity Politics in Deconstruction: Calculating with the Incalculable*. Aldershot: Ashgate.

Dominelli, L. (1989). An uncaring profession? An examination of racism in social work. *Journal of Ethnic and Migration Studies, 15*(3), 391–403.

Du Bois, W. E. B. (2007a). *The Philadelphia Negro: A Social Study*. [1899]. New York: Oxford University Press.

Du Bois, W. E. B. (2007b). *Darkwater: Voice from Within the Veil*. [1920]. New York: Oxford University Press.

Du Bois, W. E. B. (2007c). *Dusk of Dawn: An Essay towards an Autobiography of a Race Concept*. [1940]. New York: Oxford University Press.

Du Bois, W. E. B. (2007d). *The Souls of Black Folk*. [1903]. New York: Oxford University Press.
Fforde, C., Bamblett, L., Lovett, R., Gorringe, S. & Fogarty, B. (2013). Discourse, deficit and identity: aboriginality, the race paradigm and the language of representation in contemporary Australia. *Media International Australia, 149*, 162–173.
Fischetti, J. (2013). WEB Du Bois: the roots of critical race theory. In J. D. Kirylo (Ed.), *A Critical Pedagogy of Resistance: 34 Pedagogues We Need to Know* (pp. 33–36). New York: Springer.
Foley, D. (2003). Indigenous epistemology and Indigenous standpoint theory. *Social Alternatives, 22*(1), 44–52.
Fraser, N. (2000). Rethinking recognition. *New Left Review, 3*, 107–120.
Hammer, R. (2018). Bringing the global home: students research local areas through postcolonial perspectives. *Teaching Sociology, 46*(2), 135–147.
Hankivsky, O. (2014). *Intersectionality 101*. Vancouver, British Columbia: Simon Fraser University, The Institute for Intersectionality Research and Policy. Available at: http://vawforum-cwr.ca/sites/default/files/attachments/intersectionallity_101.pdf
Hollinsworth, D. (2013). Forget cultural competence: ask for an autobiography. *Social Work Education, 32*(8), 1048–1060.
Hollinsworth, D. (2016a). How do we ensure that the aim of Indigenous cultural competence doesn't reinforce racialized and essentialised discourses of Indigeneity? *Journal of Australian Indigenous Issues, 19*(1–2), 33–48.
Hollinsworth, D. (2016b). Unsettling Australian settler supremacy: combating resistance in university Aboriginal studies. *Race Ethnicity and Education, 19*(2), 412–432.
Hunter, M. A. (2016). Du Boisian sociology and intellectual reparations: for coloured scholars who consider suicide when our rainbows are not enuf. *Ethnic and Racial Studies, 39*(8), 1379–1384.
Jerabek, H. (2016). WEB DuBois on the history of empirical social research. *Ethnic and Racial Studies, 39*(8), 1391–1397.
Kowal, E. & Paradies, Y. (2005). Ambivalent helpers and unhealthy choices: public health practitioners' narratives of Indigenous ill-health. *Social Science and Medicine, 60*, 1347–1357.
Ladson-Billings, G. (1998). Just what is critical race theory and what is it doing in a nice field like education? *International Journal of Qualitative Studies in Education, 11*(1), 7–24.
Lewis, D. L. (2009). *W. E. B. Du Bois: A Biography*. New York: Henry Holt.
Long, M. & Sephton, R. (2011). Rethinking the "best interests" of the child: voices from Aboriginal child and family welfare practitioners. *Australian Social Work, 64*(1), 96–112.
López, G. R. (2003). The (racially-neutral) politics of education: a critical race theory perspective. *Educational Administration Quarterly, 39*, 68–94.
Marable, M. (2015). *WEB Du Bois: Black Radical Democrat*. New York: Routledge.
Martin, G., Nakata, V., Nakata, M. & Day, A. (2017). Promoting the persistence of Indigenous students through teaching at the cultural interface. *Studies in Higher Education, 42*(7), 1158–1173.
McAuliffe, D., Nipperess, S., Daly, K. & Hardcastle, F. (2015). New steps in the AASW reconciliation journey. In C. Fejo-King & J. Poona (Eds.), *Reconciliation and Australian Social Work: Past and Current Experiences and Informing Future Practice* (pp. 157–172). Canberra: Magpie Goose Publishing.
Morris, A. (2015). *The Scholar Denied: WEB Du Bois and the Birth of Modern Sociology*. Oakland, CA: University of California Press.
Morris, A. (2017). WEB Du Bois at the center: from science, civil rights movement, to Black Lives Matter. *The British Journal of Sociology, 68*(1), 3–16.
Mullen, B. (2016). *WEB Du Bois: Revolutionary across the Color Line*. London: Pluto Press.
Nakata, M. (2007). The cultural interface. *The Australian Journal of Indigenous Education, 36*(Suppl. 1), S7–S14.
Paradies, Y. (2006). Beyond black and white: essentialism, hybridity and Indigeneity. *Journal of Sociology, 42*(4), 355–367.
Paradies, Y. & Cunningham, J. (2009). Experiences of racism among urban Indigenous Australians: findings from the DRUID study. *Ethnic and Racial Studies, 32*(3), 548–573.
Pease, B., Goldingay, S., Hosken, N. & Nipperess, S. (Eds.). (2016). *Doing Critical Social Work: Theory in Practice*. Crows Nest, Australia: Allen & Unwin.
Rabaka, R. (2007). *W.E.B. DuBois and the Problems of the Twenty-First Century: An Essay on Africana Critical Theory*. Lanham, MD: Lexington Books.
Rabaka, R. (2010). *Against Epistemic Apartheid: W.E.B. Du Bois and the Disciplinary Decadence of Sociology*. Lanham, MD: Lexington Books/Rowman & Littlefield Publishers.

Ranzijn, R. & McConnochie, K. (2013). No place for whites? Psychology students' reactions to article on healing members of the stolen generations in Australia. *Australian Psychologist*, *48*, 445–461.

Reed, A. L. (1997). *W. E. B. Du Bois and American Political Thought: Fabianism and the Color Line*. Oxford: Oxford University Press.

Schwartz, M. (2017). Academic apartheid and the poverty of theory: the impact of scholarly segregation on the development of sociology in the United States. *The British Journal of Sociology*, *68*(1), 49–66.

Seltzer, M. (2017). The road not taken: the fate of W. E. B. Du Bois's science of society. *The British Journal of Sociology*, *68*(1), 37–48.

Singh, G. & Cowden, S. (2009). The social worker as intellectual. *European Journal of Social Work*, *12*(4), 479–493.

Swigonski, M. E. (1994). The logic of feminist standpoint theory for social work research. *Social Work*, *39*(4), 387–393.

Todd, N. & Abrams, E. (2011). White dialectics: a new framework for theory, research, and practice with white students. *The Counseling Psychologist*, *39*(3), 353–395.

Walter, M. (2010). The politics of the data: how the Australian statistical Indigene is constructed. *International Journal of Critical Indigenous Studies*, *3*(2), 45–56.

Walter, M., Taylor, S. & Habibis, D. (2011). How white is social work in Australia? *Australian Social Work*, *64*(1), 6–19.

Wilks, K. & Wilson, J. (2015). Indigenous Australia: a profile of the Aboriginal and Torres Strait Islander higher education student population. *Australian Universities' Review*, *57*(2), 17–30.

Winant, H. (2004). *The New Politics of Race: Globalism, Difference, Justice*. London: University of Minnesota Press.

Wolfe, P. (2006). Settler colonialism and the elimination of the native. *Journal of Genocide Research*, *8*(4), 387–409.

Young, S. & Zubrzycki, J. (2011). Educating Australian social workers in the post-apology era: the potential offered by a 'whiteness' lens. *Journal of Social Work*, *11*(2), 159–173.

5
Reaching higher ground
The importance of Lev Vygotsky's therapeutic legacy for social work

Katherine Reid

QUEENSLAND UNIVERSITY OF TECHNOLOGY, AUSTRALIA

Through others we become ourselves.

(Vygotsky, 1997: 105)

Introduction

Increasing global inequality presents a range of different challenges for caregivers seeking to support the social, emotional and cognitive development of their child. Neo-liberal discourses have infiltrated our expectations of children to 'self-regulate' and independently solve problems they face. Clinical discourses in social work have meant an increased focus on assessing children's developmental deficits and recommending therapeutic intervention in order to compensate for such deficits, and children are often situated as passive recipients of such therapeutic interventions. The focus of this chapter is Lev Vygotsky, a Russian psychologist who published a series of studies between the 1920s and 1930s, which presented an entirely new and ground breaking understanding of child development. The significance of his work is still very much with us today. His research was largely unknown outside of Russia due to the lack of translation of his published works. It was also unrecognised due to its challenge to dominant Western child developmental theories of the time. While Vygotskian concepts have subverted education theory and practice, their implications for social work therapeutic practice with children, caregivers and social work education has not been sufficiently explored, and it is this which is the focus of this chapter. Vygotsky points to the importance of social workers reflecting on the socio-cultural and historical context in which children are living so as to understand more fully the extent to which this context can enable or constrain higher mental functioning. Vygotsky offered a highly significant contrast to individualistic developmental theories by highlighting how learning occurs through children engaging in collaborative activities with a more capable peer or adult. It is this idea that is captured in one of his most important concepts – the 'Zone of Proximal Development' (ZPD); Vygotsky, 1978).

The chapter locates Vygotsky's key concepts in the socio-cultural and historical context of Soviet Russia. It argues how some of Vygotsky's concepts can be applied in discursive therapeutic interactions to generate agentic discourses that position children as 'active agents' in their own learning regarding the challenges they face. Through a 'conversational partnership', social workers can offer therapeutic scaffolding to stretch the child from the 'known and familiar to what is possible to know' (White, 2012). In doing this, children can reflect on their everyday experiences, to discern from categories of their experience, in order to develop abstract concepts. Vygotsky regarded this kind of concept development as crucial for children to achieve agency, to apply these concepts in future actions and shape their own lives. However, therapeutic interaction that supports children's learning and development is reliant on language and narratives being told. Problem-saturated narratives re-told in therapeutic interactions, by contrast, can be profoundly limiting for children's agency and self-identity. This chapter also draws on the work of Jerome Bruner, who was born in 1915 and died in 2016 aged over 100. Bruner built on some of Vygotsky's concepts to highlight the importance of language acquisition and narrative structure. The chapter underscores the importance for social workers to critically reflect on their own therapeutic practice, to enable the co-production of alternative narratives that make visible children's emerging knowledge. This chapter then points to the relevance of Vygotsky's concepts for social work pedagogy. By offering experiential teaching processes, social work students can be supported to critically reflect on their own discursive practice, to further discern categories of experiences, to support their own concept development in relation to discursive therapy interactions with children. These collaborative learning interactions can disrupt taken-for-granted subject positions of 'expert supervisor' and 'novice student', to instead generate learning partnerships.

Locating Vygotsky's work

To avoid misunderstanding Vygotsky's work it is important to appreciate the social-cultural and historical conditions that gave rise to his research and publications. Vygotsky was a Jewish, Marxist, Russian psychologist, who received little attention for a number of years from either Russian or Western scholars for his theories of child development. Vygotsky has left a legacy that has disrupted the 'entrenched intellectual strongholds' in various disciplines such as education and psychology (Edwards, 2007: 79). He argued that learning precedes development and recognised the 'complex interconnections of learning-and-development' (Vygotsky, 1987a: 201). Vygotsky argued that 'development based on collaboration and imitation is the source of the specifically human characteristics of consciousness that develop in the child' (Vygotsky, 1987a: 210). His collectivist notions of learning were a marked contrast to other Western developmental theorists of the time, who asserted individualistic and genetic accounts of development. He offered a sharp critique of 'old' psychologies that sought to separate the 'individual' from their social contexts. Instead, he argued that the child and their social-cultural and historic context 'mutually shape each other in a spiral process of growth' (Van der Veer, 2007: 22).

Vygotsky also pioneered a revolutionary re-conceptualisation of education – both formal and everyday educational experiences, as his perspective positioned children as active participants in their own learning. This perspective was developed in stark contrast to past and current dominant discourses within education and psychology in which the 'expert-adult' imparts their knowledge to the 'unknowing' child. Vygotsky argued that

> direct teaching of concepts is impossible and fruitless. A teacher who tries to do this usually accomplishes nothing but empty verbalism, a parrot like repetition of words by the child, simulating knowledge of the corresponding concepts but actually covering up a vacuum.
>
> *(1986: 150)*

He presented a radical challenge for pedagogy stating that

> Pedagogics is never and was never politically indifferent, since, willingly or unwillingly, through its own work on the psyche, it has always adopted a particular social pattern, political line, in accordance with the dominant social class that has guided its interests.
>
> *(Vygotsky, 1997b: 349)*

Despite growing up in a large, wealthy and well-educated Jewish family, Vygotsky experienced many hardships (Van der Veer and Valsiner, 1991; Daniels et al., 2007). He faced systemic discrimination based on his Jewish heritage. Even though he received a gold medal for excelling academically in his secondary schooling, his entry to tertiary education was not guaranteed, due to the Tsarist Russian state imposing an intake limit of 3% 'Jewish' students (Van der Veer and Valsiner, 1991). Once enrolled to study law at Moscow's University (to appease his parents), he also enrolled at the Shanyavsky People's University (Bakhurst, 2007; Kozulin, 1999). He went on to major in philosophy and history. His passion for literature and the dramatic arts saw him work in Gomel in the early 1920s, travelling around Russia to organise 'the best theatrical companies to Gomel' (Van der Veer, 2007: 24). He was well known for not only his teaching in various institutions but also his public lectures on a range of subjects and his hosting of literary nights in Gomel (Van der Veer and Valsiner, 1991). This passion for linguistics, literature, philosophy and history shaped his gradual interest in psychology.

In 1924 he relocated to Moscow to commence his research program in experimental psychology. Vygotsky researched and published the majority of his work during the 1920s, until his premature death in 1934. Daniels and colleagues explain that Vygotsky was prolific, publishing 274 titles in a short period of time, due to the 'political context in which he was writing' (Daniels et al., 2007: 8–9). He lived during a time of intense political unrest and social disruption, including the German and Ukrainian occupations, civil war, food shortage and political surveillance (Valsiner et al., 2000). This context presented safety concerns for Vygotsky, with some of his colleagues being executed by the state. Vygotsky's high volume of publications in a short period may also have been due to his ongoing battle with tuberculosis, as if he knew that his death was imminent. Vygotsky managed to achieve seminal publications, despite living in a time of 'social upheaval following the Russian Revolution' (Daniels et al., 2007: 1), in an overcrowded apartment with his wife and two daughters, and intermittent stays in also overcrowded medical facilities, due to his recurrent episodes of tuberculosis (Van der Veer and Valsiner, 1991).

Despite the political intensity, Russia also experienced a resurgence of creative pursuits during this time and novel solutions to social challenges began to emerge. One consequence of the Russian Revolution was that millions of children became homeless (Valsiner et al., 2000). Due to their social circumstances, these children were pedagogically neglected. Vygotsky played a role in responding to this significant social issue. In the latter part of his life he worked as a psychologist (Edwards, 2007). These experiences shaped Vygotsky's critique of deficit-focused discourses influencing social practices of pathologising and labelling children. He stated clearly that educational practices (in all forms) 'must, in fact, make a blind child become a normal, socially accepted adult, and must eliminate the label and the notion of defectiveness which has been affixed to the child' (Vygotsky, 1993: 108). According to Vygotsky, education in this broad sense, should not seek to compensate for a perceived 'deficit' of the child. Instead, he points to collective responses that are required in order to develop 'conditions in which culture becomes accessible to the child' (Bakhurst, 2007: 56). In fact, Vygotsky goes further to underscore 'the teacher must orient his work not on yesterday's development in the child but on tomorrow's'

(Vygotsky, 1987a: 211). From these work experiences and his experimental research, Vygotsky distilled a new way of conceptualising learning and development.

Vygotsky was compelled to understand the social formation of the mind; the process of becoming within the social-cultural and historical context. Bruner notes that Vygotsky's research findings were informed by 'incessant observations of children learning to talk and learning to solve problems' (1962: viii–ix). Even though Vygotsky did not explicitly investigate the economic conditions that either constrained or enabled children's development, he focused on the influence of collective structures in forming the mind (otherwise termed 'consciousness') (Edwards, 2007). Vygotsky's activity theory highlighted how children act in the world, and in doing so transform it by developing a more complex understanding of it (Edwards, 2007). From his view, children engage in activities with relational supports that are developmentally above their capacity by imitating others. Consequently, Vygotsky argued that assessing children on the basis of what they can do independently is insufficient. He contends that:

> The psychologist must not limit his [sic] analysis to functions that have matured. He [sic] must consider those that are in the process of maturing. If he [sic] is to fully evaluate the state of the child's development, the psychologist must consider not only the actual level of development but the zone of proximal development.
>
> *(Vygotsky, 1987a: 208–209)*

Vygotsky's key concepts: concept development and the ZPD

Much of Vygotsky's work was not translated and published in the Western world until the late 1980s. Since then, a range of Vygotsky's concepts have been taken up by Western scholars. Although this has meant the development of his ideas, it has also meant the 'assimilation of his ideas into the prevailing schema of Western social science' (Edwards, 2007: 77; Bruner, 1962). Newman and Holzman (2013) and Kozulin (1999) also contend that Western scholars have misused Vygotsky's concepts, misappropriating their meaning, and superimposing their cognitive, individualised bias. For Vygotsky, learning and development were only possible through social collaboration in the ZPD, to achieve higher mental functioning. Vygotsky defined the ZPD as 'the distance between the actual developmental level as determined by independent problem solving and the level of potential development as determined through problem solving under adult guidance or in collaboration with more capable peers' (1978: 86). Vygotsky's ZPD highlighted the role of scaffolding to enable children's learning and development to take place. The process of scaffolding is defined as this social collaboration or guidance to enable children to 'distance' (Sigel, 1993) from their current level of knowing to a 'higher consciousness' (Bruner, 1984: 94).

Many scholars have expanded the notion of what is involved in this scaffolding process. Social collaboration has been characterised by a 'unique' form of 'cooperation' between the child and the adult (Vygotsky, 1978), 'interpersonal connection' (Goldstein, 1999), 'guided participation' (Rogoff, 1990), 'active interaction', 'verbal exchanges' (Wertsch, 1984), 'assisted performance' (Bruner, 1984) and 'engaging the learner in joint meaning making' (Stone, 1998: 409). Fernández, Wegerif, Mercer and Rojas-Drummond highlight how the success of any scaffolding relates 'to the appropriateness of the communication strategies participants use to combine their intellectual resources' (2015: 57). Rogoff extends this focus on communication in the ZPD by highlighting communication that enables a resolution of challenge and 'a search for the common ground of shared understanding, to create a "reference point" for the learning interaction' (Rogoff et al., 1984: 196). Newman and Holzman (2013) are specifically concerned with research that has only focused on 'techniques' that support learning and cognitive processes. By researching in this way, Newman and Holzman argue that 'the "zone" is wrenched out of life, out of history, out of material reality, out of the social processes that produces it: the individual (or "mind") is ontologically and epistemologically separated from society' (2013: 78). They warn that the ZPD significance can be lost by a reductionist cognitive paradigm.

Vygotsky (1987a) explored how the ZPD assists the development of abstract thinking. By enabling the child to reflect on their experience and increase awareness of their own thinking, the child begins to internalise abstract concepts. Enhancing children's problem-solving strategies is a part of this process (Chak, 2001). Sigel's concept of 'distancing' highlights how adults can provide scaffolding via 'distancing acts' in the form of statements or questions that extend the child's current level slightly (1993:142). If the scaffold is not sufficiently extending, the child will potentially find the process boring and potentially disengage. If the scaffold extends the child's knowledge and skill too far, the child might respond with anxiety (Chak, 2001). Sigel (1993) highlighted how the parent or teacher, in providing attuned scaffolding, can assist a child to distance themselves from their immediate experiences, to make sense of events (past and present), enabling possibilities for future alternatives to become known. This abstraction of learning from immediate experiences leads to concept development. Once this concept has been abstracted from immediate experience children can de-contextualise the local particularities of the event, to be able to transfer these concepts when responding to other situations. Chak asserts that the original meaning of Vygotsky's theory of the ZPD characterised 'the individual as an active contributor in the dynamic person-environment relationship' (2001: 384). A co-constructivist perspective rejects the notion that learning is unidirectional, highlighting instead how both child and adult are active participants in this social collaboration. From this perspective, 'the actualization of the ZPD is not seen as a process of transmission of skills but as a transformation of skills' (Chak, 2001: 387). In its place, the ZPD is the site for the co-construction of knowledge.

In Vygotsky's seminal text 'Thinking and Speech' (1987b) he investigated the process of concept development. According to Vygotsky, concept development begins by children naming and making meaning of objects and events in their lives, by 'heaping' them into general categories. We see this when children begin to acquire language. A young child may have a furry pet dog. For this child, all 'furry' animals are then sorted into the general category 'dog'. Drawing on Vygotsky, Newman and Holzman explain how children's 'initial word placing is in relation to the object's characteristics' (2013: 113). Through engaging with their social-cultural and historic context, children begin to make meaning of their everyday activities and experiences. Vygotsky highlighted how, through the activity of fantasy role play, the child can begin to separate from their immediate experiences to ascribe words to particular roles, objects and ways of relating. He wrote:

> [In] play a child spontaneously makes use of his [sic] ability to separate meaning from an object without knowing he [sic] is doing it, just as he [sic] does not know he [sic] is speaking prose but talks without paying attention to the words. Thus, through play the child achieves a functional definition of concepts or objects, and words become parts of a thing.
>
> *(Vygotsky, 1978: 99)*

Vygotsky (1978) argued that play provides a ZPD because the child uses her/his imagination to perform roles or activities that are beyond her/his immediate developmental capacity, stating that, 'in play, it is as though he were a head taller than himself' (Vygotsky, 1978: 102). He explained how, through fantasy play, children imitate the world around them and, by engaging their imagination to perform new roles, children develop in unique and original ways. Vygotsky clarified that 'action in the imaginative sphere, in an imaginary situation [leads to] the creation of voluntary intentions, and the formation of real-life plans and volitional motives' (1978: 102–103). Vygotsky cast children as the producers of their own meaning-making process. Newman and Holzman construct this type of play as a 'revolutionary activity' as the child 'has more control in organizing the perceptual, cognitive and emotional elements' when drawing on elements from their social-cultural and historical context (2013: 102).

Through play and other concrete activities children begin to sort the characteristics of objects or events according to their emerging criteria informed by abstract 'everyday' or 'spontaneous' concepts (Vygotsky, 1987a). Further movement across the ZPD is possible when children start to discern from their 'heaped' categories of objects or events, to more refined 'complexes' or 'higher psychological functions' (Vygotsky, 1978). The development of this type of conceptual thinking takes place when the child begins to make links to the relationships between these objects and events. In Vygotsky's words, concept development 'presupposes more than unification. To form such a concept it is also necessary to abstract, to single out elements, and to view the abstracted elements apart from the totality of the concrete experience in which they are embedded' (Vygotsky, 1986: 135). In this process of abstraction, children obtain altitude from their immediate experiences, and develop an in-depth understanding of their specific, concrete experiences.

Vygotsky (1987a) differentiated 'everyday' concepts from 'scientific' concepts. He explained how these two types of concepts have different histories, with scientific concepts being predominantly taught in school by instruction. Bakhurst explains that scientific concepts are 'verbally articulated, theoretically embedded, and tightly related to many other concepts [therefore] they seem abstract, general and more remote from concrete experiences' (2007: 70). In contrast, according to Vygotsky,

> the birth of a spontaneous concept is usually associated with the child's immediate encounter with things … Only through a long developmental process does the child attain conscious awareness of the object, of the concept itself, and the capacity to operate abstractly with the concept.
>
> *(1987a: 219)*

For example, 'gentle patting' of the family pet is an everyday concept born from the child's immediate environmental experience. He exposed how 'while scientific and everyday concepts move in opposite directions in development, these processes are internally and profoundly connected with one another' (Vygotsky, 1987a: 219). Higher mental functioning for children is possible with the development of significant abstracted concepts (such as trust or social justice, for example) which act as internal tools that children can employ to actively shape their own lives. White explicitly linked concept development with children achieving agency. He asserts that through concept development 'children begin to inhabit their own lives' (2012: 125).

For Vygotsky, children develop concepts in their social-cultural and historical context via the development of word meanings. Vygotsky (1978) referred to this phenomenon as 'semiotic mediation' in which the child's engagement is mediated by the signs, symbols and words around her/him. From Vygotsky's perspective,

> when a new word has been learned by the child, [the child's] development is barely starting; as the child's intellect develops, it is replaced by generalizations of a higher and higher type – a process that leads in the end to the formation of true concepts … Real concepts

> are impossible without words, and thinking in concepts does not exist beyond verbal thinking. That is why the central movement in concept formation, and its generative cause, is a specific use of words as functional tools.
>
> *(1986: 107)*

Vygotsky goes further to clarify 'the word without meaning is not a word but an empty sound. Meaning is a necessary, constituting feature of the word itself … It is the word viewed from the inside' (Vygotsky, 1987a: 244). He highlighted how the relationship achieved between thought and words involves a process of moving back and forth between words and thought. Holland emphasises how semiotic mediation enables children to obtain control, co-ordinate and 'resignify' their own actions within their social context (2007: 115). In this way, children's concept development and language acquisition are influenced by the historical context in which they live; at the same time they co-produce their social environments.

Vygotsky demonstrated how children's inner speech is a tool they use in order to overcome challenging activities. Inner speech for Vygotsky was 'speech for oneself' (1986: 225). It was also referred to as 'egocentric speech' (initially termed by Piaget). Unlike Piaget however, Vygotsky exposed how this type of speech is social in origin and then internalised by the child. He explained how this egocentric speech is inherently linked with the child's thought processes while engaging with activity, helping the child guide their actions. Inner speech also allows children to create their own sense of self in relation to the social context in which they live. According to Vygotsky then,

> every function in the cultural development of the child appears on the stage twice, in two planes, first, the social, then the psychological, first between people as an inter-mental category, then within the child as an intra-mental category. This pertains equally to voluntary attention, to logical memory, to the formation of concepts, and to the development of will.
>
> *(Vygotsky, 1997: 145)*

Vygotsky's research made visible the interconnection between concept development within the ZPD, inner speech and the achievement of agency for children.

Bruner's key concepts: narrative structure and identity

Jerome Bruner was born in New York in 1915 and died in 2016 aged over 100. Bruner, like Vygotsky, was drawn to the generative influence of the socio-cultural and historic context on children's cognitive development and learning. He was inspired to build on Vygotsky's work through his educational psychology and language development research from the 1960s onwards. Bruner's research (1985) highlighted the importance of 'joint attention' between caregiver and infant in assisting the infant to recognise themselves through the interactions with their caregivers. He, too, understood language acquisition as being central to formation of inner speech, children's development and agency (Bruner, 1975). In the 1980s, Bruner began to immerse himself in research that explored how narratives shape our social realities. He argued that children's inner speech is inherently connected to the narratives that are available to them in their historical context. In this sense, children's inner speech is also characterised by the stories they tell themselves (Bruner, 2004). The narratives children employ to make sense of their past and current experiences will dramatically influence what kind of action (if any) is possible in order to respond to future challenges. For example, if a child has been supported to identify themselves as a child who is 'good at solving problems', the child can tell stories about these abilities, imagine and project themselves in future situations being able to face adversity of some kind or another. Children who experience deficit-focused narratives re-told about them and their problematic 'behaviour', experience themselves and their identities as 'dysfunctional'. Key people in the child's life, such as teachers, caregivers, family members and peers retell these problematic stories. This ongoing external dialogue and inner speech can present significant constraints for the child, to develop alternative ways of seeing themselves. Bruner warned that children 'become the autographical narratives' they tell themselves (2004: 694).

Bruner's work on narrative structure demonstrates how influential the social-cultural and historical context can be for children's identity formation. In this sense, a child's identity is a social achievement. Drawing on Vygotsky's concept of semiotic mediation, Bruner made explicit the role culture plays in the formation of children's identity. From this perspective, an identity 'personalizes a set of collectively developed discourses about a type and cultivates, in interaction with others, a set of embodied practices that signify the person' (Holland and Lachicotte, 2007: 134). Children find ways to navigate and negotiate their social worlds and 'they come to be able to organize and narrate themselves in practice in the name of an identity, and thus achieve a modest form of agency' (Holland and Lachicotte, 2007: 134). Bruner's work (1987) is also significant because he identified how the re-construction of children's narratives can assist them to imagine a way of addressing current and/or future predicaments they might face.

Discursive therapy as pedagogy: the 'third wave' therapeutic stance

Vygotsky's concepts are not only relevant for educational settings but they offer a significant contribution to our understanding of learning and development within discursive therapeutic interactions with children and their caregivers. The field of psychotherapy has expanded over time to include the notion of learning and education that can occur within therapeutic interaction. Discursive therapies stem from 'third wave' approaches, which can include solution-focused, narrative, and collaborative therapies that are informed by social constructionism (Strong, 2016). Discursive therapy literature conceptualises therapeutic interaction as a form of pedagogy, enabling the co-production of knowledge.

Children are referred to therapy due to some concern (usually identified by an adult), relating to their development. Vygotsky's legacy is one that reminds social workers who engage in therapeutic interaction with children of their role in children's pedagogy and how therapeutic 'joint activities' can support scaffolding in the ZPD. To achieve this, however, therapeutic interactions need to position children as 'active learners' in a 'conversational partnership', as opposed to passive recipients to therapeutic intervention (White, 2012). Children accessing therapy need to be identified as the producers of their own meaning and initiatives, within their social-cultural and historical context. To contribute to this type of partnership, social workers position themselves in a deconstructive stance to invite a less problem-saturated account of the child, to construct alternative narratives that feature the child 'as a competent social agent' (Avdi and Georgaca, 2007: 163). Yet, how can social workers co-produce agentic discourses with children that assist in children's concept development in therapeutic interactions?

Vygotsky has the potential to inspire social workers to reconsider therapeutic interactions as an opportunity to re-engage with children's imagination and fantasy play. Children are constantly making sense of their experiences, they just have different ways of expressing themselves, which may involve non-verbal actions, or demonstrating their thinking through play (Anderson and Gehart, 2007). Children's attempts at meaning-making via play or other non-verbal means can be easily dismissed. Discourses of 'professionalism' and 'therapeutic procedure' can invite social workers to disqualify the significance of joining with children in their fantasy role playing, construing it as 'just play' and not 'actual' therapy. Vygotsky and Newman remind us of how 'revolutionary' it can be when adults join children in child-led fantasy play, to enable children to put words to objects and events in their lives, in order to move across the ZPD.

In addition to child-led play-based activities, discursive therapeutic conversation can be 'playful' to richly engage with the child's meaning-making. Marsten, Epston and Markham's (2016) recent publication encourages social workers who engage in therapeutic interactions to recognise and connect with children's imaginative know-how, to find unique and creative ways for children to address the challenges they face. They remind us as social workers to 'unlock our imaginations of an intrepid child and attend to characterization more as co-authors than clinicians' (Marsten et al., 2016: 9). In such collaborative therapeutic interactions, children are exposed to activities and conversations that stretch them beyond their current developmental capacity. In these scaffolding processes, meaningful connections are developed to create collective learnings and potential development (Newman and Holzman, 2013).

For such collective learnings to occur, an astute ability to analyse power in micro interactions is required, in order to subvert any deficit-focused discourses that may be infiltrating the conversation. Power is at play in subtle yet significant ways in therapeutic interactions with children. White explained that in order to influence scaffolding in the ZPD, the social worker does not engage in 'pointing out positives', 'giving affirmations', 'illustrating strengths and resources', 'reframing' the difficult experiences of [children's] lives, 'making hypotheses', or 'delivering interventions' (2012: 123). To avoid social workers' or caregivers' agendas driving the focus of therapy, it is crucial that children are consulted about what is of concern or interest to them. Vygotsky understood that children will explore what they are interested to know, by engaging in activity. Consequently, time needs to be taken to clarify with the child what they are interested in or concerned about in relation to their lives.

Vygotsky's work highlights the need to critically reflect on how social workers can meaningfully contribute to scaffolding with the child and caregiver in therapeutic interactions. Scaffolding is possible when the social worker sensitively attunes to, and is responsive to, the child's current developmental capacities, while challenging them by stretching their concept development. White explicitly stated that a position of genuine curiosity to co-explore with the child and their caregiver is required, 'to traverse the gap between what is known and familiar to them and what it is possible for them to know and to do' (2012: 123). Drawing from Vygotsky's understanding of the ZPD, White (2012) reconceptualised therapeutic inquiry. He proposed a way to understand therapeutic practice, and outlined how a child (or any person) could be supported to move across the zone in 'manageable steps' via various levels of distancing from their immediate experiences (White, 2012: 127).

Low-level distancing tasks invite the child to characterise and link words to actual objects or events (White, 2012). Without this linking, children may speak therapeutic language that has been provided to them via 'psycho-education' provided by adults/professionals, however these words or phrases are empty, without any embodied meaning. By inviting the child to characterise problematic or preferred objects and events, and to make sense of them enables the beginning of 'everyday' concept development. Characterising objects or events, however, may be too demanding for the child at first, who may struggle to find the words. The caregiver is invited to offer tentative descriptions of key objects and events, and their observations of children's initiatives. These descriptions can act as a reflective surface from which the child can agree or disagree, to begin to discern their own preferred meaning-making. To avoid centralising the caregiver's meaning-making, the child needs to be consulted about their views of caregiver's accounts, to invite them to put alternative words (if needed) to the relevant objects and or preferred events in their lives.

Medium-level distancing tasks enable the child to discern from their experiences, to reflect on emerging categories or 'complexes' informing their understandings of such experiences. This type of conversation assists children to identify how these events and objects relate to each other (White, 2012). In practice, this means questions or statements serve as a platform to assist the child to identify and clarify what skills or practices they have been drawing on, in order to take steps in their lives. It can also involve exploring what has supported them to resist the influence of the problems they may face, to reclaim their lives from the influence of such problems. Medium- to high-level distancing tasks involve the child reflecting on the steps they have taken, to make visible what they have learned from these initiatives (White, 2012). By inviting the child to retell these events, she or he can reflect on who or what in their environment supported them in their initiatives. In doing this, the historical and relational context that supports the child, their initiative and their preferred intentions and values can become more visible, and thus replicable.

High-level distancing tasks in therapy foster reflection that abstracts learnings from the local and concrete social context that gave rise to them (White, 2012). This type of reflection enables 'everyday' concepts to more fully develop. In practice, this involves the social worker playing a key role in supporting the child to identify and unpack key intentions and values that have informed current or past action(s). Preferred events in the child's life are linked together according to key concepts, which become 'rooted in history' (White, 2007: 62). By abstracting these concepts they become generalisable and transferrable, enabling the child to draw on these local ways of knowing when facing future challenges. Very high-level distancing tasks in therapeutic interactions invite the child to consider what steps they might take in the future, in accordance with such concepts (White, 2012). In such conversational partnerships, children are supported to richly describe and characterise key objects and events, in order to reflect on 'their lived experience, to stretch their minds, to exercise their imagination, and to employ their meaning-making-resources' (White, 2007: 62).

Vygotsky and Bruner provided a crucial reminder that language used by adults in their interactions with children, particularly in a therapy context, is not neutral. Particular words and phrases obtain prominence in therapeutic interactions (Marsten et al., 2016). For instance, particular phrases, such as 'children should be seen and not heard', are born from a historical context, and constitute a discourse that identifies children and their meaning-making as less valuable. As social workers, we need to remain vigilant about whose words are being privileged in therapeutic interactions. The repetition of such words, phrases and problematic stories told about the child in therapy can serve to represent a particular view of the child as 'the truth' (Madigan, 2011). These problematic interpretations of the child and their initiatives have profound influence on her/his meaning-making, self-narratives and inner speech. We, as social workers, need to critically question if we are contributing to these dominant stories that can serve to reinforce apparently 'fixed' qualities or 'traits' of the child, or if we are actively working to make visible subordinate stories that reveal children's skills and knowledge in the face of the challenges they face.

Vygotsky's legacy to social work pedagogy

Vygotsky's key concepts offer an alternative perspective to dominant Western theories of child development for social work pedagogy. Psychology theories and concepts of child development are routinely imported into social work courses. Such courses could be sites of critical analysis, to invite social work students to interrogate psychological theories and concepts, to avoid individualist accounts remaining a taken-for-granted paradigm. The key concepts from Vygotsky and Bruner outlined earlier in the chapter provide a needed point of difference to commence a more critical engagement of child development theories to further investigate the therapeutic practice implications.

Vygotsky offers an alternative way of conceptualising teaching interactions with social work students, to offer a parallel scaffolding process of concept development in the ZPD. To go beyond the presentation and instruction of Vygotsky's concepts, discursive therapy can be taught in experiential ways, to create a collaborative learning environment in which social work students can step into practice opportunities. Such 'joint activities' serve as a foundation to support students' concept development in relation to discursive therapeutic approaches with children and their caregivers. Following practice opportunities, students are offered low-level distancing questions to critically reflect on their immediate experiences, to initially characterise and put words to their practice experiences. Other scaffolding processes can involve teaching staff offering their observations, summaries, case examples as reflecting surfaces for students to identify their own key learnings (James et al., 2008). Social work student group reflections can be facilitated to enable further discernment of ways of positioning children in therapeutic interactions to support concept development and agency. Such interactive processes serve as platforms to consolidate students' knowledge (James et al., 2008), to distance from their immediate practice experience to develop a more embodied and complex knowledge of discursive therapy. By students having first-hand experiences of collaborative learning processes that support their own concept development, social work graduates are better placed in their transition to therapeutic work with children and their caregivers.

Conclusion

In contemporary practice contexts, when clinical discourses encourage social workers to be 'behaviourally-focused', to find evidence of developmental deficits, Vygotsky provides an important reminder for social workers to gain altitude from our immediate therapeutic practice with children and their caregivers. The prevalence of social workers working therapeutically with children and their caregivers facing complex challenges is increasing. Critical pedagogy is essential to further equip social workers to optimally work with children within the institutional context of therapy. Vygotsky and Bruner's key concepts are critical in the current political environment of increased privatisation of therapeutic services for children. In this current context, social workers are expected to assess children's developmental capacities independent of their relational context, to diagnose and problematise children's developmental deficits, in order to prescribe 'needed' interventions to compensate for such deficits. These diagnoses are required in order for caregivers and children to receive government funding for therapeutic services. Vygotsky's ideas are clearly a product of his interaction with the social-cultural and historical context around him. Yet his legacy continues to remind us to consider how activity in the child's cultural and historical context shapes concept development, higher mental functioning; to enable children to reach higher ground.

The key concepts outlined in this chapter highlight the challenges children face when negotiating their social context, while at the same time demonstrating how children can transform their environments by developing a more complex understanding of it. Both theorists provide pedagogic concepts for social workers to position children in therapeutic interactions in ways that support their emancipatory transformation, enabling their achievement of learning, development and agency. To achieve this, social workers offering therapeutic interaction with children need to assume a de-constructive and curious stance. Through this stance, social workers can assist the child to distance themselves from their immediate experience, 'to stretch their minds, to exercise their imagination, and to employ their meaning-making-resources' to reach higher ground (White, 2007: 62).

References

Anderson, H and D Gehart. 2007. *Collaborative therapy: Relationships and conversations that make a difference*. New York: Routledge.
Avdi, E and E Georgaca. 2007. "Discourse analysis and psychotherapy: A critical review." *European Journal of Psychotherapy & Counselling* 9 (2): 157–176. doi: 10.1080/13642530701363445.
Bakhurst, D. 2007. "Vygotsky's demons." In *The Cambridge companion to Vygotsky*, Eds. H Daniels, M Cole and J Wertsch, 55–76. Cambridge: Cambridge University Press.
Bruner, J. 1984. "Vygotsky's zone of proximal development: The hidden agenda." *New Directions for Child and Adolescent Development* 1984 (23): 93–97. doi: 10.1002/cd.23219842309.
Bruner, J. 1985. "Child's talk: Learning to use language." *Child Language Teaching and Therapy*: 111–114. http://journals.sagepub.com/home/clt.
Bruner, J. 2004. "Life as narrative." *Social Research: An International Quarterly* 71 (3): 691–710. www.socres.org/.
Bruner, J S. 1975. "The ontogenesis of speech acts." *Journal of Child Language* 2 (1): 1–19. doi: 10.1017/S0305000900000866.
Bruner, J S. 1987. *Actual minds, possible worlds*. Cambridge: Harvard University Press.
Bruner, J S. 1962. "Introduction to LS Vygotsky." In *Thought and language*.
Chak, A. 2001. "Adult sensitivity to children's learning in the zone of proximal development." *Journal for the Theory of Social Behaviour* 31 (4): 383–395. https://onlinelibrary.wiley.com/loi/14685914.
Daniels, H, M Cole and J Wertsch. 2007. *The Cambridge companion to Vygotsky*. Cambridge: Cambridge University Press.
Edwards, A. 2007. "An interesting resemblance: Vygotsky, mean and American pragmatism." In *The Cambridge companion to Vygotsky*, Eds. H Daniels, M Cole and J Wertsch, 77–100. Cambridge: Cambridge University Press.
Fernández, M, R Wegerif, N Mercer and S Rojas-Drummond. 2015. "Re-conceptualizing "scaffolding" and the zone of proximal development in the context of symmetrical collaborative learning." *Journal of Classroom Interaction* 50 (1): 54–72. http://summon.serialsolutions.com.
Goldstein, L S. 1999. "The relational zone: The role of caring relationships in the co-construction of mind." *American Educational Research Journal* 36 (3): 647–673. doi: 10.2307/1163553.
Holland, D and W Lachicotte. 2007. "Vygotsky, mead and the new sociocultural studies of idenity." In *The Cambridge companion to Vygotsky*, Eds. H Daniels, M Cole and J Wertsch, 101–135. Cambridge: Cambridge University Press.
James, I A, D Milne and R Morse. 2008. "Microskills of clinical supervision: Scaffolding skills." *Journal of Cognitive Psychotherapy* 22 (1): 29. www.springerpub.com/journal-of-cognitive-psychotherapy.html.
Kozulin, A. 1999. *Vygotsky's psychology: A biography of ideas*. Cambridge: Harvard University Press.
Madigan, S. 2011. *Narrative therapy*. 1st ed. Washington, DC: American Psychological Association.
Marsten, D, D Epston and L Markham. 2016. *Narrative therapy in wonderland: Connecting with children's imaginative know-how*. New York: W.W. Norton & Company.
Newman, F and L Holzman. 2013. *Lev Vygotsky (classic edition): Revolutionary Scientist*. London: Psychology Press.
Rogoff, B. 1990. *Apprenticeship in thinking: Cognitive development in social context*. New York: Oxford University Press.
Rogoff, B, S Ellis and W Gardner. 1984. Adjustment of adult-child instruction according to child's age and task. *Developmental Psychology* 20 (2): 193–199. doi: 10.1037/0012-1649.20.2.193.
Sigel, I E. 1993. "The centrality of a distancing model for the development of representational competence." In *The development and meaning of psychological distance*, Eds. R R Cocking and K A Renninger, 141–158. London: Lawrence Erlbaum Associates.
Stone, C A. 1998. "Should we salvage the scaffolding metaphor?" *Journal of Learning Disabilities* 31 (4): 409–413. doi: 10.1177/002221949803100411.
Strong, T. 2016. "Discursive awareness and resourcefulness: Bringing discursive researchers into closer dialogue with discursive therapists?" In *The Palgrave handbook of adult mental health: Discourse and conversation studies*, Eds. M O'Reilly and J Lester, 482–501. New York: Palgrave Macmillan. nmXTudP8zgUy-KWoFxqbYESOcpQ2VOtGAlmcE5rj0na4CxVM-GEUezl3JYd5bZLIkImYX5DRzwe7_O2LK3LYdeA12Vt_bsS4Ubp-A3pmL_A.
Valsiner, J, R Van der Veer and V Jaan. 2000. *The social mind: Construction of the idea*. Cambridge: Cambridge University Press.

Van der Veer, R. 2007. "Vygotsky in context: 1900–1935." In *The Cambridge companion to Vygotsky*, Eds. H Daniels, M Cole and J Wertsch, 21–49. Cambridge: Cambridge University Press.

Van der Veer, R and J Valsiner. 1991. *Understanding Vygotsky: A quest for synthesis*. Oxford: Blackwell Publishing.

Vygotsky, L S. 1978. *Mind in society: The development of higher mental process*. Cambridge, MA: Harvard University Press.

Vygotsky, L S. 1986. *Thought and language*. edited by Alex Kozulin. Translation newly rev. and ed. Cambridge: MIT Press.

Vygotsky, L S. 1987a. *The collected works of LS Vygotsky: Vol. 1, Problems of general psychology (RW Rieber & AS Carton, Eds., N. Minick, trans.)*. New York: Plenum Press.

Vygotsky, L S. 1987b. "Thinking and speech." In *The collected works of LS Vygotsky. Vol 1, Problems of General Psychology*, Trans. Norris Minick and Eds. R W Reiber and A S Carton, 39–285. New York: Plenum Press.

Vygotsky, L S. 1993. *The collected works of LS Vygotsky. Vol. 2, The fundamentals of defectology (Abnormal psychology and learning disabilities)*. Translated by Aaron S Carton and Robert W Rieber. New York: Plenum Press.

Vygotsky, L S. 1997. *The collected works of LS Vygotsky. Vol. 4, The history of the development of higher mental functions*. Trans. MJ Hall and ed. RW Reiber. New York: Plenum Press.

Wertsch, J V. 1984. "The zone of proximal development: Some conceptual issues." *New Directions for Child and Adolescent Development* 1984 (23): 7–18. doi: 10.1002/cd.23219842303.

White, M. 2007. *Maps of narrative practice*. 1st ed. New York: W.W. Norton & Company.

White, M. 2012. "Scaffolding a therapeutic conversation." In *Masters of narrative and collaborative therapies: The voices of Andersen, Anderson, and White*, Eds. T Malinen, S Cooper and F Thomas, 121–170. New York: Routledge.

6

A prophet without honor
Bertha Capen Reynolds' contribution to social work's critical practice and pedagogy

Michael Reisch

UNIVERSITY OF MARYLAND, BALTIMORE, US

The spirit of the profession is embodied in … Bertha Capen Reynolds.
(Quam, 1995, p. 77)

Introduction

This chapter provides a concise overview of the life and career of Bertha Capen Reynolds, with a particular emphasis on her contributions to social work theory and pedagogy. Reynolds was a leading social work theorist and activist, who strove to integrate concepts derived from Freud and Marx into both practice and educational frameworks. The chapter places Reynolds in the context of the social and political environment in which she lived and worked. It traces her influence on the social work profession in the United States, her marginalization due to her political views and affiliations, her subsequent rehabilitation, and her legacy today.

Unlike most 'first generation' U.S. social workers, Bertha Capen Reynolds came from a family of modest means. Born in Western Massachusetts in December 1885, shortly before the establishment of the first North American social settlements and nearly a decade after the earliest Charity Organization Society appeared in the U.S., Reynolds grew up in a strict Methodist family that endured several personal tragedies and chronic financial hardship. She was educated at home until she was 12 in an intellectually supportive but emotionally distant household by her widowed mother and maternal grandparents. Although her family life lacked emotional warmth, it provided her with several valuable assets that shaped her career: moral discipline; a lifelong concern for others' well-being; and, in her mother, a strong female role model (Reynolds, 1963).

Reynolds graduated Phi Beta Kappa from Smith College, an all-female institution, in 1908, majoring in psychology, an unusual choice for a woman of her generation, one that foreshadowed her later interest in psychiatric social work. As an undergraduate, she developed a class-consciousness that influenced her entire professional life. Although she did not self-identify as a feminist or play a leadership role in women's organizations during her career, the independence and courage Reynolds displayed in the face of political and professional adversity reflected the influence of changing ideas about women's role in society and in organized efforts to effect social change.

Upon graduation, she taught for a year in an all-Black high school affiliated with Atlanta University, where she met the great African American social scientist and activist W.E.B. Du Bois. This early exposure to the social conditions affecting African Americans and to emerging views about racial equality had a subtle influence on the conceptual frameworks that formed the foundation of her views about social work practice and education. They appear in both her scholarship – e.g., the adoption of universalist theories of change, such as Marxism – and in her activism. She was a strong supporter of organized labor, particularly the multi-racial organizing efforts of the Congress of Industrial Organizations (Reynolds, 1945), and of the program of the Communist and Socialist Parties during the 1930s and 1940s, when they were among the few entities speaking out against racial inequality.

Reynolds then enrolled in Simmons College's certificate program in social work in Boston. After working five years at the prestigious Boston Children's Aid Society, Reynolds entered the first class for psychiatric social workers at Smith College, where E.E. Southard and Mary Jarrett exposed her to the then 'revolutionary content' of psychotherapy (Reynolds, 1963). She then worked as a psychiatric social worker at Danvers State Hospital and the Massachusetts Department of Mental Hygiene.

During the 1920s, Reynolds immersed herself in the study of Freudian theory and psycho-analytic methods and began to publish professional papers on these subjects. A paper she presented at the 1924 National Conference of Social Work, 'The Mental Hygiene of Children' (Reynolds, 1924), led to the offer of the Associate Director position at the Smith College School of Social Work, which she reluctantly accepted. Her ambivalence stemmed from concerns about the disease model of practice at the core of psychoanalysis that contrasted sharply with her innate humanitarianism and growing interest in social reform.

Reflecting on this tension some years later, Reynolds (1938) wrote that psychiatric social work grew in popularity during the 1920s based on an unspoken fear of social revolution if the façade of the decade's prosperity collapsed:

> Was it because of an unacknowledged fear that people who had begun to move and think in masses would not be easily silenced if they began to speak of very real wrongs? The ruthless suppression of strikes and denial of civil liberties suggest this … Studies of individual behavior may well have seemed safer than a search for the causes of sickness in society. Perhaps, after all, it was better to assume that those who agitated for reforms could be best explained, and thus silenced, by one of the terms for describing a psychopathic personality.
>
> (p. 8)

Nevertheless, the introduction of Freudian and Rankian psychology reflected a radical challenge to prevailing theories of human behavior. These ideas were particularly attractive to radical social workers from the early 1920s through at least the 1950s because they stressed 'client self-determination, clarity of agency function, and the importance of relationship' (Schwartz, 1981, p. 7). (Feminist critiques of Freudian concepts first appeared among social workers as a consequence of the emergence of second wave feminism in the 1960s.) In her review of Virginia Robinson's groundbreaking book, *A Changing Psychology in Social Casework* (Robinson, 1931), Reynolds praised its emphasis on the worker–client relationship and its recognition that 'adjustment of individuals is a *social* adjustment, never a purely individual affair' (Reynolds, 1931, pp. 543–544). Reynolds maintained this emphasis on relationship throughout her career. In her words, it 'make[s] us human and give[s] us immortality in the heritage we leave ... to future generations' (quoted in Rosen, 1963, p. 931). She combined this focus with 'consciousness of class differences and their implications for human development and professional practice' (ibid., p. 932).

In response to the widespread human tragedy produced by the Great Depression, Reynolds became active in the radical Rank and File Movement among social workers. Through its publication, *Social Work Today*, the Rank and Filers addressed issues, such as racial repression in the South that the mainstream profession largely ignored. Although she initially supported the New Deal, Reynolds soon advocated for more widespread change and collective action. In publications and presentations, she joined movement spokespersons who criticized New Deal policies from a left-wing perspective, and supported civil rights legislation (Reynolds, 1941), union organizing, and direct social action (Wenocur and Reisch, 1989). Reynolds' stature as the most published social worker of the period heightened the movement's status and legitimacy.

In the late 1930s, the newly created House Committee on Un-American Activities began to investigate 'subversives' in the Roosevelt Administration, left-wing unions, and the social work profession. In this environment, Reynolds' affiliation with the Socialist and Communist Parties and with organized labor eventually made her position at Smith untenable. Under pressure from Everett Kimball, the school's director, Reynolds resigned in 1938 and began a new career as a consultant, trainer, and lecturer (Freedberg, 1986).

The subsequent professional blacklisting of Reynolds is, perhaps, most clearly revealed in the failure of the Red Cross to respond to her application for a position, even when it desperately needed trained social workers in the aftermath of Pearl Harbor. Finally, in 1943, the left-wing National Maritime Union and the United Seamen's Service hired Reynolds to develop one of the first worker-controlled social service programs. This experience and her interaction with the union's members gave Reynolds the opportunity to refine and put into practice many of her progressive ideas about practice and education.

After the project ended in 1947, Reynolds went into semi-retirement in Massachusetts, where she continued to write and lecture. During these years, anti-Communist purges inside and outside the profession contributed to her marginalization in the increasingly conservative social work field (Reynolds, 1953). A glaring manifestation of this marginalization was the omission of her influential scholarship from histories of social work and textbooks on social work practice published in the post-war period. Another was the successful attempt by public officials to prevent her from speaking at social work conferences.

By the mid-1950s, Reynolds was living in obscurity and near poverty in her childhood home in Western Massachusetts. It was not until a new generation of activist social workers 'rediscovered' her work in the late 1960s and 1970s that she regained the professional prominence she once held. After considerable urging, she agreed to have her books and articles reprinted and, as a final symbol of her redemption, before her death at the age of 93 in 1978, a national organization of progressive social workers, the Bertha Capen Reynolds Society (now the Social Welfare Action Alliance) emerged to promote her ideas.

Key concepts

Reynolds' scholarship, teaching, and activism emphasized several key concepts. First, she believed strongly that the nation's social welfare system should combine economic supports for people's need delivered through public policy and psychosocial supports provided by social service agencies. This synthesis presaged by three decades the dual focus of empowerment theory, developed by Solomon (1976). Although Reynolds was one of the strongest critics of New Deal policies, she defended its foundational principles and the concept of universal social welfare based on a critical analysis of political-economic conditions that are eerily prescient of today's realities:

> If public assistance could be destroyed, Labor would be forced to accept wages below subsistence levels, and without recourse. If protests of organized labor could be eliminated, public assistance itself could be reduced to legalized starvation under controls approximating slavery.
>
> *(Reynolds, 1963, p. 271)*

This perspective also held important implications for social work's role in society. Reynolds argued that if the profession did not go beyond 'offering palliatives to assuage the miseries of poverty and racism, [it] was destined to carry out the designs of the ruling class and victimize clients' (Joseph, 2009, p. 122).

A natural corollary of this position was that social work needed to avoid 'the path of exploitation and [adopt] a more radical vision of society' (Reisch, 1993, p. 63). This was the basis for Reynolds' attempt to synthesize the theories of Freud, Rank, and Marx into a coherent practice framework and to reconcile the structural change goals of the Rank and File Movement with casework' (ibid.). Reynolds' view of these connections and the potential to combine concepts from Freud and Marx, which parallels similar efforts by Marcuse a generation later, was far ahead of the professional mainstream, particularly her recognition of the shared interests of workers and clients (Reynolds, 1934).

In her autobiography (1963, pp. 173–174), Reynolds summarized the Rank and File Movement's 'five simple principles':

1. Social work exists to serve people in need. If it serves other classes who have other purposes, it becomes too dishonest to be capable of either theoretical or practical development.
2. Social work exists to help people help themselves and therefore, should not be alarmed when they do so by organized means, such as client or tenant or labor groups.
3. Social work operates by communication, listening, and sharing experiences.
4. Social work has to find its place among other movements for human betterment.
5. Social workers as citizens cannot consider themselves superior to their clients as if they do not have the same problems.

Influenced by two major 20th-century Western intellectual traditions – the writings of Freud and Marx – Reynolds sought to synthesize a 'science of society' (Marx) with a science of human behavior (Freud). The so-called 'Functional School of Social Work,' based on the ideas of Otto Rank and developed at the University of Pennsylvania by Virginia Robinson and Jessie Taft, also appealed to her because it stressed the importance of the social service agency. Well before the development of 'generalist' social work, she identified the common threads in all practice modalities and the role of power in the practice relationship and society (Kaplan, 2002).

Unlike many colleagues in her era (and our own) who viewed the psychological and social dimensions of practice as distinct, Reynolds regarded them as inextricably connected to the human condition. Yet, in constructing her synthetic practice framework, Reynolds applied a critical eye even to the theories that formed its foundation. She criticized the Functional School for its rigidity, regarded Freud's bourgeois background and Eurocentric views as grounds for skepticism about the universal application of his ideas, and recognized that social justice movements, inspired by ideologies such as Marxism, could lead to the neglect of individual freedom.

Despite these criticisms, she tried to synthesize Marxism with Freudian and Rankian psychology and her Calvinist beliefs to create a revolutionary model of social work practice. Like many intellectuals and activists of her generation, Reynolds found in Marxism an explanation of social conditions that complemented the 'philosophy of growth' she had expounded as the basis for social work practice since the 1920s (Reynolds, 1963, p. 184; 1938). Marxism helped her explain the existence of poverty and the role of class divisions. Freud's ideas enabled her to analyze and forgive people. Her Methodist upbringing helped her cope with fear and hostility, forces with which she contended throughout her life and career (McQuaide, 1987, p. 273).

Decades before most of her colleagues, she recognized the mutuality of worker and client interests in the support of social reforms. In her words, social service work could 'free men from the crippling accumulations of fear and hate so that they may have energy to use what intelligence they possess ... [to work for] ... a better social order' (Reynolds, 1973[1934], p. 27). In effect, Reynolds laid the foundation for what became critical social work theory and practice in the late 20th century; half a century before it appeared (Gil, 1976; Goroff, n.d.).

By the mid-1930s, in addition to her theoretical work with Taft and Robinson and growing political and union activism, Reynolds published numerous scholarly articles about her innovative practice framework (Reynolds, 1932; Rosen, 1963). 'She believed that social workers should be, not separate from the passions of the time, but intimately involved in the restructuring of a more equitable, more humane society' (Rosen, 1963, pp. 932–933). Her attempt to integrate Marx and Freud stemmed from 'the need for close attention to social issues of exploitation, of class conflict and of helping the client to function more adequately in his [sic] social relationships' (p. 933). She believed that both inner and outer stress need to be understood 'if the individual is to be truly helped to function.' In Rosen's words, this made her 'a prophet of the profession' (p. 933).

Reynolds' interests were more than theoretical. Reynolds linked the future of casework to recognition of the roots of the Depression in the increased concentration of wealth and the need to create counter movements for democracy and the democratization of services (Reynolds, June 1938). She sought to expand the role of social welfare by recognizing the relationship between government funded economic support and the social supports provided by agencies through casework (Reynolds, 1935). She believed that social workers had to defend the socio-economic interests of their clients as part of a broader defense of welfare state provisions.

Reflecting on her career, Reynolds cited several key environmental influences on her thinking about social work practice and education. One was the repression of class-consciousness in the profession after World War I and the resultant shift in casework's clientele toward 'those whose economic needs were cared for otherwise, and who had enough leisure and verbal articulateness to explore their own personal difficulties with a skilled professional person.' Another was the challenge the Great Depression posed to the universal presumptions of Freudian theory and to the belief 'that private philanthropy could take care of almost every problem.' In order to respond to economic conditions, 'a civilized society requires both an administration efficient enough to see that thousands of mothers had income with which to care for their own children, and a skilled service available to mothers who need it.' These views inevitably led Reynolds to question the prevailing definition of social casework. 'The social casework of Mary Richmond's day could [no longer] be practiced ... Its assumption of class stratification would be considered condescending and we demand[ed] a democratic approach to people' (Reynolds, 1964, pp. 13–15).

Her revised definition focused on 'adjustment, not maladjustment, health instead of pathology' (p. 15). Its key features were (1) the importance of *social* diagnosis; (2) the importance of egalitarian relationships; and (3) recognition of the potential for change in persons and their situation.

While she believed that the current social order was fundamentally unjust, she strove to create a practice model that embodied social democratic principles on a daily basis. The essays she published in *Social Work and Social Living* (Reynolds, 1987[1951]) attempted to correct the tendency of contemporary practice to over-emphasize 'the techniques of social work and the operation of social agencies' often in harmful ways. Throughout, Reynolds posed two critical questions: 'Must it hurt to be helped?' and 'Are clients people?' These questions reflected Reynolds' view of the helping process: 'Help must be connected with increase, not diminution, of self-respect, and it must imply the possibility of a reciprocal relationship of sharing within a group to which both giver and recipient belong' (quoted in Maxted, 1952, pp. 79–80).

Based upon these values, which focused on prevention and education rather than cure, Reynolds (1987[1951], pp. 33–52) articulated four key practice principles for social service:

1   The criterion of belonging;
2   The criterion of full adult status while receiving help;
3   The criterion of mutuality, that is having a recognized capacity to repay society at some time in some way; and
4   The criterion of having no strings attached to the receipt of assistance.

She rejected the conflation of social work practice with other mental health services and underscored the *social* dimension of the profession. Unlike many of her contemporaries, Reynolds also actively resisted elite definitions of the function of social work in society (Lee, 1937). She challenged the 'sense of superiority' social workers often develop toward non-professionals and stressed how social workers could use 'their common heritage as members of communities' in order to reflect the inextricable connection between social work and social living (Chakerian, 1952, p. 392). She foresaw the potential for social workers to become agents of social control unless clients participated as full partners in the design and implementation of services (Reynolds, 1973[1934], 1942).

> Once I became sensitized to what people were doing for themselves in the struggles of the 1930s, I could not fail to see that social casework had here its greatest ally – the active will to live of humans whose intelligence could now be used in organized efforts with their fellows [sic].
>
> *(Reynolds, 1942, p. 17)*

The underlying ideas of the practice framework she developed in response to social conditions shared an emphasis on wholeness and growth. Ironically, critics from both ends of the political spectrum attacked her attempted synthesis. Those on the left chided Reynolds for refusing to repudiate Freudian psychology, while conservatives rejected her embrace of Marxism and labor activism.

She responded to her critics in two ways. To critics of her Marxism, she asserted the importance of acknowledging how political-economic forces shaped the practice environment. To those who questioned her attraction to Freudian psychology, she responded that she did not accept all of Freud's ideas and that it was possible to 'work with schools of thought … with which we do not wholly agree' (Reynolds, letter of March 7, 1950). According to Ann Hartman (1986), Reynolds was, therefore, able 'to avoid the dichotomous struggle between social action and psychotherapy' that divided the profession (pp. 88–89).

Throughout her career, Reynolds underscored the importance of understanding how unequal power dynamics influenced the social service setting. She criticized social work's uncritical embrace of the hierarchical medical model implicit in the profession's turn toward psychiatric modes of practice. By the mid-1930s, she broke openly with many of her colleagues on this issue in a manner that complemented her overall view of politics and society.

Reynolds regarded the role of social workers was to facilitate clients' development of strengths and resources to enable them to solve their problems as they defined them. The egalitarian relationship this implied anticipated both future radical models of practice (Reisch and Andrews, 2002) and the strengths perspective that became popular in the 1990s (Saleeby, 1992). The mutuality underlying this practice model provided a justification for social workers to resist the agency's authority, when necessary, to satisfy clients' needs (Reynolds, 1938).

This perspective helps explain Reynolds' attraction to Marxism. She thought

> the Marxist outlook welcomed change, instead of fearing it [and] the goal of a Marxist scientist is to work for necessary change before hate and violence so accumulate between classes that destruction is inevitable. … [This] relieved the social work profession of the 'Jehovah complex' which had always plagued it.
>
> *(Rosen, p. 932)*

Reynolds also criticized the profession for its class bias, its tendency to blame people for their problems, and its practice of 'creaming' the most verbal and compliant clients in order to create 'successful' programs and affirm their own status. She even argued that the use of the term 'client' reflected the profession's intrinsic inequality and the acquiescence of most agencies to the dominant forces in society. By contrast, she asserted, 'Social work can defend its standards only if it realizes the organized nature of the opposition to it, why these interests are opposed, and where its own allies are to be found' (Reynolds, 1987[1951], p. 166).

Reynolds repeatedly stressed that the influence of psychological theory led social workers to focus on clients' emotions and minimize the structural conditions that produced exclusion and misery. This perspective reinforced the tendency of practitioners to 'save' clients rather than acknowledge their self-determination and treat them with dignity and respect. As an alternative, she believed 'the function of social casework is not to treat the individual alone or the environment alone, but … [to recognize] … a dynamic interaction between the two' (quoted in Hartman, 1986, p. 89). In doing so, practitioners could help people cope with the forces in their environment more effectively (Reynolds, 1939).

Reynolds' concept of professionalism, therefore, differed considerably from that of her mainstream colleagues. She regarded social activism as a core component of service delivery, not an ancillary feature of practice. Without this involvement, she believed that the social work profession would never be able to achieve its foundational democratic values (Reisch, 2008). Reynolds' understanding of professionalism flowed naturally from her egalitarian view of practice and her support for social work unions 'as a tool of social change and … a guarantor of effective and ethical service' (Reisch, 1993, p. 68).

Reynolds' support for the unionization of social workers also reflected her more inclusive view of professional membership that conflicted with the narrow definition of many social work leaders (Fisher, 1980; Spano, 1982; Wenocur and Reisch, 1989). In her view, professional organizations should be educational, not gatekeeping institutions. Their goals should include acknowledging the strengths that all workers possess and facilitating their entry into the field. Otherwise, she argued, social workers would be forced 'to choose between practicing their profession ethically … or becoming slavishly obedient to powerful forces which must in the end destroy every vestige of professional integrity' (Reynolds, 1938, p. 8). These ideas ultimately led Reynolds to develop her progressive conception of social work pedagogy.

Reynolds' views of social work education

Reynolds' academic career coincided with the emergence of social work as a profession and the tumultuous events of the early and mid-20th century. She always regarded herself as both a practitioner and an educator. She felt that the latter role 'presented her with some of the most challenging and vexing problems of her professional life and … helped her mold her lifelong conceptions of what helping people was about' (Schwartz, 1981, p. 5).

The intellectual themes of the Progressive Era that influenced Reynolds' views of society and practice also shaped her ideas about social work education. She embraced 'the themes of experiential learning, action and interaction, the study of man [sic] in nature, and the values of social responsibility' (Schwartz, 1981, p. 6). Although not formally acknowledged in her writings, the concepts of progressive education developed by John Dewey are clearly apparent in her work. These included faith in science, the importance of experience, and the central role of a social vision to guide practice.

Although she was a potent intellectual and a lifelong idealist, Reynolds never lost sight of the practical in her teaching. She believed that students needed to know the objective conditions that affected the people with whom they worked. In addition to understanding how social policies affected their lives, these included such mundane information as the cost of everyday items and the major components of popular culture.

Reynolds' conception of social work education, therefore, complemented her ideas about social work practice and the process of social change. She challenged students' ideas about the prevailing casework model and taught them to maximize clients' strengths while empowering them to seek their own solutions to their problems (Kaplan, 2002). She anticipated by several decades the ideas of Paulo Freire (1971) and North American proponents of empowerment theory (Simon, 1994). Like Freire (1971), Reynolds understood that leveling the worker–client relationship was critical to the development of transformative services. Like Freire, she rejected the traditional hierarchical ('banking') model of education, substituting instead a problem-posing approach and the importance of intra-group dialogue.

In emphasizing the importance of group process and the wisdom people acquired and could share based on their lived experience, Reynolds incorporated the work of contemporaries such as Mary Parker Follett (1920), Edward Lindemann (1948), Gisela Konopka (1963), and Grace Coyle (1948). Her faith in people's ability to learn from each other bears a striking resemblance to contemporary concepts of 'strengths-based practice' (Saleeby, 1992) and assets-based community organizing (Kretzmann and McKnight, 1993). She regarded education as a cooperative and interactive endeavor and a lifelong, developmental process; this mirrored her overall egalitarian ethos (Reynolds, 1942).

Almost from the beginning of her career, and certainly by the 1930s, Reynolds regarded social work practice as a political and critical act, whether it occurred 'in the classroom, the casework interview, the group meeting … [or] … the supervisory conference' (Schwartz, 1981, p. 8). According to Reynolds, neither education nor practice could occur in isolation from the external environment. Understanding the social, economic, and political context and being an active, critical participant in that environment were, therefore, essential components of practice and the learning process. This perspective embodied her synthesis of scientific analysis and humanistic values.

Reynolds was equally critical of herself as an educator. Conscious of her relative lack of academic credentials, she struggled with finding a balance between 'structure and freedom in the educational process' (Schwartz, 1981, p. 10). While group process and dialogue appealed to her, like many contemporary educators with a progressive orientation, she reluctantly acknowledged the need to 'guide' her students more than she would have preferred, because their abilities did not match her expectations. Two methods she used to bridge this gap were the cultivation of group work skills and multiple writing exercises (comparable to journaling) that required students to integrate theory, practice, thoughts, and emotions.

Reynolds' conception of educational content paralleled her view of its overall pedagogical function. Her model curriculum consisted of four parts: supervision, group process, economics, and psychiatric methods. She also recognized the importance of helping students overcome their fear of risk-taking and their resistance to acknowledging the power dynamics involved in practice.

To do this, Reynolds applied her experiences from social casework to group work and community organization settings. She taught that social workers should 'be able to enter ... into the situation ... Not [to] disrupt what is there, but [to] enhance the ability of the people who live in it to play their part' (Smalley, 1943, p. 366). She also stressed the important role that agencies played in the relationship dynamic and the importance of teachers 'taking into account where the learner or groups of learners is' (ibid.).

Conclusion

Throughout her career, Reynolds recognized that social work practice and education were inseparable from the process of social change. She consistently emphasized that social work played a key role in both individual and institutional change, and that a false dichotomy existed between interventions to improve the distribution of vital resources and power and those designed to enhance people's quality of life. Almost 70 years ago, during an era whose political climate bears a striking resemblance to our own, Reynolds framed the options facing the social work profession in frank terms. Social workers, she asserted, faced

> a choice between contradictory forces in our society: those which are moving toward the welfare of the people ... and those which destroy human life in preventable misery and war, and relieve poverty only grudgingly to keep the privileged position they hold.
>
> *(Reynolds, 1987[1951], p. 174)*

Because she dedicated her career to helping others, particularly the marginalized and excluded, Reynolds took considerable intellectual and political risks. Not only did she frequently break with conventional social work thinking, she risked her reputation by her identification with the Rank and File Movement and the Socialist and Communist Parties. While the former contributed to her elevated status within the profession, the latter led to her blacklisting and virtual banishment from the field.

The questions she posed continue to be fundamental to the determination of social work's role (Bandler, 1979). They involve an examination of '(1) the limits of the human spirit, (2) the empowering and disempowering effects on clients of clinical social work, and (3) the ethics of politically activating – or not activating – clients' (McQuaide, 1987, p. 277). She even questioned how social workers could rationalize practice with individuals in an environment of persistent poverty and growing human need:

> Is social casework perpetuating starvation wages and degraded working and living conditions while it attempts to fill the gap until the forces of change can be made effective? Are those forces delayed for millions while social case-work relieves a little of the misery of a few hundreds? If the ability of professional social caseworkers helps a client to attain

> emotional release and a measure of personal happiness does this result in his [*sic*] being a stronger person to grapple with evils and to overcome difficulties, or does it make him [*sic*] more dependent on others in any difficulty and more submissive under exploitation.
>
> *(Reynolds, 1973[1934], p. 17)*

She pondered whether social workers would become agents of social control who doled out barely adequate resources to clients in order to placate them and thereby preserve the status quo.

> The way we do our professional work contributes inescapably to the outcomes of [the] ... struggle [for social justice]. It we think social work is not a force in the battle of ideas, the enemies of the people know better. Either we serve the people's needs or we evade them. Either we make democracy real or we reduce it to an abstraction which the foes of democracy do not object to at all. Either we use all that science can teach to help people build a genuinely good life for themselves or we build a professional cult that the place of interrelations with other advances in human knowledge.
>
> *(quoted in Quam, 1995, pp. 78–79)*

Today, the failure of the organized social work profession to articulate clearly an alternate vision of society based on a critical analysis of contemporary issues constrains educators and practitioners in their individual efforts to confront persistent racism, nativism, misogyny, and homophobia, and challenge a political-economic system that creates and rationalizes increasing inequality. The persistent attack on social welfare has corrupted the profession's vocabulary (for example, the current focus on resiliency not resistance), obscured social work's historical role in pursuing social and political change, and left many students, educators, and practitioners without the guidelines or values that would enable them to navigate today's dangerous waters.

> Reynolds' suggestions, written over 75 years ago, could fill this void: The best preparation for adapting ... social work ... [to] the future ... is to see it now, without illusions, as a part of our own time, and to face what we have with an active determination to be flexible enough ... so that we do not hold back its growth into something else. While change is inevitable, change for the better is not unless we ... understand the dynamics of growth [and] ... aid what is socially useful and try to inhibit forces that that are destructive to human well-being.
>
> *(Reynolds, 1942, p. 4)*

These prophetic words have the potential to provide a roadmap for a more progressive future.

Sources

Bandler, L. (1979). Bertha Capen Reynolds: Social worker of all times. *Journal of Education for Social Work*, 15(3), 5–12.

Chakerian, C.G. (1952). Review of Social work and social living: Explorations in philosophy and practice. *American Sociological Review*, 17(1), 392.

Coyle, G.L. (1948). *Group work with American youth: A guide to the practice of leadership*. New York: Harper & Row.

Fisher, J. (1980). *The response of social work to the depression*. Cambridge, MA: Schenkman.

Follett, M.P. (1920). *The new state: Group organization, the solution of popular government*. New York: Longmans, Green.

Freedberg, S. (1986). Religion, profession and politics: Bertha Capen Reynolds' challenge to social work. *Smith College Studies in Social Work*, 56(2), 95–110.

Freire, P. (1971). *Pedagogy of the oppressed*. New York: Seabury Press.
Gil, D. (1976, March 3). Resolving issues of "social" provision in our society: The role of social work education. Paper presented at the 1976 Annual Program Meeting of the Council on Social Work Education, Philadelphia, PA: Evelyn Butler Pamphlet Collection, School of Social Work, University of Pennsylvania.
Goroff, N. (n.d.). *A pedagogy for radical social work practice*. Unpublished paper West Hartford, CT: University of Connecticut School of Social Work. Evelyn Butler Pamphlet Collection, School of Social Work, University of Pennsylvania.
Hartman, A. (1986). The life of Bertha Reynolds: Implications for education and practice today. *Smith College Studies in Social Work*, 56(2), 79–94.
Joseph, B.R. (2009). The Bertha C. Reynolds centennial conference June 28–30, 1985: Taking organizing back to the people. *Smith College Studies in Social Work*, 56(2), 122–131.
Kaplan, C.P. (2002). An example of brief strengths-based practice: Bertha Reynolds at the National Maritime Union, 1943–1947. *Smith College Studies in Social Work*, 72(3), 403–416.
Konopka, G. (1963). *Social group work: A helping process*. Englewood Cliffs, NJ: Prentice Hall.
Kretzmann, J., & McKnight, J. (1993). *Building communities from the inside out: A path toward finding and mobilizing a community's assets*. Evanston, IL: ACTA.
Lee, P. (1937). *Social work as cause and function and other papers*. New York: Columbia University Press.
Lindemann, E. (1948, January). *Educating youth for social responsibility*. New York: Community Chests and Councils, Inc. Evelyn Butler Archive, Box 50, University of Pennsylvania.
Maxted, M.C. (1952). Review of social work and social living. *Rural Sociology*, 17(1), 79–80.
McQuaide, S. (1987). Beyond the logic of pessimism: A personal portrait of Bertha Capen Reynolds. *Clinical Social Work Journal*, 15(3), 271–280.
Quam, J. (1995). Review of an uncharted journey. *Reflections*, 1(4), 77–79.
Reisch, M. (1993). Linking client and community: The impact of Bertha Reynolds on social work. In J. L. Andrews (Ed.), *From vision to action: Social workers of the second generation* (pp. 58–74). St. Paul, MN: University of St. Thomas.
Reisch, M. (2008). The democratic promise: The impact of German Jewish immigration on social work in the United States. In *Yearbook of the Leo Baeck Institute* (pp. 169–190). London: Leo Baeck Institute.
Reisch, M., & Andrews, J.L. (2002). *The road not taken: A history of radical social work in the United States*. New York: Routledge.
Reynolds, B.C. (1924). The mental hygiene of young children. *Proceedings of the National Conference of Social Work*. Toronto, Canada: PUBLISHER.
Reynolds, B.C. (1931). Review of V. Robinson. A changing psychology in social casework. *The American Journal of Orthopsychiatry*, 1(5), 543–545.
Reynolds, B.C. (1932). An experiment in short contact interviewing. *Smith College Studies in Social Work*, 3(1), 1–101.
Reynolds, B.C. (1935). Whom do social workers serve? *Social Work Today*, 5(2), 5–8.
Reynolds, B.C. (1937). The development of a professional self. *The Family*, 18, 61–66.
Reynolds, B.C. (1938, April–June). Rethinking social casework. *Social Work Today*, 5. (Reprinted: Reynolds, B.C. (1991). Re-thinking social case work. *Journal of Progressive Human Services*, 2(2), 83–101).
Reynolds, B.C. (1939). Social casework: What is it? What is its place in the world today? In F. Lowry (Ed.), *Readings in Social Casework, 1920–1938* (pp. 136–147). New York: Columbia University Press.
Reynolds, B.C. (1941). Social workers and civil rights. In M. Van Kleeck et al. (Ed.), *Social work, peace, and the people's well-being* (pp. 19–26). New York: Astoria.
Reynolds, B.C. (1942). *Learning and teaching in the practice of social work*. New York: Russell & Russell.
Reynolds, B.C. (1945). Labor and social work. *Social Work Yearbook 1945*, 8, 230–234. New York: Russell Sage Foundation.
Reynolds, B.C. (1953). Fear in our culture. *Unpublished paper presented at the Cleveland Council of Arts, Sciences, and Professions*. Evelyn Butler Archive, University of Pennsylvania.
Reynolds, B.C. (1963). *An unchartered journey*. New York: The Citadel Press.
Reynolds, B.C. (1964, October) The social casework of an unchartered journey. *Social Work*, 9(1), 13–17.
Reynolds, B.C. (1973[1934]). *Between client and community: A study of responsibility in social casework*. New York: Oriole Press. *Smith College Studies in Social Work*, 5(1) 39–127.
Reynolds, B.C. (1987[1951]). *Social work and social living: Explorations in philosophy and practice*. Silver Spring, MD: NASW Press.

Robinson, V. P. (1931). *A changing psychology in social casework*. Chapel Hill, NC: The University of North Carolina Press.
Rosen, A. (1963). Review of an unchartered journey. *American Journal of Orthopsychiatry, 33*(5), 931–933.
Saleeby, D. (Ed.) (1992). *The strengths perspective in social work practice*. New York: Longman.
Schwartz, W. (1981). Bertha Reynolds as educator. *Catalyst, 3*(3), 5–11.
Simon, B.L. (1994). *The empowerment tradition in American social work: A history*. New York: Columbia University Press.
Smalley, R. (1943). Review of learning and teaching in the practice of social work. *The American Journal of Orthopsychiatry, 13*(2), 365–367.
Solomon, B.B. (1976). *Black empowerment: Social work in oppressed communities*. New York: Columbia University Press.
Spano, R. (1982). *The Rank and File Movement in social work*. Washington, DC: University Press of America.
Wenocur, S., & Reisch, M. (1989). *From charity to enterprise: The development of American social work in a market economy*. Urbana, IL: University of Illinois Press.

7
Reflecting on Antonio Gramsci's *Prison Notebooks*
Marxism and social work

Paul Michael Garrett

NATIONAL UNIVERSITY OF IRELAND

Introduction

In this chapter it is maintained that Antonio Gramsci (1891–1937) is a significant figure for social work educators and practitioners aspiring to shape critical pedagogies that are intent on promoting wider social change. In what follows, therefore, the focus will be on a range of interrelated Gramscian conceptualisations (see also Garrett, 2019). First, the chapter dwells on Americanism, Fordism and Taylorism and refers to how Gramsci articulated an understanding that these three 'isms' were central to how capitalist modernity appeared to be evolving. Second, his notion of hegemony – the theme Gramsci is most associated with – will be examined. Third, the related idea of 'common sense' will be discussed. Next, we will turn to explore how Gramsci endeavoured to revise understandings of the role that intellectuals fulfil. Having summarily examined some of these key conceptualisations, the remainder of the chapter begins to make the connection between Gramsci's theorisation and the pedagogical and political role of critical scholars and practitioners within contemporary social work.

Gramsci and his political context

After spending his first two decades on the remote island of Sardinia, Gramsci arrived in Turin, 'the red capital of Italy' and 'home of its most advanced industry' in 1911 (Hoare and Nowell Smith, 2005, p. xxv). In May 1919, he became one of the founders of the weekly *L'Ordine Nuovo* which became the 'intellectual voice of a revolutionary movement' and the journal of the 'factory councils' generating organised working-class opposition to capital during the period (Bellamy, 1994, p. xiii). Furthermore, the newspaper was a 'paradigmatic experiment of young intellectuals who sought to redefine their relationship with the working class in active, pedagogical terms – a relationship in which they were more often the "educated" than the "educator"' (Thomas, 2009, p. 408).

During the years of 1919–20 it seemed that an Italian socialist revolution was a distinct possibility (Bellamy, 1994). However, the shape of politics in Italy – and elsewhere in Europe – quickly began to change. Industrialists moved onto the offensive, providing financial support and tacit approval to fascist vigilantes. In October 1922, while Gramsci was in Moscow as the representative of the *Partito Communista Italiano* (PCI), Mussolini's 'March on Rome' initiated the fascist social and economic order (Bosworth, 1998). Having returned to Italy in December 1923, Gramsci became the leader of the PCI in 1924. However, on the evening of 8 November 1926, in defiance of his immunity as an elected deputy, he was arrested. At the ensuing 'trial', Michele Isgro – the prosecutor – notoriously demanded that the fascist state 'stop this brain from functioning for twenty years' (Thomas, 2009, p 104). Gramsci was to die under guard in a clinic in Rome at the age of forty-six. At his funeral, 'held as quickly as possible on 28 April 1937 the watchful police guards far outnumbered the mourners' (Buttigieg, 1986, p. 2). The product of those years of 'slow death in prison' were 2,848 pages of handwritten notes which he 'left to be smuggled out of the clinic and out of Italy' (Hoare and Nowell Smith, 2005, p. xviii).

Gramsci's *Prison Notebooks*, his 'carceral project' written between February 1929 and June 1935, present today's readers with substantial challenges (Thomas, 2009, p. 56). First, his web-like prose can seem fragmentary, even lacking coherence. A second complicating factor is that Gramsci, attentive to the censoring activity and 'malevolence on the part of the Fascist panopticon', often appeared to write in coded form (Thomas, 2009, p. 104). Third, perhaps his writings assume an understanding of the intellectual and political context in which he wrote: the struggle against fascism in Italy, the various competing political currents within the Italian Communist Party, the shifts and turns of the Communist International. Good annotated editions of his work can, however, assist in this regard. Readers new to Gramsci can find English translations of his writings in Bellamy (1994), Forgacs (1988), Hoare (1988), Hoare and Nowell Smith (2005). Fourth, related to his specific historical and cultural milieu, Gramsci can appear to present somewhat 'staid views on sexual morality, women and the family' (Forgacs, 1988, p. 276). Nevertheless, the *Prison Notebooks* are a 'classic of twentieth-century social theory' and they continue to provide fascinating insights and perspectives for those willing to explore them (Thomas, 2009, p. xvii).

Clearly, Gramsci was an 'unapologetic' Marxist, but he rejected the notion that Marx's work provided a blueprint that had to be adhered to rigidly (Crehan, 2002, p. 176). Even in his now neglected, pre-prison journalism, he asserts that the Bolsheviks were not 'Marxists' in the sense that they had used the 'Master's works to compile a rigid doctrine' since 'true Marxist thought' always 'identified as the most important factor in history not crude, economic facts, but rather men [sic] themselves, and the societies they create, as they learn to live with one another and understand one another' (Gramsci in Bellamy, 1994, pp. 39–40).

How, therefore, might the thought of this complex, intellectually brilliant figure help social work practitioners and educators gain a better understanding of their roles and of the world that they inhabit? Mohd Shahid and Manoj K. Jha (2014), for example, provide a fascinating Gramscian perspective on India, disability and Felix Biestek's (1975) social work ethics. In what follows, it will be argued that many of Gramsci's insights can assist those looking to develop alternatives to neoliberal forms of social work education and practice (see also MacKinnon, 2009; Singh and Cowden, 2009).

Analysing the trajectory of capitalist modernity: Americanism, Fordism, Taylorism

During Gramsci's era, the idea of modernity was bound up with industrialisation and the gradual introduction of mass production in factories such as those established in Italy by the car manufacturer FIAT. In this context, Gramsci was particularly fascinated with the new regulatory and surveillance practices, often originating from the United States, seeking to manage and control the body of individual workers, the pace of their work, the extent of their productivity and even their lives beyond the factory walls.

In a series of articles in the early 1920s, Gramsci was already responding to the transformations under way in industrial centres such as Turin, a city gradually metamorphosing into 'one great factory' (Gramsci in Bellamy, 1994, p. 137). In the cultural domain, he was increasingly attracted to Futurist art and its urge to declaim 'the age of big industry, of the large proletarian city and of intense and tumultuous life' (Gramsci in Bellamy, 1994, p. 74). Gramsci himself tended to be rhapsodic in his praise for the factory and the 'intense methodical life' of the factory worker who has 'shed all psychological traces of his agricultural or craft origins'. His 'life may be disorderly and chaotic where his social relations are concerned … But within the factory, it is ordered, precise and disciplined' (Gramsci in Bellamy, 1994, p. 152).

Bound up with the introduction of these new productive processes was the creation of a new type of human being with new habits and new modes of socialisation. These ruminations led Gramsci to comment on some of the innovations being introduced by Henry Ford in his car plants and on the broader question of 'Fordism'. Seeking to retain workers and increase his profitability, Ford was intent on developing a model of worker better suited to assembly line production. Acclaimed as a 'sociologist manufacturer' whose 'real business' was the 'making of men' (Grandin, 2010, p. 34), Ford also extended control over his workers well beyond the spatial confines of the factory. By 1919 Ford's 'Sociological Department' employed hundreds of agents, frequently referred to as 'social workers', asking 'questions, taking notes, and writing up personnel reports' to ensure that his employees possessed the prerequisite moral standards (Grandin, 2010, p. 38).

These preoccupations are connected to Gramsci's interest in the labour management technique known, after its founder Frederick W. Taylor, as Taylorism. Notoriously, Taylor maintained that if his techniques – which involved breaking the process of production down into a series of repetitive tasks devised by managers – were deployed, a 'trained gorilla' could undertake the work as efficiently as a human being could. Despite this observation, Gramsci's own ambivalent perspective, appearing to accept the utility of such methods within socialist industrial planning, is arguably at odds with that of Marx (1990), for whom the factory is a place of exploitation and alienation, and of other Marxist currents (such as the Frankfurt School), similarly sceptical about the progressive possibilities granted by mechanisation and technology. Pivoting on simplistic body/mind dualism, Gramsci's perception that 'modern' production techniques might engender 'new and freer forms of thought' is less than convincing (Landy, 1994, p. 229). Moreover, he does not seem to recognise the harm that a worker's involvement in production can cause, given that repetitive tasks can prove injurious to both body and mind (see also Bellamy, 1994, p. xxii). Like a number of other contemporary Marxists, such as Trotsky, Gramsci often appears to insufficiently appreciate that Taylorism was *not* socially and ethically neutral and could not be legitimately transferred to socialist forms of production. Rather, it was devised to discipline workers' bodies, control *alienated* labour and increase capitalist profits (Braverman, 1974). In more recent times, this understanding might also help us to grasp the significance and intent of neoliberal managerialism and new forms of work organisation. For example, the deployment of the so-called New Public Management (NPM) has resulted in the curtailment of professional discretion as evinced by over-reliance on metrics and measurement of 'outcomes'. The construction of 'work flows' dictating the tasks that individual workers have to complete in a particular way, subject to a particular temporal ordering, can also be associated with these NPM processes (Clarke et al., 2007). Within social work, a good example of this type of imposition was the influential 'looking after children' system, devised in the 1990s, and subsequent templates used for child-care assessments (Garrett, 2018a).

For Gramsci, the bundle of ideas and practices associated with Americanism, Fordism and Taylorism revealed the direction that capitalism – and potentially other forms of 'modernisation' – were to take. This perspective is related to his ideas around hegemony, given that it was necessary for ruling groups to win public consent to further and sustain a *particular* vision of modernity.

Analysing the capitalist social formation and constructing a socialist alternative: hegemony

On account of the existing social and economic conditions in the West at the time of his writing, Gramsci did not feel that it was feasible to embark on a frontal assault, what he called 'war of manoeuvre', against capital. This had been the tactic in the East – more precisely in Russia – where such a form of attack had cast aside a brittle and degenerating empire. According to Lenin, in fact, a revolution in Russia had proved to be 'as easy as lifting a feather' (in Thomas, 2009, p. 205). Instead, Gramsci recommended a 'war of position', a subtler form of confrontation focused on long-term, strategic struggle. Moreover, in the West, the state was simply an 'outer ditch' and those seeking revolutionary change would need to gain consent within civil society in order to begin to successfully confront the powerful defensive 'fortresses' and 'earthworks' that the bourgeoisie had at its disposal (Gramsci in Forgacs, 1988, p. 229; see also Thomas, 2009, ch. 6). Therein, Gramsci argued, lies the importance of the struggle for hegemony (see also Garrett, 2009a).

The etymology of the word hegemony relates to *hegemon*, literally meaning leader, and the concept refers to a combination of authority, leadership and domination (see also Ives, 2004a, 2004b; Anderson, 1976, 2017). Some commentators suggest that the concept of hegemony is Gramsci's 'own invention', but its roots actually lie in classical-Marxist theorisation in the years prior to the Russian Revolution (Thomas, 2009, p. 56). Hegemony signifies 'something more substantial and more flexible than any abstract *imposed* ideology' (Williams, 1973, p. 10, emphasis added). What counts is what *penetrates*, what *sticks* and what achieves some degree of explanatory power in terms of our experience of the world. Currently, for example, neoliberal compliant academics are often important figures helping to sustain neoliberal hegemony. Marnie Holborow (2015), for example, illuminates how neoliberal economics have found key supporters within universities that are increasingly likely, as is apparent from their promotional literature, to be modelled on corporate businesses. Affirming the values of the market, academic institutions amplify and mimic private sector practices circulating around themes such as 'performance', 'customer', 'employability', 'enterprise' and 'entrepreneurship' (Holborow, 2015, ch. 6; see also Williams, 1973). These keywords are augmented by an array of upbeat 'hooray words', such as 'creative', 'participation' and 'empowerment' (Cook in Holborow, 2015, p. 103).

According to Gramsci, a movement does not become hegemonic simply because it manages to manipulate 'passive masses into supporting it, nor because it manages to construct cross-class alliances at the level of elite politics' (Robinson, 2006, p. 82). No short cuts exist to achieving hegemony. For a hegemonic project to be successful it has to address and meaningfully respond to people's lived experience of the world. Both hegemonic and counter-hegemonic projects need to be embedded, nurtured and promoted. In examining hegemony, therefore, it is important to stress how a dominant class has to *organise, persuade* and *maintain* the consent of the subjugated by ensuring that its own ideas constitute the core perceptions and 'common sense' within a particular social formation (Crehan, 2011). The capitalist state is 'no longer merely an instrument of coercion, imposing the interests of the dominant class from above'. Now, in its 'integral form', it has become a 'network of social relations for the production of consent, for the integration of the subaltern classes into the expansive project of historical development of the leading social group' (Thomas, 2009, p. 143).

Hegemony is not to be understood at the 'level of mere opinion or mere manipulation. It is a whole body of practices and expectations' (Williams, 1973, p. 9). Part of the political skill integral to such an endeavour is the relentless aspiration to try to co-opt or eliminate 'alternative meanings and values' (Williams, 1973, p. 10). Hegemonic power does 'not flow automatically from the economic position of the dominated group', rather it has to be 'constructed and negotiated' (Joseph, 2006, p. 52). As Wendy Brown (2015, p. 81) makes plain, even when an explanation of a political event or social crisis becomes 'hegemonic, it carves itself against a range of other possibilities – tacitly arguing with them, keeping them at bay, or subordinating them'. Hegemonic projects do not simply seek to win over people to a particular worldview. Rather, they try to disqualify competing oppositional perspectives 'while recruiting small but strategically significant populations and class fractions into active support' (Gilbert, 2015, p. 31). What Hall (2011, pp. 727–8) refers to as the excluded 'social forces, whose consent has not been won, whose interests have not been taken into account, form the basis of counter movements, resistance, alternative strategies and visions'.

The maintenance of consent, or the calculated dispensing with consent, is 'dependent upon an incessant repositioning of the relationship between rulers and the ruled' (Jones, 2006, p. 3). This becomes especially important at specific historical 'conjunctures' (Hall and Massey, 2010). Located within a broadly Gramscian framework, conjuncture refers to the emergence of social, political, economic and ideological contradictions at a particular historical moment. At this time, 'levels of society, the economy, politics, ideology, common sense, etc., come together or "fuse"' (Hall in Hall and Massey, 2010, p. 59). Hence, a 'conjuncture' is a 'critical turning point or rupture in a political structure, primarily signifying a crisis in class relations' (Rustin, 2009, p. 18). Crises – such as a significant economic 'downturn', the outbreak of war or an event such as the recent decision to leave the EU by British voters – represent an opening to assemble a potentially new hegemonic settlement which could be either socially progressive or retrogressive depending on the political bloc emerging as dominant. Closer to professional home, within social work, it is possible to observe how the deaths of children and policy 'crisis' that evolves is often cynically manipulated to try to shape a new form of hegemony which discursively re-maps what constitutes appropriate forms of intervention in the lives of children and families (Garrett, 2009b). Relatedly, interrogation of the way that the deaths of children – such as Peter Connelly in the UK in 2007 – are presented makes it clear that integral to the public debate has often been a harsh, retrogressive and punitive anti-welfare discourse in which 'underclass' figures have featured prominently (Garrett, 2017).

As Gramsci observes, hegemonic powers seek to maintain 'the "spontaneous" consent given by the great masses of the population to the general direction imposed on social life' (in Hoare and Nowell Smith, 2005, p. 12). However, the 'apparatus of state coercive power' is empowered to 'legally' enforce 'discipline on those groups' failing to render active or passive consent (ibid.). Significantly, continues Gramsci, this latter apparatus is 'constituted for the whole of society in anticipation of moments of crisis of command and direction when spontaneous consent has failed' (ibid.). In this way, coercive power is held in reserve for those times and places when the means of generating sufficient consent *fails* (Smith, 2011). Most of the time, people would not directly be targeted or experience such a deployment of coercive power. However, some population segments – as illustrated by the concerns of the 'Black Lives Matter' protesters in the United States – are routinely confronted by the state's coercive edge in the form of lethal interventions by uniformed and militarised police (Wilderson, 2003). More theoretically, given that the state has more forceful ways to foster compliance and acquiescence, hegemony does not play out, as some misleading perceptions of hegemony are prone to imply, merely on the terrain of culture. A hegemonic apparatus is *not*, therefore, to be interpreted as the antithesis of domination or outright coercive intervention on the part of the capitalist state. Rather, as Gramsci avows,

> the supremacy of a social group manifests itself in *two ways*, as 'domination' and as 'intellectual and moral leadership'. A social group dominates antagonistic groups which it tends to 'liquidate', or to subjugate perhaps by armed force; it leads kindred and allied groups.
> *(Gramsci in Hoare and Nowell Smith, 2005, p. 57, emphasis added)*

As Thomas (2009, p. 163) further elaborates:

> Leadership-hegemony and domination are therefore conceived less as qualitatively distinct from one another, than as strategically differentiated forms of a unitary political power: hegemony is the form of political power exercised over those classes in close proximity to the leading group, while domination is exerted over those opposing it.

A palpably coercive component has, of course, been witnessed in countries such as Greece, as greater numbers of people have demonstrated and resisted EU 'austerity' diktats (Pentaraki, 2016). Over the past few decades in the UK, laws have also been enacted to curtail the right of trade unions to collectively challenge neoliberalism. However, a generalised resort to coercion hints at a loss of authority on the part of the ruling class and not, perhaps paradoxically, its omnipotence. As Gramsci remarks:

> If the ruling class has lost its consensus, i.e. is no longer 'leading' but only 'dominant', exercising coercive force alone, this means precisely that the great masses have become detached from their traditional ideologies, and no longer believe what they used to believe previously, etc. The crisis consists precisely in the fact that the old is dying and the new cannot be born; in this interregnum a great variety of morbid symptoms appear.
> *(Gramsci in Hoare and Nowell Smith, 2005, pp. 275–6)*

Indeed, the 'morbid symptoms' are certainly apparent in the present unstable conjuncture: for example, in the 2016 US presidential election in which the erratic and narcissistic Trump, lost in the 'turbid void of his own dreams and desires', was rendered triumphant (Gramsci in Hoare and Nowell Smith, 2005, p. 172). Similar 'symptoms' may also be detectable in the sheer scale of the votes garnered by the racist Marine Le Pen and the Front National in France. Elsewhere, right-wing figures including Victor Orbán (in Hungary), Jaroslaw Kaczyński (in Poland), Robert Fico (in Slovakia) and Matteo Salvini (in Italy) pollute the European social and political landscape (see also Bauman, 2016; Fekete, 2018). Relatedly, on a summer's day in June 2016, a serving member of the UK parliament was hacked to death by a professed fascist associated with the far-right Britain First Party. This 'interregnum' has also witnessed – at a personal and micro-level close to the professional concerns of many social workers – a rise in instances in self-harm and suicides. In the United States, for example, it was reported, in 2018, that

> suicide rates rose in men and women and across all age and ethnic groups, propelled by mental illness, substance use, financial hardship and relationship problems. Nationwide … the suicide rate rose by nearly 30% over the same 17-year period, 1999 to 2016.
> *(The Guardian, 2018)*

Analysing everyday understandings: 'common sense'

Unlike in English, the 'Italian notion of common sense (*senso comune*) does not so much mean good, sound, practical sense, rather it means normal or average understanding' (Ives, 2004a, p. 74). Gramsci explains that it is the 'conception of the world which is uncritically absorbed ... Common sense is not a single unique conception, identical in time and space [but] it takes countless different forms. Its most fundamental characteristic is that it is ... fragmentary, incoherent' (Gramsci in Hoare and Nowell Smith, 2005, p. 419).

For Gramsci, then, 'common sense' is 'a chaotic aggregate of disparate conceptualisations in which one can find anything one likes' (Gramsci in Hoare and Nowell Smith, 2005, p. 422). Generally averse to novelty and change, common sense tends to be 'crudely neophobe and conservative' (ibid., p. 423). This 'does not mean that there are no truths in common sense. It means rather that common sense is an ambiguous, contradictory and multiform concept' (ibid.).

As many social workers are likely to recognise, many aspects of 'common sense' contribute to people's everyday subordination and humiliation by making situations of 'inequality and oppression appear to them as natural and unchangeable' (Forgacs, 1988, p. 421). Hall and O'Shea (2015, pp. 52–3) elaborate that 'common sense' is a

> form of 'everyday thinking' which offers us frameworks of meaning with which to make sense of the world. It is a form of easily-available knowledge which contains no complicated ideas, requires no sophisticated argument and does not depend on deep thought or wide reading. It works intuitively, without forethought or reflection...Typically, it expresses itself in the vernacular, the familiar language of the street, the home, the pub, the workplace and the terraces.

Here we could add, of course, that social media increasingly fulfil an important role in forming popular views and opinions and this is recognised by massive corporate entities such as Facebook. 'Common sense' furnishes a blurred, hazy and defective lens through which to view the world because it also incorporates information that is objectively inaccurate or crucially incomplete. Beyond a Gramscian conceptual framework, Bourdieu (1996, p. 21) hints at a similar understanding when he suggests that the 'pre-notions of common sense and the folklore categories of spontaneous sociology' contribute 'to *make* the reality that they describe' (Bourdieu, 1996, p. 21, original emphasis). Common sense perceptions often cohere with the tendency of ruling elites to 'manufacture ignorance' in order to justify the way society is hierarchised, regulated and rendered unequal (Slater, 2012). This might also help explain the ascendancy of the so-called 'alt-right' in the US and its deployment of 'alternative facts' to try to craft a socially and avowedly racist hegemony (Vice News Tonight, 2017). In this context, Kate Crehan (2016) has produced a lively articulation of Gramsci's 'common sense' and related themes, applying them to the rise of the Occupy Movement in the US. Casting her analytical gaze to the political right, she also examines the ascendancy of the Tea Party Movement which was to partly provide the impetus and electoral base for Trump.

However, commentaries on Gramsci often accord insufficient attention to his assertion that within common sense is often a kernel of 'good sense' (*buon senso*) which is more than a simple reflection of the ideas of the ruling class. Far from entirely conformist, common sense 'necessarily includes elements expressing the people's genuine experiences and interests' (Snir, 2016, p. 271). Gramsci's theorisation implies, therefore, that Marxism should not simply present itself as an abstract philosophy but 'should enter people's common sense, giving them a more critical understanding of their own situation' (Forgacs, 1988, p. 421). Thus, his particular perspective on Marxism – or what he prefers to call a 'philosophy of praxis' – should tease out and elaborate 'elements of critical awareness and "good sense" which are already present within people's "common sense"' (Forgacs, 1988, p. 323). For example, many people often seem to hold onto socially progressive ideas circulating around the valorisation of 'fairness' and possess an almost intuitive or 'gut-level' sense that it is wrong, for example, that the world's eight richest billionaires control the same wealth between them as the poorest half of the earth's population (Oxfam, 2017). A Gramscian approach would, therefore, seek to nurture the development of a fuller understanding of *why* the world is economically organised in this way: whose interests does this serve and how can the system be toppled and replaced with one that is more equitable? Here, the aim is to create new forms of critical thinking within which new possibilities arise. On a micro-level, it is also possible to see how this form of critical thinking might be of use when considering certain types of social work intervention; how might those, often in contact with practitioners, rendered subservient because of, for example, masculine hegemony within particular families begin to comprehend their predicament and begin to think about alternative counter-hegemonic strategies and less oppressive futures? Indeed, although not conceptualised in Gramscian terms, the accounts of many abuse 'survivors' can be framed in this way (McKay, 1998).

Dismantling the elite intelligentsia: intellectuals

The philosopher Jacques Rancière (2014, p. xiii) asserts that the 'very idea of a class in society whose specific role is to think is preposterous and can be conceived only because we live under a preposterous social order'. Over a century ago, Gramsci similarly embarked on challenging elitist notions about intellectuals and their role in society. Gramsci is also considered the 'Marxist theorist *par excellence* of the intellectuals' and 'Marxism's contribution to this field of research in large parts' rests with him (Thomas, 2009, p. 407).

His chief emphasis is on the social location, role and function of 'intellectuals'. Underpinning Gramsci's perspective is a democratising project aiming to extend 'the concept of the intellectual beyond the received notion of an elite intelligentsia' (Martin, 1998, p. 44). He asserts that although 'one can speak of intellectuals, one cannot speak of non-intellectuals, because non-intellectuals do not exist … There is no human activity from which every form of intellectual participation can be excluded' (Gramsci in Forgacs, 1988, p. 321). Gramsci redefines 'intellectual', therefore, as 'anyone whose function in society is primarily that of organizing, administering, directing, educating or leading others' (Forgacs, 1988, p. 300). Furthermore, the 'mode of being of a new intellectual can no longer consist in eloquence … but in active participation in practical life, as a constructor, organizer, "permanent persuader"' (Gramsci in Forgacs, 1988, p. 321). Within this framework, intellectuals play a crucial role in helping to maintain or challenge a given economic and social order. That is to say, intellectuals (and here we might, following Gramsci's interpretation, include social workers and social work educators) are potentially significant actors helping to either consolidate or undermine the exercise of hegemony.

Historically, the 'most typical' intellectuals were ecclesiastics who for a

> long time … held a monopoly of a number of important services: religious ideology, that is the philosophy and science of the age, together with schools, education, morality, justice, charity, good works, etc. … ecclesiastics can be considered the category of intellectuals bound to the landed aristocracy.
>
> *(Gramsci in Forgacs, 1988, p. 302)*

Over time, we also find 'the formation ... of a stratum of administrators, etc., scholars and scientists, theorists, non-ecclesiastical philosophers, etc.' (Gramsci in Forgacs, 1988, p. 303). These '*traditional intellectuals* ... put themselves forward as autonomous and independent of the dominant social group' (ibid., p. 303, emphasis added). One of the most important characteristics of any group that is 'developing towards dominance' is its 'struggle to assimilate and conquer "ideologically" the traditional intellectuals' (ibid., pp. 304–5). However, for an oppressed group to challenge and ultimately usurp the existing order it must stop relying on intellectuals from outside its own class and create its own *organic intellectuals*. Related to this task was a related aspiration to define and nurture the creation of the 'democratic philosopher' (Gramsci in Hoare and Nowell Smith, 2005, p. 350).

Discussion

Gramsci's observations on the incursion of technology in the workplace can add to debates about contemporary developments in social work. Some complain that due to the deployment of computer technology and the greater use of centrally devised electronic templates, social work's labour processes are also becoming much more Taylorised and de-skilled (see, for example, Baines, 2004a, 2004b; Carey, 2007). We may also be able to detect traces of Ford's approach in the new fixation of the State in monitoring social workers' private lives and activity beyond the workplace (McLaughlin, 2006, 2007, 2010). Often this is done – and rightly so – to ensure the safety of the public. Nevertheless, the emerging case law relating to instances where practitioners' conduct is questioned hints at a more politically and socially ambiguous surveillance agenda. Arguably, the spectre of Henry Ford's 'Sociological Department' appears to cast a shadowy influence across the invasive activity of organisations such as the Health and Care Professions Council in the UK and its Irish equivalent, CORU (McLaughlin, 2017).

Gramsci also reminds us how the seemingly private and personal aspects of daily life are politically important. Not unlike Foucault, but adopting a different theoretical lens, he was deeply interested in the 'quotidian and molecular operations of power' and in how seemingly unrelated micro practices can be rooted in structurally embedded shaping mechanisms (Ives, 2004a, p. 71). A similar attentiveness to the everyday and the unquestioned could potentially steer social workers and educators in a more reflexive and critical direction (see also Trotsky, 1979). Emphasising that rule is constructed rather than given, Gramsci's theorisation implicitly poses key questions for us today. For example:

- As a field of practices, how does social work function in the context of specific hegemonic orders?
- How are practitioners and social work educators positioned at this particular conjuncture?
- How might a faltering neoliberal capitalist hegemony be overcome?

This form of investigation might prompt reflection – and action – as to how social workers and those in receipt of their services might coalesce to defend provision from the encroachment and ongoing commodification.

Crucially, Gramscian thinking encourages social worker educators and practitioners to question professional 'common sense' and those undisputed truths 'inherited from the past and uncritically absorbed' (Gramsci in Hoare and Nowell Smith, 2005, p. 333). This may entail, for example, a critical interrogation of the categories and categorisations we are encouraged to use (Garrett, 2003). Thinking about how hegemony works might also lead social workers to reflect on how they engage with the ethical tensions inherent to the fields in which they are situated: locations, we have seen Gramsci refer to as, the 'outer ditches', 'fortresses' and 'earthworks' of civil society. Importantly, these questions direct attention to the use of language within micro-engagements with colleagues as well as service users (Garrett, 2018b). Indeed, Gramsci 'pays great attention to language as a political issue' (Ives, 2004a, p. 5).

Language is, in fact, the very 'materiality of ideology' (Althusser in Thomas, 2009, p. 432). Thinking more deeply and politically, therefore, about how it operates within prevailing social work discourses and daily interactions requires sustained questioning of what particular words 'assume about a social totality or infrastructure, or the presumed characteristics of social actors' (Barrett, 1992, p. 202). Far from being an exercise in what is often caricatured as 'political correctness', this type of inquisitiveness can potentially help us unpick how neoliberal power relations operate through language and culture (Ives, 2006). Here, a good example is provided by the types of professional conversations that circulate around the ubiquitous words such as 'client' or 'service user'. More broadly, what I have elsewhere termed 'welfare words' can continually – but often imperceptibly – contribute to solidifying the neoliberal hegemonic order (Garrett, 2018b). Nestled within wider 'common sense' understandings, 'welfare words', such as 'resilience' and its nefarious shadow, 'welfare dependency', might also be interpreted as forming part of a wider, politically distracting 'screen discourse' (Bourdieu and Wacquant, 2001) deflecting attention from issues related to capitalism, economic exploitation and a differential distribution of power. Not only do such words reflect – or mask – how the dominant order is constructed, they contribute to its constitution and consolidation.

Hence, the need to acknowledge that the terms 'used to describe social life are also active forces in shaping it' (Fraser and Gordon, 1997, p. 122). In tune with Gramsci's approach, Fraser and Gordon's interpretation assumes the development of a 'critical political semantics' (ibid., p. 123): a practice rooted in a project to disrupt 'taken-for-granted beliefs in order to render them susceptible to critique and to illuminate present-day conflicts' (ibid., p. 122). Indeed, failure to operate in this way could be highly problematic for social workers because 'unreflective' use of words might 'serve to enshrine certain interpretations of social life as authoritative and to delegitimate or obscure others, generally to the advantage of other groups in society and to the disadvantage of subordinate ones' (ibid., p. 123).

Engaging in such oppositional activity is, of course, a far from easy task because those in positions of structural power (and invested with the power of naming and defining) seek to bolster their hegemony and identify what is permissible and what should be 'closed down'. Similar constraints apply also to social work education where the curricula mapped out by central 'authorities', are frequently grounded in a neoliberal worldview or are insidiously tilted in that direction. This is not to argue that there are no spaces for a more critical engagement. What is more, it needs to be stressed that a Gramscian approach is not exclusively preoccupied with words and discursive struggle. It remains grounded in a more orthodox Leftist politics and is committed to seeking out alternative bases (trade unions, Leftist political parties and professional associations) from which to forge counter-hegemonic strategies intent on achieving political power. In short, while Gramsci was – what we might term today – a 'cultural theorist', he remained a revolutionary socialist.

Promoting more critical forms of intellectual engagement in social work education and practice is a difficult and delicate task which needs to take into account the multifarious ways in which the profession is constructed in different national settings. Although not drawing specifically on Gramsci's thinking, there are distinct Gramscian echoes in

Gudrid Aga Askeland and Malcolm Payne's critique of a global 'cultural hegemony' within social work education, where

> those who have the resources to produce and market social work literature are able to disseminate their theoretical views and skills ... throughout the world as the way to handle social issues in a professional way, ignoring the different local contexts in which [social work literature] is produced and ... should be read.
>
> *(Askeland and Payne, 2006, p. 734)*

This pattern also relates to how discourses emanating from influential parts of the West endeavour to colonise social work education and practice (Hutchings and Taylor, 2007; see also De Sousa Santos, 2012).

Conclusion

Gramsci has been dead for over 80 years, but his complex theorisation remains vital in our troubled world. The fact that his contribution is largely ignored within the academic literature of social work is puzzling given that – arguably – Gramsci is today a more 'popular theorist in mainstream academic debates than any other thinker from the Marxist tradition, Marx and Engels themselves not excluded' (Thomas, 2009, p. 199). Perhaps this omission from the social work literature is grounded in the fact that Gramsci provides no simplistic 'blueprints'. Unfettered by the shackles of 'evidenced-based practice', his thought is not driven by 'outcomes' and cannot be 'literally or mechanically' applied (Morton, 2003, p. 121). However, what can be distilled from Gramsci's writing has the power to invigorate the way we think and practice social work, prompting us to examine the constraints and possibilities of the profession and its potential evolution as part of a more encompassing critical and emancipatory project.

References

Anderson, P. (1976) 'The antinomies of Antonio Gramsci,' *New Left Review*, vol.100, pp. 5–79.
Anderson, P. (2017) *The antinomies of Antonio Gramsci*, London: Verso.
Askeland, G. A. and Payne, M. (2006) 'Social work education's cultural hegemony,' *International Social Work*, vol.49, no. 6, pp. 731–743.
Baines, D. (2004a) 'Caring for nothing,' *Work, Employment and Society*, vol.18, no. 2, pp. 267–295.
Baines, D. (2004b) 'Pro-market, non-market,' *Critical Social Policy*, vol.24, no. 1, pp. 5–29.
Barrett, M. (1992) 'Words and things', in M. Barrett and A. Phillips (ed.) *Destabilizing theory: Contemporary feminist debates*, Cambridge: Polity, pp. 201–219.
Bauman, Z. (2016) 'How neoliberalism prepared the way for Donald Trump', *Social Europe*, 16 November, www.socialeurope.eu/how-neoliberalism-prepared-the-way-for-donald-trump
Bellamy, R. (ed.) (1994) *Gramsci: Pre-prison writings*, Cambridge: University of Cambridge.
Biestek, F. P. (1975) 'Client self-determination', in F. E. McDermott (ed.) *Self determination in social work*, London: Routledge & Kegan Paul, pp. 17–32.
Bosworth, R. J. B. (1998) *The Italian dictatorship*, London: Arnold.
Bourdieu, P. (1996) 'On the family as a realized category,' *Theory, Culture & Society*, vol.13, no. 3, pp. 19–26.
Bourdieu, P. and Wacquant, L. (2001) 'NewLiberalSpeak,' *Radical Philosophy*, Jan/Feb, vol.105, pp. 2–6.
Braverman, H. (1974) 'Labour and monopoly capital,' *Monthly Review*, vol. 26, no. 3, pp. 1–134.
Brown, W. (2015) *Undoing the demos*, New York: Zone Books.
Buttigieg, J. A. (1986) 'The legacy of Antonio Gramsci,' *boundary 2*, vol. 14, no. 3, pp. 1–17.
Carey, M. (2007) 'White-collar proletariat?,' *Journal of Social Work*, vol. 7, no. 1, pp. 93–114.
Clarke, J., Newman, J., Smith, N., Vidler, E. and Westmarland, L. (2007) *Creating citizen-consumers*, London: Sage.

Crehan, K. (2002) *Gramsci, culture and anthropology*, London: Pluto.
Crehan, K. (2011) 'Gramsci's concept of common sense,' *Journal of Modern Italian Studies*, vol. 16, no. 2, pp. 273–287.
Crehan, K. (2016) *Gramsci's common sense*, Durham, NC: Duke University.
De Sousa Santos, B. (2012) 'Public sphere and the epistemologies of the South,' *African Development*, vol.XXXV11, no. 1, pp. 43–67.
Fekete, L. (2018) *Europe's fault lines: Racism and the rise of the right*, London:Verso.
Forgacs, D. (1988) *A Gramsci reader*, London: Lawrence and Wishart.
Fraser, N. and Gordon, L. (1997) 'A genealogy of dependency', in N. Fraser *Justice interruptus*, London: Routledge, pp. 121–151.
Garrett, P. M. (2003) *Remaking social work with children and families: A critical discussion on the 'modernisation' of social care*, London: Routledge.
Garrett, P. M. (2009a) *'Transforming' children's services? Social work, neoliberalism and the 'modern' world*, Maidenhead: McGraw Hill/Open University.
Garrett, P. M. (2009b) 'The case of "Baby P": Opening up spaces for debate on the "transformation" of Children's Services,' *Critical Social Policy*, vol. 29, no. 3, pp. 533–547.
Garrett, P. M. (2017) 'Castaway categories: Examining the re-emergence of the underclass in the UK,' *Journal of Progressive Human Services*, published online 21 December, doi: 10.1080/10428232.2017.1399038
Garrett, P. M. (2018a) 'Social work and Marxism: A short essay on the 200th anniversary of the birth of Karl Marx,' *Critical and Radical Social Work*, vol. 6, no. 2, pp. 179–196.
Garrett, P. M. (2018b) *Welfare words: Critical social work and social policy*, London: Sage.
Garrett, P. M. (2019) 'Looking east: (Re-)creating a social work "industry" in the People's Republic of China,' *Critical Social Policy*, Online First, 5 June. doi: 10.1177/0261018319853492
Gilbert, J. (2015) 'Disaffected consent: That post-democratic feeling,' *Soundings*, vol. 60, pp. 29–42.
Grandin, G. (2010) *Fordlandia*, London: Icon.
The Guardian. (2018) 'US suicide rate has risen nearly 30% since 1999, federal study finds', 8 June, www.theguardian.com/us-news/2018/jun/08/us-suicide-rate-has-risen-nearly-30-since-1999-federal-study-finds
Hall, S. (2011) 'The neo-liberal Revolution,' *Cultural Studies*, vol. 25, no. 6, pp. 705–728.
Hall, S. and Massey, D. (2010) 'Interpreting the crisis,' *Soundings*, vol. 44, pp. 57–72.
Hall, S. and O'Shea, A. (2015) 'Common-sense neoliberalism', in S. Hall, D. Massey and M. Rustin (ed.) *After neoliberalism*, London: Lawrence and Wishart, pp. 52–69.
Hoare, Q. (ed.) (1988) *Antonio Gramsci: Selections from political writings (1910–1920)*, London: Lawrence and Wishart.
Hoare, Q. and Nowell Smith, G. (eds.) (2005) *Antonio Gramsci: Selections from prison notebooks*, London: Lawrence and Wishart. 10th reprint.
Holborow, M. (2015) *Language and neoliberalism*, London: Routledge.
Hutchings, A. and Taylor, I. (2007) 'Defining the profession? Exploring an international definition of social work in China,' *International Journal of Social Welfare*, vol. 16, pp. 382–390.
Ives, P. (2004a) *Language and hegemony in Gramsci*, London: Pluto.
Ives, P. (2004b) *Gramsci's politics of language*, Toronto: University of Toronto.
Ives, P. (2006) 'Language, agency and hegemony', in A. Bieler and A. Morton (ed.) *Images of Gramsci*, London: Routledge, pp. 61–75.
Jones, S. (2006) *Antonio Gramsci*, London: Routledge.
Joseph, J. (2006) *Marxism and social theory*, Houndsmill: Palgrave Macmillan.
Landy, M. (1994) *Film, politics and Gramsci*, Minneapolis, MN: University of Minnesota.
MacKinnon, S. T. (2009) 'Social work intellectuals in the twenty-first century,' *Social Work Education*, vol. 28, no. 5, pp.512–527.
Martin, J. (1998) *Gramsci's political analysis*, Houndsmill: Macmillan.
Marx, K. (1990) *Capital*,Vol. 1, London: Penguin.
McKay, S. (1998) *Sophie's story*, Dublin: Gill & Macmillan.
McLaughlin, K. (2006) 'A taste of their own medicine?', *spiked*, www.spiked-online.com/newsite/article/906#.V_3HrU0VDbA
McLaughlin, K. (2007) 'Regulation and risk in social work,' *British Journal of Social Work*, vol. 37, no. 7, pp. 1263–1277.
McLaughlin, K. (2010) 'The social worker versus the general social care council,' *British Journal of Social Work*, vol. 40, pp. 311–327.

McLaughlin, K. (2017) 'English lessons: CORU and the surveillance of practitioners', *Frontline: The Social Work Action Network (Ireland) Bulletin*, December, pp. 3–6, https://socialworkactionnetworkireland.files.wordpress.com/2016/11/frontline-dec-2016-issue.pdf

Morton, A. D. (2003) 'Historicising Gramsci,' *Review of International Political Economy*, vol. 10, no. 1, pp. 118–146.

Oxfam. (2017) '*An economy for the 99%*', www.oxfam.org/sites/www.oxfam.org/files/file_attachments/bp-economy-for-99-percent-160117-en.pdf.

Pentaraki, M. (2016) 'I am in a constant state of insecurity trying to make ends meet, like our service users,' *British Journal of Social Work*, advanced access from 31 August, doi: 10.1093/bjsw/bcw099.

Rancière, J. (2014) *Moments politiques: Interventions 1977–2009*, New York: Seven Stories Press.

Robinson, A. (2006) 'Towards an intellectual reformation', in A. Bieler and A. Morton (ed.) *Images of Gramsci*, London: Routledge, pp. 75–89.

Rustin, M. (2009) 'Reflections on the present,' *Soundings*, vol. 43, pp.18–35.

Shahid, M. and Jha, M. K. (2014) 'Revisiting the client-worker relationship: Biestek through a Gramscian gaze,' *Journal of Progressive Services*, vol.25, pp.18–36.

Singh, G. and Cowden, S. (2009) 'The social worker as intellectual,' *European Journal of Social Work*, vol. 12, no. 4, pp.1369–1457.

Slater, T. (2012) 'The myth of "Broken Britain",' *Antipode*, vol. 46, no. 4, pp. 948–969.

Smith, G. A. (2011) 'Selective hegemony and beyond-populations with "no productive function",' *Identities*, vol.18, no. 1, pp.2–38.

Snir, I. (2016) '"Not just one common sense",' *Constellations*, vol. 23, no. 2, pp. 269–281.

Thomas, P. D. (2009) *The Gramscian moment*, Leiden & Boston, MA: Brill.

Trotsky, L. (1979) *Problems of everyday life and other writings on culture and science*, New York: Pathfinder, Third Printing.

Vice News Tonight. (2017) 'Charlottesville, race and terror', 14 August, https://news.vice.com/story/vice-news-tonight-full-episode-charlottesville-race-and-terror

Wilderson, F. (2003) 'Gramsci's black Marx,' *Social Identities*, vol. 9, no. 2, pp. 225–240.

Williams, R. (1973) 'Base and superstructure in Marxist cultural theory', *New Left Review*, Nov-Dec pp. 3–17.

8

From language to art
A Marcusian approach to critical social work pedagogy

Adi Barak

BAR-ILAN UNIVERSITY, ISRAEL

> Utopia is a historical concept. It refers to projects for social change that are considered impossible. Impossible for what reasons?
>
> *(Marcuse, 1967e; p. 250)*

Introduction

Herbert Marcuse (1898–1979) was born in Berlin, Germany to a Jewish family. He completed his PhD in literature in 1922 in Freiburg, and returned to Freiburg in 1928 to study philosophy with Edmund Husserl and Martin Heidegger. In 1933, Marcuse joined the Institute for Social Research (Institut für Sozialforschung) in Frankfurt, the institutional origin of the group that was later known as the Frankfurt School (Kellner et al., 2009; see also Jay, 1996).

In 1933, Marcuse fled Germany to escape Nazism and, along with other members of the Frankfurt School, received a position at Columbia University. In 1942, he began working for the US government in the Office of War Information and then in the Office of Strategic Services, as part of a governmental attempt to research, understand, and fight fascism (Farr, 2017). In 1954 he was appointed to a position at Brandeis University (Whitfield, 2015).

During his American years, Marcuse became a leading intellectual figure who exerted a major influence on the counter-revolution of the 1960s and on the New Left movement (Salerno, 2004). In fact, Marcuse was considered by some "the guru" of the New Left, although he himself rejected this notion (Kellner, 2005). As an academic, Marcuse openly supported various protest movements, such as the protest against the Vietnam War, and the struggles of the women's movement, among other causes (see Marcuse, 1967a, 1967b).

Marcuse was a prolific philosopher, writing about many areas, and as such it is difficult to summarize his theory. However, throughout his many influential texts, one can identify his preoccupation with the concept of liberation.[1] That is, how can society be truly liberated from the constraints of an oppressive apparatus? How can individuals develop a critical consciousness: one that allows the individual to be critical and negative, intolerant of injustice, and able to identify and process dialectical contradictions, without reconciling and/or eliminating them? Marcuse also focused on the role of art, Eros, fantasy, and imagination as radical liberating forces. His many books and essays describe a grim picture of a one-dimensional society – a society that on the one hand "delivers the goods" (Marcuse, 1967c/2007; p. 77) but on the other "integrates all authentic opposition, absorbs all alternatives" (Marcuse, 1964/2013; p. 20), and thus offers no real freedom.

One-dimensional society has made its measures of domination and indoctrination of the masses more sophisticated, creating a consciousness that is tolerant of injustice and restricted in its ability to negate, criticize, or even think of alternatives. However, by describing the mechanisms of domination and the kind of suppressed individual consciousness it elicits, in great detail, Marcuse also depicted possibilities of resistance – ways to develop a critical consciousness and to engage in an uncompromising struggle against injustice – a struggle Marcuse sometimes referred to as "the Great Refusal" (see for instance, Marcuse, 1969).

Marcuse, education, and the question of critical social work

Marcuse, as is evident, was not only an academic, writing "abstract" philosophy, but also a public supporter of social change and liberation. He was also a major influencer of key pedagogical and social leaders (Reitz & Spartan, 2011). Pedagogy, for Marcuse, and within it institutions of higher education, was a place that had a moral responsibility to create critical thinkers and activists – to nurture a real opposition (Kellner, 2011).

In a lecture given at Brooklyn College in 1968, Marcuse described the goals and conditions of critical education, claiming that

> to create the subjective conditions for a free society, it is no longer sufficient to educate individuals to perform more or less happily the functions they are supposed to perform in this society, or, to extend this "vocational" education to the "masses" … [we need] to educate men and women who are incapable of tolerating what is going on, who have really learned what is going on, and why, and who are educated to resist and to fight for a new way of life.
>
> *(1965/2009; p. 35)*

Perhaps, even if unintentionally, this is what social work educators do – educate social workers to "happily" perform their task in society, regardless of how uncritical this task might be, and how it might in fact be complicit with injustice. Can we develop a critical social work pedagogy that would nurture students who are unable to tolerate injustice and oppression? Would these students be able, as such, to participate in existing social work systems? These are some of the questions that Marcuse's approach raises.

About this chapter

In this chapter I will follow up on some of Marcuse's major concepts that, to me, seem most relevant to critical social work pedagogy, based on my experience as a critical educator. Marcuse wrote about pedagogy, among other subjects, but my intention is not to elaborate in detail about his notions of education (for an overview on Marcuse and education, see Kellner et al., 2009). Rather, I wish to specifically apply some of his central concepts to critical social work pedagogy. After describing concepts that are central to Marcuse's theory, I will also suggest some pedagogical practices that could be implemented in class. These practices, which I have developed over the years, personally involve the students in the exploration of critical social work.

The pedagogical practices that I will offer here accord with Freire's famous assertion that critical pedagogy cannot be delivered as a lecture, but rather as a question, a discussion, and a reflection of both pedagogue and student (Freire, 1970/2000). Discussing fundamental questions should open a path toward eliciting critical insights about society, self, creativity, art, and social work (for a discussion on the complementary nature of Marcuse and Freire in a pedagogical context, see Van Heertum, 2009).

Perhaps, then, it would be most appropriate to begin this chapter by posing a simple yet important question that, to me, seems neglected in the context of critical social work pedagogy – a pedagogy that is often based on discussions that take place in class: What is a critical discussion?

Language and discussion

Marcuse did not necessarily provide us with a specific explanation of what a critical discussion is, but rather allowed us to realize how language operates as a mechanism of oppression, and in that sense, what prevents a critical discussion from taking place.

Within the subject of language and discussion, Marcuse was deeply concerned with the forced verbal marriage of the good with the bad. Adopting an Orwellian insight, Marcuse demonstrated how the language in advanced industrialized societies is subverted to contain, as well as to obscure, contradictions. In Orwellian language, the "positive" and the "negative" are fused together, creating a "hybrid" (e.g., love and hate), and with the acceptance of this hybrid an individual becomes less able to separate the two constructs and see each for what it is. This "unification of opposites," as Marcuse explained:

> is one of the many ways in which discourse and communication make themselves immune against the expression of protest and refusal. How can such protest and refusal find the right word when the organs of the established order admit and advertise that peace is really the brink of war, that the ultimate weapons carry their profitable price tags, and that the bomb shelter may spell coziness?
>
> *(Marcuse, 1964/2013; pp. 93–94)*

Orwellian language is used by all of us in our most intimate thinking processes. This language, as much as we see it as our "own," also represents the values and interests of the political and economic system, and via the process of constant repetition, through the media and everyday conversation, promotes a constant reproduction of this system of values. In this regard, although oppositional vocabulary does exist, and thus

> other words can be spoken and heard, other ideas can be expressed … at the massive scale of the conservative majority … they are immediately "evaluated" … in terms of the public language – a language which determines a priori the direction in which the thought process moves.
>
> *(Marcuse, 1965b; p. 42)*

Thus, language is limited in its ability to oppose and negate – that is, to be critical.

But even if we could disrupt language patterns (e.g., object to the notion that war is peace) and their counter-dialectic repetition, this disruption would not be enough to generate a critical discussion, unless we also regard the actual content of the discussion as important. What should the topics of a critical discussion be? The problem, as Marcuse asserts in his *Note on Dialectic,* is that "[t]he established reality seems promising and productive enough to repel or absorb all alternatives. Thus acceptance – and even affirmation – of this reality appears to be the only reasonable methodological principle" (Marcuse, 1960/2007; p. 64). Based on this idea, much of what we consider critical discussion might merely be a "discussion and promotion of alternative policies within the status quo" (Marcuse, 1964/2013; p. 4). Against this backdrop, Marcuse claimed that

> persuasion through discussion and the equal presentation of opposites (even where they are not really equal) easily lose their liberating force as factors of understanding and learning; they are far more likely to strengthen the established thesis and to repel the alternatives.
> *(Marcuse, 1965b; p. 42)*

Unfortunately, the institutions that could have committed to producing oppositional knowledge – that is, knowledge of the true existence of oppression in society; universities, for instance – also turn "scientific and technical progress into an instrument of domination" (Marcuse, 1964/2013; p. 18). In a lecture given at Berkeley in 1975, Marcuse pointed out that:

> [one aspect] of the management of the mind through education [is]: the liberal sublimation, that is, the ... conversion of real gut problems, gut actions, into problems of method, research, and statistics. For example, the neutralized language and syntax of false consensus, the search for exact definitions and research in what we already know. The insistence on spurious objectivity, obscuring the difference between true and false, right and wrong, by insisting on the "other side" of everything.
> *(Marcuse, 1975; pp. 40–41)*

One could note that the uber-positivist discourse of current social work scholarship might align with this description.

Applying this critique to the definition of a critical discussion, then, it is fair to say that critical social work pedagogy should make room for a discussion that is radical enough to offer alternatives that transcend the status quo, and see possibilities beyond what "reality," "professional identity," and "professional intervention" are considered to be. In order to do so, we should teach ourselves a new language that restores our ability to see the opposition between contradicting concepts in our society while at the same time insisting on reclaiming the right to be negative: that is, to reaffirm existing contradictions rather than reconcile them. Thus, "the political language of the radicals is the elemental act of giving a new name to men and things, obliterating the false and hypocritical name which the renamed figures proudly bear in and for the system" (Marcuse, 1969; p. 35).

Pedagogical practice

What would a truly critical language for critical social work be? This could be a question posed to students and educators alike. A search for a critical discussion is fundamental to any critical social work pedagogy, and yet the failure to establish one should not discourage us: defining what a critical discussion is would set the stage for finding it.

In line with Garrett (2015), critical educators could engage students in examining "keywords," that is, common expressions that are used in social work discourse and are politically charged with meaning, often implicitly reinforcing a neo-liberal order. These expressions should be reviewed so that students can see how their meaning was at no point fixed but was, rather, changed in accordance with different political viewpoints; in this way "the political, ethical, and class stakes in deploying a given term" could be exposed while at the same time students could identify "what is at stake in redefining, or keeping intact, these concepts" (Safri & Ruccio, 2013; p. 8). Critical educators could also engage students in coming up with new definitions for common social work expressions, thus exposing the underlying ideology of professional vocabulary.

In my critical social work class, I address the issue of language by, actually, bypassing language. I teach students, for instance, to interview each other about a political issue, and to take note of the resultant bodily sensations that arise, through techniques of embodiment, such as an adaptation of Augusto Boal's image theatre (Barak, 2015) or an adaptation of analogical listening (Neimeyer, 2012). These techniques entail asking oneself about where in the body a political issue is felt and focusing on that. Bypassing the particulars of day-to-day language, students are often able to more deeply understand how words mask oppression.

Society and liberation

Perhaps one of the biggest challenges in critical social work class is the crucial deciphering of the oppressive factors in society. In a talk given in London, Marcuse posed the challenge of such an endeavor, explaining that "today we have to be liberated from a relatively well-functioning, rich, powerful society" (Marcuse, 1967d/2005). It is precisely because of this, the fact that society is "affluent," that a discussion about society would immediately be countered by the assertion that the current state of affairs, although not perfect, is probably the best we could achieve.

The oppressive affluent society, as Marcuse explained, operates under the guise of true liberty; however, perhaps counterintuitively, "under the rule of a repressive whole, liberty can be made into a powerful instrument of domination" (Marcuse, 1964/2013; p. 9). What Marcuse suggests here is that under the guise of the liberties provided by an advanced capitalist society – one that deliver the goods, to use Marcuse's terminology – the individual is granted freedom of choice, but this choice is far from free, as it is a choice to elect "masters" and a choice between goods and services. Such choices maintain the social controls that reinforce a capitalist economic view of society (see Marcuse, 1964/2013; p. 10).

In *Some Social Implications of Modern Technology* Marcuse provides a striking example of this process of choice and oppression (Marcuse, 1941/1998; p. 46):

> Let us take a simple example. A man who travels by automobile to a distant place chooses his route from the highway maps ... Numerous signs and posters tell the traveler what to do and think; they even request his attention to the beauties of nature or the hallmarks of history. Others have done the thinking for him, and perhaps for the better ... He will fare best who follows its directions, subordinating his spontaneity to the anonymous wisdom which ordered everything for him ... There is no personal escape from the apparatus which has mechanized and standardized the world.

Marcuse, indeed, used the highway as a quintessential example of domination that operates under the guise of liberty. The car, an iconic symbol of American freedom, represents the ability of one to hypothetically go wherever he or she desires, with no limitations. However, this ability is constituted within a pre-determined set of choices. Freedom of choice, hence, is restricted to the offers presented by the signs and billboards on the way – all positioned by a supreme, transparent voice of "wisdom."

"Domination in the guise of affluence and liberty" (Marcuse, 1964/2013; p. 20) extends to every realm of life, even the spiritual, and thus the spiritual realm hardly represents a space of resistance. Rather, for Marcuse the "spiritual" also served as a method by which the social capitalist apparatus could retain its power. In a sardonic tone, Marcuse asks:

> Why not try God, Zen, existentialism, and beat ways of life … But such modes of protest and transcendence are no longer contradictory to the status quo and no longer negative. They are rather the ceremonial part of practical behaviourism … and are quickly digested by the status quo as part of its healthy diet.
>
> *(Marcuse, 1964/2013; p. 16)*

Society, thus, is a society that has no opposition, neither in academia nor in religion nor in spirituality, neither in regard to free will nor in regard to free speech.

Pedagogical practice

Social work students could be asked to reflect on society in light of Marcuse's insights. The Freirean concept of conscientisation (Freire, 1970) could be applied to point students' attention to their own privilege and their own role in the oppression that exists in their society (Gorder, 2008; see also, Sakamoto & Pitner, 2005). In order to decipher their role in an affluent society, students should focus their reflection on how and what they gain as individuals from the existing status quo – and how this gain affects their motivation to counter oppression. Indeed, we must reflect on our own individual consciousness, to see if we can find a critical way of resisting and finding alternatives. However, we must also acknowledge that by insisting on such reflection, we might encourage our students to pursue a practice that is very different from the one they will be expected to perform in the field (Rossiter, 2001). We should be able to address this concern in class, as well (see Barak, 2019).

In my critical social work class, I ask students to interview each other about what I call "birth of the political me." This interview focuses on the students' first remembered experience of discovering that the world is political, that there is such a thing as "politics," and that their "self" takes part in the political realm. Students almost always respond by saying that they made these discoveries at a very young age, and most of their stories connect "birth of the political me" to a traumatic experience (e.g., parents' bankruptcy; inter-racial violence in the neighborhood). After sharing their answers, students are more apt to discover their relation to the current political status quo and their place in the power grid of domination and oppression, as if acknowledging the child who once discovered politics allows the adult to re-discover it.

The happy consciousness and negative thinking

In *One-Dimensional Man*, Marcuse terms the uncritical consciousness as a "happy consciousness." The happy consciousness is a consciousness that firmly holds "the belief that the real is rational and that the system delivers the goods" (Marcuse, 1964/2013; p. 87). This belief, of course, is not "natural" but rather a belief that subjects are indoctrinated through several mechanisms that absorb all opposition into the existing modes of domination, and thus make any opposition futile.

Rationality, Marcuse explained, is a term that has been used to justify and therefore perpetuate the existing culture and society. As a result, the widespread use of the terms "rationality" or "reason" constitutes an utterly uncritical consciousness. In Marcuse's words, "individualistic rationality has developed into efficient compliance with the pre-given continuum of means and ends" (Marcuse, 1941/1998; p. 46); thus, the development of rationality in modern society is "the process by which logic became the logic of domination" (Marcuse, 1964/2013; p. 128).

Hence, what people might perceive as their own individual rational choices, and their rational deciphering of reality, is basically self-subjugation and conformity.

A "happy consciousness," or "uncritical consciousness," is learned, promoted, and indoctrinated on a large scale, through the state and capitalist economic apparatus: for instance, through the education system, and through social and cultural practices. This tendency, as Marcuse explained, produces a balanced yet utterly uncritical and de-politicized way of looking at the world. As captured by Orwellian language, "the negative features (overproduction, unemployment, insecurity, waste, repression) are not comprehended as long as they appear merely as more or less inevitable by-products, as 'the other side' of the story of growth and progress" (Marcuse, 1964/2013; p. 229). Clinging to this assumption, the inclination to see everything as a balance, a give and take, does not allow for any real critical consciousness to develop.

As may by now be evident, the absence of a truly oppositional thought was one of Marcuse's biggest concerns, a concern he wrote about extensively. Being un-contradictory necessitates a tolerance of the faults and injustices of the system, one that Marcuse defined as a repressive tolerance (Marcuse, 1965b). This kind of tolerance is not, as one might think, a typical byproduct of a dictatorship, but rather of democracies. Marcuse's analysis of modern democracies demonstrates how in order to support an unjust system, individuals tend to develop a "tolerance toward that which is radically evil" (Marcuse, 1965b; p. 34). This tolerance is promoted in educational settings when, by exposing students to all viewpoints, as if all viewpoints are equal, oppressive ideologies are legitimized (Brookfield, 2018).

By contrast, one primary way to develop a critical consciousness is through dialectics. What Marcuse suggests is that dialectical thinking identifies the contradictions and tensions within society without attempting to reconcile them. Such a process essentially involves negative thinking, as "the power of negative thinking is the driving power of dialectical thought, used as a tool for analyzing the world of facts in terms of its internal inadequacy" (Marcuse, 1960/2007; pp. 64–65). A dialectical way of looking at society, thus, is a pre-condition for any critical stance.

Indeed, an uncritical consciousness is in no way a given. Marcuse identified a different kind of consciousness, one that can develop and perform a radical liberating "Great Refusal." The great refusal, in this regard, is not a single heroic act of protest, and cannot be equated with the term "social action." Rather, the Great Refusal embodies a state of radical consciousness, which is manifested through "an emergence of different goals and values, different aspirations in the men and women who resist and deny the massive exploitative power of corporate capitalism even in its most comfortable and liberal realizations" (Marcuse, 1969; p. xii). Such a great refusal is dependent on what might be seen as the opposite of reason, as "reason was defined as an instrument of constraint, of instinctual suppression" (Marcuse, 1966; p. 159). The great refusal, and the consciousness upon which it depends, is driven by a different set of "rules" stemming from Eros.

Eros, in this sense, is a force of imagination, fantasy, and sensuality that might run contrary to the logic of "the performance principle": a reality principle, in the Freudian sense, that restricts society to the logic of labor and productivity as the sole guidelines for societal norms and thinking. Such restrictions suppress the pleasure principle, the imagination, and the instincts. Thus, Marcuse advocates for fantasy in its deeper political sense, as part of a consciousness that allows one to imagine alternative, better, utopian political realities, explaining that "in the realm of phantasy, the unreasonable images of freedom become rational" (Marcuse, 1966; p. 160).

Pedagogical practice

The questions of critical consciousness in critical social work pedagogy, then, could be about our own consciousness, both in our personal and professional lives: What restricts our consciousness from dialectical thinking? What kinds of repressive tolerances have we developed over the years? And how can we unleash the forces of imagination, bypassing the oppressive forces of the performance principle, in an attempt to imagine new forms of liberation, for ourselves and for others? Could we use our insights to imagine a radically different kind of social work? A critical social work?

One way of addressing questions of imagination and/or tolerance is through focusing on students' subjectivity. In her essay, Amsler (2011) argues that subjectivity itself should be a realm of critical education, as students' "'comfort zones' of knowledge and feeling are understood not as obstacles of systemic transformation but as sites of hegemonic struggle" (p. 57). Such pedagogy sees "encounters between the body, the biographical and the political and experiences of emotional dissonance and discontent as necessary conditions for the development of critical sensibility rather than as targets for amelioration in rationalist subject-transformation" (p. 59). Pedagogies of critical consciousness, thus, should allow critical pedagogues to recognize zones both of ideological comfort and discomfort, and, without approving or disapproving of neo-liberal sensibilities, to encourage individuals to imagine radical alternatives.

In my critical social work class, I find great importance in helping students address the emotions that are related to dominant political ideologies, as well as to their own viewpoints. One method that I have developed is what I call "emotional ideology." Through this process students are asked to interview each other about the emotions attached to their, and/or a, dominant neo-liberal political ideology. Students are provided a set of questions which they are asked to use in the process of interviewing each other:

- Can you talk about your ideological views?
- Can you describe your feelings when you think about this ideology?
- Could you tell me the story of how this ideology developed?
- Could you describe the important others in your life who are connected with this ideology?

Or, for instance:

- What do you perceive as the dominant ideological viewpoint in society?
- Can you share events or points in time in which you experienced this ideology as oppressive/difficult/different from how you felt about things?
- Can you describe your feelings when you experience/d this gap?
- Could you tell me a story about an instance when you felt this gap?
- Can you describe the ideological/political transition you went through over the years?
- What emotions were related to this transformation?

Focusing on the emotions attached to political ideology often allows students' consciousness to transcend the thin layer of "happy consciousness," enabling them to get in touch with their discomfort.

Art, creativity, and liberation

Art was considered by Marcuse to be a mechanism for a "great refusal"; that is, "the protest against that which is" (Marcuse, 1964/2013; p. 66). Indeed, the futility of language, and basically of all forms of opposition in one-dimensional society, led Marcuse to look at art as a radical alternative. As art cannot really be fully controlled by the apparatus, it might be one of the only remaining routes for staging protest and seeking liberation.

Art, in a simple manner, can provide a new language that is more suitable for describing the protest against existing forms of domination and oppression. In a public lecture titled "Art in the One-Dimensional Society" (Marcuse, 1967c/2007), Marcuse explained:

> When I saw and participated in [the] demonstration against the war in Vietnam, and I heard [demonstrators] singing the songs of Bob Dylan, I somehow felt, and it is very hard to define, that this is the only revolutionary language left today.
>
> *(p. 113)*

In this sense, art for Marcuse was an effective form of revolutionary communication that provided a way to "break the oppressive rule of the established language and images over the mind and body ... language and images which have long since become a means of domination, indoctrination and deception" (Marcuse, 1972; p. 79). This development of a new language, for Marcuse, was one of the only alternatives for liberation from a system that had absorbed all of our ability to use regular forms of expression, thinking, imagining, and expressing alternatives.

But art, for Marcuse, was not only about communication in the simple sense, perhaps because capitalist societies could void art (as they could any other form of opposition) of its radical negation and appropriate it. Marcuse referred to this process as "repressive desublimation," arguing that the process of voiding the power of works of art takes place through "their wholesale incorporation into the established order, through their reproduction and display on a massive scale" (Marcuse, 1964/2013; p. 60). What, then, makes art a powerful alternative, despite this incorporation? Or in Marcuse's words, "How could art, in the midst of the all-assimilating mechanisms of mass culture, recover its alienating force, continue to express the Great Refusal?" (Marcuse, 1945; p. 202).

In *The Aesthetic Dimension* (1978), Marcuse deepened his theory of art claiming that it is not solely the actual political content, or message of art that is revolutionary. Rather, the aesthetic dimension itself is the core of art's radical power as, "by virtue of its aesthetic form, art is largely autonomous vis-à-vis the given social relations. In its autonomy art both protests these relations, and at the same time transcends them" (Marcuse, 1978; p. ix). In this statement Marcuse points to the fact that the actual creation of an altered aesthetic dimension that is unrelated to the "social relations" is in itself a radical resistance to the power of the capitalist apparatus.

The implication, as Marcuse suggested, is that art could subvert society's social and economic order by creating an imaginary aesthetic space that escapes the "performance principle." Hence, by virtue of creating an aesthetic space, "art may promote the alienation, the total estrangement of man from his world. And this alienation may provide the artificial basis for the remembrance of freedom in the totality of oppression" (Marcuse, 1945; p. 214). Creating "an 'aesthetic' reality – society as a work of art," Marcuse asserted – is "the most Utopian, the most radical possibility of liberation today" (see, Marcuse, 1967d/2005; pp. 82–83).

It is important to note that Marcuse based this theory predominantly on what he defined as high – as opposed to grassroots – art, a concept for which he was criticized (Davis, 2005). He also placed this argument in the context of debating and offering alternatives to the Marxist approach to art – a debate that goes beyond the scope of this chapter. However, the idea that the aesthetic dimension can make space for transcendence and liberation, in a society that is otherwise "one-dimensional," was adopted by some as a way to look at critical pedagogy in general (see for instance, Brookfield, 2002). This idea is worth contemplating from a critical social work perspective.

Pedagogical practice

The question here could be, for starters, why has social work neglected art as a practice and as knowledge, given the goals of critical practice? (For a discussion on art and social work, see for instance, Sinding et al., 2014; Wehbi et al., 2016.) We could also reflect on our perspective toward the aesthetic dimension as critical social workers: Can/should we avoid this dimension? Critical social work, as much as this idea may sound unconventional, could create a space in which the aesthetic dimension is thoroughly explored, with regard to its inherent ability to transcend and resist (see, Barak & Stebbins, 2017).

Giroux (2004) identifies hope as subversive, as it connects social critique with social change. Without what Giroux calls "educated hope," important social struggle may seem futile. Critical pedagogy, thus, should find new ways to generate radical hope – with which one can imagine a radically different world (see also, Stewart-Harawira, 2005). Art should be considered a major path toward achieving just this goal.

In my critical social work class, I insist on teaching creative arts-based approaches to intervention and reflection. For instance, I teach students how to use what I call "Generative Writing" (Barak & Leichtentritt, 2016). In this method I ask students to imagine an alternative reality, one that opposes the current political and ideological status quo. Students are then asked to write about this reality, using their creative skills. Writing, in my experience, unleashes creative energy, as the medium itself allows for free association and a flow of ideas, even if these ideas seem unrealistic. Through the art of writing, thus, a radical alternative of reality is explored, and within it, sometimes, a radical, even if very fragile, hope emerges.

A conclusion: is critical consciousness enough?

Marcuse advocated for critical theory not only as theory but also as practice, criticizing those theories that remained in the realm of abstraction: "the divorce of thought from action, of theory from practice, is itself part of the unfree world" (Marcuse, 1960/2007; p. 69). However, he offered no false optimism regarding its success. By posing questions about our own consciousness, society, language, art, and the Great Refusal, we can offer a path for a different kind of consciousness to develop: a possibility for a new way of seeing the world, and in that sense, a new possibility for a critical social work.

However, having come to understand what Marcuse referred to as "the performance principle," we should be cautious about immediately translating critical insights into critical practice. Focusing on questions such as, "How could Marcuse's ideas be applied in welfare services?" might force Marcuse's insights into an uncritical framework of organizational mainstream practice. We, as critical social work educators, should be humbly reminded that it is a critical consciousness that we wish to develop, and with this consciousness students can discover their own practical path (see Barak, 2015).

These ideas should also be understood with regard to the current hegemonic neo-liberal notions that dominate higher education. Neo-liberal ideologies render critical social work contrary to the occupational goals of students, and moreover, contrary to institutions' curricula and pedagogical vision (Macfarlane, 2016). Neo-liberalism, however, should not discourage social work educators who are committed to emancipatory pedagogy as a way to move from theory to practice (MacKinnon, 2009).

There is no road map or specific practice for the achievement of this goal. Critical consciousness cannot speak a positivist means-to-an-end language. Rather, it offers a constant search for liberation, both on the professional and personal level. Marcuse himself made this point. At the end of *One-Dimensional Man*, he writes:

> the critical theory of society possesses no concepts which could bridge the gap between the present and its future; holding no promise and showing no success, it remains negative. Thus it wants to remain loyal to those who, without hope, have given and give their life to the Great Refusal.
>
> *(Marcuse, 1964/2013; p. 261)*

Notes

1 Marcuse often used the word "liberation" to refer to the general idea of gaining freedom from oppression. I therefore use this word as well, throughout the chapter, to express the same idea.

References

Amsler, S. S. (2011). From 'therapeutic' to political education: The centrality of affective sensibility in critical pedagogy. *Critical Studies in Education*, 52(1), 47–63.

Barak, A. (2015). Critical consciousness in critical social work: Learning from the theatre of the oppressed. *The British Journal of Social Work*, 46(6), 1776–1792.

Barak, A. (2019). Critical questions on critical social work: Students' perspectives. *The British Journal of Social Work*. Retrieved from https://academic.oup.com/bjsw/advance-article-abstract/doi/10.1093/bjsw/bcz026/5381115

Barak, A., & Leichtentritt, R. D. (2016). Creative writing after traumatic loss: Towards a generative writing approach. *British Journal of Social Work*, 47(3), 936–954.

Barak, A., & Stebbins, A. (2017). Re-entry as performance: Reflections from Institution X. *Critical Social Policy*, 37(2), 287–309.

Brookfield, S. (2002). Reassessing subjectivity, criticality, and inclusivity: Marcuse's challenge to adult education. *Adult Education Quarterly*, 52(4), 265–280.

Brookfield, S. D. (2018). Repressive tolerance and the management of diversity. In V. C. X. Wang (Ed.), *Critical Theory and Transformative Learning* (pp. 1–13). Hershey, PA: IGI Global.

Davis, A. (2005). Marcuse's legacies. In D. Kellner (Ed.), *Collected Papers of Herbert Marcuse: The New Left and the 1960s* (pp. vii–xiv). New York: Routledge.

Farr, A. (2017). Herbert marcuse. In *The Stanford Encyclopedia of Philosophy*. Retrieved July, 2018 from https://plato.stanford.edu/entries/marcuse/#toc

Freire, P. (1970/2000). *Pedagogy of the Oppressed*. New York: Continuum.

Garrett, P. M. (2015). Words matter: Deconstructing "welfare dependency" in the UK. *Critical and Radical Social Work*, 3(3), 389–406.

Giroux, H. (2004). When hope is subversive. *Tikkun*, 19(6), 38–39.

Jay, M. (1996). *The dialectical imagination: A history of the Frankfurt School and the Institute of Social Research, 1923–1950* (Vol. 10). Berkeley and Los Angeles, CA: University of California Press.

Kellner, D. (2005). Introduction: Radical politics, Marcuse and the new left. In D. Kellner (Ed.), *Collected Papers of Herbert Marcuse: The New Left and the 1960s* (pp. 1–37) New York: Routledge.

Kellner, D., Lewis, T., & Peirce, C. (2009). Introduction. In D. Kellner, T. Lewis, C. Peirce, & Cho. D. (Eds.), *Marcuse's Challenge to Education* (pp. 1–32). Lanham, MD: Rowman & Littlefield.

Kellner, D. M. (2011). On Marcuse: Critique, liberation, and reschooling in the radical pedagogy of Herbert Marcuse. *Estudos e Pesquisas em Psicologia*, 11(1), 23–55.

Macfarlane, S. (2016). Education for critical social work: Being true to a worthy project. In B. Pease, S. Goldingay, N. Hosken, & S. Nipperess (Eds.), *Doing Critical Social Work: Transformative Practices for Social Justice* (pp. 326–328). Sydney: Allen & Unwin.

MacKinnon, S. (2009). Social work intellectuals in the twenty-first century, critical social theory, critical social work and public engagement. *Social Work Education*, 28(5), 512–527.

Marcuse, h. (1965b). Repressive tolerance. In A. Fenberg, & W. Leiss (Eds.), *The Essential Marcuse: Selected Writings of Philosopher and Social Critique Herbert Marcuse* (pp. 32–60). Boston: Beacon.

Marcuse, H. (1941/1998). Some social implications of modern technology. In D. Kellner (Ed.), *Collected Papers of Herbert Marcuse Collected Papers of Herbert Marcuse (Vol. 1): Technology, War and Fascism* (pp. 41–65). New York: Routledge.

Marcuse, H. (1945). Some remarks on Aragon: Art and politics in the totalitarian era. In D. Kellner (Ed.), *Collected Papers of Herbert Marcuse (Vol. 1): Technology, War and Fascism* (pp. 201–214) New York: Routledge.

Marcuse, H. (1960/2007). A note on dialectic. In A. Fenberg, & W. Leiss (Eds.), *The Essential Marcuse: Selected Writings of Philosopher and Social Critique Herbert Marcuse* (pp. 63–71). Boston: Beacon.

Marcuse, H. (1964/2013). *One-Dimensional Man: Studies in the Ideology of Advanced Industrial Society*. New York: Routledge.

Marcuse, H. (1965/2009). Lecture on education, Brooklyn College, 1968. In D. Kellner, T. Lewis, C. Peirce, & Cho. D. (Eds.), *Marcuse's Challenge to Education* (pp. 33–38). Lanham, MD: Rowman & Littlefield.

Marcuse, H. (1966). *Eros and Civilization: Philosopical Inquiry Into Freud*. Boston: Beacon.

Marcuse, H. (1967a/2005). The Inner Logic of American Policy in Vietnam. In D. Kellner (Ed.), *Collected Papers of Herbert Marcuse: The New Left and the 1960s* (pp. 38–40). New York: Routledge.

Marcuse, H. (1967b/2005). The problem of violence and the radical opposition. In D. Kellner (Ed.), *Collected Papers of Herbert Marcuse: The New Left and the 1960s* (pp. 71–89). New York: Routledge.

Marcuse, H. (1967c/2007). Art in the one-dimentional society. In D. Kellner (Ed.), *Art and Liberation: Collected Papers of Herbert Marcuse* (Vol. 4, pp. 113–122). New York: Routledge.

Marcuse, H. (1967d/2005). Liberation from the affluent society. In D. Kellner (Ed.), *Collected Papers of Herbert Marcuse: The New Left and the 1960s* (pp. 76–86). New York: Routledge.

Marcuse, H. (1967e) The end of Utopia. In D. Kellner, & C. Pierce (Eds.), Collected papers of Herbert Marcuse. *Marxism, Revolution and Utopia* (Vol. 6, pp. 249–263). New York: Routledge.

Marcuse, H. (1969). *An Essay on Liberation*. Boston: Beacon Press.

Marcuse, H. (1972). *Counterrevolution and Revolt*. Boston: Beacon Press.

Marcuse, H. (1975). Lecture on higher education and politics, Berkley, 1975. In D. Kellner, T. Lewis, C. Peirce, & Cho. D. (Eds.), *Marcuse's Challenge to Education* (pp. 39–44). Lanham, MD: Rowman & Littlefield.

Marcuse, H. (1978). *The Aesthetic Dimension: Toward a Critique of Marxist Aesthetics*. Boston: Beacon Press.

Neimeyer, R. A. (2012). Analogical listening. In R. A. Neimeyer (Eds.), *Techniques of Grief Therapy: Creative Practices for Counseling the Bereaved* (pp. 55–57). New York: Routledge.

Reitz, C., & Spartan, S. F. (2011). *Critical Work and Radical Pedagogy: Recalling Herbert Marcuse*. The Authors.

Rossiter, A. (2001). Innocence lost and suspicion found: Do we educate for or against social work. *Critical Social Work*, 2(1), 1–9.

Safri, M., & Ruccio, D. F. (2013). Keywords: An introduction. *Rethinking Marxism*, 25, 7–9.

Sakamoto, I., & Pitner, R. O. (2005). Use of critical consciousness in anti-oppressive social work practice: Disentangling power dynamics at personal and structural levels. *The British Journal of Social Work*, 35(4), 435–452.

Salerno, R. A. (2004). *Beyond the Enlightenment: Lives and thoughts of Social Theorists*. Westport, CT: Greenwood Publishing Group.

Sinding, C., Warren, R., & Paton, C. (2014). Social work and the arts: Images at the intersection. *Qualitative Social Work*, 13(2), 187–202.

Stewart-Harawira, M. (2005). Cultural studies, Indigenous knowledge and pedagogies of hope. *Policy Futures in Education*, 3(2), 153–163.

Van Gorder, C. (2008). Paulo Freire's pedagogy for the children of the oppressors: Educating for social justice among the world's privileged. *Journal of Pedagogy, Pluralism, and Practice*, 4(1), 31.

Van Heertum, R. (2009) Moving from critique to hope: Critical interventions from Marcuse to Freire. In D. Kellner, T. Lewis, C. Pierce, & K. D. Cho (Eds.), *Marcuse's Challenge to Education* (pp. 103–116). Lanham, MD: Rowman & Littlefield Publishers Inc.

Wehbi, S., McCormick, K., & Angelucci, S. (2016). Socially engaged art and social work: Reflecting on an interdisciplinary course development journey. *Journal of Progressive Human Services*, 27(1), 49–64.

Whitfield, S. J. (2015). A radical in academe: Herbert Marcuse at Brandeis University. *Journal for the Study of Radicalism*, 9(2), 93–124.

9

Theodor Adorno
'Education after Auschwitz': contributions toward a critical social work pedagogy

John G. Fox

DEAKIN UNIVERSITY, GEELONG, AUSTRALIA

Introduction

Social work emerged in response to the suffering experienced in the cruel dislocations of industrialisation and immigration (internal and international) in the global North in the nineteenth century. Within the United Kingdom, the longer term impacts of the agricultural and industrial revolutions and the rapid, unplanned internal migrations to urban centres disrupted long-standing ways of living – ways of being in one's environment – and caused widespread hardship. Within the United States of America, those same forces, coupled with substantial international immigration, similarly disrupted long-standing ways of living and being and caused suffering. Systemic responses to these demands, as typified by the English Poor Laws and rationalised in classical liberal discourse, contributed to people's suffering: neglecting the impact of changing environments, they located the problem in poor character and 'blamed the victims' for their oppression.

Social work sought to address this neglect: to understand and respond to the 'person-in-environment'. Mary Richmond (1971, p. 131), one of the pioneers in systematising casework, insisted 'that society is not only the medium in which personality is developed but its source and origin'. However, Richmond's consideration of this 'wider self', while recognising the influence of the environment, tended to remain focused on the individual and their most proximate relationships, particularly their families (Richmond, 1917, 1971). Jane Addams, reflecting the Settlement House movement, took a broader approach and emphasised wider forms of interaction through industrial and social reform. Since that time critical social work has continued to seek to promote human emancipation through the critique of, and actions to change, structures of domination (Allan et al., 2009; Mullaly, 2007). Its 'common and binding theme … [has been linking] the personal with the political' (Allan, 2009, p. 87) – the relations between a person and environment – with regard to the ways power shapes them both. Most recently, that endeavour has followed the postmodern 'linguistic turn', focusing on language, narrative and discourse (Allan et al., 2009; Parton and O'Byrne, 2000).

Over the last few decades the cruel dislocations of capitalism have been reinvigorated, again with the aid of new technologies and a new or 'neo' liberal discourse. Neoliberal policies have dismantled environmental supports in education, health and social services. For those unable to bear the increased burden, we have seen increased regulation. As Henri Giroux (2016) has argued, we face an increasingly authoritarian state in many countries where liberal democratic cultures, which were believed to be an effective safeguard against oppression, have failed. For the first time in the global North since social work was established, we face an environment where many have grown up in Fukuyama's world. A world in which liberalism appears to have become so dominant that political history has ended and liberalism's grounding assumptions – particularly its emphasis on the individual – have achieved the status of common sense. One that promotes a new 'illiteracy' that isolates people, limits their ability to 'translate [their] private troubles to broader public issues', and undermines their sense of agency (Giroux, 2011, p. 83).

Theodor Adorno shared similar concerns. He reflected on Germany's insecure democracy in the 1920s and 1930s, the rise of Nazism and the subsequent horrors of the Holocaust. He considered that these were enabled by the weaknesses of Western culture that typify liberalism. For Adorno (2003, p. 19), the Holocaust revealed the failure of Western culture – the inability of Western civilisation to prevent a 'relapse' into 'barbarism'.

Theodor Adorno: a brief biography

Adorno (1903–1969) received his philosophy doctorate in 1924 and then studied musical composition. In 1931 he joined the Institute for Social Research at Frankfurt University (the 'Frankfurt School') and began the work for which he is famous. His thought draws deeply on philosophy and music, as well as other sources, such as Marxism and psychoanalysis.

The Frankfurt School sought 'to organise investigations … in which philosophers, sociologists, economists, historians, and psychologists [were] … brought together in permanent collaboration' (Horkheimer, 1993, p. 8). This endeavour became known as 'critical theory'. The critical tradition of social work locates its roots in this work.

Fleeing the Nazis, Adorno worked overseas with others to comprehend the rise of Nazism and the failure of Western culture to resist it. He returned to Germany after the war, with a keen interest in exploring the complicity of those who had remained, and the best means to prevent the repetition of Nazism's horrors. He (2003, p. 19) considered that means to be education, and that 'the premier demand on all education is that Auschwitz not happen again'. That concern informed his university teaching, his post-war publications and his public engagement through more than one hundred radio broadcasts (Parkinson, 2014).

Adorno's key concerns resonate deeply with those of the critical social work tradition. His key concern, like that of social work, was responding to unjustified suffering: to 'make suffering eloquent' (1973, p. 17). He, like critical social work, located a key cause of that suffering in the treatment of the self as independent of the environment. Adorno also considered how this approach enabled others to withhold aid to those suffering – evasions more recently considered through concepts such as privilege. He sought to replace the disinterest or independence of liberal society with an ethics founded in compassion: an ethics that shares a common orientation to that of both Mary Richmond and Jane Addams.

Key concepts

Adorno's key concern was the manner in which Western thought conceptualised a thing's being or nature as separate from or independent of other things: as a thing-existing-in-itself with an essence or substance (Fox, 2015). This assumption of independence supported the treatment of any concept as universal – if a being's substance is internally located, the context in which it is considered is of secondary importance. Adorno called this 'identity thinking' (Jarvis, 1998, p. 177): the treatment of any object as if it was identical to our concept of it. However, he (Adorno, 1997, p. 33) warned that any concept, however useful when first constructed, often cast a 'spell' over those using it. Like a magical spell, it limited a person's power to act against it – to attend to the object. This thinking without regard to context made the concept an abstraction, and necessarily incomplete, leaving what Adorno (1973, p. 5) called a 'residue'. To then treat the object without regard to that residue was to do violence to the object (O'Connor, 2013, p. 12). Adorno (1973, p. 28; 2003, p. 20) regarded this violence as characteristic of Western culture, and a key contributor to the horrors of the Holocaust, the Armenian genocide, the Asian and African colonial conflicts and the potentials for atomic warfare.

Adorno insisted that we needed to recognise the relational, limited nature of all understanding. Drawing on Hegelian dialectics, he insisted that nothing existed in isolation, but only by virtue of its ongoing relations with other, supposedly 'external', objects. Anything, including a human being, was, as Marx (1975, p. 570) put it, an 'ensemble of … relations'. The relational character of being meant that the locus or foundation of its identity was not 'internally' located but external – in those various relationships – and hence subject to change over time as those relations varied.

This relational, historical understanding prompted Adorno (2001, p. 169) to insist on the 'fallibility' of our understanding of anything and his rejection of the teleological elements of both Hegel and Marx's works. As Adorno's close collaborator, Horkheimer (1993, p. 139), insisted, an absolute confidence in the end state of history, or in any other 'lofty ideas', operated to legitimise the suffering of those who did not fit with that envisioned end state. Borrowing from Nietzsche, Adorno was concerned that any comprehensive ideology could only be secured by force. In the same way that concepts are limited, ideologies built on them are incomplete and their enforcement, ultimately, arbitrary. Instead, Adorno insisted that we construct and apply any concept with humility. Drawing on his Jewish background, he (1973, p. 207) referred to Judaism's prohibition of fixed images of God to caution against similarly fixed images of our humanity. Within the Jewish tradition (and others) any image of God would be inadequate and misleading. It could not accurately represent something that, by its nature, transcends our conceptual capacities. Rather than the confidence of certain knowledge, Adorno (2005b, p. 39) thought the most moral stance we could adopt was to 'not be at home in one's home'.

This insistence on the relational, variable nature of being founded Adorno's critique of liberalism. Contrary to the liberal vision of the independent, stable self only engaging with others to meet its interests, Adorno (1973, pp. 139, 278, 283, 162) insisted on a much more intimate relational conception: 'man never was … being-in-itself', but rather 'a mere limited moment' of 'the dialectic of individual and species', and, in turn, the broader material world. This emphasis on interdependence led Adorno to conceive of the self as inseparable from the relations that constituted that self. Relationships were not external, accidental and formed after coming into existence, but were the very gist of the self. This emphasis also led Adorno to reject a dualist characterisation of human nature. He treated bodily, aesthetic and unconscious experience as central to our humanity.

Adorno considered the non-rational to be volatile and influential. He (2006, p. 213) insisted that human beings were primarily mimetic: that thought was intimately shaped by the 'involuntary adjustment to the extramental', so much so that he located the foundations of the self, and its spontaneity or autonomy, in the 'shudder'. For Adorno (1997, pp. 245, 331; 2006, p. 216), 'life in the subject is nothing but what shudders … that shudder in which subjectivity stirs without yet being subjectivity is the act of being touched by the other … a constitutive relation … [that] joins Eros and knowledge'. So powerful were these influences that Adorno (2003, p. 30;

2006, p. 155) considered that the ensuing uncertainty, insecurity and anxiety, the efforts to repress them, and the problems that followed from those efforts, formed a key element of the history of oppression in the West.

For Adorno, that history made a central contribution to the Holocaust. He (2005a, p. 271) called the modern, rational self 'cold', having repressed the 'warmth' of non-rational influences. This repression promoted a certain rigidity and unresponsiveness. It extended to compassion, which Adorno (1973, p. 365) saw as having a bodily foundation: it sprang from a 'bodily impulse' of identification with those suffering. This disinterest is central to the liberal conception of the self as independent, with no responsibility to any other being beyond those commitments voluntarily made in its self-interest. For liberalism, the good is centred in being left alone – being free of extraneous commitments or restraints. Its consequences in relation to the Holocaust were captured by the apology given by Lutheran pastor Martin Niemoller. He stated that when the Nazis came for the Communists, trade unionists, Jewish peoples and others, he did not intervene because he did not identify with them. When the Nazis came for him, he found that he too had no one to turn to.

Adorno insisted that we could only overcome 'identity thinking' by 'giving priority to the object'. This involved a 'working back, an uncovering' (Jarvis, 1998, p. 166), a 'patient', 'uncoercive gaze' that reveals the object's dependence on relationships (Adorno, 2005a, pp. 129, 130). That attentiveness involves confronting suffering and abandoning the desire to avoid the discomfort it prompts. This insistence fuelled Adorno's (2000, p. 210) oft-misunderstood claim that to write 'poetry after Auschwitz is barbaric'. This was not a devaluation of art, but a demand that we not evade confronting the inescapable insecurities and dependencies of a human existence – and the debts we owe others by virtue of those dependencies – by indulging in some grand teleology or comforting 'lofty thoughts'.

Adorno (2003, p. 19) believed that the Holocaust had proven the modern world's faith in reason was misplaced: that reason, rather than preventing a 'relapse into barbarism', could rationalise anything. Drawing on the materialist tradition, which had long held that the senses were the 'heralds of truth' (Epicurus, cited by Schaffer, 2006, p. 43), Adorno considered that bodily, sensuous interruptions were the only mechanism that could disrupt deeply held rationalisations. He (1973, p. 365) revised Kant's categorical imperative, which had rooted ethics in independent rationality, and relocated that foundation 'in the unvarnished materialistic motive' – 'a bodily sensation'. As Snir (2010, p. 429) has observed:

> The universal validity of the new imperative … originates not from the empty universality of abstract reason but from … the concrete body – every person is bound by it because every person carries it in his body, and … is capable of feeling pain … Morality is reborn in Auschwitz because, for the first time since … the Enlightenment, it has a motive: suffering.

For Adorno, this attention to suffering had transformative potential for the very discomfort it provokes. That discomfort, because it challenges the foundation of liberal disinterest – because it prompts us to identify with others, regardless of our conception of them – has the potential to break the 'spell' of 'identity thinking'. That potential remains because the volatility of the non-rational cannot be completely repressed.

This experience contradicted 'identity thinking', which presumes difference. 'Identity thinking' treats its objects as independent of and unlike the person considering them. The common experience of bodily discomfort prompts a contradictory sense of identification. This can come from directly witnessing another person's suffering or through other, powerful, aesthetic experiences, including artworks. This 'bodily impulse' is, however, only a prompt to revise our thinking. It, too, warrants critique. Moreover, Adorno was well aware that it, alone, was insufficient to remedy the flaws of abstract conceptualisation, and that some support would be needed to 'make sense' of the sensations triggered by witnessing suffering. Absent that support – an alternate discourse – the likelihood remained that the prompt could be resolved within pre-existing ways of thought. Consistently with his understanding of thought as combining both the logical and aesthetic, Adorno suggested an alternative, more relational way of 'making sense' of experience, drawing on both dialectics and aesthetic theory.

In dialectics, every object is an 'ensemble of … relations' (Marx, 1975, p. 570). Each characteristic of the object, be that colour, weight, or any other feature, is a reference to a relation with other objects of different colours or weights. Those relations, together, comprise that object. It has no separate or inner essence or substance. Considering each characteristic enables a person to unbundle an object's constituent relations – to uncover, or recover, its intimate relationship with its environment. Adorno also drew on Walter Benjamin's concept of a constellation. Insights into an object's various relations could be assembled around it, just as 'constellations are [assembled around] … stars' (Jarvis, 1998, p. 175). Every constellation involves the selection of some – and omission of other – stars from the night sky (that is, the neglect of context). For Adorno (2000, p. 32), these constellations could be reconstructed and experimented with as 'trial combinations', with the advantage of engaging non-rational aspects of thought. Constellations operated as a form of 'associative thought' where the 'relaxation of consciousness' enabled the exploration of a range of possibilities, including those offered through 'playful', even 'clownish' engagement (Adorno, 1993, p. 141; 1973, p. 14). This experimentation, inspired by a focus on the object, had the potential to enable its better conception in the same way that the 'lock of a … safe-deposit box' can 'fly open … in response … to a combination of numbers' (Adorno, 2006, p. 149; 1973, p. 163). These ensembles of concepts could illuminate the neglected 'residue' of an object, and enable the 'recreating [and] re-weaving [of] … webs of significance' (Foster, 2007, L288–290). They enable a person, family, group or community to be better considered in their environments.

Adorno's contribution to a critical social work pedagogy

Adorno's ideas provide a framework for an adaptable, facilitative, pedagogy for critical social work, one that grounds a promising response to the influence of liberalism.

I first explored the potentials of Adorno's framework in collaborating with academic development lecturers to combine the teaching of both fundamental academic literacies and skills in critique. It appeared to us that students did 'not give weight to … context, but … [treated it] … in instrumental terms: as the dross from which the gold of knowledge has to be separated' (Fox and O'Maley, 2018, p. 1600). It appeared that the students approached their studies consistently with the dominant way of life, and of being, in capitalist, neoliberal society. The difficulties confronted in thinking critically were not that students lacked literacy, but that they were 'very literate in capitalist frames of thought' (Fox and O'Maley, 2018, p. 1600). These late capitalist literacies amplify two ways of thinking that typify liberalism, and which undermine students' sense of agency in the manner described by Giroux (2011). First, they emphasise the conceptualisation of anything as having its essence, nature, or character located internally – as independent of context. So influential is this framing, that a relationship, however important, is still seen as separate to a thing, and as secondary to understanding its character and needs. This framing renders the influence of environment, however powerful, secondary to the constitution of the thing. It always suggests that some private reserve or source of agency resides in a person that might be activated regardless of environmental obstacles. It reserves room to blame a victim for his or her suffering. Second, late capitalist literacies treat values as individual or private matters, and 'good' knowledge as objective or value-free. These two approaches are foundational elements of a 'grammar of oppression' (to borrow from the title of Axel Honneth's book, *The Struggle for Recognition: the Moral Grammar of Social Conflicts*). Adorno's ideas suggest a framework to effectively, inclusively, move from this 'grammar' toward that of the critical tradition: one in which being, and social work, are understood as interdependent with their environment.

Critical analysis

Adorno's framework, as an 'immanent' critique of any concept – one that works from within the concept's own terms – enables students to both appreciate the flaws of liberal, positivist forms of critique and to develop a greater sensitivity to the intimate influences of context. In particular, it enables students to move beyond seeing relationships with other people and the broader environment as separate to a person's constitution and thereby better grasp the depth of their impact. It also enables students to appreciate the constructed nature of all knowledge, and the central, inescapable, role of values therein. It works from where they are – from their strengths in late capitalist literacies – and scaffolds a pathway toward a more relational understanding.

The critical analysis of any proposition involves unbundling its claims, explanations, evidence and assumptions. The particular interest of critical theory is in examining these relations to reveal the falsehoods that legitimate and enable privilege and oppression. This demands a close attention to a claim's context – the recognition that it is dependent on its context, and frequently neglects contradictory or devalued 'residues'. It requires that the concept or claim not be assumed to be 'identical' to its object, but tested by playing close attention to – 'giving priority to' – that object.

Adorno's ideas provide a framework that prompts students to consider an idea or discourse in context – not merely as situated within, but dependent on, and constituted by, those relations. Students can be introduced to the framework in lectures by giving 'priority to the object', such as the concept of 'deservedness' under the Poor Laws, and then unbundling its connections to other ideas and discourses. This modelling can be both verbal and visual, with the related ideas drawn in a constellation around the central concept.

In tutorials students can immediately engage with a lecture by whiteboarding their views (or writing them up on large sheets of paper attached to a wall). They can be invited to whiteboard, in small groups, 'what struck' them. This frees them of the burden of identifying the 'correct' answers and focuses them on assembling a 'constellation' of ideas and impressions. It enables them to make connections with other perspectives (other units of study and experiences), ask questions and present challenges. Each group can then stand by their whiteboard and present their constellation to the class, and the combination of these whiteboards becomes a larger constellation again. The same activity can then be applied to that week's readings. In the course of each group's whiteboarding and presenting, tutors and others students ask questions of the group. The group then demonstrates the connection to the object being considered (that they are 'giving priority' to it) and explain the relationship between it and the point they have whiteboarded. At every step, students work to understand every point relationally – in context.

Sometimes students struggle to make the connections. In that event, Adorno's use of dialectics and aesthetic theory helps, as does his emphasis on humility.

Dialectics takes the 'guesswork' out of analysis: it provides a straightforward starting point – the object's perceived characteristics. Unbundling those characteristics provides a concrete focus, as each characteristic is a referent to a relationship – each leads a student to consider context and the depth of its influence. Dialectics also enables students to overcome the 'shock of inconclusiveness' or 'dizzying' (Adorno, 1973, pp. 33, 31) feeling that can follow from abandoning previous ideas of 'good' knowledge and critique: it provides a clear pathway or scaffolding to work within.

Aesthetic theory, on the other hand, makes some 'guess work' valuable. It enables students to start with what they think is important, even if they cannot yet explain why. They can simply whiteboard a connection in orbit around the object and follow a 'hunch' and draw dotted, squiggly or different coloured lines to work toward unbundling the relationship. Moreover, these 'hunches' are not limited to those inspired by the learning materials, but can extend to the students' own experiences and 'funds of knowledge' (Gonzalez et al., 2005).

Adorno's insistence on humility assists these explorations. To be cautious concerning the accuracy of one's ideas makes for a safe learning environment: it normalises the labour of learning. Classroom discussions can then become learning collaborations where everyone can make a contribution, and no contribution is expected to be comprehensive or 'correct'.

The greatest advantage of Adorno's framework may be its inversion of the status of values. It enables one to grasp that they are not 'dross' that obscures 'good' knowledge, but the standpoint from which any knowledge is constructed. To make 'what struck you' central to learning then promotes a more personal connection as it roots learning in a student's own values and makes that connection both legitimate and productive. It also makes the learning collective. Adorno's focus on making suffering 'eloquent' – something that cannot be ignored – resonates strongly with the value that motivates most people to study social work, namely compassion. The explicit ties in Adorno's framework between critique and responding to suffering motivate students to persevere and learn how to enact one of critical social work's key values.

Critical reflection

Adorno's framework can also assist in developing skills in critical reflection and reflexivity when the student takes him or herself as the 'object'. It can help change their sense of self or, for those already contesting liberalism, assist them in expressing their difference.

In places like Australia, liberalism promotes an understanding of oneself as independent and uninvolved, with no sense of privilege and a limited capacity to speak of oppression without sounding like a 'victim'. Adorno's ideas provide a basis for a student to consider how the very terms by which they define themselves evidence their interdependence. As they describe themselves, students can be prompted to explore how their descriptions reflect their ties to others. Masculinity, for example, is inextricably bound up with ideas about femininity. Adorno's framework, when coupled with more recent work in analysis, such as critiques of binary thinking, provides a sound foundation for reflection about privilege, oppression and intersectionality. It can enable students to realise that 'there is no alibi in being' (Bakhtin, 1993, p. 40), such that emancipation cannot be the liberal negative freedom – not withdrawal, isolation and selective, voluntary engagement, but collaboration within inescapable connections.

Adorno's framework also encourages dialogue. No one can fully know themselves independently: each self is so constituted by relations with others that knowing oneself requires knowing those others. That expanded sense of self can, in turn, be illuminated by 'giving priority' to those other people, and attending to their experiences and perspectives. It leads to a space where, for example, a man can learn from feminist insights into violence and relational ways of being. It can help promote a sense of an obligation to listen, even when what is heard is difficult or disturbing, and help promote a space in which different voices can safely be expressed. Students from indigenous cultures and non-Western cultures, for example, draw on rich, relational perspectives, but it can be difficult for them to share those perspectives within social work, given social work's liberal foundations. Adorno's framework, by directly addressing the oft-invisible 'grammar' of liberal thought, facilitates the expression of these diverse voices. It can, for example, open up spaces for non-Western ideas of parenting and attachment. It can facilitate a dialogue where commitments to care for others in a group, rather than independence, become an important goal, as it is in Aboriginal Australian and Japanese (and other Confucian) cultures (Rothbaum et al., 2000; Ryan, 2011). Adorno's framework sets the ground for respectful learning from other cultural traditions. It can contribute to the de-colonising of social work.

Adorno's framework, in prioritising attentiveness to the object, contributes to the key social work commitment to learn from others. It supports the emphasis on closely considering alternative points of view and diverse experiences, and providing students with opportunities to do so via written and other media, presentations by guest speakers and the immersive exposures of placements. It supports educating social work students in alliance with others, including organisations like the Jewish Holocaust Centre, Melbourne, Australia (JHC), and participating in their education programs, and hearing the testimony of those who have experienced oppression, such as Holocaust survivors. These collaborations, such as that with the JHC, as detailed in Fox (2017), can embody the kinds of sensual encounters that create opportunities for deep, transformational learning.

Working with difference

Adorno's framework can also help minimise the conflicts potentially involved in engaging with difference. Positivism, because it insists on one, value-free, 'truthful' view of any object, makes the confrontation with difference a zero-sum encounter: only one view can be correct. Moreover, it also suggests that the person holding the opposing view has flawed thinking. It makes difference conflictual, intimidating, shameful and silencing. Adorno's framework helps produce the opposite effect: 'classes [that] move from the shadow of stigma and shame to … tutorials of choice: a community … a joyful place' (Fox and O'Maley, 2018, p. 1598).

Adorno's framework, by highlighting the role of values, and of different standpoints, makes the constructed nature of knowledge clear: a different view is not necessarily evidence of error, but of the pursuit of different discourses and values. Difference then prompts a debate about those values, and their relative priorities, and how they do, or do not, make a contribution toward a more comprehensive understanding. This addresses the concern expressed by Eduard Lindemann (cited in Brookfield, 2005, p. 61), a professor at the New York School of Social Work (later the Columbia University School of Social Work), that most people 'are democratically speaking, illiterate'. Lindeman's use of 'literacy' is apt: if students are to learn to critique and advocate well, the ability to recognise and work with a diversity of values is fundamental. It is a capacity, as Henri Giroux (2016) has noted, that has been much diminished under neoliberalism.

Adorno's framework facilitates the exploration of difference in the classroom, but its impact goes further. In qualitative research undertaken to explore students' experience of Adorno's framework, students reported how it helped them better deal with differences in their personal lives, including discussing differences of values with their partners they previously found difficult to raise. They also reported how it changed their interest in political debates. Grasping the role of values, they found they could better understand, critique and advocate in relation to contemporary issues. As one student put it, studying politics and policy using Adorno's framework was 'life changing'. She said she now 'found [herself] leaning into the uncomfortable … shaking the system up a bit, which [was] so unlike [her], but [added]: "How could you not now?"'.

John G. Fox

A critical compass

Adorno sets the ground to up-end liberalism's distortions and emphasise the importance of values (and the care we need to take in giving effect to them). In place of liberalism's cold, disinterested emphasis on independence, Adorno's works suggest a framework that reflects critical social work's core commitment: to respond to the suffering experienced in unfair relationships between the self and environment. They also suggest some key values to guide its enactment, namely interdependence, compassion and collaboration (the latter in varying forms and durations, from temporary alliances to longer term collectivisation). These values provide a 'critical compass': a guide as to the kinds of transformations critical social work aspires to, and how to proceed in working to those ends. They promote the recognition that:

- we are all bound up together – that we are *interdependent* in multiple, intersecting, ways, and always obliged to each other for our very existence;
- this interdependence extends to the *material world*, including our corporeal bodies and the balance of the natural world and other beings inhabiting it;
- feelings of *compassion* give expression to this interdependence, found our recognition of others' suffering, and need to be critically valued and expressed as part of the way we reason about the world;
- to be interdependent is to have limited comprehension of the complexities, and variabilities, of other people and the world, such that we need to approach them *humbly*;
- to be interdependent and humble, we can only begin to respond to others' suffering by *'giving priority' to their experience* so as to allow for narrow inadequate understandings and concepts to be 'reconciled' with, and corrected by, the neglected aspects of their being and experience (the 'residue' neglected by 'identity thinking'); and
- all these things demand that we *collaborate*, ally and collectivise to better, and more fairly, give effect to our inescapable interdependence.

These concepts are only a compass. They do not provide exhaustive guidance (nor should they). They serve to provide a different 'grammar' for interaction with others – an orientation that allows for many different forms of interdependence, and so supports the recognition of those who are different on equal terms, given those interlocking dependencies.

Adorno's contribution to practising critical social work

Adorno's framework can also assist in practice.

Casework

Adorno's caution in relation to 'identity thinking' – that a concept will always omit some features of its object – enables casework to follow Mary Richmond's (1930) demand that we attend to the unique situation of each individual, and not apply some pre-existing 'wholesale' idea. Adorno, like Richmond, insisted that we 'give priority' to the object of our consideration. However, Adorno's method of doing so helps ensure that casework gives effect to the insistence of Jane Addams and others that we understand the individual as part of, and not separate to, a larger environment. Adorno's use of dialectics here operates much like postmodern social construction: it enables the tracing of the intimate links between an individual and broader social relations, and suggests points to work to change them. As noted above, Adorno's framework can then be 'fleshed out' with the aid of more recent work in relation to the particular terms of concepts and discourses dominating particular relationships. Here Adorno's insistence on humility reflects the postmodern cautions against grand narratives, but, given its foundation in dialectical analysis, adds an additional caution: to remain aware that even the most modest discourse analysis will remain incomplete and potentially in error, as the relations considered in that analysis extend toward the totality. No analysis is ever truly complete (it can never grasp the totality – that 'whole' would be 'false' (Adorno, 2005b, p. 50)). At best, an analysis serves a particular purpose or objective, and a particular set of values.

Collaboration

This central role of value choices, and the risks inherent in those choices, has long been recognised in critical social work. It drives the commitment to work in partnership with a client – to exercise power with, and not over, them. Adorno's framework supports that commitment, and its extension to work in collaboration with others, not only other human service organisations and professionals, but less common partners, such as museums. The capacity of organisations like the JHC to testify about the experience of oppression is not only relevant to social work education, but to social work at the cultural and structural levels: to community development, advocacy and activism. Here, too, Adorno's insistence that the only reliable foundation for ethics is the bodily response to witnessing others' suffering lends weight to social work's commitment to work in alliance with others. Those others can directly, credibly, testify about that suffering. This links Adorno's framework to contemporary scholarship exploring these potentialities – pedagogies of discomfort and public pedagogies.

A 'pedagogy of discomfort' is an invitation 'to engage in critical inquiry regarding values and cherished beliefs' with a 'central focus' on 'how emotions define … what one chooses to see, and … not to see' (Boler, 1999, p. 93). It is founded in the belief that dominant discourses, such as those of neoliberalism, enable people to flee the discomfort aroused by, for example, arguments that men and 'white' people are complicit in the suffering of women and people of other colours (Pease, 2011; Zembylas, 2018). These pedagogies explore the necessity to confront discomfort. 'Public pedagogies' refers to 'the various forms, processes and sites of education and learning that occur beyond the realm of formal educational institutions' (Sandlin et al., 2011, p. 4). They recognise that non-traditional institutions and practices are profoundly influential in all learning and highlight the power of sensual experiences in prompting transformational learning (Springgay, 2011). Both speak of the power of witness and the unique capacity of community groups and organisations to do so.

Ethical practice

Adorno's relocation of the foundation of ethics to the body – his insistence that we attend to our 'gut reaction' to others' suffering – can also help critical social workers resist the combined pressures of neoliberalism and managerialism. It reflects the practice wisdom that opposes instrumental rationality and its coldness. It gives expression to the imperative that drives most to become, and remain, a social worker: care, founded in the 'involuntary adjustment to something extramental' (Adorno, 2006, p. 213) we call compassion. Rather than a cause for fatigue, compassion – if enacted – operates to sustain a practitioner in the face of cold neoliberalism (Ferguson, 2008).

The same 'gut reaction' equally serves as a prompt toward critical reflection. Adorno's work makes attending to those 'gut reactions' a duty, and reminds us that their repression with the aid of some convenient conceptualisations enables injustice. Adorno's use of dialectical and aesthetic theory then supports a critical consideration of that prompt and provides a framework to do so – a critical compass and methods to explore it.

Conclusion

Adorno's framework can make a substantial contribution to critical social work pedagogy and practice. Revisiting his work is timely and relevant. His critique of the influence of liberal thought, especially its coldness and exaggerated individualism, is directly relevant to resisting neoliberalism today. His concern that the faith placed by liberalism and, more broadly, Modernity, in rationality as a bulwark against barbarism speaks directly to our moment in time, and the renewal of the right-wing threats Adorno saw succeed, with horrendous effects.

Adorno's inversion of liberalism – his emphasis on interdependence and immanent ethical obligations – directly expresses the founding commitments of critical social work. Namely, to grasp being human as intimately interwoven with our environments, and to be motivated by compassion to seek to address the suffering often experienced in the midst of those interrelationships. The exaggerations of austere neoliberalism require critical social work to revisit its original commitments, and renew its endeavours to enact them.

Adorno's framework can contribute to those endeavours. His non-teleological application of the Hegelian/Marxist dialectic, coupled with the aesthetic re-imaginings enabled by constellation-work, provide robust, flexible means to do so. Together, they reflect Adorno's keen appreciation that our concepts are no more than constructions, and remind us of the deep, often neglected, influence of fundamental values. The most profound aspect of Adorno's inversion of liberalism might lie here. By making the constructed, always limited, fallible, character of concepts so clear, Adorno highlights the influence of values. His work reminds us of the need to articulate those of the critical social work tradition with a clarity that enables their ready application in everyday practice. Adorno's works suggests such a 'critical compass': a clear set of values that directly reflect critical social work's founding, non-liberal commitments. A compass that can not only inform a pedagogy, but also practice: one that can support practitioners' artwork, and their 'gut reactions' and resistances to poor policies and practices. Adorno's framework might then be said to provide an answer to Jan Fook's (2017, p. 406) recent challenge to social work educators: that we

> ask ourselves how we create an environment which models and supports compassionate thinking and actions, and … engage in critical thinking in our own work and behaviour to ensure that we … create … environments which instil a sense of compassion in those who interact with them.

References

Adorno, TW 1973, *Negative dialectics*, Routledge, London.
Adorno, TW 1993, *Hegel: Three studies*, The MIT Press, Cambridge.
Adorno, TW 1997, *Aesthetic theory*, University of Minnesota Press, Minneapolis, MN.
Adorno, TW 2001, *Problems of moral philosophy*, Stanford University Press, Stanford, CA.
Adorno, TW 2003, 'Education after Auschwitz', In Adorno, TW and Tiedemann, R (Eds.), *Can one live after Auschwitz? A philosophical reader*, Stanford University Press, Stanford, CA, pp. 19–33.
Adorno, TW 2005a, *Critical models: Interventions and catchwords*, Columbia University Press, New York.
Adorno, TW 2005b, *Minima moralia: Reflections from damaged life*, Verso, London.
Adorno, TW 2006, *History and freedom*, Polity, Malden.

Adorno, TW, and O'Connor, B (Ed.) 2000, *The Adorno reader*, Blackwell Publishers, Oxford.

Allan, J 2009, 'Doing critical social work', In Allan, J, Briskman, L, and Pease, B *Critical social work*, 2nd edition, Allen and Unwin, Sydney, pp. 70–87.

Allan, J, Briskman, L, and Pease, B. 2009, *Critical social work*, 2nd edition, Allen and Unwin, Sydney.

Bakhtin, M 1993, *Toward a philosophy of the act*, University of Texas Press, Austin, TX.

Boler, M 1999, *Feeling power: Emotions and education*, Routledge, Hoboken.

Brookfield, SD 2005, *The power of critical theory for adult teaching and learning*, Open University Press, New York.

Ferguson, I 2008, *Reclaiming social work: Challenging neo-liberalism and promoting social justice*, Sage, London.

Fook, J 2017. 'Whither compassion?', *Affilia: Journal of Women and Social Work*, Vol. 32, Iss. 3, pp. 404–406.

Foster, R 2007, *Adorno: The recovery of experience*, State University of New York Press, Albany, NY.

Fox, JG 2015, *Marx, the body, and human nature*, Palgrave Macmillan, Basingstoke.

Fox, J 2017. 'The Jewish Holocaust Centre, Melbourne: Public pedagogies of compassion and connection', *Journal of Public Pedagogies*, Vol. 2, pp. 12–22.

Fox, J, and O'Maley, P 2018. 'Adorno in the classroom: How contesting the influence of late capitalism enables the integrated teaching of academic literacies and critical analysis and the development of a flourishing learning community', *Studies in Higher Education*, Vol. 43, Iss. 9, pp. 1597–1611.

Giroux, HA 2011, *Zombie politics and culture in the age of casino capitalism*, Peter Lang, New York.

Giroux, HA 2016, *Dangerous thinking in the age of the new authoritarianism*, Routledge, London.

Gonzalez, N, Moll, LC, and Amanti, C 2005, *Funds of knowledge: Theorizing practices in households, communities and classrooms*, Lawrence Erlbaum Associates Inc, Mahwah, NJ.

Honneth, A 1995, *The struggle for recognition: The moral grammar of social conflicts*, The MIT Press, Cambridge, MA.

Horkheimer, M 1993, *Between philosophy and social science: Selected early writings*, The MIT Press, Cambridge, MA.

Jarvis, S 1998, *Adorno: A critical introduction*, Polity Press, Cambridge.

Marx, K 1975, 'Concerning Feuerbach', In *Early writings* (Livingstone, R. and Benton, G., Trans.), Penguin Books, London, pp. 421–423.

Mullaly, B 2007, *The new structural social work*, 3rd edition, Oxford University Press, Ontario.

O'Connor, B 2013, *Adorno*, Routledge, Oxford.

Parkinson, A 2014. 'Adorno on the airwaves: Feeling reason, educating emotions', *German Politics and Society*, Vol. 32, Iss. 1, pp. 43–59.

Parton, N, and O'Byrne, P 2000, *Constructive social work: Towards a new practice*, Macmillan Press, London.

Pease, B 2011, 'Governing men's violence against women in Australia', In Ruspini, E, Hearn, J, Pease, B, and Pringle, K (Eds.), *Men and masculinities around the world*, Palgrave Macmillan, New York, pp. 177–189.

Richmond, M 1917, *Social diagnosis*, Russell Sage Foundation, New York.

Richmond, M 1971, *What is social case work?*, Arno Press & The New York Times, New York.

Richmond, M, and Greer, A (Ed.) 1930, *The long view: A selection from the Russell Sage Foundation*, Brown Reprints, Dubuque, IA.

Rothbaum, F, Weisz, J, Pott, M, Miyake, K, and Morelli, G 2000. 'Attachment and culture: Security in the United States and Japan', *American Psychologist*, Vol. 55, Iss. 10, pp. 1093–1104.

Ryan, F 2011. 'Kanyininpa (holding): A way of nurturing children in Aboriginal Australia', *Australian Social Work*, Vol. 64, Iss. 2, pp. 183–197.

Sandlin JA, Wright, RR, and Clark, C 2011. 'Reexamining theories of adult learning and adult development through the lenses of public pedagogy', *Adult Education Quarterly*, Vol. 63, Iss. 1, pp. 3–23.

Schaffer, PM (Ed.) 2006, *The first writings of Karl Marx*, Ig, New York.

Snir, I 2010. 'The "new categorical imperative" and Adorno's aporetic moral philosophy', *Continental Philosophy Review*, Vol. 43. pp. 407–437.

Springgay, S 2011. '"The Chinatown Foray" as sensational pedagogy', *Curriculum Inquiry*, Vol. 41, Iss. 5, pp. 636–656.

Zembylas, M 2018. 'Affect, race and white discomfort in schooling: Decolonial strategies for "pedagogies of discomfort"', *Ethics and Education*, Vol. 13, Iss. 1, pp. 86–104.

10
Paulo Freire's critical pedagogy for critical consciousness and practice

Stephen Cowden
COVENTRY UNIVERSITY

Nilan Yu
UNIVERSITY OF SOUTH AUSTRALIA

Wilder Robles
BRANDON UNIVERSITY, CANADA

Debora Mazza
STATE UNIVERSITY OF CAMPINAS [UNICAMP], BRAZIL

Education either functions as an instrument which is used to facilitate integration of the younger generation into the logic of the present system and bring about conformity or it becomes the practice of freedom, the means by which men and women deal critically and creatively with reality and discover how to participate in the transformation of their world.
Paulo Freire – Pedagogy of the Oppressed (1970)

Freire's life and work

Paulo Freire is arguably one of the most renowned philosophers from Latin America, but his influence is far from restricted to this region. Indeed, unlike much European-based philosophy and social theory, his legacy is truly global, and his work has influenced educational theory, policy and practice in Africa, India, Australia, Europe and North America, as well as his native Latin America. He is fundamentally known for his work in the field of 'critical pedagogy', a field he himself helped to constitute, and his book *Pedagogy of the Oppressed*, which was first published in Portuguese in 1968, is now an international bestseller, which has been published in over 18 languages, recently having its 50th anniversary. The book itself is a deeply philosophical work, but again unlike many philosophy texts, its influence extends far beyond its discipline. In this chapter we set out Freire's life and then discuss his ideas on pedagogy in the context of his life. We conclude by sketching out how these might be applied to social work practice.

Freire was born on 19 September 1921 to a middle-lower-class family in Recife, the capital of Brazil's north-eastern state of Pernambuco. He was one of four children of Joaquim Temístocles Freire, a captain in the Pernambuco Military Police, and Edeltrudes Neves Freire, a homemaker. Freire's father died when Paolo was just 13 years old. This tragic event, followed by the effects of the Great Depression of the 1930s, profoundly affected his upbringing (Araujo & Macedo, 1998; Beisiegel, 2010), as Freire came to know first-hand the frightening and dehumanising effects of poverty. He witnessed the daily struggles of his mother in raising the family on her own. Freire's own childhood experiences of difficulty gave him a lasting sense of solidarity with the poor and an unfaltering commitment to work with them toward improving their social conditions. At both a political and ethical level, this was the impetus of Freire's intellectual journey throughout his life and work (Beisiegel, 2010; Robles, 2018).

Freire completed his primary education in *Jaboatão dos Guararapes*, followed by high school in the Oswaldo Cruz Collegiate, a highly respected private school in Recife. The young Freire was granted a scholarship through Aluízio Pessoa de Araújo, the principal of the Oswaldo Cruz Collegiate. He later became a Portuguese language teacher for the lower grades. Encouraged by Pessoa de Araújo, Freire entered Recife's Faculty of Law at the University of Recife (now Faculty of Law of the Federal University of Pernambuco) in the early 1940s at the age of 22. In 1944, he married Elza Maria Costa de Oliveira, the principal of a public high school in Recife who went on to become a great influence in his life (Spigolon, 2016). The couple had five children. After finishing his law degree in 1946, Freire decided not to practice law, choosing instead to serve as a Portuguese grammar teacher at the Oswaldo Cruz Collegiate again. He also started teaching philosophy of education at the University of Recife (Araujo & Macedo, 1998; Beisiegel, 2010; Gadotti, 1994).

In 1947, Freire began working in adult education programs in Recife. These programs were sponsored by the Industry Social Service (SESI), which was linked to the National Council of Industries (CNI) and funded by the Brazilian government. The mission of SESI was to provide social programs to Brazil's marginalised classes and groups in the areas of education, health, housing, and leisure. Freire really found his métier as an adult educator, and the success and respect he earned in this area led to his becoming director of SESI's Education and Culture Department from 1954 to 1957. During these formative years with SESI, Freire came into direct contact with the socio-economic and educational realities of landless peasants, industrial workers, and shantytown dwellers. Working with some of the poorest sectors of Brazilian society, he came to understand how their impoverished social conditions could only be shifted through fundamental societal transformation, but most significantly he grasped the role education could play in this (Araujo & Macedo, 1998; Beisiegel, 2010; Gadotti, 1994; Robles, 2018). It was in the process of trying to make sense of this that Freire came into direct contact with progressive organisations within the Catholic Church and trade unions who were working with these communities. At the same time, Freire was trying to think through the work he was doing intellectually and he read widely, looking at the work of Karl Marx, Georg Wilhelm Friedrich Hegel, Jean-Paul Sartre, John Dewey, Erich Fromm, Frantz Fanon, Antonio Gramsci, György Lukács, Herbert Marcuse, and Gustavo Gutiérrez. At both the theoretical and practical level of the work he was doing, Freire developed a deeply egalitarian approach. This meant that working in partnership with the poor rather than for the poor became both a philosophical principle, as well as a practical tenet of his work. It was during this time that he began to think about the use of dialogic education as a tool to stimulate adult students' critical thinking about their social conditions. For Freire, dialogic education as a process of understanding human experience entailed both *reflection and action* oriented toward human emancipation (Beisiegel, 2010; Freire, 2012; Gadotti, 1996). His ideas earned him wide recognition as a progressive educator committed to radical social transformation (Beisiegel, 2010; Gadotti, 1996; Torres, 1996). Freire's growing intellectual stature, alongside the effectiveness of the methods of teaching he developed, led to his appointment to a full-time teaching position at the University of Recife. While teaching at Recife, he was also pursuing his doctoral degree in education, which he completed in 1959.

However, the politics of the world beyond education, so central to Freire's work, intervened within what was developing into a promising academic career in 1964. On 21 January 1964 the left-wing Brazilian President João Goulart launched the National Alphabetisation Program, which aimed to teach millions of illiterate Brazilians how to read and write. Freire had played a key role in the design of the program and had expected to play a key role in its implementation. But as literacy was the basis of having the right to vote in Brazil at this time, this campaign was perceived by reactionary forces as leading the way toward a wider democratisation of society, which they most definitely did not want. On 1 April 1964, a military coup removed Goulart from power. Two weeks after taking power, the military regime scrapped Goulart's National Alphabetisation Program, seeing Freire's work as an act of open political subversion. Facing constant political harassment and eventual persecution, Freire went into exile in Bolivia in September 1964. However, Freire's stay in this country was short-lived due to Bolivia's severe political instability. From Bolivia, Freire moved to Chile, where he was granted political asylum and continued his adult education work with peasants and workers with the tacit support of Chilean President Eduardo Frei of the Christian Democratic Party (Beisiegel, 2010; Marques de Melo, 2015). The family lived in Chile from November 1964 to April 1969. During these years, Freire wrote his magnum opus, *Pedagogy of the Oppressed* (first English edition published in 1970), which has gone on to be considered a foundational text of critical pedagogy. From April 1969 to February 1970, Freire lectured at Harvard University as a Visiting Professor. From the United States, Freire moved to Geneva Switzerland, to work for the World Council of Churches in their national literacy campaigns in many developing countries such as Angola, Cape Verde, Guinea-Bissau, and Mozambique (Araujo & Macedo, 1998; Beisiegel, 2010; Marques de Melo, 2015). Freire's wife, Elza also played an active role in these projects (Spigolon, 2016).

After 16 years of living in exile, Freire was finally allowed to return to Brazil in 1980. By this time, the military regime was no longer capable of remaining in power and was preparing the country for a return to democratic rule. Freire resumed his academic career by teaching at both the State University of Campinas (Unicamp) and the Pontifical Catholic University of São Paulo (PUC-SP). In 1986, Freire's wife Elza passed away. Two years later, Freire married Ana Maria (Nita) Araújo, daughter of Aluízio Pessoa de Araújo. In 1989, São Paulo City Mayor Luiza Erundina de Souza of the Workers' Party (PT) named Freire Secretary of Education. Two years later, Freire resigned from his position in order to continue teaching and writing. After leaving office, Freire published dozens of academic articles and several books including *Pedagogy of Hope: Reliving Pedagogy of the Oppressed* (published in English in 1994) and *Pedagogy of Freedom: Ethics Democracy and Civil Courage* (published in English in 1998), two of his best-known works. Freire died on 2 May 1997.

Paulo Freire's philosophy of education

Richard Shaull, who wrote the introduction to the English language version of Freire's *Pedagogy of the Oppressed* summarised Freire's philosophy in the book as follows:

> There is no neutral education process. Education either functions as an instrument which is used to facilitate the integration of generations into the logic of the present system and

bring about conformity to it, or it becomes the 'practice of freedom', the means by which men and women deal critically with reality and discover how to participate in the transformation of their world.

(1970: 16)

This points to two fundamental aspects of his approach – his deep egalitarianism and his commitment to the relationship between theory and practice. For Freire, theory and practice were perpetually in a conversation with each other. The diverse elements in Freire's work have already been mentioned, but what is distinctive about his work is not just this diversity, but the distinctive way in which he put these different elements together. For example, Freire was not the first thinker to synthesise Marxism and Christianity, but the way he did this was very original. In characterising this he famously stated that he 'stayed with Marx in the worldliness, looking for Christ in the transcendality'[1].

Freire rejected both a 'magical' Christianity of divine intervention, which reinforced the passivity of the poor, as well as a theology of social service, which presented itself as virtuous for the way it sought to alleviate the suffering of the poor, but which Freire saw as ethically and spiritually compromised with the dominant order for its refusal to address the forces that benefited from the poverty and exclusion of the poor and oppressed. Instead, he advocated a spirituality of human action, which sought to dismantle those oppressive forces and structures, and their impact 'on' the being of people.

This focus on the sense of 'being' reflected his spiritual beliefs, but it was in addressing the hold which the dominant order had over individual consciousness that he turned to forms of radical social theory. In another of the books he wrote in the 1973 *Education for Critical Consciousness* (2012), Freire sought to delineate what he saw as three levels of 'being' and consciousness.

1. 'Magical consciousness' characterises a situation in which the subject has no sense of being able to act independently; they see their fate as entirely controlled by outside forces against which they are powerless to intervene. Within this approach people possessed no consciousness of the socio-economic contradictions in society: they accept life for what it is, not questioning the injustices done to their lives in the face of which they are silent and docile.
2. 'Naive consciousness' is where the subject has some understanding of power relationship and a sense of 'us' and 'them', but has no sense of how they themselves could ever act in relation to that. While they are not as docile as in 'magical consciousness', people in this state are pessimistic about the possibility of social change, and prefer instead to hope for this to be done for them by some powerful outside agent, so are susceptible to belief in a strong leader to follow, who they hope will make the change which they feel unwilling or unable to initiate.
3. 'Critical consciousness' is characterised by a growing understanding of how a person's own capabilities have been defined not by their own choice, but through socio-economic contradictions in society. By looking at this reality and recognising such contradictions as something both outside themselves as social structure, but also inside themselves as a set of internalised beliefs about themselves, people come to believe that they themselves can make changes and, in fact, must play an active part in a process of change (Freire, 2012: 13–16).

The way Freire developed these ideas illustrates how he was inspired by Karl Marx's famous 'Theses on Feuerbach', and it is useful to turn briefly to Freire's understanding of Marx to see the way he incorporated this influence. In his 'Theses on Feuerbach', Marx, like Freire, is asking the question of how it is that human self-consciousness develops. Marx argues that 'the human essence is no abstraction inherent in each single individual. In its reality it is the ensemble of the social relations' (Marx, 1975: 423). What this means is that while individual subjectivity of course exists, it does not exist as an isolated abstraction, but rather is always social and contextual – and that context is the social relations which shape and inform that consciousness (Irwin, 2012: 19). Hence when Freire talked about 'magical consciousness' he was not intending to patronise the poor as being incapable of comprehending what was really going on, rather he saw 'magical consciousness' as a reflection of the real conditions of powerlessness in which impoverished people existed. However, he wanted to point out that it was the power of capitalist and patriarchal social relations, not abstract conceptions of an all-powerful God or an unknowable Fate, which determined their lack of power. These relations were not 'magical' but are real material relations created by people, and just as they were created by people, so they could be re-created. Similarly with 'naive consciousness', Freire is not using this term as a judgement; rather he wants to make the point that this naivety reflects the lack of a realisation that the power of the system over people exists precisely because they internalise its norms and maxims, however resentfully they do this. The system of power relations that dominates them could not continue to wield its power over them without their belief in their own lack of power. It is the emphasis on capitalism as a set of active and lived social relations and the way this shapes the 'being' of the working class that Freire develops from Marx here.

The sense in which Freire wanted to understand the way the oppressed *internalise* those social relations points to another major influence on Freire; Frantz Fanon's *The Wretched of the Earth* (1961). (See also Chapter 33 on Frantz Fanon by Linda Harms Smith). Fanon was a psychologist who sought to understand the impact of colonialism on the colonised, and his pioneering analysis understood this as working through the negation of the 'being' of the colonised. This had a significant influence on Freire and, in the first chapter of *Pedagogy of the Oppressed*, he characterised the disempowerment many people experience as based in what he called a 'double consciousness'. This is expressed through the way people are 'at the same time themselves and the oppressor whose image they have internalized. Accordingly, until they concretely "discover" their oppressor and in turn their own consciousness, they nearly always express fatalistic attitudes toward their situation' (Freire, 1970: 43). Freire saw this 'fatalism' as a consequence of people having internalised the dominant logic, which was based on their own 'negation'. This did not just work at the level of individual consciousness, but became part of the intrapersonal relations as people became locked into the perceptions and expectations or other people, just as at the macro level it is endlessly repeated that the existing system represents the best of all possible worlds. It is in this way that social, political, and economic structures and processes that develop and maintain social inequality, thus produce a culture of silence among the oppressed by instilling fatalism, submissiveness, and a distorted self-image that renders them incapable of recognising and escaping their domination. They internalise the worldview of their oppressor such that they see themselves as their oppressors do. In being silenced as such, they are 'prohibited from being' (Freire, 1970: 50).

'Banking education' versus 'problem-solving education'

The central feature of Freire's work lies in the way he developed a theory of education and pedagogy that was based on this material. Central to his focus on pedagogy was the way educational systems played a crucial role in constituting and reproducing this 'culture of silence'.

His critique of conventional education is expressed through the image of 'banking education', which he describes as involving

> a narrating Subject (the teacher) and patient listening objects (the students) ... His [sic] task is to 'fill' the students with the contents of his narration – contents which are detached from reality, disconnected from the totality that engendered them and could give them significance.
>
> *(Freire, 1970: 52)*

Under the banking concept, students are expected to mechanistically receive, file, store, and be prepared to retrieve and regurgitate such knowledge. Students are veritable receptacles that need to be filled with knowledge. However, this form of pedagogy was a 'practice of domination' in that it reinforced passivity and disengagement, suppressing students' capacity to generate new forms of knowledge and, in the process, become independent thinkers.

Freire (1970: 61–62) contrasts this with 'problem-posing education', which he characterises as 'acts of cognition, not transferals of information ... Through dialogue ... the teacher is no longer the-one-who-teaches but who is himself [sic] taught in dialogue with the students, who in turn while being taught also teach'. Problem-solving education was a bottom up process in which the teacher and class entered into dialogue with each other. Freire (1970: 25) saw his pedagogy as a way of making 'oppression and its causes objects of reflection by the oppressed' so that they are able to perceive their oppression and engage in the struggle against this through the development of critical consciousness. The key elements of this process are action and reflection. An iterative process of action and reflection was required to enable the oppressed to confront their systemic subordination in society. Critical consciousness is achieved through active engagement in action-reflection-action as they grapple with and seek to critically understand their social reality. However, understanding is not just important for its own sake, but it is important for the way it leads, of its own internal necessity, to action in the social:

> As we attempt to analyze dialogue as a human phenomenon, we discover something which is the essence of dialogue itself: the word. But the word is more than just an instrument which makes dialogue possible; accordingly, we must seek its constitutive elements. Within the word we find two dimensions, reflection and action, in such radical interaction that if one is sacrificed – even in part – the other immediately suffers. There is no true word that is not at the same time a praxis. Thus, to speak a true word is to transform the world.
>
> *(Freire, 1970: 68)*

Freire (2012: 15–16) referred to the process of developing critical consciousness as 'conscientisation' (derived from the Portuguese word *conscientização*) or consciousness-raising. It is important to understand that Freire never conceived critical education as the imposition of radical 'political correctness' on students by their teachers. Rather, he argued:

> the more radical the person is, the more fully he or she enters into reality so that, knowing it better, he or she can better transform it. This individual is not afraid to confront, to listen, and to see the world unveiled. This person is not afraid to meet the people or to enter into dialogue with them. This person does not consider himself or herself the proprietor of history or of all people, or the liberator of the oppressed; but he or she does commit himself or herself, within history, to fight at their side.
>
> *(Freire, 1970: 21)*

Central to Freire's approach to education was that he understood oppressive social relations never as simply external to subjective consciousness, but crucially co-existing within it – in the 'being' of the oppressed. It was for this reason that people so often conformed to the strictures of the system, a fact that Freire saw as so important within the reproduction of the status quo:

> The 'fear of freedom' which afflicts the oppressed, a fear which may equally well lead them to desire the role of oppressor or bind them to the role of oppressed, should be examined … The oppressed, having internalized the image of the oppressor and adopted his guidelines, are fearful of freedom. Freedom would require them to eject this image and replace it with autonomy and responsibility. Freedom is acquired by conquest, not by gift. It must be pursued constantly and responsibly. Freedom is not an ideal located outside of man [sic]; nor is it an idea which becomes myth. It is rather the indispensable condition for the quest for human completion.
>
> *(Freire, 1970: 28–29)*

As the process of internalisation negates the 'being' of the oppressed, the naming of that negation, both as an internal and external force, was at the heart of a critical pedagogy. In acknowledging the pain and difficulty of the naming process, Freire speaks to something many social workers will recognise from experience; that the process of naming abuse and violence to the self is traumatic and something that can only be attained through an internal struggle. This is so because naming this as violence and abuse calls on us to engage in a process of recovering a different self-consciousness, which is a difficult, painful and risky initiative, but central to the recovering of people's humanity, and Freire would argue, a more humane society. While much of the way we do this in social work at the moment is individualised in context, Freire (1970: 47) is interested in how this process of naming could become not just a collective process, but also a pedagogical process, which he characterised as 'critical and liberating dialogue, which presupposes action'. An emancipatory pedagogy thus sought to collectivise this internal struggle, pointing to the relationship between individual consciousness and wider material power relations.

Application of Freire's pedagogy in social work

We want to conclude this chapter by thinking about some of the implications of Freire's work in relation to social work. In social work we often talk about 'empowering' service users, but in the present context we are only encouraged to see this in quite individualistic ways, reflecting the individualised focus of neoliberal social policy. Freire characterised empowerment as 'the deepening and widening of the horizon of democratic practice' (Freire, 1990). A key implication of this 'deepening and widening' is the idea of social workers being able to see the humanity within a service user, even if this humanity is not always reflected in the service user's actions. Freire was distinctive for the way he combined a recognition of the real relations of power that shape individual relationships with society, alongside a sense of people always having agency, and therefore always being ethically responsible for their actions. Note the phrase in the quote above which says: 'Freedom is acquired by conquest, not by gift. It must be pursued constantly and responsibly.' Real change is never something that is 'done to' the people social workers work with – it can only come when people themselves arrive at a point where they can see that they have to do this for themselves. This is where a social work practice based within critical pedagogy can be valuable. When Freire talks about empowerment based in 'democratic practice', he is rejecting the blaming and pathologising that takes place in some social work practice today. He would see this not just as unethical, but also as wrong, as it has failed to understand the impact of the social structure on 'being'. Critical pedagogy, by contrast, focuses not just recognition of people's humanity, but also that they are citizens with political rights and with the capacity for meaningful participation. A social work practice based on critical pedagogy could, therefore, be one where a social worker initiates a dialogue that is based on uncovering or 'naming' the operations of power in their lives (including the social work role itself). In doing so, we can create a space where the people we work with can think about the way relations of power impact on them and so open the possibility of new forms of agency.

When working with disempowered and excluded people, social workers often find themselves in an 'us and them' situation with service users; something that is promoted within the blaming and pathologising language of neoliberal social policy. Freire's work offers us an alternative to this by pointing to dialogue as the basis of social work. It is important to say that entering into dialogue with service users does not imply agreeing with everything they say and do. As McLaren and De Silva argue:

> A major consideration for the development of contextual critical knowledge is affirming the experiences of [service users] to the extent that their voices are acknowledged as an important part of the dialogue; but affirming [these] voices does not necessarily mean that [social workers] should take the meaning that [service users] give to their experiences at face value, as if experience speaks romantically or even tragically for itself. The task of the critical educator is to provide the conditions for the individual to reflect upon and shape their own experiences and in certain instances transform those experiences in the interest of a larger project of social responsibility.
>
> *(McLaren and Da Silva, 1993: 49)*

This is important for the way it emphasises the importance of a critical understanding of power and disempowerment as the basis for thinking about empowerment. Social workers hold power over service users, yet that power can be used in positive ways, and it is crucial to continue to believe in this possibility when the dominant ideas are pushing us into highly instrumental and dehumanised relationships with service users. The radical theologian Cornell West argued the purpose of a critical perspective is to create a space that 'allows suffering to speak. That is, it creates a vision of the world that puts into the limelight the social misery that is usually hidden or concealed by the dominant viewpoint of society' (West, 1999: 551). A dialogic form of social work can respect someone's choices at the same time as seeking to interpolate their capacity to make different choices through developing their wider awareness of the power relations that frame their life. It is through this that we can create the possibility of other ways of being, which is the basis of a progressive social work practice. The course of action proposed above might not have a guaranteed outcome – but what interventions in social work do? In this sense it involves a risk, but not just the risk that it may be unsuccessful. It also opens up the risk that the social worker's position becomes open to interrogation from the outside, from the service user. To take this risk requires us to have confidence not just in our skills and abilities, but in the authenticity of our own critical understanding, and it is perhaps this which is the most important element in any discussion of critical pedagogy and Freire's legacy.

Conclusion

There is a formidable challenge facing the integration of critical pedagogy in the training of social workers for professional practice: the political environments in which social work is practised today are increasingly inhospitable to the values embodied in such approaches

(Saleebey & Scanlon, 2005). The largely individualist orientation of welfare policy and the weakening of the welfare state accompanying the advance of neoliberal philosophy around the world leaves ever decreasing spaces for the kind of work that Freire envisioned. But at the same time it is crucial to remember that critical pedagogy is a politics of hope. Neoliberal politics works by framing social life through an entirely individualised lens: 'I'm alright.' At the same time it is encourages collusion with a logic that people themselves know to be false and unjust – 'I don't like this any more than you do but it's how we have to do things now'. What links these together is a fatalism that smothers and stifles hope. Even though Freire conceived critical pedagogy in very different political conditions from those we face in social work today, the power of his analysis is revealed in the way his words continue to resonate as one of the most important critiques of our time. Fatalism holds us back from expressing what we really think through fear – 'we can take what you have from you' – and from taking risks (which are inherent in political change) for something that people believe can 'never happen'. More than ever, social work needs Freire's conception of radical hope. This is not about being optimistic for its own sake, but rather works by being alert to the way new possibilities for change become immanently present when oppressive relations are named, and intrapersonal relations based in dialogue are initiated. It is this close relationship between social work's fundamental conception of progressive social change and Freire's critical pedagogy that makes the interaction of the two of such ongoing significance.

Notes

1   www.youtube.com/watch?v=MF9-tZMwqjE

Further Reading on Freire and Social Work

Aambo, A. (1997). Tasteful solutions: Solution-focused work the groups of immigrants. *Contemporary Family Therapy: An International Journal, 19* (1), 63–79.
Alvarez, A. R. (2001). Enhancing praxis through PRACSIS. *Journal of Teaching in Social Work, 21* (1–2), 195–220. doi: 10.1300/J067v21n01_12.
Araujo, M., & Macedo, D. (1998). *The Paulo Freire reader.* New York: Continuum.
Beisiegel, C. (2010). *Paulo Freire.* Recife: Fundação Joaquim Nabuco/Editora Massangana.
Boal, A. (1979). *Theatre of the oppressed.* London: Pluto Press.
Bransford, C. L. (2011). Integrating critical consciousness into direct social work practice: A pedagogical view. *Social Work Education, 30* (8), 932–947. doi: 10.1080/02615479.2010.534449.
Breton, M. (1994). On the meaning of empowerment and empowerment-oriented social work practice. *Social Work with Groups, 17* (3), 23–37. doi: 10.1300/J009v17n03_03.
Brigham, T. M. (1977). Liberation in social work education: Applications from Paulo Freire. *Journal of Education for Social Work, 13* (3), 5–11.
Burstow, B. (1991). Freirian codifications and social work education. *Journal of Social Work Education, 27* (2), 196–207. Retrieved from www.jstor.org/stable/23043158.
Carroll, J., & Minkler, M. (2000). Freire's message for social workers. *Journal of Community Practice, 8* (1), 21–36. doi: 10.1300/J125v08n01_02.
Checkoway, B. (1997). Core concepts for community change. *Journal of Community Practice, 4* (10), 11–29.
Christensen, M. C. (2014). Engaging theatre for social change to address sexual violence on a college campus: A qualitative investigation. *The British Journal of Social Work, 44* (6), 1454–1471. doi: 10.1093/bjsw/bct006.
Darder, A. (2015). *Freire and education.* New York: Routledge.
Darder, A. (2017). *Reinventing Paulo Freire.* New York: Routledge.
Finn, J.L. (1994). The promise of participatory research. *Journal of Progressive Human Services, 5* (2), 25–42.
Freire, P. (1970). *Pedagogy of the oppressed.* Baltimore: Penguin Books.
Freire, P. (1985). *The politics of education: Culture, power and liberation.* London: Macmillan.

Freire, P. (1990) Interview with Carlos Torres [online] Retrieved from http://aurora.icaap.org/talks/freire.html [Accessed 23.11.2010].

Freire, P (2010) Karl Marx e Jesus Christo [online] Retrieved from: www.youtube.com/watch?v=MF9-tZMwqjE [Accessed 24/6/19].

Freire, P., & Moch, M. (1990). A critical understanding of social work. *Journal of Progressive Human Services*, *1* (1), 3–9.

Freire, P. (2012). *Education for critical consciousness*. London and New York: Continuum Press.

Gadotti, M. (1994). *Reading Paulo Freire: His life and work*. Albany, NY: SUNY Press.

Gadotti, M. (1996). *Pedagogy of praxis: a dialectical philosophy of education*. Albany, NY: SUNY Press.

Harlow, E., & Hearn, J. (1996). Educating for anti-oppressive and anti-discriminatory social work practice. *Social Work Education*, 15 (1), 5–17. doi: 10.1080/02615479611220021.

Hegar, R. L. (2012). Paulo Freire: Neglected mentor for social work. *Journal of Progressive Human Services*, 23 (2), 159–177. doi: 10.1080/10428232.2012.666726.

Hyde, C. (1989). A feminist model for macro-practice: Promises and problems. *Administration in Social Work*, *13* (3/4), 145–181.

International Federation of Social Workers. (2014, August 6). Global definition of social work. Retrieved from http://ifsw.org/policies/definition-of-social-work/

Irwin, J. (2012). *Paulo Freire's philosophy of education*. London and New York: Continuum Press.

Juliá, M., & Kondrat, M. E. (2005). Health care in the social development context: Indigenous, participatory and empowering approaches. *International Social Work*, *48*, 537–552. doi: 10.1177/0020872805055317.

Kant, J.D. (2014). Becoming a liberation health social worker. In D.B. Martinez and A. Fleck-Henderson (Eds.), *Social justice in clinical practice: A liberation health framework for social work* (pp. 29–43). Abingdon and New York: Routledge.

Kant, J. D. (2015). Towards a socially just social work practice: The liberation health model. *Critical and Radical Social Work*, *3* (2), 309–319. doi: 10.1332/204986015X14320477877474.

Kenny, S., & Connors, P. (2017). *Developing communities for the future*. South Melbourne: Cengage Learning.

Kline, M., Dolgon, C., & Dresser, L. (2000). The politics of knowledge in theory and practice: Collective research and political action in the grassroots community organization. *Journal of Community Practice*, *8* (2), 23–38. doi: 10.1300/J125v08n02_02.

Koenig, T. L., Spano, R., Kaufman, D., Leiste, M. R., Tynyshbayeva, A., Madyarbekov, G., & Makhadiyeva, A. K. (2017). A Freirean analysis of Kazakhstani social work education. *International Social Work*, *60* (1), 156–169. doi: https://doi.org/10.1177/0020872814559558.

Lewis, E. (1995). Toward a tapestry of impassioned voices: Incorporating praxis into teaching about families. *Family Relations*, *44* (2), 149–152.

Lewis, E.A. (1993). Continuing the legacy: On the importance of praxis in the education of social work students and teachers. In D. Schoem, L. Frankel, X. Zúñiga, & E. Lewis (Eds.), *Multicultural teaching in the university* (pp. 26–36). New York: Praeger.

Lockwood, D. K., Lockwood, J., Krajewski-Jaime, E. R., & Wiencek, P. (2011). University and community partnerships: A model of social work practice. *International Journal of Interdisciplinary Social Sciences*, *6* (1), 39–46.

Lundy, C. (2011). *Social work, social justice & human rights: A structural approach to practice*. North York, ON: University of Toronto Press.

Marques de Melo, J. (2015). El exilio de Paulo Freire. *Chasqui*, *2*, 6–12.

Marx, K. (1975). Theses on Feuerbach. In Coletti, L. (Ed.), *Karl Marx: Early writings* Harmondsworth: Penguin Books.

McClaren, P., & De Silva, T. (1993). De-centring Pedagogy: Critical Literacy, Resistance and the Politics of Memory. In Paulo Freire: *A critical encounter* London: Routledge.

Mizrahi, T., Davis, L. E., Oxford University Press, & National Association of Social Workers. (2008) *Encyclopaedia of social work* (20th ed.) Washington, D.C: Oxford University Press/ National Association of Social Workers.

Mullaly, B., & Dupré, M. (2018). *The new structural social work: Ideology, theory, and practice* (4th ed.). Don Mills, ON: Oxford University Press Canada.

Mullaly, B., & West, J. (2017). *Challenging oppression and confronting privilege: A critical approach to anti-oppressive and anti-privilege theory and practice* (3rd ed.). Oxford: Oxford University Press.

Narayan, L. (2000). Freire and Gandhi: Their relevance for social work education. *International Social Work*, *43* (2), 193–204. doi: https://doi.org/10.1177/002087280004300205.

Oh, H., & Solomon, P. (2013). Teaching and providing recovery-oriented care through problem-posing dialogue. *Social Work Education, 32* (7), 933–943. doi: 10.1080/02615479.2012.720251.

Robles, Wilder. (2018). Paulo Freire and education for liberation: The case of the landless rural workers movement (MST). In (Ed.), *Consciousness-raising critical pedagogy and practice for social change*. London, UK: Routledge.

Sachs, J. (1991). Action and reflection in work with a group of homeless people. *Social Work with Groups, 14* (3/4), 187–202. doi: 10.1300/J009v14n03_14.

Saleebey, D., & Scanlon, E. (2005). Is a critical pedagogy for the profession of social work possible?. *Journal of Teaching in Social Work, 25* (3-4), 1–18. doi: 10.1300/J067v25n03_01.

Sewpaul, V., Ntini, T., Mkhize, Z., & Zandamela, S. (2015). Emancipatory social work education and community empowerment. *International Journal of Social Work and Human Services Practice, 3* (2), 55–62.

Spigolon, N.I. (2016). *Pedagogia da Convivência: Elza Freire – Uma vida que faz Educação*. Jundiai: Paco Editorial.

Todd, S. (2015). Social action and social justice. In J. D. Wright (Ed.), *International encyclopedia of the social & behavioral sciences (Second Edition)* (pp. 132–138). Oxford: Elsevier.

Torres, C. A. (1996). A voz do biógrafo latino-americano: Uma biografia intelectual. In Paulo Freire. *Uma biobibliografia* (pp. 117–147). São Paulo: Editora Cortez: Instituto Paulo Freire/Editora Cortez.

Torres, C.A. (2014). *First Freire: Early writings in social justice education*. New York: Teachers College.

Tsang, N.M. (1998). Beyond theory and practice integration in social work: Lessons from the West. *International Social Work, 41* (2), 169–180.

Webb, D. (1985). Social work and critical consciousness: Rebuilding orthodoxy. *Issues in Social Work Education, 5*, 89–102.

West, C. (1999). *The Cornel west reader*. New York: Basic Civitas Books.

Yu, N.. (Ed.) (2018). *Consciousness-raising: Critical pedagogy and practice for social change*. Oxford: Routledge.

11
Teaching democracy in the social work and human service classroom
Inspiration from Myles Horton and the Highlander Folk School

Trevor G. Gates

UNIVERSITY OF THE SUNSHINE COAST, QUEENSLAND, AUSTRALIA

Introduction

The International Federation of Social Workers' (2012) *Statement of Ethical Principles* states that social workers recognize and respect the diversities of the communities in which they practice and challenge power, privilege, and other forms of oppression that threaten society. Stigmatizing attitudes about race, gender, sexual orientation, and other diversities are part of the social fabric of many societies and are part of dominant social norms with which students arrive in the classroom. Social work and human service students, though perhaps more committed to social justice than the general population of students, come to the classroom having lived experiences that might have devalued diversity and difference. Social work and human service educators must help students unlearn negative attitudes and beliefs about race, gender, sexual orientation, and other diversities, many of which they may have internalized. Additionally, social work and human service education can provide an opportunity to critique power and privilege, to correct and contradict structural inequalities, and to provide an opportunity for democratic participation.

In this chapter, I review the work of Myles Horton and the Highlander Folk School as a model for challenging power, privilege, and other forms of oppression. Highlander's mission is to serve as a grassroots organization in Appalachia and the southern United States, and to enable the people of the region to collectively address issues of justice, equality, and sustainability (Highlander Research and Education Center, n.d.). Horton's model of adult education worked to enable individuals, families, and communities to overcome histories of exclusion, stigma, and other forms of oppression. His transformative model of education is useful for a broader educational context of growing a democratic society in which every person can be an active participant. I explore how lessons learned from Myles Horton and the Highlander Folk School can be used as a model for social work and human service education and help students draw upon their experiences of racism, sexism, and homophobia that they might bring to the classroom. I argue that a social work and human service pedagogy that aims to transform society can strengthen teaching, practice, and research.

Myles Horton

Myles Horton and the Highlander Folk School (now called the Highlander Research and Education Center) played a transformational role in the 20th-century civil rights movement in the southern United States. His contributions to social justice education are well supported in the adult education and learning literature. Horton's personal history with power and privilege was central to his identity as a practitioner. However, Horton's story might be unfamiliar to some social work and human service educators. In this section, I share Horton's biographical background, as understanding his story is key to understanding the mission and strategy of Highlander.

Born in 1905 in Tennessee's Appalachia region to schoolteachers Elsie and Perry Horton, Horton's family was among the region's poor working class. Horton grew up in a community of economic poverty and a plantation-based economy that historically relied upon slave ownership and labor (Horton & Horton, 2006). During Horton's childhood, the Horton family experienced changes in their financial circumstances and went from their relatively low-paying but secure positions as teachers into unemployment and poverty (Keefe, 2015). Horton's parents obtained work as sharecroppers, an arrangement by which tenant farmers, typically former slaves or the poorest White families, lived and worked the land in exchange for providing a share of the harvest to the landowner (MacRae, 2006). Many sharecropping families barely survived under this system. The system usually allowed the families to eat but not to prosper. These childhood experiences exposed Horton to both the plight of the White working poor (of which the Horton family was a part) and the aftermath of racism and poverty among former slaves in the South (Glen, 2015; Payne, 2007; Rahimi, 2010).

Horton left home as a teenager, like many of his contemporaries, to enter the world of the working class. He began working in the sawmill factories in 1920, where he witnessed poverty, exploitation, and disempowerment. Industrial factories of this era typically required their workers to endure grueling hours with very few protections. The work was dangerous. If workers found themselves injured and unable to work, they were often unable to support their families, as there were virtually no protections for workers or any governmental safety net for injured or disabled workers. In an introduction to their edited volume *Dying for Work: Workers' Safety and Health in Twentieth-century America*, Rosner and Markowitz (1987) described the difficult and often deplorable conditions for production workers of this era:

> [U]nderpaid, overworked, and poorly fed workers were more likely to be injured or incapacitated on the job: a miner who worked 12 to 14 hours a day could not stay alert enough to avoid injury from unguarded machinery in unlighted, noisy, and humid shafts; miners found their lives constantly threatened by speed-ups, explosions, dust, and suffocation. In contrast, employers, fearing the loss of control over production and the added cost of improving work conditions, have traditionally resisted reforms.
>
> *(p. x)*

Horton managed to survive factory work but would vividly remember conditions of the factory. He closely identified with the working class. Horton used his earnings to enroll in university, which led him to a seminary to continue his studies. At Union Theological Seminary, Horton learned the theological vision for a "social gospel." Beliefs had to be connected to action—actions that improved the community, provided aid to the needy, and worked toward social justice. The social gospel movement in the United States called its followers to, not only convert to Protestant Christianity, but also to engage in social justice reform and service to the community (Rauschenbusch, 1997).

Though Horton's education did not lead him to a traditional path of ministry, lessons of the social gospel, inclusion, and reform certainly informed his career path and vocational aspirations. Horton founded the Highlander Folk School in 1932, an experimental school of adult education, which taught people how to be participants in democracy, draw upon their own experiences, and mobilize others to build upon their collective interests (Imel, 2012). At Highlander, community members themselves were the starting point for education and research, not the teacher. It was not a traditional school in that the teachers were not trained educators. They might have been seamstresses, cooks, or beauticians (Levine, 2004). Rather than privileging academic degrees and formal qualifications, Highlander valued the experience of its teachers. Their lived experience taught them about power, oppression, and privilege. It taught them about poverty, discrimination, and injustice. They were invited to Highlander because Horton believed they could help others within its programs recognize the value of their own lived experience and potential for making social change. Throughout Highlander's history, it ran various social justice programs, focusing on labor union, poverty, civil rights, and educational justice causes (Baker & Williams, 2008).

Horton was not a social worker by education or training. However, he was deeply committed to social justice. He was broadly influenced by and contributed to the shaping of social welfare and civil rights activism in the United States. One of Horton's strongest influences was Jane Addams, the founder of Chicago's Hull House. Addams is well known in social work education as bringing the settlement house movement to the United States and as being one of the foremothers of American social work (Deegan, 2010). Addams viewed Highlander's mission as being aligned with the settlement house movement—still mostly an urban effort—as well as a way to bring democratic participation to the rural American people. She saw Highlander as having the potential for bringing the settlement house movement to the South. Like Addams, Horton was accused of being unpatriotic, communist, and "un-American" due to his liberatory philosophies (Biggers, 2006; Longo, 2007).

Over time, Horton got closer to his goal of liberation and civil rights for all. During the civil rights era, Horton and the Highlander Folk School brought in several important figures in the civil rights movement in the US, including Dr. Martin Luther King, Jr., Don West, Lilian Wyckoff Johnson, Rosa Parks, Septima Clark, James Bevel, Bernice Robinson, and others (Duke, 2015; Herbers, 2015; Keefe, 2015; Payne, 2007). It was during the civil rights era that, though his work at Highlander, Horton became a noted figure in the radical education movement in the United States. Education at Highlander, from Horton's point of view, would not lead to a formal qualification. Rather, education could contribute to a radical social agenda of mobilizing people who are capable of challenging and dismantling the structures of inequality and oppression that were a part of the Appalachian experience (Hale, 2007; Highlander Research and Education Center, n.d.; Holst, 2009).

Description of use and application of key concepts

Horton's radical vision for transforming education and society envisioned a flexible pedagogy, driven by the needs of the community. The community knew what they required and just needed to be taught the skills of reflection, organizing, advocacy, and change. Education need not be prescriptive or driven by what the educator thinks the people need. Instead, education can be adjusted and adapted to the people in front of you. It is for these reasons that Highlander successfully worked on several emerging social issues, including civil rights, leadership development, environmental issues, union and labor organizing, and other issues. Were there absolute rules about pedagogies or who the "teacher" or "student" should be, Highlander might not have achieved such success. This section explores Highlander's pedagogical model and how it might be useful in a social work and human service classroom.

The radical model of education delivered at Highlander was experiential and focused on engaging participants in democratic participation and decisions about their own lives (Williams & Mullett, 2016). Horton's philosophy of education was strongly influenced by the American educational philosopher John Dewey, who valued learning-by-doing. Learning can be situated within life and need not be driven solely by the educator's priorities, as was common in many educational settings. According to Dewey, learning should be driven by what the community needs rather than what the educator perceives that they need. Dewey (1938) noted that traditional learning spaces, consisting of "desks, blackboards, a small schoolyard" where the educator is the source of knowledge and center of the classroom, represents an incomplete learning encounter (p. 14). What the educator thinks students "should" know can be secondary to what the students want and need to know. The needs, experiences, and interests of students are the central features of the classroom.

The social work and human service classroom, broadly defined, is a natural venue for experiential, democracy-focused learning. Learning in the social work and human service classroom often begins with a broad foundation of knowledge of human behavior, human rights, diversity, and ethical practice with various levels of systems, but quickly moves to a field placement that offers students opportunity to work toward real-world problems within their community (Australian Association of Social Workers, 2012; Council on Social Work Education, 2015). These real-world experiences are integral and complementary to the classroom experience, a "signature pedagogy" for social work and human services (Larrison & Korr, 2013).

Subsequent experiential learning theorists who were disciples of Dewey, such as David Kolb (1984), argued that, in order to be a meaningful learning experience, classroom lessons could connect to the problems of ordinary life for the students; authentic learning must be a "continuous process grounded in experience" (p. 27). Education is not provided for education's sake alone. Rather, it has to be bound in the present needs of the people seeking it. The social work and human service classroom can provide a venue for such learning when it enables students to draw upon their own experiences of social injustice such as experiencing poverty, racism, sexism, homophobia, and other social justice issues.

Highlander's educational programming always started with learning about the experience of the students or simply the "people," as Horton liked to think of them. Horton (1966) said in an interview that he views education as a process that always begins and ends with the people in front of the teacher, noting:

> [Highlander deals] with people who come with problems. We don't justify our existence on the basis of what happens in a week or month at Highlander. The educational process has started long before they come and continues after they leave. What we do at a typical workshop is say, "What are your problems, how do you see yourself, what do you want to do, what do you want to be?"
>
> *(p. 492)*

In the social work and human service classroom, the educator and students could, at the beginning of each learning encounter, spend time listening to one another's stories and experiences. If the educator is open to listening, the educator will learn that students come to the classroom with a deeply personal narrative of adversity and triumph. Students have borne witness to the problems in their communities. They come to the social work and human service classroom having experienced both joys and tribulations in their lives. They have been both the helpers and the recipients of help. They might have years of experience helping others, either in a formal capacity or informally as a trusted friend, family member, or member of the community. We should also acknowledge that they might come to the classroom with deeply held beliefs that are racist, sexist, or homophobic. Starting with the community's perception of their problems is only that, a starting place for conversation not the end; reflection, information gathering, and cooperation with others must follow, which Horton believed would be mutually transformative. To the extent possible, social work and human service students should be encouraged to commit to hearing different ideas while also acknowledging that everyone deserves to feel safe in the classroom.

The educator, too, occupies various privileged and oppressed identities. If the educator also comes from the local community, their understanding of the needs of the community may also be deeply personal. The educator may share anger about what has been done or left undone in the community. The educator may also occupy relative privilege and have a lived experience that shielded them from these stories. Having an open and frank conversation about who we are and how we have come to this place at this moment in time is a great equalizer that acknowledges that we all have valuable stories to tell. We need not have rigid ideas about who must learn from whom. The educator and the student are on a learning journey together, whereby both the teacher and the pupil can grow and benefit.

Sharing stories and lived experiences was not unique to Highlander but instead part of a global popular education movement. Popular education aims to liberate the community by helping its members recognize their empowerment, value their own lived experience, critique injustice, and develop a response addressing the causes of disempowerment and inequality (Bengle & Sorensen, 2017; Brookfield, 2018). The popular education movement is perhaps most associated with Paulo Freire (1970), who popularized emancipatory education in Latin America. A contemporary and friend of Freire, Horton saw the advantage of dialogue and transformation. Dialogue helps us recognize that we are all experts at our own experience (Glowacki-Dudka & Griswold, 2016; Jara, 2010). In a series of conversations with Paulo Freire (Horton & Freire, 1990), Horton discussed the importance of the educator or facilitator recognizing the expertise of the people:

> [T]hey don't need to come to Highlander to turn things over to the expert. They've got to think through the information themselves or they can't use it when they get back. It can't be part of their experience, their experience of learning, and therefore be theirs, if you deny them the right of making it theirs. If I'm the expert, my expertise is in knowing not to be an expert or in knowing how I feel experts should be used.
>
> *(p. 131)*

Social work and human service education has the potential for being far more than a system of production whereby "workers" are produced simply to deliver client systems or the human service organization a "product" or "service." It need not be narrowly focused on practice skills or functional tasks required of the human service marketplace. Instead, social work and human service education can focus on broader aims, facilitating dialogue, and creating a more just society. In the tradition of popular education at places like Highlander, social work and human service education can aim to create a more respectful, equal, and just world by engaging in using a dynamic and open flexible pedagogy that encourages participants to engage in critical analysis and dialogue (Connolly & Finnegan, 2016). This requires the educator, as well as the student, to recognize their own subjectivity as well as complicity in poverty, racism, sexism, homophobia, and other community problems. We might need to model humility for our students by admitting where we have failed and hope to do better. Doing so will likely earn us respect for being transparent, open, and willing to personally engage in the lessons we are asking of our students. Growth and development need not be one-way.

A needed step in teaching people the language of advocacy, collective agency, and social change is acknowledging our power subjectivity as well as the space that we occupy. As academics in higher education, we might have become accustomed to occupying spaces that listen to what we have to say because of our position. Our students may have not yet learned that their voice matters and that they have valid authority to speak on their own experiences. Educators might initially need to position themselves as experts in the language of social change, but students can be positioned as the experts of their own perspective and voice. Schneider (2014) argues that the education provided at Highlander

> not only helped oppressed communities recognize the transformative value of their own experiences and traditions but also to develop the various rhetorical strategies needed to agitate for social change ... to frame and mobilize their experiences as resources for social change.
>
> *(p. 2)*

In the social work and human service classroom, teaching students the language of social change enables them not only to articulate their own experiences, but to use language effectively to mobilize individuals, groups, and communities. Having good use of the language of advocacy and change can help them be more convincing when trying to engage others in their change efforts.

Social change is a long-term proposition and might require many years to materialize. Outcomes might not always be directly linked to our efforts. Highlander's efforts at creating a more respectful and equal world and to fight community problems did not always yield immediate results. For instance, Rosa Parks, the famous African American civil rights advocate, attended a serious of workshops at Highlander Folk School on the desegregation of schools in the United States (Schneider, 2014). At Highlander, she learned basic lessons of empowerment, valuing her voice, and collectively working toward solutions to inequality. Parks learned that her voice mattered and began to believe that she could take meaningful steps toward making her community a different place in which to live.

Months later, Parks refused to give up her seat to a White passenger on a Montgomery, Alabama bus and did not move to the back of the bus, as was customary for African American riders during this era (Cooperman et al., 2016). Parks went on to organize the famous Montgomery Bus Boycott. The Montgomery Bus Boycott was a concerted effort by the African American community to boycott public transportation for over a year in protest of its racist ridership policies. Neither her personal efforts nor her efforts at organizing the African American community were directly planned at Highlander. Yet, the lessons she learned at Highlander, to recognize the importance of her own story and to actively engage in democratic citizenship, enabled her to make an impromptu decision to refuse to give up her bus seat and to organize the African American community in Montgomery, to fight against a community culture that treated them as less than equal.

Applications for learning, practice, and research

Recognizing our capacity for fighting against poverty, racism, sexism, homophobia, and other community problems is difficult, but important work. When asked about her impromptu decision to refuse to give up her seat to a White passenger, Parks said, "I had given up my seat before, but this day, I was especially tired. Tired from my work as a seamstress, and tired from the ache in my heart" (Barcella, 2016, p. 43). Institutions like Highlander can inspire students, practitioners, and graduates to use that "ache in [their] heart" to recognize their agency to fight against the status quo and to work toward social change. Highlander's role in grassroots advocacy meant that its "students" were quite different from social work and human service students. However, Highlander was a leader in developing several of the strategies used by progressive educators today, which are useful in the social work and human service classroom. Students, graduates in social work and human services, and other practitioners can be taught to draw upon their voices, draw upon painful experiences, learn the language of social change, critique power and privilege, and agitate for positive social change. In this section, I explore applications for learning, practice, and research in social work and human services, using teaching techniques employed by Horton at Highlander.

Learning the language of change, how to critique power and privilege, and eventually how to agitate for positive social change is a core feature of social work and human service education. Horton, Dewey, Freire, and other contemporaries might argue life itself is what is most instructive for entering social work and human service students. Students enter the classroom having perhaps experienced various levels of power and privilege and might have already learned to respond to adversities related to poverty, racism, sexism, homophobia, and other social justice issues. Dialogue can help set the stage for participatory learning (Boone et al., 2018). At the beginning of the semester, educators can prepare students for dialogue by focusing activities on learning about one another's lived experience and learning about what students already know. During the early weeks of the semester, the educator should acknowledge that past educational experiences might not have always been pleasant. Students might be fearful of making mistakes or appearing foolish. Educators can set a tone of safety and of encouraging students to experiment with their ideas by avoiding behaviors that might be perceived as criticism of students in the classroom during the first few weeks of a semester. As trust is established through the open sharing of ideas, students can become more comfortable with receiving feedback without receiving it as personal criticism. During the initial years of a social work and human service education, students can be encouraged to begin the journey of critical reflection, to examine their experience with power and privilege, to embrace uncertainty, and to interrogate the assumptions from their lived experience that they bring (Morley et al., 2014). Social work and human service students begin to internalize their obligation to interrogate their power and privilege and structural inequalities. These skills can be developed in a classroom that uses a critical pedagogy framework and encourages a deep analysis of social structures, context, advantage, and disadvantage.

In an introduction to critical pedagogy, Crawford (2010) argues that critical pedagogy is frequently misunderstood and misconstrued as simply "critical thinking" but is far less complicated, noting:

> A lot of nonsense is written about critical pedagogy both by those who support it and those who oppose it yet the core idea is uncomplicated and almost commonplace. Critical pedagogy is grounded in the premise that there exists in society deep-seated and underlying injustices, inequality, and prejudices and that as educators we ought not to tolerate such a

situation, moreover, we have a moral, ethical, and democratic obligation to challenge inequality, injustice, and discrimination wherever and whenever we come across it.

(p. 814)

While critical thinking is an important skill for social work and human service graduates, being able to thoughtfully analyze and respond to the interaction between power, privilege, and the individual, family, group, or community's presenting issue is a core practice skill (Bailey & Brake, 1975).

Each social work and human service student is a work-in-progress, shaped by their experience, their current social and environmental context, and the classroom. They are also influenced by their past experience in democracy (or lack thereof) and their perceived access to citizenship, political influence, and civic life. Students might also come to the classroom experiencing frustration with political leaders, community problems, and other issues. They might feel excluded from the community and need convincing that they can actually be democratic participants in society. Each of these frustrations is important to acknowledge, as students can come to the social work and human service classroom feeling that they lack democratic agency. A core element of teaching for democracy is the lesson that, according to the radical education activist Bill Ayers (2009),

[we] each have a mind of our own; we are all works-in-progress swimming toward an uncertain and indeterminate shore; we can join with others in order to act on our own judgments and in our own freedom; the way things are is not inevitable.

(p. 9)

After teaching the students the core skill of critique and critical reflection about their lived experiences, Highlander worked to help students collectively craft a solution to problems as the students saw them. Highlander worked toward solving a variety of needs, uniquely framed and driven by the needs of the students. Speaking within the context of Highlander's work within the labor union movement, Horton (1990) said, "You don't just tell people something; you find a way to use situations to educate them so that they can learn to figure things out themselves" (p. 122). Problems that were situated within the individual participants and the community were drivers of the educational experience at Highlander.

Critique of inequality and injustice was only a part of the programming at Highlander. Full democratic participation meant not just an assessment of what was wrong but also action aimed at contradicting and correcting the conditions that enabled structural inequality to exist and to continue (Bassey, 2010). In the social work and human service classroom, learning to become active, democratic participants in social change can occur through practical, problem-based learning. Problem-based learning is an experience-driven teaching approach whereby students are given stimulus material approximating a real-life situation and cooperatively work together toward a solution that integrates knowledge, experience, and skills (Boud & Feletti, 2013).

Informed by the Highlander tradition, social work and human service educators can begin by helping students become democratic participants, engage in dialogue about their own experience, and identify a priority issue to work toward together. The basic problem need not be initially generated by the social work and human service educator through a case study, as is common in much of practice-based education. Rather, the educator can work with students as a facilitator—a "guide on the side" versus the "sage on the stage" (Anastas, 2010, p. 33)—helping students work together to identify a broad social issue such as poverty, racism, sexism, homophobia, and other social justice issues, situated within the context and needs of the local community.

Together, as a class, students can work toward a project aimed at solving a real problem in the community, rather than a contrived problem. This classroom activity could take the form of a whole-of-class macro project, focusing on a public issue, program, organization, or community need, working with neighborhood groups, community centers, or other coalitions to develop a community-level intervention that would be of value to the public (Kasper & Wiegand, 1999). Wherever possible, these efforts can be coordinated with field organizations, community leaders, and students completing advanced placements who may be more aware of ongoing projects and needs. They may have insight about the priorities of the community—what will work and will not work. Not only will involvement encourage students to strengthen relationships with community leaders, but it will also help provide needed oversight to the project.

Social work and human service education can be transformative for students and empower them to work toward solving real-world issues within their communities. They inspire students and may function as cultural activists that "kindle fire, arouse the imagination, and rally the troops" (Erenrich, 2013, p. 86). To Horton, the transformation of the student, community, and society was the real purpose of education. In a famous series of interviews with Bill Moyers (1982) during the final years of Horton's life, Horton articulated a vision for transformative education:

> [W]ho's been telling you what to do—teachers, preachers, politicians—and did it work? Was it good advice, did it work for you? I don't know, but you wouldn't be here, if that worked. Because you've had plenty of advice, you've had plenty of people telling you what to do. So we're not going to do that, we're not going to compound that. We're going to try something else—we're going to try to build on what you know, and your experiences, and help you understand that your neighbors have some experiences, and that other people in another place, maybe in another country, have some experiences that relate to this.
>
> *(p. 260)*

Pedagogies that teach social work and human service students how to critique power and privilege, to contradict and correct the conditions that enable structural inequality, to promote democratic participation, and to value the lived experience of people have advantages outside of the classroom. Recipients or clients of social work and human services, or simply "people" as Horton would think of them, can be taught to reflect upon their lived experience and to craft solutions to their problems. Practitioners engaging people in services should acknowledge that, while they may come to a human service organization after experiencing discrimination, stress, pain, or loss, they come with valuable ideas, experiences, motivations, and competencies that enable them to craft a sustainable solution (Munford & Sanders, 2005; Saleebey, 2009).

People engaged in services can be brought together to cooperatively work toward a solution that integrates a critique of power and privilege, drawing upon experience of the collective (Boud & Feletti, 2013). The experience of the community might include formal degrees, qualifications, or other experience. It might also include experience of living with the label of a mental illness or the responsibility of caring for a loved one with such a label. Each person's experience is unique, and their expertise of various kinds can be useful to the group. By drawing on the group's collective experience, the community can work toward sustained change. The practitioner is an educator who can see themselves as a facilitator of the process rather than the expert. The people are the experts.

Practitioners who engage in research as their primary area of practice can also draw upon the pedagogies taught by Horton at Highlander. The methods that Horton espoused have influenced not only adult educators but also researchers, especially participatory action researchers

(Shosh, 2017). Today, Highlander, through its participatory action research program, disrupts the idea that "only academics or trained professionals can produce accurate information" and instead aim to produce research that is driven by the needs and problems of the people (Highlander Research and Education Center, n.d.). Participatory action research is consistent with Horton's original philosophy of viewing expertise as lying primarily with the people, with the educator, practitioner, or researcher functioning as a consultant.

Summary

In this chapter, I explored the story of Myles Horton and Highlander, arguing for a social work and human service pedagogy that values the experience of students, teaches them how to engage in critical dialogue, and helps them acknowledge their power in working toward social change; this best prepares them for practice, broadly defined. Social work and human service education can serve a purpose greater than preparing technician-practitioners capable of performing functional roles such as case management, counseling, or other interventions. Instead, social work and human service education, inspired by the lessons learned from Highlander, can aim to create practitioners who can facilitate transformation and democracy, driven by the needs, abilities, and desires of the community.

References

Anastas, J. W. (2010). *Teaching in social work: An educator's guide to theory and practice*. New York: Columbia University Press.

Australian Association of Social Workers. (2012). Guideline 1.2: Guidance on field education programs. Retrieved from www.aasw.asn.au/document/item/3553

Ayers, W. (2009). Teaching in and for democracy. *Curriculum and Teaching Dialogue*, 12 (1/2), 3–10.

Bailey, R., & Brake, M. (1975). Introduction: Social work in the welfare state. In R. Bailey & M. Brake (Eds.) *Radical social work* (pp. 1–12). New York: Pantheon.

Baker, C., & Williams, L. (2008). 75 years of empiricism and empowerment: The Highlander Research and Education Center. *Humanity & Society*, 32 (2), 197–203. doi: 10.1177/016059760803200206.

Barcella, L. (2016). *Fight like a girl: 50 Feminists who changed the world*. San Francisco: Zest Books.

Bassey, M. O. (2010). Education for civic citizenship and social justice: A critical social foundations approach. *Education as Change*, 14 (2), 247–257. doi: 10.1080/16823206.2010.522062.

Bengle, T., & Sorensen, J. (2017). Integrating popular education into a model of empowerment planning. *Community Development*, 48 (3), 320–338. doi: 10.1080/15575330.2016.1264441.

Biggers, J. (2006). *The United States of Appalachia: How Southern mountaineers brought independence, culture, and enlightenment to America*. Emeryville: Shoemaker and Hoard.

Boone, K., Roets, G., & Roose, R. (2018). Social work, participation, and poverty. *Journal of Social Work*, Advance online publication. doi: 10.1177/1468017318760789.

Boud, D., & Feletti, G. (2013). Changing problem-based learning. In D. Boud & G. Feletti (Eds.) *The challenge of problem-based learning* (pp. 1–14). New York: Routledge.

Brookfield, S. (2018). Critical adult education theory: Traditions and influence. In M. Milana, S. Webb, J. Holford, R. Walker, & P. Jarvis (Eds.) *Palgrave international handbook on adult and lifelong education and learning* (pp. 53–74). London: Palgrave.

Connolly, B., & Finnegan, F. (2016). Making hope and history rhyme: Reflections on popular education and leadership following a visit to Highlander. *Adult Learning*, 27 (3), 120–127. doi: 10.1177/1045159516651611.

Cooperman, R., Patterson, M., & Rigelhaupt, J. (2016). Teaching race and revolution: Doing justice to women's roles in the struggle for civil rights. *Political Science & Politics*, 49 (3), 558–561. doi: 10.1017/S1049096516000986.

Council on Social Work Education. (2015). *2015 Educational policy and accreditation standards*. Retrieved from www.cswe.org/Accreditation/Standards-and-Policies/2015-EPAS

Crawford, K. (2010). Active citizenship education and critical pedagogy. In T. Lovat, R. Toomey, & N. Clement (Eds.) *International research handbook on values education and student wellbeing* (pp. 811–823). New York: Springer.

Deegan, M. J. (2010). Jane Addams on citizenship in a democracy. *Journal of Classical Sociology, 10* (3), 217–238. doi: 10.1177/1468795X10371714.

Dewey, J. (1938). Experience and education [public domain version]. Retrieved from http://ruby.fgcu.edu/courses/ndemers/colloquium/experienceducationdewey.pdf

Duke, D. C. (2015). *Writers and miners: Activism and imagery in America*. Lexington: University Press of Kentucky.

Erenrich, S. J. (2013). Funding leadership-development training for cultural activists: A reflective essay. *Foundation Review, 5* (2), 84–95. doi: 10.4087/FOUNDATIONREVIEW-D-13-00001.1.

Freire, P. (1970). *Pedagogy of the oppressed*. New York: Continuum Publishing Company.

Glen, J. M. (2015). *Highlander: No ordinary school*. Lexington: University Press of Kentucky.

Glowacki-Dudka, M., & Griswold, W. (2016). Embodying authentic leadership through popular education at Highlander Research and Education Center: A qualitative case study. *Adult Learning, 27* (3), 105–112. doi: 10.1177/1045159516651610.

Hale, J. N. (2007). Early pedagogical influences on the Mississippi freedom schools: Myles Horton and critical education in the Deep South. *American Educational History Journal, 34* (1/2), 315–329.

Herbers, M. S. (2015). Progressive era roots of Highlander Folk School: Lilian Wyckoff Johnson's legacy. In B. G. Bond & S. W. Freeman (Eds.) *Tennessee women: Their lives and times* (pp. 337–359). Athens: University of Georgia Press.

Highlander Research and Education Center. (n.d.). Mission & methodologies. Retrieved from www.highlandercenter.org/our-story/mission/

Holst, J. D. (2009). Conceptualizing training in the radical adult education tradition. *Adult Education Quarterly, 59* (4), 318–334. doi: 10.1177/0741713609334140.

Horton, J. O., & Horton, L. E. (2006). *Slavery and the making of America*. New York: Oxford University Press.

Horton, M. (1966). An interview with Myles Horton: 'It's a miracle—I still don't believe it'. *Phi Delta Kappan, 47* (9), 490–497.

Horton, M. (1990). *The long haul: An autobiography*. New York: Doubleday.

Horton, M., & Freire, P. (1990). *We make the road by walking: Conversations on education and social change*. Philadelphia: Temple University Press.

Imel, S. (2012). Civic engagement in the United States: Roots and branches. *New Directions for Adult and Continuing Education, 2012* (135), 5–13. doi: 10.1002/ace.20021.

International Federation of Social Workers (2012). Statement of ethical principles. Retrieved from www.ifsw.org/statement-of-ethical-principles/

Jara, O. H. (2010). Popular education and social change in Latin America. *Community Development Journal, 45* (3), 287–296. doi: 10.1093/cdj/bsq022.

Kasper, B., & Wiegand, C. (1999). An undergraduate macro practice learning guarantee. *Journal of Teaching in Social Work, 18* (1/2), 99–112. doi: 10.1300/J067v18n01_09.

Keefe, D. (2015). Andragogy in the appalachians: Myles Horton, the Highlander Folk School, and education for social and economic justice. *Journal of Adult Vocational Education and Technology, 6* (3), 16–30. doi: 10.4018/IJAVET.2015070102.

Kolb, D. A. (1984). *Experiential learning: Experience as the source of learning and development*. Englewood Cliffs: Prentice Hall.

Larrison, T. E., & Korr, W. S. (2013). Does social work have a signature pedagogy? *Journal of Social Work Education, 49* (2), 194–206. doi: 10.1080/10437797.2013.768102.

Levine, D. P. (2004). The birth of the citizenship schools: Entwining the struggles for literacy and freedom. *History of Education Quarterly, 44* (3), 388–414. doi: 10.1111/j.1748-5959.2004.tb00015.x.

Longo, N. V. (2007). *Why community matters: Connecting education with civic life*. Albany: SUNY Press.

MacRae, A. C. (2006). Country goods and looking glasses: An Appalachian community moves to a free economy. *Journal of Appalachian Studies, 12* (1), 102–110.

Morley, C., MacFarlane, S., & Ablett, P. (2014). *Engaging with social work: A critical introduction*. Melbourne: Cambridge.

Moyers, B. (1982). The adventures of a radical hillbilly an interview with Myles Horton. *Appalachian Journal, 9* (4), 248–285.

Munford, R., & Sanders, J. (2005). Working with families: Strengths-based approaches. In M. Nash, R. Munford, & K. O'Donoghue (Eds.) *Social work theories in action* (pp. 158–173). Philadelphia: Kingsley.

Payne, C. M. (2007). *I've got the light of freedom: The organizing tradition and the Mississippi freedom struggle.* Oakland: University of California Press.
Rahimi, S. (2010). Myles Horton. Peace Review, *14*(3), 343–348. doi:10.1080/1367886022000016910
Rauschenbusch, W. (1997). *A theology for the social gospel.* Westminster: John Knox Press.
Rosner, D., & Markowitz, G. E.. (Eds). (1987). *Dying for work: Workers' safety and health in twentieth-century America.* Bloomington: Indiana University Press.
Saleebey, D. (2009). Introduction: Power to the people. In D. Saleebey (Ed.) *The strengths perspective in social work practice* (pp. 1–23). Boston: Pearson.
Schneider, S. A. (2014). *You can't padlock an idea: Rhetorical education at the Highlander Folk School, 1932-1961.* Columbia: University of South Carolina Press.
Shosh, J. M. (2017). Toward the construction of a local knowledge base on teaching and learning by and for teachers and learners. In L. L. Rowell, C. D. Bruce, J. M. Shosh, & M. M. Riel (Eds.) *Palgrave international handbook of action research* (pp. 647–665). New York: Palgrave Macmillan.
Williams, S., & Mullett, C. (2016). Creating highlander wherever you are. *Adult Learning, 27* (3), 98–104. doi: doi:10.1177/1045159516651591.

12
Pedagogy and power through a Foucauldian lens

Julie King

QUEENSLAND UNIVERSITY OF TECHNOLOGY, AUSTRALIA

Introduction

Social work immerses practitioners in the social world of the people they work with; a world where disempowerment and helplessness are common feelings (Carter, Jeffs and Smith, 1995). While personal circumstances are many and varied, it is inevitable that at least some of these feelings result from interactions with sources of power in society such as police and government agencies. The analysis and interpretation of the roles of these sources in relation to the experiences of people often involve an implicit or explicit analysis of power relationships, a judgement by the social worker regarding the justifiability of the policies, procedures and actions of these agents, and an assessment of the outcomes in terms of the balance between the benefits received in relation to need, and the compromises involved. In an exploration of some of the historical roots of social work, Beddoe (2017: 125) states that social work is recognised "as intrinsically preoccupied with the alleviation of suffering at individual, family and community levels, while acknowledging that social change is needed to reduce health inequalities". This is essentially critical analysis, although in practice the analysis may be informal and informed more by sentiment than by a coherent analytical framework.

Critical theory (drawing on a Marxist approach) has an obvious role in a more formal analytical approach to mapping and exposing power relationships that affect social work clients, and indeed Beddoe (2017) emphasises the role of power relationships as a defining characteristic of the context of social work. However, critical Marxist analyses often take a specific position on the use of power, casting people as victims and systems as perpetrators of the exertion of power. In such discourses, the exertion of power is axiomatically unfair, if not malevolent.

This chapter sets out to provide an alternative view of power, drawing on Michel Foucault's writings. They present a less uniformly negative and more productive perspective on the nature and use of power. This alternate view can play an important role in re-visioning critical pedagogy, both in providing a more nuanced understanding of the role of power in students' future social work practice, and in developing the relationship between teacher and students in the pedagogical process, as will be illustrated with examples drawn from Australian social work education (that will be applicable in similar Western settings).

In doing so, this chapter addresses an important distinction between modernist and postmodernist/poststructuralist accounts of the relation between power and knowledge. Modernism envisages a gradual improvement in human welfare through increasing, general, reliable knowledge achieved via the exercise of reason and the application of scientific methods (Fook, 2016). Under this view, knowledge exists in a hierarchy with structures such as disciplines that organise knowledge. Postmodernist approaches challenge the validity of these structures and hierarchies, instead seeing a multiplicity of perspectives and means of generating knowledge. Chambon and Irving (1999) highlight this aspect of Foucault's work and its disruptive influence on the practices that enact knowledge. A criticism of postmodern and poststructural approaches is that they are too passive, in the sense that they acquiesce to a narrative that accepts the exertion of power to enforce social compliance rather than challenging it (Morley, 2016); however, it is the disruptive influence of critical reflection on the power–knowledge–practice relationship that can avoid this criticism by generating alternative practices.

Foucault's biographical context and concept of power

Michel Foucault was a French historian, social theorist and philosopher whose works have been widely translated. He was born Paul-Michel Foucault in France in 1926. His father was a wealthy surgeon who was rather authoritarian and prescriptive about his son's future. Foucault was an excellent student, and at 17 rebelled against his father's wishes to pursue a demanding academic career which matured into an interest in philosophy, drawing on influences from Hegel, Heidegger, Nietzsche, Sartre and Husserl, among others. The demands of his studies to reach university, and the difficulties of being homosexual (from both a family and societal perspective), contributed to suicide attempts that led to his exposure to the mental health system. This early experience focused his philosophical interests onto the relationship between bodies of knowledge and their practices, in particular the way in which they acted together to police compliance with discourses of normality. While at university, Foucault joined the Stalinist French Communist Party but was not very committed and swiftly became disenchanted with the negative way that Marxism was expressed and used (Horrocks and Jetvic, 2004). However, he remained engaged politically, and became increasingly activist following the Paris riots of 1968. Both politically and intellectually he focused on social justice, with his intellectual contribution being the evolution of a structuralist approach to the constitution of truth and knowledge in society (O'Farrell, 2006). Starting from his exploration of psychiatry, he developed a historical and (following Nietzsche) "genealogical" approach to modern discourse, tracing the evolution of ideas and their use exerting power (Horrocks and Jetvic, 2004; O'Farrell, 2006). He is considered to be a highly influential leader in social theory in the 20th century, who saw himself as a "historian of systems of thought", whose aim was to deconstruct discourses of power (Powell, 2013). He died from the complications of HIV infection in 1984 (Powell, 2013).

After a period of popularity both before and after his death, Foucault's influence waned somewhat, but has seen a resurgence because of the continued relevance of his ideas in understanding the neoliberal world in which we live (Burman, 2016). Foucault's epistemological work is ultimately about the relationship between knowledge and power, although Foucault arrived at this point via an examination of the historical evolution of how society deals with mental illness (Martin, 1988) and the punishment of criminals (Foucault, 1995). On the one hand, Foucault saw a progressive increase in the exertion of state power over individuals, while on the other hand the rationale for this exertion of power shifted discontinuously (Hutton, 1988). His focus was therefore on the state, in particular "the disciplining of human affairs by public and quasi-public agencies" (Hutton, 1988: 126).

Consistent with the familiar view of power as oppressive and dominating, Foucault referred to it in relational terms (Powell, 2013), as hierarchies of force relations: "power means relations, a more-or-less organised, hierarchical, coordinated cluster of relations" (Foucault, 1980: 198), and "must be understood in the first instance as the multiplicity of force relations immanent in the sphere in which they operate and which constitute their own organization" (Foucault, 1984: 92). However, and more importantly, Foucault's concern with the use of power was intimately entwined with his views on the privileging of knowledge: "power and knowledge directly imply one another, there is no power relation without the correlative constitution of a field of knowledge, nor any knowledge that does not presuppose and constitute at the same time power relations" (Foucault, 1995: 27). For Foucault, knowledge is constituted through practices such as those of social work (Chambon, 1999), so that power, knowledge and practice are interrelated (Powell, 2013).

Barker (1993: 77–78) abstracted six "working hypotheses on power" from Foucault's writings:

1   Power and social existence go together, so that there is no social space which is free of power.
2   Power relations are a part of other relations in society, such as work, family, sex, etc.
3   Power relations are not just about repression but are also productive, and there are many kinds of power relationship.
4   A person is part of many power relationships as both the dominator and the dominated, these relationships intersect in many ways and have an overall effect, as do the different tactics and strategies of the exercise of power, and the way this exercise of power is resisted.
5   Power relations are used because they serve strategic purposes for everyone, and are not just the way political and economic entities achieve their ends.
6   The exercise of power always engenders resistance at the point it is exercised – at multiple levels, with the individual resistances contributing to a global picture.

The general thrust is that human existence is pervaded by power relationships, so that to be a human being is to be part of a network of power relationships. The word "domination" therefore follows naturally, in that all people will in some way and at some time be the inferior in some kind of power relationship. The patterns of power relationships, then, describe society at all levels.

Power and the operation of the state

Foucault inquired into the way power was applied historically (Barker, 1993: 48). Taking the view that social order and the exercise of power amount to the same thing, he inquired into the ways that the methods of domination and control had changed over time, and this led him to a view of the way that society now operated. He referred to the emergence in the 17th and 18th centuries of "a new technology of the exercise of power" aimed at "obtaining productive service from individuals in their concrete lives" (Foucault, 2006b: 159–161). This he saw as the exertion of control over the bodies of individuals and their behaviours, and as having an administrative function in relation to the population and its health and welfare (Powell, 2013).

This process is often labelled *governmentality*. Foucault explains (2006a) that he is inquiring into an ongoing problem for government in the exercise of power: that while political power applies to the nation as legal subjects, there is also a welfare power aimed at improving people's individual lives, caring for them, etc., an aim clearly relevant to social work. He goes on to say that, based on his reading of European history in the 17th and 18th centuries, he sees two doctrines as the basis on which government operates: *reason of state*, which means rational government as opposed to arbitrary rule of a sovereign, and *policing*, which is a broad term including administration, education, regulation of trade and crafts, etc., as well as the narrower law enforcement role we associate with policing in the English language today. This puts the government in a position of "surveillance" (monitoring, supervision) and control with respect to citizens.

One way Foucault's approach has been interpreted has been to refute the notion that the growth of the state, and in particular its welfare component, is a benign, well-meaning process – it is simply yet another manifestation of dominating and coercive power. However, a consequence of Foucault's approach to power-knowledge is that domination exists everywhere, all the time, as is clear in his references to power cited above. Further, while "domination" has a negative connotation, Foucault has a more optimistic view because he sees the exercise of power as – by definition – engendering resistance, and it is this resistance that fosters creativity: "Where there is power, there is resistance, and yet, or rather consequently, this resistance is never in a position of exteriority in relation to power" (Foucault, 1984: 95–96).

While it appears that Foucault's central interest with governmentality is the operation of the state, he saw this as being connected with individual experience. In other words, the world of social experience and the use of power by the state are continuous with each other, rather than being separate arenas. Late in his life Foucault acknowledged this, while introducing the concepts of "technologies of individual domination" and "the technology of the self" (Foucault, 1988: 19). He defines four "technologies", though it is the latter two that are relevant here:

> [T]echnologies of power, which determine the conduct of individuals and submit them to certain ends or domination, an objectivising of the subject; (and) technologies of the self, which permit individuals to effect by their own means or with the help of others a certain number of operations on their own bodies and souls, thoughts, conduct, and way of being, so as to transform themselves in order to obtain a certain state of happiness, purity, wisdom, perfection, or immortality.
>
> *(Foucault, 1988: 18)*

This means that, while the state establishes categories for people, labels them, applies rules to them and polices compliance with the rules, it also relies on people to internalise those categories and rules and to self-enforce them, exerting power upon themselves.

Hancock (2018) explains the top-down and bottom-up ways that power can be considered. In social work, the state, through its social welfare schemes and various forms of aid assistance, uses its power to constitute people as clients of different kinds – unemployed, single parent, pensioner, etc. In taking a critical approach to the social and economic context in which social work clients' experience is embedded, it is easy to see governmentality (the operation of the state) as the technology of domination. However, Foucault stresses a subtle but important difference by focusing on the outcome of governmentality, i.e. management of individuals both within and outside formal institutions. Governmentality achieves this through the interaction between technologies of domination and technologies of self. Foucault is distinguishing between technologies as "what is done" – domination of others and domination of the self as processes or activities – and the outcome of these forms of domination for the individual. Governmentality is, therefore, not the same as the "technologies of power" which "objectivise the subject", and the "technologies of self" with which individuals effect changes upon themselves – it is in fact the outcome for the individual of the combined action of the technology of domination and the technology of self. Hancock (2018) notes that, through the technologies of self, people exercise agency in developing and maintaining their own sense of self, not merely as the self defined by the power of government programs.

One feature of governmentality (expressing the technologies of domination) is that the bodies of people in a society become formally constructed by government institutions and subject to surveillance and control (Powell, 2013), for example through institutionalised medical systems (Nettleton and Bunton, 1995; Gignac and Cott, 1998; Lupton, 1999). The expression of the technologies of the self is less obvious: instead of government explicitly undertaking surveillance and control, social and political processes have led to people monitoring themselves and controlling their own behaviour in response to a moral enjoinder to be a "worthy citizen". For both types of technologies, resistances would be expected to emerge at the same sites where power is being exerted. For example, Foote and Frank (1999) note that since the exertion of power starts in the body, so does resistance, and provide examples where older people resist discourses of grieving by adopting complicated forms of mourning: "these people use their bodies to disrupt normal expectations, including emotional restraints, diet, sexuality and work" (p. 175).

How a Foucauldian approach extends critical theory

Because Foucault deals with power and how it structures experience, there is an obvious overlap with critical theory. However, Ingram (1994) and Sawicki (1994) point out that Foucault's approach, while critical, differs from mainstream critical theory on an important point: he does not assume that there is a Marxist (or Freudian) nirvana, absent of domination. Instead, power is always exercised, domination always occurs. For the same reason, Foucault's approach is reflexive, in that any knowledge generated in relation to a subject must in some way involve domination.

The Marxist model of social analysis sets up an oppositional framework where government and social order are seen as oppressors to be acted against until freedom is achieved. This contrasts with Foucault's view that power is exercised everywhere, all the time, and can even be liberating and afford a spark for creativity. A key element of Foucault's conceptualisation is the emergence of resistance wherever power is exercised (Barker, 1993). By "resistance" Foucault does not mean just active and organised rejection of oppression, but also the many and varied forms of noncompliance, passive as well as active, of which human beings are capable (as in the example of complicated mourning above). Further, a better appreciation of Foucault's notion of the technologies of self as a contributor to governmentality opens up new insights into the emergence of resistance at the inter- and intra-personal levels.

How Foucauldian analysis can contribute to social work teaching

Social work is one of several professions that enact the welfare aims of the state, yet at the same time social work maintains a focus on the empowerment of the individual and a constituting of the individual as agent. Social work education is the milieu in which we should expect future social workers to understand this apparent conflict, and a Foucauldian analysis provides an ideal way of doing so. Smith, Jeffery and Collins (2018) define critical pedagogy as "a variety of teaching practices employed by educators to help destabilize seemingly normal or neutral knowledge" and use Foucault's governmentality as a theoretical basis to inform social work education. Morley (2016) points out that learning about and practicing critical reflexivity is central to assisting social work students and practitioners to understand the social construction of knowledge and therefore its contested nature. Applying critical reflection within the framework of governmentality should, therefore, foster agency.

Australian social work students come from many backgrounds, but are usually of Australian origin. As a colonised country, Australia has discourses about Indigenous Australians that have become multiple as newer discourses have challenged older ones. Australia is also a country of immigrants, whose dominant countries of origin (and their associated cultures and religions) are continuously changing, again contributing to a multiplicity of discourses. Certain of these discourses may be considered privileged, with some being seen as more "common sense" than others, such as neoliberal discourses on the economy, work and individual responsibility. Others are less entrenched; however, people tend to mix with others who share similar assumptions and values.

At this broad level, a Foucauldian analysis via critical reflection should have the effect of destabilising and denaturalising perceptions of the "matter-of-fact" discursive themes of Australian culture and society (Burman, 2016), shedding light on how subjectivity is constituted and developing a more open approach to the expectations and assumptions that social work clients will bring to the social worker–client relationship. In particular, through an understanding of governmentality and the technologies of power, such a deconstruction would illustrate how the state acts through its welfare objectives to constitute people in relation to welfare needs defined by the state. For example, it would uncover and enable questioning of attitudes toward Indigenous Australians, responses to asylum seekers, and dominant culturally laden discourses around family structure. This approach is taken in the author's course on human rights, where the introduction of technologies of power is used to spur discussion of power, and revisited through the course.

Further examples can be found in research the author conducted on the lived experience of disability among Indigenous Australians (King, 2010; King, Brough and Knox, 2014). A central finding of the research was that Indigenous Australians with a disability constructed themselves as Indigenous above all, despite the pressure from formal institutions to enforce "person with disability" as the dominant category to achieve its welfare aims among Indigenous people with disability, a prime example of the controlling of bodies inherent in governmentality. The research also provided examples of more specific forms of resistance to the exertion of power by the state by Indigenous Australians with a disability, and by the Indigenous organisations that supported them. While the label "disability" conflicted with the Indigenous holistic construction of health (King, 2010; King, Brough and Knox, 2014), "disability" categories were adopted for instrumental reasons, in order to gain access to resources, but without the appropriation of the constructs. Part of the research took place at a centre that operated within a government framework, but subverted the formal and less formal constraints of role and accountability to provide a service more in keeping with the needs of their "clients", similar to the examples of resistance cited by Powell (2013) among social workers. These instances provide examples of a creative, subversive response to the exertion of power, at the sites where it was exerted. Not only does this provide a richer picture of the operation of power than a typical critical analysis, it also presents a more hopeful and positive perspective on how oppressions and victimhood are resisted.

The Foucauldian perspective can be applied to social work pedagogy in other ways and is frequently (perhaps most frequently) used to understand the influences of technologies of power on the pedagogical process in neoliberal societies (e.g. Smith, Jeffery and Collins, 2018). At the same time Foucauldian concepts are often included in social work curricula, often as a means of showing students how the process of governmentality constitutes categories of individuals in society, the ostensible purpose of thus constituting them, and how this disempowers, racialises and genders them. Foucault's dissection of power and discipline in the experience of subjectivity may also provide insights for people who often come into contact with social workers, such as people with mental health issues, helping them to make sense of their experiences with doctors, therapists and agencies, and with the politicisation of them as people and members of a socially constituted category (or categories) (Burman, 2016).

As noted above, critical reflexivity is advocated as the means of ensuring that social work pedagogy achieves the aim of destabilising dominant discourses. In this regard, Morley (2016) places Foucault's approach among "the combination of critical modernist and poststructuralist theories ... that distinguishes critical reflection from reflection" (p. 27). She emphasises the need for such reflection to lead to change, rather than reinforcing existing patterns of discourse and power. Drawing on the literature on critical reflection in pedagogy, Morley outlines the deconstruction and reconstruction phases that provide an opportunity for students to gain a sense of agency. A key element is the identification of discontinuities and contradictions in dominant discourses that provide an opportunity for resistance. In this sense, the exertion of power expressed in a dominant discourse can thus engender resistance at the very site it seeks to dominate.

Various techniques in critical pedagogy have been adopted to teach critical reflection, for example Fook and Askeland (2007) describe their method of asking students to focus on a critical incident in professional practice. Translation of the critical incident model into social work teaching is not necessarily straightforward, as noted by Giles and Pockett (2013) and Savaya (2013) in relation to cases in their respective studies. In both studies, practical constraints meant students addressed critical incidents presented to them, rather than their own, and using someone else's critical incident might not have the same benefits because there is less need for introspective reflection. In the Giles and Pockett (2013) study, this was partially addressed by having students critically reflect on their interactions with their groups, and this seemed to be successful; in Savaya's (2013) study it was considered that the specific context of the learning – a Master's course – was characterised by cultural and contextual factors that enhanced the success of the exercise in spite of the use of a third person's critical incident. Baikie, Campbell, Thornhill and Butler (2013) report an online undergraduate course that enabled the use of personal critical incidents; it appears to have had mixed success, suggesting that there might be a pedagogical trade-off between the personal relevance of the critical incident and the immediacy of the reflective interactions.

As a cautionary footnote, it is often asserted that Foucault's focus was on the trajectory of European society, so one criticism of the argument presented here is that it only pretends to universal applicability across social work. This extends a criticism that was applied to social work itself in the past, prior to the efforts of the International Federation of Social Work (IFSW) to arrive at a global definition of social work that avoided colonialist, Westernising discourses (Hutchings and Taylor, 2007). However, research and analysis conducted by Hutchings and Taylor (2007) on social work in China led them to the conclusion that the IFSW definition remains embedded in Western discourses. For example, the very use of the concepts of empowerment and social change is problematic in China because they imply a criticism of socialism and potentially call for disruption of the existing social order. Therefore, the conclusion reached in this chapter, about the value of a Foucauldian understanding of social work through critical reflection, might be of most value in neoliberal states that represent the progression of governmentality traced by Foucault. Certainly, this has been the author's experience in teaching human rights to social work students.

Concluding remarks

At this point it is appropriate to raise the need for caution in how Foucault's concepts and Foucauldian approaches are used in social work education. As Burman (2016: 2–3) notes, it would be hoped that Foucault "helps us know ourselves better, situating what we know of ourselves and how we know this within cultural-historical conditions of possibility", but it is also possible that "like good neoliberal entrepreneurial subjects, we know or 'make up' our own individualised, personalised version of his ideas" that make us feel comfortable in the lives constituted for us by the state. A different point is made by Badwall (2016), whose research with social workers in Canada found that the practice of critical reflexivity, which is typically central to the implementation of a Foucauldian approach by social workers, can inadvertently reinforce the constitution by social workers of clients as disempowered. Since this taps into the state constitution of social work clients as recipients of defined forms of welfare, not as agents, there is a distinct risk that social workers will gravitate along the cultural line of least resistance.

Interestingly, some of the author's research threw up a challenge for a Foucauldian interpretation, because governmentality is seen as operating in one direction – toward greater control of individuals by the state by constructing their bodies as Indigenous, disabled, unproductive, unhealthy, poor, etc. – whereas among the participants in the author's research the policing of Indigeneity was a form of self-discipline that operated in the opposite direction. Two questions arise here: (1) is this particular form of self-discipline better characterised as resistance? and (2) has this problem arisen because of the specific set of circumstances? i.e. Indigenous communities themselves police the Indigeneity of individuals, while at the same time the communities exist in a broader white state that exercises power, so that governmentality is operative at more than one level. These questions point to the need for Foucauldian governmentality to be better elaborated.

However, there is no doubt that Foucault's conceptualisation of power gives a different perspective from earlier constructions on the role of power (of state actors, other entities and individuals) in people's lives. Power is not necessarily seen as oppressive, since the operation of power is ubiquitous, being a part of everyday interactions between people. Simply appreciating this can be empowering for social work students, because it presumes that the exertion of power is not synonymous with inevitable victimhood. Instead, the exertion of power engenders resistance, and resistance (or subversion) can be creative and empowering. The author's experience with social work students shows that an analytical understanding of Foucault's conceptualisation of power contributes to an appreciation of how power and agency can combine in unexpected ways to benefit individuals and societies and can empower individuals in their fight for human rights. Many Australian students arrive at university accepting much of the dominant discourse on social justice and human rights as rational and objective, until encouraged to critically reflect on the assumptions underlying this discourse and the consequences it has for individuals. The shift in their understanding is expressed in their assessments (reports and posters), tutorial discussions, and the addition to their phones of apps such as Human Rights Watch and Aljazeera.

The process of deconstructing the "matter-of-factness" of one's own culture is an enlightening experience for social work students, because it opens up the possibility of alternative solutions at several levels. Whether the focus is on the needs of a particular client, or advocacy about the operation of a policy or program, or a political program being promoted by a party or government, an understanding of the logic in terms of governmentality can give a coherent context to the way that power is being leveraged to pursue state interests and objectives.

Finally, the pedagogical process itself can convey the essence of the Foucauldian conceptualisation of power, by demonstrating how the teacher–student relationship can foster productive learning and empower students, without oppressing them. The teacher–student relationship is based on a power dynamic that is explicitly linked to the privileging of knowledge, however in the arena of social experience there would also be space to enable articulation of themes of resistance and/or subversion of accepted knowledge. Not only does this benefit students, but also the practice of social work pedagogy and the social work educators themselves.

References

Badwall, H. (2016). Critical reflexivity and moral regulation. *Journal of Progressive Human Services*, 27(1):1–2. doi: 10.1080/10428232.2016.1108169.

Baikie, G., Campbell, C., Thornhill, J. and Butler, J. (2013). An online critical reflection dialogue group. Ch. 18 In J. Fook and F. Gardner (Eds.) *Critical Reflection in Context: Applications in Health and Social Care*. Oxford: Routledge. pp. 219–230.

Barker, P. (1993). *Michel Foucault: Subversions of the Subject*. New York: St Martin's Press.

Beddoe, L. (2017). Field, capital and professional identity: social work in health care in S. Webb (Ed.) *Professional Identity in Social Work*. Oxon UK: Routledge. Chapter Nine: pp. 122–135.

Burman, E. (2016). Knowing Foucault, knowing you: 'raced'/classed and gendered subjectivities in the pedagogical state. *Pedagogy, Culture & Society*, 24(1):1–25. doi: 10.1080/14681366.2015.1057215.

Carter, P., Jeffs, A. and Smith, M.K. (1995). Making sense of social working. Ch. 12 In P. Carter et al. (Ed.) *Social Working*. Basingstoke: Macmillan. pp. 165–180.

Chambon, A.S. (1999). Foucault's approach: making the familiar visible. Ch. 3 In A.S Chambon, A. Irving and L. Epstein (Eds.) *Reading Foucault for Social Work*. New York: Columbia University Press. pp. 51–81.

Chambon, A.S. and Irving, A. (1999). Introduction In A.S Chambon, A. Irving and L. Epstein (Eds.) *Reading Foucault for Social Work*. New York: Columbia University Press. pp. xiii–xxx.

Fook, J. (2016). *Social Work: Critical Theory and Practice, 3rd Edition*. London: Sage.

Fook, J. and Askeland, G.A. (2007). Challenges of critical reflection: 'nothing ventured, nothing gained'. *Social Work Education*, 26(5):520–533.

Foote, C.E. and Frank, A.W. (1999). Foucault and therapy: the disciplining of grief. Ch. 7 In A.S Chambon, A. Irving and L. Epstein (Eds.) *Reading Foucault for Social Work*. New York: Columbia University Press. pp. 157–187.

Foucault, M. (1980). *Power/Knowledge: Selected Interviews and Other Writings*. New York: Pantheon.

Foucault, M. (1984). *The History of Sexuality Vol. 1*. New York: Vintage.

Foucault, M. (1988). Technologies of the self. Ch. 2 In Martin, L.H., Gutman, H. and Hutton, P.H. (Eds.) *Technologies of the Self: A Seminar with Michel Foucault*. London: Tavistock Publications. pp. 16–49.

Foucault, M. (1995). *Discipline and Punish: The Birth of the Prison*. New York: Vintage Books.

Foucault, M. (2006a). "Omnes et singulatim". Ch. 5 In *The Chomsky-Foucault Debate on Human Nature*. New York: The New Press. pp. 172–210. Originally Appeared in *Power: Essential Works of Foucault, 1954–1984*, published by The New Press in 2001.

Foucault, M. (2006b). Truth and power. Ch. 4 In *The Chomsky-Foucault Debate on Human Nature*. New York: The New Press. Originally Appeared in *Power: Essential Works of Foucault, 1954–1984*, published by The New Press in 2001.

Gignac, M.A.M. and Cott, C. (1998). A conceptual model of independence and dependence for adults with chronic physical illness and disability. *Social Science and Medicine*, 47(6):739–753.

Giles, R. and Pockett, R. (2013). Critical reflection in social work education. Ch. 17 in J. Fook and F. Gardner (Eds.) *Critical Reflection in Context: Applications in Health and Social Care*. Oxford: Routledge. pp. 208–218.

Hancock, B.H. (2018). Michel Foucault and the problematics of power: theorizing DTCA and medicalized subjectivity. *Journal of Medicine and Philosophy*, 43(4):439–468. doi: doi:10.1093/jmp/jhy010.

Horrocks, C. and Jetvic, Z. (2004). *Introducing Foucault*. London: Icon Books.

Hutchings, A. and Taylor, I. (2007). Defining the profession? exploring an international definition of social work in the China context. *International Journal of Social Welfare*, 16:382–390.

Hutton, P. (1988). Foucault, Freud, and the technologies of the self. Ch. 7 In Martin, L.H., Gutman, H. and Hutton, P.H. (Eds.) *Technologies of the Self: A Seminar with Michel Foucault*. London: Tavistock Publications. pp. 121–144.

Ingram, D. (1994). Foucault and Habermas on the subject of reason. Ch. 9 in Gutting, G. (ed.) *The Cambridge Companion to Foucault*. Cambridge: Cambridge University Press.

King, J.A. (2010). *Weaving Yarns: The lived Experience of Indigenous Australians with Adult –Onset Disability in Brisbane*. Unpublished PhD Thesis, Queensland University of Technology https://eprints.qut.edu.au/34447/

King, J.A, Brough, M., and Knox, M. (2014). Negotiating disability and colonisation: the lived experience of Indigenous Australians with a disability. *Disability & Society*, 29(5):738–750.

Lupton, D. (1999). Introduction: risk and sociocultural theory In Lupton, D. (Ed.) *Risk and Sociocultural Theory: New Directions and Perspectives*. Cambridge. pp. Cambridge University Press.

Martin, R. (1988). Truth, power, self: an interview with Michel Foucault, October 25, 1982. Ch. 1 In Martin, L.H., Gutman, H. and Hutton, P.H. (Eds.) *Technologies of the Self: A Seminar with Michel Foucault*. London: Tavistock Publications. pp. 9–15.

Morley, C. (2016). Critical reflection and critical social work. Ch. 2 In B. Pease, S. Goldingay, N. Hosken and S. Nipperess (Eds.) *Doing Critical Social Work: Transformative Practices for Social Justice*. Crows Nest NSW Australia: Allen & Unwin. pp. 25–38.

Nettleton, S and Bunton, R. (1995). Sociological critiques of health promotion. Chapter 4 In Bunton, R, Nettleton, S, Burrows, R (Eds.) *The Sociology of Health Promotion: Critical Analyses of Consumption Lifestyle and Risk*. London: Routledge. pp. 41–58.

O'Farrell, C. (2006). Foucault and post modernism. *The Sydney Papers*, 18(3-4):182–194.

Powell, J.L. (2013). Michel Foucault. C4 In Gray, M. and Webb, S.A. (Eds.) *Social Work Theories and Methods*. London: Sage. pp. 46–62.

Sawicki, J. (1994). Foucault, feminism and questions of identity. Ch. 11 in Gutting, G. (ed.) *The Cambridge Companion to Foucault*. Cambridge: Cambridge University Press.

Savaya, R. (2013). Critical reflection training to social workers in a large, non-elective university class. Ch. 15 in J. Fook and F. Gardner (Eds.) *Critical Reflection in Context: Applications in Health and Social Care*. Oxford: Routledge. pp. 181–195.

Smith, K., Jeffery, D. and Collins, K. (2018). Slowing things down: taming time in the neoliberal university using social work distance education. *Social Work Education*, 37(6):691–704. doi: 10.1080/02615479.2018.1445216.

13

'A social work counter-pedagogy yet-to-come'

Jacques Derrida and critical social work education and practice

Peter Westoby

QUEENSLAND UNIVERSITY OF TECHNOLOGY, AUSTRALIA

Introduction

> That [social work] died yesterday ... and [social work] should still wander toward the meaning of its death – or that it has always lived knowing itself to be dying; that [social work] died one day, within history, or that it has always fed on its own agony.

This is the kind of thing Derrida *might say*. He used these words, but about philosophy (replace social work with philosophy) early in his career, writing an essay on Emmanuel Levinas in the journal of his day, *Critique*. Like such a provocation to philosophy, Derrida's deconstruction invites a critical reflection on social work pedagogy.

The word deconstruction, as used by Derrida, is a play on Heidegger's *destruktion* – which in German and French is not so much about destroying, but about a critical re-constituting. For Derrida, the deconstructive task is not so much destroying but about opening up text, programmes and institutions – not with the purpose of anarchy, but with a view to *more just* programmes and institutions (Smith, 2005, p. 11).

Derrida's deconstructive episteme is understood to be messianic in the sense that it is one of profound affirmation about a future yet-to-come. If he pronounced the death of social work he would be inviting a social work, and for this chapter, a social work counter-pedagogy, that is 'yet-to-come'. As he said in his final interview, 'deconstruction is always on the side of the yes, on the side of an affirmation of life' (Derrida, 2007, p. 51). As Smith argues, quoting Derrida directly, 'I cannot conceive of a radical critique which would not be ultimately motivated by some sort of affirmation' (Smith, 2005, p. 12). Hence, the title of this chapter is an affirmative and life-giving suggestion of 'a social work counter-pedagogy yet-to-come'.

Why the need for a 'social work yet-to-come'?

Peter Westoby

Deconstructive episteme as Derrida's key contribution

I opt for the term 'deconstructive episteme' as opposed to deconstruction in honour of Derrida's dislike of the latter term, a noun, implying deconstruction as a 'thing'. In contrast, deconstructive episteme implies *a way of knowing, a sensibility or sensitivity*. As will become clear in this chapter, deconstruction as an episteme is oriented around re-thinking language, ethics and politics, *focused on reforming institutions.*

One institution he often had his eye on was the university (because he loved it dearly), always reaching for a reformation of the university and particularly the way philosophy was understood and taught within it. Derrida yearned for a university-yet-to-come, a key institution in what he talked about as the 'democracy-yet-to-come' (Derrida, 2005, p. 41; Smith, 2005, p. 84) – one more fully alive to justice than ever before. In his final interview he referred to this university as the 'university of tomorrow' (Derrida, 2007, p. 47) which must

> take on the mission inscribed in its very concept ... a modern concept that ordered the university to organise its search for truth without any conditions attached. That is, to be free to know, criticise, ask questions, and doubt without being limited by any political or religious power ... In the originary concept of the university is this absolute claim to an unconditional freedom to think, speak and critique.
>
> *(ibid., p. 48)*

This paragraph holds substantive ideas – for example, the 'orginary concept of the university' – yet, within the text is also a way of reaching into Derrida's deconstructive episteme.

Cutting to the chase, the take home message of his episteme of deconstruction is that there are *at least* two readings of any text – or for this chapter – the texts of the university institution and social work pedagogy. The first reading is reading for the Truth, which reaches for the author's intent – or as per the above paragraph – the originary concepts of the institution. In contrast, the second reading is a reading for the contradictions, fissures and tensions within any text or institution – for Derrida they are always there, undermining, or bringing more complexity to the so-called Truth of the first reading. This second reading is also an affirmation of something new, something that can arrive from a fresh living encounter with the text or institution – e.g. the 'university of tomorrow'. Importantly, this new reading, as per Derrida's *hauntology* (a term that we will come to), is also one that is haunted by the summons of justice.

In the same way that Derrida loved philosophy and the university, in this chapter I make the case that Derrida *would* (for he never talked of social work) love social work as a professional or programme and the university that teaches it as an institution, to be subject to the minimal 'two readings'. The first, a reading that reaches for the Truth of the university and social work (their 'originary concepts' and traditions), delving into the traces of life that live deep within their traditions. Perhaps we could trace the traditions of the university as a critical commons and social work as the kind of practice of solidarity and service embodied in the Settlement House work of Jane Addams? More or less re-stating the Derrida paragraph above, 'in principle, the university remains the only place where critical debate must remain unconditionally open' (Derrida, 2007, p. 49). What would be the equivalent for social work?

Then the second reading is *both* critical – seeing the multiplicities, tensions and fissures within the university and social work, acknowledging there is no Truth – *and* affirmative, reaching for a social work-of-tomorrow and university-yet-to-come. In terms of the critical – the multiplicities, tensions and fissures – there are many kinds of social work, conservative through to more critical, social work that has become an 'agent of the state' and social work that holds to emancipatory aspirations. In terms of the affirmation, Derrida would insist that our love of the social work profession and the university institution ensures we deconstruct them, reaching for a social work counter-pedagogy that is haunted by the call for justice. Clearly, a kind of deconstruction has been going on for 100 or so years, as per the architecture of social work evidenced in journals, conferences, and so forth.

For Derrida, within this constantly reforming process, to not be haunted by the summons of justice would be to slip into a deadened position and perspective – which echoes the thinking of Wittgenstein who argued that universities are full of people whose thinking is ossified. It would be, using the idea of philosopher Francois Jullien, to 'become settled' which is to enter a state of decay (Jullien, 2016).

Derrida's contrast to death, decay or a deadened settling, is to always affirm the 'Yes', in fact making the case for what he referred to as a 'second yes' and even a 'third yes'. This affirmation, sitting at the centre of his final interview, recorded in the gem of a book *Learning to Live Finally* (Derrida, 2007), is an affirmation of the constant inauguration of a commitment. To affirm that a social work-of-tomorrow and the university-yet-to-come are haunted by the call to justice is a 'yes'. But – and here is Derrida's key point – tomorrow we must wake up and affirm it again – a 'second yes', and then again we must awake with a 'third yes'. And onwards, always with the inauguration of reform – the messianic-like *telos* that drives Derrida, that haunts him, and should each of us.

If we are not haunted by the spectre of justice, then it would be best to walk away from the university and social work, to leave it alone, to do no more damage.

The deconstructive double reading is also the way I will try to read Derrida for this chapter. The first reading is a careful scholarly reading of aspects of Derrida, looking for the Truth that Derrida is trying to communicate. Yet, the second reading is *my engagement with Derrida* – a reading that is not so much seeking a 'fusion of horizons' – a dialogue between my and Derrida's Truth (that approach would be the Gadamer-inspired hermeneutical circle) – but is instead seeking to riff off a more nuanced reading of Derrida with all the potential contradictions, fissures and tensions within his work. Yet, this second reading is also reaching into new territory that can affirm a social work counter-pedagogy that is 'yet-to-come'.

Note, this 'yet-to-come' is not a vision of a social work or university that is constructed by neoliberal logics (because that is a likely 'to come' if powerful interests are not thwarted). Quite the contrary, Derrida's thought is radical in the sense of reaching for the roots of the university and social work – the traces of those originary concepts – which are not neoliberal.

His work has had a powerful influence on critical theory, 'such as post-colonial theory, feminist theory or critical race theory' (Smith, 2005, p. 12), and the last 20 years of his life and writing were dedicated to the more explicit theorising of what deconstruction meant for radical politics. His radical politics was always reaching for a politic that I argue has two key dimensions – first, the already mentioned 'summons to justice', and second, being attuned to 'vigilance for the other'. These two key political principles underpin his yearning for a democracy-yet-to-come, more radically alive to justice than anything we have yet seen.

A sketch of Derrida's life

Approaching Derrida's life in such a small chapter is obviously fraught. We are talking here of an intellectual rock-star, one who brought philosophy back to life in an era where it was in decay. This is a thinker who split the Academy in half, some arguing that Derrida was a 'monster' destroying the Academy and reading, while also obscuring his own writing in ways that made it almost impossible for others to read (so true of many not versed in continental philosophy). Yet the other half argued that he was rescuing philosophy from its own inherent decay and irrelevance, bringing it back to life and renewing its relevance to practical and political life.

Many a reader can find biographies of Derrida. I have read three such biographies and there will be plenty more to come, but the question is, how to read his life in a way that gives life to our question of a social work counter-pedagogy-yet-to-come? Furthermore, to be transparent, I can only now read him through three lenses. First, my encounter with him in Johannesburg in 1998, where he was in dialogue with a colleague and friend of mine Verne Harris (now with the Nelson Mandela Foundation) around the topic of memory, archive and the Truth and Reconciliation Commission, as alluded in Derrida's book *Archive Fever*. Second, Verne Harris's interpretation of Derrida for the purposes of memory work and justice, which I have been reading, and in conversation with, for years. And third, John Caputo's tireless scholarly work on what Derrida means for a radical hermeneutic.

But, returning to Derrida's biography, there are a few angles I want to draw on. The first is an unusual recognition by an intellectual that biography counts. He was one of the few intellectuals who left behind many fragments of auto-biography or memoir, including two films, books such as 'Circumfession', *The Post Card*, *Veil*, *Memoirs of the Blind* and *Counterpath*, along with many interviews (e.g. *The Last Interview*, cited above). Importantly, he himself argued that 'you must put philosophers' biographies back in the picture and the commitments, particularly the political commitments' (cited in Peeters, 2013, p. 1). So, this brief biographical sketch counts. It is not just background fluff. Read Derrida asking what his commitments were. Also, know that this is a sketch, and like any biography I choose what to presence and absence – in some ways it is as much fiction as truth. *So read him yourself* (imagine that as capitalised, as me shouting, 'read him yourself').

The second angle, and perhaps the most significant, is that he often was, and felt to be, an outsider. Shaped as both an Algerian-born Jew, but living most of his life in France; and also an outsider to the Academy who was never quite accepted by the gate-keepers of orthodoxy, he lived with a profound sense of exclusion. This embodied experience of often feeling like the outsider was crucial in his theorising of what he called alterity, or the 'other' – hence that principle of 'vigilance for the other'. The 'other' is an important element to his deconstructive episteme and how his philosophical sensibility played out in many disciplines and fields of practice – from law to architecture. Deconstruction as a vigilance to the 'other', and deconstruction is being open to the disruption of the 'other'.

Derrida was born into a Jewish family in July 1930, in Algeria. As per his experiencing of being the 'other' he, along with many Jewish children, was expelled from school around the age of 12 as a result of French Algeria's newly passed anti-Semitic laws restricting the number of Jewish children allowed in its schools. Derrida himself described this expulsion as 'one of the earthquakes in his life' (Peeters, 2013, p. 19). This expulsion lasted two years, which severely disrupted his schooling, and also led to many years of enjoying an easy life of football, basketball and playing around at the beach.

At the time of expulsion Derrida was the top student at his academy, yet here he was, thrown, along with his family, into turmoil. Derrida's family also lost its citizenship after five generations of living in France, and it is clear that from here on, Derrida began to think of himself as an outsider.

One of the upshots of this experience, a key third angle for this biographical sketch, was also a commitment against communitarianism. I am conscious, as a community development scholar, that he was very ambivalent about the idea of 'community', living with the spectral haunting of the *dangers of community*. He explicitly shared how 'I don't much like the word community. I am not sure I even like the thing' (Derrida's lectures, in Caputo, 1997, p. 107). Community as unity or uniformity smelled of danger for Derrida, which makes sense in the context of his biographical experiences of anti-Semitism. Alternatively, he talked of 'community as hospitality' always arguing for an opening of the social, never allowing it to be closed (as it often does in the name of community) (ibid., pp. 109ff). Linking the third biographical angle to the second, he was for a community always open to the 'other'.

As an adolescent Derrida took an interest in both literature and philosophy, particularly falling in love with the literature of Andre Gide and Albert Camus, but then also the literature-philosophy of Jean-Paul Sartre. His curiosity stirred, Derrida began reading the works of German philosopher Friedrich Nietzsche and French philosophers such as Jean Jacques Rousseau.

He turned to academia and earned admittance to France's most prestigious college, the École Normale Supérieure in Paris. While there he met Marguerite Aucouturier, who was studying to become a psychoanalyst. With some time together living in the USA, they married there in 1957 and eventually had two sons. Derrida earned his philosophy degree in 1956 and around 1960 he began teaching philosophy and logic at the Collège de Sorbonne in France. By 1965 he was teaching at the École Normale Supérieure and contributing to many journals, among them the influential leftist magazine *Tel Quel*.

Derrida upended the intellectual community in the 1960s with deconstruction, which turned much philosophy on its head, prodding for the multiplicity within all text – as opposed to unity. This deconstructive episteme provoked controversy as it spread through college campuses in the 1960s, 70s and 80s, earning Derrida both reverence and contempt for the remainder of his life.

In 1966 Derrida introduced his episteme to the United States during a symposium at Johns Hopkins University. He gained more attention the following year when he published three groundbreaking works, *Writing and Difference* (1967), *Speech and Phenomena* (1967) and *Of Grammatology* (1967). Their publication touched off animated debates in intellectual circles around the globe, and served to further Derrida's argument that a text can never have a single, authoritative meaning in and of itself.

Over the next decades Derrida's work deepened and expanded. He mixed and mused with many of the 'greats' including Pierre Bourdieu, Michel Foucault, Emmanuel Levinas (author of *The Trace of the Other* (1986), which clearly influenced Derrida profoundly), Hélène Cixous (who was to become a close friend), Jean Genet, and so many more.

Of importance for this chapter, 1989 represented a key turning point in Derrida's career, signalled with a lecture he gave in Greenwich Village, New York at the Cardoza Law School – a well-known school of radical legal theory, of which most graduates become defenders of the poor against the rich (Caputo, 2018, p. 191). This lecture represented a turn toward more practical things – ethics, justice, politics – which occupied him for the last 20 years of his life. You could more or less say that he was taking his radical deconstructionist episteme into the practical and political realm of public life. From here on he published work on issues as wide as the law and justice, memory work, refugees and hospitality, the death penalty, and so much more.

Three threads of thought crucial for social work

Following the biographical sketch, I foreground three key threads, all equally important, all interlinked, all briefly mentioned already, but needing expansion as we consider the implications for a social work counter-pedagogy 'yet-to-come'. These include: deconstruction as 'opening up' institutions; the 'passion of not knowing' – on alterity, the 'other' and hospitality; and the hauntology of justice, the imperative to activism.

Deconstruction as 'opening up' texts, programmes and institutions

As already stated, deconstruction sits at the heart of Derrida's contribution to philosophy with its diffused influence in so many other fields and disciplines. Often derided, mostly misunderstood, deconstruction is a disruptive episteme that threads its way through all Derrida's work. Building on the introductory description, as per Heidegger and *destruction*, 'in a nutshell', deconstruction is an episteme – a way of reading, a way of viewing, or being in the world, a practice, a sensibility – that insists, or summons the reader/practitioner to be disrupted or to disrupt. In using the word disruption, I am not necessarily meaning being a trouble-maker, albeit deconstruction is often a pre-cursor for trouble – but it is to move into a mode of a kind of interpreting writing, or ideas, or programmes (that of the university or social work and so on) that does not settle for the familiar or easy.

As mentioned earlier, one of Derrida's key texts is the seminal *Of Grammatology*. Written earlier in his career it sets out what might be understood as his rules of reading or interpreting. The rules are those of at least two readings, as already briefly explained. While the first reading looks for the Truth – the essence of what an author was trying to say – and again thinking of Gadamer's famous work on hermeneutics *Truth and Method*, this is a reaching for the whole, the essence, and then a fusion, a dialogue, a dialectic between what the author is intending and the reader is experiencing – the second deconstructive reading instead seeks out the contradictions, the tensions, the multiplicity, within the reading, along with the affirmation. This reading recognises there is no whole (as Gadamer argued), but there are multiple centres, many truths, many marginal possibilities. In contrast to Gadamer's fusion this Derridean reading looks for the fissures, the cracks.

You can imagine how many in the Academy (and many others) were rather upset, angry, fearful even. Imagine an episteme that supports many readings, multiple possibilities – that legitimises a search not for *the Truth* of a text, but *the multiple truths*.

Derrida did go further, more or less arguing that there is a third interpretation, somewhere between the two – that in fact any real reading – as encounter, as summons, something alive – requires the interplay of the minimal two readings. Without this interplay something deadens, or again using the language of Wittgenstein, ossifies.

Part of this alive summons is to move beyond deadening binaries, which means, for Derrida, inhabiting binaries in a nuanced different way. For Derrida, living much of his life during an era where you had to be either for-or-against Marx, the deconstructive episteme reached beyond the binary, offering a way to re-imagine a hauntology of Marx. In previous work I have applied this idea to the social, suggesting the concept of 'deconstructive movements' (Westoby and Dowling, 2013, p. 16). The concept of deconstructive movements provides an opportunity to remain open to complexity, refusing to practise the tyranny of simplifying 'readings' of a text or a social phenomenon (in much the same way that Derrida was refusing to simplify reading a text). The notion of deconstructive movement also invites pulling apart or destabilising simplistic ways of thinking about social work practice and pedagogy. For example, the splitting of theory and practice, human and environment, local and global, mind and body, worker and service user, the structural and the personal.

Derrida's deconstructive episteme suggests that not only are phenomena often reduced to such simplistic binaries, but often within those binaries there is an explicit, or usually implicit, hierarchy. In referring to a couple of the binaries mentioned above, and notwithstanding significant progress in re-imagining practice, many social work practitioners would prioritise practice over theory, mind over body, local above global, and the human as more important than the environment. Instead, Derrida's deconstruction insists on disruption of such hierarchies and a re-constitution of new ways of thinking, such as embodied intelligence (collapsing the mind–body dualism) or praxis (collapsing the practice–theory dualism). The implication of collapsing such binaries requires much more consideration in the field of social work practice and pedagogy. For example, binary thinking could be replaced by logics of dialogue, as per Buber's work (Buber, 1947), or logics of dialectic (see Freire, 1970; Sennett, 2012), or even the logics of polarity (Kaplan, 2002). Finally, in avoiding any simple rejection of opposites, for Derrida, instead there is a play with what he referred to as spectrality, demonstrating how one 'opposite' opens up the 'other', and how each bifurcates endlessly – and why the trace, for Derrida, is a way of not reversing the binaries but juxtaposing or occupying terms differently.

The 'passion of not knowing': on alterity, the 'other' and hospitality

To not settle is crucial. Deconstruction as an episteme, an attitude, a sensibility, a practice, also feeds what is important within Derridean thinking – what Caputo calls the 'passion of not knowing' (Caputo, 1997, p. 338). Modernist thinking loves to understand and explain, and then to provide the final word and sure solution – again, that Truth that Derrida talked about in more traditional hermeneutics, and which many are willing to settle for within institutional life. Yet, in contrast, Derrida's hermeneutics and deconstructive episteme called for the constant re-reading of text, or re-constitution of programmes and institutions, driven by a 'passion of not knowing'.

A key lens to enable this constant re-reading and re-constituting – mobilised by a passion of not knowing – is the lens of alterity, or the 'other'.

Deconstruction then, in practice, is to maintain the lens of being open to alterity – always reaching for the 'other' which disrupts our taken-for-granted. It is to encounter the 'other' within a text, or a programme or institution, including, for this chapter, the institution of social work.

As already mentioned, hospitality toward the 'other' is also his definition of community. He argued in his work on refugees and asylum seekers that there is a paradigmatic struggle occurring within the idea of community – based on those for hospitality, and those *against* welcoming the 'other' (Derrida, 2001). Embedded within the idea of hospitality is a stance that constantly welcomes the stranger. If such an idea of hospitality is combined with the passion of not knowing, then the only possible trajectory for social work practice and pedagogy is both more dialogue, opening up space for possibility, imagination, critical thinking and freedom to ask any question; and a constant endeavour to 'open' community up to those who have historically been excluded.

Crucially, this 'passion of not knowing', mobilised by a sensitivity to alterity is also a knowing that includes blindness and tears. Most clearly articulated in *Memoirs of the Blind*, Derrida talks of the 'blindness of tears' (Derrida, 1993), in which he disrupts the binary of knowing/sight and ignorance/blindness. Instead, the moment of really seeing also requires the seer to be blinded by tears – and the point he is making is that seeing and knowledge is not simply a function of reason, but *also of passion*. In this, the alterity of blindness (at the moment of tears we usually cannot see), usually understood as not-seeing, is returned to a central place in Derrida's calling for a knowing that beings head, heart and soul together (Harris, 2002, p. 77). Here is an invitation in social work practice and pedagogy to integrate theory (ideas), practice (the doing with an idea of our intention) with passion, or emotion. Derrida is suggesting this integration is a place of real seeing, or real knowing, one that again displaces the implicit binary of thinking versus feeling.

Peter Westoby

The hauntology of justice, the imperative to activism

Importantly, Derrida argues that everything is open to deconstruction *except justice*. In fact, he argued deconstruction is justice (Caputo, 2018, p. 201). Many sceptics of Derrida's philosophy thought deconstruction was a form of anarchy – anything goes – yet later in his life Derrida clarified his thinking and writing, making the case that deconstruction is justice. In this case he argued that all 'things' are deconstructable – e.g. the law, ethics, professional practices – *but that justice is not a thing*. Justice instead is 'an appeal', an imperative – 'it is like a ghost' (ibid., p. 203). In this sense, as an example, the law is a thing as a historical construction, as is a social work programme and pedagogy. These 'things' can always be deconstructed, which is a good thing, and is the basis for constant reform. But, and here is the crux of it for Derrida, we reform the law, social work and the university, and all things in the light of the call, imperative, or summons to justice – this undeconstructable haunting presence. Together, the deconstructability of social work and the undeconstructability of justice go hand in hand to make up deconstruction (ibid., p. 205). The imperative of justice puts pressure on social work to be in constant reform.

Weaving this thread with the previous one, for Derrida, deeply indebted to Levinas, this presence of justice is also a relation to the presence of the 'other'. Again, justice not as a thing, but a living spectral, relational presence.

Derrida alluded to this idea of hauntology in the title of his book *Spectres of Marx* (Derrida, 1994, p. 10). Justice is spectral, always haunting, ghost like, never quite present, but always inviting presence. From a hermeneutical, or interpretive perspective, Derrida is asking people always to interpret the law while reaching for justice, or 'under the call of justice' (Caputo, 2018, p. 197). He is trying to disrupt the tendency for people in the legal field to run on auto-pilot, assuming the law, or their orthodox interpretations of law, equate with justice. In *Spectres of Marx* he explicitly gives some reference points for this haunting justice:

> No justice ... seems possible or thinkable without the principle of some *responsibility*, beyond all living present, before the ghosts of those who are not yet born or who are already dead, be they victims of war, political or other kinds of violence, nationalist, racist, colonialist, sexist, or other kinds of exterminations, victims of the oppressions of capitalist imperialism or any of the forms of totalitarianism.
>
> *(Derrida, 1994, p. xix)*

The imperative is to do justice then, and parallel to the law, to reconstruct social work as an activist project foremost. This implies not getting stuck in familiar tropes and arguments, undone by meaningless binaries that distract from the serious work of responsibility toward those who are oppressed and marginalised.

Yes, social work is a professional project – yes, it increasingly reaches to a practice grounded in evidence – that is, with claims to be scientific, yet the relevance of Derrida's episteme is an insistence that all such endeavours be trumped by social work as an activist project responding to the call to justice. Any calls for efficiency, or economic imperatives, or profit-making must be haunted by the call to justice. Any deep mythologies that mask our ability to penetrate any damaging logics of social work need to be seen clearly. This implies a paradigmatic shit-fight, one that unmasks the university as an institution being re-shaped for profitable purposes; and potentially unmasks social work as a programme of state control of the marginals and 'wasted lives' (Bauman, 2003), or social work as a misplaced new enterprise of individual economic empowerment.

Contributing to a social work pedagogy

Having considered three key threads of Derrida's work, and their relevance to social work, I now suggest a way forward for a social work *counter-pedagogy* – one foregrounding an ethic of learning, a recognition of the 'event' of learning, and an obligation to read and listen in a particular way.

An ethics of learning

Applying Derrida's episteme to social work pedagogy specifically, I first foreground what I call a deconstructive ethics of learning. Referring to the traces of thought articulated above, I am reaching for parallels in the space of social work pedagogy. In the same way that Derrida's deconstruction is a way of unsettling those of the legal profession, never equating law with justice, so deconstruction disrupts any settling of the social work profession, and those who educate social workers. Social work learning programmes can easily lead to auto-pilot learning, unable to disrupt the student's world-view, hardly ever unlocking a 'passion of not knowing', lacking a way of bringing forth learning of *heart and head* (those tears that accompany real seeing), and rarely transforming the social work student into an activist.

Derrida's philosophical imperative is to always keep programmes and institutions 'open'. He asks the question, how open is social work and the accompanying pedagogy to being re-radicalised? He does not want learning programmes or institutions to ossify, to become satisfied in a set pedagogy, which ultimately lead to them decaying. He is trying to both honour the traditions of the past in any institution yet keep them open to the new.

Social work, as an institutional and programme, yet ethical project in and of itself, recognises the spectral haunting calls of its traditions – those 'originary concepts'. For example, social justice, democracy and equity – and yet reaches into the new, being open to new ethical calls – for example, toward the non-human world, and new kinds of collective work, or being 'for the commons' in a world being commodified and enclosed by corporations. At the same time, social work educators, like practitioners, in their everyday practice, doing ethics work (Banks, 2019), cannot afford to sit back in the comforts of any code, rules of conduct, or programmes.

However, an ethics of learning is also a call to justice. This must be clear to the reader by now. A Derridean take on an ethics of learning insists on disrupting the institution of social work and the university – and this is particularly true in an era of the university as enterprise, or the neoliberal university (Bottrell and Manathunga, 2018). Derrida is *against* the neoliberal university and any attempts to reconstruct educational pedagogy in its own image (a neoliberally oriented curriculum). Derrida is for a university that is constantly open, disrupted by a justice that is responsive to the 'other', and therefore must be open, or hospitable to the 'other'. It is a university for the commons, open to those who want a world open to others.

Responding to the summons of the learning moment

While Derrida's deconstruction insists on renewing social work as an activist project, it also invites a counter-pedagogy that is alive to the singular moment. For Derrida, the idea of event is crucial. As Caputo summaries, 'When an event happens in education, it may be that no one knows it' (Caputo, 2018, p. 238). Trying to measure this invisible process – that no one knows – is more or less impossible. Ultimately no one knows when the teaching event, the learning moment really arrives. It is a singular moment, determined by a confluence of curiosity, real critical reading and listening, and so on. Therefore, any attempts to evaluate education or design pedagogy by measurable outcomes – often linked to endless testing or assessment – is a distortion of the event, and as Caputo reminds us, 'a disaster for education' (ibid.). For Derrida, the event is what we must be open to, recognising the summons of unknowing (un-doing ignorance) and new knowing.

Drawing on Derrida's approach, I offer these two *aporias* (points of difficulty or undecidability) for social work educators reaching for an ethical counter-pedagogy sensitive to the 'event'. First is 'the suspension of the rule'. Derrida argues 'each case is other, each decision is different and requires an absolute unique interpretation' (Derrida, 2002, p. 252). In educational practice this means not abolishing a way of teaching, a clear pedagogy, but acknowledging that any approach has to be held lightly, perhaps in 'mid-air', such that the educator-practitioner can see the singularity of the teaching situation. The point being, every teaching moment or situation is singular, requiring its own unique and open response – that alterity we have talked of. To walk into a classroom or lecture room is to walk into a singular space requiring an alive responsivity to the moment, the people, the context – but, as per Derrida's hospitality or alterity, it is to respond to the summons of the 'other' that is always present. Alluding to George Lakey's work on the mainstream and the margins (Lakey, 2010) – which are always present in any teaching moment – Derrida insists on allowing the margins, as other, to become visible, disrupting the mainstream's lens (including the educators). It is to bring alterity into the centre of a counter-pedagogy.

The second *aporia* is 'the undecidable', which entails recognising that any approaches can conflict with one another. True care of the singular educational moment requires recognising sometimes following the rule of the vocation with its call to justice rather than the code of any pedagogical commitment. You could say that for Derrida justice always trumps pedagogy.

The obligation to listen (and read) critically in a particular way

If the first point above is aimed at social work educators and the university institution as a whole, and the second point is aimed at the social work educator-in-the-moment of teaching, this third point is aimed at the reader. Recognising that a social work counter-pedagogy-to-come will need readers and reading, I argue that a Derridean contribution obliges the reader to listen (and read) critically *in a particular way*. This particular kind of listening (to text and teacher) and reading (of text) recognises that a deconstructive hermeneutic always is an intervention, an interruption, a disruption – an 'encounter' summonsing action. Again, this is to contrast with a more traditional Gadamer-inspired hermeneutic that would invite a way of reading and listening with the intention of a fusion of horizons (dialogue) between the author's intent and the reader's world. Gadamer yearns for dialogue between the two. Derrida comes with a sword – he does not want dialogue – he wants disruption. He wants the reader to have an encounter with text, and to then be summonsed.

'Summonsed to what?' we might ask. This is unanswerable because it is singular, but again the Derridean *aporias* would include an opening to the 'other'. It would be to have the reader's world disrupted by an encounter with a profoundly different perspective. Rather than 'eating the other' (hooks, 1992), as bell hooks put it when thinking of how mainstream culture consumes black African-American culture, it could be to 'apprentice oneself to the other' (Bywater, 2005, p. 305).

The *aporias* also imply a disruption that leads to the reader re-constituting themselves as a social work activist. To be a professional social worker is to engage in the becoming process – for it also implies a yes, a second yes and a third yes – that constant inauguration to becoming an activist when the hegemonic *habitus* is toward a settled, familiar, deadening conservatism.

In conclusion

In moving toward a conclusion, I riff off the earlier words of Derrida about justice, and quote Verne Harris, given in a 2013 lecture *Antonyms of our Remembering*, to archivists:

> Friends, we are called by the ghosts of the living, of those not yet born, and those already dead. They call us to take responsibility before them. In front of them. Seeing them, re-specting them. They call us to take responsibility for making a just society. We honour the ghosts, we offer them hospitality, we promise them peace, by taking responsibility for making a just society. This is a calling to all human beings. But is, in my view, the calling to we who work with archive.
>
> *(cited in Harris, 2014, p. 4)*

And of course, I add, 'the calling to we who work with social work, and with the university'. The call is to do justice to the ghosts of those gone, those still with us, yet marginal and invisible, rendered as other, and those ghosts yet-to-come – the future generations. Social work has a role to play, and a counter-pedagogy for teaching social work in the 'university of tomorrow' is crucial. Without a radical re-constituting of pedagogy – a deconstructive task – social work ossifies into a programme that is no longer haunted by justice, is no longer mobilised by the 'passion of not knowing' and is no longer vigilant toward the 'other'. In contrast, this chapter offers a way forward for a social work counter-pedagogy, one foregrounding an ethic of learning, a recognition of the 'event' of learning, and an obligation to read and listen in a particular way.

References

Banks, S. (2019). 'Ethics, Equity and Community Development: Mapping the Terrain', In Banks, S. & Westoby, P. (eds). *Ethics, Equity and Community Development*. Bristol: Policy Press, pp. 3–36.
Bauman, Z. (2003). *Wasted Lives: Modernity and Its Outcasts*. Cambridge: Polity Press.
Bottrell, D & Manathunga, C. (eds). (2018). *Resisting Neoliberalism in Higher Education Volume I: Seeing through the Cracks*. Palgrave Critical University Studies series.
Buber, M. (1947). *Between Man and Man*. London and New York: Routledge & Kegan Paul.
Bywater, B. (2005). 'Goethe: A Science Which Does Not Eat the Other', in *Janus Head*, 8(1). pp. 291–310.
Caputo, J. (1997). *Deconstruction in a Nutshell: A Conversation with Jacques Derrida*. New York: Fordham University Press.
Caputo, J. (2018). *Hermeneutics: Facts and Interpretation in the Age of Information*. UK: Pelican Books.
Derrida, J. (1967a). *Writing and Difference*. Paris and France: Editions du Seuil.
Derrida, J. (1967b). *Of Grammatology*. Paris and France: Les Editions de Minuit.
Derrida, J. (1967c). *Speech and Phenomena*. Paris and France: Presses Universitaires de France.
Derrida, J. (1993). *Memoirs of the Blind: The Self-Portrait and Other Ruins*. Chicago: University of Chicago Press.
Derrida, J. (1994). *Spectres of Marx*. London and New York: Routledge.
Derrida, J. (2001). *Cosmopolitanism and Forgiveness*. London and New York: Routledge.
Derrida, J. (2002). *Negotiations: Interventions and Interviews: 1971-2001*. USA: Stanford University Press.
Derrida, J. (2005). *Rogues*. USA: Stanford University Press.
Derrida, J. (2007). *Learning to Live Finally: The Last Interview*. New Jersey: Melville House Publishing.
Freire, P. (1970). *Pedagogy of the Oppressed*. London: Penguin Books.
Harris, V. (2002). 'A Shaft of Darkness: Derrida in The Archive', in Hamilton, C, Harris, V., Pickover, M., Reid, G. & Saleh, R. (Eds.). *Refiguring the Archive*. Cape Town: David Philip, pp. 61–82.
Harris, V. (2014). 'Antonyms of Our Remembering', in *Archival Science*, 14, pp. 3–4.
hooks, bell (1992). 'Eating the Other', in *Black Looks: Race and Representation*. Boston: South End Press, pp. 21–39.

Jullien, F. (2016). *The Philosophy of Living*. London: Seagull Books.
Kaplan, A. (2002). *Development Practitioners and Social Process: Artists of the Invisible*. Chicago and London: Pluto Press.
Lakey, G. (2010). *Facilitating Group Learning: Strategies for Success with Diverse Learners*. San Francisco: Jossey-Bass.
Levinas, E. (1986). 'The Trace of the Other', In Taylor, M (Ed.). *Deconstruction in Context*. Chicago: University of Chicago Press, pp. 345–359.
Peeters, B. (2013). *Derrida: A Biography*. Cambridge: Polity Press.
Sennett, R. (2012). *Together: the Rituals, Pleasures and Politics of Cooperation*. London: Allan Lane/Penguin Books.
Smith, J. (2005). *Jacques Derrida: Live Theory*. New York and London: Continuum.
Westoby, P. & Dowling, G. (2013). *Theory and Practice of Dialogical Community Development: International Perspectives*. New York and London: Routledge.

14
From privileged irresponsibility to shared responsibility for social injustice
The contributions of Joan Tronto and Iris Marion Young to critical pedagogies of privilege

Bob Pease

DEAKIN UNIVERSITY, VICTORIA, AUSTRALIA

Introduction

For some years now, I have been involved in teaching members of privileged groups about their/our unearned advantages. While much of this work has taken place within social work education, I have also undertaken workshops with men outside of social work and outside of the academy to encourage them to acknowledge their male privilege within gendered relations of power. The pedagogical challenge in working with members of privileged groups on issues of social injustice is to overcome obstacles that prevent them from seeing how they are implicated in social practices that contribute to social inequality. In undertaking this work, I acknowledge my own privilege as a white male academic who is located in the West.

Increasingly, critical social workers recognise that they must address privilege as well as oppression in their work, as well as acknowledge their own structural positioning in the systems that oppress the people they work with. In this chapter, I outline how the ideas of Joan Tronto and Iris Marion Young provide important insights into pedagogical strategies for naming and addressing privilege and complicity in the social practices that produce social injustice.

Naming oppressive social practices

I have previously identified social practices as habitual activities that normalise privilege and oppression (Pease 2010). Social practices are practices governed by principles and rules that frame what we say and do. They enable us to make sense of our lives. So in this context, oppressive actions by individuals are legitimated by these wider social practices. The issue of responsibility for oppressive acts, then, is not just in relation to individual actions but also in relation to the practices that shape them (O'Connor 2002). In this view, responsibility moves beyond the individual to collective and shared responsibility (May 1993) or what Card (2002) calls 'relational responsibility' where the wider community of individuals need to address their support for those practices.

The question arises, however, as to how conscious individuals are of supporting oppressive social practices. O'Connor (2002) discusses how some oppressive attitudes and actions are habituated to the extent that individuals are not aware of holding or expressing them. If that is so, the question is raised about the extent to which individuals can be held responsible and culpable for them.

Calhoun (1989) observes that social acceptance of oppressive practices often prevents individuals being aware of the harmful consequences of these practices. So the issue is how much responsibility individuals have to see through these socially constructed determinants that normalise oppressive social practices. If individuals are not responsible than we cannot defend our use of moral reproach to challenge such practices.

Individuals will need to acknowledge their responsibility for oppression that occurs at the level of social practice if they are going to be able to listen to moral reproach for their actions. In this chapter I argue Joan Tronto and Iris Marion Young contribute to critical pedagogies that assist individuals to recognise these practices and the role they play in reproducing oppressive structures.

Joan Tronto and the critical ethics of care

Joan Tronto is an Anglo-American Professor of Political Science at the University of Minnesota. Her research traverses the fields of political theory, gender and ethics of care with a particular focus on theoretical explorations about the nature of care. Her two most important single-authored books are *Moral Boundaries: A Political Argument for an Ethic of Care* (1993) and *Caring Democracy: Markets, Equality and Justice* (2013).

Tronto's work is located within an international body of scholarship concerned with the moral implications of care (Williams 2001; Robinson 2010; Hankivsky 2014; Barnes et al. 2015). Tronto (1995) argues that care has the potential to interrogate relationships of power to reveal how current institutional arrangements support inequality and injustice. Within this context, she has advanced a feminist democratic ethic of care, whereby caring becomes a central principle for democracies (Tronto 2013). Her work has addressed the unequal burden of care across gender, class and race lines and it has interrogated the ways in which some people are able to neglect their caring responsibilities. In her view, the more that people become aware of their interconnectedness with other people, the more they will become responsible. To care well, in Tronto's view, requires an understanding of care as relational.

A key focus of Tronto's work is on the gendered basis of caring and the mechanisms by which men absent themselves from their caring responsibilities. They do so in part through framing their role as protectors of women and through their production roles in the economy; a protection pass out and a production pass out, respectively. Men use their protective and productive roles to exclude themselves from the daily activities of caring for others. I have used Tronto's work to illustrate the ways in which gender norms are reproduced or transformed through caring practices and to explore the ways in which men's caring practices create new forms of masculinities and/or reproduce traditional forms (Pease 2018a).

In this chapter I take some of Tronto's ideas about responsibility for caring and consider what they mean for critical pedagogies in social work education and social activist workshops. I argue that Tronto's notion of privileged irresponsibility, in particular, can assist people in privileged groups to see how their inactivity on issues of social justice makes them complicit in the reproduction of that injustice. Such a notion also enables educators to encourage students and workshop participants to see beyond neoliberal conceptions of personal responsibility which ignore the social context and social relations within which individuals are embedded (Zembylas et al. 2014).

Tronto's concept of privileged irresponsibility

Tronto (2013) uses the notion of privileged irresponsibility to describe the process by which those who receive care fail to acknowledge their dependence on the care provided by others. As such, members of dominant groups argue that they do not need to concern themselves with hands-on caring activities. By ignoring their dependence on others, those in privileged groups are able to reproduce their privilege. Zembylas et al. (2014) note the origins of the term in a little-known paper titled 'Chilly Racists', presented at the American Political Science Association Conference in 1990. Focusing on racism, Tronto used the term to describe the ways in which white people ignored the exercise of their power to reproduce their white privilege. Privileged irresponsibility is closely connected to hegemonic masculinity and the power of dominant groups of men to exclude themselves, not only from caring responsibilities, as Tronto (2013) notes, but also from wider engagements in social relations of power.

I have published elsewhere about how members of privileged groups fail to acknowledge their privileges and seek ways to avoid taking responsibility for the consequences of their privileges for others (Pease 2010). However, at that time of writing I was unaware of Tronto's work on privileged irresponsibility and its usefulness in elucidating the processes of denial and ignorance.

Tronto (2013) argues that ignorance is one of the main ways in which people avoid responsibility. If you do not know about a problem, you can absolve yourself from taking action to address it. This ignorance is sustained by broader social, political and cultural processes that obscure the workings of power. Tronto is concerned with the conditions under which people come to see and understand their responsibilities for others.

Tronto suggests that one way of understanding the complicity of members of privileged groups with normative and exploitative practices is through the scholarship on epistemologies of ignorance (Sullivan & Tuana 2007). Members of privileged groups, even when they have good intentions, can reproduce social inequalities through various forms of ignorance. The way in which epistemologies of ignorance operate is that members of privileged groups generally do not know the extent to which they do not know.

Thus it can be argued that there is an epistemology of ignorance in relation to structural forms of privilege. Such ignorance is systemically reproduced through the attempts by some members of privileged groups to deflect attention away from the social processes that produce privilege. Members of privileged groups have an interest in staying ignorant because it allows them to avoid facing their moral complicity in the reproduction of social inequality (Applebaum 2013).

I believe that Tronto's concept of privileged irresponsibility can be used to analyse how privileged groups reproduce their own privilege. Although Tronto is primarily concerned with how the notion of privileged irresponsibility functions in relation to care and caring responsibilities, I find the concept very useful in describing more generally how privileged groups fail to acknowledge their responsibilities. For example, I recently presented a paper titled 'Privileged Irresponsibility and Global Warming' to an audience predominantly comprised of emergency services workers at a Diversity in Disaster Conference in Melbourne (Pease 2018b), where I outlined how the concept of privileged irresponsibility could be utilised to interrogate climate debt and corporate environmental crime. The concept was useful in illuminating how conservative white corporate men enacted ecologically destructive practices and ignored their responsibility to address them. I have received numerous requests for copies of the paper and in the conference evaluation, sixty per cent of conference participants said it was the most interesting and provocative paper presented at the conference. I mention this not to exaggerate the importance of my own work but to illustrate the value of Toronto's concept of privileged irresponsibility in elucidating the nature of privilege.

The challenge that is not fully addressed by Tronto is how to overcome privileged irresponsibility. This is where I believe Iris Marion Young's work is of immense value.

Iris Marion Young and responsibility for justice

Iris Marion Young, who died in 2006, was an Anglo-American feminist political theorist who focused on the nature of justice and difference. She was the author of twelve key books concerned with justice, difference, oppression, intersectionality, structural injustice and social responsibility. One of her contributions was her model of the 'five faces of oppression' (Young 1990) where she articulated five types of oppression: exploitation, marginalisation, powerlessness, cultural domination and violence. In her view, these five dimensions of oppression each needed to be addressed to achieve a socially just world. However, the main text that I draw upon in this chapter is her posthumously published *Responsibility for Justice* published in 2011, five years after her death. The main focus of her book is on how to understand responsibility for structural inequality.

Young (2011) identifies the limitations of what she calls the liability model of responsibility whereby specific individuals are held to be legally or morally responsible for isolated instances of wrongdoing. The most common understanding of responsibility is that based on the assumption that society consists of individuals who are unconnected to their historical and social contexts. In this view, perpetrators of racism, or violence against women or other abusive practices, are prejudiced and ignorant individuals. The approach focuses on the mind of the individual perpetrator. Applebaum (2006) argues that we need to develop new forms of responsibility that are less focused on the acts of individual perpetrators and more able to identify the contribution that members of privileged groups make to the structural patterns of privilege and oppression.

Boyd (2004) raises the question of whether the conception of the subject that underlies the notion of the liberal individual who has moral responsibility for individual actions obscures systemic oppression and protects members of privileged groups because of the focus on individual intention. In the liberal conception, the individual is isolated from others, exercises rational choice and is able to transcend structural constraints in the exercise of agency.

The model of responsibility that is based on the premise of the liberal individual conceals the complicity of members of privileged groups in the perpetuation of privilege and oppression (Boyd 2004). There is a need to challenge this concept of the liberal individual if people are to be encouraged to recognise their complicity. This means that it is important to focus less on individual responsibility and more on collective responsibility to challenge the structural dimensions of inequality. This is where Young's work is important in critical pedagogies of privilege.

I have previously criticised men's behaviour change programs for their premise that individual men are solely responsible for the violence they perpetrate and that they can change their attitudes and behaviour (Pease 2004/2005). Although I was unfamiliar with Young's work on shared responsibility at the time, drawing upon Hearn (1998), I argued that in such programs, the violent man was portrayed as 'a rational free actor' who engaged in violence in a calculated and utilitarian way. I argued that such programs mystified men's power and obscured the extent to which men's violence was embedded in the structures of patriarchal society. Young's identification of the limitations of the liability model of responsibility provides a valuable way of naming this individualising of responsibility. For in Young's view, the liability model is unable to address structural forms of injustice.

Young argues that structural injustice is produced by large numbers of people through their adherence to normative rules and practices. It is one's position within social structures that implicates one in injustice. This is because people are connected to the harm that is caused by these structures. If we are socially connected to the harm, through our participation in those structures, we have an obligation to challenge the injustice. In Young's view, even if one is innocent of directly perpetrating an injustice, if they are connected to processes that facilitate the injustice, they still bear some responsibility. Consequently, we all have an obligation to work with others to change the structural processes that produce the unjust outcomes.

Young's social connection model of responsibility

To address responsibility for injustice, Young develops a model of shared responsibility that includes: locating people in terms of their capacity to influence the social injustice, their privilege and the benefits they receive from the injustice, and the interest people have in changing the injustice. The focus of Young's work is on encouraging individuals to take action against structural injustices that they are connected to.

For Young, political responsibility can only be enacted collectively. However, McKeown (2014), rightly in my view, notes that before collective action can be undertaken, individuals must learn about their own complicity in social injustice and convince other members of the privileged group that they share this responsibility.

To confront our responsibility for structural injustice, we must at first acknowledge how we are implicated in the processes that produce it (Schiff 2008). However, it is difficult to know how we are implicated when the wider context obscures these processes. Young draws upon Bourdieu's (1977) notion of 'habitus' to describe how members of privileged groups reproduce the behaviours that are connected to their social position. It is through the un-reflexive and often unconscious actions of individuals that are routinised and habitual that structural inequalities are reproduced (McKeown 2014).

Young identifies a number of strategies that people use to avoid their responsibility to address these injustices: reifying social processes, denying that they are connected to the injustice, claiming that we are only responsible for those in our immediate circle, and arguing that addressing social injustice is the work of others.

Young notes that structural injustices not only produce victims, but also those who benefit from the injustices and who are consequently privileged by them. Payson (2009) makes the point that because one was born into systems of privilege and oppression, does not mean that one has no responsibility to challenge them. The structures of inequality are not self-perpetuating. They are rather reproduced by individual participants, especially those who are members of privileged groups. The burden of responsibility to promote social justice should fall more heavily on those who benefit most from their complicity than on those who are non-beneficiaries (Young 2011).

Thus, those who benefit from privilege have more responsibility to challenge the structures that produce this privilege. However, they have less interest in doing so, compared to the victims of injustice (Langlois 2014). Those with privilege will lose some of their privileges. McKeown (2014) says that they should nevertheless take action in the name of social justice. Whereas, Brazzell (2015) suggests that they will need to see how their own quality of life and relationships are damaged by an oppressive society if they are to challenge structural injustice. I have addressed this issue of motivation of privileged group members to challenge social injustice elsewhere (Pease 2002). I have also emphasised that in undertaking this work, members of privileged groups should develop relationships of accountability to those who are oppressed (Pease 2017).

I believe that Young's social connection model of responsibility can be a valuable way of challenging privileged irresponsibility named by Tronto. Hölscher et al. (2014), for example, have used Young's social connection model of responsibility to address the ways in which social workers are implicated in social injustices associated with South Africa's refugee receiving program. I have used Young's model to argue that men have a responsibility to get involved in challenging men's violence against women because they are causally embedded in processes that produce such violence (Pease 2015). Parekh (2011) further argues that moving beyond the liability model of responsibility enables us to assign responsibility to states for creating some of the injustices that inform men's violence against women.

Contributions of Tronto and Young toward a pedagogy of the privileged

Much of critical pedagogy has focused on the engagement of those who are oppressed and marginalised. There has been less attention given to interrogating the privileged positioning of members of dominant groups. While social change should be driven by the oppressed, the responses to members of dominant groups to the challenges to their privilege will either hinder or support liberation movements from below. This is the basis for the case to critically engage members of dominant groups in reflecting upon their practices that perpetuate social inequalities (Bacon 2015).

This emerging field of scholarship moves beyond Paulo Freire's (1970) focus on oppressed populations to engage members of privileged groups to become allies against social injustice (Curry-Stevens 2010). In the context of social work education, this means not only engaging with the intersections of gender, class, race and sexuality, etcetera as they apply to the people social workers work with. It also means interrogating the positional privilege of professional social work itself in the context of the Eurocentric knowledge and practices.

Professional privilege is a relatively neglected area of study (Weinberg 2015). However, social workers who are committed to the radical and critical tradition in social work need to reflect upon their own positioning in systems of inequality. Social workers are beneficiaries of the systems that oppress the people they work with. They are part of a professional-managerial class who occupy contradictory class locations (Wright 1978) and those who are also white, male, heterosexual and able-bodied receive further benefits from the unjust system they oppose.

How might social workers who adopt a critical perspective, unwittingly reproduce systemic oppression, while espousing social justice and human rights? How might they be complicit in the reproduction of patriarchy, white supremacy, class domination and other systems of inequality? Probyn (2004) challenges us to consider the connections between the work we do on social justice issues and the privileged positions we occupy. This means that social workers will need to become more cognisant of their complicity and challenge it in others. We will also need to develop strategies and skills to develop critical practices that encourage responsibility for exposing this complicity.

It is the process of developing a critical consciousness of members of dominant groups about their privilege that has led to the emergence of a pedagogy for the privileged (Curry-Stevens 2004, 2007) and a pedagogy of the oppressor (Lee 2002; Breault 2003; Kimmel 2003; Fruch 2007; Van Gorder 2007). These developments provide us with a conceptual and pedagogical framework for engaging members of privileged groups about their unearned entitlements.

Much of this work also takes these strategies out of the university classroom and into government and community-based forums where privilege holders can be challenged about their unearned advantages.

Curry-Stevens (2007) identifies six steps in educating members of privileged groups about oppression and privilege: (1) developing awareness of the existence of oppression; (2) understanding the structural dynamics that hold oppression in place; (3) locating oneself as being oppressed; (4) locating oneself as being privileged; (5) understanding the benefits that accrue to one's privileges; and (6) understanding oneself as being implicated in others' oppression and acknowledging one's oppressor status. She notes that the latter stage is perhaps the most difficult task to take on because it requires acknowledging one's culpability in the oppression of others.

This is where I find Tronto's concept of privileged irresponsibility and Young's social connection model of responsibility valuable in doing critical pedagogy with members of privileged groups. Such concepts enrich the process of assisting people to overcome their complicity in the oppression of others. In 2007, Curry-Stevens lamented that pedagogy for the privileged was under-theorised. Eleven years later at the time writing, this is still the case. While this work has drawn from critical pedagogy principles and theories of privilege, it has not been informed by wider critical social theories. Enter Joan Tronto and Iris Marion Young.[1]

Zembylas et al. (2014) have explored the implications of Tronto's ideas for critical pedagogies of emotion, whereby her critical ethics of care framework assists educators to expose the relationship between power, complicity and emotions. Pogge (2010) illustrates how Young's social connection model of responsibility can illuminate complicity in the international context, where people have some level of culpability in perpetuating an unjust global social order. Pogge suggests that people in the global North are complicit in the actions of their governments in relation to the global South. Such people should understand the ways in which their affluent country maintains its affluence at the expense of underdeveloped countries. We can see this clearly in relation to climate debt (Warienius 2017). These ideas illuminate and frame pedagogical interventions I have used in working with members of privileged groups.

Critical pedagogy with men in relation to men's violence against women

Encouraging men to recognise their complicity in the perpetuation of patriarchy is notoriously difficult to do. Part of the process of understanding patriarchy for men is becoming more aware of the consequences for women and to become conscious of the significance of our own involvement in those processes that result from our structural location within it. Below, I provide an example of a workshop exercise I have used in encouraging men to recognise their complicity in the oppression of women.

I am sitting with a group of men in a circle and I roll out a long sheet of paper, which has a timeline from 5000 years BC to the present day. I scatter some felt-tipped pens across the paper and I say to the men:

> What I would like you to do is to think about ways in which men have used their power over women. This may be in the form of violence, discrimination or unequal treatment. It can include something that impacts on all women or just some women or just one woman. It can include an event that you remember from history or a recent or contemporary event that you remember being reported in the media. It can also include something that impacted on a woman in your life. You may also want to consider whether there is anything that you do not feel particularly proud of in terms of your own behaviour in relation to a woman in your life. You may not choose to disclose this. But I want you to think about it.

I give the participants a few minutes to think and I then invite them to come forward and name the event they want to record on the timeline and the date on which it occurred. After recording the event on the timeline, they return to their seats. Participants come forward as many times as they want, until there is nothing more they want to record. I do not allow any discussion during the exercise. At the end of the exercise, the timeline is covered with numerous incidents of violence and abuse against women, including personal disclosures about women in their own lives who have been affected by violence and it sometimes includes self-disclosure by the men about their own complicity in the abuse of women.

When the timeline is completed, we sit silently to reflect on the events that the participants have recorded. From my experience in running the workshops over a number of years, the exercise always evokes emotional responses in the men, ranging from sadness and distress to anger as they reflect on the extent of the processes of victimisation and violence against women throughout history, in contemporary society and in their own lives and the lives of women they love.

This exercise provides an example of how men's emotional investments in privilege can be disrupted. If men are to be engaged in promoting gender equality, they need to recognise the role that emotions play in sustaining their privilege and address the barriers that inhibit them from experiencing compassion, empathy and sadness in response to the suffering of others. When men are emotionally engaged in the injustices experienced by women, they are more likely to interrogate their own complicity in women's oppression and to recognise their responsibility to challenge their own unearned advantages (Pease 2012). I argue that this strategy of engaging men emotionally in addressing violence against women is also applicable with other privileged groups in relation to, for example, racism, homophobia and class elitism.

Following the timeline exercise above, I introduce participants to the key ideas of Tronto and Young to illuminate how men's privileged irresponsibility and complicity reproduce patriarchy and men's violence against women. These ideas resonate when men's emotions have been engaged and they are more open to recognising their complicity with the various forms of everyday sexism.

Much complicity by members of privileged groups is lawful and manifested, for example, in the forms of everyday sexism and everyday racism that aggravates harm but is not criminalised. As Card (2010) notes, these forms of everyday oppressive practices create the climate in which physical violence against women and other socially marginalised groups is legitimated and excused. Card uses the language of 'enablers' to describe those men who are not physically violent but are connected to men who are violent without challenging them.

Applebaum (2007) is concerned with the question of how 'good white people' reproduce racism while believing that they are not racist. Such people see themselves as part of the solution, while denying that they are part of the problem. Applebaum aims to develop a conception of moral responsibility that implicates all white people in the reproduction of racism, while at the same time encouraging them to understand their complicity and to develop strategies to work against it. Tronto and Young inform the development of this moral responsibility.

Conclusion

Critical pedagogy with members of privileged groups has not been without critiques. A number of commentators (Leonardo 2004; Smith 2013; Margolin 2015) argue that white privilege pedagogy, for example, distracts attention away from structural forms of racism and white supremacy. Their concern is that it individualises privilege instead of understanding it as a structural phenomenon. Margolin (2015) argues that focusing on the experiences of whites coming to terms with their privilege has the unintended effect of supporting white privilege rather than encouraging taking action to address it. This is because, he argues, it seems more concerned with white identity than institutionalised racism. In acknowledging our racism, whites may come to see themselves as egalitarian and anti-racist and consequently innocent of actions that reproduce racism.

To focus on the exploration of whites' racist attitudes and consciousness is seen to keep the focus on them and away from the structures of racial injustice. However, this becomes more of a problem if whites believe that they can personally repudiate the advantages of their whiteness without taking action against structural racism. I argue that if we keep the focus on complicity with systems and structures of inequality, as advocated by Tronto and Young, we avoid this danger. As Smith (2013) suggests, rather than presume we are exempt from the structures of oppression, we should presume that we are complicit in those structures as a starting point. From this premise, we can then develop strategies to undo our complicity by transforming our subjectivities and practices. I believe that Joan Tronto and Iris Marion Young provide important theoretical contributions to understanding and addressing this complicity.

Notes

1 I would like to thank Vivienne Bozalek, who, upon reading my earlier work, *Undoing Privilege* (Pease 2010), recommended that I read the most recent publications of Iris Marion Young and Joan Tronto. She recognised, before I did, the importance of their contributions to critical pedagogies of privilege.

References

Appelbaum, B. 2010. *Being White, Being Good: White Complicity, White Moral Responsibility, and Social Justice Pedagogy and Social Justice Pedagogy*. Lanham: Rowman & Littlefield.
Appelbaum, B. 2006. "Race ignore-ance, Color talk and White Complicity: White is … White isn't." *Educational Theory* 56 (3): 345–362.
Appelbaum, B. 2007. "White Complicity and Social Justice Education: Can One Be Culpable Without Being Liable?" *Educational Theory* 57 (4): 453–467.
Appelbaum, B. 2013. "Vigilance as a Response to White Complicity." *Educational Theory* 63 (1): 17–34.
Bacon, C. 2015. "A Pedagogy for the Oppressor: Re-invisioning Freire and Critical Pedagogy in Contexts of Privilege." In *Revisioning Paradigms: Essays in Honour of David Selvaraj*, edited by M. Kappen, M. Selvaraj and T. Baskaran, 226–237. Bangalore: Visthar.
Barnes, M., Brannell, T., Ward, L. and Ward, N. (eds) 2015. *Ethics of Care: Critical Advances in International Perspective*. Bristol: Policy Press.
Bourdieu, P. 1977. *Outline of a Theory of Practice*. Cambridge: Cambridge University Press.
Boyd, D. 2004. "The Legacies of Liberalism and Oppressive Relations: Facing a Dilemma for the Subject of Moral Education." *Journal of Moral Education* 33 (1): 3–22.
Bozalek, V. 2015. "Privilege and Responsibility in the South African Context." In *Ethics of Care: Critical Advances in International Perspective*, edited by M. Barnes, T. Brannelly, L. Ward and N. Ward, 83–94. Bristol: Policy Press.
Brazzell, M. 2015. "Positioning Ourselves Intersectionally: Reading Iris Marion Young on Shared Responsibility for Oppression." *Humboldt-Universitat zu Berlin*. http:responsibilityintheglobaleconomy.files.wordpress.com
Breault, R. 2003. "Dewey, Freire and a Pedagogy for the Oppressor." *Multicultural Education* 10 (3): 2–7.
Calhoun, C. 1989. "Responsibility and Reproach." *Ethics* 99 (January): 389–406.
Card, C. 2002. "Responsibility, Ethics, Shared Understanding and Moral Communities." *Hypatia* 17 (1): 141–155.
Card, C. 2010. *Confronting Evils: Terrorism, Torture, Genocide*. Cambridge: Cambridge University Press.
Curry-Stevens, A. 2004. "Pedagogy for the Privileged: Building Civic Virtues in Political Leaders." *Unpublished paper, University of Toronto*.
Curry-Stevens, A. 2007. "New Forms of Transformative Education: Pedagogy for the Privileged." *Journal of Transformative Education* 5 (1): 33–58.

Curry-Stevens, A. 2010. "Journeying Toward Humility: Complexities in Advancing Pedagogy for the Privileged." *Reflections (Winter)*: 61–72.
Freire, P. 1970. *Pedagogy of the Oppressed*. New York: Continuum.
Fruch, J. 2007. "Challenging Nationalism from a Position of Privilege." *Paper presented at the International Studies Association Conference*, Chicago, IL, March.
Hankivsky, O. 2014. "Rethinking Care Ethics: On the Promise and Potential of an Intersectional Analysis." *American Political Science Review* 108 (2): 252–264.
Hearn, J. 1998. *The Violences of Men*. London: Sage.
Hölscher, D., Bozalek, V. and Zembylas, M. 2014. "Assuming Responsibility for Justice in the Context of South Africa's Refugee Receiving Regime." *Ethics and Social Welfare* 8 (2): 187–204.
Kimmel, M. 2003. "Toward a Pedagogy of the Oppressor." In *Privilege: A Reader*, edited by M. Kimmel and A. Ferber, 1–10. Boulder, CO: Westview Press.
Langlois, A. 2014. "Social Connection and Political Responsibility: An Engagement with Iris Marion Young." *St. Antony's International Review* 10 (1): 43–63.
Lee, R. 2002. "Pedagogy of the Oppressor: What was Freire's Theory for Transforming the Privileged and the Powerful?" Paper presented at the Annual Meeting of the American Educational Research Association, New Orleans, April 1-5.
Leonardo, Z. 2004. "The Color of Supremacy: Beyond the Discourse of White Privilege." *Educational Philosophy and Theory* 36 (2): 137–152.
Margolin, L. 2015. "Unpacking the Invisible Knapsack: The Invention of White Privilege Pedagogy." *Cogent Social Sciences* 1 (1). doi: http://dx.doi.org/10.1080/233/1886.2015.1053183.
May, L. 1993. *Sharing Responsibility*. Chicago: University of Chicago Press.
McKeown, M. 2014. "Responsibility Without Guilt: A Youngian Approach to Responsibility for Global Justice." *UCL, School of Public Policy, PhD thesis*.
O'Connor, P. 2002. *Oppression and Responsibility: A Wittgensteinian Approach to Social Practices and Moral Theory*. University Park, PA: Pennsylvania State University Press.
Parekh, S. 2011. "Getting to the Root of Gender Inequality: Structural Injustice and Political Responsibilit." *Hypatia* 26 (4): 672–689.
Payson, J. 2009. "Moral Dilemmas and Collective Responsibilities." *Essays in Philosophy* 10 (2): 1–23.
Pease, B. 2002. "(Re)Constructing Men's Interests." *Men and Masculinities* 5 (2): 165–177.
Pease, B. 2004/2005. "Rethinking Profeminist Men's Behaviour Change Programs." *Women Against Violence: An Australian Feminist Journal* 16: 32–40.
Pease, B. 2010. *Undoing Privilege: Unearned Advantage in a Divided World*. London: Zed.
Pease, B. 2012. "The Politics of Gendered Emotions: Disrupting Men's Emotional Investments in Privilege." *Australian Journal of Social Issues* 47 (1): 125–140.
Pease, B. 2015. "Disengaging Men from Patriarchy: Rethinking the Man Question in Masculinity Studies." In *Engaging Men in Building Gender Equality*, edited by M. Flood and R. Howson, 55–70. Newcastle upon Tyne: Cambridge Scholars' Press.
Pease, B. 2017. *Men as Allies in Preventing Violence Against Women: Principles and Practices for Promoting Accountability*. North Sydney: White Ribbon Research Series, White Ribbon Australia.
Pease, B. 2018a. "Do Men Care? From Uncaring Masculinities to Men's Caring Practices in Social Work." In *Critical Ethics of Care in Social Work: Transforming the Politics and Practices of Caring*, edited by B. Pease, A. Vreugdenhil and S. Stanford, 186–196. London: Routledge.
Pease, B. 2018b. "Privileged Irresponsibility and Global Warming." Invited plenary paper presented at the Diversity in Disaster Conference, Melbourne, 17–18 April 2018.
Pogge, T. 2010. *Politics as Usual*. Cambridge: Polity Press.
Probyn, F. 2004. "Playing Chicken at the Intersection: The White Critic of Whiteness." *Borderlands E-Journal* 3 (2): 1–42.
Robinson, F. 2010. "After Liberalism in World Politics? Towards an International Political Theory of Care." *Ethics and Social Welfare* 4 (2): 130–144.
Schiff, J. 2008. "Confronting Political Responsibility: The Problem of Acknowledgement." *Hypatia* 23 (3): 99–117.
Smith, A. 2013. "'Unsettling the Privilege of Self-Reflexivity'." In *Geographies of Privilege*, edited by F. Twine and B. Gardner, 263–279. Hoboken: Taylor and Francis.
Sullivan, S. and Tuana, N. (eds) 2007. *Race and Epistemologies of Ignorance*. Albany: State University of New York Press.

Tronto, J. 1990. "Chilly Racists." Paper presented to the Annual meeting of the American Political Science Association, San Francisco, California, August 30–September 2.
Tronto, J. 1993. *Moral Boundaries: A Political Argument for an Ethic of Care.* New York: Routledge.
Tronto, J. 1995. "Care as a Basis for Radical Political Judgements." *Hypatia* 10 (2): 158–171.
Tronto, J. 2013. *Caring Democracy: Markets, Equality and Justice.* New York: New York University Press.
Van Gorder, A. 2007. "Pedagogy for the Children of the Oppressors." *Journal of Transformative Education* 5 (1): 8–32.
Warienius, R. 2017. "Decolonizing the Atmosphere: The Climate Justice Movement on Climate Debt." *The Journal of Environment and Development* 27 (2): 131–155.
Weinberg, M. 2015. "Professional Privilege, Ethics and Pedagogy." *Ethics and Social Welfare* 9 (3): 225–239.
Williams, F. 2001. "In and Beyond New Labour: Towards a New Political Ethics of Care." *Critical Social Policy* 21: 467–493.
Wright, E. 1978. *Class, Crises and the State.* London: New Left Books.
Young, I. 1990. *Justice and the Politics of Difference.* Princeton, NJ: Princeton University Press.
Young, I. 2011. *Responsibility for Justice.* Oxford: Oxford University Press.
Zembylas, M., Bozalek, V. and Shefer, T. 2014. "Tronto's Notion of Privileged Irresponsibility and the Reconceptualization of Care: Implications for Critical Pedagogies of Emotion in Higher Education." *Gender and Education* 26 (3): 200–214.

15
Critical social work education as democratic *paideía*
Inspiration from Cornelius Castoriadis to educate for democracy and autonomy

Phillip Ablett

UNIVERSITY OF THE SUNSHINE COAST, AUSTRALIA

Christine Morley

QUEENSLAND UNIVERSITY OF TECHNOLOGY, AUSTRALIA

Introduction

At the heart of social work education there have always been tensions reflecting the contested purposes of the profession since it arose in response to the social problems of modernity in the late 19th century. Social work, of course, is an explicitly value-driven profession whose international and national bodies persistently define its core mission in terms of 'social change' for 'the empowerment and liberation of people', based on principles such as 'social justice, human rights, collective responsibility and respect for diversities' (IFSW, 2014). These values are also reflected in attempts to formulate global standards for social work education (IASSW, 2018; IFSW, 2014; Sewpaul and Jones, 2005). Therefore, one would expect these values to translate into the primary content and conduct of social work education, producing 'critically self-reflective practitioners' (Sewpaul and Jones, 2005: 221) and citizens, with a 'critical understanding' (ibid.: 220–221) of society (including the role of their own discipline) and how society might be changed to realise the espoused principles. Such ethical and pedagogic considerations are also deeply implicated in the contested development of 'democracy' in contemporary societies. However, social work practice and education are simultaneously overshadowed by the demands of globalising neoliberal capitalism, where service provision is increasingly disciplinary and higher education policy deems pedagogy subservient to the imperatives of a digitised economy rather than democratic accountability. Accordingly, many discussions and formal reviews of social work education are pragmatic, dealing with government and industry requirements, identifying lowest common denominator skillsets within delimited fields of practice or refining the techniques and technologies of knowledge transfer (Hanesworth, 2017; Morley, Macfarlane and Ablett, 2017; Reisch, 2013). Consequently, the question of education for democratic 'empowerment and liberation', and how this might guide pedagogic practice is seldom raised and extremely challenging for social work education today.

This chapter takes up the proposal of Bouverne-De Bie et al. (2014) that social work, through its educational practices, can deliver on its promise of becoming a 'democratic practice' (both in the education of practitioners and in influencing the wider society). In developing this line of argument, we concur with Bouverne-De Bie et al. (2014: 43) that social work's contribution to 'learning democracy' can be best achieved by treating 'democracy as an open and on-going process, and not as a predefined project'. Additionally, we contend that such a process and its embodiment in institutions cannot exist without the formation of radically democratic subjects, people capable of questioning dominant social forms, their own practice within such forms, and of creating new forms and practices. Thinking through the educational implications of this for social work, we draw on the work of the revolutionary social theorist, Cornelius Castoriadis (1921–1997), whose philosophy accords a crucial role to democratic pedagogy (*paideía*) as an essential form of praxis in the creation of a radically democratic, egalitarian and sustainable society. In particular, we elucidate his idea (against (neo) liberal individualisation) that 'autonomy' is simultaneously an individual and social project that begins in, and is always dependent upon, individual and collective self-reflection. To illustrate this argument, we give examples from our own classroom experiences in teaching both critical reflection and critical social theory to social work students in Australian universities, on the premise that both are indispensable in social work education as a democratic practice for 'empowerment and liberation'. We begin with a brief discussion of Castoriadis, his main ideas and the pedagogic dimensions of his philosophy before bringing the latter to bear on our teaching experiences.

Cornelius Castoriadis

Cornelius Castoriadis (1922–1997) was a Greco-French philosopher, social theorist psychoanalyst and revolutionary. Born in Constantinople (Istanbul) in 1922, Castoriadis grew up in Greece amid dictatorship, invasions and civil war (Ablett, 2016). He studied politics, economics and law at the University of Athens; and joined the Greek Communist Party in 1941 who resisted the Nazi invasion but later joined the Trotskyists at great personal risk (Memos, 2014). After the Second World War, Castoriadis studied philosophy in Paris, where he broke with Trotskyism and co-founded (with Claude Lefort) the libertarian socialist group and journal *Socialisme ou Barbarie* (*Socialism or Barbarism* – 1949–1967), many of whose ideas influenced the May 1968 Paris uprising (Cohn-Bendit and Cohn-Bendit, 1968). Prior to gaining French citizenship in 1970, Castoriadis led a revolutionary's double life, working professionally as a senior OECD economist while agitating under various *noms de plume* (Curtis, 1992). As the journal's leading theoretician, he launched a series of thorough going internal critiques of the Marxist tradition. Against top-down models of socialism equated with state planning and nationalization, Castoriadis advocated workers' self-management, which he developed into the radically egalitarian and democratic *project of autonomy*. By the time *Socialism or Barbarism* disbanded in 1967, Castoriadis announced having 'to choose between remaining Marxist and remaining revolutionar[y], between faithfulness to a doctrine ... and faithfulness to ... a radical change of society' (1987: 14).

Castoriadis' mature work, beginning with *The Imaginary Institution of Society* (first published in 1975 in French) and voluminous essays, stages an original, philosophical and political critique of contemporary capitalist modernity. In doing so, he formulates an alternative to both foundationalist social science and poststructural relativism (Breckman, 1998); to reenvisage revolution 'as transforming society through the autonomous action of people and at establishing a society organized to promote the autonomy of all its members' (1987: 95). In addition to Marx and Trotsky, Castoriadis' thinking was influenced by Max Weber, Freud, Heidegger, Arendt, Merleau-Ponty, the biologist Francisco Verela, German Idealism and the Ancient Greeks (particularly Plato and Aristotle). After 1970, Castoriadis retrained as a psychoanalyst but also served as director of studies at the Écoles des Hautes Études. Politically, he supported various movements he saw as furthering the project of autonomy through expanding direct democracy, notably the European Green parties and the participatory budgeting movement initiated by the Brazilian Workers Party (De Souza, 2000). Castoriadis died in December 1997 in Paris after complications following heart surgery at the age of 75 (Agora International, 2014).

Main ideas: underdetermination, creation, social imaginary and the project of autonomy

Castoriadis was an ontological thinker who, against the dominant modes of Western thought (including social work thought), posits a fundamental indeterminacy or *underdetermination* in the nature of being (both social and natural). This view challenges the exhaustive knowledge claims of objectivist determinism or what Castoriadis defines as 'identitarian-ensemblistic' logic: the idea that being consists exclusively in a rationally or empirically identifiable set of determinate objects (ideal or material) related through inevitable chains of cause and effect. According to Castoriadis, causal sequences represent only one determinate layer of being but do not exhaust it. There is another indeterminate layer, evident in such things as 'undecidable propositions' in mathematics or the 'uncertainty principle' in quantum physics (Castoriadis, 1984). In the social realm, Castoriadis locates underdetermination in the creative imagination; in both the personal (*radical imaginary*) and collective (*social imaginary*) domains of human existence, and the creations these bring forth. A *creation*, Castoriadis insists (1997b: 3), is not a *cause* in the usual determinist sense nor an *effect* that can be calculated from a pre-existing set of elements but consists rather in the radical rupture and positing of a new form (*creation ex nihilo*). Such creations might be a neologism, a new law, the invention of the wheel or a new social policy, none of which were inevitable based on the conditions specifiable prior to their making.

For Castoriadis, imagination enables people to transcend the empirically given and functional by invoking images, to 'see in a thing that which is not or not yet' (Castoriadis, 1987: 104). It is not simply illusions but the ability to see things otherwise than what is and so 'provide new responses to the "*same*" situations or create new situations' (1987: 44). Consequently, Castoriadis conceives of social institutions as the collective creations of a social imaginary in action. A social imaginary for Castoriadis refers to the constantly changing and unstable '*magma*' of cultural meanings that give a society its broadest interpretive schema or world-view. No world-view is ever entirely rational or empirically based but depends on the creation of *imaginary significations* (e.g. God, the ancestors, the market, the Crown, etc.) invested in and cohering its practices. In this way, Castoriadis' social theory resists all attempts to subsume meaningful social practices into a determinism of underlying forms (as in functionalism, structuralism, systems theory, orthodox Marxism, neuroscience, etc.). Any such forms only make sense and have efficacy within the context of a given social imaginary. Society (*the sociohistorical*), therefore, is not a system but a contested interplay between the already *created* array of symbolically mediated, institutions and the *creating* of new ones; 'the union *and* the tension of instituting society and of instituted society, of history made and of history in the making' (Castoriadis, 1987: 108). This also means that institutions, as social imaginary creations, cannot be completely 'explained' by determinate causes, structures or functions but always require an *elucidation* of the *social significations* that validate their practices or transform them (Joas, 1989: 1191).

Understanding society as an imaginary creation does not mean that everyone within it is aware of, or participates equally (democratically) in, this creation (Ablett, 2016). On the contrary, since the rise of sedentary civilisations, most societies have been predominantly characterised by *heteronomy* (i.e., 'rule of the other'), in which the imaginary of the dominant group is instituted as natural, inevitable, or divinely sanctioned (Castoriadis, 1987: 155). Heteronomous imaginaries are ideological, they justify disparities in power and wealth, while concealing the arbitrary, socially constructed and oppressive nature of these divisions. It is only in exceptional circumstances that most members of a society become conscious of its self-institution and struggle for collective governance. *Autonomy* (self-determination), therefore, is an imaginable possibility for the individual and society but never guaranteed.

Castoriadis contests the contemporary (neo)liberal ideal of an exclusively individual autonomy as lop-sided and illusory. An individual as a social creation cannot be free in an unfree society like capitalism, where people surrender their agency to the heteronomy of 'representative' democracy (which Castoriadis calls 'liberal oligarchy') and market despotism. Autonomy, as self-governance (Gr. *Auto* = self; *nomos* = rule), is a reciprocally interdependent, individual and social ideal (Castoriadis, 1987: 107). *Social autonomy* means a society being able to self-consciously institute and revise its own laws with the maximum, equal participation of its members (Castoriadis, 1997a: 405). This can only happen in a society whose democratic practice goes beyond formal voting elections and allows the participation of all its members in making the decisions that affect them. The project of autonomy begins whenever a subordinate group begins questioning the dominant imaginary that constructs their subservience as inevitable and seek to create alternative imaginaries based on equal participation. This exceptional form of deliberate and directly democratic, self-creation, which depends upon the mutual autonomy of others, Castoriadis characterises as *autonomous revolutionary praxis*. Historically, partial approximations of this praxis would include the Ancient Greek democracies, medieval Italian communes, modern workers' councils and many social movements. It follows that movements or 'societies that [can] call themselves into question means that there are individuals capable of putting existing laws into question' (Castoriadis, 1997b: 311).

Individual autonomy cannot be fully realised without social autonomy, but likewise begins in critical self-reflection, bringing one's socially constructed self and motives into question, envisaging alternatives and taking responsibility for enacting them. This too is a form of *praxis*, of conscious, reflexive and creative activity directed toward self-determination and of being accountable to oneself for one's actions (Castoriadis, 2007). Castoriadis argues that while revolutionary praxis is decisive for social autonomy, there are other complementary forms of praxis, namely in critically reflective dialogues (such as critical psychoanalysis) and education, which can facilitate autonomy. While analytic treatment is for the few who seek it, an autonomous society requires the self-reflexive education of all its members. Indeed, direct democracy would soon fail without it: 'There can be no democratic society without democratic *paideía*' (Castoriadis, 1997c: 10).

Ideas on education: democratic *paideía*

Castoriadis' ideas have influenced a number of social science disciplines but only negligibly in social work to date (Shuttleworth, 1992, 2013; Madhu, 2005; Ablett and Morley, 2019). In relation to education, Ingrid Straume says Castoriadis conceived his work as part of the 'Western tradition, where education and philosophy are two sides of the same coin' (2014a:

106) and, to date, she is the most systematic expositor of his educational thought (Straume, 2013, 2014a, 2014b, 2015, 2016). Castoriadis is also part of a tradition that stresses the intrinsic nexus between education and politics (stretching from Plato to Rousseau, and through Dewey to Freire); particularly that stream which advocates the desirability of radical participatory democracy and the critical pedagogy required to institute and sustain it. His influence can be seen in the works of Giroux (2002, 2010), Fotopoulos (2005), Nikolakaki (2011) and Wustefeld (2018). Although less developed than his works on revolution and psychoanalysis, Castoriadis saw education (specifically *paideía*), as central to any durably just and democratic transformation of society.

According to Castoriadis (2012) there are two senses in which the Ancient Greeks used the term *paideía*. First, in a broad generic sense, 'there is a "part" of almost all institutions that aim at the nurturing, the rearing, the education of the newcomers – what the Greeks called *paideía*: family, age-groups, rites, schools, customs, laws, etc.' (1991: 149). This sort of education is akin to socialisation and helps reproduce the existing social order without questioning its basis or inequalities; and increasingly relies heavily on technical knowledge. However, there is a second, stronger sense of *paideía*, which Castoriadis says originated in Ancient Athenian democracy, that is not simply reproductive of the status quo but is a form of creative and critically transformative praxis. As a form of praxis, this critically creative *paideía* might employ technical skills and knowledge but is never simply the reductive sum of techniques or know-how. Rather, this *paideía* is a 'collective, self-reflective, and deliberate activity', integral to the creation of an autonomous society of activist citizens capable of governing themselves and altering their institutions (Castoriadis, 1997a: 132). Consequently, democratic *paideía* instils an *ethos* of care for society insofar as democratic citizens recognise society as their own collective creation and responsibility. According to Straume, in forming responsible citizens, democratic *paideía* creates not merely a socialised individual but rather an autonomous 'subject', a 'reflexive agent capable of questioning' (2014a: 106–107) themselves and the world.

Historically, social work has exhibited both (the reproductive and creative-democratic) forms of *paideía* and continues to reflect the tensions between them. The social work value statements referred to at the start of this chapter exhibit the ethos of taking responsibility for society and (for one's actions in) addressing social suffering. However, despite rhetorical gestures to the contrary, the *paideía* of professional and institutional reproduction is dominant in social work education and risks further marginalising critical content (Beddoe, 2019; Hanesworth, 2017; Morley et al., 2017; Reisch, 2013). Despite this, both authors of this chapter have persisted in attempting to employ something like what Castoriadis calls democratic *paideía* in social work education programs in Australia. Like Castoriadis, we believe autonomy is a worthy project for human beings and, while we do not expect a revolution tomorrow, 'the seeds of autonomy … are still alive', even within 'some aspects of … formal institutions' (Castoriadis, 2007: 97). As educators who identify with the critical social work tradition (Morley and Ablett, 2016), the question for us is how do we 'preserve and develop those seeds' (Castoriadis, 2007: 97) through social work education and practice? We contend that for social workers to become democratic subjects capable of questioning heteronomous social forms (discourses and structures) and creating new forms with others; their education must at least contain two foundational and synergistic curricula components. These are critical reflection and critical social theory (including social policy analysis) aimed, respectively, at fostering individual and collective self-reflection for autonomy. This is what we have each taught and we offer the following examples to illustrate their transformative potential.

Seeds of autonomy: critical reflection and critical theory in social work education

Critical reflection

In the context of social work education, critical reflection can be practised in a manner analogous to Castoriadis' idea of individual self-reflection for autonomy. That is, critical reflection is a basic mode of connecting people with their individual agency against disempowering, heteronomous social constructions or *significations* (Morley, 2011).

One of the authors (Christine) has developed a range of units (e.g. on organisational practice, social research, and working in groups, teams and communities) that draw on critical reflection to enact what Castoriadis might see as critically democratic aims for education. Critical reflection has been deployed in these units as the main pedagogic strategy to assist students in grappling with issues which they have experienced as blocks, challenges and/or dead ends for a critical, or in Castoriadis' view, autonomous form of social work practice.

The process begins when students are invited to bring their most difficult dilemmas to class in the form of a critical incident from their practice. Many draw upon a placement experience for this task. Almost always, the critical incident encapsulates the frustration of not being able to directly enact critical practice in their workplace. Students run up against heteronomous organisational policies, legislation, and/or broader structural forces, often in clinical or medicalised settings, that restrict their capacities to work with integrity, as critical practitioners. This often results in students feeling as though the critical aims they seek to implement into practice are unachievable and so have little relevance for contemporary practice contexts, ultimately manifesting in a sense of alienation from the means of change.

The aim of critical reflection, in such situations, is to find ways to reconnect students with a sense of autonomous agency in working toward social change in seemingly conservative, imposed and unyielding contexts (Morley, 2016). In utilising Castoriadis, Christine stresses the skepticism he shares with poststructuralists against singular, foundational truths and structural determinism, without embracing relativism. Following Ojeili (2001: 225), she sees Castoriadis' work as 'simultaneously modern and postmodern', in that it acknowledges both the modernist veracity of empirical and rational knowledge but simultaneously the postmodern concern that such truths are partial, incomplete and always situated and interpreted within the multiple significations of contested discourses or (for Castoriadis) social imaginaries. This version of critical reflection also retains critical theory's commitment to the emancipatory significations of individual and social autonomy.

Castoriadis' non-structural understanding of society as an ever-shifting constellation ('magma') of contested and co-constructed, imaginary significations; enables the positioning of students' initial accounts of their challenging practice incidents, as one possible construction among others. In most cases, students present a challenging practice situation as a *fait accompli* (highlighting their lack of agency to challenge oppressive and undemocratic policies and practices). However, Castoriadis' theory of social imaginaries, enables the creative positing of alternative elucidations of the situation.

Again, for Castoriadis, the purpose of education is to become a critical subject, one that can bring themselves into question and critically analyse their society and its problems, with others. This requires students to re-imagine an apparently immutable situation, institution or structure as contested, fluctuating and open-ended. It invites them to question received ideas that do not necessarily serve them, or the people with whom they work. One student, for example, said she felt powerless to offer a socially informed analysis to medical professionals, in the context of undertaking a placement in an acute mental health setting. She then used critical reflection to deconstruct her assumptions about the social work student identity she had assumed within the dominant medical imaginary, which gives power to others (heteronomy) rather than seeing oneself as an active participant in that construction. Through questioning the construction of her identity in terms of the dominant imaginary (medical expertise and service user passivity, dependency and compliance), she recognised that the powerless positioning she had accepted was not conducive to advocating around the impact of severe inequality, poverty and consequent trauma that she had observed in her service user's experience of domestic violence. So, she began to imagine other ways of expressing this perspective, outside of medicalised significations and the psychiatrist's overt attempts to silence her (Morley and Stenhouse, unpublished). What Castoriadis adds to this process is an appreciation of our potential creativity, of invoking or inventing an alternative imaginary; one in which there is shared power to negotiate different points of view.

Another student spoke of her lack of autonomy in the context of working in child safety where decisions are seemingly mandated by legislation, and coming to recognise that there was 'wiggle room' in her interpretation of the legislation. The example that prompted this shift in thinking arose in conversation around a policy that exists at Christine's institution to award a grade of zero if students submit assessments one second after the digitised deadline. Academics do not have the technological or administrative agency to stop or reverse this process once it has been applied, even if they regard it as authoritarian, oppressive and undemocratic. Nor do they have license to grant extensions as this, too, is managed by a central administration. The possibilities for autonomy, however, lie in the capacity for academics to simply not impose a late penalty in the digital learning platform settings in the first place. Hence, a student who has been consistently engaged throughout the semester and done the required work to be assessed, does not automatically fail if they have mistaken the submission deadline, or experienced a technological malfunction at the time of submission. In translating this example to her own experience, the student began to imagine the possibilities for some autonomous agency or at least discretionary space, within the context of child safety legislation, to mitigate the destructive effects of unreflectively applying formal rules.

Castoriadis' ideas can also be used to inform how social work educators undertake social research. Rather than simply documenting the problem as it is represented in the dominant social imaginary, Castoriadis' perspective can help connect research participants with a sense of agency that transcends the original construction of the problem by connecting them with critical reflection. While transformation is not necessarily the goal of a traditional research process, when used with social work practitioners, such a goal can have emancipatory implications. For example, Christine's PhD research focused on the hopelessness, fatalism and despair that many sexual assault practitioners experience in supporting victims/survivors of rape through the legal process. She witnessed the misogynist and patriarchal legal norms and outcomes that regularly play out in court processes while supporting victims/survivors following sexual assault, and how these heteronomous processes produce the sense of powerless and fatalism in practitioners. This is fueled by a sense of disconnection from the determining elements such as legislation and the implementation of this by legal practitioners who are often influenced by a victim-blaming rape mythology. This research project (Morley, 2014) while not explicitly informed by Castoriadis, drew on analogous ideas of critical reflection, particularly in connecting practitioners with the means to challenge and change. The research unearthed many strategies that practitioners could engage in that existed outside the dominant social imaginary that enabled them to more proactively support victims/survivors through the contestation of discourse, and even to potentially alter unjust legal findings (Morley, 2014). An example of this came from a practitioner who talked about her sense of powerlessness in observing legal processes such as cross-examination that further victimise complainants of sexual assault. Part of the way cross-examination processes do this is to activate patriarchal significations about sexual assault that blame victims, minimise or deny violence and exonerate perpetrators. Through a process of critical reflection, and the idea that power operates through signifying practices, this practitioner was freed to imagine requesting the prosecution to subpoena her as an expert witness so that she could expose and counteract the effects of pervasive but contestable significations around gender. In effect, she used the opportunity to educate the court by introducing a counter-imaginary concerning rape as a violating abuse of power (rather than anything to do with the survivor's sexuality), replete with the latest empirical studies around sexual violence.

In facilitating critical reflection among social work students, and the creativity and civic courage (*parrhesia*) it can foster, it needs to be acknowledged that such reflection has its limits in terms of what it can change, especially when practised as an individual exercise. Liz Beddoe has recently written that critical reflection is 'at the heart of so much of what we do as [social work] educators … but reflection … can fall short of critical analysis' and so she proceeds to make 'a case for strengthening critical analysis, with contemporary political discourse' (Beddoe, 2019: 105) to better equip practitioners for the pursuit of social justice and human rights in a power-divided world. We concur regarding the crucial role of critical reflection in social work and, like Beddoe, insist that this must always be related to critical social analysis, particularly social policy analysis, if social work education is to foster practice for emancipatory social change. However, we would add that both critical reflection and critical analysis require anchoring in critical theory as a collective democratic exercise if they are to produce an autonomous society.

Critical social theory (including critical social policy analysis)

By critical theory we mean, echoing Marx, practical theory that seeks to 'overthrow all conditions under which humankind is an oppressed, enslaved, destitute and a despised being' ([1843] 1977: 220). In other words, critical theory is not just the criticism of flawed ideas but of flawed social-power relations. Moreover, it seeks emancipation from social suffering by exposing oppressive conditions from which human subjects seek redress and posits alternatives. In social work, Karen Healy has written that critical theories 'are concerned with possibilities for liberatory, social transformation … not just to understand the world but to change it' (2000: 13). Castoriadis (1987: 57) would agree:

> We are not in the world to look at it or submit to it; our fate is not servitude; there is a type of action that can be based on what is, in order to bring into existence what we want to be.

In this 'type of action', theory is a moment of lucidity about our context and actions but Castoriadis rejects the idea that it can ever be exhaustive or provide the prescriptive 'rational mastery' (really 'pseudo-mastery') that characterises the heteronomous imaginaries of managerial domination (which we see in claims to 'evidence-based practice' or 'early intervention science' in social work today). Nor can critical theory be undertaken by isolated intellectuals as a contemplative enterprise. Castoriadian critique is conceived as part of autonomous democratic practice, involving individual and collective self-reflection, and not the imposition of a 'predefined project' or 'pushing through one's pre-given convictions' (Hammond, 2018: 1).

Both of us teach critical theory and Phillip has run courses with this as their main focus. In Phillip's case he teaches critical social theory with a view to bringing students into a 'conversation' with a range of critical philosophies and world views; and then asking the students to deliberate on how they may (or may not) use these in investigating, navigating and possibly changing their world. Change is conceived at many levels but his principal focus has been on macro-practice (social policy) and macro-level change, where collective self-reflection as part of democratic mobilisation and decision-making is foregrounded. However, he also presents examples from local practice settings to demonstrate the connections between differing levels of practice, from case-work to community work to policy practice, social movement activism and legislative change.

Both undergraduate and Master's social work units begin with the traditional lecture format to articulate contexts, key terms and the organising themes of the course. This includes a vividly storied presentation starting with Socrates (and other philosophers) on terms like the relation of 'theory' to 'practice', what is meant by words like 'critical', 'power', 'truth', 'science', and why they might be important in 'practice' or 'praxis'. Key organising themes such as 'knowledge and power'; 'oppression and emancipation'; 'identity and difference'; 'social change'; and the quest for the 'good society' are also introduced. The students are encouraged to explore different social models from the dominant imaginary of neoliberal capitalism. For example, they are referred to works on participatory budgeting, citizens' assemblies, basic income guarantees, permaculture, producer cooperatives and stakeholder grants. The lecture is as interactive as possible with an effort to share the questioning time equitably.

The first major assessment is to work collaboratively in groups to select a contemporary social issue (typically found in the media), to research the issue, and then using the ideas of an early social theorist, also chosen by the group (from a menu of Karl Marx, Max Weber, W.E.B. Du Bois, Charlotte Perkins-Gilman or Jane Addams), to critically analyse the issue and suggest ways of addressing its problematic features. The whole exercise is designed to encourage collective decision-making, research skills and develop an initial facility in the use of conceptual tools in creating a wider understanding of complex social problems, beyond the framing of the prevailing social imaginary. The students present their analysis in the form of a creative artefact, which they present and explain to the class in a brief presentation. The presentations are typically diverse in subject matter and choice of visual media. The groups go to a lot of trouble in attending to the intellectual coherence, empirical support and aesthetics of their presentations. Each presentation ends with the group soliciting questions from the floor about the social issue and asking what the class would recommend. Every attempt is made in the presentation forum to create a space where students feel free to exercise collective responsibility and rehearse the freedom for dissent and deliberation, which would be expected in an autonomous society. Interestingly, many students from countries whose governments are noted for human rights abuses, chose of their own unsolicited volition to explore topics like environmental protest and sustainability options or industrial action by unions and worker-run enterprises, which would most likely incur disapproval or possibly repression in their country of origin.

In relation to Castoriadis' views about the purpose of education being to promote a democratic society, Christine uses an exercise in first year teaching that invites students to identify and critically theorise a social justice issue of their choosing. This assessment task requires students to define why their issue is a social justice issue (in terms of either rights, access, participation and/or equity) (Morley et al., 2019) and then to develop critical practices to respond to the issue, in a manner outside of the dominant social imaginary (Castoriadis, 1987). This exercise is used as an introduction to social work education at both undergraduate and post-graduate qualifying levels. At the Master's qualifying level, the classes are constituted by students from many countries around the world, with differing understandings of what is meant by 'social justice'.

A few semesters ago, Christine met with a group of diverse international students after the first lecture and they reported that they did not understand the relevance of global social forces (such as neoliberalism, capitalism, managerialism, nationalism, racism, etc.) to the concept of social justice for service users. These students also talked of their fears at not being able to identify a social justice issue because they were unfamiliar with the Australian context (most of these students had arrived in Australia less than two weeks prior). In democratising the curriculum, Christine clarified that they could choose social justice issues from their own countries of origin, which seemed to allay immediate anxieties. As the projects began, different narratives started to emerge from the students about internal conflicts, gendered violence and persecution of same sex attracted people from their homeland. Another example that one student raised, which affected all the overseas cohort, was the inequity in tuition fees required for international students compared to domestic students. This was a point of discussion that all the students felt that they could identify with (including the locals, who could see the impact of these inequities on their classmates). In time, they also began to connect social justice with a critical analysis of the social forces and institutions that created the injustices. These discussions moved from being formal presentations to become lively forums, exploring the connections between personal grievances on one or another of the broader social forces and what might be done about it.

The weekly forum around social justice issues did not stop at critical consciousness raising, the students were keen to 'practice' or 'do something' about certain issues. This desire was consistent with Castoriadis' point that one must be able to 'do democracy' in learning to become an autonomous subject. Many students were highly critical of the fact that they were able 'to talk about' social justice but 'had to do' case management activities in other classes and field placement. From their placement experiences, they could see that case management did not solve anything other than immediate problems, and often created new ones for service users. They wanted to know what else social workers could do in terms of promoting social justice and human rights? Christine encouraged them to use this as a learning opportunity for thinking about what they might do otherwise and so various political lobbying or social action scenarios were canvassed, although, putting them into effect was not always feasible within the classroom. However, on one occasion the prime minister was in the government buildings in Brisbane to attend a luncheon near to the campus where these classes were conducted. A major issue of the time was the Australian Federal Government's legislation (being debated in the Senate) to uncap university fees to let market forces do their work. As it happened, the National Union of Students (NUS) and the National Tertiary Education Union (NTEU), aware of the prime minister's schedule, had organised (as part of an ongoing nationwide campaign) to hold a rally and march in the city protesting the fees hike that deregulation would incur. Instead of the regular class, Christine announced that here was an opportunity to bridge the gap between professional practice and the activism associated with exercising democratic power. Most of the class, based on what they had been discussing about social justice, were keen to join the action. So, at lunchtime, many of the students attended the rally with their educator for a lesson in direct political action in solidarity with others about an issue affecting all of them. In class reflections the following week, several students spoke of how this was their first ever demonstration and that it would not be their last. Subsequently, the proposed deregulation legislation was defeated in the Senate but the class had concluded the semester. On the basis of their final reflections, however, at the very least, we believe that by participating self-consciously in the rally the students gained a sense of what might be achieved through critical analysis, reflecting openly on social issues as a group and acting collectively for change.

Conclusion

This chapter has examined how the educative practices of social work could benefit from an engagement with Castoriadis' idea of democratic *paideía* in forming critically reflective practitioners, committed to promoting a more just, sustainable and democratic (autonomous) society. Indeed, we argued that if social work is to act in accordance with its espoused emancipative goals, then its educative role must centre on democratic *paideía* and resist the retreat into technical standards, subject to the demands of the neoliberal market imaginary and its reproduction. The latter promises only a nihilistic vision of endless production and consumption, in a divided and unsustainable world. While avoiding the hubris of heroic agency, social work education can do better than abetting that vision.

Further to this, we examined Castoriadis' idea that 'autonomy' is simultaneously an individual and social project that begins in, and is always dependent upon, individual and collective self-reflection. This argument was illustrated by examples from the authors' classroom experiences of teaching both critical reflection and critical social theory (with policy analysis) to social work students in Australian universities, on the premise that both are indispensable in social work education as a democratic practice for 'empowerment and liberation'. These examples showed students readily exposing the heteronomous constraints of the dominant social imaginary in their critical self-reflections and the analysis of their social contexts. It also indicated how in modest measure this enabled students to regain a sense of their own individual and collective agency in relation to social and political institutions by creatively formulating alternative significations for the world they want for themselves and their constituencies.

Acknowledgements

Some of the biographic and 'main ideas' sections of this chapter draw upon an earlier version of similar sections published in Ablett (2016). Permission to re-use this material here in modified form is gratefully acknowledged (License Number 4407890517249).

References

Ablett, P. (2016) 'Cornelius Castoriadis (1921–1997).' In *The Blackwell Encyclopedia of Sociology*, Second Edition (Ed. George Ritzer). Honken, NJ and Oxford: John Wiley & Sons, Ltd.. DOI: 10.1002/9781405165518.wbeosc010.pub2.

Ablett, P. and Morley, C. (2019) 'Social Work as Revolutionary Praxis? The Contribution to Critical Practice of Cornelius Castoriadis' Political Philosophy.' *Critical and Radical Social Work*, 7(3): 1–6. DOI: 10.1332/204986019X15695800764884.

Agora International. (2014) 'About Cornelius Castoriadis.' Available at http://agorainternational.org/about.html (accessed August 23, 2019).

Beddoe, L. (2019) 'Social Work Education: Shifting the Focus from Reflection to Analysis'. *Australian Social Work*, 72(1): 105–108. DOI: 10.1080/0312407X.2018.1533028.

Breckman, W. (1998) 'Cornelius Castoriadis contra postmodernism: beyond the "French Ideology"'. *French Politics and Society*, 16(2): 30-42.

Bouverne-De Bie, M., Roose, R., Coussée, F. and Bradt, L. (2014) 'Learning Democracy and Social Work'. In *Civic Learning, Democratic Citizenship and the Public Sphere*, (Eds. Gert Biesta, Maria De Bie, and Danny Wildemeersch). Dordrecht, the Netherlands: Springer, pp. 1–10. DOI: 10.1007/978-94-007-7259-5_4.

Castoriadis, C. (1984) *Crossroads in the Labyrinth*. trans. K. Soper and M. Ryle Cambridge: MIT Press.

Castoriadis, C. (1987) *The imaginary institution of society*. trans. K. Blamey Cambridge: Polity.

Castoriadis, C. (1991) *Philosophy, Politics, Autonomy: Essays in Political Philosophy*. Oxford: Oxford University Press.

Castoriadis, C. (1997a) *World in fragments. Writings on politics, society, psychoanalysis, and the imagination*. ed. and trans. D. A. Curtis Stanford: Stanford University Press.

Castoriadis, C. (1997b) *The Castoriadis Reader*. ed. and trans. D. A. Curtis, Oxford: Blackwell Publishers.

Castoriadis, C. (1997c) 'Democracy as Procedure and Democracy as Regime'. trans. David Ames Curtis *Constellations*, 4(1): 1–18. DOI: 10.1111/1467-8675.00032.

Castoriadis, C. (2007) *Figures of the Thinkable*. trans. H. Arnold Stanford: Stanford University Press.

Castoriadis, C. (2012) '*Paideía* and Democracy'. *Counterpoints*, 422: 71–80. Retrieved from www.jstor.org/stable/42981755

Cohn-Bendit, D. and Cohn-Bendit, G. (1968) *Obsolete Communism: The Left-Wing Alternative*, (trans A. Pomerans). New York: McGraw-Hill.

Curtis, D. A. (1992) 'Cornelius Castoriadis.' In *Social Theory: A Guide to Central Thinkers*, (ed. Beilharz, P.) Sydney: Allen and Unwin.

De Souza, M. (2000) 'Urban development on the basis of autonomy: a politico-philosophical and ethical framework for urban planning and management'. *Philosophy & Geography*, 3(2): 187–201. DOI: 10.1080/13668790008573712.

Fotopoulos, T. (2005) 'From (Mis)education to Paideía'. *The International Journal of Inclusive Democracy*, 2(1): www.inclusivedemocracy.org/journal/vol2/vol2_no1_miseducation_paideía_takis.htm

Giroux, H. (2002) 'Educated Hope in an Age of Privatized Visions'. *Cultural Studies - Critical Methodologies*, 2(1): 93–112. DOI: DOI: 10.1177/153270860200200111.

Giroux, H. (2010) 'Neoliberalism as Public Pedagogy'. In *Handbook of Public Pedagogy: Education and Learning Beyond Schooling*, (Eds. Sandlin, J., Schultz, B. and Burdick, J.). New York: Routledge, pp. 486–499.

Hammond. (2018) 'Deliberative democracy as a critical theory'. *Critical Review of International Social and Political Philosophy*, DOI: 10.1080/13698230.2018.1438333.

Hanesworth, C. (2017) 'Neoliberal Influences on American Higher Education and the Consequences for Social Work Programmes'. *Critical and Radical Social Work*, 5(1): 41–57.

Healy, K. (2000) *Social Work Practices: Contemporary perspectives on change*. London: Sage.

IASSW. (2018) Global standards for the education and training of the social work profession. *International Association of Schools of Social Work*. www.iassw-aiets.org/wp-content/uploads/2018/08/Global-standards-for-the-education-and-training-of-the-social-work-profession.pdf

IFSW. (2014). 'Global Definition of Social Work.' *International Federation of Social Workers* www.ifsw.org/what-is-social-work/global-definition-of-social-work/

Joas, H. (1989) 'Review Essay: Institutionalization as a Creative Process: The Sociological Importance of Cornelius Castoriadis' Political Philosophy.' *American Journal of Sociology*, 94(5): 1184–1199.

Madhu, P. (2005) *Towards a Praxis Model of Social Work: A reflexive account of 'Praxis Intervention' with the Adivasis of Attappady'*. unpublished PhD Thesis, Kerala: Mahatma Gandhi University.

Marx, K. ([1843] 1977) *Critique of Hegel's Philosophy of Right*. ed. J O'Malley Cambridge: Cambridge University Press.

Memos, C. (2014) *Castoriadis and Critical Theory: Crisis, Critique and Radical Alternatives*. Basingstoke: Palgrave MacMillan.

Morley. (2016) 'Promoting activism through critical social work education: The impact of global capitalism and neoliberalism on social work and social work education'. *Critical and Radical Social Work*, 4(1): 39–57. DOI: 10.1332/204986016X14519919041398.

Morley, C. (2011) 'How Does Critical Reflection Develop Possibilities for Emancipatory Change? An Example from an Empirical Research Project'. *The British Journal of Social Work*, 42(8): 1513–1532. DOI: https://doi.org/10.1093/bjsw/bcr153.

Morley, C. (2014) *Practising Critical Reflection to Develop Emancipatory Change: Challenging the Legal Response to Sexual Assault*. Surrey UK: Ashgate.

Morley, C. and Ablett, P. (2016) 'The Renewal of Critical Social Work'. *Social Alternatives*, 35(4): 3–6.

Morley, C., Ablett, P. and Macfarlane, S. (2019) *Engaging with Social Work: A Critical Introduction*, 2nd ed. Cambridge: South Melbourne.

Morley, C., Macfarlane, S. and Ablett, P. (2017) 'The Neoliberal Colonisation of Social Work Education: A Critical Analysis and Practices for Resistance'. *Advances in Social Work and Welfare Education*, 19(2): 25–40.

Nikolakaki, M. (2011) 'Critical Pedagogy and Democracy: Cultivating the Democratic Ethos'. *Journal for Critical Education Policy Studies*, 9(1): 48–70.

Ojeili, C. (2001) 'Post-Marxism with Substance: Castoriadis and the Autonomy Project'. *New Political Science*, 23(2): 225–239.

Reisch, M. (2013) 'Social Work Education and the Neo-Liberal Challenge: The US Response to Increasing Global Inequality'. *Social Work Education*, 32(6): 715–733. DOI: 10.1080/02615479.2013.809200.

Sewpaul V, and Jones D. (2005) 'Global Standards for the Education and Training of the Social Work Profession'. *International Journal of Social Welfare*, 14: 218–230.

Shuttleworth, R. (1992) The imaginary institution of a geropsychiatric rehabilitation program. *The Social Construction of Symptom, Cause and Cure, 91st Annual Meeting of the American Anthropological Association*, San Francisco, CA, December.

Shuttleworth, R. (2013) 'Conceptualising Disabled Sexual Subjectivity'. In *The Politics of Recognition and Social Justice: Transforming Subjectivities and New Forms of Resistance*, (Eds. M. Pallotta-Chiarolli and B. Pease). London: Routledge, pp. 77–90.

Straume, I. (2013) 'Castoriadis, Education and Democracy'. In *Creation, Rationality and Autonomy: Essays on Cornelius Castoriadis*, (Eds. Straume, I. and Baruchello, G.). Denmark: NSU Press, pp. 203–228.

Straume, I. (2014a) 'Cornelius Castoriadis'. In *Encyclopedia of Educational Theory and Philosophy*, (Ed. D. C. Phillips). London: Sage, 106–107.

Straume, I. (2014b) 'Education in a Crumbling Democracy'. *Ethics and Education*, 9(2): 187–200. DOI: 10.1080/17449642.2014.921973.

Straume, I. (2015) 'The Subject and the World: Educational Challenges'. *Educational Philosophy and Theory*, 47(13-14): 1465–1476. DOI: 10.1080/00131857.2014.951596.

Straume, I. (2016) 'Democracy, Education and the Need for Politics'. *Studies in Philosophy and Education*, 35(1): 29–45. DOI: 10.1007/s11217-015-9465-4.

Wustefeld, S. (2018) 'Institutional Pedagogy for an Autonomous Society: Castoriadis & Lapassade'. *Educational Philosophy and Theory*, 50(10): 936–946. DOI: 10.1080/00131857.2016.1266923.

16
Sociology for the people
Dorothy Smith's sociology for social work

Michelle Newcomb

GRIFFITH UNIVERSITY, QUEENSLAND, AUSTRALIA

Introduction

Dorothy Smith is a Marxist, feminist sociologist who rejected traditional sociology and instead developed a sociology 'for the people' which could be used to examine power and oppression within organisations and institutions. Critical to her work is understanding how the day-to-day activity of people reveals social and institutional power as privileged sources of knowledge (Smith, 2004). Smith is renowned for her use of standpoint theory and the development of institutional ethnography; a method of sociological inquiry and research that examines how dominant ideologies are exercised within organisations and institutions (Smith, 2005). This approach has been distinctive in the way it has examined managerialist processes and procedures within organisations, observing the way regimes of power and control operate. This can most clearly be done through analysis of organisational texts, such as case files, assessment forms or funding applications, which privilege information that maintains hegemonic social order. This chapter explains Smith's sociology with reference to her use of standpoint theory and institutional ethnography, to examine how power and discrimination are often replicated unknowingly by social workers. By critically reflecting upon these organisational processes it is hoped social workers, educators and researchers can engage in transformative social change which is, in Smith's (2005, p.10) words, 'by the people for the people'.

The activities of social workers are often complex, multi-layered and contradictory. While these professions strive for social justice, the actualisation of these goals is often hampered by neoliberal, managerialist processes (Bhuyan et al., 2017). Within these contexts unexamined power is often enacted through language and professional processes. In such environments social workers may unwittingly perpetuate oppression by undertaking practice that ignores the standpoint of those they are working with, who may be experiencing oppression. However, analysis and reflection on organisational processes using Dorothy Smith's sociology can also offer the opportunity for progressive social change. This chapter will provide a brief biographical overview of Dorothy Smith and outline how her use of standpoint theory and creation of institutional ethnography can be used within social work education. This chapter seeks to give a sense of Smith's contribution to sociology and how this can be applied to social work to unlock and reveal processes of oppression.

Dorothy Smith

Dorothy Edith Smith was born in 1926 and is a Marxist, feminist sociologist specialising in the examination of how power is exercised through language, action and social relations. Smith was born into an upper middle-class family in North Yorkshire to a militant suffragette mother and grandmother (Smythe, 2009). At the age of eighteen Smith worked in a factory post World War Two and described this as a pivotal experience in developing her social justice framework (Carroll, 2011). Smith originally trained as a social worker, undertaking her practicum in impoverished areas of Sheffield but left the profession as she felt it would not allow her to undertake radical social change (Carroll, 2011). She moved to London, where she became involved in the trade union movement and undertook a Bachelor's degree at the London School of Economics (Carroll, 2011). Later Smith moved to Berkeley California completing a PhD supervised by Erving Goffman (Carroll, 2011). She became a lecturer at Berkeley while simultaneously becoming a single parent; the dual occupation of these roles became central to the later development of her sociological argument. Smith became Associate Professor at the University of British Columbia in 1968, also becoming involved in feminist activism including setting up the Women's Research Centre in Vancouver (Carroll, 2011). Smith later moved to Toronto to take up a professorship with the Ontario Institute for Studies in Education (Carroll, 2011).

The contribution of Dorothy Smith

Smith's sociology is grounded in her highly original reading and interpretation of Marx, which contributed to the development of Marxist feminism (Carpenter & Mojab, 2008). Different from previous interpretations, Smith (2004, p. 446) is interested in Marx's 'method of inquiry rather than an explication of this theory'. Through the examination of Marx's method of inquiry Smith suggests that social inquiry should start with the real, material processes of people's day-to-day life (Carpenter, 2012; Carpenter & Mojab, 2008; Smith, 2004). Smith (2004) proposes that social reality is constructed by the cooperative social activity of people rather than through the academic abstraction. This is important because: 'real people, philosophers or jurists, are at work; they are active in the context of definite social relations; their experience in those relations is formulated in concepts or theories; hence the concepts or theories reflect those relations' (Smith, 2004, p. 451).

Smith's interest in how real people experience the power embedded in social relations led her to develop two key areas of work: standpoint theory and institutional ethnography. Her sociology has provided important contributions to social work's understanding of how the standpoint of those in power is used, often textually to impose *ruling relations*. Smith (2005, p. 10) describes ruling relations as an 'extraordinary yet ordinary complex of relations that are textually mediated, that connect us across space and time and organise our everyday lives'. *Ruling relations* show how the standpoint of the powerful is often privileged over others, and this concept demonstrates the innovative way Smith develops Marx's ideas. Smith's development of this perspective urges the reader to consider the world from the 'standpoint' of the less powerful, questioning existing, often patriarchal and hegemonic processes. To uncover the ruling relations within organisations Smith later developed institutional ethnography, which can be used as both a theoretical and methodological framework. Smith (2005, p. 31) describes institutional ethnography as: 'beginning in the actualities of the lives of some of those involved in the institutional process and focus on how those actualities were embedded in social relations, both those of ruling and those of the economy.'

This exploration of institutional practices has resonance for contemporary social work education and practice where procedural or skill-based ideas are increasingly privileged over critical approaches (Bhuyan et al., 2017; Morley et al., 2014). Smith's (2004) work calls upon practitioners to question the way in which administrative and procedural processes are used to justify the work of social workers while often simultaneously reasserting dominant power structures. Smith's contribution has allowed exploration of how processes and procedures such as assessment and planning, the writing of case notes or court documents enact and replicate ruling relations in social work practice. Written processes, such as the completion of case reports or notes, within systems such as criminal justice or mental health are structured so major items of information predicate the individual subject of the report (Smith, 1974b, p. 263). For example, within psychiatry this is visible in the way the language of diagnosis can be used to prescribe or compel individuals into regimes of treatment (Burstow, 2016). In this way documents do not present the experience of a social work client, but rather the language, meaning and ruling relations of organisations and institutions.

During her lifetime Smith produced a range of journal articles and books explaining her sociology. Her influential books include:

- *The Everyday World as Problematic: A Feminist Sociology* (1988). This text incorporates Marxist and feminist theory to examine the everyday world and the social relations used within it.
- *The Conceptual Practices of Power: A Feminist Sociology of Knowledge* (1990). In this book Smith examines sociology's practices of reasoning and conceptualisation which lacks subjects and subjectivity. She explores these concepts within the realm of feminism.
- *Institutional Ethnography: A Sociology for People* (2005). This text culminates with an examination and explanation of institutional ethnography as both a research approach and a mechanism for social change.

This chapter will explore two key areas of Smith's sociology; standpoint theory and institutional ethnography and their utility within social work practice and education.

Standpoint theory

Smith's sociology began with an adaptation of standpoint theory which she uses to explain and explore power within sociology. Standpoint theory identifies the importance of social positioning of subjects, and the difference between the knower and the creator of knowledge (Harding, 2004; Smythe, 2009). Smith (2004) was interested in epistemology derived from Marx, which sought to understand the views of sociological subjects rather than those creating knowledge. Marx (1970, p. 92) believed the ideas of the ruling class permeated every epoch of the ruling ideas. The class that has economic and material control of society also has control of intellectual thought and development (Marx, 1970). Ruling ideas simply become an expression of dominant material relationships which can be transformed into intellectual pursuits and meaning (Marx, 1970, p. 93).

This understanding of power extended beyond social class, including gender in Smith's development of standpoint theory. Early standpoint theorist Sandra Harding (1986) argued that men's dominating social position led to only partial understandings of social life, whereas women's understandings were more complete due to their subjugation (Harding, 1986). Smith's views varied, believing women's standpoint began in the experience of being a housewife and that, prior to the women's movement, the standpoint of women existed but had not yet been formulated (Smythe, 2009).

At the time, Smith's contribution was significant as structural, functionalist perspectives, such as the work of Talcott Parsons, had been deemed superior. Structural functionalists felt the researcher should be objective, viewing people as subjects (Parsons, 1967). Smith radically contested this approach by arguing that the notion of 'standpoint' creates a point of entry into exploring the social without subordinating or objectifying others (Smith, 2005). Rather than viewing people from 'above', sociologists should view them from the 'street level' (Smith, 2008). Standpoint theory allows a position of examination to be taken by anyone in society, allowing power and inequality to be examined and interrogated. This resonated with second-wave feminists as Smith (1988, p. 61) describes sociology as a discipline in which women had experienced 'virtual exclusion from positions of influence … which has meant that we have been unable until very recently to give themes and topics to sociological discourse'.

Smith viewed traditional, structural, functionalist sociology as limited and unable to capture the practices of people, groups and organisations, due to its propensity to reduce them to observable data. Smith dubbed these data points as *observables* and claimed they were reductionist, objectifying people without truly conveying the depth or actual activities of people's lives (Smith, 1990, 2008). In observing people in this manner, Smith (2008) argues traditional sociology relies on the domination of 'ordinary' language, a focus that looks at social phenomena through selecting fragments. This approach ends up replicating ruling relations. By contrast, Smith (2008) argued that sociological study could be a driver for social change by seeking the examination of ruling relations and the way these were produced and reproduced within organisations and institutions. In using standpoint theory, Smith questioned the validity of past sociological enquiry to uncover the truth of people's lives (Carroll, 2011).

Standpoint theory and feminism

Central to the way Smith uses standpoint theory is to uncover how sociology replicates the ruling relations of patriarchy by excluding women. She argued that traditional sociology had produced an 'ideology of knowledge, and culture of means that our experience, our interests, our ways of knowing the world have not been represented in the organisation of our ruling not in the systematically developed knowledge that has entered into it' (Smith, 1988, p. 17). Smith (1988) believed traditional, contemporary sociology othered the experience of women while simultaneously celebrating men's presence and work as vital and necessary to the world (Smith, 1974a). She argued our understanding of the social world had been built until this point on methods, schemes and theories made for and devised by men (Smith, 1974a, 1988). Smith (1974a) saw men as occupying institutions that replicate the ruling relations that lock women into gender-based discrimination and exclusion. The institutions that use, develop and examine sociology, such as universities, also define which topics are relevant and which are not, and in doing so are deciding whose experience 'matters'. Within such institutions the lived experience of women, and the day-to-day experiences they had of being treated as the inferior gender, could be disregarded as unreliable or irrelevant in traditional sociology. It was in this way that traditional sociology excluded women from the development of sociological knowledge, meaning women's ways of knowing and experience were not represented (Smith, 1988). Feminist standpoint theorists such as Smith, position their analysis from the perspective of women, claiming the view of the oppressed allows for a deeper understanding of social problems (Burstow, 2016). Her book *The Everyday World as Problematic* became a feminist classic due to its ability to link dominant ruling relations to the actual position of women within society.

Smith's experience of patriarchal oppression within the academy and broader society informs much of her work. In juggling her roles as a single parent and a full-time scholar, Smith developed the term *bifurcated consciousness*. Smith (1990, p. 27) explains 'women's situation in sociology discloses to us a typical bifurcate structure with the abstracted, conceptual practices on one hand and the concrete realisations, the maintenance routines ... on the other'. In using standpoint theory Smith argues that women experience a contradiction between ruling relations and the actual activities of their lives, leading to them inhabiting a double existence between these two worlds. Men, on the other hand, experience a clear separation between the world of work and the world of home: so men's private life is separated from their working one (Smith, 1974a). Interrogating this separation between paid and unpaid work led Smith to categorise all activities that take time, effort and intent as *work* (Lund, 2012; Smith, 2005). This was a radical shift in sociological thinking which laid the basis for the ongoing development of feminist perspectives in sociology.

Smith also examined the types of paid work women do. In undertaking roles that are considered traditionally 'feminine' such as clerical work, nursing, social work, human services and administration, they enable the work of men in traditionally more senior roles such as managers, doctors or politicians (Smith, 1988). These traditional paid roles mediate men's workplace roles allowing conceptual ideas to be transformed into concrete action (Smith, 1974a). Put simply, men's roles could not be performed without the work of women, despite the lower status and wage applied to women's roles. Smith (1974a) suggests that no matter how hard women work in traditional 'support' roles, they simply strengthen a system that simultaneously oppresses women. Even when women enter into a traditionally male role in the workplace, they do not do so on the same terms as men due to the bifurcation of consciousness (Smith, 1974a) as the ruling relations of society require her consciousness to be divided within two places; the home and work. This divided activity ensures traditional, patriarchal processes of power continue.

However, Smith's interpretation of standpoint theory was subsequently critiqued by the emergence of intersectionality theory within feminist sociology. This critique argued that Smith presented all women as one group, devoid of racial or class differences (Clough, 1993). Smith (1988, p. 78) rightly responded to this stating that this was a selected reading of her work and later noting that 'standpoint does not imply a common viewpoint among women'. It is argued that standpoint theory is entirely capable of incorporating experiences of working class, black, lesbian and disabled women precisely because of its emphasis on everyday experiences, and the way being a woman is known and experienced differently from the different positions within it (Kearney et al., 2018; Smith, 1974a).

Standpoint theory has made a massive contribution to feminism and sociology, but also more broadly to social work. In fact, the work of second-wave feminists such as Smith is often taken for granted in social work education, although it is considered essential for the development of empathy or understanding of lived experience (Phillips & Cree, 2014). Smith's use of standpoint theory also paved the way for her development of future work analysing institutions and the way people are coordinated within them.

Institutional ethnography

In her later work, Smith further developed this sociological focus on understanding the everyday experience of people through institutional ethnography; which is distinctive for the way it represents both a theory and a research methodology. Smith (2008, p. 420) explains this concept as 'recognising that our everyday doings are coordinated with those of others in relation of which we are generally only marginally, if at all, aware'. Institutional ethnography involves understanding how people interact with institutions through their day-to-day lives through the analysis of texts. Interviews, observations and document analysis are used in institutional ethnography to analyse the ruling relations in a range of settings including health systems, domestic and family violence, community services funding regimes, disability rehabilitation, employment services, academia, psychiatry and social work education (Breimo, 2015; Burstow, 2016; Hosken, 2018; Hughes, 2014; Kearney et al., 2018; Lund, 2012; Ng et al., 2017; Nichols, 2016; Prodinger & Turner, 2013; Sinding, 2010). Rather than seeking out the opinions, beliefs and values that people hold, institutional ethnography examines what people do in their actual day-to-day work (Ng et al., 2017). By examining how people use and interact with institutional texts, the ruling relations between people can be found (Walby, 2013). Using institutional ethnography allows texts to be examined, showing how people are coordinated and controlled. Additionally, interviews or observations can be conducted to see how people work with texts to recreate ruling relations within organisations (Walby, 2013). Within social work, institutional ethnography can also be used as a research approach allowing researchers to work alongside individuals, groups and communities to create social change (Nichols, 2016). Using this approach in social work settings allows for an examination of how power is used and exercised, enabling feasible and meaningful change to occur (Lund, 2012; Ng et al., 2017).

Ruling relations and text

Analysing how organisations create reality through texts is a central tenet of institutional ethnography. Reporting and recording socially organised practices can create a *documentary reality* where texts become the key medium for coordinating the ruling relations of institutions and large-scale organisations (Kearney et al., 2018; Smith, 2004). Factual documents such as medical files, case notes or court proceedings are a form of social organisation. Within business, government and welfare agencies, documents construct problems but also advise on our responses to them. They create a reality between the reader and 'what actually happened/what is' (Smith, 1990, p. 89). The knowledge created by such documents affords them status as a source of knowledge and as a social product (Smith, 2004).

The information recorded in formal documents is read as a fact simply because of the status of knowledge accorded to it. Factual documents act as an interpretive schema for how the reader can name, analyse and assemble what has happened (Smith, 2004). The facts apparent in such documents are desired to 'tell' us what happened, privileging what should be considered relevant. This allows what we have learned about individuals to be categorised and treated as personal characteristics, with assigned social desirability or beliefs (Kearney et al., 2018). Important for social work is understanding that the complexities and challenges of individuals' lives are often lost within the process of categorising or documenting their experiences (Prodinger & Turner, 2013). In highlighting certain 'facts' the writer can be acting on regulatory procedures that allow social organisation to occur (Smith, 2004). Institutional ethnography attempts to find the concealed standpoint that exists within language that is considered descriptive and neutral within institutions (Lund, 2012). Within a social work context it allows for an understanding of the institutional experience of practice to be examined (Ng et al., 2017).

The material entered into social work clients' files or case histories provide material to academic and professional discourses. As well as being an administrative process and function, case histories and records form a knowledge base to social work (Smith, 1990). The process of recording client details risks becoming standardised, potentially limiting the recognition of individuals' experiences. Certain information is deemed important or factual, ignoring alternative understandings of client situations (Smith, 1990). Through reading, hearing, seeing and speaking about texts, a *sequence of action* occurs which coordinates individuals' and agencies' activities (Lund, 2012). Practitioners may not always be aware of how such texts connect to each other or create outcomes for clients (Ng et al., 2017). Certain sections of documents may not be consistently completed or adhered to, showing potential bias within the process of completing texts (Sinding, 2010). An example of this is research within Canadian hospitals using institutional ethnography which revealed a tendency for physicians and allied health staff to prioritise efficiency over patient care (Webster et al., 2015). Informally some patients were described by staff as 'failing to cope' when they stayed in the emergency department longer than prescribed (Webster et al., 2015). This can lead to patients or social work clients being viewed as units of work, rather than as individuals in need of support. Wider processes are at work in the construction of factual documents in social work, describing the world as it is for those who rule it, rather than a world for those who are ruled (Smith, 2005).

In responding to standardised assessments or plans, clients' voices can be undermined. The information provided by clients is not considered objective, it only exists to reassert the ruling relations held within social work. The organisation of social work in this manner seeks to separate the person from the individual contexts in which their actions have arisen (Smith, 1990). The organisation of texts within social work is taken for granted, assumed to be beneficial for both clients and practitioners. However, this ignores the power relations, division of labour and work organisation in the settings where these texts are produced (Smith, 1990, p. 93). This contradicts the foundations of social work which often proclaims to understand the person within their environment (Harms, 2007). The continued reliance on documenting reality using set texts questions the ability of social workers to effectively undertake this mission. Creating a reality by using texts risks clients becoming the object of practice, rather than active participants in the process of change. Clients can become marginalised; associated with behaviours rather than being complex and diverse individuals. The texts used within social work organisations offer a mechanism for power to enter unseen into professional practice, despite an espoused focus on social justice.

Ruling relations in the translocal

Smith (2008) argues that in studying the everyday we can see how people's local doings replicate ruling relations. While ruling relations can occur within local settings, *translocal* interactions exist that may occur in other local settings where others are, or have been, at work (Smith, 2008, p. 420). In *translocal* contexts, standardised and generalised operations are products of the ruling elite and are shown in government policies, laws, regulations and professional and academic discourses (Lund, 2012). The increasing use of information management systems and call centres in social work practice, highlights how ruling relations can occur in translocal settings (Burton & Diane van Den, 2009). For instance, a translocal connection may exist between a social work client in a local community centre who might be impacted by the text-based decision of a civil servant in a geographically distant location. Both exist within local communities, but their everyday activities and existence impacts on the other. The power used by the civil servant in making decisions about a service user's eligibility for resources is an example of how the power of a ruling elite is used in a translocal setting. Further research has examined the impact of translocal connections in social work practice, such as the case study provided below.

Michelle Newcomb

> ### Case study: health care for the homeless
>
> In 2013, Canadian researcher Naomi Hughes published her doctoral research using institutional ethnography to examine the health care experiences of 27 homeless people in Greater Toronto, Ontario, Canada. In Toronto accessing health care is dependent on having an Ontario Health Insurance Card, requiring a fixed address, which rough sleepers do not have. To uncover the ruling relations Hughes interviewed homeless people but also analysed a range of texts such as agency letters, cards, forms and documents to uncover the ruling relations within the health care system. She found texts were used to control, coordinate and operationalise the activities of homeless individuals.
>
> Participants expressed displeasure at filling out invasive, non-client friendly forms and applications to simply access health care. While some people felt pushed out by health providers, others opted out due to not wanting to engage with bureaucracy. Those with skills in organisational literacy, such as being able to use the internet, were able to read into texts and understand the ruling relations of a multi-layered health care system, a skill not all participants possessed. Hughes reveals the translocal connections between homeless people and broader neoliberal ideologies and health care policies. Policies that were created and operationalised in translocal settings were often invisible, despite the startling impact they have on individuals' lives. Hughes found neoliberal policies and directives mean marginal groups, such as the homeless, are not only economically disadvantaged but have restricted access to health care within Toronto. Ultimately, homeless people's experiences of health care were silenced and invisible due to the ruling relations within the health system (Walby, 2013).

The work of Dorothy Smith in developing standpoint theory and institutional ethnography enables social work practitioners and students to analyse and understand how it is that power imbalances are played out at the level of the everyday. Understanding differing views or standpoints due to social oppression is an important concept for social work. In a profession that strives to understand and authentically connect with people, rather than simply observe their experience of disadvantage, standpoint theory offers a crucial contribution. Institutional ethnography also offers valuable contributions to how social workers and students can interrogate and thereby deconstruct and understand power in the context of organisations, social policies and institutions.

Applying Smith's sociology to social work education

The prescribed goal of social work is social justice and actions of practitioners should be congruent with this (Bhuyan et al., 2017). However, the process of translating these abstract aims into concrete processes is something we think of much less in social work. Smith's work can be important in helping us think about how the 'doing' of social work impacts on people by providing the basis through which we can examine the way power and inequality are produced for service users and practitioners within organisations. This is important to consider as neoliberal, managerialist policies and processes have become widespread in social work practice. It can be particularly difficult for those in statutory roles or roles funded by government departments to be aware of the ways in which these agendas are changing the impact that social work can have

(Morley et al., 2014). Opportunities for critical practice can be constrained for these workers, leading to more traditional, conservative social work practice. Social work curricula and teaching have exacerbated this situation by emphasising the development of skills over critical social work approaches (Bhuyan et al., 2017). Such processes risk conservatising social justice rhetoric without providing students with the skills to engage in transformational social change. To challenge unjust practices, social work students need to be equipped with analytic tools to undertake an examination of power. The use of Smith's sociology can help students to understand how experiences of poverty, discrimination and dispossession create unique, often silenced standpoints. Furthermore, institutional ethnography provides skills and tools for the analysis and understanding of harmful institutional processes. The work of Dorothy Smith can allow social work students to understand ruling relations. It also offers the opportunity for expanding and developing students' ability to engage in deep, critical reflection about their practice.

Assisting students to develop critical understandings of organisations

Organisations that employ social work graduates may replicate the ruling relations of broader society. Institutional ethnography can enable students to gain a critical understanding of how this occurs within organisations by providing a rich and deep analysis of how social issues impact clients. Becoming a social worker involves learning how to navigate systems, processes, legislation, policies and practices across a range of service systems, organisations and environments (Ng et al., 2017). Institutional ethnography offers a unique perspective of how inequality is enacted by organisations, allowing students to develop skills and knowledge applicable to anti-oppressive practice (Ng et al., 2017; Sinding, 2010). In exploring and changing language, the processes attached to embedded power structures can be destabilised, which has been illustrated in the area of mental health, for example.

Psychiatry and mental health service provision have received considerable attention from institutional ethnographers (Burstow, 2016; Simon, 2017; Smith, 1990). Burstow's (2016) anthology, which uses institutional ethnography, explores how texts and practice within psychiatric settings recreate ruling relations. In removing people from their own environments and taking away control of their own lives, psychiatry can be understood as a form of extreme social control. This form of control is often presented as treatment, which is required due to a 'diagnosis'. Burstow (2016) suggests dominant interests such as pharmaceutical companies and medical bodies are served by psychiatry over the needs of those diagnosed with a mental illness. Using institutional ethnography within psychiatric contexts can involve deconstructing terminology, particularly labels attributed to certain behaviours.

By examining how language and discourse replicates ruling relations in psychiatry, mainstream practices can be questioned. The continued development and proliferation of recovery-based mental health movements serve as a testament to the oppression and othering faced by many in psychiatry (Burstow, 2016). The application of institutional ethnography to psychiatry can be used as an insightful educative tool in social work, showing students how accepted forms of language and behaviour can harm rather than help those seeking services.

Assisting students to develop critical understanding of policy

Social and organisational policy can also be examined and rewritten using institutional ethnography. Within social work, social policy is often taught as an area of knowledge that can be applied to specific clients or organisational settings (Zubrzycki & McArthur, 2004). However, institutional ethnography offers an example of how policy and practice interact on a day-to-day level. In examining texts the problems and tensions faced by practitioners can be empirically understood, leading to recommended changes (Ng et al., 2017). While institutional ethnography can inform practitioners of the lived reality of the disadvantaged, the responsibility for changing these systems lies with those working in oppressive institutions, such as social work graduates (Nichols, 2016). Those using institutional ethnography need to consider how the process of examining and researching institutions can also lead to wider social change.

Hosken (2018) used institutional ethnography to examine the processes of inclusion and exclusion used within Australian social work education. Her research found that despite social work's aim for social justice the implicit curriculum and standardised rules for the delivery of course and practicums reasserted ruling relations in social work education. Courses replicated existing power structures, emphasising the presence of white, middle-class, urban, heterosexual practitioners, educators and students. Hosken's (2018) analysis revealed the ruling relations within Australian social work education by uncovering a disconnect between the rules set by the governing body for social work education, the Australian Association of Social Workers (AASW), and their own espoused requirements in relation to social justice and human rights. This study highlights the implicit nature of power even within institutional settings which strive for social justice. Such unjust policies and processes, when left unexamined, can proliferate. Like much of the social work sector, the AASW has engaged in a managerial, business discourse in setting social work course requirements (Hosken, 2018). Rather than simply focusing on skills-based competencies, social work education needs to also engage students in critical thinking, political knowledge and diverse strategies for engaging in policy and organisational change (Zubrzycki & McArthur, 2004). However, a central tenet to both social work and institutional ethnography is the ability to engage in critical reflection, in relation to both the self and wider social forces.

Assisting students to develop skills in critical reflection

The ability to reflect upon oneself and the organisational setting is an important aspect of practice and routinely taught within social work courses. Critical reflection can enable students to engage in more than rote learning and instead investigate why certain judgements, strategies and theories are used. This approach to learning and practice is opposed to more managerialist approaches which require students to develop technical rationality through skills-based acquisition. Institutional ethnography offers a mechanism for critical reflection where students can move beyond describing events and experiences of clients to understanding the deeper ruling relations and implicit standpoints occurring with their practice. In reflecting on how ruling relations occur within organisations, students are also encouraged to develop the ability to solve problems and collectively respond to inequality.

The processes in institutional ethnography can also allow students and practitioners to limit taking on institutional discourses, allowing for more reflective practice to be developed. Institutional ethnography enables a deconstruction of ruling relations, leading to resistance through not participating or even attempting to change these processes. Nichols (2016) suggests using a process of reflexivity to unpack and make visible the ruling relations of organisations, allowing for policy and practice changes to take place. This allows those in social work to understand and examine the broader social relations that are coordinating the actions of both staff and clients (Nichols, 2016). Such reflection may allow students, especially those on field placement to not unthinkingly accept the words, concepts, ideology and actions of agencies (Burstow, 2016). By avoiding this process of *institutional capture*, practitioners and students can reject dominant discourses that seek to replicate unfair social structures (Smith, 2005). This is not without challenge as participation in the institutional discourse and language is a key feature of professionalism or workplace cultures. However, left unexamined, discriminatory or oppressive terminology and subsequent actions may continue to occur. Collective engagement and understanding in institutional ethnography would, however, enable future practitioners to develop a collective response to change discriminating practices. Uncovering how ruling relations are replicated, resisted and transformed by people provides a basis for social change by social work graduates (Nichols, 2016).

Many of Smith's ideas are used within mainstream social work education, yet little credit has been given to her work within these disciplines. Despite her pioneering influence on sociology, her work and contribution remains largely unrecognised outside of her adopted Canada. Standpoint theory is at the heart of much social work, enabling students to understand and empathise with those experiencing disadvantage. The use of institutional ethnography also allows a deeper, nuanced exploration of organisational and professional power in social work. Smith's sociology should have a place in social work education in teaching students about the disconnect that occurs between theory and practice. In using Smith's sociology, organisational culture, social policy and critical reflection can be advanced, ensuring students develop a deep understanding of power and oppression which can occur within society and welfare agencies.

It is ironic that Dorothy Smith's work, which seeks to provide voice to those who are oppressed, has to a large degree been ignored by social work despite its goal of social justice. Her sociology offers innovative but practical mechanisms for understanding power across a range of settings and institutions. Further incorporation of her work into social work practice, research and education has the power to subvert, resist and change current neoliberal discourses. Standpoint theory offers an opportunity to provide a voice to the voiceless, the keystone to advocacy and the advancement of a fairer society. Institutional ethnography is an underutilised but powerful tool for examining how power lies within the day-to-day functions and relations of organisations. In contemporary times, when social work agencies work within ever more restrictive, neoliberal environments, the need to acknowledge different ways of being, doing, knowing and exploring is more evident than ever. Dorothy Smith offers practitioners, researchers and educators the chance to not work above the people but to ensure social change is by the people and for the people.

References

Bhuyan, R., Bejan, R., & Jeyapal, D. (2017). Social workers' perspectives on social justice in social work education: When mainstreaming social justice masks structural inequalities. *Social Work Education*, *36*(4), 373–390.

Breimo, J. (2015). Captured by care: An institutional ethnography on the work of being in a rehabilitation process in Norway. *Journal of Sociology and Social Welfare*, *42*(2), 13–29.

Burstow, B. (Ed.). (2016). *Psychiatry interrogated an institutional ethnography anthology*. doi: 10.1007/978-3-319-41174-3

Burton, J., & Diane van Den, B. (2009). Accountable and countable: Information management systems and the bureaucratization of social work. *The British Journal of Social Work*, *39*(7), 1326–1342.

Carpenter, S. (2012). Centering Marxist-feminist theory in adult learning. *Adult Education Quarterly*, *62*(1), 19–35.

Carpenter, S., & Mojab, S. (2008). *Institutional ethnography: Pursuing a Marxist-feminst analysis of consciousness*. Paper presented at the 30th Annual SCUTREA Conference, University of Edinburgh. www.leeds.ac.uk/educol/documents/172300.pdf

Carroll, W. K. (2011). 'You are here': An interview with Dorothy E. Smith. *Socialist Studies/Études Socialistes*, *6*(2), 9–37.

Clough, P. T. (1993). On the brink of deconstructing sociology: Critical reading of Dorothy Smith's standpoint epistemology. *The Sociological Quarterly*, *34*(1), 169–182.

Harding, S. G. (1986). *The science question in feminism*. Ithaca: Cornell University Press.

Harding, S. G. (2004). A socially relevant philosophy of science? Resources from standpoint theory's controversiality. *Hypatia, 19*(1), 25–47.

Harms, L. (2007). *Working with people: Communication skills for reflective practice.* South Melbourne, VIC: Oxford University Press.

Hosken, N. (2018). Practices of exclusion and injustices within social work education. *Social Work Education, 37*(7), 825–837.

Hughes, N. R. (2014). Are institutional health policies exclusionary? *Qualitative Health Research, 24*(3), 366–374.

Kearney, G., Corman, M., Gormley, G., Hart, N., Johnston, J., & Smith, D. (2018). Institutional ethnography: A sociology of discovery—In conversation with Dorothy Smith. *Social Theory & Health, 16*(3), 292–306.

Lund, R. (2012). Publishing to become an "ideal academic": An institutional ethnography and a feminist critique. *Scandinavian Journal of Management, 28*(3), 218–228.

Marx, K. (1970). *The german ideology.* London: Lawrence & Wishart.

Morley, C., Macfarlane, S., Ablett, P., & Ife, J. W. (2014). *Engaging with social work: A critical introduction.* Port Melbourne, VIC: Cambridge University Press.

Ng, S. L., Bisaillon, L., & Webster, F. (2017). Blurring the boundaries: Using institutional ethnography to inquire into health professions education and practice. *Medical Education, 51*(1), 51–60.

Nichols, N. (2016). Investigating the social relations of human service provision: Institutional ethnography and activism. *Journal of Comparative Social Work, 11*(1), 38-63.

Parsons, T. (1967). *Sociological theory and modern society.* New York, NY: Free Press.

Phillips, R., & Cree, V. E. (2014). What does the 'fourth wave' mean for teaching feminism in twenty-first century social work? *Social Work Education, 33*(7), 930–943.

Prodinger, B., & Turner, S. M. (2013). Using institutional ethnography to explore how social policies infiltrate into daily life. *Journal of Occupational Science, 20*(4), 357–369.

Simon, A. (2017). Crazy making: The institutional relations of undergraduate nursing in the reproduction of biomedical psychiatry. *International Journal of Nursing Education Scholarship, 14*(1), 65–76.

Sinding, C. (2010). Using institutional ethnography to understand the production of health care disparities. *Qualitative Health Research, 20*(12), 1656–1663.

Smith, D. E. (1974a). Women's perspective as a radical critique of sociology. *Sociological Inquiry, 44*(1), 7–13.

Smith, D. E. (1974b). The social construction of documentary reality. *Sociological Inquiry, 44*(4), 257–268.

Smith, D. E. (1988). *The everyday world as problematic: A feminist sociology.* Milton Keynes [England]: Open University Press.

Smith, D. E. (1990). *The conceptual practices of power: A feminist sociology of knowledge.* Boston: Northeastern University Press.

Smith, D. E. (2004). Ideology, science and social relations: A reinterpretation of marx's epistemology. *European Journal of Social Theory, 7*(4), 445–462.

Smith, D. E. (2005). *Institutional ethnography: A sociology for people.* Walnut Creek, CA: AltaMira Press.

Smith, D. E. (2008). From the 14th floor to the sidewalk: Writing sociology at ground level. *Sociological Inquiry, 78*(3), 417–422.

Smythe, D. (2009). A few laced genes: Women's standpoint in the feminist ancestry of Dorothy E. Smith. *History of the Human Sciences, 22*(2), 22–57.

Walby, K. (2013). Institutional ethnography and data analysis: Making sense of data dialogues. *International Journal of Social Research Methodology, 16*(2), 141–154.

Webster, F., Rice, K., Dainty, K., Zwarenstein, M., Durant, S., & Kuper, A. (2015). Failure to cope: The hidden curriculum of emergency department wait times and the implications for clinical training. *Academic Medicine, 90*(1), 56–62.

Zubrzycki, J., & McArthur, M. (2004). Preparing social work students for policy practice: An Australian example. *Social Work Education, 23*(4), 451–464.

17
Henry Giroux's vision of critical pedagogy
Educating social work activists for a radical democracy

Christine Morley
QUEENSLAND UNIVERSITY OF TECHNOLOGY, AUSTRALIA

Phillip Ablett
UNIVERSITY OF THE SUNSHINE COAST, QUEENSLAND, AUSTRALIA

Introduction

This chapter discusses Henry Giroux's vision of critical pedagogy and its implications for social work education and practice. Giroux, a public intellectual, who coined the term "critical pedagogy" (Amsler, 2013), offers a rich, philosophical and political approach to education that can be applied to help reinvigorate social work as a critical project. His vision is committed to creating citizen activists, who are cognisant of structural oppression, yet also connected with a sense of agency to work toward a radically democratic and just society. In applying Giroux's critical pedagogy to social work education, we explore the example of teaching social work practice skills and contrast this with instrumental or *technicist* approaches to education, elucidating the implications for practice. We begin this exploration with a biographical overview, followed by an outline of Giroux's critique of neoliberalism, particularly showing how it degrades education. We then turn our attention to Giroux's critique of technicist education, which is increasingly relevant for social work, and explore the need for theory—particularly critical theories of education—highlighting their fundamental importance for social work. As part of Giroux's critical pedagogy, we also briefly explore his concepts of educated hope and agency, and examine his reconceptualisation of critical pedagogy beyond the classroom that potentially includes all aspects of social and cultural life.

Henry Giroux

Henry A. Giroux (b. 1943) is Chair for Scholarship in the Public Interest and The Paulo Freire Distinguished Scholar in Critical Pedagogy at McMaster University, Canada. Acclaimed as "one of the foremost critical educators of his time" (Peters, 2012, p. 688), Giroux is an internationally renowned scholar and cultural critic, best known for his ground-breaking work in public pedagogy, cultural studies, youth studies, media studies, the impact of neoliberalism on education, and his more recent work critiquing authoritarian populism (epitomised by the Trump regime) in American society. Giroux's scholarly output is diverse and challenging, leading peers to describe him as a "man on fire" (Barto and Whatley Bedford, 2013, p. 61). Initially denied tenure in his fist academic post at Boston University for his politically unpopular and radical views on education, Giroux has since received many prestigious accolades. Among such honours, he received the "Changing the World Award" and "The Paulo Freire Democratic Project Social Justice Award", both from Chapman University in 2015.

American born, Canadian-based Giroux is a prolific writer who, to date, has authored 68 books and several hundred journal articles and book chapters. He is one of the most cited academics in the humanities throughout the world. While much of Giroux's work is relevant to social work education and practice, in this chapter we focus particularly on his critical pedagogy.

While Giroux does not write specifically about social work education, the parallels between his vision of critical pedagogy and the espoused values of social work are deeply connected. His pioneering work on critical pedagogy holds clear implications for reinvigorating social work education and the pedagogic functions of social work practice, as politically emancipatory endeavours. As he states, "[e]ducation is not only about issues of work and economics, but also about questions of justice, social freedom, and the capacity for democratic agency, action, and change as well as the related issues of power, exclusion, and citizenship". Consequently, Giroux contends educational issues "should be addressed as part of a broader concern for renewing the struggle for social justice and democracy" (Giroux, 2014, p. 121).

Giroux came from a working-class background, growing up in Rhode Island in the 1950s and 1960s, where he developed an appreciation of solidarity being linked to agency and freedom. He attended a high school that was divided along the lines of class and race, which was formative in his sense of a social justice that "began at that moment when the lived experience of solidarity and loyalty rubbed up against … [his] own unquestioned racism and sexism, which had a long history in the daily encounters of [his] youth" (Giroux in Peters, 2012, p. 690). This period was also foundational in his development of a critical analysis and commitment to inclusive democratic agency. As he explains: "I moved through high school, met black men and women who refused … stereotypes and had the kindness and intelligence to open my eyes through both their own lived experiences and their access to a critical language that I lacked" (Giroux in Peters, 2012, p. 690). Later, he described how his teacher education influenced his development of critical pedagogy because he "quickly realized the ethical and political dimensions of teaching and how important the issue of developing a critical consciousness and formative culture was to any viable democratic society" (Giroux in Peters, 2012, p. 690).

Giroux's interest in critical pedagogy emerged from his experiences of teaching in a secondary school. His discovery of Freire's *Pedagogy of the Oppressed* sowed the seeds for his own engagement with the development of critical pedagogy (Peters, 2012). As he states:

> Crucial to my own conception of pedagogy is that I saw it as a moral and political practice that was not only about analyzing classrooms and schools. Pedagogy for me was central to proclaiming the power and necessity of ideas, knowledge and culture as central to any viable definition of politics, and living in a just world with others.
>
> *(Giroux in Peters, 2012, p. 696)*

This highly original conceptualisation of critical pedagogy formulated by Giroux will be explored, particularly in relation to its implications for social work practice later in this chapter.

Giroux's critique of neoliberalism

Giroux offers a powerful critique of neoliberal authoritarianism and its degradation of education and democracy that holds direct implications for social work. For Giroux, neoliberalism as a "crushing form of economic Darwinism" (2014, p. 2) and "predatory" global force is

> an ideology marked by the selling off of public goods to private interests; the attack on social provisions; the rise of the corporate state organized around privatization, free trade, and deregulation; the celebration of self-interests over social needs; the claim that government is the problem if it gets in the way of profits for the megacorporations and financial services; the investing in prisons rather than schools; the modelling of education after the culture of business; the insistence that exchange values are the only values worthy of consideration; the celebration of profit making as the essence of democracy coupled with the utterly reductionist notions that consumption is the only applicable form of citizenship.

In sum, Giroux identifies the chief problem with neoliberalism is that it "upholds the notion that the market serves as a model for structuring all social relations: not just the economy, but the governing of all social life" (Giroux, 2015, p. 126). Scathing about the "survival of the fittest" mentality this produces, and consistent with a critical social work analysis, Giroux identifies the consequences of neoliberalism as including the concentration of economic and political power with the elite, and "a ruthless attack on the welfare state", without any concern for ethical breaches or the social costs involved in manifesting such profound inequalities (Giroux, 2015, p. 126). He identifies the direct social problems emerging from this as: "immense suffering", "misery", the production of widespread "serious mental health crises", and increased suicide rates due to people being robbed of their economic security "and dignity", which he points out creates a "very bleak emotional and economic landscape for … 99% percent of the population" (Giroux, 2015, p. 126).

Giroux (2014, p. 2) explains that neoliberalism is "almost pathological in its disdain for community, social responsibility, public values and the public good"—the social attributes at the heart of social work. Similarly, neoliberalism "thrives on a kind of social amnesia" that aims to "erase" cornerstones of the foundational knowledge base for social work, such as "critical thought, historical analysis, and any understanding of broader systemic relations … by eliminating those public spheres where people learn to translate private troubles into public issues" (Giroux, 2014, p. 2).

Giroux argues public schools and universities have been particularly targeted in this war against public welfare and democracy (Giroux, 2006c), as they represent "one of the few public spheres left where people can learn the knowledge and skills necessary to allow them to think critically and hold power and authority accountable" (Giroux, 2014, p. 34). An effective way to arrest the counter-hegemonic potential of education is to reduce public spending on higher education, which has resulted in the corporatisation of universities. This has fundamentally changed the role of higher education in society, from one of public obligation and democratic responsibility to one of consumption and profit generation (Giroux, 2006c). Hence, within neoliberal contexts, education is important only "to the extent that it drives economic growth, technical innovation, market transformation and promotes national prosperity" (Giroux in Peters, 2012, p. 693). The impact of neoliberalism on higher education has effectively positioned university governance, priorities, funding and purpose as an "adjunct [to] corporate values and interests … undermining the civic and intellectual promises that make higher education a public good" (Giroux in Peters, 2012, p. 693). The palpable changes/impediments to critique, analysis and structural-level thinking include "balloon[ing]" class sizes, "an increased emphasis on rote learning and standardized testing" at the expense of critical forms of education, and the "skyrocket[ing]" of enrolment fees, "making it impossible for thousands of working-class youth to gain access to higher education" (Giroux in Peters, 2012, p. 693). Consequently, Giroux points out that universities are increasingly being degraded as spaces of critical questioning and open debate that challenges the status quo. According to Robbins (2009, pp. 462–463), who draws on Giroux, this

> orients students (and faculty) to particular sets of questions, particular futures, and thus particular forms of subjectivity and agency, where affective investments are made in merely repaying egregiously high student loans and getting a job, rather than with learning how to be critical, independent thinkers, gaining civic power and contributing to public life.

Nevertheless, Giroux points out that neoliberal corporatism needs "a culture of cynicism, insecurity, and despair" (2011, p. 133) to survive. This point galvanises his central thesis that posits critical pedagogy as vital in challenging the neoliberalisation of schooling and higher education. Despite the adverse impacts of neoliberalism, which represents a long-standing theme in Giroux's work, he maintains higher education is a contested space, characterised by pockets of resistance that provide students and educators with the opportunity to develop the critical thought essential for democratic participation and leadership. Giroux's vision of critical pedagogy necessitates academics' defence of higher education as a space for critical debate, self-reflection and social transformation (Giroux, 2006c). As he explains: "One way of challenging the new authoritarianism is to reclaim the relationship between critical education and social change" (Giroux, 2014, p. 23). Furthermore, he argues "Critical thought and the imaginings of a better world present a direct threat to a neoliberal paradigm in which the future replicates the present in an endless circle" (Giroux, 2014, p. 31). To this end Giroux views pedagogy as

> a mode of critical intervention, one that endows teachers with a responsibility to prepare students not merely for jobs but for being in the world in ways that allow them to influence the larger political, ideological, and economic forces that bear down on their lives.
>
> *(Giroux, 2014, p. 37)*

Giroux's vision of critical pedagogy: citizen activists for a radical democracy

A critique of technicist education

Giroux's vision of critical pedagogy offers a critique of technicist (technique-driven) approaches to education, instead emphasising the need for theory—particularly critical theories to inform pedagogic practices. As he notes, "Approaching pedagogy as a critical and political practice suggests that educators refuse all attempts to reduce classroom teaching exclusively to matters of technique" (Giroux, 2011, p. 79).

For Giroux, pedagogy is inherently political and fundamental in shaping knowledge, power, citizens and society. As he explains:

> Far from [objective or] innocent, pedagogical practices operate within institutional contexts that carry great power in determining what knowledge is of most worth, what it means for students to know something, and how such knowledge relates to a particular understanding of the self and its relationship to both others and the future.
>
> *(Giroux, 2011, p. 123)*

In the context of social work education, pedagogy shapes the theoretical and political orientation of future practitioners, impacting whether graduates see their role as agents of genuine change in the lives of the people they work with, or rather as essentially administrators of welfare regimes (Morley et al., 2019). Pedagogy in this sense is linked with questions of ethical responsibility.

Given the political potency of critical pedagogy to counteract neoliberalism, its contemporary eschewal in mainstream education is perhaps not unexpected. Conversely, we see that ascendance of technicist pedagogies that promote "a narrow sense of leadership, agency, and public values [that are] largely indifferent to those concerns that are critical to a just society" (Giroux, 2011, p. 116). While skills acquisition is an essential part of social work education, it becomes a problem when this process is separated off from ethical questions about the ends to which skills are being acquired. Again, while it is crucial that social work education has an evidence base, it is really important that ostensibly objective scientific methods do not objectify service users and individualise the difficulties and suffering they face. Equally, there is a danger the use of new technology can result in work processes driven by cost cutting, but gaining legitimacy among social workers by masquerading as pedagogic innovation. Giroux (2011, pp. 75–76) suggests educators should "resist all calls to depoliticize pedagogy through appeals to either scientific objectivity or ideological dogmatism" (Giroux, 2011, pp. 75–76), and reject "modes of pedagogy that embrace an instrumental rationality in which matters of justice, values, ethics, and power are erased from any notion of teaching and learning" (Giroux, 2011, pp. 3–4). This is crucial for social work education, which arguably places disproportionate emphasis on the learning and teaching of "practice" skills that are often treated as separate from, and more important than, other theoretical applications of knowledge within social work programs. This is problematic because within a technicist construction, practice skills are reduced to disembodied techniques that are related predominantly to micro-practices involved in direct service, such as counselling or interviewing. Without critical analysis, these practices are usually underpinned by hegemonic assumptions (see, for example, Morley et al., 2019; Reisch, 2013), and promoted at the expense of a broad range of social work practices that can be harnessed for progressive social change. The learning and teaching of these skills in social work education is often undertaken using role-plays, in which techniques are decontextualised and presented as apolitical and atheoretical with the ostensibly neutral goal of improving communication. If other critical curricula exist alongside the practice skills courses within social work programs, they are often marginalised in comparison, for these technical skills are seen as the real work of social work.

Alternatively, for Giroux (2011; Keller, 2001), among the skills that students develop when exposed to critical pedagogy are: critical thinking; the questioning of power and authority; analysing and challenging dominant power structures and relations; deconstructing language; connecting private troubles with public issues; critical reflection; and promoting democratic agency. The tendency to conceptualise the teaching of social work practice in terms of the acquisition of micro-skills, undercuts social work educators' intentions to produce practitioners committed to social justice through upholding the rights of service users. Giroux's concern is that by subjugating the skills he identifies as synonymous with producing critical citizens and activists capable of fostering a democratic society, we lose the fundamental sense of what the purpose of education actually is (Giroux, 2011). In articulating his concerns about the limitations of technicist approaches to teaching the communication skill of argumentation, he states:

> In spite of the professional pretense to neutrality, academics need to do more pedagogically than simply teach students how to be adept at forms of argumentation. Students … need

much more from their educational experience ... in and of itself [it] guarantees nothing in terms of furthering a critical agenda.

(Giroux, 2011, p. 147)

In the context of social work education, learning micro-skills associated with interviewing and counselling, or the steps associated with the latest crisis intervention model, in a technical fashion, may completely miss the core issues of power, oppression, inequality, discrimination and other social injustices embedded in the person's experience, along with the structural causes of their misery and misfortune, including the roles of capitalism, patriarchy, colonisation, xenophobia and other global forces implicated in producing ostensibly "private" troubles. As Giroux insists, education should provide students with "alternative modes of teaching, social relations, and imagining rather than those that merely support the status quo" (Giroux, 2011, p. 6).

In addition to obscuring the moral, political and social implications of practice, technicist pedagogy uses what Paulo Freire calls a "banking model", where the educator transfers knowledge deposits to students, as if they are passive and empty receptacles of this information (Freire, 1972). It is perhaps not surprising, then, that some social work practitioners also engage in similar information dumps with their clients. In highlighting the manifest limitations of such an approach, Giroux points out that education should not simply involve students "consum[ing] knowledge", as in learning technique, but requires both educators and students to "actively transform knowledge" (Giroux, 2011, p. 7). Giroux (2011, p. 154) was inspired by Freire, whom he knew personally. Giroux explains that Freire "believed that education was part of a project of freedom in its broadest sense and eminently political because it offered students the conditions for self-reflection, a self-managed life, and empowering forms of critical agency" (Giroux, 2011, p. 154). He further explains that "[p]edagogy in this sense connected learning to social change; it was a project and provocation that challenged students to critically engage with the world so they could act on it" (Giroux, 2011, p. 154). Without this, education is stripped of "public values, critical content, and civic responsibilities" to instead foster neoliberal goals of "creating new subjects wedded to the logic of privatization, efficiency, flexibility, the accumulation of capital, and the destruction of the social state" (Giroux, 2011, p. 123). Hence, for Giroux, critical pedagogy serves the dual purposes of social work education and practice, providing "not only important thoughtful and intellectual competencies; it also enables people to intervene critically in the world" (Giroux in Peters, 2012, p. 694). Giroux's vision of critical pedagogy is thus entirely compatible with the espoused goals of social work and holds important implications for the purpose of social work education and the design of curricula. Importantly, "This is a notion of education that is tied not to the alleged neutrality of teaching methods but to a vision of pedagogy that is directive and interventionist on the side of reproducing a democratic society" (Giroux, 2011, p. 147). For Giroux, "[t]his is what makes critical pedagogy different from training" (Giroux, 2011, p. 147).

The application of critical theory to education

Giroux's vision of "critical pedagogy" therefore provides a robust and much needed, alternative paradigm to the technicist "conservative revolution" (Garrett, 2010) currently being fostered by neoliberalism in both social work education and practice. Central to this for Giroux is critical theory, because critical theory is the "enemy of common sense" and a nemesis to the "anti-intellectual authoritarianism" promulgated by neoliberalism (Giroux in Peters, 2012 p. 697). Accordingly, critical theory helps us "develop better forms of knowledge, promote more just social relations, and search for new understandings regarding the task of developing new modes of agency, power, and action in the service of connecting theoretical rigor with social relevance" (Giroux in Peters, 2012, p. 697).

In relation to the example above about teaching practice skills, Giroux points to the importance of praxis (i.e. the connection between theory and practice/action) over and above technicist approaches to micro-skills. Giroux's approach seeks to critically engage students in questioning the social dimensions of power and knowledge, and create opportunities to work in ways that "overcome those social relations of oppression that make living unbearable for those who are poor, hungry, unemployed, refused adequate social services, and under the aegis of neoliberalism, viewed largely as disposable" (Giroux, 2006b, p. 210).

Giroux's vision of critical pedagogy includes creating the classroom conditions that enable: the critical questioning of power and authority; the challenging of hegemonic structures; an interrogation of the use of language; elucidation of the connections between the personal with the political; use of critical analysis and reflection; and other skills essential for exercising democratic agency (Giroux, 2011). Hence, informed by Giroux's critical pedagogy, role-plays, for example, are not simply used to enable students to develop technical skills necessary to engage in communication, but to develop a capacity to link critical theory to practice. This may involve students critically questioning and analysing the role of dominant power relations and structures in creating oppression; thinking beyond dominant constructs; critically questioning their own use of language and the language embedded within the narratives of other practitioners, clients and dominant discourses that construct experience; and considering the potential advocacy, research, policy, community development and activist practices needed, beyond communication techniques, to work toward a more democratic and socially just society. As Giroux suggests, "We need to make connections, build broad social movements, make pedagogy central to politics and dismantle the reactionary forms of neoliberalism, racism and media culture that have become normalized" (quoted in Peters, 2012, p. 698).

Critical pedagogy similarly holds implications for how role-plays are taught and assessed. A technicist approach to the learning and teaching of practice skills through role-plays may involve interviews of counselling sessions being pre-recorded and subsequently assessed independently by the marker, who engages in evaluation of the role-play without dialogue with the student. By contrast, Giroux's theorised approach to critical pedagogy recognises the importance of context, interpretation and dialogue in making meaning. Using Giroux's principles, an alternative approach may be to engage in live, immediate and negotiated feedback with students in order to co-construct learning experiences and assessment. As Giroux (2011, p. 156) explicates:

> Central to such a pedagogy is shifting the emphasis from teachers to students and making visible the relationships among knowledge, authority, and power. Giving students the opportunity to be problem-posers and engage in a culture of questioning in the classroom foregrounds the crucial issue of who has control over the conditions of learning and how specific modes of knowledge, identities, and authority are constructed within particular sets of classroom relations. Under such circumstances, knowledge is not simply received by students, but ... open to be challenged, and related to the self as an essential step towards agency, self- representation, and learning how to govern rather than simply be governed.

In our own experiences of teaching "practice", we have found using role-plays as a stimulus to facilitate critical analytic and reflective conversations with students to be one of the richest opportunities for learning that effectively links critical theory with social work practice in transparent and accessible ways. Drawing on Giroux, Guilherme (2006, pp. 185–186) provides a pertinent description of this process in which both educators and students "become critical agents actively questioning and negotiating the relationship between theory and practice, critical analysis and common sense, and learning and social change".

An important component of this experience involves "students also learn[ing] how to engage others in critical dialogue and be held accountable for their views" (Giroux, 2011, p. 156). In this way, students are encouraged to think critically about a range of social issues, power dynamics and the political and ethical dimensions of their practice, and to engage in learning that is transformative, rather than simply rote learning techniques, which are then mistaken as social work practice.

His vision includes the view that: "we need to educate students to be critical agents, to learn how to take risks, engage in thoughtful dialogue and address what it means to be socially responsible" (quoted in Peters, 2012, p. 694). For Giroux, then, critical education is essential to foster critical, self-reflective, morally agentic and knowledgeable citizens who have tools to "unsettle common-sense assumptions, theorize matters of self and social agency and engage the ever-changing demands and promises of a democratic polity" (Giroux, 2011, p. 3). Such qualities and tools, he argues, are central to the survival of democratic society and indeed humanity (Giroux, 2011, p. 3).

Giroux's ideas combine theoretical insights from the works of Gramsci, the Frankfurt School, Freire and poststructuralists such as Derrida and Foucault (each addressed separately in this volume). As with critical approaches to social work, Giroux draws on progressive elements from a range of critical theories (e.g. radical theories, feminism, postmodernism, poststructuralism, neo-Marxism, etc.). His earlier work criticises the way reproduction theories of education (e.g. Bourdieu and Passeron, 1977; Bowles and Gintis, 1976) construct a rigid, totalitising narrative of powerlessness; while traditional resistance theories over-emphasise individual choice and experience, thus ignoring the impact of power structures and systems. Giroux argues that both approaches engage in producing an unhelpful structure–agency dichotomy. Instead, he proposes that educators need to transcend this artificially constructed divide between structure and agency because material domination is always already cultural and discursive. Therefore, Giroux has posited a more dialectical theory of resistance, which Robbins (2009, p. 433) sees as highlighting "the limits and possibilities of agency within specific historical and institutional contexts by dignifying students' (and teachers') resistance to the commands of seemingly fixed structures". In articulating how this informs critical pedagogy, he suggests, "We need to combine the modernist emphasis on the capacity of individuals to use critical reason to address the issue of public life with a critical post-modernist concern with how we might experience agency in [the] world" (Giroux, 2006a, p. 49).

Educated hope

One expression of this theoretical combination is Giroux's concept of "educated hope", which involves not only critique, but the creation of conceptual space to imagine alternative futures that might lead to social transformation. Educated hope contests the assumption that existing social structures cannot be challenged and enables students to envision alternative ways of living and organising society (Giroux, 2006c). Giroux (2012, p. 38) suggests:

> Hope makes the leap for us between critical education, which tells us what must be changed; political agency, which gives us the means to make change; and the concrete struggles through which change happens. Hence, hope is more than a politics, it is also a pedagogical and performative practice that provides the foundation for enabling human beings to learn about their potential as moral and civic agents.

For social work, the concept of educated hope opens multiple possibilities and practices to resist, contest and dismantle unjust structures in society. Moreover, educated hope challenges us to "reclaim social agency within a broader discourse of ethical advocacy" in our pedagogic practices without neglecting the impact of structural forces such as global capitalism and neo-liberalism (Giroux, 2006c, p. 272), and provides both students and educators with a language of resistance and possibility (Giroux, 2006a).

Combining ethics with politics, this pedagogic strategy connects individual agency with social change and, in the context of social work, can, for example, be used to uncover social work practitioners' and educators' capacity to contest hegemonic discourses, and neoliberal organisations that seek to restrict critical practices. This is perhaps why Giroux has described educated hope as a potentially "subversive" practice (see, for example, Giroux, 2012). As he further explains:

> Hope as a form of militant utopianism … is one of the pre-conditions for individual and social struggle, and the ongoing practice of critical education in a wide variety of sites—the attempt to make a difference by being able to imagine otherwise in order to act in other ways.
>
> *(Giroux, 2006c, p. 270)*

Critical pedagogy beyond the classroom

A vital contribution of Giroux's vision of critical pedagogy is his conceptualisation of education beyond the classroom. This holds significant implications for social work practice. As he notes:

> The articulation of knowledge to experience, the construction of new modes of agency, the production of critical knowledge, the recovery of critical histories, and the possibility of linking knowledge to social change cannot be limited to the students we encounter in our classes.
>
> *(Giroux in Peters, 2012, p. 695)*

Giroux reconceptualised pedagogy as a mode of social transformation not limited to formal educational settings, but as any practices "that shape, mold, socialize and educate individuals" (Keller, 2001, p. 224), which potentially occur within multiple sites for various social purposes. Influenced by Gramsci's (1971, p. 350) work on hegemonic domination, and how "every relationship of 'hegemony' is necessarily an educational relationship" (p. 350), Giroux notes that the most effective educators today have been multi-national companies and governments promoting conservative agendas for profit and power. However, critical theory can be mobilised as a counter pedagogy to resist racism, sexism, homophobia, class oppression, ableism and other harmful social divisions. Translating this conceptualisation of pedagogy into social work practice: every interaction social workers engage in has pedagogic functions, whether practitioners are aware of this or not. In social workers' practice with citizens, do we educate for progressive social change? Or do the types of conversations with the people with whom we work serve to maintain an inequitable status quo? Giroux's critical pedagogy enables social workers to appreciate the pedagogic dimensions of neoliberal welfare regimes, for example, and how our own practice responses may be complicit in denigrating and disciplining impoverished and otherwise marginalised populations, or in championing their rights. In case managing clients, for example, how do practitioners engage with service users about the injustices associated with austerity measures and many managerial organisational practices? Many social workers feel themselves constrained by the professional role to articulate their own concerns here, and while questions of roles are important in social work, it is crucial not to lose sight of the ethical dimension of critical pedagogy here. This commitment could allow us to find ways to connect with service users with regard to organisation against unjust social policies. What Giroux reminds us of is the need not to fall into fatalistically using pedagogic practices to quiet dissent and seek compliance with unjust resourcing and problematic (in)eligibility assessment schemes. For example, do we participate in psychoeducation about hegemonic psychiatric constructions of mental illness, do we raise consciousness about how rates of mental illness are distributed along the lines of disadvantage, while seeking to depathologise personal responses to inequality, precarity, exclusion and oppression? Hence Giroux's work on critical pedagogy and neoliberal critique provides vital lessons for social work practice and education within and beyond the classroom.

Within the classroom:

> Pedagogy is a mode of critical intervention ... that endows teachers with a responsibility to prepare students not merely for jobs but for being in the world in ways that allow them to influence the larger political, ideological, and economic forces that bear down on their lives and the lives of clients.
>
> *(Giroux, 2014, p. 37)*

Within the domain of social work education, Giroux's influence seeks to create social work practitioners who are citizen activists (Giroux, 2011). As he explains:

> We need to link knowing with action, learning with social engagement, and this requires addressing the responsibilities that come with teaching students and others to fight for an inclusive and radical democracy by recognizing that education in the broadest sense is not just about understanding, however critical, but also about providing the conditions for assuming the responsibilities we have as citizens to expose human misery and to eliminate the conditions that produce it.
>
> *(Giroux, 2011, p. 148)*

In this sense, education is not simply about critical questioning, but intimately connected to "recognizing the value of a future in which matters of liberty, freedom, and justice play a constitutive role" (Giroux, 2011, p. 125). Within this vision, the point of social work education is not simply to transmit knowledge but to "create the conditions in which forms of agency are available for students to learn how not only to think critically but to act differently" (Giroux, 2011, p. 125). Our own experiences of researching the use of critical pedagogy in social work education indicate that it can have quite direct impacts on interests and capacities to become activists (Morley, 2016, 2019; Morley and Macfarlane, 2014; O'Connor et al., 2016). This includes engaging in social action and protest, as one student states, for example: "I now see activism as a fundamental part of social work practice. I see it as my responsibility. I didn't think that before my degree" (Morley, 2016, p. 50). Another student similarly shared: "As soon as I started to engage with this learning and the links between personal and political, I started to become an activist" (Morley, 2016, p. 50).

Activism can also be enacted through more covert practices, such as bringing a critical analysis to the conceptualisation of social problems that clients present with, ethical advocacy to facilitate more socially just outcomes for clients, and contesting organisational practices that contradict the espoused values of social work. As this student states: "Critical social work education has given me the skills to challenge neoliberal constructs; to resist by advocating for change, at structural and systemic levels instead of just looking at individuals for the answer" (Morley, 2016, p. 50). Others talked about their need to "voice concerns and advocate more effectively for the needs of community members" and "challenge practices th[ey] believe to be unethical within organisation[s]" (Morley and Macfarlane, 2014, p. 348), for example.

Conclusion

Ultimately, in this chapter we have argued that Giroux's vision of critical pedagogy offers vital lessons for the revivification of social work education and practice as emancipatory projects. This vision is underpinned by an ethical, pedagogic commitment to combatting inequality and oppression, while fostering a radically democratic and just society. Such a vision can be greatly assisted by social workers, educated in, and educating for, critical and dialogical participation (with their constituents) in the public sphere, "unsettling common-sense assumptions" about our social problems and linking structural critique with personal agency, as agents for a democratic polity (Giroux, 2011, p. 3). As Giroux argues, this democratic agency simultaneously necessitates the creation of conditions that foster transformative learning, within and beyond the classroom. In this, Giroux positions critical pedagogy and the educated hope it embodies, as a counter pedagogy to the hegemonic order, and therefore a "potentially energizing practice that gets students to both think and act differently" (Giroux, 2011, p. 14). Within social work education, critical pedagogy can enable students to link critical social theory with practice, and in doing so develop a much broader, reflexive and ethically robust practice framework. This can result in producing citizen activists and critical practitioners who are prepared to fight for justice rather than reproducing the status quo. Having elucidated the implications of Giroux's critical pedagogy for social work education and practice, we conclude with Giroux's (2003, p. 483) summation of what is at stake for critical educators in the context of today's neoliberal universities:

> Finding our way to a more human future means educating a new generation of scholars who not only defend higher education as a democratic public sphere, but also frame their own agency as both scholars and citizen activists willing to connect their research, teaching and service with broader democratic concerns over equality, justice, and an alternative vision of what the university might be and what society might become.

In essence, then, Henry Giroux's visionary pedagogy is a moral and political call to civic courage that has implications for every aspect of social work education in fostering critical notions of professionalism and citizenship.

Acknowledgements

With kind acknowledgements to Dr Selma Macfarlane (of Deakin University) and Jessica Fox (of Queensland University of Technology) who assisted us with library research for this chapter.

References

Amsler, S. (2013). Criticality, pedagogy and the promises of radical democratic education in, against and beyond the university. In S. Cowden & G. Singh (Eds.) *Critical pedagogy in, against and beyond the university* (pp. 67–84). New York and London: Bloomsbury.
Barto, M., & Whatley Bedford, A. (2013). Henry Giroux: Man on fire. In J.D. Kirylo (Ed.) *A critical pedagogy of resistance: 34 pedagogues we need to know* (pp. 61–64). Rotterdam: Bloomsbury.
Bourdieu, P., & Passeron, J. (1977). *Reproduction in education, society and culture*. London: Sage.

Bowles, S., & Gintis, H. (1976). *Schooling in capitalist America: Educational reform and the contradictions of economic life*. Chicago, IL: Haymarket Books.

Freire, P. (1972). *Pedagogy of the oppressed*. London: Penguin.

Garrett, P. M. (2010). Examining the 'conservative revolution': Neoliberalism and social work education. *Social Work Education*, 29(4), 340–355.

Giroux, H. (2003). Dystopian nightmares and educates hopes: The return of the pedagogical and the promise of democracy. *Policy Futures in Education*, 1(3), 467–487.

Giroux, H. (2006a). Border pedagogy in the age of postmodernism. In C. Robbins (Ed.) *The Giroux reader* (pp. 47–66). Boulder, CO: Paradigm Publishers.

Giroux, H. (2006b) Cultural studies, critical pedagogy, and the responsibility of intellectuals. In C. Robbins (Ed.). *The girous reader* (pp. 195–215). London: Paradigm Press.

Giroux, H. (2006C). Youth, higher education, and the crisis of public time: Educated hope and the possibility of a democratic future. In C. Robbins (Ed.) *The Giroux reader* (pp. 253–277). Boulder, CO: Paradigm Publishers.

Giroux, H. (2011). *On critical pedagogy*. New York: Continuum.

Giroux, H. (2012). When hope is subversive. *Tikkun*, 19(6), 38–39.

Giroux, H. (2014). *Neoliberalism's war on higher education*. Chicago, IL: Haymarket Books.

Giroux, H. (2015). *Dangerous thinking in the age of new authoritarianism*. Boulder, CO: Paradigm Publishers.

Gramsci, A. (1971). *Selections from the prison notebooks*. New York: International Press.

Guilherme, M. (2006). Is there a role for critical pedagogy in language/cultural studies?. In C. Robbins (Ed.) *The Giroux reader* (pp. 181–193). Boulder, CO: Paradigm Publishers.

Keller, D. (2001). Critical pedagogy, cultural studies and radical democracy at the turn of the millennium: Reflections of the work of Henry Giroux. *Cultural Studies—Critical Methodologies*, 1(2), 220–239.

Morley, C. (2016). Promoting activism through critical social work education: The impact of global capitalism and neoliberalism on social work and social work education. *Critical and Radical Social Work*, 4(1), 39–57.

Morley, C. (2019). Social work education and activism. In S. Webb (Ed.) *Routledge Handbook of Critical Social Work* (pp. 437–448). London: Routledge.

Morley, C., & Macfarlane, S. (2014). Critical social work as ethical social work: Using critical reflection to research students' resistance to neoliberalism. *Critical and Radical Social Work*, 2(3), 337–356.

Morley, C., Macfarlane, S., & Ablett, P. (2019). *Engaging with social work: A critical introduction* (2nd ed.). South Melbourne: Cambridge University Press.

O'Connor, D, Thomas, E., White, K & Morley, C. (2016). The challenges, triumphs and learning from participating in an Australian social work students' activist group. *Critical and Radical Social Work*, 42(2), 289–299.

Peters, M. (2012). Henry Giroux on democracy unsettled: From critical pedagogy to the war on youth—An interview. *Policy Futures in Education*, 10(6), 688–699.

Reisch, M. (2013). Social work education and the neoliberal challenge: The US response to increasing global inequality. *Social Work Education*, 32(6), 715–733.

Robbins, C. (2009). Searching for politics with Henry Giroux: Through cultural studies to public pedagogy and the 'terror of neoliberalism'. *Review of Education, Pedagogy, and Cultural Studies*, 31(5), 428–478.

18

Social work through the pedagogical lens of Jacques Rancière

Stephen Cowden

COVENTRY UNIVERSITY, ENGLAND

Introduction

> Equality is not a goal to be reached. It is not a common level, an equivalent amount of riches or an identity of living conditions that must be reached as the consequence of historic evolution and strategic action. Instead it is a point of departure. This first principle immediately ties up with a second one: equality is not a common measure between individuals, it is a capacity through which individuals act as the holders of a common power, a power belonging to anyone.
>
> (Rancière, 2017)

This chapter explores the idea of equality through the prism of a case study from practice, by drawing on the pedagogical lens of Jacques Rancière. It highlights the complexities of power relations inherent in social work practitioners' relationships with service users and points to the implications for a critical pedagogic approach to social work education.

As a student social worker in London in the early 1990s there was a particular case I had on my first placement that really stayed with me. The placement was a social services office in south London – it was a typical inner London borough prior to the gentrification that later took over; very ethnically mixed, poor, scruffy looking, but also with a kind of vibrant energy. One of the pieces of work given to me by my Practice Teacher was writing court reports for various young men who had been in trouble with the police. There was one sixteen-year-old man, David F, who was a complex character and someone who intrigued me. His mum was a single parent to him and his younger half-sister. His mum was studying accountancy to try to improve the family's situation, but this seemed to mean that while she was out most evenings attending classes, the care of his younger half-sister, who was aged 10, was left to a large extent with David. He was extremely attentive to her; he would cook for them both, help her with her homework, and was in general very caring and protective toward her. I was really surprised (and impressed) by the way he helped her so much with her homework, as he was himself 'persistently truanting' at the time. This was one of the reasons he was referred to me. The context for his unlawful activity was a gang he was part of. He was the only white boy in a gang made up of all young black lads; something he was quite proud of. The gang used to go around stealing portable radios and CD players from cars. David's nickname was 'lightning' as he claimed he was able to smash car windows and remove these from cars faster than anyone else in the gang. He claimed he was able to do this in 30 seconds. Sometimes the gang would also attempt to rob kebab shops in their local areas, so while he justified his robbery of cars on the basis that the owners would 'get it all back on insurance', he was also involved in some nasty aggression with shop owners. When I had put all this information together, I felt a real sense of contradiction in my feelings about him. I really disliked the aggression and violence he was involved in, yet I did not feel that completely defined him. I struggled with the idea of what my role was in writing a Court Report on his behalf, and when I took this to my Practice Teacher, he explained that our role here was to speak for people who were not able to be 'the judge of their own best interests' – yet I felt very unsure how I was supposed to be playing that role. On a practical level I was aware that the violence and aggression he was involved with were really wrong, but at the same time a trajectory into the criminal justice system would only brutalise him still further, emphasising all the worst aspects of his character, as well as taking him away from his half-sister; a relationship that seemed to have brought out the best in him. I did the work as well as I could – as it was, the magistrate brushed over my report in seconds and made the decision herself, but the case stayed with me for the issues it raised about the nature of the social work role.

The International Federation of Social Work defines social work as

> a practice-based profession and an academic discipline that promotes social change and development, social cohesion, and the empowerment and liberation of people. Principles of social justice, human rights, collective responsibility and respect for diversities are central to social work. Underpinned by theories of social work, social sciences, humanities and indigenous knowledge, social work engages people and structures to address life challenges and enhance wellbeing.
>
> *(IFSW, 2014)*

For me, this summarises the social work mission at its most positive. But experience demonstrates that the reality of doing social work is not only a lot more mundane, but also could be often quite removed from these principles. When you are a social work practitioner, this is the contradictory space that you occupy, and the work I was doing with David seemed to embody those contradictions. I was attracted to social work because it seemed to allow the possibility of doing work based on ideals of 'equality and social justice', and the material I was studying on the social work course also promoted this as the basis of the profession. Yet I was also acutely aware that when you were out in practice, there were real questions about how those commitments were realised. Not only are there a whole series of organisational and institutional structures and imperatives that you are working within – and there were issues about how well and how badly some social workers negotiated these – but there was also a real question about what judging someone else's 'best interests' actually meant. Social work's claim to being a profession is based on the application of specialist knowledge – and I do not want to suggest for a moment that this is not important. But what I was really struck by was how differently this assessing the 'best interests' of another could play out with different social workers in different situations. This seems to me to express a tension between those aspirations to social justice, and the need to 'get on with the job'. As someone coming into social work at the height of the Thatcher period, I was also really conscious of the way an emerging anti-state welfare rhetoric coming from the Tory government grabbed onto a lot of these tensions around the power differential between professionals and service users through a language of service users now needing to be 'in control'. This was the beginning of what we would now call 'neoliberalism' (though that word was not used until quite a bit later), and I felt that Stuart Hall was really insightful in the way he used the term 'authoritarian populism' (Hall & Jacques, 1983) to describe Thatcher's stance toward social welfare. She always positioned herself as 'out there with the people', which also always meant she was with them *against* the welfare state and the 'nosey' professionals who worked within it. This appeal to the idea of 'people wanting to stand on their own two feet' instead of being 'dependent on' or controlled by the state became the basis of the way the Tories created a social consensus for retrenching and privatising social welfare. However, rather than address the issue of the power professionals had in relation to service users, the imposition of neoliberal principles onto social work has made the tensions between professionals and service users much worse. A recent report from the UK Family Rights Group about the experiences that families had with social workers, epitomises this. It noted that 'while there are structural problems that make everyone feel overstretched, families face a system which is not just at crisis point, but one where everyday humanity can be forgotten' (Community Care, 2018). This is one small instance of the way neoliberal managerial imperatives which dominate now are crushing the soul of social work. At the same time, however, it is important not to blame everything on neoliberalism, as many of the contradictions involved here already existed, as they were to a large extent built into the way social work was constituted in the UK in the period after the Second World War.

Social work developed as a salaried profession in the process of social rebuilding that took place at this time, which in Britain saw the creation of the welfare state through massive increases of state investment in education, health and social services. These represented huge social advances, which improved life expectancy, social mobility, employment opportunities and prosperity for many, but it was also the case that poverty and exclusion were contained rather than eradicated. Social work's ideological framework, as it grew in this period, came from the philosophy of Fabianism – an evolutionary and gradualist form of socialism. As Fred Powell (2001:46) has noted, at the centre of this reformist tradition in social policy was the concept of social obligation – that public services represented a social contract between the citizen and state, whose good intentions the individual was expected to respect, as the basis of being entitled to assistance. While rhetorically collectivist, the social work practice that grew out of this represented 'an essentially individualised response based on humanistic values, rather than structural change.' Taylor et al. (1995:12–13) point to some further implications of this when discussing the growth of social work during the 1960s:

> Social work treatment, however much it can be described as being in the client's own interest, could often result in spiral of further labelling, further deviant commitment, and finally the irreversible channelling of individuals into careers in prison, mental hospitals or skid row. Placing the activities of social welfare agencies into political and ideological context, it is easy to see that the everyday decisions of workers in those agencies, flow not from an ill-informed understanding of 'deviant' or 'maladjustment' but from a clearly formulated, Fabian-conformist, and essentially *liberal* ideology … – the encouragement 'to adjust', 'to encourage good citizenship' to 'mature' – and indeed to accept the good offices of the helping agencies themselves.

It was the gap between David F as he sat in front of me, with all his particular experience of life, and this notion of 'good citizenship' that I was supposed to be promoting that seemed most problematic to me at the time, and it is this that brings me to a discussion of the meaning of the 'equality' in social work, which is the focus of this chapter. I want to open this up through a discussion with the work of the French philosopher Jacques Rancière (1940–present), someone who has written extensively on the meaning and significance of equality. At the time of being a social work student, I was not aware of the Rancière's work. That came quite a bit later, but Rancière's work links with this case that I have discussed above because of his very original ideas about how teachers, and other professionals by implication, work with their students or service users in situations like the one I have been describing. He is also really interested in the way professionals such as social workers can profess a belief in 'empowerment and liberation' but, in reality, be doing something not that much like that, not always in a bad way – but I still think it is important to try to understand why that happens as it does. It is in this sense that I think Rancière's theories offer a unique way to understand social work, as well as allowing us to think about how we can deal with these contradictions in practice. As noted, Rancière's work is intensely preoccupied by the question of equality, but the way he approaches this is very distinctive. Rather than stating what equality stands for as a positive value, which is like the IFSW statement, his work comes out of a tradition of negativity in critical thinking. What this means is that Rancière works by delving into an abstract concept, such as equality, and trying to figure out what that actually means at the level of everyday life for people. This tradition of negativity in critical thinking contrasts with the way the process of defining an abstract concept is usually approached. So in dominant conceptions of political citizenship, the starting point will be the meaning of equality as a positive ideal; Rancière's approach, by contrast, sees equality as what happens when people reject or come out *against something*. In this chapter I want to point to the ways we in social work can engage with these ideas. I begin with a discussion of his approach to philosophy and politics, moving to an outline of his distinctive ideas about equality in one of his most important books, *The Ignorant Schoolmaster* (1991).

Against abstraction: Rancière's conception of equality

Jacques Rancière was born in 1940 in Algiers, which was still a French colony at that point. He entered the elite *École Normale Supérieure* University in Paris in 1960 and became a student of Louis Althusser, who was at that stage France's leading Marxist and Communist Party intellectual. This was at a time when the Communist Party in France gained around 20% of the overall vote in elections, as well as being highly influential in the trade union movement. In 1965, Rancière was invited to join a seminar group, which became hugely influential in the humanities and among Leftist thinkers. The group's work was published in French in 1965 as the book *Reading Capital*, with Louis Althusser as the main author, and other members of the group also writing chapters (see Althusser et al., 2016). Althusser's central project in doing this work was to establish that Marxism was a 'science' and, in order to achieve this, the group undertook a densely theoretical re-reading of Marx's *Capital*. Rancière contributed a chapter to this book and during this stage was very much a loyal disciple of Althusser.

However, all of this changed when the student protests and their violent repression by the authorities exploded onto the streets of Paris in May 1968. Although the Parisian university, where all these Marxist intellectuals were based, was one of the key places where the action began, Althusser refused to join in or support the protests; instead he dismissed them as not revolutionary at all, initiated as they were by 'petit-bourgeois' students, at a time when the working class was 'not yet ready' for a revolution. Yet Althusser's proclamations were made as students were already in the process of linking politically with workers in the streets outside the *École Normale Supérieure*, an alliance that went on to build the biggest general strike in French postwar history (Figure 18.1).

Social work and Rancière's pedagogy

Figure 18.1 Factory occupied by the workers
Source: BeenAroundAWhile at en.wikipedia, CC BY-SA 3.0, https://commons.wikimedia.org/w/index.php?curid=47397033

Althusser's failure to engage with the reality of what was going on around him shocked, disappointed and angered Rancière, who by contrast threw himself into support of this new political movement. It also led to him thinking about how Althusser could be a great Marxist intellectual, but at the same time, entirely unable to grasp the significance of the unfolding developments among students and workers that were happening right in front of him. (This sense of the emerging political process represented by May 1968 is captured wonderfully by Kristin Ross in her book *May '68 and Its Afterlives* [2002]). Rancière went on to argue that at the core of Althusser's understanding of Marxism was an idealised notion of 'the proletariat', which ordinary flesh and blood workers had failed to live up to; that for him, the working class were not so much people as an abstraction, an idealised philosophical category. For Rancière these problems were amplified by the elevated social status of intellectuals. In his book *Althusser's Lesson* (2011), Rancière vociferously attacked his former teacher, arguing that the privileged position of theory, even really radical theory, had the effect of hugely reinforcing the privileged position of intellectuals; not just over students, but within political movements, and within society as a whole. Through getting directly involved in the protests of '68, Rancière came to experience the way intellectuals like himself

> had no specific place in May, no particular role; they were like everyone else, part of the crowd … like everyone else, they did not represent a concrete social category, but merely an agent at work with other agents, on the street, inscribed in the same project.
>
> *(Ross, 2002:174)*

It is important to note that Rancière was not being simply anti-intellectual here; it was rather about how making sense of this whole experience was central in allowing him to re-think differently what the role of intellectuals in political movements should be. This experience was pivotal for Rancière as it informs so much of the work he went on to produce, as well as setting out the kind of 'contrary' intellectual he went on to become. In this sense the May '68 events and his split with Althusser, form the essential background of one of his most important books, *The Ignorant Schoolmaster* (1991).

Against explication: *The Ignorant Schoolmaster*

The Ignorant Schoolmaster (1991) is fundamentally a book about the kinds of social relationships in which we find ourselves when 'education' takes place. While the focus of the book is education, Rancière wanted to make the point that it is not just something that happens in schools, colleges and universities; instead this is what happens whenever you are in any situation when you have to be shown how to do something you have not done before. This could be becoming part of a band, joining a political party, starting a new job, having a child and so on. In this sense the politics of education are the politics of society as a whole, as though society is like a big school. *The Ignorant Schoolmaster* (1991) does not involve Rancière setting out his views directly; rather, Rancière's views are expressed through an account of an unusual and once famous eighteenth-century Enlightenment educator, Joseph Jacotot (1770–1840). Although Jacotot's influence was huge in his day, his writings had been largely forgotten until their resuscitation by Rancière.

As a young man Jacotot had been actively involved in the French Revolution, and during the very open and experimental period of the revolution, he worked as an educator at the École Polytechnique in Dijon. While working here Jacotot began to conduct experiments in 'democratic teaching methods' which were highly regarded by students and staff. The success of these brought him into politics and in 1815 he was elected to the Chamber of Deputies in the French parliament. However, with the restoration of the Bourbon monarchy to power in France, the tide turned against this radicalism and Jacotot was forced into exile in Belgium in 1819, where in his changed circumstances he had to accept 'a position of Professor at half-pay' at the University of Louvain (Rancière, 1991:1). Here he was given the job of teaching French to Flemish-speaking students, only there was one fairly enormous problem – he spoke no Flemish and the students spoke no French. Faced with what might have seemed to many teachers an insurmountable problem, Jacotot improvised a solution. He managed to obtain a set of copies of a bilingual edition of a French novel called *Les Aventures de Télémaque* (which recounted the travels of Telemachus, son of Ulysses) and made these available to his students. He then experimented with a method of teaching where instead of explaining to his students how the French language worked grammatically, structurally, linguistically as the vast majority of language teaching does, he adopted a highly unorthodox method of asking his students to learn to recite this book in French, section by section, building up to a recitation of the entire book. What he discovered, to his own astonishment, was that the experiment was more successful than he could have imagined; as his students went through this book, they figured out themselves how to speak French. As Rancière (1991:4) notes:

> Jacotot had not explained spelling or conjugations to them. They had looked for the French words that corresponded to the words they knew and the reasons for their grammatical endings by themselves. They had learned to put them together to make, in turn, French sentences by themselves; sentences whose spelling and grammar became more exact as they progressed through the book.

It was out of this that Jacotot developed a method that came to be known as 'Universal Teaching'. Rancière described the emancipatory power of Jacotot's method of 'Universal Teaching', as an experiment that demonstrated:

> One can teach what one doesn't know if the student is emancipated, that is to say they are obliged to **use** their own intelligence ... To emancipate an ignorant person, one must be, and only need be, emancipated oneself, that is to say conscious of the true power of the human mind. The ignorant person will learn by themselves what the master doesn't know if the master believes they can and obliges them to realise their capacity.
>
> *(Rancière, 1991:15)*

Jacotot's method was one in which instead of presuming his students' ignorance, which he needed to address through an extensive process of explanation, Jacotot presumed their capacity; that is, their ability to themselves establish the connections on which their learning was based. Of course, the teacher still had a role to play, but this was not one of knowledge transmission. Rather, the teacher's role lay in requiring the student to pay attention to their intellect, as well as that of others, and in this way 'realise their capacity'. In developing a pedagogical method based on this, Jacotot radically overturned the dominant conception of the pedagogical relation. Rancière characterises this as the initiation of a *presumption of equality* within the classroom. This approach to equality was also not simply theoretical or rhetorical, but deeply practical – and indeed the method developed had a highly successful outcome. It was the way Jacotot inverted the presumption of ignorance into a presumption for capacity that Rancière seized upon as a means to critique contemporary pedagogy and the power relations that surround it.

This is significant because the vast bulk of contemporary learning theory gestures to an ideal of educational equality, but in practice defers this as an ideal to aspire to – as something that can only be approached when the students have diligently listened to and absorbed that which their teacher has explained to them. What Rancière saw in Jacotot was the way this assumption was turned on its head – so instead of being something to be aimed for, the enacting of equality became the very basis of the process and practice of teaching. As Rancière puts it, 'equality exists as the ensemble of practices that mark out its domain; *there is no other reality of equality than the reality of equality*' (1991:79, italics added). Thus it was the presupposition of equality *at the outset* that made a democratic pedagogy possible. In developing these radical conclusions, we can see how Rancière was drawing on his experience with Althusser, the revolutionary intellectual who was afraid of what would happen to his own power as an intellectual by getting involved in an actual revolution. In this book Rancière returned Jacotot to the present, as someone who was able to show that intellectual discovery is not something conferred by the master onto the student; it is instead something that needs to be appropriated by the student through an act of 'transgressive will':

> To explain something to someone first of all is to show them they cannot understand it by themselves. Before being the act of the pedagogue, explication is the myth of pedagogy, the parable of a world divided into knowing ones and ignorant ones, ripe minds and immature ones, the capable and the incapable, the intelligent and the stupid.
>
> *(Rancière, 1991:6)*

Rancière's conception of the role of the teacher is thus not the person who graciously shares their knowledge with the uneducated. It is rather that of a person who insists that education is what happens when students begin to pay attention to the development of their own and others' intellects. This is the process Rancière tries to capture when he describes work of the teacher as 'revealing intelligence to itself' (Rancière, 1991:28). The method of equality demands that the capacity for intellectual engagement is taken as a starting point, rather than as something that can only be achieved through quantitative or qualitative changes in consciousness in the student, which must be led by the all-knowing teacher. A pedagogy that is not 'stultifying' is one that brings forth the capacity for intellectual engagement and knowledge formation which every human being possesses, and it is this deeply democratic and egalitarian dimension of the Enlightenment that Rancière wants to return to as a means of challenging the assumptions of contemporary educational and pedagogical practice. On a number of occasions throughout the book, Rancière reiterates one of the key principles of Jacotot's 'Universal Teaching' method; that 'everything is in everything' (Rancière, 1991:41). What this means is that it is in the process of discovering the connections between one thing and another that students discover not just their own intelligence, but the joy of intellectual discovery. In describing Jacotot as an 'ignorant schoolmaster' Rancière is of course being ironic. The method of 'Universal Teaching' that Jacotot developed through his experiments came from a huge amount of effort, commitment and insight. But the word 'ignorant' articulates the idea that the job of the educator is not to explain, but rather to compel the will of the student to take seriously their own intellect, and those of others, and in doing so uncover their own capacity for independent critical thought.

Against knowing best: the ignorant social worker

At the beginning of this chapter I talked about my work with David F and I want to return to the discussion of him and his situation as a way of thinking about what all this means for social work. I previously discussed the way the magistrate brushed over my report and made her own decision regarding David, and the decision she made was not to give him a custodial sentence. However, she did require him to return to attending school, a decision that was seen as a process of re-integrating him into some kind of normal path for a young man. My Practice Teacher at the social services office where I was based explained to me that the job of making this school re-integration happen now fell to me, and it was with considerable self-doubt and dread as to how I was ever going to achieve this, that I began this work. As I noted earlier, David had been 'persistently truanting' from school for at least a year, and more to the point, was manifestly disinterested in attending again. Indeed, I could see that my many entreaties to him about the benefits of doing so, and numerous meetings set up to appeal to him to do that, were having zero impact. The problem for me was that I could see at the outset that re-integration into the existing system was not going to work, not because he was not capable of learning, but because the manner and attitudes he had were entirely contrary to those which schools require of their pupils. My placement was nearing its conclusion and I really wanted to leave having offered him something, but I was, at the same time, uncertain as to what I was going to be able to do if he simply continued to reject everything that was on offer. With nothing organised, I could see the streets and career criminality beckoning. I decided to work with something he had consistently told me he felt really passionate about – music. Eventually I came across a further education course that would accept him for a programme in music production. When I introduced him, the teachers there evinced a scepticism of having seen 'people like him' many times before, to which he responded by slouching on the chair, looking out of a window and confirming every pre-conceived idea they already had about him. But as I left, they said to me that they would do what they could in working with him, and it was clear that they were really passionate teachers who cared about what they did. They also said to me that my enthusiasm for his success was all very good but at the end of the day he had to attend and do the work if he wanted to stay there.

It was at that point that my placement ended and so did my contact with him. However, the conclusion to this story came in the form of a letter to me, which arrived about a year later, right at the end of my course. It had been sent to the university and eventually arrived in my tutor's in-tray after having been sent around to various locations within the university. It was from his mother; someone whose earlier communications with me were, at the very least, dismissive of the possibility that he was ever going to 'make anything of himself'. She had told me when I first met her that David had had social work input before me – which she described as 'useless' – and the fact that he now had a student allocated to him showed how much of a priority he was. The letter was brief and to the point, thanking me for finding David a course that he had not only stayed on and really loved, but that it had been one of the first times he had found a group of peers who were 'not criminals' – I 'must have done something right' she concluded. At the time I received this I was really pleased, but I was also confused in feeling that I was not sure what it was that I had done right. It is this question that my encounter with Rancière's work has helped me think through and, by way of concluding, I want to sketch out how the ideas in *The Ignorant Schoolmaster* might be applied to social work. Much of the time I was working with David I felt incredibly 'ignorant'; not just of the world he was part of, but also about how I was going to do something that would improve his situation. In spite of this, I must have conveyed to him something about the fact that he did have alternatives other than career criminality, and that these options were things he was capable of. This is, I think, how we can read Rancière when he says that 'one can teach what one doesn't know' (1991:15). The point is that while I was very inexperienced in working with young people in David's situation, what I did do was to provide a space where he could think about what he was going to do with his life in a way that allowed him to make the connections between doing something different and the kind of person he did and did not want to be. As I noted earlier, the gap between a conception of 'judging the best interests of another person' and that person's entirely different sense of their own situation, were all too apparent to me when I was working with him. In his book *Short Voyages to the Land of the People*, Rancière (2003:122) comments on exactly this issue:

> All teleologies and all images of coming-to-consciousness are founded on a certainty of distribution: some people's mission is to speak for others who know not what they do. Such is ... the point of view of mistrust: behind things are where their reasons lie.

What Rancière is pointing to here is that knowing best for other people involves a 'distribution' of power. He wants to question the assumption of virtuousness that is associated with those who dedicate themselves to 'speaking for others', and this parallels the way he questions the role of the teacher in *The Ignorant Schoolmaster*. When he talks about the 'certainty' of this distribution, he is referring to the way the person seen to be in need of help comes to be defined inherently as 'less than' the person who has taken on the role of the helper. So there are some teachers and social workers who espouse a desire to 'make a difference' to the people they work with, but end up feeling quite contemptuous toward them. What is this about? I think Rancière is suggesting to us that this reflects their personal investment, encouraged by the social position they occupy, in the idea that change will come through the people they work with accepting that they 'know best'. This embodies 'mistrust' of those people but it also fails to grasp how real change happens. The alternative to this, as with the teaching relation, lies in an inversion of that relationship. Hence, for Rancière, important change is not about imposing or cajoling someone toward a positive ideal of what you think their place in the world should be; it lies instead in the insistence that they pay attention to finding and creating an alternative – even if the shape of this is as yet unknown. Just as Rancière saw the role of the teacher not in transferring knowledge but in compelling students to take themselves seriously as thinkers, we can see the social work role in the same way. In the violently unequal, dangerous and horribly unhealthy world we live in, we need the kind of social work that works at the level of relationships. In those relationships, we really do need to 'be there' for the people we work with, but Rancière is saying something more than that. I would sum this up in the idea that an emancipated social work is one freed from the idea that we have to know best for other people. This 'knowing best' manifests a 'mistrust'; that is a false sense of the kind of distance between ourselves and the people we work with, as well as embodying a power relation that inhibits the development of the process of change that it claims to want. We might not know all that much about what it is like to live in the shoes of our service users – we are after all only making short visits to their land – but we can still play a really important role in their lives. What does matter is being there for someone through a time of difficulty and insisting on their engagement with the meaning of this difficulty, even if neither you nor they know what the 'solution' is going to be. This strikes me as a really good way of talking about what the social work relationship can offer. Even better would be to have this kind of social work positioned within a democratised and publicly accountable conception of public service, but one which takes equality rather than deficit as its point of departure.

References

Althusser, L., Balibar, E., Establet, R., Macherey P. & Rancière, J. (2016) *Reading Capital – The Complete Edition.* London: Verso.
Community Care (October 2018) [online] 'Humane' practice crucial to successful social work, study argues Available at: www.communitycare.co.uk/2018/10/29/humane-practice-crucial-successful-social-work-study-argues/ [Accessed 14/5/19].
Hall, S. & Jacques, M. (1983) *The Politics of Thatcherism.* London: Lawrence and Wishart.
International Federation of Social Work (2014) [online] Available at: www.ifsw.org/what-is-social-work/global-definition-of-social-work/ [Accessed 14/5/19].
Powell, F. (2001) *The Politics of Social Work.* London: Sage.
Rancière, J. (1991) *The Ignorant Schoolmaster: Five Lessons in Intellectual Emancipation.* CA: Stanford University Press.
Rancière, J. (2003) *Short Voyages to the Land of the People.* CA: Stanford University Press.
Rancière, J. (2011) *Althusser's Lesson.* London: Continuum.
Rancière, J. (2017) '*Jacques Rancière: reflections on equality and emancipation*' in *Autonomies* 5/8/2017 [online] Available at: http://autonomies.org/2017/08/jacques-ranciere-reflections-on-equality-and-emancipation/[Accessed 14/5/19].
Ross, K. (2002) *May '68 and its Afterlives.* Chicago: University of Chicago Press.
Taylor, I., Walton, P. & Young, J. (1995) 'Critical criminology in Britain: review and prospects', in Taylor, I., Walton, P. and Young, J. (eds) *Critical Criminology.* Routledge Kegan Paul Publishers: Abingdon, 6–62.

19
Giorgio Agamben
Sovereign power, bio-politics and the totalitarian tendencies within societies

Goetz Ottmann and Iris Silva Brito

AUSTRALIAN COLLEGE OF APPLIED PSYCHOLOGY, SYDNEY, AUSTRALIA

Introduction

This chapter focuses on Giorgio Agamben's work on power, sovereignty, bare life, and bio-politics. Agamben's work achieved recognition beyond the discipline of philosophy during the 1990s and 2000s when a range of policy decisions taken in the name of 'counter terrorism' and 'homeland security' (i.e. the defection of the United States from human rights norms during the 'war on terror' leading to the internment of prisoners of war at the Guantanamo Bay detention camp, the legitimation of 'enhanced interrogation techniques' by the George W. Bush administration, and incidents of torture and abuse at a number of prisoner of war camps) lent credence to his argument that the modern state is not premised on a contract underpinned by universal humanism but on the pure violence of the sovereign that is visible in its unbridled, murderous form during the state of exception, a period when all rules that guide human social and political life are suspended (Boukalas, 2014; Lewis, 2006; Rigi, 2012; Taylor, 2009; Yamaguchi, 2012). Agamben's work has found only marginal application within a social work context. Nevertheless, his ideas have entered social work discourses on post-colonialism, the refugee crisis, and physical oppression (Tangenberg & Kemp, 2002; Trista Lin et al., 2018; Zavirsek, 2017). In this chapter we provide a brief summary of Agamben's thought, describe a number of key concepts that Agamben developed in his nine-volume *Homo Sacer* project that have proven useful within a critical social theory context, and finally focus on the relevance of Agamben's work for social work practitioners.

It is important to mention upfront that Agamben's work is at odds with key tenets in critical social work. And those readers who approach Agamben with an expectation to glean from it pearls of wisdom that might advance the cause of human rights or the excluded will walk away perplexed if not frustrated. Agamben is deeply sceptical about the power of humanism and its associated human rights discourses and forms part of a group of post-humanist thinkers that attempt to develop a new ethics that is not grounded in humanism but in human life stripped of all of its socio-political significance. However, Agamben's work can make a crucially important contribution to critical social work theory inasmuch as it offers an ontology that enables us to perceive and denounce the totalitarian structures that criss-cross the democratic state. It alerts us to the fact that the repressive violence of the state takes many guises that, if unchallenged, become a permanent fixture of the politico-normative fabric of society. His political philosophy, and particularly his work on sovereign power, offers a radical critique that traces the root cause of the totalitarian horrors committed by modern democratic states to contradictions and paradoxes at the core of the very structures and processes that constitute it. Yet he has only little to say about the politicians, lawyers, public servants, and social workers that potentially enable and unleash the pure violence at the core of the state. Nevertheless, his work can be used to philosophically ground and amplify discussion focusing on critical multiculturalism and potentially makes an important contribution to critical social work.

Biographical background

Born in Rome in 1942, Giorgio Agamben studied law and philosophy at the University of Rome. In 1965, he completed a thesis on the political thought of Simone Weil, a French philosopher. Among the influences during his early career were Martin Heidegger and Walter Benjamin, followed later by Michel Foucault (bio-politics), Carl Schmitt (the foundation of the state of law), and Hannah Arendt (totalitarianism). He collaborated with film makers, writers, and poets such as Pier Paolo Pasolini, Italo Calvino, Ingeborg Bachmann, Guy Debord, Jacques Derrida, Anonio Negri, Jean-François Lyotard, and others. Elements of the radical approach he applies to the *Homo Sacer* project from the 1990s onwards are already visible in his earlier work on metaphysics and the philosophy of language (Agamben, 1991 [1982], 1993 [1978]) and his work on political communities (Agamben, 1993 [1990]). *Homo Sacer: Sovereignty Power and Bare Life* (Agamben, 1998 [1995]) is Agamben's best-known work within the context of critical social and political theory published in English. In it, he delineates a powerful critique of modern democracies, pointing at totalitarian residues of the 'camps' (a reference to the concentration camps during the Third Reich) within them deploying Foucault's concept of 'bio-politics'. He revisited and expanded these themes in other well-known publications such as *Remnants of Auschwitz* (Agamben, 1999) and *State of Exception* (Agamben, 2005 [2003]).

While Agamben characterises his own approach as an 'ontology of potentiality', authors, such as Antonio Negri, have critiqued it, arguing that Agamben succumbs to a negative ontology – an ontology grounded in a fundamental contradiction (Negri, 2011). This tension foreshadows the main critique of his work, namely that his ontology does not give rise to a positive, nourishing vision that could realistically inform the construction of new socio-political structures and processes.

Agamben held teaching positions at a range of prestigious universities in Europe and has held visiting appointments at prestigious US-based universities, such as the University of California, Berkeley and the Northwestern University, and the New School at New York University.

Foundations

Agamben regards all forms of structures (e.g. communal, social, and political) as potentially repressive. For example, during infancy, un-structured forms of being (in-fancy) are repressed when the child comes into language (when the largely unmediated world of the infant encounters the structuring power of language). It is toward the end of infancy that the child experiences the structure and power of language that enables her to say 'I'. However, because subjectivity is mediated by the structure of language, this leads to a re-framing and repression of more instinctive forms of being (Agamben, 1991 [1982], 1993 [1978]). Becoming a member of a collective (e.g. family, community, society) involves a transition that constitutes persons as social-political beings, delivering them from their mere biological existence. However, the construction of a collective in the form of the administrative and legal structures of the modern state generates potentially repressive forces that can de-humanise citizens by stripping them of their rights, voice, entitlements, and community membership. Indeed, Agamben argues that the very basis of our democratic legal order – and Western modernity more generally – is the state of exception and, associated with it, the possibility of pure, unrestrained violence (Agamben, 1998 [1995], 2005 [2003]). Symbolic institutions (signification, moral norms, and political laws), he argues, 'rely on the repression or exclusion of that which makes them possible' (Agamben cited by Deranty, 2007, p. 175). Agamben anchors the democratic state in a logical figure in which exclusive inclusion (i.e. of citizens) contains the potential of inclusive exclusion of persons (e.g. of refugees, terrorists, etc.) who, for some reason, do not fit the order created by the state. This inclusive exclusion can give rise to a 'zone of indistinction' (where there is no difference between citizens and dehumanised beings) 'where the law of exception – that is to say the possibility of total violence – is sovereign' (Deranty, 2007, p. 176). Agamben uses this logical figure to explain the horrors of Auschwitz, the internment of prisoners of war at Guantanamo Bay, the indeterminate detention of refugees, and the indiscriminate retention of DNA in databases (including the DNA of those not convicted of a crime) in the name of national security.

State of exception

Agamben argues that the state of exception is a condition where legal norms no longer order social life, creating a kind of no-man's-land where rules are made by those in charge. For Agamben it is the original political relation that underpins the workings of the modern state. An example of this state of exception is the concentration camp, a place where human beings whose political rights are for some reason forfeited are being stored and often destroyed. The camp is a place where persons are stripped of their humanity, their rights (including the right to take their own life), social roles, and dignity. It is a place where persons are reduced to non-persons or what Agamben terms 'bare life'. It is the pure violence unleashed during the state of exception that reduces humans to 'bare life', someone that has lost all socio-symbolic significance – including the right to a name (in camps, inmates are often referred to as numbers). The structure of the camp, Agamben states, survives in the modern democratic state where it has mutated into many different forms. In *State of Exception* (Agamben, 2005 [2003]), he describes how during the First and Second World Wars the executive powers in European nations were expanded way beyond their initial democratic remit (often in the name of the protection of democratic society), highlighting that such an expansion is often legally legitimised and that the resulting state of exception retains features of a democracy while creating parallel structures that circumvent the application of democratic processes.

The result is a political space (e.g. Camp X-Ray at Guantanamo Bay, refugee centres on Nauru and Manus Island) that is created by law where democratic laws and norms are suspended. This often means that access to persons held within this space (e.g. by social workers, medical professionals, human rights lawyers) is tightly controlled by the administrators of that space. Furthermore, the state often seeks to control information that emanates from the camp, attempting to keep secret its very existence and the conditions suffered by the people within it. In order to enforce an information embargo, the state often forces contractors working within the space to sign non-disclosure agreements whose breach potentially carries a prison term. Agamben highlights the role of law scholars, public servants, and other agents of the state in creating and running these totalitarian spaces of exception (Agamben, 2005 [2003]). At the core of the *Homo Sacer* project, he urges us that 'it is this structure of the camp that we must learn to recognise in all its metamorphoses' (Agamben, 1998 [1995], p. 113). Hence, a strength of Agamben's radical deconstructive ontology is its potential to unmask and denounce (to bear witness to) the remnants of Auschwitz, the varied forms of the state of exception that survive within modern democratic states. In this sense, Agamben's *Homo Sacer* project seeks to identify foundational structures that help us to critique totalitarian power structures within modern states.

More importantly still, Agamben's work brings into focus that states of exception are often created at a minor scale. His work suggests that the camps represent but one extreme example among less extreme forms that have been habilitated to such a degree that they form a widely accepted part of contemporary governance. Indeed, traces of 'zones of exception' exist throughout the human services and beyond. Agamben points out that within zones of exception, conditions largely depend on the humanity of those who have a say in these zones. Indeed, social workers often find themselves in positions where they have considerable powers to determine who is to be subjected to involuntary interventions and how these interventions are to play out. They often occupy positions that define or decide whether a threshold has been breached and what is to happen as a result; their professional identity is often tied to the belief that there is a threshold. Agamben asks us to consider the possibility of a society without threshold.

Bare life

Agamben differentiates between the socio-political persona and the biological persona. Bare life, in Agamben's work, refers to the person that has been stripped of all of her political and social status; it refers to the characteristics of a non-person, someone who has been reduced to her biological persona. People reduced to bare life are without any social or political protection. Their life is terrifyingly fragile as they can be killed without punishment; yet, because of its fragility, bare life is metaphysically regarded as sacred. Bare life is the result of pure violence unleashed by the sovereign state of exception. It signifies the 'abandonment to an unconditional power of death' (Agamben, 1998 [1995], p. 60). The concept of bare life highlights Agamben's scepticism of the idea that universal rights and a social contract constitute the founding elements of modern democratic states. He argues that

> the very rights of man that once made sense as the presupposition of the rights of the citizen are now progressively separated from and used outside the context of citizenship, for the sake of the supposed representation and protection of bare life which is more and more driven to the margins of the nation states, ultimately to be recodified into a new national identity.
>
> *(Agamben, 1998 [1995], p. 85)*

In Agamben's analysis, the democratic state, particularly when under threat (fictively or actually), has a tendency to separate civic rights from citizenship. It increasingly relegates civic rights to the realm of charitable humanitarianism rather than political citizenship. As a result, the civic rights of citizens can no longer be redeemed (see also Standing, 2011). Modern states, he argues, are increasingly abandoning life as bare existence 'to the force and act of the sovereign' (Colebrook & Maxwell, 2016, p. 77). With this in mind, Agamben suggests that it might be time to re-build political philosophy, starting with the figure of the refugee – the non-person that symbolises bare life – rather than the citizen with elusive rights.

At a more general level, Agamben's post-humanist reconstruction aims at a threshold that operates at the core of rights-based political philosophy as he argues that it is this philosophy that constitutes bare life. Agamben explains this by holding up the concept of 'the people'. He argues that the concept of the people results in a bio-political fracture separating those who belong from those who do not. That is, 'the people' that are supposedly the sovereign citizens of the modern state can only be constituted at the exclusion of those who do not belong (i.e. foreigners, dissidents, refugees, people on welfare, drug users, etc.) (Agamben, 1998 [1995], pp. 113–114). Ultimately, the authority deciding over who belongs and who does not is the state. By relinquishing the old notions of universal rights, and by starting with bare life, Agamben hopes to create the possibility of a political order without a social division at its core – a people without threshold.

The modern state routinely creates structures in which the 'normal order' is suspended. These zones of exception are generally produced at the point at which 'the political system of the modern nation state … enters into a lasting crisis, and the state decides to assume directly the care of the nation's biological life as one of its proper tasks' (Agamben, 1998 [1995], p. 112). For example, the neo-liberal state is awash with threshold criteria – often in the form of bio-markers – that separate those that act 'responsibly' from those that act 'irresponsibly', imposing behavioural sanctions upon the latter. These behavioural sanctions represent a suspension of the normal order and the opening of a zone of exception. Agamben's work allows us to understand how people that are forced into these zones are abandoned both socially and politically. How they are stripped of their humanity and rendered mute, how the last vestiges of their dignity are stripped from them, and why – when finally able to bear witness because they have been released from the state of exception – their accounts sound unbelievable and seem to fail to make sense (Agamben, 1999). Indeed, the accounts of witnesses that have survived the extermination camp of Auschwitz quoted by Agamben (Agamben, 1999) seem to agree on one point: the one thing that makes it difficult to understand – or even believe that Auschwitz happened – is that the horrors and cruelty inflicted upon them were utterly senseless and that what happened is therefore unimaginable. What is more, the only ones that could truly bear witness to the abandonment of bare life are those who did not survive. To bear witness, Agamben argues, is therefore difficult if not impossible (Agamben, 1998 [1995]).

Bio-politics

Agamben argues that the political rights and entitlements of citizens are defined by a politico-legal threshold. On one side of the threshold, the law potentially maintains the rights of citizens, on the other side, they are mere human bodies that have no political persona and, as a result, have no rights. Within our modern societies, Agamben warns, this threshold 'no longer appear[s] as a stable border dividing two clearly distinct zones' (Agamben, 1998 [1995], p. 78). On the one hand, this is because humanitarianism is increasingly becoming divorced from politics, turning politics into a machinery of cold instrumental rationality. On the other, it is the result of the rise of bio-politics. With the rise of bio-politics, Agamben argues, 'we can observe a displacement and gradual expansion beyond the limits' of decisions that define the threshold (Agamben, 1998 [1995], p. 78). In other words, in the absence of a public debate on the use of technology in the service of governance (public or private), bio-politics has enabled the state to expand its executive powers by putting technocrats in power of managing society. Bio-politics is a form of politics where the state steps in to make decisions that directly affect the biological body of persons, often without giving them any effective avenue for recourse. Bio-politics is a formidable instrument allowing the state to manage the behaviour of its population, rendering them docile (see the discussion of Foucault in Chapter 12) often without citizens being conscious of it (Colebrook & Maxwell, 2016). Bio-politics often suspends socio-political rights, treating humans as mere biological bodies. Bio-politics also highlights that sovereignty in the modern democratic state is dispersed. It rests with decision makers who hold powers that can fundamentally alter a person's life. To restate this in Agamben's terms: 'In modern bio-politics, sovereign is he who decides on the value and non-value of life as such' (Agamben, 1998 [1995], p. 91).

Bio-politics draws on Foucault's notion of bio-power which Foucault defined as operating by 'knowing, analysing, and managing an underlying substance of life' (Colebrook & Maxwell, 2016). It is the application of modern science to administration and government. In Foucault's work, bio-power is often a benign force (i.e. it is used to produce and sustain life rather than to exclude or abandon it) that contains mediated and defused residues of pre-modern sovereignty. In Foucault's work, bio-politics is used to produce life, maintain health and wellness, control illnesses, and manage behaviour that is defined as irresponsible because it is deemed to produce social, medical, psychological, or economic outcomes that are not desirable. 'Life becomes the substance to be constantly monitored' (Colebrook & Maxwell, 2016, p. 59). In Agamben's work, by contrast, bio-politics retains the pure violence that inhabits sovereign force that still lurks behind the façade of the modern democratic state (Colebrook & Maxwell, 2016). Agamben problematises bio-politics by highlighting that bio-power has not displaced sovereignty in modern society but that it has indeed intensified and extended the reach of sovereign power. Through the use of bio-power, the state is biologically fracturing individuals, producing new biological tropes of inclusion/exclusion juxtaposing newly constituted bodies and bare life. Increasingly, bio-power is used to monitor all aspects of life, turning all citizens into bare life, subjected to the exclusionary regime of thresholds as defined by the state (Agamben, 1998 [1995]; Colebrook & Maxwell, 2016).

Resisting the machine

One critique of Agamben's work aims at the radical negative ontology that underpins large segments of his work. Commentators have argued that his radical deconstruction leads to a very dark place from which escape seems only possible in the form of more philosophy (Deranty, 2007; Prozorov, 2014; Ziarek, 2008). The only escape from these repressive structures Agamben offers is their suspension, the rendering inoperative of the apparatus of power, to step out of the logics of law and sovereignty (Agamben, 1998 [1995]). Many commentators doubt that this theoretical approach can be fruitfully translated into practice and argue that it results in political paralysis (Deranty, 2007; Deutscher, 2008; Prozorov, 2014; Ziarek, 2008). In particular, critics bemoan the fact that Agamben dissolves any basis for collective resistance without providing an ethics that could be the source of practical change (Deranty, 2007; Ziarek, 2008). Deranty expertly summarises this critique when he writes that:

> Ethics becomes a practice that is not practical: it involves no action and only contingently attitudes towards others. It is a normative attitude beyond the normative, an experience of the subject's relation to itself, where the latter speaks its own impossibility. ... Politics is a practice where the notion of praxis is supposed to have been made redundant, a historical experience beyond history, a communal action that rejects the notion of community, a challenging of the law beyond the notion of the law.
>
> *(Deranty, 2007, p. 184)*

There can be little doubt that Agamben's work, while offering an answer to the question of how the contradictions at the core of modern democratic systems can be resolved (Prozorov, 2014), does not readily provide a platform for emancipatory collective action that is organised along the lines of a clearly demarcated ethics, praxis, and identity (Deutscher, 2008; Ziarek, 2008). There is no easily identifiable agent in Agamben's work that could take control of historicity (see, for example, discussion of Touraine in Chapter 38). However, this does not mean that the potentiality contained within Agamben's work cannot be observed and enacted in practice. Within this post-modern political moment, political formations enabled by social media often fall into categories that could be loosely described in terms of Deranty's above-stated critique. Indeed, the rebellion against liberalism that we are witnessing, in which right-wing populists play the lead role, is based on a radical rejection of conventional politics and the humanist values associated with post-Second World War social democracy (Noble & Ottmann, 2018). This conflict over inclusion/exclusion that is again dominating political debates over societal values has the capacity to undo old political alliances, normative premises, and political praxis. Yet while on the one side of politics, movements that thrive on exclusionary solidarity seem to rip apart the very fabric of inclusive democratic societies, demanding from the state new zones of exception and the de-humanisation of those that have been identified not to belong, on the other hand, online collectives have sprung up around the ideal of an inclusive solidarity that seems to resonate with Agamben's society without threshold (Agamben, 1998 [1995]). For example, in Germany, the #unteilbar (undividable) hash tag has created an online collective whose several million members rally around the idea of solidarity and against exclusion. For some commentators, this foundation of social inclusion and acceptance of difference without grounding in a more traditional emancipatory politics may resemble a normative attitude beyond the normative and a politics of non-praxis. Yet on 13 October 2018, #unteilbar enticed some 250,000 people from a wide range of social backgrounds onto the streets of Berlin. This suggests that it is much too early to dismiss the emancipatory force of online collectives, such as #unteilbar.

Agamben's ontology of potentiality appears to be able to theoretically capture key elements of ephemeral movements such as #unteilbar. The question whether such movements have the capacity to stand up to a totalitarian state, and whether Agamben's politicisation of bare life will provide a useful anchor point for the new movements that will follow in their footsteps, remains unanswered. It seems pointless, however, to search in Agamben's work for a premise for new rights-based movements that somehow recreate the emancipatory achievements of movements of past decades. The potentiality of Agamben's work is inextricably bound up with a radical pluralistic politics and the creation of a society without thresholds. The importance of this project cannot be lost on social workers at this political juncture.

Implications for social work education

Recent contributions to the field of multiculturalism (see, for example, Nipperess & Williams, 2019) represent a powerful alternative to Agamben's departure from a human rights-based approach. Indeed, critical multiculturalism makes use of theoretical lenses (i.e. identity, citizenship, human rights, power, privilege, intersectionality, critical reflection as practice, etc.) that are familiar entities in critical social work education. This raises the question what Agamben's work has to offer that has not been already covered by such texts. And perhaps more importantly still, is Agamben's work a mere distraction from the emancipatory humanist project embodied in critical multiculturalism?

A tentative answer to these questions could highlight that Agamben's work makes an important contribution to critical reflection as practice theory in as much as it brings to the fore the totalitarian seeds within the modern democratic state. He critically highlights the role of agents of the state in fertilising these seeds. A critical reflection that takes into account this fundamental tendency could lead to a more radical critique of social work practice within the context of the welfare state. Particularly when read in combination with Arendt's 'banality of evil' thesis (Arendt, 1963), Agamben's work manages to impress upon us that zones of exception are a common feature in modern democratic societies – we have just gotten used to them to a point where we are no longer able to distinguish them. Agamben's work provides us with an impetus to become more aware of zones of exception; he shows us how to recognise them. Indeed, recognition can be a difficult process, particularly when our workplace is located within a zone of exception.

The *Homo Sacer* project could lead to a critical reflection that focuses more squarely on the role of social workers as agents of the state and how social workers can become implicated in the de-humanisation process, socio-political exclusion, and the production of bare life. Such a reflection might include a focus on how social workers enable zones of exception by defining or policing thresholds and by sanctioning those that transgress. This, in turn, might stimulate a debate that re-defines what anti-oppressive practice ought to look like when social workers are asked to assume the role of an agent of the state and develop strategies that might enable them to effectively advocate for their closure. His work could stimulate a critical reflection on the deployment of bio-politics within a social work context, highlighting how social workers are increasingly involved in the implementation of bio-political governance. Such a reflection is particularly timely in the current neo-liberal context in which bio-politics is closely associated with a new authoritarianism (comprised of IT-enabled surveillance and punitive welfare conditionality) that blames people on the other side of the threshold (i.e. the unemployed) and forces them to change their behaviour. Agamben's work might lead to greater awareness of how bio-politics has become the machinery that potentially turns persons into non-persons, devoid of the right to make decisions that shape their lives.

Agamben could assist social work students to become more aware of the importance of creating a society without threshold. His work can be used to foster a commitment to a radical pluralism that could underpin critical multicultural social work practice. To be sure, Agamben needs to be read with a good dose of pragmatism, as his work cannot be easily translated into the canon of critical social work education. However, when read alongside contributions to critical multiculturalism (see, for example, Nipperess & Williams, 2019; Nylund, 2006), Agamben's work provides a powerful and important critique of the modern state and beyond. His work offers a different perspective to what it means to be human and to have 'rights'. It explains how 'rights' lose their meaning within zones of exception, and how social workers can turn into wardens of bare life when the demands of their work undermine their anti-oppressive practice and, ultimately, their humanity.

Conclusion

Agamben's post-humanist deconstruction is powerful because it resonates strongly and perhaps paradoxically with the humanist framework it tries to leave behind. When reading Agamben's rendering of systemic contradictions that define our modern political and administrative systems, the reader is waiting for the rise of a political actor, an actor/fixer that will ensure the return to the rule of law and the re-instatement of civic rights, to do away with the state of exception, and to outlaw de-humanising forms of bio-politics. Yet, this hero makes a rather tentative appearance in Agamben's account; her actions/non-actions are vague and seem strangely empty of the agency and collective action for the greater good that inspire the rhetoric of human rights-based movements. His work highlights systemic flaws in modern democracy rather than moral flaws in political leaders, economic elites, or agents of the state. Indeed, for an account of the 'banality of evil' that brings into focus the role of individuals in totalitarian states, we have to visit thinkers such as Hannah Arendt (Arendt, 1963). Yet Agamben's account is powerful precisely because it delineates the mercilessly cold mechanism of the apparatus that many social work clients are exposed to. His radical critique of modern Western thought and institutions produces a sense of desolation that screams out for action.

For students of critical social work, Agamben's insistence that zones of exception have become an accepted part of our politico-normative fabric and can be encountered in a variety of guises within our modern democratic state is a wakeup call. Agamben's work urges social workers to reflect more carefully on the structures within which they are embedded and the roles they occupy within those structures. His work highlights the structures and processes that make it difficult to practise social work in an anti-oppressive fashion. Becoming more acutely aware of what it means to be an agent of the state charged with defining and policing thresholds and enforcing sanctions if thresholds are breached, should make us uneasy about our role. It will force us to consider a social work practice that is cognisant of the fact that the term 'person' is a 'hierarchical and elevated notion' (Colebrook & Maxwell, 2016) and that our clients' rights to personhood are in danger when they approach a threshold controlled by social workers. This insight makes it more difficult to resort to easy fixes and has the potential to ground anti-oppressive practice in bare life – in the non-person, in the refugee. In this chapter we have argued that Agamben's work could stimulate a critical reflection that could potentially form the basis of a critical multicultural approach to social work.

References

Agamben, G. (1991 [1982]). *Language and Death: The Place of Negativity*. MI: University of Minnesota Press.
Agamben, G. (1993 [1978]). *Infancy and History*. London, UK: Verso.
Agamben, G. (1993 [1990]). *The Coming Community*. MI: University of Minnesota Press.
Agamben, G. (1998 [1995]). *Homo Saccer: Sovereign Power and Bare Life*. Palo Alto: Stanford University Press.
Agamben, G. (1999). *Remnants of Auschwitz*. New York: Zone Books.
Agamben, G. (2005 [2003]). *State of Exception*. Chicago: University of Chicago Press.
Arendt, H. (1963). *Eichmann in Jerusalem*. New York: The Viking Press.
Boukalas, C. (2014). No exceptions: Authoritarian statism. Agamben, Poulantzas and homland security. *Critical Studies on Terrorism*, 7(1), 112–130.
Colebrook, C., & Maxwell, J. (2016). *Agamben*. Cambridge: Polity Press.
Deranty, J. P. (2007). Witnessing the In human: Agamben or Merleau-Ponty. *The South Atlantic Quarterly*, 107(1), 165–186.
Deutscher, P. (2008). The inversion of exceptionality: Foucault, Agamben, and 'reproductive rights'. *South Atlantic Quarterly*, 107(1), 55–70.
Lewis, T. E. (2006). The school as an exceptional space: Rethinking education from the perspective of the biopedagogical. *Educational Theory*, 56(2), 159–176.
Negri, A. (2011). *Art and Multitude: Nine Letters on the Arts*. Cambridge: Polity Press.
Nipperess, S., & Williams, C. (2019). *Critical Multicultural Practice in Social Work: New Perspectives And Practices*. East Melbourne, VIC: Allen & Unwin.
Noble, C., & Ottmann, G. (2018). Nationalist populism and social work. *Journal of Human Rights and Social Work*, 3(3), 112–120. doi: 10.1007/s41134-018-0066-3.
Nylund, D. (2006). Critical multiculturalism, whiteness, and social work: Towards a more radical view of cultural competence. *Journal of Progressive Human Services*, 17(2), 27–42. doi: 10.1300/J059v17n02_03.
Prozorov, S. (2014). *Agamben And Politics: A Critical Introduction*. Edinburgh: Edinburgh University Press.
Rigi, J. (2012). The corrupt state of exception: Agamben in the light of Putin. *Social Analysis*, 56(3), 69–88.
Standing, G. (2011). *The Precariat*. London: Bloomsbury Academic.
Tangenberg, K., & Kemp, S. (2002). Embodied practice: Claiming the body's experience, agency, and knowledge for social work. *Social Work*, 47(1), 9–18.
Taylor, M. L. (2009). *Today's State Of Exception: Abu-Jamal, Agamben, Jan Mohamed and the Democratic State of Emergency Political Theology*. London, UK: Equinox Publishing.

Trista Lin, C.-C., Minca, C., & Ormond, M. (2018). Affirmative biopolitics: Social and vocational education for Quechua girls in the postcolonial "affectsphere" of Cusco, Peru. *Environment and Planning D: Society and Space, 36*(5), 885–904.

Yamaguchi, K. (2012). Rationalization and concealment of violence in American response to 9/11: Orientalism(s) in a state of exception. *Journal of Postcolonial Writing, 48*(3), 241–251.

Zavirsek, D. (2017). The humanitarian crisis of migration versus the crisis of humanitarianism: Current dimensions and challenges for social work practice. *Social Work Education, 36*(3), 231–244.

Ziarek, E. P. (2008). Bare Life on Strike: Notes on the biopolitics of race and gender. *The South Atlantic Quarterly, 107*(1), 89–106.

20
Avishai Margalit's concept of decency
Potential for the Lived Experience Project in social work?

Lorna Hallahan

FLINDERS UNIVERSITY, AUSTRALIA

Introduction

In *The Decent Society*, Israeli philosopher Avishai Margalit (trans. Naomi Goldblum, Harvard University Press, 1996) provides a compelling indictment of the privacy-impinging, bureaucratic functions of the welfare state that humiliate dependent citizens, contributing, alongside other institutions, to the emergence of an indecent society. Margalit charges a society with indecency if it uses its institutions to humiliate people. Humiliation is 'the rejection of a person from the human commonwealth and the loss of basic control' (Margalit, 1996, p. 3).

This chapter takes Margalit's concept of an indecent society as a starting point to critique the Lived Experience Project in social work education. The Lived Experience Project is widely prescribed in education and accreditation standards in social work education. The *Global Standards for the Education and Training of the Social Work Profession*, released by the International Federation of Social Workers in 2012, refer to the involvement of service users in the design and delivery of academic and field education topics as well as in the selection of students. Translated into the Australian setting, these standards are grounded in *The Ethical Guidance: Using client information for research and educative purposes* issued by the Australian Association of Social Workers (last modified July 2016). It states: 'It is often very useful to bring the voices of clients and those with personal experiences of social issues to the fore in an educational way through workshops, conferences or lectures at universities where the clients are physically present' (AASW, 2016, p. 5). The chapter looks at aspects of the Lived Experience Project in relation to people with disability and the positioning of our needs in all aspects of welfare, including social work education. Drawing on my experience in the disability rights movement, I offer an alternative to the narrative of neediness that is elicited in an uncritical approach to using clients in social work education.

The Australian *Ethical Guidance* applies liberal research ethics, with a strong emphasis on proceeding in the best interests of a client, addressing processes of gaining free and informed consent, briefing and debriefing, and referral to trauma supports. The educator is also advised to facilitate the process carefully and to establish audience ground rules around questions and reactions to the input of the person. The link to the Australian Association of Social Workers Code of Ethics (2010), through expectations of respecting clients and their data and boundaries protection, is made explicit. Implicitly, therefore, the Australian *Ethical Guidance* affirms the liberal ethics ground of social work ethics in Australia. This chapter reframes the proposal in order to disrupt the assumptions that could lead to unacceptable moral hazards in social work education. In its widest form, moral hazard occurs when one person carries a risk and bears a burden for another, unburdened person's benefit. Its opposite is honouring the person, allowing them self-respect and autonomy. Margalit implicates welfare as a major social institution that can operate to humiliate citizens, especially via the use of tests of eligibility and compliance regimes. Setting aside, as erroneous, the claim that poverty, illness or unemployment are themselves degrading and humiliating, Margalit focuses on how charities and state welfare can impose a loss of self-respect on people rendered dependent on services. Here I implicate social work assessment approaches in eliciting narratives of neediness, suffering and insufficiency (especially when presented to gain access to services and supports) as potentially humiliating and link these mechanisms to a naive approach to the Lived Experience Project in the education of student social workers. Such an approach perpetuates a potential source of humiliation as the person is positioned solely as exemplar 'client', and as representative of a class of citizens.

Further, I contemplate whether such lived experience testimonies are educationally beneficial or could serve to reinforce otherness and a professional gaze that serves the humiliating welfare regime. If the threat of humiliation lies within the scope of the Lived Experience Project, the protections of liberal research ethics might not be sufficient to sustain self-respect and autonomy; nor the questionable benefits of this approach sufficient to offset the threat of humiliation. I conclude by proposing alternative non-humiliating models of engagement in the Lived Experience Project that are potentially ethically and educationally viable.

The decent society: its form and it critics

Emeritus Professor Avishai Margalit (born 1939) has an outstanding academic career starting in 1970 and including positions of leadership in philosophy departments in Israel and the United States. He is a founding leader of the *Peace Now* movement in Israel and, as an activist-academic, contributes to peace-making and human rights defence in the Occupied Territories. Now in late career, his capacity to speak authoritatively on the moral dimensions of social inequality and injustice is born from decades of scholarship and a commitment to maintain a clear and ethical gaze on non-ideal dimensions of societies and social interactions.

Margalit, in *The Decent Society* (1996), is writing against the backdrop of the Holocaust and subsequent developments in Palestine/Israel as well as cultural conflicts in a divided Europe. At the heart of his work lies the normative claim that people should be respected by virtue of their humanity. Viewed as an austere approach, this work is not laden with the arcane language so prevalent in contemporary academic philosophy writing. The text reveals that he knows and understands the liberal arguments about respect, rights and human dignity; but he does not dedicate space to elucidating these ideas and debates. He states his case graphically and confidently, at times compared to the style of Isaiah Berlin or George Orwell. Margalit is therefore open to criticism from two sides. First, he does not ground his work empirically, favouring an observing commentator approach to advance his view of social conditions. This looks too light when trying to gauge the scale and detailed nature of the social phenomena he challenges. Conversely, Margalit does not use an insider philosopher language that meticulously advances finely grained arguments. His style is sweeping and at times declamatory; showing little of the equivocation found in contemporary political philosophy. Yet, its immediate appeal lies in its normative stance: an unabashed commitment to justice, decency and civility.

This authorial assuredness is at once comforting in its assertions while being confronting in its apparent lack of uncertainty. The text's accessibility is seen by some as evidence of thin thought. Close reading reveals this is not the case. To dismiss these arguments, however, as light-weight or poorly considered because they are presented in a long plain-language essay, rather than an analytical philosophy monograph, would be disingenuous, unfair and unwise. Margalit is genuinely wrestling with big ideas in the service of those who are typically the clients of social workers; the users of human services; and those who are incarcerated or socially excluded. Margalit's ideas about societies that use their welfare institutions to humiliate their citizens, while being characterised by disrespectful exchanges between its citizens (described as incivility), are compelling and challenging for social workers as the key workers in welfare bodies. Further, Margalit's work is aimed at action; it does not become as Cavel (1971, p.131) describes: 'that philosophy [which] seems so often *merely* to nag and to try no special answers to the questions which possess us – unless it be to suggest that we sit quietly in a room.'

Margalit first analyses the semantic field, asking 'what meanings might these words (respect, rights, humiliation, honour, citizenship) carry?' in order to build a framework that he uses to put certain institutions to the test. Next he explores decency as a social concept, in particular examining the role of loss of privacy as a key aspect of humiliation, which is, in turn, seen in the operations of bureaucracy. Moving onto analysis of particular social institutions, Margalit draws on historic and present examples of the operations of certain institutions, including welfare. Rather than pile data to advance his arguments he gives us a brief history of the emergence of the welfare state and its operations. This contextual approach is eminently suitable for social work: critical reflection on potentially damaging consequences of our well-intentioned intrusions into the lives of those considered vulnerable to 'the second class citizenship of the needy and giving them the practical status of nonadult human beings' (Margalit, 1996, p. 224). Margalit's argument about humiliation, decency and civility brings us right to the normative heart of social work and the integrated values of commitment to respect human dignity and pursue social justice (AASW, 2010).

The Decent Society is a contextual philosophical exploration of respect and humiliation grounded in observable social conditions. A contextual philosophy never strays far from human experience, moving back and forth to theories to locate and challenge ideas and to position new propositions. For social workers carrying out the daily face-to-face professionalised interactions with clients of health and human services, the option of sitting quietly in a room is rarely available. Practice demands decisions and it demands actions, even in unfavourable conditions. Margalit also shows us how a negative (in the sense of an absence) condition, i.e. non-humiliation, is a worthy goal and necessary step in pursuit of a just and decent society. Margalit (1996, pp. 10–11) describes a decent society in these ways:

> A decent society is one that fights conditions which constitute a justification for its dependents to consider themselves humiliated. A society is decent if its institutions do not act in ways that give the people under their authority sound reasons to consider themselves humiliated.

Lorna Hallahan

Introducing notions of humiliation, decency and civility within the welfare society

Margalit is at pains to identify a particular understanding of humiliation, which he defines as: 'any sort of behaviour or condition that constitutes a sound reason for a person to consider his or her self-respect injured '(Margalit, 1996, p. 9). This is not simply how one feels but rather it is normative and focused on the behaviour of another. His model requires the existence of a humiliator (Margalit, 1996, p. 10). Note the focus on humiliating actions, distinguished sharply from the motives of the humiliating institution. It is what follows from conditions that arise through nature or social conditions, in relation to the behaviour of others and social institutions, that constitutes the humiliation. According to Margalit (1996) the society that allows this to happen is an indecent society.

This claim is considered a smaller, less optimistic idea than a vision of a just society, but Margalit argues that a just society (viewed in Rawlsian terms), in which people have access to the resources necessary to support their reasonable needs, can still be an indecent society, especially through the ways that welfare provision is meted out to those who show sufficient neediness and become subject to loss of autonomy and, at times, self-respect. As Leadbeater (1996, p. 21) sums it up:

> Theorists such as Rawls concentrate on calculating the just distribution of income and rights. Margalit argues that is not enough: we also need to examine how justice is delivered. A centrally planned economy or a welfare state might deliver a just distribution of income and benefits, but only at the cost of a highly intrusive, de-humanising bureaucracy, which humiliates people by turning them into little more than 'numbers'.

Civility, according to Margalit, takes this need for humanisation into interpersonal interactions. A civilised society is therefore one in which the citizens do not humiliate each other. It is possible to build a decent society by forging respectful institutions while not living in a civilised society, because violence and uncivility have not been eradicated in intimate and social group relations. Sadly, however, the two are likely to be present at one time. For example, a woman subject to violence experiences the 'uncivility' of control, cruelty and abuse within her home, but will also experience the humiliating impact of social institutions when pursuing her rights through the court system. She will face additional humiliation if she seeks income and housing support in a bureaucratised welfare system that is accustomed to intruding into matters considered private, distrusting her motives, questioning her financial independence from sexual partners, and scrutinising her capacity to parent safely.

Margalit's concepts of humiliation and uncivility, grounded in his links between privacy, bureaucracy and the operations of welfare, provide a framework to look at the positioning of 'needs and neediness' in the Lived Experience Project in social work education. Margalit does not expressly focus on the identification of needs and production of neediness by the welfare state, but his focus on the compromise of privacy by welfare bureaucracies takes us to the core of assessment of need by social workers and other welfare officials. His criticism of the disrespectful relationship that those who become dependent on welfare (understood here as both income support and human service users) are manipulated into when seeking support, gives graphic intensity to views that we know are widely held in contemporary Australian (and many other Western capitalist) societies. Media coverage of the Business Expenditure Review initiated by the Abbott-Hockey Coalition Government in Australia in 2014, carrying headlines such as: 'Tony Abbott's razor gang considered welfare crackdown on "job snobs" under 30' (ABC, 29 Jan.

2018), reveals enduring notions of the deserving and undeserving poor. Identifying the emergence of the contemporary welfare state in the Poor Law Reforms of 1834, Margalit captures the 'Dickensian' undercurrents of much welfare provision in the current era, saying:

> Suspicion of the sham poor, who are nothing but lazy exploiters dipping their vampiric fingers into the public's pockets, still nourishes opposition to the welfare state and those who need it. The desire to put the needy to humiliating tests of entitlement is not entirely a thing of the past.
>
> *(Margalit, 1996, p. 224)*

Inflammatory language and negative images abound here, but not because Margalit (1996) himself is anti-welfare; he is resolutely committed to building just societies, but they must be decent as well. Social work does not sit outside the welfare system (Margalit, 1996, p. 237). Viewed in this light, social work is a professional creature of the extension of state power into the lives of people deemed the potential or actual clients of health and human services. It becomes clear that social work education, insofar as it is shaped by the expectations of the profession codified into standards and accreditation regimens, is also a part of the welfare system and subject to the same scrutiny for its potential to produce and reproduce humiliating practices. This is where *The Ethical Guidance: Using client information for research and educative purposes* (AASW, 2016) is directly pertinent.

Our question is, therefore, are these humiliating processes (testing entitlement) replicated in the use of the 'client' in educational settings to inform student social workers of the conditions that drive people into welfare service use (statements of neediness, suffering and insufficiency)?

Becoming 'client': what does it require?

Margalit does not provide details of the imposts of bureaucratised welfare through its eligibility tests, but we can draw on other theorists to see how this works. Rose, O'Malley and Valverde (2006), reworking the Foucauldian notion of governmentality of the self, point to the language and technologies that a person or group of persons must use to render themselves eligible for an allocation of resources or access to the professional knowledge of the welfare practitioner. This is seen as a shift from rigid state authority through to the power of professions such as social work in shaping the identity and expectations of the client. Rose et al. (2006, p. 101), say:

> We need to investigate the role of the gray sciences, the minor professions, the accountants and insurers, the managers and psychologists, in the mundane business of governing everyday economic and social life, in the shaping of governable domains and governable persons, in the new forms of power, authority, and subjectivity being formed within these mundane practices. Every practice for the conduct of conduct involves authorities, aspirations, programmatic thinking, the invention or redeployment of techniques and technologies.

The art and science of social work assessment is extensively addressed in the academic and professional literature, and embedded in all services where social workers establish entitlement to service, and then conduct more thorough assessment in order to plan and monitor their interventions with the person or family. While each assessment method is linked to a theory of change, in social work it is often co-opted to establish eligibility or to provide a rationale for referral to another service.

All of these 'mundane' processes turn on the person seeking service and submitting to eligibility testing providing three related narratives about their condition: a narrative of neediness, which is substantiated by a narrative of insufficiency in self and in one's immediate world, and an associated narrative of suffering (Margalit calls it an elicitation of pity (1996, p. 231)). It is these intensely personal accounts, gathered by an official violation of privacy (Margalit, 1996, p. 207) that are translated into measures of the merit of the claim. While Rose et al. (2006) see this as the terrain of welfare professional discretionary power, Margalit (1996) draws our attention to how prospective clients experience it as rigid, unresponsive to individual conditions and highly controlling.

There is a further twist here. Introducing people with disability as a significant population among those who rely on welfare and other human services, we can see that it is fundamentally and predictably difficult for a person who is living with significant lifelong impairment, the consequences of stigma and a probable trauma history, to free themselves from the terrain of low expectations and hopelessness via a process of rendering themselves needy, even pathetic. Their goal of accessing the supports they need in order to flourish turns into acquiring the impairment points they need to get into the system. This is called 'adaptive preferencing' (Nussbaum, 2001, p. 79). While this may mark a distortion of 'genuine' need in order to access services, the centrality of understandings of positioning need remains crucial for detecting the humiliating aspects of establishing welfare entitlement by combining the intrusion into privacy and the bureaucratic dimensions of welfare processing. Direct treatment of need is neglected in Margalit's work so it is necessary to locate related approaches, which can help chart a way to overcome the moral hazards attached to the Lived Experience Project in social work education.

In 2012, Nancy Fraser republished an earlier essay (1989) called 'Struggle over Needs: Outline of a Socialist-Feminist Critical Theory of Late-Capitalist Political Culture'. She attributes adaptive preferencing to two main interwoven processes. First, the consolidation, for administrative purposes, around consensus such as the capture of rights claims by notions of service-dependency and enduring non-participation; and second, by professionalised problem solving, often therapeutic approaches which are tied to diagnosis. So, its practice can quickly morph into suspicion of claimants, rigidity of eligibility criteria, and shallow decision-making related to performance pressure for the welfare bureaucrat or professional. This translates into distancing tactics (the best of which is seeing a person only as a representative of a class), excessive surveillance, and regimens of accountability for resource use (compliance) focused on users rather than on providers. These processes add humiliation at every step as the person is obliged to reveal more and more about themselves (their struggles, transgressions, fears, etc.) while accepting increasing oversight of their daily actions.

Margalit (1996, p. 239) goes on to warn, however, that we must not become trapped by powerful stereotypes. As he states:

> [O]n the one hand, good-hearted social workers [are] unconditionally devoted to the families they take care of; and on the other hand, brutal night visits by supervisory authorities [are carried out] at the homes of single mothers to check whether there is a man hiding under the bed.

Margalit's point underlines his intention to explore the ideal type of the welfare society, not to enunciate whether individual instances of support are rendered respectfully or not. This, however, is a useful warning for social work educators: just as we must not allow these stereotypes to drive our analysis of the operations, humiliating or not, of a contemporary welfare system, neither must we employ powerful stereotypes to drive our use of narratives of neediness, insufficiency and suffering in educational settings.

Becoming an expert in lived experience: what are the hazards?

To find a way through that brings those with lived experience into a genuine critical partnership in social work education, we need to go beyond the protections provided in the Australian *Ethical Guidance*. These are, after all, the ostensive protections against humiliation that exists in indecent social work service provision (and social science research). They are, however, indirectly implicated as inadequate within Margalit's (1996) condemnation of the indecency of welfare.

A useful comparison for the Lived Experience Project in social work education is the role of testimony and witness in public enquiries such as Royal Commissions, which appear with regularity throughout the almost 200 years of state-sponsored welfare provision in the UK and the colonies. Here we see the operation of a romantic notion of the emancipated subject, advancing their tales of oppression and suffering, in order to confront the very forces that produced the inhumanity. Added to this is a therapeutic goal through which the emancipated subject is healed and their dignity restored by bringing their suffering to light. Perhaps this is closer to the guest lecture in the university course, delivered by a person positioned as a service user, for the benefit of the learners in the audience. Margalit does not directly address this move into the testimonial aspect of public enquires, but it is justified by his attention to stigma, and the habituated ways in which we stigmatise others. He describes the defensive techniques that some groups (such as Jewish people in the Diaspora) develop to defuse the existential burden of dehumanisation, and to preserve self-respect, stating (1996, p. 123) that these 'cannot uproot the humiliating situation. At most they may mitigate it somewhat.' Perhaps the purest expression of his position is found here (1996, pp. 124–125):

> Even if the humiliated person has no doubt that she has incurred an appalling injustice, whereas she is just as human as anyone else, she cannot ignore how others treat her in shaping the way she regards herself ... the attitude of others is built into the very concept of the value of humans which the bearer of self-respect is supposed to adopt with regard to herself.

This is what Margalit calls 'the paradox of humiliation' (1996, pp. 115–129). Taking this point further, we can see it explicated in the literature about public testimonies of suffering and injustice. Auerhahn and Laub (1990, p. 447), reflecting on Holocaust testimonies, describe these as ambivalent expectations:

> [A]ll forms of the survivor's testimony depend on invoking presence out of absence, continuity out of discontinuity, and identity out of difference – to that extent, they are healing and necessary. However, there are ambivalences in the structure of testimony: Testimony covers over the opposite possibility, that of the absence of the other, and hence contains negative valences that make it threatening and dangerous.

Extending their perspective on the person giving the testimony, Auerhahn and Laub (1990) also take the position that we cannot solely deal with the public meaning construction – we are dealing primarily with personal, existential meaning construction as well. While this raises the potential for re-traumatisation, foreshadowed in *The Ethical Guidance*, it becomes a more direct moral hazard as well. Here we shift to the other side of the dynamic of the paradox of humiliation identified by Margalit. In a perhaps genuine effort to face painful realities, listeners/learners could create and reinforce the 'client as victim' role, robbing informants of their humanity, because all we choose to see is their suffering. The depth of their suffering elicits 'ooh ah' responses in listeners. This can be the most painful form of binding the tongues of people – to make them permanent victims. At its worst, it can be exploitative because it only pretends to 'ground' the claim for justice in their life.

Gilmore (2003) writes about the denial of truth in public testimonies, especially if they are heard in a court. Often, the story is rejected as untruthful: too confronting, too demanding, or too backward looking, too staccato, internally contradictory and/or dismissed as the unreliable memories of fevered accusing minds. Even when there is recognition that the fractured account is evidence of the trauma, the person is potentially pathologised and their account discredited as unhistorical. Alternatively, the story may be appropriated and distorted. Sometimes the story is taken from the teller and used to promote other people's righteous actions. Relatedly, we can see in the form of consultation, that public testimony is enlisted to ensure government legitimacy in certain decision-making rather than to honour the voice of those who are afflicted and to advance their claim for justice and decency. This is perhaps the most likely outcome from the testimonial of clients within social work educational spaces, as educators use accounts to add value to lessons about social policy and social work practice.

These are hazards that all social work educators should resolve not to realise in their practices as they aim to add depth and pungency to their teaching, bringing students into close, vivid and convincing accounts of clienthood. This animates the Lived Experience Project, with its aim to move narratives from the 'twilight of knowing' (Anna Haebich, 2000, p. 563) into public testimony; stories revealed in therapeutic space are moved into public space via understandings of private pain and public issues (Mills, 1959). Yet, social work educators genuinely committed to emancipatory transformation of individuals and societies are left with these questions: Do these risks constitute a sufficient concern to question the liberatory potential of a testimonial Lived Experience Project? Is the threat of humiliation too real and/or too great to advocate a continuation of the project? Margalit is harsh in his critique of humiliating situations such as this. As he states (1996, p. 128):

> [S]ince we are concerned with institutional humiliation – whose agents are clerks, police, soldiers, prison warders, teachers, social workers, judges and all the other agents of authority – we can ignore the subjective intentions of the humiliators in examining whether their actions are degrading.

Margalit goes on to say that humiliators are not absolved of the moral responsibility for their deeds (1996, p. 128), but that a focus on the humiliating situation (in our case the welfare system) provides rational grounds for the person to legitimately consider themselves humiliated through their contact with the indecent institution. Perhaps perversely, this provides an excellent opportunity to shift the Lived Experience Project toward emancipation and away from potential humiliation.

In the interests of charting another way, grounded in a respectful silence and attentive listening, I present an example from the Australian disability rights movement that offers the opportunity of honouring voice without recapitulating the conditions for humiliation. This takes up Margalit's injunction to focus on the humiliating dynamics of the indecent institution, especially exposing the links among privacy violation, bureaucracy and the positioning of needs and neediness within the welfare system. This expands the potential for student social workers and their educators to learn without undermining our collective commitment to building emancipatory approaches to respect and justice.

Engaging with emancipatory social movements and activists: a disability example

Nancy Fraser's focus on needs talk, rather than privileging an empirical documentation of needs, provides a pertinent development out of Margalit's understanding of the humiliating exchange in advancing needs claims in welfare systems. Fraser (1989) describes a set of processes through which social movement struggles over needs and rights interpretation are politicised and transformed into management of need satisfactions by the formal political-administrative sphere. The mid-2000s in Australia saw what she calls 'a discourse of runaway needs interpretation' (Fraser, 1989, p. 300) break free from the service system that had held sway from the late 1980s. Multiple voices in a politicised disability movement were amplified through the debates about the United Nations Convention on the Rights of Persons with Disabilities; the Rudd Government's national consultations leading to the release of the *Shut Out Report* (2009), which led to the development of the National Disability Strategy 2010–2020. *Shut Out* condemned the existing services system as broken and broke, failing in its goal to increase community participation; having morphed over time into highly restrictive services that offered little flexibility and personalisation.

Within a year the encompassing goals of the National Disability Strategy 2010–2020 with its focus on rights, economic and social participation and community development, were swamped by this service discourse, feeding into the introduction of the National Disability Insurance Scheme (Hallahan, 2015). Fraser would agree that while the demand for service transformation was probably the clearest point of consensus in this large and multi-vocal social movement, she would also point out that economic forces were particularly potent at this point. Indeed, she would align the economic and social here, seeing how the call for personalised services and individualised funding, genuinely fuelled by a desire for liberation from excessive social over-protection, was met by and engulfed by the changes in late capitalism that bring the market to all spheres of economic, social and political life. Margalit (1996) is less inclined to focus on the economic–social nexus, favouring a more cultural-social framework for analysing the indecency in welfare systems. He is, however, clear that even when the service provision occurs through private/commercial means, the welfare claimant must undergo eligibility tests in order to access the funds for the purchase of service (Margalit, 1996, p. 214). For him, welfare, even in its current market manifestation, always starts in the public bureaucracy (Margalit, 1996, p. 216).

There is nothing new in cementing the nexus between public bureaucracy and private sector for welfare provision, but it is new in its manifestation in disability services. Fraser (1989, p. 228) declares this approach destructive of social bonds, arguing that 'untrammelled marketisation endangers the fund of capacities available to create and sustain social bonds'. Fraser (1989) goes on to propose that our actions must be directed against domination wherever it roots; for example, in disembedded markets or exclusionary institutions (such as the education system); or uncivil communities wanting nothing of those who confront us with the certainty of human frailty. Following Fraser's attention to emancipatory movements, not considered in Margalit's work, we can listen closely for the runaway needs interpretations. In the current disability space this includes: a call to transform and democratise, not to eradicate social protections; to use market-thinking to open up fresh opportunities and potentiate creative, entrepreneurial ways of driving change in work and community; and to insist on full membership of society by pressing for universal access to communication, education, transport, housing, etc.

How can we heed the runaway needs interpretations while addressing adaptive preferencing and not automatically privileging our professional 'I know better' stance? Margalit does not take us into solutions, but his conclusions point us in useful directions. Recognising that it is institutions and situations that produce the humiliation in welfare systems, not necessarily the intentions of individual operators in these settings, we are initially drawn to focus on analysis and reform at systems' levels. Margalit is positive about the possibility of doing better in this arena but does not give a program of reform. He warns against using words such as decency, respect and honour as 'aiming for the sublime that is used in moral and political discourse' (1996, p. 289). He says he is not presenting a theory, which is tested reflexively according to its need for consistency. Instead he wants to tell a story about the decent society (Margalit, 1996, p. 289). While this may be seen as a weak point in his work, it also opens opportunities for the voices of those people who know about the humiliation to take centre stage in new ways. He has stayed away from telling the humiliated how to speak back to the system.

As a starting point, in order to bring his insights to our present aim, which is to carry out the Lived Experience Project in social work education in non-humiliating ways, we must look for sites where that story of decency is being developed. Learning from social movements (as the site of emerging runaway needs discourses), we can see that any reform needs to begin in a new place: one of optimism, of respect and of releasing and building capability. Being able to hear diverse expressions of runaway or oppositional needs interpretations is to be courageous enough to offer a respectful and emancipatory engagement with the person who lives through these discourses. Looking at the example of the voices of people with disability, it is difficult for welfare organisations and educational institutions to heed this social conversation with them when they are only related to as clients whose resistance is ascribed to diagnosis and addressed by behavioural interventions. Yet social work educators and their institutions can do this differently.

Margalit (1996, p. 28) asserts that 'the enterprise of a decent society has meaning only relative to a society with a clear notion of rights'. Investing in and supporting movement-level activities and capacity-building will lead to a clearer, more comprehensible engagement with those who voice both discontent with the present and articulate a vision that is more aligned to full citizenhood, defended rights and autonomy; and provision of supports that serve flourishing. In particular, it is important to listen closely for those calling for establishment and renewal of community bonds and for transformation in the practice models used in our work alongside those relying on services. For Margalit (1996, p. 40) this brings into sharper focus a society's potential to preserve civil rights but to continue to humiliate people because they are considered second class citizens. The focus, therefore, on restoring citizenhood to people who have been humiliated, becomes a necessary companion to the work of rights defence.

Listening carefully to the disability rights movement, to the person and those who love them, will unfold a story that reveals both the damaging and uplifting forces that give us something to work with as we commit to shining goals, to thoughtful, doable mid-range goals, to building capacity, to protecting autonomy, to shaping opportunities for self-determination and to hearing the life-story of the person in order to support their healing from rejection, shame and trauma and the trap of adaptive preferencing. For Margalit (1996), in his concluding remarks about 'sensibility', about feelings associated with concepts, we can see the importance of linking sensibility with moral concepts that are not conventionally seen as emotive. For him the central concepts of *The Decent Society* are focused around sensibility (1996, p. 290). We can feel and see humiliation. Its antidote in decency must also have this awareness that lives need not be shaped by shame and despair, and that the respect related to decency is felt and observed. This is the ground in which we grow as citizens in a democracy. This is the ground in which families can rest with a confident hope for a future not haunted by the risk of abandonment. It is hard and rewarding work so far from the current functionalism, systematic utilitarianism, professional dominance and aggressive governmentality that is emerging in the Australian welfare system.

Privileging narratives of refusal, resistance and rights

Social work education's critical and emancipatory turn requires engagement with those whose lived experience teaching is formed around recognition and denunciation of the humiliating and dehumanising aspects of welfare, not a submission to it. The message of criticism and insight is, therefore, one of refusal to be limited to clienthood and its associated adaptive preferencing;

and resistance to the situational and wider social forces that reduce demands for rights, resources, belonging and respect to stifled hopes contained in service plans and paid relationships. This goes to the heart of Margalit's thoughts about respect and why it is a justified expectation. After exploring a number of options, he argues, consistent with his reasoning throughout the text, that we must maintain a focus on why it is wrong to humiliate human beings (Margalit, 1996, p. 57). This is what he later calls 'being beastly to humans' (Margalit, 1996, p. 89), arguing that treating humans as non-human is a feature of rejecting people from the human commonwealth. Many who are relegated to service world are able to tell just this story.

Timothy Garton-Ash, writing on free speech in 2016, quotes the German political theorist Kurt Tucholsky: 'Nothing is more difficult and nothing requires more character than to find yourself in open contradiction to your time and to loudly say: No' (p. 371). He goes on to explain that it is intellectually and psychologically difficult to step outside the received wisdom of your time and place ... to resist the 'normative power of the given' (Garton-Ash, 2016, p. 371). An emancipatory approach to social work education offers opportunity for educators and students to join this resistance to the normative power of the given with those who call for an honest appraisal of how risk in services is analysed and addressed. In disability services the biggest risk is the corruption of care; a growing tolerance of limiting people's rights, autonomy and free expression; and a growing tolerance for brutal ways of governing behaviour. This occurs alongside a community with a seemingly endless capacity for rejection; the twin breeding grounds of trauma. In doing this, we must also acknowledge the courage it takes for oppositionalised 'disabled' people and their close associates to call out the humiliation.

Margalit (1996, p. 290), forever cautious and reflexive, warns that:

> There is a danger implicit in the concepts used in this book. They are taken from the rhetoric aiming for the sublime that is used in political and moral discourse. The arousing function of concepts such as honor and humiliation is liable to turn discussions of the decent society into a lot of hot air ... Another danger is that the discussion will become mired in a sticky morass of sermonising ... I believe that an intelligent form of discourse is possible that is not theoretical, yet is far from sticky sermonising or hot air.

This chapter has drawn on my reflections as an activist-academic involved, over many years, in the disability rights movement. The disability rights movement is not the only site of refusal and resistance from which strong voices emanate, offering critique and vision; condemnation and hope; rights claims and respect. It links to all those with a vision of social justice, a commitment to the value of respect and the capacity to instruct the open-minded through their accounts of struggle, organising and victory. If diverse and intersecting movement voices are consciously brought into social work education through history, testimony, text, film, philosophy, literature and political action, student social workers will find themselves equipped to continue the work of emancipation in their professional lives. Without this approach, the moral hazard inherent in seeking narratives that unintentionally reinforce the humiliation of the welfare system will leave students social workers with a view that their role permits them to act upon others in ways that reproduce clienthood in those they serve.

The Australian Social Work *Ethical Guidance: Using client information for research and educative purposes* is grounded in the integrated values of respect for individuals and pursuit of social justice. Margalit (1996) provides a way into understanding this integration by simultaneously exposing the humiliation generated by the welfare system while declaring a decent society a realisable goal. In this way he moves the goal of building a decent society away from simply evaluative (good or bad) to being a regulative idea (remote or realisable). This realisation is within the reach of an emancipatory and critical social work practised in solidarity with those who actively resist the predations of indecency. As Margalit says (1996, p. 284):

> It is doubtful whether the decent society is a low peak on the mountain ridge that has to be climbed by anyone striding toward the high peak of the just society, it is quite possible that the political strategy for the realization of the decent society is very different from that intended to bring about the just society, even if a just society is necessarily a decent one. A decent society is a worthy ideal to be realized.

When we pay attention to strategies that will promote a decent society, we will select interlocutors who can address student social workers and educators and otherwise front the service system with a life-expanding vision, grounding their self-concept in rights claims as citizens. In short, we start by believing and then acting on the belief that we are here to support the person to strive for rights protection, meaning and purpose in their lives, as well as joy and connection and self-respect.

References

Auerhahn, Nanette and Laub, Dori. (1990) Holocaust testimony. *Holocaust and Genocide Studies*, 5 (4): 447–462.
Australian Association of Social Workers. (2010) *Code of Ethics*. Melbourne: AASW.
Australian Association of Social Workers. (last modified July 2016) *The Ethical Guidance: Using Client Information For Research And Educative Purposes*. Melbourne: AASW.
Australian Government. (2009) *Shut Out: The Experience of People with Disabilities and their Families in Australia*. National Disability Strategy Consultation Report prepared by the National People with Disability and Carers Council. Canberra, ACT: AGPS.
Cavel, Stanley. (1971) 'Must we mean what we say?' In Lyas, C.. (ed). *Philosophy and Linguistics. Controversies in Philosophy*. Palgrave, London, p. 131–165.
Fraser, Nancy. (1989) Talking about needs: Interpretive contests as political conflicts in welfare-state societies. *Ethics*, 99 (2): 291–313.
Garton-Ash, Timothy. (2016) *Free Speech: Ten Principles for a Connected World*. New Haven, CT: Yale University Press.
Gilmore, Leigh. (2003). Jurisdictions: "I, Rigoberta Menchu", "The Kiss", and scandalous self-representations in the age of memoir and trauma. *Signs*, 28 (2): 695–718.
Haebich, Anna. (2000) *Broken Circles: Fragmenting Indigenous Families 1800–2000*. Fremantle WA: Fremantle Press.
Hallahan, Lorna. (2015). Disability policy in Australia: A triumph of the scriptio inferior on impotence and neediness. *Australian Journal of Social Issues*, 50 (2): 191–208.
Leadbeater, Charles. (Oct 11, 1996) Just be decent: (Tony Blair's view of social justice) new statesman. 9 (424): 21. London.
Margalit, Avishai. (1996 translated Naomi Goldblum) *The Decent Society*. Cambridge, MA: Harvard University Press.
Mills, C. Wright. (1959) *The Sociological Imagination*. London: Oxford University Press.
Nussbaum, Martha. (2001) Adaptive preferences and women's options. *Economics and Philosophy*, 17: 67–88.
Rose, Nikolas, O'Malley, Pat, and Valverde, Mariana. (2006) Governmentality. *Annual Review of Law and Social Science*, 2 (1): 83–104.

21

The relevance of Nancy Fraser for transformative social work education*

Dorothee Hölscher

GRIFFITH UNIVERSITY QUEENSLAND AUSTRALIA

Vivienne Bozalek

UNIVERSITY OF THE WESTERN CAPE, SOUTH AFRICA, AND

Mel Gray

UNIVERSITY OF NEWCASTLE NEW SOUTH WALES, AUSTRALIA

Introduction

It is a well-established tradition in social work to define itself, *inter alia*, by its commitment to principles of justice. Yet, there appears to be little agreement about the concept of justice itself, and about what practices would most suitably be employed to furthering its ends (Hugman, 2008; Ife, 2008; Solas, 2008a, 2008b). Accordingly, there is little clarity around the kinds of educational content and pedagogical practice required to enable social work students to contribute to advancing just social arrangements and just ways of relating, beyond the classroom, especially in the face of escalating crises of injustice in which social, cultural, political and ecological dimensions have been shown increasingly to be intertwined (see Chapters 17 and 18 in this volume). Hence, questions arise around *what* should be taught and *how* it is taught. This chapter proposes that the work of political philosopher and critical theorist, Nancy Fraser, holds potential to enrich both *content* (theoretical positions and frameworks) and *process* (how pedagogy and scholarship is enacted in social work) of transformative social work education, aspects of justice which, Fraser's theorising demonstrates, are interlinked.

Following a brief biography, this chapter traces the development of key concepts in Fraser's work over the past 30 years. It begins with a presentation of Fraser's early scholarship, which was concerned particularly with the politics of *needs interpretation* and ideologies of *dependency* in contemporary constructions of welfare. This work culminated in Fraser's formulation of *seven principles of gender justice*, upon which she then developed her multidimensional *theory of justice*. Fraser structured this theory around her idea of participatory parity as a central principle and standard of justice. With this, she articulated (in)justices as structural processes spanning the global and local levels of discourse and practice in the economic, cultural and political spheres of social life. Thereafter, the chapter briefly presents Fraser's recent work on the capitalist crisis in the 21st century, which forms the backdrop against which her concepts of abnormal justice and transformative practices are discussed. The implications of Fraser's scholarship for social work education are articulated thereafter and discussed with reference to several years of educational research and practice with higher education students, including students of social work. Throughout the chapter, examples are used to illustrate how the concepts under discussion illuminate the kinds of injustice to which present-day social work ought to respond. The chapter concludes that Fraser's work can equip social work students with an integrative framework to make sense of the complex and changing dynamics of injustice that surround and implicate the profession in multiple ways. This can be taught in a manner that encourages them to act upon their understandings and to think creatively about the evolving meanings of social justice and its moral and political implications for their emerging practice.

Nancy Fraser

Nancy Fraser was born in 1947, received her bachelor's degree in 1969 and, in 1980, was awarded her PhD at the Graduate Center of the City University of New York. Fraser specialises in critical social theory and political philosophy. She is Henry A. and Louise Loeb Professor at the New School for Social Research, a Visiting Research Professor at Dartmouth College and holds an international research chair at the Collège d'études mondiales, Paris. Fraser holds six honorary degrees and was recently awarded the Nessim Habif World Prize, the Havens Centre Lifetime Award for Contribution to Critical Scholarship, and the status of 'Chevalier' of the French Legion of Honour. She is also a past President of the American Philosophical Association, Eastern Division. Fraser's work has been translated into over 20 languages and was cited twice by the Brazilian Supreme Court in decisions upholding marriage equality and affirmative action.

Fraser is well respected for her sustained work around the concept of justice, which she developed, over three decades, in relation to global capitalism's developments from World War II to date. Over 30 years, she traced capitalism's relation to diverse struggles for democracy and against domination, including race-, class- and gender-based oppression and imperialism. More recently, her attention has turned to the intersection of economic crisis, ecological crisis, and crisis of social reproduction under conditions of global capitalism in the 21st century. Her work has been published in a series of interconnected essays in the *New Left Review* and *Critical Historical Studies* and as a collection in *Fortunes of Feminism: From state-managed capitalism to neoliberal crisis* (2013). Previous books include *Capitalism: A conversation in critical theory*, with Rahel Jaeggi (2018); *Domination et Anticipation: Pour un renouveau de la critique*, with Luc Boltanski (2014); *Transnationalizing the Public Sphere: Nancy Fraser debates her critics* (2014); *Scales of Justice: Reimagining political space for a globalizing world* (2008); *Adding Insult to Injury: Nancy Fraser debates her critics*, edited by Kevin Olson (2008); *Redistribution or Recognition? A political-philosophical exchange* (2003) with Axel Honneth; *Justice Interruptus: Critical reflections on the 'postsocialist' condition* (1997); and *Unruly Practices: Power, discourse and gender in contemporary social theory* (1989). Her most recent book, entitled *Feminism for the 99%: A Manifesto* and co-authored with Cinzia Aruzza and Tithi Battacharya, was published in 2019 (Aruzza, Battacharya & Fraser, 2019).

In *Fortunes of Feminism*, Fraser (2013) grouped her writings into three phases. The first phase, from 1989 to 1997, involved a radical critique of 'male domination in state-organised capitalist societies' in a postwar era of social democracy (Fraser, 2013, p. 1). In the second phase, from 2003 to 2009, Fraser developed an expansive theory of justice, examining how concerns of redistribution were challenged by competing and complementary calls for recognition, as well as considering the relevance of the political dimension of justice for calls for recognition and redistribution to succeed. The third phase (from 2007 onwards) examines the nature and dynamics of capitalist crisis in the contemporary neoliberal era and the implications thereof for emancipatory movements across the world.

Needs interpretation, dependency, and Fraser's principles of gender justice

In 1989, Nancy Fraser published a landmark concept, the *politics of needs interpretation* (Fraser, 1989). This concept enabled her to highlight problems with welfare professionals' tendency to construe service-user needs as 'self-evident', rather than socially constructed and structurally determined. Fraser (1989) saw needs interpretation as a contested practice and site of power struggles. To elaborate, she highlighted what she labelled the Juridical-Administrative-Therapeutic nature of the welfare system:

- The *Juridical* element referred to service-user's welfare rights and claims;
- *Administrative* decisions determined their entitlement, or not, to benefits and services based on needs interpretation;
- *Therapy* referred to the assumption that mental health and behavioural issues required therapeutic intervention.

Referring to US state organisations, she showed how this system was coded by gender and race with:

> An implicitly 'masculine' social insurance subsystem tied to 'primary' labor-force participation and historically geared to (white male) 'breadwinners'; and an implicitly 'feminine' relief subsystem tied to household income and geared to homemaker-mothers and their 'defective' (female-headed) families, originally restricted to white women, but subsequently racialized.
>
> *(Fraser, 1989, p. 156)*

Fraser argued that, together, these historically specific valuations of gender roles, a gendered (and racialised) division of labour, and a gendered (and racialised) understanding of needs, constitute the underlying assumptions that structure the ways in which the state – and social workers in its employ – continue to determine service-users' needs.

Linked to this is Fraser's (1989) conceptualisation of *the social*, which constitutes the terrain in which social work operates to date. For Fraser (1989), this is a site of discourse about those needs that states consider problematic. Fraser (1989) identified several competing discourses about such 'problematic' needs in the terrain of 'the social': the *needs discourse of experts* provides social workers' *raison d'être*, which is to intervene in 'problematic' situations. Against this, the term *oppositional needs discourse* refers to the efforts by social movements to confront and disrupt hegemonic interpretations of the identities, roles, vices, and needs attributed to, for example, racialised people, women, gendered and sexualised minorities, workers, and social service-users. The third discourse is what Fraser (1989) called the *reprivatisation discourse*, which serves to curtail public welfare spending by shifting responsibility for social service provision to the private and market spheres. These three discourses re-appear in Fraser's interpretation of the roles of social movements under conditions of capitalist crisis.

The concept, *politics of needs interpretation*, remains relevant to date, given that categorising (assessing) and responding to human needs continues to be central to social work practice (Dover, Hunter & Randall, 2008; Towle, 1945/1973). It points to the mechanisms by which social workers are often implicated in the surveillance of, rather than care for, their service-users. It also alerts social workers to the way public discourses on needs often represent the interests of dominant groups, rather than those of the marginalised groups from which most service-users stem. Consequently, service-users risk internalising hegemonic need interpretations even as they are disadvantaged by them. Cruikshank (1999) later highlighted that because they have a vested interest in keeping their jobs, middle-class professionals, such as social workers, play a willing role in this dynamic, in a way that kept the welfare apparatus intact (see also Bozalek & Lambert, 2008).

In this context, Fraser and Gordon's (1994; Fraser, 2013) *genealogy of* the term *dependency* shows that from a concept describing social relations of subordination (such as a child's legal dependence on an adult), the term 'dependency' has become a psychologised label to designate 'deviant and incompetent individuals' (Fraser & Gordon, 1994, p. 108), thereby denoting inherent personality characteristics of certain (stigmatised) persons and groups, such as teenage mothers, and people who engaged in (unacknowledged and devalued) caring work, such as mothers or grandmothers providing the unpaid work of caring for children. Fraser and Gordon's (1994; Fraser, 2013) genealogy highlights how the idea of *welfare dependency* has provided politicians with a terminology that can be used to legitimise cuts to welfare services, stunt new demands for public welfare expenses, and justify attacks on social security provisions for people who are not economically independent. It also shows that this idea has impacted social work service provision by feeding into distinctions between those considered deserving or undeserving of services and helping to sustain prevailing hierarchies, rather than enabling service providers and users to relate on more equal terms. As such, the notion of welfare dependency continues to undermine social workers' abilities to respond to service-users' *felt* rather than *imposed* definitions of needs.

Fraser and Gordon (1994) noted that such revised understandings of dependency were informed by the ideal of an *ideal human being* as rational, autonomous, economically independent, unencumbered, middle-class, white, and male. This ideal person does not exist, since all human beings are dependent on one another and 'independence' is predicated on a range of invisible support over a lifetime. Yet, it continues to bolster social, economic, and cultural hierarchies; with everyone who deviates from this ideal being seen as 'less than' and at risk of being pathologised. Fraser's (1994, 2013) seven normative *principles of gender justice*, mounted upon her critique of needs interpretation and welfare dependency, provide social workers with a sound set of guidelines to respond to this flawed notion of independence and its unjust social, political, economic, and cultural outcomes:

1 *Anti-poverty:* addressing social arrangements that leave people's basic needs unmet.
2 *Anti-exploitation:* recognising that people with unmet needs are vulnerable to exploitation. Fraser (2013) argued that support of such groups is their right, not a privilege: 'When receipt of aid is highly stigmatised or discretionary, the anti-exploitation principle is not satisfied' (p. 117).
3 *Addressing income equality:* advocating against unequal pay, based on gender, for similar work, or the devaluation of caring labour and skills.
4 *Leisure-time equality:* recognising that unpaid care work robs carers of leisure time, thus promoting social arrangements that equalise caring work for all involved.
5 *Equality of respect:* promoting social arrangements that prevent the objectification and depreciation of women or trivialise their activities and contributions, such as caring work.

6 *Anti-marginalisation:* acknowledging that social policy arrangements should make it possible for women to participate fully, on a par with men, in all aspects of social life, thus advocating, for example, for public child care, elderly care, and the dismantling of 'old boys clubs' and masculinist work cultures.

7 *Anti-androcentrism:* decentring unequal gender norms and masculinist policies, norms, values, and practices: needed are social policies that support both giving and receiving care, with a view to subverting men's life patterns as the norm to which women must assimilate in order to flourish.

Though Fraser (1994, 2013) articulated these principles in relation to the post-industrial welfare state, they are equally relevant to countries in the Global South that have emerged from, or remain invested in, concepts of the developmental state. The following sections demonstrate how, globally, neoliberal ideologies, policies, and practices have eroded previous gains won by feminist and other emancipatory movements, suggesting that Fraser's principles for gender justice remain as relevant for contemporary critical social work practice as when they were conceived 25 years ago. As a substantive contribution to the social work curriculum, therefore, Fraser's early scholarship can assist social work students and practitioners in interrogating many of the often unquestioned assumptions and implicit accusations permeating welfare practice and in explaining the profession's continued implication in some of the gender injustices that prevail in the sector. It can serve, further, to remind social workers of their responsibility to help change, rather than uncritically embrace, an ideology that continuously works to (re-)create conditions that stigmatise, marginalise, and undermine the well-being of much of their service-user base.

Redistribution, recognition, and the development of participatory parity as a standard and process of justice

During the second phase of her work, Fraser (2003) developed a *multidimensional, multilevel theory of justice*, which has the potential to highlight injustices that commonly escape public attention, thereby contributing significantly to critical theorising and transformative practices in social work across the globe. To pull together a wide array of social (in)justices in relation to one central norm, Fraser (2003) proposed the principle of *participatory parity*, which she later explained as follows:

> The most general meaning of justice is parity of participation. According to this radical-democratic interpretation … of equal moral worth, justice requires social arrangements that permit all to participate as peers in social life. Overcoming injustice means dismantling institutionalised obstacles that prevent some people from participating on a par with others, as full partners in social interaction.
>
> *(Fraser, 2009a, p. 16)*

According to this principle, social arrangements can be considered 'just if, and only if, they permit all the relevant social actors to participate as peers in social life', whereas norms can claim to be 'legitimate if, and only if, they can command the assent of all concerned in fair and open processes of deliberation, in which all can participate as peers' (Fraser, 2007, p. 29). The concept of participatory parity, then, enables at once an analysis both of existing social arrangements and of the norms legitimising them, thereby helping to illuminate their underlying dynamics. Such an analysis provides activists (including, if they so wish, educators, practitioners, and students of social work) with a key prerequisite for addressing their 'root causes' of prevailing injustices (Bozalek & Hochfeld, 2016, p. 201; see also Leibowitz & Bozalek, 2015).

Fraser (1997) began by developing the economic and cultural dimensions of justice, calling this a *two-dimensional approach*. This *perspectival dualism* serves to identify two types of power relations, which, albeit substantially different, are nonetheless 'ineluctably entwined' (McNay, 2008, p. 283). According to this bifocal view, both *redistribution*, located in the economic dimension of contemporary societies, and *recognition*, located in the cultural dimension of social life, are required for participatory parity, with neither being reducible to the other (Fraser, 2000, 2003). Fraser continued to subscribe to the view held by Marxists, socialists, and social democrats that justice is a matter of a just distribution of economic rights, opportunities, and resources. Questions of 'how much economic inequality does justice permit', and 'how much redistribution is required, and according to which principle of distributive justice' remained important to her because 'economic structures that deny [people] the resources they need to interact with others as peers' constituted important impediments to justice (Fraser, 2009a, pp. 15–16). These, she referred to as *maldistribution*, thus denoting many of the issues to which social workers must respond, such as poverty, hunger, and rampant inequality.

Yet, Fraser (2009a) also shared the understanding, mainstreamed by feminist, anti-racist, and anti-imperialist movements that identity, too, mattered to questions of justice: to ask 'what constitutes equal respect' and 'which kinds of differences merit public recognition, and by what means' is instructive because 'institutionalised hierarchies of cultural values that deny [people] the requisite standing … to interact with others as peers' constitute equally important 'obstacles to participatory parity' as do economic injustices (Fraser, 2009a, pp. 15–16). Fraser (2009a) called these kinds of injustices *misrecognition*, thereby denoting a common dynamic underlying a wide array of discriminatory practices, such as ageism, classism, ethnocentrism, nationalism, racism, and sexism, all of which social workers are expected to challenge (IFSW/IASSW, 2014). Importantly, Fraser intended the term to reference a *status subordination*, located at a macro level of society (Fraser & Honneth, 2003, p. 30). In other words, Fraser (in McNay, 2008) never conceived misrecognition

> as a psychological dynamic, but as institutionalised cultural value patterns that have discriminatory effects on the equal standing of social actors. Status subordination takes the concrete forms of juridical discrimination, government policy, professional practice, or sedimented moral and ideological codes.
>
> *(p. 284)*

Fraser's (2009b, 2013) political analysis of post-World War II feminist theorising and practice is instructive of her understanding of injustice as a deep structural process. Adopting a historical perspective, Fraser (2009b, 2013) traced feminism's post-World War II alignments with other 'New Left' movements (for example, anti-racism, anti-imperialism), and showed that feminist critique pioneered an *intersectional* reading of gender injustice, which regards 'women's subordination' as 'systemic, grounded in the deep structures of society' (Fraser, 2013, pp. 214–215) that cannot be separated from a broader capitalist critique. However, such comprehensive analysis and the activism it informs have been gradually displaced by feminism's turn to an *identity politics* which prioritises cultural over all other justice concerns. This changing emphasis is best understood in relation to the ascendance, from the early 1970s onwards, of neoliberalism as an ideology and economic policy framework, in that the increasing tendency of feminism and other social movements to foreground cultural critiques began to be impacted by a rising ideology that worked to repress 'all memory of social egalitarianism' (Fraser, 2013, p. 219). Consequently, the idea of (mis)recognition became 'unmoored from the critique of capitalism' (Fraser, 2013, p. 219), with the term *recognition* understood increasingly to signify individual ambitions and interpersonal concerns, while *misrecognition* came to represent merely individual hurts and interpersonal afflictions. In short, matters of recognition were being privatised. This development unfolded alongside similar changes in other domains of social reproduction, where responsibilities for welfare, education, and health were being returned to individuals and families, even as their ability to meet them was being undermined by a deepening and widening neoliberal ordering of societies at a global scale.

Social work's professional discourse, analyses, and practices have been affected profoundly by these individualised and privatised notions of culture and justice. For example, in a predominantly female profession, the personal ambitions of many practitioners and academics may be well-served, at least to the extent that they are able to benefit from a growing consensus that people should not be disadvantaged on account of their identities, instead requiring positive discrimination and support to overcome historical limitations. Yet, such privatised readings of recognition may also have contributed to the profession's commitment to justice becoming disjointed from equally important concerns for economic maldistributions within and across societies. This slimmed-down politics of recognition fails to illuminate the extent to, and ways in which, the economic and cultural dimensions of justice are entwined. Likewise, these changes in consciousness have resulted in a general failure to appreciate how individual acts of misrecognition within interpersonal relationships are connected inseparably to the broader contextual conditions that enable interpersonal slights and oversights in the first place.

To the extent then that social work has embraced and subscribes to this limited understanding of the requirements of justice and prioritises identity issues over other justice concerns, the profession may not be alert to a much wider range of injustices, instead overlooking the extent to which the multiple forms of discrimination that social workers are to challenge, are in fact structural, macro-level concerns. Thus, a failure to consider that economic and cultural injustices are irreducible yet complementary processes undermines the profession's ability to formulate, let alone act upon, a critique that is appropriate to the complexities of contemporary injustices. Against this, Fraser's concepts of misrecognition and maldistribution can alert social workers to the ways in which structural forms of injustice are woven into people's everyday lives and the political responsibilities to which this gives rise.

Representation, framing, and justice as a multilevel phenomenon

Fraser (2005a, 2005b) began to expand her previous, bifocal conceptualisation into a *trivalent theory of justice*, based on her contention that a third dimension was needed to match the complexities of the injustices brought to the fore by globalisation, and to help devise practices capable of protecting, widening, and deepening justice in their wake (Fraser, 2005a, 2005b, 2009a). She explained that the *political dimension*

> [f]urnishes the stage on which struggles over distribution and recognition are played out. Establishing criteria of social belonging and thus determining who counts as a member, the political dimension specifies the reach of ... [the] other dimensions. It tells us who is included in, and who is excluded from, the circle of those entitled to a just distribution and reciprocal recognition. Establishing decision rules, the political dimension likewise sets the procedures for staging and resolving contests in both the economic and the cultural dimensions. It tells us not only who can make claims ... but also how such claims are to be mooted and adjudicated.
>
> *(Fraser, 2009a, p. 17)*

Due to her observation that it was as common as it was misleading to conflate the concept of justice with the construct of the nation state, Fraser (2005b, 2009a) asserted that simply adding another dimension to her theory would not suffice. From the emergence of nation states as the dominant means for organising economic, political, social, and cultural life, there was a widely shared consensus that arguments about, and claims for, justice pertained either to relations between citizens, or to their relations with the state to which they 'belonged'. Fraser (2009a) called this the *Keynesian-Westphalian frame* of justice. However, with the global spread of neoliberalism as a political ideology and economic policy framework, it became increasingly obvious that pertinent forms of injustice, whether economic, ecological, social, political, cultural, and/or military, unfold across national boundaries. Thus, Fraser (2005b, 2009a) contended that any conceptualisation of justice that fails to critique the Keynesian-Westphalian frame itself will fall short analytically and cannot adequately inform efforts to protect, widen, and deepen relations of justice. This is important for a profession that has struggled to move beyond the still-dominant conflation of the idea of justice with nation states, as the latter continue to finance, either directly or indirectly, most social work services provided within their respective realms.

Thus, Fraser (2005a, 2005b) made the additional case for the political dimension of her expanded theory to be conceptualised across three interconnected levels. On the first level, the political, like the economic and cultural dimensions, concerns substantive questions of justice. Describing these as matters of *ordinary-political (mis)representation*, Fraser (2005a, 2005b) contended that such substantive concerns are about the terms of engagement in a given political community. For her, the question was whether these terms 'accorded' its members 'equal voice in public deliberations and fair representation in public decision-making' (Fraser, 2009a, p. 18). *(Mis)framing*, as a 'second order' (in)justice (Fraser, 2009a, p. 15), is a matter of scope in that it pertains to 'the question of who does, and who doesn't count as [a] subject of justice' (Hölscher, 2014, p. 23). In other words, framing decisions are about admission criteria and procedures concerning the award or denial of membership and thus constitute an important aspect of what Fraser (2009a) called *the grammar of justice* (p. 21). Examples for this are the layered form of in-/exclusion of non-citizens, from undocumented migrants to permanent residents, in the country in which they reside (Hölscher, 2014), or the financial exclusion of university students unable to raise funds for their study fees or to access bursaries or loans (Bozalek & Boughey, 2012). Fraser (2009a) contended that frame-setting decisions could result in particularly grave injustices by 'constituting both members and non-members in a single stroke' (p. 19):

> When questions of justice are framed in a way that wrongly excludes some from consideration, the consequence is a special kind of meta-injustice, in which one is denied the chance to press first order [that is, substantive] claims in a given community.
>
> *(Fraser, 2009a, p. 19)*

To qualify what she meant by wrongful exclusion, Fraser (2009a) proposed the *all-subjected principle*, which denotes the idea that 'all those who are subjected to a given governance structure have moral standing in relation to it' (p. 63). Rather than either asserting or disputing the nation state as the relevant frame for justice, this principle provides guidance for working out who has a substantive claim in relation to whom. If membership and subjection to governance matter in relation to questions of justice, then it follows that the way membership is framed and questions of ordinary-political representation are settled are equally important to a theory of justice. This understanding led to Fraser's (2009a) articulation of the third level of her expanded model, which concerns matters of process, that is, questions of *meta-political (mis)representation*. The importance of participatory parity as an overarching framework for Fraser's conceptualisation of justice is evident again at this level, in that Fraser's (2009a) stated aim was to contribute to a democratisation of global affairs.

The significance of the second and third levels of Fraser's theory for social work can be illustrated with reference to the specialised field of social work with cross-border migrants (Hölscher, 2014). To date, much of social work discourse continues to accept, at face value, the dominant ideology that cross-border migrants could be divided usefully along the binary of *voluntary* versus *forced* migration. Following Fraser, scholars, practitioners, and students of social work would do well to ask questions such as these: What historical and geopolitical dynamics underlie contemporary forms of mass-migration, and who bears responsibility for these? Who should respond when such migrants, en route to their hoped-for destinations are imprisoned, encamped, enslaved, tortured, and traumatised? Who should bear the costs of responding to their needs for protection and care? What legal standing should such migrants at their various stop-over or destination points possess? To what extent are these matters of, or matters that exceeded, national sovereignty? Who takes the decisions in relation to any of these conundrums, and according to what parameters and decision-making rules? Are current decision-making models, rules, and processes enough, and are responses adequately resourced? Similar questions arise in relation to all major and historical lines of injustice, including, but not limited to, colonialism and racism, poverty and exploitation, and patriarchy and gender violence. They point to the importance of social work scholars and practitioners being attentive to how macro-level structures, dynamics, and processes can impact their everyday work, while simultaneously entangling them in global regimes of injustice.

In short, matters of ordinary and meta-political representation and framing are relevant for social work as they impact on the kinds of work that practitioners are called upon and often consent to perform, and on the ways in which this is done. Few would seriously question justice as a value in broad and general terms or argue that gender justice did not matter, that cultural concerns of recognition were unimportant, that poverty constituted an injustice, or that cross-border migrants did not have human rights. However, beyond such broad-brush ideas, there appears to be little consensus on the meaning or scope of justice (Fraser, 2009a). This is where Fraser's *multidimensional, multilevel theory of justice* holds utility for social work education: it can provide students with a conceptual grid to help develop shared understandings of contemporary forms of injustices and their common, underlying dynamics, as well as the kinds of responsibilities the profession holds in relation to them.

Crisis of capitalism, abnormal justice, and the call for transformative practices in social work education

Recently, Fraser (2012) turned her attention to the *crisis of capitalism in the 21st century*, which she described as one of great severity and complexity and unprecedented intricacy and brutality, for which we lack a conceptual framework to interpret or resolve it 'in an emancipatory way' (p. 4) (see also Fraser, 2016a, 2016b; Fraser & Jaeggi, 2018). Importantly, Fraser (2012) noted that this crisis is 'multidimensional, encompassing not only economy and finance, but also ecology, society, and politics' (p. 4), and that the *crisis nodes* in these respective spheres are interlinked on a global scale. With this, Fraser aligned her scholarship with that of an increasing number of critical theorists, who have turned their attention to the question of ecological justice and its connection to other dimensions of justice (see also Chapters 17 and 18 in this volume).

Fraser (2012) contended that contemporary social struggles unfolding around major crisis nodes in the ecological, economic, and sphere of social reproduction 'must be analysed as a *triple movement* in which … struggles for *emancipation* alongside those for *marketisation* and *social protection* … combine and collide' (p. 12, emphasis added). According to Fraser (2012), struggles for *emancipation* comprise a diverse set of anti-capitalist, feminist, anti-racist, anti-imperial, decolonial, and environmentalist movements in regions of both the Global North and South. Struggles for *marketisation* are being waged by forces representing neoliberal interests in governments, international governance structures, and the corporate sector worldwide, among other places. Struggles for *social protection*, finally, are pursued by formations as diverse as social-democratic parties and trade-union movements on the one hand and a range of (re-)emerging nationalist movements on the other, who operate from assumptions that protectionist measures around national boundaries might shield their constituencies from un- and under-employment and buffer existing social security systems against being eroded; that cultural insecurities might be contained by limiting or, better still, reversing the presence of *Others* in their communities; or that the continued extraction of minerals and fossil fuels from the earth around them might advance, rather than undermine, their followers' interests and well-being (see Fraser, 2012, 2016a, 2016b; Fraser & Jaeggi, 2018). In saying, furthermore, that these three lines of struggle can combine as well as collide, Fraser alerts her readers that simplistic left–right cartographies of the contemporary political space can be shown to be increasingly inadequate. In the case of women, for instance, emancipation continues to require the right to sell labour, thus aligning this interest with some of the demands of free marketeers (see above), yet potentially pitting women against the agendas of social protectionists. Meanwhile, demands for social protection that go together with calls for the subjugation and exclusion of *Others* are anti-emancipatory (see above), while consent to the continued destruction of the natural environment is apt to strengthen neoliberal and neocolonial agendas (see Fraser, 2012, 2016a, 2016b; Fraser & Jaeggi, 2018).

Given this analysis, Fraser's (2009a) observation of a diminishing of consensus concerning both meaning and scope of justice is perhaps unsurprising. Fraser (2009a) referred to this as *abnormal justice*, that is, a historical moment when public debates about justice 'increasingly lack the structured character of normal discourse', instead assuming a progressively 'freewheeling character' (p. 49). In other words, the idea of abnormal justice refers to a situation where there are insufficiently shared normative understandings concerning the issues being deliberated upon. This then makes consensus hard to conceive and difficult to attain. Conditions of abnormal justice can be said to prevail when calls for social protection are made both by movements clamouring for the opening of national boundaries and those demanding the opposite; when struggles for women's emancipation align with economic agendas that serve also to retain poor and racialised women in positions of powerlessness and exploitability; and when fears of economic marginalisation and loss of social protection prompt the consent of communities to the continued exploitation of natural resources at the cost of undermining the sustainability of life itself. When such shared understandings are lacking, Fraser (2009a) contended, 'contests over basic premises [of justice] proliferate [and] deviation becomes ... the rule' (p. 50). The idea of abnormal justice, therefore, alerts social work that contemporary political, economic, social, cultural, and ecological crises need not necessarily lead to emancipatory outcomes generally, or within social work discourse and practices more specifically. However, it does make room for the possibility that, and enable imaginations of how, different social movements might align and combine in myriad ways to advance emancipatory ends. It is the task of social work education to equip students to navigate this increasingly complex terrain.

Thus, incorporating the concept of abnormal justice into social work education could contribute to students developing critical reflexivity around their roles and responsibilities in relation to contemporary expressions and experiences of injustice. This is because it opens possibilities and creates an imperative for activists, including social workers, to try to (re-)inscribe egalitarian values – that is, the principle of participatory parity – into debates on the implications and requirements of justice in a world seemingly spinning out of control. It also brings the transformative potential of Fraser's multidimensional notion of social justice to the fore: in claiming the right to participate on a par, activists can work to advance a comprehensive notion of justice that attends at once to the question of *what* is at stake, *who* should participate in deliberations about this, and *how* decision-making rules have come into being and may need to be changed to ensure that *all subjected* to the fallout from the unfolding ecological, economic, social, and political crises can have a say in resolving them. In other words, social work education needs to meet the requirements of Fraser's (2003, 2009a, 2013) notion of *transformative practices*, that is, a form of activism directed at changing 'the deep grammar' of injustice 'in a globalising world' (Fraser, 2009a, pp. 23–24). Just how can such a notion of *justice as a transformative practice* be shared and explored in a way that is directly relevant to students' lived experiences and, rather than abstract ideas, is tangible and meaningful within their personal and emerging professional horizons? This is the concern of the chapter's final section.

Transformative practices in social work education: a case study from South Africa

As highlighted in the introduction and preceding sections, Fraser contended that the concept of justice generally, and its central norm of participatory parity specifically, denote both substantive and procedural concerns, thereby drawing attention to the content and process of social work education. This understanding guided several years of higher education research and practice in South Africa, including in the field of social work (Bozalek, 2014; Bozalek et al., forthcoming; Hölscher, 2018; Hölscher & Chiumbu, forthcoming). The research focused, among other things, on 'students' experiences' of 'participatory parity' and how the use of 'transformative pedagogical practices' might make it possible for them to 'participate as equals' in their education (Bozalek, 2014, p. 6). As part of this research, students from 'nine differently placed public universities' (Hölscher, 2018, p. 32) conducted a range of Participatory Learning and Action activities, including drawing their personal life lines and visual representations of their respective communities, and producing photovoice stories (Bozalek, 2011, 2013; Chambers, 2006; Wang, 2006). They presented and discussed these with one another in recorded focus groups. In several instances, students proceeded to analyse their respective artworks and discussions, compiling their findings using Fraser's theory of justice as their framework (see, for example, Hölscher, 2018). One social work student described her experience of the process as follows:

> We shared thoughts and experiences as well as ideas ... using the different symbols ... It was the first time I could talk about my experiences and ... I felt ... like ... a rock ... [had] been removed from my shoulders ... I also listened to others' stories which then made me ... feel better ... I used to not [be] proud of who I am ... but ... being in a participatory group is the most amazing feeling because we all feel equal and no one is better than the other.

As students shared and reflected upon forms of injustice they had encountered across their life spans and discussed the different ways in which they had tried and often failed to cope with and resist them, they discovered a similarity of experiences, which signified the structural injustices embedded in South African society. Issues that came to the fore included experiences of poverty as structural violence, sexual exploitation, the dynamics of academic and financial exclusions from higher learning, and the frequent student protests in which most had taken part (Bozalek et al., forthcoming). In addition, the social work students discovered and explored the extent to which they continued to share in the experiences of the communities in which they had grown up and from where many of their future service-users would come (Hölscher & Chiumbu, forthcoming). Furthermore, students were able to use Fraser's concepts to articulate and interpret their experiences within their broader context of South Africa's historical struggle for liberation and emancipation (see, for example, Caluza, 2015). These concepts assisted the students in developing shared understandings of citizenship, their expectations of the university as an institution to which they could belong, and what this meant for them as future social work practitioners (see, for example, Khoza, 2016; Magubane, 2015). Importantly, the methodology prompted social work participants to consider different forms of political action in response to the forms of injustices they had encountered. Activities that students explored and, where feasible, implemented in the wake of their research included: exhibiting their artefacts and research findings and initiating monthly 'talking sessions' between different stakeholders in social work education to address collaboratively concerns around gender violence, poverty, and financial exclusion from higher learning (Hölscher, 2018, p. 45); conducting mutual support schemes, writing to the press and relevant government ministers, and organising public protests (Hölscher & Chiumbu, forthcoming). Finally, it has been possible to demonstrate the capacity of the participating students to contribute to critical theorising in social work (Hölscher & Chiumbu, forthcoming).

Within the context of this research project, Nancy Fraser's concepts and the modes of engagement which they inspired were shown to have transformative potential in terms of how students positioned themselves, related to, perceived, interpreted, understood, and acted upon important injustices in their lives. Participating students experienced what it meant to engage as equals within the contexts they described, overall, as structurally unjust. This, in turn, encouraged them to explore different ways in which they could claim voice and demand recognition of the challenges they faced and contributions they could make as students and future social workers. By situating their personal experiences within South Africa's historical struggles, the students did not retreat into an identity politics that focused merely on their individual claims as members of 'black' or 'female' or 'poor' constituencies. Instead, they drew links between one another and in relation to their communities of origin and future service-users. They were able to articulate the underlying dynamics, or deep grammar, connecting them. The research pointed to the possibility that to the extent to which students could experience the transformative power of engaging as equals, they might also be open to what would be involved in engaging with future service-users as their equals and explain why they should want to do this.

In all these respects, the research suggests that educational interventions which incorporate the principle participatory parity both in terms of substantive contents and pedagogical style might help enable and inform future social workers' critically reflexive engagement around the profession's roles in perpetuating prevailing regimes of injustice, their responsibility to resist this, and ways of doing so creatively. None of this suffices, on its own, to resolve the intricacies of contemporary crises of justice. It might, however, contribute to avoiding a social work education that reproduces a depoliticised acceptance of the world as it is, pathologises the vulnerable and poor, and attempts to ameliorate problems in a way that, ultimately, contributes to maintaining the *status quo*. It might, thus, provide social work students with a conceptual and normative compass to navigate an increasingly complex terrain in a manner that may be considered *just*.

Conclusion

This chapter sought to demonstrate the relevance of Nancy Fraser's lifetime work on justice for social work education, in terms of content and pedagogical practices. It presented the historical depth and conceptual scope of Fraser's work on justice as a matter of substance and process through her concepts of *needs interpretation*, *dependency*, and *gender justice*; *participatory parity* and the *economic* and *cultural dimensions of justice*; the *political dimension of justice* as a set of structural processes spanning three interconnected levels; and *abnormal justice* in the context of *capitalist crisis*, as signified by deepening and escalating nodes of injustice. Finally, it explicated Fraser's emphasis on the need for *transformative practices* to change the deep grammar underlying the breadth and depth of contemporary forms of injustice. In this respect, it argued that, overall, its critical and radical traditions notwithstanding, social work has fallen short in its mission to eradicate injustice. It posited that this is possibly due to its affinity to *expert* discourses, its readiness to embrace *reprivatisation*, and its longstanding discomfort with *oppositional discourses* on the needs of those who use and depend on its services. Further, it argued that the implications for social work education and practice inhere in Fraser's insights on social justice within a complex and rapidly changing world. Fraser invites students to attend to injustices of maldistribution, misrecognition, misframing, misrepresentation, and reprivatisation and their effects on service-users and providers in the Global North and South under conditions of capitalist crisis. Taking the principle of participatory parity seriously means supporting students in finding – and demanding – their own voice so they might articulate and deliberate on their experiences of injustice, their visions of justice, and their ideas on how social work might contribute to advancing justice in a deep, transformative way. Transformative pedagogical practices of this nature facilitate and extend practices of participatory parity *in* the classroom and provide students opportunities to explore and develop the confidence to engage in transformative practices *beyond* it. This would enable future social workers to contribute to emancipatory movements responding to contemporary crises of economic, ecological, social, political, and cultural injustice.

Notes

* Dedicated to the memory of our friend and colleague Tessa Hochfeld. Thank you, Tessa, for your feedback on this chapter, which was as invaluable as were the many other ways in which you have touched our lives.

References

Aruzza, C., Battacharya, T., & Fraser, N. (2019). *Feminism for the 99%: A Manifesto*. New York: Verso Books.
Bozalek, V. (2014). *Detailed proposal for the project, participatory parity and transformative pedagogies for qualitative outcomes in higher education* (NRF Grant No. 90384). University of the Western Cape: Directorate of Teaching and Learning.
Bozalek, V., & Boughey, C. (2012). Misframing higher education in South Africa. *Social Policy and Administration*, 46(6), 688–703.
Bozalek, V., & Hochfeld, T. (2016). The South African Child Support Grant and dimensions of social justice. In J. Drolet (Ed.), *Social development and social work perspectives on social protection* (pp. 195–212). London: Routledge.
Bozalek, V., Hölscher, D., & Zembylas, M. (Eds.). (forthcoming). *Nancy Fraser and participatory parity: Reframing social justice in South African higher education*. London: Routledge.
Bozalek, V., & Lambert, W. (2008). Interpreting service users' experiences of service delivery in the Western Cape using a normative framework. *Social Work/Maatskaplike Werk*, 44(2), 107–120.
Bozalek, V. G. (2011). Acknowledging privilege through encounters with difference: Participatory learning and action techniques for decolonizing methodologies in Southern contexts. *International Journal of Social Research Methodology*, 4(6), 465–480.
Bozalek, V. G. (2013). Participatory learning and action (PLA) techniques for community work. In A. K. Larsen, V. Sewpaul & G. O. Hole (Eds.), *Participation in community work: International perspectives* (pp. 57–71). London: Routledge.
Caluza, L. (2015). *Understanding the experiences of financial hardship amongst social work students*. Unpublished Research Report. University of KwaZulu Natal.

Chambers, R. (2006). *Notes for participants in PRA-PLA familiarisation workshops in 2006*. Institute of Development Studies. University of Sussex. Retrieved February, 2017, from www.ids.ac.uk/ids/particip/

Cruikshank, B. (1999). *The will to empower: Democratic citizens and other subjects*. Ithaca, IL: Cornell University Press.

Dover, M. A., Hunter, B., & Randall, J. B. (2008). Human needs: Overview. In T. Mizrahi & L. E. Davis (Eds.), *Encyclopedia of social work* (20th ed., pp. 398–406). New York: Oxford University Press and National Association of Social Workers.

Fraser, N. (1989). *Unruly practices: Power, discourse and gender in contemporary social theory*. Oxford: Polity Press.

Fraser, N. (1994). After the family wage: Gender equity and the welfare state. *Political Theory*, 22(4), 591–618.

Fraser, N. (1997). *Justice interruptus: Critical reflections on the 'postsocialist' condition*. London: Routledge.

Fraser, N. (2000). Rethinking recognition. *New Left Review*, 3(May/June), 107–120.

Fraser, N. (2003). Social justice in the age of identity politics: Redistribution, recognition and participation. In N. Fraser & A. Honneth (Eds.), *Redistribution or recognition: A political-philosophical exchange* (pp. 7–109). London: Verso Books.

Fraser, N. (2005a). Mapping the feminist imagination: From redistribution to recognition to representation. *Constellations*, 12(3), 295–307.

Fraser, N. (2005b). Reframing justice in a globalising world. *New Left Review*, November–December, 69–88.

Fraser, N. (2007). Re-framing justice in a globalising World. In T. Lovell (Ed.) *(Mis)recognition, social inequality and social justice: Nancy Fraser and Pierre Bourdieu*. Abington and New York: Routledge, 17–35.

Fraser, N. (2009a). *Scales of justice: Reimagining political space in a globalising world*. Cambridge: Polity Press.

Fraser, N. (2009b). Feminism, capitalism and the cunning of history. *New Left Review*, March–April, 97–117. NLR 36.

Fraser, N. (2012). Can societies be commodities all the way down? Polanyan reflections on capitalist crisis. *Hal Archives-Ouvertes*. Retrieved from https://halshs.archives-ouvertes.fr/halshs-00725060

Fraser, N. (2013). *Fortunes of feminism: From state-managed capitalism to neoliberal crisis*. London: Verso Books.

Fraser, N. (2016a). Expropriation and exploitation in racialized capitalism: A reply to Michael Dawson. *Critical Historical Studies*, Spring 2016 163–178.

Fraser, N. (2016b). Contradictions of capital and care. *New Left Review*, July–August, 99–117. NLR 100.

Fraser, N., & Gordon, L. (1994). A genealogy of dependency: Tracing a keyword of the U.S. welfare state. *Signs: Journal of Women and Culture in Society*, 19(2), 309–336.

Fraser, N., & Honneth, A. (2003). *Redistribution or recognition? A political-philosophical exchange*. London: Verso Books.

Fraser, N., & Jaeggi, R. (2018). *Capitalism: A conversation in critical theory*. Cambridge: Polity Press.

Hölscher, D. (2014). Considering Nancy Fraser's notion of social justice for social work: Reflections on *misframing* and the lives of refugees in South Africa. *Ethics & Social Welfare*, 8(1), 20–38.

Hölscher, D. (2018). Caring for justice in a neoliberal university. *South African Journal of Higher Education*, 32(6), 31–48.

Hölscher, D., & Chiumbu, S. (forthcoming). Anti-oppressive community work practice and the decolonisation debate: A contribution from the Global South. In S. Todd & J. Drolet (Eds.), *Community practice and social development in social work*. New York: Springer.

Hugman, R. (2008). Social work values: Equity or equality? A response to Solas. *Australian Social Work*, 61(2), 141–145.

Ife, J. (2008). Comment on John Solas: 'What are we fighting for?'. *Australian Social Work*, 61(2), 137–140.

International Federation of Social Workers/International Association of Schools Of Social Work (IFSW/IASSW) (2014). *Global definition of social work*. Retrieved October 30, 2019 from http://ifsw.org/get-involved/global-definition-of-social-work/

Khoza, X. L. (2016) *Understanding social work level 4 students' lack of political action in the face of unemployment: Reflection on identity and oppression*. Unpublished Research Report. University of KwaZulu Natal.

Leibowitz, B., & Bozalek, V. (2015). Foundation provision: A social justice perspective. *South African Journal of Higher Education*, 29(1), 8–25.

Magubane, N. P. (2015) *The (mis)recognition of economic differences: Understanding the experiences of social work students at the University of Kwa-Zulu Natal Durban, South Africa*. Unpublished Research Report. University of KwaZulu Natal.

McNay, L. (2008). The trouble with recognition: Subjectivity, suffering and agency. *Sociological Theory*, 26(3), 271–296.

Solas, J. (2008a). Social work and social justice: What are we fighting for? *Australian Social Work, 61*(2), 124–136.
Solas, J. (2008b). What kind of social justice does social work seek? *International Social Work, 51*(6), 813–822.
Towle, C. (1945/1973). *Common human needs.* London: George Allen & Unwin.
Wang, C. C. (2006). Youth participation in photovoice as a strategy for community change. *Journal of Community Practice, 14*(1–2), 147–161.

22
Roberto Esposito, biopolitics and social work

Stephen A. Webb
UNIVERSITY OF GLASGOW, SCOTLAND

Introduction

Intended both as an introduction to the thought of the Italian philosopher Roberto Esposito and as a mapping of current biopolitical analysis, this chapter traces the contributions of recent Esposito scholarship to widen perspectives in social work education and critical pedagogy to the nuances of contemporary theory. The chapter offers a summary of Esposito's insight into the biopolitical nature of social work and its implications for pedagogy. As one colleague recently remarked to the author, "social work is the biopolitical project *par excellence*". Social work is a striking illustration of the neoliberal biopolitical strategy of governing "from below" whereby agents of the state are intimately connected with calculation or control and direction as micro practices of self-reflection. Social work articulates neoliberalism's normative attempts of mobilising social agents as reflective instruments of control. It will be shown how adopting a critical pedagogical approach among social work educators, researchers and students can educate and strengthen tactics of resistance (Webb, 2019). Drawing on Esposito's work, this can be achieved by a pedagogy that critiques professional normalisation as a negative protection, and the way this conditions front-line power relations with service users and carers. As a part of this biopolitical regime, a primary function of social work is to safeguard (negatively) individual, family and community life. From an education standpoint biopolitical analytics can focus social workers on investigating the network of power relations, knowledge practices and modes of subjectification evident in change processes and modes of surveillance.

Biographical details of Roberto Esposito

Italian theory is attracting increasing attention around the world. Roberto Esposito is one of the most prominent contemporary living Italian political philosophers. However, his work, compared to that of Michel Foucault, for example, is largely unknown to the social work readership. His influence on Anglophone social work has been late in arriving. Born in 1950, Esposito is a professor at the Italian Institute for the Human Sciences in Naples where he lectures contemporary philosophy along with other subjects including political theory and history. He questions the traditional categories of political thought in light of the emergence of biopolitics. Esposito's work is also concentrated on works of Foucault, Deleuze, Negri and Agamben. He has coined a number of critical concepts in current debates about biopolitics – from his work on the implications of the etymological and philosophical kinship of community and immunity, to his theorisations of the impolitical and the impersonal. He embarks on the project of providing an affirmative biopolitics. Esposito is an author of over 20 books with the most important translated into English, *Communitas: The Origin and Destiny of Community*; *Immunitas: The Protection and Negation of Life*; *Bìos: Biopolitics and Philosophy*; *Third Person: Politics of Life and Philosophy of the Impersonal*; and perhaps his most influential and accessible, *Terms of the Political: Community, Immunity, Biopolitics*. His 2012 monograph, *Living Thought: The Origins and Actuality of Italian Philosophy* (trans. Zakiya Hanafi), is dedicated to Italian philosophical thought, and aims at creating a historical and theoretical background for the definition of the notion of "Italian Theory".

Applying Esposito's key concepts for social work education

Situating Esposito with theories of biopolitics

The term biopolitics is attracting widespread attention in the social sciences, and particularly in sociology, cultural students, political theory, geography and education. It has far reaching explanatory power and is used to discuss, for example, political asylum policies, as well as race policy, the prevention of AIDS and questions of demographic change. "Biopolitics may refer to issues as diverse as financial support for agricultural products, promotion of medical research, legal regulations on abortion, and advance directives of patients specifying their preferences concerning life-prolonging measures" (Lemke et al., 2011: 1). Broadly speaking it is an interdisciplinary concept which refers to life as an object of politics. However, as Rabinow and Rose put it:

> [W]hen Foucault introduced the term [of biopolitics] in the last of his Collège de France lectures of 1975–6, *Society must be defended* (2002), he is precise about the historical phenomena which he is seeking to grasp. He enumerates them: issues of the birth rate, and the beginnings of policies to intervene upon it; issues of morbidity, not so much epidemics but the illnesses that are routinely prevalent in a particular population and sap its strength, requiring interventions in the name of public hygiene and new measures to coordinate medical care; the problems of old age and accidents to be addressed through insurantial mechanisms.
>
> *(Rabinow & Rose, 2006: 199)*

The work of Foucault in these Collège de France lectures on biopolitics are important because it is from these that Esposito draws his own reflections in *Bìos*, the conceptual centrepiece; his first book to be translated into English and one of the most influential. It is here that he reconstructs the negative biopolitical core of Nazism. The deadliest excess of the biopolitical regime is signalled, for Esposito, by Hitler's telegram sent from his bunker just prior to his suicide, where he

> ordered the destruction of the conditions of subsistence for the German people who had proven themselves too weak. Here the limit point of the Nazi antinomy becomes suddenly clear: the life of some and finally the life of the one, is sanctioned only by the death of everyone.
>
> *(2008: 116)*

For Esposito, we need to account for Nazism as a turning point in biopolitics.

Anyone who has followed the development of biopolitical theory knows, however, that two other Italian figures dominate contemporary discussion in this area: Giorgio Agamben and

Antonio Negri. Alongside, Esposito, Agamben and Negri offer the most influential contemporary interpretations, elaborations and critiques of Foucault's seminal studies on biopolitics. While it is beyond the scope of this chapter to enter into a detailed discussion about the scholarly contributions of Agamben and Negri – or perhaps other less prominent Italian thinkers such Paolo Virno, Christian Marazzi and Sandro Mezzadra, Maurizio Lazzarato and Franco Berardi Bifo – it is important to indicate to the readership this fertile intellectual diaspora of Italian thought.

The biopolitical function of social work

Biopolitical analysis has yet to fully enter the field of social work education and pedagogy. In this chapter the writings of Esposito are introduced to lay the foundation for an educational biopolitics in social work as a theoretical framework to understand processes of subjection, negative protection and relations of power. Put differently, it attempts to unravel the logics of biopower as a power over life in modern societies. In the last sections I turn to consider an affirmative educational biopolitics which entail a different operation of exploring processes of political subjectivation, in which subjectivity breaks with the nexus of power relations and produces new knowledge, new politics and, in turn, new, affirmative and collective subjectivities (Hardt & Negri, 2017).

We saw in the previous section the indebtedness of Esposito to biopolitical theorists such as Foucault and Agamben. In this section I shall outline more specifically the entangled relation between biopolitics and social work. Biopolitics in its crudest formulation is the exercise of modern forms of power (McNay, 2009). What distinguishes it from previous technologies of power is its new preoccupation with the management, regulation and administration of populations. Biopolitics is the moment "when politics assumes life as an object of direct intervention" and reduces it "to a state of absolute immediateness" (Esposito, 2008: 17). It attempts to administer, capture, control, mediate and seize all aspects of modern forms of life. It is a power that becomes embedded, dispersed, and regularised throughout society and its populations. An example of the articulation of biopolitics is easily seen through the operations of the nation state in defining itself in terms of the connection between birth, reproduction rights and territory – the foundation of sovereignty. Belonging to a community is directly identified with possession of national citizenship and usually place of birth (John-Richards, 2014). In literal terms, biopolitics signifies a form of politics that deals with the management of life (Greek: *bios*). It is a political rationality that takes the administration of life and populations as its subject and is comprised of ground-level strategies and mechanisms through which human life processes are managed under regimes of authority over knowledge, power and processes of subjectivation. The intimate relation between biopolitics and social work can easily be traced through the writings of Esposito, as interventions based on a complex series of mediations able to solve the problem of safeguarding life and the avoidance of risk, threat and danger.

Let us look more closely at a few examples of how this plays out in social work. In her analysis of working with older people Tomkow (2018) shows how the concept of frailty is locked into biopolitical regimes of classification. By narrating older people as a cost, a threat or a burden, increasing age is commonly constructed in relation to risk, which augments the discourses around older people's vulnerabilities representing both a burden and a threat. Frailty is presented as a "truth discourse" which supposedly describes an objective condition for older people. She argues that this is driven by the ability of frailty measurements to predict risk of costly adverse outcomes; the capability of frailty scores to enumerate complex needs; and the scientific legitimacy frailty affords to geriatric medicine. Consequently, frailty has become pervasive, knowable and measurable (Tomkow, 2018: 5).

Esposito teaches us that any biopolitical field of intervention, such as social work, is characterised by specific forms of "expert" knowledge, classification and method. According to Esposito this exhibits an internal logic that helps it perform biopolitical functions of normalisation, regulation and control. Expert responses to sex offending and sexual abuse, for example, fit within this biopolitical schema. In relation to work with sex offenders there has been an intensive growth of systems of measurement, tracking processes, surveillance management technologies and an increasing integration of data processes. Based on the principle of pre-emption those at risk of sex offending are targeted. This involves the prior construction of risk profiles out of a pool of information about suspect identities and risky individuals. In Scotland, MAPPA (Multi-Agency Public Protection Arrangements) is the process through which the police, social work, probation and prison services work together with other agencies to manage the risks posed by violent and sexual offenders living in the community in order to protect the public. In reflecting the biopolitical preoccupations with territory, the housing and accommodation of the sex offender figure centrally in the logic of risk regulation. MAPPA reports that there is clear and consistent advice from experts that stable housing arrangements and effective monitoring make a key contribution to minimising the risks sex offenders under MAPPA may pose. Different agencies can be involved in the risk assessment alongside criminal justice social work and housing, for example local authority children's services in social work and education. The checks undertaken will depend on the offender, but could include information retrieved from:

- the System for Tasking and Operational Resource Management (STORM);
- the Scottish Intelligence Database (SID);
- the Violent and Sex Offenders Register (VISOR);
- Local Police Systems;
- Police National Computer (PNC);
- Criminal History System (CHS);
- Vulnerable Persons Database (VPD);
- Crime Management System;
- Community Police information.

If sex offenders are characterised as a risky population management problem that needs to be solved, then the respective elaborate administrative structures, data bases, information retrieval systems and devices of calculation can be seen as increasingly bleeding into one another. Surveillance and biopolitics work hand-in-hand in this context to enable a comprehensive, effective and unitary management of the category of the sex offender.

In surveying the language, knowledge, research, professional identity, practice interventions and mandatory responsibilities, it is possible to identify a particular biopolitical logic at work in the way social work functions as part of the modern state apparatus. It is this central issue that I turn to in the next section on negative protection and immunisation.

Social work as negative protection and immunisation

A central feature of the biopolitical function of social work is found in the processes of immunisation; that is, the immunisation of those sectors of society that are perceived as the most vulnerable, dangerous, risky and in need of protection. The logic at work is to protect them from themselves, in order to protect others from any contamination. The host (variously described normatively as the modern state, the capitalist system, the community and the family) must be protected from infection. This is why safety, risk, and notions of troubling and threatening figure so prominently in social work discourse. Esposito (2008) argues that the immunitary *dispositif* has spread from biomedics and law to all sectors and discourses of our modern lives. The legal definition of immunity is the exemption to the common law. More generally, the externalisation of other forms of life in the process of immunisation is crucial to the biopolitics of governance.

In developing the "immunity paradigm", for Esposito (2008), just as the human body's immune system protects the organism from deadly incursions by viruses and other threats, social work also ensures the safety of individuals and community in various threatening situations. Through the process of immunisation, it protects and secures a normative form of social order. But the biopolitical function of social work as immunisation points to a more disturbing set of considerations. Like the individual body, the collective body can be immunised from the perceived danger only by allowing a little of what threatens it to enter its protective boundaries. Immunity, as we know from the discourse of medical science, incorporates a small dose of the threat it intends to ward off – and by such incorporation, it takes an external threat and brings it inside, making the threat internal to itself, a part of itself, and thereby reorganises, redefines and rearticulates itself. Social work functions in this manner whereby the service-user is immunised in a dual process of inclusion and exclusion.

In order to escape the clutches of risk, insecurity or danger, the service-user is forced to incorporate within themselves the meanings of those dangers and risks, by accommodating the newly discovered normative principles of social work judgement. Thus, immunity is both a legal and a medical term that implies the negative protection of an agent who, for purposes of that protection, ceases to be bound to certain obligations. In political-juridical language, immunity alludes to a temporary or definitive exemption on the part of the subject (service-user) with regard to concrete obligations or responsibilities that, under normal circumstances, would bind one to others. The immunity politics relies on social work to reproduce its functional role as a decision-making institution. Donald Trump's recent "Make America Great Again" trade tariff protectionist war against China, Canada and Europe is a typical example of the immunity principle at work through the negative protection of American manufacturing trade.

Luhmann was also drawn to the persuasive nature of the immunisation construct. To say, as he does, that "the system does not immunize itself against the no but with the help of the no" or "to put this in terms of an older distinction, it protects through negation against annihilation", means getting right to the heart of the question, leaving aside the apologetic or at least the neutral connotations in which the author frames it (Luhmann, 1995: 371–372). As Esposito (2008: 49) notes, his "thesis that systems function not by rejecting conflicts and contradictions, but by producing them as necessary antigens for reactivating their own antibodies, places the entire Luhmannian discourse in the semantic orbit of immunity." Immunity is the foundational dimension in which human life is inscribed, constituted and recognised within the modern socio-political order. It is modernity that witnesses the entrance of *the power to preserve life itself* into the domain of politics as an object of care (Bazzicalupo, 2006). Thus, we need to examine the extent to which social work's paradoxical function within the state apparatus is keenly involved in the modern apparatus of immunity – through the governance of vulnerability as a protective regime of safety. That is, to what extent is the function of social work based on the immunity paradigm, in which immunisation alludes to a particular situation that protects someone from a risk; a risk to which an entire community is exposed (Richter, 2019).

Historically, we can see how the institutions of the state are premised on the principle of the need to protect humans from the excesses of greed and exclusion. The administration of poor relief in its late Victorian charity organisation guise is emblematic of this original immunity impulse at work. Developing important aspects of this historical lineage, Abbott's (1988) study locates the construction of personal problems to the rising concern with social order in the last quarter of the nineteenth century. This is exactly the same period social work emerged on the modern landscape as charity work. He identifies the professionally defined epidemic of "nerves", bad nerves and nervous ailments as central to the need for intervention in personal affairs during this period (Abbott, 1988: 280–295). Psychiatry emerged later in the 1920s and psychoanalysis in the 1930s. Abbott (1988: 303) notes, "By the 1930s, a firm subjective structure was created that would not require serious attention until the renewed competition of psychology and social work forced a rebiologizing of personal problems in the 1970s". Nevertheless, social work was heavily dependent on psychiatry for its increased professional status and legitimacy. As Abbott (1988: 302) further explains: "Social workers were finding individual approaches to personal problems far more congenial than the social diagnosis approach bequeathed on them by Mary Richmond. The individual approaches, which they borrowed directly from psychiatry offered therapeutic answers that casework did not." Abbott (1988) shows how the normalising role of social work increasingly individualised personal problems by borrowing heavily from psychiatry. As he states: "How much more attractive to deal with the individual or family as a self-enclosed unit to be adjusted to society, rather than society to it" and "Psychiatric social work flourished during the twenties, becoming the most prestigious of the social work specialities" (Abbott, 1988: 303). Social work takes place in this paradoxical movement of separating or dividing life from itself in order to protect it (Giorgi & Pincus, 2006). It provides a shelter of immunity from the excesses of the competitive markets and the economics of calculation but in turn demands a regulative, moral and legal role in the governance of vulnerability and need. It is for this reason that the juridico-moral character of the service-user is so critical for social work in attempting to install its normative regime. From here we can move to further situate social work within the immunity paradigm of Esposito. Accordingly, Esposito (2006: 24) notes:

> From this perspective, we can say that immunization is a negative [form] of the protection of life. It saves, insures, and preserves the organism, either individual or collective, but it doesn't do so directly or immediately; on the contrary it subjects the organism to a condition that simultaneously negates or reduces its power to expand.

Esposito (2013: 59) further states: "Immune is he or she who breaks the circuit of social circulation by placing himself or herself outside it." As Lewis (2009: 487) summarises: "Immunization enables us to understand the internal complexity of this relationship as both affirmative/productive and equally negative/lethal." In immunising the service-user, social work temporarily breaks the circuit of production, placing both the service-user and social worker outside of it. To immunise a service-user, social work must classify the person into a "property with a problem" (e.g. a troubled family or a career criminal). Even when referring to a collective, immunity always belongs to someone. It is thus anti-social or anti-communal, an exceptional quality that defines whoever is immune as belonging in some way outside the community. We can detect the immunity apparatus at work most acutely in social work's preoccupation with risk management and protection with work with children, drug dependency and mental health. Social work is increasingly cast as a security regime with the primary focus of managing risky populations (Webb, 2006). It is as if, rather than adjusting the level of protection to the effective nature of the risk, what is adjusted is the perception of the risk to the growing demand for protection, which is to say risk is artificially created in order to control it, as insurance companies routinely do (Esposito, 2008: 115). Thus, social work as part of the state apparatus continuously performs the reciprocal strengthening between risk, protection and insurance. This preoccupation with self-protection as immunity is distinctive in characterising an essential function of social work.

From this point of view, the immunity function is more than a defensive apparatus superimposed on the individual or community, but a core internal mechanism of social work. The normative immunising character of social work is an *ethos* of biopolitical governance from the inside, by the inside. As a central component of social work's internal architecture, the system of immunity must also simultaneously immunise itself from those given care and protection under its auspices. It is under these conditions that expert systems such as evidence-based practice, risk management and new communication technologies for casework emerge. Their purpose is precisely to formally "bracket off" the service-user within a regime of professionalised expertise.

The safeguarding agenda in social work is a good example of biopolitical functioning. Indeed, safeguarding might be couched as the liberal biopolitics of securing life for children through social work intervention. Biopolitics seeks to secure life by creating a binary division within populations: the "good" part of the population that must be looked after, and the "bad" part of the population that must be eliminated for the "good" part to live (Foucault, 2004: 254–255). We have seen an increasing use of "practice for safeguarding professionals" over the past decade in the UK. Safeguarding is symptomatic of the construction of personhood today in which it is often made or unmade in an instant, creating regimes of persons, liminal persons and non-persons (terrorists or migrants with no recourse to public funding). Increasingly personhood is framed in terms of "vulnerable individuals" and "at risk of harm" through social work assessments. It is increasingly incumbent on social workers to safeguard against ideological abuse and encourage resilience. Indeed, the safeguarding agenda has been extended in the UK PREVENT policy to include social work intervention with radicalism and potential terrorism. The state's education initiatives are direct here, and as McKendrick and Finch (2016: 5) explain:

> In the wake of the war on terror, and in response to attacks on the British mainland, the British government produced a policy document in 2003, referred to as CONTEST (HM Government, 2011), which was its counter-terrorism policy. Out of this general policy strategy, the British government developed a series of policies aimed at preventing vulnerable people from being "drawn into terrorism". The UK PREVENT strategy thus aimed to identify those at risk of extremism and radicalisation. PREVENT describes extremism as "vocal or active opposition to fundamental British values, including democracy, the rule of law, individual liberty and mutual respect and tolerance of different faiths and beliefs."

Those at risk of radicalisation are immunised by social work intervention aimed at protection, risk and security. Charlotte Heath-Kelly (2013) explains this well as follows:

> Safeguarding against terrorism now refers to the identification of ideological abuse which prefigures terrorism. "Radicalisation", in the Prevent review, has been reframed as a form of abuse that vulnerable children and adults can suffer, much like the domestic and sexual abuse which healthcare professionals are already required to notice and act upon within their "safeguarding" protocols.

Here we can detect the way in which biopolitical logic immunises terrorism by depoliticising it with the safeguarding agenda. Bigo (2006) argues that social work is increasingly required to perform practices of surveillance that aim to avoid infiltration of "the bogus" among the citizens and immigrants, while at the same time advocacy discourses serve a process of normalisation of immigrants as "victims". Age assessments of migrant child refugees is a typical device aimed at detection of "bogus" status. In addition, across Europe, it is likely social work will increasingly be involved in "bordering practices". Social workers can be powerful gatekeepers in relation to everyday bordering practices with destitute migrants, criminal gang members, Roma people and undocumented asylum seekers. These are administrative and street-level practices implemented by various state and non-state actors which regulate migrants' residence permits and their access to health care, schooling, accommodation and welfare benefits. Health and social care practitioners also frequently refer Roma to immigration authorities such as the UK Home Office (e.g. NHS Digital and NRPF Connect database which allows the sharing of intelligence regarding cases supported, identify potential fraud and joint resolution of cases). "Deportability" is at the heart of the unequal power relations associated with bordering practices of state and non-state gatekeepers. Social workers are charged with upholding the internal boundaries of the nation state by enforcing policies that are often expressly designed to avoid creating "incentives" for unwanted migrant populations in what is described as a hostile environment in the UK. The Home Office (2014) hostile environment policy is a set of administrative and legislative measures deliberately designed to make staying in the UK as difficult as possible for people without leave to remain, in the hope that they might "voluntarily leave" (Kirkup & Winnett, 2012: 8). Farmer (2017) has shown that social workers conceptualise destitute migrant family members in terms of their immigration status and their subsequent entitlements, often at the expense of considerations about the welfare of children. In doing so they reify government policy in their decision-making processes. Farmer demonstrates how the hostile environment creates tensions between immigration legislation and social services' statutory duty to safeguard and promote the welfare of destitute families with children. Under the hostile environment, fear and penury are systematically imposed on undocumented homeless migrants (Broomfield, 2017). This can be described as "everyday bordering"; processes by which state bordering practices extend into everyday life (Tervonen et al., 2018: 139). With biopolitics, the border is a membrane device. It is not about the blocking of motion and the absolute division of political space, but rather an active process of bifurcation that does not simply divide once and for all, but continuously redirects flows of people and things across or away from itself. Social workers are border guards with migrants and radicalised groups governed by instrumentalising subjective states to ensure the vigilance required to secure security and prevent foreseeable risk. Bordering practice is a concrete example of Esposito's (2008) immunity paradigm in action.

In summary, it can be shown how enacting the immunity logic in social work is two-fold: both real and symbolic; both constitutional and normative. By this I mean immunisation is a normalisation process which is most apparent: as a front-line praxis, which regularises while containing, secures while engineering, legislates while restricting. It regulates, prohibits and disciplines lifestyles, by winning cooperation of those who are being controlled; with the threat of accusations of "disguised compliance" should things not go to plan (Bazzicalupo, 2006: 113). The normalising function rests on the closed circuit of self-reproduction such as Fahlberg's (1991) "good enough parenting" and attachments, and Erikson's linear lifecycle model of human growth and development.

The analysis of social work as a biopolitical apparatus allows us to take an important step in tracking the developmental nature of social work in relation to its biopolitical function. Esposito's analysis of immunisation brings to the fore the way in which biopolitics consists in the protection of life through the contradiction of it: the protection of life relies on a strong dose of uncertainties, threats and dangers that risk security, precisely to generate the protection against these dangers. We have seen how in Esposito's (2008) sense social work is a form of negative protection. Social work is given the role of protecting and safeguarding against the state's own constituent negativity that places people in danger in the first place. The immunity function of social work drives its governance role into the unfolding logics of security and regulation as part of the project of biopolitical modernity.

Stephen A. Webb

Transformative aspects of Esposito's work for pedagogy

Biopolitics has a distinctive speculative and experimental dimension: it does not affirm what is but anticipates what could be different (Lemke et al., 2011: 123). This is one reason why it lends itself so well to thinking about critical pedagogy and social work. However, most of the scholars of biopolitics have been less than optimistic with respect to the transformations in politics and governance they have analysed. There is a distinct pessimism in their writings about the possibilities of an emancipatory project, a militant activism or a liberating series of events. For Agamben (2009) there is a violent inner logic of biopolitics, exemplified in the horror of the concentration camp, that cannot be dispensed with. Indeed, for most biopolitical theorists the ascendancy of biopolitics in the late-modern politics renders democracy meaningless or at least reduced to a merely a formal arrangement of organising government. Yet, for all their criticism, these authors nonetheless approach biopolitics as the inescapable tendency of late-modern politics that can be transformed only its own terrain and in its own terms. Esposito is one of the few biopolitical theorists who deliberately sets out to envisage an "affirmative biopolitics", whereby the power of life is reclaimed from governmental apparatuses. With Esposito's affirmative biopolitics the decision on the proper form of life is removed from the field of expert knowledge, government and management and restored to popular sovereignty (Prozorov, 2019). Against an antagonistic politics of hegemony, he develops "a vision of democratic biopolitics where diverse forms of life can coexist on *the* basis of *their* reciprocal recognition as free, equal and in common" (Prozorov, 2019: 5). In the concluding sections the implications of Esposito's affirmative biopolitics are discussed in relation to social work education.

Affirmative biopolitics and critical education

According to Esposito (2008), there is an emancipatory potential within biopolitics that is yet unrealised. Whereas Foucault (2004) links biopolitics to the rise of racism and the state management of the population, Esposito (2008) believes biopolitics also provides opportunities for an affirmative politics of life. This, however, needs to be understood not as moral theory of resistance, but a political theory of transformation. By proposing an "affirmative biopolitics" and locating it, as Timothy Campbell (2008: 15) writes in his introduction to *Bíos: Biopolitics and Philosophy*, in "the continuum of *immunity* and *community*", Esposito both differentiates himself from other theoreticians of biopolitics and "synthesizes Agamben's negative vision of biopolitics with Hardt and Negri's notion of the common as signalling" precisely "a new affirmative biopolitics". Prozorov (2017: 803) summarises Esposito's affirmative biopolitics:

> Accordingly, Esposito's affirmative biopolitics ventures to temper this immunitary drive by restoring its relation to the communitarian principle of exposure to the other from which it arises and seeks to efface. While the immunitary logic is plagued by the paradox of negating the immanent negativity of life that only plunges it further into the negative, Esposito seeks to attain the self-suppression of the negation itself whereby this immanent negativity is rethought as an essential part of life, without which it would lose its self-generating potential.

Esposito (2008) thus seeks to undermine and weaken biopolitical rationalities through an *inversion* of the state's and government's immunising powers. The inversion of the immunity paradigm points Esposito into considerations of other forms of life such as "common life" or the "good life". An example of an inversion of immunity politics would be to work on an activist platform that states "immigration is not a problem" and stress a commonality of interest between "native" workers and immigrant workers. Suffice to say, Esposito's affirmative biopolitics is rather abstract and disconnected from practical politics. Some might go so far as to say it resembles a diagnosis with no practical solution. Critical pedagogy must find its force in the actuality of practice, in asking how Esposito's key insights are elaborated in practical terms, and how they are at stake in particular reforms, events and institutions.

Impersonal education and the commons

As we have seen, immunity is a condition of particularity: whether it refers to an individual or a collective, it is always "proper", or property in the specific sense of "belonging to someone" and therefore "un-common" or "non-communal". Effective political engagement requires radical educators in social work to abandon an uncritical adherence to liberal sensibilities. This means not only examining the process of subjectification and its individualistic leanings in social work curricula, such as empathy skills, life cycle and human growth, but also the very foundations of the "liberal subject", such as the self and the person. Epistemologies drawn from the discipline of psychology, with their focus on resilience, vulnerabilities, self-actualisation, self-esteem and practitioner self-care, only serve to harden these liberal sensibilities. Lewis (2017) examines the hidden politics behind this most common and taken-for-granted concept: the priority of education for personhood. Indeed, the personalisation policy introduced over a decade ago in UK social work is predicated on self-determination, choice and individual autonomy. On both the right and the left of educational theory and policy, Lewis (2017) shows ubiquitous references to personal development/growth, personal security, personalisation and personality. Personhood is an artificial entity (Esposito, 2012). Drawing on Esposito's politics of immunisation, he argues that the person is always already predicated on the externalisation of otherness. Lewis (2017) proposes an impersonal education that breaks with this implicit endorsement of immunisation and, in the process, radically democratises education for anyone at all. For Esposito the alternative is to develop a critical pedagogy which shifts from the personal to the impersonal, thereby retrieving what is lost in liberal education, the body, the outside, the recognition of the Other. It is only by making such a radical shift that we can begin to envisage a critical pedagogy of the commons for social work. This would combine critical pedagogy with a place-based approach to social work education.

References

Abbott, A. (1988) *The System of Professions: An Essay in the Division of Expert Labour*. Chicago, University of Chicago Press.
Agamben, G. (2009) *What is an Apparatus?*. Stanford, Stanford University Press.
Bazzicalupo, L. (2006) The ambivalences of biopolitics. *Diacritics*, 36(2): 109–116.
Bigo, D. (2006) Protection: Security, territory and population. In Huysmans, J., Dobson, A. and Prokhovnik, R. (eds.) *The Politics of Protection: Sites of Insecurity and Political Agency*, pp.84–100, London, Routledge.
Broomfield, M. (2017) How Theresa may's "hostile environment" created an underworld. *New Statesman*, 19th, December. www.newstatesman.com/2017/12/how-theresa-may-s-hostile-environment-created-underworld[12thMarch 2019].
Giorgi, G. & Pincus, K. (2006) Zones of exception: Biopolitical territories in the neoliberal era. *Diacritics*, 36(2): 99–108.
Esposito, R. (2006) The immunization paradigm. *Diacritics*, 36(2): "Bios," (Summer, 2006) 23–48.
Esposito, R. (2008) *Bios: Biopolitics and Philosophy*. Minnesota, University of Minnesota Press.
Esposito, R. (2012) *Third Person: Politics of Life and Philosophy of the Impersonal*. Zakiya Hanafi (tr.), Cambridge, Polity Press.

Esposito, R. (2013) *Terms of the Political – Community, Immunity, Biopolitics*. New York, Fordham University Press.

Fahlberg, V.I. (1991) *A Child's Journey through Placement*. London, BAAF.

Farmer, N. (2017) No recourse to public funds', insecure immigration status and destitution: The role of social work?. *Critical and Radical Social Work*, 5(3): 357–367.

Foucault, Michel (2004) *Society Must Be Defended. Lectures at the College de France, 1975-76*. translated by David Macey. London, Penguin Books.

Hardt, M. & Negri, A. (2017) *Assembly*. Oxford, Oxford University Press.

Heath-Kelly, C. (2013) Counter-terrorism and the counterfactual: Producing the radicalisation discourse and the UK PREVENT Strategy. *British Journal of Politics and International Relations*, 15(3): 394–415.

John-Richards, S. (2014) Asylum and the common: Mediations between Foucault, Agamben and Esposito. *Birbeck Law Review*, 2(1): 13–36.

Kirkup, J. & Winnett, R. (2012) Theresa may interview: 'We're going to give illegal migrants a really hostile reception'. *Telegraph*, 25 May.

Lemke, T., Trump, E., Casper, M., & Moore, L. (2011) *Biopolitics: An Advanced Introduction*. New York and London, NYU Press. Retrieved from www.jstor.org/stable/j.ctt9qg0rd.

Lewis, T.E. (2009) Education and the immunization paradigm. *Studies in the Philosophy of Education*, 28(1): 485–498.

Lewis T.E. (2017) Impersonal education and the commons. In Means A., Ford D. and Slater G. (eds.) *Educational Commons in Theory and Practice*, pp. 95–108, New York, Palgrave Macmillan.

Luhmann N. (1995) *Social Systems*. Stanford, CA, Stanford University Press.

McKendrick, D. & Finch, J. (2016) 'Under heavy manners?': social work, radicalisation, troubled families and non-linear war. *British Journal of Social Work*, 47(2): 308–324.

McNay, L. (2009) Self as enterprise: Dilemmas of control and resistance in Foucault's the birth of biopolitics. *Theory, Culture & Society*, 26(6): 55–77.

Prozorov, S. (2017) Foucault's affirmative biopolitics: Cynic parrhesia and the biopower of the powerless. *Political Theory*, 45(6): 801–823. doi: 10.1177/0090591715609963

Prozorov, S. (2019) *Democratic Biopolitics: Popular Sovereignty and the Power of Life*. Edinburgh, Edinburgh University Press.

Rabinow, R. & Rose, N. (2006) Biopower today. *Biosciences*, 1(2): 195–217.

Richter, H. (2019) Beyond the 'other' as constitutive outside: The politics of immunity in Roberto Esposito and Niklas Luhmann. *European Journal of Political Theory*, 18(2): 216–237.

Tervonen, M., Pellander, S. & Yuval-Davis, N. (2018) Everyday bordering in Nordic Countries. *Nordic Journal of Migration Research*, 8(3): 139–142.

Tomkow, L. (2018) The emergence and utilisation of frailty in the United Kingdom: A contemporary biopolitical practice. *Ageing and Society*. doi: 10.1017/S0144686X18001319 Published online: 08 October 2018.

Webb, S.A. (2006) *Social Work in a Risk Society*. London, Palgrave Macmillan.

Webb, S.A. (2019) Resistance, biopolitics and radical passivity. In Webb, S.A. (ed.) *The Routledge Handbook of Critical Social Work*, pp.148–161, London, Routledge.

23
Gilles Deleuze
Social work from the position of the encounter

Heather Lynch
GLASGOW CALEDONIAN UNIVERSITY

Introduction

Gilles Deleuze's philosophical work continues to have a distinct influence on a wide range of disciplines from education to environmental studies and from politics to fine art. However, his influence, to date, in social work is minimal. This chapter draws on creative encounters with two adults who have lifelong experience of social services to argue that Deleuze's thought is highly relevant for social work practice. His key concept "the dogmatic image of thought" is used to discuss the ways in which common sense can have a detrimental influence on engagement with people diagnosed with autism and complex disability. His concepts of "affect", "minor" and "rhizome" are employed to articulate how oppressive norms might be countered and lead to meaningful relations with people who are perceived as difficult to engage. It is ultimately argued that Deleuzian thought has the potential to inform the minute detail of personal interaction and, in doing so, challenge the micro politics of systemic social work norms. This holds impactions for both practice and education.

Gilles Deleuze was a continental philosopher (born Paris 1925; died Paris 1995) whose radical work has influenced a wide range of disciplines across social science, humanities, material science, technology and applied disciplines such as education, architecture, art and design. Many in social work will have an affinity with the way that his difficult early experience informed his values and activism. His childhood was defined by the traumatic loss of his brother Georges; a fighter for the French resistance during the Second World War who died while being transported to a German concentration camp. Deleuze's parents idolised his older brother and left him feeling overlooked. As a result, he rejected family life and his parents' right-wing political views and developed an affinity with the growing strength of the working class. His earliest work poses questions of widely held views on religion, gender and capitalism. As a student he defined his own path, exploring unfashionable scholarship and troubling accepted norms. He rejected elitism based on economic structures, cultural hierarchies and intellectual practices which limit imagination and freedom (Dosse, 2010).[1] This radical position defined the catalogue of work which he would go on to produce alone and with his collaborator Felix Guattari. He published volumes on philosophers Bergson, Nietzsche, Kant and Hume; artists Proust, Artaud and Bacon, each of whom provided the inspiration for his distinctive thought. More than any, he used the work of the 17th-century rationalist philosopher Baruch Spinoza whom he described as the "Christ of philosophers". His most widely influential work *Capitalism and Schizophrenia* (1983, 1987) was co-authored with Felix Guattari. Its two volumes overturn the dominant voices of Marx and Freud, offering a different perspective on resistance to inequality; one which is based in creative affirmation. His intention to disrupt habits of thought is conveyed by the unusual terminology he used to express his ideas—the lexicon of "war machines", "bodies without organs", "nomads", "assemblages", "rhizomes" and "planes of immanence".

Drawing on Spinoza, Deleuze poses the question "what can a body do?" (Deleuze, 1990, p. 226). In this he is probing the potentiality of every organism or entity, not defining it by a limiting identity but by seeking to understand its possibilities yet to be realised. This might be considered a radical position on non-judgement, a value held in high regard by social work practitioners. His process-based philosophy considers life as dynamic and constantly in the making. It therefore focuses on flow and inevitable change. This relates to social work's aspiration toward the possibility of progress even for those in the most challenging circumstances. For Deleuze, philosophy is a creative endeavour and it is perhaps for this reason that Deleuzo-Guattarian thought has had such huge traction in the practice-based disciplines of art, design, architecture (Radman and Sohn, 2017) and education (Allan, 2004; Semetsky, 2013). However, it is, by the same token, surprising that his work has had such negligible influence in the social work literature. This chapter will allude to some of the reasons why Deleuze has been largely ignored in social work while establishing his potential relevance. Following an introduction to some of the central themes that weave through his work, the body of the chapter will outline the relevance of his resistance to "the dogmatic image of thought" through discussion of two case studies involving Robert and Norma, two people diagnosed with disabling conditions. The final section indicates how such an approach is useful for a radical social work pedagogy.

Key concepts

Deleuzian concepts are often neologisms that work by seeking to provoke new ways to think. His ideas are challenging as he forces the reader to understand the world differently and not to lapse into the laziness of habitual thought which he sees as simply reproducing its own logic. Deleuze rails against foundational Western philosophy that follows Enlightenment philosopher Dèscartes. Dèscartes' "cogito" famously declares "I think therefore I am". This claim creates two powerful assumptions. First it separates mind and matter in a move that privileges mind; second it produces anthropcentricism[2] as human reason is prioritised over other ways of knowing. Deleuze rejects these assumptions, for him there is no separation between mind and matter. The mind *is* matter and is affected by physical interactions with environment which include objects and animals as much as humans. Within Deleuzian philosophy, human life is not placed above other forms of life but is interwoven within an integrated ecology where human and non-human factors influence each other, creating tiny and sometimes significant changes. It is these forces and unique interactions in place and time that Deleuze focuses on. His interest is in process, how subjects come to presence and dissolve, this is a focus on "difference and becoming". Deleuze does not see difference as "the other" but as how "bodies" become different to themselves as a result of interaction with other bodies. A body could be a human/animal body, an organism, an institution of micro or macro scale. Each body is itself constituted by bodies operating in relation to each other. You might think of the human body as made up of different facets, organs, blood, lungs which interact with each other, affecting each other but also affected by the factors such as air we breathe and the surrounding temperature. This complex view of interacting dynamic relationships affords an understanding of life as always in flux. This abstraction of the various factors that influence within any context draws attention to the specificity and unique interaction within any situation. Deleuze states that assumptions and pre-given understanding limit our ability to connect with the real of the here and now. This is a pertinent point for social work, which Gray and Webb (2013) have brought out when they question social work's over-reliance on models, arguing that these limit rather than connect with the specificity of experiences and events.

However, without doubt, the decentring of the individualised rational human is challenging for social work. Social work developed from the modernist tradition with an interest in human relations (Lorenz, 2012), human wellbeing and the potential of human reason to change the circumstances of people and communities. It is perhaps for this reason Deleuzian thought has not proved as influential as it has across other theoretical and applied disciplines. This is a loss. I will go on to outline some of Deleuze's key concepts, demonstrating how these can be used in social work settings. Two case studies which summarise the experience of different individuals diagnosed with disabling conditions demonstrate how some of Deleuze's central concepts support the development of meaningful interactions which not only have relevance on the micro level of one-to-one encounters but also challenge prevalent discourses. Through this discussion I aim to establish that Deleuze's radical posthuman thought offers something original and significant for social work practice and has implications for what we teach students about practice.

The "dogmatic image of thought"

Deleuze describes habitual understanding as the "dogmatic image of thought" (Deleuze, 1995). This calls into question everyday categories that are used to understand and communicate. Deleuzian scholar Daniel Smith (2012, n.p.) describes this as "the oppression of common sense", and this is similar to the way Gray and Webb (2013) talk about the way social workers need to think outside of "common sense". Deleuze rails against common-sense thought and argues that it generalises and produces a disconnection from the real and unfolding forces active in any discrete situation (Snir, 2018). For Deleuze (1994, p. 131), common sense enshrines what he calls "dogmatic, orthodox or moral image". These are the representations of identities and objects which provide a shorthand for sensemaking. We therefore have ready-formed images for categories such as man, woman, sun, apple and so on, which each come with a range of inbuilt assumptions that transcend their specific context. While such shorthand may speed our ability to read situations quickly, in doing so it overlooks and obscures the particulars or—in Deleuzian terms—singularities of any situation. This matters for social work as a practice grounded in ethics, which centres values of being non-judgemental and anti-oppressive (Dominelli, 2002; Thompson, 2012). Above all, within a context of equalities, social workers set out to recognise and value people who are disadvantaged as a result of differences such as disability, ethnicity, age, gender, etc. Thinking with Deleuze through Robert and Norma's experience illuminates the ways in which the categories that we use to promote understanding are themselves oppressive.

Comprehension which is pre-given in the form of a thought formed outside of the context to which it is applied is oppressive as it fails to account for the real and differentiated forces active within any situation. According to Daniel Smith, the "error of the dogmatic image of thought is not to deny diversity, but to tend to comprehend it only in terms of generalities or genera" (Smith, 2012, n.p.). The key point that is being made here is that generality hides or obfuscates difference. In the dogmatic image of thought it is the "*same* self that breathes, sleeps, walks, eats; and objectively the same object that is seen remembered and imagined" (Smith, 2012, n.p.). This tethers thought to existing forms of identity and representation. For Deleuze, concepts are not objects but events. This means that ideas are generated through embodied awareness, not simply cognition, and this relates to the earlier point I made about the push in social work education toward reliance on pre-existing models and methods.

Identity categories are frequently used in social work assessment. We attribute difference based on gender, ethnicity, colour, age, disability and an assortment of medical diagnoses. While these may have a general function of helping us to recognise patterns in populations, these are crude. If we build a profile of an individual in their context based on such generalities then we might miss entirely all that is active in their material present. We might also be tempted to emphasise one facet of their presentation as this is what is foremost in our given models of thinking. This risks losing sight of their complex multifaceted experience that does not stand still but changes within and across contexts in relation to different human and material influences. Deleuze forces us to engage with such complexity, even though this can be disorientating. Such uncertainty is the basis of active thought. The case studies of Robert and Norma provide an opportunity to explore what this means in the context of disability and institutional care.

Using Deleuze in social work practice

Robert

Robert was in his early 60s when I knew him. He had an autism and non-specific learning disability diagnosis. He had spent most of his life in a mental health institution for people with a learning disability. He was moved from this institution into a community setting as a result of changes in Scottish legislation. The Community Care (Scotland) Act 1999 echoed the calls of disability activists that people who have a disability should not be shut out of society and pathologised but recognised for their value and included in mainstream life. He lived in a group home with two other people who had also recently left institutional care and was supported by a team of carers whose role was to provide care and facilitate his inclusion in community life.

Notwithstanding the clear affirmative action which this change in legislation and distribution of funding took, the staff supporting Robert stated that realising "inclusion" was extremely challenging. An ongoing issue was how to help him to integrate and fully participate in "the community". This shift in policy toward inclusion casts the nebulous and idealised status of community into sharp focus. Who and where was the community to which Robert should now belong? Support staff saw it as their role to find or create a network of people through which Robert could start to build a life outside of the institution. The challenges were that Robert's general disinterest in contact with other people and very limited verbal communication made this difficult. It certainly seemed that staff were trying to coach him into socialising with others but were often frustrated that Robert resisted this. They were, therefore, pleased to find an arts initiative that offered workshops for people with a learning disability diagnosis.

In contrast with his limited interest in human connection, Robert communicated with materials, paint, pastels, charcoal like they were old friends. He crafted and moulded the paint, coaxing it into desired shapes and contours. He sculpted with masking tape, teasing each length in minute detail. His main artistic preoccupation was with the sun. He produced hundreds of studies of the sun at different times of year, positions in the sky and weather conditions. Robert would work attentively for time spans of 4–6 hours absorbed in the minutiae of each coloured seam of light, attentive to the changes in the clouds. Robert rarely communicated verbally or sought the company of others while in the studio. Robert's social work staff were pleased that his time was occupied in an activity that he clearly enjoyed but found evidence of a lack of creativity in his consuming interest in the sun. They claimed that this confirmed his autism, as a lack of creativity and preoccupation with a singular subject are components of the autistic profile. These tensions in Robert's experience were not dissimilar to many of the people with whom I worked.

Norma

Norma was a woman with a diagnosis of profound and complex learning disability, with whom I worked on a project that aimed to support the resettlement of people living in long-term institutional care. Now aged 66, she had lived in the institution, according to records, since early childhood and had no family contact. She was one of the many children who lived out their lives in such institutions (SCLD, 2014). While she was fully dependent on social care staff to ensure that her basic needs were met she did not communicate verbally and showed no interest in contact with other people. She folded herself into her wheelchair in a pose that seemed to limit as much as possible the amount of contact she had with the world beyond her skin. She wrapped herself in her own arms in a posture that resisted all forms of connection. Her pending move to a house in a community setting challenged social work staff who wanted to include her as much as possible in this process yet struggled to find channels of communication.

Without a glimmer of reciprocal communication, assessments of Norma were largely technical accounts based on observation and reports from nursing staff. These observational accounts have a value, but without comprehension of Norma's interests, likes and dislikes it was impossible to plan for her future in any meaningful way. My task was to engage with her and find an opening that would allow her some involvement in this resettlement process. On first meeting she showed no interest in me, my words, my presence in the room, my array of coloured and textured material, my sounds and rhythms. I felt irrelevant, superfluous, invisible in the space. Her occasional groans and rocking actions appeared in no way connected to my attempts to arouse her interest. This persisted for a number of sessions. One windy day a leaf blew through the doorway. Norma's head lifted, I was conscious of her attention drawn to this subtle rustling motion. I sat beside her and gave the leaf my attention. We were together in those moments, connected through the motion of the leaf. This became the basis of our developing relationship. I sought other objects that might be gently wafted across the table and floor so that we could enjoy the sensory subtlety of their movement together. I learned to echo Norma's attention and learned about her interests in these shared encounters. This experience provided a form of orientation to being with Norma, that may not have met the requirements of deciding which colours to paint her kitchen but it provided the possibility of understanding through shared presence within material environment, not just observation.

Encountering difference

The resettlement programmes in long-term institutions in Scotland which took place in the late 1990s and early 2000s were underpinned by the consultation report *Same as You* (Scottish Government, 2000). This report was published when the closure of long-term institutions for people who have a learning disability was well under way. Keeping people who have a learning disability cut off from wider society had been viewed as archaic by many for decades at this time. "Care in the community" was a UK government policy which was taking time to have real effect within the field of learning disability. A central aim of *Same as You* was to "help them (people who have a learning disability) lead lives which are as normal as possible" (Scottish Government, 2000, p. 4). Furthermore, associated legislation, the Adults with Incapacity (Scotland) Act 2000, states that any actions taken on behalf of a person must benefit them. Few argue that these intentions were not worthy and a vast improvement on an institutional model of care that segregated and limited the lives of those living in such places. However, I felt that my work with Robert and Norma, people who experienced this transition, exposed some of the problems of enacting these intentions. Deleuzian concepts provide a means of scrutinising common-sense terms such as "normal", "community" and the micro politics of decisions around what "benefit" means.

The oppression generated by categories of identity and representation was evident in my encounters with Robert and Norma in different ways. Robert's autism diagnosis created a lens through which his behaviour and expression were understood by the staff who supported him. While this diagnosis has benefits in bringing a health rather than "problem" view of his behaviour which did not conform to norms, this also obstructed a meaningful understanding of Robert's particular interests. His disinterest in human interaction was perceived by staff as a lack of communication skills and his interest in the sun as an unhealthy obsession that exemplified a lack of creativity. This view obscures other possible ways to understand his interest and therefore generated problems and solutions that were remote from Robert's experience. The primary focus of staff was how he could be encouraged to interact more with people and to show an interest in subject matter that was not the sun. Engaging with Robert beyond this pre-given frame generated a very different understanding which led to deeper connection with the problems that motivated Robert.

Kuppers (2015) states that Deleuzian thought counters the common-sense proposition that people with autism are not enough in the world by arguing that "some of the specific aesthetics and somatics of autism place people deeply into the world" (p. 410) much more so than those with a neurotypical[3] view. Deleuze's rejection of dominant norms of thought, therefore, enabled me to connect with Robert's actual engagement unfiltered by notions of the pre-given normal by which his interest was generally assessed. Robert's adept handling of materials demonstrated his remarkable ability to respond to and interact with substances. He sculpted complex layers of paint in response to changing light, which demonstrated his ability to connect with minute environmental changes and express these on paper and canvas. Far from a deficiency of communication, his ability to ally with and respond to environment was accomplished. He immersed himself in the detail of minute environmental shifts, which grounded him in the world as it unfolded. Attention to this involved decentring human relationships and respecting the sensory, material connections that Robert valued.

Erin Manning is a Deleuzian scholar who has worked extensively with people who have an autism diagnosis, and she uses Deleuze to disrupt dominant ways of understanding people diagnosed with this condition. In her work, Manning (2016) further develops the affordances of sensory awareness drawing on the Deluzian concept of "affect". For Deleuze, to be alive is the capacity to affect and be affected. All forms of life brush, sometimes collide into, each other, shaping their capacity for action in ways that expand or limit. Deleuzian affect does not pertain to emotion but the clashing and colluding of forces in the unfolding of life. All bodies have capacity to affect and to be affected. Manning notes that people who participate in her work do not rush to find resolution but instead linger in the affective flow of their sensory relations with material, more than human environment. Robert's attention to the sun was a shared intensity without intention. He was drawn to the sun in a way that allowed him to hold to every change of light. He had no interest in the production of art as artefact to be consumed by others and his volumes of artwork were effectively a by-product of his interaction with sunlight. He radiated the sunlight through the movement of his hand-brushes. This understanding shifts attention toward what Robert valued in his interaction with light, and away from a view that might emphasise the paintings themselves as artefacts. In doing so it enabled me to engage with Robert's values, interests and indeed the non-human communication issues which he perceived as problems to be overcome.

Obsessive preoccupation with a particular interest is one of the three defining characteristics of autism, as is a lack of creativity (Van Wijngaarden-Cremers et al., 2014). Robert's care staff's overview of his considerable volume of work was the result of an obsessive preoccupation with the sun and an inability to extend beyond this. A typical comment from care staff was "all he does is the sun", and "he needs to expand his interest". From this vantage point his extensive body of work was reduced to one image, the sun. This dogmatic image of autism as obsessive and uncreative obscured the creative attention in his encounters with sunlight and material. Robert did not see the sun as one static entity, but as a movement of light in a changing landscape. His attention followed the composition of gases in perpetual flux, changing times of year and day, weather, and any number of factors that were acting together to generate the sun at any given moment. Deleuze's concept of "difference" helps to understand Robert's view. Deleuze (1994) does not collapse difference into identity, where entities perceived as static are defined in opposition to each other. Deleuze's process philosophy challenges us to consider the perpetual flux of all that is, grasping the reality that what appears static is constantly changing. Difference, rather than dividing separate entities from each other, points to how they differ from themselves. Robert's paintings evidence his ability to understand difference not as a category of identity but as a situated shift in the ongoing movement of life, the sun differs from itself, as it is affected by and affects all that it encounters in landscapes and movements in spacetime. Attention to these minute shifts alongside the interaction of different elements, which produced difference in sunlight, enabled Robert to produce a diverse collection of paintings which were, in every respect, a study of difference, not sameness.

Understanding the problems that concerned Robert created an opening for parity of engagement. Rather than encouraging him to abandon his problem of closer connection with the sun, in favour of normative expectations for human sociality, I could work toward consideration of his interests, by stepping into his affective realm. This did not mean less engagement, but more. Moving into Robert's rhythm was slower and more focused on material, environmental relations than I was used to. It put me into a place of discomfort, not knowing, following change rather than guiding or nudging it in a particular direction. I had a sense of this connection when he drew my attention to the minute changes that he was interested in and trying to express. Social practice in the UK is dominated by assessment and intervention formats, which have a particular end-view in sight (Featherstone et al., 2012). These might well be accompanied rhetorically by social work values of person-centred practice. However, if assessment criteria and outcomes are configured outside the context of the encounter then it is unlikely that these can prioritise difference. Thinking with Deleuze generates a critical awareness of just what this requires.

Minor connections with Norma

Both the medical and social care systems in operation throughout Norma's resettlement process were embedded in regulatory frameworks, schedules and timeframes. A generic infrastructure aimed to make sure that the many people resettled[4] went through a clearly articulated process. The resettlement machinery required operational decision making which, in turn, released funding for community residence and support staff. Working to the externally set hospital closure time frame, patients came through the list and moved through this system from preparation to relocation. Legislative and policy attention to person-centred values meant that professionals involved aimed to include the individuals subject to resettlement as much as possible. A major frustration of the team of clinical staff who worked with Norma was how to achieve this. They had a remit to involve her and yet it was clear that they did not know her or, more importantly, how to know her. The operational worlds of resettlement management and Norma's world seemed very far apart. These appeared as two different systems that clashed rather than enabled.

Deleuze provides a language that supports understanding of the operations of systems and how they might be disrupted to create new connections. He differentiates the regulatory operations of the "molar" with the transformative motion of the "minor" (Deleuze and Guattari, 1987). The planning process is a "molar" order which articulates the path which leads between one molar point—the hospital—and another, its care regimes to the community. Molar milestones are stages within a process, which led Norma to her new home. There was a sense of exasperation within the multi-professional group that this process was stuck due to an inability to get some meaningful input from her. My challenge was to find a means of connecting Norma to this process. The approach, however, could not be found in "molar order" but in the disorder of the "minor". Deleuze and Guattari's (1986) work on the author Franz Kafka explores the potential of what he calls "minor language"; which he sees as words that disturb the dogma of the molar. It has three components. It does not speak definitively but, instead, stutters and stammers. It is always political as it undoes molar architecture. It paves the way for a people to come so is always collective.

Stuttering is widely considered "broken speech" (Eagle, 2013), it therefore operates in the register of "abnormal". It is an attempt to communicate that is immediately limited and partial. It operates from a position of not knowing but experimenting with possibility. The motion of stuttering does not know where it might lead, unlike the molar, which has its landing point in sight. My stuttering involved experimentation with gesture, sounds and sensations, variations on tapping, humming, moving and generating images, which I undertook in an attempt to create dialogue with Norma. I felt foolish at times, clueless as to how or why these motions might have any relevance to her. The first sense of shared presence was indicated by her attentiveness to the action of blowing a leaf across the floor. She lifted her head and made some squeals, she became part of the event of the movement of the leaf and the sounds of the breath that blew. Manning (2016, n.p.) refers to such action as the minor gesture:

> The minor gesture, allied to Gilles Deleuze and Felix Guattari's concept of the minor, is the gestural force that opens experience to its potential variation. It does this from within experience itself, activating a shift in tone, a difference in quality.

This act, which was found through a commitment to interaction in the moment, became the basis through which we could relate. The intensity of the sensation was a connection that we extended through variations on this movement in different settings. This shared language, which was not known to either of us, was generated through experimentation and response. The minor syntax, of sound, breath and subtle movement allowed a mode of sharing experience if not the form of information sought by those planning Norma's move. What was clear is not how this could be understood, but that Norma, my breath and the leaf had become the apparatus of something new, which altered Norma's and my connection to the world and to each other. Our sessions with each other developed these sensory connections which allowed me to make the case that communication with Norma was indeed possible, but time, creativity and a commitment to entering creatively and humbly into a sensory realm were required. These experiential encounters did not complete the resettlement process checklist but did expose the problems of such an approach.

These problems lead to a second point, which is that, the minor is always political and leads to a disruption of the molar. This was the case on an individual professional level as my experience with Norma challenged my vocabulary as a practitioner. I was constantly placed in the position of novice seeking participation without prospect of mastery. It also challenged the multi-agency team responsible for Norma's care to grapple with how they might learn from and adjust their understanding through consideration of her expression. The politics of "minor" communication are rigorously explored in Petra Kuppers' Tiresias project. Tiresias is a research project that involves people who identify as disabled coming together to experiment with forms of communication and expression that challenge ableist practices. Kuppers builds on Deleuzian ideas of the minor to promote productive connections, which are not configured by the dominant communication norms. Kuppers states, "I lead a session that undoes that unawareness" (Kuppers, 2015, p. 405). These sessions make visible societal blindness to the oppression of normative communication practices. Verbal language is not central, touch and movement have a much greater role in communication. Some of the exercises involve a degree of physical contact that disrupts personal space. These sessions make you acutely aware of the invisible boundaries that you present. Standard expectations of communication, such as the SOLER model (Egan, 2018)[5] taught regularly to social work students, have no place in this environment. In this movement, as with the movement of the leaf, the register of representation is undone by the register of the real, and in their place is a stuttering participation in the event of encounter.

On the third point, this work calls into presence the possibility of a people to come as Kuppers (2016) asks how might discourse change if we entered into dialogue with the non-verbal? What might multi-agency meetings become with professionals prepared to dialogue in minor language? This was a challenge to the multi-professional group working on Norma's resettlement, which included social workers, psychiatrists, nurses, a physiotherapist and a speech therapist. Norma was often wheeled into the room while her case was discussed, but the standard rhetoric of the professional meeting offered no meaningful mechanism to communicate with her. Meaningful inclusion of Norma in this meeting would have required a radical shift in established professional communication practices and a loss of control of the prefigured agenda. Embracing this level of discomfort was too challenging to contemplate for those involved.

This level of discomfort, for some, may allow them some insight into the sense of exclusion that many disabled people experience. Cockain's (2018) poignant narrative of walking with Paul, a man with a severe learning disability diagnosis, calls stark attention to the way Paul's everyday minor gestures present in the world create the possibility of different environments, different modes of interaction and different worlds. Manning (2016, n.p.) states in her introduction that:

> The minor gesture is not the figure of the marginal, though the marginal may carry a special affinity for the minor and wish to compose with it. The minor gesture is the force that makes the lines tremble that compose the everyday, the lines both structural and fragmentary, that articulate how else experience can come to expression.

The minor gesture is a challenge to dominant communication as it undoes normative dogmatic syntax, disrupting the comfort of the known as it calls the new into presence. Such an approach aligns with a social work commitment to egalitarian ethical approaches. It reveals just how challenging this is in practice, particularly where professionals are expected to take the minor position of not knowing.

Deleuzian pedagogy

Deleuze makes concepts that promote action, unlike conventional philosophers of logic who present a critique of other philosophers. Understanding concepts such as stuttering, depends on enactment and experimentation. Deleuze has no interest in determining outcomes, only in provoking actions that resist oppressive norms and generate difference. This is not a model based on the transfer of knowledge from one mind to another; what Deleuze would term "arborescent" knowledge. He and Guattari state, "we are tired of trees" (Deleuze and Guattari, 1987, p. 15); trees are hierarchical and point to point structures. Deleuze favours the botanical metaphor of the rhizome, as it foregrounds the creative potential of multiplicity. According to him, it points to "new connections, new pathways, new synapses produced not through any external determinism, but through a becoming that carries the problems themselves along with it" (Deleuze, 1995, p. 149). Arborescence relies on binaries normal/abnormal; good/bad; right/wrong, but rhizomic learning validates the inclusive generative potential of not knowing. Education scholar Julie Allan (2011, p. 156) states that "rhizomic learning is always in process, having to be constantly worked at by all concerned and never complete. This in-betweenness is an inclusive space in which everyone belongs and where movement occurs." Rhizomic learning calls on a practice constantly alert to the oppressive risks of arborescent thought that constrains. As Deleuze and Guattari (1987, p. 9) state:

> That is why one can never posit a dualism or a dichotomy, even in the rudimentary form of the good and bad. You may make a rupture, draw a line of flight, yet there is still the danger that you will still encounter organisations that re-stratify everything, formations that restore power to a signifier, attributions that reconstitute a subject—anything you like from Oedipal resurgences to fascist concretions.

A rhizomic approach to learning honours the complexity and messiness of everyday life. Rather than attempting to impose order it works from *the position of the encounter*. Social work, which intends to work with people from where they are, and support them to progress in their own direction have much to learn from such thought. Despite a rhetorical value of individual difference and empowerment, social work too often, as in the situations described, operates within a molar order. A focus on such pre-planned futures for service users can overlook where they are situated and what they value. Pedagogical spaces informed by Deleuzian thought create openings for the new; they also validate uncertainty and not knowing as vital components in a process of emancipatory resistance to oppressive common sense.

Thinking with Deleuze generates a challenge to many social work norms. Devices and models that provide much relied upon blueprints for assessment and intervention become facets of an oppressive apparatus that obscures difference. In turn, this creates both challenges and opportunities for social work pedagogy. This short analysis has three implications for critical learning and teaching. First, a social work pedagogy informed by Deleuze's ideas is resistant to any type of thinking that is not situated in the material, more than human specificities of any discrete context. This requires a situated pedagogy that promotes curiosity of details and how they interact. Second, this social work pedagogy will involve modes of learning that are embodied and therefore generate awareness of the affects of material and more than human actors which are not subject to human intention. This requires a refocusing away from an anthropocentric view. Third, such an embodied social work pedagogy will involve awareness of the speeds and slownesses of different situations and how to navigate rhythms that feel alien and uncomfortable. Such a pedagogy promotes awareness of sensibilities and how they interact. A critical Deleuzian social work pedagogy challenges models and techniques of assessment and intervention that afford comfort and technical expertise. Operationalising such a pedagogy invites students to become aware of their embodied sensibilities and the agency of more than human actors; to manage discomfort; to linger in the position of not knowing in order that they might connect with the motion of the multiple forces active in the real lives and environments of the people they seek to work with.

Conclusion

Deleuze promotes not knowing and, therefore, not just gives licence to but anticipates a connection with the uniqueness of each encounter. In this chapter I have discussed relations in the context of institutions and disability, however this orientation to how we connect with the worlds of others has much wider relevance. Deleuze does not simply state that each situation is unique, he provides a language and a means of working through contingency. This is strengthening for social work practice which often succumbs to behavioural science which reduces unique, contingent experience to a checklist. He forces us to become immersed in the details, in sweeping aside all that would offer accessible explanations and to engage with the complexity of the real. This is surely the basis of ethically balanced relationships.

Notes

1. François Dosse's (2010) biography of Gilles Deleuze and Félix Guattari provides a detailed account of the influence of Deleuze's early life.
2. This means prioritising human life above other forms of life.
3. Neurotypical is a word widely used with autistic communities to describe people who are not diagnosed with autism—a resistance through counter othering.
4. Over 2,000 in the greater Glasgow area at the time.
5. SOLER was designed to promote awareness of non-verbal communication in relationships between counsellor and client. It assumes encounters take place between people seated beside each other and focused largely on verbal exchange.

References

Allan, J. (2004). Deterritorializations: Putting postmodernism to work on teacher education and inclusion. *Educational Philosophy and Theory*, 36(4), 417–432.
Allan, J. (2011). Complicating, not explicating: Taking up philosophy in learning disability research. *Learning Disability Quarterly*, 34(2), 153–161.
Cockain, A. (2018). Walking small with 'Paul', a man with 'severe learning difficulties': On (not) passing in purportedly public places. *Disability & Society*, 33, 5.
Deleuze, G. (1990). *Expressionism in Philosophy: Spinoza*. New York: Zone Books.
Deleuze, G. (1994). *Difference and Repetition*. New York: Columbia University Press.
Deleuze, G. (1995). *Negotiations*. New York: Columbia University Press.
Deleuze, G. and Guattari, F. (1983). *Anti-Oedipus: Capitalism and Schizophrenia*. trans R. Hurley, M. Seem & H. Lane Minneappolis: University of Minnesota Press.
Deleuze, G and Guattari, F. (1986). *Kafka: Toward a Minor Literature*. trans Dana Polan Minneappolis: University of Minnesota Press.
Deleuze, G. and Guattari, F. (1987). *A Thousand Plateaus: Capitalism and Schizophrenia*. trans B. Massumi Minneappolis: University of Minnesota Press.
Dominelli, L (2002). *Anti-Oppressive Social Work Theory and Practice*. Basingstoke: MacMillan.
Dosse, F (2010). *Gilles Deleuze and Félix Guattari: Intersecting Lives*. New York: Columbia Press.
Eagle, C. (2013). Literature, speech disorders, and disability: Talking normal. In *Literature, Speech Disorders, and Disability: Talking Normal* (4–25). New York: Routledge.
Egan, G. (2018). *The Skilled Helper : A Client-Centred Approach*. Second edition, EMEA edition. Andover, United Kingdom: Cengage Learning EMEA.
Featherstone, B., Broadhurst, K., & Holt, K. (2012). Thinking systemically — thinking politically : Building strong partnerships with children and families in the context of rising inequality. *British Journal of Social Work*, 42, 618–633.
Gray, M. & Webb, S. (2013). *Social Work Theories and Methods*. 2nd edition. London: SAGE.
Kuppers, P. (2015). Occupy the WEFT: Choreographing factory affect and community performance. *Contemporary Theatre Review*, 25(3), 401–416.
Kuppers, P. (2016). Diversity: Disability. *Art Journal*, 75(1), 93–97.

Lorenz, W. (2012). Response: Hermeneutics and accountable practice. *Research on Social Work Practice*, 22(5), 492–498.

Manning, E (2016). *The Minor Gesture*. ebook London: Duke University Press.

Radman, A. and Sohn, H. (2017). *Critical and Clinical Cartographies Architecture, Robotics, Medicine, Philosophy*. Edinburgh: Edinburgh University Press.

Scottish Government (2000). *Same as You*. Edinburgh: Scottish Office.

Semetsky, I. (2013). Deleuze, edusemiotics, and the logic of affects. In I. Semetsky & D. Masny (Eds.). *Deleuze and Education*. Edinburgh: Edinburgh University Press. 215–234.

Smith, D. (2012). *Essays on Deleuze*. ebook Edinburgh: Edinburgh University Press.

Snir, I. (2018). Making sense in education: Deleuze on thinking against common sense. *Educational Philosophy and Theory*, 50(3), 299–311.

Thompson, N. (2012). *Anti-Discriminatory Practice: Equality, DIversity and Social Justice*. 5th ed.. Basingstoke: MacMillan.

Van Wijngaarden-Cremers, P. J. M., van Eeten, E., Groen, W. B., Van Deurzen, P. A., Oosterling, I. J., & der Gaag, R. J. (2014). Gender and age differences in the core triad of impairments in autism spectrum disorders: A systematic review and meta-analysis. *Journal of Autism and Developmental Disorders*, 44(3), 627–635.

Part II
Specific applications
Fields of practice, postcolonial and Southern voices, practice methods, and fields of practice

24
Donna Haraway
Cyborgs, making kin and the Chthulucene in a posthuman world

Jim Ife

WESTERN SYDNEY UNIVERSITY

Introduction

The crises facing humanity, and indeed the world itself, in the early twenty-first century require radical analysis and radical action. Climate change is seen by increasing numbers of people as posing an existential threat to humanity, and this threat is reinforced by other crises no less urgent and no less serious: loss of biodiversity, political instability, the over-fishing of the oceans, increased inequality, desertification, the impossibility of perpetual 'growth', deforestation, economic instability, the threat of nuclear war, loss of community, toxic waste, land degradation, and so on (Angus 2016; Bonneuil & Fressoz 2015; Hamilton 2017; Kingsnorth 2017). Indeed these crises are interrelated; there is little point concentrating only on climate change, for example, while ignoring the others, as the other crises both contribute to and result from climate change (Eisenstein 2018; Kingsnorth 2017). A much more holistic understanding is needed, and this requires radical change not only in government policies, but in the way we understand humanity and its place in the world. The need for this is increasingly recognised within the physical sciences, with the idea of the Anthropocene (Angus 2016; Bonneuil & Fressoz 2015), but also in the humanities and the social sciences with the interest in the 'posthuman' (Braidotti 2013; Grusin 2015; Heise Christensen & Niemann 2017). No discipline or profession that claims to be concerned with the values of humanity – including social work – can afford to ignore this area of scholarship if it is to remain relevant in the period of crisis which lies ahead. The future cannot be a simple continuation of the present, and we cannot pretend otherwise. And it will require a fundamental rethink of 'humanity'; we can no longer afford to think of ourselves, our futures, our relationships, our cultures and our politics in isolation from the non-human world, ignoring and mistreating the other species, and the 'natural world', that sustain us (Jensen 2016). And we can no longer ignore the impact of human industrialisation and technology – including digital technology – on humanity itself; humans are not simply inventing and defining technology, but that technology is redefining humanity (Bridle 2018).

In this context, posthuman theorists are of importance for social workers, as they can contribute to the reconfiguring of 'humanity' that is now imperative. The idea of humanity has remained largely unproblematic for social workers – we have assumed that we know what 'human' means – but the Enlightenment Modernity construction of humanity that has been taken for granted in Western discourse can no longer remain unexamined. Donna Haraway is an essential contributor to this reconfiguring of humanity. Posthuman scholarship extends further to include other perspectives (Braidotti 2013; Grusin 2015) and it might be argued that Donna Haraway is not strictly a posthuman theorist. She rejects the label of 'post-humanist', and much of her important work was done before the idea of the posthuman became popular. Nevertheless, her work is foundational for the posthuman movement, and is widely cited by posthuman scholars.

Donna Haraway

Donna Haraway was born in 1944. Her academic career has always traversed the boundaries between the sciences and the humanities, and this gives her work a particular relevance at a time when it has become clear that both the sciences and the humanities need each other if they are to remain relevant to the human condition. She triple-majored in zoology, philosophy and literature in her undergraduate degree at Colorado College, and did her PhD at Yale in 1970, writing her dissertation on the use of metaphor in shaping experiments in experimental biology. This was later published as a book, *Crystals, Fabrics, and Fields: Metaphors of Organicism in Twentieth-Century Developmental Biology*. Such scholarship in the 1970s was indeed revolutionary, and this multi-disciplinarity, drawing from both the sciences and the humanities, is reflected throughout Donna Haraway's work, and provides a strong basis for the kind of theorising that is so important at the present historical moment.

Although strongly influenced by feminism, and identifying herself as a feminist, a major theme in Donna Haraway's work has been the elaboration of *affinity* rather than *identity* (Haraway 2016b). This is, of course, not necessarily incompatible with feminism, but it does move feminism beyond the easy label of 'identity politics'. While identity is readily focused on the individual and individual consciousness, affinity is concerned with relationships, especially relationships with those that are different. I can hold an identity as an individual, but affinity is something I can only hold with others. Haraway has explored the importance of relationships with other animals (remembering that humans themselves are animals), and also with the mechanical and the technological. But the word 'relationship' in this context does not imply the depth of connection that Haraway explores. She uses the phrase 'making kin with' to describe the deep interconnection, at an ontological level, that she sees as important (Haraway 2016b, 2016c, 2018). Making kin with another is much more than a simple 'relationship'; it implies an embeddedness in the other, deep obligations and a sharing of being, rather than the boundaries established by a 'sense of identity'. For Haraway, this kind of thinking is essential if we are to move beyond the anthropocentrism that has transformed into the Anthropocene. We will return to her ideas about the Anthropocene later in this chapter.

Among Haraway's earlier work, her *Cyborg Manifesto*, first published in 1985 as an essay entitled 'Manifesto for Cyborgs: Science, Technology, and Socialist-Feminism in the 1980s' (see Haraway 2004, 2016a) and her subsequent publication *Simians, Cyborgs and Women: The Reinvention of Nature* (1991) created particular attention through her use of the cyborg metaphor. The relationship between humans and machines, or technology, has been a longstanding topic for science fiction writers, aware of how humans and machines are not merely interrelated, but can become fused in the form of the cyborg. For the modern Western human, the mechanical and technological are now so much part of life that they have become essential to the achievement of a 'full humanity'. Glasses are widely used in order to see, and many people have hearing aids in order to hear, to the extent that moderate vision and hearing impairment are no longer regarded as 'disabilities'. And people with conditions or impairments that are still commonly understood as 'disabilities' have had their lives enormously enriched by technology in many different forms. People are using an increasing variety of artificial body parts in order both to stay alive and to function as a modern human. We use motor vehicles to move, computers to think and calculate, smartphones to communicate and indeed we use them to define our humanity. Those who say 'I couldn't live without my smartphone' are telling a truth about human existence in the global North, and increasingly elsewhere. Humans, in the global North at least, are heavily dependent on machines and on technology to achieve what they see as their 'humanity'. In the future this interconnection with technology seems set to increase, with implanted microchips, artificial intelligence, genetic modification, and so on. We have reached a point where technology, instead of being generally seen as benign and advancing 'humanity', now raises both great possibilities but also increasing concern about its darker side as enabling further surveillance, manipulation and control by the powerful (Bridle 2018; Zuboff 2019). Technology does not emerge from nowhere, but is created within a cultural, social and political context; a context where increased control and exploitation has been allowed to flourish (Zuboff 2019). As such, it has thus far remained a product of human activity, but we are now reaching a point where, through the application of artificial intelligence, it can develop its own autonomy and agency. Our relationship to technology is now being transformed.

In this context, Haraway's metaphor of the cyborg (Haraway 2004, 2016a) has become more relevant and immediate. To Haraway, this presents an opportunity to rethink humanity. The advantage of a cyborg is that it can understand both the world of people and the world of machines, which is consistent with her own intellectual roots in both the sciences and the humanities. To be a human is to be a cyborg, to be at home in both worlds, and to understand each in terms of the other. She is arguing for a reformulation of the human away from the individualism of 'identity' and toward affinity. In this case affinity is with machines rather than living beings: a startling idea until we remember that we are making this a reality in our increasingly mechanised world.

But Haraway sees the cyborg metaphor as more than this. She sees it as holding the potential to move to more collective consciousness, with the erosion of the individual human subject, and hence moving beyond the divisions of class, gender and race, none of which readily apply to cyborgs. In this sense she sees the cyborg metaphor as having positive potential, rather than the negative connotations of the cyborg as commonly understood in science fiction. The cyborg metaphor is a way to progress beyond the nature/culture dualism that has been at the heart of human degradation and exploitation of the 'natural world' (Heise Christensen & Niemann 2017), and similarly it transcends the binaries of gender, class and race. It is a political project, not merely an academic analysis. This gels with Haraway's feminism and her general commitment to social justice goals and to social activism. Donna Haraway is no disengaged scholar; she has been an active participant in social movements and activist struggles in relation to class, race, gender and the environment. She sees the need for continuous action toward a better world, and regards this is an ongoing human responsibility in the here-and-now, without necessarily articulating any long-term utopian ideal as the unachievable endpoint of activism. In one of her U-Tube Videos[1] she has used the metaphor of how we have to keep cleaning the toilet; it is an ongoing task of humanity to keep cleaning up our mess so we can keep living.

Donna Haraway does not confine herself to 'making kin' with machines. She is also concerned for the non-human animal world and sees it as important for humans to be making kin with other animal beings. She describes her important relationship with her dog and talks about how dogs and humans have evolved together, with each adapting to the needs of the other (Haraway 2004, 2016a). But she is concerned with far more than dogs, emphasising our one-ness with other beings and asking us to establish an ontology that has us embracing, and being embraced by, non-human animals. She uses the metaphor of the tentacles of sea creatures such as octopus and squid, to describe this 'tentacular' embracing, and indeed enfolding and enclosing (Haraway 2016b). This is not simply establishing relationships with the non-human world, but is about immersing ourselves in it and becoming one with it. It is a natural extension of Haraway's feminism and social justice commitments, as such an ontological immersion moves beyond, or at least renders less significant, the inequalities and oppressions of class, race and gender.

Haraway is one of the scholars who has questioned the use of the term *Anthropocene* to describe the world which has been so damaged and altered by human activity (Haraway 2016c). The broad thrust of this critique is that the damage to the earth and the biosphere has not been caused by all of humanity, and so blaming 'humanity' through the use of the term 'Anthropocene' unfairly reflects on the vast majority of humans who have lived over tens if not hundreds of thousands of years with minimal impact on the earth and its living systems. A common alternative name is 'Capitalocene', suggesting, along with Naomi Klein (2014) and others (Moore 2016), that it is the capitalist system rather than 'humanity' that has been responsible for the parlous state of the planet. This of course does not take account of the devastating environmental record of the Soviet bloc in the years of communism, and maybe it is more appropriate to blame industrialisation and/or patriarchy rather than capitalism, though the growth imperative has been so central to capitalist ideology, and so necessary for capital accumulation, that it can certainly be argued that capitalism should take most of the blame. Donna Haraway, while accepting the critique outlined in the 'Capitalocene' argument, has proposed that we should seek to move to a new way of being, characterised by the awkward word 'Chthulucene' (Haraway 2016b, 2018). This derives from the Greek *chthonios*, meaning 'of, in or under the earth and the seas'. It implies that we are bound to the earth, it evokes the ontological oneness with other beings, and, to use a favourite phrase of Haraway's, to 'staying with the trouble'.

Haraway's advocacy of 'staying with the trouble' suggests that we should not be exerting a lot of energy on articulating and realising utopian futures, but rather should stay with the present, doing our bit to make things better, by helping other beings as well as ourselves to live well, within ecological constraints. But this is not to deny the seriousness of the challenges facing humanity, and the political crisis that has exacerbated them. Rather it is an argument to address those challenges from a deep respect for the world in which we find ourselves, and the other beings with whom we share it.

It is, of course, impossible to do justice to the nuance and complexity of the work of a scholar such as Donna Haraway, in a few pages. Haraway is a complex, challenging and at times perplexing thinker, whose work is well worth exploring in greater depth, and readers wishing to further explore her thinking are referred to her various publications. *The Haraway Reader* (2004) is a good source for her earlier writing, as is *Manifestly Haraway* (2016a); both collections include the *Cyborg Manifesto*. Her more recent work is best understood by reading *Staying with the Trouble: Making Kin in the Chthulucene* (2016b). She also discusses her work in several YouTube clips which can be readily accessed.[2]

Donna Haraway and social work

Donna Haraway is not a social worker, nor does she mention social work in her writing. There are several ways in which her work resonates with social work, and other ways in which her work presents a challenge for social workers trapped within an anthropocentric paradigm.

The sciences

One particularly important area for social work is its relationship to the natural sciences. The natural sciences might seem of little relevance to social work, but in the contemporary world the natural sciences, the social sciences and the humanities are coming together in some surprising and fruitful ways. Climate scientists have realised they need to understand politics, economics and social change if they are to see their dire warnings listened to and acted on. They have also been made aware of the social justice implications of climate change, and have started to talk about class, race and gender. Economists are finally realising that some knowledge of ecological limits is important in shaping economic policy. Indeed, no social scientist can afford to be ignorant of ecological challenges such as global warming, biodiversity loss, land degradation, food and water crises, and so on. The humanities have always had a connection to science (e.g. science fiction) but recently the existential challenge of the ecological crisis and the Anthropocene has received increased attention from humanities scholars (see Ghosh 2016; Heise Christensen & Niemann 2017). The urgent need to adopt a less anthropocentric world view requires a synergy between the humanities, social sciences and natural sciences that was largely missing in the twentieth century, as famously identified by C.P. Snow in his essay on 'two cultures' (1959), though in earlier times the intellectual connection between the sciences and the humanities was better appreciated (Holmes 2008). Social work, if it is to remain relevant to the contemporary world and its challenges, must seek to incorporate this synergy. Social work has largely confined itself to a social science knowledge base, though it has also been able to include the humanities. But it can no longer afford to ignore the natural sciences, especially ecology, earth system science (Hamilton 2017), and the new biology (Margulis 1999; Weber 2016). These are important in understanding social issues, understanding the ways ecological systems impact social work service recipients, formulating effective and genuinely sustainable social policies, encouraging community-level initiatives, and helping people cope with the multiple crises threatening all societies in the relatively near future. This is seen in the emerging literature on Green social work (Dominelli 2018), and Donna Haraway's work adds to this as she has always been concerned with undoing the boundary between the natural sciences and the humanities.

Relationships

Social work has been centrally concerned with relationships; they form the essence of 'the social'. The dominant narrative of individualism, a central tenet of neo-liberalism, has eroded the importance of relationships, yet it is in relationships that we define and experience reality (Gergen 2000; Spretnak 2011). Donna Haraway not only emphasises the importance of relationships, she forces us to rethink the idea of relationship, in terms of 'making kin' (Haraway 2016b). The idea of making kin is much deeper than most social work understandings of 'relationship-building'. It implies strong networks of obligations to each other, and clear expectations on how we should relate to each other, in ways that resonate with the understandings of Indigenous peoples. It is a connection not just in terms of behaviours, but an ontological connection, where our very being is experienced in 'kinship' with others. Haraway requires us to take the idea of 'kin' out of the confines of Anthropology, and to take it seriously as a way of relating to each other and defining our humanity in relation to others. Social work might be thought of as the art of helping people 'make kin'. To do this, it is clear that social workers need to learn from Indigenous traditions, where the powerful connections of kin are understood in an ontological sense, and have not been weakened by centuries of industrialisation, capitalism and individualised Modernity (Sveiby & Skuthorpe 2006; Turner 2010). Donna Haraway's work clearly gives social workers good reason to take Indigenous knowledges seriously, and to rethink their superficial understanding – at an ontological level – of the idea of relationship.

Non-humans

It is important to emphasise that Haraway talks about 'making kin' not just in human-to-human interactions, but also in terms of relationships between humans and non-human species. Social work has taken responsibility for non-human beings seriously only in recent years, and it still remains a marginal interest for the profession (Ryan 2011). Yet the current crises facing humanity require a less anthropocentric perspective, and it will be important for social work to move more seriously in this direction. This requires us to understand relationships as not just being human-to-human, but also involving relationships with non-human animals, and indeed also with plants, whose intelligence is only now being realised by science (Mancuso 2017), and with non-living entities such as rivers, mountains, beaches and oceans. Haraway not only moves us in this direction, but also insists that in 'making kin' with the non-human world we seek to do this at an ontological level, where we are sharing our existence and our being. This is a big ask for social work.

Social work concern for animals has largely been confined to recognising animal cruelty (e.g. abuse of the family pet), and to the use of animals such as dogs and horses (the two species with which humans can most readily find emotional connection) in therapy. Haraway is asking for much more, both in terms of the variety of species, and in terms of the depth of the relationship. Again, a way forward can be found in taking Indigenous knowledge systems seriously. Indigenous people typically see their interactions with 'nature' in this way (Sveiby & Skuthorpe 2006), and indeed the very construction of 'nature' which effectively others the non-human world from the validity of human experience, needs to be seriously questioned. Indigenous world views see non-human species very differently, and are starting to form the basis of a social work that accepts, explores and affirms this aspect of our humanity, understanding that we can really only achieve our humanity in kinship with other species.

Affinity

Haraway's notion of 'affinity' as opposed to 'identity' represents another challenge to a taken-for-granted assumption in social work. The idea of 'identity' is controversial in the era of 'identity politics', though it is a term that is commonly used by social workers, often without an awareness of the complexity of the idea. Although identity can be understood collectively, it is more commonly thought of as an individual attribute – we 'own' an identity, or we individually identify with a particular group, for example as a woman, a person of colour, a gay man, a person with a disability, or an older person. Individualised identity is one of the legacies of the individualism of capitalism and neo-liberalism, and so we often ignore the more collective elements of identity. Haraway, however, argues for affinity rather than identity. This emphasises relationship, and the inclusion of others in how one identifies oneself. The difference can be understood by simply considering the term 'affinity politics' rather than 'identity politics'. Such a perspective can readily retain the social justice dimensions of identity, but does so in a way that requires the inclusion of others, and the importance of one's relationships with others in defining one's humanity and identity. We cannot exist in isolation, and it is only in deep relationship with others (both human and non-human) that our humanity derives meaning and authenticity. Can we therefore think of 'affinity-based' social work? Community-based social work can, and frequently does, encourage people and communities to think about their affinities, rather than their identities, which is important in building community, collective consciousness, and embracing other beings. This aspect of Haraway's work represents a promising direction for those people and groups seeking to 'rediscover' their humanity in a fragmented neo-liberal world.

Technology

Social workers have had to adapt to the world of technology, and social workers tend to reflect the range of opinions within the wider society regarding the benefits and the costs of technological innovations. Social workers' doubts about technology tend to focus on the loss of face-to-face human interaction as the primary experience of the social, given that human-to-human relationships are increasingly mediated through information technology, social media, and so on. This is seen by many social workers as a cause for regret, and as eroding the social and devaluing the realisation of humanity in social relationship with other humans. Donna Haraway requires us to think rather differently about technology. Her metaphor of the cyborg suggests that a fusion of the human and the mechanical is not necessarily new, or nasty, but becomes a way of thinking differently about the world. Rather than simply regretting the decline of unmediated human–human interaction, Haraway asks us to understand our relationships as not just with other humans, but with non-humans and particularly with the technology itself. Our relationship with the mechanical and technological is in itself potentially enriching, and can be understood at an ontological level. The cyborg can see the world 'from both sides' – the human and the non-human – because in itself it is neither human nor non-human but both, dismantling a binary that has been uncritically accepted within Modernity, and enabling us to step outside the confines of anthropocentrism. Seeing the world from the non-human perspective is the challenge that Haraway sets; it is to recognise that we have a non-human, or trans-human, side, and to look at our humanity from 'outside' the human. Technology becomes more than just a tool for humanity to use, but also gives us a different standpoint to view the world. This, in turn, allows a new appreciation of humanity, understood both collectively and individually.

Seeing things from both sides has always been an important aspect of social work, and extending that to include a non-human and mechanical/technological perspective is both challenging and potentially rewarding. Social workers need to understand the importance not just of relationships between humans, or between humans and the non-human world, but also between humans and technology. We have relationships with our computers, our cell phones, our cars, our kitchen appliances, our TV screens and the various other technological and mechanical 'necessities' of modern life. Simply labelling them as 'necessities' shows an assumption of their central importance in our humanity, and to lose them would be to give up part of what we have come to accept as the 'human' experience. And, at the most fundamental level, we have relationships with, and physically incorporate, various artificial body parts, be they glasses, contact lenses, pacemakers, hearing aids, artificial limbs, walking aids, dentures, surgical implants or, in the near future, implanted microchips. The vast majority of people, in the global North at least, and increasingly also in the global South, will require at least one of these mechanical/technological extensions of their bodies over the course of their lives, if they are to see themselves as 'fully human'. We are already cyborgs, part-human, part mechanical, and Haraway encourages us to think about what this means for 'humanity' in an increasingly posthuman world. This of course has relevance for social workers themselves, as they confront the reality of their humanity and their personal and professional identities, but also for those with whom social workers work. Social workers often work in this space, and many of the people with whom social workers work are actually experiencing some difficulty in their relationships with their computers, glasses, cars, walking aids, and so on. Such practice is not new for social workers, but Haraway can help us to understand that people have *relationships* with these things, that those relationships are important, and that they help to define one's humanity. They are not just 'resources' to be 'accessed', but become connected to us in such a way that they are part of our human experience. This means more than simply saying that these things are necessary to help us overcome 'disadvantage', but rather that they change our very experiences of being 'human' and our ways of knowing and being in the world.

Dualisms

Like many postmodern and posthuman scholars, Haraway is concerned with unsettling and transcending the dualisms that are characteristic of Modernity. Critical and postmodern social workers have also been concerned with transcending dualisms that so pervade social work discourse: worker/client, professional/personal, private/public, personal/political, man/woman, straight/gay, structural/poststructural, oppressor/oppressed, psychological/sociological, reform/revolution, top-down/bottom-up, macro/micro, and so on. Haraway requires us to consider other dualisms that have not been so central to social work, most importantly the human/non-human. Her work explores the non-human both in terms of the mechanical/technological, and also in terms of non-human living species, with whom she urges us to 'make kin' in the Chthulucene.

The challenging of dualisms is not new to social work, but Haraway forces us to consider other dualisms that have been largely unexamined in the discourse of Western Modernity, but which are vital for a viable posthuman future. Here the term 'posthuman' does not mean a world without humans, but rather a world where human privilege is challenged (Jensen 2016), and where humanity is embedded in, rather than separate from, the world of other species and of the mechanical/technological (Braidotti 2013). Social workers strongly affirm the values of something called 'humanity', and Haraway (as well as other posthuman writers) challenges what 'humanity' means. This can help social workers move beyond the Western Enlightenment view of the autonomous 'human' which is hardly consistent with the reality of the Anthropocene or the Chthulucene.

Indigenous epistemologies

In facing Haraway's challenge, the area of inquiry that is perhaps most familiar to social workers is the interest in Indigenous epistemologies. The world views of Indigenous people certainly resonate with Haraway's ideas of 'making kin' and 'affinity', and the way in which Indigenous epistemology firmly embeds the human within 'nature' and not separate from it, is consistent with Haraway's Chthulucene (Haraway 2016b). For Indigenous people, in many different Indigenous cultures, humans have strong interdependence with other living (and indeed non-living) beings, including networks of obligations and understanding of non-human beings as kin (Turner 2010). This is perhaps best understood in the idea of totem (Sveiby & Skuthorpe 2006).

An Australian Indigenous person is allocated a totem and has special responsibilities to understand and care for the habitat of the totem. If your totem is, say, an emu, you must learn everything you can about the life and habitat of emus, you must respect emus and always look after their welfare and their habitat. You have a strong kinship with emus, you must never eat emu meat (though others in your group will), you must try to think like an emu, you may represent emus in dance, and in a sense you 'become' an emu. As other members of your group will have different totems (snake, kangaroo, possum, lizard, etc.), there is a collective sense of deep kinship with and responsibility for other species; quite consistent with Haraway's Chthulucene. And even in terms of the cyborg, Indigenous people may have special and deep relationships with their own technologies: hunting implements, utensils, fire, and so on. Indeed, the common Indigenous practices of body painting and wearing of elaborate ritual clothing can represent an extension of the human body to include additional body parts which have deep significance, and which are to some degree analogous with the cyborg. Indigenous people would, in all likelihood, find Haraway much less challenging and closer to their own epistemological and ontological traditions. Social workers have had particular interest in exploring and using Indigenous knowledge systems – they are even named in the *Global Definition of Social Work* – and so perhaps they represent a way for social workers to begin to explore Donna Haraway's work.

Whither human rights?

Human rights have been seen as central to social work practice and identity (Ife 2012). Like Indigenous knowledge as discussed above, human rights are seen as important enough to be named in the *Global Definition of Social Work*, and there is now a considerable literature on human rights as a basis for social work practice. Much of this literature, while exploring the idea of *rights*, pays little attention to the idea of *human*. Haraway is one of a number of authors in the posthuman tradition who turn a critical lens onto the idea of 'human' and refuse to accept 'human' as non-problematic.

In the light of Haraway's work and the work of other posthuman scholars, anyone wishing to consider seriously the idea of 'human rights' must accept that the 'human' is not a simple empirical entity, on whose meaning we can all agree, but rather is a contested construction, understood differently in different contexts, with decidedly permeable boundaries. We must now question whether an idea such as 'human rights' is compatible with the world of Indigenous cultures, and the world of the Chthulucene.

Given the ecological insanity of contemporary Western 'civilisation', and the imperative to rethink its taken-for-granted anthropocentrism if some form of 'civilisation' is to survive, ideas of rights and obligations need to be rethought, from what Haraway (2016b) calls a 'tentacular' perspective, as we live sharing ontological space with other beings. Increasingly, the rights of non-humans are being seen as significant in the treatment of 'rights'. Animal rights have been of concern for a considerable time, and more recently ideas of the rights of the earth, or the 'rights of Mother Nature', have received increasing attention (Boyd 2017). Questioning anthropocentrism, as Haraway and others demand, requires a reformulation of the taken-for-granted assumptions about human rights, to include the rights of non-human animals, the rights of the earth, and indeed the rights of those mechanical and technological devices with which we interact. What does the metaphor of the cyborg suggest about the nature of the 'human' who has the rights?

Toward a posthuman future for social work

Much of the most significant critical thinking about the ontological crises facing humanity, the posthuman, and the need to dismantle anthropocentrism has come from the humanities. The sciences have provided the empirical evidence for a world in crisis (climate, oceans, water, desertification, agriculture, pollution, and so on), but have only been able to prescribe technical-rational 'solutions' often without due consideration for social, cultural, ideological and political contexts. The social sciences have been concerned with these latter issues, researching climate justice, recognising neo-liberal patriarchal capitalism as a major driver of unsustainability, allowing for cultural diversity, and looking either for more relevant policies within the existing order, or, more radically, alternative forms of social and political organisation.

The humanities, however, have been concerned with the epistemological and the ontological dimensions of the crisis currently facing the human species. The idea of the 'posthuman' had its origins in the humanities, through the work of Donna Haraway and others such as Rosi Braidotti (2013), Timothy Morton (2017) and Richard Grusin (2015). These scholars have articulated a world view that is far more radical and challenging than anything undertaken within the physical or social sciences, as it questions the very idea of humanity and the human. For such exploration, it is the humanities – with centuries of wrestling with the human condition – that can address the radical ontological questions posed by the crisis of the Anthropocene. Donna Haraway is one of these scholars, whose work has an added impetus because of her disciplinary background in the sciences and her ability to straddle the world views of both the sciences and the humanities.

For social work to address these challenges, the work of Donna Haraway provides a different way of thinking about social work's value base of 'social justice and human rights', a phrase often glibly recited without deep critical reflection. Donna Haraway is very committed to these values – she is not an armchair theorist but also a committed activist – but insists that we reconceptualise them in ways that make sense in the turbulent world of the twenty-first century. While, as indicated above, social work's concern for Indigenous epistemologies is a good entry into this way of thinking, there is also room for a wider engagement with the humanities, the disciplines most concerned with exploring what it means to be 'human'. Inclusion, not only of Donna Haraway but a wider critical humanities disciplinary framework in social work curricula, is essential if social work is to remain relevant to the needs of a perplexed humanity. It can be argued that social work has paid too little attention to the humanities as part of its knowledge base, even though the humanities are also mentioned in the *Global Definition*, and engagement with Haraway and other posthuman humanities scholars should emphasise the significance of a broader and deeper inclusion of humanities scholarship in social work education.

The field of humanities does not only include philosophy, history and literature. It also includes the arts in their various forms. It is often artists – poets, novelists, painters, sculptors, musicians, dancers, film-makers – who are most successful at challenging world views and providing the stimulus for people to dare to dream of something different, and again, it can be suggested that the arts have not occupied the place in social work that they deserve. Donna Haraway certainly refers to artists in her writing, recognising their importance in exploring and expanding the boundaries of the 'human', and social work could draw on her work in this regard. Again, it is perhaps through the interest that social workers have shown in Indigenous epistemologies and world views that there is a possibility to engage with the artistic, and this represents another way that Haraway's work can influence social work.

Donna Haraway certainly does not provide 'answers', nor does she seek them, as the search for the ready answer is increasingly a futile one in the complexity of a world experiencing multiple crises. This is also true of social work and of the crises facing those with whom social workers work. The neat answer, which is the implicit goal of social work that is 'solution-focused', is seldom clear or attainable. Much social work practice, however, has the less ambitious goal of 'staying with the trouble', and looking at ways to encourage 'affinity' and to 'make kin', in recognition of the seismic changes happening around us. Donna Haraway's work suggests that this is an ontologically radical perspective, and reflects the perplexing but also exciting reality of contemporary social work theory and practice.

Notes

1 www.youtube.com/watch?v=GrYA7sMQaBQ
2 www.youtube.com/watch?v=GrYA7sMQaBQ
   www.youtube.com/watch?v=fWQ2JYFwJWU
   www.youtube.com/watch?v=Q9gis7-Jads
   www.youtube.com/watch?v=IXQTex0a3dc

References

Angus, I. (2016), *Facing the Anthropocene: Fossil Capitalism and the Crisis of the Earth System*, New York: Monthly Review Press.
Bonneuil, C. & Fressoz, J-P. (2015), *The Shock of the Antrhopocene*, London: Verso.
Boyd, D. (2017). *The Rights of Nature: A Legal Revolution That Could Change the World*, Toronto: ECW Press.
Braidotti, R. (2013), *The Posthuman*, Cambridge: Polity Press.
Bridle, J. (2018), *New Dark Age: Technology and the End of the Future*, London: Verso.
Dominelli, L. (ed.) (2018), *The Routledge Handbook of Green Social Work*, London: Routledge.
Eisenstein, C. (2018), *Climate: A New Story*, Berkeley CAL: North Atlantic Books.
Gergen, K. (2000), *Relational Being*, New York: Oxford University Press.
Ghosh, A. (2016), *The Great Derangement: Climate Change and the Unthinkable*, Chicago: University of Chicago Press.
Grusin, R. (ed.) (2015), *The Nonhuman Turn*, Minneapolis: University of Minnesota Press.
Hamilton, C. (2017), *Defiant Earth: The Fate of Humans in the Anthropocene*, Sydney: Allen & Unwin.
Haraway, D. (1991), *Simians Cyborgs and Women: The Reinvention of Nature*, London: Free Association Books.
Haraway, D. (2004), *The Haraway Reader*, New York: Routledge.
Haraway, D. (2016a), *Manifestly Haraway*, Minneapolis: University of Minnesota Press.
Haraway, D. (2016b), *Staying With the Trouble: Making Kin in the Chthulucene*, Durham: Duke University Press.
Haraway, D. (2016c), 'Staying With the Trouble: Anthropocene, Capitalocene, Chthulucene', in Moore, J. (Ed.) *Anthropocene or Capitalocene: Nature, History and the Crisis of Capitalism*, Oakland CAL: PM Press, pp. 34–76.
Haraway, D. (2018), 'Making Kin in the Chthulucene: Reproducing Multi-Species Justice', in Clarke, E. & Hararway, D. (Eds.) *Making Kin Not Population*, Chicago: Prickly Paradigm Press, pp. 67–100.
Heise, U, Christensen, J. & Niemann, M. (eds.) (2017), *The Routledge Companion to Environmental Humanities*, London: Routledge.
Holmes, R. (2008), *The Age of Wonder: How the Romantic Generation Discovered the Beauty and Terror of Science*, London: Harper.
Ife, J. (2012), *Human Rights and Social Work: Towards Rights-based Practice*, Melbourne: Cambridge University Press (3rd ed.).
Jensen, D. (2016), *The Myth of Human Supremacy*, New York: Seven Stories Press.
Kingsnorth, P. (2017), *Confessions of a Recovering Environmentalist*, London: Faber & Faber.
Klein, N. (2014), *This Changes Everything, Capitalism Versus the Climate*, London: Penguin.
Mancuso, S. (2017), *The Revolutionary Genius of Plants: A New Understanding of Plant Intelligence and Behaviour*, New York: Atria Books.
Margulis, L. (1999), *Symbiotic Planet: A New Look at Evolution*, New York: Basic Books.
Moore, J. (ed.) (2016), *Anthropocene or Capitalocene: Nature, History and the Crisis of Capitalism*, Oakland CAL: PM Press. pp. 34–76.
Morton, T. (2017), *Humankind: Solidarity with Non-Human People*, London: Verso.
Ryan, T. (2011), *Animals and Social Work: A Moral Introduction*, London: Palgrave.
Snow, C.P. (1959), *The Two Cultures*, London: Cambridge University Press.
Spretnak, C. (2011), *Relational Reality: New Discoveries of Interrelatedness that are Shaping the Modern World*, Topsham MA: Green Horizon Books.
Sveiby, K. & Skuthorpe, T. (2006), *Treading Lightly: The Hidden Wisdom of the World's Oldest People*, Sydney: Allen & Unwin.
Turner, M. (2010), *Iwenhe Tyerrtye: What it Means to be an Aboriginal Person*, Alice Springs NT: IAD Press.
Weber, A. (2016). *The Biology of Wonder: Aliveness, Feeling and the Metamorphosis of Science*, Gabriola Island USA: New Society Publishers.
Zuboff, S. (2019), *The Age of Surveillance Capitalism: The Fight for a Human Future at the New Frontier of Power*, New York: Public Affairs.

25
Critical (animal) social work
Insights from ecofeminist and critical animal studies in the context of neoliberalism

Heather Fraser

QUEENSLAND UNIVERSITY OF TECHNOLOGY, AUSTRALIA

Nik Taylor

UNIVERSITY OF CANTERBURY, NEW ZEALAND

Introduction

Ecofeminism and critical animal studies (CAS) have much to offer social workers interested in transformative social change that includes non-human animals, built and natural environments. Inequality on the basis of species and gender—particularly as they intersect with neoliberal rhetoric—are major points of our discussion. The chapter is organised into five overlapping sections: ecofeminism; critical animal studies; ecological/green social work; critical (animal) social work in the context of neoliberalism; and transformative education and the joy of animal connections. We draw ideas most from Val Plumwood and Vandana Shiva (representing ecofeminism), Carol J. Adams (vegan ecofeminism), Steve Best (CAS), Fred Besthorn (ecological social work) and Lena Dominelli (green social work). We have chosen ecofeminism and CAS as they are important and complementary bodies of thought and impetus for action, with earliest iterations of CAS having its intellectual roots in ecofeminism, anarchism and radical ecology (Best, Nocella, Gigliotti & Kemmerer, 2007; Twine, 2014).

Our primary focus is on how the central ideas from ecofeminism and CAS can inform non-anthropocentric social work, that is, social work that does not assume human superiority or governance over other animals, nature and the environment. Our interest is to outline how these schools of thought indicate the necessity of challenging anthropocentric and neoliberal ideologies and practices that have infiltrated social work education and practice. This is because both neoliberalism and anthropocentrism are intertwined, complicit in, and dependent upon, the exploitation of the earth, human beings and other species. Our aim is to use ideas from ecofeminism and CAS (as well as others) to underline the importance of transformative education for social work, a profession dedicated to the pursuit of social justice and recognition of oppression and privilege. To meet these aims we consider the epistemological foundations of (Western) knowledge, which have shaped the development of social work in Anglo-dominated countries such as Australia. This is necessary because, as we outlined above, these epistemological foundations are built upon a veneration for the hierarchical and binary (or dualistic) modes of thought that maintain systemic privilege and oppression (including the exploitation of the earth and other species).

A note of caution: While this chapter follows the format of others in this collection, it is imperative to note that our consideration of 'key' scholars in these areas should not be taken to suggest they are 'leaders'. As Twine (2014, p. 30) notes, 'CAS is critical of the notion of the heroic masculinised competitive lone scholar model of research'. Following this line of thought we present key thinkers in this chapter as those who contributed to the emergence of their respective schools of thought but note that (1) this does not mean all their ideas are unproblematic and (2) they are not 'experts' in the neoliberal sense. Rather, they are people whose ideas have shaped our own work as senior feminist and critical animal scholars working in social work and human services (Fraser, 2008; Fraser & Taylor, 2016, 2019; Fraser, Taylor & Signal, 2017).

Ecofeminism

Ecofeminism dates back to the early 1970s where it emerged from both academic feminism and the social justice movements of the time that began to formulate the idea of linked oppressions between women, nature and other marginalised categories such as race, colonialism, capitalism and species (e.g., Griffin, 1978). As discussed below, key texts pointed to 'the male ideology of transcendent dualism' (Ruether, 1975, p. 195) as the main mechanism of this oppression. Following these early ideas and associated activism was a period of feminist activism in the 1980s that 'linked militarism, corporatism, and unsustainable energy production by joining together the antinuclear protests and the peace movement' (Gaard, 2012a, p. 28) extending the purview and popularity of ecofeminist ideas. Throughout the 1980s more attention was paid to the ways in which race and environmental destruction are connected, historically (e.g. Spiegel, 1988) and through colonial processes and ideologies (e.g., Shiva, 1988).

Val Plumwood: how dualisms reproduce intersecting oppressions

Val Plumwood (b. 1939–2008), an Australian feminist philosopher, produced compelling arguments about dualisms and the role they play reproducing intersecting oppressions and injustice. Dualisms occur when related phenomena (such as reason/emotion) or beings (such as men/women, humans/animals) are placed in opposition to, or split from each other with one assumed better, or more important, than the other (see Plumwood, 1991, 1993, 2002). This splitting matters because such dualisms are founded on hierarchies that overvalue men, humans, reason and progress as superior and devalue women, animals, emotions and nature as inferior. As Plumwood argued:

> Reason in the western tradition has been constructed as the privileged domain of the master, who has conceived nature as a wife or subordinate other encompassing and representing the sphere of materiality, subsistence and the feminine which the master has split off and constructed as beneath him. *The continual and cumulative overcoming of the domain of nature by reason engenders the western concept of progress and development.*
>
> (Plumwood, 1993, p. 3, italics added)

Western notions of progress and associated ideas about (capitalist) development have been historically lauded and continue to dominate mainstream Australia and beyond, despite their legacy of environmental destruction and decay. One of the problems is the embeddedness of dualisms in our thinking. As Plumwood explains (2000, p. 315),

> most of us are still to some degree entrapped by dualistic conceptual structures and assumptions that are part of the legacy of the western worldview ... The dominant way of thinking about these problems in the western tradition has been in terms of human/nature dualism as elaborated in the narrative of the sanctity human life, a narrative of personal justice and salvation, carried over from Christianity into humanism, in which we humans are irreplaceable and unique individuals, who gain our right to sacrifice other species from our rational superiority.

Vandana Shiva: mobilising opposition to corporatisation

Indian activist-scientist Vandana Shiva (b. 1952) offers an inspiring example of ecofeminism focusing on women in the developing world. In 1988 she analysed the connections between nature and femininity and the domination and degradation of both (Shiva, 1988). In *Close to Home*, Shiva ([1994]2014) showed how grassroots women's groups were taking action against environmental degradation and toxic pollution, through community development. In 2002, Shiva showed how the trading of water and ensuing water wars have negatively affected communities, particularly poorer communities, through the privatisation of water. In *Ecofeminism*, Shiva and Mies (2014) consider how social movements can mobilise opposition to patriarchal oppression and the inherent violence of the privatisation and corporatisation of life-sustaining public resources. Food distribution networks are analysed in *Who Really Feeds the World*, where Shiva (2016) asks critical questions about the causes of world hunger and destruction of environment through capitalist agribusiness, refuting the idea that the further industrialisation of agriculture and extensions of genetically modified foods, are healthy and viable solutions. Shiva's work has much to offer transformative social work education and practice, not only because of her unwavering commitment to examining the effects of neoliberal corporatisation on the outcast and impoverished, but also because her work challenges dominant ideas about nature, society and knowledge.

However, in our view another major step is still required. Contemporary social work needs to do more than conceptualise the environment in relation to nature and its effects on humans. It needs to consider other species as individuals, as opposed to as part of 'nature' as many ecofeminists do. These non-human animals are so dominated and commodified for human use through practices normalised in speciesist and carnist cultures (Ryan, 2011; Wadiwel, 2015) that even social progressive social workers may roll their eyes at the mention of animal exploitation and the sexual politics of meat eating.

Carol J. Adams: the sexual politics of meat

In many ways, animal ecofeminism prefigured CAS. Consider, for instance, that it is nearly thirty years ago that Carol J. Adams published *The Sexual Politics of Meat*, a pioneering ecofeminist book examining the links between the patriarchal oppression of women and (non-human) animals, including the patriarchal nature of meat and dairy eating (Adams, 1990). In this book she made the case for the 'absent referent', a notion that, when applied to meat eating, points to the deliberate fragmentation, removal, separation or disassociation of meat eating from the facts of animal cruelty and slaughter so as to avoid feelings of discomfort (Adams, 1990). For instance, meat and dairy eaters, who in other areas of their lives might be committed to social justice and interested to learn about domination and abuse, often (still) say words to the effect of, 'Don't tell me, you'll spoil my dinner/bbq/celebration', even when discussions are not taking place during such times. (Certainly, we have had students say this to us in the classroom, at the first sign of discussion about animal agribusiness and slaughter.) Adams (1990) also made the case that women were often absent referents in advertising, pornography and other dominant representations that dismembered, objectified and sexualised bodies, with few traces of the whole remaining visible.

By 1991 Adams had published the paper 'Ecofeminism and the Eating of Animals', noting that ecofeminism: (1) does not accept the human domination of animals; (2) is concerned with the environmental consequences of farming and consuming animals; (3) argues against animals being seen as unthinking and unfeeling machines; (4) refutes the construction of animals as natural edible resources designed for human use, and the assumption that humans need to eat meat; (5) does not accept the legitimacy of hunting, especially in the name of sport; and (6) seeks to reposition human–animal relationships to prioritise egalitarianism and solidarity across differences (Adams, 1991). By the mid-1990s Adams explained how much more expansive *animal ecofeminism* was than feminisms that focused exclusively on humans. She wrote, '[ecofeminism] proposes a broader feminism, a radical cultural feminism, which provides an analysis of oppression and offers a vision of liberation that extends well beyond the liberal equation, incorporating within it, other life forms as well as human beings' (Adams & Donovan, 1995, p. 3).

As we will explain later in this chapter, animal ecofeminism has much to offer transformative social work that refuses to ignore the plight of (other) animals. It is based on the idea that 'all forms of social domination are feminist concerns' (Besthorn, 2003, p. 78), and that one form of domination cannot be eradicated without removing them all (also see Besthorn, 2003).

However, as Gaard (2012a) chronicles, the 1990s saw a backlash against ecofeminism with critics charging it with essentialism. Despite this, a specific branch of 'animal ecofeminism' (Gaard, 2012a) was developing at this time (e.g., Adams & Donovan, 1995) building on earlier foundations that noted links between speciesism, sexism and the control or mastery of nature.

Critical animal studies

Acknowledged or not, CAS scholars draw on ecofeminism to highlight the role that dualistic, binary, post-Enlightenment paradigms have played in creating and maintaining the oppression of vulnerable groups by marginalising and othering them. CAS draws from these ecofeminist roots (as well as others, e.g., the Frankfurt School, Best, 2006) but adds a specific focus on both advocacy (for animals and against capitalism) and the material and symbolic oppression of other species at the hands of humans. Where ecofeminism focuses on 'nature'/'environment' broadly, CAS has other species as its central point of reference, and it is also worth noting that not all CAS scholars consider themselves ecofeminists or, indeed, acknowledge the intellectual roots of feminism in their work. Arguably CAS scholars (e.g., Best, 2013; Nibert, 2003) are also more focused on the role capitalism plays in normalising the domination of other species than ecofeminists, and their main preoccupation is with species, as opposed to environment and/or nature (Taylor & Twine, 2014; Wadiwel, 2015). CAS scholars investigate the mechanisms that lead to human prerogative and exceptionalism reifying the human being at the expense of all other beings and while this includes 'nature' broadly conceived, the central focus is animals. Key to this is the idea of total liberation developed by Best (2011a, 2011b) that reorients notions of progress (back) to social justice:

> A postmodern, posthumanist concept of progress repudiates the zero-sum game of winners and losers. The only meaningful definition of progress refers to improvements in life

> for all—not just 'all' humans but all species and individuals—and does not sanction the exploitation of the majority for the benefit of a minority. This new concept breaks with domineering and dualistic views that define human interests in opposition to other species and the natural world, rather than understanding humans as inseparably involved with the vast biocommunity and entire globe. This equal consideration extends in principle not only to all human interests (and therefore requires a theory of global justice), it also gives equal consideration to the interests of animals and the requirements of ecological integrity and balance.
>
> *(Best, 2011a, n.p.)*

This idea, based on the centralisation of countering the material and symbolic oppression of other animals, extended traditional ecofeminist ideas and (while not always acknowledged) built upon ecofeminist ideas of interlinked oppressions and the black feminist concept of intersectionality.

Intersectionality (Crenshaw, 1991) was originally conceived of as a way of understanding the interlocking oppressions that black women faced but has, over the last few decades, been extended to encompass other sites of marginalisation such as class, religion, dis/ability and increasingly species (Cho, Crenshaw & McCall, 2013; Kemmerer, 2011). While a useful concept—for both theory and pedagogy—one problem with intersectionality is it grew from post-modernism with its stress on difference and fragmentation. While there are some strands of ecofeminism that mirror this, it is problematic for scholars interested in linked oppressions to follow this slavishly. This is because theories that stress individual differences among humans, or identity, or fragmentation, are incapable of grappling with structurally embedded inequality. For animals (as well as oppressed/disenfranchised human groups) it is the structurally embedded ideologies that lead to institutionally approved abuses that are precisely the problem. It is profoundly important, then, that we address how structural oppressions intersect each other to produce normative experiences and frameworks that allow and encourage exploitation and oppression.

Both CAS and ecofeminism share a commitment to intersectional analyses of power. That is, both point to the role of binary and hierarchical thinking (man/woman; human/animal), in particular the culture–nature binary, that sits at the heart of (mainstream) Western intellectual paradigms. Linked to this is a critique of the reification of rationality and objectivity that subordinate women and animals by positing them as 'closer to nature', which is cast in opposition to assumed, superior, 'civilisation.' As Best (2013), wrote:

> Following the lead of historicists, poststructuralists, postmodernists, feminists, and others who 'deconstructed' binary oppositions pivotal to Western ideology and hierarchical domination (e.g.: mind vs. body, reason vs. emotion, and men (the masculine) and women (the feminine)), animal studies theorists rearranged the conceptual furniture in the house of humanism.

Steven Best: animal liberation and the ALF

Steven Best (b. 1955) is an American philosopher and animal rights activist. He co-founded International Critical Animal Studies (ICAS) and the Animal Liberation Press Office, and in the early 2000s he produced a series of papers concerned with 'radical' animal liberation ideas and practices. This includes the book he coedited (with Anthony Nocella) *Terrorists or Freedom Fighters: Reflections on the Liberation of Animals* (2004), where they explained that

> [t]his is a book about a new breed of freedom fighters—human activists who risk their own liberty to rescue and aid animals imprisoned in hellish conditions. Loosely bonded in a decentralised, anonymous, underground, global network, these activists are members of the Animal Liberation Front (ALF). Their daring deeds have earned them top spot on the FBI 'domestic terrorist' list as they redefine political struggle for the current era.
>
> *(p. 11)*

Urging direct action not just activist talk, Best and others in the ALF have attracted public attention, police, federal intelligence and immigration surveillance, particularly in relation to their arguments about the justified use of violence to release animals from the harm humans inflict on them through agribusiness, fast food corporations and vivisection (using animals to test medications, cleaners and cosmetics). They describe how

> ALF activists operate under cover, at night, wearing balaclavas and ski masks, and in small cells of a few people. After careful reconnaissance, skilled liberation teams break into buildings housing animal prisoners in order to release them (e.g. minks and coyotes) or rescue them (e.g. cats, dogs, mice, and guinea pigs). They seize and/or destroy equipment, property and materials used to exploit animals and they use arson to raze buildings and laboratories. They have cost the animal exploitation industries hundreds of millions of dollars. They wilfully break the law because the law wrongly consigns animals to cages and confinement, to loneliness and pain, to torture and death.
>
> *(Best & Nocella, 2007, p. 12)*

While not all who identify with ideas from CAS support the views of Best and other members of the ALF, they/we conduct structural analyses of power, pointing to the ways in which systems of domination and oppression overlap and are mired in anthropocentric worldviews that see humans as superior to nature and men as superior to women.

It is important to note, however, that early iterations of ecofeminism, specifically 'animal ecofeminism', such as those of Carol J. Adams, Josephine Donovan and Greta Gaard, are the intellectual antecedents of CAS. This is not always acknowledged within CAS circles, however, where some seemingly fall into the trap of traditional 'animal rights' scholars who ignore the ground-breaking work of feminist thinkers, leading to the pervasive idea that animal liberation has 'fathers' such as Singer and Regan and no 'mothers' (Adams, 2014, p. 2). As Adams points out in an intersectional argument that resonates with CAS scholars, 'separating animal liberation from feminism and other social justice issues promotes social injustice' (Adams, 2014, p. 3). Gaard (2012a, p. 42) also notes that

> scholars in fields outside of feminism—such as posthumanism … , postcolonial ecocriticism … , and animal studies … —are moving forward with ideas initially developed in feminist and ecofeminist contexts, often without acknowledging those contexts as foundations for the work'. It might be that scholars in these fields are uncomfortable being associated with feminism and/or are blind to the work women scholars and activists have produced today and in the past.

Ecological and green social work

In mainstream social work that has been historically influenced by psychodynamic and systems approaches, 'the environment' often stands for local interpersonal relations, such as those relating to individual families, local schools, churches and, on occasion, policing. Social work references to the environment do not ordinarily evoke notions of nature, geography, physicality and embodiment, such as the impact of land use, water quality and food systems on health and wellbeing across species. Noteworthy silence usually surrounds species recognition, flora and fauna, habitat, animal rights and protection. Yet, the way we conceive of and relate to 'the natural world' has consequences, as Besthorn well understands.

Fred Besthorn: ecological social work

American social work professor Fred Bestorn (b. 1951) made the case for social work to engage with environmental issues (natural/physical not just social and cultural environments), to extend social work's historical notion of person-in-environment (Besthorn, 2012). More than two decades ago he explained that an alienated humanity has produced not just a significant and diverse range of ecological problems but also a raft of familial, emotional and social problems (Besthorn, 1997). He wrote that social work needs to adopt a 'person-with-environment perspective' that allows the profession to see these issues holistically, thus including the human/nature relationship in social work (Besthorn, 1997, p. 356).

Besthorn warned against mechanistic expressions of social work: 'Direct knowing, intuitive grasp, and subjective experience of *the other*, especially nature, has been replaced with a reverence for numbers, mechanistic metaphors and individualized treatment plans' (Besthorn, 2003, p. 82).

Such a mechanistic outlook, as ecofeminists such as Shiva, Adams and Plumwood have long pointed out, is the basis of a post-Enlightenment, neoliberal, positivist orientation to the world that stresses mastery over nature rather than connection between all living things, normalising hierarchy, mastery and oppression (also see Besthorn & McMillen, 2002). For Besthorn (2003, p. 81), what is needed is for the discipline of social work to focus on the connections between people and the environment, and 'fully recognizing and appropriating this connection means more than simply adding another theoretical framework to the way social work understands human identity. It challenges the core assumptions and distinctions that have principally shaped the social work agenda'. This is similar to the argument made by Ryan (2011) who points out that social work's own humanist intellectual history has led to animals being invisible to the profession. This is untenable given 'human beings and domestic animals form a genuine community and that a concern for animals is an inherent feature of human moral sensibility, as is sensitivity to their suffering' (p. 156).

Lena Dominelli: green social work

Lena Dominelli (b. 1922), a Canadian social work professor who lives in the UK, is well known for her work on feminist, anti-racist and anti-oppressive practice social work perspectives (Dominelli, 2013, 2014, 2017). With Besthorn, Dominelli's *Green Social Work* (2012) challenges the silencing of 'nature' in social work. Green social work takes up questions of environmental injustice, which Dominelli (2014, p. 339) defines as, 'society's failure to ensure the equitable distribution of the Earth's resources in meeting human needs, simultaneously providing for the well-being of people and planet Earth today and in the future'. Although still mostly focused on human societies in relation to the physical/natural environment, she calls for the greening of the profession (Dominelli, 2013) and for 'social workers [to] have a role … formulating alternative models of socio-economic development by promoting environmental justice and organizing and mobilizing communities in meeting human need' (Dominelli, 2014, p. 339).

Both Besthorn and Dominelli appreciate the need for social work educators, practitioners and students alike to move beyond limiting dominant discursive paradigms, including those relating to neoliberalism. For instance, as Dominelli (2014, p. 195) wrote:

> In trying to transcend the limitations of neoliberal capitalism through an inclusive egalitarian framework predicated on social and environmental justice, green social workers adopt an explicitly political stance, rather than the covert one inherent in neoliberal ideology in which the current political regime is seen as non-political or neutral.

Yet, many of the people we currently teach in higher education have never known anything but a neoliberal world and so exposing them to alternate viewpoints is crucial. Key to this is helping them to understand the exclusionary paradigms that neoliberalism has made utterly—and depressingly—normal.

Critical (animal) social work in the context of neoliberal compliance

In this section we consider the difficulties inherent to incorporating non-anthropocentric ideas, that are fundamentally challenging to the status quo, into social work pedagogy as currently constituted under neoliberal regimes. Our reference to Critical (Animal) Social Work brackets animals because we are not proposing that a branch of critical social work be dedicated to animals. Rather, we are arguing that social work as a discipline and profession, especially that which is designated as critical and transformative, needs to pay attention to the plight of non-human animals, their often-brutal interactions with humans, and the often-restricted social and physical environments in which they live and die.

We make these arguments knowing that social work is a values-based profession committed to social equality and collective wellbeing and rights (AASW, 2010). Our value position is that social and educational arrangements founded on neoliberal ideologies and practices are socially unjust, based on domination, if not prone to bullying, and environmentally unsustainable (Fraser & Taylor, 2016).

Neoliberalism—itself a contested and arguably over-used term—is used here to refer to, 'a set of policies, a development model, an ideology, and an academic paradigm' (Boas & Gans-Morse, 2009, p. 140). Across the world, the neoliberalisation of public utilities (welfare, health and education) has meant an active and deliberate deviation away from notions of the collective good to promote the business interests of efficiencies, protection of reputation—of 'the brand'—and the regulation of workers through the commercialisation, instrumentalisation, proceduralisation and bureaucratisation of health, welfare and education (Ferguson, Ioakimidis & Lavalette, 2018; Fraser & Taylor, 2016; Spolander, Engelbrecht & Sandsfacon, 2016). This shift has been seismic, for the senior staff who are now likely to be called managers and directors, the workers (including social work educators) otherwise called 'talent', and the students and clients, who in neoliberal vernacular are called 'customers' or 'units of consumption'. Neoliberalism promotes the idea that everything, including services and individuals, can and should be treated as if they have an exchange value (Connell, 2013; Gonzales & Nunez, 2014). This is tied to positivist, quantitative epistemologies and the uncritical adoption and adulation of metrics. In turn, this is predicated upon and leads to the marginalising of other forms of knowledge relevant to, produced by, or that argue for the liberation of subjects that are not human, white, middle class, heterosexual, able bodied and male (Fraser & Taylor, 2016).

Corporatism, not just capitalism, is a key part of neoliberalism, and has been shown to have close ties to the authoritarianism some argue is constitutive of totalitarianism (Connell, 2013) and fascism (Pinto, 2017). In the higher education system of Australia (as well as beyond) and the provision of social services, corporate compliance has a habit of cleverly shutting down dissent, often under the guise of accountability (see Connell, 2013). In the context of neoliberalism, it can be precarious and risky trying to integrate critical ideas into social work curricula and research agendas. This is especially the case for work that *fundamentally* challenges the intellectual—humanist—paradigms upon which our discipline (and indeed the majority of Western thought) is built. As Twine (2014, p. 31), another CAS scholar explained:

> CAS should act as a mirror to all academics whose work somehow involves other animals, and it does offer an important set of distinct questions and perspectives not found elsewhere. These include such points as represented in the principles as a stronger commitment to intersectionality which concertedly attempts to account for the shaping of human/animal relations by political economy; a suspicion of abstracted as opposed to engaged theory; a commitment to rethinking the academy; and the promotion of a relationship of mutuality between critical theory and radical politics.

However, finding the time and space for critical and/or revolutionary ideas can be logistically not just ideologically difficult, both in terms of research and teaching—especially in large and work intensified social work programs. As Best (2013) notes, even though CAS has the potential for 'progressive change in public attitudes and policies toward nonhuman animals, its academic proponents can only advance it within tight institutional constraints and intensive normalising regimes that frequently demand conformity, "neutrality," disengaged detachment, and activism within narrowly accepted limits.'

However, it is worth remembering that across fields and modes of practice, social work is and has always been, a contradictory profession, especially in relation to the politics of voice, dissent and silence (Dominelli, 2017; Ferguson et al., 2018). Neoliberalism has extended and embedded this inclination toward compliance but historically social work has been bounded by longstanding dilemmas associated with care/control, and the need for social change compared to individuals having to adjust to unfair and harmful living conditions (Dominelli, 2017; Ferguson et al., 2018). It is, therefore, in some ways surprising that social work has not considered 'the animal question' sooner (Ryan, 2011) yet not surprising that many social workers have embraced the ideas of green or animal-based social work so enthusiastically over the last few years. Yet, there are still several challenges when it comes to thinking about animals and social work.

Neoliberalism celebrates commercially defined forms of 'innovation' but largely expects it to occur within the organisational context of maintaining the status quo and displaying loyal servitude. This has resulted in animal-assisted social work being defined primarily in anthropocentric terms, with many applauding the numerous benefits animals can bestow on humans with often little consideration of the animals themselves (Taylor et al., 2016). Read through a CAS and ecofeminist lens, this posits the animals as passive beings exploited by a system that uses their bodies for human care. Their bodies and their labour are further exploited when they are co-opted by academics in order to leverage research funding that meets neoliberal education systems imperatives. Humans and other animals alike are caught up in the neoliberal injunction to be loyal for their 'masters'. Loyal servitude is anathema to social equality and transformation because, by its very nature, it involves passivity and compliance. Student and staff silence, compliance—and ultimately their (sometimes unknown or unrecognised) collusion with injustice—can occur for many ostensibly plausible reasons. Social work students whom we teach often emphasise that they are powerless given the assessment power of their teachers; that they are powerless to effect change in their field placement agencies because they might be negatively assessed to be 'trouble makers'. New graduates can make the same argument, noting their newness in practice and limited job options. Casual academics can fear the negative repercussions of speaking out on future employment arrangements often dictated by the discretion of individual academics with more tenure. Mid-career and later career staff may emphasise how speaking out could jeopardise their promotion prospects and/or their mental health. Chief Executive Officers may say that their hands are tied due to existing and future funding arrangements. There are many more reasons not to speak up, advocate for others or agitate for transformative change.

In and beyond social work, we know that finding ways to subvert this dominant ideology is difficult and at times perilous in terms of job security and mental health. So normalised and pervasive has neoliberalism become in higher education that those who offer challenge to it risk being seen as dissenters by management and colleagues alike (Davies & Bansel, 2010; Fraser & Taylor, 2016; Slaughter & Rhoades, 2004). In such a climate, finding ways to introduce critical pedagogy into social work teaching can be treacherous but is more important than ever. As Best (2013) argues so passionately:

> By definition, nature, and goals, CAS can only be developed by radicals, activists, engaged intellectuals, controversial thinkers, defiant teachers, audacious authors, and courageous educators who know their rights and will defend them in mutual solidarity against threats and intimidation. CAS calls on radical writers, academics, teachers, and intellectuals to apply their critical thinking, research, and communicative skills—mining the rich theoretical insights and political potency of the animal standpoint—to promote systemic social transformation. CAS demands a break from positivism and the bogus 'neutrality' that favours the dominator culture in order to openly ally with the oppressed (human and nonhuman animals) and establish themselves as 'organic intellectuals' in the tradition of Antonio Gramsci and Paulo Freire (and thus always operating in the dual role of teacher and student, speaker and listener).

Transformative education and the joy of animal connections

A focus on other species and our relationships with them, perhaps especially those close, intimate, loving relationships many of us have with companion animals, can be one of several keys to transformational learning. Experiencing living, breathing animals not as oppressed others, but as agentic beings with their own lives and concerns can be key to understanding ecofeminist and CAS concepts of interlocking oppressions.

> Transformative learning involves experiencing a deep, structural shift in the basic premises of thought, feelings, and actions. It is a shift of consciousness that dramatically alters our way of being in the world. Such a shift involves our understanding of ourselves and our self-locations; our relationships with other humans and with the natural world; our understanding of relations of power in interlocking structures of class, race, and gender; our body awarenesses, our visions of alternative approaches to living; and our sense of possibilities for social justice and peace and personal joy.
>
> *(O'Sullivan, Morrell & O'Connor, 2002, p. 11)*

One of the most important identified aspects of transformative education is the relationship between student and educator, as well as between students, along with hands-on experiences in safe, trusting, non-judgemental environments (Taylor & Snyder, 2012). Focusing on other species can help create many of these aspects, including pleasure which has also been shown to be important for transformational learning (Tisdell, 2008). The presence of other animals has repeatedly been shown to improve learner outcomes in a variety of settings, as well as promoting empathy for other humans and other animals (Daly & Suggs, 2010; Fraser, Taylor & Signal, 2017; Friesen, 2010) and has led to a resurgence of interest in humane education. Humane education is 'a process that promotes compassion and respect for all living things by recognising the inter-dependence of people, animals and eco-systems' (Jane Goodall Institute, 2017) and, as such, is indicative of ecofeminist and CAS principles, even if not explicitly stated.

In this final section we share some of our own experiences and classroom strategies aimed at disrupting hegemonic speciesism. We do this in our classrooms as an end in itself but also to help students see, critique and move beyond the dualistic thinking that underpins the neoliberal, individualistic, anti-environment, anti-animal status quo. In one class on animals and society, one of us (NT) asks students what they think the guidelines for discussion should be, after noting that the class covers extremely contentious topics. After assembling a list together that the entire classroom can see (on a white board, or the pc projector, for example), she then asks them how they feel about deciding to ban all eaten animal products from the classroom (so they cannot bring in coffee with cow's milk for instance) and about the idea that in the last class of the semester everyone brings in a plate of vegan food to share. This elicits a lot of discussion and almost always brings up the idea of 'personal choice'. This allows—usually hearty and robust—deconstructions of the idea of personal choice and shows how, in the case of consuming animals' bodily products, it hides systems of oppression. Students clearly embrace the confrontational nature of the idea, meaning it works well as a pedagogical device. They are then asked, following class and further reflection, to post their thoughts to an online forum. The posts clearly show that this simple question and following discussion allows them to understand—what are for many of them advanced—concepts of structural speciesism, hegemony and intersectionality as well as interrogate their own complicity in such systems as the three examples below show:

> An aspect of class that I found really interesting this week was how strongly society is constructed to disconnect people from where the meat on their plate really comes from, through things like the absent referent.

> Discussing the class situations of the slaughterhouse workers, the issues of gender (masculinity, femininity, social roles, etc.) and more that come into play when we argue that 'eating meat is manly' or 'hunting is manly' or 'preparing food is a woman's role' particularly caught my attention as an intersectional feminist—it made me consider the intersectionality that we must have in veganism/animal activism. Beginning to look past the mere idea that 'meat eating is wrong', and really dissecting where and whom is influenced by the social, cultural and physical process of eating and 'producing' animal products is highly interesting.

> I'm also getting a clearer understanding of the power of discourse and that language is a major tool in normalising eating meat by separating the meat-eater from the animals.

Concluding comments

In the context of growing social inequality, international conflict and environmental disasters (see Dominelli, 2013; Ferguson et al., 2018), the importance of an animal-inclusive, intersectional pursuit of justice cannot be overstated, that is, one that considers human, environmental and animal justice. This must include a redefinition of what we mean by 'social' and social justice, inclusive of other animals and the environment, in pursuit of Vandana Shiva's notion of earth democracy. We must also do more than think and talk about justice. Of particular importance to transformative social work is the focus on praxis—on 'the necessary linkage of intellectual, political, and activist work' (Gaard, 2012b, p. 15) common to eco/feminism, CAS and green social work. Using ecofeminist and CAS frameworks that explain how capitalism and its current iteration neoliberalism are both based on and maintain (il)logics of domination exposes students to different ways of looking at the world—crucial if we are to contest the prevailing hegemony. This has to include reflection on our own ideologies as well as those that permeate our institutions, practices and classrooms.

Because higher education and other public utilities have been so dramatically reconfigured away from notions of the public good to narrowly defined commercial interests, transformative critical social work education and practice is needed today, more than ever. Ecological and animal feminists, along with CAS scholars have much to offer social work because, as they well understand, social justice and social equality cannot be truly realised if they exclude natural not just lived environments, and the rights and needs of (other) animals, not just humans.

References

Adams, C. (2014) Foreword: Connecting the dots. In W. Tuttle (Ed.), *Circles of compassion: Essays connecting issues of justice* (pp. 10–18). Danvers, MA: Vegan Publishers.
Adams, C., & Donovan, J. (Eds.). (1995). *Animals and women: Feminist theoretical explanations.* Durham, NC: Duke University Press.
Adams, C. J. (1990). *The sexual politics of meat: A feminist-vegetarian critical theory.* New York: Continuum.
Adams, C. J. (1991). Ecofeminism and the eating of animals 1. *Hypatia*, 6 (1), 125–145.
Australian Association of Social Workers. (2010). Code of ethics. Retrieved 20/7/18, www.aasw.asn.au/document/item/1201.
Best, S. (2006). Rethinking revolution: Animal liberation, human liberation, and the future of the left. *The International Journal of Inclusive Democracy*, 2 (3), 1–24.
Best, S. (2011a). Total liberation and moral progress: The struggle for human evolution. Retrieved from http://drstevebest.wordpress.com/2011/06/22/total-liberation-and-moral-progress-the-struggle-for-human-evolution-3/, Accessed 4/11/19.
Best, S. (2011b). Manifesto for radical liberationism: Total liberation by any means necessary. Retrieved from http://drstevebest.wordpress.com/2011/07/14/manifesto-for-radical-liberation-ism-total.
Best, S. (2013). The rise (and fall) of critical animal studies. *Liberazioni: Associazione.* Retrieved from www.liberazioni.org/articoli/BestS-TheRise(and%20Fall)ofCriticalAnimalStudies.pdf. last accessed 28 November 2018.
Best, S., & Nocella, A. J. (Eds.). (2004). *Terrorists or freedom fighters?: Reflections on the liberation of animals.* New York: Lantern Books.
Best, S., & Nocella II, A. J. (2007) Behind the mask: Uncovering the animal liberation front, In S. Best & A. Nocella (Eds.), *Terrorists or freedom fighters? Reflections on the liberation of animals* (pp. 9–63). New York: Lantern Books.
Best, S., Nocella, A.J. II, Kahn, R., Gigliotti, C., & Kemmerer, L. (2007). Introducing Critical Animal Studies. *Journal for Critical Animal Studies*, 5 (1), 4–5.
Besthorn, F. (2003). Radical ecologisms: Insights for educating social workers in ecological activism and social justice. *Critical Social Work*, 3 (1), 66–106.
Besthorn, F., & McMillen, D. P. (2002). The oppression of women and nature: Ecofeminism as a framework for an expanded ecological social work. *Families in Society: The Journal of Contemporary Social Services*, 83 (3), 221–232.
Besthorn, F. H. (1997). *Reconceptualizing social work's person-in-environment perspective: Explorations in radical environmental thought.* Unpublished doctoral dissertation. Lawrence: University of Kansas.
Besthorn, F. H. (2012). Deep ecology's contributions to social work: A ten-year retrospective. *International Journal of Social Welfare*, 21 (3), 248–259.
Boas, T., & Gans-Morse, J. (2009). Neoliberalism: From new liberal philosophy to anti-liberal slogan. *Studies in Comparative International Development*, 44 (2), 137–161.

Cho, S., Crenshaw, K., & McCall, L. (2013). Toward a field of intersectionality studies: Theory, applications, and praxis. *Signs*, 38 (4), 785–810.

Connell, R. (2013). The neoliberal cascade and education: An essay on the market agenda and its consequences. *Critical Studies in Education*, 54 (2), 99–112.

Crenshaw, K. (1991). Mapping the margins: Intersectionality, identity politics, and violence against women of color. *Stanford Law Review*, 43 (6), 1241–1299.

Daly, B., & Suggs, S. (2010). Teachers' experiences with humane education and animals in the elementary classroom: Implications for empathy development. *Journal of Moral Education*, 39 (1), 101–112.

Davies, B., & Bansel, P. (2010). Governmentality and academic work: Shaping the hearts and minds of academic workers. *Journal of Curriculum Theorizing*, 26 (3), 5–20.

Dominelli, L. (2012). *Green social work: From environmental crises to environmental justice*. London: Polity.

Dominelli, L. (2013). Environmental justice at the heart of social work practice: Greening the profession. *International Journal of Social Welfare*, 22 (4), 431–439.

Dominelli, L. (2014). Promoting environmental justice through green social work practice: A key challenge for practitioners and educators. *International Social Work*, 57 (4), 338–345.

Dominelli, L. (2017). Social work challenges in the second decade of the 21st Century: Against the bias. *Affilia*, 32 (1), 105–107.

Ferguson, I., Ioakimidis, V., & Lavalette, M. (2018). *Global social work in a political context: Radical perspectives*. New York: Policy Press.

Fraser, H. (2008). *In the name of love: Women's narratives of love and abuse*. Toronto: Women's Press/Canadian Scholars Press.

Fraser, H., & Taylor, N. (2016). *Neoliberalization, universities and the public intellectual: Species, gender and class and the production of knowledge*. London: Palgrave.

Fraser, H., & Taylor, N. (2019). *Companion animals and domestic violence: Rescuing me, rescuing you*. London: Palgrave.

Fraser, H., Taylor, N., & Signal, T. (2017). Young people empathising with other animals: Reflections on an Australian RSPCA Humane Education Programme. *Aotearoa New Zealand Social Work*, 29 (3), 5–16.

Friesen, L. (2010). Exploring animal-assisted programs with children in school and therapeutic contexts. *Early Childhood Education Journal*, 37 (4), 261–267.

Gaard, G. (2012a). Ecofeminism revisited: Rejecting essentialism and re-placing species in a materialist feminist environmentalism. *Feminist Foundations*, 23 (2), 26–53.

Gaard, G. (2012b). Feminist animal studies in the U.S.: Bodies matter. *DEP - Deportate, Esuli E Profughe*, 20, 14–21.

Gonzales, L., & Nunez, A. (2014). The ranking regime and the production of knowledge: Implications for academia. *Education Policy Analysis Archives*, 22 (31), 1–24.

Griffin, S. (1978). *Woman and nature: The roaring inside her*. New York: Harper & Row.

Jane Goodall Institute. (2017). *Humane education*. Retrieved from www.janegoodall.org.au/humane-education/.

Kemmerer, L. (2011). *Sister species: Women, animals and social justice*. Urbana, Chicago and Springfield: University of Illinois Press.

Nibert, D. (2003). Humans and other animals: Sociology's moral and intellectual challenge. *International Journal of Sociology and Social Policy*, 23 (3), 4–25.

O'Sullivan, E., Morrell, A., & O'Connor, M. (Eds.). (2002). *Expanding the boundaries of transformative learning: Essays on theory and praxis*. New York: Palgrave Press.

Pinto, A. C. (Ed.). (2017). *Corporatism and fascism: The corporatist wave in Europe*. New York: Routledge.

Plumwood, V. (1991). Nature, self, and gender: Feminism, environmental philosophy, and the critique of rationalism. *Hypatia*, 6 (1), 3–27.

Plumwood, V. (1993). *Feminism and the mastery of nature*. London: Routledge.

Plumwood, V. (2000). Integrating ethical frameworks for animals, humans, and nature: A critical feminist eco-socialist analysis. *Ethics and the Environment*, 5 (2), 285–322.

Plumwood, V. (2002). *Environmental culture: The ecological crisis of reason*. London and New York: Routledge.

Ruether, R. (1975). *New woman, new earth*. New York: Seabury Press.

Ryan, T. (2011). *Animals and social work: A moral introduction*. Basingstoke, UK: Palgrave Macmillan.

Shiva, V. (1988). *Staying alive: Women, ecology and development*. London: Zed Books.

Shiva, V. (2002). *Water wars*. London: Zed Books.

Shiva, V. (2016). *Who really feeds the world?: The failures of agribusiness and the promise of agroecology*. Berkeley, CA: North Atlantic Books.

Shiva, V. ([1994] 2014). *Close to home: Women reconnect ecology, health and development*. London: Routledge.
Shiva, V., & Mies, M. (2014). *Ecofeminism*. London: Zed Books.
Slaughter, S., & Rhoades, G. (2004). *Academic capitalism and the new economy: Markets, state and higher education*. Baltimore, MD: Johns Hopkins University Press.
Spiegel, M. (1988). *The dreaded comparison: Human and animal slavery*. New York: Mirror Books.
Spolander, G., Engelbrecht, L., & Pullen Sansfacon, A. (2016). Social work and macro-economic neoliberalism: Beyond the social justice rhetoric. *European Journal of Social Work*, 19 (5), 634–649.
Taylor, E., & Snyder, M. (2012). A critical review of research on transformative learning theory, 2006–2010, In E. Taylor and P. Cranton *Handbook of transformative learning: Theory, research, and practice* (pp. 37–55) New Jersey: John Wiley & Sons.
Taylor, N., & Twine, R. (2014). *The rise of critical animal studies: From the margins to the centre*. Vol. 125 London: Routledge.
Taylor, N., Fraser, H., Signal, T., & Prentice, K. (2016). Social work, animal-assisted therapies and ethical considerations: A programme example from Central Queensland, Australia. *The British Journal of Social Work*, 46 (1), 135–152, https://doi.org/10.1093/bjsw/bcu115
Tisdell, E. J. (2008). Critical media literacy and transformative learning. *Journal of Transformative Education*, 6 (1), 48–67.
Twine, R. (2014). Review: Defining critical animal studies – An intersectional social justice approach for liberation. In Anthony J. Nocella II John Sorenson, Kim Socha and Atsuko Matsuoka (Eds.), *Animal Studies Journal*, 3 (2), 30–35 Available at http://ro.uow.edu.au/asj/vol3/iss2/6.
Wadiwel, D. (2015). *The war against animals*. Boston and Leiden: Brill.

26
Thomas Piketty's inequality and educational convergence concepts for transformative social policy practice

Jenni Mays

QUEENSLAND UNIVERSITY OF TECHNOLOGY, AUSTRALIA

Introduction

French economist, Thomas Piketty's *Capital in the Twenty-First Century*, is a detailed historical narrative and economic analysis of the developments in the accumulation and distribution of capital spanning two centuries. As he states:

> I am interested in contributing ... to the debate about the best way to organize society and the most appropriate institutions and policies to achieve a just social order ... see justice achieved ... under a rule of law, which should apply equally to all and derive from universally understood statutes subject to democratic debate.
>
> *(Piketty, 2014a, p. 31)*

His work reveals how wealth accumulation (or "super-wealth") within "patrimonial societies" (Milanovic, 2014; Piketty, 2014a) perpetuates burgeoning inequalities. Rapidly increasing inequalities originate from the convergence between political institutions, social and economic forces, and belief systems (such as "meritocratic extremism") that perpetuate unequal wage and capital distribution (Piketty, 2014a). In these circumstances, the rate of return on capital far exceeds the growth rate of the economy, leading to an unequal concentration of wealth at the top 1 per cent of economic elites. Refusing both Marx's thesis of inevitable pauperisation and Kuznets's faith in the egalitarianism of economic growth, Piketty argues the solution to increased inequality is redistribution through mechanisms of state regulation, tighter fiscal control and a progressive global wealth tax. More recently, he has lent support to a group advocating a form of basic income. While not an educational theorist or social worker, Piketty's work offers both a provocative challenge and powerful resource for social work education, particularly for those concerned with teaching social policy and promoting literacy among future social workers in political economy. This chapter provides examples of the use of Piketty's economic analyses in social work and human services education; and critically evaluates Piketty's claim that education is a "force for convergence", for countering the increasing divergence of global economic inequality.

Thomas Piketty

Capital in the Twenty-First Century reflects Thomas Piketty's (2014a) long-term commitment to the scholarship of the economics of income distribution, wealth inequality and the political economy. Born in 1971, in Clichy, France, he has dedicated his academic scholarship to studying historical and contemporary global trajectories of capital wealth to reveal structural inequities over time. He is a Professor at École des Hautes Études en Sciences Sociales (EHESS) and the Paris School of Economics, having taught economics at the Massachusetts Institute of Technology. Piketty's (2014a) doctoral study on economics and wealth distribution, awarded in 1993, earned him the French Economics Association's award for the "best thesis of the year" (Hopkins, 2014). The achievement is remarkable given that he earned his doctorate at just 22. Piketty has since achieved other distinguished awards for outstanding theoretical and applied research contributions to the study of economics (Hopkins, 2014).

Much of his deep commitment to economics, an egalitarian social state, and improving society, stems from having revolutionary parents. Their socialist influence over time, together with major global events during the 1980s and 1990s (Gulf War and oil crisis), political shifts and ensuing widening inequalities, combined to have a profound impact in shaping his intellectual pursuit of economics and a just democratic society (Piketty, 2015). *Capital in the Twenty-First Century* emerged from a decade-long compilation of extensive research and forms an essential *oeuvre* on wealth distribution and inequality. His narrative, supported by empirical evidence, is inspiring for educators committed to critical pedagogy and transformational change. As Piketty (Piketty, 2014a, p. 2) reflected on the consequences of inequality he suggested, "the distribution of wealth [therefore] is … of interest to everyone", especially in the current neoclassical economic climate.

Capital in the Twenty-First Century has established Piketty (2014a) as a highly renowned global authority on the political economy of inequality and the study of the historical dynamics of wealth inequality. Such a comprehensive book builds on the established inequality research by other notable critical theorists such as Stiglitz (2013) and Wilkinson and Pickett (2009). Yet, *Capital in the Twenty-First Century* is inherently distinctive in its return to the detailed writing traditions of classical theorists, including Thomas Robert Malthus and Karl Marx (Hopkins, 2014; Piketty, 2014a, 2014b, 2015). Piketty (2014a, 2015) also credits French classical thinkers, François Simiand (1932), Ernest Labrousse (1933), Simon Kuznets (1953), Adeline Daumard (1973), Anthony Atkinson and Alan Harrison (1978), and Pierre Bourdieu (1986) as his dominant influences. Thomas Piketty's (2014a) influential work has brought the political economy of inequality and policy into mainstream debates on income distribution. Although Piketty (2014a) makes direct reference to the political philosophy, history, economics and social science (sociology) disciplines, his work is also highly informative for social work education and policy teaching (hereafter called policy education. The term policy scholars is also used in this chapter to refer to educators and students in social work and human services).

Piketty: philosophy, radicalism and embedding the political economy in policy education

Within the contemporary context of social struggles surrounding the intensification of capitalism in crisis,[1] Thomas Piketty's *Capital in the Twenty-First Century* (2014a) is a classical, modernist text with transformative potential. Not since economic theorists such as David

Ricardo, Karl Marx, Simon Kuznets and Anthony Atkinson has such an extensive historical and economic analysis of the post-industrial developments associated with the accumulation and distribution of capital been undertaken. *Capital in the Twenty-First Century* is a pivotal challenge to the entrenched assumptions of neoclassical economics and contemporary neoliberal orthodoxy. Piketty makes no apologies for his political stance (see Piketty, 2014a, pp. 20, 35). He provides a conceptual framework for understanding how inequalities created by capitalism undermine democracy, and this holds direct implications for social work education and practice.

Piketty (2014a) begins *Capital in the Twenty-First Century* with a contextualisation of the academic and public debates concerning income and wealth distribution. He states, "the distribution of wealth is one of today's most widely discussed and controversial issues" (2014a, p. 1). Piketty is right to make this claim. In this era of globalisation, distinguished by rapidly growing inequality (Piketty & Saez, 2014; Stiglitz, 2013), the dominant neoclassic economic approach to wealth capitalism has dominated political debates and policy responses. Yet, neoclassic economics and its approach to solving inequality is antithetical to democratic society and egalitarian forms of wealth distribution (Hopkins, 2014). Inequality, therefore, is a contentious issue because of the conflicting and competing normative (moral) requirements that shape policy responses to wealth and income distribution debates. His narrative sets the scene for Piketty to pose critically reflective (normative) questions. He asks:

> But what do we really know about its evolution over the long term? Do the dynamics of private capital accumulation inevitably lead to the concentration of wealth in ever fewer hands as Karl Marx believed in the nineteenth century? What do we really know about how wealth and income have evolved since the eighteenth century, and what lessons can we derive from that knowledge for the century now under way?
>
> *(Piketty, 2014a, p. 1)*

For policy education, such deep reflective questions are necessary. These questions represent a moral compass for guiding critical thinking about the social justice norms required to underpin redistributive mechanisms (social state and social protections) for addressing inequality. Piketty's questions direct students to reflect on the normative dimensions underpinning distributive justice, the problems of inequality and the associated political processes that shape income and wealth distribution. As such, Piketty advances our understanding of the historical dynamics affecting wealth distribution, consequences of inequality and the types of policy responses required to reduce inequality (Piketty, 2014a; Weiss-Gal, 2016), which is vital knowledge for social work educators and practitioners concerned with social justice.

Piketty, political economy and the politicisation of policy education

Piketty (2014a) presents a compelling case for using the political economy tradition in education as an approach to critically analysing inequality in wealth and income distribution. The global dominance of neoclassic economics during the past five decades demands a reinvisioned way to critique narrow conceptions of economics and inequality in wealth distribution (Preston & Aslett, 2014). And this is precisely the intent behind Piketty's claim for embedding the political economy in education. For Piketty (2014a), the political economy tradition helps frame his conceptual framework that can be used in education.

Piketty (2014a) argues for the positioning of the political economy approach to be at the forefront of inequality analyses. He emphasises that the political economy approach is relevant because "the history of the distribution of wealth has always been deeply political, and it cannot be reduced to purely economic mechanisms" (as has been the case in Western capitalist economies since the 1970s) (Piketty, 2014a, p. 20). His argument lends itself well to inform a critical pedagogical approach to policy education. Such an approach helps to orient educators and students to adopt a political stance in relation to conceptualising the political, historical and contemporary dynamics of inequality, and in analysing policy responses adopted during particular eras (Apple, 2016; Boone et al., 2019; Hopkins, 2014; Weiss-Gal, 2016).

Piketty (2014a) also advocates for the embedding of a structural critique of the political economy, in part as a rejoinder to Simon Kuznets' (1953) "inequality curve" theory and principle of natural egalitarianism of economic growth. Kuznets' (1953) theory of the inequality (illustrated by a bell-shaped curve), promoted the assumption that within capitalist societies, when the economy grows, incomes may at first become more unequal, however over time, they will become more equal (Piketty, 2014a). In stark contrast, Piketty's (2014a, 2014b) research shows, "there is no natural, spontaneous process to prevent destabilizing, inegalitarian forces from prevailing permanently" (Piketty, 2014a, p. 20). Piketty found that any stabilisation or reduction of inequality in effect manifested, not from capitalist market mechanisms, but from government and nation-state policies that strengthened national social programs to manage global shocks (for example, the post war expansionist policies) (Piketty, 2014a, 2014b). In making this claim, Piketty reveals a fundamental contradiction prevalent in modern capitalist societies that is useful for policy educators: that Western capitalist countries ignore sharply rising inequalities and focus only on economic growth, free-market and industrialisation policies. Acknowledging the pre-eminence of strong economic growth and industrialisation, at the expense of nation-state interventions to stabilise and reduce inequality is instructive for understanding the causes of rising rates of poverty, to which front-line human service and social work practices must respond (Gray et al., 2015).

The political economy tradition embedded in policy education is useful for orienting policy scholars to the task of disrupting the limitless growth of inequality. In finding that capitalism and market forces cannot resolve the growing problems of inequality confronting modern society, Piketty (2014a) reminds us we need to act politically and intervene (hence the political economy approach). Nevertheless, his conceptual framework captures the essentials of the political economy tradition. It is by applying Piketty's conceptual framework and his associated concepts ($r > g$ inequality equation as a force of divergence; meritocratic wealth extremism; and educational convergence through diffusion of knowledge) that policy education can find possibilities for an alternative vision of democratic society. Each of these concepts will now be discussed.

The $r > g$ equation as a force for divergence

Piketty (2014a) explains the relevance of the $r > g$ inequality equation, which is useful for informing policy education. The inequality equation provides a conception that broadens understanding of the nature of the burgeoning capitalist crisis, and its consequences for those groups who do not hold power or wealth. In tracing the historical, political and economic trends over time, Piketty (2014a) points out that when the rate of return on capital (r) (accumulated wealth through profits, dividends, interests, rents or other forms of income from capital), exceeds the growth rate of the overall economy (g) (accumulated wealth from increases in income or outputs), then vast concentrations of income and wealth ($r > g$) are held within the hands of a few dominant elites (Hopkins, 2014; Piketty, 2014a, 2015). The result, if sustained over lengthy periods of time, is a tendency toward a burgeoning gap between rich and poor ($r > g$ inequality equation) (Piketty, 2014a, 2014b, 2015;Tarlau, 2016). If there is a greater difference in r – g, then divergent forces will function more powerfully as a destabilising effect on democracy (Hopkins, 2014; Piketty, 2014a). He states:

> If the fortunes of the top decile or top centile of the global wealth hierarchy grow faster for structural reasons than the fortunes of the lower deciles, then inequality of wealth will of course tend to increase without limit. This inegalitarian process may take on unprecedented proportions in the new global economy.
>
> *(Piketty, 2014a, p. 431)*

Thus, Piketty (2014a, p. 25) views the r > g equation as a fundamental force for divergence and capitalist contradictions that maintain inequalities in wealth, power and status in modern capitalist society (Apple, 2016; Hopkins, 2014; Piketty, 2014a, p. 25).

Forces of divergence are those mechanisms that push in opposite directions, creating momentum toward greater inequalities in wealth distribution over lengthier periods (Hopkins, 2014; Piketty, 2014a, p. 25). Indeed, when global wealth distribution surpasses equilibrium distribution (stabilising forces), and continue to do so without regulated capital growth, the consequence is limitless growth of wealth in capital accumulation (burgeoning inequality). The threat is revealed in the way wealth accumulates faster than output and wages. The consequence, as Piketty's (2014a) research shows, is stark, ever-growing divisions between those who control the production and wealth (higher incomes; the top 1 per cent dominant elite) and the other 99 per cent who possess nothing but their labour potential (Blume & Durlauf, 2015).

The implications for policy education and practice are significant. His r > g equation and forces of divergence conception, translated to policy education, provide one way to detect underlying inequality dynamics (history of inequality, capital and power) and hidden forces of divergence, to shed new light on how these dimensions work to sustain inequality (Piketty, 2014a; Tarlau, 2016). Exploring the divergent (political and economic) forces assists in explaining institutional change and inequality dynamics (inequality equation) (Piketty, 2015). Piketty (2015) adds that in exploring the forces of divergence in policy research, attention needs to be given to the structural dimensions of inequality (such as class, age and gender). In exploring structural dimensions, a deeper, systematic approach to policy research can emerge for gleaning insights into the implications for particular disadvantaged groups (Piketty, 2015). His message is especially crucial for policy education given that "it would be a mistake to believe that the forces of modern growth and competitive markets are sufficient to address these challenges" of technological advancement and precarity (Piketty, 2015, p. 525). Thus, the inequality equation and forces of divergence formula help detect and explain the dynamics of inequality, to help us consider why it is that extreme accumulation and concentration of wealth prevails and what are the impacts on different groups.

Using conceptions of meritocratic extremism to unmask the ideology of capitalism

The distribution of income and wealth, social order and implications are at the heart of Piketty's (2014a) economic analyses. The way the r > g inequality and forces of divergence play out in a given society, "gives rise to different representations and belief systems about social inequality, which in turn shape institutions and public policies affecting inequality dynamics" (Piketty, 2015, p. 523). Piketty (2014a, 2014b) found that belief representations, based on meritocratic (wealth) extremism, interacted with the forces of divergence to justify rising inequality and vast concentrations of wealth (Gale et al., 2017). For Piketty, exploring the belief representations associated with the dynamics of inequality and institutional arrangements is essential for revealing the interaction between history, politics, inequality and power, and explaining wealth concentration. He states, "I believe that the analysis of representations and beliefs systems about income and wealth is an integral and indispensable part of the study of income and wealth dynamics" to make sense of the way belief representations shape and influence government policy, institutions and structural arrangements (such as the labour market) (Piketty, 2015, p. 518).

Piketty (2014a) states that meritocratic wealth extremism has become a prevailing and entrenched belief system in modern capitalist economies. Piketty describes meritocratic wealth extremism as a "set of strong statements about the fact the losers deserve to lose, so to speak. The future structure of inequality might bring together extreme forms of domination based simultaneously on property and culture" (Piketty, 2015, p. 523). Therefore, in modern capitalist economies, meritocratic wealth extremism functions to establish and justify new structural/institutional arrangements in society (deregulation and corporatisation) and legitimise greater economic privilege, status and reward to the newly formed dominant wealthy groups (super managers) (Piachaud, 2014; Piketty, 2014a, pp. 8, 378).

Meritocratic wealth extremism helps explain the associated rise of the super manager and potentially "medium rentiers", in conjunction with neoliberal orthodoxy, as the newly formed meritocratic order of society during the late twentieth and early twenty-first centuries (Gale et al., 2017; Piketty, 2014a). The modern neoclassic reconstruction of meritocracy is different from nineteenth-century wealthy rentiers in patrimonial societies (where associated status, privilege and opportunity were attributed to inherited wealth, title and background); and the modern post war era to the 1970s (meritocracy based on social justice, egalitarianism and equality of opportunity) (Piketty, 2014a). Piketty (2014a, p. 334) found that meritocratic extremism reflected a newly formed belief representation that justified a new meritocratic order (hierarchy) in capitalist society. Under neoclassic economics, meritocratic wealth extremism perpetuated the belief that super managers possessed specific talents or expertise that were seen as greater than the qualifications or skills of others in the labour pool and therefore, super managers should receive greater privilege, status, and salaries and bonuses (Gale et al., 2017; Piketty, 2014a). The ideological function of the meritocratic wealth belief representation also corresponded with major structural adjustments in the labour market and taxation system, including financial deregulation (Blume & Durlauf, 2015). The consequence, as Piketty (2014a) reveals, has been an unprecedented, dramatic increase in income and wealth concentrated at the top that has not been in parallel, nor equitable with, increased wage or job mobility for the rest of the population (Piketty, 2014a, p. 299). Thus, while widening disparities have resulted in growing gaps between rich and poor, meritocratic discourses are used to justify and legitimate the privileged position of so-called "winners" in society (Gale et al., 2017). This research about wealth and income distribution in modern capitalist society is invaluable for exploring in policy education (Hopkins, 2014).

Exploring the ideological functions of meritocratic wealth extremism helps reveal the way it has legitimised greater financial rewards and status to particular groups (the dominant elite 1 per cent) over other groups (the other 99 per cent), and simultaneously restricted social mobility (Blume & Durlauf, 2015). As Piketty (2014a) states, such exposure brings to the fore of analysis the way "modern economic growth [has] … not modified the deep structures of capital and inequality" (Piketty, 2014a, p. 1). For policy education, such a formula makes visible belief representations and forces of divergence that reinforce and sustain unjust, oppressive policies (Boone et al., 2019; Preston & Aslett, 2014; Zubrzycki & McArthur, 2004). In doing so, the dominant individual self-sufficiency or deficit conceptualisations underpinning wealth distribution policies can be exposed and challenged.

Applying educational convergence through diffusion of knowledge for structural change

Social policy courses have long been a central pillar in the human services, community welfare and social work programs in education (Boone et al., 2019; Preston & Aslett, 2014; Reisch, 2013; Reisch & Jani, 2012). Piketty's (2014a, 2014b) work is invaluable to the teaching of social policy because it raises educators', students', and practitioners' critical consciousness about people in poverty, communities and vulnerable groups. Piketty (2014a, 2015) argues that if there is no intervention and the dominant neoclassic policy responses to inequality remain unchallenged, then the result is "potentially threatening to democratic societies and to the values of social justice on which they are based" (Piketty, 2014a, p. 398). As Piketty argues, "if democracy is someday to regain control of capitalism, it must start by recognizing that the concrete institutions in which democracy and capitalism are embodied need to be reinvented" (Piketty, 2014a, p. 570). Piketty's insights point to the need for deeper structural change, which can be found in his policy solutions that promote socially just redistribution. Such proposals are relevant to policy education because they point to the need for mechanisms of state regulation (modernising the state), tighter fiscal control and a progressive global wealth tax. Piketty (2017) has recently given weight to the credibility of basic income as part of the overall strategy in the pursuit of structural change. As Piketty (2014a) points out,

> if we are to regain control of capitalism, we must bet everything on democracy … The nation-state is still the right level at which to modernize any number of social and fiscal policies and to develop new forms of governance and shared ownership … which is one of the major challenges for the century ahead.
>
> *(p. 523)*

Education through diffusion of knowledge is the force for convergence that can help achieve this aim of progressing egalitarian structural change "to regain control of capitalism" (Piketty, 2015, p. 526).

Applying Piketty's (2014a) educational convergence through diffusion of knowledge to policy education, therefore, strengthens a critical pedagogical approach to policy. In creating space in the curriculum for Piketty's solutions, possibilities can emerge that help progress structural change (Piketty, 2015; Weiss-Gal, 2016). As Piketty cautions, if there is no attention to egalitarian solutions as part of a radical democratic strategy for change, then "there can be no economic [or social, political] democracy" (Piketty, 2015, p. 526). Such a potential outcome is important for policy education. Piketty also notes, "the twentieth century is not synonymous with a great leap forward in social justice" (Piketty, 2014a, p. 350). Policy education therefore plays an important political role in adopting his solutions to reinvision democratic futures.

Piketty (2014a) also explains that education can function as a powerful force for convergence through diffusion of knowledge. Educational convergence does this by using mechanisms such as diffusion of knowledge to produce new knowledge and approaches concerning "what public policies and institutions bring us closer to an ideal society?" (Piketty, 2014a, p. 574). Diffusion of knowledge refers to the central force pushing toward the reduction of inequality and creating fairer societies through knowledge dissemination and action in democratic spaces. Diffusion of knowledge, for Piketty, is not simply the passive transfer of knowledge in education. Piketty views diffusion of knowledge in terms of being a political and civic act; that is, a process for transmitting and sharing knowledge with an aim to bring about change. Knowledge diffusion creates the conditions for political engagement, and in turn prompts policy action to be enacted both within an educational setting and beyond to public policy spheres (Piketty, 2014a, p. 574). As Piketty suggests, "the analysis of representations and beliefs systems about income and wealth is an integral and indispensable part of the study of income and wealth dynamics", and diffusion of knowledge helps facilitate democratic engagement in the classroom environment and beyond (Piketty, 2015, p. 518). The curriculum and teaching space are critical pedagogical sites for creating the space for sharing knowledge (policy research and discussion) and participating in in-class activities (engaging in policy debates and role plays, or taking field trips to Parliament House) and applying insights in assignments (policy research paper, policy submission or policy brief). For Piketty, educational convergence through diffusion of knowledge is the stabilising force of convergence to translate theory into action.

In translating Piketty's (2014a) educational convergence to my own teaching of social policy within human services and social work education, I apply diffusion of knowledge to extend beyond traditional passive forms of knowledge transfer. Informed by Piketty's concepts and solutions, I have designed policy curricula, content and interactive activities that facilitate orienting students to the study of income and wealth dynamics, the analysis of divergent forces and corresponding belief representations to position Piketty's solutions as the central strategies for structural change. During early phase policy workshops, foundations are set by sharing lecture content on Piketty's formula and then engaging with students in discussions on the dynamics of wealth inequality and problems with hyper wealth and meritocratic wealth extremism. This assists in forming connections between Piketty's concepts and destabilising forces that erode democracy and the commitment of citizens to cooperate socially (Piketty, 2014a). This approach contributes to the creation of new knowledge around inequality dynamics and the way the history of wealth distribution is shaped and influenced by structural dimensions. In classes, current media articles, readings from Piketty and related others, lecture content, and excerpts from policy speeches, are used to frame small-group activities that support students' deeper level insights into inequality dynamics, divergent forces and potentialities for change. Critical questions are posed during activities to guide students in exploring the forces of divergence and the dominant viewpoints on what is considered just and also unjust, together with power dynamics and resultant policy outcomes (Piketty, 2015, p. 518). Diffusion of knowledge used in this way facilitates educator and students' critical thinking on the forces of divergence, destabilising features and structural dimensions of inequality based on historical trends (not individual self-sufficiency or deficit conceptualisations) associated with wealth and income distribution in modern capitalist society (Hopkins, 2014).

In furthering translating Piketty's (2014a) political approach, his policy solutions are applied to activities and discussions to help students conceptualise "what public policies and institutions bring us closer to an ideal society?" (Piketty, 2014a, p. 574), and the relevance of his change strategies for achieving "just" policy solutions that are both aspirational and concrete, are explicated. Piketty's solutions are essential for capturing concrete policy mechanisms that can progress structural change. His solutions offer an alternative vision that is a credible way forward for policy education to challenge increased inequality. This is especially crucial during the modern era where the problem of burgeoning inequality can appear to be unresolvable (as Piketty also indicated). Piketty's (2014a) solutions consist of redistribution through mechanisms of state regulation, tighter fiscal control and a progressive global wealth tax. Extending this, I have included universal basic income as part of the overall inequality-reducing mechanisms (similarly taken up by Piketty in 2017). He argues that incorporating basic income as part of the overall change strategy "implies re-thinking a whole set of institutions and policies which complement one another. These include a new system of basic income (*revenue universel*) which is more automatic and more efficient" (Piketty, 2017, para. 14). As a complementary mechanism, basic income provides an unconditional, regular payment (provision) to all citizens, regardless of being rich or poor, and with no strings attached (Widerquist, 2013). As a whole, these solutions disrupt neoclassic economics and unequal structures of society to forge new public policies and institutional arrangements grounded in social justice, egalitarianism and democracy (Mays et al., 2016). Piketty's (2014a) solutions are powerful resources for policy educators, students and practitioners to draw on, in the pursuit and application of strategies for structural change.

In consolidating the use of Piketty's (2014a) educational convergence through diffusion of knowledge, I have prescribed a policy submission assignment, with related in-class interactive activities, for supporting efforts toward policy change and engagement in democratic policy debate. The initial activity involves students and the educator participating in a field trip to Parliament House during a parliamentary session. The field trip provides an opportunity to observe an instance of knowledge diffusion in a democratic public space. Observation of such a session helps students to make sense of the forces of divergence in the contested space of policy debate, which are crucial for discerning contested ideas (belief representations) in the policy setting. Immersion in the parliamentary setting also reveals insight into the challenges of designing and implementing policy change and thinking through, how can Piketty's solutions be implemented (Piketty, 2014a). At a subsequent workshop, a follow up (parliamentary) role-play activity is implemented to give context, meaning and deeper insight into parliamentary processes, policy submission processes, political choices and policy outcomes. I have also introduced a role-play that helps position Piketty's solutions in the broader political context to anticipate barriers and challenges to policy implementation. This facilitates the practice of policy debate for policy persuasion. Piketty views participation in public democratic debates in policy spheres as central to the change process. Therefore, providing students with opportunities to practise debating, not only aligns with Piketty's vision, but also better prepares students for influencing policy debates.

Diffusion of knowledge is extended by supporting students to share insights within a group process. In assignment groups, students work together to develop a policy submission that contains a critical analysis and recommendations for policy change. Diffusion of knowledge occurs through sharing Piketty's (2014a) solutions for redistribution (state regulation, tighter fiscal control, a progressive global wealth tax and universal basic income) and exploring the way each solution represents an inequality-reducing mechanism that is socially just. Each of Piketty's solutions reflects a mechanism that redresses structural inequality, disadvantage and unequal societies. As policy mechanisms for change, his solutions redistribute wealth (social state and progressive taxation), rein in capitalism through fiscal controls (such as government regulations), and introduce universal schemes for the benefit of all in society (basic income), not just the wealthy few (Piketty, 2015). Piketty's (2014a) solutions applied in the classroom demonstrate concrete examples of mechanisms that promote inequality reduction, equality of opportunity, safeguarding of rights and equity in wealth distribution. As an invaluable resource, Piketty's solutions can be enacted in the students' policy submissions through the recommendations and strategies for change. In the current neoliberal political climate, such egalitarian solutions that offer concrete potentialities, are crucial for modifying, disrupting and transforming the deep structures of capital and inequality.

In sum, Piketty's (2014a) final suggestion for diffusion of knowledge, is taking action in intellectual and public policy spheres (that is, engagement in democratic debate). Following the completion of the policy submission assignment, students are supported to engage in public debates through presentation of their policy document to policy leaders, peak advocacy agencies or the community. They are supported to speak at public forums (rallies, public meetings) and to lobby government (Piketty, 2014a). Applying Piketty's approach and solutions reflect the goal of critical pedagogy in action.

Conclusion

On the surface, it may at first appear that Piketty's (2014a) *Capital in the Twenty-First Century* is an unlikely book for policy education and critical pedagogy in social work and human services. Yet, it is precisely his clear messages about the dynamics of inequality and need for structural change that makes Piketty's economic analyses an invaluable resource for policy education. His conceptual framework, based on the political economy tradition, contributes to forging a greater understanding of the dynamics of inequality. In building a conceptual picture for explaining structural inequality in wealth distribution, Piketty (2014a) also directs attention to the necessary solutions required for transforming the dominant neoclassic economic order that has entrenched inequality in Western capitalist economies. Here, Piketty (2014a) provides renewed socially just visions and egalitarian measures for structural change that challenge the established unequal social order (where greater concentrations of wealth remain in the hands of a wealthy few). Indeed, Piketty's (2014a) call for embedding the political economy in education and making explicit a political standpoint, is essential for those policy educators and students concerned with redressing burgeoning inequalities and fostering an egalitarian, just society.

This chapter shows how Piketty's (2014a) economic analyses and philosophical vision of an ideal society, when applied in the teaching within social work and human services space and beyond, function as forces for educational convergence. Seeking alternative egalitarian policy responses to dominant neoclassic economic policies is one such force for educational convergence. Using Piketty's (2014a) approach as a force for educational convergence becomes a process of political and critically informed discovery. Such discovery happens through the application of his concepts to address the seemingly insurmountable problem: inequality in wealth distribution. Translating Piketty's concepts helps uncover and make visible the destabilising divergent forces ($r > g$ inequality equation) and belief representations (meritocratic wealth extremism), which are the major threats to democratic society and socially just policy responses. He extends this approach further by illustrating how his egalitarian solutions for redistribution through mechanisms of state regulation, tighter fiscal control, a progressive global wealth tax and universal basic income are central mechanisms for countering and redressing inequality (Piketty, 2014a).

In the context of social work policy education, his conceptual framework is crucial for bringing about "real improvement in the living conditions of the least advantaged" (Piketty, 2014a, p. 336). For policy education, Piketty's diffusion of knowledge and guidance regarding solutions as change mechanisms, facilitates the discovery of alternative visions of society that can be used to inform broader public debate. In this way, Piketty's (2014a) approach functions as a critical pedagogy in policy education (Behring, 2018; Morley & Ablett, 2016, 2017). Unless there is disruption to neoclassic economics and growing inequality, then "it is almost inevitable [that the] … concentration of capital will attain extremely high levels—levels potentially incompatible with the meritocratic values and principles of social justice fundamental to modern democratic societies" (Piketty, 2014a, p. 26). Yet, Piketty's approach is necessary for informing structural analyses and change efforts because it presents possibilities for "avoiding an endless inegalitarian spiral" and reflects one way to reclaim "control over the dynamics of accumulation" to progress to a just society (Piketty, 2014a, p. 572).

Notes

1 The notion of capitalism in crisis refers to the modern capitalist conceptualisation of crisis (different from historical Marxist theorising around crisis of capitalism) whereby there are stark distinct features in contemporary Western industrial societies characterised by neoliberalism, minimal state regulation, political forces, beliefs and representations and structural adjustments that perpetuated

the concentration of wealth within the hands of a few wealthy people or corporations. The growth rate reached higher levels than the rate of return (Piketty, 2014a). These features together with the global financial crisis in 2008, decline of manufacturing, attacks on democracy, and an emerging robot economy and gig economy have generated greater levels of precarity, higher levels of unemployment, financial meltdowns, environmental crisis, food crisis, and growing poverty and inequality (Amin, 2010). The injustice of burgeoning inequality, if remaining unchecked, has dire consequences on the vast percentage of the population who do not share in the amassed wealth, that is, precarity and greater financial insecurity. Piketty (2014a) illustrates such a point in his claims that following a brief stabilisation between 1940 and 1970, the recent rapid rise in inequality and extreme growth of top incomes (wealth extremism) occurring since the 1980s is an intense contest for hegemonic power and control played out in the context of capitalism in crisis (Piketty, 2015). The broader global and national climate of economic stagnation, precarity through increased unemployment, underemployment or job insecurity, erosion of wages, pensions and benefits and reduction of public sector spheres has produced unparalleled challenges for social work education and professional practice.

References

Amin, S. (2010). Exiting the crisis of capitalism or capitalism in crisis?. *Globalizations*, 7 (1-2), 261–273.
Apple, M. W. (2016). Piketty, social criticism, and critical education. *British Journal of Sociology of Education*, 37 (6), 879–883.
Atkinson, A., & Harrison, H. (1978). *Distribution of personal wealth in Britain, 1923–1972*. Cambridge: Cambridge University Press.
Behring, E. (2018). Marx's influence on brazilian social work. *Critical and Radical Social Work*, 6 (2), 215–229.
Blume, L. E., & Durlauf, S. N. (2015). Capital in the twenty-first century: A review essay. *Journal of Political Economy*, 123 (4), 749–777.
Boone, K., Roets, G., & Roose, R. (2019). Raising critical consciousness in the struggle against poverty: Breaking a culture of silence. *Critical Social Policy*, 39 (3), 434–454.
Bourdieu, P. (1986). The forms of capital In J. G. Richardson Ed., *Handbook of theory and research for the sociology of education* 241–258. New York: Greenwood Press.
Daumard, A. (1973). *Les Fortunes françaises au XIXe siècle: Enquête sur la répartition et la composition des capitaux privés à Paris, Lyon, Lille, Bordeaux et Toulouse d'après l'enregistrement des déclarations de successions*. Paris: Mouton.
Gale, T., Molla, T., & Parker, S. (2017). The illusion of meritocracy and the audacity of elitism: Expanding the evaluative space in education In S. Parker, K. Gulson and T. Gale Eds., *Policy and inequality in education* 7–21. Education Policy and Social Inequality 1.. Singapore: Springer.
Gray, M., Dean, M., Agllias, K., Howard, A., & Schubert, L. (2015). Perspectives on neoliberalism for human service professionals. *Social Service Review*, 89 (2), 368–392.
Hopkins, J. (2014). The politics of Piketty: What political science can learn from, and contribute to, the debate on capital in the twenty-first century. *The British Journal of Sociology*, 65 (4), 678–695.
Kuznets, S. (1953). *Shares of upper income groups in income and savings, 1913–1948*. New York: National Bureau of Economic Research.
Labrousse, E. (1933). *Esquisse du mouvement des prix et des revenus en France au 18e siècle*. Paris: Alcan.
Mays, J., Marston, G., & Tomlinson, J. (2016). Neoliberal frontiers and economic insecurity: Is basic income a solution? In J. Mays, G. Marston and J. Tomlinson Eds., *Basic income in Australia and New Zealand: Perspectives form the neoliberal frontier* 1–25. New York: Palgrave Macmillan.
Milanovic, B. (2014). The return of "patrimonial capitalism": A review of Thomas Piketty's capital in the twenty-first century. *Journal of Economic Literature*, 52 (2), 519–534.
Morley, C., & Ablett, P. (2016). A critical social work response to wealth and income inequality. *Social Alternatives*, 35 (4), 20–26.
Morley, C., & Ablett, P. (2017). Rising wealth and income inequality: A radical social work critique and response. *Aotearoa New Zealand Social Work*, 29 (2), 6–16.
Piachaud, D. (2014). Piketty's capital and social policy. *British Journal of Sociology*, 65 (4), 696–707.
Piketty, T., & Saez, E. (2014). Inequality in the long run. *Science*, 344 (6186), 838–843.
Piketty, T. (2014a). *Capital in the Twenty-First Century*. Translated by Arthur Goldhammer. Cambridge: Harvard University Press.

Piketty, T. (2014b). Capital in the Twenty-First Century: A multidimensional approach to the history of capital and social classes. *The British Journal of Sociology*, 65 (4), 736–747.

Piketty, T. (2015). Capital, inequality, and power. *Journal of Ethnographic Theory*, 5 (1), 517–527.

Piketty, T. (2017 February 13). Is our basic income really universal? Le blog de Thomas Piketty [Web log post]. Retrieved from www.lemonde.fr/blog/piketty/2017/02/13/is-our-basic-income-really-universal/

Preston, S., & Aslett, J. (2014). Resisting neoliberalism from within the academy: Subversion through an activist pedagogy. *Social Work Education*, 33 (4), 502–518.

Reisch, M. (2013). Social work education and the neo-liberal challenge: The US response to increasing global inequality. *Social Work Education*, 32 (6), 715–733.

Reisch, M., & Jani, J. S. (2012). The new politics of social work practice: Understanding context to promote social change. *British Journal of Social Work*, 42 (6), 1132–1150.

Simiand, F. (1932). *Le Salaire, l'évolution sociale et la monnaie*. Paris: Alcan.

Stiglitz, J. (2013). *The price of inequality*. New York: Penguin.

Tarlau, R. (2016). If the past devours the future, why study? Piketty, social movements, and future directions for education. *British Journal of Sociology of Education*, 37 (6), 861–872.

Weiss-Gal, I. (2016). Policy practice in social work education: A literature review. *International Journal of Social Welfare*, 25 (3), 290–303.

Widerquist, K. (2013). *Independence, propertylessness and basic income*. Basingstoke: Palgrave Macmillan.

Wilkinson, R., & Pickett, K. (2009). *The spirit level: Why more equal societies always do better*. London: Allen Lane.

Zubrzycki, J., & McArthur, M. (2004). Preparing social work students for policy practice: An Australian example. *Social Work Education*, 23 (4), 451–464.

27
The radical potential of Carl Jung's wounded healer for social work education

Selma Macfarlane

DEAKIN UNIVERSITY, VICTORIA, AUSTRALIA

Introduction

Research indicates that social work students and practitioners come to the profession at least partly due to their own adverse experiences in childhood or adult life (see for example, Jarldorn et al., 2015; Newcomb et al., 2015). However, what they (students, who are emerging social workers) and we (social work educators) 'do' with this aspect of identity is not often explored, except to caution against over-identification with clients, warn against the dangers of self-disclosure, and highlight potentially increased vulnerability to vicarious trauma and burnout. While these are important concerns, in this chapter I consider the radical possibilities of more fully acknowledging and exploring our 'adverse life experiences' as part of social work education and critical anti-oppressive practice.

My interest has been prompted by my own experiences and by what Bachelor of Social Work (BSW) and qualifying Master of Social Work (MSWQ) students have shared, as they engage in increasingly complex activities of critical reflection as part of their studies and assessment tasks. This might begin with a simple exploration of their responses to challenging material in the curriculum. Later, it might include a more structured and in-depth exploration of assumptions that underpin practice in specific incidents and how one considers their positioning in terms of power and identity, such as the process put forward by Jan Fook (see, for example, Fook, 2016). In their critically reflective writing, many students reveal trauma, violence, abuse, and/or mental health struggles in their past and present, which, while having strong resonance with their experience as social work students and sense of self as emerging practitioners, are often perceived as 'no-go' areas within their formal social work education.

This chapter begins with a brief discussion of Carl Jung's concept of the wounded healer as expressed in his own work and in literature about his ideas. The discussion that follows, which comprises the bulk of the chapter, takes extensive liberties in spring-boarding from Jung's original concept to consider how the basic idea of a wounded healer can illuminate, inform and expand critical social work pedagogy and praxis.

Jung and the wounded healer

Carl Jung might not seem like a prime candidate for a chapter in a book on theorists or philosophers relevant to critical social work education. According to Jung himself, 'I am first and foremost a doctor and practising psychotherapist, and all my psychological formulations are based on the experiences gained in the hard course of my daily professional work' (Jung, 1937/2016, p.xiii). It is possible that critical social workers will cringe at the presumption that psychotherapeutic concepts have relevance to emancipatory social justice-oriented education and practice; even the use of the word 'healer' may be considered offensive, inappropriate or oppressive. However, Jung's body of ideas and published work is vast, and I believe there is value in considering this particular concept of the wounded healer in relation to critical social work. The word 'healer' will be used in this chapter, although 'worker' will be used more regularly; it is up to the reader to consider if and how they are different.

The concept of the wounded healer – 'the notion that people who have faced and overcome adversity might have special sensitivities and skills in helping others' – has deep historical roots (White, 2000, p.2). Jackson (2001) traces the notion that a healer's own suffering and vulnerability contribute to their ability to heal others: from Greek mythology, through Indigenous shamanism, Renaissance humanism, Christian pastoral care and more recent self-help movements. White (2000) observes that it may have been the emergence of psychotherapeutics and psychoanalysis in the late 19th and early 20th centuries, particularly the work of Sigmund Freud and Carl Jung, that enabled the concept to be more formally articulated.

Carl Jung was born to a poor family in a small village in Switzerland in 1875; his father was a parson who taught him Latin at an early age; his mother, a housewife, fostered his interest in the occult. Jung was haunted by his dreamworld from an early age as he realised his secret inner life of imagery and contemplation, and outer life as a confident schoolboy, were quite separate and different. At age 20, Jung received a grant to study medicine, with additional courses in science, philosophy, archaeology and history; his doctoral thesis was entitled 'On the psychology and pathology of so-called occult phenomena' (Dunne, 2000). In science, Jung said, he 'missed the factor of meaning; and in religion that of empiricism' and was 'torn between these two poles' (cited in Dunne, 2000, p.42). By age 25 he had been rapidly promoted to Deputy Director of a Zurich hospital and a lectureship at the University of Zurich. He worked with patients experiencing psychic disorders and 'unlike most practitioners of his day, he actually listened to their personal stories, paid attention to the context of their fantasies, discussed their dreams' (Dunne, 2000, p.43); the crucial point being, according to Jung, 'that I confront the patient as one human being to another' (cited in Dunne, 2000, p.44).

In the early 1900s Jung became a follower and supporter of Sigmund Freud, considered the founder of psychoanalysis, and a strong relationship ensued as the two corresponded over some years, eventually growing apart as their ideas clashed. Jung was delving into new studies around the collective unconscious as expressed in mythology, shamanism and primal culture and he wrote of his own painful journey toward self-realisation. His therapeutic approach with others focused on words and their underlying meanings, body language and dreams to discover the individual's own truth (Dunne, 2000). His studies in world religions, alchemy and archetypes continued as the great wars swept across the world, seeking to know more about the development of the internal spiritual self. Despite his achievements, which included many publications, Jung, in his late seventies, faced bouts of depression and self-doubt and craved silence and solitude. One of his most well-known books, *Man and His Symbols*, was his last work, completed ten days before his death in 1961 (Dunne, 2000).

The concept of the wounded healer was but one of many in Jung's vast repertoire of ideas, and while Jung speaks of physicians, healing, therapy and patients, as per his profession, in this lengthy quote we can grasp the essence of the concept under discussion:

> The intelligent psychotherapist has known for years that any complicated treatment is an individual, dialectical process, in which the doctor, as a person, participates just as much as the patient ... The patient ... can win his own inner security only from the security of his relationship to the doctor as a human being ... a good half of every treatment that probes at all deeply consists in the doctor's examining himself, for only what he can put right in himself can he hope to put right in the patient.
>
> *Jung (1953/1982, p.116)*

He further explains: 'it is his own hurt that gives the measure of his power to heal. This, and nothing else, is the meaning of the Greek myth of the wounded physician' (Jung, 1953/1982, p.116).

Jung's explication of the wounded physician, often referred to in more general terms as the wounded healer, has been taken up by some in 'helping professions' such as nursing, psychology, medicine and social work, who suggest that all humans – including 'helpers' – are wounded and have experienced various degrees of trauma and disturbance (Christie & Jones, 2014; Cvetovac & Adame, 2017; Jarldorn et al., 2015; Newcomb et al., 2015). Moreover, they suggest, these experiences can be drawn upon in the interests of those we intend to assist or support. Within those professions there are also concerns around this woundedness, ranging from potential damage to the worker–client relationship through over-identification, to very real fears that revealing one's own wounds (such as past traumas, past or current mental health struggles) will create negative consequences for professionals themselves. While these concerns are valid, they will not be the focus of this chapter. In the next section, I turn to a brief examination of those who enter higher education, and social work education more particularly, as a contextual element in this discussion.

Student demographics, social work and today's university

As access to higher education in Western societies, such as Australia, has widened in recent years, student diversity has increasingly included those who are described variously as 'first in family', from 'low socio-economic-status' backgrounds, 'culturally and linguistically diverse', or coming via 'non-traditional pathways'. Some educators have described this shifting demographic as a time when more university students have 'special needs ... broken wing students' (Morgan 2000, cited in Ejsing, 2007, p.240), engendering greater distances between students themselves and between teachers and students (Bleich, 1993, p.44). McArdle and Mansfield (2007, p.487) observe that despite growing diversity in universities, the mainstream or 'middle-class' orientation of the classroom continues to devalue or silence diverse voices, despite university rhetoric around inclusiveness. It is clear that diversity has become a natural feature of today's world where people from vastly different places cross paths and where increasingly fewer fixed truths, divisions and ways of making meaning are relevant (Belenky & Stanton, 2000). 'Building discursive bridges' to span potential gaps between Western academia and the socio-cultural and experiential world of students is a growing topic in literature discussing changes in higher education and the pedagogical approaches such changes require (see, for example, Booth, 2012; Jarldorn et al., 2015). In relation to social work, Jarldorn et al. (2015) comment that, while the discipline has always drawn students who have experienced, and may continue to experience, hardship, distressing life disruptions and disadvantage, the new demographic of students means that more are coming in with personal experiences of adversity or service use, which have often been instrumental in their choice to study social work.

At the same time that diversity in the classroom is increasing, trends to buffer students from exposure to anything different from themselves, particularly 'people and ideas one might find uncongenial or wrong' have been identified (Lukianoff & Haidt, 2015, p.45). Students are paying for their degree, and academics are under increasing scrutiny and pressure to ensure 'student satisfaction'. The movement to 'scrub campuses clean of words, ideas and subjects that might cause discomfort or give offense' is, according to Lukianoff and Haidt (2015, p.44) a form of misguided protectiveness that poorly prepares students for professional life and engagement with a range of people and ideas. Freire and Macedo (2001, cited in Van Gorder, 2007, p.9) refer to this as the 'anesthetization of the mind', which is particularly worrying for social work: if students cannot engage with challenging materials, experiences or concepts in the classroom; it raises questions about their potential ability to listen and respond to service users in professional practice (Tew et al., 2012) and to engage in active critical reflection on themselves as practitioners.

Critical social work education rejects this anesthetisation and is aligned not only with social work values and priorities, but also with critical pedagogy more generally. As the discussion proceeds, teasing out various elements of critical social work education, I increasingly make conceptual links with Jung and the resonance of the wounded healer concept.

Critical social work pedagogy and education

Whether explicitly acknowledged or not, higher education is always based on wider social purposes – all educational structures and theories are political (Leibowitz et al., 2010; McArthur, 2010) and connected 'to social change and to issues of power' (McArthur, 2010, p.304). Campbell (2002) observes that while working with difference is a core concept within anti-oppressive approaches, teaching and learning about difference is not necessarily experienced first-hand in the classroom. She suggests five strategies of anti-oppressive pedagogy to guide classroom practice: modelling anti-oppressive practice, deconstructing traditional knowledge claims, promoting self-awareness in the exploration of identity, supporting and valuing affective learning, and negotiating power and authority. In the 'liberatory social work classroom', students 'experience first the concepts and principles they are expected to apply in their work with clients: awareness of feelings, validation of life experience and holding the theories being taught up to the light of one's own experience'. The classroom, says Campbell (2002, p.38), is our practice location, where we can 'demonstrate effective anti-oppressive practice and prepare students for action as well as abstraction'.

Education for social justice, according to Van Gorder (2007, p.16), encourages students of diverse backgrounds to hear each others' stories and to learn in contexts of difference. This can often be emotional and discomforting for students (and educators) from both marginal and dominant groups. A 'pedagogy of discomfort invites students to critique deeply held assumptions and destabilise their view of themselves and their world'; it includes a moral and emotional component, calling students to take responsibility for their self – to acknowledge their location and their agenda (Leibowitz et al., 2010, p.84). A critical theory of adult learning, according to Brookfield (2005, pp.144–5), considers how students become aware of their power and 'what happens to them when they do'. Here and now moments that reveal vulnerability or woundedness can provide opportunities for students to become aware of their own social location, validate life experience as a legitimate form of knowledge, and feel their power to be effective as they practise anti-oppressive skills (Campbell, 2002). Conversations, for example about race and white privilege, require courage and commitment; rather than closing down difficult discussions. Singleton and Hayes (2013) suggest that we engage *more deeply* when people speak their truth, drawing on skills of active listening, inquiring and responding.

Askeland (2003, p.357) observes that 'what people take in and make their own is most likely that to which they react emotionally, whatever the feelings are'. Expressions of emotions such as fear, guilt, uncertainty or anxiety are anathema to neoliberal tenets in which 'mastery, instrumentality, invulnerability, and emotional self-control' are valorised (Gannon et al., 2015, p.193). Conversely, Jung's notion of the wounded healer is prefaced on an understanding of the worker/therapist/helper as vulnerable, and that this vulnerability – 'wholeness rather than "clean hands" perfection' – is a source of strength in assisting others and contributing to one's own transformation (Wheeler, 2007, pp.246–7). Wheeler describes vulnerability as 'being real – the capacity to feel at a deep level [and] openness to pain and the experience of others' (2007, p.247). In social work, we often talk about our clients as 'vulnerable,' connoting disempowerment; on the odd occasion when we use the word to speak of ourselves, it is as something to be wary of, such as vulnerability to burnout, over-identification with clients, or weakness.

Gilson (2011) observes that denial of human vulnerability is not only oppressive, but ethically and politically dangerous – its pursuit a form of ignorance. 'Being vulnerable', she says,

> makes it possible for us to suffer, to fall prey to violence and be harmed, but also to fall in love, to learn, to take pleasure and find comfort in the presence of others, and to experience the simultaneity of these feelings,

Enabling us to '[be] affected and affecting in turn' in both positive and negative ways (Gilson, 2011, p.310). Projecting vulnerability onto others and de-identifying with those vulnerable 'others' she says, can be 'motivated by the desire – conscious or not – to maintain a certain kind of subjectivity privileged in capitalist socioeconomic systems, namely, that of the prototypical, arrogantly self-sufficient, independent, invulnerable master subject' (Gilson, 2011, p.312).

Woundedness implies vulnerability, which is viewed and experienced as a common bond among humans whether workers or clients or both, not only personally, 'but also about the way we are in communities, the way we relate to our planet' and the way we go on as 'the randomness of the universe continues to ricochet through all our lives' (Martin, 2011, p.14). This sense of common humanity and vulnerability is a powerful challenge to paternalistic or stigmatising constructions of others as 'projects' or as 'objectified victims floundering in an identity limited to oppression alone' (Freire, 1970/1990, cited in Van Gorder, 2007, p.16).

Unfortunately, much social work literature – consciously or unconsciously – constructs the identity of worker and client as binary opposites: identities that are relatively fixed and mutually exclusive. This can be unconsciously reflected and reinforced in the classroom as our emancipatory intentions are compromised by the 'dominance protecting mechanisms' of professions, including social work. We become complicit in consigning 'the client population' to 'the eternity of a client identity' (Lorenzetti, 2013, p.52) whose status is ascribed 'through the prism of one aspect' of their life (McLaughlin, 2009, p.1108), that is constructed as 'other' to our own.

It is possible that this dichotomisation of identities has, paradoxically, been reinforced as social work educators have increasingly brought service users, particularly those involved with mental health services, into the classroom, so students can learn from their experiences. Responses are generally positive, with students indicating the experience 'provided a link with the real world' (Irvine et al., 2015, p.138). This practice is well intentioned, given that mental health professionals, including social workers, still hold stigmatising attitudes toward people experiencing mental illness despite their commitment to empowering relationships (Zellmann et al., 2014).

The image of the wounded healer 'tells us that the patient has a healer within, as much as the healer has a patient within' (Benziman et al., 2012, n.p.). Bharati Sethi identifies herself as a consumer of mental health services as well as a provider, a student, and a professor, a social worker and a client. She contends that

> although listening to the stories of the clients we meet ... is integral to creating individual and structural changes and raising awareness of mental health issues, ... it is just as important to share our own personal and collective stories of mental health, stigma and recovery.
> *(2013, p. 175)*

This sharing, she believes, challenges the divide that continues to characterise social work education and practice – the 'us/them' split between service provider and service user, and the expert and the client.

Identities, according to Clarke (2009) are both given (by oneself and others) and achieved within processes of becoming. Critical social work education aims for students to engage in potentially transformative experiences – becoming allies in struggles for social justice (Curry-Stevens, 2007, p.33). This involves 'unlearning domination', a form of spiritual awakening 'that allows learners to expand their circle of compassion while at the same time feeling profoundly interconnected with others' (Curry-Stevens, 2007, p.40). This feeling of interconnection with others poses a critical challenge to oppressive neoliberal discourses of individualism, commodification and static, polarised identities.

Within Jung's archetype, woundedness alone does not make a helping professional into a healer: it is not the degree of woundedness that holds healing power 'but the ability to draw on woundedness in the service of healing' (Zerubavel & Wright, 2012, p.482). Central to Jung's interpretation was a process of ongoing transformation 'in order to be enlightened by the experience of trauma or adversity' (Newcomb et al., 2015, p.57). The wounded healer, Zerubavel and Wright (2012) stress, is not the same as the 'impaired professional', whose personal distress impacts negatively on their work with others. Christie and Jones (2014, n.p.) describe 'the walking wounded', in contrast to the wounded healer, as those professionals who 'project their woundedness on both patients and colleagues while considering themselves unharmed'.

Given the prevalence of adverse experiences in both social work student and practitioner cohorts, how can we acknowledge and play some part, as social work educators, in this potentially transformational process? (How) can we assist students to learn how their experiences might interact with their professional development? (Newcomb et al., 2015, p.58). (How) can we acknowledge that personal experience as a potential resource for constructing professional identity and assist emerging practitioners to understand 'how and when to draw on personal history and experience'? (Seden 2011, cited in Wiles, 2013, p.861). How can the process of transformation from 'the walking wounded' to a 'wounded healer' (Christie & Jones, 2014) be facilitated, and (how) can it be addressed in critical social work education?

Taking it to the classroom

Individual and collective storytelling in social work education has the potential to change the vocabulary and the discourse style of our classrooms, providing a basis in human experience with our engagement in practice (Bleich, 1993). A 'pedagogy of disclosure needs and asks to know who is in class with us ... [believing] that what each person brings to the classroom must become part of the curriculum for that course' (Bleich, 1995, p.47). This, Bleich (1995, p.49) suggests, creates a 'collective accomplishment' that enfranchises everyone's need to learn from each other. The sharing of stories by lecturers and students can contribute to an anti-oppressive environment by engaging in mutual consciousness-raising and reducing power differentials – although this is not without risk – while modelling the sorts of collaborative partnerships that extend beyond the classroom and into practice (Campbell, 2002). Our classrooms could be a place 'where we can demand of ourselves and our comrades an openness of mind and heart … as we collectively imagine ways to move beyond boundaries' (hooks, cited in Campbell, 2002, p.39).

Debates in professional practice realms are mirrored in the educational context: views on the use of self-disclosure range from being considered 'strictly taboo' to being viewed as an important element of genuineness, connectedness, power sharing and mutual consciousness-raising. Students, new graduates and experienced practitioners may have widely divergent opinions around the appropriateness of self-disclosure in education or in critical practice, and justifiably so; self-disclosure can be risky, particularly if it involves 'weakness' or woundedness. Bleich (1995, p.44) observes that practising self-disclosure carries personal, professional and political ramifications that need to be anticipated if exchanging parts of our 'inner or unapparent lives' with others. Critical consciousness does not come easily; we have a duty of care for students. Increasingly, we are urged to include 'trigger warnings' in our teaching to reduce potential harm to students around confronting classroom content. Students are encouraged to 'do what they have to do' to take care of themselves (Kafer, 2016, p.5).

As previously discussed, bringing real-world experience – stories of woundedness and/or resilience – into the classroom can bring strong emotions, which are sometimes difficult or uncomfortable. However, these emotions can result in powerful and transformative learning outcomes, giving voice and validity to stories that might otherwise be excluded (Booth, 2012): 'stories of suffering and revival … are transformative in nature, a protest against silence and a call for personal and political change' (Berman, 2001, cited in Lucas, 2007, p.370). Indeed, the word 'voice' rather than 'self-disclosure' has been proposed, as a way of reducing power differentials in the classroom and modelling a learning partnership that could carry through into professional practice (Zapf, 1997, cited in Campbell, 2002, pp.35–6).

The sharing of stories by educators and students, for example, by using experiential exercises that involve 'self-disclosure, personal narrative and humour' might be a way of making content more relevant to students from diverse backgrounds, creating a 'pedagogical bridge' between one's own world and the learning material (Ejsing, 2007, p.238). For social work education, we want to avoid unintentionally fostering environments where 'students and the content of the lectures remain strangers to each other, except that each student has become the owner of a collection of statements made by somebody else' (Fromm, 1976, cited in Brookfield, 2005, p.167). The creation of 'authentic learning activities' has received much rhetorical attention in recent years at universities, with the aim of integrating 'real-world' relevance into the classroom and deepening student engagement (Booth, 2012, p.7). On a deeper and more challenging level, Booth (2012, p.8), referring to Mezirow, suggests this creates transformative learning, as 'individuals' critically reflect on their experiences, beliefs and assumptions and thus change their frames of reference.

Froggett et al. (2015, p.135) contend that 'students need to think *from* experience with concepts which help them think *about* experience'; ideally this involves having students become 'more aware of their psychological selves in relation to the work they do, whilst maintaining a socially critical stance' (Froggett et al., 2015, p.140). Froggett et al. (2015, p.144) work with students to help them come to an appreciation of 'how practice nearness' and 'practice distance are distinct and complementary roles'. Newcomb et al. (2015, p.65) observe 'the personalisation of theory allows for authentic learning' allowing past difficulties to be 'reframed as a stepping stone towards the development of professional resilience'. Meekums (2008) describes an autobiographical process in which she traced the development of her identity and her wish to be a counsellor/trainer, reflecting on her past life experiences to find that certain elements of her identity enabled her to productively transform other less empowered elements. She discovered that all the elements combined to form a rich tapestry. Her love of writing – her 'embodied wordsmith identity' – transformed her experience of woundedness due to disability, 're-authoring the story to contain and contextualise it, thus detoxifying and depersonalising the narrative' so that she no longer felt 'compelled to relive it' (Meekums, 2008, p.291). By asking 'How did I get here?' in relation to her professional choice, she was able to identify 'what was it in my body's story that led me here and offered something valuable in my new role' (Meekums, 2008, p.288). In her words, this exploration allowed her to 'reposition myself with one eye on my own story and another on a sociological and political analysis' (Meekums, 2008, p.289). Engaging in this process enabled her to feel a greater sense of confidence in her present multifaceted identity and the rich experiences she brought to her work.

According to Ejsing (2007, p.237), because 'self-disclosure engages students so effectively, the post-disclosure learning process is perhaps the time when students' minds are most receptive'. When students are confronted by 'critical engagement with the material in front of them', educators can purposefully guide them through the tension that may arise between comfort and discomfort, generating an atmosphere where ideas become real. When theory becomes connected to experience, 'learners have only entered the space where they are ready to learn, just as teachers have only entered the space where they must be prepared to teach' (Ejsing, 2007, p.242); this can be a challenging experience for educators. However, this space of 'critical consciousness' is one that, according to Gramsci, is necessary to enter into authentic self-directed learning, comprised of the adult student's 'perception of herself as an outsider ... a basic sense of independence and separateness ... followed by a consciousness of one's own place in a hegemonic or counterhegemonic group' (Brookfield, 2005, p.107).

The sharing and hearing of these stories, Lucas (2007) suggests, may require nothing other than an empathic and non-judgemental response; however, while the act of teaching in the 'contact zone' is one where 'no one is excluded', it may also be one where 'no one [is] safe' (Pratt 2002, cited in Lucas, 2007, p.377). So, how do we protect students against harmful reactions from others while providing them with the tools they need to critically engage with material that straddles the realms of comfort and discomfort (Ejsing, 2007)? Equally important, how do we create a classroom culture in which diverse stories of privilege and oppression, woundedness, vulnerability and healing can be shared in ways that promote mutual consciousness-raising and transformation? What does it mean for a classroom to be both 'safe' and critical?

A safe classroom, according to Holly and Steiner (2005, cited in Nicotera & Kang, 2009, p.193) is 'one in which students are able to openly express their individuality, even if it differs dramatically from the norms set by the instructor, the profession, or other students'. Supportive spaces where this can occur can be developed, as can unsupportive spaces, although the former requires more conscious effort. A safe critical space is one where students and educators can engage in genuine examination of their own assumptions, experiences and social locations, as well as those deeply embedded in social work theory and practice. Sharing stories of being and becoming, finding and expressing voice are not meant to serve as confessionals, but contribute to the creation and evolution of a learning environment where students are active 'co-investigators who learn to take multiple perspectives on their own prior knowledge and beliefs, on each other's viewpoints and on the course content' (Rasmussen & Mishna, 2003, p.40).

In a 'pedagogy of disclosure', sharing information about oneself is not forced, but because 'each member of a classroom actually has an individual history, habitual and scholarly reference to it becomes part of the process of presenting, opinions, interpretations and reports of other things' (Bleich, 1993, p.48). A pedagogy of disclosure, according to Bleich (1993, p.49), honours students by having their own histories and cultures recognised in the classroom, helping to teach students to demand 'non-alienated work, to make their work more a part of their identities, their identities more connected to others, and their vocations more palpably implicated in society and in other people's needs'. This process is one that mirrors and actively addresses the transformation from walking wounded to wounded healer, or, in terms more aligned with critical social work, the incorporation of intersecting elements of one's identity into one that is critically engaged with power, intersectionality and meaningful challenge to oppressive and exclusionary discourse.

Merlinda Weinberg (2015) observes that one of the difficult tasks for critical social work education is balancing emerging social workers' sense that they have knowledge and skills that are useful in the service of others, while avoiding the assumption of some sort of superiority in which service users become passive recipients of their expertise. She uses an experiential exercise to help students realise the complexity of the helper/helped binary and reduce potential for 'othering' that is rife in human services and social policy. She acknowledges with her students that many of those in the classroom have their own experiences as service users and that she wants to give an opportunity to hear those experiences. She asks students to privately contact her to discuss the story the student wishes to share, what it might be like to do so, and whether the material is too raw to share. Before the student shares their story, she reiterates rules about confidentiality with the class. After the presentation, she goes around the group to hear what they have taken away from the experience. She has found students consider this one of the most meaningful and useful experiences they have had, realising they are not different from the clients they work with. Weinberg (2015, p.236) concludes by emphasising the importance of trust in the classroom, but at the same time, she says,

> 'safety' is problematic as a term to describe the environment, since shaking up basic assumptions and beliefs is a key component of critical education ... when students come to me and say they are confused and distressed by what they are learning, I applaud and suggest that this may be a sign they are really grappling with material ... trust rather than safety is the intended environment.

She does not always use this exercise, depending on the cohesion and dynamic of the class.

The creation of a 'holding environment' is important for all concerned; Ward (2008) describes the anxieties experienced by students in his social work seminar series when he asked them to compile a lifeline listing the main events of their lives and identify the emotions they associated with some of them. Some chose not to participate as they thought there was a risk of stirring up powerful feelings that they preferred not to revisit; some describe feeling shocked by what their personal and family histories revealed; others were concerned they would be 'found out' as less than professional; while others were dismayed that their personal issues were following them into the academic world. At the same time, the majority of students reported they had found the exercise valuable to their professional learning. In evaluating their seminars, Ward and his colleagues developed a number of key themes about how to create a holding environment: combining the sense of an open space to explore the overlaps between personal, professional and intellectual learning with a sense of that space being structured sufficiently to prevent anxiety taking over; a sense of a process of learning evolving through time and within 'unfolding relations', a message that strong emotions 'which may arise from examining one's personal experience in the context of professional development will be respected, validated and "contained" by both peers and tutors' (Ward, 2008, p.80).

Conclusion

This chapter has invited consideration of whether, and how, critical social work education can draw on Jung's concept of the wounded healer to challenge binary oppositional thinking, learn from diverse knowledge sources and bring anti-oppressive practice into our classrooms. As outlined earlier, many social work students are motivated by their own challenging or adverse experiences to enter the profession. Jung believed that these experiences of woundedness could enhance one's ability to 'heal' if engaged with transformatively. In today's neoliberalised and risk-averse society that locates the causes of social problems in individual deficiency, which has (unfortunately) been transferred into social work education and practice, it might be hard to consider anything that would 'rock the boat' or suggest that there is not a clear delineation between the helped and the helpers. The issue for social work educators to consider, is whether there is a role for critical social work educators in traversing the helper/helped divide, in actively bringing the personal and the political together in our classrooms and being part of the transformative experience that enables our lived experiences to be validated and theorised as part of the process of becoming critical social workers.

References

Askeland, G 2003, 'Reality-play – Experiential learning in social work training: a teaching model,' *Social Work Education*, 22 (4), pp 351–362.

Belenky, M & Stanton, A 2000, 'Inequality, development and connected knowledge,' In J. Mezirow & Associates, ed., *Learning as transformation: critical perspectives on a theory in progress*, Jossey-Bass, San Francisco, pp 71–102.

Benziman, G, Kannal, R & Ahmad, A 2012, 'The wounded healer as cultural archetype,' *Comparatie Literature and Culture*, 14 (1).

Bleich, D 1995, 'Collaboration and the pedagogy of disclosure,' *College English*, 57 (1), January 1993, pp 43–61.

Booth, M 2012, 'Boundaries and student self-disclosure in authentic, integrated learning activities and assignments,' *New Directions for Teaching and Learning*, 131, Fall 2012, pp 5–14.

Brookfield, S 2005, *The power of critical theory for adult learning and teaching*, Open University Press, Maidenhead.

Campbell, C 2002, 'The search for congruency: developing strategies for anti-oppressive social work pedagogy,' *Canadian Social Work Review*, 19 (1), pp 25–42.

Christie, W & Jones, S 2014, 'Lateral violence in nursing and the theory of the nurse as wounded healer,' *Journal of Issues in Nursing*, 19 (1), January 2014, pp n.p.

Clarke, M 2009, 'The ethico-politics of teacher identity,' *Educational Philosophy and Theory*, 41 (2), pp 185–200.

Curry-Stevens, A 2007, 'New forms of transformative education: pedagogy for the privileged,' *Journal of Transformative Education*, 5 (33), pp 33–58.

Cvetovac, M & Adame, A 2017, 'The wounded therapist: understanding the relationship between personal suffering and clinical practice,' *The Humanistic Psychologist*, 45 (4), pp 348–366.

Dunne, C 2000, *Wounded healer of the soul: Carl Jung*, Parabola Books, USA.

Ejsing, A 2007, 'Power and caution: the ethics of self-disclosure,' *Teaching Theology and Religion*, 10 (4), pp 235–243.

Fook, J 2016, *Social work: a critical approach to practice*, (3rd edn.), SAGE Publications, London.

Froggett, L, Ramvi, E & Davies, L 2015, 'Thinking from experience in psychosocial practice: reclaiming and teaching 'use of self',' *Journal of Social Work Practice*, 29 (2), pp 133–150.

Gannon, S, Kligyte, G, McLean, J, Perrier, M, Swan, E, Vanni, I, & van Rijswijk, H 2015, 'Uneven realities, collective biography, and sisterly affect in neoliberal universities,' *Feminist Formations*, 27 (3), pp 189–216.

Gilson, E 2011, 'Vulnerability, ignorance and oppression,' *Hypatia*, 26 (2), Spring 2011, pp 308–332.

Irvine, J, Molyneux, J & Gillman, M 2015, '"Providing a link with the real world": learning from the student experience of service user and carer involvement in social work education,' *Social Work Education*, 34 (2), pp 138–150.

Jackson, S 2001, 'Presidential address: the wounded healer,' *Bulletin of the History of Medicine*, 75 (1), pp 1–36.

Jarldorn, M, Beddoe, L, Fraser, H & Michell, D 2015, 'Planting a seed: encouraging service users towards educational goals,' *Social Work Education*, 34 (8), pp 921–935.

Jung, CG 1937/2016, *Psychological types*, Routledge, Great Britain or UK.

Jung, CG 1953/1982, 'The practice of psychotherapy: The collected works of C.G. Jung, volume 16: Practice of psychotherapy,' In Adler R. F. C. Hull, ed., *Series: collected works of C.G. Jung*, Princeton University Press, Princeton, New Jersey, USA.

Kafer, A 2016, 'Un/safe disclosures: scenes of disability and trauma,' *Journal of Literary & Cultural Disability Studies*, 10 (1), pp 1–20.

Leibowitz, B, Bozalek, V, Rohlder, P, Crolissen, R & Swartz, L 2010, '"Ah, but the whiteys love to talk about themselves:" discomfort as a pedagogy for change,' *Race Ethnicity and Education*, 13 (1), pp 83–100.

Lorenzetti, L 2013, 'Developing a cohesive emancipatory social work identity: risking an act of love,' *Critical Social Work*, 14 (2), pp 48–59.

Lucas, J 2007, 'Getting personal: responding to student self-disclosure,' *TETYC*, 34 (4) May 2007, pp 367–379.

Lukianoff, G & Haidt, J 2015, 'The coddling of the American mind,' *The Atlantic*, September 2015, pp 42–52.

Martin, P 2011, 'Celebrating the wounded healer,' *Counselling Psychology Review*, 26 (1), March 2011, pp 10–19.

McArdle, K & Mansfield, S 2007, 'Voice, discourse and transformation: enabling learning for the achieving of social change,' *Discourse: Studies in the Cultural Politics of Education*, 28 (4), December 2007, pp 485–498.

McArthur, J 2010, 'Time to look anew: critical pedagogy and disciplines within higher education,' *Studies in Higher Education*, 35 (3), pp 301–315.

McLaughlin, H 2009, 'What's in a name: 'client,' 'patient,' 'customer,' 'consumer,' 'expert by experience,' 'service user,' – What's next?,' *British Journal of Social Work*, 39, pp 1101–1117.

Meekums, B 2008, 'Embodied narratives in becoming a counselling trainer: an autoethnographic study,' *British Journal of Guidance & Counselling*, 36 (3), pp 287–301.

Newcomb, M, Burton, J, Edwards, N & Hazelwood, Z 2015, 'How Jung's concept of the wounded healer can guide learning and teaching in social work and human services,' *Advances in Social Work & Welfare Education*, 17 (2), pp 55–69.

Nicotera, N & Kang, H 2009, 'Beyond diversity courses: strategies for integrating critical consciousness across social work curriculum,' *Journal of Teaching in Social Work*, 29 (2), pp 188–203.

Rasmussen, B & Mishna, F 2003, 'The relevance of contemporary psychodynamic theories to teaching social work,' *Smith College Studies in Social Work*, 74 (1), pp 32–47.

Sethi, B 2013, 'Reclaiming self,' *Journal of Progressive Human Services*, 24 (3), pp 175–186.

Singleton, G & Hayes, C 2013, 'Beginning courageous conversations about race,' In M. Pollack, ed., *Everyday anti-racism: getting real about race in school*, The New Press, New York, pp 18–23.

Tew, J, Holley, T & Caplen, P 2012, 'Dialogue and challenge: involving service users and carers in small group learning with social work and nursing students,' *Social Work Education*, 31 (3), pp 316–330.

Van Gorder, A 2007, 'Pedagogy for the children of the oppressors: liberative education for social justice among the world's privileged,' *Journal of Transformative Education*, 5 (8), pp 8–32.

Ward, A 2008, 'Beyond the instructional mode: creating a holding environment for learning about the use of self,' *Journal of Social Work Practice*, 22 (1), pp 67–83.

Weinberg, M 2015, 'Professional privilege, ethics and pedagogy,' *Ethics and Social Welfare*, 9 (3), pp 225–239.

Wheeler, S 2007, 'What shall we do with the wounded healer? The supervisor's dilemma,' *Psychodynamic Practice*, 13 (3), August 2007, pp 245–256.

White, W 2000, 'The history of recovered people as wounded healers,' *Alcoholism Treatment Quarterly*, 18 (1), pp 1–23.

Wiles, F 2013, '"Not easily put into a box:" constructing professional identity,' *Social Work Education*, 32 (7), pp 854–866.

Zellmann, E, Madden, E & Aguiniga, D 2014, 'Bachelor of social work students and mental health stigma: understanding student attitudes,' *Journal of Social Work Education*, 50, pp 660–677.

Zerubavel, N & Wright, M 2012, 'The dilemma of the wounded healer,' *Psychotherapy*, 49 (4), pp 482–491.

28
Embedding the queer and embracing the crisis
Kevin Kumashiro's anti-oppressive pedagogies for queering social work education and practice

Jen Kaighin
QUEENSLAND UNIVERSITY OF TECHNOLOGY, AUSTRALIA

Introduction

This chapter draws on the work of Kevin Kumashiro to examine the implications of his work for how we prepare social work students to work with the queer community. It will also explicate the relevance of Kumashiro's concepts to social work education and practice more broadly. Specifically, this chapter will discuss four distinctive approaches to anti-oppressive education that Kumashiro both summarises and critiques. These are: education for the 'other'; education about the 'other'; education that is critical of privileging and othering; and education that changes students and society (Kumashiro, 2000a). This chapter discusses the challenges and opportunities that might lie within each approach for a queer social work education and practice. In examining these approaches I will also discuss some of Kumashiro's key concepts, including embedding the queer, embracing crisis, troubling the comforting act of repetition, moving through 'stuck' places in engaging with ideas, and the transformative potential that can be found in the space between what is taught and what is learned.

Kevin Kumashiro is an American educator. He was born in Hawaii and identifies as Asian American and Queer. Kumashiro has taught in schools and colleges across the United States and is the Former Dean of the School of Education at the University of San Francisco. Kumashiro received his PhD from the University of Wisconsin-Madison in 2000 and has gone on to publish ten books as well as dozens of articles and essays. Kumashiro is a founding member of The Center for Anti-Oppressive Education; Education Deans for Justice and Equity; the California Alliance of Researchers for Equity in Education; and Chicagoland Researchers and Advocates for Transformative Education. He is now a consultant, educator and activist and a frequent commentator and critic of education 'reforms' in the Trump era.

Kumashiro, uses the term queer in his writings to refer to people who are lesbian, gay, bisexual, transgender, intersexed, or in other ways 'queer' because of their sexual identity or gender orientation. I also use the term queer throughout this chapter, apart from when citing the works of authors who use LGBTIQ and variations of this. Kumashiro refers to queer for its inclusiveness, but also for its 'pedagogical and political significance' (2001a, p.26). He states that the term invokes a history of bigotry and hatred, which continues, however, it also signifies a rejection of normative sexualities and genders and has been used as an empowering term in the reclamation of identities and of ideas. Willis (2007) agrees, stating that 'queer' has been reclaimed by activists and academics 'both as an umbrella term for representing all non-normative sexualities and gender positions, and as a body of critical theory'. Kumashiro argues that the notion of queer is inherently uncomfortable. Queerness is often constructed as a binary opposite to 'normal'. Kumashiro suggests that being normal is similar to doing what is common sense, conforming, comfortable. A goal for anti-oppressive teaching is to disrupt normative ideas, and this process can be uncomfortable for both students and educators. As queerness is positioned within the mainstream as anti-normative, teaching queer ideas is often avoided. However, anti-oppressive education involves constantly looking beyond what we teach and learn (Kumashiro, 2001a) and being queer, rather than being abnormal can be disruptive and empowering, For social work education, Kumashiro offers a path toward embedding queer teaching and learning practices that will build students' capacity to not only work with queer individuals and communities, but also work toward social justice and personal transformation.

The silencing of queer in social work education

Anti-oppressive practice lies at the heart of social work, as is espoused by the Australian Association of Social Workers (AASW). This is evident in its embrace of core values including respect and social justice, and its focus on 'the empowerment and liberation of people' (AASW, 2010, p.10). However, the espoused theory and practice of social work do not always align. Dominelli (2002) argues that social work has been reluctant to explicitly embrace an anti-oppressive mantle, despite its history of defending the interests of the underdog. Rossiter (1997, p.32) similarly laments,

> the ideal of 'real' social work is the establishment of empirically tested theory; generation of practice principles that match the theory; and teaching those principles to students, whose clients then need to alter their perspectives in relation to the reigning theory.

The challenges become larger in the face of neoliberal and managerial policies that favour technicist approaches, rather than critical practice (Morley, Macfarlane & Ablett, 2014). The aim of social work practice to promote positive change (Chenoweth & McAuliffe, 2018) often locates the need for change at the individual level rather than the systemic level. Increasingly, social work education falls into line, teaching theories and strategies that lull students into a false belief that while social work is complex, the complexity can be managed; the chaos can be ordered through, for example, using evidence-based interventions, refining our risk assessment techniques and following proceduralised practice manuals. Within this conservative (mainstream) construction of social work, a successful outcome sees the 'client' fitting in – realigning themselves with dominantly accepted 'social arrangements' (O'Connor, Wilson, Setterlund & Hughes, 2008). In other words: data forms filled in; boxes ticked; case closed. Next!

This form of social work practice and education is troubling, especially if social work education claims to be critical, anti-oppressive and transformative while remaining complicit in oppression and silencing; failing to question the 'hidden curriculum' (Giroux, 1978) and failing to create space for other voices, perspectives, ways of seeing and knowing. How can we hope that social work graduates will align their espoused critical theory with a critical practice if, as educators, we do not do the same?

This chapter positions 'queer' as a concept that remains problematic in social work education and practice. While queer theories are not highlighted and queer ways of knowing and seeing are not identified, students who identify as queer do not feel safe, and service users who identify as queer remain problematised by mainstream social work (Craig, McInroy, Dentato, Austin & Messinger, 2015; Roberts, 2005; Wagaman, Shelton & Carter, 2018). Given that Education and Accreditation Standards state that, for example: 'It is expected that social work programs will promote sensitivity to, and incorporate content on culture, ethnicity, race, gender and sexual orientation' (Australian Association of Social Workers, 2008, p.6), it is unacceptable that queer issues have not been well integrated into social work curricula (Roberts, 2005). As Roberts (2005, p.44) contends: 'A one off lecture on gay or lesbian issues will not address the heterosexism weaved both obviously and subtly throughout the remainder of a four year undergraduate course.' Wagaman et al. (2018) similarly suggest that the lack of LGBTIQ-specific content in social work courses limits social work education's capacity to prepare students to practice effectively, and that this is reinforced by limited field education opportunities in this area. Related to this, MacKinnon (2011, p.142) argues that anti-oppressive social work education has had the unintended consequence of reinforcing differences between heterosexual and non-heterosexual sexualities, particularly when applying an identity-based oppression model where 'LGBT people are constructed as melancholy subjects, carrying out difficult lives in the pages of a social work text'.

Alarmingly, social work students in a class that I teach purported to value respect, yet were still troubled by the idea of marriage equality. Further evidence of heterosexism and homophobia are present when they remark that they have yet to meet a gay person (despite as their lecturer, openly identifying as a lesbian). Even more concerning are the queer social work students who report homophobic and trans-phobic bullying by their social work student colleagues. It becomes clear that even among those who espouse a commitment to social work values, the word 'queer' and the idea of queer remain problematic for some.

Developing a critical understanding of queer and the ways it can not only inform social work practice with queer people and communities, but also the implications queer ideas have for disrupting heteronormative and cis-gendered ideals, and therefore transforming society, requires access to 'ideas, practices, practitioners and institutions tied to and rooted in queerness' (Greteman, 2018, p.2). Kumashiro engages us in a critical exploration of anti-oppressive education strategies that can move beyond seeing queer as 'other' to embracing queer as a part of a practice that changes students and society.

Education for the other: anti-oppressive practices toward safety and inclusion

The first approach to anti-oppressive education Kumashiro (2000a) discusses is 'Education for the "Other"'. In this, he is referring to education practices that improve the experiences of students who are 'othered' or in some way oppressed. Kumashiro (2000a) identifies multiple ways this oppression occurs: from blatant discrimination, to policies that privilege the (heterosexual) mainstream, to assumptions about particular cohorts of students based on stereotypes.

There has been no research examining the experiences of queer social work students in social work courses in Australia, however a number of North American studies have found that despite an espoused commitment to social justice, equity and respect being core social work values, social work students who are queer do not experience the classroom, or the content, as safe, inclusive or affirming (Chinell, 2011; Chonody, Woodford, Brennan, Newman & Wang, 2014; Craig et al., 2015; Wagaman et al., 2018). One North American study highlights that one-third of the 1,018 queer social work students surveyed reported experiencing homophobia in their social work programs and that one-fifth felt that 'faculty behaved and spoke in ways that reflected their own homophobia and/or bias' (Craig et al., 2015, p.7). Another found that 14.5% of heterosexual social work faculty hold negative views toward gay men, and 13.9% toward lesbians (Chonody et al., 2014). It is the responsibility of teaching staff who set the content and facilitate the culture of the classroom to ensure that the classroom is safe, and that students see themselves reflected in affirming ways in course content and classroom practices. When teaching staff hold negative views or do not challenge homophobia within their classroom then queer students will continue to feel unsafe (Chinell, 2011; Wagaman et al., 2018). A lack of safety, invisibilising and silencing within social work courses also contributes to queer social work students struggling to integrate their queer identity with their social work professional identity. This affects not only their academic performance but also their preparedness for practice, with students wondering if it will be safe, or professionally accepted to be 'out' (Craiq, Ianoco, Paceley, Dentato and Boyle, 2017). These studies demonstrate that an 'education *for* the "other"' (Kumashiro, 2000a, p.26) is not how queer social work students experience the classroom. On the contrary, the curriculum, the classroom and responses by faculty all contributed to an invisibilising and silencing, and at times a lack of safety for queer social work students.

Kumashiro (2002a) identifies that, typically, anti-oppressive teaching strategies to address othering include educators acknowledging the diversity within their cohorts of students and tailoring teaching to be inclusive of all students. However, he highlights a number of key concerns with such strategies. While acknowledging that some students are harmed by various forms of oppression, he cautions against focussing on the negative experiences of the 'other'; the weakness of focussing on the individual, rather than the structural. A further concern is that this approach can essentialise the experience of the 'other', rather than recognise the multiple and diverse experiences within groups. Kumashiro (2000a, p.30) states that 'the multiple and intersecting identities of students make difficult any anti-oppressive effort within the classroom that revolves around only one identity and only one form of oppression'. Such consideration requires a constant looking beyond the margins, to see who is being silenced or excluded and what assumptions are being made. In order for queer social work students to feel safe and supported in their classrooms, work must be done in understanding and challenging heterosexism, cis-genderism and homophobia, not only outside the classroom, but also within it. This work needs to be driven by social work educators and supported by the institution, and this requires educators and the institution to engage in challenging their own complicity with oppression. This challenge will be discussed in a later section of this chapter.

Education about the 'other': reinforcing the queer/straight binary

Kumashiro's (2002a) second critique concerns 'Education about the "Other"' that incorporates educational strategies including specific units of study focussing on the 'other'. It is here that the single class on working with queer individuals and communities or the unit on working with people from a refugee background might appear. Additional strategies aim to integrate otherness throughout the curriculum, potentially enabling educators to address intersections of different identities and forms of oppression experienced. However, as Kumashiro (2000a) argues, this remains problematic: first, teaching may present a dominant narrative of the 'other's' experience; second, 'otherness' becomes essentialised as different from the norm; and third, teaching about the 'other' will always be partial as knowledge about the 'other' is always incomplete or distorted, often coming from an uncritiqued place of privilege. Again, a problem with this approach is that it does not call for structural change of heterosexual normativity. It does not disrupt the processes that differentiate the 'other' from the 'normal'.

Education about the 'other' is deeply embedded in traditional social work education. McPhail (2008, p.4) states that 'in social work theory, practice and education, people are generally classified by their membership in groups … and that these group statuses are often divided into binary categorisations'. Much of social work education draws on case studies and practice examples that highlight the experiences of the 'other', as well as identifying the issues and interests of marginalised groups as being the target for policy and practice. Much of social work theory and research eschews queer theory, and, where queer is mentioned, it is in the context of 'cultural competence' or LGBT-affirming practices (Hicks & Jeyasingham, 2016, p.2361). Anti-oppressive social work education can unintentionally reinforce differences between heterosexual and non-heterosexual identities, assuming that hetero identities are both normal and dominant, while positioning queer identities as 'requiring better understanding' (MacKinnon (2011, p.140).

In the same way, essentialising of queer identities becomes problematic in an education *for* the 'other', it is also a concern in the process of educating *about* the 'other'. Kumashiro (2000a) suggests that a one-off lesson fails to examine the intersecting identities and the oppressions that might encompass these identities. Kumashiro (1999) points to the intersections between race and sexuality as a site of oppression where anti-racist and anti-heterosexist teaching strategies revolve around normative conceptualisations of race and queer. He cites examples whereby in teaching about queer, the queers being talked about are white, and when race is discussed there is an assumption of heterosexuality (Kumashiro, 1999). Poon (2011) argues that social work education reduces people who are racialised and queer in social work education to bodies with fixed attributes that can be examined and categorised. The assumption is that with 'proper' knowledge people who are racialised and queer can be 'managed' by people with the 'right' skills, knowledge and values (Poon, 2011, p.148).

Rather than a focus on teaching about the 'other', Kumashiro (2000a) calls for an education that challenges normalcy, and works against privileging certain groups and the essentialising of certain identities. It is the social work educator's job to teach students to think critically about essentialising and problematised constructions of identity, including queer identities. As Kumashiro (2000a, p.34) states: 'Changing oppression requires disruptive knowledge, not simply more knowledge.'

Education that is critical of privileging and othering: complicity, crisis and the 'stuck' place

In Kumashiro's (2002a) third approach, 'education that is critical of privileging and "othering"', we see more possibility for critical pedagogy to emerge in social work education; and approaches that advocate a critique and transformation of hegemonic structures and ideologies. In order to engage with this process, education is not simply about the 'other', rather, the form of education makes explicit the processes by which some are 'othered', while others are normalised. Kumashiro (2000a, p.37) says that 'teaching critically involves unmasking or making visible the privilege of certain identities and the invisibility of privilege'. In doing this, students learn not only about the dynamics of oppression, but also about themselves. This might include seeing themselves in the identities and experiences of those being studied, and also seeing the ways in which they might be (often unknowingly) complicit with, and even contributing to, forms of oppression. Therefore, the goal of critical education is both critique and transformation of structural oppression. However, Kumashiro (2002b) questions the assumption that knowledge automatically leads to transformation – the assumption that students (who occupy identities of heterosexual privilege) might choose to act differently than before. Kumashiro (2000b) suggests that the process of unlearning could lead students into a state of crisis, whereby they become stuck, or unable to actively resist. Kumashiro (2015, p.52) suggests that barriers to addressing queer issues (particularly for heterosexual students), exist because we search for comfortable ways to do this work.

Critical approaches to learning are necessarily discomforting because we often desire teaching and learning that affirms hegemonic views about society and views that do not challenge our ideas about the way society is, or is supposed to be. Kumashiro (2001b) asks us to imagine an alternative. He wonders what might happen if learning uncovered that everything we think of as normal is really a social construct maintained through othering, and that we are complicit in this. Many students resist such ideas because they trouble how we think and feel, not only about the 'other', but also about ourselves (Kumashiro, 2001b). Queer theory disrupts existing knowledge: it challenges binary thinking and it recognises that identity can be dynamic and fluid (Butler, 1990; Willis, 2007). Kumashiro (2001b) suggests that it is this discomfort that leads to reluctance on the part of many educators to engage with queer theory, primarily because the definition of straight requires the existence of queer, so changing what it means to be queer, by centring it rather than othering it, simultaneously changes what it means to be straight, which can be an uncomfortable realisation for some educators and students (Kumashiro, 2001b).

Kumashiro reflects on a classroom experience where he used the word queer in discussion about oppression. Students became stuck on 'queer' claiming he should use homosexual or gay. Kumashiro writes that on one hand, 'queer' confronted students with the fluidity of sexuality, which therefore suggests that one's own sexual orientation is not fixed. Queer also, he argues, invokes a history of ignorance, bigotry and hatred that homosexual or gay does not, primarily because homosexual has a medically pathologising history, and gay an assimilationist history (Kumashiro, 2001b). Kumashiro (2001b, p.6) highlights the challenges in stating: 'although my students desired to learn, their desire for normalcy and for affirmation of their belief that they do not oppress others was stronger.'

Although social work students typically begin a social work course because they want to 'help' people (Chenoweth & McAuliffe, 2018), very early in their studies, their notions of 'helping' become, or should become, challenged. Their ideas about their own value system is ideally disrupted. From a critical perspective, they should be subject to an education that challenges the notion that values they hold, particularly those that do not align with social work values, can simply be 'left at the door' and will not impact on their practice (Morley et al., 2014). Kumashiro (2002a) suggests that we resist knowledge that reveals our complicity with racism, homophobia and other forms of oppression. Unlearning one's worldview can be upsetting and even paralysing for students, leading them to simultaneously become both unstuck (moving away from previous thinking that may be complicit with oppression); and stuck (intellectually paralysed by needing to work through their thoughts and feelings before moving on) (Kumashiro, 2002b). This is particularly evident for students who believe their values align with ideas of anti-oppressive practice, when there are clear gaps.

An example of this was shared by a student in an undergraduate social work course I teach. This student was journaling about a youth work tutorial where learning was supported by an ongoing case study. The subject of the case study was a 14-year-old transgender young person named Jaimie. This student writes:

> I finished reading the first part of Jaimie's story when I caught a glance of my reflection in the window. I was frowning and pulling the strangest face! 'What's going on?' I thought.

> 'Am I uncomfortable by this story? There have been many similar and more complex cases presented throughout the degree which have not triggered feelings like this. Why am I feeling this way?' At this point I realised I was totally confronted and that unconscious opinions and underlying issues I was completely unaware of were surfacing! It was a long time before I engaged with this task again as there was a great deal of thinking that I needed to do. This case has raised many different feelings for me ranging from anger and frustration to deep sadness, to confusion, inspiration and motivation. It has challenged my underlying constructed ideas, beliefs and perceptions about gender, sexuality and identity and what these mean to me, my life and others around me.

Another student was more explicit about what she saw as a potential challenge to her beliefs and values

> We met our young person today. Jaimie is a 14-year old transgender person. I am a Christian. Help.

Kumashiro (2002b) argues that in challenging hegemonic assumptions about gender and sexuality as part of anti-oppressive teaching, the ways we think and act can be experienced as oppressive by students. Because of this, educators should expect their students to experience a sense of crisis when their worldview is questioned. Therefore, educators need to create space in the curriculum for students to work though crisis, or moments of discomfort and their 'stuck' place. While he states that crisis can lead toward a transformation in thinking, he warns that it can also lead toward more entrenched resistance (Kumashiro, 2000b). Therefore, as social work educators, we need to create space for discussion, so students do not become stuck in a place of resistance to new ways of thinking. For social work students who struggle with ideas about Jaimie, I found the need to more explicitly create spaces to engage in discussion – not just about 'the issues' but about how students were feeling; how they were being challenged by the story; how their responses might be located in thinking and practice that did not honour and support Jamie's fluid and changing identity, and what these responses ultimately said about how they saw themselves as social work practitioners.

It must also be emphasised that while creating space for discussion and critique is essential, the goal is not necessarily to provide a 'safe' space. As (Allen, 2015) states, all spaces of learning are risky; what is educative makes us anxious. Indeed, Allen (2015, p.767) suggests that a 'truly queer pedagogy might embrace a lack of "safety" as pedagogically productive'. Kumashiro (2002b) addresses concerns that leading students into crisis might be seen as unethical. Rather, he believes leaving students in harmful repetition is unethical. Allen (2015) explores the pedagogical potential of discomfort, yet highlights that higher education values happy students who are satisfied and engaged. She suggests that this provides a quandary for queer pedagogy's intent to expose and disrupt normalcy, as doing so creates discomfort, leaving students potentially ill at ease. Allen (2015) argues that this might result in queer pedagogy being seen as failing, in institutional terms, to meet the standards of 'success'. Students feel challenged and potentially uncomfortable, and this might then result in negative feedback through the various student evaluations of teaching. This resonates with my own experience as an educator, as I have received negative feedback from students about 'pushing my own agenda', or aiming to alienate males in the classroom when I draw on queer or feminist ideas.

A further challenge with queer pedagogy is that it can simply replace a socially hegemonic framework with an academically hegemonic one: one in which students read and write what they think they should, rather than engage critically with the ideas. As Kumashiro (2001b, p.8) notes, 'To read critically is not merely to read texts that say critical things'. Kumashiro (2000a) argues that an education that invites critical thinking allows students to critique that which is being taught for what it says and makes possible, as well as what it leaves unsaid and unthinkable. This can present a challenge to educators who assume a position of expert. Critical social work education encompasses the practice of critical reflection (Morley et al., 2014). Kumashiro's work is calling on students and educators to engage in critical and reflective practices to disrupt comforting knowledge and to examine positions of privilege and power that create a safety barrier of professional or academic 'expertise' that we can hide behind. Queer pedagogies can help us emerge from behind this barrier and confront our own complicity in oppression. As confronting as this challenge might be, it is a necessary one if we wish to become critical practitioners in our work with and for queer individuals and communities.

Education that changes students and society: repetition and the transformative possibilities of the 'space between'

The fourth approach that Kumashiro outlines is education that changes students and society, drawing on poststructuralism to help students understand the importance, not only of what is said, but also what is left unsaid. Kumashiro (2000a) urges us to look beyond the repetition of common sense and tradition that can perpetuate multiple forms of oppression. He argues that oppression has its origins in the citing of discourses that frame how people think, feel, act and interact, and that these might not always be clear or overt. Kumashiro (2000a) argues for the importance of labouring to stop the repetition of harmful discourses. He provides the example of the work among people who identify as queer to disrupt the harmfulness of the term queer, and to reclaim it as an empowering term. However, Kumashiro (2002b) laments that ultimately what often happens in classrooms is repetition and comfort, rather than discomfort and change. Repetition is comforting for educators because it removes uncertainty. Britzman (1995) suggests that teaching practice can be influenced by that which we consciously, or unconsciously, desire not to know. Indeed, Kumashiro (2003, p.366) suggests that 'being a university professor often requires repeating what others have already asserted to be the best or most important ways to research, teach and serve'. He states that asking students to critique what is being taught, and to challenge the partial nature of knowledge, requires a level of unpredictability and uncertainty (Kumashiro, 2003). Repetition is both comfortable and comforting for students and educators, however repetition does not lead to transformation.

All students come to class with partial knowledges, drawn from stereotypes, lived experience and notions of 'common sense'. Ellsworth (1997) argues that there is always a space between the learner and the educator, and that the goal of education is typically to narrow the gap between what the teacher knows and the student learns. However, rather than reduce the gap (and control where and how the student is changed), the aim of education should be to explore the space in between the known (by the teacher) and the yet to be learned (by the student), 'to explore the possibilities of disruption and change that live in the unknowable' (Kumashiro, 2000a, p.46). This requires a recognition that all knowledge is partial, and that repetition does not challenge the partial nature of knowledge. Kumashiro (2002a) suggests that even in anti-oppressive teaching practices, some forms of repetition may be interrupted, but others remain invisible and so remain unquestioned, and repeated. Within social work education, the research is clear that queer is taught only within certain parameters (Hicks & Jeyasingham, 2016; Poon, 2011; Wagaman et al., 2018). Indeed increased claims of lesbian and gay equality in social work are characterised by homonormativity, where lesbians and gay men become closer to heteronormative ideas of traditional nuclear families and relationships, and therefore become less threatening to normative ideas about family (Hicks & Jeyasingham, 2016). Such attempts to normalise are evident in marriage equality debates and in legal recognition of same-sex parenting. These rights claims and 'wins' have extremely important practical and symbolic gains for same-sex relationships and families, yet nonetheless affirm relationships that mimic traditional nuclear heterosexual relationships and family forms, rather than open the space to recognise the transformative potential to 'do family differently' (Kaighin, 2011). Kumashiro (2003) argues that a project of queer theory must be to problematise the ways we might unintentionally normalise certain ways of being queer. As he states: 'we see queerness as ideals that never solidify, because once grasped they tend towards normalcy' (Kumashiro, 2003, p.367). Queer theory, as argued by Britzman (1995), offers a critique of the repetitions of normalcy and allows for an imagining of difference on its own terms. The inclusion of queer theory and queer knowledges into social work teaching will broaden the scope of ideas available to social work students. Creating space in the curriculum to critically examine the ideas emerging from queer theory will challenge both heteronormativity and homonormativity, and from this critical space emerges the potential for better practice with queer people and queer communities.

Ultimately, Kumashiro (2000a) calls on educators to make use of an amalgam of the four approaches. However, as this chapter has explored, there are challenges inherent within this because of: resistance to learn that which may cause discomfort; the desire to only learn and teach that which affirms our sense that we are good people; and the paradox that teaching can simultaneously bring some marginalised voices to the fore, while silencing others. Such challenges result in anti-oppressive teaching that reflects the first two, rather than the last two approaches presented above. This pattern is evident in social work education that draws on establishment theories that reinforce difference, and operate to identify the 'other' as a target for empathy and change, rather than seeking to critique and transform students, systems and ourselves (Morley et al., 2014) Consequently, establishment social work education prepares students to fit into a managerialist practice framework in which targets, data forms and achieving outcomes are prioritised, and where workers and service users comply with the status quo (Morley et al., 2014). However, social work education also claims to be critical, inclusive and transformative, and so cannot continue to invisibilise, or actively silence queer voices, queer students and queer knowledge. Hence Kumashiro's work on queering holds direct relevance for social work.

Queering social work knowledge and practice

Teaching practice can often be focussed on certainty and control. This need for certainty is reflected by students in a desire to focus on what they need to know to pass an assessment, rather than the learning required to be critical practitioners. In many ways this assessment-driven focus is supported by the neoliberal higher education environment, where students are paying fees and juggling work, and engaging with ideas beyond assessment is simply asking too much (Hil, 2012). This dilemma is at the heart of the challenge; it is easier for educators to fit in, to give students what they desire, to meet the requirements of accrediting bodies and the university. Kumashiro (2015) suggests that, as academics, we can fall into a trap of believing that the social justice curriculum comes at the expense of academic rigour, however he counters this, arguing that 'if the curriculum is unable to be applied to creating a more humane and just society and world, it is not academically rigorous' (Kumashiro, 2015, p.140). The space to teach queer has narrowed in higher education, and this has much to do with accreditation by professional bodies limiting and shaping the curricula around expected skills and knowledges required by the profession (Allen & Rasmussen, 2015). Kumashiro (2015, p.54) says that if the norms of teaching position it as neutral and objective, then any teaching which is non-neutral is 'pretty queer'. The word queer reminds Kumashiro to never stop asking what is problematic with the norm. Therefore, queering teaching reminds us to question the ways anti-oppressive approaches might be contributing to oppression by silencing or making invisible other sites for oppression. A challenge in social work education is recognising that queer theory is not exclusively for the study of people who identify as queer (Allen & Rasmussen, 2015). A queer social work recognises that queerness is more than a problem requiring intervention, a queer social work seeks to challenge and disrupt hegemonic ideas about identity and normalcy, a queer social work centres social justice and social transformation.

A queer pedagogy is one that 'begins with an ethical concern for one's own reading practices, one that is interested in exploring what one cannot bear to know, one interested in the imagining of a sociality unhinged from the dominant conceptual order' (Britzman, 1995, p.165). Kumashiro (1999) suggests that changing the discourses of normalcy changes the communities' reading practices – how an individual within a community reads others and themselves, 'therefore reworking discourse involves changing one's identity' (Kumashiro 1990, p.506). Queer theory offers social work a pedagogical tool in discussions beyond LGBT identity categories, including exploring the 'yet to be revealed queerness of heterosexual subjectivities' (MacKinnon, 2011, p.143). As Kumashiro (1999, p.506) argues, this may seem threatening to some people as it aims to disrupt 'how things are, and who I am'.

Engaging in queer theory-making involves work; the labour that Kumashiro (2000a) refers to in his fourth approach, looking at how queer theory can be used to critique discourses, not just about gender and sexuality but about structural inequality and the construction of norms. In calling for a decolonising queer pedagogy, Smith (2013, p.469) urges students to 'think through the ways they can take action to disrupt the lock step of unanimity found in monolithic systems, institutions and in their own lives'. This approach aligns itself with critical social work theories that work toward emancipatory personal and social change, challenging dominant assumptions and working toward greater social justice (Pease & Nipperess, 2016). Kumashiro (2015) suggests that, as educators, we need to challenge the institutional practices that perpetuate an oppressive norm, and challenge our own emotional discomfort with things that are queer. We need to create the conceptual space in which alternatives can be raised and challenged if we seek to be socially transformative (Poon, 2011). Queer theories provide tools to challenge neoliberal regimes and their effects on social welfare. Hicks and Jeyasingham (2016) argue that a (post) queer theory encompassing race, class, the neoliberal state and anti-normativity may well invigorate social work theory and practice.

A social work that centres social justice must challenge the partial nature of knowledge, and must actively insist that students engage in challenging how issues are constructed, and how the ideas are being taught. If social work education is simply repetition, then social work itself fails to learn from its own complicity in oppression. Kumashiro does not seek to provide strategies. Instead he encourages educators to reflect on our assumptions, to rethink our practices, and to constantly look for new insights. Disruptive knowledge is not an end in itself, but a means toward always wanting to learn more (Kumashiro, 2002b). For social work educators, a queer approach to education reminds us never to stop asking what is problematic with the norm, addressing the resistance, the discomfort and our own uncertainty. A queer pedagogy will support students to become more critical practitioners, not just in work with queer individuals and communities, but more broadly in challenging dominant discourses, disrupting hegemonic ideas and working toward social justice. If social work education is to be truly anti-oppressive then embedding the queer, and embracing the crisis, is a necessary project.

References

Allen, L (2015) 'Queer pedagogy and the limits of thought: teaching sexualities at university', *Higher Education Research & Development*, 34:4, 763–775, doi: 10.1080/07294360.2015.1051004.

Allen, L, & Rasmussen, M L (2015) 'Queer conversation in straight spaces: an interview with Mary Lou Rasmussen about queer theory in higher education', *Higher Education Research & Development*, 34:4, 685–694, DOI: 10.1080/07294360.2015.1062072

Australian Association of Social Workers (2008) *Australian social work education accreditation standards*. (January 2010 update) Canberra: AASW.

Australian Association of Social Workers (2010) *Code of ethics*. Canberra: AASW.

Britzman, D (1995) 'Is there a queer pedagogy? or, stop reading straight', *Educational Theory*, 45:2, 151–165.

Butler, J (1990) *Gender trouble feminism and the subversion of identity*. London: Routledge.

Chenoweth, L, & McAuliffe, D (2018) *The road to social work and human service practice* (5th ed). South Melbourne: Cengage Learning Australia.

Chinell, J (2011) 'Three voices: reflections on homophobia and heterosexism in social work education', *Social Work Education*, 30:7, 759–773, doi: 10.1080/02615479.2010.508088.

Chonody, J, Woodford, M, Brennan, D, Newman, B & Wang, D (2014) 'Attitudes toward gay men and lesbian women among heterosexual social work faculty', *Journal of Social Work Education*, 50:1, 136–152, doi: 10.1080/10437797.2014.856239.

Craig, S, Iacono, G, Paceley, M, Dentato, M & Boyle, K (2017) 'Intersecting sexual, gender, and professional identities among social work students: the importance of identity integration', *Journal of Social Work Education*, 53:3, 466–479, doi: 10.1080/10437797.2016.1272516.

Craig, S L, McInroy, L B, Dentato, M P, Austin, A & Messinger, L (2015) *Social work students speak out! the experiences of lesbian, gay, bisexual, transgender, and queer students in social work programs: a study report from the CSWE council on sexual orientation and gender identity and expression*. Toronto: Author.

Dominelli, L (2002) *Anti-oppressive social work theory and practice*. Hampshire: Palgrave MacMillan.

Ellsworth, E (1997) *Teaching positions: difference, pedagogy, and the power of address*. New York: College Press.

Giroux, H (1978) 'Developing educational programs: overcoming the hidden curriculum', *The Clearing House: A Journal of Educational Strategies, Issues and Ideas*, 52:4, 148–151, doi: 10.1080/00098655.1978.10113565.

Greteman, A (2018) 'Sexualities and genders in education : towards queer thriving', In W Pinar, N Rodriguez & R U Whitlock *Queer studies and education series*. Cham: Palgrave Macmillan.

Hicks, S & Jeyasingham, D (2016) 'Social work, queer theory and after: a genealogy of sexuality theory in neo-liberal times', *British Journal of Social Work*, 46, 2357–2373, doi: 10.1093/bjsw/bcw103.

Hil, R (2012) *Whackademia: an insiders account of the troubled university*. Sydney: UNSW Press.

Kaighin, J (2011) 'Different ways of 'doing family' in Australia: queerying the impact of same- sex law reform', in B Scherer & M Ball (Eds.) *Queering paradigms II; interrogating agendas* (pp 259–274). Bern: Peter Lang.

Kumashiro, K (1999) 'Supplementing normalcy and otherness: queer Asian-American men reflect on stereotypes, identity and oppression', *International Journal of Qualitative Studies in Education*, 12:5, 491–508, doi: 10.1080/095183999235917.

Kumashiro, K (2000a) 'Toward a theory of anti-oppressive education', *Review of Educational Research*, 70:1, 25–53.

Kumashiro, K (2000b) 'Teaching and learning through desire, crisis and difference: perverted reflections on anti-oppressive education', *Radical Teacher*, 58, 6–12.

Kumashiro, K (2001a) 'Queer students of color and antiracist, antiheterosexist education: paradoxes of identity and activism', In Kumashiro K (Ed.) *Troubling intersections of race and sexuality: queer students of colour and anti-oppressive education* (pp 1–25). New York: Rowman & Littlefield Publishers.

Kumashiro, K (2001b) '"Posts" perspectives on anti-oppressive education in social studies, English, Mathematics and Science classrooms', *Educational Researcher*, 30:3, 3–12, doi: 10.3102/0013189X030003003.

Kumashiro, K (2002a) *Troubling education: "queer" activism and anti-oppressive pedagogy*. New York: Routledge.

Kumashiro, K (2002b) 'Against repetition: addressing resistance to anti-oppressive change in the practices of learning, teaching, supervising and researching', *Harvard Educational Review*, 672:1, 67–92.

Kumashiro, K (2003) 'Queer ideals in education', *Journal of Homosexuality*, 45:2-4, 365–367, doi: 10.1300/J082v45n02_23.

Kumashiro, K (2015) *Against common sense: teaching and learning towards social justice* (3rd ed). New York: Routledge.

MacKinnon, K V R (2011) 'Thinking about queer theory in social work education: a pedagogical (in) query', *Canadian Social Work Review*, 28:1, 139–144.

McPhail, B (2008) 'Re-gendering the social work curriculum: new realities and complexities', *Journal of Social Work Education*, 44:2, 33–52, doi: 10.5175/JSWE.2008.200600148.

Morley, C, Macfarlane, S & Ablett, P (2014) *Engaging critically with social work: an introduction*. Cambridge & Melbourne: Cambridge University Press.

O'Connor, I, Wilson, J, Setterlund, D & Hughes, M (2008) *Social work and human service practice* (5th ed). Frenchs Forest: Pearson Education Australia.

Pease, B, & Nipperess, S (2016) 'Doing critical social work in the neoliberal context: working on the contradictions', in B Pease, S Goldingay, N Hosken & S Nipperess (Eds) *Doing critical social work; transformative practices for social justice* (pp 3–24). Crows Nest: Allen & Unwin.

Poon, M K L (2011) 'Writing the racialized queer bodies: race and sexuality in social work', *Canadian Social Work Review*, 28:1, 145–150.

Roberts, R (2005) 'Social work with gay men and lesbians', In M Alston and J McKinnon (Eds.) *Social work fields of practice* (pp 32–47). South Melbourne: Oxford University Press.

Rossiter, A (1997) 'A perspective on critical social work', *Journal of Progressive Human Services*, 7:2, 23–41, doi: 10.1300/J059v07n02_03.

Smith, K (2013) 'Decolonizing queer pedagogy', *Journal of Women and Social Work*, 28:4, 468–470, doi: 10.1177/0886109913505814.

Wagaman, A, Shelton, J & Carter, R (2018) 'Queering the social work classroom: strategies for increasing the inclusion of LGBTQ persons and experiences', *Journal of Teaching in Social Work*, 38:2, 166–182, doi: 10.1080/08841233.2018.1430093.

Willis, P (2007) '"Queer eye" for social work: rethinking pedagogy and practice with same-sex attracted young people', *Australian Social Work*, 60:2, 181–196, doi: 10.1080/03124070701323816.

29

The panopticon effect

Understanding gendered subjects of control through a reading of Judith Butler

Jamilla Rosdahl

KARLSTADS UNIVERSITY, SWEDEN

Introduction

Domestic violence is the most common form of violence against women (Our Watch, 2019). In Australia, domestic violence is so prevalent that one woman a week is murdered by a current or former male partner (Australian Institute of Health and Welfare, 2019). Statistics reveal that women are almost three times as likely as men to experience violence from their partner (Our Watch, 2019). One in four women has experienced emotional abuse by a current or former male partner (Our Watch, 2019). As recently as last year, Australian researchers declared domestic violence against women a 'national crisis' and 'hidden epidemic' (Mao, 2019). Australia is currently in its fourth and final phase of a twelve-year national action plan initiated by state and federal governments. The *National Plan to Reduce Violence against Women and their Children* (Department of Social Services, 2019) proposed the introduction of sweeping changes to be implemented through a series of action plans with the vision that 'Australian women and children live free from violence in safe communities'. After almost a decade of action and more than 700 million dollars spent, new reviews are raising concerns about the effectiveness of the plan (Meyer, 2018).

Unfortunately, efforts to change cultural attitudes toward domestic violence, such as ascribing blame to women victims, have also not been successful (Diemer et al., 2018). Alarmingly, recent studies reveal that many Australians still hold outdated beliefs on sexual assault and violence against women (Meyer, 2018). Two in five Australians believe 'women make up sexual assault reports just to punish men' (Australian Institute of Health and Welfare, 2019). One in three believe 'a woman is responsible for experiencing domestic violence if she doesn't leave her abusive partner' (Australian Institute of Health and Welfare, 2019). Forty-three per cent of men think 'women make up claims of domestic violence when going through custody battles to improve their case' (Australian Institute of Health and Welfare, 2019). 'One in three young people do not believe controlling someone is a form of violence' (Australian Institute of Health and Welfare, 2019). Apart from domestic violence advocates such as Rosie Batty, and a small number of female journalists who have called on Australia's leaders to address the cultural crisis, 'the governments, media as well as the wider public have remained mostly silent on the crisis' (Meyer, 2018).

Jamilla Rosdahl

This chapter introduces the reader to the *panopticon effect*, and how the concept can be used to gain a deeper understanding of the complex relationship between gender and coercive control. Further, it attempts to explain why a majority of Australians are not recognising domestic violence as a problem despite the large body of evidence presented by victim testimonies, academic research, editorials and national government reports. Influenced by Michel Foucault (1971, 1979), this chapter begins from the premise that violence is a discursive project that produces and reinscribes specific theories and politics that effectively conceal relations of power, control and domination enacted out against already precarious bodies and lives. Through a reading of Judith Butler's (1990, 2004) critical social theory on *gender performativity*, *heterosexual matrix* and *normative violence*, this chapter applies the *panopticon effect* to the contemporary themes of stalking and custody control. Drawing on victim accounts, it reveals how gender norms reinforce masculine violence expressed through control mechanisms and instruments of discipline, surveillance and self-surveillance, with the effect of trapping women within an invisible prison. In this way, individual subjects are not only the effects of specific cultural and historical practices and relations of power, but gender enables and shapes everyday power relations which masks acts of control. Through a rethinking of gender and the protected status of violence, this chapter provides social work students and practitioners with tools for understanding the invisibility of masculinity and heterosexuality as normative categories that serve to perpetuate violence norms. The *panopticon effect* contributes to social work theory, teaching and practice with the aim of facilitating the emancipatory transformation of individuals and societies. The chapter concludes by arguing for the need, not only to critique established institutions and practices that support normative violence, but to transform those institutions and practices – with the ultimate goal of transforming society itself.

Coercive control

Cultural narratives on domestic violence are propped up by a persistent myth that domestic violence is only *real* or serious when physical violence is present. Contrary to popular beliefs, a growing body of research reveals that coercive control is just as serious as physical violence and more pervasive (Fisher, 2011). The stereotype of domestic violence – 'the woman with the black eye – really misses the dynamic', argues Fisher (2011, p. 3). In most industrialised Western countries, socio-legal conceptualisations of, and responses to, domestic violence rely on a violence model, adapted from the criminal justice system that equates partner abuse with discrete acts or threats of assault or physical violence in the pursuit of legal substantiation for such acts (Stark, 2012). Evan Stark (2007), in his critique of the model, maintains that it only applies to a minority of situations where abuse is limited to physical assaults and threats of physical abuse. It ignores the large majority of cases where physical assaults are not present. Non-violent tactics are much more devastating and salient to victims (Stark, 2007). Mounting evidence also suggests that the level of control in abusive relationships is a better predictor than prior assaults of future assault and of severe and fatal violence ending in murder (Stark, 2012).

We need to focus on the coercive control exercised by the domestic perpetrators, not on the acts of violence that might or might not accompany the control (Hill, 2019). Coercion can be described as 'the use of force or threats to compel or dispel a particular response' (Short and Wilton, 2016, p. 89), while control refers to 'structural forms of deprivation, exploitation, and commands that compel obedience indirectly' (Short and Wilton, 2016, p. 89). Control techniques include

> forms of constraint … monitoring and/or regulation of commonplace activities of daily living, particularly those associated with women's roles as mothers, homemakers and sexual

> partners and run the gamut from their access to money, food and transport to how they dress, clean, cook or perform sexually.
>
> *(Herring et al., 2015, p. 220)*

When coercion and control occur together, the result is a 'condition of unfreedom' (DeShong, 2015) experienced as regulation, confinement, imprisonment and entrapment.

The tactics used in coercive control have no legal standing, are rarely identified as violence and are almost never targeted by intervention (Stark, 2012). Yet the large majority of women survivors of domestic violence across the world identify multiple forms of restriction, isolation, power and control as the primary form of violence (Butterworth and Westmarland, 2015). In international surveys, women survivors regularly identify control techniques that range from the constraints partners place on their time, economy, parenting, socialising, dieting, or other facets of everyday living (Butterworth and Westmarland, 2015). For many, the most terrifying and threatening experiences of control may never be recorded by police or identified as a crime by a court. As Hill (2019, p. 18) explains, after all

> it's not a crime to demand that your girlfriend no longer sees her family. It's not a crime to tell her what to wear, how to clean the house, and what she's allowed to buy at the supermarket.... to convince your wife she's worthless, or to make her feel like she shouldn't leave the children alone with you. It's not a crime to say something happened when it didn't – to say it so many times that you break her sense of what's real. You can't be charged by turning someone's entire family against them. And yet, these are the ... controlling behaviours that show up as red flags for domestic homicide. By the time that crime occurs, it's too late.

Coercive control, when read through the dominant paradigm, renders invisible the oppression women regularly experience within domestic violence relationships.

The role of gender in domestic violence work

Men's violence against women has reached epidemic proportions and yet the role of gender and control within intimate relationships continues to be sidestepped during public discussions on domestic violence. Despite the overwhelming evidence on the impact of gender on cultural understandings, attitudes and expressions of men's violence against women, very little work has examined in detail the ways in which gender enables and shapes everyday power relations and masks acts of coercive control. Gender within domestic violence work, research and education continues to be a contentious and debated term, and gender inequalities are deeply embedded in the very language and structures that practitioners, police and even representatives of law rely on in their assessments of domestic violence (Pease, 2017). What is more, public servants like some domestic violence practitioners, still have very little knowledge about the structural causes of men's violence and this often works to reproduce structural gender relations and patriarchal discourses which in turn continue to enable men's violence against women (Pease, 2017).

Gender is a valuable and critical tool for violence work, feminist theory and politics. Gender, shaped by interlaying systems of power and inequalities, along with other relations of domination and submission, impact on how violence is perceived, experienced, enacted and responded to. Although studies highlight that gender dynamics play a role in domestic violence, they do not address the complex relationship between gender and coercive control (Wright, 2015). Gender serves to disguise patterns of control by male perpetrators (Stark, 2012). 'In the name of sustaining traditional male privileges', perpetrators of coercive control make each household 'a patriarchy in miniature complete with its own web of rules or codes, rituals of deference, modes of enforcement, sanctions, and forbidden places' (Stark, 2007, p. 67). Stark's framework of coercive control has been challenged by writers such as Anderson (2009) who argue that his theory fails to adequately explain the gendered nature of violence against women. Although Stark's (2007) theory has been vital in advancing an understanding of the powerful forces of control in oppressing women, it sidesteps the importance of gender for understanding how control both creates and is the outcome of violent gender norms.

For over 40 years, feminist researchers, theorists and activists have emphasised the role of gender and power within domestic violence, explaining that domestic violence is a manifestation of male power in a patriarchal society (Dobash and Dobash, 1979; Hearn, 1998). Despite the overwhelming evidence on the impact of gender on men's understandings, attitudes and expressions of violence against women, children and other men, the relationship between gender and coercive control remains marginalised within domestic violence work. The *panopticon effect*, influenced by Butler's (1990) gender theory, directs our analytical focus to the taken-for-granted assumptions about gender and violence, providing us with a conceptual framework for understanding the invisibility of masculinity and heterosexuality as normative categories serving to perpetuate violence norms.

The remainder of this chapter is divided into three parts. The first part introduces and explains the *panopticon effect* as a tool and mechanism demonstrating the theoretical foundations of the concept, describing a selection of Butler's main ideas including (1) *performativity*, (2) *heterosexual matrix*, and (3) *normative violence*. The second part explains the application of the *panopticon effect*. Here, Butler's theoretical insights are utilised and the section details how we can employ the *panopticon effect* to gain a deeper understanding of gender-based control within intimate relationships. The chapter concludes by exploring critical pedagogy as essential for critical social work practice, research and education within domestic violence work.

Influences from Foucault: panopticism, discipline, surveillance and self-surveillance

In my earlier work, *Reflections on Power, Gender and Violence* (Rosdahl, 2017), I argued that Michel Foucault's (1971, 1972) extensive work on *genealogy*, *discourse* and *power/knowledge* provide important theoretical frames through which we can begin to problematise violence as a distinct modern project. Further, I argued that violence produces and reinscribes very specific ideas, theories and politics that reinforce gender norms that conceal relations of power and domination enacted out against already precarious bodies and lives (Rosdahl, 2017). As a result, and as I continue to argue here, social practices including heteronormative relationships and gender identities regularly and successfully conceal coercive control techniques. In this way, individual subjects are not only the effects of specific historical, cultural practices and relations of power, but *gender performativity* enables and shapes everyday power relations that conceal acts of coercive control.

The *panopticon effect* is particularly influenced by Foucault's (1971, 1979) ideas on *genealogy*, *power/knowledge* and *discourse* and loosely inspired by his concept *panopticism*. In *Discipline and Punish* (1979), Foucault details how power relations become inscribed and ensured through different types of instruments such as the operations of disciplinary power and processes of normalisation. He traces a historical genealogical account of a production of new kinds of norm-governed individuals through disciplinary technique: a power not exercised through physical violence directed at the body but a form of subject defining punishment that is individualising, monotonous, invisible and continuous (Foucault, 1979). This new form of power 'cannot be exercised without knowing the inside of people's minds, without exploring their souls, without making them reveal their innermost secrets. It implies a knowledge of the conscience and a capacity to direct it (Foucault, 1982b, p. 783). It has the ability to manipulate and extend control of individuals' minds and bodies, securing their submission.

According to Foucault (1979), disciplining techniques for managing and normalising individuals instil controlling habits and value-sustaining self-representations through a form of surveillance that can be likened to a panopticon. Foucault uses Jeremy Bentham's model design of the panopticon, the idea of an ideal prison, as a symbol for his argument. The panopticon is a creation that relies on forms of surveillance and training techniques directed at an individual to shape, correct and

> Induce ... a state of conscious and permanent visibility that assures the automatic functioning of power ... the surveillance is permanent in its effects, even if it is discontinuous in its action; that the perfection of power should tend to render its actual exercise unnecessary; that this architectural apparatus should be a machine for creating and sustaining a power relation independent of the person who exercises it.
>
> *(Foucault, 1979, p. 201)*

The aim of the panopticon is pervasive management gained through enabling as well as restrictive conceptions, definitions and descriptions that support norm-governing behaviours that intrude into every space of an individual's life and psyche.

The *panopticon effect* as a mechanism for discipline, surveillance and self-surveillance

In order to elucidate the concept of the *panopticon effect* as a different way of seeing and understanding control, I draw loosely on Foucault's *panopticism* as a metaphor to explain an effective but invisible form of violence; part of a brutal system of masculine power and domination. This is designed to discipline individuals as subjects, inflicting suffering and misery through observation and normalising judgement. The *panopticon effect* is a conceptual tool that can be used to explain a type of disciplinary mechanism, a generative matrix and system as a social force, an apparatus of power relations that produces powerful, threatening and controlling processes through instruments of discipline, surveillance and self-surveillance (Rosdahl, 2017). Both project and machine, it acts as an invisible prison that can be operated, reworked, extended and mobilised by agents or subjects and larger structural systems and institutional processes. The *panopticon effect* is generated within and supported by culture, language, beliefs, symbols and knowledges and through systems and institutions of which power relations and gender already form a part. It is, therefore, also a social process, a transferable practice enacted and embodied by different subjects and instruments. In this way, it is not a thing in itself; it is not an agency, an innate condition nor a structure; it shape-shifts; as it is an amalgamation of accepted cultural forms, understandings and truths, imagined relationships, social stories and myths.

The *panopticon effect* presupposes that we are all exposed to neoliberal, masculinist and masculine, paternalist and late capitalist organisations and structures as well as ideological political state apparatuses. We are also vulnerable to the discourses, symbolic systems and social forms that proceed our entrance into this world and subjugate and structure how we think, act, move, love and identify, as well as how we define ourselves as individual subjects. It is a process that is dynamic and manifold that begins even before masculinist or patriarchal speech games are evoked or expressed. Thus, the *panopticon effect* is durable and can be described as attaching itself to and shaping dominated subjects. The dispositions of the dominated are a function of the *panopticon effect*, intricately connected to power and domination. It becomes lodged within individuals, internalised as dispositions, and largely determines the limited actions and choices subjects can make. The *panopticon effect* produces experiences in the dominated, which disciplines subjects into accepting their lack of agency and potential for action within the constraints placed upon them. During their training in becoming docile, the subjects are under constant surveillance and regulation, but in ways that are subtle and thereby seemingly invisible. This leads to states of normalisation of such conditions of existence in contiguous experiences of subordination. The *panopticon effect*, as a methodological approach influenced by poststructuralist feminist accounts of gender, offers a particular understanding of coercive control as a contingent and historical but effective and efficient instrument for domination and oppression. Judith Butler's work is instructive for social work here.

Judith Butler

Judith Butler is an American philosopher and gender theorist. Her critical work can be connected to influences such as Lacanian psychoanalysis, German Idealism, Phenomenology, and the Frankfurt School, while her later work has been indebted to the intellectual writings of thinkers such as Michel Foucault (1979), Hannah Arendt (1958), Giorgio Agamben (1999) and Emmanuel Levinas (1982). Butler is one of the most widely cited philosophers and has made a profound influence on feminist and political theory and queer scholarship (Lloyd, 2007). Butler (1990) is best known for her work *Gender Trouble: Feminism and the Subversion of Identity* in which she develops her theory of *gender performativity*, questioning the seeming fixity of bodies and gender. Here she argues that the 'naturalness' of female and male sexed bodies is the effect of repeated performances that are culturally constructed, discursively produced and therefore open to contestation.

Butler's theoretical toolbox

Judith Butler's (1990) theory of *performativity* centres on the notion that gender is constructed and repeatedly performed according to normative cultural and historical frameworks making individuals believe that gender identity is real. The performance of binary genders such as masculinity and femininity, reconfirms the binary order and heteronormative power and thus repeats oppressive and painful gender norms (Butler, 2011). The concept *heterosexual matrix* refers to this hegemonic and discursive grid of cultural intelligibility that naturalises specific bodies, sex and genders through the compulsory practice of heterosexuality (Butler, 1990, p. 151). Butler's concept *normative violence* describes the violence of norms; a violence that is primary and, therefore, not physical violence per se; rather, the norm produces various forms of violence that are not an essential or structural feature of their function (Chambers, 2007). In other words, although norms potentially operate through violence, it must be seen as a historically and socially contingent phenomenon. Butler's account of norms is to expose the conditions under which norms operate through violence or with violent effects.

Performativity: stalking and surveillance

Central to Butler's notion of gender is the position that what individuals experience as an interior essence of gender, is a 'performative' and 'repetitive act' made to feel real through the very desire to express a culture's constructions of gender. Gender can thus be understood as:

> a stylized repetition of acts ... which are internally discontinuous ... [so that] the *appearance of substance* is precisely that, a constructed identity, a performative accomplishment which

the mundane social audience, including the actors themselves, come to believe and to perform in the mode of belief.

(Butler, 1988, pp. 519–520)

Performativity, therefore, means that gender exists only to the extent that it is performed, generating a collection of performative 'effects'. For Butler (1990), identities such as masculinity and femininity and their various shapes, are continuously performed and 'permanently problematic'. Over time, these identifications and self-expressions create illusions of gendered selves with deeply felt emotions, needs, beliefs and attitudes. These are repeatedly created through everyday social and cultural practices as effects of discursive relations of power (Butler, 1990). Gender is, therefore, constructed through a set of acts that are in compliance with dominant and violent societal norms.

By employing the *panopticon effect*, we can explain how *performativity* enables and shapes everyday power relations that mask male perpetrators' use of coercive control such as stalking. The relationship between gender and stalking, however, is not straightforward. When we examine stalking behaviours, we must remember that not only are cultural ideas of gender taken up as a ritualistic performance by individual subjects, but gender is influenced by powerful, dispersed and shifting nexuses of social power that form part of larger discourses on violence, sex and sexuality (Foucault, 1982b). The act of stalking, as a corporally enacted practice, is thus always and already made sense of within culture and larger society. This affects how stalking can be conceptualised, theorised, carried out and experienced. To begin to understand how a discursive deployment of hegemonic masculinity works on and through male perpetrators' bodies that are infused with prevailing, historical forms of gestures and movements, we must explore how gender conventions structure the way their bodies are performed and perceived in their relations and interactions with women's bodies.

Stalking, one of the most misunderstood acts of control, is particularly interesting for what it reveals about gender, control, domination and violence norms. Perpetrators of domestic violence regularly use control techniques such as stalking to maintain power and control. Stalking is the act of repeated, unwanted contact or communication with a person, causing distress, anxiety and fear in the victim (Cox, 2015). The perpetrator might begin by slowly introducing forced, unwanted communications with the victim through repeated phone calls and text messages, insisting the victim call back immediately or respond frequently. This is often coupled with unrequested contacts where the perpetrator shows up unannounced or uninvited with gifts or claiming he can be of assistance (White Ribbon Australia, 2019).

Stalking acts are very difficult to detect since they are not only romanticised within popular culture and media, and made invisible through violence myths, but they are further made incoherent by male perpetrators who regularly perform gendered identities that imitate familiar and dominant conventions of masculinity. By drawing on heterosexual romance stereotypes, clichés and familiar gendered narratives in their interactions with victims, perpetrators trap victims within a complex web of deceit and mastery. Testimonies from women victims reveal how male perpetrators frequently engage in acts of more 'typical' heterosexual romance such as flattery in order to make unwanted contact to scare, threaten, control and isolate victims. Perpetrators initially make contact with victims bearing gifts such as flowers, sweets, notes and cards or to offer assistance (The National Domestic Violence Resource Centre Victoria, 2013):

> Valentine's Day, he showed up with an engagement ring. I cannot state strongly enough that we had no type of reconciliations, we never once, there's police involvement, it's done and so that thinking really scared me badly.

> The day that I moved in I got, there was flowers on my doorstep. Roses on my doorstep. And it says, welcome home.

> He would drop off flowers or he would drop off food or whatever. I would always give the flowers away. I never took them home. Not once.

> He left flowers at my door. I was flattered at first. But then he started coming by unannounced …

Perpetrators regularly excuse, justify and minimise coercive control techniques such as stalking by utilising familiar language and behaviours that mirror stereotypical heterosexuality and masculinity. These performances eventually transform into more regular, identifiable acts of control designed to isolate, coerce, monitor and discipline victims.

> He would text me over and over saying 'you just aren't used to real romance, you need me to take care of you. You need a real man'. But then he'd text and say, 'what are you doing now? Where have you been? Why didn't you answer when I called?' I just started feeling awful all the time. Just awful … like he was always there somehow … always controlling me.
> *(The National Domestic Violence Resource Centre Victoria, 2013)*

Perpetrators are also skilled at performing an aspired hegemonic masculinity in public to prop up the image that they are good men, fathers or husbands. These acts work to obscure and cover up coercive control techniques such as stalking and other forms of violence:

> He messaged me up to thirty times a day, stalked me for years, stopped me from seeing my friends, raped me and forced me to do disgusting things. After I left him, he went to my family and told them I'd taken money from him, that I was a sexual freak, that I was psychologically unstable, that I hated men, that I used him, that I was a terrible mum, and how I didn't like my family. My family believed him and sided with him … All they heard and saw was this friendly, charming man who sent me flowers, who cooked for them when they visited, proposed to me with an expensive ring. When I tried to tell my sister about what he'd done to me, she said, 'I don't believe you. I've seen him out with his daughter at the shops and he holds her hand and everything just like any great dad'. I was horrified.
> *(The National Domestic Violence Resource Centre Victoria, 2013)*

Violence associated with masculinity, is not used to express anger or frustration, rather it is motivated by power and control (Wright, 2015). In this way, perpetrators are skilled at hiding their abuse in public.

Contrary to popular beliefs, perpetrators often appear charming and friendly, impersonating identities that are at odds with the control techniques used against victims. These techniques are hidden within a cultural imaginary of heterosexuality and gender norms, which shape the way disciplinary techniques are enacted, interpreted and experienced:

> When we first met, he made me a candle-lit dinner, took me to restaurants. He told me I 'deserved a real man' who respects me. He bought me flowers and gifts … but he became increasingly controlling. He said I had to delete my male friends from facebook, he said I could only wear certain clothes. He told me to post a photo on facebook of the flowers he got me. When I asked why, he said other women show how much they love their men and

I needed to do the same to convince him that I loved him! I posted a photo of the flowers and wrote something like, 'I am so lucky and feel so special' ... I guess I just didn't want him to keep bringing it up. I just wanted him to stop.

(The National Domestic Violence Resource Centre Victoria, 2013)

Perpetrators regularly draw upon heterosexual stereotypes and clichés about romance in their interactions with victims to trap them:

He told me he 'trusted our love', that we were 'soulmates', that 'other couples weren't connected the way we were'. But then he would sit in his car and watch me outside the cafe whilst I was having coffee with my mum. He told me I had 15 minutes. He even messaged me whilst I was in there. I could see him through the window of the cafe. I left mum after 15 minutes because I didn't want him to get mad again.

(The National Domestic Violence Resource Centre Victoria, 2013)

Performing gender is a culturally enforced effect that regularly goes unnoticed (Butler, 1999). For male perpetrators, gender both hides and excuses control:

He started coming by even when I said I was busy. He would use any excuse like 'oh, I was just driving past' or 'I just picked up some lunch and thought you might want some'. He would come by and mow my lawn when I wasn't home. He left flowers at my door saying things like, 'I thought it would cheer you up' even though I told him I needed space. After I broke up with him and moved house to hide from him! he came by and mowed my lawn when I was out! It made me feel absolutely sick.

(The National Domestic Violence Resource Centre Victoria, 2013)

The heterosexual matrix: discipline masked as public displays of affection

Butler (1990) interprets any unconscious compulsion that seeks to render gender identity uniform, as a normalising and naturalising practice; part of a powerful, repetitive heterosexual system that regulates and reproduces cultural identities and practices. Drawing from Monique Wittig's (1992) notion of the *heterosexual contract* as a system of discursive violence, Butler in her earlier writing describes this system as a *heterosexual matrix*. The system can be conceived of as a hegemonic grid of cultural intelligibility that coheres bodies, genders and desires as naturalised; made to appear and feel real (Butler, 1990, p. 151). Butler (1990, p. 194) defines this grid as a

model of gender intelligibility that assumes that for bodies to cohere and make sense there must be a stable sex expressed through a stable gender (masculine expresses male, feminine expresses female) that is oppositionally and hierarchically defined through the compulsory practice of heterosexuality.

To guarantee the reproduction of a specific culture, normative gender identities are inextricably tied to ideas, norms and behaviours of dominant notions of heterosexuality (Butler, 1990). Being a 'man' or a 'woman' involves investing in and actively pursuing compulsory heterosexual identities, attitudes and relations within the confines of a heterosexually based system. This system requires taboos and a punitive regulation of reproduction to guarantee the production, reproduction and maintenance of heteronormative culture (Butler, 1990). To be recognised as normative individuals, contemporary gender subjects must perform a gender that matches the sexed body and desire the said opposite sex. The policing of the sex-gender-sexuality matrix coerces subjects into heterosexual positionings while deviating from this cultural system causes consternation, othering, normative violence and precarity.

Read through the lens of the *panopticon effect*, we can begin to explain how sexuality norms shape control techniques with the effect of trapping women victims into an invisible prison. As Butler (1988, p. 526) maintains, 'the act that one does, the act that one performs is, in a sense, an act that's been going on before one arrived on the scene'. In this way, perpetrators who perform acceptable masculinity, are not only well-versed in acceptable forms of cultural behaviours and regular day-to-day social interactions, but their acts form part of a larger, familiar cultural pattern which has been performed repeatedly; stabilising the act as a natural occurrence that appears to be in natural relationship with a female body. This *heterosexual matrix* regularly interrupts victims' and onlookers' ability to identify the perpetrator's gender performance as forms of coercive control:

> When we'd go out with my family and friends, he would cook barbecue food for everyone and be all friendly and nice. But then when no one was close by, he would put me down like saying I wasn't cutting the bread rolls properly. In the beginning I didn't notice all these little controlling things he started doing. I even started cutting the bread rolls his way.
> *(The National Domestic Violence Resource Centre Victoria, 2013)*

Cultural beliefs about male dominance, violence and heterosexual masculinity shape and conceal coercive control tactics that perpetrators employ within their intimate relationships. Dominant norms surrounding masculinity, such as 'men are in charge of the barbecue', create specific ideas about what it means to be a 'man' or woman within the schema of everyday life. These regular performative roles within a heterosexual grid of cultural intelligibility, not only work to impress bodies with narrow and regulatory forms and gestures, structuring the way bodies and behaviours are perceived, but they serve to enforce men's power and control over women and women's subservient status to men. Within this matrix, perpetrators perform roles that are part of unequal sexual relations that function to control, discipline and dominate women within heterosexual relationships, yet these violence techniques often go unnoticed as they are idealised and reinstituted in and through the daily social rituals of bodily life. These interconnected power structures and patterns push and entangle women, sustain gender dominance and gender inequality, often exposing women to further dangerous and exploitative systems, precarious positionings, situations and experiences.

Normative violence: custody stalking and self-discipline

To Butler (2004), norms can be conceived as mechanisms of social power that make the social field intelligible and recognisable, constituting different types of subjects, lives, practices and forms of action. In this sense, norms produce and organise social life, regulating 'what will and will not appear within the domain of the social' (Butler, 2004, p. 42). Although norms usually remain hidden and unquestioned as they operate implicitly in daily life, they are 'discernible most clearly and dramatically in the effects … they produce' (Butler, 2004, p. 41). Norms function within social practices as the implicit standard of normalisation. As mechanisms of social power, norms not only produce subjects but they also act forcefully on the bodies and lives of these subjects (Butler, 2004). Norms thus assign individuals to social categories such as gender and produce standards and ideals that regulate, often through violence and exclusion, those kinds of subjects and lives that are regarded as possible.

A common approach is to read Butler's notion of norms in terms of what academics have termed 'normative violence' (Lloyd, 2007). Employing the *panopticon effect* with the insight of Butler's notion of *normative violence*, it becomes possible to identify how norms and conventions are reproduced by regulative discourses through the implicit standard of normalisation. Norms surrounding family and parenting, including joint parental practice, work to support coercive control techniques such as 'custody stalking' within heterosexual domestic violence relationships. Custody stalking can be defined as

> a malevolent course of conduct involving the use or threatened use of legal and other bureaucratic proceedings … to obtain, or attempt to obtain, care time with … children far in excess of … involvement with them prior to separation.
>
> *(Elizabeth, 2017, p. 187)*

In a recent study by Vivienne Elizabeth (2017), custody stalking illuminates women's post-separation experiences of coercive control. The study reveals how the losses suffered caused the mothers tremendous grief, damaged their psychological wellbeing and had a detrimental effect on their mothering relationships (Elizabeth, 2017). According to Elizabeth (2017, p. 187), 'custody stalking, described as a form of malevolent attack, is not well recognised and mothers' resultant losses are largely culturally invisible'. Custody control instils feelings of anxious dread in mothers who are its targets.

With the help of the *panopticon effect*, it is possible to explain how custody stalking as a form of coercive control instils feelings of anxious dread and self-discipline in mothers who are targets, locking the women into ongoing and far-reaching power relations. Custody stalking, via custody litigation and/or reports of suspected abuse or neglect to child protection agencies, affords coercively controlling fathers with culturally and legally legitimate channels through which they can attack mothers (Elizabeth, 2017; Watson and Ancis, 2013). Custody stalking, similar to other forms of stalking, is a type of attack on women's psychological integrity which disciplines women victims, who are also mothers, into a restricted space, often with severe consequences. Elizabeth's study (2017) tells a story of one of the informants, Jamila, a Māori woman, and her experience of coercive control by her former partner Pita. Jamila's experiences of maternal loss brought through custody stalking are associated with experiences of high levels of distress, overwhelming sorrow and extended states of grief.

Custody stalking is but one volatile example of how gender and coercive control shape men's violence against women. *Normative violence* sets the conditions for an invisible form of violence that is not socially recognised as violence. Custody stalking as a form of coercive control is the result of normative violence embedded in the imposition of gender. The normative structure of gender is determined through the naturalisation of norms and the reproduction of these norms by society. Through the use of the *panopticon effect*, we can expand our understanding of the persistence of *normative violence* and how it is possible to problematise performative acts of masculinity, heterosexual contracts and violence norms in order to identify the ways in which they create, enable and sustain masculine control and domination over women.

Rethinking domestic violence work as the practice of individual and social responsibility

Women's struggle for support, protection, acknowledgement and existence across the public and political spheres affects all spheres of social work. Domestic violence must be considered central to social work education, for developing practice that is critical and reflective and to advance knowledge of coercive control within social work. A critical approach to social work teaching, research and practice settings within domestic violence work necessarily begins with a positioning that refuses what Giroux, following writer Georges Didi-Huberman (2008), and within a different frame of reference, speaks of as the 'disimagination machine'; that is a critical approach where all forms of violence are confronted as part of a larger commitment to political accountability, community and the importance of positive effect for belonging and change. To writers such as Morley et al. (2019, p. 3), a critical approach to social work is necessarily a form of social work that is aligned with the people whom social workers claim to work with – 'those who experience social or socioeconomic disadvantage, those who are marginalised and those who experience oppression'. It is about acknowledging the limitations of our world and exposing oppressive conditions that impede human freedom and social justice.

It is crucial for social work educators, practitioners and students to engage in the ongoing political and moral project of what Giroux speaks of as 'critical pedagogy'. To Giroux (2011), critical pedagogy must be seen as a political and moral practice, a movement and an ongoing struggle for education as a force for strengthening the imagination and expanding democratic and public life. Critical pedagogy can thus provide the knowledge skills and social relations that enable students to engage critically in social life. Extending the work of thinkers such as Paulo Freire (1970) and later advancing his work alongside writers such as Roger Simon (1987a), David Livingstone (1986) and Joe Kincheloe (2008), Giroux (2011) argues that critical pedagogy draws attention to questions such as who has control over the conditions for the production of knowledge, values and skills, and illuminates how knowledge, identities and authority are constructed within social relations. To writers and thinkers who support social work education and practice as a larger project of freedom justice, moral judgement and individual and social responsibility, critical pedagogy goes to the very heart of what it means to address real inequalities of power at the social level and to conceive of education as a project of freedom (Giroux, 2011).

Critical pedagogy, in this instance, insists on the fundamental task of educators to ensure that the future points to a more socially just world (Giroux, 2011). As a practice of individual and social responsibility, it has direct implications for educators, students and practitioners of critical social work who are situated within domestic abuse work. Critical pedagogy as a practice of combating masculine control is not only important but a crucial site of struggle. An understanding of our current political situation demands attentiveness to these normative frames that surround and condition men's dominance and violence against women. It is about an act of moral imagination that forces the critical social worker within domestic violence work to think otherwise in order to act otherwise to expose, resist and finally counter all forms of normative violence practised everyday against women and their children.

Concluding remarks

This chapter has applied the work of Judith Butler and the *panopticon effect* to demonstrate its significance for critical social work and its broader relevance for attempting to explain the role of gender and violence norms in shaping masculine control and domination. By drawing on Butler's (1990, 2004) work on *gender performativity*, *heterosexual matrix* and *normative violence*, this chapter applies the *panopticon effect* to shed light on the invisible and difficult normative acts of violence that form part of an insidious social practice, within a modern system of violence, that sanctions the control, harm and murder of women. The *panopticon effect* is of political importance because it highlights victims' struggles for safety, protection and recognition within the context of very powerful norms that restrict women's intelligibility as human beings, and therefore has direct implications for social work education and practice, which can be a vehicle to challenge the normalisation of masculine control and dominance, including regular cultural stories that obscure appropriate recognition and response to men's violence against women.

Acknowledgements

I would like to thank Dr Phillip Ablett and Professor Christine Morley for their helpful feedback on an earlier draft of this chapter.

References

Agamben, G. (1999). *The Man Without Content*. Unites States: Stanford University Press.
Anderson, K. (2009). 'Gendering Coercive Control', *Violence Against Women* 15, (12), 1444–1457.
Arendt, H. (1958). *The Human Condition*. United States: University of Chicago Press.
Australian Institute of Health and Welfare. (2019). *Family, Domestic and Sexual Violence in Australia*. [Online]. Available at www.aihw.gov.au/reports/domestic-violence/family-domestic-sexual-violence-in-australia-2018/contents/summary [Accessed 2 January 2019].
Butler, J. (1988). 'Performative Acts and Gender Constitution: An Essay in Phenomenology and Feminist Theory', *Theatre Journal* 40, (4), 519–531.
Butler, J. (1990). *Gender Trouble: Feminism and the Subversion of Identity*. London: Routledge.
Butler, J. (2004). *Undoing Gender*. London: Routledge.
Butler, J. (2011). *Gender Trouble: Feminism and the Subversion of Identity*. London: Routledge.
Butterworth, K. and Westmarland, N. (2015). 'Victims' Views on Policing Partner Violence', *European Police Science and Research Bulletin* 13, 60–63.
Chambers, S. (2007). 'Normative Violence after 9/11: Rereading the Politics of Gender Trouble', *New Political Science* 29, (1), 43–60.
Cox, P. (2015). *Sexual assault and domestic violence in the context of co-occurrence and re-victimisation: State of knowledge paper*, ANROWS Landscapes, 13/2015. Sydney, NSW: ANROWS.
Department of Social Services. (2019). *The National Plan to Reduce Violence against Women and their Children 2010–2022*. [Online]. Available at www.dss.gov.au/women/programs-services/reducing-violence/the-national-plan-to-reduce-violence-against-women-and-their-children-2010-2022 [Accessed 4 January 2019].
DeShong, H. (2015). 'Policing Femininity, Affirming Masculinity: Relationship Violence, Control and Spatial Limitation', *Journal of Gender Studies* 24, (1), 85–103.
Didi-Huberman, G. (2008). *Images in Spite of All: Four Photographs from Auschwitz*, trans. Shane B. Lillis. Chicago: University of Chicago Press.
Diemer, K., Powell, A., and Webster, K. (2018). *Four in Ten Australians think Women Lie About Being Victims of Sexual Assault*. [Online]. Available at https://theconversation.com/four-in-ten-australians-think-women-lie-about-being-victims-of-sexual-assault-107363 [Accessed 5 January 2019].
Dobash, R. E. and Dobash, R. (1979). *Violence Against Wives*. New York: The Free Press.
Elizabeth, V. (2017). 'Custody Stalking: A Mechanism of Coercively Controlling Mothers Following Separation', *Feminist Legal Studies* 25, (2), 185–201.
Fisher, S. (2011). *From Violence to Coercive Control*. White Ribbon Research Series 3. Retrieved 10 April 2019 from https://www.whiteribbon.org.au/wp-content/uploads/2016/10/From_violence_to_coercive_control_Fisher_2011.pdf.
Foucault, M. (1971). 'Nietzsche, Genealogy, History'. In: Rabinow, P. (ed.), *The Foucault Reader*. (pp. 76–100). New York: Pantheon Books.
Foucault M. (1972) *The archaeology of knowledge*, Tavistock Publications, London.
Foucault, M. (1979). *Discipline and Punish: The Birth of the Prison*. New York: Vintage Books.
Foucault, M. (1982a). 'On the Genealogy of Ethics: An Overview of Work in Progress'. In: Dreyfus, H. L. and Rabinow, P. (eds.), *Michel Foucault: Beyond Structuralism and Hermeneutics*. (pp. 229–252). Chicago: University of Chicago Press.
Foucault, M. (1982b). 'The Subject and Power', *Critical Inquiry* 8, 777–795.

Freire, P. (1970). *Pedagogy of the Oppressed*. New York: Herder and Herder.
Giroux, H. (2011). *On Critical Pedagogy*. USA: Bloomsbury Publishing.
Hearn, J. (1998). *The Violences of Men: How Men Talk About and How Agencies Respond to Men's Violence to Women*. Sweden: Orebro University.
Herring, J., Probert, R., and Gilmore, S. (2015). *Great Debates in Family Law*. England: Palgrave Macmillan.
Hill, J. (2019). *See What You Made Me Do: Power, Control and Domestic Abuse*. Australia: black Inc.
Kincheloe, J. (2008). *Critical Pedagogy Primer*. 4th ed. New York: Peter Lang.
Levinas, E. (1982). *Ethics and Infinity*. Pittsburgh: Duquesne University Press.
Livingstone, D. (1986). *Critical Pedagogy and Cultural Power*. United States: Praeger.
Lloyd, M. (2007). *Judith Butler: From norms to Politics*. Lloyd. USA: Polity Press.
Mao, F. (2019). *How Dangerous is Australia for Women?* [Online]. Available at www.bbc.com/news/world-australia-46913913 [Accessed 2 February 2019].
Meyer, S. (2018). *After a Deadly Month for Domestic Violence, the Message Doesn't Appear to be Getting Through*. [Online]. Available at https://theconversation.com/after-a-deadly-month-for-domestic-violence-the-message-doesnt-appear-to-be-getting-through-105568 [Accessed 12 January 2019].
Morley, C., Ablett, P., and Macfarlane, S. (2019). *Engaging with Social Work: A Critical Introduction*. 2nd ed. London: Cambridge University Press.
Our Watch. (2019). *Facts and Figures*. [Online]. Available at www.ourwatch.org.au/understanding-violence/facts-and-figures [Accessed 12 January 2019].
Pease, B. (2017). *Men as allies in preventing men's violence against women: Principles and practices for promoting accountability*. Sydney: White Ribbon Australia.
Rosdahl, J. (2017). *Reflections on Power, Gender and Violence*, SCEaT Workshop report 2B Brisbane: SCEaT.
Short, E. and Wilton, L. (2016). *Talking About Structural Inequalities in Everyday Life*. USA: Information Age.
Stark, E. (2007). *Interpersonal violence. Coercive control: How Men Entrap Women in Personal Life*. New York: Oxford University Press.
Stark, E. (2012). Re-presenting battered women: Coercive control and the defense of liberty. In conference Violence Against Women: Complex Realities and New Issues in a Changing World, Les Presses de l'Université du Québec, Québec.
The National Domestic Violence Resource Centre Victoria. (2013). *True Stories*. [Online]. Available at www.dvrcv.org.au/stories [Accessed 5 June 2019].
Watson, L. and Ancis, J. (2013). 'Power and Control in the Legal System: From Marriage/Relationship to Divorce and Custody', *Violence Against Women* 19, (2), 166–186.
White Ribbon Australia. (2019). *Understanding Domestic Violence* [Online]. Available at www.whiteribbon.org.au/understand-domestic-violence/types-of-abuse/stalking/ [Accessed 1 July 2019].
Wittig, M. (1992). *The Straight Mind and Other Essays*. Boston: Beacon Press.
Wright, H. (2015). *Addressing Notions of Masculinity that Drive Conflict*. UK: Safeworld.

30
Disrupting ableism in social work pedagogy with Maurice Merleau-Ponty and critical disability theory

Lisa Stafford

QUEENSLAND UNIVERSITY OF TECHNOLOGY, AUSTRALIA

Introduction

Cultural and institutional forms of discrimination toward people with diverse "non-normative" bodies continue to be perpetuated in society through dominant normative discourse and images. Ableism is a key form of prejudice underpinning discrimination which has largely gone unchecked (Campbell, 2009; Goodley, 2014). This has resulted in the devaluation and dehumanisation of bodies that differ from the "standardised" body form – aka the *normate*. This normative body form is superimposed upon all bodies, regardless of the diversity of narratives those bodies present (Stafford & Volz, 2016). Added to the normative body type, is also the dominant Cartesian view of the body as thing, permitting objectification (Moran, 2000).

Yet the post-war, French phenomenological philosopher, Maurice Merleau-Ponty's (1908–1961) work contests this dominant view, instead viewing the body as lived – our embodied form of agency in the world. Merleau-Ponty (2012) felt that the body, when viewed as "lived", takes on a new position in the mind of people, that is "the body as valued and respected" (Moran, 2000, p. 45). Through understanding the body as lived, Merleau-Ponty, 2012 argues that we come to recognise and understand the everyday: taken-for-granted connections with our world; our perception; our consciousness of the world. We also importantly come to understand the world's influence and impact on our embodied or disembodied felt experiences of the world (Stafford & Volz, 2016). That is, our being-in-the-world plays out within social, cultural, temporal and material context. As Matthews (2002, p. 9) noted, "Our lived experience is thus lived out against the background of a certain social reality, and cannot be understood except by taking into account social reality". Here, Merleau-Ponty contended that "social and political involvement is a necessary part of our being-in-the-world" (Matthews, 2002, p. 9).

Merleau-Ponty's scholarship and doctrine regarding embodiment and perception unfolded during a complex time of war and post-war Europe during the early to mid-twentieth century. His thinking was influenced by a cross-section of thinkers in existentialism, phenomenology, gestalt psychology and political theory. Henry Bergson and Edmund Husserl had a profound influence on his thinking early on, along with his tenuous friendship with Jean-Paul Sartre. The idea of being-in-the-world proposed by Martin Heidegger (a German phenomenology philosopher) also interested Merleau-Ponty – so much that he adopted the term but expanded the ideas through perception, embodiment and a non-dualist lens. From this work, he went on to produce his famous doctoral thesis and published book, *Phenomenology of Perception*, in 1945. This and his other works raised critical insights into our human existence and freedom – that is, our being-in-the-world is embodied and cannot be understood separate to our social-physical-political world. His work has inspired scholarship across many areas including feminism, politics, arts and architecture. These continuities are thanks to more recent translations of this work, which have raised awareness of the significance of his thinking.

Merleau-Ponty's theorising about embodiment provokes deeper ways of understanding the body-in-the-world. Embodiment became a critical lens in feminism and disability studies as a way of illustrating and contesting how our lived bodies are influenced by "physical and socio-cultural paradigms that are enacted in everyday spaces" (Stafford & Volz, 2016, p. 1). It is through our body-world experience that we are able to expose certain "meanings and understandings attached and inscribed about the body" (Stafford & Volz, 2016, p. 1), including entrenched ableist thinking.

Within social work discourses, ableism and the devaluing of non-normative bodies persists in both subtle and, at times, overt ways. This is evident in the prolonged existence of medical discourse that focuses on deficits of non-normative bodies; probing and problematising "non-standardised" ways they move, think, speak and act; and the practices of non-normative bodies being assessed, classified and managed in neoliberal systems (Meekosha & Dowse, 2007; Roulstone, 2015; Shakespeare et al., 2016). This occurs despite the social model and critical disability theorising contesting the medicalisation of disability since the 1980s (Barnes, 2000, 2012; Hughes & Paterson, 1997). In addition, how diverse bodies are positioned in social work and human services suggests subtle and overt forms of ableism toward the body. For example, mainstream social work responses often exclude disability and treat it as something different or special, yet disability cuts across age, class, gender and race. Further adding to this othering, is the historical lack of presence and recognition of disability alongside class, race, gender and age in social theory.

In order to genuinely promote critical thinking and anti-oppressive practice, social work pedagogy must embrace the lived body and critical disability studies as part of the mainstream. This chapter will argue that the aim of creating a more just society is contingent upon social work students and practitioners developing a critical understanding of disability, the human experience and socio-politics of bodies, access and inclusion. To begin we start with exposing ableism in society, perpetuated through the normate – the normative body form. It will then turn to theorising the body through Merleau-Ponty's Phenomenology of the Body, illustrating the body is not some inanimate object, it is lived and agentic. His works also show how certain bodies' agency might be limited due to interaction with an ableist world underpinned by historical socio-cultural context (Weiss, 2015). Understanding and adopting this way of thinking is critical for social workers working with individuals and families with disabilities, in order to address the entrenched prejudice of ableism.

Introducing the normate and ableism: oppressive normative body representation

Society holds dominant beliefs and images of what is a normal and able body. These images – or representations – of "stereotypical" bodies have persisted over time throughout society, with only slight modifications in style preferences (Butler, 1990; Garland-Thomson, 2002). Garland-Thomson (2017, p. 8), describes the dominant representation held about the body as the *normate*, "the social figure through which people can represent themselves as definitive human beings". This social figure against which bodies are measured is male, upright, white and of a mesomorphic physique. Such a representation was noted by sociologist Erving Goffman in his early work on stigma (see Goffman, 1989) – describing extremely narrow representation of what is deemed the normative body – "a young married white urban heterosexual protestant, father, college educated, fully employed of good complexion weight and height and sporty" (Goffman, 1989; Garland-Thomson, 2017, p. 8). Power in terms of authority and status is attributed to anyone who fits such bodily configuration (Weiss, 2015).

There is a long history of images of standardisation of body form conveyed and reinforced through society and space (Imrie, 2003; Stafford & Volz, 2016). This is no more evident than in art and architecture works such as Leonardo Da Vinci's interpretation of *The Vitruvian Man* in the sixteenth century, Charles-Édouard Jeanneret-Gris' (better known as Le Corbusier) 'Modular' body of the twentieth century, and Neufert's (2012) *Metric Handbook* for anthropometric data in the twenty-first century (Stafford & Volz, 2016). These idealised proportions of the body are imbued in everyday life spaces, where power and status are mediated spatially to normative bodies while subjugated bodies are devalued, precluded and/or exploited in everyday life (Garland-Thomson, 2002; Weiss, 2015).

The normate's status and power are so embedded and accepted as a societal norm that it is in need of explicitly exposing and "calling out". As Garland-Thomson (2017) describes:

> The normate subject position emerges, however only when we scrutinise the social processes and discourse that constitute physical and cultural otherness. Because figures of otherness are highly marked in power relationships, even as they are marginalised, their cultural visibility as these deviant obscures and neutralises the normative figure that they legitimate.
>
> *(pp. 8–9)*

Exposing this normative conception of the body and the power it holds has been undertaken by feminist, race, queer and disability scholars (Weiss, 2015). Feminist scholars have shown how masculine-dominated medicine systems judge and measure women's bodies against the normate, rendering female bodily difference as helpless, dependent, weak, vulnerable and incapable (Butler, 1990; Grosz & Eisenman, 2001; Weissman, 1992). Race theorists, particularly black feminist scholars such as hooks, have also shown not only how body gender has been used to determine worth and power, but so too body colour (Hooks, 1981). As Fanon's classic work contends: "being viewed and treated as a normal" body is not everyone's birthright, rather it is an inherited privilege assigned to white bodies (Fanon, 2008, cited in Weiss, 2015, p. 86). Crip Queer theory has also exposed the rights and freedom that the image and gait of the heterosexual able body is granted, at the same time revealing the ridicule and wounding assigned to queer bodies (McRuer, 2005).

The social-cultural-material processes upholding the normate while othering non-normative bodies have been further progressed by disability scholars through the concept of ableism.

Ableism: prejudice against non-normative bodies

Ableism is a prejudice that preferences "normative" standardised body form while subjugating non-normative bodies. According to Chouinard (1997, p. 380), who was one of the early theorists of ableism, this form of prejudice is based on "ideas, practices, institutions, and social relations that presume ablebodiness, and by doing so construct persons with disabilities as marginalized … and largely invisible 'others'". It is a set of beliefs, processes and practices about the kind of body that holds value and worth (Wolbring, 2008).

Identity, abilities and markets have all been linked to this deeply rooted form of prejudice (Campbell, 2009; Wolbring, 2008). Campbell (2009) suggests that such ableist thinking and systems have led to the re-produced idea of the "typical" self and body that personifies being human. In this sense, "it is a trajectory of perfection, a deep way of thinking about bodies and wholeness, ... moves beyond the more familiar terrority of social inclusion and usual indices of exclusion" (Campbell, 2014, p. 80). Campbell explicitly links ableism with the intersection of identities, and discusses the internalised ableism encouraged by social, economic and political systems (Campbell, 2009).

Specific body attributes and abilities are particularly valued by systems according to Wollbring (2007, p. 1, cited in Goodley, 2014, p. 22), who defines ableism as "favouritism for certain abilities for example cognition, competiveness or consumerisms and the often negative sentiments towards the lack of favoured abilities". Assumptions about competencies have been linked to the body for some time (James, 1993; Toombs, 1997). James (1993, p. 105) contends "height, shape, appearance, gender and performance" are five features of the body that are the basis of judgements of capability. This was reinforced by disabled feminist scholars Chouinard (1997), Scully (2008) and Toombs (1997) illustrating how one's value and recognition are tied to the corporeal form, and illuminating how the "normal" body (upright, forward-facing) is assigned value and autonomy, whereas bodies that vary from this norm lose autonomy and value (Stafford, 2013). A person whose body differs from what society conceives as "normal", often encounters exclusion and discrimination because of assumptions made about their body's capabilities (Scully, 2008; Hughes et al., 2005; Hughes & Paterson, 1997; Toombs, 1997). Such acts of prejudice have meant that many people with non-normative bodies have to "manage" negative experiences and devaluations attached to corporeality (Imrie & Kumar, 1998).

The market plays a particular role in determining what bodily attributes are of value, such as those relating to mind and agility. Goodley (2014) explicitly links ableism to one's value determined through the markets. This is reflected in Gleeson's earlier work (Gleeson, 1999) illustrating the influence industrialisation and capitalism have had on determining a body's economic value. Economic value is predicated on ableist "normative" body-mind requirements declared to be productive in meeting deemed working rates set for profit by economic systems (Gleeson, 1999). Under the Capitalist system, non-normative bodies that speak, move, think, feel, sense and act in ways that contest the "norms" of bodies, are devalued and viewed as burdensome and dependent – not profitable (Taylor, 2004). Or as Garland-Thomson (2002) notes, such bodies are often labelled as "Misfits" (2002).

Ableism is used to exert power over non-normative bodies deemed as burdens and unproductive. According to Wollbring (2007, p. 1, cited in Goodley, 2014, p. 22), ableism is used "by various social groups to justify their elevated level of rights and status in relation to other groups ... the system from which forms of disablism, hetero/sexism and racism emanate and has in mind a 'species-typical' human being". Acts of discrimination based on abilities and appearances continue to be perpetuated toward people with non-normative bodies. Goodley (2014) notes that the form of oppression that stems from the normative discourse privileging "ablebodiness" is understood as disablism. As outlined by Thomas (2007, p. 73), "disablism is a form of social oppression involving the social imposition of restrictions of activity on people with impairments and the socially engendered undermining of their psycho-emotional wellbeing". This form of oppression results in disabled people being excluded in all aspects of everyday life – social, political, cultural and psycho-emotional (Goodley, 2014).

The concept of ableism is important as it helps to expose and explain the normative arrangement of bodies embedded in everyday life spaces, systems and discourses (Shakespeare, 2005; Holt, 2003, 2004; Allen, 2004). However, to start to disrupt normative body representation and discourses and the privilege and power they yield, we need to re-establish non-normative bodies as valuable, embodied, knowing forms of agency. This counter narrative can be assisted through the work of Maurice Merleau-Ponty (2012).

The lived body

Merleau-Ponty (2012) argues that we come to recognise and understand the everyday world – the taken-for-granted connections with our world; our perception; our consciousness of the world through our body (Carman, 2008, 1999; Cerbone, 2006; Thomas, 2005). The key to understanding experience, Merleau-Ponty (2012) argues, is through the body, which gives meaning to the space around itself (Cerbone, 2006; Thomas, 2005). The body not only plays an essential role with respect to the constitution of other categories of objects but is itself constituted in experience as a categorically distinct kind of entity (Cerbone, 2006, p. 103).

Merleau-Ponty rejected the distinction between body and mind conveyed in the influential work of René Descartes, who was a French philosopher of mathematics and science in the seventeenth century. Referred to as "Cartesian" philosophy, the mind is considered as the key to understanding experience, while the body is seen as simply an inanimate object (Thomas, 2005). Merleau-Ponty felt that Cartesian objectification of the body led to it being detached, dehumanised and inanimate (Cerbone, 2006; Moran, 2000; Thomas, 2005). However, Merleau-Ponty felt that the body when viewed as "lived", takes on a new position in the mind of people, that is "the body as valued and respected" (Moran, 2000, p. 45). This is reinforced by Moran (2000, p. 415) who notes that when the "body is viewed as sacred, then it is impossible for society to treat the face or body, or even dead body, like a thing". But this must extend to all bodies, which means the normate representation needs to be contested, and all bodies are to be viewed as sacred and knowing.

Bringing attention back to all bodies as lived is needed to contest an ableist view of the body as it persists in society (Thomas, 2005; Imrie, 2001). Merleau-Ponty's non-dualist approach to the body-world relationship is an important frame through which to build an understanding of embodiment of our experiences with our world (Smith, 2008), and from which to understand and disrupt dominant representations of the body imbued in an everyday life world. Such life world interactions are where inclusion and exclusion of particular bodies are constantly being mediated.

Corporeal schema and forms of bodily self-expression

Central to Merleau-Ponty's philosophy, is the argument that integrity of perception is informed by and founded on the integrity of bodily self-experiences (Merleau-Ponty, cited in Cerbone, 2006, pp. 119–120). Key to this understanding is the *corporeal schema*, which is understood as the body's previous experience of space, producing a corporeal system of possible movement, thus enabling the body-subject to adjust unthinkingly (without the mind) to the demands that space places on it during everyday activities (Carman, 1999). As Carman (1999, p. 220) describes: "The body schema is the bundle of skills and capacities that constitute the body's precognitive familiarity with itself and the world it inhabits." The body scheme is thus the state of knowledge: "I am conscious of my body via the world and I am conscious of the world through the medium of my body" (Merleau-Ponty, 1962, p. 82).

According to Merleau-Ponty (2012), the lived body has two forms of "bodily self-expression", that is, *habitual body* and *body-at-this-moment*. The two levels are considered important dimensions to meaning and movement in the world – in particular, exercising spatial agency.

The habitual body is characterised as the person's habitual actions and the routines the person performs fluently on a regular basis (Cerbone, 2006; Seamon, 1980, 2002). Habitual movement was considered by Seamon (2002, p. 44) as the "routine sequence in daily movement patterns that are pre-conscious", that is, the body instinctively knows what to do without the need for conscious awareness or thought (Seamon, 1980, 2002). An example of habitual routine is the act of driving the same route home and on arrival wondering how one got home; it is the sensation of being on automatic pilot (Seamon, 2002, 1980).

The habitual body enables people to perform routine movements without the need to think and plan every single movement within a routine (Seamon, 2002), where "the body-subject is considered to be 'stabilizing force' in which people gain the freedom to extend their world horizons" (Seamon, 2002, p. 44). In other words, the body takes over and performs these routine movements without conscious thought, enabling the person to proceed through their lifeworld (Cerbone, 2006). Here the body itself is understood as an "experiencing agent" (Hughes & Paterson, 1997, p. 329; Seamon, 2002) that facilitates interaction and movement in spaces we inhabit. For example, Allen's (2004) geographical study of young people with visual impairment, and Valentine and Skelton's (2003, 2007) geographical study of deaf children, both illustrate how a child's body is the foundation of their spatial agency.

Body-at-this-moment, is bodily self-experience, that is the "layout of the body" in the current situation (Thomas, 2005, p. 71), otherwise known as the body position. An example of the body-at-this-moment is sitting on the bus. Where conflict occurs between the habitual body and body-at-this-moment, the body generally adjusts to the situation unthinkably. An example of this is when you are walking on a footpath and someone is walking on the wrong side and coming toward you; you unconsciously move to the other side to avoid a collision. However, if the body cannot adjust to the situation the effect can be profound. According to Thomas (2005, p. 71), "when the relationship with the body and world is disturbed, a person's existence is profoundly shaken". Merleau-Ponty (2012) felt that such clashes or conflicts between the two levels of bodily self-experience, habitual body and body-at-this-moment, provide an insight into taken-for-granted bodily self-expression and world relationships.

People with impairments or "non-normative" bodies encounter such clashes on a daily basis, not because of lack of agency by the habitual body (a person's unique embodied way of being-in-the-world), but because the body-at-this-moment encounter is frequently based upon the normate body-in-the-world. Such clashes convey the non-normative bodies as the "misfits" in this situation; rather than the prejudicial ableist world and systems built upon these normative ideas that restrict the habitual bodies of disabled people. How restricted body agency and disembodiment in the world unfolds, was illustrated by Merleau-Ponty (2012) in cases of people with impairments. He importantly showed how "non-normative" bodies do have agency through their habitual body, it is only when the body in a particular setting is not permitted their way of being-in-the-world that the habitual body becomes immobilised (enforced immobility), because it cannot adjust unthinkingly to an ableist body-world clash at that point in time (Merleau-Ponty, 2012; Thomas, 2005).

This enforced immobility and loss of spatial agency have been further illustrated in disability geography studies (Moore et al., 2008). For example, the studies mentioned above, such as Allen (2004) and Valentine and Skelton (2003, 2007), found young people's embodied agency collapsed due to unexpected changes to familiar routes, exclusionary spaces and other people's actions. The clash reveals social-spatial conditions impeded the person's habitual way of being mobile, thus forcing immobility and diminishing agency. The conflicted experience conveys deeper meanings embedded in the world – particular historical sociocultural representations of the body which maintain ableism.

The philosophical position of Merleau-Ponty brings attention back to our body as lived embodiment with agency. The lens makes known that our understanding of our experiences with the world becomes known through our body's relationship with the spatiality of the world. The lived body also conveys socio-cultural meanings held about the body and world. We importantly come to understand the world's influence and impact on our embodied or disembodied felt experiences of the world through our body-world interactions (Stafford & Volz, 2016). This is expanded further by Grosz and Eisenman, who view the body as "the primary sociocultural product" (2001, p. 32) shaped by "physical and sociocultural paradigms that are enacted in everyday spaces" (Stafford & Volz, 2016, p. 1). Through the body-world experience we can reveal "meanings and understandings attached and inscribed about the body" (Stafford & Volz, 2016, p. 1), including entrenched ableism. Applying Merleau-Ponty's thinking can help to expose ableist Cartesian ideas that operate in both overt and covert ways in social work and human services praxis. This is illustrated in the next section.

Able body discourse othering people with impairments in social work and human service praxis

Social work and human services prides itself on the pursuit of social justice for people and groups experiencing injustice and inequality due to oppressive cultures and structures. Yet, social work and human services praxis can be part of the oppression of people with impairments when dominant normative discourse and representations go uncontested. The body, and particularly "the able body" discourse is one such area that has gone largely uncontested in social work and human service as evident in praxis regarding disability. This lack of disruption of ableism occurs despite decades of scholarly advancement in disability studies and the enactment of the UN Convention of Rights of Persons with Disability (CRPD) in 2006.

Teaching how ableism works in social, economic and political systems is critical to address subtle and overt forms of oppression that continue toward diverse bodies (Roulstone, 2012). For too long now disability has been treated as something separate – not part of mainstream social work (Meekosha & Dowse, 2007; Roulstone, 2012) – which has meant that ableism has gone unchecked in disability praxis. Part of this problem carries over from the historic dominant medicalisation approach toward people with impairments, but it also links back to the lack of presence and recognition of disability alongside class, race, gender and age in social theory. To address ableism we must expose how it pervades in programmes of practice to understand how to disrupt it from a critical social work lens with a focus on the lived body. We do this by examining how unruly bodies are being dealt with in systems in which social work and human services operate. This will be followed by a call to action to disrupt ableism through embedding the lived body and critical disability studies in mainstream social work and human service pedagogy.

Medicalisation of bodies teamed up with neoliberalism

Disability is still often understood in social work and human services as a deficit – of biological and psychological processes – rather than a social structural creation (Goodley, 2014; Roulstone, 2012). Praxis in disability is dominated with ideas and discourse of impaired bodies in need of assessment, treatment and management (Meekosha & Dowse, 2007; Roulstone, 2012). The medical individualised model influence has intensified with the domination of neoliberalism underpinning social service systems. For example, bodies are being classified and categorised in terms of their degree of "functional deficit" in how they move, think, feel and act, in order to determine their deservingness to access to supports (Meekosha & Dowse, 2007;

Roulstone, 2012; Shakespeare et al., 2016). Access is mediated through two notions: deservingness and paternalism.

The notion of *deservingness* is said to be "central to the moral framework of distributive justice and social welfare in a modern liberal state" (Soldatic & Pini, 2009, p. 83). As noted by Soldatic and Pini (2009, p. 83) this conceptualisation has "meant structural disadvantage has been reframed as an internal affect" resulting from the individual's poor behaviour, thus rendering them unworthy and undeserving (Stafford et al., 2019). Whereas, the new paternalism concept suggests "those who are impoverished suffer from defects of reason and/or character" and are less willing to comply with societal norms and expectations (Marston et al., 2016, p. 401). Bodies determined by systems as undeserving or, worse, "suspect" are managed through compliance measures with which social and human service workers are complicit (Meekosha & Dowse, 2007; Shakespeare et al., 2016).

Applying deservingness and paternalism within a medicalised model of disability has been implemented by many OECD countries to justify a reduction of welfare spending, and to arbitrate access to income and disability supports (Soldatic & Pini, 2009; Roulstone and Prideaux, 2012; Spagnuolo, 2016). In Australia, access to welfare and social services continues to be mediated by deservingness/undeservingness through external assessment processes. For example, access to the disability support pension is mediated through work capacity assessment linked to the Welfare to Work Policy and Disability Employment/Job Access Services (Stafford et al., 2019). Another example is the National Disability Insurance Scheme (NDIS) introduced in 2012, which is one of the most significant reforms to disability support to occur in Australia. Despite the NDIS shifting to a social model of disability that promotes choice and control, access to the system is still mediated through eligibility processes based on body deservingness – type of condition and severity of functional capacity (how bodies think, talk, feel, move or act) determined by assessments such as WHO Disability Assessment Schedule 2.0 (WHO, 2012). Bodies scoring less than the deservingness benchmark must fend for themselves.

These systems favour technocratic practices of professionalism and managerialism to mediate access and compliance (Marston et al., 2016; Shakespeare et al., 2016). It is important to unpack these practices to illustrate how far we are from Merleau-Ponty's thoughts about the body. These systems do not acknowledge or permit the person's own body knowing and embodiment in decisions about itself and the supports it needs to contest the ableist world it finds itself in.

Access to support mediated by "independent" body assessments

Coding and classifying body function has been an ongoing assessment mechanism used in disability and income support service systems for some time (Stafford et al., 2019). This practice has not been removed with the introduction of the United Nation's CRPD in 2006, or replaced with self-determination of access to support based on lived body-world knowing. No – instead, assessment mechanisms continue to be used as divisive and deterrence measures to meet economic rationalist priorities. This is supported by Grover and Piggott (2015, pp. 1–2), who believe assessments are mechanisms to "curtail the growing number of disability pensions", because such supports are pushed as unsustainable under austerity rhetoric conveyed by governments (Grover & Piggott, 2015). This concern was also observed by Garsten and Jacobsson (2013) in their review of the processes undertaken in the Swedish system. Yet Spagnuolo (2016, p. 90) argues that "the scarcity of resources" rationale being used to justify such approaches must be challenged, rather than accepted. Because Spagnuolo (2016, p. 90) argues that "by accepting we are permitting the categorisation of disabilities" and upholding deserving and undeserving rhetoric (Stafford et al., 2019).

Research has shown that coding and sorting deservingness of "disability" is problematic (Garsten & Jacobsson, 2013; Marston, 2013; Roulstone, 2015; Soldatic & Pini, 2009; Spagnuolo, 2016). Such processes operate from a paternalist positioning of people with impairments in the assessment process, preferencing professionalism over a person's own body knowing (Barnes, 2000; Marston, 2013; Roulstone, 2015; Shakespeare et al., 2016; Spagnuolo, 2016). This exposes the ableist and Cartesian view of the body underpinning disability systems.

Professionalism enacted as an "expert-led" approach is also problematic as it not only shifts power away from the knowing person with the disability to the professional "expert" (Shakespeare et al., 2016), but also reframes the social production of disability into medical deficit issues, thus requiring expert technical knowledge input (Barnes, 2000; Schoeman & Schoeman, 2002). A study by Shakespeare et al. (2016) demonstrated the significant issues that occur in the work capacity assessment process when dominated by the expert narrative. First, the government's nominated allied health professional is deemed the expert to determine the work capacity of a person with impairments (Shakespeare et al., 2016). The individual's known health providers, such as general practitioners, are excluded from undertaking the assessment with the person, rather it is performed on them by an unknown "expert" (Shakespeare et al., 2016). According to Grover and Piggott (2009, cited in Shakespeare et al., 2016, p. 27) this was because "Drs were considered too soft" in their assessment of work capacity.

Management of unruly bodies

Another practice occurring in OECD countries such as Australia, is mutual obligation requirements being placed upon non-normative bodies deemed capable of working in order to access income support, e.g. disability support pension or newstart (Marston, 2013; Stafford et al., 2019). This is a practice noted by Grover and Piggott (2015, p. 1) occurring in the United Kingdom (UK):

> A reorientation of welfare benefit support for disabled people that has emphasised a contractual, rather than rights-based approach and which as a consequence has increased the expectation that in order to receive support, individuals will have to act in a pro-social manner, most notably through attempts to re-enter wage work at earliest opportunity.

Compliance of deemed-capable non-normative bodies is administered by social and human service workers tasked with ensuring contractual arrangements for support are adhered to. Non-normative bodies deemed capable are constantly threatened with breaching if they dare not to comply with job-seeking orders. Managerialism of bodies is also found in practice language – "good patient"/"bad patient", compliant/non-compliant (Mallett & Runswick-Cole, 2014). These systems and practices transfer the socio-cultural oppression experienced by non-normative bodies to the individual – as a deficit problem. This is predicated by ableism informed by socio-cultural views of the body and capitalism. Here we can see Marxist influences, where Merleau-Ponty contends that there are conditions to our embodiment, which set limits to our freedom (Matthews, 2002). These conditions are influenced by our being in a social and political world in which our individual lives play out. For non-normative bodies, the condition of ableism operating in a capitalist world has a profound effect on one's embodiment, personhood and freedom.

The persistence of this medical individualised view of disability in a neoliberal service context, suggests that despite decades of strong disability activism and scholarship contesting such views, ableism and an objectified view of the body persist. A significant praxis shift is required to disrupt ableism and neoliberalism which is a powerful influence in mediating access to disability services. As noted by Campbell (2009), contesting the biomedical models of disability must be progressed through models of disability which are more aligned with critical, anti-oppressive practice that links "the designation 'disability' to capitalist economy and social organisation" (Campbell, 2009, p. 78). This is important, as the rights of non-normative bodies continue to be contested – being subject to scrutiny, surveillance and control by oppressive systems and practices. Social work and human services education must confront this normative way of thinking through Merleau-Ponty's understanding of our being-in-the-world, as it ensures we understand experience in relation to our world that is imbued with social, temporal, cultural and political influences that favour the dominant and oppress others. We cannot be complacent because reform is occurring, as these conditions to embodiment and freedom persist. Social work pedagogy must instil in students a critical gaze to working with these systems, in order to resist and disrupt oppressive practice toward non-normative bodies.

Ensuring lived bodies and critical disability studies are located centrally in social work pedagogy

Disability scholars have illustrated that disability is a social construct, not the inevitable consequence of impairment (Oliver, 2009); yet Roulstone (2012) notes that an examination of social work university course content, quickly reveals how much the medical and paternalistic view of disability prevails. This is despite decades of disability scholarship illuminating how disability is a social disadvantage experienced by disabled people because of the physical, institutional and attitudinal environment which fails to meet the needs of people who do not match the social expectations of "normalcy" (Goodley, 2014; Hosking, 2008; Mallett & Runswick-Cole, 2014).

Critical disability studies has been instrumental in probing some of the tensions between medical and social dualism that seem to exist in academia (Goodley, 2014; Mallett & Runswick-Cole, 2014). Such tensions could also be influencing curricula in social work and human services. Critical disability studies presents a much more complex account of disability that reflects the diversity of how disability is constructed and experienced (Goodley et al., 2017; Hosking, 2008; Meekosha & Shuttleworth, 2009). Goodley (2013) suggests critical disability studies advances theorising of disability through concepts of materialism, bodies that matter, inter/trans-sectionality, global disability studies, and self and Other. Hosking (2008, pp. 7–8) expands upon Goodley's key themes, outlining that the critical lens permits the questioning of concepts of personal independence and interdependence, the social construction of non-disability as well as disability, the concept of normalcy, fundamental values of individual dignity and respect in democratic societies, and issues at the intersection of disability with class, gender, race, sexual orientation, ethnicity and other socially constructed categories. The lived reality of people with disabilities alongside the social and political understandings based on societal power relations is fundamental to this critical frame (Goodley, 2013). Social work and human services must engage in critical disability studies, to overcome the prolific yet subtle prejudice against diverse bodies due to privileging "Normal and Able" discourse and approaches.

Bodies have a central role in critical disability studies (Goodley, 2014); the aim being to counter the persistent narrative of ableism, and notions of deservingness and paternalism enacted toward non-normative bodies in the social welfare sector. Merleau-Ponty's philosophy of the body can be particularly helpful to contest the body as an object. Shifting the mindset toward the body as lived is a critical step in changing the paradigm. This lived body – our unique embodiment in the world – possesses knowledge and agency only known to oneself, including the constraints placed on it by the world. People with non-normative bodies are the experts.

Our body has the insider knowledge that can never be captured or understood by an "independent expert" assessor.

Meekosha and Dowse (2007) presented a challenge back in 2007 in Australian social work education regarding disability and the need to adopt a critical disability studies approach. How far have we really come since this time? Are we educating students with a critical lens so they can understand and identify the complex socio-cultural production of disability, diverse identities in disability and various experiences of disablement to disrupt ableist practice? Or are we just continuing ableism in education through teaching the "impairment bus tour" approach to non-normative bodies? Is disability taught as a one-off subject in isolation? Or worse, not taught at all? How disability is taught and positioned in a four-year undergraduate programme or two-year Master's programme is a clear indication of the value held about diverse bodies. If embedded, then it demonstrates a commitment to the intent and progression of the rights of disabled people, the disruption of ableism, and instilling critical disability thinking and anti-oppressive practice.

Starting points to disrupt ableist pedagogy

Challenge 1. An important starting point is to do an audit of your social work courses, both undergraduate and Master's, to determine if and how disability and the body are being conveyed in curricula. Is there a unit/course? If yes, what is the dominant discourse and model of disability being conveyed? Does it have the dominant overview of impairment types? To start shifting the paradigm toward a more critical approach, revise units/courses to align with a critical disability studies approach. Use key concepts as a starting point – do we discuss ableism/disablism, models of disability including history; rights, "voice" and citizenship; identity politics, advocacy and activism; diversity, culture and intersectionality? Furthermore, embedding disability throughout the programme will help to transform praxis. Disability intersects all fields of practice as well as cutting across age, race, class, gender and sexuality. An important starting point for embedding across the programme is to check if and how other academics are conveying disability in other units – such as child and family, youth services, domestic violence, age care.

Challenge 2. Who is conveying the information about disability? Is lived experience and leadership from disabled people prioritised in course content and delivery? This is crucial for students' learning to disrupt ableism. As a privileged disabled academic myself, I am always aware of the importance of ensuring multiple experiences and perspectives are presented. One of the many ways I have done this was through having five young women with diverse impairments provide a lectorial on the experience of growing up with impairments in an ableist world. Young women were positioned as the experts of their experiences and students were able to listen and ask questions in informal circles with the young women, which was a novel experience for both, breaking down stigma.

Conclusion

Merleau-Ponty dedicated his life's work to thinking about human existence. His philosophy of being-in-the-world challenged dominant Cartesian thinking that preferences the mind and objectifies the body. Merleau-Ponty not only showed how the body is lived, agentic and knowing, he also illustrated that our being is embodied and cannot be understood without the world. That is, our being occurs in the world, and this world has social, historical and political context. Merleau-Ponty's theorising about embodiment provokes deeper ways of understanding the body-in-the-world. His work has also been used to poignantly illustrate how non-normative bodies' agency and knowing are often oppressed – not due to the body itself, but due to being in a world underpinned by ableism. And such ableist thinking toward non-normative bodies has been shown to operate in social systems and approaches in social work. By adopting Merleau-Ponty's thinking of bodies as lived, agentic and knowing within a critical disability studies approach, we can begin to disrupt and shift unchecked ableism that exists in everyday social work praxis. This is an essential approach in order to achieve anti-oppressive practice.

References

Allen, C. (2004). Merleau-Ponty's Phenomenology and The Body-in-Space Encounters of Visually Impaired Children. *Environment and Planning D: Society and Space* 22: 719–735.
Barnes, C. (2000). A Working Social Model? Disability, Work and Disability Politics in the 21st Century. *Critical Social Policy* 20(4): 441–457.
Barnes, C. (2012). Disability Work and Welfare. *Sociology Compass* 6(6): 472–484.
Butler, J. (1990). *Gender trouble: Feminism and the Subversion of Identity*. New York: Routledge.
Campbell, F. K. (2009). *Contours of Ableism: The Production of Disability and Ableness*. London: Palgrave Macmillan.
Campbell, F.K. (2014). Ableism as Transformative Practice. In C. Cocker & T. Hafford Letchfield (Eds). *Rethinking Anti-Discriminatory and Anti-Oppressive Theories for Social Work Practice*. (pp. 78–92). Palgrave, 2014.
Carman, T. (1999). The Body in Husserl and Merleau-Ponty. *Philosophical Topics* 27(2): 205–226.
Carman, T. (2008). *Merleau-Ponty*. Hoboken: Routledge.
Cerbone, D. R. (2006). *Understanding Phenomenology*. Durman. GB: Acumen.
Chouinard, V. (1997). Making Space for Disabling Differences: Challenging Ablest Geographies. *Environment and Planning D: Society & Space* 15: 379–387.
Fanon, F. (2008). *Black skin White Masks. Trans Richard Philcox*. New York: Grove Press.
Garland-Thomson, R. (2002). Integrating Disability, Transforming Feminist Theory. *NWSA Journal* 14(3): 1–32. doi: 10.2979/NWS.2002.14.3.1.
Garland-Thomson, R. (2017). *Extraordinary Bodies: Figuring Physical Disability in American Culture and Literature* (Twentieth anniversary edition). New York: Columbia University Press.
Garsten, C., & Jacobsson, K. (2013). Sorting People in and out: The Plasticity of the Categories of Employability, Work Capacity and Disability as Technologies of Government. *Ephemera* 13(4): 825–850.
Gleeson, B. (1999). *Geographies of Disability*. London: Routledge.
Goffman, E. (1989). *Stigma: Notes on The Management of Spoiled Identity*. New York: Simon & Schuster, Touchstone.
Goodley, D. (2013). Dis/entangling Critical Disability Studies. *Disability & Society* 28(5): 631–644.
Goodley, D. (2014). *Dis/ability Studies Theorising Disablism and Ableism* (1st ed.). London: Routledge.
Goodley, D., Lawthom, R., Liddiard, K., &. Cole, K.R. (2017). Critical Disability Studies. In Gough, B. (Ed.) *The Palgrave Handbook of Critical Social Psychology*. (pp. 499–512). Palgrave Macmillan, London.
Grosz, E., & Eisenman, P. (2001). *Architecture from the Outside: Essays on Virtual and Real Space*. Cambridge: MIT Press.
Grover, C., & Piggott, L. (2015). *Disabled People, Work and Welfare: Is Employment Really the Answer?*. Bristol: Policy Press.
Holt, L. (2003). (Dis)abling children in primary school micro-spaces: geographies of inclusion and exclusion. *Health & Place* 9(2): 119–128.
Holt, L. (2004). Children with mind-body differences: Performing disability in primary school classrooms. *Children's Geographies* 2(2): 219–236.
Hooks, Bell. (1981). *Ain't I a Woman: Black Women and Feminism*. Boston, MA: South End Press.
Hosking, D. L. (2008). Critical Disability Theory. *A Paper Presented at the 4th Biennial Disability Studies Conference at Lancaster University*, UK, September 2-4. http://lancaster.ac.uk/fass/events/disabilityconference_archive/2008/abstracts/hosking.htm
Hughes, B., & Paterson, K. (1997). The Social Model of Disability and the Disappearing Body: Towards a Sociology of Impairment. *Disability & Society* 12(3): 325–340.
Hughes, B., Russell, R., & Paterson, K. (2005). Nothing to be Had "Off the Peg": Consumption, Identity and the Immobilisation of Young Disabled People. *Disability & Society* 20(1): 3–17.

Imrie, R. (2001). Barriered and Bounded Places and the Spatialities of Disability. *Urban Studies* 38: 231–237.

Imrie, R. (2003). Architects' Conception of the Human Body. *Environment and Planning D: Society and Space* 21: 47–65.

Imrie, R., & Kumar, M. (1998). Focusing on Disability and Access in the Built Environment. *Disability & Society* 13(3): 357–374.

James, A. (1993). *Childhood identities: Self and Social Relationships in the Experience of the Child*. Edinburgh: Edinburgh University Press.

Mallett, R., & Runswick-Cole, K. (2014). *Approaching Disability: Critical issues and Perspectives*. Abingdon, Oxon: Routledge.

Marston, G. (2013). Frontline Workers as Intermediaries: The Changing Landscape of Disability and Employment Services in Australia. In Brodkin EZ & Marston G (Eds.) *Work and Welfare State: Street-level Organizations and Workfare Politics*. (pp. 209–225). Georgetown University Press, Washington.

Marston, G., Cowling, S., & Bielefeld, S. (2016). Tensions and Contradictions in Australia Policy Reform: Compulsory Income Management and the National Disability Insurance Scheme. *Australian Journal of Social Issues* 51(4): 399–417.

Matthews, E. (2002). Merleau-Ponty in Context. In *Philosophy of Merleau-Ponty*. (pp. 1–22). McGill-Queen's University Press. Retrieved from http://jstor.org.ezp01.library.qut.edu.au/stable/j.ctt81dhr.4. Online: https://www.mqup.ca/philosophy-of-merleau-ponty--the-products-9780773523845.php?page_id=46&.

McRuer, R. (2005). Crip Eye for the Normate Guy: Queer Theory and the Disciplining of Disability Studies. *PMLA. Publications of the Modern Language Association of America* 120(2): 586–592. Available at: http://search.proquest.com/docview/214765756/.

Meekosha, H., & Dowse, L. (2007). Integrating Critical Disability Studies into Social Work Education and Practice: An Australian Perspective. *Practice* 19(3): 169–183. doi: 10.1080/09503150701574267.

Meekosha, H., & Shuttleworth, R. (2009). What's so 'Critical' about Critical Disability Studies?. *Australian Journal of Human Rights* 15(1): 47–75.

Merleau-Ponty, M. (1962). *Phenomenology of Perception* (Trans. Colin Smith). London: Routledge & Kegan Paul. (Reprinted from Phénoménologie de la perception, by M. Merleau-Ponty, 1945, Paris: Gallimard).

Merleau-Ponty, M. (2012). (Trans Donald A. Landes) *Phenomenology of Perception* Oxon: Routledge. (Reprinted from Phénoménologie de la perception, by M. Merleau-Ponty, 1945, Paris: Gallimard).

Moore, S., Melchior, L., & Davis, J. M. (2008). "Me and the 5 P's: Negotiating Rights-based Critical Disabilities Studies and Social Inclusion. *International Journal of Children's Rights* 16: 249–262.

Moran, D. (2000). *Introduction to Phenomenology*. London: Routledge.

Neufert, E 1936 (2012). *Architects' Data* (4th ed.). West Sussex, UK: Wiley-Blackwell.

Oliver, M. (2009). *Understanding Disability: From Theory to Practice* (2nd ed.). London: Palgrave Macmillan.

Roulstone, A. (2012). "Stuck In The Middle With You": Towards Enabling Social Work with Disabled People. *Social Work Education* 31(2): 142–154.

Roulstone, A. (2015). Personal Independence Payments, Welfare Reform and the Shrinking Disability Category. *Disability & Society* 30(5): 673–688.

Roulstone, A., & Prideaux, S. (2012). New Labour and Clauses for Conditionality: Activating Disabled Citizens. In *Understanding Disability Policy*. (pp. 79–100). Policy Press, Bristol.

Schoeman, M., & Schoeman, M. (2002). Disability and the Ideology of Professionalism. *International Journal of Special Education* 17(1): 14–20.

Scully, J. (2008). Disability and The Thinking Body. In K. Kristiansen, S. Vehmas & T. Shakespeare (Eds.) *Arguing about disability: Philosophical perspectives*. (pp. 57–73). Routledge, Hobooken.

Seamon, D. (1980). Body-subject, Time-space Routines, and Place-ballets. In A. Buttimer & D. Seamon (Eds.) *The Human Experience of Space and Place*. (pp. 148–165). Crom Helm, London.

Seamon, D. (2002). Physical Comminglings: Body, Habit, and Space Transformed into Place. *Occupation, Participation and Health* 22(10): 42S–51S.

Shakespeare, T. (2005). *Life as a disabled child: A qualitative study of young people's experiences and perspectives: ESRC Full Research Report (Research no. L129251047)*. Swindon: ESRC. Retrieved from http://www.esrc.ac.uk/my-esrc/grants/L129251047/outputs/Read/96fce713-c2fb-4352-8d59-270ecacf3ec2

Shakespeare, T., Watson, N., & Abu Alghaib, O. (2016). Blaming the Victim, All Over Again: Waddell and Aylward's Biopsychosocial (BPS) Model of Disability. *Critical Social Policy* 37(1): 22–41.

Smith, D. (2008). Phenomenology. In Edward N. Zalta (Ed.), *The Stanford Encyclopedia of Philosophy*. Stanford: Stanford University. Retrieved from http://plato.stanford.edu/entries/phenomenology/

Soldatic, K., & Pini, B. (2009). The Three D's of Welfare Reform: Disability, Disgust and Deservingness. *Australian Journal of Human Rights* 15(1): 77–96.

Spagnuolo, Natalie (2016). Political Affinities and Complex Identities: Critical Approaches to Disability Organizing. *Canadian Journal of Disability Studies* 5(2): 72–97.

Stafford, L. (2013). The Journey of Becoming Involved: The Experience of Participation in Urban Spaces by Children with Diverse Mobility. *PhD thesis*, Queensland University of Technology.

Stafford, L., Marston, G., Chamorro-Koc, M., Beatson, A. T., & Drennan, J. In press (2019). Interpretative Accounts of Work Capacity Assessment Policy for Young Adults with Disabilities. *Disability & Society* doi: 10.1080/09687599.2018.1561356.

Stafford, L., & Volz, K. (2016) Diverse Bodies-space Politics: Towards a Critique of Social (in)justice of Built Environments. *TEXT, Special Issue,* 34. Available at: http://textjournal.com.au/speciss/issue34/Stafford&Volz.pdf (accessed 23 August 2017).

Taylor, S. (2004). The Right Not to Work: Power and Disability. *Monthly Review* 55(10): 30–44.

Thomas, C. (2007). Swain, J., French, S., Barnes, C., & Thomas, C. *Disabling Barriers - Enabling Environments* (2nd ed.). London: Sage.

Thomas, S. (2005). Through the Lens of Merleau-Ponty: Advancing the Phenomenological Approach to Nursing Research. *Nursing Philosophy* 6: 63–76.

Toombs, S. K. (1997). Taking the Body Seriously. *Hastings Center Report* 27(5): 39–43.

The United Nations. (2006). *Convention on the Rights of Persons with Disabilities.* http://ohchr.org/english/law/disabilities-convention.htm.

Valentine, G., & Skelton, T. (2003). Living on the Edge: The Marginalisation and Resistance of d/deaf Youth. *Environment and Planning A* 35: 301–321.

Valentine, G., & Skelton, T. (2007). Re-defining 'Norms': D/deaf Young People's Transition to Independence. *The Sociological Review* 55(1): 106–123.

Weiss, G. (2015). The Normal, The Natural and The Normative: A Merleau-Pontian Legacy to Feminist Theory, Critical Race Theory and Disability Studies. *Continental Philosophy Review* 48(1): 77–93.

Weissman, L. K. (1992). *Discrimination by Design: A Feminist Critique of the Man-Made Environment.* Urbana: U of Illinois.

Wolbring, G. (2008). The Politics of Ableism. *Development* 51(2): 252–258.

World Health Organisation (2012) WHO Disability Assessment Schedule 2.0 (WHODAS 2.0). Retrieved from: https://www.who.int/classifications/icf/whodasii/en/

Postcolonial and Southern pedagogies

31

No more 'Blacks in the Back'

Adding more than a 'splash' of black into social work education and practice by drawing on the works of Aileen Moreton-Robinson and others who contribute to Indigenous Standpoint Theory

Jennie Briese and Kelly Menzel

DEAKIN UNIVERSITY, VICTORIA, AUSTRALIA

Acknowledgements

We would like to pay our respect to our Elders, past and present; the warrior women and men who came before us, who laid the way so that we may follow. We hope we make you proud.

We also pay our respect to the Traditional Custodians of the land on which we walk, work and write this piece, and their Elders past and present, the Wadawurrung people of the Kulin Nation in Victoria, Australia.

Introduction

As Indigenous[1] scholars, we have a responsibility to confront discrimination and work toward equity for our communities. Therefore, we challenge the status quo and urge others to consider Indigenous ways of knowing, being and doing (Martin & Mirraboopa 2003). We consider that many western scholars write from an unearned position of privilege (Moffatt 2016). There is nothing inherently wrong with writing from this position, if the writer concedes bias and acknowledges their privilege. This requires critical reflection of one's own complicity in dominant power relations, and how assumptions and values underpin practice. The aim of this chapter is to de-objectify the scholar and concede bias. This is a very Indigenous approach to writing, researching and teaching. We will highlight the contributions of Aileen Moreton-Robinson and other Indigenous scholars contributing to the development of Indigenous Standpoint Theory, and the furthering of Indigenous knowledges. As early career academics, the significant role played by people such as Aileen Moreton-Robinson and others shapes us as educators and researchers. The 'shoulders' they provide, in the generosity of knowledge articulated in their work, allows us a privilege that is critical to the development of our voices. Earlier battles mean we now have the opportunity to work on more than identity debates, if we so choose. Hence, the imperative is to utilise 'positioning' as a finely nuanced indicator of the insider/outsider paradigmatic shift. Further to this, we discuss the complexities of decolonising university curricula for Indigenous students, Indigenous ways of knowledge-sharing and the relevance of this for critical social work practice.

In the western academy, it is not common for scholars to write by placing themselves central to their work. Positionality, within western paradigms, particularly in research, is about scholars locating themselves and acknowledging their personal journey. Positionality 'refers to the stance or positioning of the researcher in relation to the social and political context of the study – the community, the organisation or the participant group' (Cunneen & Rowe 2014:2). The dominant paradigm is often very technical and written from an academic, Eurocentric place, automatically separating us into groups of those who do, and those who do not, understand the language (Carter, Lapum, Lavallée & Schindel Martin 2014:362). As such, positionality requires an acute awareness of one's social background, and political and ideological assumptions.

For an Indigenous person, positionality is much deeper and more significant than this definition. Writing, researching and teaching from an Indigenous perspective is to continually challenge dominant, western, patriarchal structures and agendas in order to reframe, reimagine and decolonise (Russell-Mundine 2012). The goal is to reframe historical and current colonial-centric and exploitative paradigms, and to privilege the voices of Indigenous peoples. As Indigenous women, we position ourselves within our ancestral, family and community lineage before introducing our professional selves. To us, all these elements that make us whole, are inextricably linked, fundamental to our being, and influence how we experience the world. Thus, our positionality shapes how we teach, research and write.

Positionality statements

Jennie

I (Jennie) identify as an Indigenous Australian woman. I am a daughter, mother and grandmother who has not always known who I am, yet always knew that I did not 'fit' in my western adoptive family. I was told that my 'natural' parents were probably Greek or Italian because of my rich olive skin-tone and darker eye colour (in those days it was all about certain cultural groups looking a 'particular' way). I heard music in the trees, saw people who others could not (and interacted with those people), and dreamed of places and faces that I did not yet know. I was never frightened of these experiences and recently discovered that the family I interacted with regularly were not visible to others. As an adult I have realised my ancestors were guiding me throughout my childhood, and continue to guide me now.

I was born on Yuggera Country (Brisbane, Queensland) in the late 1960s and spent my childhood on Giabal Country (Darling Downs, Queensland), where I felt nurtured and in tune with my surroundings. This Country protected, healed and sang to me. As a child I did not understand the significance of this. However, discovering my cultural identity makes sense of this, and me. I am grateful that my ancestors were guiding me and pushing me along my life path, and continue to do so.

I struggle to articulate how I locate myself culturally, as I do not yet have all the answers required to confidently discuss the relational lineage of my belonging. My identity has been formed within the context of my family and community – my lived experience. In this, I do not need to conform to external constructions of Indigeneity. The journey of identity discovery is exciting and ongoing, although there are also many moments of feeling a great sense of loss around what I was culturally denied throughout my earlier life years. I now know my biological mother. She is strong, resilient and full of love for her children, of which I am the second. My mother does not know our stories/histories, but supports and walks with me in my/our ongoing identity search. It is comforting to know I am not alone in this.

I have experienced great privilege in access to western education, health care and other social opportunities that many are denied. Although I did not complete high school and spent many years 'off the rails', I had a solid education foundation to fall back on when I decided I wanted more than welfare dependency for my life. It is this privilege that I share now, as a social worker and new academic. I am grateful for the guidance of the many Elders who have, and continue to guide me in sharing this privilege, particularly my knowledge of western education.

Kelly

I (Kelly) am the youngest and only girl in my family. I am a Bohemian Ngadjuri woman from South Australia. My father's family are from Bohemia and my mother's family are very old, Australian. Being a Bohemian Black has always made me feel pretty cool, which in reality, I am not. I was born in Adelaide, on Kaurna Country, as was my mother. My mother's father's birth was registered in Adelaide but I am not sure where he was born. My family has always known we are Aboriginal. I have always known I am Aboriginal. But we did not talk about it. My grandfather said we were 'licked by the tar brush'. Afterwards he would laugh hysterically. We were 'black Irish', he said. Then he would wink. Being black had consequences. He was called 'Aboriginal Keith' by his peers. He was a violent man. His Aboriginality caused him great shame. So, he drank to suffocate his shame and to obscure the violence he had endured. He did this by acting out violently toward his wife and children. He was also a very difficult man when sober, which was not often. He and my mother were estranged at the time of his death. Because of her upbringing, my mother knew very little about her Aboriginality and I learned to not ask questions about my Aboriginality. I always felt unfinished and incomplete.

I have always had feelings of loss and disconnection, but for a long time, I did not know why I was lost and what I felt disconnected from. All I knew was I did not quite fit in. I grew up with an uncertainty of what it meant to be Aboriginal. I did not learn like 'normal' people. I did not see the world like 'normal' people. I was the 'other' and I did not understand why. There was a void, which was impossible to fill. I could not fill it with alcohol, sex or drugs, although I certainly made a concerted effort to do so. I continued to feel lost.

It was not until an Aboriginal Elder from Cherbourg and a Torres Strait Islander Elder sat and talked with me that I began to learn and feel connected to culture. I will be forever grateful to Aunty Mischa and Aunty Dot. I have learned that I grieve for the loss of my ancestors' language. I grieve for the loss of my ancestors' country. I grieve the loss of my ancestors' culture. I grieve the loss of my ancestors' stories.

I have since been able to connect with other Ngadjuri people and the community and I have developed a deep connection to wider Aboriginal and Torres Strait Islander communities and culture. This has assisted me to heal, learn and grow and I will continue to do this for the rest of my life.

I am Aboriginal, I am fair skinned with green eyes, which are apparently my grandfather's eyes. I acknowledge this has sometimes put me in a position of privilege and I acknowledge this privilege. I have received different treatment than some of my family members and peers simply based upon the colour of my skin. I have also received negative treatment based upon the colour of my skin. I am very aware of lateral violence – 'internalised colonialism' (Australian Human Rights Commission 2007; Fanon 1963; Freire 1970) – in the Indigenous community, however these comments affect me very deeply as I am proud of both my Indigenous and non-Indigenous ancestry.

I am an Aboriginal nurse, teacher, researcher and writer. I was privileged to enter university straight from high school and although I am a nurse, both of my parents are teachers and, as such, I finally succumbed and entered the 'family business' – because it is in my blood.

Key theorists

We acknowledge the many Indigenous voices that contribute to the richness of Indigenous Standpoint Theory, all worthy of mention in their own right for their particular contributions. Indigenous Standpoint Theory can be enriched by tracing the lineage of the ideas of all of these thinkers, but obviously this cannot be done in one chapter. Therefore, for the purposes of this chapter, as Indigenous women, and because we are discussing Indigenous Standpoint Theory, we will be addressing the work of Aileen Moreton-Robinson, an exemplar of this approach, in the context of other voices that contribute to Indigenous Standpoint Theory.

Aileen Moreton-Robinson

Distinguished Professor of Indigenous Research, Office of the Provost, Indigenous Research and Engagement Unit at Queensland University of Technology, Aileen Moreton-Robinson (1950s) is a Goenpul woman from Minjerribah (Stradbroke Island), Quandamooka First Nation (Moreton Bay) in Queensland, Australia (QUT 2019). Moreton-Robinson experienced significant racism and discrimination at school yet excelled as a student. Because of this racism, however, she left school prior to graduating and became a political activist engaging in the issues of land rights and human rights for Aboriginal people (Moreton-Robinson 2019). Moreton-Robinson writes from an Indigenous women's standpoint and her work is a compelling analysis of whiteness. Moreton-Robinson (cited in Walter & Baltra-Ulloa 2019:70) describes whiteness as 'the invisible norm, a set of invisible benchmarks that are used to measure everyone in subtle and nuanced ways'. Having written extensively on the experience of Indigenous Australians post-invasion and colonisation of Australia, and issues of race and whiteness studies, post-colonialism, Indigenous feminism, Indigenous studies, native title law and Aboriginal land rights, Moreton-Robinson's major contribution to Indigenous Standpoint Theory is a series of articles compiled into a book titled *The White Possessive* (2015). This work explores the links between race, sovereignty and possession through themes of property, owning property, being property, and becoming propertyless. The nation, Moreton-Robinson (2015) argues, is socially and culturally constructed as a white possession.

In this chapter, along with Moreton-Robinson, we have referred to Indigenous theorists such as Atkinson, Grant, Grieves, Kovach, Nakata, Rigney, Smith and Yunkaporta. Indigenous knowledges are plural and we are not boxed in by Eurocentric ideals and colonial discourse (Yunkaporta 2019). There are subtle differences in each theorist's standpoint and articulation of such. However, all contribute to the collective voice that enriches and strengthens Indigenous Standpoint Theory. There is unity in a theorist's message, especially from an Indigenous women's standpoint, which is the standpoint we take. We are Aboriginal women. We can be nothing other than this. Moreton-Robinson (2013:331) states it is important to acknowledge that Indigenous women's individual experiences will differ due to intersecting oppressions produced under social, political, historical and material conditions that we share consciously or unconsciously. These conditions and the sets of complex relations that discursively constitute us in the everyday are also complicated by our respective cultural differences and the simultaneity of our compliance and resistance as Indigenous sovereign female subjects.

Our standpoint is also informed by our day-to-day lives, our communities, collective knowledges, politics and history (Nakata 2007). Further, Moreton-Robinson (2011:413) states in the last 10 years there has been an increase in the number of Indigenous women scholars reflecting our 'respective embodied standpoints and disciplinary training'. She argues the production of this body of work has transpired during a period of neoliberalism that normalises a

> discourse of Aboriginal pathology to increase state surveillance of Aboriginal bodies, lands and lives. The majority of this work is produced through an episteme that does not privilege white patriarchal knowledge even though it is informed by its disciplinary knowledges.
> *(2011:413)*

Therefore, our work as Indigenous women scholars must challenge the negative, prevailing constructions of Indigeneity, thus causing disruption and 'discomforting systemic, white ignorance' (Moreton-Robinson 2011:414).

Indigenous knowledges are anti-oppressive and are deeply rooted in decolonising current western, patriarchal paradigms. Simply being Indigenous makes us political. Therefore, value-neutral teaching, research and writing is unlikely to be our position or experience (Kovach 2015). As such, we teach, research and write from an anti-oppressive and emancipatory stance, and all that we do is done with the knowledge that benefits our community, and is undertaken for and with our communities' needs and interests and priorities (Moreton-Robinson 2013). However, much of the anti-oppressive stance has been 'defined within an epistemological framework of Whiteness, arising predominantly from western European culture and thought' (Kovach 2015:46). This dominant western paradigm is philosophically, axiologically, ontologically and epistemologically quite different from an Indigenous approach. So we need to 'promote continued discussion on Indigenist methodology as a step toward assisting Indigenous theorists and practitioners to determine what might be an appropriate response to de-legitimate racist oppression in research and shift to a more empowering and self-determining outcome' (Rigney 1999:110).

To understand Indigenous knowledges and methodologies one must understand the history of invasion and colonisation of Australia: the impact of this on Indigenous people and the subsequent movement toward de-colonisation (Moreton-Robinson 2003; Rigney 1999). Fundamentally, the process of de-colonising falls back to challenging deep-seated colonial racism, a racism that is alive and well, and institutionally entrenched. Rigney (1999:113) argues 'the cultural assumptions throughout dominant epistemologies in Australia are oblivious of Indigenous traditions and concerns. The research academy and its epistemologies have been constructed essentially for and by non-Indigenous Australians'. This is why it is paramount that Indigenous knowledges, axiological, ontological and epistemological practices have a collective voice in social work education. We, as Indigenous scholars, whether teaching, researching or writing, need the freedom to legitimise our Indigenous experience. Rigney (1999:114) states:

> Racism will not be overcome by simply changing the attitudes and values of researchers, nor will it be overcome by simply adding Indigenous researchers to the academy of

research and stirring. Indigenous Peoples must now be involved in defining, controlling, and owning epistemologies and ontologies that value and legitimate the Indigenous experience. Indigenous perspectives must infiltrate the structures and methods of the entire research academy.

Indigenous Standpoint Theory itself is an enmeshing, or layering, of a collective voice. Although difficult to delineate the contributions of specific theorists to this collective tradition, as Indigenous women, Moreton-Robinson's Indigenous Women's Standpoint Theory supports 'how' we see the world, and in this, how we see and experience the deeply entrenched colonialism within social work education.

Where and how we work

We work in a space where students all identify as Indigenous Australian Peoples. Most social work students are first in family to attend university, mature-aged, and many have internalised an ascribed identity about who they are in a western education setting. That is, an identity ascribed by others about who they are, and what they are and are not capable of, in a space that historically benefits middle-class, Anglo, male school leavers (Brookes & Waters 2011; Sharma 2008). Many students feel they have no educational capital and often find themselves feeling like an intruder in a space not intended for their participation. Indigenous students also often have many competing commitments, such as family, work and community obligations. These competing commitments can affect students' ability to remain engaged in higher education and studies are sometimes interrupted, ceased, or progressed over extended periods of time (Green et al. 2013). Further, historical contributions of social work to Indigenous peoples' experiences of 'intrusive, judgmental, controlling and harmful' interactions with social workers (Green et al. 2013:207) pose a particular set of tensions for students. Therefore, we as educators need to take care with our language and approaches, couch things in positive ways, and ensure that we are facilitating processes that support the building of student identities through culturally appropriate knowledge-sharing. To ensure we do not reinforce an intruder identity, we Indigenise the content and remove anything reinforcing negative stereotypes and power relations.

Students study through mixed-mode delivery and are geographically located Australia-wide. Delivery is flexible, meaning students study online while continuing to reside in their communities, and visit the university campus to undertake 'intensive knowledge-sharing blocks' several times each trimester. While on campus, students are housed in a residential block with other Indigenous students and attend an institute space where Indigenous culture, shared knowledge and histories, and local knowledges inform the operations of all that occurs. This means students undertake their qualifications in a culturally appropriate learning environment. That is, students study online at home, in their own community and attend their 'intensives' in a space where Indigenous cultural protocol is 'the norm'. This flexible model of delivering higher education to Indigenous Australians means that Indigenous Australian communities have increased capital and are strengthened; benefiting all Australians. In turn, this increases the cultural capital of students, their families and their communities (Jenkins 2002).

This is similar to the First Nations Control of First Nations Education approach (AFN 2010). This approach enables Indigenous communities to access education independently from mainstream course delivery in order to reclaim education in a self-determined way. Because students remain in their communities, they can apply what they learn within their communities, thereby incorporating praxis into the educational experience. In this approach both Indigenous Knowledge and western knowledge systems are valued, and students, Elders and teachers are all learners and educators (AFN 2010).

For us, equal acknowledgement of both western and Indigenous Knowledge systems is vital. Success in western institutions requires demonstration of competence in traditional academic discourse. However, this should not be at the exclusion of Indigenous Knowledge. McGregor (2004:387) describes Indigenous Knowledge as follows:

> In conventional Eurocentric definitions of Indigenous Knowledge it is presented as a noun, a thing, knowledge; but to Indigenous people, it is much more than knowledge. Indigenous Knowledge cannot be separated from the land/environment/Creation. Furthermore, Indigenous Knowledge does not lend itself to being fragmented into various discrete categories. No separation of science, art, religion, philosophy or aesthetics exists in Indigenous thought. Such categories do not exist.

To guard against homogenisation, Pewewardy and Hammer (2003) recognise that cultural inclusiveness in the classroom rests with the teaching staff. Thus there is a requirement for culturally aware, knowledgeable and literate staff. The main factors potentially leading to culturally inclusive education are the acknowledgement of systemic racism, removal of institutional barriers, and addressing the general lack of understanding of cultural values or norms and negative attitudes that are rife within institutions and systemically perpetuated (Moreton-Robinson 2013; Womack 1997). These barriers remain very real for Indigenous students, and applying decolonising strategies is imperative (Moreton-Robinson 2013). When in the classroom, the space created must be culturally safe so students can speak freely and discuss issues relevant and meaningful to them. As Indigenous teachers, we believe it is paramount to create a place of reciprocal knowledge-sharing. Our students bring with them a wealth of cultural knowledge that is valuable and must be treated with respect, and if appropriate can be utilised in the classroom to create a unique, Indigenous learning framework and environment. The key to this is not to expect the student to change their behaviour, rather to provide a safe, inclusive education space and changing and Indigenising the curriculum, knowledge-sharing strategies and, if possible, the assessment methods to meet the needs of our students (Moreton-Robinson 2013; Womack 1997).

Most social work students in our higher education space work in human service roles in their own communities. Many students have worked in their respective roles for a substantial time but are denied a voice in decision-making processes within their respective organisations. Students often disclose that they watch 'young big-city fresh graduates' arrive in remote communities, make 'text-book' decisions around what Indigenous people 'need', unravel and unsettle the locals, realise the complexities of working in remote communities, and leave; leaving these student-workers and other Indigenous workers to 'clean up the mess'. This political posturing of services in Indigenous communities acts to perpetuate the ongoing silencing of Indigenous voices and knowledges, while feeding the colonial agenda of ongoing legal guardianship and control 'over' Indigenous Peoples. Non-Indigenous social workers are often unaware of racist and colonising assumptions underpinning practice. Moreton-Robinson (2000, 2006) and Moreton-Robinson and Walter (2011) argue it is essential that there be a paradigmatic shift. There needs to be a greater understanding of Indigenous approaches and much of the onus of this falls to non-Indigenous practitioners and educators.

Indigenous higher education

As mentioned in our positionality statements, Jennie is a social work academic and Kelly is a nursing academic. Indigenous perspectives are trans-disciplinary and contribute to emancipatory pedagogies across all education spaces. The reality of our lived experience within academia is that institutional decolonisation is required, and is not exclusive to social work. It is the invisibility of whiteness entrenched institutionally, that perpetuates Eurocentric curricula, where Indigenous knowledges are often 'slotted' into the curriculum in particular weeks (Walter & Baltra-Ulloa 2019). This understanding leads us to unite in sisterhood to highlight not only the value of Indigenous Standpoint Theory in social work teaching pedagogies, but to challenge the structural and placial whiteness (Walter & Baltra-Ulloa 2019) that we see existing within higher education spaces regardless of the discipline.

To further unpack this concept of placial whiteness:

> Whiteness, like 'colour' and 'Blackness,' are essentially social constructs applied to human beings rather than veritable truths that have universal validity. The power of Whiteness, however, is manifested by the ways in which racialized Whiteness becomes transformed into social, political, economic, and cultural behaviour. White culture, norms, and values in all these areas become normative natural. They become the standard against which all other cultures, groups, and individuals are measured and usually found to be inferior.
>
> *(Tator & Henry 2006:46–47)*

For Indigenous Australian students, the ongoing practice of being benchmarked against Eurocentric standards means that students are assessed against standards devoid of Indigenous ways of knowing, being, and doing (Martin & Mirraboopa 2003); including language, cultural and practical considerations. There is no meritocracy in this. Rather, this is an agenda where Indigenous students are expected to assimilate into only western styles of knowledge acquisition, while evidencing their knowledge growth through processes excluding these 'other' ways of knowing and doing. Our hope is that our contribution can be used across disciplines for the emancipation of all Indigenous higher education students.

Racist policies, processes and behaviours that assert and maintain colonial power are deeply embedded in Australian systems (Anderson 2006). In addition to current practices in the delivery of education within all levels, the ongoing effects of multi-generational trauma (Green et al. 2013) significantly influence many Indigenous Australians' access to equitable education, health and wellbeing. Racism continues to have a considerable influence on the unacceptably large socioeconomic, education and health gap between Australia's Indigenous and non-Indigenous population. Arabena (2013:22) argues:

> [R]acism has had and continues to have a real and damaging impact on the health of Aboriginal and Torres Strait Islander people. [It is] embodied in dubious practices, disparities in access and subtle variations in effort within health and other institutions and programs [and] it is clear that full health equity cannot be achieved until racism … can be overcome.

To encourage more Indigenous students into higher education it is necessary to facilitate student empowerment by removing institutional barriers and addressing systemic racism. Therefore, curricula used for teaching Indigenous students need to be flexible, holistic, and provide opportunities for collective working while avoiding linear teaching processes. Bowman (2003),

Hilberg and Tharp (2002), Weaver (2001), Demmert (n.d.) and Nichol and Robinson (2000) all recommend applying specific strategies to support the success of Indigenous students, such as western and Indigenous Knowledge systems being embedded within curricula, and using holistic learning approaches and group learning activities.

Having said that, Australian academia still predominantly operates within a western, male-dominated paradigm because 'political, religious and economic histories of western civilization have shaped the philosophies, values and organizational patterns evident in today's western educational programs' (Woolsey Des Jarlais 2009:1) and in the institutions that run them. Western cultural aspects are favoured, such as individualism, homogenisation, universalism, meritocracy and rationalisation (Woolsey Des Jarlais 2009). These values do not align with Indigenous values. It is argued that the dominant western educational paradigm is damaging to Indigenous communities and societies (Yunkaporta 2009). Additionally, it is asserted they are actually damaging and unsustainable for any culture (Reynar 1999; Semali & Kincheloe 1999; Shiva 1993). Clearly, culturally appropriate pedagogies addressing Indigenous exclusion in higher education are required.

How we share knowledge

It is our responsibility to disrupt dominant discourses by decolonising the curriculum, making it accessible for students. As stated above, it is preferable that curricula already be Indigenised. However, in reality it is far from culturally safe and inclusive. An Inquiry-Based Learning (IBL) approach is employed across the social work and nursing curriculum where we work. However, it is still culturally unsafe and lacks meaning for Indigenous students, placing the burden on Indigenous teaching staff and Indigenous students to adapt and change to 'fit' the curriculum available. This is diametrically opposed to culturally inclusive education and places the onus on the already marginalised group, rather than where the onus actually lies. Using an IBL approach means that students' prior knowledge is validated and it becomes more of a process around marrying what students already know and do (their prior knowledge), with western academic expectations. Doing this, however, requires that we challenge dominant, white, patriarchal discourses. Moreton-Robinson (2013a:331) argues the need for this is to contest 'the colonial institutional relations and practices that have constituted Indigenous peoples as objects ... rather than as authorities about their own ways of knowing, being and doing'. Our ways of knowing, being and doing include how we learn, teach, process and translate information. This has been taught to us by our Elders to allow us, and our students, the ability to navigate the space between two worlds and maintain our connection to country and cultural practices. This is the crux of an Indigenous approach.

Yarning is a particularly Indigenous manner of conversation (Bessarab & Ng'andu 2010; Drawson, Toombs & Mushquash 2017). Ostensibly, yarning is a process of telling stories and sharing information. Walker, Fredericks, Mills and Anderson (2014:1216) define yarning as 'a conversational process that involves the sharing of stories and development of knowledge. It prioritizes Indigenous ways of communicating, in that it is culturally prescribed, cooperative, and respectful'. There are protocols for yarning when discussing, collecting and analysing culturally specific information that needs to be observed (Laycock, Walker, Harrison & Brands 2011). Generally speaking, it is considered polite to begin with some social yarning to establish a connection with a person. This can be followed by more specific yarning such as information yarning, which is still relaxed but more purposeful and introduces the person to the ideas and concepts. Collaborative yarning can then follow, facilitating deep explorations of ideas and concepts. Finally, therapeutic yarning may occur. Therapeutic yarning is when someone discloses deeply personal information (Bessarab & Ng'andu 2010). Yarning can facilitate in-depth discussion and produce deep, significant information and is always done in a relaxed manner (Drawson, Toombs & Mushquash 2017). Yarning is always reciprocal and promotes the building of relationships as an important consideration in education spaces. As teachers, we often expect our students to lay themselves bare and to expose their vulnerabilities. To expect this of our students means we must also lay ourselves bare. Reciprocity and relationality are essential.

From a methodological perspective, Indigenous Knowledge systems are guided by Indigenous Knowledge Paradigms. This paradigmatic approach is centred in an Indigenous belief system and is, at its core, a relational understanding and accountability to the world. Thus Indigenous axiological, ontological and epistemological practices are seen and demonstrated from a different cultural and theoretical standpoint (Martin & Mirraboopa 2003). Relationality is paramount in acquiring Indigenous Knowledge. To understand relationality from an Indigenous perspective one needs to see and accept the

> interconnected ways in which relationality provides the necessary epistemological scaffolding to actualize the underlying motives, concerns, and principles that characterize decolonizing methodologies. Relationality draws attention to the multiple intersecting influences that shape research and knowledge itself, emphasizes reciprocity, and is compatible with many Indigenous worldviews.
>
> *(Gerlach 2018:1)*

Relationality requires accountability. Moreton-Robinson (2013:340) states:

> Indigenous women's standpoint is ascribed through inheritance and achieved through struggle. It is constituted by our sovereignty and constitutive of the interconnectedness of our ontology (our way of being); our epistemology (our way of knowing) and our axiology (our way of doing).

Indigenous women's standpoint acknowledges Indigenous women's experience and knowledge as it relates to dominant, western, patriarchal paradigms. Due to varied levels of oppression, Indigenous women's ontology, epistemology and axiology will be affected by individual experiences through collective, shared experiences of colonisation that have emerged 'under social, political, historical and material conditions that we share either consciously or unconsciously' (Moreton-Robinson 2013:340).

We use this particular standpoint because we are Indigenous women. However, we acknowledge that our individual experiences are (respectively) ours alone, but that we also have shared experiences with other Indigenous women. Further to this, we believe this standpoint is useful for our teaching because we teach in an Indigenous space. Indigenous learning values, Indigenous ontology, epistemology and axiology are a paradigmatic approach that value an Indigenous perspective.

Conclusion

Embedding Indigenous Standpoint Theories as a central component of any teaching or practice framework is crucial to decolonising the academy and social work practice. Indigenous perspectives are trans-disciplinary and can be used to disrupt, challenge and erode Eurocentrism, particularly when one's social positionality and privilege are understood, owned and acknowledged. We urge educators and practitioners to challenge dominant, western, patriarchal structures and agendas by re-framing, re-imagining and decolonising their understandings of ongoing colonial discourses that continue to place Indigenous Australian Peoples and knowledges as 'the other'. This challenge begins with accepting the value and legitimacy of Indigenous ways of knowing, being and doing, such as yarning and inquiry-based approaches to knowledge-sharing, and adopting such values into teaching and practice actions.

Notes

1 We use the term 'Indigenous' to respectfully represent all Aboriginal and/or Torres Strait Islander people.

References

Anderson, W. (2006). *The cultivation of whiteness. Science, health, and racial destiny in Australia*. Basic Books, New York.

Arabena, K. (2013). 'Future initiatives to improve the health and wellbeing of Aboriginal and Torres Strait Islander peoples', *Medical Journal of Australia*, 199 (1), p. 22 [cited 26 Feb 19].

Assembly of First Nations. (2010). *First nations control of first nations education*. AFN, Canada.

Australian Human Rights Commission. (2007). *Social justice report 2007*. Chapter 3: The Northern Territory 'Emergency Response' intervention. AHRC, Sydney.

Bessarab, D. & Ng'andu, B. (2010). 'Yarning about yarning as a legitimate method in indigenous research', *International Journal of Critical Indigenous Studies*, 3 (1) DOI: https://doi.org/10.5204/ijcis.v3i1.57.

Bowman, N. (2003). 'Cultural differences of teaching and learning', *American Indian Quarterly*, 27 (1/2), pp. 91–102.

Brookes, R. & Waters, J. (2011). *Student mobilities, migration and the internationalization of higher education*. Palgrave Macmillan, Basingstoke Hampshire, UK.

Carter, C., Lapum, J. L., Lavallée, L. F. & Schindel Martin, L. (2014). 'Explicating Positionality: A Journey of Dialogical and Reflexive Storytelling'. *International Journal of Qualitative Methods*, 13 (1), pp. 362–376 https://doi.org/10.1177%2F1609406914013001 18

Cunneen, C. & Rowe, S. (2014). 'Changing Narratives: Colonised Peoples, Criminology and Social Work'. *International Journal for Crime, Justice and Social Democracy*, 3 (1), pp. 49–67 http://dx.doi.org/10.2139/ssrn.2257364

Demmert, W. Jr. (n.d.). *Improving academic performance among native American students: A review of the research literature*. ERIC, Clearinghouse on Rural Education and Small Schools, Charleston, WV.

Drawson, A., Toombs, E., & Mushquash, C. J. (2017). 'Indigenous research methods: A systematic review', *The International Indigenous Policy Journal*, 8 (2) DOI: 10.18584/iipj.2017.8.2.5.

Fanon, F. (1963). *The wretched earth*. Grove Weidenfeld, New York.

Freire, P. (1970). *Pedagogy of the oppressed*. The Continuum International Publishing Group, New York.

Gerlach, A. (2018). 'Thinking and researching relationally: Enacting decolonizing methodologies with an indigenous early childhood program in Canada', *International Journal of Qualitative Methods*, 17, pp. 1–8 DOI: 10.1177/1609406918776075.

Green, S., Bennett, B., Collins, A., Gowans, B., Hennessey, K., & Smith, K. (2013). 'Walking the journey: The student experience', in B. Bennett, S. Green, S. Gilbert & D. Bessarab (eds), *Our voices. Aboriginal and Torres Strait Islander social work*. Palgrave Macmillan, South Yarra, Victoria, pp. 206–247.

Hilberg, R & Tharp, R. (2002). 'Theoretical perspectives, research findings, and classroom implications of the learning styles of American Indians and Alaska native students', ERIC Digest, EDO-RC-02-03.

Jenkins, R. (2002). *Pierre Bourdieu*. Routledge, London.

Kovach, M. (2015). 'Emerging from the margins: Indigenous methodologies', In S. Stega & L. Brown (eds), 2nd edition, *Research as resistance. Revisiting critical, indigenous and aniti-oppressive approaches*. Canadian Scholars' Press, Women's Press, Toronto, pp. 19-36.

Laycock, A., Walker, D., Harrison, N., & Brands. (2011). *Researching indigenous health: A practical guide for researchers*. The Lowitija Institute, Melbourne.

Martin, K. & Mirraboopa, B. (2003). 'Ways of knowing, Ways of being and ways of doing: A theoretical framework and methods for indigenous research and indigenist re-search', in K. McWilliam, P. Stephenson, & G. Thompson (eds), *Voicing dissent. New talents 21C. Next generation Australian studies.* Vol. 76, pp. 203–214 https://doi.org/10.1080/14443050309387838.

McGregor, D. (2004). 'Coming full cycle: Indigenous knowledge, environment and our future', *American Indian Quarterly*, 28 (3/4), pp. 385–396.

Moffatt, M. (2016). 'Exploring Positionality in an Aboriginal Research Paradigm: A Unique Perspective'. *International Journal of Technology and Inclusive Education*, 5 (1), pp. 763–768.

Moreton-Robinson, A. (2000). *Talkin' up to the white woman: Aboriginal women and feminism.* Univ. of Queensland Press, Brisbane.

Moreton-Robinson, A. (2003). 'I still call Australia home: Indigenous belonging and place in a white postcolonising society', in Ahmed, Sarah (ed), *Uprootings/regroundings: Questions of home and migration.* Berg Publishing, Oxford, pp. 23–40.

Moreton-Robinson, A. (2006). 'How white possession moves: After the word', in Lea, T., Kowal, E., & Cowlishaw, G (eds), *Moving anthropology: Critical indigenous studies.* Charles Darwin University Press, Australia, Northern Territory, Darwin, pp. 219–232.

Moreton-Robinson, A. (2011). 'The White Mans Burden', *Australian feminist studies*, 26 (70), pp. 413–431, DOI: 10.1080/08164649.2011.621175.

Moreton-Robinson, A. (2013). 'Towards an Australian indigenous women's standpoint theory', *Australian Feminist Studies*, 28 (78), pp. 331–347, DOI: 10.1080/08164649.2013.876664.

Moreton-Robinson, A. (2013a). 'Unspeakable things: Indigenous research and social science. Socio La nouvelle revue des sciences sociales', pp. 331–348 DOI: 10.4000/socio.524

Moreton-Robinson, A. (2015). 'The white possessive: Property, power, and indigenous sovereignty', University of Minnesota Press. Retrieved from www.jstor.org/stable/10.5749/j.ctt155jmpf

Moreton-Robinson, A. (2019). 'QUT | staff profiles | Aileen Moreton-Robinson', Queensland University of Technology. Retrieved 24 July 2019.

Moreton-Robinson, E. & Walter, M. (2011). *Leadership in Indigenous research capacity building: Implementing and embedding an Indigenous research methodologies masterclass module.* Australian Learning and Teaching Council, Sydney, NSW.

Nakata, M. (2002). 'Indigenous knowledge and the cultural interface: Underlying issues at the intersection of knowledge and information systems', *IFLA Journal*, 28 (5/6), pp. 281–293.

Nakata, M. (2007). *Disciplining the savages: Savaging the disciplines.* Aboriginal Studies Press, Canberra.

Nichol, R. & Robinson, J. (2000). 'Pedagogical challenges in making mathematics relevant for indigenous Australians', *International Journal of Mathematical Education in Science and Technology*, 31 (4), pp. 495–504. DOI: https://doi.org/10.1080/002073900412606.

Pewewardy, C. & Hammer, P. (2003). 'Culturally responsive teaching for American Indian students', ERIC Digest, EDO_RC_03_10.

QUT (2019). Distinguished Professor Aileen Morton Robinson, Office of the Provost, Indigenous Research and Engagement Unit. Staff Profile. Retrieved from https://staff.qut.edu.au/staff/a.moreton-robinson.

Reynar. R. (1999). 'Indigenous people's knowledge and education: A tool for development?' in L. Semali & Joe Kincheloe (eds), *What is indigenous knowledge? Voices from the academy.* New York, Palmer Press, pp. 285–304.

Rigney, L. I. (1999). 'Internationalization of an indigenous anticolonial cultural critique of research methodologies: A guide to indigenist research methodology and its principles', *Wicazo Sa Review*, 14 (2), Emergent Ideas in Native American Studies (Autumn, 1999), pp. 109–121.

Russell-Mundine, G. (2012). 'Reflexivity in indigenous research: Reframing and decolonising research?' *Journal of Hospitality and Tourism Management*, 19 (Issue 1), pp. 85–90.

Semali, L. & Kincheloe, J. (1999). 'Introduction: What is indigenous knowledge and why should we study it?' in L. Semali & J. Kincheloe (eds), *What is indigenous knowledge? Voices from the academy.* New York, Falmer Press, pp. 3–58.

Sharma, R (2008), 'The Australian perspective: Access, equity, quality and accountability in higher education', *New Directions for Institutional Research*, Winter edn., pp. 43–45.

Shiva, V. (1993). *Monocultures of the Mind: Perspectives on biodiversity and biotechnology.* Zed Books, London.

Tator, C. & Henry, F. (2006). *Racial profiling in Canada: Challenging the myth of a "few bad apples".* University of Toronto Press, Toronto.

Walker, M., Fredericks, B., Mills, K., & Anderson, D. (2014). '"Yarning" as a method for community basedealth research with indigenous women: The indigenous women's wellness research program', *Health Care for Women International*, 35 (10), pp. 1–11 https://doi.org/10.1080/07399332.2013.815754.

Walter, M. & Baltra-Ulloa, J. (2019). 'Australian social work is white', in B. Bennett & S. Green (eds), *Our voices. Aboriginal social work*, 2nd edition. Red Globe Press, UK, pp. 6–19.

Weaver, H. (2001). 'Indigenous nurses and professional education: Friends or foes?' *Journal of Nursing Education*, 40 (6), pp. 252–258.

Womack, R. (1997). 'Enhancing the success of native American nursing students', *Nurse Educator*, 22 (4). http://gateway.ut.ovid.com/gw1/ovidweb.cgi.

Woolsey Des Jarlais, C. L. (2009). 'Cultural characteristics of western educational structures and their effects on Local ways of knowing', Graduate Student Theses, Dissertations & Professional Papers. 1301. https://scholarworks.umt.edu/etd/1301.

Yunkaporta, T. (2009). 'Aboriginal pedagogies at the cultural interface', Professional Doctorate (Research) thesis, James Cook University.

Yunkaporta, T. (2019). *Sand Talk. How Indigenous Thinking Can Change the World*. Text Publishing, Melbourne, VIC.

32
Healing justice in the social work classroom
Engaged Buddhism, embodiment, and the legacy of Joanna Macy

Loretta Pyles

UNIVERSITY AT ALBANY, SUNYUSA

Introduction

Social workers and activists are beginning to realize the importance of both inner and outer work for a global and transformative practice. Social movements of the past attended primarily to changing political and material conditions. Today, a new generation is inquiring into and attempting to heal internalized oppression and intergenerational trauma as exemplified by the healing justice movement (Brown, 2017; Pyles, 2018). Activist Tanuja Jagernauth (2010) notes that healing justice work "recognizes that we *have* bodies, minds, emotions, hearts, and it makes the connection that we cannot do this work of transforming society and our communities without bringing collective healing into our work." Feminist and other post-colonialist thinkers have theorized embodiment, something that previously has been ignored by scholars and educators, affirming that oppression has a somatic dimension and that embodied interactions reflect structured realities (Price and Shildrick, 2010). Healing justice is thus a practice of attention and connection to the body and other parts of the self and a liberatory pathway that asks social practitioners "to cultivate the conditions that might allow them to feel more whole and connected to themselves, the world around them, and other human beings" (Pyles, 2018, p. xix). Healing justice also means using a critical lens to understand the economic, political, and systemic forces at work in oppression and human suffering, while also invoking the body-mind-spirit to heal and forge a new way forward in communities. Healing justice is vital to transformative justice which seeks to radically change the existing systemic arrangements as we radically change ourselves.

One of the early progenitors of this kind of work was Joanna Macy, who has taught transformative and empowering practices to environmental and anti-war activists for decades, drawing from Engaged Buddhism, deep ecology, and systems theory. Her book, *Mutual Causality in Buddhism and General Systems Theory: The Dharma of Natural Systems* (1991), is a multilayered scholarly analysis that brings together esoteric Buddhist philosophical perspectives with scientifically based general systems theory. Its premise is that the self is not a self-existent entity but fluid, interdependent, and co-arising with everything. Thus, she argues, healing the world, each other, and ourselves, are multiple dimensions of a cohesive reality. It is worth noting that some of these "non-Western" ideas that emphasize mutuality, permeability, and collectivity are now being confirmed by science (see for example, Hanson, 2009).

I had Macy's book checked out from my university's library virtually the entire time I was in my doctoral program and it became a symbol for the kind of work I wanted to do. Her ideas overturned the scientific materialism that tends to dominate the social work profession, scholarship, and education, disrupting the traditional divide between knower/known, body/mind, self/other, and doer/deed. Moreover, it filled a gap that the critical, postmodernist, and post-colonialist thought of the time was giving only scant consideration to, namely attention to the body-mind-spirit and non-Western perspectives. While manifesting these ideas in my scholarship and pedagogy has been an unfolding process as I have forged my way through the academic ranks, Macy and other teachers such as Mirabai Bush (Barbezat and Bush, 2014), Paulo Freire (1970), and Becky Thompson (2017) have continued to inspire me on a pathway as a critical, feminist, and transformative educator.

The key intellectual forces that ennoble Joanna Macy's work are Engaged Buddhism, general systems theory, and deep ecology. These mutually reinforcing living traditions have informed her scholarship, activism, and pedagogy. The body of wisdom that she has created, with collaborators such as Chellis Glendinning, John Seed, Chris Johnstone, David Korten, and Molly Brown, has impacted literally thousands of activists, facilitators, and teachers around the world. It is the work that she considers necessary as we transition in what has been called a "Great Turning" from an "Industrial Growth" society to a "Life Sustaining" society.

The work began as "Despair and Empowerment Work" in the 1970s as she and her co-facilitators began holding space for people to feel their despair for the planet and for social injustice that no one was talking about. The model drew from spiritual principles, group counseling methods, ritual and myth, and play to help individuals break out of despair and denial. Drawing from the inspirations of deep ecology, her work evolved into the "Council of All Beings," a psycho-drama which invites participants to enact the voices and roles of all planetary beings, who are otherwise silenced. Eventually called the "Work that Reconnects" in the late 1990s and 2000s, a vast network of facilitators and participants continue to refine the methods as they go deeper into issues of power and privilege and work more proactively with diverse communities.

I have been fortunate to be able to incorporate the spirit and methods of Macy's pedagogy into my teaching, as my students and I engage in theater, ritual, despair/grief and empowerment work, and mindfulness and yoga on the university campus and in social justice and social work spaces in the community. In western countries, academia is predominantly a patriarchal, capitalist, and white supremacist space (Thompson, 2017) and many of us have internalized resistance to such embodied forms of working in the classroom. Mentors are necessary for this kind of work and thus Joanna Macy holds a central place in the development of critical pedagogy for healing justice, specifically in terms of helping teachers facilitate more interconnected and generative learning spaces, which can animate the practice of healing justice.

The widening circles of Joanna Macy

Joanna Macy is an activist, writer, teacher, and systems thinker. Her intellectual contributions have been wide ranging, from her translations of Rilke's poetry to her philosophical essays to her books on popular education for movement building, to her own memoir, *Widening Circles*

(2000). Throughout these texts, a core teaching is that humans can attend to and move beyond the limits of the individual self in order to take action on behalf of the ailing planet and suffering humans. Macy's message is that as we work on behalf of the planet, we can nourish and replenish our own spirits as well. Though she does not use the term "healing justice," she believes that something positive happens

> when we pay attention to the inner frontier of change, to the personal and spiritual development that enhances our capacity and desire to act for our world. By strengthening our compassion, we give fuel to our courage and determination. By refreshing our sense of belonging in the world, we widen the web of relationships that nourishes us and protects us from burnout. In the past, changing the self and changing the world were often regarded as separate endeavors and viewed in either-or terms. But in the story of the Great Turning, they are recognized as mutually reinforcing and essential to one another.
>
> *(Macy and Johnstone, 2012, p. 32)*

To know Macy's work is to know her as a poet and storyteller. She tells new and old stories like an ancient Greek lyrical poet with the rhythmic cadence of her voice drumming the words "like the heartbeat of our living universe" (Macy and Fleming, 1988, p. 57), as if from both ancient and future times simultaneously. In her workshops and in the story, "Life with Gaia" (1988), she recounts the history of the Earth, a story not so much about humans but of the Earth herself, Gaia's story. This story teaches that humans did not appear until very late on the scene in Gaia's history, and that "Gaia is becoming aware of herself, she is finding out who she is" (Macy and Fleming, 1988, p. 61). This and other stories serve a pedagogical purpose and provide a clarion call to activists. She writes:

> So, we are now at a point unlike any other in our story. I suspect that we have, in some way, chosen to be here at this culminating chapter or turning point. We have opted to be alive when the stakes are high, to test everything we have ever learned about interconnectedness, about courage – to test it now when Gaia is ailing and her children are ill … When you go out from here, please keep listening to the drumbeat. You will hear it in your heart … When you return to your communities to organize, saying no to the machinery of death and yes to life, remember your true identity … Out of that knowledge you can speak and act. You will speak and act with the courage and endurance that has been yours through the long, beautiful aeons of your life story as Gaia.
>
> *(Macy and Fleming, 1988, pp. 63–65)*

It is this kind of careful attention to embodiment in Macy's work that nourishes the spirit and sustains activists in social change work.

Born Joanna Rogers in California in 1929, her family's roots were on the East Coast of the United States. She spent significant time growing up in New York City, but her memories of her grandfather's farm in Western New York and the legacy of preachers on that side of the family were very influential to her. She recalls the quiet solitude of the maple tree on her grandfather's farm which offered respite from the conflict between her parents and the abuse she experienced from her father. As she states:

> I entered the solitude that was more than my own. It was a protected solitude, like the woods near the north pasture, but different because here one single, living being was holding me. My hands still remember the feel of her: the texture of the gray bark, the way it

rippled in folds near the joints, its dusting of powder. As I climbed up into her murmuring canopy, my heart quickened – from fear of falling, and from awe. Caution felt like reverence.
(Macy, 2000, p. 2)

From the beginning, the contemplative life has been central to who she is; a life of engagement with Mother Earth, visceral and embodied ("it rippled in folds near the joints"). This is clearly one of the things that sets Macy apart from other critical educators. As she engages with the world and community around her, her Earth-centered spiritual life remains central.

Macy was born in an era where being a daughter, wife, and mother were prioritized over the development of a woman's individual self. This context was a source of catapult and conflict for her throughout her life. Her marriage to Fran Macy, a Russian scholar, diplomat, and anti-nuclear activist, is a significant part of her narrative, as is the story of their children and the family's travels. Her memoir, *Widening Circles* (2000), depicts her worldly explorations, some of Fran's choosing and some of her own, and the ever-widening circles that she found herself in, from Washington DC to Europe to Nigeria to India to Sri Lanka.

Macy was also profoundly shaped by her interactions with Tibetan Buddhist teachers, Khamtrul Rinpoche and Choegyal Rinpoche, and the story of the Shambhala warrior.[1] The vision of the Shambhala warrior is a prophecy that arose in Tibet over twelve centuries ago from the *Calchakra Tantra*. It is, in essence, the story of the Bodhisattva, a being who devotes their energy to the awakening of all beings while delaying their own. The kingdom of Shambhala emerges at the point in history "when the future of all beings hangs by the frailest of threads" and "life on Earth is in danger. Barbarian powers have arisen. Although they waste their wealth in preparations to annihilate each other, they have much in common: weapons of unfathomable devastation and technologies that lay waste the world" (Macy, 2002, p. 161). The Shambhala warrior goes into the heart of power and dismantles the weapons of the oppressor with their own weapons – wisdom and compassion.

It is this message of wisdom and compassion that permeates Macy's workshops, as she helps participants to non-judgmentally listen and hold space for one another through difficulty, while at the same time tapping into an ancient wisdom and creative force that can transform our way of living. I surmise that the silences around the abuse that was occurring in Macy's own family of origin and the pain that caused for her, have been part of the inspiration for her willingness to bear witness to other people's despair and pain. While her initial wound was for her mother, her family, and herself, she was also drawn to people who, like her, felt pain for the planet and society, inspiring her to be a midwife for the creation of something better and more humane.

Buddhist thought, systems theory and deep ecology in Macy's work

Joanna Macy is a founding mother of the Engaged Buddhist movement. The Buddhist concept, *paticca samuppada*, or interdependent co-arising (also, dependent co-arising), was fleshed out by Macy, to show how every person, object, feeling, and action is influenced by a complex web of interconnected causal factors. If one looks at something as simple as a chair, one will see the wood, the tree, the sun, the rain, and the people who cut the tree, milled the wood, and built the chair. Referring to systems thinker von Bertalanffy's work, she writes that "the person is an irreducible and dynamic whole, in open interaction with their world, sustaining and organizing herself through appropriation, transformation and differentiation of meanings and symbols" (Macy, 1991, p. 80).

This metaphysical view has significant implications for morality and values. Macy writes: "In the Buddha Dharma, concern for other beings, which is integral to the perception of the dependently co-arising nature of reality, finds purest expression in *metta*, 'loving-kindness'"

(Macy, 1991, p. 195). *Metta*, also translated as "good will," can be illuminated by a passage from Buddha's text, *Karaniya Metta Sutta* (Thanissaro Bhikku, 2004):

> With good will for the entire cosmos,
> cultivate a limitless heart:
> Above, below, & all around,
> unobstructed, without enmity or hate.

Macy's groundbreaking approach to activist pedagogy in the environmental justice movement has encouraged grief and despair work for what we have lost and are losing, sought to widen the sense of self beyond western individualism, and supported by the cultivation of what Tibetan Buddhists refer to as *bodhichitta*, the innate impulse toward compassion and liberation. She says that without this, "all striving and all uses of the intellect are not worth much. But with it, aahh, everything self-realizes; you're already home. So, compassion is key" (Macy, 1991 p. 160).

Macy's translation of the concept of interdependent co-arising, or what Thich Nhat Hanh calls "interbeing," is the linchpin for all of her work. Disentangling the western philosophical divide between self and other, or self and society, interdependent co-arising is philosophically commensurate with the principles of deep ecology and the Gaia principle, i.e. that we are the Earth and the Earth is us. This Buddhist perspective on the self, which is essentially the idea of "no-self," is also commensurate with the conclusions of postmodern philosophy in that the self is socially constructed and fluid and can never be fully pinned down (Loy, 2003). These ideas are reflected in her essay, "The Greening of the Self" (Macy, 1990), promoting the transformation of an ego-based self to an eco-self. She writes:

> [O]nce we stop denying the crises of our time and let ourselves experience the depth of our own responses to the pain of our world – whether it is the burning of the Amazon rainforest, the famines of Africa, or the homeless in our own cities – the grief or anger or fear we experience cannot be reduced to concerns for our own individual skin. It can never be the same.
>
> *(Macy, 1990, p. 56)*

This is an essay that my students read every year and it seems to express an idea that a new generation is at least interested in learning more about, if not learning how to come to embody. Importantly, the deep empathy that social work students need to cultivate, is not just for the planet, or people on the other side of the globe, or people on the other side of the tracks in their own cities, but also for people on the "other" side of the political spectrum. Always inspired by the father of Engaged Buddhism, Vietnamese Zen Master Thich Nhat Hanh, Macy (2007, p. 29) cites his poem, "The Old Mendicant" to illustrate these principles:

> You have manifested yourself
> As trees, grass, butterflies, single-celled beings,
> And as chrysanthemums.
> But the eyes with which you looked at me this morning
> Tell me you have never died.

The Buddha's emphasis on interdependence and the collective in his spiritual community, known as a *sangha*, was particularly inspiring for Macy. She describes the dimensions of this in *World as Lover, World as Self* (2007) as she articulates the Buddha's emphasis on social inclusiveness and his rejection of caste discrimination and the egalitarian composition of the Sangha; his distrust of private property and the establishment of voluntary poverty, sharing, and alms-begging in the Sangha; his advocacy of government by assembly and consensus; and the Sangha's rules for debate and the settlement of differences.

(Macy, 2007, pp. 45–46)

While there is a strong emphasis on collectivity and the consensus decision making of Buddha's monastic order who strived, in the face of competing views, to be "in concord," Macy believes that we are still held individually responsible for our own awakening and the outward expression of political commitments to transformation, thus affirming her belief in human agency.

Racialized people have played critical roles in environmental justice organizing, including, for example, the development of principles of environmental justice at the First National People of Color Environmental Leadership Summit in 1991 in Washington, DC. And yet, the environmental justice movement also has been appropriately criticized for its lack of racial diversity and lack of racial analysis (Johnson, 2019). Macy's work is not immune to such criticism as her pro-active analysis of race, as well as other interlocking oppressions, at least historically, could be described as latent, at best. Fortunately, in more recent years, she and her colleagues, are addressing white supremacy through the 'Work that Reconnects'.[2] Without a robust racial analysis, the environmental justice movement will continue to perpetuate white supremacy. Central to any transformative justice and healing justice pedagogy must be opportunities to inquire into the ways that intersecting oppressions manifest personally, inter-personally, and structurally (Pyles and Adam, 2016).

Macy's key pedagogical innovations and their implications for social work pedagogy

Macy's signature pedagogies, which have been utilized in hundreds of workshops with thousands of participants, are easily translatable into the social work classroom, despite the fact that her work has focused most robustly on issues of peace and environmental justice. With a few exceptions, social workers have primarily focused on issues of poverty, violence, mental and physical health, and other forms of social injustice. Social work has only been tangentially focused on environmental justice though there is new vigor as climate change looms and social work gatekeepers are making strong statements about environmental justice[3]) thus making Macy's work all the more salient in this moment.

As non-western and indigenous body-mind-spirit practices begin to take hold in a variety of social work settings (Lee et al., 2009), classrooms become an important space for engaging in inquiry into the impacts that oppressive social systems have on the whole self (Pyles and Adam, 2016). Students are beginning to be taught the vital skills of mindfulness of the whole self, including body, mind, heart, spirit, community, and the natural world, so that they are more equipped to engage in resistance to patriarchal, capitalist and racist systems and cultures that promote disconnection and domination. Below I discuss several of Macy's signature pedagogies, showing how they are relevant for social work classrooms.

Despair work

Apathy, numbing, and despair are just some of the reactions that humans can have to the perils of the planet and its people. But Macy (2007, p. 93) notes that:

> The refusal to feel takes a heavy toll. It not only impoverishes our emotional and sensory life – flowers are dimmer and less fragrant, our loves less ecstatic – but also impedes our

capacity to process and respond to information. The energy expended in pushing down despair is diverted from more creative uses, depleting the resilience and imagination needed for fresh visions and strategies.

Though the prospect of connecting with deeply painful feelings is daunting, Macy invokes the idea of Polish psychiatrist Kazimierz Dabrowski, "positive disintegration," to explain that entering the chaotic darkness of the (individual and collective) self, allowing things to fall apart, actually serves an evolutionary purpose and is, indeed, healthy and creative. Despair and grief work is essentially a radical truth-telling in a ritualized group setting. Macy offers several versions of this work. For example, she invites participants to work with partners and take turns completing sentences such as: "What concerns me most about the world today is …. Feelings about all this, that I carry around with me, are …. Ways I avoid these feelings are …. Some ways I can use these feelings are …" (Macy and Brown, 1998, p. 99). These kinds of inquiry practices have been central to various Eastern traditions, including jnana yoga and various Buddhist traditions. Another method is the truth mandala wherein participants sit in a circle divided into four quadrants and in each quadrant a symbolic object is placed: a stone (representing fear), dead leaves (grief), a stick (anger), and an empty bowl (deprivation, emptiness). Hope is represented by the very ground of the mandala. The participants are invited to take turns picking up an object and expressing the various emotions. For instance, picking up the stone, one might say, "I am afraid of the policies on immigration and deportation. Will my family be next?" After each person speaks, the group responds, "We hear you." The facilitator ends by reminding participants that each symbolic object is like a coin with two sides – a stone representing fear but also the trust it takes to speak it. Because we only grieve over who we love, the dead leaves represent both sorrow and love. The anger of the stick springs from a passion for justice and the emptiness of the bowl implies space for the new (Macy and Brown, 1998).

Though social work students tend to be empathetic and engaged, with proper guidance students can face hidden feelings of despair and other feelings about the suffering and social injustices in their communities. Social work scholar and educator Ben Shepard (2016) writes about the ways that he uses the pain and suffering of the moment in his community of Brooklyn, New York, USA as fodder for connection, dialogue, interaction, and action in and out of the classroom. Topics have included the perils of gentrification, the killing of a local student by police, or the grief that he himself experienced when he found himself teaching the day after his own father's death. He writes about how his class spent the entire class talking about grief and pain and loss:

> Some students talked about loved ones who had passed. Others reflected on other kinds of pain they had experienced and the ways they did or did not confront it, or the pain of loss and trauma … I was different in the classroom, more open, more interested in hearing and being in the listening process while students felt like it was a time for them to be honest and make sense of their lives without judgment, to be better people, better human beings, not just better students. Many talked about those people who had helped them along the way.
> *(Shepard, 2016, pp. 109–110)*

Besides the difficulties of coping with compassion fatigue and secondary trauma, I find that many of my students are holding onto grief, despair, and cognitive dissonance over the contradictions of social services and social justice work. Many of them feel a call to help and to uplift human dignity, and yet they are working in neoliberal social services organizations that may be privileging the bottom line, responsibilizing clients, and grinding their own staff down (Reisch,

2013; Schram, 2011). Through guided inquiry processes, I hold space for my students to feel this sense of despair and disappointment that they might be experiencing about the social work profession. This opens up pathways for generating new visions of what transformative social services organizations could look like.

The council of all beings

Deep ecologist, Arne Naess, advocated for a form of community therapy or experiential process whereby people could embody the teachings of deep ecology (Macy and Fleming, 1988). Toward this end, the Council of All Beings, a ritual and set of practices performed by a group of people wishing to connect more deeply with the experiences and voices of Earth's elements and creatures, was originated in Australia in 1985 with Macy, John Seed, and other Australian colleagues. The purpose of the Council of All Beings is "to heal our separation from the natural world, or to know our interexistence with all beings, or to find in the web of life the power that will help us act in its self-defense" (Macy and Brown, 1998, p. 150). In the ritual, participants create masks reflecting a being of the universe (e.g., a mountain, or an eagle) and then spontaneously speak the truths of those beings. It is an opportunity to express the confusion, fear, grief, and hope of the times.

Such practices can also help people to feel previously unfelt grief for the planet and its species. In a practice known as the Bestiary, names of threatened and endangered species are read aloud followed by the sound of a drum or clacker, simulating a funeral-type ritual. The point is not to focus on guilt, but to honor the lives of species lost, and to open to the grief. Toward the end of the process, participants are invited to name other things that are disappearing from their world. People say things such as "clean beaches," "safe food," or "hope."

These and other rituals and enactments are apropos for social work students. Social work students have been engaging in role playing as part of their educational process for decades, but not necessarily in transformative/healing ways or toward transformative/healing ends, but rather for the purpose of professional skill building (Pyles and Adam, 2016). With transformative intentions, expanding this practice to include masks, props, and elements of ritual can help students in deepening their understanding, expanding their empathy, and engaging in their own healing in embodied ways. Today there are social work educators who are innovating exercises from *Theatre of the Oppressed* or other forms of theater in order to create learning spaces that allow students to embody and express oppression and liberation (Boal, 2002; Pyles and Adam, 2016). Social work educator Uta Walter (2016) utilizes what is known as "the clown bow" to help students overcome fear and to promote risk-taking: something that is essential for transformative justice. She describes it as "the boisterous, happy, and proud raising of the arms after 'failing' or when feeling embarrassed accompanied by a loud call of 'whoo-hoo!' and a big bow, which is cheered and applauded by the group" (Walter, 2016, p. 168). The purpose is not to "shrink in shame" when a mistake is made, but to "make themselves physically and emotionally big" (Walter, 2016, p. 168). This kind of joy in transformative education is something Macy, too, has encouraged her students to embrace; not as self-indulgent but essential to a life sustaining society (Macy and Johnstone, 2012).

Storytelling

Humans have always been storytellers. Indeed, according to cognitive science, the frames and images that storytelling conjure are likely more powerful in changing people's minds about key social issues than statistics and "facts" (Lakoff, 2004). According to Brown and Macy [4]:

> It is deep in the human psyche and the vast panoply of human cultures to tell ourselves stories about our world. A story is the lens by which a group interprets and controls its experience, creating meaning according to the values its members hold and most deeply believe. A story may be largely unconscious and unquestioned, and even assumed to be the only reality, although no story is inherently complete.
>
> *(https://workthatreconnects.org/choosing-the-story-we-want-for-our-world/)*

Economist David Korten reminds us that "when the stories a society shares are out of tune with its circumstances, they can become self-limiting, even a threat to survival" (cited in Macy and Johnstone, 2012, p. 13). Thus, like all critical pedagogies, the work is to uncover marginalizing stories so that new ones can be identified.

In Macy's workshops, she describes the three stories that are happening in the current moment – the story of Business as Usual; the Great Unraveling; and the Great Turning. The story of Business as Usual is the story of the Industrial Growth society that continues to perpetuate power and wealth accumulation for the few. In this story, there is no acknowledgment of any problems with the status quo, and the solution offered for any problem is to "grow the economy." The Great Unraveling is the story told by climate scientists, journalists, and activists who shed light on the degradation and collapse of biological and social systems. This story brings attention to the collapse of bee colonies, natural disasters, flare ups in longstanding divides including racism, and the coming of the sixth extinction. The Great Turning is told by people who do not want the great unraveling to have the last word. It is a story of the creative human response and new structures being forged through cooperation and respect toward a sustainable planet. My students read short versions of each of the three stories and they are invited into inquiry (e.g., journaling or partner discussion or expressing in a physical posture) about which stories they tend to embrace and to explore any shifts in their stories throughout the semester.

I remember an experience I had in a workshop in Calgary, Canada with Joanna some years back. She asked everyone to sit in two large circles one inside of the other, with the inner circle facing out, and the outer group facing in so that we were face to face with someone. The inner circle was asked to tell this person in the outer circle, who represented a future generation (100 years into the future), what we were doing during the time of the Great Turning. The outer circle represented a generation who had survived climate change and were very grateful to the current generation for making the changes it made. The current generation in the inner circle talked about what we were doing in our activism, in our communities, in our homes, and in our relationships. The process invited us to acknowledge what we were currently doing, but also to imagine what we could be doing differently or more of, dreaming a successful outcome into existence. Social work educators and students also use storytelling as a way to leverage political action. Mizrahi et al. (2016) discuss how they work with community organizing students to help them to consider how the narratives of community organizations are a form of storytelling, and a form of political education that can bridge divides and build coalitions.

Widening circles

Perspective taking is considered a key dimension of human empathy. The ability to widen and shift perspective is critical to transformative justice work as well, in order to disrupt the human tendency toward narcissism and ethnocentrism and to gain deeper understanding and connection across difference. Drawing from the Rilke poem: "I live my life in widening circles/ that reach out across the world … And I still don't know/Am I a falcon, a storm,/or a great song"? (cited in Macy and Brown, 1998, p. 121), Macy invites participants to sit in groups of four and identify an issue that concerns them. After a moment of silence, each takes a turn to speak, describing the issue from four different perspectives: (1) their own perspective, including feelings about the issue; (2) the perspective of a person whose views are very different or even adversarial to the issue; (3) the view of a non-human that might be affected by the issue; and (4) the perspective of a future human who will be affected by the issue. The activity ends with de-briefing. It could be adapted so that social work students focus on a pressing issue such as mass incarceration or discrimination against immigrant families, taking on their own perspective as well as that of someone directly impacted, someone adversarial to the issue, and a voice from the future. The key here is not that students only discuss the issue from these other perspectives, but that they *embody* a different role. This is where the transformative and healing power of embodiment lies. This creative process, an act of "moral imagination" (Macy and Brown, 1998, p. 122), is a somatic experience permitting the participant to potentially feel the emotional tones of the perspective and its impacts in the body.

Conclusion

In her book, *Teaching with Tenderness*, Becky Thompson (2017) writes about embodied teaching, noting that "our bodies include our unconscious selves – the self that goes deeper than words. This is the realm we need to be willing to communicate with when we teach, particularly about subjects that are considered taboo, sensitive, or too touchy" (Thompson, 2017, p. 40). Macy has been at the forefront of such education, as she invites participants into embodied activity for engaging with difficult subjects, deepening relationship, and maintaining collective spaces. It is the work of healing justice and a methodology that can help social work students to become holistically engaged and transformative practitioners.

Joanna Macy has given people the permission, inspiration, and tools to be with the pain of the planet, the dysfunction of human-made systems, and the internalized suffering in the human psyche. It is only through such processes that we can even begin to imagine something different. Her teacher, Choegyal Rinpoche, reminded her that the weapons of the old society are *"manomaya,* mind-made. This is very important to remember, Joanna. These weapons are made by the human mind. So, they can be *un*made by the human mind!" (Macy, 2000, p. 162). And with this idea, hope is also central to the critical and social constructionist projects. Her work inspires us to disentangle the complex trauma unleashed by the Industrial Growth society on the Earth and its inhabitants, and at the same time envision and practice a sustainable way forward. It is never a complete throwing out of the old but a kind of composting of it. The Buddha articulated this idea through his image of the lotus flower in the *Dhammapada* – "as in a pile of rubbish cast by the side of a highway, a lotus might grow, clean-smelling, pleasing the heart" (Thanissaro Bhikku, 1998, p. 17).

Notes

1 The Shambhala concept was formalized into the Shambhala community in the West by Chogyam Trungpa Rinpoche and later by his son, known as Sakyong Mipham. Both men have been accused of egregious sexual and other forms of misconduct in this community – www.nytimes.com/2018/07/11/nyregion/shambhala-sexual-misconduct.html. I think it is important that this information be transparent and studied further in order to understand the ways that spiritual and religious ideas can cause harm.
2 https://workthatreconnects.org/
3 https://libres.uncg.edu/ir/uncg/f/M_Powers_Social_2017.pdf
4 https://workthatreconnects.org/choosing-the-story-we-want-for-our-world/

References

Barbezat, D.P. and Bush, M. (2014). *Contemplative Practices in Higher Education: Powerful Methods to Transform Teaching and Learning*. San Francisco, California: Jossey-Bass.

Bhikku, T. (1998). *Dhammapada: A Translation*. Barre, MA: Dhamma Dana Publications.

Bhikku, T. (2004). *Karaniya Metta Sutta: Good Will*. www.accesstoinsight.org/tipitaka/kn/snp/snp.1.08.than.html

Boal, A. (2002). *Games for Actors and Non-actors* (2nd ed.). London: Routledge.

Brown, A.M. (2017). *Emergent Strategy: Shaping Change, Changing Worlds*. Chico, CA: AK Press.

Freire, P. (1970). *Pedagogy of the Oppressed*. New York: Herder and Herder.

Hanson, R. (2009). *Buddha's Brain: The Practical Neuroscience of Happiness, Love, and Wisdom*. Oakland, CA: New Harbinger Publications.

Jagernauth, R. (2010). *Just Healing. Organizing Upgrade*. http://archive.organizingupgrade.com/index.php/modules-menu/community-care/item/91-jagernauth-just-healing.

Johnson, S.K. (2019). *Leaking Talent: How People of Color are Pushed Out of Environmental Organizations. Green 2.0*. www.diversegreen.org/leaking-talent/.

Lakoff, G. (2004). *Don't Think of an Elephant!: Know Your Values and Frame the Debate : The Essential Guide for Progressives*. White River Junction, VT: Chelsea Green Publishing Company.

Lee, M.Y., Ng, S., Leung, P., and Chan, C. (2009). *Integrative Body-mind-spirit Social Work an Empirically Based Approach to Assessment and Treatment*. Oxford; New York: Oxford University Press.

Loy, D. (2003). *The Great Awakening: A Buddhist Social Theory*. Boston: Wisdom Publications.

Macy, J. (1990). The Greening of the Self. In *Dharma Gaia: A Harvest of Essays in Buddhism and Ecology* (pp. 53–63). Berkeley, CA: Parallax Press.

Macy, J. (1991). *Mutual Causality in Buddhism and General Systems Theory: The Dharma of Natural Systems*. Albany, NY: State University of New York Press.

Macy, J. (2000). *Widening Circles: A Memoir*. Gabriola Island, BC: New Catalyst Books.

Macy, J. (2002). *The Shambhala Warrior*. www.awakin.org/read/view.php?tid=236

Macy, J. (2007). *World as Lover, World as Self*. Berkeley, CA: Parallax Press.

Macy, J. and Brown, M.Y. (1998). *Coming Back to Life: Practices to Reconnect Our Lives, Our World*. Gabriola Island, BC, Canada; Stony Creek, CT: New Society Publishers.

Macy, J. and Fleming, P. (1988). Guidelines: For a Council of All Beings Workshop. In Seed, J., Macy, J., Fleming, P. & Naess, A. (Eds.), *Thinking like a Mountain: Towards a Council of All Beings*. Philadelphia, PA: New Society Publishers.

Macy, J. and Johnstone, C. (2012). *Active Hope: How to Face the Mess We're in without Going Crazy*. Novato, CA: New World Library.

Mizrahi, T., Martell, E., Cavanagh, K., and Weingarten, A. (2016). Learning in Community: A Transformative Healing Model for Teaching Community Organizing. In Pyles, L. and Adam, G. (Eds.), *Holistic Engagement: Transformative Social Work Education in the 21st Century* pp. (57–82). New York: Oxford University Press.

Price, J. and Shildrick, M. (2010). *Feminist Theory and the Body: A Reader*. New York: Routledge.

Pyles, L. (2018). *Healing Justice: Holistic Self-Care for Change Makers*. New York: Oxford University Press.

Pyles, L. and Adam, G. (2016). *Holistic Engagement: Transformative Social Work Education in the 21st Century*. New York: Oxford University Press.

Reisch, M. (2013). Social Work Education and the Neo-Liberal Challenge: The US Response to Increasing Global Inequality. *Social Work Education*, 32(6), 715–733. https://doi.org/10.1080/02615479.2013.809200.

Schram, S.F. (2011). *The End of Social Work: The Neoliberalization of Doing Good. Silverman Graduate School of Social Work and Social Research (SSRN Scholarly Paper No. ID 1901020)*. Retrieved from Social Science Research Network website: https://papers.ssrn.com/abstract=1901020

Shepard, B. (2016). Conversation and Dialogue in Social Work Education. In Pyles, L. and Adam, G. (Eds.), *Holistic Engagement: Transformative Social Work Education in the 21st Century* (pp. 101–114). New York: Oxford University Press.

Thompson, B. (2017). *Teaching with Tenderness: Toward an Embodied Practice*. Urbana, IL: University of Illinois Press.

Walter, U. (2016). Improvisation: A Practice for Praxis. In Pyles, L. and Adam, G. (Eds.), *Holistic Engagement: Transformative Social Work Education in the 21st Century* (pp. 157–174). New York: Oxford University Press.

33
Frantz Fanon's revolutionary contribution
An attitude of Decoloniality as critical pedagogy for social work

Linda Harms Smith

ROBERT GORDON UNIVERSITY, ABERDEEN, SCOTLAND

Introduction

There are many reasons why Frantz Fanon's work is relevant to social work today. He wrote in a very specific socio-historical period, but given ongoing Coloniality evident in global power asymmetries and neoliberal economic arrangements with grave levels of global (and within-state) inequality, Fanon's (1986) characterisation of racist colonisation, oppressive power relationships and their intrapsychic impact, remain relevant. Fanon acknowledges the rootedness of his own work in his temporal context and states in *Black Skin, White Masks* that "The architecture of [his] work is rooted in the temporal. Every human problem must be considered from the standpoint of time" (Fanon, 1986, p. 5). However, as a Martinican living in Algeria and working as a psychiatrist, his work as a post-colonial theorist is said to be as important and relevant today as it was during the 1950s and 1960s (Gibson, 2008; Guegan, 2015).

His work confronted the brutal asymmetrical power relationships of colonialism, critically interrogating these on levels of the psychological, social, material, cultural and political. Fanon's (1986) politics and struggle was "not that of socialism against capitalism but that of poor against rich and, at some level, the derided racial category of 'blackness' against that of 'whiteness', African culture versus European" (Hook, 2004a, p. 123). As a post-colonial critique, his work brings together many philosophical, psychological and cultural theories with personal anecdotes and illustrations from practice relevant to the colonial context. In so doing, Fanon lays bare the "forms of discrimination and disempowerment that would have otherwise remained effectively invisible, indiscernible, 'naturalised' within a society" (Hook, 2004a, p. 123).

The impact of oppressive racist power relationships exerts a similar impact today as during the colonial era, from the perspective both of the similarity of these dynamics and through intergenerational transmission of collective trauma (Hilton, 2011; Hoosain, 2018; Masson and Harms-Smith, 2019). Fanon's key texts, all of a liberatory, anti-colonial and revolutionary nature, included *Black Skin, White Masks* (1952, translated into English in 1967, 1968); *A Dying*

Colonialism (1959, translated into English in 1965); *The Wretched of the Earth* (1961, translated into English in 1963) and *Toward the African Revolution* (1964, translated into English in 1969).

Fanon starts *Black Skin, White Masks* (1986, p. 1) with a quotation from Césaire (2000),[1] the anti-colonial theorist and his former teacher: "I am talking of millions of men [sic] who have been skillfully injected with fear, inferiority complexes, trepidation, servility, despair, abasement." His work is described as seminal, a key text, a bible of the anti-colonial liberation movements, a theory of the psychic life of colonial man [sic], and one of the most important contributions to anti-colonial studies, liberation and revolutionary social change (Burawoy, 2011; Flores-Rodríguez & Jordan, 2012; Guegan, 2015; McCulloch, 1983). When regarded in this way, his work clearly has an extensive reach, both contextually, politically and philosophically.

When considering critical pedagogy as an important project of liberatory education in social work, its value in providing experiential learning for social work students for their work with people at all levels of practice, is immense. McCulloch (1983, p. 69) argues that the position of critical theorists is that people are "essentially unfree and inhabit a world rife with contradictions and asymmetries of power and privilege", and that the critical educator engages with theories that see societal problems as relating to the interaction between individual struggles and those of the social structure (McCulloch, 1983). For the critical social work practitioner, it is therefore those emancipatory experiences in the "classroom" context that inform the strategies and content of what is required in the context of practice. With respect to the oppressive nature of ongoing Coloniality, race-, class- and gender-based socioeconomic inequality, intersections of oppression, and institutional and structural racism, it is argued here that Fanon's many propositions provide a rich and valuable resource for critical engagement with these conditions. For example, psychopolitics and sociogeny; the impact of colonisation; internalised oppression; negritude; disalienation and liberation; the importance of affect; and an attitude of Decoloniality, provide rich ground for liberatory and conscientising encounters in an environment of critical pedagogy and critical social work.

Frantz Fanon

Frantz Omar Fanon was born on 20 July 1925 in Fort de France, Martinique. Bulhan (2004, p. 15) states that Fanon was "inextricably bound to the social dialectic he studied and sought to transform". His own lived experience as a colonial subject in Martinique and later France and Algeria, encountering the destructive and dehumanising racism of colonialism and the psychological trauma of denigration of identity, language and culture, provoked a consciousness that a "comprehensive understanding of racist trauma under colonialism is unthinkable without attention to psychological *and* political processes" (Desai, 2014, p. 64). Having grown up in Martinique with a strong French identity, for Fanon's family the World War II period was transformative. Experiencing severe anti-black racism by the occupying French soldiers, he later, together with other Caribbean volunteers for France, experienced "personal humiliation and disillusionment" on the ships transporting them to North Africa. As Antillean soldiers in Casablanca they were treated by local white settlers as wild savages or at best domesticated servants (Bulhan, 2004).

Fanon was also influenced by the philosophy of negritude and the challenge of Aimé Césaire (who had also been one of his school teachers); namely, "Black was not only beautiful, he declared, but the heart of such darkness – Africa – was also its majestic center at which aesthetic and spiritual emancipation awaits" (Gordon, 2015, p. 11). Fanon, at the age of 17, driven by his commitment to liberty for all, joined the French army to fight in Algeria, "witnessing colonial oppression of a sort he had never seen before, and then in Eastern France where he discovered the meaning of metropolitan racism" (Burawoy, 2011, p. 3) in the sense that he encountered racist disregard for his French status as a Martinican and interiorisation as a black man. Having experienced such racist humiliation and indignity for black soldiers fighting for France, Fanon turned to radical politics after his return to Martinique (Gordon, 2015).

It is, however, the period when he returned to France to study medicine and psychiatry in Lyon, France, that he encountered what is described as traumatogenic racialisation through alienation and inferiorisation as a colonial subject (Burman, 2016). These experiences led him to reflect on and investigate the pathologies of colonised–coloniser encounters and racist structures (Desai, 2014) using individual psychological analyses within the context of sociopolitical structures (Desai, 2014; Hook, 2004a). The work that would later become his book *Peau noire, masques blancs* (*Black Skin, White Masks*, published in 1952 when he was 27 years old), was initially proposed as the content of his thesis. However, this was turned down by his doctoral supervisor and so he went on to produce his new thesis on "Mental Illness and Psychiatric Syndromes in Hereditary Cerebral Spinal Degeneration" within two weeks (Gordon, 2015).

Fanon arrived in Algeria in 1953 after accepting a position as a psychiatrist at the Blida-Joinville psychiatric hospital, at a time when it was beginning to engage in the violent anti-colonial struggle and revolution against France. His role at the hospital was such that he became head, where he encountered the lived experiences of patients in the hospital and it is said that "through his patients he vicariously experiences the traumas of colonial violence" (Burawoy, 2011, p. 3). His exposure to the oppressive inequality and racist treatment of the Algerian people by the French and their brutal and repressive response to the uprisings, led him to support the Algerian National Liberation Front (FLN) from 1954, and later to resign his post as psychiatrist in 1956 to join the liberation struggle and become one of its leading figures (Sardar, 2008). He is said to have chosen to fight injustice, and "viewed the revolutionary insurrection in Algeria as the logical consequence of an attempt to oppress, decerebralise and alienate an entire people" (Lamri, 2019, p. 1). After his expulsion from Algeria in 1956 he left for Tunis to continue his psychiatric work and become an ambassador for the FLN in various parts of North and West Africa. He died of leukemia in 1961, before Algeria's independence.

Key transformative and critical concepts relevant to critical pedagogy in social work education

There are many reasons for claiming the importance of Fanon's work today. Among the contributions of his work to liberatory and critical anti-racist praxis, is its psychopolitical emphasis. This emphasis provides a psychological analysis of the political which explores the significance of the sociopolitical and departs from traditional Western psychoanalytical perspectives (Hook, 2004a; McCulloch, 1983). Fanon foregrounds issues such as "cultural dispossession, colonial violence, racism and racial identity" (Hook, 2004a, p. 123).

The nature of colonisation and Coloniality as a form of racist brutalization, is described by Fanon as being related to the way in which it was a "systematic negation of the other and a frenzied determination to deny any attribute of humanity to millions of people" (Fanon, 1963, p. 82). The relationship between the coloniser and the colonised is one of domination and negation of humanity of the colonised (Fanon, 1963, p. 195).

Fanon provides a descriptive analysis, using a phenomenological approach that includes socio-politic realities, describing his own lived experiences as well as those of his patients. He is influenced by a large number of theorists including Sartre, Hegel and Marx. His analysis exposes and addresses the problems of racist colonialism and the way in which structural dominance is maintained through the racist structures of Europe (Sardar, 2008); it emphasises the need for continuous action to transcend the reality of the inhumanity of racist exploitation; it warns of complacency against the "European unconscious … and the idea of progress where everyone climbs up towards whiteness and light and is engulfed by a single, monolithic notion of what it means to be human" (Sardar, 2008, p. xix); and it provides mechanisms for the achievement of humanisation and Decoloniality through resistance against structurally determined internalised and material oppression.

Psychopolitics and sociogeny

Fanon's (1986) contribution to understanding, resisting and challenging the brutality of racist colonialism that was, and continues to be, imposed on 'black' people, lies in his resolution of the dichotomy between the psychological and the political. Fanon (1986) explains that the struggles of 'black'[2] people are far better explained by a sociopolitical framework than by individual psychological factors and goes on to introduce the idea of sociogeny – that which is to be found between approaches of the specific individual and the structural or political. The psychopolitical framework should be "with reference to violence, power and subordination" (Hook, 2004a, p. 85). Fanon's (1986) work demonstrates how the human psyche is closely linked to sociopolitical and historical forces. Not only does Fanon's psychopolitics mean that psychology should be expanded to explore the political, but "a second route of psychopolitics lies in employing psychological concepts and explanations to describe and illustrate the workings of power" (Hook, 2004a, p. 115).

In order to understand the alienation and oppression of the black colonised person, Fanon (1986) proposes a sociogenic approach, which he describes as that which lies between the phylogenic (study of a species' evolutionary development as a whole) and ontogenic approaches (the focus on the individual, specific experience). He maintains that Freud's psychoanalysis was such an attempt to substitute the phylogenic approach with an ontogenic, individual perspective. However, he argues that neither of these positions is adequate, and that "It will be seen that the black man's alienation is not an individual question. Beside phylogeny and ontogeny stands sociogeny … let us say that this is a question of a sociodiagnostic" (Fanon, 1986, p. 4).

The dichotomy of agency and structure is, therefore, dealt with by a sociogenic approach. It is no longer necessary to adopt an either/or approach to social change and liberation from oppressive power relationships, as the "sociodiagnostic" or sociogenic position of understanding provides for the interaction between the individual and the structural. Gordon (2005, p. 2) explains that "the sociogenic pertains to what emerges from the social world, the intersubjective world of culture, history, language, economics" that is brought about by human beings. It is these social structures that are the cause of the internal conflict (Fanon, 1986, p. 75).

Impact of colonisation

Fanon (1986) demonstrates that "the colonial encounter is unprecedented: the epistemic, cultural, psychic and physical violence of colonialism makes for a unique type of historical trauma" (Hook, 2012, p. 17). The colonised therefore became psychologically, physically and materially dehumanised through colonisation. This was achieved through violent colonial conquest which included annexure of land and people, together with "hypocritical Euro-centricity that justified the negation of the Other, thus alienating the mind and spirit" (Guegan, 2015, p. 169). Fanon argued that because colonialism in fact was a determined and systemic negation of the humanity of the other, it "forces the people it dominates to ask themselves the question constantly: 'Who am I?'" (1963, p. 249).

Wa Thiong'o (1986) similarly describes the most important area of colonisation as that of the control of "the mental universe of the colonised", which meant the destruction and undervaluing of their language and culture, and of how they perceived themselves. This meant the "destruction and deliberate undervaluing of a people's culture, their art, dances, religions, history, geography, education, orature and literature, and the conscious elevation of the language of the coloniser" (Wa Thiong'o, 1986, p. 16).

That the domination and exploitation of colonisation was achieved through violence is regarded by Burawoy (2011) as the first of his "theses on colonialism", which analyse the domination of colonialism, the struggles against it and its overthrow. He states that, for Fanon, in *Black Skin, White Masks* (1963), the colonial is characterised by segregation, dehumanisation and dispossession of land, and that it is only through revolution which transforms consciousness and builds solidarity that the colonial order can be overthrown.

It is useful, however, to explore the difference between colonialism and Coloniality. Maldonado-Torres (2017) maintains that colonialism denotes a political and economic relation in which the sovereignty of a nation or a people rests on the power of another nation, which makes such nation an empire. Coloniality, instead, refers to long-standing patterns of power that emerged as a result of colonialism, but that define culture, labour, intersubjective relations, and knowledge production well beyond the strict limits of colonial administrations. It is this Coloniality, as ongoing relations of power asymmetry, that remains present and ubiquitous in the world today.

Internalised oppression

Burawoy (2011, p. 13) argues that the idea of internalised oppression relates to a "psychoanalytical understanding of the internal dynamics of racial domination in which the colonized internalizes the social structure and wrestles to find his or her place in that structure". It is important, however, to note that Fanon's understanding of the development of a so-called "inferiority complex" resulting from racialisation is not an internal, pathological process arising from within the racialised individual but rather as "pathologizing forces that, while they infect black bodies, do not come from within them, but are rather produced and circulated in the situation of colonial racism" (Whitney, 2015, p. 50).

Internalisation of oppression and racialisation is a process engaging both intrapsychic and sociopolitical processes. The dynamics through which colonial oppressors exert dominating and subordinating power is through the restriction of material resources and "by implanting in the subordinated persons or groups fear or self-deprecating views about themselves" (Prilleltensky and Gonick, 1996, p. 130). Oppression at the intrapsychic level is therefore interlinked and affected by the structural and political forces at the interpersonal level, exacerbated by the use of force when attempts are made to challenge authority (Prilleltensky & Gonick, 1996).

Internalisation is, furthermore, said to occur not only at an individual level, but also with respect to the colonised country collectively. Sadar (2008, p. ix) argues in the foreword to *Black Skin, White Masks* that the colonial context of struggle meant that a colonised country had "lost its own cultural bearings and internalized the idea of the inherent superiority of the colonizing culture". This may be seen as a form of genuflection to such Western/American/European cultures. Much work around particularly epistemic Decoloniality relates to, for example, positioning Africa as the centre and "provincialising" or "indigenising" Europe as a strategy to reclaim histories and narratives of the previously colonised (Ndlovu-Gatsheni, 2018). This is not a process of rejection of all that is Western, and as this process unfolds and the richness of culture, history and language is embraced and celebrated, that which is of value should be chosen and incorporated.

Negritude

Although Fanon at times acknowledged the importance of negritude as a movement as a "subjectively necessary counter to the psychologically damaging influence of colonial deculturation" (McCulloch, 1983, p. 50), he also dismissed it as a social force because it inadequately addresses the material conditions of social and economic inequality. He is also said to have been ambivalent toward the movement, as he disagreed with it as a response to the problems of black identity, as racialisation had been imposed by the colonial order (McCulloch, 1983). However, later in his writing, in *The Wretched of the Earth*, he acknowledged that the reclaiming of a "worthwhile historical past" and national culture was important, especially for black intellectuals (McCulloch, 1983). In keeping with his sociogenic approach, the value of negritude is to be found both for the psychological struggle of colonial subjugation as well as for the solidarity that promotes the demands for structural social change (McCulloch, 1983).

Fanon's (1963) view described in *The Wretched of the Earth*, about the value of the negritude movement is that it has a rehabilitative function to claiming historical national culture as a way of providing hope for a national culture in the future. Fanon argues that it also important for achieving "psycho-affective equilibrium" (McCulloch, 1983, p. 49). Fanon, therefore, seems to have supported the philosophy of negritude for its temporary therapeutic value. This includes the importance of reclaiming narratives and rewriting history to counter that which was imposed by colonising nations.

In coloniser/colonised situations, it is argued, as part of such a therapeutic phase, the subjugated group develops an "essentialist identity to promote group pride and unity, to advance and achieve specific, socio-political goals, and to foster healing" (Spivak, 2006, cited by Nielsen, 2011, p. 372). Fanon, problematising negritude for its essentialising blackness, is able to reject these essentialised notions and agree with the central aspects of Césaire's Negritude, which include "the development and continued fostering of a positive, black, social identity, a non-repetitive 'return' to and ongoing reappropriation of African values, and a revolutionary call to decolonization" (Nielsen, 2011, p. 372).

Fanon (1963), toward the end of *The Wretched of the Earth*, writes about the importance of the embrace of culture in such processes. He argues that the struggle for liberation and emancipation from dehumanising colonial oppression, cannot be successfully achieved, "save in the expression of exceptionally rich forms of culture … [and that] the future of national culture and its riches are equally also part and parcel of the values which have ordained the struggle for freedom" (Fanon, 1963, p. 246).

Disalienation and liberation

Fanon (1986), in his introduction to *Black Skin, White Masks*, explains the importance of the recognition of both social and economic realities in the process of disalienation. He argues against the existence of an inferiority complex situated and produced internally within the psyche of a black person. He writes that the so-called inferiority complex arises from both the external reality of economic oppression as well as its psychological internalisation, and that

> the effective disalienation of the black man entails an immediate recognition of social and economic realities. If there is an inferiority complex it is the outcome of a double process: primarily, economic; subsequently, the internalization or, better, the epidermalization – of this inferiority.
>
> *(Fanon, 1986, p. 4)*

Wynter (1999, p. 12) argues that what must then be understood is that the internal psychological condition of inferiority arises from material realities and that "the second part of the process [i.e. internalisation] is no less objectively structured, even where subjectively experienced, than is the first [i.e. economic]" (Wynter, 1999, p. 12).

As described in the section on sociogenic analysis, this alienation of the "black" person is not only an individual problem and cannot be explained in only psychoanalytic (or ontogenic) terms (Wynter, 1999). The "black" person will therefore be able to achieve liberation only if war may be waged at two levels – at the material and structural level manifested in the socio-economic, and at the level of the sociogenic (Fanon, 1986). Because each level has historically impacted and shaped the other, Wynter (1999, p. 13) argues that resolution at only one level would be incomplete and that "a solution will have to be supplied both at the objective level of the socioeconomic, as well as at the level of subjective experience, of consciousness, and therefore, of identity".

Fanon (1963) emphasises the depth of struggle of alienation at the level of racist economic exploitation in *Black Skin, White Masks*. He compares the alienation experienced by, for example, a black doctor at an "almost intellectual level" where he regards European culture as a means of being rid of his racialisation, with that of a black person who is "a victim of a system based on the exploitation of a given race by another, on the contempt in which a given branch of humanity is held by a form of civilization that pretends to superiority" (Fanon, 1963, p. 224). It is this depth of alienation that must be struggled against through a "refusal to accept the present as definitive" (Fanon, 1963, p. 226) in order to achieve disalienation and true liberation.

Importance of affect in experiences of racialised oppression and racism

Ideas about the micro and structural onslaught and aggression of racism, and particularly colonial racism, frequently elide the depth of psychic pain and deep affective injury (Charania, 2019). Fanon (1986, 1963) himself frequently expresses his own anger and in this regard Sardar (2008, p. vii) argues that such anger does not arise suddenly or spontaneously, but is "borne out of grinding exxperience, painfully long self-analysis and even longer thought and reflection.".

Colonisation and post-colonial racism and dehumanisation, as powerful forms of damage at an intrapsychic level, are experienced at both a cognitive and affective level. Hage (2010) argues that Fanon's theory was grounded on the inclusion of the affective dimension in the analysis of the psychological and political. These experiences impact on the psyche of both the individual and the collective. Fanon, in his psychoanalytical positioning, argues that these racialising and racist experiences which accompany the negation of being, occur so overtly and at such conscious levels, that they do not find relief through the usual Western "white" psychological mechanisms of suppression into the unconscious through neuroses (Fanon, 1986). It is evident, therefore, that experiencing and recalling such oppressive racism will, of necessity, occur at both a cognitive and affective level, and thus be accompanied by strong emotions.

Fanon (1986) argues that psychopathology in the colonised person is a product of their particular sociocultural reality that results from the colonial experience of racialisation, inferiorisation and negation of being. The hyper-arousal or affective erethism that may manifest, are part of the response to this culturally induced situation. Fanon explains that these postulates by means of various forms of media such as film, books, advertisements and even school, confront the "black" child and adult and "work their way into one's mind and shape one's world view of the group to which one belongs. In the Antilles, that world view is 'white' because no black voice exists" (Fanon, 1986, p.118). This colonial racialisation and inferiorisation thus give rise to a deep psychic pain of otherness and dehumanisation at both an individual and collective level.

Zembylas (2012, p. 116) maintains that Fanon provides a most powerful depiction of racialising and racist embodiment and affectivity, and cites Srivastava (Srivastava in Zembylas, 2012, p.116) in arguing that such accounts expose the "deep emotional undercurrents and foundations of racial conflict". Hook (2004b), too, highlights the role of the affective, and argues that colonisation and racialisation are phenomena that are as political as they are affective, discursive, psychological and ideological. These affective states, in the current context, are often contested and challenged by dominant groups as too emotional (Essed, 1991, p. 282).

Importance of an attitude of Decoloniality

Fanon (1986) argues that the collective unconscious and attitudes are not formed by cerebral heredity, but are acquired by cultural imposition collectively – and in the case of the colonised, the denigration of all that is "black" and an extolling of all that is "white" and European: "the collective unconscious, without our having to fall back on the genes, is purely and simply the sum of prejudices, myths, collective attitudes of a given group" (Fanon, 1986, p. 145). This attitude is, therefore, not a psychological reaction that develops within the individual alone, but, as Maldonado-Torres (2017, p. 434) argues, arises from structural conditions and power struggles: "for Fanon, social structures both reflect and reinforce collective attitudes, both of which play a role in the formation of subjectivity." This subjectivity is therefore reflective of an attitude of Coloniality, imposed by the structural forces of inferiorisation and materiality in which the individual and the collective find themselves.

It is from this perspective of both the subjective, internal disposition as well as the collective response to structural realities, that Fanon (1986) stresses the importance of "attitude" as a means to achieve liberation from all that is imposed onto the psyche of the colonised. In fact, Fanon appeals for a development of an attitude of Decoloniality rather than a focus on a method or strategy for achieving transformation and liberation from Coloniality (Fanon, 1986; Maldonado-Torres, 2017).

This attitude of Decoloniality, which arises through both action and reflection, is demonstrated by Fanon (1963), who shows the importance of both action and intellectual reflection through his witnessing of, and direct involvement in, the anti-colonial struggle, and in his writings (Guegan, 2015). Freire (1972) similarly describes this circular process of action, reflection and action as praxis and essential for the development of critical conscientisation in order for liberation and humanisation to be achieved.

Facilitation of emancipatory transformation in social work education

The importance of Fanon's (1986, 1963) work as a holistic approach to work with people living in conditions of socioeconomic inequality, hardship, and oppressive, racist social structures, cannot be overemphasised. The applicability and strength of Fanon's work is to be found in the sociogenic or psychopolitical emphasis: it is neither only the individual intrapsychic, nor only the political context that is deemed crucial to understanding – it is the interplay between both (Hook, 2004a; McCulloch, 1983). The dichotomy of agency and structure; micro and macro; or clinical and structural approaches is eliminated as the practitioner is guided to a critical understanding and consciousness of both the political context and psychological dynamics of the person and the collective.

In the South African context more specifically, social work is indicted with a general focus, historically, on status quo maintenance and colonising knowledge and practice (Harms Smith, 2013). The Apartheid era acted as a silencing of those social work voices that challenged and resisted, "contributing to the ongoing colonising nature of social work itself" (Harms Smith & Nathane, 2018, p. 15). Despite a transformation of the welfare system toward a developmental approach after the end of the liberation struggle and transition to democracy, ongoing inequality stratified by race, transformative and liberating social work has been constrained by neoliberal economic policies (Sewpaul, 2006).

Frantz Fanon's revolutionary contribution

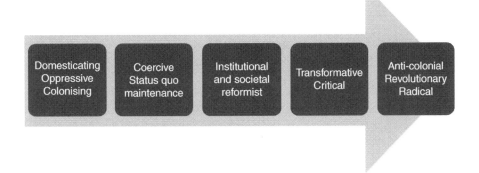

Figure 33.1 Continuum of social work knowledge and discourse.
Source: Harms Smith (2013, p. 92)

It is also argued that so-called "indigenisation" and Africanisation merely obfuscate the underlying conservative and colonial nature of knowledge generally (Mbembe, 2015), and social work knowledge and discourse specifically (Harms Smith & Nathane, 2018; Mathebane & Sekudu, 2017): "What is required is a transformed curriculum committed to a position of Decoloniality" (Harms Smith & Nathane, 2018, p. 15).

Taking into account ideologies underlying and supporting social work, as well as the historical complicity of social work with conservative and oppressive practices (Smith, 2008; Harms Smith, 2013), social work knowledge and discourse may be described as being positioned on a continuum from domesticating, oppressive and colonising, through to revolutionary, radical and anti-colonial (See Figure 33.1).

It is crucial, therefore, that as students are prepared for social work practice through the theory and discourse of their curriculum, they are exposed to appropriate critical and anti-colonial content (Harms Smith & Nathane, 2018), not only at a cognitive but also at an experiential level. However, where students themselves live within a post-colonial context and realities of socioeconomic inequality and intergenerational transmission of collective trauma, they will need to work through issues of Coloniality and internalised oppression (Smith, 2008; Harms Smith & Nathane, 2018). Developing an attitude of Decoloniality (Fanon, 1986) is therefore critical. Using Fanon's concepts to engage with individuals, families or communities, therefore, enables social work practice that has the potential to be transformative, decolonising and liberatory. However, it is social work students themselves that need to experience the development of an attitude of Decoloniality; critical conscientisation about their own internalised oppression and other materialist/structural oppression at all levels; explore racism and anti-racist positions; explore the mutuality of intrapersonal and structural dynamics; and reclaim narratives, cultural histories and languages as a means of centring the local (African-centred).

Sociogenic analysis

A focus on internalised oppression and "colonisation of the mind" must of necessity also pay attention to the material reality of oppressive socioeconomic structures. Such efforts must include work toward change in these conditions. Working on a project, for example, of community development in the context of material conditions of severe poverty, cannot therefore engage only with people's attitudes and behaviours. Working toward facilitating the development of a critical consciousness and understanding of the conditions in which people live, is insufficient if there are no projects of advocacy that challenge injustice perpetuated, for example, by local government.

Students, during their field placements, often encounter the realities of gross, socioeconomic inequality and suffering of whole communities living in so-called informal settlement areas (not formal housing but small plots of allocated land with basic sewerage services and perhaps a running tap at every fifth plot), and are therefore often impelled to explore socioeconomic and structural factors contributing to these conditions beyond the individualist, intrapersonal explanations of the causes of problems. Fanon's sociogenic analysis serves them well in developing understanding of these contexts.

Reclaiming historical narratives and celebrating cultural practices and languages

Black consciousness and negritude, seen as part of a process of reclaiming cultures, narratives, histories and language as well as dignity and pride, are an important part of critical Decoloniality work both in social work education, as well as in practice. For any individual, group or community struggling with dynamics of oppression and racism, the development of pride and celebration of culture are crucial. The imposition of Western universalism and inferiorisation of culture is wholly implicated in the dynamics of oppression and racism. In post-colonial contexts, where Western culture and language remain dominant, and local cultural practices and languages are repressed, this becomes important anti-racist and anti-oppressive practice. As part of developing an attitude of Decoloniality, cultural practices, histories and languages that are seen to be "indigenous" should be reframed as valid, with the imposed cultural practices and languages reframed as being indigenous to contexts of origin (Ndlovu-Gatsheni, 2018). Emancipatory social work education, if it is to facilitate an attitude of Decoloniality within social work students and, in turn, within the communities where they intervene, requires the celebration and embracing of culture. There should, however, be caution that such efforts at reclaiming culture and histories are not framed as "indigenisation", "celebration of diversity" and "cultural competence" which provide a liberal mask for dominance, "othering" and racism (Pon, 2009). In post-colonial contexts where Western knowledge systems have been imposed, denigrating local culture, traditions and histories, these narratives must be reclaimed and centred, in order for these to take central positions within these societal contexts. It is only after such a process of Decoloniality that external, Euro-centric and Western influences should be re-incorporated (Comaroff & Comaroff, 2012; Ndlovu-Gatsheni, 2018).

The role of language, as a bearer of culture, is exceptionally important. Where educators, for example, are not fluent in the first languages of students, higher education institution language communication policies, such as proficiency of educators in such languages or presence of interpreters in the classroom setting, may need to be revisited. Failing adequate arrangements, there should be discussions around these issues.

The importance of engaging with the affective

Critical interventions around oppression, internalised racism and inferiority that seek to facilitate an attitude of Decoloniality, will of necessity connect with the emotional aspects attached to these issues. Zembylas (2012, p. 117) describes the need to acknowledge and explore the "emotional undercurrents and foundations of race and racism, and develop pedagogical strategies to unearth the powerful affective component in the ubiquitous manifestations of racial practices". Especially in the presence of institutional racism, the encouragement of discussion and development of consciousness might be resisted and denied among "white" students or community members, and could elicit strong emotions. Boler and Zembylas (2003) argue that a pedagogy of discomfort is required in order to explore the emotional aspects of racism, whether in the role of the recipient or perpetrator of racism.

It is imperative that "black" students or community members are able to express the depth of psychic pain and anger that is part of their daily living and experience. Any process of working toward Decoloniality or anti-racism must include attention to the affective dimensions of the experience of being in the position of the oppressed and the oppressor. In the South African context, where historic colonial and Apartheid oppression divided communities according to categorisations of colour, all those categorised as not being "white" were structurally and institutionally discriminated against. While there is thus an ongoing need for the celebration of cultural diversity, this does not achieve anti-racism (Nylund, 2006; Pon, 2009).

During class discussion and individual and group activities, the value of personal individual reflection and then sharing in a group context, of early experiences of discrimination and racism lead to emotional self-disclosures. Students discover the validity of anger at their own experiences of racist oppression and racially stratified socioeconomic inequality. Rather than having to minimise, control and "soften" their own emotional responses, these kinds of exercises allow for a cathartic expression of what is often repressed emotional pain (Smith, 2008).

Conclusion

Working toward Decoloniality beyond the context of social work education, means that conscientisation, resistance and challenge of oppressions arising from ongoing Coloniality of power; political conflict; the impact of global neoliberalism; right-wing conservatism; and racism should be ongoing. Social work ideals around social justice, human and non-human animal dignity, care for the planet and the belief that a better world is possible, must be sustained, and it is for this reason that a pedagogy of hope must be retained.

The revolutionary potential of Fanon's work as a critical theorist for a critical pedagogy of hope lies in its contextual and temporal relevance – for post-colonial and socially unjust contexts. Interrogating and engaging with some of his thinking, offers important material for students' own journeys through the consequences and impact of historical colonisation and ongoing Coloniality – in their roles and identities as oppressors and oppressed, privileged and disadvantaged. These opportunities for engagement at a cognitive and affective level, offer experiences of liberatory education. The dynamics of historic colonial racism evident in ongoing power asymmetries of Coloniality which extend beyond, but include, those related to race, demand interrogation, resistance and challenge. As stated by Freire (1972), no education is neutral and so it is with critical pedagogy, that students may be introduced to conscientisation around dynamics and processes of oppressive power relationships, Decoloniality, and liberation from personal and collective oppression. In so doing, these students may be equipped to intervene in similar contexts. With Decoloniality currently being a global imperative, neglecting Fanon in social work education would mean that social work finds itself on the domesticating, oppressive and colonising side of the continuum of knowledge, discourse and practice, while it is called upon to provide hope and strategies for radical and even revolutionary change. Fanon urged generations to come, to strive toward humanisation and liberation and argued that "each generation must out of relative obscurity discover its mission, fulfil it or betray it" (1963, p. 206). It is the discovery and working toward fulfilment of this mission that is essential for relevant and transformative social work.

Notes

1 Aimé Césaire was a celebrated anti-colonial Martinican philosopher, writer, politician and revolutionary and regarded as one of the foremost French poets of the 20th century. He was a friend and mentor of Fanon's. His book, *Discourse on Colonialism* is regarded as seminal in relation to *negritude* (Hobs, 2018). This work presented the horrors and brutality of colonialism, and the role of negritude, surrealism and a revised form of Marxism in the achievement of humanisation.
2 The use of racialised categories are used in keeping with Fanon's writing. However, the terms are placed in single quotation marks to acknowledge that "race" and its labels are contested and constructed terms. Furthermore, Fanon's writing is gendered as masculine, and where this is evident in direct quotations, it is denoted as such by the insertion of [sic] to denote the author's disagreement with the style.

References

Bhabha, H.K. (1986). Forward to the 1986 edition: Remembering Fanon: Self, psyche and the colonial condition. In Frantz Fanon (Ed.), 1986[1967]. *Black skins white masks*. London: Pluto Press, xxi–xxxvii.
Boler, M and Zembylas, M. (2003). Discomforting Truths: The Emotional Terrain of Understanding Difference. In Peter Pericles Trifonas (Ed.), 2003 *Pedagogies of difference: Rethinking education for social change*. London: Routledge, 116–139.
Bulhan, H. A. (2004). *Frantz Fanon and the psychology of oppression*. New York: Plenum Publishing Company.
Burawoy, M. (2011). IV: Colonialism and revolution: Fanon meets Bourdieu. http://burawoy.berkeley.edu/Bourdieu/5.Fanon.pdf
Burman, E. (2016). Fanon's Lacan and the traumatogenic child: Psychoanalytic reflections on the dynamics of colonialism and racism. *Theory, Culture & Society*. 33(4): 77–101. 10.1177/0263276415598627
Césaire, Aimé. 2000 [1955]. *Discourse on Colonialism*. Monthly Review Press, New York.
Charania, G.R. (2019). Revolutionary love and states of pain: The politics of remembering and almost forgetting racism. *Women's Studies International Forum*. 73: 8–15.
Comaroff, J. & Comaroff, J.L. (2012). Theory from the South: Or, how Euro-America is Evolving Toward Africa. *Anthropological Forum*. 22(2): 113–131. 10.1080/00664677.2012.694169
Desai, M.U. (2014). Psychology, the psychological, and critical praxis: A phenomenologist reads Frantz Fanon. *Theory and Psychology*. 24(1): 58–75. 10.1177/0959354313511869
Essed, P. (1991). Sage series on race and ethnic relations Vol. 2. *Understanding everyday racism: An interdisciplinary theory*. Thousand Oaks, CA, US: Sage Publications, Inc.
Fanon, F. (1963). *The Wretched of the Earth*. trans. Constance Farrington with a preface by Jean-Paul Sartre New York: Grove Press.
Fanon, F. (1986). 1967 *Black skins white masks*. London: Pluto Press.
Flores-Rodríguez, D. (Guest Editor) & Jordan, J. (Guest Editor) (2012). Introduction: The continuing relevance of fanonian thought: Remembering the life and work of Frantz Fanon. *The Black Scholar*. 42: 3–7.
Freire, P. (1972). *Pedagogy of the oppressed*. translated by Myra Bergman Ramos New York: The Seabury Press.
Gibson, N. (2008). Upright and free: Fanon in South Africa, from Biko to the shackdwellers' movement (Abahlali baseMjondolo). *Social Identities*. 14(6): 683–715. 10.1080/13504630802462802
Gordon, L. (2005). Through the zone of nonbeing: A reading of Black Skin, White Masks in celebration of Fanon's eightieth birthday. *Worlds and Knowledges Otherwise (WKO)*. Duke, Trinity College of Arts and Sciences 1(3): 1–30. https://globalstudies.trinity.duke.edu/sites/globalstudies.trinity.duke.edu/files/file-attachments/v1d3_LGordon.pdf.
Gordon, L. (2015). *What Fanon Said: A philosophical introduction to his life and thought*. New York: Fordham University Press.
Guegan, X. (2015). Frantz Fanon's the wretched of the earth: Embodying anti-colonial action In Rachel Hammersley (Ed.), 2015 *Revolutionary Moments Reading Revolutionary Texts*. Bloomsbury Academic. 167–174. www.bloomsburycollections.com/book/revolutionary-moments-reading-revolutionary-texts/ch20-frantz-fanon-s-embodying-anti-colonial-action
Hage, G. 2010. The Affective Politics of Racial Mis-interpellation, *Theory Culture & Society*, 27(7-8):112–129.
Harms Smith, L. (2013). Unpublished PhD Thesis: Social work education: Critical Imperatives for social change. *University of the Witwatersrand*. https://core.ac.uk/download/pdf/39671629.pdf
Harms Smith, L. & Nathane, M. (2018). #Notdomestication #Notindigenisation: Decoloniality in social work education. *Southern African Journal of Social Work and Social Development*. 30(1): 1–18.

Hilton, B. (2011). Frantz Fanon and Colonialism: A psychology of oppression. *Journal of Scientific Psychology.* December 2011, 45–59. www.psyencelab.com/uploads/5/4/6/5/54658091/frantz_fanon_and_colonialism.pdf

Hobs, D.A. (2018). At the living heart: Translating Aimé Césaire. *The Nation.* July 30 – August 6 Issue. www.thenation.com/article/at-the-living-heart/

Hook, D. (2004a). Frantz Fanon, Steve Biko, 'psychopolitics' and critical psychology. In D. Hook, N. Mkhize, P. Kiguwa & A. Collins (Eds.), *Introduction to critical psychology.* Cape Town: UCT Press, pp. 84–114.

Hook, D. (2004b). *Fanon and the psychoanalysis of racism.* online]. London: LSE Research Online. Available at: http://eprints.lse.ac.uk/2567 Available in LSE Research Online: July 2007.

Hook, D. (2012). *A critical psychology of the postcolonial: The mind of apartheid.* London: Routledge.

Hoosain, S. (2018). Decolonising social work research with families. *Southern African Journal of Social Work and Social Development.* 30(1): 1–18.

Lamri, R. (2019). An urgent, necessary homage: "Fanon: Yesterday, Today" by Hassane Mezine. *Ceasefire.* June 2019. https://ceasefiremagazine.co.uk/fanon-yesterday-today-hassan-mezine/?sfns=xmwa

Maldonado-Torres, N. (2017). Franz Fanon and the decolonial turn in psychology: From modern/colonial methods to the decolonial attitude. *South African Journal of Psychology.* 47(4): 432–441.

Maldonado-Torres, M. (2017). Outline of Ten Theses on Coloniality and Decoloniality. *Franz Fanon Foundation* http://frantzfanonfoundation-fondationfrantzfanon.com/article2360.html

Masson, F and Harms Smith, L. (2019). Colonisation as collective trauma: Fundamental perspectives for social work In Tanja Kleibl, Ronald Lutz, Ndangwa Noyoo (Eds.), *Handbook of Post-Colonial social work.* Routledge pp.13–26.

Mathebane, M. and Sekudu, J. (2017). A contrapuntal epistemology for social work: An Afrocentric perspective. *International Social Work.* 55(2): 155–167.

Mbembe, A. (2015). "Decolonising Knowledge and the Question of the Archive." *Unpublished Paper: Public Lecture, WISER, University of the Witwatersrand.* Accessed 21 August 2017. http://wiser.wits.ac.za/system/files/Achille%20Mbembe%20-%20Decolonizing%20Knowledge%20and%20the%20Question%20of%20the%20Archive.pdf

McCulloch, J. (1983). 2002 edition *Black soul, white artefact: Fanon's clinical psychology and social theory.* Cambridge: Cambridge University Press.

Ndlovu-Gatsheni, S. (2018). Dynamics of epistemological decolonisation in the 21st century: Towards epistemic freedom. *Strategic Review for Southern Africa.* 40(1): 16–45 Accessed 2 December 2018 from www.up.ac.za/media/shared/85/Strategic%20Review/vol%2040(1)/Ndlovu-Gatsheni.pdf

Nielsen, C. R. (2011). Resistance through re-narration: Fanon on de-constructing racialized subjectivities. *African Identities.* 9(4): 363–385. 10.1080/14725843.2011.614410

Nylund, D. (2006). Critical multiculturalism, whiteness, and social work. *Journal of Progressive Human Services.* 17(2): 27–42. 10.1300/J059v17n02_03

Pon, G. (2009). Cultural competency as new racism: An ontology of forgetting. *Journal of Progressive Human Services.* 20(1): 59–71. 10.1080/10428230902871173

Prilleltensky, I. and Gonick, L. (1996). Polities change, oppression remains: On the psychology and politics of oppression. *Psychology.* 17(1): 127–148.

Sardar, Z. 2008. Forward to the 2008 edition. In: Fanon, F. (ed.), 1952 [2008]. *Black skin, white masks.* New York: Grove Press.

Sewpaul, V. (2006). The global-local dialectic: Challenges for African scholarship and social work in a post-colonial world. *British Journal of Social Work.* 36: 419–434.

Smith, L. 2008. South African Social Work education: Critical imperatives for social change in the post-apartheid and post-colonial context. *International Social Work,* 51(3): 371-383.

Wa Thiong'o, N. (1986). *Decolonising the mind: The politics of language in African literature.* London: J. Curry.

Whitney, S. (2015). The affective forces of racialization: Affects and body schemas in fanon and Lorde. *Knowledge Cultures.* 3(1): 45–64. www.ceeol.com/search/article-detail?id=413134

Wynter, S. (1999). Towards the Sociogenic Principle: Fanon, The Puzzle of Conscious Experience, of "Identity" and What it's Like to be "Black" In Mercedes Durán-Cogan and Antonio Gómez-Moriana (Eds.), 1999 *National Identities and Sociopolitical Changes in Latin America.* University of Minnesota Press. www.coribe.org/PDF/wynter_socio.pdf

Zembylas, M. (2012). Pedagogies of strategic empathy: Navigating through the emotional complexities of anti-racism in higher education. *Teaching in Higher Education.* 17(2): 113–125. doi:10.1080/13562517.2011.611869

34

Samkange's theory of *Ubuntu* and its contribution to a decolonised social work pedagogy

Jacob Mugumbate

SCHOOL OF HEALTH AND SOCIETY, FACULTY OF SOCIAL SCIENCES, UNIVERSITY OF WOLLONGONG, NSW, AUSTRALIA. FORMERLY AT BINDURA UNIVERSITY, ZIMBABWE

To be human is to affirm one's humanity by recognizing the humanity of others and, on that basis, establish respectful human relations with them.

(Samkange & Samkange, 1980, p.6)

Introduction

How relevant are Western pedagogies that dominate African social work today? This, and many other pedagogical questions have been debated by social workers in both the global North and South. Midgley (1983), for example, questioned the relevance of Western-originated social work that is prevalent in the global South, referring to the situation as 'professional imperialism'. Midgley (1983) recommended a social development approach; an idea that has been expanded by several authors who argued for decolonised social work (Kaseke, 2001; Razack, 2009), indigenous social work (Gray et al., 2009; Pawar, 1999) and developmental social work (Mupedziswa & Sinkamba, 2014). The argument has been that the Western-oriented social work training that emphasises the remedial approach, has not been very effective in the context of professional practice in Africa. Hence, there is a need for community as an indigenous guiding principle (Gray et al., 2009; Mupedziswa & Sinkamba, 2014). Developmental social work would be consistent with the clarion call to indigenise or decolonise social work in Africa and this resonates with the philosophy of *Ubuntu*. African indigenous knowledge such as that entailed in *Ubuntu* is not widely recognised and used in present-day educational systems (Gade, 2017; Hapanyengwi-Chemhuru &, Makuvaza, 2014). Yet, adoption of *Ubuntu* has the capacity to decolonise African social work from dominant Western pedagogies. In this chapter, Samkange's theory will be used as a case study to show how the philosophy of *Ubuntu* can help in efforts to decolonise social work pedagogy in Africa.

Ubuntu is a symbol of African identity among the indigenous Black populations of Africa (Metz, 2007; Sibanda, 2014, p.26). Many writers agree that the Black African population share commonalities in terms of philosophy, cultures, languages and religions (e.g. Chilisa, 2012;

Metz, 2007; Mugumbate & Nyanguru, 2013; Oelofsen, 2015; Ramose, 1999) but a few others argue that *Ubuntu* is not common (e.g. Gade, 2017). Despite the downplay, Gade (2017) acknowledges that *Ubuntu* has deep historical roots. *Ubuntu* was transmitted from generation to generation through observation, experience, language and art (Sulamoyo, 2010). Public and intellectual figures later transformed *Ubuntu* into written literature. In South Africa, *Ubuntu* or *botho* was popularised by Jordan Kush Ngubane in his novels (e.g. *An African Explains Apartheid*, 1963 and *Conflicts of Minds*, 1979) and articles in the *African Drum* and *Inkundla Ya Bantu* magazines. In Tanzania, the notion of *Ubuntu* or *untu* was popularised by Mbiti (1969) whose framework, often termed the 'African view of man' (*sic*) says: 'What happens to the individual happens to the whole group, and whatever happens to the whole group happens to the individual. The individual can only say: "I am because we are; and since we are, therefore I am"' (Mbiti, 1969, p.106).

In Zimbabwe, Samkange and Samkange (1980) defined *Ubuntu* or *hunhu* as African humanism in 'the first book to be published specifically on Ubuntu' (Gade, 2017, p.12). Nziramasanga (1999) reinforced the views of the Samkanges. *Ubuntu* acquired prominence in the liberation struggles of the 1960s to the 1990s as part of movements for Africanisation and decolonisation (Mtumane, 2017). The concept has subsequently been renewed, elaborated and contested as an educational, political, social, economical, environmental and theological philosophy (Mangena, 2012; Mtumane, 2017; Muvangua & Cornell, 2012; Oelofsen, 2015; Ramose, 2003). *Ubuntu*'s elaboration in recent African thought is ontological, epistemological, axiological and methodological (Chilisa, 2012; Ramose, 1999). The authors seem to agree that *Ubuntu* defines the African philosophy and a true African prior to colonisation, or as Sibanda said, *Ubuntu* reflects 'a true African society' (Sibanda, 2014, p.26). When Africans talk of decolonisation, they are referring to going back to *Ubuntu*. Therefore, decolonising social work pedagogy resonates with *Ubuntu*.

In the next section, a biography of Samkange will be provided, followed by a discussion of how his writing and life contributes to a decolonial pedagogy. Stanlake Samkange wrote one book with his wife Tommie Samkange, the rest of his work was done alone. In addition to exploring this body of work, more examples and nouns will be drawn from the Zimbabwean Shona culture to reflect my (the writer's) background and experience.

Samkange's biography

Stanlake Samkange was born in Mariga village, Zvimba area of Mashonaland region of Zimbabwe (named Southern Rhodesia by the colonial regime) in 1922, about 40 years after the area was taken over by the British South Africa Company, which was founded by Cecil John Rhodes, a British colonialist. Samkange's father was a politician and a minister of religion in the British colony, and his mother an Evangelist, both in the Methodist Church. After primary education at Waddilove Methodist Mission in Zimbabwe, Samkange left for Adams College (an institution then well known for Black student activism) in Natal in South Africa for secondary education, and proceeded to obtain an Honours degree in history at the University of Fort Hare in the same country in 1947 (Cary & Mitchell, 1977). At that time, the University of Fort Hare was the only institution of higher learning that accepted Black students in Africa. When he graduated, he became the first Black college graduate in his home area of Mashonaland. Samkange returned home to work as a teacher at Mzingwane Government School, but later left to start his own school, the Nyatsime College in Chitungwiza, near Harare. He went for studies on a scholarship to the USA where he obtained a Master of Science degree at Syracuse University in 1957 before going back home for political action. In 1966 he returned to the USA for further studies, culminating in a Doctor of Philosophy degree from Indiana University. While in the USA, he taught African history at Harvard University and Northeastern University. At Northeastern University he was Professor of African American studies. Samkange's career also included journalism and public relations.

Samkange was a politician, largely influenced by his father. Further influence might have come from Adams College where he was educated. The college nurtured several African nationalists. In Zvimba, where he was born, there were other nationalist and liberation war leaders such as Robert Mugabe and James Chikerema. Robert Mugabe was to become Prime Minister and later President of Zimbabwe from independence in 1980 until 2017. One of his friends, Molefi Kete Asante, said Samkange was also influenced by Black consciousness leaders. When Asante visited Samkange's bookstore in Harare named the Little Professor, he saw pictures of Marcus Garvey on the wall (Asante, 2015). After a discussion about the pictures, and other issues, Asante concluded that Samkange was inspired to be a pan-Africanist and nationalist supporting decolonisation of Black people by the likes of Garvey, Martin Luther King Jnr, Kwameh Khrumah and Malcolm X.

Politically, Samkange started as a liberal (interested in liberty and equality) in Rhodesian White politics in the 1950s and 1960s, before becoming a nationalist (interested in national independence), after realising that the minority White population was not interested in sharing or giving power back to the Black majority. As a Black politician doing 'White' politics, Samkange was part of a group of people called 'teaboys', simply meaning Blacks who advanced the interests of Whites so that they could get tea or White privileges. Samkange, like other 'teaboys', attracted hatred from the community for dining with a colonial regime that was repressive. Being labelled a teaboy probably influenced Samkange to leave White politics to join African Black politics. He joined the Zimbabwe African People's Union led by Joshua Nkomo and then the United African National Council led by Bishop Abel Muzorewa. He held high ranks in these parties. In 1979 Samkange left politics to concentrate on writing, a year before Zimbabwe gained independence from Britain. By the time he left politics, he was still disillusioned by the regime's control of politics and education. In education, the regime created bottlenecks for Blacks, preventing the most talented students from attaining primary, secondary or higher education. These bottlenecks reduced the number of critical thinkers or writers of books from a Black African perspective.

In spite of the handicaps imposed by colonialism, Samkange was described by Asante (2015) as a critical thinker and a smart person. He was one of the few Black Africans of his generation who was able to obtain an education and to write historical novels in the English language. The novels were critical of the regime. *On Trial for My Country* (1966) and *Origins of Rhodesia* (1966) were banned in Rhodesia (De Baets, 2002). The other book that he wrote with his wife, *Hunhuism or Ubuntuism: A Zimbabwean Indigenous Political Philosophy* (1980) is acclaimed as the first book on *Ubuntu* (Gade, 2017). In writing about *Ubuntu*, his main argument was that Western philosophies that were taught or practised in Zimbabwe were not the only philosophies, and that Africans needed to learn, write and practice their own values and beliefs.

As stated earlier, his other major achievement was the founding of Nyatsime College, a school for Black students, as a strategy to counter the shortcomings of colonial education in 1960. The college was the first private school run by Blacks in Zimbabwe. Samkange was concerned with the administration, staffing, literature, activities and curriculum at colonial schools because they promoted Western philosophies. The schools, including those he attended or taught, were administered by the colonial government or missionaries. The staff were mostly White with the exception of a few teaboys. The activities at these schools reflected those of schools in the West. Most books and syllabi came from Britain. This frustrated him.

Stanlake Samkange died of heart and lung disease at the age of 65 years in 1988 in Harare, Zimbabwe. He lived a short life, but his contribution to African literature, philosophy, education and politics is still felt strongly and appreciated today.

Samkange's contribution to the African philosophy of *Ubuntu*

> Hunhuism or Ubuntuism is … a philosophy that is the experience of thirty five thousand years of living in Africa. It is a philosophy that sets a premium on human relations.
> *(Samkange & Samkange, 1980, p.34)*

This statement affirms that *Ubuntu* was the way of life of Africans before colonisation and that *Ubuntu* had survived several years of existence. Writing on *Ubuntu* in 1980, the Samkanges gave life to an indigenous philosophy that had been sidelined for about a century, yet it was central to the life of colonised Black Africans. The Samkanges believed that African indigenous knowledge such as *Ubuntu* was not recognised in educational systems of the day. Their book sought to promote *Ubuntu* in order to transform and decolonise the legacy of a Rhodesian educational system. Samkange and Samkange (1980) defined *Ubuntu* as African humanism classified into three maxims elaborated below.

The first maxim says: 'To be human is to affirm one's humanity by recognizing the humanity of others and, on that basis, establish respectful human relations with them' (Samkange & Samkange, 1980, p.6). This maxim was further expressed in this statement: 'The attention one human being gives to another: the kindness, courtesy, consideration and friendliness in the relationship between people; a code of behaviour, an attitude to other people and to life, is embodied in *hunhu* or *Ubuntu*' (Samkange & Samkange, 1980, p.6).

According to Samkange and Samkange (1980) being human is shown through acts of sharing, respect, harmony and communalism, evident in the statement above. Samkange gave several examples to illustrate this, including a traveller passing through foreign lands who would not go hungry or be denied a place to sleep at night because the people value helping visitors freely. Through similar acts of kindness and sharing, children whose parents die, never become orphans because they are looked after or adopted by relatives. In a family, each child has several mothers, not just one. An illustration of communalism is when individuals are given a community or family identity, instead of an individual one. Often, people are called by their clan names, such as Madiba for former South African President Nelson Mandela, or Musoni for myself. Respectable references such as *Mzee* are prevalent for adults in some communities. This is done to emphasise community or family identity. Further, acts such as kneeling or clapping hands when greeting elders, reflect deep respect. Samkange and Samkange believed that each individual was an ambassador of their family, culture, community or society. This ambassadorial role is reflected through *hunhu*. By writing about living amicably with neighbours, or discouraging Western ideas of private land ownership, Samkange stressed communal values. For Samkange, the family and community were responsible for education, hence most schooling occurred in the family and community.

The second maxim states that: 'If and when one is faced with a decisive choice between wealth and the preservation of the life of another human being, then one should opt for the preservation of life' (Samkange & Samkange, 1980, p.7). This maxim means that life is important above everything else, including wealth, and was supported by Samkange's view of *ngozi*, avenging spirits. The spirits become angry when someone is killed. If there is no acceptance of wrongdoing and compensation, then a spell will be cast on the individual and/or their family. As the Samkanges said, a crime committed by one is a crime committed by family, community or society. This idea exemplifies the spiritual nature of *Ubuntu* too (Chimuka, 2001).

The third and last maxim focuses on status, power and leadership. It says: 'The king owes his status, including all the powers associated with it, to the will of the people under him' (Samkange & Samkange, 1980, p.7).

Samkange and Samkange argued this maxim reflected a principle deeply embedded in traditional African political philosophy. Leaders are expected to consult widely, live with the people and share the same lifestyles. These thinkers asked whether there was a philosophy or ideology that would help Zimbabwe, as it transitioned from colonial rule in 1980; the same year the book was published. The answer provided in the book was that hunhuism or Ubuntuism could best guide and inspire thinking in post-colonial Zimbabwe. However, this maxim does not only apply to political parties and government, but to all institutions including the home, the school, village, community, kingdoms or chiefdoms.

Often Samkange encountered people who did not know about African philosophies; people who perhaps believed that Africans had no ideologies of their own. In one instance, cited in Gade (2017, p.13), Samkange said:

> Whose fault is it if no one knows about the philosophy of your grandfather and mine? Is it not your fault and mine? We are the intellectuals of Zimbabwe. It is our business to distill this philosophy and set it out for the world to see.

Again, Samkange was stressing that Black African people have their own philosophies that they inherited from their ancestors, and that each has a role to promote those philosophies.

Samkange acknowledged that *Ubuntu* attributes are not exclusive to Africans (Sibanda, 2014). Referring to Zimbabwe, Samkange and Samkange (1980, p.77) note that 'It does not follow that certain traits/attributes which are readily identifiable with *Ubuntu/hunhu* cannot be found among other peoples who are not of Bantu origin'. This was an acknowledgement that other people had their own philosophies, but philosophies share commonalities.

Other intellectuals and public figures have presented complementary views of *Ubuntu* focusing on similar or different aspects of the philosophy. Nziramasanga (1999) cited in Sibanda (2014, p.27), for example, focused on *Ubuntu* as denoting a 'good citizen' as a 'morally upright person who is characterised by responsibility, honesty, justice, trustworthiness, hardwork, integrity, cooperative spirit, solidarity, hospitality and devotion to the family as well as community welfare'. Dolamo (2014) argues that *Ubuntu* was adopted and popularised as a social and political ideology by African freedom fighters and promoters of the liberation struggle. They would always tell communities that they were fighting so that Africans could reclaim their humanity.

In this conceptualisation of *Ubuntu*, the liberation movement emphasises possession (as opposed to dispossession and colonialism), liberty, self-determination, empowerment, respect, recognition, justice, cohesion, forgiveness and communalism among other virtues. Such statesmen and liberators include: Kwameh Nkrumah of Ghana, who promoted a pan-Africanist ideology now known as Nkrumaism; Julius Nyerere of Tanzania who popularised *ujamaa* (which refers to community self-help); Robert Mugabe of Zimbabwe, who promoted total independence; Kenneth Kaunda of Zambia who promoted humanism; Jomo Kenyatta of Kenya, who promoted *harambee* (which means pulling together as a community); Nelson Mandela of South Africa who focused on freedom; and Samora Moises Machel, who promoted social justice and self-reliance. Archbishop of Cape Town, Emeritus Desmond Tutu, popularised *Ubuntu* through efforts to reconcile Black and White South Africans after centuries of colonialism, dispossession and apartheid (Battle, 1997; Tutu, 2000). For Maphalala (2017), *Ubuntu* is interpersonal values (regard for others), intrapersonal values (regard for self) and environmental values (regard for environment). In their analysis of *Ubuntu*, Mugumbate and Nyanguru (2013) noted that the philosophy could improve social work education, practice and research, concurring with Ramose (1999) and Chilisa's (2012) frameworks that view *Ubuntu* as ontological (having philosophical assumptions about the nature of reality), epistemological (a way of knowing) and axiological (forming ethics and values). It could be added that *Ubuntu* is methodological. Despite its richness, *Ubuntu* is often ignored or dismissed as simple African thinking (Chilisa, 2012; Chimuka, 2001; Maphalala, 2017).

In concluding this section, it is stated again that Samkange offered us a view of *Ubuntu* that focuses on *humanity*, *sanctity of life* and *people-centred status*. While Samkange focused largely on *Ubuntu* as a political philosophy, others have used *Ubuntu* to describe African moral, educational, social, economical, environmental and theological standpoints. It seems, what is lacking presently is an integrated framework of *Ubuntu*; one that would bring all these facets together. To me, the integrated framework would explain *Ubuntu* as something experienced or expressed at the level of the individual, family, community, society, environment and spirit. I argue here that *Ubuntu* is practised everyday; it is present and I have encountered it myself when I travelled across Africa or when I interacted with people from different African nations. I grew up in *Ubuntu*, it is in my family, village, chiefdom and country. The views of Samkange on *humanity*, *life* and *status* are supported by other writers on the subject such as Chilisa (2012), Dolamo (2014), Maphalala (2017), Nziramasanga (1999) and Ramose (1999). The views are still very relevant today and have a part to play in decolonising pedagogy in Africa.

Contribution to decolonised pedagogies

Returning to the philosophy of the colonised

Samkange and Samkange argued that through colonialism Africans were forced to adopt foreign philosophies, and African learners were taught that their ancestors had no teachings of their own. They challenged this notion, arguing that before colonisation, the overarching philosophy of Black people in Africa was *Ubuntu* (Samkange & Samkange, 1980). As shown in the preceding section, for the Samkanges, this philosophy was represented by values guiding humanity, life and status. Their argument was for a return to these original values.

Although Samkange's writing was not directly on social work, his ideas and life could be used to transform the legacy of colonialism in contemporary African social work education and practice. Western methods of social work used in former colonies, are rooted in Western culture, creating a bias when applied in other cultures. Samkange argued that the process of decolonising will not be complete until indigenous knowledge systems take their place, replace or truly integrate with colonial systems, especially in education. For this assertion, Samkange had support from many writers. Muwanga-Zake (2009) argued that if African values are not used in educating Africans, this is akin to re-colonisation. Thus, *Ubuntu* is a tool for decolonising learning to come up with a decolonised learner (Sibanda, 2014). Muwanga-Zake (2009, p.413) argued that indigenous knowledge from Africa is submerged, diminished and misrepresented by Western approaches. Hapanyengwi-Chemhuru and Makuvaza (2014, p.1) said:

> It is therefore essential to search for a philosophy that will bring relevance to the education system – an education system that emanates from the existential historical circumstances of the people. We argue that for the education system at any level to be relevant, it must have its foundations in the philosophy of *hunhu*.

The effective incorporation of indigenous African literature and methods of information storage and dissemination of theories, books, journals and articles is desirable in the decolonisation and promotion of *Ubuntu*. During my social work studies, as well as teaching social work in Zimbabwe, I often had limited access to local literature. This was because for most subjects, local literature was not available. The libraries were stocked with literature from the West. Indeed, as Mupedziswa and Sinkamba (2014, p.141) have argued:

> Research done in this regard (social work literature in Africa) also made some disturbing discoveries with respect to literature used in social work education and training in Africa. Most African schools of social work were found to be dependent on Western social work literature and, sadly, few efforts had gone into developing indigenous teaching materials.

This is a challenge for African social workers who wish to contribute to the production and use of indigenous literature. The starting point, as Pawar (1999) proposed, is to acknowledge that we are using a foreign pedagogy, and then to establish our own pedagogy before integrating with, or replacing, colonial pedagogies. Samkange's theory provides us with an opportunity to value our own philosophy and to see that the dominant philosophies we are using were externally imposed, and are therefore limited for the needs of an African pedagogy in social work. The Samkanges (1980) also reminded us that even non-written sources can be useful.

Valuing non-written and local sources of information and 'informal' education

One pedagogical lesson from Samkange was that although written literature was powerful, *Ubuntu* existed in non-written formats that were equally powerful. *Ubuntu* is largely not written but is 'tacit, sacred and imbedded in practices, relationships and rituals' (Muwanga-Zake, 2009, p.414). In agreement, Gikandi (2003) argued that 'orature' (oral literature) is passed through the spoken word and thrives in communities when it is practised or lived. *Ubuntu* existed in African orature for a long time, possibly centuries, prior to colonial records. Most of it is not written, hence the use of the term orature, which was coined by Ugandan theorist Pio Zirimu (Gikandi, 2003). In Zimbabwean Shona culture, *Ubuntu* is communicated in folklore (*ngano*), songs (*nziyo*), stories (*nyaya*), poems (*detembo*), teasing (*zvituko*), epics, jokes or humour (comic/funnies) (*nyambo*), metaphor or idiom (*dimikira*) and proverbs (*tsumo*) and riddles (*zvirahwe*). It is a rich oral tradition and a lived experience which forms part of the African culture. By writing the first book on *Ubuntu*, Samkange transformed orature into literature and showed that non-written sources were just as important, especially in communities that did not have a tradition of writing.

In teaching social work, we need to value people who are regarded as knowledge holders in the family or community as well as other non-written sources. The founders of social work education in Africa, most of them European, did not seem to value local sources. Instead, they imported social work books from Britain and the USA. My own experience of undertaking social work training at the University of Zimbabwe, was that the literature used in the School of Social Work, mostly came from Britain, and the library had only a few books written by locals. This British dominance reflected the founder's background. The founder, Ted Rogers, a Catholic Jesuit, was British and so were many of the founding lecturers. They did a commendable job in introducing social work in Zimbabwe in 1964 but their pedagogy supported Western ideals; hence most of the social workers they trained could only effectively work in urban areas where lifestyles are highly Westernised or in Western countries themselves (Chogugudza, 2008; Kaseke, 2001).

For Kaseke (2001), the challenge with the colonial education was that it responded curatively to social ills of unemployment and delinquency that were in urban areas, but neglected structural and developmental issues that are important for masses of poor people in rural, farming and mining communities. I am an example of that failure, so are my many other colleagues working mostly in the UK and Australia.

Samkange argued that most of the education in Africa takes place in the home and community, and this is often termed 'informal' education from the colonial perspective. In social work, we need to acknowledge the role played by the family and community in education. We should seek not to replace or ignore the knowledge gained outside the formal classroom, but to build on it. The missionaries and colonisers misconstrued home and community education, labelling it informal education and equating it with lack of education. As Ocitti (1994, p.14) cited in Hapanyengwi-Chemhuru and Makuvaza (2014, p.2) said, the missionaries argued that the children 'have no nurseries, no tea parties, no birthdays and no instruction from their parents. They are there and that is all. Their lives are one big nothing'. However, the communities did not value or need nurseries, tea parties or birthday celebrations, they had numerous ways of instructing their children and their lives were valuable. The environment was the children's playground and classroom.

Promoting communalism and humane relationships

Ubuntu places emphasis on collectivity and communalism as opposed to individualism. These are the values that Samkange promoted. Metz (2007) and Maphalala (2017) agreed with Samkange and Samkange (1980) that *Ubuntu* is about relationships, and that we become human through others. *Ubuntu* creates a learner who says, 'I achieve because of others; others achieve because of me'. Using *Ubuntu*, the classroom (and indeed the school or college) would be seen as an *ujamaa* community in Tanzania or *harambee* community in Kenya. These are communities in which every member has a role to play for the achievement of the other. *Ujamaa* stresses sharing knowledge or resources and not just accumulating it for individual use. *Ubuntu* does not promote individual champions or heroes ahead of their family or community. In the case of Zimbabwe, strategies of *Ubuntu* include *dare* (a groupwork strategy used for discussions) and *nhimbe* (a community strategy used for cooperative work). *Dare* is similar to sharing or yarning circles where each person gets a turn to contribute to a discussion without interruption. In a *dare*, questions and answers wait until your turn. A *nhimbe* could be used to assist one family (or person) to cope with the demands of work or it could be used for community projects (Muyambo, 2017).

According to Samkange, *Ubuntu* is relational and it stresses the need for humane relationships. Social work includes the development of professional relationships between learner and educator, learner and supervisor, learner and learner, learner and service users, and supervisor and educator. Strong reciprocal relationships are important if social work teaching and learning are to be fruitful. Students work with service users during fieldwork, demonstrations and simulations. It is important that students have appropriate values to engage each other, teachers, supervisors and service users in a humane way. *Ubuntu* fosters respectful communication in teaching and learning situations; for example, using respectful language in their emails or when addressing colleagues. In building relationships, we can recognise the potential for leadership within everyone. Samkange's view was that the leader respects his people, and this is an important lesson for leadership in social work education, lecturers and leaders of programmes or classrooms.

Promoting Ubuntu research

Social work education includes research training, especially for Honours, Master's and Doctoral students. Samkange's view of *Ubuntu* offers lessons for research. For example, as indicated earlier, Samkange was concerned with creating respectful, humane relationships and avoiding harm – values that are important in research design. Writers have used the term '*Ubuntu* research', as a way to use *Ubuntu* principles to set research agendas in relation to ethics and methodology (Mugumbate & Nyanguru, 2013; Seehawer, 2018). Many other writers have supported *Ubuntu* research (Maphalala, 2017; Muwanga-Zake, 2009). Maphalala (2017, p.102) argued: 'If educationists continue to use Western lenses to examine African phenomena and ideologies they will see no value nor will they reap any benefit from them.' This argument was supported by Muwanga-Zake (2009) who noted that the use of Western lenses is dominant because indigenous knowledges are not valued, and research is evaluated on how it contributes to existing Western knowledge, which is regarded as the universal truth (Muwanga-Zake, 2009).

Research questions are framed by the dominant ideology, and there is need to ask questions that help to decolonise (Muwanga-Zake, 2009). *Ubuntu* research philosophy gives the research processes a humane face, as opposed to top-down imposed research processes, and advocates collaboration with the participants and community humanely, with respect to their spirituality, values, needs, norms and mores. The researcher becomes a *munhu* (humane person), thus removing power imbalances. Being a *munhu* means greeting participants the *Ubuntu* way, understanding their needs, joining them in their chores and providing them information about researcher's background (Muwanga-Zake, 2009). *Ubuntu* research accepts that knowledge is co-created; hence the need for participation and collaboration. It acknowledges that researchers, just like the researched, do not know everything. *Ubuntu* impacts the researcher, the researched and their communities. In other words, it could be said *Ubuntu* presents an ontology that is relational, an epistemology that is co-creational, a theory that is humane and a methodology that is collaborative (Chilisa, 2012; Ramose, 1999). This means that through the process of research, the researcher and the researched learn new ways of doing things for both their communities, and not just the researched community.

Combining politics, writing, practice and founding a school

There is much to learn from Samkange's work. Samkange was a politician, an educationist, a founder of a school and a writer. In doing all this, he had one theme in mind: that complete decolonisation was necessary. Complete decolonisation meant a decolonised school syllabus, decolonised educational institutions, decolonised educators and educational leaders. By opening a school, Samkange taught about the need for decolonised educational institutions. Samkange believed that the educator was an instrument of colonisation, therefore, there was a need to have decolonised teachers. This is the reason why he founded Nyatsime College.

What are the implications of Samkange's life for social workers? In my view, as social workers we are politicians due to the nature of our work which promotes social justice. Extending Samkange's ideas to a social work context, if need be, we have to take up political activism and political office. Another important lesson is that we need institutions that are decolonised, and if these are not there, we have to create them. We also need decolonised educational content, and if this is not there, we have to create it. Indeed, Samkange proved to us that this is achievable. In my social work learning, *Ubuntu* was not on the list of theories; we had Western theories like psychodynamic theory that focused on the individual. As Mupedziswa and Sinkamba (2014, p.146) described the dominant liberal tradition:

> Western models are narrow, remedial and curative in nature; that these models tend to ignore the issue of traditional forms of welfare and hence they come short as they are not rooted in local culture, that they focus on individual pathologies (e.g. crime, prostitution, delinquency etc.) at the expense of structural issues imbued in the rubric of poverty, i.e. issues like homelessness, unemployment, etc.
>
> *Mupedziswa and Sinkamba (2014, p.146)*

As learners in Africa, we were not exposed to anti-oppressive, relational, cross-cultural, indigenous, critical, radical or developmental social work. We had views that went against our own culture; for example in counselling we were taught to look people in the eye, to hug them, to exclude family members during appointments, to use their first names even when they are adults, to hide our emotions, to avoid counselling relatives. Such an approach fails to incorporate local ways of counselling by privileging other Western techniques. Despite this silencing, *Ubuntu* has found its way into African social work and it now influences ethics, education and social services, as shown below.

Promoting Ubuntu ethics and values

Samkange's views on *Ubuntu* are consistent with social work practice. As an example, the Council of Social Workers (CSW) of Zimbabwe and the Department of Social Development in South Africa use *Ubuntu* in their work. The Code of Ethics of Social Workers in Zimbabwe produced by the CSW describes *Ubuntu* as humaneness. The code says: '*Ubuntu*/unhu/humaneness includes the stipulations of the philosophy that: " … places emphasis on values of human solidarity, empathy, human dignity and the humaneness in every person, and that holds that a person is a person through others"' (CSW, 2012, p.1). It further states that the mission of social work includes promoting social justice, *unhu/Ubuntu*, human rights, positive change, problem solving and improvements in individual and community relationships and the development of society in general (CSW, 2012, p.2). According to CSW, *Ubuntu* is a core value of social work. The CSW expects social workers to recognise and promote *unhu/Ubuntu*, and appreciate the dignity and value inherent in each person. It stresses that social workers must recognise that each person deserves respect and that each person exists within a cultural setting and a community, and that the individual and community shape, influence and benefit from each other (CSW, 2012, p.3). In agreement, South Africa's White Paper for Social Welfare states that social development is guided by key principles such as democracy, partnership, *Ubuntu*, equity, and inter-sectoral collaboration, among others (Government of South African, 1996). The paper describes *Ubuntu* as the principle of caring for each other's well-being and fostering the spirit of mutual support. One hopes that all ethics and values used in professional social work in Africa will one day resonate with *Ubuntu* as a way to decolonise the profession.

Conclusion

The process of decolonising social work will not be complete until indigenous knowledge systems take their place, subvert, replace or truly integrate with colonial systems. Like other African knowledge systems, *Ubuntu* is often neglected, even by Africans themselves, in favour of Western knowledge systems, in the process advancing professional imperialism. This is because of limited written literature or underutilisation of indigenous knowledge systems, often as a consequence of colonialism. Hence, more literature needs to be published to simplify *Ubuntu* and make it more accessible to communities, students, intellectuals, public figures, practitioners, researchers and policy makers. Samkange, an educationist, a *hunhuist* and politician, argued for complete decolonisation of education. To him, this process begins by acknowledging that indigenous systems exist, then, replacing colonial systems with indigenous ones. Social work education, especially in Africa, has much to benefit from the work of Samkange. As Samkange said, the world would be a better place if we all recognise the humanity of others, the sanctity of life, and if we become people-centred. Such a philosophy is vitally important for social work pedagogy.

References

Asante, M. K. (2015). *As I run toward Africa*. London: Routledge.
Battle, M. (1997). *Reconciliation: The Ubuntu theology of Desmond Tutu*. Cleveland: Pilgrim Press.
Cary, R. & Mitchell, D. (1977). African nationalist leaders in Rhodesia: Who is who. Available at www.colonialrelic.com/biographies/dr-stanlake-john-william-samkange/#sdfootnote2sym Accesed 01 February 2019.
Chilisa, B. (2012). *Indigenous research methodologies*. Los Angeles: Sage.
Chimuka, T. A. (2001). Ethics among the Shona. *Zambezia, XVVIII(i)*, 23–37.
Chogugudza, C. (2008). Social work education, training and employment in Africa: The case of Zimbabwe. *Ufahamu: A Journal of African Studies, 35(1)*, 1–9.
Council of Social Workers (CSW). (2012). Social workers code of ethics. *Statutory Instrument 146 of 2012*.
De Baets, A. (2002). *Censorship of Historical Thought: A World Guide, 1945–2000*. Westport: Greenwood.
Dolamo, R. T. H. (2014). Botho/Ubuntu: Perspectives of black consciousness and black theology. *Studia Historiae Ecclesiasticae, 40(Suppl. 1)*, 215–229.
Gade, C. B. N. (2017). *A discourse on African philosophy: A new perspective on Ubuntu and transitional justice in South Africa*. New York: Lexington Books.
Gikandi, S. (Ed). (2003). *Encyclopedia of African literature*. London: Routledge.
Government of South African. (1996). White paper on welfare. Government Gazette Number 16943.
Gray, M., Coates, J., & Bird, M. L. (2009). *Indigenous social work around the world: Towards culturally relevant education and practice*. Southermpton: Routledge. (ebook).
Hapanyengwi-Chemhuru, O., & Makuvaza, N. (2014). Hunhu: In search of an indigenous philosophy for the Zimbabwean education system. *Journal of Indigenous Social Development, 3(1)*, 1–15.
Kaseke, E. (2001). Social work education in Zimbabwe: Strengths and weaknesses, issues and challenges. *Social Work Education, 20(1)*, 101–109. doi:10.1080/02615470020028409
Mangena, F. (2012). Towards a Hunhu/Ubuntu dialogical moral theory. *Phronimon: Journal of the South African Society for Greek Philosophy and the Humanities, 13(2)*, 1–17.
Maphalala, M. C. (2017). Embracing Ubuntu in managing effective classrooms. *Gender and Behavior, 15*, 10237–10249.
Mbiti, J. S. (1969). *African Religions and Philosophy*. London: Heinemann.
Metz, T. (2007). Towards an African moral theory. *The Journal of Political Philosophy, 15(3)*, 321–341.
Midgley, J. (1983). *Professional imperialism: Social work in the third world*. London: Heinemann.
Mtumane, Z. (2017). The practice of Ubuntu with regard to amaMfengu among amaXhosa as Depicted in S. E. K. Mqhayi's Ityala Lamawele. *International Journal of African Renaissance Studies - Multi-, Inter- and Transdisciplinarity, 12(2)*, 68–80. doi:10.1080/18186874.2017.1392146
Mugumbate, J., & Nyanguru, A. (2013). Exploring African philosophy: The value of Ubuntu in social work. *African Journal of Social Work, 3(1)*, 82–100.
Mupedziswa, R., & Sinkamba, R. P. (2014). Social work education and training in southern and east Africa: Yesterday, today and tomorrow. In C. Noble, H. Strauss, & B. Littlechild (Eds.), *Global social work: Crossing borders, blurring boundaries* (pp. 141–153). Sydney: Sydney University Press.
Muvangua, N. & Cornell, D. (2012). *Ubuntu and the law : African ideals and post apartheid jurisprudence/edited by Drucilla Cornell and Nyoko Muvangua*. New York: Fordham University Press.
Muwanga-Zake, J. W. F. (2009). Building bridges across knowledge systems: Ubuntu and participative research paradigms in Bantu communities. *Discourse: Studies in the Cultural Politics of Education, 30(4)*, 413–426.

Muyambo, T. (2017). Indigenous knowledge systems: A haven for sustainable economic growth in Zimbabwe. *Africology: the Journal of Pan African Studies, 10(3)*, 172–186.

Nziramasanga, T. (1999). *Report of the presidential commission of inquiry into education and training.* Harare: Curriculum Development Unit (CDU).

Ocitti, J. P. (1994). *An Introduction to Indigenous Education in East Africa: a study in the Cultural Foundations of Education.* Bonn: Institute for International Zusammenarbeit.

Oelofsen, R. (2015). Decolonisation of the African mind and intellectual landscape. *Phronimon, 16(2)*, 130–146.

Pawar, M. S. (1999). Professional social work in India: Some issues and strategies. *Indian Journal Social Work, 60(4)*, 566–586.

Ramose, M. B. (1999). *African philosophy through Ubuntu.* Harare: Mond Books.

Ramose, M. B. (2003). The philosophy of Ubuntu and Ubuntu as a philosophy. In P. H. Coetzee & A. P. J. Roux (Eds.), *The African philosophy reader* (2nd ed., pp. 230–238). New York/London: Routledge.

Razack, N. (2009). Decolonising the pedagogy and practice of international social work. *International Social Work, 52(1)*, 9–21.

Samkange, S. & Samkange, T. M. (1980). *Hunhuism or Ubuntuism: A Zimbabwean indigenous political philosophy.* Salisbury: Graham Publishing.

Seehawer, M. K. (2018). Decolonising research in a Sub-Saharan African context: Exploring Ubuntu as a foundation for research methodology, ethics and agenda. *International Journal of Social Research Methodology, 21(4)*, 453–466.

Sibanda, P. (2014). The dimensions of hunhu/Ubuntu (humanism in the African sense): The Zimbabwean conception. *Journal of Engineering, 4(1)*, 26–29.

Sulamoyo, D. (2010). "I am because we are": Ubuntu as a cultural strategy for OD and change in Sub-Saharan Africa. *Organization Development Journal, 28(4)*, 41–51.

Tutu, D. (2000). *No future without forgiveness: A personal overview of South Africa's truth and reconciliation commission.* London: Rider Random House.

35
The relevance of Gandhi for social work education and practice

Lata Narayan

FORMERLY TATA INSTITUTE OF SOCIAL SCIENCES (TISS), MUMBAI, INDIA

A leader of his people, unsupported by any outside authority: a politician whose success rests not upon craft nor the mastery of technical devices, but simply on the convincing power of his personality; a victorious fighter who has always scorned the use of force; a man of wisdom and humility, armed with resolve and inflexible consistency, who has devoted all his strength to the uplifting of his people and the betterment of their lot; a man who has confronted the brutality of Europe with the dignity of the simple human being, and thus at all times risen superior.

Generations to come, it may be, will scarcely believe that such a one as this ever in flesh and blood walked upon this earth.

(Einstein, 1950, cited in Gandhi, 2017: 21)

Introduction

The objective of this chapter is to draw out the relevance of Mohandas Karamchand Gandhi, person, thinker and practitioner, for contemporary social work education and practice. This chapter is not a theoretical discourse but focuses on a few major concepts and strategies used by Gandhi. Rather than undertake an exegesis of Gandhian thought as seen in the texts of his time, I have chosen to concentrate on the writings of present-day commentators and relevant practices for social work practitioners. Gandhian values and practices are either explicitly stated or implied in these contemporary practices. Most importantly, they suggest ways in which Gandhian thought (which might have been considered outdated) might be concretely brought into present-day social work education and practice.

The chapter begins with a brief profile of Gandhi, followed by an understanding of the present social context, within which the social work profession operates. The chapter then discusses the key concepts, values and strategies propagated and practiced by Gandhi. The application of Gandhian thought and practice in the modern world, through innovative practice and perspectives is also included. The relevance of Gandhian thought and practice in social work education and practice is then further deliberated upon.

Mohandas Karamchand Gandhi

Mohandas Karamchand Gandhi (1869–1948) is known in India as the 'Father of the Nation' and 'Mahatma' (great soul) due to his leadership and mobilization of the Indian people to achieve independence from British rule in 1947. Though primarily hailed as a political leader, he has been called a practical idealist, a socio-political reformer (Rai, 2000).

His mobilization of the people for freedom ignited a revolution through specific strategies, which forced the British to leave India. He developed his strategies based on his experiences with oppressive governments, prison life, and work with the masses in poverty, which gives a realistic dimension to his discussions. An amalgamation of his strategies, actions, practice and philosophy are often termed as Gandhism, though he ridiculed the idea, stating that there was nothing new in what he was saying or doing and one of his kind was enough! (Leon, 2016).

Gandhi was born into an affluent family in the state of Gujarat, India. The major influences in his life were his mother, religious teachings of Hinduism and specifically the holy text, the Bhagvad Gita, Jainism, Christianity, Islam, and the writings of Ruskin, Thoreau, and Tolstoy among many others (Rai, 2000: 30). He went to England for his higher education in law and returned to India to practice. He was married at the age of 13 years to Kasturba who played a very key role in supporting him in his work.

He spent some years in South Africa, where an experience of racial discrimination proved to be a turning point in his life. When traveling from Durban to Pretoria, he was pulled out of the train at Maritzburg and not allowed to travel first class, as in those days, colored men were not permitted to travel in the first class. This incident of injustice due to color prejudice, angered and pained him, and goaded him into the political arena.

On his return to India in 1915, he was fully involved in the political struggle for freedom. His primary goal in pre-independent India was to obtain freedom for the country from British rule. Hence, all his work was linked to his political goals, i.e., (a) freedom for India, (b) a plan for a post-independent India, based on his vision of society. His strategies for social justice were guided primarily by Indian philosophy and thought and based on strong values, which included a strong sense of morality. He was assassinated in 1948 by a Hindu, and ironically, for his secular views on Hindu-Muslim unity. Since he died soon after India attained independence, one cannot perceive how Gandhi may have influenced the growth of India, post-independence.

He wrote extensively on nearly every topic, all related to his vision for a free India. The modern edition of his complete works runs into one hundred volumes. His principles and strategies, with emphasis on non-violence, have also inspired other movements and leaders such as Martin Luther King, Jr., Nelson Mandela, and the current Dalai Lama. In India, the initiative of Anna Hazare in Ralegaon Siddhi,[1] is an example where Gandhism has been practiced. Following Gandhi's principles and strategies, right after World War II, the movement against nuclear weapons gained momentum with 'Operation Gandhi' in London in 1952. Unfortunately, social work education and practice, including in India, has yet to give adequate attention to his work and the wealth of learning that he has to offer.

Contemporary context

While historical forms of injustice such as caste, class and gender continue to prevail in Indian society, in the last decade there has been a sharp increase in inequities and oppressive forces. The consequences of globalization have become ingrained into the social and ecological fabric of society. The overconsumption of resources concentrated in urban industrialized locations and developed nations has led to conflicts for access to water, food, soil, fuels and housing within and between nations and regions (Dominelli, 2012). In his book, *The Dream of the Earth*, Berry (1990) refers to the dynamics of our consumer society as the supreme pathology of all history, a pathology in which humanity has virtually defined consumption as the highest human purpose (cited in Korten, 2010).

On the one hand, there is a perception of the nation and the world as one community, and simultaneously, a strong polarisation on multiple narrow identities such as language, territorial identification, religion and ethnicity is evident. There is also a gradual increase of sensitive responses to social ills, where people are coming together to respond to protect local ecosystems and communities by building more localized, place-based economic and social structures (Norberg-Hodge, 2016 in Narayan & Pandit, 2017). The next section briefly describes Gandhi's vision for society and his concept of sustainable development.

Gandhi's vision for a sustainable world

Gandhi believed in an alternative development model based on agrarian society. He did not have faith in power being invested in the state, as it represents violence in an organized form. He prescribed a non-violent society based on voluntary organizations as the substitute for the state. Gandhian economics propagate decentralization. The rural village was visualized as the basic unit connecting to earth and nature, a bottom-up participation of all villages and persons, and that every village would be a republic having full power (Rai, 2000: 27). An integral part of Gandhian economics is his concept of bread labor, according to which every human being should earn his daily bread by his own labor. Gandhi recognized physical labor as a biological necessity, as much as one needs food, air and water. Though not against technology and mechanization, he was against mass production and strongly believed in localization of production and consumption. According to him, machinery should aid labor, not displace it. His ideal was a classless, stateless society, and if that was not feasible, then the second best ideal was a democratic state rooted in truth and non-violence.

Gandhi's philosophy for change was based on the belief that sustainable change was only possible if the emphasis was on collective social justice, as we are all connected with life in all forms. Hence, inclusion of the dimensions of spirituality (experiencing self as part of the whole of creation) and ecology were essential for sustainable growth. He rejected the theory of survival of the fittest, and believed that all life is connected, and the goal is collective transformation.

Relevance to contemporary society

Korten (2010) states that the conventional paradigm of development has been a dismal failure, and a choice for status quo solutions could lead to the end of human civilization and even the extinction of our own species. He further advocates that sustainable social practice must decentralize and distribute economic power to facilitate the reconnection of spiritual connection between humans and nature and community. This is similar to Gandhi's principle of decentralization of power, including economic power, to the smallest unit, the village community.

Localization is one perspective practiced today which also emphasizes the processes of decentralization and rebuilding connections between humans and nature. It is a process that aims to shorten the distance between production and consumption and to build more self-reliant local economies and communities. Gandhi's extensive work in localization has been acknowledged in this process (Norberg-Hodge, 2016). Localization is seen in initiatives related to local food movement, community-supported agriculture, education that promotes local traditional skills and self-reliance; and traditional and complementary medicine (Norberg-Hodge, 2016).

Social permaculture is a creative design process based on whole-systems thinking for ecological and sustainable living, integrating plants, animals, buildings, people and community. This approach offers guidance to mimic the patterns and relationships found in nature and can be applied to all aspects of human habitation, from agriculture to ecological building, from appropriate technology to education, community building and even economics (Holmgren, 2011). Gift economy (Eisenstein, 2011) is another perspective that states that a community is broken due to the framework which results in the monetization and commodification of most of the things we need for living, including relationships. When healing this damage, and building community, it is critical to transit to a more connected, ecological and sustainable way of being. The four shifts required in this process are: (a) consumption to contribution; (b) transaction to trust; (c) isolation to community; and (d) move from a mindset of scarcity to abundance.

Values practiced by Gandhi

Gandhi was clear that no change or progress could happen without a spiritual dimension to the task undertaken, and hence, all his work had a strong emphasis on the values he practiced and professed.

Spirituality

Gandhi is also called a 'spiritual activist', as every action had a strong foundation of spiritualism. Hinduism formed the core of his religious beliefs. He believed that formal religion was the space where ritual practices diverged, and the eternal where all faiths had common goals. However, for him, spirituality was far beyond religion; it represented truth, soul force, training of the heart (Gandhi, 1962) and the practice of morality. The key values he upheld are described below.

Truth

Gandhi believed that the purpose of life was to strive for the realization of truth, and he measured all decisions against truth. He viewed injustice, oppression and violence as untruthful, and hence, to be opposed. His autobiography was titled *My Experiments with Truth*. He was a humanist, and for him patriotism was equivalent to humanity (Gajendragadkar, 1970).

Sarvodaya

Gandhi introduced this concept, which means universal uplift or welfare of all. It is a Sanskrit term made up of two words, *sarva* meaning one and all, and *uday* meaning welfare or uplift. This was an inclusive philosophy, in which the individual was as important as the collective, as the happiness of the individual is integral to the happiness of the collective.[2] In this context, he made the removal of untouchability a central focus of his campaign for human rights and inclusion of all in India (Axelrod, 2010: 51). For *sarvodaya* to be a reality, Gandhi believed that only love could be the basis for social justice and is the subtlest force in the world (cited in Axelrod, 2010). It is interesting to note that other revolutionaries, such as Che Guevara for example, have also stated that 'at the risk of seeming ridiculous, the true revolutionary, is, motivated by love' (Che cited in Lewis, 2011: 1). Freire, in his *Pedagogy of the Oppressed* (1972: 22), stresses that true liberation is an act of love.

Gandhi expected his people and volunteers (*satyagrahis*) to uphold and practice five ethical and moral principles: *satya* (truth); *ahimsa* (non-violence); *brahmacharya* (celibacy) – with an emphasis on self-control; *asteya* (non-stealing); *apigraha* (non-possession). He knew that the desire to amass wealth, in a situation where resources are limited, would lead inevitably to violence both at the individual and societal levels. Hence, he constantly pleaded for a lifestyle of simplicity and self-control.

Ahimsa or non-violence

Ahimsa is another popular and well-known feature of Gandhi's philosophy. *Ahimsa* as a concept is built on the spiritual tradition of India, having a spiritual base in Hinduism, Buddhism and Jainism: religions practiced in India. But non-violence was largely practiced in relation to food and diet. However, Gandhi applied non-violence to the social scale and made it a powerful force in his strategy, calling it the strength of the weak and the masses. He saw non-violence not just as a personal virtue, but a social virtue, which could be the expression of functioning extended to the whole world (Gandhi, 1939 cited in Prabhu & Rao, 1960).

Ahimsa was not just absence of violence,

> but involved changing one's whole way of life and consciousness, remaining in communion with nature and feeling that the whole world is throbbing with the divine spirit of which an individual is a small part. It was not ahimsa if compassion, forgiveness and equality were absent.
> *(Gandhi, 2017: 133)*

He further states: 'It is never the intention of the Satyagrahi to embarrass the wrongdoer. The appeal is never to his fear, it is, must be, always to his heart. The Satyagrahi's object is to convert, not to coerce the wrong-doer' (Gandhi, 1939, Harijan, March 25, cited in Xaxa & Mahakul, 2009: 48).

Today we find the concept of *Spiritual Activism* used and defined as the spiritual underpinning of *action* for social and ecological justice (McIntosh & Carmichael, 2015). Spiritual perspectives are, today, arising in science (quantum physics, neuroscience, chaos theory, creativity studies, biology, ecology), art and alternative healing, and these are also enriching our understanding of the spiritual dimension outside of traditional religious formulas (McKernan, 2005).

Dimension of ecology in Gandhian thought

Ecology is defined as the science of interdependence of living things and their environmental habitat. Within each ecosystem, each living member must act in a way that is compatible with the continued existence of that system and therefore of the organism itself (Commoner, 2011).

Gandhi could be deemed to have the closest resemblance to the philosophical presuppositions of deep ecology which is a holistic approach to facing world problems that brings together thinking, feeling, spirituality and action (Lal, 2015). Arne Naess (1974), who is associated with the concept of deep ecology, combined his ecological perspective with Gandhian non-violence.

Social justice

As stated earlier in this chapter, Gandhi believed in collective justice, and he believed that injustice was not ordained, but happened due to the way the dominant class (oppressors) suppressed and weakened the oppressed classes (Gandhi, 1962). He emphasized the need to have faith in the masses, and when in doubt, he advised a journalist to call to mind, 'the face of the poorest and the weakest man whom you may have seen, and ask yourself if the step you contemplate is going to be of any use to him' (Axelrod, 2010: 22).

It was through this innate faith in people's capacities and wisdom that Gandhi derived the two principles of *swarajya*, which meant self-governance, and *lokniti*, meaning people's policies, which were used to denote freedom from foreign rule. Gandhi repeatedly clarified that these were not just political principles, but self-rule or self-control can only truly happen if people cultivate and nurture their spiritual selves in a self-disciplined manner.

Satyagraha

Gandhi's major strategy for confronting injustice with the practice of *ahimsa*, was *satyagraha*. He coined the term in South Africa, *satya*-(truth), *agraha*-(insistence or determined pursuit or holding on to the truth). It is based on three basic tenets: *satya*, which implies openness, honesty and fairness; *ahimsa*, which is a refusal to inflict injury on others; and *tapasya*, conveying willingness for self-sacrifice and patience (Xaxa & Mahakul, 2009).

Satyagraha was a technique to practice active non-violence, based on the moral principle that one cannot be non-violent about one's own activity of oneself and violent about others. Non-violence is the weapon of choice – not to injure or destroy the opponent, but to convert him and turn him into an ally. It was a new technique of 'spirituality in action' (Munshi, 1967: 136). Gandhi used the moral weapon of *satyagraha* for social, political, economic, religious and cultural problems and conflicts (Pyarelal, 1953; Rai, 2000). *Satyagraha* and *ahimsa* apply to the nation as well as the individual – relations with the family, authority, subordinates and all other relationships. Gandhi used several strategies and techniques within the ambit of *satyagraha*. These include investigation, negotiation, publicity, self-purification, temporary work stoppages, picketing, boycotts, non-payment of taxes, non-cooperation, civil disobedience and fasting (Sharp, 1967).

Non-cooperation and *civil disobedience:* One of his chief techniques of *satyagraha* was to break laws that were unjust. He believed that breaking the law through civil disobedience was an inherent right of the individual and is never followed by anarchy. However, breaking the law through criminal disobedience, 'can lead to it' (Axelrod, 2010: 49). One of his most famous actions was when Gandhi led Indians in protesting the national salt tax with the 400 km Dandi Salt March in 1930, and later initiating the Quit India movement demanding that the British leave India immediately in 1942, during World War II.

Swadeshi: Swadeshi is the Hindi term for self-sufficiency and was an important technique to break the economic dependence on foreign goods. Spinning was considered a symbol of India's backwardness, exploitation and slavery, and he made it a symbol of non-violence, and self-sufficiency.

Fasting: Gandhi used to fast often to protest against injustice and as a non-violent tool/weapon. Fasting is still practiced as the method of protest in India by social activists to protest a glaring injustice in society.

Peaceful protests for social justice have been used over decades and are practiced today also. Gandhian inspiration and ideology strongly re-emerged on a global scale at the end of the 1990s when the People's Global Action against the World Trade Organisation (WTO) and Free Trade centered on the principles of non-violence and refusal to cooperate as the main tools in the struggle against the neoliberal world order. The Farmers' Protest in Mumbai (2018) and the Dacota Access Pipeline or the Standing Rock movement in USA (Wehlie, 2016), are two events that followed the strategies and values of Gandhism.

Farmer's protest in Mumbai: An estimated 35,000 farmers (men and women, young and old) marched into Mumbai, India, walking 180 km from another city, Nashik. In support of their demands, and the sense that farmers are those who are the producers of food, both urban and rural citizens welcomed them with food, water, footwear and medical aid. The farmers had decided to walk the whole night to reach their destination, near the government headquarters in Mumbai, so as to avoid obstruction of traffic during the day and inconvenience to the students in their final year of school and junior college who had their final board exams on that day. This struck an emotional chord with all the citizens of Mumbai (NDTV, 2018).

Innovative practices for non-violent social justice

Restorative justice is a new movement in the fields of victimology and criminology. It is a theory of justice that emphasizes repairing the harm caused or revealed by criminal behavior. It seeks to replace the values of vengeance and retribution with a more humane and morally defensible stance of restoration, healing and forgiveness (Besthorn, 2004).

Deep democracy: Practices, such as world work, which is a process-oriented psychology, have been applied to a range of conflict situations such as terrorism, climate change, government leadership, school conflicts and so on. Deep democracy is the core principle and practice of world work (Mindell, 2014).

Circle work is the peacemaking circle process, which brings together individuals for conflict resolution, healing, support, decision making, by creating a space of trust and respect. It is also used as an alternative to traditional sentencing and other criminal justice mechanisms for responding to violence and harm (Boyes-Watson, 2008).

Non-violent communication, sometimes referred to as compassionate communication, is the process developed by Rosenberg (2003), which involves both communication skills that foster compassionate relating and consciousness of the interdependence of our well-being and using power with others to work together to meet the needs of all concerned (Rosenberg, 2003).

Having discussed the key concepts of Gandhi, the next section reflects on the relevance of Gandhi for social work in today's times.

Relevance of Gandhi in social work: some reflections

Having explored the key tenets of Gandhi's perspective, values and strategies, this section reflects on the relevance of these concepts for social work education and practice. Gandhi called education 'the spearhead of a silent social revolution' and emphasized the all-round development of the person – body, mind, heart and spirit. Social work education also aims at preparing students for social change by providing a holistic education.

Social work as a profession (including both practice and education) is also evolving and challenged to meet the demands of the external environment. This has necessitated development of new perspectives in social work that redefine human relationships to the social and ecological environment through a rediscovery and recognition of indigenous worldviews and a reflection of social work education in ongoing post-colonial settings (Dominelli, 2012). The Institutions of Social Work Education (ISWE) have a major role in reviewing the existing perspectives of social work and introducing the new perspectives that are more relevant in today's context.

Perspective

Since the 1970s, countries in Asia, Africa and Latin America have oriented their programs toward social development (Hokenstad et al., 1992), as the context necessitated the adaptation to a community and collective approach. This perspective advocates 'people-centered development', which emphasizes process over outcomes, and represents faith in people (Cox, 1998). Emerging perspectives in social work such as ecological social work, spiritual social work (Besthorn, 2002; Dudley, 2016; Groen, Graham and Coholic, 2012;; McKinnon & Alston, 2016), green social work, anti-oppressive social work (Dominelli, 2012), the strengths perspective (Saleebey, 1996) and the *samagratha* perspective (Narayan & Pandit, 2017), incorporate the vision, values and strategies of Gandhian thought. However, in contemporary contexts where abuse of the habitat, violence, unemployment and migration are common global concerns, it seems imperative that Gandhi's perspective and strategies need to be given emphasis in social work curricula for visioning and strategizing for a sustainable planet. Some of the areas in which Gandhian thought and strategies can be integrated into social work education are given below.

Culture of the ISWE

The essential prerequisite for introducing the Gandhian perspective in social work training is that the perspective and values taught are practiced in the institutional ethos, or else it could generate cynicism among the students. This includes the practices adopted in running the institution, e.g., awareness of consumeristic practices, adopting eco-friendly practices, the nature of communication between those in the ISWE, and participatory mechanisms to ensure that democratic spaces are provided.

It would be also necessary for the perspective to be interwoven into the courses taught, the fieldwork placements, the research themes encouraged, the positions taken by the ISWE on local and national issues, the development networks with whom the institute and faculty associate, and the role modeling of the faculty. There is a need to see whether the 'spaces' available to the academic institutions are fully used, and academic activism is promoted. It is only then that students can be truly aware of, and experience, the philosophy of Gandhi, and the pedagogy can be truly transformatory.

Curriculum

Gandhi's perspective, vision, values and strategies could find a place in the different courses of social work. Courses on critical perspectives, values and social work methods, especially those related to social action and community work, would be enriched by including the strategies of Gandhi. For example, there can be dialogues on the use of non-violent strategies when working through conflict. In a society where violent means, such as war, gun shootings and road rage in daily life, are on the increase, finding alternatives is a must. Exposure to peace initiatives and spiritual values that help to co-create strategies for protest, and do not lead to violence and hatred, need to be emphasized as a real possibility and not just as empty rhetoric. For example, strategies used by the Green Peace movement, organize international protests with a strong emphasis on non-violence. Other practices and examples are provided in the sections that follow.

Spirituality in social work

There is often apprehension about including spirituality in social work as it is equated to religion, and thus, not considered secular (Narayan & Pandit, 2017). Now, however, the spiritual dimension is recognized as an important resource, rather than as a problem, in social and therapeutic work (Becvar, 1998). A spiritual dimension needs to be acknowledged and taught as an integral dimension of human life, and as being subjectively experienced by social workers and the people/populations with whom we engage. It is well recognized and documented that attending to the self and adopting spiritual principles is essential for: (a) personal well-being and effectiveness, as well as collective capacities as social workers; (b) practicing values that one would like to see in the world; and (c) building partnerships and solidarity for bringing about change (Halpern, 2008, cited in Narayan & Pandit, 2017: 540–541).

Inculcating values

The core values of the social work profession all over the world may be considered spiritual and similar to the thoughts of Gandhi, as these profess to uphold human dignity and human rights, right to participation, self-determination, equality, freedom and social justice (IFSW and IASSW, 2004). One of the most important learnings from Gandhi is the importance of inculcating values and the application of these in daily life. In today's context, enabling students to build connections of love and compassion across populations and internalize the sense of interdependence and responsibility with all life, has become a key purpose of social work education. Inculcating and assimilating the values mentioned in the earlier sections is part of the internal personal journey of an individual, which is a lifelong process. Discussions of social justice are usually accompanied by confronting issues related to conflict and violence and the student is often required to deal with this at the personal and professional levels. Hence, it is crucial that time and a nurturing, non-judgmental space is provided in the educational process (classroom and fieldwork), to enable students to identify, reflect and make choices, as they transition from personal values gained as part of their life socialization processes and attempt to assimilate values expected of a trained social worker. Spiritual values such as compassion, love, courage and inclusion would form the guiding attributes, which would underlie all actions of social justice and change, when providing illustrations from the field.

Social work education could reflect on whether adequate emphasis and opportunities are provided to students for 'training of the heart', as Gandhi (1962) called it. Spiritual practices enable the person to develop a wide perspective, a universal outlook, by which they can develop a more all-encompassing and unconditional inclusion of all life. Some of the practices mentioned in this chapter, such as mindfulness, gratitude and non-violent communication have been initiated and tried out in certain ISWE and other development fields with very positive outcomes, and can also be introduced in other ISWE (Halpern, 2008; Magee, 2016; Wong, 2013).

Gandhi emphasized the importance of social responsibility toward society and people without expectations of any rewards. Social work is a profession, and hence, social workers do expect financial benefits from the work they do. Yet, emphasizing the spirit of volunteerism where they can contribute as citizens to a cause that they are passionate about, is important for students and faculty members.

Ahimsa in social work

Presently, the need to emphasize *ahimsa* as an inherent value and practice for social work education and practice has become crucial. Gandhi knew that the desire to amass wealth in a situation where resources are limited would lead inevitably to violence both at the individual and societal levels. Hence, he constantly pleaded for a lifestyle of simplicity and self-control. It may not be feasible for all to adhere to the strict discipline and rigour by which Gandhi expected his people to practice non-violence, and hence, attempts have been made to classify non-violence for the present context (Paullin, 1944; Sibley, 1944 cited in Sharp, 1967). Sharp (1967: 38) provides nine types of generic non-violence practices, in order of increasing activity, which are: non-resistance, active reconciliation, moral resistance, selective non-violence, passive resistance, peaceful resistance, non-violent direct action, *satyagraha*, and non-violent revolution. *Ahimsa* can no longer be taught as a conceptual discourse, but needs to be practiced as a personal and institutional value.

Ecology in social work

The environment and the habitat have been given significant importance in social work, especially in rural development, community development and social action. However, there is a growing sense of alarm at the rate at which humans are degrading the planet and its ecology. The time has come when social work education needs to understand the urgency of including the ecological dimension in all socio-politico-cultural analyses. Opportunities need to be provided to students to reflect on the relationships between their habitat, and issues of urbanization, migration, employment and violence and so on. Students can also be exposed to innovations and perspectives of localization, social permaculture, the eco-justice movement and paradigms of deep ecology, eco-psychology and eco-feminism, and the application of these perspectives to their personal and professional lives. Opportunities to reconnect with nature through various activities are essential for students, as they strengthen their awareness and relationships with our physical bodies and our larger ecological body, the earth. Wilderness practices, experiencing clay and mud and the other creative arts, like music and dance, encounters with plants, pets, are some of the practices which can be introduced in ISWE whereby a transformative self can emerge.

Satyagraha and social work

Four inspirations of Gandhi that have been used in social work, especially community work and social action, are: boycott against oppressive regimes; *padyatras* or long marches linked to direct action; intervention by direct non-violent intervention in conflicts, and mass support for constructive programs to give humanitarian support to liberation movement territories (shodhganga.inflibnet). These often involve the ISWE initiating discussions and asking pertinent questions about whose side we are on, and supporting social workers who are willing to engage in social action.

Field education

Placements often provide the most hard-hitting experiences for many students, as they confront social realities and the marginalized populations, with whom social work swears an allegiance. This can be one of the most powerful exposures to develop their personal and professional selves. The choice of fieldwork agencies, the tasks and processes of engagement and the quality of field supervision can all provide the students the live experience of practicing Gandhism. Locations such as trade unions, social movements, and unstructured open communities, all provide the opportunities for experiencing social work beyond traditional structured agency fieldwork placements.

Research

The type of research studies undertaken by students for their Master's and Doctoral studies, and faculty as part of their work, are determined by the philosophy of the ISWE. Studies on Gandhism could add knowledge and understanding about Gandhian strategies used by social workers and development workers, the values practiced in the field, challenges faced, and so on.

Social work has a wide array of skills for working with people, and hence, for social justice. Yet, there is some soul searching required when applying these techniques in rapidly changing contexts. Are we reaching out to the most oppressed populations in our specific contexts in our engagements with social issues? We need to express solidarity with oppressed groups and initiate/support them to avail of their rights. Engaging in academic activism is another way in which institutions have responded to social issues. Another question that needs to be asked is: how necessary is it to translate social justice in terms of collective justice versus individual justice?

Conclusion

Gandhism, which is a process of change based on ethical, non-violent and democratic values, is extremely relevant for social work, but difficult to emulate in all aspects. However, exposing students to Gandhi's perspective and strategies is important, as he continues to be a role model, and an icon of non-violence. His values and strategies can be part of classroom learning, fieldwork, research, campus culture and role modeling by faculty and supervisors.

The relevance of *satyagraha* is being recognized both as a way of life and as a weapon for evolutionary social change, are being used successfully by people all over the world. Gandhi's insistence on the resolution of all conflicts by peaceful means is also an important aspect of his teaching, and his declaration that war and violence never solve any problems is still relevant. Yet, there is probably a gap between the intellectual discourse of these concepts and the practice of Gandhism. It is possible that social work educators need to review and retrain themselves in strategies and skills in order to make practice more relevant for the fast-changing social realities.

This chapter ends with a quote by Aruna Roy, a well-known social activist in India:

> Gandhi is irrevocably and absolutely relevant, especially in 3 areas: bringing ethical responsibility into public life- no public figure anywhere in the world has examined himself so thoroughly in public view; bringing a moral position into the economic debate; and, his position against communalism, about the equality of all religions.
>
> *(Roy, 2006: 33)*

Notes

1 Ralegaon Siddhi – A sustainable village model for the country. Anna Hazare, a Gandhian in heart and practice, changed the extremely poor and unsustainable village of a population of about 2,500 into a self-sustaining model of development with maximum voluntary involvement of the people in developmental activities and the introduction of scientific agricultural practices. He ensured that the government schemes were implemented with the best example of watershed management in the country. The World Bank group has concluded that the village of Ralegaon Siddhi has demonstrated that it is possible to rebuild natural capital in partnership with the local economy and is a model for the rest of the country.
2 Gandhi's first encounter with this concept was in John Ruskin's book, *Unto This Last* which he read in South Africa in 1904, and its powerful impact on Gandhi was a lifechanging experience for him.

References

Axelrod, A. 2010. *Gandhi, CEO*, New York: Sterling Publishing Co.
Becvar, D. 1998. 'Soul Healing and the Family', *Family, Spirituality and Social Work* (Vol. 2 4, pp. 1–11). New York: The Haworth Press.
Berry, T. 1990. *The Dream of the Earth*, San Francisco, CA: Sierra Club Books.

Besthorn, F. H. 2002. 'Transpersonal Psychology and Deep Ecological Philosophy: Exploring Linkages and Applications for Social Work', *Journal of Religion and Spirituality in Social Work: Social Thought*, 20(1–2), 23–44.

Besthorn, F. H. 2004. 'Restorative Justice and Environmental Restoration – Twin Pillars of a Just Global Environmental Policy: Hearing the Voice of the Victim', *Journal of Societal and Social Policy*, 3(2), 33–48.

Boyes-Watson, C. 2008. *Peacemaking Circles and Urban Youth: Bringing Justice Home*, St. Paul, MN: Living Justice Press, www.livingjusticepress.org

Commoner, B. 2011. *Ecology and Social Action*, googleweblight.com/i?u=http://climateandcapitalism.com/2011/12/20/barry-commoner-ecology-and-social-action/

Cox, D. 1998. 'Towards People-Centred Development: The Social Development Agenda and Social Work Education'. In Desai, M., Monteiro, A., Narayan, L. (Eds.) *Towards People – Centred Development* (pp. 512–530, Part 2). Mumbai: Tata Institute of Social Sciences.

Dominelli, L. 2012. *Green Social Work: From Environmental Crisis to Environmental Justice*, Cambridge: Polity Press.

Dudley, J. R. 2016. *Spirituality Matters in Social Work: Connecting Spirituality, Religion and Practice*, Oxon: Routledge.

Einstein, A. 1950. *Out of My Later Years: The Scientist, Philosopher and Man Portrayed Through His Own Words*, New York: Philosophical Library.

Eisenstein, A. 2011. *Sacred Economics: Money, Gift and Society in the Age of Transition*, California: Evolver Edition.

Freire, P. 1972. *Pedagogy of the Oppressed*, New York: Penguin Books.

Gajendragadkar, P. B. 1970. *'Preface', Research on Gandhian Thought*, Mumbai: Khadi and Village Industries Commission Centenary Celebrations Committee.

Gandhi. 1939. *Harijan*, January 7th Poona: The Servants of Untouchables Society.

Gandhi. 1962. *True Education*, Ahmedabad: Navjivan Publishing House.

Gandhi, R. 2017. *Why Gandhi Still Matters – An Appraisal of the Mahatma's Legacy*, New Delhi: Aleph Book Company.

Groen, J. R., Graham, J. E., & Coholic, D. (eds.) 2012. *Spirituality in Social Work and Education: Theory, Practice, and Pedagogies*, Canada: Wilfrid Laurier University.

Halpern, C. 2008. *Making Waves and Riding the Currents: Activism and the Practice of Wisdom*, California: Berrett-Koehler Publishers, Inc.

Hokenstad, M. C., Khinduka, S. K., & Midgley, J. (eds.) 1992. *Profiles in International Social Work*, Washington, DC: NASW Press.

Holmgren, D. 2011. *Permaculture: Principles and Pathways Beyond Sustainability*, England: Permanent Publications.

IFSW and IASSW. 2004. *Ethics in Social Work. Statement of Principles*, iassw-aiets.org/wp-content/uploads/2015/10/Ethics-in-Social-Work-Statement-IFSW-IASSW-2004.pdf

Korten, D. C. 2010. *Economy, Ecology and Spirituality: A Theory and Practice of Sustainability*, Living Economics Forum, jointly produced by Asian NGO Regional Fellows Program held in Baguio, Phillipines, davidkorten.org/economy-ecology-spirituality/

Lal, V. 2015. 'Gandhi and the Ecological Vision of Life: Thinking beyond Deep Ecology', satyagrahafoundation.org/wp-content/uploads/2015/03/Environ.pdf

Leon, S. 2016. *Gandhi's Choices for Non-Violence, Road to Peace Films*, roadtopeacefilms.com/road-to-peace/gandhis-choices/

Lewis, W. 2011. 'Che Guevara: True Revolution is Love', *Elephant Journal*, elephantjournal.com/2011/03/che-guevara-true-revolution-is-love/

Magee, R. V. 2016. 'Martin Luther King Jr. Offers Insight into 'Justice for All''', *ABA Journal*, Chicago, IL: American Bar Association.

McIntosh, A., & Carmichael, M. 2015. *Spiritual Activism: Leadership as Service*, Cambridge: Green Books, alastairmcintosh.com/spiritualactivism/

McKernan, M. 2005. 'Exploring the Spiritual Dimension of Social Work', *Critical Social Work*, 6(2), uwindsor.ca/criticalsocialwork/exploring-the-spiritual-dimension-of-social-work

McKinnon, J., & Alston, M. 2016. *Ecological Social Work: Towards Sustainability*, London: Palgrave Macmillan.

Mindell, A. 2014. *The Leader as Martial Artist: An Introduction to Deep Democracy, Techniques and Strategies for Resolving Conflict and Creating Community*, California: Deep Democracy Exchange.

Munshi, K. M. 1967. 'The Spiritual Base of Satyagraha'. In Guha, R., & Mahadevan, T. K. (Eds.) 1967 *Gandhi – His Relevance for Our Times* (pp. 134–137). New Delhi: Gandhi Peace Foundation.

Naess, A. 1974. *Gandhi and Group Conflict: An Exploration of Satyagraha – Theoretical Background*, Oslo: Universitietsforlaget.

Narayan, L., & Pandit, M. 2017. '*Samagratā* Framework for Social Work', *Indian Journal of Social Work*, 78(3), 533–560. Mumbai, India: Tata Institute of Social Sciences.

NDTV. 2018. 'Walking 180 kms., 35,000 Farmers Reach Mumbai for Debt Waiver, Fair Play', March 12th, ndtv.com/mumbai-news/mumbai-braces-for-jams-ahead-of-big-farmers-march-35-000-join-in/

Norberg-Hodge, H. 2016. *Localisation: Essential Steps to Economics of Happiness*, USA: Local Futures, www.localfutures.org/

Paullin, T. 1944. *Introduction to Nonviolence*, Pennsylvania, PA: Pacifist Research Bureau.

Prabhu, R. K., & Rao, U. R. 1960. *The Mind of Mahatma Gandhi*, Ahmedabad: Navjivan Trust.

Pyarelal. 1953. *Gandhian Techniques in the Modern World*, Ahmedabad: Navjivan Trust Publishing House.

Rai, A. S. 2000. *Gandhian Satyagraha an Analytical and Critical Approach, Gandhian*, Studies and Peace Research Series No. 14, New Delhi: Concept Publishing Company.

Rosenberg, M. 2003. *Non-Violent Communication, A Language of Life: Life Changing Tools for Healthy Relationships*, California: Puddle Dancer Press.

Roy, A. 2006. 'Gandhi, A Second Coming'. In *Outlook*, September 11th 2006: 33, Outlook Publishing (India) Limited, New Delhi.

Saleebey, D. 1996. 'The Strengths Perspective in Social Work Practice: Extensions and Cautions', *Social Work*, 41(3), 296–303.

Sharp, G. 1967. 'A Study of the Meanings of NonViolence'. Ramchandran, G., & Mahadevan, T. K. (Eds.) *Gandhi – His Relevance for Our Times* (pp. 31–76). New Delhi: Gandhi Peace Foundation.

Sibley. 1944. *The Political Theories of Modern Pacifism: An Analysis and Criticism*, Pennsylvania, PA: Pacifist Research Bureau.

Wehlie, B. 2016. 'Sacred Ground- Inside the Dakota Pipeline Protests', *CNN World*, https://edition.cnn.com/interactive/2016/12/us/dapl-protests-cnnphotos/

Wong, Y. R. 2013. 'Returning to Silence, Connecting to Wholeness: Contemplative Pedagogy for Critical Social Work Education', *Journal of Religion and Spirituality in Social Work: Social Thought*, 32(3), 269–285.

Xaxa, J., & Mahakul, B. K. 2009. 'The Contemporary Relevance of Gandhism', *The Indian Journal of Political Science*, 70(1), 41–54, (January–March 2009): Indian Political Association on JSTOR, https://www.jstor.org/journal/indijpoliscie

Practice methods

36
Teaching community development with Hannah Arendt
Enabling new emancipatory possibilities

Uschi Bay

MONASH UNIVERSITY MELBOURNE, AUSTRALIA

Introduction

This chapter will highlight Hannah Arendt's key concepts of 'political action', 'natality', 'plurality' and 'publicness', and then discuss their applicability to teaching community development as part of social work education from a critical pedagogical perspective. After introducing Arendt briefly through outlining her biographical background and some of her key texts, I will also draw on some of the secondary literature that applies Arendt's concepts to explore her notions of political storytelling and what it means to think and act politically (Bay, 2014; Disch, 1993, 1994). Arendt herself did not explicitly articulate her own methodology for facilitating critical situated thinking and the forming of political judgment through political storytelling, but rather showed this throughout her many writings. Next, I will illustrate how Arendt's political concepts are highly relevant to teaching and practicing community development in transformative ways in the current neoliberal context (Bay, 2018).

Hannah Arendt

Hannah Arendt (1906–1975) was born in Hanover Germany in 1906 and studied with several key German philosophers: notably Martin Heidegger in Marburg and Carl Jasper in Heidelberg. She completed her doctoral thesis on the concept of love in the thought of Saint Augustin in 1929. As a German Jew, Arendt was forced to flee Nazi Germany in 1933 after she had been interrogated by the Gestapo for eight days. She made it to France and worked as a 'social worker' to relocate Jewish youth to Palestine. Later, still in France, Arendt was detained in an internment camp as a German refugee, but fortunately managed to escape to the United States in 1941. Overall, Arendt spent 18 years as what she called a stateless person (Bernstein, 2005).

In response to her lived experiences, Arendt described a deep need to understand how the world had lost its bearings and broken with traditional morals in Nazi Germany and Stalin's Russia (Bernstein, 2005, p. 46). Arendt (1963a) considered that traditional philosophy did not provide guidance on, nor could it provide the answers to, her questions about what it means to be human after this massive rupture. In effect, Arendt (1951, 1958) proposed that Nazi Germany and Stalin's Russia were novel forms of governance that decisively and fundamentally altered the world, thus requiring a reclaiming of political action, respect for the individual uniqueness of each person and the capacity of each of us to act anew into the common and shared world.

Arendt (1951, 1958), from then on, identified herself not as a philosopher nor even as a political philosopher, but rather as a political theorist whose work focused on the need to understand how to maintain, enliven and value the public realm and not allow it to be destroyed by totalitarianism. In order to answer her questions on how to continue in the world, motivated by the 'love of the world', she examined the essence of totalitarianism and published *The Origins of Totalitarianism* (1951), *The Human Condition* (1958), *Between Past and Future* (1961a), *On Revolution* (1963c), *Eichmann in Jerusalem* (1963a), and *On Violence* (1970) among many other publications that followed. Arendt also wrote specifically on school education in two essays: 'The Crisis in Education' (1961b) and 'Reflection on Little Rock' (1959) in ways that can be related to teaching adults about community development (which is discussed later in this chapter).

Arendt is widely known as one of the most influential and original political thinkers of the 20th century. In recent times, there has been an extraordinary revival and interest in her work (Bernstein, 2018). In part, this is due to the relevance of her political concepts for understanding modern events and ideologies. Her unique use of concepts such as 'political action', 'natality', 'plurality' and 'publicness' – terms she added to the political lexicon – can assist social workers in making sense of the world (Levinson, 2010). Her concern for political freedom requires a commitment to continually re-create a public space where the exercise of 'common sense' and solidarity is made possible through 'acting in concert' with plural others (Arendt, 1951, 1958). The way Arendt uses her political concepts offers powerful counterpoints to the current rise of world-alienation and loneliness in the Western world (Cane, 2015; Levinson, 2010). Further, Arendt's use of political storytelling based on lived experience, adds another layer to her rich analysis of totalitarianism, statelessness and human rights (Disch, 1993). This kind of political storytelling can provide conditions for students to make links between their own personal positioning, identities and identifications to question and critically engage social and political change (Giroux, 2015). Arendt's method of political storytelling promotes the capacity to make political judgment a necessary element in community development. To explain Arendt's unique and complex political lexicon and the implications for critical pedagogy in community development, I will outline some of her key concepts in the next sections.

Political action

In *The Origins of Totalitarianism* (1951), one of Arendt's most well-known books, she addressed the degradation that happens to people when they are made politically superfluous. She explored the dire impact on human beings when they are stripped of their legal, civil and political rights. Arendt (1951, p. 428) considered the concentration camps operated as experiments that reduced human beings into 'subhuman, creatures without the capacity of action and choice'. In effect, Arendt (1951, p. 300) argued that 'it seems that a [human being] who is nothing but a [human being] has lost the very qualities which make it possible for other people to treat [them] as a fellow-[human]'. Arendt's (1951) novel argument here was that universal human rights do not hold or protect people in circumstances where the state, nation or political community does not recognise a person as having legitimate membership in the political community. The loss of this right to belong to a political community is what expels a person from humanity and makes them vulnerable to all kinds of mistreatment, disconnection, dispossession and killing by the state or others (Arendt, 1951). This process of de-recognition of sub-populations within Nazi Germany and Stalin's Russia was described by Arendt as a deliberate mechanism or strategy, and one element of totalitarianism.

Further, Arendt's (1951) contention was that totalitarianism has not been eradicated for all time, but rather that each of us needs to be politically informed and vigilant to resist totalitarianism in all its guises, and also within ourselves. Importantly, Arendt identifies loneliness as fertile ground for the growth of totalitarianism. Arendt considered that:

> While isolation concerns only the political realm of life, loneliness concerns human life as a whole. Totalitarian government, like all tyrannies, certainly could not exist without destroying the public realm of life, that is, without destroying, by isolating men, their political capacities. But totalitarian domination as a form of government *is new* in that it is not content with this isolation and destroys private life as well. It bases itself on loneliness, *on the experience of not belonging to the world at all*, which is among the most radical and desperate experiences of man.
>
> *(Arendt, 1951, p. 173, my italics)*

Based on her analysis of totalitarianism, Arendt aimed to reconstruct the notion of political action for the 'love of the world'. In her book *The Human Condition* (1958), Arendt set out to find a new model for rethinking political action. One of the main storylines of this book was that philosophy went astray when Plato, after Socrates' death, advocated for the life of the mind and a contemplative life rather than a politically active life. In Arendt's (1958) opinion, it is the plurality of ideas in public spaces that prevents tyranny from taking hold. In order to reclaim an active political life, Arendt outlines three main kinds of activities human beings engage in as part of living in this world: labour, work and action. She assesses each of these activities for their relevance as a model for political action. Labour is all the activities that sustain life – cooking, cleaning, growing food – which are necessary for human biological survival. These tasks need to be repeated daily, and in this sense, are endless and consumed without permanent trace. Work is considered the making of things, such as a home, furniture and poetry: all those things that are necessary to make a home on this earth; which have some permanence and are not consumed immediately. However, more recently with mass production and consumption the line between labour and work is becoming more blurred. Also, labour has become, much to Arendt's (1958) dismay, elevated as 'a noble and worthwhile way of life' in our mass consumerist societies, at least in the West. Whereas, action as highlighted by Arendt (1958) is the human activity that creates and makes new things happen in inter-connection with others, and as such is the most likely model for politics.

Political action is where individuals converse and argue and keep open a space of diverse political opinion. Political action importantly also means being able to hold each other accountable for the consequences of our actions, and provides us with the opportunity to reveal 'who' we are – uniquely through our speech, our actions, our consent and our dissent. Political action creates a space where one can be judged according to *who*, and not merely *what*, one is positioned to be. It means that one can be recognised based on one's words and deeds and not just as a member of a particular category (Arendt, 1958). Her point here assists community developers, teachers and practitioners to recognise that political identity, or identity politics (what we are, or the categories we are positioned into) is not the basis of political action. Rather it is our capacity to engage as 'who' we are that makes political action possible.

In community development teaching and practice, it also means that we are not bound to 'what' others see us as, individually or as a group (Meyer & Fels, 2013, p. 308). It also means being able to align ourselves with those groups that are being persecuted, discriminated against or treated unfairly or unjustly on the basis of belonging to this group or sub-population. We can act in solidarity; as our own political identity is not a barrier for taking actions or standing beside others.

Arendt (1951) considered strong political engagement with each other as necessary to prevent terror, loneliness and isolation. Terror, loneliness and isolation are also the pre-conditions for the rise of widespread totalitarianism and, some would argue, for right-wing populism today (Brooks, 2018). Community development with its emphasis on mutual rights and responsibilities can promote inter-connection with others to create 'a place where one is recognised and included' (Ife, 2009, p. 10). Community development might be part of the pre-condition for preventing social isolation, loneliness and exclusion in society. Teaching community development through engaging with the principles of political action, however, first requires us to engage with Arendt's (1958) understanding of plurality and natality.

Natality

Arendt (1958, p. 9) contends that natality is 'the capacity of beginning something new, that is, of acting'. Arendt (1958, pp. 176–77) compares natality to a second birth in that we can insert ourselves into the world and take it on ourselves to make an appearance 'explicitly' in the world, through speech and action. Arendt (1958, p. 9) wrote, '[T]he new beginning inherent in birth can make itself felt in the world only because the newcomer possesses the capacity of beginning something anew, that is of acting'. Thus, natality refers to 'our capacity to take initiative in relation to the world' (Levinson, 2010, p. 476). Arendt (1958) considered natality a condition of our birth: it is a given, a fact; the fact of our arrival in the world. We are a new beginning and have the potential to participate, to make anew and take responsibility for shaping our collective life with others. Arendt describes this human condition of natality as:

> The fact that ... [people are] capable of action means that the unexpected can be expected from him[/her], that he[/she] is able to perform what is infinitely improbable. And this again is possible only because each ... [person] is unique, so that with each birth something new comes into the world.
>
> *(1958, p. 178)*

Arendt's notion of natality suggests that humans can transcend human-made structures and create something new, as being human 'always maintains a difference – that individuals cannot be reduced to the human condition or to the power structures in which they reside' (Gordon, 1999, p. 206).

Arendt (1958) strongly advocated for the human capacity to intervene in events that seem inevitable, predetermined or inescapable. This capacity to augment and bring novelty to current arrangements is thus inherent in each of us (Bay, 2014). One of the decisive factors in all political organisations is the capacity 'to receive new beginners into a communal pattern that is more permanent than each of them' (Disch, 1994 p. 32). 'Thus, each encounter is an invitation for us to renew ourselves, to reconsider our actions, to recognize that we might, in the presence of a newcomer, become other than what we currently are' (Meyer & Fels, 2013, p. 306).

This openness to others means being willing to extend mutual regard to other political actors even without personal knowledge of them, to treat each actor as equal and not as means to an end. Respecting the integrity of the person and their speech and actions, can also be related to not splitting the means and ends of actions more generally. As Ife (2009, p. 37) highlights, one of the community development principles is that 'the means is as important as the end, and that the end does not necessarily "justify" the means'. Arendt would agree that either treating the other as a means to an end in political action or splitting the means and ends of action are both flawed and dangerous in community development teaching and practice.

The promise of natality is tempered by the fact that we are born into a world that pre-exists us and that will exist after we are dead. This means that any of our efforts to 'initiate something new occurs in the thick of other acting beings' (Meyer & Fels, 2013). As Arendt (1958, p. 184) stated, 'already existing webs of relationships with its innumerable conflicting wills and intentions [means] that action almost never achieves its purpose'. However, there is also a burden that action carries in that it can be irreversible and is unpredictable. And Arendt has been critiqued for promoting amoral political action because of her acknowledgment of action's boundlessness (Cane, 2015). However, Arendt (1963c) also outlines a range of political principles such as honour, courage, virtue (which in political terms refers to a love of equality as well as the equal status of each of us as distinct actors), and solidarity meaning standing alongside others. These principles inspire action and also allow for and facilitate critical judgment of political action, in that these as principles are either enacted or not, to a lesser or greater extent, in the events that unfold (Arendt, 1963c).

According to Arendt (1958), there is also the need for a capacity for making and keeping promises, that applies to political action in human plurality. Hence, for Arendt (1958, p. 237) there is a necessity for 'being forgiven, released from the consequences of what we have done, [otherwise] our capacity to act ... could never recover' when taking political action. Again, Arendt has been critiqued for this position as indicating any action can be forgiven. However, Arendt does draw a distinction between the kinds of actions that can be forgiven and those that cannot. Those actions that are arguably miscalculations or erroneous acts can be forgiven, whereas acts like those of Eichmann, who efficiently enabled the transport of Jews to the death camps, for instance, were deemed to be much more significant, deliberate and thus unforgiveable (Arendt, 1963a). Eichmann also was not willing to be accountable for his actions but continued to argue that he was merely 'following orders', that all fault lay with the political leadership and that his only flaw was obedience (Arendt, 1963b). He claimed he was not guilty of killing anyone. According to Arendt (1963a), Eichmann indicated that he was not able to understand himself as politically responsible, as an agent in the events of the Holocaust. Even as Eichmann was aware of the significance of his job, and the terrible consequences of his carrying out the commands, he failed at the trial to admit his wrong-doing and hence could not be released from his deeds through forgiveness. Further, Arendt (1958, p. 241) considers the Holocaust a crime against humanity and as outside the realm of political action, as it exceeds this realm of humanity in which forgiveness can take place.

In political action, forgiveness is not to be expected, rather it is like all action, unpredictable. Forgiveness is thus not a reaction, but a new action, unconditioned by the act that provoked it. Forgiveness sets both the one who forgives and the forgiven free (Arendt, 1958). Forgiveness allows for the mutual regard and courage necessary between people to continue acting into the world, while knowing that action is unpredictable and that often the consequences will only become clear in hindsight. As Arendt (1958) indicated, we can use political principles to guide our actions, but are still not able to predict the outcomes of our actions. Acknowledging the unpredictability of political action is a valuable notion in community development education, as political and human affairs are enacted by a plurality of people, who through speech and action and this plurality are both the reason and the need for politics.

Plurality

Plurality was used distinctively by Arendt (1958, p. 7) as a political category that recognises that we exist on the planet in relation to others, not just in the sheer multiplicity of human beings, but also in reference to our diversity and our individual uniqueness. Famously, Arendt (1958, p. 8) stated, '[W]e are all the same, that is, human, in such a way that nobody is ever the same as anyone else that ever lived, lives, or will live'. Disch (1994, p. 32) takes this to also mean that 'the possibility of community is never simply given or essential to human being but must, rather, be built by speech and action'.

Community is thus an event, a becoming, and not an object or something that can be had or held, but a being and (be)coming together. Community development education can gain from this insight that community is not an object, a geographical location nor a predetermined identity group, but a process that requires human interaction and is dependent on unique individuals coming together and engaging through their interactions in continuously constructing the common realm or common world. Sometimes, Arendt (1951, 1958) referred to 'common sense' as co-original with the common world, as the 'situatedness of understanding' (Borren, 2013, p. 225). Specifically, Arendt (1958, pp. 57–58) claimed that 'the presences of others, who see and hear what we hear assures us of the reality of the world and of ourselves'.

From a critical pedagogical perspective, what is crucial here is that to belong, people have to come to terms with and reconcile themselves to reality, that is, try to be at home in the world (Arendt, 1958). This does not mean that citizens need to adapt and reconcile themselves to injustices, inequality, or a lack of human freedom. Rather, to attain and develop the capacity for critical reflexivity and analysis of how people are situated in the world, by both being shaped and shaping the world, requires the decisive factor of intersubjective communication, elaborating the different perceptions and perspectives people have.

Plurality also refers to the web of human relationships whenever people live together. Thus, plurality is an experience of 'both equality and of distinction; [in that] we are all human, and we are all separate individuals' (Canovan, 1992, p. 206). Politics takes place in the space *between* plural human beings and power is understood here as something that 'springs up in between' people 'when they act together' (Arendt, 1958, p. 182). This is what Arendt (1958) means by 'acting in concert'; power for her is defined as the capacity of people to 'act in concert'. Her metaphors here are based on performativity, like people playing instruments together, and once the performance is over, the moment has passed. Similarly, power that springs up between people vanishes once their acting together is completed.

This notion of plurality reinforces that community is comprised of peers and that political action is a shared concern.

> Because we are plural, *action in politics is not a matter of lonely heroes but of interaction between peers*; because we are plural, even the most charismatic leader cannot do more than lead what is essentially a joint enterprise; because we are plural, human beings are at their most glorious not when their individuality is lost … but when they are revealing their unique identities on the public stage.
>
> *(Canovan, 1992, p. 205, my italics)*

This notion of plurality is thus a key concept for community development. As Ife (2009, p. 47) warns, it 'is so easy for a community worker to assume superior knowledge and wisdom and to seek to impose their world view on others, with the best of intentions'. For

Arendt (1963c), heroes are the ones who contribute to the construction of the public sphere. This contribution is heroic as it requires what, for Arendt, is the most political of emotions: courage.

Publicity or maintaining the common world

Publicity is more than the common world and much more fragile than the world; 'it is a place of discourse and action' where very importantly 'reality discloses itself' (Canovan, 1992, p. 111). It is the plurality of human beings in an authentic public realm that creates a space for 'reality to appear in its many sidedness' according to Canovan (1992, p. 117).

The polis, according to Arendt,

> is not the city-state in its physical location: it is the organization of the people as it arises out of acting and speaking together, and its true space lies between people living together for this purpose, no matter where they happen to be.
>
> *(1958, p. 198)*

Arendt was always concerned that the realms of 'the social' and 'the political' were not made distinct and that by carelessly interchanging these two terms, politics was disregarded. Her critiques of mass society and consumerism are contrasted with her advocacy for political action as a way of keeping open, and making available to each other, the common world, through people exchanging varied opinions and perspectives on events. This space Arendt calls variously the 'interspace', 'in between' or 'inter-est, which lies between people and therefore can relate and bind them together' (1958, p. 182).

Before discussing further how Arendt's key political concepts are relevant to teaching community development in social work education, it is worthwhile to consider Arendt's understanding of political storytelling as an important element for achieving this aim.

Political storytelling

In effect, Arendt devised a distinctive form of political storytelling in her efforts to explore the unprecedented occurrence of totalitarianism as a novel and modern phenomenon. Arendt's storytelling was an innovative approach to critical understanding that Disch (1993, p.666) called 'situated impartiality', where the validity of the account does not rely on a disembodied voice and vision from nowhere, nor does it claim 'the experience of subjugation' as a privileged perspective on 'structures of domination'. Rather, the intent is to 'tell provocative stories that invite contestation from rival perspectives' (Disch, 1993, p. 667). In community development education, the forming of political opinions that are intersubjective and relate to real events in the world is part of the engagement educators facilitate with their students to explore the world as it is.

Arendt (1961a, p. 6) was particularly concerned about the conditions in Nazi Germany, for instance, where 'thought and reality have parted company'. This kind of incongruence is currently evident in this era of on-going political lying, fake news and corporate unaccountability including the spreading of false science on issues such as tobacco smoke and global warming (MacKenzie & Bhatt, 2018; Oreskes & Conway, 2010). Arendt's (1958) style of political storytelling pays attention to reality or *the world as it is*, and aims to inspire critical thinking in its audience. Arendt (1961a) argued that to understand a phenomenon like totalitarianism it is best not to start with categories or formulas or traditional concepts but with stories that are situated, and by paying attention to events from multiple perspectives.

Arendt (1961a) challenges us to think 'without banisters'; without the crutches of prior categories or concepts in order to deal with and understand unprecedented and unfamiliar events. This kind of storytelling, according to Disch (1993, p. 669), invites critical situated thinking by engaging its audience to think within the dilemma in a way that is different from an argument. In community development, storytelling may be used more as a project to develop community members' confidence, recognition, or to reduce inter-group conflict, to express and contain emotions and to help build networks. Storytelling can also be used as a therapeutic and awareness-raising tool, or to explore conflict and diversity between ethnic groups and intergenerational groups (Horsley, 2007). Whereas, Arendt's storytelling about totalitarianism (1951) and Eichmann's trial (1963a) was not to 'compel assent but, rather, [aims to and] stirs people to think about what they are doing' (Disch, 1993, p. 671). Arendt wanted to ground her storytelling in experience to understand political events and the world *as it is* in ways that inspire critical thinking in her audience (Disch, 1993, p. 681).

Arendt (1963b), in reporting on the Eichmann trial in Jerusalem, considered that one of Adolf Eichmann's many failings was that he was a thoughtless bureaucrat, a 'functionary' who could not imagine what the other person was experiencing (in this case the many Jews transported to their deaths). Arendt's (1963a) subtitle of her book on the trial was 'the banality of evil'. This phrase has been highly controversial, but was received by many intellectuals as a new insight into a novel modern kind of evil (Miller, 1998). Evil had, until that time, been associated with strong passions and with murderous monsters. For Arendt (1963a) to call evil 'banal' was to locate it as part of an ordinary, mundane and unthinking man's daily job. It highlighted the possibility that any bureaucrat, or indeed human generally, could, without thinking, cause harm to others; to commit crimes against humanity. To prevent this from happening, Arendt (1961b) called on people to enlarge their thinking and 'to train "one's imagination to go visiting" which involves evoking or telling yourself multiple stories of a situation from the plurality of conflicting perspectives that constitute it' (Disch, 1993, p. 686). In effect, asking 'how would the world look to *you* if you saw it from this position?' (Disch, 1993, p. 687).

Arendt (1994) was careful to distinguish between empathy here, which would erase all difference, and visiting another place to experience what the world looks like from different perspectives. This implies that the storyteller, at times, looks into themselves to go visiting in one's imagination, and also engages in testing one's perspective against the perspectives of others. For Arendt, the 'point of storytelling is not consensus or accuracy but plurality and accountability' (Disch, 1993, p. 688). Arendt made it clear that it is not easy to think about 'what we are doing' (Arendt, 1958, p. 5). However, this seems a most apt question for teaching community development with the purpose of promoting emancipatory possibilities.

Applying Arendt's key concepts to community development

'Community development is both a professional practice and a political practice' (Shaw, 2008, p. 26; Bunyan, 2010). Arendt's (1958) political lexicon adds much to community development teaching in its focus on valuing political action, and by reinforcing the role of community development as enhancing people's agency and critical situated understanding. In teaching community development, Arendt's (1994) practice of political storytelling as situated critical thinking, can mean learning a community (and the way it has been constituted in policy and program or neighbourhood terms) and its many structural issues by engaging with various people from a range of different groups. The further challenge, then, is in applying a critical pedagogical lens to these differing views in teaching community development as part of social work education, given the Australian Association of Social Work's Code of Ethics (AASW, 2010) is not politically neutral but has an explicit commitment to social justice, self-determination, equality, fairness and non-discrimination.

For this reason, the classroom needs to be structured by the educators and students together in such a way that it generates political principles as outlined by Arendt (1963c), as these can yield a robust political ethics. These political principles, such as: the 'innate value of every human being'; 'solidarity' by standing alongside others as equals; interconnectedness through the principle of mutual promise and common deliberation; sharing perspectives on the 'common world'; public and political freedom; and respecting the right to consent and to dissent, are worldly principles that can guide political action and can also be used as evaluative standards (Arendt, 1963c). It is also important in the community development curriculum, and the interactions between students and teachers, to name and recognise degenerative political principles such as: rage, charity, distrust (includes lying and dishonesty) and hatred. These degenerative political principles need to be explored also for their ability to destroy and annihilate the 'common world' and political spaces (Arendt, 1958). Arendt's (1963c) political principles can be a basis for exploring the common world and specific events happening in relevant communities, as well as the interactions between students and their educators.

These political principles also facilitate critical political judgments about whether a particular goal or action exemplifies or can sustain these principles. Further, these political principles need to resist any means-ends reasoning (Arendt, 1963c), such as currently applies to political rationalities such as neoliberalism (Bay, 2018). For instance, the political principle of solidarity means that community development needs to address poverty and its stigma, as solidarity requires standing alongside others as equals. Discussion of these principles, in the classroom or in online forums, offers students the opportunity to develop political ways of thinking in order to consider issues from multiple perspectives, and to make political judgments about the importance of addressing such issues as inequality, unfairness, injustice and hatred. By encouraging enlarged mentality through representative thinking and the exertion of imagination, students can be asked to consider any worldly events in their multilayered aspects. However, to make a political judgment also needs the presence of others. To think politically means encouraging practitioners, students and teachers to engage with injustice, inequality, hatred, lying and its impact on communities and to address any specific events that arise from such degenerative principles in interaction with each other.

Arendt, in her essay 'The Crisis of Education' (1961b), also makes it clear that it is not possible to *teach* adults. Rather, when teaching community development with adults, their life experiences, capacities and abilities to 'imagine visiting others' in a current situation to promote 'enlarged thinking', are already present. Educators can encourage students through critical situated thinking to articulate political opinions to the group as part of the learning in community development classes. Specifically, critical reflection as part of critical situated thinking can be taught

> to assist students to recognise their own and other people's frames of reference, to identify the dominant discourses circulating in making sense of their experience, to problematise their taken-for-granted 'lived experience', to reconceptualise identity categories, disrupt assumed causal relations and to reflect on how power relations are operating.
>
> *(Bay & Macfarlane, 2011, p. 745)*

The likely conflicting views between students as well as educators, can then fuel the discussion about how to engage across these differences rather than to avoid them. This is vital learning for students in holding space for conflictual views in community development practice. For when political spaces are absent, 'the distinct perspectives our locations allow become indiscernible, and, again, both plurality and commonality are at risk and with them our political agency and the capacity to thoughtfully effect the conditions of our lives' (Orlie, 1997, p. 86).

As Arendt (1958) stated, we need to preserve the notion of natality and teach the world not as we as educators would like it to be, but rather we need to take responsibility for teaching the world *as it is* and encourage newcomers to begin anew in sharing and shaping the world with others – as it could be. According to Shaw, the same dilemma is true for community development itself, in that it

> contains within its own terms an unavoidable choice: it can act as a mirror, *simply reflecting back an image of 'the world as it is'*, in the process reinforcing existing unequal and divisive social relations of power, *or it can provide a lens through which existing structures and practices can be critically scrutinized* in order to find ways to create a more equal, supportive and alternative – 'the world as it could be'.
>
> *(Shaw, 2008, p. 34, my italics)*

Conclusion

Arendt's (1958) theorising adds to community development teaching the notion of natality, of agency and of the ability and capacity of the newcomers to work out how the world should be, or could be, as a transformative possibility. Rather than community development teachers pre-determining and teaching how the world should be, students are encouraged to take a lead in this regard based on an engagement with generative political principles and critical situated thinking. As when teachers take the lead, Arendt (1961b, p. 196) considered they might 'short-circuit the genuine motor of social progress' and 'strike from [the young's] hands their chance of undertaking something new, something unforeseen by us'.

Arendt's (1958) concept of natality also means that no one is tied to their identity in order to be included in politics; rather, political action asks us not 'what' we are but 'who' we are. The capacity to act comes from being with plural others and 'acting in concert' with them. Arendt, in thinking politically, makes it clear that the frailty of human affairs can only be tackled through 'acting in concert' with others, as power is 'never the property of an individual; it belongs to a group and remains in existence only so long as the group keeps together' (Arendt, 1970, p. 44). It is 'when individuals bind themselves together by means of promises and engage in concerted action, [that] they become powerful' (Allen, 1999, p. 113). This emphasis on political action is what Arendt (1958) brings to teaching community development. Her idea of political action is partly based on her understanding that the political is necessary for everyone's self-fulfilment and self-discovery, and both 'require interaction with other people, perspectives and principles' (Topolski, 2008, p. 277). '[P]articipation is a key feature of community development' (Ife, 2009, p. 40), and students' participation in classroom discussions, whether online, by Distance Education mode, or face-to-face, needs to be structured by the educators and students together in such a way that it generates political principles, situated political judgment and promotes political action.

References

Allen, A. (1999) Solidarity after Identity Politics: Hannah Arendt and the Power of Feminist Theory. *Philosophy & Social Criticism* 25(1), pp. 97–118.
Arendt, H. (1951) *The Origins of Totalitarianism*. Harcourt. Brace and Co.: New York.
Arendt, H. (1958) *The Human Condition*, 2nd ed. University of Chicago Press: Chicago.
Arendt, H. (1959) Reflections on Little Rock. *Dissent* 6(1), pp. 45–56.
Arendt, H. (1961a) *Between Past and Future: Eight Exercises in Political Thought*. Penguin: New York.
Arendt, H. (1961b) The Crisis in Education. In *Between Past and Future: Eight Exercises in Political Thought*. Penguin: New York, pp. 173–196.
Arendt, H. (1963a) *Eichmann in Jerusalem: A Report on the Banality of Evil*. Viking Press: New York.
Arendt, H. (1963b) Eichmann in Jerusalem-V. *The New Yorker*, March 16.
Arendt, H. (1963c) *On Revolution*. Penguin: London.
Arendt, H. (1970) *On Violence*. A Harvest Book, Harcourt Inc.: New York.
Arendt, H. (1994) Understanding and Politics. In Kohn, J. (ed.) *Essays in Understanding*. Schocken: New York, pp. 307–327.
Bay, U. (2014) *Social Work Practice: A conceptual Framework*. Palgrave Macmillan: South Yarra.
Bay, U. (2018) Neoliberalism as an Art of Governance: Reflecting on Techniques for Securing Life through Direct Social Work Practice. *European Journal of Social Work* 22(2), pp. 201–211 (online: 13 Oct).
Bay, U. & Macfarlane, S. (2011) Teaching Critical Reflection: A Tool for Transformative Learning in Social Work. *Social Work Education* 30(7), pp. 745–758.
Bernstein, R. (2005) Hannah Arendt on the Stateless. *Parallax* 34, pp. 46–60.
Bernstein, R.J. (2018) *Why Read Hannah Arendt Now*. Polity Press: Cambridge.
Borren, M. (2013) A Sense of the World': Hannah Arendt's Hermeneutic Phenomenology of Common Sense. *International Journal of Philosophical Studies* 21(2), pp. 225–255.
Brooks, A.C. (2018) How Loneliness is Tearing America Apart. *The New York Times*, Opinion piece. November 23.
Bunyan, P. (2010) Broad-based Organizing in the UK: Reasserting the Centrality of Political Activity in Community Development. *Community Development Journal* 45(1), pp. 111–127.
Cane, L. (2015) Hannah Arendt on the Principles of Political Action. *European Journal of Political Theory* 14(1), pp. 55–75.
Canovan, M. (1992) *Hannah Arendt: A Reinterpretation of Her Political Thought*. Cambridge University Press: Cambridge.
Code of ethics. (2010) *Canberra ACT: Australian Association of Social Work*.
Disch, L.J. (1993) More Truth Than Fact: Storytelling as Critical Understanding in the Writings of Hannah Arendt. *Political Theory* 21(4), pp. 665–694.
Disch, L.J. (1994) *Hannah Arendt and the Limits of Philosophy*. Cornell University Press: New York.
Giroux, H.A. (2015) The Curse of Totalitarianism and the Challenge of Critical Pedagogy. *Truthout*. https://truthout.org. Accessed 26 May, 2019.
Gordon, N. (1999) Social Control in Democracies: A theoretical analysis. *Unpublished doctoral thesis*. University of Notre Dame: Notre Dame.
Horsley, K. (2007) Storytelling, Conflict and Diversity. *Community Development Journal* 42(2), pp. 265–269.
Ife, J. (2009) *Human Rights from Below: Achieving Rights Through Community Development*. Cambridge University Press: New York.
Levinson, N. (2010) A "More General Crisis": Hannah Arendt, World-Alienation, and the Challenges of Teaching for the World. *As It Is. Teachers College Round*. 112(2), pp. 464–487.
MacKenzie, A. & Bhatt, I. (2018) Lies, Bullshit and Fake News: Some Epistemological Concerns. *Postdigital Science and Education*. 10.1007/s42438-018-0025-4
Meyer, K.A. & Fels, L. (2013) Imagining Education: An Arendtian Response to an Inmate's Question. *Canadian Journal of Education* 36(3), pp. 300–316.
Miller, S. (1998) A Note on the Banality of Evil. *Wilson Quarterly* 22 (Autumn), pp. 54–59.
Oreskes, N. & Conway, E.M (2010) *Merchants of Doubt: How a Handful of Scientists Obscured the Truth on Issues from Tobacco Smoke to Global Warming*. Bloomsbury Press, New York.
Orlie, M.A. (1997) *Living Ethically, Acting Politically*. Cornell University Press: London.
Shaw, M. (2008) Community Development and the Politics of Community. *Community Development Journal* 43(1), pp. 24–36.
Topolski, A. (2008) Creating Citizens in the Classroom: Hannah Arendt's Political Critique of Education. *Journal of the European Ethics Network* 15(2), pp. 259–282.

37

The transformation and integration of society

Developing social work pedagogy through Jürgen Habermas' theory of communicative action

Rúna í Baianstovu
ÖREBRO UNIVERSITY, SWEDEN

Phillip Ablett
UNIVERSITY OF THE SUNSHINE COAST, QUEENSLAND, AUSTRALIA

Introduction

Social work is a globalised field of action, facing theoretical, practical, ethical and pedagogical challenges caused by major global transformations, that have given rise to an increasing diversity of socioeconomic, national, ethnic, racial and religious divisions. This context poses anew the question of the possibility of interconnectedness over or between these divisions. It prompts us to ask, *inter alia*, do we have to share the same life, the same experiences, the same class, nationality, ethnicity, race or religion to achieve solidarity and mutual understanding? The German philosopher, sociologist and critical theorist, Jürgen Habermas has shown that this increasing diversity calls for a specific kind of communication to reach mutual understanding and the emancipatory possibilities this entails. He also states that our possibilities for communication are often systematically obstructed. However, Habermas has not been content with stating the problem, he also offers a way to create mutual understanding and cohesion in a rapidly changing world. In such a context, the stakes for social workers (both as practitioners and educators) to communicate or facilitate mutual understanding over socioeconomic, cultural, religious and normative divides, are extraordinarily high. In this chapter the pressing needs of communication across difference and the obstacles to it will be examined in the light of Habermas' *Theory of Communicative Action* (TCA).

Several researchers in social work have drawn on Habermas' work while studying the possibilities of mutual understanding in different areas of social work such as social justice and communicative responsibility (Rossiter 1997; Lorenz 2006), health, family and caregiving

(Hagen et al. 2012), family group conferences (Hayes & Houston 2007, 2009; Houston 2010, 2013), higher education and rethinking the relation between spirituality, religious thought and values in social work practice (Gray & Lovat 2008). A reoccurring argument in these works is that Habermas' theories deliver a rational basis to social work for egalitarian dialogical practices in times of rapid change and distorted communication (e.g. Rossiter 1997; Houston 2008; Gray & Lovat 2008; Houston 2013).[1] A number of education scholars have also drawn upon Habermas' work to theorise critical approaches to transformative learning in the context of building a more just society (Ewert 1991; Torres & Morrow 1998; Welton 2005; Mezirow 2009). However, this chapter is not so much a discussion of educational processes or methods in social work as it is concerned with imparting or advocating a particular content in social work education. As another critical educationalist, who draws upon Habermas, reminds us: 'Teaching critically is not just a question of how we teach. It is also about what we teach' (Brookfield 2005, p. 349).

The usefulness of Habermas' work became clear to the lead author during a study of how social workers in social services in Sweden understand and handle cultural diversity (Baianstovu 2012). The social workers in this study conceived communication as the most distinctive feature of social work and the most important tool of the profession. In interviews, the social workers revealed notions of success and shortcomings in their inquiry and decision-making with families. In the Swedish context, the notion of success relates to achieving consensus, in contrast to the enacting of temporary coercive measures (under the Social Service Act §1). The interviews showed that coercion most often is enacted toward families that explicitly declare religious, conformist and patriarchal norms. In a comparative perspective, Sweden is a relatively secular society, whereas most often these families have roots in the Middle East and Africa where traditional religion and gender inequalities are stronger (Zuckerman 2007; WEF 2018).

Consensus in a service delivery context, requires that every person be afforded the opportunity for his or her personal situation and needs to be voiced and heard. Nevertheless, social workers in public institutions are not given the options of communicating with clients in the varying ways needed to reach mutual understanding across socioeconomic, cultural, religious and normative differences. A market-oriented style of governing social services, under the rubric of New Public Management (NPM), has become an obstacle to the communication between social worker and diverse clients. NPM is characterised by bureaucratic ritualism around 'customer service' and narrow economic performance frameworks derived from business management; and is something with which social workers in most Western societies struggle (Lorenz 2006; Rogowski 2010).

The core of the social workers' narratives about communicative success or failure can be better understood by employing the concepts of integration, intersubjectivity, lifeworld, system, and discourse ethics from the TCA. The concepts reveal the logics, powers and actions involved in the structuring of communicative interactions at individual, organisational and societal (moral/legislative) levels. They function as analytical tools for understanding communication in contemporary social work in a globalised world, and the challenges it is facing. These concepts also highlight an indispensable communicative practice that provides the ground for the contribution social work makes to inclusion and integration in welfare systems today, as well as the obstacles to it. Habermas' work further provides a conceptual map, guiding the analysis of the social, economic and political landscape in which social work operates, and the communicative interactions so central to its practice. For this reason, we argue that the basic elements of the TCA should form an essential part of the analytical frameworks taught to future practitioners in their social work education and provide an example of how this is being done by one of the authors.

Rúna í Baianstovu and Phillip Ablett

Jürgen Habermas

Born in Düsseldorf, Germany, on June 18, 1929, but growing up in Gummersbach where his father was director of the local Bureau of Industry, Habermas was raised in the era of Nazi rule by the totalitarian political party NSDAP (*Nationalsozialistische Deutsche Arbeiterpartei*), under Adolf Hitler 1933–1945. Like other boys in Germany at the time, he held a mandatory membership of the *Hitlerjugend* (Hitler Youth). It was during his young adult life, listening to broadcasts of the Nuremburg trials and viewing documentaries on the concentration camps, that Habermas was awakened to the tactics employed by the Nazi party in securing mass support, and the horrors of the concentration camps (Kellner 1996; Restorff 1997). These formative experiences have shaped the focal point of his work on how totalitarianism can be kept at bay, and a strong democracy developed and sustained.

Habermas began university studies at Göttingen in 1949, completing a dissertation at Bonn (1954) and then worked as a journalist for two years. Attracted to the critical renewal of Marxism, particularly the critical theory inaugurated by Adorno and Horkheimer at Frankfurt, Habermas commenced his doctorate under Adorno in 1956 (Kellner 1996). He also became active in the student and anti-nuclear movements. After disagreements with Horkheimer, Habermas completed his doctorate at Marburg and with the recommendation of Hans George Gadamer, obtained a professorship at Heidelberg in 1962 before returning to Frankfurt as Horkheimer's successor in 1964. Subsequently, his ideas have significantly influenced several areas, e.g. philosophy, sociology, political-legal thought and theology. However, he is not only known for academic research, but is an outstanding public intellectual, often involved in and commenting on actual events in Germany and elsewhere (Bohman & Rehg 2017).

Habermas gained public notoriety with the book *Structural Transformation of the Public Sphere* (Habermas 1962/1989) but his magnum opus is *The Theory of Communicative Action* (1984).[2] His works are linked together by an interest in exploring and explaining the interconnectedness between social life, morality, law, social cohesion and democracy in modernity, a line explored more deeply in *Between Facts and Norms* (1996). In recent years, the study of religion has become a focus in Habermas' work. He holds that orthodox religion, believed to be steadily losing influence during the 1900s, has made a comeback in European countries in recent decades, increasingly influencing society and democracy (Habermas 2008; Gray & Luton 2008). The resurgence of religion is a potential threat to democracy because 'opinion- and will-formation within the democratic, public arena can function only if a sufficiently large number of citizens fulfil specific expectations concerning civil conduct even across deep religious and ideological divides' (Habermas 2008, p. 4). Civil conduct involves culture, or in Habermas' terms, norms.

Habermas continues working in the tradition of critical theory and the Frankfurt School, of which he is the most widely influential scholar today. Philosophically, Habermas also stands in a Kantian tradition in which a specific moral principle must be fulfilled for a norm to have validity: 'Do to others whatever you would like them to do to you' (Habermas 1983, p. 103). Although this moral principle has roots in a religious context, it is not confined to religion. It finds its secular equivalence in Kant's categorical imperative: 'Act only according to that maxim by which you can at the same time will that it should become a universal law' (Kant 1785/2009).

The TCA emerged from Habermas' radical 'reconstruction' of Marxian historical materialism as a critical theory of modernity, aimed in part at 'a redirection rather than an abandonment of the project of enlightenment' (Habermas 1984a, p. viii). By making 'communication' the key category of this theory, Habermas claims to restore the centrality of language, counterbalancing Marx's one-sided reliance on material production, in explaining praxis, power and societal development. Communicative action is cooperative and deliberative action motivated by an urge to deliver on modernity's intrinsic promises of democracy and critical thought. Habermas has taken a stand as 'the last' defender of modernity, stressing that scholars and politicians on the left and the right have prematurely abandoned the emancipatory dimension of modernity, long before ever reaching it (D'Entrèves & Benhabib 1996).

For Habermas, modernity holds the capacity of freedom from the tyranny of tradition, and totalitarianism. Following Émile Durkheim's analysis of the shift from traditional authoritarian societies to more diverse, egalitarian, and democratic societies (Durkheim 1893/1984), Habermas understands modernity in terms of such transformation. He builds on ideas from the Enlightenment, understanding modernity as striving for freedom from all forms of arbitrary power.

Habermas assumes that the viability of democracy demands that every person develops and constantly reassesses their ability to be critical toward rules and norms, and follows no authority other than the reasoned will to freedom. Critical thought in this sense means awareness of the rules you live by, which you should not follow solely because such authorities as parents, church, ideology or organisational rules, say so. This critically reflective quality also needs to be central to the education and practice of social workers if their profession is to be effective in realising the goal of extending social citizenship, espoused in the national and international mission statements of social work associations since the days of Jane Addams (Ferguson 2008; IFSW 2014; Lorenz 2016).

The theory of communicative action

We now turn to the Theory of Communicative Action (TCA) in which valuable insights for the education and practice of social workers are to be found.

Although starting with Marx, the TCA is derived from a combination of sociological theories (e.g. Durkheim, Weber and Mead) together with pragmatism, phenomenology, hermeneutics and linguistics. The relation envisaged between the Habermasian concepts employed here is that *integration* is the problem and the goal, while *deliberative democracy* is the procedural ideal. Furthermore, *discourse ethics* delivers the communicative tools necessary to achieve democratic integration across difference. Finally, the concepts of *lifeworld* and *system* describe the basic dimensions of the social domain in which communicative action occurs. Through TCA, Habermas explores the conditions for a consensual and democratic integration in differentiated societies.

Integration

The concept of *integration* is necessary for the understanding of communicative action, as it is both the problem and the means to solving it. For Habermas, integration refers to a constantly ongoing deliberative process inherent in the need for social cohesion of modern, democratic society (cf. Durkheim 1893/1984). This contrasts with contemporary political discourses, where integration often refers to the assimilation of foreigners (or Indigenous peoples) into the dominant order.

In this context, democracy refers to the integration processes of articulating and deliberating upon the justification of norms (Habermas 1984a, 1984b, 1995). The basic assumption is that the greater the part that communication, deliberation and reflection play in public activities, the more democratic the society will be (Durkheim 1893/1984; Habermas 1995; Benhabib 2002). Ultimately, democracy is concerned with the ability of politics and legislation to acknowledge, encompass and integrate a variety of groups' and individuals' diverse wills and life projects

(Habermas 1996). Understood in this way, democracy is continuous action and only genuinely exists to the extent that people act democratically in public and everyday life.

Doing democracy as a conscious action and participating in the normative processes requires critical consciousness. Which conditions must be present to enable critical participation in the normative processes of society? According to the basic idea of deliberative democracy, every moral creature with the ability to feel, speak and act is a potential participant in the deliberation (Benhabib 2002). This presupposes equality in the moral and political spheres, regarding the ability and the opportunity to choose and act on the terms of one's own identifications – rather than on the terms of categorisation. Such an ability demands a certain disposal of material resources as well as access to education, professional development, public institutions and places (ibid.). The Catch 22-like problem of such a suggestion is that not everybody possesses the necessary resources for participation in the deliberative processes.

Democracy is characterised by diversity and cohesion simultaneously, which creates a deep need for constant communicative deliberation on the rules and norms at all levels of society in order to constantly renew them. In this sense, communicative action has a collective pedagogic dimension or entails what Habermas calls 'social learning processes' (1984a). Moreover, for integration and democracy to exist, every member of society must feel like a subject who is taking part in the creation of the norms underlying its legislation.

To not become objectified, but remain free, acting subjects, we need to experience that the demands (rules, norms and laws) that society places on us are just. We also need to perceive ourselves as the authors of these demands (Habermas 1996a). This means that if you and I are to be convinced that a specific rule, norm or law is worthy of respect, we must feel that we could have formulated it ourselves. When we feel that, the norms of society are legitimate, meaningful and natural to us. They have become justified parts of our lifeworld because they are an expression and extension of ourselves (ibid.). As a value-driven institution in society, social work within the social services is of great importance to these processes.

Social work has been shaped in this constantly ongoing communicative ordering and reordering of social life (Lorenz 1994, 2006). Hence, social work is strongly linked to the internal stability that nation states need to achieve cohesion, which creates an intimate connectedness between the state and social work. This lends a double and problematic function to social work: it must advocate the rights of vulnerable groups and individuals and integration on equal terms, while representing the cohesive and often assimilatory projects of the nation state (Lorenz 1994, 2006). This makes social work partly a state-centered work with potentially discriminatory effects for vulnerable groups, blurring the differences between integration and assimilation (ibid.).

Habermas suggests that 'the professional divisions of the modern occupational system should form the point of departure for universally, justified normative regulations' (1984b, p. 117). Viewing social work as one of these professions, social work becomes irreplaceable in the democratic consolidation processes of society. This is why the double nature of it as either *advocating and integrative* or *assimilatory and coercive*, is deeply challenging.

Social work as conducted in modern, democratic nation states today is a victim of the consequences of the economic, political and social globalisation (cf. Castells 2009). Consequently, at the same time that social work is profoundly changing due precisely to the *economic* and *political* aspects of globalisation; it faces challenges in communicating with the *embodied representation of social globalisation* due to migration (Baianstovu 2012, 2017, 2018). The effects of these simultaneous processes of globalisation are (i) high demands on the capacity of social workers to communicate dialogically with their constituents, at the same time as (ii) their communicative capacity is obstructed (Baianstovu 2012, 2017, 2018; Lorenz 2006) by managerial and administrative proceduralism. The concepts of lifeworld and system illuminate this dialectic.

Lifeworld and system as analytical tools

Central to Habermas' TCA are the concepts of lifeworld and system, derived from his synthesis of two traditionally opposed epistemological paradigms, namely the interpretive (historical-hermeneutic) and positivistic (analytic-empiricist) traditions (Habermas 1971), which he incorporates into critical theory. Lifeworld and system represent two dimensions of all societies or, more precisely, two different modes of logic of action that become increasingly differentiated (uncoupled) in late capitalist modernity, with significant consequences for individuals, groups and society. Some social work interpreters of Habermas, have tended to equate the lifeworld and system with empirical entities, suggesting that the lifeworld represents the family and the system the state (Houston 2010), or that social workers should act in some field between lifeworld and system, drawing on both (Rode 2016). However, for Habermas, lifeworld and system are modes of action that are rarely if ever exhaustive in empirical situations of action. While certain institutions may exhibit the preponderance of one mode more than another, lifeworld and system remain co-extensive conceptual types of social being, suitable for analysing the complexity of actions in a variety of situations (Carleheden 1996). They offer tools for analysing all social situations, from face-to-face interactions in everyday life to the logic of action at different levels in organisations and political systems.

The lifeworld

The lifeworld is the everyday world in which cultural and moral life is lived, understood and expressed, and the sphere in which connectedness and mutual understanding is created; it is life in its most organic and varying forms. The lifeworld takes place in the morally guided, linguistically transmitted, and norm-producing interactions of social life (Habermas 1984b). A *moral action* for Habermas is defined by the disciplining of the individual will under collective representations; it is value- or belief-oriented (Wertrational) and relates to others as subjects.

The lifeworld is constituted through intersubjectivity. Intersubjectivity is a universal human, social condition that all human beings potentially possess. Nevertheless, it is not always fully attainable in interactions because its universality does not guarantee a shared world of meaning between all actors in every, particular context. Intersubjectivity also means that our private 'inner world' is attached to the 'outer world' and social context. Intersubjectivity consists of interactions between sensuous, embodied beings, and is therefore both inner and public at the same time. Intersubjectivity is also open to consciousness about other human beings, to alterity (Habermas 1984a). Intersubjectivity is interwoven with human action, particularly speech in which meaning is embedded (Habermas 1984a; Crossley 2007). Intersubjectivity includes the desire for self-consciousness and recognition, both of which require a strong sense of reciprocity and equality:

> It is not only the slave who suffers in the master/slave relation […] The master suffers because they are only recognised by a slave, who is unworthy of bestowing recognition since they are not recognised themselves. To be recognised by a slave is to achieve slavish consciousness, not full self-consciousness. Recognition is only satisfactory if one is recognised by those whom one recognises as worthy as recognising one.
>
> *(Crossley 1996, p. 18)*

The reason why self-consciousness demands equality is that equality is required for the mere existence of recognition, because both parts in an unequal relation are deprived of the recognition they desire.

The moral principle 'Do to others whatever you would like them to do to you' (Habermas 1983, p. 103), mentioned above, presupposes a symmetrical relation between equals without one-sided domination as in the master/slave relationship for a given norm to have legitimacy. The practical effect of this moral principle for Habermas (1983, 1984a, 1984b) is that a disputed norm can only be valid when everyone can accept its consequences and side effects without force. In other words, the principle presupposes intersubjective relations between people in the sense that two different subjects can meet without losing their diversity, because real nearness between two subjects requires that they stay diverse in their fellowship and solidarity vis-à-vis each other. If the diversity is lost, the subject is not meeting the other – it only meets itself as in a mirror (Habermas 1983). Hence, the baseline of the moral principle is everyone's right to remain equal strangers to each other within community.

Communicative action requires intersubjective communication, which is never simply an isolated interaction between two people but always already involves the groups, identities and categories that individuals refer to as they communicate (Habermas 1984a). As they meet, cultures, societies and power structures also meet. Hence, norms and values are inevitably involved in the interaction situation (Durkheim 1912/1965; Habermas 1984a, 1984b, 1971). This is because language is filled with conviction and imagination lending meaning to our words. Our words become *collective representations* (Durkheim 1912/1965). Therefore, when we truly communicate, we activate the common stock of knowledge that is carried by the language available to us.

The *lifeworld* is the culturally organised and linguistically transmitted *patterns of interpretation* that hold meaning, identity and community. Language connects individuals to each other as the collective representations produce intersubjectivity and unity that representations mediate. Therefore, the lifeworld is what we understand society to be in its most common sense (Habermas 1984b).

The system

According to Habermas, social integration requires not only normative consensus-making but, following Marx, a system for the production and reproduction of material life. This system is concerned with the coordination and control mechanisms required to meet the needs of increasingly complex societies. Therefore, actions within the system are guided by the technical, economical, administrative and juridical rules which are decoupled from the intersubjective logic of the lifeworld (Habermas 1984a, 1984b). The system is developed from the rationalisation of functions in society – for example, from the industrialisation of production, bureaucratic administration and urbanisation, leading to instrumental action in areas such as communication which is becoming increasingly technical (Habermas 1968/1984). These processes lead to the domination of instrumental or goal-rational (Zweckrational) action, organising social life on the basis of an efficiency of means and inputs to maximise the achievement of amoral ends (ibid.). In relational terms, this risks converting others from being free and acting subjects into mere means and objects necessary to one's ends. Hence the system is utilitarian and goal-oriented. It also lacks intersubjectivity, entangled as it is with egocentric calculation (Habermas 1984b). The system does not require communicative action, only readymade rules and strategies.

The colonisation of the lifeworld by the system

Habermas' lifeworld/system distinction provides us not only with tools for the analysis of our actions, but also points toward what he sees as the fundamental contradiction of late capitalist modernity. In short, his analysis shows an increasing breech between the lifeworld and the system, whereby the system contributes to the enforced decomposition of the lifeworld – which inherently needs constant and organic reconstitution – resulting in growing economic, social, cultural and religious divides. These divisions engender antagonism and disintegration rather than any cosmopolitan pluralism and so reduce the possibilities of integration around deliberative democratic norms.

The complexity of the lifeworld and the rationality of the system have expanded continuously over the past century, leading to the social and moral dimensions of society becoming subordinate to the logic of the system. During this process, the mechanisms of the system are separated from the social structures that give rise to culture and shape the normative direction of social integration (Habermas 1984b). Therefore, the system operates more or less autonomously, eluding the morally driven integration in the lifeworld. In the system, social relations are basically regulated by money and unilateral power. At the same time, the lifeworld remains the field in which the patterns of social life are defined (ibid.). In a practical context, this means that societal integration through reflective, moral action in the lifeworld is obstructed, or even repealed, due to the abrogation of sociality by the system (Habermas 1984b).

Habermas' concepts help us understand the specific threat to democracy and freedom expressed as the 'colonisation of the lifeworld' by the system, which means that our daily life actions are increasingly directed by technical rules, which abolish morality. 'When stripped of their ideological veils, the imperative of autonomous subsystems make their way into the lifeworld from the outside – like colonial masters coming onto a tribal society – and force a process of assimilation upon it' (Habermas 1984b, s. 355).

The system's colonisation of the lifeworld is a great disadvantage for any genuine consensual integration in society, because communicative action is a prerequisite for such consensus and solidarity between citizens or residents, across lines of diversity. *Communicative action* also has a socialising effect that is indispensable for the individual development of identity because the lifeworld is mediated to new members of society at the same time as it is creating continuity between the consciousnesses of different members of society (Habermas 1984b). Communicative action simultaneously contributes to mediating the cultural stock of knowledge and renewing it (ibid.).

So, the concepts of lifeworld and system distinguish between two aspects or forms of communication. The first is communication in the lifeworld, where the reciprocal interpretation of situations and practical understanding are paramount. This is (or should be) particularly evident in the socialisation of new generations and the renewal of national communities through immigration. The second form of communication, however, expresses the logic of the system and is aimed at technical control, at implementing actions according to a utilitarian criteria and whereby teleological ends are deemed to justify the means (Habermas 1984b). Accordingly, in communicative terms, the consequences of the system colonising the lifeworld means that practical and negotiated, intersubjective communication, is subjected to technically oriented, unilateral and objectifying relations in which others become the means to preconceived ends. This, of course, undermines the emancipative potential of modernity that demands equality and mutual recognition.

In social work, the colonisation of the lifeworld is most evident in situations where rigid administrative rules and economic calculation dictate what rights clients have and what social workers ought to do. The logic of the system is empirically featured by NPM, which has become increasingly dominant since the 1980s in the UK (Rogowski 2010), Sweden (Baianstovu 2012) and many other neoliberal welfare states (Lorenz 2006). This same logic is evident not only in welfare practice settings but also in the restructuring of social work education to meet systemic imperatives in the welfare and educational sectors (Wagner & Yee 2011). The incursion can be seen in the shift in social work's knowledge base from critical social science and the humanities to psychology and management; the reduction of educational quality to performance metrics and market demand; an increase in standardised testing at the expense of imparting critical analysis or dialogical learning; a focus on techniques at the expense of engaging and reflectively conversing with people; the increasing mediation of technology in teaching at the expense of face-to-face interaction; and the reduced autonomy of social work educators in having to comply with managerial systems of reporting and audit that leave little time for creative curricular development (Hanesworth 2017; Morley et al. 2017).

Stripped of everything else, the essence of deciding whether an action is guided by the lifeworld or the system lies in assessing to what degree others are treated as subjects in their own rights or as mere means to someone else's ends. For example, when a social worker is forced to use a manual that does not address the specific needs of a particular service user, the help takes shape not in the form of meeting the client's need but in trying to make the client's need fit into the help provided (Baianstovu 2012).

Discourse ethics on the road toward mutual understanding

Ideally, *communicative action* is a non-coercive means of carrying out integration processes, potentially involving everyone (every citizen or citizen-in-the-making) who, in this joint dialogical effort, can renew norms and values cooperatively through critically reflective and transparent processes (Habermas 1984b). It does so on the basis of respect for the diversity and individual life projects of the actors involved (Habermas 1995). That is why communicative action is of central importance for bridging norms and mitigating moral divides between groups (Habermas 1984b). As communicative action is applied in democratic practices, there is always a risk that the power relations underlying the complexity and diversity of views involved in different situations will not be satisfactorily explicated or problematised (Habermas 1995). A way of overcoming these difficulties or barriers to understanding in the lifeworld is what Habermas (1984b) calls *discourse ethics*.

Discourse ethics refers to basic rules that must be realised for a communicative situation to be trustworthy and just. The normative basis for this is that social integration and consensus in a democratic society should be characterised by mutually intelligible and open communication. However, achieving consensus across difference is never a simple process. In the usual course of conversation, any individual speaker's proposal(s) may be affirmed, partly modified, dismissed, or questioned by the other participants. According to Habermas (1984b), the ideal communicative situation depends on three basic criteria being met:

- *Truth claims.* The utterance must be true in the sense that what it refers to exists, i.e. that it can be observed or verified from all the lifeworld perspectives that the participating actors may hold.
- *Validity claims.* The utterance should actually consider the legitimate normative context to which it must apply.
- *Honesty claims.* The intent that the speaker manifests must be uttered with a certain degree of sincerity.

(Habermas 1984b, p. 188f)

The more these criteria can be met in each situation or practice, the greater the possibility is for communicative action to create a *consensus*. While Habermas sees communicative action informed by discourse ethics as a requisite of democratic citizenship, the implications for professional practice, and social work in particular, are instructive. As previously indicated, communicative action requires *reciprocity* and *equality*, which means striving to achieve horizontal power relations. As such, it is a way of consciously mitigating vertical power. It presupposes that every actor recognises every other actor as a speaking and listening subject, simultaneously, and not as speaking *or* listening in a vertical power relation. There is of course a sizeable, critical social work literature regarding the need to reduce, as much as practicable, power differentials between practitioners and service users (Fook 1993; Ferguson 2008). Habermas' theory helps illuminate the communicative dimension of such power relations, and the need to foster communicative practices oriented to practical dialogue rather than those aimed simply at control and compliance.

An equal communicative relation for Habermas is founded upon intersubjective reciprocity because as actors recognise each other intersubjectively, they can examine each other's validity claims and mutually criticise what is being said. This can only happen when everyone recognises that every single actor who speaks and listens is a member of a social group that he or she identifies with. In the case that the social group is defined categorically, i.e. by others in an asymmetric power relation, rather than by the participant him- or herself, normative agreements cannot take place, because integration only happens when the communicating parts mutually recognise each other, both as individuals and as collective beings (Habermas 1984b).

This is where democracy and communicative action reveals its extremely demanding character. Arguably, the recognition of the other as a social being is usually less complicated when the participants refer to and hail from the same social groups in an intersectional perspective (e.g. combinations of ethnicity, gender, nation, race, religion), and complicated when multidimensional differences are at stake.

When people reach mutual understanding, and consensus reached is based on people's identities rather than on categorisations and stereotypes, social change is promoted. And, when the actors in the interaction situation strive for an understanding of which social groups and categories other participants are identifying with as actors, the participants stand out as visible, real actors. They are not just individuals taking part in the interaction, but also the social groups to which every single one of them is referring. This creates the foundations on which the participants can enrich each other with knowledge about the collective identities. In the end, the norms and convictions that the participants are presenting in the interaction situation become visible.

The framework of discourse ethics, of course, cannot handle acute crisis or violent situations, because the emergency must be managed before the situation can pass into the domains of discourse ethics. In difficult communication situations, where people perceive each other as standing far apart and where strong conflicts of values seem inevitable, it can be tempting for actors to advance communication without involving their own lifeworld or moral convictions, feigning accommodation to achieve an advantage that would have been jeopardised by honesty. Such communication has no value as discourse ethics because the consensus achieved is superficial and instrumental, and hence invalid (Habermas 1998).

Discourse ethics can be applied when we want to understand what happens when we communicate face-to-face as well as via texts on paper or digitally, and when organisations and groups are involved. TCA connects the needs, the reasons and the methods for democratic participation at individual, group and societal levels. Ideally, all groups can participate in this communicative practice comprising governmental levels, public boards, welfare institutions and their clients, the average citizen, immigrants, researchers or – simply put, the entire population with its variety of functions, preferences and identities.

Discourse ethics demands recognition of the other both as an individual and a collective being. The recognition can be uncomplicated when the participants refer to the same social group, but most interactions in social work – especially when they are carried out under coercive frames – are characterised by multidimensional differences between the actors. Through communicative action and open-mindedness toward the identities and categories involved in the interaction situation, actors can receive a mutual understanding of who the participants are and what is at stake for each of them. By focusing on discourse ethics, the prerequisites for a communicative situation to function as a recourse are created. This stimulates social change, inclusion and democracy.

Lifeworld, system and discourse ethics in social work practice and education

Where is the need for discourse ethics (truth, validity and sincerity) to be found in the communicative practices of social work? On the basis of the research referred to at the beginning of this chapter, it appears that social workers view their ideal mode of action as being horizontal and communicative, while they stress that, in practice, their freedom of action (discretion) is extremely limited. Despite system incursions, social workers are still educated to establish communicative contact with the clients' lifeworld, attempting to achieve an interaction situation where intersubjective communication is possible (Baianstovu 2012). The prerequisite for such a communicative situation to arise is that the social worker is empathetic and open to getting to know the other's lifeworld.

When social workers refer to *genuine* communicative situations, they describe situations resembling and coinciding with *discourse ethics* (Baianstovu 2012). These situations occur whenever the client and the social worker achieve mutual understanding of what the problem is and how it could be solved but in difficult communicative situations where inaccuracy, value conflict or manipulation prevail, these criteria cannot be fulfilled. For example, in terms of *truth claims*, if the subject is abuse, participants first need to agree on whether it has taken place or not. When the social worker and the client(s) agree on the truth, namely the verifiable facts that a specific action took place, the next challenge for the participants is whether they can agree in an analogous manner on *validity claims*, concerning how the action should be ethically valued. This raises the question of whether the action represents a violation against shared (or shareable) norms by all those affected. In situations in which social workers and clients take different stands about the value of the action, for instance if a client claims the rightfulness of an act of physical abuse, discourse ethics – based on consensus – will fail and the possibility of coercion emerges. If through conversation, however, norms (and their consequences) can be agreed upon by all parties then non-coercive, practical action is more likely to ensue (Habermas 1991). This will only occur, though, if concomitant *honesty claims*, based on mutual trust and sincerity in reaching consensus about truth and validity, are likewise established. If one of the actors is lying, another foundational premise for discourse ethics fails and any agreement reached is invalidated.

Basic obstacles to discourse ethics

The social workers interviewed in the research undertaken by the lead author explained that often the conditions needed to reach mutual understanding are lacking because one or all criteria are unfulfilled. The reason for the lack of communicative action can be found in a set of conditions that together constitute the interaction situation: (1) the client and the environment of the client, (2) the social workers' knowledge and attitudes, (3) administration and local politics.

The first obstacle for discourse ethics arises when clients, for example, invoke moral arguments to defend violence and inequality within the family, or by other arguments, and do not have, or at least do not appear to have, the capability of understanding when they are acting harmfully toward their children, spouses or others.

The second obstacle arises through the social workers' own shortcomings, in terms of their own prejudices and lack of knowledge about the situation of the clients, be it socioeconomical, racial, ethnic, cultural, religious, functional, or sexual factors, or a mix of them. The challenges of dealing with increasing cultural diversity and complexity are mirrored in social work education and must be addressed. One of the authors of this chapter has developed a pedagogical sequence aiming at understanding diversity as a source of knowledge in communicative situations in the lifeworld, comprising workshops and lectures. It provides a collection of experiences including conflicts between worldviews in the lifeworld, but also conflicts between the logics of the lifeworld and the system. The first workshop builds upon the presupposition that the variety of students' life experiences and the emotions connected to them contain rich material for developing knowledge by communication. The workshop theme is injustice and it is carried out in the following steps:

1 Individual work: Think of an injustice in personal and professional situations that you or someone else have been subject to or have committed. Describe the situation and the emotions attached to it on post-it notes. Put them on the walls. Silently read them.
2 Groupwork (4–6): Choose one situation and discuss it: What made it especially interesting? What kind of problem is it? Can exclusion/inclusion be identified in it based on nation, ethnicity, race, religion or something else? What would you have done in the situation?
3 Whole group discussion.
4 Finally: Did we treat the situations in accordance with truth? Were we able to approach various normative validity claims? Were our discussions honest and sincere?

The workshop is followed up by lectures about social justice, equality and democracy and a final workshop aiming at practicing the discourse ethics in communicative situations. Here students debate difficult themes such as the complex relations between racism and diverse perceptions about family violence and crime and how to reach mutual understanding about social change in difficult situations in casework, groupwork and community work.

The third and most important obstacle to discourse ethics lies in the administrative system. The prescriptive *form of the work* makes it increasingly difficult to obtain knowledge about the lifeworld of the client. This can be related to strictly formalised procedures, such as time factors, communication tools, treatment options, and other issues. Furthermore, the social worker might not have the necessary time to understand the client, and vice versa. Pure linguistic divides must also be considered. Cognitive and intellectual capacities due to differences in schooling, education and other experiences are also factors (Baianstovu 2012).

The obstacles to communication are framed here as a conflict between the lifeworld vs. system, empirically experienced as professional knowledge vs. the rigidity of NPM.

If social services are to contribute to the consensual integration of a just and deliberative society, social workers need to strive for equality rather than sameness in all fields of practice. This means that social workers must meet different people in different ways to achieve the same goal. However, the homogenising, top-down style of the system logic, becomes an obstacle to communication in the lifeworld, making it difficult to meet the clients' increasingly varying needs. As we said, at the same time as the lifeworld and the system are separating, each of them is also becoming increasingly complex. In practical terms, this means that as the demand of communicative action increases, the possibility for putting it into action in the daily work decreases. The dominance of the system logics threatens to destroy the socially transformative and progressive potential of communicative action. Nevertheless, education, including social work education, is one modest platform for promoting critical analysis and the fostering of alternative practices and policy ideas that might translate back from the lifeworld into the system if a public consensus in their favour can be achieved.

For social workers reflecting on their own professional situation, discourse ethics and the obstacles to it, helps us to understand the conflicts between themselves, the logic and role of administrative bodies, as well as conflicts between practitioners and clients.

Conclusion

Despite the apparent banality of Habermas' discourse ethics, it offers the possibility of a critical analysis of complex communicative situations and knowledge of what is at stake for every actor. Social work education, drawing upon Habermasian thinking, could play an important role in sensitising future practitioners to these different modes of communication at play in practice situations, and their consequences. At the very least, the student or practicing social worker can draw benefit from the key concepts in the TCA as thinking tools in their daily duties, be it in their studies or practical work when planning and analysing an interaction situation. Awareness about the conditions of communication is a vital ingredient in establishing communication situations that are characterised by practical understanding and consensus-making, even when the actors present are initially distant from each other, and where the cultural complexity might seem overwhelming. The obstacles to communicative action in the social services and its role in the education of practitioners are many, nevertheless Habermas' TCA provokes possibilities for emancipative practice that social workers, in dialogue with service users, can productively scrutinise, trial, embrace, reject or trial again.

Notes

1 At the same time, a social work critique of Habermas' work is made by Garrett (2018) regarding its insufficient explication of power relations in the lifeworld. The critique mirrors a discussion from the 1980s between the French philosopher Michel Foucault and Habermas himself (e.g. Kelly 1994).
2 It was originally published in Germany 1981.

References (in English)

Baianstovu, R. (2012): *Diversity as a Challenge for Democracy. Doctoral dissertation, Social Work*, Örebro: Örebro University.
Baianstovu, R. (2017): *Honour. Honour related Violence, Oppression and Social Work*. Lund: Studentlitteratur.
Baianstovu, R. (2018): 'Communication and Power in Complex Communicative Situations in Social Work', in B. Anders & Källström, Å. (eds.) *Relationships in Social Work at the Borderland of Profession and Person*. Stockholm: Liber, 76–90.
Benhabib, S. (2002): *The Claims of Culture. Equality and Diversity in the Global Era*. Princeton, NJ: Princeton University Press.
Bohman, J. & Regh, W. (2017) 'Jürgen Habermas', in E.N. Zalta (ed.) *The Stanford Encyclopedia of Philosophy* (Fall Edition). https://plato.stanford.edu/archives/fall2017/entries/habermas/
Brookfield, S. (2005) *The Power of Critical Theory: Liberating Adult Learning and Teaching*. New York: Wiley.
Castells, M. (2009): *Network Society. The Power of Identity*. New Jersey: Wiley-Blackwell.
Crossley, N. (1996): *Intersubjectivity*. London: Sage.
Crossley, N. (2007) *Intersubjectivity. The Fabric of Social Becoming*. Newbury Park, CA: Sage.
D'Entrèves, M. & Benhabib, S. (ed.) (1996): *Habermas and the Unfinished Project of Modernity*. Cambridge: Polity Press.

Durkheim, É. (1893/1984): *The Division of Labor in Society*. Glencoe, IL: Free Press.
Durkheim, É. (1912/1965): *The Elementary Forms of Religious Life*. New York: Free Press.
Ewert, G. (1991). 'Habermas and Education: A Comprehensive Overview of the Influence of Habermas in Educational Literature', *Review of Educational Research*, 61(3): 345–378.
Ferguson, I. (2008). *Reclaiming Social Work: Challenging Neoliberalism and Promoting Social Justice*. London: Sage.
Fook, J. (1993) *Radical Casework: A Theory of Practice*. St Leonards: Allen & Unwin.
Garrett, P. M. (2018): 'Thinking with Jürgen Habermas', in P.M. Garret (ed.) *Social Work and Social Theory*. Chicago, IL: Polity Press, 153–166.
Gray, M. & Lutan, T. (2008): 'Practical Mysticism, Habermas, and Social Work', *Journal of Social Work*, 8(2): 149–162. Los Angeles, CA, London, New Delhi and Singapore: Sage Publications.
Habermas, J. (1991): *Moral Consciousness and Communicative Action*. Cambridge, MA: MIT Press.
Habermas, J. (1962/1989): *The Structural Transformation of the Public Sphere*. Cambridge: Polity Press.
Habermas, J. (1971): *Knowledge and Human Interests*. Boston: Beacon Press.
Habermas, J. (1984a): *The Theory of Communicative Action* (Part I. GB). Cambridge: Polity Press.
Habermas, J. (1984b): *The Theory of Communicative Action* (Part II. GB). Cambridge: Polity Press.
Habermas, J. (1995) *Diskurs, rätt och demokrati: politisk-filosofiska texter*. Göteborg: Daidalos (*Discourse, Justice and Democracy: Political-Philosophical texts*. Gothenburg: Daidalos).
Habermas, J. (1996): *Between Facts and Norms*. Cambridge, MA: The MIT Press.
Habermas, J. (2008): *Between Naturalism and Religion*. Cambridge: Polity Press.
Hagen, N., Lundin, S., O'Dell, T. & Petersén, Å. (2012) 'For Better or for Worse: Lifeworld, System and Family Caregiving for a Chronic Genetic Disease', *Culture Unbound*, 4: 537–557.
Hanesworth, C. (2017). 'Neoliberal Influences on American Higher Education and the Consequences for Social Work Programmes', *Critical and Radical Social Work*, 5(1): 41–57.
Hayes, D. & Houston, S. (2007). '"Lifeworld", "System" and Family Group Conferences: Habermas's Contribution to Discourse in Child Protection', *British Journal of Social Work*, 37(6): 987–1006.
Houston, S. (2008) 'Communication, Recognition and Social Work: Aligning the Ethical Theories of Habermas and Honneth', *The British Journal of Social Work*, 39(7): 1274–1290.
Houston, S. (2010) 'Further Reflections on Habermas's Contribution to Discourse in Child Protection: An Examination of Power in Social Life', *The British Journal of Social Work*, 40(6): 1736–1753.
Houston, S. (2013): 'Jürgen Habermas', in Gray, M. & Webb, S. A. (eds.) *Social Work Theories and Methods*. London: Sage Publications, 13–24.
IFSW, (2014). 'Global Definition of Social Work', *International Federation of Social Workers*. www.ifsw.org/what-is-social-work/global-definition-of-social-work/ (Accessed 9/06/2019).
Kant, I. (1785/2009): *Groundwork of the Metaphysics of Morals*. New York: HarperCollins.
Kellner, D., (1996) 'Jurgen Habermas', in Kuper, A. & Kuper, J. (eds.) *The Social Science Encyclopedia*. London/New York: Routledge. https://pages.gseis.ucla.edu/faculty/kellner/essays/habermas.pdf
Kelly, M. (1994): *Critique and Power. Recasting the Foucault/Habermas Debate*. Cambridge, MA: MIT-Press.
Lorenz, W. (1994): *Social Work in a Changing Europe*. London: Routledge.
Lorenz, W. (2006): *Perspectives on European Social Work*. Farmington Hills, MI: Barbara Budrich Publishers.
Lorenz, W. (2016) 'Rediscovering the Social Question', *European Journal of Social Work*, 19(1): 4–17.
Mezirow, J. (2009) 'An Overview on Transformative Learning', in K. Illeris (ed.) *Contemporary Theories of Learning*. London and New York: Routledge, 90–105.
Morley, C., Macfarlane, S. & Ablett, P. (2017) 'The Neoliberal Colonisation of Social Work Education: A Critical Analysis and Practices for Resistance', *Advances in Social Work and Welfare Education*, 19(2): 25–40.
Rode, N. (2016): 'Defining Social Work is a Neverending Story', *European Journal of Social Work*, 20: 64–75, 2017.
Rogowski, S. (2010): *Social Work. The Rise and Fall of a Profession*. Cambridge: Policy Press.
Rossiter, A. B. (1997): 'A Perspective on Critical Social Work', *Journal of Progressive Human Services*, 7(2): 23–41.
Torres, C. & Morrow, R. (1998) 'Paulo Freire, Jürgen Habermas, and Critical Pedagogy: Implications for Comparative Education', *Melbourne Studies in Education*, 39(2): 1–20.
Wagner, A., & Yee, J. (2011). 'Anti-Oppression in Higher Education: Implicating Neo-Liberalism', *Canadian Social Work Review/Revue Canadienne De Service Social*, 28(1): 89–105. Retrieved from http://www.jstor.org/stable/41658835

WEF. (2018) 'The Global Gender Gap Report 2018', *World Economic Forum*, Geneva, Switzerland. www3.weforum.org/docs/WEF_GGGR_2018.pdf (Accessed 2/8/2019).

Welton, M. R. (2005). *Designing the Just Learning Society: A Critical Inquiry*. Leicester: Niace.

Zuckerman, P. (2007). 'Atheism: Contemporary Rates and Patterns', in M. Martin (ed.) *The Cambridge Companion to Atheism*. Cambridge: Cambridge University Press, 47–68.

References (in Swedish)

Carleheden, M. (1996): *Det andra moderna*. Göteborg: Daidalos.

Habermas, J. (1983): *Moralbewusstsein und Kommunikatives Handeln*. Frankfurt am Main: Suhrkamp.

Habermas, J. (1968/1984): '"Technik und Wissenschaft als "Ideologi"', in *Den rationella övertygelsen*. Stockholm: Akademilitteratur.

Habermas, J. (1998): 'Wahrheit und Rectfertigung', in *Deutsche Zeitschrift für Philosophie*.

Habermas, J. (1996a): 'Über den internen Zusammenhang von Rechtsstat und Demokratie', in *Die Einbesiehung des Anderen*. Frankfurt am Main: Suhrkamp.

Restorff, M. (1997): *Die Politische Theorie von Jürgen Habermas*. Marburg: Tectum Verlag.

38
Alain Touraine
The politics of collective action

Goetz Ottmann
AUSTRALIAN COLLEGE OF APPLIED PSYCHOLOGY, SYDNEY, AUSTRALIA

Carolyn Noble
AUSTRALIAN COLLEGE OF APPLIED PSYCHOLOGY, SYDNEY, AUSTRALIA

Introduction

This chapter explores Alain Touraine's work on 'new' social movements and how social change occurs. Briefly, Touraine's work focuses on how people come together to challenge and alter cultural and socio-political boundaries of a social, institutional or political system deemed to be discriminatory or oppressive. In the text below, we provide a brief historical background to his opus before delineating core elements of Touraine's theory of new social movements, his social change strategy and how his work can be applied to contemporary social work practice and education. We do this based on our experiences as practitioners and activists, in Australia and Europe with a view to similar socio-political conditions elsewhere. We argue that Touraine's social movement theory can be used to:

a. Develop and articulate an agenda for social work in post-industrial societies that contributed to an emancipatory social work practice;
b. Deploy a socio-cultural critical lens that analyses social change in terms of equality, self-realisation, quality of life, emancipation, human rights and individuals as actors;
c. Describe fundamental social changes that sparked significant developments in community and activist social work; and
d. Foster a teaching philosophy and critical pedagogy that is able to enhance individuals to become activists for a democratic public life and agents of hope for the future.

(Touraine, 2000, p. 284)

Regarded as a maverick by his Marxist colleagues, Touraine wanted to change social norms 'from within', by concerted social action, relegating institutional politics to a secondary and subordinate role. As an influential theorist of social movements and social change, Touraine's work can shape the teaching and practice of community development and social action and frame a critical pedagogy to advance a more progressive, transformative social work education and practice.

Who is Alain Touraine?

Alain Touraine is still regarded as the most influential writer, researcher and one of the most widely read sociologists on 'new social movements' today. He was born in 1925 in Hermanville-sur-Mer, a small coastal village in France's Normandy region – one of the main landing sites of allied forces in 1944. He was 20 at the end of WWII and would have experienced first-hand the havoc that fascism wrought in Europe. This experience had a lasting influence on his work. He completed his studies at the École Normale Supérieure, a prestigious Parisian 'ivy-league' university traditionally associated with a career in the public service. Reflecting on his formative years at university as a period during which he became aware of a massive gap between the way the social sciences explained social events and the actual world around him, he says

> I discovered in becoming an adult that between the social and academic world in which I was reared and the reality of the world itself there was nothing in common ... my society ... smelled to me like a bag of garbage ... But at the same time, I forced myself to be forever conscious of being responsible, devoted to intellectual work, and to knowledge as to that which is beyond society and which can vindicate it.
> *(Touraine – Reflections on Sociology's Raison d'Être (1981), cited in Kerr, 1997, p. 72)*

Experiencing the actual world was important to Touraine. After leaving the École Normale Supérieure, he worked in the mines in northern France, spent time in Hungary to learn, from the outside and inside, about the transition to socialism, and he studied the solidarity movement while in Chile (Litmanen, 2010, p. 229). He witnessed the wild and unruly student movements in France and across the western world (1968–1970) and the popular resistance to military coups in Latin America. These experiences and events shaped his intellectual endeavours. In 1950, he became a professor of history. Subsequently he held numerous senior academic and research positions. In 1970, he founded the Centre for Studies on Social Movements and in 1981, the Centre of Sociological Analysis and Intervention (CADIS), an important research hub that still exists today (currently under the leadership of well-known sociologist Michel Wieviorka).

This work led to three decades of research dedicated to the study of social movements. Touraine's pioneering role in sociology is based on his ideas on how history is made by people, especially people engaged in collective action, thus giving social movements a central role in the workings of society. In seeking to discover the conditions that can produce social relations in which freedom, equality, self-realisation and support for human rights prevail rather than repression or subjugation, he drew attention to the impact powerful identity-based collectives had on social change. By focusing squarely on identity and cultural politics, his ideas on new social movements introduced a new element largely overlooked by other sociologists. He argued that it is possible to understand social conflict through both the objective and subjective analysis of social movements, which heralded him as a courageous and innovative thinker willing to plough new ground both conceptually and methodologically (Touraine, 1980, 1988). Touraine's work is important and, although controversial, and often criticised, few academic commentators, including those in social work, would deny that Touraine's work on social movements was and is still highly influential.

Touraine's social movement theory

Backdrop

The 1960s and 1970s was the period when corporations in the 'developed world' began to relocate their industrial production to Eastern Europe and increasingly to Asia; at the same time they were shifting from an industrial to a post-industrial or, what Touraine (1980) called, 'programmed' society. As a result the traditional powerbase of the 'old' worker-led, labour movements was undermined and was becoming politically and industrially powerless in the face of this industrial transformation (Touraine, 1980). Touraine was worried that the fading from the political scene of the old workers' movement would lead us back to an era of 'domination of empires and the reinforcement of social control, of propaganda, and of repression' (Touraine, 1980, p. 8); still a worry today that many progressive scholars share in light of the growing technological surveillance and the political popularity of the extreme right in various western societies.

For Touraine, the key question was (and still is), if the class-based conflict between the workers' movement and moneyed elites that dominated industrial societies (and gave rise to the welfare state) was waning, what would take its place? What kind of movements would emerge in a post-industrial society that could replace the workers' movement and ensure that democratic freedoms would survive? Who would be the next actors that would challenge the state and vested interests within this new political constellation (Touraine, 1981, p. 24)? To address these questions Touraine's analysis moved away from class-based, anti-capitalist struggles toward new social movements whose anti-system and, more specifically, counter-cultural or identity-based struggles were emerging as the new key actors in social change activism. Indeed, he presented social movements as *the* central actor in creating change by drawing attention to the impact of 'new social movements' (Litmanen, 2007, p. 4). He did this when outbreaks of civil unrest were deemed a symptom of the alienated masses acting out of control or as pocketed reactions to structural changes in society and were, therefore, considered tangential to the social and political struggles emerging at the time.

New social movements

Significantly, Touraine regarded the new social movements as important actors at the heart of society itself. Such movements, he argued, play a key role in the workings of a functioning society, and understanding these social movements and the social conflict they generate would explain how social activists can mobilise societal norms toward a desired social change. For Touraine, social conflict ranged from low-level collective routines, pressure group actions and political party conflict to large-scale social movements, most evident during the 1960s and 1970s. The idea of individuals banding together in collective action to protest perceived injustices was not a new one. However, what was new was that the civil unrest of the 1960s and 1970s focused on issues beyond social class and on the mobilisation of resources. New social movements, Touraine argued, asserted the significance of social divisions based on gender, sexuality, race, ethnicity, age and ability (Mullaly, 2010; Noble, 2007) and their role in maintaining oppressive social relations (Touraine, 1980, 1985, 1988).

It was these movements that he regarded as the most important and influential form of social change (1985, 1988). The rise of civil protest from feminist, environmentalist, anti-nuclear, gay and lesbian rights, or life-style/health/consumer movements were, according to his analysis, potent expressions of marginalised voices challenging an increasingly controlling technocratic state and assuming a new agency in civil society. It was these new socio-cultural confrontations with civil society that would overturn exclusionist and discriminatory practices by inventing and instituting new norms, new institutions, new social, political and cultural practices that reflect the new actors' ideology and life-style politics. To be effective, social change activism needed to shift away from relations of production and the state to civil society and culture (Touraine, 1988). New movement activism was aimed to re-invigorate and re-charge civil society, creating the capacity to challenge the state as well as influential elites. In his analysis, these popular movements, located in civil society and bypassing the state, emerged to fight against the pervasiveness of neo-liberalism, political and cultural imperialism, patriarchy and colonialism that had become, in the 1990s, more demonstrably evident in undermining the very basis of a socially just and equal society (Gray & Webb, 2013; Noble, 2007). Concerned with the concept of a 'greater good', these collective actors challenged social injustice, inequity and a-moral control by creating safeguards against more authoritarian, violent forms of social conflicts which, according to Touraine were always just lying below the surface of modern life. Change would come about through negotiated settlement rather than revolution.

Touraine's work on new social movements became the focal point of the hope of the political left in search of an actor that would continue the struggle against the power of vested interests and institutionalised inequality once the class-based and union-supported activism lost its currency. His work was also influential in the social sciences academy where the study of social movements heralded a new area of social theory scholarship.

Coincidentally, Touraine's work on social justice and resistance against structural oppression was also evident in critical social work, emerging at this time (see Bailey & Brake, 1975; Moreau, 1979). Critical social work posited a commitment to work toward social justice, equality for those oppressed and marginalised in society. It argued, and continues to argue, for a commitment to work alongside the oppressed and marginalised; to question the status quo and dominant assumptions and beliefs and analyse power relations that serve to oppress populations in society (Gray & Webb, 2013). Importantly, its orientation is toward emancipatory personal and social change. Its practice also provides an important source of resistance to neo-liberalism's disdain for democracy, the social good and the social contract (Mullaly, 2010).

Social change: how does it come about?

The most challenging questions for critical thinkers to address are: How does social change come about? What are the key conflicts that shape the cultural fabric of our society (i.e. conflicts around the social choices that we believe we have and the choices we believe are realistic)? Who are the actors and what is the desired outcome? Here, Touraine's work goes a long way to answer these questions. Inevitably, he argues, change is possible when the struggle for societal, cultural and symbolic rights, and recognition by marginalised or *subjugated voices* (Touraine's term) comes into conflict with the established sets of relations, institutions, cultural signs and symbols, and a resolution is needed to avoid societal conflict or break-down.

Collective action is how excluded and marginalised voices find their societal and political expression and make their demands on the cultural and social fabric. He did not regard the state as *the* fundamental driving force of social, cultural and political relations but civil society and the market (Litmanen, 2007). His fight was against social determinism. For Touraine, social structures are not fixed or immovable, but fluid and contradictory; held together by the dominant 'rules of the game' (e.g. meta-social forces). These forces are many – from class power, educational, economic, cultural, symbolic, historical and information systems that make up social life. The battle, if you like, is for actors to influence these meta-forces, infusing them with new societal norms and cultural patterns.

Touraine's actors have the capacity to act freely and responsibly, to be innovators and be able to resist forces and pressure. They are creators of their own environment in the struggle for freedom (2000, p. 909). They are autonomous individuals acting in concert to broaden the field of acceptable social and cultural norms and collective choices. Actors 'are not defined by their conformity to rules and norms, but by a relation to themselves, by their capacity to constitute themselves as actors capable of changing their environment and of reinforcing their autonomy' (Touraine, 2000, p. 902). He called this process *historicity*.

Historicity for Touraine is the ability of actors to initiate and shape their own future; to gain control over cultural patterns as well as transform these patterns (Touraine, 1985, 1988). For Touraine, new social movements transform society by spreading and legitimising ideas and values in the practices of everyday life. They are assigned the role of producing a social identity (e.g. LGBTI+; Strong women, Black Lives Matter) that is potent enough to galvanise the masses to agitate for social change. They must avoid being dominated by party political interests if they are to maintain this role because the compromises that underpin institutionalised politics undermine a movement's cultural transformative capacity. What is essential is the idea that by assuming control of historicity, the social movement, through its conflictual action, impacts on the whole of society, and shapes and structures it in line with activists' demands (Wieviorka, 2016). He shares the idea with Marx's conflict theory in that there is always a struggle and divergence of interest in which the stakes are not goods but identities.

In summary, then, for Touraine the aims of social movements to change society are cultural rather than directly political; they operate in civil society rather than institutionalised politics; they are concerned with life-style and quality of life issues rather than political and economic issues of distributive justice; and they draw on and embrace the creativity of the actor, seeing this as a central ingredient for re-imagining society (Touraine, 1988). So how do these actors create a movement strong enough to press for social change?

Sociological intervention as part of social change strategy

We glean more about how social change can occur from Touraine's important and possibly more controversial work – his 'sociology of action'. He argued that at this time in history the most important task of sociology is to study how society is being produced. According to Litmanen, Touraine's work was inspired by the ambition to follow Marx's dictum 'that the reason for understanding the world is to change it' (2007, p. 3). Touraine wants a fairer, more just and democratically egalitarian world for all.

Touraine argued that this is best done by focusing on the various conflicts that underpin the production of society and that shape most social choices available to us. Society is a product of a conflict or constant negotiation of competing historical actors linked to a cultural model (patriarchy, liberalism, capitalism, class system). Because of this, he argued, it is impossible for researchers to be 'detached'. Rather, he assigned an active role to the researcher; on the premise that it is better to be involved than merely to observe, theorise and comment. More precisely, Touraine stated that involvement, theorisation and comment ought to be interrelated and informing each other. Involvement should be prior to theorisation and comment, and those who are on the front line of conflict must be actively involved as theorisers and commentators on their actions. In this way, theorisation and comment could be harnessed to sharpen social action, assisting in the development of strategies and in the identification of overarching concerns (Touraine, 1985, 1988).

Touraine saw the role of social research as critical to this process. For him, the role of the social researcher is to assist social movements to break down dominant norms, imaginaries, or ideologies and informing new social norms and cultural practices by means of a 'sociological intervention' or 'sociology of action'. This intervention consisted of several methodical strategies. The first stage is to invite movement actors to meet with key stakeholders, ranging from allied movements to civil servants, politicians, to corporate leaders. The objective here is to encourage actors to engage with representatives of different perspectives of the struggle to learn more about these perspectives. The co-facilitator/researcher would then assist movement actors to reflect on and analyse these interactions.

In the second phase, the co-facilitator/researcher co-creates with movement actors hypotheses that might lead to deeper insights of the conflicts and their role within it. A strategy here is to encourage movement actors to invite interlocutors into the group, who confront the group with alternative analyses – ultimately aiming at higher levels of abstraction of the conflict that might facilitate the identification of a common aim and an alliance of likeminded movements. Confronting the group and its many players, as well as possible opponents, brings out the field of their struggle. The researcher also presents the group with facts and ideas that are external to the group and challenges the group on its aim, direction and forward proposals. The co-facilitator/researcher supports the actors to examine how social alternatives emerge, how they are being articulated, and how they are responded to by allies as well as adversaries (Touraine, 1980, 1988).

This co-facilitation approach is likened to a form of consciousness-raising analogical to the women's movement's desire to make 'the personal political'. The co-facilitator/researcher seeks to assist actors to analyse what direction they should take, what the main problems are, what key conflicts need to be addressed, and what choices need to be made. Furthermore, Touraine hoped that the approach would assist participants to overcome phases of poor morale and self-confidence, facilitating a return to action (Touraine, 1980). From a research perspective, Touraine argued that this sociological intervention allowed researchers to penetrate the ideological discursive layers of collective behaviour, allowing them to observe the actions and reactions of participants in response to the wider contested space in which collective action takes place (Touraine, 1980). The group's life is analogous to the movement's activism. Understanding this process and being a co-facilitator gives an insight as to how social change activism unfolds and the important role an insider can play.

Implications for social work education and practice: application to collective, social action education

The significance of Touraine's theory of social movements, we argue, lies in its capacity to bridge the gaps between social activism, critical social work practice and social work education (see, for example, Baines, 2017). Touraine's work offers a new analytical lens to critical social workers, bringing into focus and illuminating the social conflicts that underpin contemporary struggles around welfare provision and service users' struggle to get their voices heard and their needs met against competing socio-cultural discourses (see, for example, Cherrier & Murray, 2002; Dowse, 2001; Martin, 2001; Pease, 2013).

For Touraine, social movements cannot be separated from the representation of society as a social system in which there is always competition for control over cultural norms (1988). This struggle over cultural values, norms and ideals occurs against the backdrop of older social conflicts whose mediation gave rise to current social institutions (Touraine, 1984). Shifting from a functional analysis of social systems to a study of social conflict at a cultural level, Touraine enables critical practitioners to make sense of the way these conflicts shape social norms and ideals, changing the way they think about their impact, for example, on the environment, the economic system, gender and/or sexual identification. Touraine enables us to see the features of the modern welfare state as the result of a social conflict that shaped society in a way that created a social consensus around their desirability and explains why the welfare state is under pressure from conservative collective forces.

Community activism, social change and social work

Community action remains a crucial vehicle for resistance to reduce current forms of oppression (Ife, 2013; Kenny & Connors, 2017) and continues to be an integral part of the social work curriculum and practice in Australia and elsewhere (ASWEAS, 2012; IASSW, 2004). Commonly it requires work at both the individual and societal level to challenge the way social systems produce and reproduce disadvantage, oppression and subordination, employing social markers such as class, gender, 'race' and ethnicity, age, disability and sexual orientation.

Touraine was strongly opposed to neo-liberalism (and globalisation) as it fragments society and fosters individualism. Like critical social work, he suggested a new focus on human rights is needed and a *new* social movement activism toward social change. Touraine's work on new social movements was regarded by Mullaly as a practice area where critical (or what Mullaly terms 'structural') social work could work collectively outside the state apparatus and against the severe discrepancies of wealth and power, the domination of economics and politics by giant corporations, the dependence on industrial production that pollutes the environment, and the patriarchy, racism and ageism that oppress particular groups in society (Mullaly, 2010, p. 332). Social advocacy involves social agents working collectively in various ways on a common project that emerges out of dissatisfaction with a form of life by seeking and promoting alternative social and political life choices (Baines, 2017; Morley et al., 2014; Mullaly, 2010). It provides a response to the lament that social work, despite its 100-year history, has done nothing to change the structural inequality causing the oppression of people who are considered outside the dominant cultural and social norms defining privilege. As a result, Touraine's concern with the politics of values and norms helps us to crack open social work's paternalist, pathology-focused discourses.

Touraine's work on collective action harbours the promise that all individuals and groups can develop a platform to speak for themselves, in their own voice and ultimately have that voice accepted as authentic and legitimate. Touraine leads us to a new epistemological premise (Powell, 2001, p. 9) that encourages us to celebrate differences. This premise forces social workers to construct their practice in a *socially inclusive* way that is grounded in social work's more critical analyses. Reflexivity and reciprocity in social relations are encouraged, so too are respect for difference and support for the inclusion of multiple subject positions such as indigenous peoples, women, children, lesbians and gay men, ethnic groupings and multicultural voices previously defined as outside the dominant discourse. Consequentially these marginalised communities are encouraged to take on a social activist platform for themselves (Touraine, 1988).

By calling for an emancipatory politics that frees people from dogma and authorisation control, we can directly ascertain that his work on social movements helps community activists see that large-scale change in social values and norms, cultural practices, law and policy is indeed possible. Although protests can work informally to improve living conditions, environmental justice, affordable housing, etc., in the main, social change groups can be strategically effective if they form part of more general, overarching social movements such as the women's movement, the peace and environmental movements, trade union and labour movements, gay and lesbian rights movements and human and animal rights movements. These movements have played a significant role is securing the presence of a social justice agenda in many countries this century (Noble, 2007).

Touraine's sociology of intervention is also analogous with how social workers involved in community development and advocacy organise and reflect on strategies and action for social and political change. Community development workers work alongside and with disaffected populations. They engage in self and group reflection as a continuous process to assess effectiveness and strength of the action to achieve the desired change (Kenny & Connors, 2017). Community work is much more than 'just doing it'; it demands a praxis that involves a constant state of doing, learning and critical reflection so each stage informs the others and the three 'effectively become one' (Ife, 2013, p. 304). Touraine's de-integrating the activist subject parallels Freire's notion of 'conscientisation', albeit through social movements. It is a process by which theory and practice are built simultaneously. The worker and the community are actively encouraged to engage in this reflection during the whole process of engagement in the action. The worker is not detached but plays many roles; one key role is to bring critical connections with local and structural issues to help develop innovative ideas for the group to explore (Ife, 2013).

Consciousness-raising is central to community development and is an important part of the process (Kenny & Connors, 2017; Ife, 2013). Engaging in reflection and critical questioning of the action for the purpose of raising people's level of consciousness to reflect on their own situation and the oppressive structures and discourses that impact on their lives, enables such action to lead to social change. In this sense, self-reflection is crucial as it helps social work activists to avoid slipping back into a non-committal state of acquiescence maintaining the tension between the commitment to social change amid the multiple demands of everyday life.

For Touraine, social action campaigns require specific human attributes such as: the courage to challenge powerful vested groups and risk defeat; commitment and perseverance to see the campaign through; the acumen to adapt and respond creatively to changing circumstances; and the capacity to cooperate and draw strength from others closely associated with the campaign (1980, 1988). Individual campaigns form a key activity to bring about specific societal change outside mainstream political channels and institutions for socially marginalised values and ideas (i.e. social justice).

The scholarship of new social movement activism also brought new tactics and strategies to community development and social action. For example, centralised systems of welfare were challenged and replaced with spontaneous, decentralised grassroots action and organisation. These alternative services and organisations (such as women's refuges, welfare rights groups, rape crisis centres, LGBTI+ associations, Alcoholics Anonymous and prisoners' support groups, etc.) sprung up as responses from disaffected peoples and their ongoing struggle for redistribution of power at all levels, including their own destiny, identity and political and cultural power (Cho, 2010, 2013; Martin, 2001; Mullaly, 2010). Their success also depended on building coalitions and working together for larger political change in the belief that single-issue activism is more effective when shared with other groups seeking to change social and cultural norms or create an entirely different social order or some aspects of that order (Kenny & Connors, 2017; Mullaly, 2010).

In adapting Touraine's thesis and its adoption in community development and social work activism, we can identify several strategies that are useful for a critical practice. They include:

1 Being located within civil society as a method to generate social capital for disaffected peoples and strengthen social cohesion;
2 Prioritising social norms, culture and structure in the analysis of social problems – rather than individual pathologies;
3 Developing egalitarian, democratic interaction and decision making;

4   Redistributing resources more equitably and sustainably (Healy, 2000, p. 240);
5   Embracing complexity, choice, difference and respect (Kenny & Connors, 2017);
6   Promoting collective development and adoption of strategies that challenge oppressive structures (Pease, 2000) and democratise access to human service;
7   Exploring the role of the social worker in activist practice;
8   Focusing on empowerment and community autonomy, thus seeking independence from the state rather than state power (Mullaly, 2010);
9   Suggesting that actors on the front line of conflict must be actively involved as theorisers and commentators on their actions; and
10 Embracing a practice that includes a global and local analysis.

(Noble, 2007; Dominelli, 2012)

In using Touraine's work, Noble (2007) characterises social action as using either oppositional or confrontational tactics. In doing so, social action groups claim a moral superiority of their position over those espoused by their opponents or claim the congruence of their goals with key social values such as justice, participatory democracy, environmentalism, human rights, aestheticism or conservation. Furthermore, the achievement of such goals by progressive activists (including critical social workers) will involve social action groups (organised formally or informally) working between and across time and place to achieve social change.

Touraine, critical pedagogy and social work education

Touraine paradoxically supports the purpose of higher education (although a conservative institution) in its capacity 'to enhance individuals to become Subjects of their own personal life-project' (2000, p. 273). What he means by this Subject-hood is not capitulation to liberal individualism or becoming mindless consumers but, rather, cultivating the capacity to become activists for a democratic and pluralistic public life in which 'the Other enjoys the same freedom' (2000, p. 284) as we do.

In terms of a critical pedagogy, Touraine's work helps us to recognise that, while power pervades pedagogy, 'the inequalities of power and cultural differences between lecturers and students and students and students need (should) not be oppressive if we recognize the fostering of student capabilities as core to any progressive pedagogical project' (Walker, 2006, p. 143). This pedagogic project is underpinned by an inclusive conception of emancipation that combines an ethic of distributive justice with a politics of recognition. In other words, the notion of justice Touraine supports, engenders

> a struggle to place limitations on all forms of power by demanding the recognition of both social rights, which can be defined in terms of justice and fairness, and cultural rights, which can be formulated in terms of identity and difference.
>
> *(Touraine, 2000, p. 302)*

Bringing these ideas together, we can refashion a critical pedagogy for use in critical social work education. Like Touraine's work, critical pedagogy emerged as a reaction against, or corrective effort as a counter to, economic, social and political determinism (Giroux, 2011; hooks, 2003). Its focus is to democratise learning, to explore different pedagogical arrangements and introduce a learning culture to empower students and transform classroom conditions tied to hegemonic processes that perpetuate the social, economic and cultural marginalisation of subordinate groups (Cho, 2013). It speaks to resistance and social change. It is cultural politics in action. Like Touraine's new social movements, a critical pedagogy is largely orientated to the sphere of knowledge, language, representation, discourse and ideology rather than economy or social institutions – a reflection of new social movements' *raison d'être* (Cho, 2010, 2013; Giroux, 2011). Touraine's rebellion against conformity to the system and his critique of the cultural and spiritual deadness of post-modern life converge with the reflexive politics in critical pedagogy. In summary, we can see Touraine's work as abetting a critical pedagogy as it:

1 Uses the politics of the everyday as the basis of an alternative emancipatory education. Individual subjective experiences, voices and resistances are validated in creating an awareness of each actor's role (both individuals and collectivities) in the social struggles that shape history.
2 Is anti-structure, anti-system, especially emphasising anti-hierarchical pedagogy, non-hierarchic forms of authority and participatory democracy in the post-modern world.
3 Is a project entirely focused on inclusion, entailing guarantees of equal opportunity and equal power for the underprivileged, oppressed and marginalised or subjugated in societal terms. It embraces differences, multiculturalism and rights-based liberalism as ultimate goals of the practice.

Conclusion

Touraine's body of work alerts us to the fact that societies are constantly changing and that the next historical moment, despite technological advances, might not necessarily be equated with social or economic progress – moreover, there is no society without humanity and humanity is very much under threat.

Touraine's work tells us that each historical moment is likely to give rise to new collective actors that redefine rationality, organisation and collective action (Ife, 2013) and are thus capable of shaping societies, creating hope that there might be a way to overcome the challenges we are facing today for the greater global good (Noble, 2007). As we enter a new epoch of geological change and endangered human-ecological existence – the Anthropocene – Touraine's (2000) work forecasts new challenges (such as global warming, health and ageing issues, pollution and overcrowding, and possible shortages of safe food and water) alongside the old (such as increasing levels of poverty, the rising gap between levels of income and economic reward, the threat of nuclear war and ongoing violence against women and children). What we need are strategies for unsettling forces that arrest our development of a new radical humanist consensus (in working for the common good), if current and future social work practitioners are to be equipped to tackle the problems service users, their families and communities face.

This imperative to collaborate and work for a greater good is now defined in global terms and clearly spells out the need to reform our current capitalist system. The great scramble for resources and jockeying for political advantages has begun bringing out the worst (but also the best) in terms of domestic and international geo-politics. Touraine (1988) asks us to take globalisation seriously and reconceptualise a politics of resistance and hope for a better future within this terrain.

Recent examples of collective action with a global focus still target issues that emerged during the 1960s but with a much broader reach. Social media and a massive increase in digital communication outlets mean that social activism can reach more people and possibly be more effective than ever before. We also see the re-emergence and re-invigoration of old as well as new actors, e.g. eco-feminism, indigenous land and culture rights and environmental justice movements. These collective action groups enable the new politics of action whose aim is to challenge neoliberal states, market despotism and vested interests within this global political constellation (Noble, 2007). Indeed, we can easily discern the impact of social movements on our society in the form of new widely accepted social and cultural norms (i.e. same-sex marriages, supported decision making for people living with disability, support for carbon emission reductions).

Based on Touraine's analysis, this radical resistance *can* rethink and then redraw the social norms, cultural symbols, texts and signs upon which gender, sexuality, ability and class-based inequalities and other forms of discrimination are based. We can do this by applying new social movement theory to our critical practice and a critical pedagogy in our curricula.

References

ASWEAS. (2012). *Australian Social Work Education and Accreditation Standards*. Canberra: Australian Association of Social Workers.
Bailey, R., & Brake, M. (Eds.) (1975). *Radical Social Work*. London: Edward & Arnold.
Baines, D. (2017). *Doing Anti-Oppressive Practice: Social Justice Work*. Nova Scotia: Fernwood Publishers.
Cherrier, H., & Murray, J. (2002). Drifting Away from Excessive Consumption: A New Social Movement based on Identity Construction. *ACR North American Advances*.
Cho, S. (2010). Politics of Critical Pedagogy and New Social Movements. *Educational Philosophy and Theory*, 43, 3. doi: 10.111/j.1469-5812.2008.00415.x
Cho, S. (2013). *Critical Pedagogy and Social Change: Critical Analysis on the Language of Possibility*. New York: Routledge.
Dominelli, L. (2012). *Green social work: From environmental crises to environmental justice*, Polity Press, London.
Dowse, L. (2001). Contesting Practices, Challenging Codes: Self Advocacy, Disability Politics and the Social Model. *Disability & Society*, 16(1), 123–141. doi: 10.1080/713662036
Giroux, H. (2011). *On Critical Pedagogy*. New York: Continuum.
Gray, M., & Webb, S. A. (2013). *The New Politics of Social Work*. Basingstoke: Palgrave Macmillan.
Healy, K. (2000). *Social Work Practices: Contemporary Perspectives on Change*. London: Sage.
hooks, b. (2003). *Teaching Community: A Pedagogy of Hope*. New York: Routledge.
IASSW. (2004). *Global Standards for the Educatio and Training of the Social Work Profession*. Adelaide, SA: International Association of Social Workers and International Federation of Social Workers.
Ife, J. (2013). *Community Development in an Uncertian World: Vision, Analysis and Practice*. Melbourne: Cambridge University Press.
Kenny, S., & Connors, P. (2017). *Developing Communities for the Future.5^e*. South Melbourne: Cengage Learning Australia.
Kerr, C. (1997) *The Academic System in American Society Alain Touraine*. New York: Routledge.
Litmanen, T. (2010). Deconstructing Touraine: The Radical Sociologist for the Sake of Social Actors and Society. In G. Martin, D. Houston, P. McLaren & J. Suoranta (Eds.), *The Havoc of Capitalism*. Rotterdam: Sense Publishers, pp. 229–252.
Martin, G. (2001). Social Movements, Welfare and Social Policy: A Critical Analysis. *Critical Social Policy*, 21(3), 361–383.
Moreau, M. (1979). A Structural Approach to Social Work Practice. *Canadian Journal of Social Work Education*, 5(1), 78–94.
Morley, C., Macfarlane, S., & Ablett, P. (2014). *Engaging with Social Work: A critical Introduction*. Melbourne: Cambridge University Press.
Mullaly, B. (2010). *Challenging Opression and Confronting Privilege: A Critical Social Work Approach*. Ontario: Oxford University Press.
Noble, C. (2007). Social Work, Collective Action and Social Movements. In L. Dominelli (Ed.), *Revitalising Communities in a Globalising World*. Aldershot: Ashgate, pp. 95–104.
Pease, B. (2000). Researching Profeminist Men's Narratives. *Practice and Research in Social Work: Postmodern Feminist Perspectives*, 138–161.
Pease, B. (2013). A History of Critical and Radical Social Work. In M. Gray & S. Webb (Eds.), *The New Politics of Social Work*. New York: Palgrave Macmillan, pp. 21–43.

Powell, F. (2001). *The Politics of Social Work*. London: Sage.
Touraine, A. (1980). The Voice and the Eye: On the Relationship between Actors and Analysts. *Political Psychology*, 2(1), 3–14.
Touraine, A. (1981). The New Social Conflicts: Crisis of Transitions. In C. Lemart (Ed.), *French Sociology: Rupture and Renewal Since 1968*. New York: Columbia Press, pp. 313–331.
Touraine, A. (1984). Social Movements: Special Area or Central Problem in Sociological Analysis? *Thesis Eleven*, 9(1), 5–15.
Touraine, A. (1985). An Introduction to the Study of Social Movements. *Social Research*, 52(4), 749–787.
Touraine, A. (1988). *Return of the Actor*. Minneapolis: University of Minnesota Press.
Touraine, A. (2000). *Can We Live Together? Equality and Difference*. Cambridge: Polity Press.
Walker, M. (2006). *Higher Education Pedagogies: A Capabilities Approach*. New York: McGraw Hill Education.
Wieviorka, M. (2016, 11 May). Alain Touraine and the Concept of Social Movement. *Interventions*. Retrieved 18 June 2018, 2018, from https://wieviorka.hypotheses.org/318

39
Boal and Gadamer
A complementary relationship toward critical performance pedagogy in social work education

Jean Carruthers

QUEENSLAND UNIVERSITY OF TECHNOLOGY, AUSTRALIA

Phillip Ablett

UNIVERSITY OF THE SUNSHINE COAST, QUEENSLAND, AUSTRALIA

Introduction

Increasingly, the climate of social work education is influenced by the current neoliberal context whereby practice is individualised and disciplined according to the interests of capitalism. The pedagogic aim of neoliberal, capitalist regimes is to acculturate students and practitioners to the needs of the market economy, thus supporting the accumulation of wealth at the expense of those whom social workers are supposed to serve through extending social citizenship (Giroux 2011; Morley et al. 2019). This context has promoted an instrumental reduction and 'dumbing down' of social work education to a technical or skills-based endeavour with a heavy reliance on avowedly 'evidence-based' approaches. Due to the dominance of neoliberalism, pedagogic responses tend to compartmentalise and depoliticise social work rather than foster the critical and creative agency required to confront the complex social, economic and political realities faced by the people we work with (Healy 2014; Morley & O'Connor 2016). Accordingly, it is now, more than ever, necessary to develop critical and creative pedagogies that open up and foster counter hegemonic alternatives.

In an unusual pairing, this chapter will explicate the value of Augusto Boal's and Hans-Georg Gadamer's philosophical interpretations of art (more specifically performing arts) in theorising the use of *critical performance pedagogy*, as a platform for transformative education in social work. Boal was a visionary theatre artist/practitioner, activist and educator from Brazil, whose philosophy supported the development of what he termed a *Theatre of the Oppressed* (*Teatro del Oprimido*; hereafter TO) (1974). He characterised his work as a 'rehearsal for revolution'; a means to practice or play with ways we might 'act' to change the oppressive conditions of an unjust society (Boal 2000, p. 141). We explore how Boal's theatrical approach might be complemented by

Gadamer's hermeneutics, which likewise construes the arts as a mode of interpretive-pedagogic exploration and transformation that resists technical reductionism, reinvigorating learning spaces. Specifically, Gadamer's notion of 'play' in art, including performing arts, supports the imaginative experimentation central to Boal's political dramaturgy, recollecting and extending emancipatory elements in social work 'traditions'. This notion of play amid intersecting and contested traditions can be utilised in educational endeavours, such as performative (in a theatrical sense) assessments, to support student learning for personal and social transformation.

The term *critical performance pedagogy* (CPP) was derived from the auto-ethnographic work of Norman Denzin (2003) and Dwight Conquergood's notion of *Critical Performative Pedagogy* (1998), which comprehensively explores the emergence of politically situated performance and performativity. CPP, as loosely defined here, refers to performative processes (in this example the development and performing of a play), in an educational setting, as a vehicle to facilitate critical learning in social work, whereby the 'performative and political intersect' (2007, p. 129). Denzin (2007, 2003) acknowledges that performance pedagogy draws its inspiration from Augusto Boal's TO, as well as creative and Indigenous knowledges that are often marginalised in academic settings. In a hermeneutic sense the use of the term CPP simply provides a language to assist social work education when using performative platforms that are critically engaged.

An example of this kind of performative assessment has been used in a social work program at a university in Australia (see Morley & Ablett 2017). It reflects an applied performance approach, a theatrical form, for students to explore, compare and critique a range of theoretical perspectives associated with social work, making relevant links between theory and practice in a critically conscious way. Students, as part of a whole-tutorial collaborative assessment, develop a play and perform this in front of their student cohort. Each tutorial group showcases their group's understanding of social work theory and practice, as a way to creatively and collectively share knowledge across the cohort. Students develop a case-scenario and use existing narratives such as fairytales, gameshows, reality television, cultural stories or other creative frames to playfully demonstrate their interpretation and embodiment of different theoretical perspectives as they apply and respond to the social justice concerns within the case-scenario. Boal's TO performance pedagogy and Gadamer's hermeneutics of play underpin this educational approach. Accordingly, the proceeding discussion highlights the relevant aspects of both thinkers' philosophies as a critical and creative pedagogy that refuses the reduction of education to technique.

The philosophical concepts explored in this chapter appropriated by Boal and Gadamer provide a basis to validate forms of pedagogy that are often marginalised in academic settings. The value of this, albeit odd, yet complementary pairing is that it disrupts dominant forms by which educational endeavours are prescribed, drawing on critical knowledges and the arts as legitimate educational traditions in academia. For students, especially those who struggle with more traditional approaches to learning, based on efficiency measures and hierarchical determinants, CPP is a breath of fresh air. In the form of the performance assessment, it is a means to invigorate learning in ways that students are not conditioned to, but will certainly benefit from on their learning journey. As one student suggests:

> Engaging in that performance. Applying this theory to pop culture but still a real-life situation and then acting it out, using my body, using my mouth and then also viewing other groups' performances. There was a whole visual aspect to that … there was humour used and drama as well. So, it is a far more engaging platform than the chalk and talk or the power points … engaging in the [performance assessment] to learn critical theory, I really wanted to be at every class … that set me up I think. I hardly ever missed classes for the next four years.

Following is a brief historical overview and detailed analysis featuring aspects of Boal's and Gadamer's work that are fundamental to CPP. Included is a demonstration of how these apsects apply to the performance assessment used in social work education. From Boal, the concepts derived from TO include: the aesthetic space, action-oriented critical analysis, working collectively with the people, and the role of the joker/facilitator. From Gadamer, ideas associated with hermeneutics, namely, prejudice and tradition and the notion of play, act as a catalyst for that transformative learning in social work that will be explored.

Augusto Boal

Augusto Boal (1931–2009) was born in Brazil and raised in Rio De Janeiro. From a very young age theatre and writing were part of Boal's everyday existence. In order to please his father, Boal completed a degree in chemical engineering in 1952. Even in this field, Boal found ways to bring theatre into his life, directing his path to study theatre at Columbia University (Boal 2001). From 1956 to 1971, he was the director for Arena Theatre in São Paulo (1956–1971). This time was instrumental in the development of the aesthetic philosophy that underpins his major work *Theatre of the Oppressed* (TO). Boal's philosophy has had an extraordinary impact on mainstream theatre and, beyond this, an activist influence against the repressive political upheaval of the time in Brazil from the late 1960s to the early 1970s (Schutzman & Cohen-Cruz 2002). Consequently, an enforced military coup lasting a decade led to extreme censorship in theatre and imprisonment and death of many in theatre and political regimes viewed as subversives. As a result, in 1971 Boal was kidnapped, tortured and imprisoned for three months before being exiled to Argentina (Babbage 2004; Boal 2001). This displacement lasted until 1986 when, upon the restoration of democratic government in 1985, Boal was invited to return. When he returned, he introduced his TO arsenal. Ironically referring to the use of the word 'arsenal' – a collection of weapons and military equipment was fitting in response to this repression (Babbage 2004). He was considered the father of Theatre of the Oppressed (see Boal 2002) publishing his first book of the same name in 1973 (Boal 1979).

TO has been recognised for its infusion in many parts of the world as a platform for theatre makers and educators to implement approaches as a form of active participatory dramaturgy or critical pedagogy. Its reach extends to fields such as medicine (nursing), social work education and practice, schools and universities, community development, youth engagement, mental health, corrections and so on (Schutzman & Cohen-Cruz 2004). According to Schutzman & Cohen-Cruz (2004), Boal's work is known for its ability to effect change within individuals and within society, personally, socially and politically. Taussig and Schechner (2004, p. 17) describe TO as 'embodied techniques that activate passive spectators to become spect-actors – engaged participants for personal and social change'. Taussig and Schechner (2004, p. 17) highlight that those who aspire to critical approaches in numerous fields have adapted Boal's work to address social and political concerns such as racism, sexism, alienation, political impotence and so on. Mark Geisler (2017, p. 347) a social work educator who uses Boal's techniques, proposes TO can be applied in social work education to raise students' awareness of self and other, which in turn can bring into sharper focus concepts such as empowerment, empathy and social change. Geisler (2017) further proposes that when Boal's theory and methods are brought into the social work classroom, it offers a means to radicalise social work pedagogy in creative and performative ways.

Some of the key influences of Boal's philosophical teachings, supporting the radicalisation of his artistic pursuits, include Machiavelli's poetics of virtue, Hegelian and Marxist poetics, Brechtian theatre and Freire's critical pedagogy. Aspects of Boal's performance pedagogy that most relate to CPP include: his notion of aesthetic space, use of action-oriented approaches to critical analysis, doing theatre with people rather than for people, and the role of the joker/facilitator in political engagement. These aspects are outlined below with an explanation of how they apply to CPP in social work education.

The aesthetic space

The aesthetic space is a sensory, artistic space that provides the conditions for critical exploration and a means to foster new ways of thinking and acting. Winnicot (cited in Feldhendler 2004, p. 104) suggests '[a]esthetic space is where symbolic realisation takes place before it is transferred to everyday life'. It is the space where the imaginary and reality intersect (Feldhendler 2004), and where creative exploration beyond words on paper or in dialogue can be fostered and interpretation is put into action in a form that is both creative (the collaborative creation of a play) and performative (the embodied performance of a play). In social work education, this space can assist students to creatively problematise social concerns, exploring conceptual links between theory and practice and invoking critical analysis and critique in performative ways. Furthermore, through both the creative and performative process, students are actively sharing knowledge with their peers within the cohort. According to Boal, watching the performance should invoke the same ideas, emotions and insights that led to its creation. This suggests that students do not have to be actual performers in the play to gain educational benefits in the aesthetic space.

The need to recognise and respond to oppressive social conditions can easily be overlooked in approaches to social work education that rely heavily on rationalisation, for example, development of technical skills that seek to depoliticise and compartmentalise social work interventions by separating out theoretical understanding from practice (Healy 2014; Morley & O'Connor 2016). Boal (in Boal & Jackson 2006, p. 15) suggests 'words are the work of instruments of reason: we have to transcend them and look for forms of communication which are not just rational, but also sensory – aesthetic communications'. This would suggest it is not enough for students to think about practice purely as a rational application of knowledge through conservative academic assessments (such as exams, essays, lectorial and technical demonstrations), students require opportunities to theorise, feel, express, imagine and embody the complexity of applying different theoretical perspectives to practice scenarios and to discover the implications these might have in a real situation. Theatrical performative expression, in its sensory modality, has enormous potential in bringing to light the detrimental impact of oppressive social conditions and demonstrating ways to 'act' to emancipate people from these conditions in creative ways (Geisler 2017). This form of aesthetic 'transcendence of reason', according to Boal and Jackson (2006), is the reason we have the arts and is key to moving toward an aesthetic educational space. As an alternative to rational and technical approaches to social work education, fostering an aesthetic approach might be an effective means to invigorate this space.

Action-oriented critical analysis

In its commitment to social justice, political analysis and critical reflexivity, Boal's work is complementary to the ethos of critical social work and therefore recognised as a good fit for social work education that is critically aligned. Babbage (2010, p. 305) refers to TO as a way to encourage individuals and groups to 'participate actively in socially engaged, critically reflexive theatre processes and, by extension, to recognise their dynamic and transformative potential in society'. Taussig and Schechner (2004) have made suggestion of a critical and postmodern theoretical lens, most notably in relation to forum theatre (a form within TO). They speak of the interplay between modern and postmodern thought, proposing that Boal's tendency to draw on Brecht and other critical thinkers, such as Marx and Freire, positions TO as a form of critical modern analysis (Boal 2008; Taussig & Schechner 2004). The additional features of forum theatre, whereby audience members can participate to try out different ways to change a situation within the performance (see Boal 2002), although not representative of CPP (as ascribed in the performance assessment) is relevant to this analysis. This feature has resonance to a student adopting a critical postmodern theoretical lens when contemplating how to respond to a social justice issue related to social work. Taussig and Schechner (2004, p. 39) suggest, 'it is a great exercise to see theatre and at the same time think through the categories by which one acts as a modernist critic' and then to 'take this modernist form and treat it in a postmodern way' (Taussig & Schechner 2004, p. 39). The influence of Boal's approach, in terms of links to performing politically engaged analysis, suggests an action-oriented critical analysis that can be utilised in social work education. In some regards it would be synonymous to the deconstruction and reconstruction process of critical reflection (as espoused by Jan Fook (2012)), only through an embodied theatrical frame.

Given the role social work plays in negotiating institutional power in society, recognising the complexities and oppressive nature of helping institutions is paramount to students' development of critical analysis. Geisler (2017) highlights that, in addition to recognising the potential to oppress, it can be challenging for students to recognise their own agency and their capacity to effect change. Boal's pedagogical influence in CPP has the potential to support students to move beyond paternalistic assumptions associated with 'helping people' (see Allan et al. 2009) and gain a deeper more nuanced analysis of social work. The complexity of assisting students to bridge the gap between theory and practice, and the creativity required to do so, are ever present (Hick et al. 2010, p. 40). To actively interrogate social work practice through a platform that allows students to 'rehearse', not just skills or techniques, but the critical embodiment of theoretical analysis and action has enormous potential as a transformative educational approach.

Working collectively with 'the people'

Boal believed that theatre was a vocation that all human beings could partake in (Gökdag 2014). He was committed to working consistently toward the liberation of those who are oppressed. He aspired to do this by delivering performances that spoke to the oppression of those he referred to as 'the people'. In early times, often the people he was referring to were missing from the audience of his theatrical endeavours as theatre in modern society was the indulgence of the rich (Boal 2001). In line with his Marxist roots and affiliation with Freirean philosophy, Boal sought to liberate 'the people', realising that in order to do so they needed to participate fully in the creation and outcome of this liberatory process (Boal 2001).

In terms of CPP in social work education, the circumstances are somewhat different. The people within this context are university students studying social work, and the intention is to develop a critical understanding of social work theory and practice. It is relevant to point out, the clients/service users students might work with in their future practice are anecdotally implicated in their exploration through the use of a case-scenario. In this regard, although having similar intentions to Boal's notion of working with 'the people' and the creation of theatre toward a liberatory outcome, CPP (in the example of the performance assessment) has two main distinctions. First, social work students are not fundamentally oppressed, as such, and second, those who are impacted by the oppressive conditions (the clients/service users) are merely anecdotal in their participation.

Aside from these distinctions, what Boal's vision does offer is a collectively engaged pedagogic space. Within this space, social work students are able to actively problematise practice with the support of educators (their tutors) who are invested in the value of critical pedagogy. Through embodied action and critical reflection, rather than being told what to think about issues related to social work by an expert (Geisler 2017), students are able to develop their own capacity for critical development and collaboration within a creative and performative structure (i.e. developing and performing a play). Students in this process have the potential to gain transferable skills, for example in collaboration, democratic decision making, inclusive leadership, advocacy, activism and so on; all important aspects of the role of social work (AASW 2010). The investment in students' ability to learn from each other in solidarity and to share the knowledge they have gained through performing to their student colleagues has significant resonance to Boal's notion of theatre 'by the people for the people'.

Following Boal's example to work with people in ways that support their liberation and the liberation of others is not necessarily realised in more traditional approaches to education. Educators attest to their belief in students' capacity to take on a whole-tutorial collaborative task and through this make critically engaged democratic decisions and deliver a performative piece of assessment, ultimately sharing their creation with student colleagues for their educational benefit. The following quote from one educator is a testament to this engagement:

> Then the magic happens … they are connecting with each other, they are on Facebook, they are talking to each other outside. There are costumes being made over in one section and then you will see students rehearsing their performances outside of class for those who can make it … it is all building their engagement with each other, their engagement with the university, their commitment and their immersion in the material. Then you see them perform and it all comes together on the stage.

The role of the joker/facilitator

Boal discovered that when working in solidarity, you must be willing to take the same risks as those you are intending to educate (2001). What this points to is the importance of the role the educator plays when guiding the pedagogical process. In the development of TO, Boal established a foundational theoretical methodology called the joker system, with the joker/facilitator at the centre of this system (see Boal 2008; Gökdag 2014). The joker system is a non-traditional approach to theatre – 'dramaturgy and staging techniques' (Boal 2008, p. 150), designed to support the synthesis of Boal's ideas and discussions and coordinate them into a way to 'present in the same spectacle the play and its analysis' (Gökdag, 2014, p. 36); a kind of theatrical praxis. Often seen as part of but also sitting outside of the process, the joker role is likened to that of a facilitator. The joker is considered a contemporary and neighbour to spectators (the link between the performers and the audience) and an exegete between the theatrical and analytical aspects of the form (Boal 2008, p. 152). The term 'joker', according to Boal's interpretation, is synonymous to the role of the joker in a card game, having more mobility than any other card in the deck. Within the role of creating theatre, the 'joker' may hold a variety of positions, including director, referee and workshop leader, a conduit for possibilities and adaptation within the performance process (Boal 2008; Gökdag 2014).

In a similar sense to that of the joker in TO, the educator in CPP is required to be reflexive within but also sit outside of the performance and take on a number of roles within the context of the performance assessment. These might include: facilitating the development of the play, providing direction in the decision-making process, negotiating roles, navigating power in the educational space, and so on. Educators are required to be critically active with regard to students' development of social work values, awareness of social and cultural protocols, notions of power and privilege, discourse and ideology, theory and practice (Allan et al. 2009; Morley et al. 2019; Mullaly 2010). Although this is a somewhat student-led process, this is not a passive role for the educator. The educator directs performative discussions to intentionally politicise the practice of social work toward revolutionary praxis, 'the collective capacity to fundamentally transform oppressive social structures to further human emancipation' (Morley et al. 2019, p. 190), for example, exposing students to ways to disrupt hegemonic norms in social work as a means to resist complicity with measures of social control which, if unquestioned, can cause further harm for the people social workers work with. The opportunity for students to experience what it feels like to practice in both oppressive and emancipatory ways can be useful, albeit not always comfortable. This approach has similarities to the way the joker in TO intentionally facilitates theatrical possibilities to address the oppressive circumstances in forum theatre as part of a 'rehearsal for revolution' (Boal 2000, p. 141). It is important that facilitation is supported by critically sensitive dialogue based on ethical decision making, values of social justice and human rights, especially since those who are most vulnerable (clients/service users) are not actually part of the process. As Boal suggests, to work in solidarity with students the educator needs to take the same risks. This means when advancing a critical agenda in social work education the educator must also be willing to critically reflect on their own shortcomings within such an intimately collaborative approach.

Boal's TO influence in CPP provides a relevant platform for the performance assessment in social work education. Fundamentally, it offers a creative and performative space for students to critically explore the links between theory and practice, actively develop social and political analysis, and apply this to a social justice issue. Boal's notion of working collectively to address social concerns supports CPP's commitment to sharing knowledge across the cohort. Similarities between Boal's joker system and the educator's role as a facilitator of CPP has been demonstrated, highlighting ways educators can actively support students through critical engagement. Educators' investment in students' educational development and their commitment to uphold social justice principles and work toward emancipatory change is paramount.

Hans-Georg Gadamer

Hans-Georg Gadamer (1900–2002), a renowned hermeneutical philosopher, was born in Marburg Germany into a conservative protestant family. Drawn to the humanities, Gadamer became an academic in the 1930s, lecturing in aesthetics and ethics in a number of universities including Marburg, Frankfurt, Leipzig and Heidelberg. His interests included poetry, ontology, epistemology, language, aesthetics and metaphysics. Studying among colleagues such as Hannah Arendt and Leo Strauss, he became a student of Martin Heidegger who was considered one of the most significant philosophers of the twentieth century with his major work *Being and Time* (Heidegger 1996, originally published 1927). Although subject to many influences, Heidegger was most important in the development of Gadamer's hermeneutic philosophy (Barthold, n.d.; Polt 2001). Like Heidegger (and the neo-Marxist Frankfurt School), Gadamer came to believe that the modern, technological worldview of the Enlightenment, culminated in the dominance of a narrow, instrumental rationality that impoverishes both culture and the richness of human understanding (Kelly 2015). Following Heidegger, Gadamer's philosophy can be seen as a quest to redeem other forms of understanding or interpretive (hermeneutic) practices, such as literature and the creative arts, which he shows can reveal vital and transformative truths about the world (Being) that evade science and technology.

However, Gadamer did not follow Heidegger's political trajectory in lending support for the Nazi regime (De Cesare 2013, pp. 14–15). A political liberal, he found the regime abhorrent and sought to protect Jewish friends (Grondin & Plant 2003, pp. 153–154; Palmer 2002) but made the accommodations necessary to keep his job. His conduct in this period has been criticised as too compliant (Orozco in Krajewski 2005; Wolin 2000) but most scholars maintain he avoided political complicity as much as anyone could short of joining the resistance (Grondin 2003; Palmer 2002).

Gadamer was most recognised for the originality of his work *Philosophical Hermeneutics* (1977) and his magnum opus *Truth and Method* (1989; originally published in German in 1960, revised in 1975). The publication of the latter established him as a major thinker and led to his engagement with the leading critical theorist of the Frankfurt School's second generation, Jürgen Habermas. Against Habermas' insistence that the basis for emancipatory critique must be anchored outside any historical or cultural tradition, Gadamer countered that 'tradition' is always contested and 'exists only in constantly becoming other than it is' (1990, p. 288), thereby providing a basis for critique from within existing or recoverable traditions (e.g. Indigenous traditions, the arts). Gadamer's writings on philosophical hermeneutics, most significantly the relationship between hermeneutics and aesthetics, and his notions of play and transformation, offer an ontological window into how CPP might work within social work education.

The historical and cultural traditions within academia significant to Gadamer's argument are reflected in the role that CPP plays in social work education. Gadamer's notion of tradition, on the one hand, allows a contestation of dominant conservative pedagogies in academia making way for new or revived knowledges to be valued (e.g. artistic and Indigenous knowledges). These knowledges are recognised as fundamental to CPP. On the other hand, Gadamer's notion of tradition offers a revaluing of historically relevant, radical and postmodern critique in academia that has been subjugated or marginalised by neoliberal dogma. As Ablett and Dyer (2009, p. 288) point out, in contrast to the common view, 'traditions already contain within themselves the moral resources for critique and renewal' rather than simply reproducing a conservative status quo. Tradition, understood in this way, can support the critical potential for social work education and augment CPP as an activist approach in its ability to question and change the dominant interpretation of pedagogy in academia.

In a somewhat similar vein to Boal, albeit not in a political sense, Gadamer speaks of the value of the arts (aesthetics), as a means for transformative and embodied expression. What is notable and relevant to Gadamer's usefulness for CPP is his philosophical hermeneutic position. Gadamer (1977) suggests that hermeneutics is a means to bridge the gap of interpretation in an attempt to make visible that which is foreign or unfamiliar and revealing its presence (Gadamer 1977). The following quote from Bernstein (cited in Gray & Webb 2013, p. 75) informed by Heideggerian thought encapsulates this understanding by suggesting:

> Our common ways of 'thinking' have become so familiar and entrenched that they conceal what needs to be unconcealed. It is only by showing how the familiar and the correct appear strange and uncanny … that thinking can be called forth.

The neoliberal influence that is central to our thinking is often present in students' initial assumptions about what social work is, based on limited constructions informed by 'common sense' and public opinion (Healy 2014; Morley et al. 2017). Often there is resistance from students when attempting to deconstruct these assumptions in social work education. Gadamer's philosophy supports ways to counter the resistance when engaged in critically questioning implicit unproductive and potentially oppressive views of social work. The two main concepts associated with Gadamer's hermeneutics relevant to CPP are his interpretations of the relationship between tradition and prejudice, and the notion of aesthetic experience through play, as outlined below.

Tradition and prejudice

Gadamer (1989) refers to the dominant assumptions held by individuals as 'prejudice', not as a necessarily distorted or negative interpretation as it is commonly understood but rather as a form of pre-judgment. Gadamer (1989, p. 267) asserts, 'a person who is trying to understand is exposed to distraction from fore-meanings that are not born of themselves'. These fore-meanings are informed by what is 'assumed' to be accurate knowledge, according to earlier interpretations of what is believed to be true. According to Gadamer (1989, p. 270), '[i]t is the tyranny of hidden prejudice that makes us deaf to what speaks to us in tradition'. Gadamer is suggesting these fore-meanings are barriers to embracing new ways of knowing (i.e. critical understandings of social work). As pointed out earlier, this is reflected in social work education whereby students often come with preconceived ideas of what social work is according to dominant or universal ideas of what social workers do. These understandings are affirmed through neoliberal, technical-rational and evidence-based appropriations to which students are often exposed prior to attending university or, more disappointingly, in their first year of study in social work (Morley et al. 2017). When students are then required to engage in dialogue and adopt a critical lens to examine practice, it can be challenging to bypass the distraction of these firmly established 'prejudices'.

For some students, it is their investment in the quest for certainty and the desire to know the 'best' or 'right' way to do social work that constitutes their leading prejudice. Some students are intimately invested in their early assumptions of what social work is based in allegedly universal values and apolitical representations, and thus are reluctant to critique the possible limitations of their position. Furthermore, in some instances students associate critical education with negative outcomes, suggesting it is 'too' subversive to take on board (Brookfield 2005; Morley et al. 2014). What Gadamer (1989) proposes is that our fore-meanings are not neutral. To become open to other ways of knowing, students first need to become conscious of their own bias (within their pre-judgments) as these are what distract them from taking in new knowledge. Drawing on Gadamer's notion of tradition and prejudice can assist educators to recognise this resistance as an inevitable part of the process of transformation (Ablett & Dyer 2009; Gadamer 1989). Using hermeneutic understanding, such as notions of tradition and prejudice, is a means to sensitively question firmly held assumptions and, furthermore, draw on alternative traditions, such as the arts, to counter resistance through play.

Aesthetic experience through play

Rasmussen and Gürgens (2006, p. 236) profess that Gadamer's teachings help us to understand that 'aesthetic experience through art is the eminent way of hermeneutically knowing what we would otherwise know through verbal language and communication'. With familiarity to earlier appropriations by Boal, Gadamer proposes 'the arts', or more specifically play, open a way for hermeneutic understanding constituting both verbal (linguistic) and bodily (aesthetic) channels and, as such, is a catalyst for transformative learning. This is because play, according to Gadamer, can enable experience of an embodied form of ontology (Barnett 2008), of 'being in' or becoming that which one is learning. Aesthetic experience through play can be a way to unearth embedded assumptions by distracting people from their prejudice and, therefore, create openness to developing new meaning which speaks to the potential for transformation.

When contemplating the purpose of play, Gadamer refers to its contemporaneousness, the immediacy of being in the moment of play that provides the opportunity to try on new ways of being. Gadamer (1989, p. 110) asserts it is not about altering one's understanding, 'what is altered remains the same'. For Gadamer (1989), this means that what is being transformed is now, as a whole, something different and thus represents its true being that is now entirely different to what it was before. Brookfield (2003, p. 142) relates this to critical education, suggesting transformative learning is 'learning in which the learner comes to new understanding of something that causes a re-ordering of the pragmatic assumptions she holds and leads her life in a fundamentally different way'. Possibly in its most profound sense, Gadamer's notion of play suggests a sense of freedom and curiosity that allows people to suspend disbelief in a meaningful way, stimulating openness to new ways of thinking and being, to be transformed. This notion of 'suspending disbelief' can be useful in helping students to expand their conceptual frame of practice by putting aside what they already think they know and ontologically experiencing other ways of being and knowing.

For social work students, the opportunity to play with existing narratives such as a fairytale, gameshow, reality television show and so on, to demonstrate their understanding of social work theories and their relationship to practice, provides an openness to question and challenge the legitimacy of taken-for-granted assumptions about social work practice, making room for and literally 'trying out' new perspectives, in line with the values of social justice and human rights. The following quote from a social work educator describes how this notion of play can support a critical exploration of social work theory and its application in practice:

> Students actually became the character. So if it was Goldilocks they became Goldilocks and Goldilocks was part of the case study. Goldilocks was a homeless young girl, who broke into someone's house because she was hungry ... [T]hat was the case study ... [T]hen the three bears came home and each bear was a different theory ... and basically offered her [Goldilocks] ways that she could help herself or what they could do for her from [each] theoretical perspective and then Goldilocks just talks back to the theory and critiques the theory and says yes that would be helpful or no that is not.

As demonstrated in this example, Gadamer's understanding of play moves beyond the 'playful' behaviour of the play (performance) and suggests a seriousness, even a sacredness of play and the transformative nature of this endeavour. Although again not in the same political sense as Boal, Gadamer (1989) proposes that seriousness is an important dimension of creative play. If play is not taken seriously in the sense that the player loses himself in a purposeful way, then the value of play is not embodied. If students are open to seriously embrace the arts and play through their participation in the performance assessment as an alternative to traditional approaches to assessment, the potential for students to experience transformative outcomes is likely.

The idea that students can begin to make critical links between theory and practice through a critical, performative and collaborative experiential process, supported by educators who are primed to critically question taken-for-granted assumptions, is a hopeful opportunity for the future of social work. The opportunity to integrate ways to think and act has implications for who students might become as emerging social workers and the critical intentions this invokes. The broader recognition that CPP might not only provide a transformative alternative to conventional education in social work but also potentially lead to ways we perform social work differently into the future has exciting possibilities.

In social work education, the philosophical ideas of Augusto Boal and Hans-Georg Gadamer point to modes of understanding and learning anchored in the creative arts, that stand in radical contrast to those promoted by current neoliberal educational regimes. CPP in particular draws on the political and theatrical foundations of Boal's TO arsenal as a complementary pedagogy in social work education and a means to support students to think and act creatively about social work theory and practice. Notions of the aesthetic space, action-oriented critical analysis, working collectively with 'the people', and the role of the joker/facilitator to achieve this, have been highlighted. In a less overtly political, yet comparable manner, Gadamer's hermeneutic notions of tradition, prejudice and play, highlight the way the arts can provide a platform for social work students to playfully discover new and meaningful interpretations of theory and practice. As Giroux (2011, p. 157) urges, educators have the task of 'educating students to become critical agents who actively question and negotiate the relationships between theory and practice, critical analysis and common sense, and learning and social change'. In order to accomplish this in social work education, creative platforms such as CPP can play a vital role in invigorating the educational space and working toward a more socially just society.

References

Ablett, P. G. & Dyer, P. K. (2009). Heritage and hermeneutics: towards a broader interpretation of interpretation. *Current Issues in Tourism*, 12(3), 209–233.
Allan, J., Briskman, L. & Pease, B. (2009). *Critical Social Work: Theories and Practices for a Socially Just World* (2nd edn.). Crows Nest, NSW: Allen & Unwin.
Australian Association of Social Workers. (2010). *Code of Ethics*, Canberra ACT, cited 7 June 2019, www.aasw.asn.au/document/item/1201
Babbage, F. (2004). *Augusto Boal*. New York, USA: Routledge.
Babbage, F. (2010). Augusto Boal and the Theatre of the Oppressed. In A. Hodge (ed.), *Actor Training* (2nd edn.). (pp. 305–323). New York, USA: Routledge.
Barnett, R. (2008). *A Will to Learn: Being a Student in an Age of Uncertainty*. Maidenhead, Berkshire: Open University Press.
Barthold, L. S. (n.d.). Hans-George Gadamer (1900–2002). *Internet Encyclopaedia of Philosophy*. Retrieved from www.iep.utm.edu/gadamer/
Bernstein, R. J. (2013). *The New Constellation: The Ethical-Political Horizons of Modernity/Postmodernity* (4th edn.). Massachusetts, USA: Polity Press. Retrieved from https://ebookcentral.proquest.com/lib/qut/reader.action?docID=1602907&ppg=3
Boal, A. (1974). *Theatre of the Oppressed*. Trans. Charles McBride and Maria-Odilia Leal McBride. London: Pluto.
Boal, A. (1979, 2000, 2008). *Theatre of the Oppressed*. London, UK: Pluto Press.
Boal, A. (2001). *Hamlet and the Baker's Son: My Life in the Theatre and Politics*. London, UK: Routledge.
Boal, A. (2002). *Games for Actors and Non-Actors* (2nd edn.). New York, USA: Routledge.
Boal, A. & Jackson, A. (2006). *Aesthetics of the Oppressed*. Retrieved from https://ebookcentral.proquest.com/lib/qut/detail.action?docID=268601
Brookfield, S. (2003). Putting the critical back into critical pedagogy: a commentary on the path of dissent. *Journal of Transformative Education*, 1(2), 141–149.
Brookfield, S. (2005). *Power of Critical Theory for Adult Learning and Teaching*. New York, USA: Open University Press.
Conquergood, D. (1998). Beyond the Text: Towards a Performative Culture of Politics. *The future of performance studies: Visions and revisions* 25–36. Retrieved from www.kineticnow.com/wp-content/uploads/2014/12/conquergood-1998beyond-the-text.pdf.
De Cesare, D. (2013). *Gadamer: A Philosophical Portrait*. Indiana: Indiana University Press. pp. 14–15.
Denzin, N. K. (2003). *Performance Ethnography: Critical Pedagogy and the Politics of Culture*. New York, USA: Sage Publications.
Denzin, N. K. (2007). The politics and ethic of performance pedagogy: toward a pedagogy of hope. In P. McLaren & J. L. Kincheloe (eds.), *Critical Pedagogy: Where Are We Now?* (pp. 127–142). New York, USA: Peter Lang Publishing.
Feldhendler, D. (2002). Augusto Boal and Jacob L. Moreno: theatre and therapy. In M. Schutzman & J. Cohen-Cruz (eds.), *Playing Boal: Theatre, Therapy, Activism* (pp. 87–109). New York, USA: Routledge.

Fook, J. (2012). *Social Work: A Critical Approach to Practice*. London, UK: Sage.
Gadamer, H. (1990). Reply to my critics. In G. Ormiston & A. Schrift (eds.), *The Hermeneutic Tradition*. (pp. 273–297). Albany: SUNY Press.
Gadamer, H. G. (1975, 1989). *Truth and Method, Crossroad,* New York.
Gadamer, H. G. (1977). *Philosophical Hermeneutics*. California, USA: University of California.
Geisler, M. (2017). 'Teaching note – theatre of the oppressed and social work education: radicalising the practice classroom', *Journal of Social Work Education*, 53(2), 347–353.
Giroux, H. A. (2011). *On Critical Pedagogy*. New York, USA: Continuum.
Gökdag, E. (2014). Augusto Boal's the joker system. *Idil*, 3(4), 27–37.
Gray, M. & Webb, S. A. (2013). *Social Work Theories and Methods* (2nd edn.). London, UK: Sage Publications.
Grondin, J. & Plant, K. (2003). *The Philosophy of Gadamer*. London, UK: Routledge.
Healy, K. (2014). *Social Work Theories: Creating Frameworks for Practice*. London, UK: Palgrave MacMillan.
Heidegger, M. (1996). *Being and Time*. New York, USA: State University New York Press.
Hick, S., Peters, H., Corner, T. & London, T. (2010). *Structural Social Work in Action: Examples from Practice*. Ontario, Canada: Canadian Scholars Press.
Kelly, S., 2015. 'Hermeneutics and genocide: Giving voice to the unspoken'. *Palgrave Communications*.
Krajewski, B. (2005). Hans-George Gadamer: a biography (review). *Common Knowledge*, 11(2), 353.
Morley, C & Ablett, P. (2017). Designing assessment to promote engagement among first year social work students. *Journal of Business, Education and Scholarship*, 11(2), 1–14.
Morley, C. Macfarlane, S. & Ablett, P. (2014). *Engaging with Social Work: A Critical Introduction*. Sydney, NSW: Cambridge University Press.
Morley, C., McFarlane, S. & Ablett, P. (2017). The neoliberal colonisation of social work education: a critical analysis and practices for resistance. *Advances in Social Work and Welfare Education*, 19(2), 25–40.
Morley, C., Macfarlane. S. & Abblett, (2019). *Engaging with Social Work: A Critical Introduction*, Cambridge University Press, UK.
Morley, C. & O'Connor, D. (2016). Contesting field education in social work: using critical reflection to enhance student learning for critical practice. In I. Taylor, M. Bogo, M. Lefevre & B. Teater (eds.), *International Handbook of Social Work Education*. (pp. 220–231). London, UK: Routledge.
Mullaly, R. P. (2010). *Challenging Oppression and Confronting Privilege: A Critical Social Work Approach*, Don Mills, ON: Oxford University Press.
Palmer, R. E. (2002). 'A response to Richard Wolin on Gadamer and the Nazis'. *International Journal of Philosophical Studies*, 10(4), 467–482.
Polt, R. (2001). Martin Heidegger. In A. Elliot & B. Turner (eds.), *Profiles in Contemporary Social Theory* (pp. 9–91). London, UK: Sage.
Rasmussen, B. & Gürgens, R. (2006). Art as part of everyday life: understanding applied theatre practices through the aesthetics of John Dewey and Hans George Gadamer. *Theatre Research International*, 31(3), 235–244.
Schutzman, M. & Cohen-Cruz, J. (2002). *Playing Boal: Theatre, Therapy, Activism*. London, UK: Routledge, Taylor & Francis.
Taussig, M. & Schechner R. (2004). Boal in Brazil, France, the USA: an interview with Augusto Boal. In M. Schutzman & J. Cohen-Cruz (eds.), *Playing Boal: Theatre, Therapy, Activism* (pp. 17–34). New York, USA: Routledge.
Wolin, R. (2000). Nazism and the complicities of Hans-Georg Gadamer: untruth and method. *New Republic*, 15 May 2000, 222(20), 36–45.

40
Critical transformative learning and social work education
Jack Mezirow's transformative learning theory

Peter Jones

JAMES COOK UNIVERSITY, QUEENSLAND, AUSTRALIA

Introduction

The impact of neoliberal ideology on higher education has been noted by many authors (e.g. Dunn & Faison, 2015; Lucal, 2015). This impact is not simply a matter of educational policy or institutional practice. As educators we increasingly see students overwhelmed with the responsibilities of care and work, struggling economically and unsupported by the state, who have bought the message of education as a vocational commodity. Such students are often willing to take on huge student debts in the hope that a degree will buy a better life for themselves and their families. For many it seems like learning itself, and particularly critical learning, is hardly on the agenda. At the same time, as educators, we experience higher workloads, fewer resources, increasing amounts of administrative work and intrusive institutional surveillance, all of which have a grindingly accumulative and negative effect on our ability to do the kind of work we would like to be doing (Hanesworth, 2017; Jovanovic, 2017).

Social work education has not been immune to these developments, as we see pressure to move toward more technically oriented, competency-based approaches to education, producing practitioners well-suited to upholding the neoliberal status quo. As Macfarlane (2016, p. 326) notes, this approach,

> rather than critically analysing and challenging inequitable social structures and power relations, reshapes social work education towards conservative, market-led demands. This is aimed at producing technically proficient practitioners who conform to existing systems, who are unable to see the broader (moral and political) implications of their work.

The current context is particularly challenging for educators with a critical, emancipatory orientation. The critical perspective has always been a significant voice in social work, highlighting the structural nature of social disadvantage (Hosken, 2016). The critical perspective represents a call to action, pointing to the need for social change to address issues of oppression that are social and ideological in origin (Allan, 2003; Mullaly, 2007). Pease and Nipperess (2016, p. 4) have characterised this critical perspective in social work as 'a group of approaches ... that are diverse but share a common commitment to both personal and structural change'. For critical social work educators, translating this emancipatory orientation into educational practice is a significant challenge. Pedagogies that support a critical approach to education and learning are therefore of great importance, providing both tools for understanding students' experiences but also for facilitating educational practices that promote critical consciousness and action for social change.

Transformative learning theory, as developed by Jack Mezirow, is one such pedagogy. There are many points of congruence between transformative learning theory and the concerns of critical social work education. It can be argued that these congruencies make transformative learning approaches particularly valuable for critically oriented social work educators (Jones, 2009; Witkin, 2014).

Jack Mezirow (1923–2014)

The late American educational theorist Jack Mezirow began developing ideas around transformative learning in the mid-1970s (Mezirow, 1975, 1978). Mezirow worked as an educational consultant with the United Nations before taking up a professorial position at Teachers College, Columbia University. Drawing on the personal experience of his wife, Edee, Mezirow conducted a number of research studies into the experiences of women returning to study at community colleges. This research was the genesis of transformative learning theory. He has generally been regarded as the primary spokesperson in the field of transformative pedagogy, and much of the research and thought that has emerged over the last 30 years has been influenced in some way by his work (Baumgartner, 2012; Hoggan, 2016; Kitchenham, 2006).

For Mezirow, the process of transformation, producing a shift in the way we see and make meaning of the world, was at the heart of adult learning. He described it as

> The process of learning through critical self-reflection, which results in the reformulation of a meaning perspective to allow a more inclusive, discriminating, and integrative understanding of one's experience. Learning includes acting on these insights.
>
> *(Mezirow, 1990a, p. xvi)*

And later as:

> Learning that transforms problematic frames of reference – sets of fixed assumptions and expectations (habits of mind, meaning perspectives, mindsets) – to make them more inclusive, discriminating, open, reflective, and emotionally able to change. Such frames of reference are better than others because they are more likely to generate beliefs and opinions that will prove more true or justified to guide action.
>
> *(Mezirow, 2003, pp. 58–59)*

Mezirow's transformation theory represents an attempt to account for the development and nature of adult learners' meaning structures, and the processes involved when those structures are challenged and changed.

Meaning structures and meaning perspectives

Transformative learning theory is grounded in a constructivist interpretation of learning (Fosnot, 2005). This constructivist paradigm is the basis for Mezirow's articulation of the nature of the meaning structures that form a central feature of his theory. Meaning structures, according to Mezirow, consist of meaning perspectives, or frames of reference, and their component parts. A frame of reference, is:

> the structure of assumptions and expectations through which we filter sense impressions. It involves cognitive, affective and conative dimensions. It selectively shapes and delimits perception, cognition, feelings, and disposition by predisposing our intentions, expectations, and purposes. It provides the context for making meaning within which we choose what and how a sensory experience is to be construed and/or appropriated.
>
> *(Mezirow, 2000, p. 16)*

According to Mezirow, meaning perspectives therefore operate as filters selectively influencing what we attend to and how we make sense of sensory experiences. These perspectives are built up over time through processes of socialisation and acculturation (Mezirow, 2000, 2012). They are usually acquired in an uncritical manner and may therefore be seen to reflect the dominant social and cultural concerns. For critically oriented educators, this is a particularly important observation, as it relates directly to the impact of the dominant neoliberal social context in which social work students (and educators) are immersed. When a meaning perspective becomes consolidated over time, it can be thought of as constituting a personal paradigm, or worldview, and increasingly less amenable to change. These meaning perspectives are underpinned by sets of unquestioned assumptions about the way the world is. Meaning perspectives, therefore, often include distorted views of reality.

Mezirow described a number of specific categories of distorted assumptions (Mezirow, 1990b, 1991). These include: epistemic distortions, or distorted assumptions about the reasoning process; sociocultural and sociolinguistic distortions, relating to issues of power and social relationships and the way these are delineated by language; and psychic or psychological premise distortions. Transformative learning, then, is the process by which such meaning structures are changed to become more open, inclusive and integrative, which Mezirow described as

> the process of becoming critically aware of how and why our assumptions have come to constrain the way we perceive, understand and feel about our world; changing these structures of habitual expectation to make possible a more inclusive, discriminating, and integrative perspective; and, finally, making choices or otherwise acting upon these new understandings.
>
> *(Mezirow, 1991, p. 167)*

Processes of transformation

Mezirow argued that such transformations usually occur in response to a disorienting dilemma, an event or series of events, which provide the impetus for critical reflection on our existing perspectives (1990a, 2012). A disorienting experience is the foundation for transformation. This transformation becomes possible where an experience that is incongruent with our existing meaning structures leads to critical reflection upon previously taken-for-granted assumptions (Mezirow, 1990a, 1991, 2000). However, according to Mezirow, simply reflecting upon or even changing one's meaning perspective is not sufficient for transformative learning to have taken place. Action is also required, in the sense of the enactment of the altered perspective in the social world.

The experience of a disorienting dilemma can be dramatic and singular, such as the death of a loved one, or can be subtler and more incremental, such as the exposure to new ideas through a course of study (Taylor, 1998). For educators this raises the potential of intentionally 'creating' experiences for students that might act as the disorienting catalysts for transformative learning. Mezirow's theory gives particular prominence to two important dynamics as part of the transformative process. Critical reflection and critical-dialectical discourse are, he argued, central to understanding the conditions that make the critical examination of meaning perspectives, and therefore transformation, possible.

Critical reflection and critical-dialectical discourse

Mezirow and others have argued that critical reflection is the central process in transformative learning (Kasworm & Bowles, 2012; Lundgren & Poell, 2016; Mezirow, 2012). Mezirow has suggested two key types of reflection: first, critical reflection of assumptions (objective reframing), which involves critically reflecting on the assumptions of others, and second, critical self-reflection of assumptions (subjective reframing), which involves critical self-reflection on one's own assumptions and, in particular, the ways in which one's world view might be limited and distorted (Mezirow, 2000). According to Mezirow, it is the critical self-reflection of assumptions that is more likely to be involved in a perspective transformation.

The second of the key processes of transformative learning relates to the role and importance of critical-dialectical discourse (1991, 2003). Mezirow's argument here, building on the work of Habermas (1971, 1984), is that critical reflection on underlying assumptions is not a solitary activity but takes place through discourse, or dialogue, with others. In particular, he was concerned with dialogue devoted to assessing contested beliefs, arguing that it is through such discourse that the process of transformation is developed and enacted (Mezirow, 2012). Mezirow recognised that in order for learners to engage in such discourse they must possess two distinct adult learning capacities: the ability to become critically self-reflective, and the capacity for reflective judgement (2003). Promoting and supporting the development of such capacities, therefore, emerges as a key concern for critically oriented social work educators.

The question of how adult educators might facilitate transformative learning has been explored in the transformative learning literature (e.g. Brooks & Adams, 2015; Dahl & Millora, 2016; Hoggan & Cranton, 2015), and a range of specific approaches and strategies have emerged. Mezirow's primary concern was to identify the conditions and capacities required for transformations to occur, with a focus on developing the skills and attitudes required for critical reflection. This critical questioning of previously taken-for-granted assumptions is the key to developing a critically reflective capacity and therefore essential to transformative learning.

Social change

For Mezirow, transformative learning was not necessarily linked directly and inevitably to broader social change. Perspective transformation may, for instance, relate to epistemic or psychic distortions, and while transforming these existing presuppositions will entail taking action in the social world, such action may relate more to individual behaviour than direct, collective, social action (Mezirow, 1991).

However, Mezirow argued that processes of transformative learning help to create the conditions that are necessary for emancipatory social transformation and engagement in participative, democratic processes (2003). In other words, while some experiences of transformative learning may lead individuals to emancipatory social action and some may not, all perspective transformations, by nature of the shift toward more critical, open and inclusive frameworks, contribute to creating the conditions for fuller participation in democratic citizenship (Mezirow, 2003, 2012) and social change. A transformed frame of reference allows the learner to see more clearly the operation of oppressive ideology that may previously have been uncritically accepted.

Mezirow's work has also acted as the foundation for more explicitly emancipatory expressions of transformative learning (e.g. Brookfield, 2005, 2012) and a number of writers have attempted to directly address issues of structural inequality and power differentials using a transformative learning approach congruent with Mezirow's conceptualisation (e.g. Barraclough & McMahon, 2013; Lorenzetti, Azulai, & Walsh, 2016).

Freire, Habermas and critical social theory

In describing the foundations of his theoretical work, Mezirow acknowledged the influence of writers in a wide range of disciplines, including psychology, sociology, philosophy, linguistics, neurobiology, religion and education (1991). In assessing the utility of Mezirow's work for social work education, three particular influences are notable. These are the work of Freire (1970, 1973), of Habermas (1971, 1984, 1987) and, more broadly, the body of work referred to as critical social theory (Bronner, 2011; Tyson, 2012).

Freire argued that education can never be a politically neutral activity, and that traditional education that lays claim to such neutrality, is simply 'a convenient alternative to saying that one is siding with the dominant' (Freire, 1985, cited in Mayo, 1999, p. 60). In essence, Freire argued for the educational goal of political literacy, through processes of conscientisation, involving critical reflection and dialogue (1998). Such learning at the individual level was, in Freire's view, always related to the sociocultural context in which it occurs and, through praxis, to the broader goal of social transformation.

Mezirow's work has strong parallels with that of Freire, as well as some significant differences. Mezirow noted that, for Freire, transformation invariably means 'social' transformation, where it is the oppressive operation of ideology that acts to limit the consciousness of learners. This contrasts with Mezirow's argument that distorted assumptions may also be of an epistemic or psychological nature, potentially, but not necessarily, leading to social change. Essentially, Mezirow distinguished between processes of critical reflection and processes of social transformation, and argued that one does not necessarily lead to the other.

Jürgen Habermas has also been recognised as one of the most influential thinkers of recent times (Segre, 2014). His philosophical work (1971, 1984, 1987) has exerted considerable influence since the 1970s. There are two aspects of his work that can be highlighted as having had a significant impact on Mezirow's development of transformation theory. The first of these is Habermas' work on epistemology and the sociology of knowledge, highlighting the role of ideology in leading to distortions in communication and understanding (Habermas, 1971), and the second has been his work in the area of communicative action (see in particular Habermas, 1984; 1987).

Habermas argued that human beings are active participants in the social construction of knowledge, and that the production of knowledge is structured by cognitive interests. Each of these cognitive interests, with their respective sphere of action or experience, is related to a specific form of knowledge. These are empirical-analytical (instrumental);

historical-hermeneutic (communicative); and critical-dialectic (emancipatory) (Habermas, 1971). It is emancipatory knowledge, according to Habermas, which, through the operation of social critique and reflexive awareness, enables people to perceive their world in an undistorted fashion (Habermas, 1971).

The difference between instrumental and communicative learning, as proposed by Habermas (1971, 1984), is recognised by Mezirow as a key proposition underpinning transformative learning theory (1990a, 1997, 2003). Unlike instrumental learning, testing the validity of communicative learning is not amenable to empirical evaluation, or an appeal to tradition or authority. Rather, validity must be assessed through consensual validation, that is, through engaging in rational, or critical-dialectical discourse (Habermas, 1987). Habermas' conception of emancipatory learning embraces the notion of ideological critique, the ability to recognise and criticise the distortions created by the operation of ideology. Mezirow's transformation theory argues that transformative learning fosters the development of the qualities and skills required for critical reflection and critical-dialectical discourse, both of which are essential in promoting participation and democracy (2003, 2012).

While Mezirow's theory drew on the work of Habermas it did not constitute an extension of the development of critical theory and the work of the Frankfurt School. Critical theorists are primarily concerned with understanding and exposing relationships of power as they exist in society and generating insight into the systems of their reproduction (Elliott, 2009). This perspective has been influential in education, with a number of prominent theoreticians, practitioners and advocates of critical and radical pedagogy emerging, including hooks (2004), McLaren (2015), Apple (2006), Giroux (2004) and Brookfield (2012). The transformation theory of Mezirow can be thought of as sitting within the broader tradition of these critical approaches. Mezirow is not exclusively concerned with learning processes that operate to reveal the hegemonic operation of oppressive ideology. However, this can be one of the functions of transformative learning. In Mezirow's work, perspective transformation leads to more critically aware, integrative and open frames of reference, an essential precondition, he argues, for democratic participation (2012). Perspective transformations of a specifically sociocultural nature may also involve a particular component of ideology critique and, through praxis, subsequent engagement in social action and social change. For social work educators, a focus on sociocultural perspective transformation would most clearly align with critical and emancipatory orientations.

Transformative learning theory and social work education

A consideration of Mezirow's transformative learning theory reveals a number of points of congruence between this approach and social work education. Both transformative learning theory and social work education are primarily focused on the interactions of the individual in the social world. In social work education the acquisition of new skills and knowledge, and the socialisation into social work values and ethics, is primarily directed at equipping learners to become effective practitioners, that is, to translate theory and knowledge into action in the social world.

Social work education is concerned with the centrality of the experiential as a source of learning and has a strong tradition of facilitating such learning through field education and experiential approaches to the classroom. Such experience is central to transformative theories as the starting point for learning and transformation. Similarly, critical reflection and reflective dialogue have been identified as essential components of the transformative process and are also usually regarded as essential aspects of social work education.

Social work education and transformative learning theories are also both concerned with issues of change. This may involve change at the level of the individual as learner or the support and facilitation of change in others. Both are also concerned with broader social change. The emphasis placed on the centrality of such social change varies among transformation theories, and this is also the case with social work education and practice, where critical/radical approaches place greater emphasis on this aspect of education and practice. The inclusion of social change as a focus is, however, indicative of the importance of the emancipatory tradition present in each.

Interest in transformative learning theory and the work of Mezirow can be identified in a number of different ways in the social work education literature. Given the importance ascribed to critical reflection it is not surprising that Mezirow's work is often referenced in this literature (e.g. Bay & Macfarlane, 2011; Fook, 2016; Ixer, 2016). Morley (2008, 2012) and Morley and Dunstan (2013) have made more explicit links between critical reflection and critical approaches to social work, arguing that this is a connection that has not been given the attention that it deserves. Morley (2012) discusses critical reflection as a process of deconstruction and reconstruction and notes the significance of Mezirow's work in this second stage particularly. She echoes the transformative learning process outlined by Mezirow in noting that reconstruction, as a part of the reflective process,

> involves taking the awareness gained from the deconstruction process about the political processes and power dynamics implicated in the construction of knowledge and meaning and using this insight to (i) develop revised interpretations of experiences and to (ii) enable alternative understandings and courses of action to emerge.
>
> *(Morley, 2012, p. 1525)*

Mezirow's work also emerges more specifically in literature with an orientation toward critical and emancipatory social work. In these instances, transformative learning theory is clearly being considered in its emancipatory iteration, whereby individual perspective transformation is clearly linked to efforts to expose and oppose dominant discourses (e.g. Desyllas & Sinclair, 2014; Owens, Miller, & Grise-Owens, 2014). A number of authors have also used ideas drawn from transformative learning theory in either understanding social work students' experiences on field placement (Papouli, 2014), while engaged in international study experiences (Roholt & Fisher, 2013), and as a tool for designing field activities with a transformative intent (Pockett, 2015). Transformative learning theory has also been used as an analytical tool in researching aspects of social work education (McCusker, 2013).

Some accounts of the design and application of specific pedagogical strategies based on transformative learning theory, or shaped by such theory, also appear in the social work education literature (e.g. Chan, Lam, & Yeung, 2013; Grise-Owens, Cambron, & Valade, 2010). Transformative learning has also begun showing up in discussions of how social work education might begin to engage more effectively with issues of environment and sustainability (e.g. Crawford et al., 2015; Gray & Coates, 2015; Jones, 2009, 2012).

Some of the discussion regarding transformative learning theory and social work education adopts a broader approach, surveying social work education in general, or suggesting broader pedagogical models or frameworks drawing on transformative learning theory (e.g. Blunt, 2007; Mackinlay & Barney, 2014). Witkin (2014) argues the need for a transformative orientation in social work education as a whole. In doing so, he considers the ways in which the term 'transformation' has become overused and over-inclusive, making the case for a more specific and particular understanding of transformative learning, aligned with that articulated by Mezirow.

Witkin proposes a conceptualisation of transformation for use in social work education, emphasising the importance of creativity and imagination, and problematising and questioning.

Transformative learning theory in practice

An example of an initiative within social work education that draws explicitly on the work of Mezirow to design an intentionally transformative learning experience for students is the work that has been done at James Cook University (JCU) in the area of intercultural learning and international student mobility (Jones & Miles, 2017). A team of researchers drawn from JCU and a number of universities in Australia, Thailand and India conducted research looking at the nature of international student exchange programs in Australian social work education.[1] Such programs have become increasingly popular, particularly in the light of Australian government support available through the New Colombo Plan, and involve a range of practices including short-term mobility projects, field education placements and semester-long study abroad options.

While the learning benefits for students participating in such international exchange projects have been recognised and well documented in the literature (Dorsett, Clark, & Phadke, 2017; Walters, Charles, & Bingham, 2017), there have also been criticisms of the uncritical approaches that often characterise such programs, and in particular concerns about the reproduction of the oppressive colonialist relationships that exist between countries of the majority and minority worlds (Razack, 2009; Wehbi, 2009). Faculty at JCU who were involved in developing and facilitating a range of international mobility programs were particularly concerned with this critique and with finding a more critically conscious approach to conducting such programs, with a focus on avoiding the reproduction of oppressive and inequitable relationships. Research had highlighted that there was considerable variation in the way Australian social work educators were preparing students for international exchanges, but that often such preparation adopted an instrumental approach, giving little or no consideration to critical issues. Drawing on Mezirow's transformative learning theory, an approach to conducting international mobility programs was developed, with an explicitly critical and transformative orientation.

Previous practice experience indicated that travel to culturally unfamiliar destinations increases the likelihood of students experiencing 'disorienting dilemmas'. However, the mere experience of such disorientation does not inevitably lead to transformative learning, and certainly not to critically transformative learning. According to Mezirow, opportunities for critical reflection and critical-dialectical discourse are also essential. From a critical social work perspective, such reflection and dialogue should be focused on exposing unexamined assumptions relating to the operation of power and ideology, or, in Mezirow's terminology, to identify and challenge the limiting sociocultural distortions that may be part of our uncritically acquired frames of reference. This is particularly important in our current context, where the dominance of neoliberal ideology has reached the point where, for many students, and others, it is virtually invisible.

To this end, JCU faculty developed a pre-travel preparation resource for students engaging in international mobility projects. The resource is in the form of an open access eBook (Jones, Miles, & Gopalkrishnan, 2018) which presents students with a range of stimulus material and reflective tasks focused on a critical consideration of the topics of culture, racism, imperialism, privilege and intercultural practice. These preparation materials, and the reflective tasks associated with them, are designed to equip students with a critical lens through which to view their international experiences and to identify and interrogate their own taken-for-granted worldviews and frames of reference. The centrality and importance of reflection through dialogue is further emphasised by the commitment within the JCU approach to fully facilitated travel, where a JCU faculty member accompanies students on their international trip and facilitates daily focused group reflections. This dialogical process reflects Mezirow's belief in the value of discourse that is devoted to assessing contested beliefs, where such critical discussion promotes, develops and enacts transformation. Students are then encouraged to enact their learning not only through their actions while on the trip, but also to consider how an altered frame of reference may shape future learning and practice and social action. This dimension of the transformative process is the focus of post-trip group debriefing and reflection sessions.

This approach to international student mobility is an attempt to use Mezirow's transformative learning theory as an explicit pedagogy with a critical, emancipatory intent. By equipping students with a critical conceptual lens, the potential for disorienting cultural experiences to lead to critical reflection on existing worldviews is greatly enhanced. In particular, such an approach increases the likelihood that existing, taken-for-granted assumptions relevant to issues around power and ideology in an intercultural context will be identified and challenged (Jones & Miles, 2017).

Conclusion

The significance of this particular example can be set within a wider consideration of the purposes of social work education, and the ways in which Mezirow's transformative learning theory might provide useful guidance for critically oriented educators. There is no question that the dominance of neoliberal ideology within society, the higher education sector, and social work as a profession has led to an increasing focus on technical and instrumental approaches to education. Without exposure to alternative discourses, and without support to develop the conceptual tools and skills required for a critical analysis of both self and society, there is a risk that students' unquestioned frames of reference simply reflect dominant neoliberal ideologies, thereby reproducing and reinforcing relationships of oppression, domination and inequity.

Transformative learning theory argues that, as educators, we can challenge this situation through critically intentional pedagogy. In a practical sense this means being prepared to create disruptive, disorienting learning experiences, and equipping students with the skills required to then use those challenging experiences to look critically at society, but also to examine their own taken-for-granted assumptions and worldviews through critical reflection. Opportunities for such reflection must be built into the curriculum and enhanced by ensuring that reflection is not a solitary experience but rather one that is part of a dialogical and critical process of engaging with others to explore and question contested beliefs. Mezirow argued the outcome of such intentionally transformative educational practice is students whose frames of reference are more open, inclusive and critically aware. A critically transformative approach to social work education might, therefore, help to create the foundation for future social work practice which is oriented toward the progressive and emancipatory.

Note

1   http://goingplaces.edu.au

References

Allan, J. (2003). Theorising critical social work. In J. Allan, B. Pease, & L. Briskman (Eds.), *Critical social work: An introduction to theories and practices* (pp. 32–51). Crows Nest: Allen and Unwin.

Apple, M. (2006). *Educating the 'right' way: Markets, standards, God, and inequality*. New York: Routledge.
Barraclough, L. & McMahon, M. (2013). U.S.-Mexico border studies online collaboration: Transformative learning across power and privilege. *Equity & Excellence in Education*, 46(2), 236–251.
Baumgartner, L. (2012). Mezirow's theory of transformative learning from 1975 to present. In E. Taylor, P. Cranton & Associates (Eds.), *The handbook of transformative learning: Theory, research, and practice* (pp. 99–115). San Francisco, CA: Jossey-Bass.
Bay, U., & Macfarlane, S. (2011). Teaching critical reflection: A tool for transformative learning in social work? *Social Work Education*, 30(7), 745–758. doi:10.1080/02615479.2010.516429
Blunt, K. (2007). Social work education. *Journal of Teaching in Social Work*, 27(3–4), 93–114. doi:10.1300/J067v27n03_07
Bronner, S. (2011). *Critical theory: A very short introduction*. Oxford: Oxford University Press.
Brookfield, S. (2005). *The power of critical theory for adult learning and teaching*. Berkshire: Open University Press.
Brookfield, S. (2012). Critical theory and transformative learning. In E. Taylor, P. Cranton & Associates (Eds.), *The handbook of transformative learning: Theory, research and practice* (pp. 131–146). San Francisco, CA: Jossey-Bass.
Brooks, K., & Adams, S. (2015). Developing agency for advocacy: Collaborative inquiry-focused school-change projects as transformative learning for practicing teachers. *The New Educator*, 11(4), 292–308. doi:10.1080/1547688X.2015.1087758
Chan, E., Lam, W., & Yeung, S. (2013). Interprofessional competence: A qualitative exploration of social work and nursing students' experience. *Journal of Nursing Education*, 52(9), 509–515.
Crawford, F., Augustine, S., Earle, L., Kuyini-Abubakar, A., Luxford, Y. & Babacan, H. (2015). Environmental sustainability and social work: A rural Australian evaluation of incorporating eco-social work in field education. *Social Work Education*, 34(5), 586–599. doi:10.1080/02615479.2015.1074673
Dahl, K., & Millora, C. (2016). Lifelong learning from natural disasters: Transformative group-based learning at Philippine universities. *International Journal of Lifelong Education*. Advance online publication. doi:10.1080/02601370.2016.1209587
Desyllas, M., & Sinclair, A. (2014). Zine-making as a pedagogical tool for transformative learning in social work education. *Social Work Education*, 33(3), 296–316. doi:10.1080/02615479.2013.805194
Dorsett, P., Clark, J. & Phadke, S. (2017). India gateway program: Transformational learning opportunities in an international context. *International Social Work*, 60(4), 883–896. doi:10.1177/0020872815580041
Dunn, A., & Faison, M. (2015). The shuttering of educational studies: Neoliberalism, the political spectacle, and social injustice at a 'world class' university. *The Journal of Educational Foundations*, 28(1–4), 9–30.
Elliott, A. (2009). *Contemporary social theory: An introduction*. London: Routledge.
Fook, J. (2016). *Social work: A critical approach to practice*. London: Sage.
Fosnot, C. (2005). *Constructivism: Theory, perspectives, and practice*. New York: Teachers College Press.
Freire, P. (1970). *Pedagogy of the oppressed*. New York: The Seabury Press.
Freire, P. (1973). *Education for critical consciousness*. New York: The Seabury Press.
Freire, P. (1985). *The politics of education: Culture, power, and liberation*. Hadley, MA: Bergin & Garvey.
Freire, P. (1998). *Teachers as cultural workers: Letters to those who dare to teach*. Boulder, CO: Westview Press.
Giroux, H. (2004). *Take back higher education: Race, youth, and the crisis of democracy in the post-civil rights era*. New York: Palgrave Macmillan.
Gray, M., & Coates, J. (2015). Changing gears: Shifting to an environmental perspective in social work education. *Social Work Education*, 34(5), 502–512. doi:10.1080/02615479.2015.1065807
Grise-Owens, E., Cambron, S., & Valade, R. (2010). Using current events to enhance learning: A social work curricular case example. *Journal of Social Work Education*, 46(1), 133–146. doi:10.5175/JSWE.2010.200800062
Habermas, J. (1971). *Knowledge and human interests*. Boston: Beacon Press.
Habermas, J. (1984). *The theory of communicative action, (Vol 1): Reason and the rationalization of society*. (T. McCarthy, Trans.). Cambridge: Polity Press.
Habermas, J. (1987). *The theory of communicative action, (Vol 2): Lifeworld and system: A critique of functionalist reason*. (T. McCarthy, Trans.). Cambridge: Polity Press.
Hanesworth, C. (2017). Neoliberal influences on American higher education and the consequences for social work programmes. *Critical and Radical Social Work*, 5(1), 41–57. doi:10.1332/204986017X14835298292776
Hoggan, C. (2016). A typology of transformation: Reviewing the transformative learning literature. *Studies in the Education of Adults*, 48(1), 65–82. doi:10.1080/02660830.2016.1155849

Hoggan, C., & Cranton, P. (2015). Promoting transformative learning through reading fiction. *Journal of Transformative Education*, 13(1), 6–25. doi:10.1177/1541344614561864

hooks, B. (2004). *The will to change: Men, masculinity, and love*. New York: Washington Square Press.

Hosken, N. (2016). Social work, class and the structural violence of poverty. In B. Pease, S. Goldingay, N. Hosken, & S. Nipperess (Eds.), *Doing critical social work: Transformative practices for social justice* (pp. 104–119). Crows Nest: Allen & Unwin. doi:10.1080/02615479.2012.734803

Ixer, G. (2016). The concept of reflection: Is it skill based or values? *Social Work Education*. Advance online publication. doi:10.1080/02615479.2016.1193136

Jones, P. (2009). Teaching for change in social work: A discipline-based argument for the use of transformative approaches to teaching and learning. *Journal of Transformative Education*, 7(1), 8–25.

Jones, P. (2012). Transforming the curriculum: Social work education and ecological consciousness. In M. Gray, J. Coates & T. Hetherington (Eds.), *Environmental social work* (pp. 213–230). New York: Routledge.

Jones, P. & Miles, D. (2017). Transformative learning in international student exchange: A critical perspective. *Advances in Social Work & Welfare Education*, 19(2), 47–60.

Jones, P., Miles, D. & Gopalkrishnan, N. (2018). *Intercultural learning: Critical preparation for international student travel*. Sydney, Australia: UTS ePress.

Jovanovic, S. (2017). Speaking back to the neoliberal agenda for higher education. *Cultural Studies – Critical Methodologies*, 17(4), 327–332. doi:10.1177/1532708617706125

Kasworm, K., & Bowles, T. (2012). Fostering transformative learning in higher education settings. In E. Taylor, P. Cranton & Associates (Eds.), *The handbook of transformative learning: Theory, research, and practice* (pp. 388–407). San Francisco, CA: Jossey-Bass.

Kitchenham, A. (2006). Teachers and technology: A transformative journey. *Journal of Transformative Education*, 4(3), 202–225.

Lorenzetti, L., Azulai, A. & Walsh, C. (2016). Addressing power in conversation: Enhancing the transformative learning capacities of the world café. *Journal of Transformative Education*, 14(3), 200–219.

Lucal, B. (2015). Neoliberalism and higher education: How a misguided philosophy undermines teaching sociology. *Teaching Sociology*, 43(1), 3–14. doi:10.1177/0092055X14556684

Lundgren, H. & Poell, R. (2016). On critical reflection: A review of Mezirow's theory and its operationalization. *Human Resource Development Review*, 15(1), 3–28. doi:10.1177/1534484315622735

Macfarlane, S. (2016). Education for critical social work: Being true to a worthy project. In B. Pease, S. Goldingay, N. Hosken, & S. Nipperess (Eds.), *Doing critical social work: Transformative practices for social justice* (pp. 326–338). Crows Nest, NSW: Allen & Unwin.

Mackinlay, E., & Barney, K. (2014). Unknown and unknowing possibilities: Transformative learning, social justice, and decolonising pedagogy in Indigenous Australian Studies. *Journal of Transformative Education*, 12(1), 54–73. doi:10.1177/1541344614541170

Mayo, P. (1999). *Gramsci, Freire and adult education: Possibilities for transformative action*. London: Zed Books.

McCusker, P. (2013). Harnessing the potential of constructive-developmental pedagogy to achieve transformative learning in social work education. *Journal of Transformative Education*, 11(1), 3–25. doi:10.1177/1541344613482522

McLaren, P. (2015). *Pedagogy of insurrection: From resurrection to revolution*. New York: Peter Lang Publishers.

Mezirow, J. (1975). *Education for perspective transformation: Women's re-entry programs in community colleges*. New York: Centre for Adult Education, Columbia University.

Mezirow, J. (1978). Perspective transformation. *Adult Education*, 28, 100–110.

Mezirow, J. (1990a). How critical reflection triggers transformative learning. In J. Mezirow & Associates (Eds.), *Fostering critical reflection in adulthood: A guide to transformative and emancipatory learning* (pp. 1–20). San Francisco, CA: Jossey-Bass.

Mezirow, J. (1990b). Toward transformative learning and emancipatory education. In J. Mezirow & Associates (Eds.), *Fostering critical reflection in adulthood: A guide to transformative and emancipatory learning* (pp. 354–376). San Francisco: Jossey-Bass.

Mezirow, J. (1991). *Transformative dimensions of adult learning*. San Francisco, CA: Jossey-Bass.

Mezirow, J. (1997). Transformative learning: Theory to practice. *New Directions for Adult and Continuing Education*, 74, 5–12.

Mezirow, J. (2000). Learning to think like an adult: Core concepts of transformation theory. In J. Mezirow Associates (Eds.), *Learning as transformation: Critical perspectives on a theory in progress* (pp. 3–34). San Francisco, CA: Jossey-Bass.

Mezirow, J. (2003). Transformative learning as discourse. *Journal of Transformative Education*, 1(1), 58–63.

Mezirow, J. (2012). Learning to think like an adult: Core concepts of transformation theory. In E. Taylor & P. Cranton (Eds.), *The handbook of transformative learning: Theory, research and practice* (pp. 73–95). San Francisco, CA: Jossey-Bass.

Morley, C. (2008). Teaching critical practice: Resisting structural domination through critical reflection. *Social Work Education*, 27(4), 407–421. doi:10.1080/02615470701379925

Morley, C. (2012). How does critical reflection develop possibilities for emancipatory change? An example from an empirical research project. *British Journal of Social Work*, 42, 1513–1532. doi:10.1093/bjsw/bcr153

Morley, C., & Dunstan, J. (2013). Critical reflection: A response to neoliberal challenges to field education? *Social Work Education*, 32(2), 141–156. doi:10.1080/02615479.2012.730141

Mullaly, B. (2007). *The new structural social work* (3rd ed). Ontario: Oxford University Press.

Owens, L., Miller, J., & Grise-Owens, E. (2014). Activating a teaching philosophy in social work education: Articulation, implementation, and evaluation. *Journal of Teaching in Social Work*, 34(3), 332–345. doi:10.1080/08841233.2014.907597

Papouli, E. (2014). Field learning in social work education: Implications for educators and instructors. *Field Educator*, 4(2), 1–16.

Pease, B., & Nipperess, S. (2016). Doing critical social work in the neoliberal context: Working on the contradictions. In B. Pease, S. Goldingay, N. Hosken & S. Nipperess (Eds.), *Doing critical social work: Transformative practices for social justice* (pp. 3–24). Crows Nest: Allen & Unwin.

Pockett, R. (2015). 'Health in all placements' as a curriculum strategy in social work education. *Social Work Education*, 33(6), 731–743. doi:10.1080/02615479.2013.874411

Razack, N. (2009). Decolonizing the pedagogy and practice of international social work. *International Social Work*, 52, 9–21.

Roholt, R., & Fisher, C. (2013). Expect the unexpected: International short-term study course pedagogies and practices. *Journal of Social Work Education*, 49(1), 48–65. doi:10.1080/10437797.2013.755416

Segre, S. (2014). *Contemporary sociological thinkers and theories*. Surrey, UK: Ashgate.

Taylor, E. (1998). *The theory and practice of transformative learning: A critical review*. Ohio: ERIC Clearinghouse on Adult, Career, and Vocational Education.

Tyson, L. (2012). *Critical theory today: A user friendly guide*. Hoboken: Taylor & Francis.

Walters, C., Charles, J. & Bingham, S. (2017). Impact of short-term study abroad experiences on transformative learning: A comparison of programs at 6 weeks. *Journal of Transformative Education*, 15(2), 103–121. doi:10.1177/1541344616670034

Wehbi, S. (2009). Deconstructing motivations: Challenging international social work placements. *International Social Work*, 52(1), 48–59.

Witkin, S. (2014). Change and deeper change: Transforming social work education. *Journal of Social Work Education*, 50(4), 587–598. doi:10.1080/10437797.2014.947897

41
bell hooks trilogy
Pedagogy for social work supervision

Carolyn Noble

AUSTRALIA COLLEGE OF ALLIED PSYCHOLOGY, SYDNEY, AUSTRALIA

Introduction

bell hooks (b.1952) is an influential feminist educator and socio-cultural critic who has taught most recently at Berea College in Kentucky, where she is Distinguished Professor in Residence. She has authored a long list of scholarly articles addressing feminism, men and patriarchy, sexuality and love, cultural criticism, media and film studies and a delightful array of children's books.

It is her theories, stories and pedagogical examples that can be read across the boundaries of race, gender, class and educational levels that this chapter explores. Her teaching trilogy – *Teaching to Transgress: Education as the practice of freedom* (1994); *Teaching Community: A pedagogy of hope* (2003) and *Teaching Critical Thinking: Practical wisdom* (2010) encapsulate her ideas of anti-racist, anti-colonial, multi-cultural, and critical and feminist pedagogies. Her work promotes community, a pedagogy of hope, self-reflection, critique of power in and outside of the classroom and, importantly, critical thinking, as key qualities to undergo a transformative learning experience. These ideas are extremely relevant to social works' desire to teach critical thinking and to foster transformational learning. Her pedagogical approach is particularly pertinent to social work supervision. Employing an engaged pedagogy in supervision sessions and giving practitioners tools to employ a critical lens on their practice can play a key role in embedding a critical view of the world for current and future practitioners.

Early life

From her early career, hooks wanted to become a critical thinker and writer. The seeds were sown in her primary school years growing up in the American south where she recalls the empowering experience of being educated in an all-black school. Her black women teachers were committed to nurturing intellect so that the students would become scholars, thinkers and cultural workers; in her words, to become 'black folks who used our "minds"' and 'to develop our own authentic voice' (hooks, 1994, 2003). She discovered early that her devotion to learning, to a life of the mind was a counter-hegemonic act; a fundamental way to resist every strategy of racist colonialisation that existed at the time. The teachers were there to guide the students and show them the way to freedom. For her, experiencing the classroom as a place of ecstasy and pleasure was a revolutionary pedagogy that was anti-colonial because it was rooted in anti-racist struggle. It was where she first learnt to experience learning as revolution (hooks, 1989, 1994).

Despite the positive experience of her early education, hooks was confronted by the constraints of her race, gender and class in what she calls the 'apartheid South'. In the quest for a writer's life she quickly realised that this path required her to enter academe, to become a teacher herself. Moving from an all-black educational setting to a de-segregated, predominately white college and graduate school, she found that her teachers merely exulted the upper-middle-class values and social norms of the white supremacist patriarchy (hooks, 1994, p.49). Attending a de-segregated school meant responding and reacting to white folks. In college she was amazed to find teachers derived pleasure by exercising their authority and power 'crushing our spirits and dehumanising our minds and bodies' (hooks, 1994, p.2). Education, she found, was reinforcing domination, rather than continuing the empowering experience of her early school years. She quickly learnt that attending college, rather than a 'paradise of learning', was a place where students were taught obedience to authority; and where teachers viewed black students as inferior and incapable of learning (hooks, 1994, p.2). In particular, she writes that graduate college was experienced as a prison, a place of punishment and confinement rather than a place of promise and freedom. As a black American woman in prestigious (white) colleges (she attended four) she felt that she was not there to learn but to prove she was of equal value to the white teachers. Furthermore, she found that knowledge was not contextualised within the framework of black student lives, but that lectures, textbooks, curricula and personal experience only served to reinforce stereotypes about black Americans.

During her studies she encountered bored teachers and bored students contrasting with her desire for knowledge and engagement with learning as a place of wonderment and imagination. Gone was the messianic zeal to transform student minds and selves she experienced as a young student. Knowledge was sharing of information without a critical lens. She was to learn obedience, that too much eagerness from her and her black students could easily be regarded as a 'threat to white authority'; while their non-conformity was viewed as a way of hiding their inferiority or incompetence (hooks, 1994, p.3). The curricula, she argued, had no relation to the way people lived, especially those who were marginalised, oppressed and discriminated against. Conformity to the status quo of 'white, mostly male authority and privilege' was the norm; to her utter dismay she found that education and the language used were not about the practice of freedom but merely to reinforce domination (hooks, 1994, p.4). Being constantly confronted by biases that hid undercurrents of discrimination and exclusion, which in turn created additional stress in her life, meant that her adult learning experiences were undermined.

Academic endeavours

While the 1960s and 1970s were heralding a climate of radical change, proclaiming the rise of equality and democratic education, hooks found that in reality and in the classroom old hierarchies of class, gender and race were untouched by the radical politics of the time, especially for black students who had to traverse the ambiguity of aspiration and reality. While she wanted to become a teacher in order to help students become self-directed learners, she found that the abuses of power were still in place and the challenge for her was how to address them. Not defeated by her experiences and the feeling of stress coupled with the ever-present boredom and apathy, she used these emotions and experiences as her inspiration that learning could be different!

Against the odds she gained a BA in English Literature at Stanford (1973), an MA at University of Wisconsin (1976) and a PhD at UCLA (1983), and secured a teaching position at Yale. These academic achievements did not eliminate the racist, elitist culture of education endemic at the time or her experiences of discrimination, nor did it dampen her love of learning, nor undermine her love of teaching which she continues to do today (Wisnesky, 2013).

Teaching career

It was serendipitous that her first teaching job was in a feminist classroom, and on black women writers from a feminist perspective, which enabled her to begin her exploration of pedagogical paradigms to critique the politics of domination in academic culture. Thanks to women studies programs that emerged across the college campuses in the 1980s and 1990s, feminist classrooms were the only place where pedagogical practice was 'allowed' to be interrogated. Students could raise critical questions about pedagogical processes where it was 'safe' and almost expected.

In this teaching space she began to explore a blueprint for her own pedagogical practice. Encountering Paulo Freire, she found a mentor, a guide, and someone who understood that learning could be liberatory (hooks, 1994). Black feminist and abolitionist Sojourner Truth, civil rights leader and community activist Martin Luther King, Jr. and Buddhist teacher, Thich Nhat Hanh were influential in helping weave her ideas to formulate a blend of critical pedagogies. From Freire she adopted his critical thinking and reflection (conscientisation), and his concept of banking (memorising and regurgitating information for later recall). From Truth and King Jr. she incorporated community and politics of hope and Hanh a sense of spiritualism and teaching as healing practice to develop classroom communities that 'cultivate engagement in authentic learning whose purpose is to transgress the class, sexism and racist boundaries' imbued in the education system (Brosi & hooks, 2012).

It was not a smooth journey. hooks' initial attempt to create and sustain a learning community met with strong resistance. Students did not want to learn new pedagogical practices and did not want to be in a classroom that differed from the norm; transgressing boundaries was frightening. Students were reluctant to place themselves and their emotions in view and for reflection; let alone for interrogation. It was enough, the students said, to hear from a disruptive black writer and her feminist ideas, without having to enjoy this unsettling experience. Introducing the notion of pleasure and excitement, making room for spontaneous eruptions of thought, to challenge the current student teacher hierarchical arrangements, to challenge their reliance on expert knowledge and to make this critique fun was considered, by her students, a transgression beyond accepted boundaries, a tough gig at that! (hooks, 1994, 2003). Her non-conformity and scepticism of the educational machine were viewed with suspicion. She had few academic colleagues who supported her critique. A smart, black woman academic was an anomaly in a mainly white college (hooks, 2003, p.97).

Things began to change when she stepped from the formal role of teacher to engage with the students as intellectuals and the classroom as one of mutual engagement. She then embarked on her journey to record and reflect on her experience. Her first book, *Teaching to Transgress: Education as the practice of freedom* (hooks, 1994) (and what was to become the first in a trilogy) outlines her attempts to transform the classroom from the stuffy, conservative, assembly-line approach to education, and seek ways to make learning more exciting and relaxing. In embarking on this project, hook deliberately eschews academic language proffering the use of the vernacular of colloquial speech and unstylised language and to use autobiography and storytelling as teaching tools.

Her thesis is that for the educational experience to be authentic it should help students become 'whole' human beings, striving not only for knowledge but knowledge of how to live in the world; to enable them to 'come to voice' and have their views acknowledged and affirmed (Bauer, 2000, p.270). She muses that a lot of effort is needed to entice every student to be fully engaged in the classroom dynamics. Quite a lot of effort is required for the teacher to engage the student in her/his context and language. Quite a lot more effort, she continues, is needed to encourage students to willingly make themselves vulnerable to challenges, questions and scrutiny, especially with students who come from privileged white backgrounds. She notes that while oppressed or colonised students seem to find a new sense of power and identity in freeing themselves from the colonised mind, privileged white students are (often) resistant to acknowledging their role in the domination of others to their advantage and instinctively resist the challenge to critical reflect on their privilege and its rewards (hooks, 1989, 1994).

hooks also makes the argument that to teach democratically demands that action moves beyond the classroom. Education is not just about acquiring a job or receiving information or exploring new ideas. It is about healing and wholeness. It is about empowerment, liberation, finding and claiming oneself and one's place in the world (2003, p.43). Keeping knowledge sharing just in the classroom devalues it and sets up splitting between what is colloquially called the 'town versus the gown' (Noble, 2016). It is about taking the classroom knowledge into the community and embracing a lifelong commitment to learning and sharing knowledge. It is about the promise of a more inclusive multi-cultural curriculum. This means including diversity in the choice of readings and discussion topics that address issues of race, class and gender. She invites teachers to extend the discourse of race, gender, class and nationalism beyond the classroom into everyday situations of learning; into the community. These ideas are further explored in her next book, *Teaching Community: A pedagogy of hope* (2003).

In *Teaching Community: A pedagogy of hope*, she continues her theme of seeking an alternative learning culture. Still using autobiography and storytelling and writing in laypersons' language, hooks calls on teachers to teach democratically, to approach teaching as an art form, a vocation, an exercise in free speech for all. Teaching can happen anywhere, not just the classroom – in churches, libraries, in homes and bookstores, anywhere people gather together to learn and share ideas that affect their daily lives. The performative aspect of teaching can be used to create space for invention, spontaneous shifts and as a catalyst for drawing out unique elements of everyone in the classroom. To do this helps create and build a community (hooks, 2003).

She encourages students and teachers to form a partnership by sharing experiences (good and bad). There is no better place, hooks argues, than the classroom where students are invited to challenge, to confront and change the hidden trauma of feeling different or stigmatised. For hooks, conveying genuine respect and care for students, especially those deemed 'other' or 'different', can affirm everyone's right to self-determination; to self-actualisation. In moving from the trauma of feeling marginalised or different in a classroom to experience the power of recognition and respect and to be fully present in a place where all voices are deemed worthy, is education as the practice of freedom and hope (2003, p.103). This process calls for a recognition of the experience that is humanising. Palmer (1993) calls it the 'intimacy that does not annihilate difference'.

Education as the practice of freedom enables teachers and students to confront feelings of loss and restore a sense of connection. 'It teaches how to create community' not only in the classroom but a feeling of connection and closeness 'with the world beyond the academy' (hooks, 2003, p.103). For example, hooks notes that the progressive study of race and gender in the academy had impact beyond the classroom as social justice movements for race and gender equality changed both the academy and the broader political stage beyond the classroom. In challenging the way imperialist notions of white supremacy, of nationalism and of patriarchy have created biases in teaching material and teaching styles, curricula, and other educational material, required teachers to not only incorporate diversity of readings and discussion topics but to teach from a standpoint that includes awareness of race, sex and class in conjunction with a multi-cultural curriculum (Bauer, 2000; hooks, 1989, 2003). This is what she means by creating a community (hooks, 2003).

For hooks, uniting feminist and anti-racist theory with practical application has been a challenge (hooks, 2003). Much of the academic theorising about feminism and anti-racist discourse, she argues, is complex and exhibits a class bias since the ideas and critiques have little relationship to the lived experiences of most women and 'black folks', particularly those who come from marginalised groups, many of whom are illiterate and lack access to higher education. Similar to Freire's literacy campaign in Brazil in the 1960s before the Junta came to power, hooks was a fierce advocate for literacy classes in her community, the lack of which she regarded as the biggest impediment to education for most black students. This lack of access excludes many from contributing to political, academic, scientific and intellectual life (hooks, 2003). To address this lack, hooks adopted a non-conventional scholarly format in her writing style motivated by the desire to be as inclusive as possible, to as many readers as possible. For hooks the use of language is important.

For hooks the use of the vernacular speech, languages other than standard English, was a key pedagogical tool and valued for its diversity and inclusiveness. To be inclusive and non-elitist, her scholarship includes essays, stories, interviews and conversations, self-dialogues, testimonials, class lessons and anecdotes, eschewing formal academic avenues of scholarship. In these texts she discusses and presents her ideas, always finding a link with her experiences and that of her audience (hooks, 1994, 2003). She is not fazed by the criticism that her work is not scholarly enough, but insists her desire to be accessible outweighs any criticism from the academy (although the lack of references, for example, makes it hard to see who influences who in this area of critical educational discourse).

Her third book, *Teaching Critical Thinking: Practical wisdom* (2010) continues her work to make the classroom a place of fierce engagement and intense learning. Reintegrating much from the other two books she expands on her experiences and, still using testimonials of herself and transcripts of conversations with students and colleagues, she lays herself open, exposing her life story as each of her books asks the reader to share and even join in the ongoing story line of her life and work (Öhman, 2010, p.287). It is her individual quest to explore the longing to know, to understand how life works, that she presents to her audience. Located in her lived experience and with examples from her teaching she makes her arguments seem refreshingly original and confrontingly candid.

Critical thinking

As hooks is notorious for the absence of citations in her work it is hard to judge how she was influenced by critical educational theorists' writing and researching about critical thinking and pedagogy before, during and since her project began. To my reading there is much overlap with Freire, Giroux and Brookfield who do reference her work. There are ideas in hooks' books that could come directly from either one and vice versa, especially Freire (1972, 1974), Apple (1990), Giroux (2010, 2011, 2012, 2014), Apple and Au (2014) and Brookfield (2012) whose actual terminology is evident in hooks' work (e.g. educating for freedom, politics of hope). But the way she presents her pedagogical practice in her trilogy is her original contribution on teaching critical thinking and employing an engaged pedagogy. Its uniqueness is in its direct applicability to the experiences, challenges and choices she has faced both in the classroom and in her life to date.

She states that critical thinking involves discovering the who, what, when, where and how of things and then utilising that knowledge in a manner that enables one to determine what matters most (hooks, 2003, 2010). Critical thinking requires all participants in the classroom process to be actively engaged. It demands everyone keeps an open mind and not stay attached to or protective of one's viewpoint in such a way as to rule out all or any other possibilities or perspectives. As an interactive initiative, its aim is to understand core, underlying truths, not the superficial, knee-jerk reactions or those most obviously visible. In one word it involves 'deconstruction' of any given fact, truth or information. It demands students and teachers to think long, hard and critically, to unpack, to move beneath the surface, to work for knowledge. Thinking is action. For her the shape of knowledge constantly shifts and changes as the teacher and student interrogate ideas, facts, options and positions. Therefore, it calls for an openness from everyone. Teachers and students are encouraged to cross the boundaries of class, race, gender and circumstance to move beneath the surface, to work for knowledge. For hooks, to think critically about the self and identity in relation to one's political circumstance is the essence of a truly liberatory experience (hooks, 2010).

A core component of her classroom activity involves the use of conversations, stories, personal narratives and reflections, songs and poems where, as a result, the classroom resonates with ideas and raw unmediated emotions – where each voice is heard. She says 'students listen to one another's stories with an intensity that is not always present during a lecture or discussion' (hooks, 2010, p.51). Stories help students connect to a world beyond the self and in making connections with other stories we can make powerful connections with a diverse world. Stories, hooks argues, are a way of knowing; they contain both the power and the art of possibility … 'we need more stories', she laments (2010, p.53).

In sharing stories, along with other teaching materials it is crucial for both teacher and student to review the assumptions, predilections, thoughts and actions embedded in the content through as many different theoretical and experiential lenses as possible. This, for hooks, is how an authentic learning community is built and maintained. In the unpacking of ideas, of curricula, of stories, of assumed knowledge and 'fact', students share the process of thinking and critiquing in an open manner; there is no failure, everyone is participating in order to 'enlarge consciousness' (2010, p.17). The aim is for students to leave the classroom knowing that critical thinking empowers everyone. As hooks states, 'When we only name the problem, when we only state complaint without a constructive focus on resolution, we take away hope' (hooks, 2003, p.xix). Not resolving the issues or finding a way forward, such critique can become 'merely an expression of profound cynicism, which then works to sustain dominator culture' (2010, p.xiv)

Just recognising the problem is not enough. What is also needed, she argues, is to fully and deeply articulate what is needed to do that will work to address and resolve issues that will generate and inspire a spirit of ongoing resistance. A pedagogy that denounces all systems of domination creates a sense of hope. Living in hope, hooks provides a way out, a way forward, a path worth travelling toward a hopeful, more just future. For hooks and her mentor Freire (1972) and other such critical thinkers such as Apple (1990), Giroux (2011, 2014), Brookfield (2012) and Apple and Au (2014), a sense of hope empowers teachers to work for justice even as the forces of injustice continue. Teachers connecting with these issues and practicing an engaged pedagogy bring this hope into the classroom. In emphasising well-being for all students, an engaged pedagogy is, however, more demanding than conventional teaching but, according to hooks, the only hope for an education that promises hope of a better future for students, especially those marginalised from the current socio-political, cultural and educational discourse. In the three books addressed in this chapter it is the current social, political and cultural power relations of the hegemonic state that explain her experiences as a black woman in the USA. For hooks, knowledge is embedded in the politics of imperialist, white-supremacist capitalist patriarchy (hooks, 2010, p.29). Indeed, for all critical educationalists the capitalist, imperial, patriarchal system of domination is still the current challenge today (Apple, 1990; Brookfield, 2012; Connell, 2019; Freire, 1972, 1974, 1994; Giroux, 2011, 2014).

Current context of higher education

Despite the ongoing critique from hooks and her critically informed colleagues to hold back the tide of oppressive hegemonic curricula and culture, we find culture and politics are inseparable and in many higher education institutions curricula are still pre-determined and lecture halls are basically 'containers for empty vessel pedagogy on a grand scale' (Connell, 2019). In many institutions the standard practice for 'knowledge transfer' still relies on lectures, textbooks, prescribed readings, pre-planned discussions, quizzes and exams. hooks is not alone in her quest to challenge institutions of learning to break open these hegemonic practices and curricula. Giroux (2012, 2014); Brookfield (2012) and Connell (2019) agree with hooks (and vice versa) that for the 'good university' to grow and flourish, the power structures need to be constantly and consciously challenged. As Connell states as currently as 2019:

> We need to break down race, class and caste exclusions, patriarchal privilege and the links between elite universities and corporate power. Within universities we need to end managerial control, the selling of assets, the commercialisation of knowledge, and the culture of lying.
>
> *(Connell, 2019, p.187)*

And Giroux in 2012: '[We need to resist university] administrators who lack either a broader vision or critical understanding of education as a force for strengthening the imagination and expanding democratic public life' (Giroux, 2012, p.715).

Connell (2019, p.53) in applying hooks' politics of hope to the current higher education culture, argues that learning with excitement and hope – Connell uses the metaphor 'catching fire' – does not make teaching obsolete but changes its logic. By engaging with hooks and other critical theorists, Connell (2019) reminds us that teaching and learning with a critical lens is about challenging the social limits embedded in the hegemonic curriculum in order to build a democratic society free from oppression (Giroux, 2014; hooks, 2010; Öhman, 2010). If it were not critical or reflective, pedagogy would continue to be part of the hyperconsumerism of oppressive neoliberalism without any pushback or seeking of alternatives (Giroux, 2011, 2014; hooks, 2010). It would continue to serve and reproduce the oppressive power relations embedded in late capitalism, imperialism and patriarchy which dominated educational cultures.

Critical pedagogy's strength is in positing that knowledge cannot be separate from experience. By creating a world where there is a union between theory and practice, one can fully engage with ideas and create a learning environment that is pursuing a democratic purpose for the whole society (hooks, 1994, 2003, 2010). It is about combining student initiatives, post-colonial perspectives, feminist analysis, environmental knowledge, including alternative knowledge formations, alternative media and practical applications. That is, it needs to be informed by critical theory and be transferable into practice. Herein lies a perfect segue to link hooks' pedagogical project with that of critically imbued social work supervision; whose focus is to link theory with practice and practice with theory; to foster reflection *in* practice and thread critical theory *within* its praxis.

Critically informed social work

Social work works in the 'social' spaces that society labels as marginal; tangential to its effective operation. It works with the groups considered least popular; the poor, unemployed, the homeless, the aged, migrants and asylum seekers, women, the young and Aboriginal and Torres Strait peoples (it is quite a big population really!). These groups exist on the borderland of invisibility; and when visible, often wear the tag 'dole bludgers', 'no hopers', 'welfare cheats' and the like (Noble et al., 2016). Their social stigma and oppression are a result of what hooks calls the politics of imperialist, white-supremacist, capitalist patriarchy, where white, Anglo men become the beneficiaries of social, political, cultural and economic power and its rewards (hooks, 2003, 2010).

Social work's critical agenda, then, is to challenge the social spaces of marginality, stigma and oppression by working collectively and individually to empower and liberate people from the yoke of their oppression; from being denied justice and human rights, and to understand and challenge systems, processes and people in surrounding contexts that contribute to their oppression (Morley, Macfarlane & Ablett, 2019). This critical analysis fuels the values and mission of social workers to provide a vision of a society better than the one we presently have (Noble et al., 2016). It demands a deconstruction of present socio-political, economic and cultural relations and their supporting structures and discourses for a more humane and just, democratic society. This is where hooks' work on engaged pedagogy and critical thinking can be translated into social work's mission to educate critical social workers. In its progressive discourse, social work education is viewed as a deeply civic, political and moral practice (Morley et al., 2019). So, to make the transition to a critically informed practitioner the profession needs to employ a critical lens in social work supervision sessions and practice as key sites for this activity (see Noble et al., 2016). That is, the development of critical practitioners needs a critically informed pedagogy for its use.

Critical social work supervision: applying an engaged pedagogy

As supervision is often a highly individualised endeavour (even in group settings, the focus is on the individual) it is strategically a key practice area that can provide the supervisors and supervisees (practitioners and or students) with the opportunity to develop, explore, enrich their practice and integrate theory with practice and vice versa. As a teaching space it can provide social workers with a safe and confidential environment to name and address the tensions, contradictions, ambiguities and conflicts encountered in practice situations and workplaces. For supervisors to help interrogate the many dimensions of disengaging from oppressive practices and for critical supervision to support the development of critical practitioners, we can draw on hooks' critical pedagogy to apply it in practice.

Indeed, hook's critical pedagogy can be readily applied to all the areas of study linked to social work's emancipatory mission, which is to create critical thinking and interweave it within its context, content and praxis. A critical perspective is about creating 'big picture' practitioners, who see and consider surrounding contexts of their practice and the broader context in which organisations function, service users live, practitioners work and the interplay within and among them. Moving the lens from the immediate circumstances of their practice to the wider 'webs of connection' to see all influencing dynamics in play enables practitioners, supervisors and students to understanding the nature of oppression, both their own and that of others and how the knowledge created from this analytical lens might free them from the dominant hegemony that both perpetrates and supports their oppression.

hooks knew that developing a critical educational practice is not done as a single event. Critical supervisors know that forming a critical lens to understand practice and effect change is a lifelong practice that demands a conscious commitment (also see Noble et al., 2016, p.145).

Like hooks' attempts in the classroom, using an engaged pedagogy in supervision is not a benign activity; it assumes a political, determinative and non-neutral stance in the world. While social, political or educational change may be illusive and/or difficult, the ability to understand those contexts in which power dynamics work and the ways challenge is possible can create a greater sense of purpose imbued with future possibilities (hooks, 2003, 2010). There are many sites in which this activity can occur, including individual, group, peer and community-based supervision. Organisational support is also important. However, without the appropriate tools and skills used in a particular way, critical supervisors and supervisees might not achieve their intention. Significantly, working critically needs a pedagogy.

Critical (engaged) pedagogy for use in supervision sessions: how?

Critical pedagogy for supervision involves a combination of critical questioning and analysis, critical reflection, critical reading, critical deconstruction and reconstruction and having critical conversations before, in and after practice moments. For supervision, applying a critical lens means reflecting on the particular interpretations of the helping relationship and power relations embedded within the interactions between the supervisor and supervisee as well as exploring the content, structure, associated tasks and assessments used in supervision sessions with the same critical lens.

In hooks' terms it means democratising the supervision process while also valuing differences in experiences and interpretations. Issue-based and solution-focused learning, critical reflection, critical incidents analysis, critical reading of case notes, research studies, critical literature, constructionist learning and use of narratives including autobiographical texts, journaling, storytelling, talking circles, hunting for false narratives, and ambiguous situations and other creative artistry are suitable tools for developing a critical pedagogy (see chapters 10 and 11 in Noble et al. (2016) for using the process and practice examples). Exploring the pedagogical tools listed above enables supervisors and supervisees to look deeper into the nature and function of their work and the context in which they practice and on how they reflect on service users lives and conditions and how that critique and reflection will inform a critically informed practice response. To be effective, critical supervision must be transformative; for supervisees, students and ultimately the service users who are impacted by social work interventions.

For hooks, exploring and shining a light on places of marginalisation (for herself as well as her students and community) become sources of resistance and optimism. hook places students and teachers in a partnership, critical supervisors place service users as well as supervisees as equal partners exploring the ways, for example, in which people come to adopt and be silenced by dominant ideologies, to awaken possibilities for change and transformation. It is built on resistance by querying features and obstacles in daily life that get in the way of fair treatment and those most affected by injustice and seeking actions to address these inequities. It can also re-instil a politics of hope. By employing the pedagogy of hope we move from a position of defeat and powerlessness to one of belief and optimism in the possibilities of change and resistance.

Engaging in open and inclusive dialogues to help those who seek greater control over their lives; to envisage a better future, for curricula to achieve their goal, they need to be linked to the emancipatory project of social justice, human rights and anti-oppressive social work practice. Developing a critical pedagogy means centring on the interactive aspects of practice experiences and situations in the socio-political, economic and cultural relations of power. It also means becoming theory literate and keeping up-to-date with new critiques about social-political relations and new spheres of concern such as the environment, sustainability and newly emerging critique of post-conventional, post-human social work.

In the supervision session and classroom components, the focus of an engaged pedagogy is to make the learning space a safe place; provide supervisors, supervisees and students with a life-sustaining, mind-expanding opportunity to learn and share the learning. In focusing on mutuality between the supervisor, supervisee and service user as well as the learning environment, participants are encouraged to work together in partnership to create a community of scholars; to experience a sense of profound hope for the future where, through education, individuals can transform their lives. That is, to 'learn why the world wags and what wags it' (hooks, 2003, p.43). According to hooks, learning should be joyous and steeped in political commitment, it should be unashamedly connected to anti-racist and feminist struggles – struggles she maintains have mainly paid off (Bauer, 2000; hooks, 2003, 2010).

A critical pedagogy when applied to social work supervision can set a curriculum that forges an expanded notion of politics and agency through a language of scepticism and possibility, and a culture of openness, debate and engagement (see Noble et al., 2016). When applied to supervision, an engaged pedagogy can foster a holistic experience where teachers and students, supervisors and practitioners share stories from their lives, listen and reflect on the voices of others and enter difficult discussions to create a narrative of life that is uplifting. Sharing knowledge fosters the development of new ideas which then circulate from classmate to classmate to teacher and back again to create a common thought, eschewing the obsession with experts owning ideas. Ideas rarely originate and are fostered in a vacuum (hooks, 2003; Noble, 2011, 2011a).

In conclusion

Critical thinking and exploring an engaged pedagogy in social work supervision practice as an interactive process demands active and self-reflective participation on the part of supervisors, supervisees and students alike. When modelled in the practice of supervision, the social workers', the students' and the service users' voices and socio-political and cultural content become centre stage. Calling attention to race, gender, class or sexual preference illuminates the markers that situate and locate the person in their true essence. By applying hooks' engaged pedagogy as a basis for a transformational learning for supervision, supervisors, students and practitioners are provided with both the theory and skills to practice critically and model a critical practice when a progressive transformative response to the current practice context and social issues is most needed. An engaged pedagogy is pivotal to a transformative approach to social work supervision, especially as the current student population is increasingly multi-cultural and with varying levels of educational competence and positional power.

References

Apple, M. (1990). *Ideology and curriculum*. New York: Routledge.
Apple, M., Au, W., (2014). *Critical education*. London: Routledge.

Bauer, M. (2000). Implementing a liberatory feminist pedagogy: Bell hooks's strategy for transforming the classroom. In *MELUS. 25(2/4)*. (Fall/Winter). 265–274.

Brookfield, S. (2012). *Teaching for critical thinking: Tools and strategies to help students question their assumptions*. San Francisco: John Wiley & Sons, Inc.

Brosi, G., & hooks. b. (2012). *The Beloved community: A conversation with bell hooks*. https://muse.jhu.edu/article/488754

Connell, R. (2019). *The good university: What universities do and why it's time for radical change*. Clayton, Melbourne: Melbourne University Press.

Freire, P. (1972). *Pedagogy of the oppressed*. Harmondsworth: Penguin.

Freire, P. (1974). *Education for critical consciousness*. New York: Continuum.

Freire, P. (1994). *Pedagogy of hope*. New York: Continuum.

Giroux, H. 2010. Rethinking education as the practice of freedom: Paulo Freire and the promise of critical pedagogy. *Policy Futures in Education. 8(6)*. 715–720.

Giroux, H. (2011). *On critical pedagogy*. New York: Continuum.

Giroux, H. (2012). When hope is subversive. *TIKKUN*. 19(6). 38–39.

Giroux, H. (2014). *Neoliberalism's war on higher education*. Chicago, USA: Haymarket Books.

hooks, b. (1989). *Talking back: Thinking feminist, thinking black*. Toronto, ON: Between the Lines.

hooks, b. (1994). *Teaching to transgress: Education as the practice of freedom*. New York: Routledge.

hooks, b. (2003). *Teaching community: A pedagogy of hope*. New York: Routledge.

hooks, b. (2010). *Teaching critical thinking: Practical wisdom*. New York: Routledge.

Morley, C., Macfarlane, S., & Ablett, P. (2019). *2e, Engaging with social work: A critical introduction*. Port Melbourne: Cambridge University Press.

Noble, C. (2011). Field Education: Supervision, curricula and teaching methods. In C. Noble & M. Henrickson (eds). *Social work field education and supervision across the Asia Pacific*, Sydney University Press, Sydney, NSW. 3–22.

Noble, C. (2011a). Ways of thinking about field education and supervision; building a critical perspective. In C. Noble & M. Henrickson. (eds). *Social work field education and supervision across the Asia Pacific*, Sydney University Press, Sydney, NSW. 299–320.

Noble, C. (2016). Social work and community welfare: Taking the community-campus engagement agenda forward. In C. Pratt (ed). *The diversity of university-community engagement: An international perspective*, D&D Digital Printing, Melbourne. 67–75.

Noble, C., Gray, M., & Johnston, L. (2016). *Critical supervision for the human services: A social model to promote learning and value-based practice*. London: Jessica Kingsley.

Öhman, A. (2010). Bell hooks and the sustainability of style. *NORA. Nordic Journal of Feminist and Gender Research*. 18(4). 284–289.

Palmer, P. (1993) *To Know as We are Known: Education as a Spiritual Journey*, Harper Collins e-books.

Wisnesky, D. (2013). bell hooks: Scholar, cultural critic, feminist and teacher. In J.D. Kirylo (ed.). *A critical pedagogy for resistance: 34 pedagogues we need to know*, Sense Publications, Boston. 73–76.

42
Navigating the politics and practice of social work research
With advice from Pierre Bourdieu

Mark Brough

Rod Kippax

Barbara Adkins

QUEENSLAND UNIVERSITY OF TECHNOLOGY, AUSTRALIA

Introduction

Social workers occupy a challenging space within the politics of knowledge. They draw on a range of knowledges to inform their practice, including a diverse set of social sciences, but also a variety of experiential knowledges derived from their day-to-day work with diverse communities. While social work does its best to synthesise this knowledge within an overarching commitment to social justice, questions remain about who decides if this commitment is realised (Spolander et al., 2016). Not least among the complicating forces here is the tension between structure and agency. Dominant neoliberal regimes of contemporary institutions are crafted to provide an individualised analytic of social problems (Lorenz, 2005). In this frame, poverty is transformed to an individual deficit 'solved' via better skills in budgeting; or health inequality is understood at the level of individual behaviour rather than in terms of race, class and gender. Knowledges to inform critical social work research are contested by a dominant discourse founded on the depoliticisation of social problems (Garrett, 2010). Even so, this realisation is insufficient to capture the contemporary political dilemma facing social work. Drawing on commitments to social justice neatly positions social work as a progressive agent of change mobilised to act against forces of oppression. Yet social work must contend with its own potential to oppress. The workings of power and inequality do not stop at the borders of social work, hence any account of social work research based on a political analytic of society must also include a reflexive capacity. The sociologist, Pierre Bourdieu explored this dilemma for all social researchers and we look to him in this chapter to navigate a path forward.

We begin by outlining the work of Bourdieu before turning to three significant matters that continue to confront social work—the structure/agency tension, the reflexive turn, and the meaning of research within social work. We position the pedagogy of social work research as a somewhat neglected area of the social work curriculum. This neglect is no doubt partly a function of the social work identity where the 'work' is about being a 'practitioner' not a 'researcher' (e.g. see Crisp, 2000; Ryan & Sheehan, 2009; Brough et al., 2013 for accounts of this tension within the Australian context). However, this is a shifting field too, since social workers are increasingly asked to show the evidence behind their practice (Plath, 2006). How then might a critical social worker engage in research?

Pierre Bourdieu

Pierre Bourdieu (1930–2002) was born in Denguin, France. His mother and father both worked in a post office. In 1951 he was accepted into the prestigious École Normale Supérieure where he completed his studies in philosophy and became a teacher. Having been called to military duty in Algeria in 1955, he was to publish his first book in 1958, *Sociologie de l'Algérie* (Sapiro, 2015). This proved to be the beginning of a prolific academic career in which he published 30 books and 340 papers. Bourdieu substantially impacted on the social sciences not only in his own country of France, but also across the English-speaking world (Shusterman, 1999). The influence in social work appears to be more nascent, with a common tone of describing what Bourdieu might offer the discipline (e.g. see Garrett, 2007a, 2007b) rather than the matured status of a significant 'back catalogue' of achievement. Given the volume of his work and the extent of his influence, perhaps the most remarkable feature of Bourdieu's contribution is the difficulty in neatly categorising his work. Rather than an overarching theory of society, Bourdieu's work has developed a series of 'thinking tools' which emerged from his empirical investigations into a variety of questions.

Bourdieu, reflexivity and the social work research

Bourdieu's work is preoccupied with inequality and power. However, rather than see the sociologist's role in defining and discussing this as self-evident, Bourdieu centralises how we talk about this in the process of his sociological investigation. A concept key to this is the term 'reflexivity' which essentially means a capacity to see oneself within the production of knowledge (Morley, 2015). Bourdieu interrogates how power is stratified directly into the researcher space (Wacquant, 1989, p. 55, cited in Swartz, 1997, p. 11). For Bourdieu this is a matter of ensuring a sound epistemological foundation for knowledge. Importantly, it is also a key component of emancipatory research (Swartz, 1997, pp. 11–12).

The neoliberalisation of higher education research pedagogy privileges techniques. Increasingly, research is seen as a set of methods, commonly categorised in a neat qualitative/quantitative binary with little or no commitment to the politics of knowledge. In this frame, even where a commitment to social justice is claimed, it is contained within borders of the topic rather than connected to a critical understanding of the contours of power. This would never be enough for Bourdieu, for whom questions of epistemology are core to a serious reckoning of social justice. How we think about 'problems' and how we embed social justice within social work research-mindedness is fundamental here. One of the keys to answering these fundamental questions is through reflexivity.

While a pervasive term in social work, the term reflexivity is used in a variety of ways (see D'Cruz et al. (2007) for a review of social work's usage of the term). Not only is the term used inconsistently, the term is also often used interchangeably with similar sounding words, such as 'reflection', 'reflectivity' and 'critical reflection' (D'Cruz et al., 2007). This is not the place to review the multitude of formulations of reflexivity in social work, however it is worth noting that Bourdieu is highly critical of the limitations of notions of reflexivity tied to personal accounts of social positioning. Bourdieu argues this is a limited strategy since it ignores wider complexities of power. Here it is essential to begin to mobilise one of Bourdieu's key concepts—habitus. We elaborate this concept in more detail later, but for now it is essential to acknowledge the everyday ways in which power is exercised through habitus. For example, the mundane ways we eat, talk or dress, are understood as saturated with power, thus almost everything comes into view (Mol, 1991, pp. 1019–1020). For Bourdieu, habitus is an outcome of social structure as well as a generator of social practices that reproduce structures. Habitus transcends the individual/institutional dichotomy to embrace a diverse set of windows into the workings of power and inequality (Swartz, 1997, p. 89). Social work is of great interest at this juncture, since it attempts to read and resist the dominant structures of society that produce social injustice, but simultaneously must also be understood in terms of the multitudinous, and at times mundane, daily work practices that reinforce rather than resist oppressive structures.

For Bourdieu, dominating classes impose their cultural values, standards and tastes on society, or at least create standards of what is the highest, best or most legitimate. Unpacking habitus must involve a reflexive core, since to unpack the other's habitus without recognition of one's own habitus is a flawed enterprise. Thus, habitus is a useful concept for not only exploring the client communities that social workers engage with, but also for examining the habitus of social work itself. Indeed, it is in the relational aspects of social work practice involved in this nexus that habitus becomes most useful. A Bourdieu-inspired study of homeless shelters by Emirbayer and Williams (2005) revealed the dialectic at work between homeless clients and a range of shelters and the different configurations of social work. For example, some shelters were found to be rich in the capital of 'authenticity' while others were rich in the capital of 'order'. Rather than reduce understanding of this difference to idiosyncrasies of management, through Bourdieu it was possible to dissect the workings of power through an analysis of field and habitus. Pertinent here is Bourdieu's concern for how the study of a field (in this case homelessness) needs to be understood as a *refraction* not simply a reflection of wider social forces. There's no separation here of 'micro', 'mezzo' and 'macro', rather habitus provides a means to describe structures but without losing the human-ness of their invention.

Power and pedagogy

In taking up the need for reflexivity in research—the capacity to incorporate an understanding of oneself in the production of knowledge—the personal confessional, we emphasise the contemporary historical moment of the discipline. Parton and Kirk (2010) posit that, unlike some older professions (e.g. medicine, law, teaching, pharmacy and engineering), social work did not emerge until the second half of the nineteenth century. This occurred at a time of rapid social change catalysed by industrialisation. Social work continues to expand in response to global economic, political and social changes and upheavals associated with war and conflict. Parton and Kirk cite Jordan (1997) in positioning social work as 'shor[ing] up social order and also compensat[ing] their most vulnerable members in the face of the socially undesirable consequences of capitalist contractual relations' (2010, p. 4). This role leads to a clear tension central to social work practice: 'While it emerges primarily in contexts where market-orientated economic individualism becomes the dominant form of social relations, its values are informed by those of a caring, inclusive, reciprocal community that wants to take collective responsibility for its members' (Parton & Kirk, 2010, p. 4). This tension inhabits contemporary social work research in navigating the connections between the profession and the social 'system' and clearly also the 'lifeworld' of the people it serves. The following section describes a central theme throughout Bourdieu's work in the analysis of suffering, symbolic power and symbolic violence, and the development of a set of concepts dedicated to identifying the full set of relationships that give rise to these.

Bourdieu, suffering and symbolic power

Bourdieu foregrounds the need to address social suffering by developing a comprehensive and systematic analysis of the conditions that give rise to domination. In so doing, Bourdieu asks us to consider that suffering extends well beyond the circumstances of material poverty (*la grande misère*). He argues:

> [U]sing material poverty as the sole measure of all suffering keeps us from seeing and understanding a whole side of the suffering characteristic of a social order which, although it has undoubtedly reduced poverty overall … has also multiplied the social spaces (specialized fields and subfields) and set up the conditions for an unprecedented development of all kinds of ordinary suffering (la petite misère).
>
> *(Bourdieu et al., 1999, p. 4)*

In addition to the highly visible deprivations associated with material poverty, Bourdieu is drawing our attention to the less apparent 'psychic wounds' associated with deprivations of value and meaning (Peters, 2011, p. 71). These deprivations can clearly have a basis in people's level of access to resources such as income, education and employment but are crucially overlaid by a system of symbolic power that categorises individuals and groups, ascribes social value to positions and practices and creates conditions favouring compliance with this symbolic ordering. These processes of domination can be insidious and difficult to identify, often leaving those who are disadvantaged by this system to ascribe their problems to themselves. For Bourdieu, this amounts to symbolic violence. Suffering is very importantly understood as a product of this system of symbolic power and symbolic violence (Schubert, 2014). Schubert charts this theme as the key implicit reason evident throughout Bourdieu's work for studying society at all.

The analysis of the system of cultural tastes and their implications for ordering and symbolic power in his book *Distinction* (1984) stands as an example of how tastes and lifestyles constitute a system of signs based on social difference and distinction which favours some groups over others. The capacity to use consumption to represent oneself positively through commitment to the symbolic and the appropriation of appearances (Bourdieu, 1984, p. 253) is not available to all. If one's life revolves around securing basic necessities, this is attended by a habitus that embeds the requirement to submit to necessity in the bodily dispositions enacted in daily life through 'the practical and tacit adaptation of subjective expectations to objective chances'—one that rejects or refuses an emphasis on appearance and pretension (Peters, 2011, p. 76). Symbolic violence occurs as a result of the classification and hierarchisation of these different approaches to culture that enables the tastes and practices of some to be classified as 'common', thus ascribing a negative value to popular tastes.

Bourdieu et al. (1999) turns more explicitly to the analysis of social suffering in *Weight of the World*. This book was written after his studies discussed above that sought to develop models of the conditions that perpetuate disadvantage through the analysis of survey data complemented in places by ethnographic description. By contrast, *Weight of the World* examines these relationships through intensive examination of the experiences and circumstances of individuals. Social workers figure explicitly in the worlds of research participants as experiencing the frustrations of having to 'expend a lot of energy for often derisory results, with the wider mechanisms ceaselessly undoing what they are trying to do' (Bourdieu et al., 1999, p. 58). They are depicted as having to undertake 'the often-endless missions entrusted to them' with 'the paltry means granted to them', and as implicated in a system that raises the hopes of the disadvantaged, which are subsequently often dashed by the inequities of the education system (Bourdieu et al., 1999, p. 184).

The circumstances and problems described by study participants represent a microcosm of how symbolic power operates in the relationships between habitus, field and capital and how pain and suffering are associated with symbolic violence. For example, Bourdieu reports on his interview with Ali and François, two young men aged in their twenties, who live in 'one of the worst buildings of a project with a bad reputation'. Ali is the son of Moroccan immigrants and François is a 'native' of France. Both have reputations for toughness and possibly problems with the law. Bourdieu describes the relationships at school as behind their rejection of education and the adoption of toughness. He analyses Ali's positioning of himself as a product of his social and symbolic position in the school system:

> Everything suggests that the organizing principle behind his rejection of school and the defiant attitudes that lead him toward, and gradually trap him in, the role of the 'tough' is the desire to avoid the humiliation of having to read out loud in front of the other student.
> *(Bourdieu et al., 1999, p. 61)*

It is clear that François is also responding to a similar kind of symbolic power and symbolic violence. In fact, Bourdieu observes: 'they share every trait except ethnic origin' and therefore have a mutual understanding based on a shared 'destiny effect'. They share a sense of 'the obviousness of this form of collective bad luck that attaches itself, like a fate, to all those that have been put together in those sites of social relegation' (Bourdieu et al., 1999, p. 64).

Bourdieu's analyses and the pedagogy of social work research

The above account illustrates three consistent threads through Bourdieu's work. The first is a focus on symbolic power and symbolic violence as a central rationale for his studies. This resonates with those in social work research who conduct their investigations at the interface of market-oriented individualism and oppression.

Second, *Weight of the World* illustrates how Bourdieu's framework is oriented to locating a specific problem in the full set of relationships that produce it. The analysis captures the complex and diverse relationships that produce symbolic violence, including the way people are positioned in the fields of economic life, education and urban life, and the habitus that becomes attuned to their positioning in these fields by adopting a specific way of 'making do', making a virtue of necessity through toughness. This analysis serves our understanding of the nexus between the practices of the research participants and surrounding structures of power. Further, it also resists reduction of practices through categorising, stereotyping and othering. Bourdieu's framework is oriented to doing justice to the worlds of those we study by resisting a substantialist mode of thinking, i.e. refusing an approach that treats the phenomena of their lives as discrete things, for example, unemployment or exclusion from school. Rather, following Bourdieu, we must understand suffering through a relational analysis that brings together habitus, field, capital and symbolic power.

Third, this example of Bourdieu's analysis illustrates his requirement for an approach to be 'reflexive'. Reflexivity is needed to 'free our thinking of the implicit' that follows from our shared implication in the social world. In place of an assumed privileged insight on the part of the knowing subject, we must build into inquiry an interrogation of three different orders of presuppositions (Bourdieu, 1997, p. 10) that we hold by virtue of social position, of the field we subscribe to in our research and of the scholastic point of view (Schirato & Webb, 2003, p. 539).

These sorts of considerations need urgent attention in social work research. Otherwise, ironically, social work research risks reliance on a conceptually undercooked understanding of reflexivity, which cannot therefore adequately describe reflexivity, either in practice or teaching and—worse still—cannot thoughtfully locate the kind of reflexive practice capable of overcoming the very non-consciously socialised dominant presuppositions that generate oppression. We can see this relatively undetermined understanding of reflexivity invoked whenever social workers are implored to simply 'self-reflect' on how their personal values and social positioning intersect with their practice. The assumption that it is possible to 'pull ourselves up by our own bootstraps', or even to know what boots to pull up, is itself an arrogant proposition of self-knowing. The heuristic and ethical risk becomes especially pressing if we consider that the whole point of reflexivity is, arguably, to foster research that is not held hostage to non-conscious presuppositions, including ideologically rooted presuppositions serving ideological interests perpetuating social injustice.

It is in this under-conceptualised space that Bourdieu's theorising of knowledge can make an ethical and practical contribution. This is because Bourdieu's work provides a reflexive way of thinking about the relationships that constitute 'reflexivity' itself—both what counts as being reflexive and what social conditions are necessary for reflexivity to occur. More specifically, because it rests on a careful theorising of the 'knowing subject', necessary to any meaningful 'reflexivity', Bourdieu's theorising of knowledge makes a consciously controlled practice of reflexivity more possible by describing the determining relationships comprising the 'subject' and the 'subject's' knowledge of the world. By theorising the 'knowing subject' Bourdieu makes possible a more rigorous conceptualisation of the inherent limits to knowledge construction by 'knowing subjects' and hence ultimately what it takes to overcome these limits in 'seeing oneself in the act of knowledge construction'.

Critical here is transformation of 'reflexivity' beyond a simple sense of psychoanalytic reflection (Bourdieu, 1998, p. 1). Bourdieu encourages us to appreciate the socially structured constitution of, and limits to, knowing imposed by the dialectic relationship between objective social structures and ordinary subjective experience. This is to acknowledge the primacy of social structural relations, which recognises that while 'subjects' undoubtedly construct their social reality, and commensurately their knowing of that social reality, from a specific point of view, the constitutive principles, and therefore the limits of this point of view and knowing, are determined by social structural relations (Bourdieu, 1998, p. 2). Importantly, for Bourdieu, the constraining force of these social structural relations on knowing operates both historically, in the genesis of the 'subject' and the 'subject's' viewpoint, and contemporaneously through the social conditions, which are themselves constituted by a history of structural relations, in which that viewpoint is applied. Accordingly, for Bourdieu (1987, p. 305), the knowing 'subject's' knowledge of the world is simultaneously constituted and constrained by the dialectic between the history of objective social structures and the history of the 'subjective' point of view.

In theorising this dialectic, Bourdieu again references habitus and field. In terms of the former, Bourdieu proposed that it was as if objective conditions constituted by social structures, for example the material conditions associated with class, particularly those of early experience, became physically inscribed in individuals (Bourdieu, 1981, p. 84, 1990a, pp. 128–129, 1990b, pp. 54–55; Mahar et al., 1990, pp. 13–14). With respect to a conceptualisation of 'fields', Bourdieu proposed habitus has no independent existence apart from its application in 'fields', that is, social domains of activity defined by the production and reproduction of specific kinds of capital such as education, culture or social work (Adkins, 1997, p. 36; Hanks, 2005, p. 72). By extension, Bourdieu theorised fields can be understood as a configuration of hierarchically structured 'positions', codified within institutions and located within specific fields, e.g. 'caseworker' or 'casework manager' or 'client', but also less formally further differentiated, e.g. 'problem client', 'good caseworker', 'bad caseworker' (Adkins, 1997, p. 37). According to Bourdieu (1987), positions are defined by historically objectified requirements for specific ways of acting, thinking, perceiving and appreciating, that is, requirements for specific dispositions. These requirements, however, are not randomly arranged. Instead social power relationships tend to ensure that the dominant symbolic order, reflecting the dominant group's habitus, is imposed within and across fields via historically objectified structures, including requirements of position (Bourdieu, 1987, 1990a, pp. 131–139; Bourdieu & Passeron, 1990, pp. 6–8). It is the theorisation of fields in these terms that reveals the value in understanding the practice of knowledge construction and knowing as a dialectical encounter between, or meeting of, two histories deeply enmeshed within symbolic power relations—the objectified history of positions and the embodied history of habitus, that is, of positions and dispositions (Bourdieu, 1987).

The relationship between habitus and field then lends itself to a theorisation of the limits to ordinary knowing and the sources of these limits. The initial source lies in the genesis of the habitus. As Bourdieu (1990b, p. 55) notes: 'As an acquired system of generative schemes, the habitus makes possible the free production of all the thoughts, perceptions and actions inherent in the particular conditions of its production—and only those.' This perhaps would be less limiting if it were not for subjects' non-consciousness of these limits. Bourdieu (1990b, p. 73) explains this is because the habitus is inscribed in the body through a physical immersion in practices, from practice to practice, beneath the level of consciousness and in the absence of a consciously controlled reflexive step. For instance, no parent teaches the objective truth that particular practices being 'taught', such as the individualisation that occurs with separate rooms for children and parents, represents an arbitrary cultural arrangement among a number of possible alternative arrangements. In this sense, the knowing associated with the habitus is 'not something that one has, like knowledge that can be brandished, but something that one is' (Bourdieu, 1990a, p. 73). Added to this is the effect of the complete congruence between the mental structures of subjects through which they apprehend the social world—the product of an internalisation of external structures—and the external structures they encounter, of which they are the product (Bourdieu, 1990b, pp. 25–26). For example, thoughts and practices accruing to particular notions of individualised selfhood are seamlessly mirrored in the physical arrangements, language and practices within households. The result is that 'subjects' have a 'doxic' relationship to their particular mental structures, which are non-consciously 'misrecognised' as *universally* valid, self-evident and natural (Bourdieu, 1990b, pp. 25–26). As a consequence, both the 'unthought' schemes of thought, perception and evaluation associated with a particular habitus, and any schemes of thought, perception and evaluation lying outside of that habitus, are unavailable for 'self-reflective' inspection, given any ordinary inspection rests on and is limited to our 'own innate wisdom rooted in familiarity' (Bourdieu et al., 1991, p. 15; Bourdieu, 1990b, p. 14).

A second limitation is associated with misrecognition of the limits to knowing. There are two aspects to this. In the first instance fields, including institutions within fields, by and large require an 'entry fee' where the requirements of position restrict entry to all but those who are predisposed to meet those requirements in terms of their dispositions (Bourdieu, 1987, 1990a, pp. 194–196). That is, where the 'same history inhabits both habitus and habitat, both disposition and position' such that, 'history communicates with itself; history as subject discovers itself in history as object' (Bourdieu, 1987, p. 306). Consequently 'subjects', as the non-conscious embodiment of the field's objective structures, can be said to be 'possessed' by the field because they are, through prior experience, non-consciously and non-reflexively predisposed to recognise and 'misrecognise' it (Bourdieu, 1981, pp. 307–308, 1998, p. 3). The second aspect involves what Bourdieu refers to as 'symbolic violence'—objectively, the imposition of 'cultural arbitrary', that is the meaning system or system of dispositions associated with a group's culture, including class culture, by an 'arbitrary power' (Bourdieu & Passeron, 1990, pp. 1–15). And given the dominant group is likely to have a monopoly on symbolic violence, this tends to be the imposition of the dominant group's meaning system (Bourdieu, 1990a; Wacquant, 1998).

Bourdieu's thesis of 'ordinary knowing'—the ordinary experience of being caught up in non-conscious limits to thought imposed by the dialectic relationship between disposition and position—discovers its anti-thesis in Bourdieu's conceptualisation of 'reflexive knowing'. Namely, that reflexive knowing requires a conscious apprehension of the relationships between one's own habitus and field and one's own practices within those fields to systematically explore the 'unthought categories of thought which delimit the thinkable and predetermine thought' (Bourdieu & Wacquant, 1992, p. 40; Schirato & Webb, 2003, p. 544). For Bourdieu, this means the practice of reflexivity cannot be an academically private exercise in self-reflection, not the least because any such self-reflection is inevitably rooted in epistemologically circumscribed familiarity, and demands a true conversion (Bourdieu, 1991, p. 15, 1975, p. 19). So that, on the one hand, it demands a reformation of the habitus, a cultivation of a truly reflexive disposition that constantly interrogates accepted doxa (Bourdieu & Wacquant, 1992, p. 40). Further, it demands a 'conversion of interest'—'an interest in truth, instead of having, as in other games, the truth which suits their interests' (Bourdieu, 1975, p. 31), that is, the truth that suits 'our'/'social work' interests in the struggle for position, status and capital in a field. Thus, reflexivity is inseparably a 'disillusioning' stance in fields defined by a break with all doxa, including cultural and personal beliefs, values and presuppositions, and simultaneously a social break with ordinary affiliations reciprocally bound to the reproductive interests of the field (Bourdieu, 1990a, pp. 177–197; Bourdieu et al., 1991, p. 72). This is not to say reflexivity marks some kind of Paulian conversion. The formation of a reflexive disposition does not somehow magically escape the operations of the field. Ironically, apart from the idiosyncratic case highly contingent on individual history, the field itself must provide the conditions of possibility for reflexivity (Bourdieu, 1975; Bourdieu et al., 1991, pp. 3, 70–75).

The conceptualisation of reflexivity in the above terms has significant pragmatic and ethical upshots for social work practice, research and teaching. Foundationally this is because it requires recognition that: (a) the principles at work in the field of social work are identical to other fields—doxa, struggle for position and capital, symbolic violence, reproduction; and (b) social workers are a 'cultivated subject of a particular culture' (Bourdieu et al., 1991, p. 73). So, if 'clients', 'students', 'research subjects' and/or 'social problems' can be seen as 'objects' of social work research and/or intervention, then the measure of reflexivity becomes 'how far the objectifier is willing to be caught up in the work of objectification' (Bourdieu, 1990b, p. 20). Consequently, what is necessary is an 'objectification of the objectifying relationship' that subordinates social work practice and the social relations that make it possible, using the critical reflexive thinking tools suggested by Bourdieu's theorising of knowledge (Bourdieu, 1990b, pp. 20–21; Bourdieu et al., 1991, pp. 11–39).

These thinking tools, which include an epistemological framework and an interrogation of language, mark the practical contribution of Bourdieu's theorising for a reflexive social work project. Their principles can be understood as an imperative to incessantly guard against presuppositions forced on the social worker by the meeting of two histories—presuppositions that arise from relationships between the habitus and the field (Bourdieu et al., 1991, pp. 73–74). Foremost among these tools is an epistemological framework that questions dominant positivist philosophies that, by resonating and reinforcing normative dominant ideologies, smuggle those dominant mental structures into social work research, practice and teaching, while simultaneously disguising deeper social relational mechanisms driving the reproduction of social injustice. For example, it can be argued that the dominant, misrecognised German Protestant prenotion of personhood, imagining human action as the self-evident conscious expression of individual deliberative subjects, philosophically rediscovers itself in the hyper-empiricism of positivism, which subsequently generates self-evident 'facts' according to those solutions within the normative paradigm according to only those problems identifiable by the normative paradigm (Bogardus, 1997, pp. 79–84; Bourdieu et al., 1991, p. 38). In opposition to the dangers inherent in hyper-empiricism, Bourdieu calls for an epistemological program that effectively problematises doxic or taken-for-granted conceptions of social problems by reflexively reconstructing them within a theoretical set of social relationships that give rise to them (Bourdieu et al., 1991).

The interrogation of ordinary language represents a second and arguably the most fundamental set of thinking tools for the reflexive project. This is because an interrogation of ordinary language, including the classifications and classificatory practices we adopt, provide perhaps the most pragmatic means of miraculously raising into consciousness, as if from the dead, non-conscious presuppositions. A systematic interrogation of our classifications or categorisations through, for example, discourse, membership categorisation and/or conversational analysis, provides a consciously controlled means of uncovering the non-conscious operations of the habitus. This is especially the case where misrecognised 'universally self-evident' visions of the world can be juxtaposed against the visions of the other, which can often be the subjects of study or intervention, such as occurs with the reinterpretation of alternative visions of 'mental disorder' or 'uncivilised' or 'hysteria' (Kippax, 2019). As such, the interrogation of language is an indispensable tool in severing those representations and reversing the non-conscious relationship to doxa and habitus and the relationships between them (Bourdieu et al., 1991, p. 14).

Conclusion

By defining reflexivity, Bourdieu exposes the dangers in producing reflexive knowledge by resorting to what he labels as 'methocracy', that is, an overestimation of the importance of methodological tools. Clearly, a reliance on methodological tools in the absence of a reflexive interrogation of the conceptualisation of the problem is likely to lead to a displacement of epistemological rigour (Bourdieu et al., 1991). Perhaps the timing of the current influence of Bourdieu is fortuitous, since the neoliberal project has many tentacles, not least within the world of social research, which is critical of the forces of neoliberalism, and must also contend with the realisation that social work is itself a refraction of neoliberalism.

References

Adkins, B. (1997). *Cultural inclusion and exclusion in youth performance arts.* Unpublished doctoral dissertation Brisbane: University of Queensland.
Bogardus, J. (1997). *Ordering conduct, conducting order: Conduct disorder and the production of knowledge.* Unpublished doctoral dissertation Burnaby: Simon Fraser University.
Bourdieu, P. (1958). *Sociologie de l'Algerie.* Paris: Presses Universitaires de France.
Bourdieu, P. (1975). The specificity of the scientific field and the social conditions of the progress of reason. *Social Science Information*, 14(6), 19–47.

Bourdieu, P. (1981). Structures, strategies, and the habitus. In C. Lemert (Ed.), *French sociology: Rupture and renewal since 1968* (pp. 86–96). New York: Colombia University Press.

Bourdieu, P. (1984). *Distinction: A social critique of the judgement of taste*. London: Routledge.

Bourdieu, P. (1987). Men and machines. In K. Knorr-Cetina & A.V Cicourel (Eds.), *Advances in social theory and methodology: Toward an integration of micro and macro sociologies* (pp. 304–317). London: Routledge & Kegan Paul.

Bourdieu, P. (1990a). *In other words: Essays towards a reflexive sociology*. Stanford, CA: Stanford University Press.

Bourdieu, P. (1990b). *The logic of practice*. Cambridge: Polity Press.

Bourdieu, P. (1997). *Pascalian meditation*. Stanford, CA: Stanford University Press.

Bourdieu, P. (1998). *Practical reason: On the theory of action*. Stanford, CA: Stanford University Press.

Bourdieu, P. et al. (1999). *The weight of the world: Social suffering in contemporary society*. Cambridge: Polity Press.

Bourdieu, P., Chamboredon, J., & Passeron, J. (1991). *The craft of sociology: Epistemological preliminaries*. Berlin: Walter de Gruyter.

Bourdieu, P., & Passeron, J. (1990). *Reproduction in education, society and culture*. (2nd ed., R. Nice, Trans.). London: Sage Publications.

Bourdieu, P., & Wacquant, J. (1992). *Invitation to reflexive sociology*. Chicago, IL: University of Chicago Press.

Brough, M., Wagner, I., & Farrell, L. (2013). Review of Australian health related social work research 1990-2009. *Australian Social Work*, 66(4), 528–539.

Crisp, B. (2000). A history of Australian social work practice research. *Research on Social Work Practice*, 10, 179–194.

D'Cruz, H., Gillingham, P., & Melendez, S. (2007). Reflexivity, its meanings and relevance for social work: A critical review of the literature. *British Journal of Social Work*, 37, 73–90.

Emirbayer, M., & Williams, E. (2005). Bourdieu and social work. *Social Services Review*, 79(4), 689–724.

Garrett, P. (2007a). The relevance of Bourdieu for social work: A reflection on obstacles and omissions. *Journal of Social Work*, 7, 355–379.

Garrett, P. (2007b). Making social work more Bourdieusian: Why the social professions should critically engage with the work of Pierre Bourdieu. *European Journal of Social Work*, 10(2), 225–243.

Garrett, P. (2010). Examining the 'conservative revolution': Neoliberalism and social work education. *Social Work Education*, 29, 340–355.

Hanks, W.F. (2005). Pierre Bourdieu and the practices of language. *Annual Review of Anthropology*, 34, 67–83.

Jordan, B. (1997) Social work and society. In M. Davies (Ed.), *The Blackwell Companion to Social Work*. Oxford: Blackwell Publications.

Kippax, R. (2019). *Disrupting schools: The institutional conditions of disruptive behaviour*. New York: Peter Lang.

Lorenz, W. (2005). Social work and a new social order: Challenging new liberalism's erosion of solidarity. *Social Work and Society*, 3, 93–101.

Mahar, C., Harker, R., & Wilkes, C. (1990). The basic theoretical position. In R. Harker, C. Mahar, & C. Wilkes (Eds.), *An introduction to the work of Pierre Bourdieu: The practice of theory* (pp. 1–25). London: Macmillan Press Ltd.

Mol, T. (1991). Appropriating Bourdieu: Feminist theory and Pierre Bourdieu's sociology of culture. *New Literary History*, 22(4), 1017–1049.

Morley, C. (2015). Critical reflexivity and social work practice. In N.J. Smelser & P.B. Bates (Eds.), *International encyclopedia of the social and behavioural sciences* 2nd ed. (pp. 281–286). Amsterdam: Elsevier.

Parton, N., & Kirk, S. (2010). The nature and purposes of social work. In I. Shaw, E. Briar-Lawson, J. Orme & R. Ruckdeschel (Eds.), *The SAGE handbook of social work research* (pp. 23–36). London: Sage.

Peters, G. (2011). The social as heaven and hell: Pierre Bourdieu's philosophical anthropology. *Journal for the Theory of Social Behaviour*, 42(1), 63–86.

Plath, J. (2006). What's happening in health: Progress and prospects for social work. *Australian Social Work*, 52, 3–7.

Ryan, M., & Sheehan, R. (2009). Research articles in Australian social work from 1998-2007: A content analysis. *Australian Social Work*, 62(4), 525–542.

Sapiro, G. (2015). Bourdieu, Pierre (1930–2002). In *International Encyclopedia of the social and behavioural sciences* (2nd ed., pp. 777–783). Amsterdam: Elsevier.

Schirato, T., & Webb, J. (2003). Bourdieu's concept of reflexivity as meta-literacy. *Cultural Studies*, 17(3/4), 539–552.

Schubert, J.D. (2014). Suffering/symbolic violence. In M. Grenfell (Ed.), *Pierre Bourdieu: Key concepts* (pp. 179–194). Durham, NC: Acumen Publishing.

Shusterman, R. (ed.) (1999). *Bourdieu: A critical reader*. Oxford: Blackwell.

Spolander, G., Engelbrecht, L., & Pullen Sansfacon, A. (2016). Social work and macroeconomic neoliberalism: Beyond social justice rhetoric. *European Journal of Social Work*, 19(5), 634–649.

Swartz, D. (1997). *Culture and power: The sociology of Pierre Bourdieu*. Chicago, IL: The University of Chicago Press.

Wacquant, J. (1989). Toward a reflexive sociology: A workshop with Pierre Bourdieu. *Sociological Theory*, 7(1), 26–63.

Wacquant, J. (1998). Forward. In P. Bourdieu (Eds.), *The state nobility: Elite schools in the field of power* (pp. ix–xxii). Cambridge: Polity Press.

43
Stephen Brookfield's contribution to teaching and practising critical reflection in social work

Christine Morley

QUEENSLAND UNIVERSITY OF TECHNOLOGY, AUSTRALIA

We teach to change the world.

(Brookfield, 1995, p. 1)

Introduction

This chapter will draw predominantly on two key works from critical educationalist Stephen Brookfield to explicate how his scholarship can enhance teaching one of the most highly prized skills in social work: critical reflection. Brookfield has surveyed the work of several leading critical theorists (including Marx, Gramsci, Foucault, Habermas and Marcuse—all of whom are addressed separately in this volume) to distil the relevance of ideas for teacher and adult education (Brookfield, 2005). He also provides a highly accessible framework for educators to become critically reflective (Brookfield, 1995, 2017). Brookfield's (2005) work across both of these related domains holds direct implications for the practice of social work educators, while simultaneously outlining a transformative learning process for social work students, that has direct relevance for practice. In this chapter, I argue that Brookfield's work is particularly important for practising and teaching critical reflection *critically*, and illustrate this by providing an example of my work with a student to facilitate critical reflection in the context of my teaching, while also demonstrating a parallel critically reflective process on my own teaching practice (Brookfield, 2016).

Critical educators face many challenges in teaching critical approaches to social work. Students often have difficulty seeing the relevance of theory to practice in a profession that can appear entirely practical. Sometimes, students learn the social justice values of social work, but struggle to implement these into practice, so the values remain at the level of aspirational rhetoric, disconnected from action. Other students, who embrace social work's values and vision for emancipatory change, may feel overwhelmed and disempowered by structural analyses, believing that they will never be able to practise critically within contemporary contexts that are dominated by neoliberalism and managerialism. Other unintended manifestations of critical social work education include that students can presume they have discovered "the truth" (a function on modernist universalist thinking), and seek to use critical theory in combative ways to "educate" those who they imagine are less enlightened, in ways that contradict the emancipatory intentions of critical theory (Morley, 2016). In this chapter I argue that Brookfield's critical philosophical approach to critical reflection can provide a powerful antidote to address these issues

Stephen Brookfield

Stephen Brookfield was born in Liverpool, England in 1949. He is a leading educational scholar who specialises in adult learning. His transformative approach to education, emphasises critical thinking and critical reflection that are firmly informed by critical theory. Originally a teacher, Brookfield has worked in England, Canada, Australia and the United States as a critical adult education scholar, where he is currently employed as the Distinguished Professor at The University of St Thomas in Minneapolis St Paul, Minnesota. He has written, co-written or edited eighteen books that have received international acclaim and been translated into numerous languages. His most cited books include the *The Skillful Teacher* (Brookfield, 2015) (first published in 2006) in which he candidly shares his own experiences of teaching, including his feelings of what he refers to as "imposter syndrome", and *Teaching for Critical Thinking* (Brookfield, 2012), which particularly addresses the importance of role modelling critical thinking in the classroom. In this chapter, I predominately draw on *The Power of Critical Theory for Adult Learning and Teaching* (2005), which explores the work of a range of prominent critical theorists, while expounding the implications for education. He does this through the explication of central themes including: ideology, hegemony, power, alienation, liberation, reason and democracy; hence putting the "*critical* back into *critical thinking* by emphasising how thinking critically is an inherently political process" (Brookfield, 2005, p. vii, italics in original). Given the critical reflection focus of this chapter, I have also emphasised Brookfield's *Becoming a Critically Reflective Teacher* (1995, 2017), which offers important insights for educators who seek to adopt a critically reflective practice in their own teaching.[1] While Brookfield is writing predominately for teachers and students in the discipline of education, his work is instructive for the teaching practices of social work educators, while simultaneously providing insight into critical pedagogical processes that are transformative for social work students.

A theorised, critically reflective approach to education

Brookfield proposes four lenses to evaluate our practice as educators: personal experience; the students' eyes; our colleagues' perceptions; and theoretical and research literature (Brookfield, 2017). He suggests being a critically reflective educator begins with recognising the ideological basis that underpins all teaching. He notes that what we choose to teach as educators represents contested decisions of which the outcomes "reflect the interests and agendas of specific people in specific situations" (Brookfield, 1995, p. 40). No educator can escape this reality: there is no neutral knowledge; there is no apolitical education. Translating the implications of this to social work education, means each time decisions are made about the content that is included in social work programs, we simultaneously make decisions about what knowledge is excluded. Such decisions have direct implications for whether students are educated as potential agents of change and are equipped to challenge injustice, or whether they accept as normal, existing inequalities that characterise our social world, and simply seek to ensure people learn to adapt to, or cope better with disadvantage. For Brookfield, these pedagogic decisions are intrinsically political, and rooted in the theories that underpin our practice as educators. As he states: "Theory is a dangerous word, one that should not be used lightly" as it "always [operates] in the midst of practice, of action, of judgment and decision" (Brookfield, 2005, p. 4).

In writing for teachers, in a way that democratises knowledge by demystifying critical theory and making it accessible, he cautions against "the unjustified valorization or reification of theory, [and] against the idea that theorizing is a high-status endeavor" (Brookfield, 2005, p. 2), or an "intellectual process restricted to a talented few" (Brookfield, 2005, p. 3). Such reassurance is also necessary for many social work students (and educators), who may struggle to make the links between theory and practice. For Brookfield (2005, p. 3) "[t]heory is eminently practical". As he explains, practising and theorising are "two processes" that are "conjoined; on the one hand, all practice is theoretically informed, on the other hand, theory always contains practical implications" (Brookfield, 2005 p. 352). Hence, he argues that "the idea that theory and practice exist on either side of a great and unbridgeable divide is nonsense" (Brookfield, 2017, p. 172).

Brookfield explicitly adopts critical theories over other theoretical perspectives, on the basis they can help us understand "not just how the world is but also how it might be changed for the better" (Brookfield, 2005, p. 7). A better world, according to Brookfield and the critical theorists such as Mezirow (1991) and Gramsci (see for example, 1957) who inform his thinking, is one in which "adult education can contribute to building a society organized according to democratic values of fairness, justice, and compassion" (Brookfield, 2005, pp. 7–8). Therefore, one of the main goals of education, informed by critical theory, is that it will "prompt social and political change, often of a revolutionary nature" (Brookfield, 2005, p. 7). Brookfield adopts a Marxist approach to critical theory in examining "the ways in which people accept as normal a world characterized by massive inequities and the systemic exploitation of the many by the few" (Brookfield, 2005, p. 2). The role of education then, is to raise students' consciousness about these inequalities, and equip them with the analysis and skills to promote social change. As he notes, "critical theory and its contemporary educational applications such as critical pedagogy are grounded in an activist desire to fight oppression, injustice, and bigotry and create a fairer, more compassionate world." He further elucidates that "c]entral to this tradition is a concern with highly practical projects—the practice of penetrating ideology, countering hegemony, and working democratically" (Brookfield, 2005, p. 10).

In relation to the teaching and practice of critical reflection, Brookfield suggests theory can assist in several ways: it "drops bombs of productive dissonance" (upsets unproblematised and settled understandings), "opens new worlds" of understanding, "helps us recognise ourselves" (by clarifying what we may have thought or felt that had not yet been put into conscious thought), and "stops us accepting groupthink" (Brookfield, 2017, pp. 173–8). The critical theory component of critical reflection is fundamental for Brookfield, albeit "with the explicit social and political critique, and activism, this implies" (Brookfield, 2005, p. 376). As he explains: "Reflection in and of itself is not enough; it must always be linked to how the world can be changed" (Brookfield, 1995, p. 217). For reflection to be *critical* it must serve two purposes: (1) to "uncover how educational processes and interactions are framed by wider structures of power and dominant ideology"; and (2) "to uncover assumptions and practices that seem to make their teaching lives easier but that actually end up working against their own best long-term interests" (Brookfield, 2017, p. 9).

To support this kind of learning, Brookfield (2005) is clear that teaching critical reflection and critical thinking are not merely pedagogic processes. He maintains the content we use to inform these processes, and indeed our broader curricula should be catalysts for challenging social divisions in the existing status quo. As he states: "Critical thinking framed by critical theory is not just a cognitive process. It is inevitably bound up with realizing and emphasizing common interests, rejecting the privatized, competitive ethic of capitalism, and preventing the emergence of inherited privilege" (Brookfield, 2005, p. 354). Hence, like social work, Brookfield's understanding of critical pedagogy is explicitly value-driven. As he further explains:

> [T]o teach informed by critical theory is, by implication, to teach with a specific social and political intent ... Informed by a critical theory perspective, students learn to see that capitalism, bureaucratic rationality, disciplinary power, automation conformity, one-dimensional thought, and repressive tolerance all combine to exert a powerful ideological sway aimed to ensure the current system stays intact.
>
> *(Brookfield, 2005, p. 353)*

From Brookfield's perspective, the fundamental purpose of adult education, or of facilitating students' engagement in the processes of critical reflection and critical thinking, "is to enable them to create true democracy" (Brookfield, 2005, pp. 353–4).

Critical theory

Critical theory is indispensable to this aim. Brookfield (2005) examines the scholarship of several prominent critical theorists to extract their key contributions to education, noting he is influenced by four traditions in criticality including psychoanalysis and psychotherapy, analytic philosophy and logic, and pragmatist constructivism, yet the overwhelming contribution to his work is from Marxist and the Frankfurt School scholars on critical social theory (Brookfield, 2005, p. 12).

In overviewing the ideas of these theorists, Brookfield explicates critical theory as a body of work predicated on three fundamental assumptions about how the world is structured:

1   That apparently open, Western democracies are actually highly unequal societies in which economic inequity, racism, and class discrimination are empirical realities;
2   That the way this state of affairs is reproduced and made to seem normal, natural, and inevitable (thereby heading off potential challenges to the system) is through the dissemination of dominant ideology;
3   That critical theory attempts to understand this state of affairs as a necessary prelude to changing it.

(Brookfield, 2005, p. viii)

According to Brookfield, some defining characteristics of critical theory are:

1   Its firm grounding in political analysis, primarily around "the conflicting relationship between social classes within an economy based on the exchange of commodities" (Brookfield, 2005, p. 23);
2   Its concern "to provide people with knowledge and understandings intended to free them from oppression" (Brookfield, 2005, p. 25); and
3   Its proclivity not only to criticise current society, but also to envisage "a fairer, less alienated, more democratic world" (Brookfield, 2005, p. 27).

In applying the work of critical theorists to education, Brookfield makes a key contribution to critical pedagogy (Brookfield, 2005). According to Brookfield (2005, p. 39), education informed by critical theory involves: "learning to recognize and challenge ideology ... learning to uncover

Stephen Brookfield's contribution

and counter hegemony, learning to unmask power, learning to overcome alienation ... learning to pursue liberation, learning to reclaim reason, and learning to practice democracy." Critical pedagogy therefore has a "transformative impetus" that begins with "developing students' powers of critical thinking so that they can critique the interlocking systems of oppression embedded in contemporary society" (Brookfield, 2005, p. 353). Given it is "highly directive", it is "inherently political" and "makes no pretence of neutrality" because it is centrally concerned with freedom, as a key tenet of critical theory (Brookfield, 2005, p. 354).

In surveying the work of critical theorists, Brookfield notes that there are no specific methods or techniques for doing critical pedagogy. However, he does identify some prominent pedagogic themes that emphasise:

1 "The importance of teaching a structuralized worldview", which links the personal with the political and views personal experiences as "structurally produced" (Brookfield, 2005, p. 355);
2 The need to foster "abstract, conceptual reasoning", which enables students to explore ethical questions about how to treat others and organise society equitably, for example (Brookfield, 2005, p. 356);
3 The need for students to become "uncoupled from the stream of cultural givens" (Brookfield, 2005, p. 356) and with practices infused with these; and
4 The need for dialogic discussion to foster democracy (Brookfield, 2005, p. 357).

Using practice incidents as a stimulus for critical reflection: an example of an application

Brookfield argues strongly for the importance of learning through experience (Brookfield, 2017). He suggests one strategy for beginning to engage in critical reflection is to choose specific incidents in recent practice that exemplify both highs and lows—experiences one was "proud of" as well as those when one felt they had "fallen short" (Brookfield, 2017, p. 122). It should be noted, a similar approach to critical reflection, beginning with examination of a critical incident, was first introduced into social work by Jan Fook (2002), who drew from a range of traditions, including critical educational scholars such as Brookfield, to develop this model for social work.

The following narrative represents my recollection of a critical incident a student presented in an undergraduate class I teach on critical reflection, which occurs during the final year of their studies in between two field education placements. Students choose an incident from their practice significant to them and present it to their tutorial. The other class members and I then ask questions to assist the presenter to engage in critical reflection. The presentation forms part of their assessment for the course in which they can use the feedback they receive to inform a critical reflection essay they will complete at the end of the semester. I selected this example because it contains a combination of the elements above, and because the description of practice provided by the student also became an incident that prompted the need for me to critically reflect on my practice as an educator.

The student described an example from a field education placement in which he was placed in a family support organisation. He described his work with an "Aboriginal woman" who had recently moved to the area. According to the student, the woman had "mental health" issues. The house she was living in was "a mess" and his supervisor had asked him to help clean up some of the rubbish, sweep the floor and wipe over surfaces. The student described feeling "annoyed" by this. After all, he was not studying a Master of Social Work qualification to become a cleaner! He also felt he was denying the woman "self-determination" by doing her housework. However, as he was in the role of a "student", he decided to comply, but privately questioned the value of the work he was doing, and the value of the field education experience. As he recited his narrative about this incident, additional information came to light, including: the woman had no support system locally, was experiencing overwhelming grief and sadness at the sudden death of a close family member, was "struggling to cope", and was a sole parent for a six-year-old child.

The student stated he had informally undertaken a risk assessment of the situation, noting the "lack of hygiene" and the woman's "failure" to provide appropriate care for the child. He felt an ethical course of action would be to make a notification to child safety about the woman's negligence to care for her child, evidenced by her "lack of motivation" and "lack of capacity" to provide appropriate "sanitary" living conditions. He indicated that he was using a strengths perspective and felt his work reflected the values of self-determination and empowerment, given his outward display of non-judgmentalism toward the woman.

As he presented his critical incident, I became aware of my own discomfort and concern about his narrative. Although I assure students that I assess their capacity for critical reflection, not the brilliance of their practice, in this situation I felt the practice was grossly inadequate and potentially dangerous and unethical. I would have perhaps felt less disturbed by the description of practice, had he demonstrated some beginning capacity for critical reflection, but in my view, this was completely absent. I felt an acute sense of responsibility as a critical educator to radically change his view—and fast! I felt a responsibility to protect the woman he was working with. However, I also recognised the need to temper my response, which I understood was being fuelled by my own emotional reaction to the content of his presentation. I did not want to counter what I perceived as oppressive practice, by enacting similarly judgmental and oppressive practice toward the student, and thereby potentially abusing my power in my role as an educator.

Teaching critical reflection

Brookfield suggests that "whenever possible teachers should initially model for students whatever it is they wish those students to do" (Brookfield, 2017, p. 3). I sometimes use my reflection on the example above when students are wrestling with imposing their "truth" onto others in a way that potentially undermines their anti-oppressive intentions. It can be tempting for both educators and students who draw on critical theory to develop "an overconfidence" about the accuracy and relevance of their approach, which may "translate into an attitude of condescension toward those whose consciousness has yet to be raised" (Brookfield, 1995, p. 35). How do we create an educational environment that is empowering and respectful of diverse viewpoints while also challenging hegemonic assumptions that lead to potentially oppressive practices and unjust outcomes? Brookfield suggests, "[a] lecture in which a teacher questions her [or his] own assumptions, acknowledges ethical dilemmas hidden in her [or his] position ... and demonstrates an openness to alternative viewpoints encourages students to do likewise" engenders a great capacity to foster transformative learning (1995, p. 4).

Because of this, I always begin teaching a unit on critical reflection by modelling a critical reflection process I have engaged in. This includes my presentation of a critical incident from my own practice, then deconstruction and articulation of assumptions I had made which have tripped me up (this includes my misassumptions, gaps between theory and practice, errors in judgment, mistakes, practices that have failed or went wrong, and so on); some of these I have written about elsewhere (see for example Fook & Morley, 2005; Morley, 2007, 2009). I then outline my subsequent learning and identification of what has changed about my practice. Brookfield (1995, p. 259) reinforces the importance of modelling the critical reflection process, as educators "have to earn the right" to ask others to "think critically about their practice" and share this with us. Further, Brookfield (2017, p. 115) observes critical reflection is best practised as a collective endeavour, a collaborative process in which people gather to ferret out assumptions, challenge groupthink, and consider multiple perspectives on common experiences in ways that can lead to changed practice. To ask students to demonstrate the courage and humility required to engage in critical reflection, educators must first demonstrate these qualities themselves and position themselves as co-learners alongside students in order to develop credibility. As Brookfield (1995, p. 259) notes, "[t]o skip an initial modelling of the process is a grave tactical error".

Other strategies Brookfield employs, which I have adopted, include spending the first few minutes of each class time on "troubleshooting"—where students can raise any issues, questions, comments about any aspect of the course. Another method he uses is to ask students toward the end of the term to write a "letter to successors" telling future students what they should know about how to "survive and flourish" in the class (Brookfield, 2017, p. 112). I share these letters from past students with new students at the beginning of a new semester, and refer back to relevant examples throughout. Brookfield also notes the importance of providing students with a rationale for the course and why you have approached it the way you have. Hence, I always begin my classes at the start of each semester explicitly noting the critical underpinnings of the units I teach, and providing a justification for this, that includes highlighting the connection between the espoused values of social work with critical theory and pedagogy. Before engaging with the critical incident presentations, as Brookfield (1995, p. 146) suggests, we also "creat[e] ground rules for critical conversation[s]" which involve asking participants to engage in an analysis of what makes conversation in groups work well (or otherwise); reassuring students "that reflection groups are not angst-ridden ordeals involving uncomfortable disclosures of personal tragedies". After selecting an incident that typifies practice, Brookfield (1995, p. 88) suggests we should "then analyse it in terms of how we have constructed its meaning and significance, what is missing from our construction and who this does and does not benefit".

This process relies on postmodernism, which, according to Brookfield, contends that "the world is essentially fragmented and that what passes for theoretical generalizations [and truths] are really only context-specific insights produced by particular discourse communities" (Brookfield, 2005, p. 1). This positions particular accounts of critical incidents as one possible construction among a sea of possibilities. Hence, "reality" is understood to be an interpretation, and "facts" as social constructions.

Brookfield suggests one of the most distinctive features of critical reflection is the "hunting [of] assumptions that frame our judgments and actions" (Brookfield 2017, p. 21). This process can assist students and educators to develop an awareness of how their tacit assumptions are implicated in how they think and act. The assumptions we make are directly implicated in the interpretation we choose to represent as our view of truth. "Ideology critique" is an important part of this process of identifying assumptions, and involves "people learn[ing] to recognize how uncritically accepted and unjust dominant ideologies are embedded in everyday situations and practices" (Brookfield, 2005, p. 35). It "focuses on helping people come to an awareness of how capitalism [and other dominant forces] shape social relations and impose—often without our knowledge—belief systems and assumptions (that is, ideologies) that justify and maintain economic and political inequity" (Brookfield, 1995, p. 13). The notion of hegemony is central to ideology critique. Brookfield, in drawing on Gramsci, defines hegemony as "the process by which we embrace ideas and practices that keep us enslaved" (Brookfield, 2005, p. 5). Hegemony explains why people are swayed to take on dominant ideologies as if they serve their own interests, and the interests of the people with whom they work (Brookfield, 2005, p. 13).

A critical perspective highlights that the student's narrative in the example described above was imbued with a number of hegemonic assumptions, or what Mezirow, who Brookfield credits as "probably the most influential contemporary theorist of adult learning" (also addressed separately in this volume), would refer to as "sociocultural distortion" (Mezirow, 1991b cited in Brookfield, 2005, p. 13). These can result in conservative/potentially harmful practices. Brookfield explains that critical pedagogy positions the educator as infiltrator of false consciousness, yet assuming another's view to be false because it differs from your own seems incongruent with an anti-oppressive approach. The student's presentation of his incident was critical for me because I felt a responsibility to challenge what I perceived as the imposition of harmful hegemonic assumptions, and yet in being committed to fostering egalitarian power relations, I did not feel it would be appropriate to simply impose my view.

Brookfield's wisdom was helpful in working through this dilemma because he points out that much adult learning is idealised as being self-directed; however, ideology critique questions the belief that adults "make free, unfettered choices regarding their learning that reflect authentic desires felt deeply at the very core of their identity", pointing out that we are embedded within "dominant social, cultural and politic streams within which we swim" (Brookfield, 1995, p. 84). One of the key challenges of being a critical educator, then, is to balance "respect [for] the agendas adults bring to a democratic negotiation of curriculum whilst contradictorily challenging those agendas by offering (and sometimes insisting on) radically different politically contentious options for study" (Brookfield, 1995, p. 170). Brookfield suggests that sometimes "fully participatory, inclusive conversation[s]" are possible, and as the "cornerstone of democracy ... [we] can play a role in teaching adults the dispositions necessary to conduct such conversations" (Brookfield, 2005, pp. 357–8). However, other occasions will call for a "strongly interventionist" approach, which involves taking more of a leadership role to influence the criticality of the discussion (Brookfield, 2005, p. 358). In the example above, my judgment was that the student's presentation of the critical incident constituted one of the latter occasions, which then influenced how I worked with the student.

Brookfield describes teaching critical reflection as a "connected activity" in which our "dance is the dance of experimentation and risk" (Brookfield, 1995, p. 42) as we seek to try to understand student experience and create more democratic classrooms (Brookfield, 1995, p. 44). He also emphasises that "speaking authentically" is at the heart of critically reflective process (Brookfield, 1995, pp. 45–7).

In attempting to facilitate the student's critical reflection in the example presented above, some of the questions I crafted to unsettle hegemonic assumptions included:

- What information did you choose to privilege in your account? Why? What dominant discourses do your assumptions reflect? What purpose does this serve?
- Why did you name the cultural identity of the woman, but not anyone else in your story (such as your supervisor—whose gender and cultural identities remain unknown)?
- How did your feelings of being shocked and overwhelmed influence your construction of the state of the home? What assumptions do you make about the presentation of a house? Do you assume these assumptions and values are universal? How else might you understand this? How might dominant discourses about gender be influencing your interpretation of the situation?
- What assumptions did you make about your role? How do these affect your practice?

- What information was left out from your assessment? Why? What are the implications for your practice?
- How might your assessment change if you conceptualised the woman's story within a broader social context? For example, how might her experience of grief, social isolation, poverty, and single parenting without support networks, impact on her presentation and on her interest or capacity to maintain a house to your standards?
- How do you imagine these contextual issues might impact on her receiving a mental health diagnosis?
- Why do you assume that her capacity to maintain a clean house (according to your standards) is directly related to her capacity to care for her child? Where might these assumptions originate from? Are these assumptions consistent with your espoused framework and the values of social work?
- Have you conflated her "opportunity to clean the house" with "self-determination"? What might be lacking from this construction of self-determination, from a social justice perspective?
- You stated you were annoyed about being asked to help with the housework. What assumptions have you made about this? What does this construction miss? How are neo-liberal discourses of individual responsibility embedded in your practice? How are similar discourses used to justify the cutting of resources and removal of support from people who need it? How might a critical perspective view such assumptions? Do they assist you to work toward emancipatory outcomes?
- How do you imagine racism and Australia's history of colonisation might play out in this woman's life?
- How do you think it would affect the woman if you made a notification to child safety? How would you feel if you were in her situation? Would you perceive your response as helpful? What might be particularly problematic about involving child safety from a critical perspective? What impact do you think it might have on your relationship with the woman?—and on your capacity to build trust/rapport and reduce power differentials between her and yourself?
- Do these outcomes reflect your intended practice?

The questions aimed to unearth alternative, counter-hegemonic interpretations of the woman's experience and the role of social work in this situation. They aimed to expose the privileged position of the student and the impact of cultural identity, gender and class position of both the woman and the student, ultimately seeking to raise the student's consciousness about the structural dimensions of the woman's situation, and the operation of power between social workers and the people we work with. They aimed to highlight the potential harms associated with the perceived expert role of the worker, and the problems inherent in involving child protection without adequate justification. As Brookfield states (1995, p. 117) based on a Gramscian analysis, "The overall task of adult education [is to] fight a war of position in which adults are helped to acquire a consciousness of their [privilege and] oppression and to organize in solidarity to struggle against adversity" (Brookfield, 2005, p. 117). As he notes, "Learning to think critically about power and control and learning how to recognize one's class position, [other indicators of privilege] and true political interests are major adult learning projects for Gramsci" (Brookfield, 1995, p. 104).

The questions also aimed to disturb what Fromm talks about as "automation conformity", which is a "pervasive element of alienation" that involves a "process of social manipulation that results in the adult striving to be exactly the same as he or she imagines the majority to be"

(Brookfield, 1995, p. 170). This leads to a "decline in originality of thought and decision [and] inevitably works to kill individual conscience and with it the possibility of morally inspired revolution" (Brookfield, 2005, pp. 172–3). Critical reflection aims to challenge this suppression of critical thinking, instead enabling students, to critically analyse the implications of interpreting people's situations through the lens of dominant ideology and conformity. In this situation, the deconstruction questions sought to highlight the limitations of privileging risk assessment and other punitive modes of surveillance, such as invoking a child protection investigation, over demonstrating compassion and respecting her rights.

A crucial role for adult education, then, is to teach "a structuralized worldview … that emphasizes how individual decisions are framed by much broader social structures and economic forces" (Brookfield, 2005, p. 174). The questions inviting a critical analysis on the impact of social structures (racism, colonisation, patriarchy, capitalism) were designed to counteract the othering and individualisation of social problems that occur as a result of distorted (hegemonic) reasoning. As Brookfield states, we need "An awareness of how ideology, culture and economics shape individual lives", which, for Fromm, is a precursor to "people deciding that alienating social arrangements could be reshaped by individual and collective will … [Thus,] adult education can lay foundations for social action" (Brookfield, 1995, p. 175). For this to happen, students need to be provided an opportunity to disengage themselves from the tacit assumptions of discursive practices. This requires social work educators to challenge and resist the uncritical embrace of hegemonic assumptions, automation conformity, internalisation of sociocultural distortions, etc. by supporting learning that fosters awareness of how these processes operate, and practices of resistance.

According to Brookfield (2005, p. 8), critical reflection also cultivates "the promise of social transformation" (Brookfield, 2005, p. 13). The purpose of critical theory is to help adults realise the ways dominant ideology limits what people feel is possible, then raises awareness of how this happens, which provides "the necessary theoretical opening for understanding how an educative process might enable people to give up their illusions" (Welton, 1995, p. 13, cited in Brookfield, 2005, p. 8). For social work students who are educated and freed in this regard, the hope is this impetus for liberation will be transferred to their work with people and communities. Brookfield's (2005, pp. 8–9) view is that "[c]ritical theory can be deemed effective to the extent that it keeps alive the hope that the world can be changed to make it fairer and more compassionate".

For Brookfield (2017), critical reflection also involves imagining new, more socially just and democratic structures and processes. Concerning the student's example above, some of the questions I posed to support transformative learning included:

- How does your understanding of the woman's situation change if you take account of the social structures impacting on her experience?
- How might your narrative about this situation change if you emphasised some of the woman's strengths?
- How might your practice change if you perceived helping with housework tasks as an opportunity to connect with the woman, gain greater understanding and appreciation of her experiences and support her while she is dealing with grief, poverty and social isolation?
- How might your practice be different if you saw that demonstrating compassion and treating her with dignity and respect were more important than risk assessment?
- How else might you understand her mental health diagnosis, given all that she is managing presently? And how does your construction of her "struggling to cope" change when you consider her ability to relocate and connect with services in the context of overwhelming grief?

The student's consideration of the initial questions indicated he felt significantly influenced and restricted by dominant discourses: discourses about how ostensibly objective professionals operate, the kinds of information they privilege in their assessments (which were also presumed to be objective); judgments made on the basis of presumed normative standards about household cleanliness/presentation and risk. His account highlighted the dominance of individualising discourses that depoliticise social problems such as the impact of poverty, a lack of social support, and her experience of grief, which was medicalised and constructed as a "mental health" problem. Similarly, the student's disregard of the impact of colonisation on the woman's situation, including the eschewal of any consideration of being a white worker, working within a largely white, mainstream government organisation implicated in producing the stolen generations and associated trauma (Bennett et al., 2013), was also unmasked. Consideration of the missing discourses allowed the subjugated critical analysis to emerge and offered a radical reconceptualisation of what constituted ethical practice in that context.

Brookfield (2005, p. 118) identifies that "unmasking power" is a key component of critical pedagogy and critical reflection. For many students, overcoming the constructed identity of "powerless student" is an important part of the critically reflective process. While the student in the example above experienced a sense of powerlessness in not being able to challenge his supervisor about doing the housework, critical reflection was not used to embolden his sense of power to challenge this on this occasion (as it is in many other scenarios). Instead, questions for this student focused on reconceptualising the meaning of housework in this context, and developing a broader understanding of the social work role. The reflection also aimed at assisting the student to develop an awareness of his own professional power and the potential to cause great harm to the people we claim to serve, if this power is misused. Then, in gaining the capacity to think outside hegemonic constructions and resist thoughtlessness and conformity, students can begin to connect with their capacity to become agents of progressive social change. As Brookfield explains in drawing on Foucault: students need to recognise "that they are themselves agents of power, perpetually challenging [or reinforcing] disciplinary power" and "also possessing the capacity to [support or] subvert dominant power relations" (Brookfield, 1995, pp. 144–5). As he notes, Foucault "sketches out a theory of power as a circular flow that draws all into its currents. Choosing whether or not to exercise power is, in his eyes, an illusion. In reality we are fated to exercise power" (Brookfield, 1995, pp. 144–5).

Because risk assessment is embedded in contemporary dominant paradigms about how social workers assess and manage others (Webb, 2006), and constructed as a core competency for social work practice, the student felt it would impress his supervisor to offer a risk assessment of the individual's situation (that excluded structural factors). However, in highlighting the ways in which the "family support" organisation that he was placed within could assist, rather than surveillance the family, he noted his level of perceived risk reduced dramatically. Being able to assist the woman with some basic house tidying may reduce the visible signs that could be misconstrued by workers as not coping and/or being an uncaring parent. His preparedness to assist also demonstrates his solidarity with the woman, while creating opportunities for connection, rapport building and understanding, which may reduce her sense of social isolation.

In this way, critical reflection can connect students (and practitioners and educators) with a sense of agency to make change. Using a modernist structural framework on its own can feel disempowering in disconnecting people from the means of change. As Brookfield notes, "When we start to analyse the power and persistence of dominant ideologies, we can quickly reach the conclusion that there is little anyone can do to stand against the massive twin pillars of capitalism and bureaucratic rationality" (Brookfield, 1995, p. 8). However, critical theory informed pedagogy, which uses a critical version of poststructuralism, such as critical reflection, can offer us a form of "radical hope that helps us stand against the danger of energy-sapping, radical pessimism" (Brookfield, 1995, p. 9). As Brookfield (1995, p. 209) reminds us: "The point of education [and indeed of social work] is not just to understand the world, but to change it, often through collective endeavour."

Conclusion

In an attempt to capture the spirit of Brookfield's critical contribution to education, this quote by him speaks volumes: "We teach to change the world" (Brookfield, 1995, p. 1). Brookfield's synthesis and application of key critical social theorists to education "relocate[s] critical thinking and critical reflection squarely in the tradition of critical theory, with the explicit social and political critique, and activism, this implies" (Brookfield, 2005, p. 376). In this chapter, I have argued Brookfield's work holds significant relevance for social work education and practice through the description of a student's critical reflection process, and my own parallel critically reflective process. Brookfield ultimately argues that living and teaching without critical reflection

> is to see yourself as a victim of fate, to be open to exploitation, to live with no sense of promise or forward movement, to be unable to say why what you're doing is important, and to think that what you do when you show up to teach makes little difference to anyone or anything.
>
> *(Brookfield, 1995, p. 263)*

In this way, he highlights the fundamental importance of the contribution of critical theorists to critical reflection, and of critical reflection to our own teaching practice, while simultaneously outlining a critical pedagogical process to inspire transformative learning in social work students.

Notes

1. Both editions of *Becoming a Critically Reflective Teacher* are drawn upon in this chapter because the 1995 edition has informed my teaching over the past two decades. While the core thesis of the second (2017) edition is the same as the first, the book has been completely rewritten. I have deliberately chosen to include some material from the 1995 edition, as it is particularly relevant to this chapter, while also including some material from the newer edition.

References

Bennett, B., Green, S., Gilbert, S., & Bessarab, B. (2013). *Our voices: Aboriginal and torres strait islander social work*. South Yarra: Palgrave Macmillan.
Brookfield, S. (1995). *Becoming a critically reflective teacher*. San Francisco, CA: JosseyBass Publishers.
Brookfield, S. (2005). *The power of critical theory for adult learning and teaching*. Maidenhead: Open University Press.
Brookfield, S. (2012). *Teaching for critical thinking: Tools and techniques to helpstudents question their assumptions*. San Francisco, CA: Jossey-Bass.
Brookfield, S. (2015). *The skillful teacher: On technique, trust, and responsiveness in the classroom* (2nd Ed.). San Francisco, CA: Jossey-Bass.
Brookfield, S. (2016). So what exactly is critical about critical reflection? In J. Fook, V. Collington, F. Ross, Gillian, R & L. West (Eds.), *Researching critical reflection: Multidisciplinary perspectives*. London and New York: Routledge, pp. 11–22.
Brookfield, S. (2017). *Becoming a critically reflective teacher* (2nd Ed.). San Francisco, CA: Jossey Bass Publishers.

Fook, J. (2002). *Social work: A critical approach to practice* (3rd Ed.). London: Sage.
Fook, J., & Morley, C. (2005). Empowerment: A contextual perspective. In S. Hick, J. Fook, & R. Pozzuto (Eds.), *Social work: A critical turn* (pp. 67–85). Canada: Thompson Education Publishers.
Gramsci, A. (1957). *The modern prince and other writings*. New York: International Publishers.
Mezirow, J. (1991). *Transformative dimensions of adult learning*. San Francisco, CA: Jossey-Bass.
Morley, C. (2007). Engaging practitioners in critical reflection: Issues and dilemmas. *Journal of Reflective Practice*, 8(1), 16–74.
Morley, C. (2009). Using critical reflection to improve feminist practice. In J. Allan, L. Briskman & B. Pease (Eds.), *Critical social work* (2nd Ed., pp. 145–159). Crows Nest: Allen & Unwin.
Morley, C. (2016). Critical reflection and critical social work. In B. Pease, S. Goldingay, N. Hosken & S. Nipperes *Doing critical social work* (pp. 25–38). Crows Nest: Allen & Unwin.
Webb, S. (2006). *Social work in a risk society*. Houndmills: Palgrave Macmillan.

Index

Note: page numbers in italic type refer to Figures.

AASW (Australian Association of Social Workers) 198, 334; Code of Ethics 234, 447; Education and Accreditation Standards 335; *Ethical Guidance, The: Using client information for research and educative purposes* 233–234, 237, 239, 243
Abbott, A. 264–265
Abbott, Edith 37
Abbott, Grace 37
ableism 359, 360, 365, 367, 368, 369; and the normate 360–361; prejudice against non-normative bodies 361–363; and social work practice 365–369; *see also* disability
Ablett, Phillip 1–16, 176–188, 201–212, 477–488
abnormal justice 246, 254–255, 257
Aboriginal and Torres Strait Islanders 50, 382; history of invasion and colonisation of Australia 379; and yarning 383–384; *see also* Indigenous Australians; Indigenous knowledge
absent referent 298, 299, 306
action, and Arendt 441
activists, social workers as 210–211
Adams, Carol J. 296, 298–299, 301, 302
Adams College, South Africa 413, 414
adaptive preferencing 238, 241
Addams, Jane 6, 7, 32, 42, 108, 109, 116, 133, 154, 184, 453; background and context 32–34; biography 34–35; founding of Hull House 25–27; philosophy of 33, 37–40; and social work education 40–42
Adding Insult to Injury: Nancy Fraser debates her critics (Fraser) 246
Adkins, Barbara 8, 512–522
Adorno, Theodore 6, 10, 118; biography 109; critical social work pedagogy 112–116; critical social work practice 116–118; and Habermas 452; key concepts 109–112
adult education 530, 531, 532; and critical theory 525, 526; *see also* Highlander Folk School; Horton, Myles; transformative learning
Adults with Incapacity (Scotland) Act 2000 275–276

'adverse life experiences' of social work students 322, 327, 331
Aesthetic Dimension, The (Marcuse) 104
aesthetic theory 112, 113, 114, 118
"affect" 271, 276
affinity 286; and social work 290–291; with technology 287
"affirmative biopolitics" 268–269
Agamben, Giorgio 8, 223–224, 230–231, 260, 261, 262, 268; bare life 225, 226–227, 230; biography 224; bio-politics 227–228, 230; and Butler 350; foundations 224–225; implications for social work education 229–230; resistance 228–229; states of exception 225–226
agency 8, 126; and technologies of the self 146
agency/structure dichotomy 402
agriculture 298
ahimsa (non-violence): and Gandhi 426, 428, 429; in social work 432–433
Algeria 400, 401
alienation 405
Aljazeera 150
Allan, J. 108, 280
Allen, L. 339
all-subjected principle 252
alterity 156, 159
Althusser, Louis 216, 217, 218, 219
Althusser's Lesson (Rancière) 217
American Civil Liberties Union 33
Americanism 84–85, 86
Amsler, S.S. 103
'anaesthetization of the mind' 325
analogical listening 100
Anderson, D. 383
Anderson, K. 348
animal ecofeminism 298, 299, 301
Animal Liberation Press Office 300
animals/non-human species 298, 306–307; animal rights movement 293, 471; animal-assisted social work 304; human relationships with 286, 287–288; and

transformative education 305–306; *see also* CAS (critical animal studies)
Anthropocene 286, 288, 292, 294, 474
anthropocentrism 293, 296
anti-nuclear movement 467
anti-oppressive pedagogy 325; *see also* Kumashiro, Kevin
anti-oppressive social work 431
Apple, M.W. 48, 505, 506
Applebaum, B. 168
Arabena, K. 382
Araújo, Ana Maria (Nita) 122
"arborescence" 279–280
Archive Fever (Derrida) 156
Arendt, Hannah 2, 8, 178, 224, 230–231, 448; application of key concepts to teaching community development 439, 446–448; biography 439–440; and Butler 350; and Gadamer 483; natality 439, 440, 442–443, 448; plurality 439, 440, 444–445; political storytelling 440, 445–446; publicness 439, 440, 445
Aristotle 10
"Art in the One-Dimensional Society" (Marcuse) 104
Artaud, A. 271
artificial body parts 287, 291
arts, the 10, 294, 477–478, 484; and Marcuse 103–105; *see also* CPP (critical performance pedagogy); TO *(Theatre of the Oppressed/Teatro del Oprimido)* (Boal)
Aruzza, Cinzia 246
Asante, Molefi Kete 414
Askeland, Gudrid Aga 93, 149, 326
assessments in welfare systems 234, 237–238, 241; and disability 366–367
Atkinson, Anthony 311, 312
Atlanta University, Georgia 46
Au, W. 505, 506
Aucouturier, Marguerite 157
Auerhahn, Nanette 239
Auschwitz 225, 226, 227; *see also* Holocaust, the; Nazi Germany
austerity policies 3, 5
Australia 3; democratic *paideía* in social work education 180, 181–185, 186; domestic violence 345; history of invasion and colonisation of 379; institutional ethnography of social work education 198; social work education 147–148, 150, 369, 496–497; welfare system discourses 236–237; welfare systems and disability 366, 367; *see also* Aboriginal and Torres Strait Islanders; Indigenous Australians
Australian Association of Social Workers *see* AASW (Australian Association of Social Workers)
'authoritarian populism' 215
autism, people with 274–275, 276–277

autonomy 177, 179, 181, 182, 186
Ayers, Bill 138

Babbage, F. 480
Bachmann, Ingeborg 224
Bacon, F. 272
Badwall, H. 150
Baianstovu, Rúna í 8, 450–464
Baikie, G. 149
Bakhurst, D. 63
Baldwin, James 47
'banality of evil' thesis 230–231, 446
'banking' model of education 10, 78, 124–125, 206
Barak, Adi 6, 96–107
bare life 225, 226–227, 230
basic income 310, 317–318
Battacharya, Tithi 246
Batty, Rosie 345
Bay, Uschi 2, 439–449
Becoming a Critically Reflective Teacher (Brookfield) 524
Beddoe, Liz 143, 183
Being and Time (Gadamer) 483
being-in-the-world 359–360, 368, 369
Benjamin, Walter 112, 224
Bentham, Jeremy 349
Benziman, G. 327
Bergson, Henry 271, 359
Berlin, Isaiah 234
Bernstein, R.J. 484
Berry, T. 426
Bertha Capen Reynolds Society 73
Best, Steven 8, 296, 299, 300–301, 304, 305
Besthorn, Fred 296, 302, 303
Between Facts and Norms (Habermas) 452
Between Past and Future (Arendt) 440
Bevel, James 133
Biestek, Felix 84
Bifo, Franco Berardi 262
bifurcated consciousness 193
Bigo, D. 266
biopolitics 224, 227–228, 230, 261–262; "affirmative biopolitics" 268–269; and social work 260, 262–263
bio-power 228
Bìos: Biopolitics and Philosophy (Esposito) 261, 268
Black Skin, White Masks (Fanon) 399, 400, 401, 403, 404, 405
black students 502–503, 505; HBC (historically black colleges) 46, 47
black women, and intersectionality 300
Bleich, D. 327–328, 330
Bler, M. 117
Boal, Augusto 10, 100, 486–487; TO *(Theatre of the Oppressed/Teatro del Oprimido)* 477–478, 479–483; action-oriented critical analysis 480–481, 487; aesthetic space 480, 487;

Index

biography 479; joker/facilitator role 482–483, 487; working collectively with 'the people' 481–482, 487

bodies: bodily self-expression 363–365; corporeal schema 363–364; economic value of 362; Merleau-Ponty's theory 359–360, 363–365, 367, 368, 369–370; prejudice against non-normative bodies 361–363

bodily impulse (Adorno) 111–112

body-at-this-moment 363, 364

Boler, M. 409

Boltanski, Luc 246

Booth, M. 328

bordering practices, and immigration 267

Boston Children's Aid Society 72

Bourdieu, Pierre 8, 89, 157, 169, 512–513; biography 513; pedagogy of social work research 516–520; and Picketty 311; reflexivity and social work research 513–514; suffering and symbolic power 515–516

bourgeoisie, Marx on 22, 23

Bouverne-De Bie, M. 177

Bownam, N. 382–383

Boyd, D. 168

Bozalek, Vivienne 7, 245–259

Braidotti, Rosi 294

Braverman, Harry 27

Brazilian Workers Party 178

Brazzell, M. 169–170

Brecht, B. 479, 481

Breckinridge, Sophonisba 37

Briese, Jennie 7, 375–387

Britain First Party 88

Britzman, D. 340, 342

Brookfield, Stephen 10, 325, 328, 329, 451, 486, 505, 506, 507, 523, 534; biography 524; critical theory 525, 526–527; critically reflective approach to education 524–526; practice incident example 527–528, 530–531, 532–533; teaching critical reflection 528–534

Brough, Mark 8, 512–522

Brown, Molly 389, 394, 395–396, 397

Brown, Wendy 87

Bruner, Jerome 59, 61, 67, 68; key concepts 64–65

Buddhism 7, 391–393; *see also* Engaged Buddhism

Bulhan, H.A. 400

Burawoy, M. 401, 403

Burnam, E. 149–150

Burstow, B. 197

Bush, Mirabai 389

Business as Usual story 396

Butler, Judith 8, 149, 350; *gender performativity* 346, 348, 350–353, 356; *heterosexual matrix* 346, 348, 353–354, 356; *normative violence* 346, 348, 354–355, 356

Butts, R. 9

CADIS (Centre of Sociological Analysis and Intervention) 466

Calhoun, C. 166

California Alliance of Researchers for Equity in Education 333

Calvino, Italo 224

Campbell, C. 149, 325

Campbell, F.K. 362, 368

Campbell, Timothy 268

Camus, Albert 157

Canovan, M. 444, 445

Capital (Marx) 22, 26, 216

Capital in the Twenty-First Century (Picketty) 310, 311–312, 319

capitalism 297–298; and CAS (critical animal studies) 299; crisis of 246, 253–255, 257; global nature of 24; and human nature 27; Marx on 19, 21–25, 27; and meritocratic extremism 314–315; and racial oppression 46

Capitalism: A conversation in critical theory (Fraser and Jaeggi) 246

Capitalocene 288

Captalism and Schizophrenia (Deleuze) 272

Caputo, John 156, 159, 161, 162

Card, C. 166, 172

Cardoza Law School, New York 157

"care in the community" policy 275

care, Tronto's critical ethics of 166–167

Caring Democracy: Markets, Equality and Justice (Tronto) 166

Carman, T. 363

Carruthers, Jean 10, 477–488

"Cartesian" philosophy 363

CAS (critical animal studies) 296, 297, 298, 299–300, 304, 305, 306, 307

case histories and records 191, 194–195

Castoriadis, Cornelius 11, 186; biography 177–178; critical reflection and critical theory in social work education 181–185; on education 179–180; main ideas 178–179

Cavel, Stanley 235

Center for Anti-Oppressive Education, The 333

Centre for Studies on Social Movements 466

Centre of Sociological Analysis and Intervention (CADIS) 466

Césaire, Aimé 400, 404

Chak, A. 62

Chambon, A.S. 144

change 184; critical theory as catalyst for 6–9; *see also* social change

Changing Psychology in Social Casework, A (Robinson) 72

Chicagoland Researchers and Advocates for Transformative Education 333

Chikerama, James 414

child development 224; and Vygotsky 58–59, 61–64, 65–68

child labor 39
children: as active participants in learning 59–60; agency of 59, 64–65
'children of empire' scandal 29
Chilisa, B. 417
China 24
Choegyal Rinpoche 391, 397
Chomsky, N. 42
Chouinard, V. 361, 362
Christianity 37, 123
Christie, W. 327
Chthulucene 288, 292, 293
circle work 430
civil disobedience, and Gandhi 429
civil rights movement, US 132, 133
civil society 468; *see also* new social movements
Civil War, US 35, 37
civilised society 236
civility 235, 236
Cixous, Hélène 157
Clark, Septima 133
Clarke, M. 327
classroom environment, self-disclosure in 327–330, 409
'client' terminology 92
climate change 23, 285, 289
Close to Home (Shiva) 298
CNI (National Council of Industries) 121
Cockain, A. 279
coercion, in social work 451
coercive control 346–347, 348, 355, 356
coercive power 87
Cohen-Cruz, J. 479
Colebrook, C. 228
Collège de Sorbonne, Paris 157
Collège d'études mondiales, Paris 246
Collins, A. L. 50
Collins, K. 147
colonialism 7, 51; impact on the colonised 124; *see also* Fanon, Franz
Coloniality 401, 403, 406, 407, 409
Columbia University 96, 490; School of Social Work 115
commodification 28
common sense: and Arendt 444; and Deleuze 273, 276
communalism, in *Ubuntu* 415, 419
communicative action *see* TCA (Theory of Communicative Action) (Habermas)
Communist and Socialist Parties 72, 73, 79
Communist International 84
Communist Manifesto (Marx and Engels) 21, 24
Communist Party, US 46
Communitas: The Origin and Destiny of Community (Esposito) 261
community: community activism 471; Derrida on 156–157; *see also* new social movements

Community Care (Scotland) Act 1999 274
community development: and Arendt 442, 444, 446–448; and plurality 444–445; and political principles 447; principles of 443; and storytelling 446; and Touraine 472–473
concentration camps 225–226, 268; *see also* Holocaust, the; Nazi Germany
concepts: concept development 59, 62, 63, 64, 68; and identity thinking 109–110
Conceptual Practices of Power, The: A Feminist Sociology of Knowledge (Smith) 191
Conference on Charity and Correction 38
Conference on Social Work, 1920 40
Congress of Industrial organizations 72
conjunctures 87
Connell, R. 507
Connelly, Peter 87
Conquergood, Dwight 478
conscientisation 101, 125, 472, 503
consensus 458–459
constellations 112, 181
consumer movements 467
consumerism 28
contradiction 20, 21
Conventions of Rights of Persons with Disability (CPRD) (UN) 365, 366
corporatism 303–304
corporeal schema 363–364
CORU, Ireland 91
Costa de Oliveira, Elza Maria 121, 122
"Council of All Beings" 389, 395
Council of Social Workers (CSW), Zimbabwe 421
Council on Social Work Education (CSWE) 40–41
counter-hegemony 6, 86
Cowden, Stephen 8, 10, 120–130, 213–222
Coyle, Grace 78
CPP (critical performance pedagogy) 478–479, 480, 481–482, 482–483, 484, 486–487
CPRD (Conventions of Rights of Persons with Disability) (UN) 365, 366
Crawford, K. 137–138
creation 178
creativity, Marcuse on 103–105
Crehan, Kate 89
Crip Queer theory 361
crises, and hegemony 87
'Crisis in Education, The' (Arendt) 440, 447
critical animal studies *see* CAS (critical animal studies)
critical consciousness 11–12; and education 41, 102–103; and Freire 123, 125; and Marcuse 97, 102; and privileged groups 170
critical incidents in social work 149; critical reflection example 527–528, 529, 530–531, 532–533

539

critical pedagogy 6, 10–12, 137–138, 356, 400, 409; "affirmative biopolitics" 268–269; and Brookfield 527; and Castoriadis 180; and Freire 120, 122–126, 128; and hooks 507–508, 508–509, 510; importance of for social work 1–2, 127; and supervision 509–510; and Touraine 73–474

critical performance pedagogy *see* CPP (critical performance pedagogy)

'critical political semantics' 92

critical poststructuralist theories 8, 13

critical race theory 48

critical reflection 11–12, 229–230, 523–524; and Brookfield 524–526; and democratic *paideía* 180, 181–185; and institutional ethnography 198–199; practice incident example 527–528; teaching of 528–534; and transformative learning 492, 494, 496

critical reflexivity 149, 150

critical social policy analysis 183–185

critical social theory: and democratic *paideía* 180, 183–185

critical social work 489–490, 496; and Du Bois 52–54; and hooks 508–510; and Touraine 468, 470

critical (animal) social work 296, 303–305

critical social work pedagogy 325–327, 523–524

critical theory 13, 143; and Brookfield 525, 526–527; as catalyst for change 6–9; and Derrida 155; and Foucault 147; and Mezirow 493, 494; and social work education 209

critical thinking 5, 137–138; and hooks 505–507, 510; tradition of negativity in 216

critical-dialectical discourse 492, 496, 497

'critique' 6

Crossley, N. 455

Cruikshank, B. 248

Crystals, Fabrics, and Fields: Metaphor of Organicism in Twentieth-Century Developmental Biology (Haraway) 286

CSW (Council of Social Workers), Zimbabwe 421

CSWE (Council on Social Work Education) 40–41

Curry-Stevens, A. 171, 327

custody control 346, 354–355; *see also* domestic violence

Cyborg Manifesto (Haraway) 286, 288

cyborg metaphor (Haraway) 286, 287, 291

Dabrowski, Kazimierz 394

dairy food eating 298–299; *see also* CAS (critical animal studies)

Dalai Lama 425

Daniels, H. 60

Darkwater: Voices from Within the Veil (Du Bois) 47

Dartmouth College 246

Daumard, Adeline 311

David F. case study 213–214, 220–221

Davis, A.F. 34

De Silva, T. 127

Debord, Guy 224

decency 235, 236, 242, 243–244

Decent Society, The (Margalit) 233, 234–235, 242

Decoloniality 400, 402, 403, 406, 407, 408, 409

decolonisation 7, 376, 379, 381, 382, 383, 413; decolonised pedagogies 417–421; decolonised social work 412

deconstruction 153, 157, 158–159, 160

deconstructive movements 158

deep democracy 430

deep ecology 388, 389, 392, 395, 428

Deleuze, Gilles 7, 260, 271, 281; application in social work practice 274–279; biography 271–272; "dogmatic image of thought" 271, 272, 273–274; key concepts 272–273; pedagogy 279–280

deliberative democracy 453, 454

Demmert, W. Jr. 383

democracy: 'brokenness' of 9; and critical theory 6; deep democracy 430; deliberative 453, 454; and education 5–6, 9, 41–42; and Habermas 453–454, 459

democratic *paideía* 177, 179–180, 186; and social work education in Australia 180, 181–185, 186

Denzin, Norman 478

Department of Social Development, South Africa 421

dependency 245, 248, 256

Deranty, J.P. 228, 229

Derrida, Jacques 8, 153, 163; and Agamben 224; biography 155–157; deconstructive episteme 154–155; and Giroux 208; key concepts for social work 157–160; and social work pedagogy 161–162

Descartes, R. 272, 363

deservingness, and disability 366, 367

"Despair and Empowerment Work" 389

despair work 393–395

developmental social work 412

Dewey, John 6, 9, 11, 34, 78, 134, 137; and Freire 121; pragmatist philosophy 37, 38

dialectic method 20

dialectical thinking 102

dialectics 113–114

dialogue, use of in social work 127

Didi-Huberman, Georges 356

"difference" 277

disability 7, 238; critical disability theory 360, 368–369; and Indigenous Australians 148; medicalisation of 360, 365–366, 367–368; and the normate 360–361; prejudice against non-normative bodies 361–363; social model of 360; and social work 360, 368–369; *see also* ableism

Disability Assessment Schedule 2.0 (WHO) 366
Disability Employment Job Access Scheme, Australia 366
disability geography studies 364
disability rights movement 233, 243; Australia 240–242
disablism 362
Disch, L.J. 444, 445, 446
disciplinary power 533
Discipline and Punish (Foucault) 348–349
discourse 348
discourse ethics 451, 453, 458–460, 460–462
discursive therapy 65–67, 68
disorientating dilemmas 491–492, 496
distancing 62, 67, 68
Distinction (Bourdieu) 515
distorted assumptions 491
distributive justice 473
diversity 451, 461
DNA databases 225
documents 194–195; *see also* institutional ethnography
Dolamo, R.T.H. 416
domestic violence 345–346, 356–357; Butler's theories 346, 348, 350–355, 356–357; coercive control 346–347, 348, 355, 356; Foucault's theories 346, 348–349; *gender performativity* 346, 348, 350–353, 356; *heterosexual matrix* 346, 348, 353–354, 356; *normative violence* 346, 348, 354–355, 356; *panopticon effect* 346, 348, 349–350, 351, 354, 355, 356–357; role of gender in 346, 347–348; and social work education and practice 355–356
Domination et Anticipation: Pour un renouveau de la critique (Fraser and Boltanski) 246
Dominelli, Lena 52, 296, 302–303, 334, 473
Donovan, Josephine 301
double consciousness 45, 48–49, 50, 53, 54, 124
Down, B. 5
Dowse, L. 369
Dream of the Earth, The (Berry) 426
Du Bois, W.E.B. 7, 45, 72, 184; and Australian Aboriginal studies courses 45, 49, 50–52; biography 45–47; contemporary issues of identity, privilege, standpoint and critical social work 52–54; double consciousness 45, 48–49, 50, 53, 54; intersectionality 49–50; social work practice and social justice 54–55; sociology and social work education 47; the veil, and race as a social construction 45, 47–48, 50, 53, 54
dualisms 292, 297–298
Dunstan, J. 495
Durkheim, Émile 453
Dusk of Dawn: An Essay towards and Autobiography of a Race Concept (Du Bois) 47
Dyer, P.K. 484
Dying Colonialism, A (Fanon) 399–400

Eagleton, Terry 26
earth democracy 307
earth, rights of 293
ecofeminism 296, 297–299, 300, 301, 302, 304, 305, 306, 307
Ecofeminism (Shiva and Mies) 298
École des Hautes Études en Sciences Sociales (EHESS) 311
École Normale Supérieure, Paris 157, 216, 466, 513
Écoles des Hautes Études 178
ecological/green social work 289, 296, 301–303, 307, 431
ecology 433; deep ecology 388, 389, 392, 395, 428; and Gandhi 428
Economic and Philosophical Manuscripts (Marx) 28
economic cycles in capitalism 23, 25
educated hope 105, 208–209, 211
education 2; and Addams 34, 41–42; and Adorno 109; colonial 418–419; and critical theory 9, 206–208; decolonising of 376, 379, 383; and democracy 5–6, 9; and Dewey 34, 41–42; education convergence through diffusion of knowledge 316–318; educational services and global capitalism 23–24; as a force for convergence 311; and Marcuse 97; reduction of to 'training' 10; role of in critical theory 525; teacher's role in 219–220; and Vygotsky 59–60, 60–61; *see also* critical pedagogy; Kumashiro, Kevin; pedagogy; social work education; teaching; technicist education, Giroux's critiques of; transformative education
Education Deans for Justice and Equity 333
Education for Critical Consciousness (Freire) 123
'egocentric speech' 64
EHESS (École des Hautes Études en Sciences Sociales) 311
Eichmann, A. 443, 446
Eichmann in Jerusalem (Arendt) 440
Einstein, A. 424
Eisenman, P. 365
Ejsing, A. 329
eligibility tests and assessments in welfare systems 234, 237–238, 241; and disability 366–367
Elizabeth, Vivienne 355
Elliott, L. 22
Ellison, Ralph 47
Ellsworth, E. 340
emancipation 253, 254
emancipatory knowledge 494
embodiment 360, 388, 390; embodied teaching 397
Emirbayer, M. 514
employment insecurity 3
empowerment 126; critical pedagogy as source of 12; empowerment theory 73, 78; as a social work value 2–3; terminology of 12
encounter, the 280
Engaged Buddhism 388, 389, 391–393

Index

engaged pedagogy 508–509, 510
Engels, F. 21, 24, 93
Enlightenment 6
environmental destruction 298; and capitalism 23, 25
environmental injustice 302
environmental issues 285, 301–302; *see also* ecofeminism; ecological/green social work
environmental justice 393
environmental movement 467, 471
'epistemological ignorance' 11–12
Epston, D. 66
equality: and Rancière 216–218, *217*; in social work 213, 216, 220–222
eros 102
Esposito, Roberto 12, 260; application of key concepts to social work education 261–267; biography 260–261; transformative aspects of work for pedagogy 268–269
essentialism 49
Ethical Guidance, The: Using client information for research and educative purposes (AASW) 233–234, 237, 239, 243
ethics: and Adorno 117–118; of learning 161
'everyday' concepts 63, 66, 67
Everyday World as Problematic, The: A Feminist Sociology (Smith) 191, 192
experiential learning 134

Fabianism 215
Fahlberg, V.I. 267
family, the: Marx's perspective on 20–21; *see also* domestic violence
Fanon, Franz 7, 124, 361, 399–400, 409; affect, in racialised oppression and racism 405–406, 408–409; biography 400–401; Decoloniality 400, 402, 403, 406, 407, 408, 409; disalienation and liberation 404–405; and emancipatory transformation in social work education 406–409, *407*; and Freire 121; impact of colonisation 402–403; internalised oppression 403; key concepts 401–406; negritude 404; psychopolitics 401, 402, 406
fantasy 102
fantasy role play, children's learning through 62–63, 65–66
Farmer, N. 267
Farmers' Protest, Mumbai 429–430
fasting, and Gandhi 429
fatalism 124, 128
feminism 7, 467, 471, 505; and Addams 38, 39; critiques of Freud 72; and Haraway 286, 287; second-wave 72, 192, 193; and standpoint theory 192–193; on women's bodies 361
Feminism for the 99%: A Manifesto (Aruzza, Battacharya and Fraser) 246
feminist teaching 503, 505

Ferguson, Iain 25, 29
Fernández, M. 61
Fico, Robert 88
field 517–518
Finch, J. 266
First National People of Color Environmental Leadership Summit, 1991 393
First nations control of first nations education (Assembly of First Nations) 380–381
Fischer, M. 41
Fisher, S. 346
Fisk University, Nashville, Tennessee 45
Fleming, P. 390
FLN (National Liberation Front), Algeria 401
Follett, Mary Parker 78
Fook, Jan 118, 149, 322, 527
Foote, C.E. 147
Fordism 85, 86, 91
forgiveness 443
Fortunes of Feminism: From state-managed capitalism to neoliberal crisis (Fraser) 246–247
Fotopoulos, T. 180
Foucault, Michel 8, 91, 120, 143–144, 157, 228, 237, 261, 262, 268, 523, 533; and Agamben 224; application for social work education 147–150; biographical context 144; and critical theory 147; and domestic violence 346, 348–349; and Giroux 208; and Habermas 462n1; and power 143–144, 144–147, 150
Fox, John G. 6, 108–119
Foxxcon Technology Group 24
frailty concept, and older people 262
(mis)framing 252
Frank, A.W. 147
Frankfurt School, The 6, 85, 96, 109, 526; and Gadamer 483, 484; and Giroux 208; and Habermas 452; and Mezirow 494
Fraser, Heather 5, 7, 296–309
Fraser, Nancy 7, 92, 238, 240–241, 245–246; abnormal justice 246, 254–255, 257; biography and work 246–247; crisis of capitalism 246, 253–255, 257; dependency 245, 248, 256; gender justice principles 245, 248–249, 256; needs interpretation 245, 247–248, 256; participatory parity 249–250, 252–253, 254, 255, 256–257; theory of justice 245, 249–253; transformative practices 246, 255–256, 257
Fredericks, B. 383
freedom 26; fear of 126
Frei, Eduardo 122
Freire, Paulo 10, 11, 12, 78, 98, 101, 127–128, 135, 137, 170, 206, 305, 325, 356, 389, 406, 409, 427, 472, 505, 506; application to social work 126–127; and Boal 479, 481; and Giroux 202, 206, 208; and hooks 503; life and work 120–122; and Mezirow 493; philosophy of education 122–126

French Communist Party 144, 216
Freud, Sigmund 323, 402; and Castoriadis 178; feminist critiques of 72; and Reynolds 71, 72, 74, 75, 76
Froggett, L. 328
Fromm, Eric 121, 531, 532
Front National, France 88
'Functional School of Social Work' 74

Gaard, Greta 297, 301, 307
Gadamer, Hans-Georg 10, 158, 162, 477–478, 486–487; biography 483–484; and Habermas 452; play 478, 479, 485–487; prejudice 485, 487; tradition 484–485, 487
Gade, C.B.N. 413, 416
Gaia principle 392
Gandhi, Mohandas Karamachand 7, 424, 434; biography 425; and ecology 428; relevance in social work 430–434; and satyagraha 429–430; and social justice 428–429; values practiced by 427–428; vision for a sustainable world 426–427
Gannon, S. 326
Garland-Thomson, R. 360–361, 362
Garrett, Paul Michael 6, 12, 83–95, 99
Garsten, C. 366
Garton-Ash, Timothy 243
Garvey, Marcus 414
Gates, Trevor G. 6, 131–142
gay and lesbian rights movement 467, 471
Geisler, Mark 479, 481
gender: and care responsibilities 166; and critical theory 7; discriminatory attitudes towards 131, 135, 137; gender justice principles 245, 248–249, 256; *gender performativity* 346, 348, 350–353, 356; role of in domestic violence 346, 347–348
Gender Trouble: Feminism and the Subversion of Identity (Butler) 350
genealogy 348
general systems theory 388, 389, 391
"Generative Writing" 105
Geras, N. 26
Gerlach, A. 384
Ghana 416
Gide, Andre 157
gift economy 427
Gikandi, S. 418
Gilbert, J. 87
Gilded Age, US 32, 34, 35, 36
Giles, R. 149
Gilmore, Leigh 240
Gilson, E. 326
Giroux, Henry 2, 5, 10, 105, 109, 112, 115, 180, 201–202, 211, 356, 487, 505, 506, 507; application to social work education 205–206, 209–211; critical pedagogy 201, 202, 204–209, 211; critique of neoliberalism 203–204

Gleeson, B. 362
Glendinning, Chellis 389
Global Standards for the Education and Training of the Social Work Profession (IFSW) 233
globalisation 474
Goffman, Erving 190, 361
Gonick, L. 403
Goodley, D. 362, 368
Gordon, L. 92, 248, 402
Goulart, João 122
governmentality 145–147, 148, 150; of the self 237
grammar of justice 252
Gramsci, Antonio 6, 10, 83, 93, 305, 523, 525, 529, 531; biography and political context 83–84; and capitalist modernity 84–86; and 'common sense' 83, 86, 89–90, 91; and Freire 121; and Giroux 208, 209; hegemony 6, 11, 83, 86–88, 91–92; role of intellectuals 83, 90–91; and social work practice 91–93
Gray, Mel 4, 7, 245–259, 273
Great Depression 73–74, 75
"Great Refusal" 97, 102, 103
Great Turning 389, 390, 396
Great Unravelling story 396
Greece 88
Greek Communist Party 177
Green parties, European 178
green social work *see* ecological/green social work
Green Social Work (Dominelli) 302
grief 394
Griffin, Susan 7
Grosz, E. 365
Grover, C. 366, 367
Grusin, Richard 294
Guantanamo Bay detention camp 223, 225
Guattari, Felix 271, 272, 278, 280
Guegan, X. 402
Guevara, Che 427
Guilherme, M. 207–208
Gürgens, R. 485
Gutiérrez, Gustavo 121

Habermas, Jürgen 8, 10, 11, 450–451, 492, 523; application in social work practice and education 460–462; biography 452–453; deliberative democracy 453, 454; discourse ethics 451, 453, 458–460, 460–462; and Gadamer 484; integration 451, 453–454; intersubjectivity 451, 455, 456, 459; lifeworld 451, 453, 454, 455–456, 456–458, 461; and Mezirow 493–494; system 451, 453, 454, 455, 456–458, 461; Theory of Communicative Action (TCA) 450–451, 452–460
habitual body 363, 364
habitus 169, 514, 517–518
Hage, G. 405
Haidt, J. 325

543

Index

Hall, S. 87, 89, 215
Hallahan, Lorna 12, 233–244
Hamilton, Alice 37
Hamington, M. 39
Hammer, P. 381
Hammer, R. 51
Hancock, B.H. 146
Hanesworth, Carolyn 6, 32–44
Hankivsky, O. 53
Hapanyengwi-Chemhuru, O. 417, 419
happy consciousness 101–102
Haraway, Donna 294; biography and key concepts 286–288; implications for social work 288–293; and a posthuman future for social work 293–294
Haraway Reader, The (Haraway) 288
Harding, Sandra 191
Hardt, M. 268
Harms Smith, Linda 7, 124, 399–411
Harris, Verne 156, 163
Harrison, Alan 311
Harvard University 46, 122, 414
hauntology 154, 160
Hayes, C. 326
Hazare, Anna 425
HBC (historically black colleges) 46, 47
healing justice 388
Health and Care Professions Council, UK 91
Healy, Karen 183
Hearn, J. 168
Heath-Kelly, Charlotte 266
Hegel, Georg Wilhelm Friedrich 6, 20, 110, 118, 144, 401, 479; and Adorno 110, 118; and Boal 479; and Freire 121
hegemony 6, 11, 209, 529–530
Heidegger, Martin 96, 144, 153, 158, 178; and Agamben 224; and Arendt 439; and Gadamer 483, 484; and Merleau-Ponty 359–360
Henry, F. 382
Herring, J. 346–347
heterosexual matrix 346, 348, 353–354, 356
heterotonomy 179
Hicks, S. 342
higher education: contemporary student demographics and context 324–325, 507–508; decolonising of 376, 379, 383; Indigenous 382–383; and neoliberalism 86, 176, 203–204, 304, 305, 489, 513–514; and Touraine 73–474; *see also* universities
Highlander Folk School 131–132, 133, 134–135, 136, 137, 138, 139–140
Hilberg, R. 383
Hill, J. 347
historical materialism 20, 21
historically black colleges (HBC) 46, 47
historicity 469
Holborrow, Marnie 86

'holding environment' 330
Holland, D. 64, 65
Hollinsworth, David 7, 45–57
Holmes, Oliver Wendell Jr. 37
Holocaust, the 109, 111, 115, 225, 226, 227, 234, 239, 443, 446, 452
Hölscher, Dorothee 7, 170, 245–259
Holzman, L. 61–62, 63, 66
homeless people, health care case study 196
Homo Sacer: Sovereign Power and Bare Life (Agamben) 223, 224, 226, 230–231
homophobia, in social work education 132, 335, 336, 338
honesty claims 458, 460
Honneth, Axel 113, 246
Hook, D. 399, 401, 402, 406
hooks, bell 7, 12, 361, 501, 510; academic endeavours 502–503; biography 501–502; critical social work supervision 508–510; critical thinking 505–507; critically informed social work 508; and the current higher education context 507–508; teaching career 503–505
hope: critical pedagogy as source of 12; Giroux's educated hope 105, 208–209, 211
Horkheimer, M. 110, 452
Horton, Myles 6, 131–132; applications for social work education, practice and research 135–136, 137–140; biography and work 132–133; key concepts 133–136
Hoskin, N. 198
Hosking, D.L. 368
hospitality 159
hostile environment policy, UK Home Office 267
House Committee on Un-American Activities 73
Hull House, Chicago 32, 33, 34, 39, 133; founding of 35–37; *see also* Addams, Jane
Human Condition, The (Arendt) 440, 441
human nature, Marx on 25–26
human rights 293, 471
Human Rights Watch 150
humanity 285–286, 288, 292
Hume, D. 271
humiliation 233, 234, 235, 236–237, 240, 242, 243; paradox of 239
Hunhuism or Ubuntism: A Zimbabwean Political Philosophy (Samkange and Samkange) 414
Hunter, M.A. 47
Husserl, Edmund 96, 144, 359
Hutchings, A. 149

IBL (Inquiry-Based Learning) 383
ICAS (International Critical Animal Studies) 300
identity 286, 327; categorisation in social work assessments 274; and Du Bois 52–54; and justice 250; misrecognition of 53
identity politics 250, 286, 290
identity thinking 109–110, 111

Ife, Jim 2, 285–295, 443, 444, 448
IFSW (International Federation of Social Workers): *Global Definition of Social Work* 3, 5, 149, 214, 293, 294; *Global Standards for the Education and Training of the Social Work Profession* 233; *Statement of Ethical Principles* 131
ignorance 12; and privileged irresponsibility 167
Ignorant Schoolmaster, The (Rancière) 218–220, 221
image theatre 100
Imaginary Institution of Society, The (Castoriadis) 177–178
imagination 178
immigrants: and biopolitics 266–267; social work with 253
immunisation/immunity paradigm 268–269; and social work 263–267
Immunitas: The Protection and Negation of Life (Esposito) 261
imperialism 51
"imposter syndrome" 524
incivility 235, 236
indecent institutions 240
indecent society 233, 236
India 425–426, 429; *see also* Gandhi, Mohandas Karamachand
Indiana University 413
Indigenous Australians 49, 50, 52–54, 115, 148, 292–293; history of invasion and colonisation of Australia 379; multi-generational trauma 382; and yarning 383–384; *see also* Aboriginal and Torres Strait Islanders; Indigenous knowledge
Indigenous communities 150
Indigenous cultures 418; and colonialism 403, 404, 408; non-written and local sources of information and 'informal' education 418–419; students from 114–115 (*see also Ubuntu*)
Indigenous knowledge 7, 290, 292–293, 294, 375–378, 384–385; and CPP (critical performance pedagogy) 478; Indigenous higher education 382–383; methods of sharing 383–384; and Moreton-Robinson 375–376, 378–380, 381, 383, 384; and social work education 380–381
Indigenous Knowledge Paradigms 384
Indigenous language, and colonialism 403, 408
Indigenous people, 'othering' of 45
indigenous social work 412
Indigenous Standpoint Theory 375, 378, 380, 382, 384–385
Indigenous Women's Standpoint Theory 380
individual autonomy 179
'individual responsibility' doctrines 3, 5
individualism 289
industrial production systems 84–86, 91
industrial working conditions 132
industrialisation, and the development of social work 108

Industry Social Service (SESI) 121
inequality 3, 22, 25, 41, 250; "inequality curve" theory 313
inferiority complex 403, 404, 405
inner speech 64–65
Inquiry-Based Learning (IBL) 383
Institute for Social Research (Institut fur Sozialforschung), Frankfurt 96, 109
institutional capture 198
Institutional Ethnography: A Sociology for People (Smith) 191
institutions, as social imaginary creations 178–179
Institutions of Social Work Education (ISWE) 430, 431
integration: TCA (Theory of Communicative Action) (Habermas) 451, 453–454
International Congress of Women, The Hague, 1915 33
International Critical Animal Studies (ICAS) 300
International Federation of Social Workers *see* IFSW (International Federation of Social Workers)
International League for Peace and Freedom 33
intersectionality 193, 250, 300; and Du Bois 49–50
intersubjectivity 451, 455, 456, 459
Irving, A. 144
isolation, and totalitarianism 442
ISWE (Institutions of Social Work Education) 430, 431
Italian Institute for the Human Sciences, Naples 260
Italy: twentieth-century political situation 83–84

Jackson, A. 480
Jackson, S. 323
Jacobsson, K. 366
Jacotot, Jacques 218–219
Jaeggi, Rahel 246
Jagernauth, Tanuja 388
Jaldorn, M. 324–325
James, A. 362
James, William 37
Jarrett, Mary 72
Jasper, Carl 439
JCU (James Cook University) transformative learning case study 496–497
Jeffery, D. 147
Jewish communities, discrimination against 60; JHC (Jewish Holocaust Centre), Melbourne, Australia 115, 117; *see also* Holocaust, the
Jeyasingham, D. 342
Jha, Manoj K. 84
JHC (Jewish Holocaust Centre), Melbourne, Australia 115, 117
Jim Crow era, US 46
Johnson, Lilian Wyckoff 133

545

Index

Johnstone, Chris 389, 390, 396
Jones, Peter 10, 11, 489–500
Jones, S. 87, 327
Jordan, B. 514
JPA (Juvenile Prosecution Association) 37
Jullien, Francois 155
Jung, Carl 12, 322–324, 326–327, 328, 331
Juridical-Administrative-Therapeutic nature of the welfare system 247
just society 236
justice 160, 161; abnormal 246, 254–255, 257; Fraser's theory of 245, 249–253; responsibility for (Young) 168–169
Justice Interruptus: Critical Reflections on the 'postsocialist' condition (Fraser) 246

Kaczyński, Jaroslaw 88
Kafka, Franz 278
Kaighin, Jen 7, 333–344
Kang, H. 329
Kant, Immanuel 6, 111, 271
Kaseke, E. 419
Kaunda, Kenneth 416
Kelley, Florence 37
Kellner, D. 6, 7, 8, 9
Kenya 416, 419
Kenyatta, Jomo 416
Kerr, C. 466
Keynesian-Westphalian frame of justice 252
"key-words" 99
Khamtrul Rinpoche 391
Khrumah, Kwameh 414
Kimball, Everett 73
Kincheloe, Joe 356
King, Julie 8, 143–152
King, Martin Luther Jr. 133, 414, 425, 503
Kippax, Rod 8, 512–522
Kirk, S. 514
Klein, Naomi 288
knowledge: diffusion of 316–318; ordinary knowing 518, 519; reflexive knowing 519; *see also* Indigenous knowledge
Kolb, David 134
Konopka, Gisela 78
Korten, David 389, 396, 426
Kovach, M. 379
Kowal, Emma 53
Kozulin, A. 61
Kumashiro, Kevin 7, 333–334; Education about the "Other" 336–337; Education for the "Other" 335–336; education that changes students and society 340–341; education that is critical of privileging and othering 337–340; queering social work knowledge and practice 333, 341–342
Kuppers, Petra 276, 279
Kuznets, Simon 311, 312, 313

labour, and Arendt 441
Labrousse, Ernest 311
Lachicotte, W. 65
Lakey, George 162
language: and colonialism 403, 408; and discussion 98–100; and social change 136, 137; use of in social work 12, 92, 127, 189, 191, 197, 198–199, 520; vernacular 505
language acquisition 59, 63–64, 224
Lathrop, Julia 37
Laub, Dori 239
Lavalette, Michael 6, 11, 19–31
Lazzarato, Maurizio 262
Le Corbusier (Charles-Édouard Jeanneret-Gris) 361
Le Pen, Marine 88
Leadbeater, Charles 236
learning: 'learning democracy' 177; learning moments 161–162, 163; learning-by-doing 134; *see also* education; pedagogy; transformative learning; ZPD (Zone of Proximal Development)
learning disabilities, people with 274–278
Learning to Live Finally (Derrida) 155
Lefort, Claude 177
Lemke, T. 261
Lengermann, P. 7
Lenin, V.I. 86
Leonardo Da Vinci 361
Les Aventures de Télémaque 218–219
Levinas, Emmanuel 153, 157, 160, 350
Lewis, David 48
Lewis, T.E. 265, 269
LGBTIQ communities *see* queer communities
liberal individual 168
liberalism, and Adorno 109, 110–111, 118
liberation, and Marcuse 96, 103–105
"Life with Gaia" (Macy) 390
lifeworld 451, 453, 454, 455–456, 456–458, 461
Lincoln, Abraham 34, 35
Lindemann, Edward 78, 115
literacy classes 505
Litmanen, T. 469
Lived Experience Project in social work education 233, 234, 236, 238, 239, 240, 242
Living Thought: The Origins and Actuality of Italian Philosophy (Esposito) 261
Livingstone, David 356
localization 426
London School of Economics 190
loneliness, and totalitarianism 441, 442
López, G. R. 54
Lorenz, Walter 1
Lorenzetti, L. 326
love, and Gandhi 427
Lucas, J. 328, 329
Luhmann, N. 264
Lukács, György 121

Lukianoff, G. 325
Lynch, Heather 7, 271–282
lynchings, US 46
Lyotard, Jean-François 224

Macedo, D. 325
Macfarlane, Selma 12, 322–332, 447, 489
Machaivelli, N. 479
Machel, Samora Moises 416
MacKinnon, K.V.R. 335
Macy, Fran 391
Macy, Joanna 7, 388–389, 389–390; biography 390–391; Buddhist thought, systems theory and deep ecology 391–393; "Council of All Beings" 395; despair work 393–395; pedagogical innovations and implications for social work pedagogy 383–397; storytelling 395–396; widening circles 396–397
'magical consciousness' 123, 124
Makavaza, N. 417, 419
'making kin with' 286, 289–290
Malcolm X 414
Maldano-Torres, M. 403, 406
maldistribution 250
Malthus, Thomas Robert 311
Man and His Symbols (Jung) 323
Mandel, Ernest 24
Mandela, Nelson 415, 416, 425
Manifestly Haraway (Haraway) 288
Manning, Eric 276, 278
Maphalala, M.C. 416–417, 419
MAPPA (Multi-Agency Public Protection Arrangements), Scotland 263
Marazzi, Christian 262
Marcuse, Herbert 6, 10, 96–98, 105–106, 523; art, creativity and liberation 103–105; and Freire 121; happy consciousness and negative thinking 101–103; language and discussion 98–100; pedagogical practices 97–98, 99–100, 101, 102–103, 105; society and liberation 100–101
Margalit, Avisha 12, 233, 234; decent society 234–235; disability rights example 240–241; eligibility and assessment 237–238; hazards of lived experience expertise 239–240; humiliation, decency and civility in welfare society 236–237; refusal, resistance and rights 242–244
Margolin, L. 172–173
marketisation 253, 254
Markham, L. 66
Markowitz, G.E. 132
marriage equality 246, 335, 341
Marsten, D. 66
Martin, P. 326
Marx, Karl 6, 10–11, 19, 183, 184, 312, 401, 469, 523; and Adorno 110, 112, 118; and alienation 19, 25–28; biography 19–21; and Boal 479, 481; and capitalism 19, 21–25, 27; and Castoriadis 177, 178; and Freire 121, 123–124; and Gramsci 84, 85, 89–90, 93; and Picketty 311; and Reynolds 71, 74, 75, 76, 77; and Smith 190, 191; and social work 28–30
masculine hegemony 90
materialism, Marx on 20
Matthews, E. 359
Maxwell, J. 228
Mays, Jenni 11, 310–321
Mazza, Debora 10, 120–130
Mbiti, J.S. 413
McCullogh, J. 400, 404
McGregor, D. 381
McKendrick, D. 266
McKeown, M. 169
McLaren, P. 127
McMaster University, Canada 201
McPhail, B. 337
Mead, George Herbert 37
meaning perspectives 491
meaning structures 491
means of production, Marx on 22, 23
meat eating 298–299; *see also* CAS (critical animal studies)
Meekosha, H. 369
Meekums, B. 329
Memoirs of the Blind (Derrida) 159
men: avoidance of caring responsibilities 166–167; behaviour change programs 168–169; privileged irresponsibility 172; violence against women 168–169, 171–172; *see also* gender
Menand, L. 37
mental health services, and institutional ethnography 191, 197
mental illness 144, 210, 265
Menzel, Kelly 7, 375–387
Mercer, N. 61
meritocratic extremism 314–315
Merleau-Ponty, Maurice 7, 178; and social work practice 365–369; theory of the body 359–360, 363–365, 367, 368, 369–370
meta-political (mis)representation 252, 253
Metz, T. 419
Mezirow, Jack 10, 11, 525, 530; application to social work education 494–496; critical reflection 492, 494, 496; critical-dialectical discourse 492, 496, 497; JCU (James Cook University) case study 496–497; meaning perspectives 491; meaning structures 491; social change 492–493, 495; transformation processes 491–492; transformative learning theory 328, 490–497
Mezzadra, Sandro 262
Midgley, J. 412
Mies, M. 298
migrants: and biopolitics 266–267; social work with 253

Index

Mills, C.W. 25
Mills, K. 383
"minor" 271, 278–279
Mishna, F. 327–330
misrecognition of identities 53, 250
Mizrahi, T. 396
modelling, in critical reflection teaching 528–529
modernism 7, 8, 13, 143–144
modernity 453
"molar" 278
money, Marx on 28
Montgomery Bus Boycott 136
moral action 455
Moral Boundaries: A Political Argument for an Ethic of Care (Tronto) 166
moral hazards, in social work education 234, 239
moral principle 456
Moran, D. 363
Moreton-Robinson, Aileen 7, 375–376, 378–380, 381, 383, 384
Morley, Christine 1–16, 2, 10, 11, 147, 149, 176–188, 201–212, 356, 495, 523–535
Morrell, A. 305
Morris, Aldon 47, 49
Morton, Timothy 294
Moyers, Bill 139
Mugabe, Robert 414, 416
Mugumbate, Jacob 7, 412–423
Mullaly, B. 471
Multi-Agency Public Protection Arrangements (MAPPA), Scotland 263
multiculturalism 229
Mupedziswa, R. 418, 421
Mutual Causality in Buddhism and General Systems Theory: The Dharma of Natural Systems (Macy) 388–389
Muwanga-Zake, J.W.F. 417, 420
Muzorewa, Abel 414
My Experiments with Truth (Gandhi) 427

NAACP *(National Association for the Advancement of Colored People)* 46
Naess, Arne 395, 428
'naive consciousness' 123, 124
Nakata, M. 52
naming 126, 127; of oppressive social practices 165–166
Narayan, Lata 7, 424–436
narrative structure 59, 64–65
natality 439, 440, 442–443, 448
National Alphabetisation Program, Brazil 122
National Association for the Advancement of Colored People (NAACP) 46
National Conference on Social Work 37
National Council of Industries (CNI) 121
National Disability Insurance Scheme (NDIS), Australia 366

National Disability Strategy 2010-2020 (Australian Government) 241
National Domestic Violence Resource Centre Victoria 351, 352, 353, 354
National Liberation Front (FLN), Algeria 401
National Maritime Union 73
National Plan to Reduce Violence against Women and their Children (Department of Social Services, Australia) 345
nature 290
Nazi Germany 261, 445, 452, 484; and Adorno 109; and Arendt 439–440, 440–442, 443; *see also* Holocaust, the
NDIS (National Disability Insurance Scheme), Australia 366
needs and neediness 238, 240–241; needs interpretation 245, 247–248, 256
Negri, Antonio 224, 260, 262, 268
negritude 404
neoliberalism 6, 86, 105, 120, 128, 249, 250; critical (animal) social work 296, 303–305; higher education 86, 176, 304, 305, 489, 513–514; medicalisation of disability 360, 368; social work 3–6, 108–109, 189, 196–197, 215, 296, 477; social work education 4–6, 489; welfare regimes 209–210
Neufert, E. 361
New Colombo Plan 496
New Deal 73–74
New Left movement 96
New Public Management (NPM) 2, 85, 451, 457, 461
New School for Social Research 246
new social movements 465, 466, 467–468, 471, 472–473, 474, 475
New York School of Social Work 115
Newcomb, Michelle 7, 189–200, 328–329
Newman, F. 61–62, 63, 66
Ngubane, Jordan Kush 413
Nhat Hanh, Thich 392, 503
Nichol, R. 383
Nichols, N. 198
Nicotera, N. 329
Niebrugge, G. 7
Nielsen, C.R. 404
Niemoller, Martin 111
Nietzsche, Friedrich 110, 144, 157, 271
Nikolakaki, M. 180
Nipperess, S. 490
Nkomo, Joshua 414
Nkrumah, Kwameh 416
Nobel Peace Price, award of to Jane Addams 32–33
Noble, Carolyn 1–16, 7, 9, 11, 12, 465–476, 473, 501–511
Nocella, Anthony 300–301
non-cooperation, and Gandhi 429

non-humans: rights of 293; and social work 290; *see also* animals/non-human species; CAS (critical animal studies)
non-violence: and Gandhi 426, 428, 429; innovative practices for 430; non-violent communication 430; in social work 432–433
Norma case study 275, 277–279
normative violence 346, 348, 354–355, 356
Northeastern University 414
NPM (New Public Management) 2, 85, 451, 457, 461
Nyanguru, A. 417
Nyatsime College 414, 420
Nyerere, Julius 416
Nziramasamga, T. 413, 416, 417

Occupied Territories 234
Occupy Movement, US 89
Ocitti, J.P. 419
O'Connor, M. 305
O'Connor, P. 166
Of Grammatology (Derrida) 157, 158
Ojeili, C. 181
older people, frailty concept of 262
O'Malley, Pat 237, 238
On Revolution (Arendt) 440
On Trial for My Country (Samkange) 414
On Violence (Arendt) 440
One-Dimensional Man (Marcuse) 101, 106
one-dimensional society 97
Ontario Institute for Studies in Education 190
oppositional needs discourse 247, 257
oppression: everyday 172; Young's 'five faces' of 168–169
oral literature 418
Orbán, Victor 88
ordinary knowing 518, 519
ordinary-political (mis)representation 252, 253
Origins of Rhodesia (Samkange) 414
Origins of Totalitarianism, The (Arendt) 440–441, 442
Orlie, M.A. 448
Orwell, George 234; Orwellian language 98, 102
O'Shea, A. 89
O'Sullivan, E. 305
Oswaldo Cruz Collegiate 121
other, the 156, 159, 162
Others 254
Ottmann, Goetz 8, 11, 223–232, 465–476
Oxfam 22

paideía 180; *see also* democratic *paideía*
pan-Aboriginality 49
Pan-African movement 46
panopticon effect 346, 348, 349–350, 351, 354, 355, 356–357
Paradies, Yin 49, 52

Parekh, S. 170
Paris School of Economics 311
Park, Robert 47
Parker, P. 145
Parks, Rosa 133, 136, 137
Parson, Talcott 192
participation, terminology of 12
participatory action research 140
participatory parity 249–250, 252–253, 254, 255, 256–257
Partito Communista Italiano (PCI), Italy 84
Parton, N. 514
Pasolini, Pier Paulo 224
'passion of not knowing' 159, 163
paternalism, and disability 366, 368
Pawar, M.S. 418
Payne, Malcolm 93
Payson, J. 169
PCI *(Partito Communista Italiano)*, Italy 84
peace movement 471
Peace Now movement, Israel 234
peaceful protests, and Gandhi 429
peacemaking circles 430
Pease, Bob 7, 11, 165–175, 490
pedagogy 9–10; decolonised 417–421; engaged pedagogy 508–509, 510; and power 514; *see also* critical pedagogy; social work pedagogy
'pedagogy of disclosure' 329–330; *see also* self-disclosure, in classroom context
Pedagogy of Freedom: Ethics Democracy and Civil Courage (Freire) 122
Pedagogy of Hope: Reliving Pedagogy of the Oppressed (Freire) 122
Pedagogy of the Oppressed (Freire) 10, 120, 122, 124, 202, 427
people, the, Agamben's concept of 227
'people-centred development' 430
People's Global Action against the World Trade Organisation (WTO) and Free Trade 429
"performance principle" 102, 103, 104, 105
Perkins-Gilman, Charlotte 184
personalisation policy 269
Pessoa de Araújo, Aluízio 121, 122
Pewewardy, C. 381
Phenomenology of Perception (Merleau-Ponty) 360
Philadelphia Negro, The (Du Bois) 47
Philosophical Hermeneutics (Gadamer) 484
Piaget, J. 64
Pickett, K. 311
Picketty, Thomas 310–311, 319; biography 311; education convergence through diffusion of knowledge 316–318; meritocratic extremism 314–315; political economy and policy education 312–313; r>g equation as a force for convergence 313–314
Pierce, Charles 37, 38
Piggott, L. 366, 367

Index

Piketty, Thomas 11
Pini, B. 366
plants 290; *see also* non-human species
play, and Gadamer 478, 479, 485–487
Plumwood, Val 296, 297–298, 302
plurality 439, 440, 444–445
Pockett, R. 149
Pogge, T. 171
policing (Foucault) 145–146
policy, and institutional ethnography 197–198
policy education 312–313, 319
polis, the 445
political action, and Arendt 439, 440–442, 448
political economy 312–313
political storytelling 440, 445–446
politics of recognition 53
Pontifical Catholic University of São Paulo (PUC-SP) 122
Poon, M.K.L. 337
poor, the, discourses on in Australia 237
popular education movement 135
populism 2, 229, 442
positionality 136; and Du Bois 48; and Indigenous knowledge 376–378; self-reflection on 54
"positive disintegration" 394
positivism 115
posthuman, the 285–286, 292
post-industrial society 467
postmodernism 7, 143, 144, 529
poststructuralism 7, 8, 143, 144
poverty: and capitalism 23, 25; discourses on the poor in Australia 237
Powell, Fred 215
power 143; ableism 361; biopolitics 262; and Foucault 143–144, 144–147, 150; intersectional analyses of 300; and pedagogy 514; and social work 127, 143, 146, 213, 215, 221–222; and students 533
Power of Critical Theory for Adult Learning and Teaching (Brookfield) 524
power/knowledge 348
practice, relationship with theory in Freire's thought 123
pragmatism 11, 37–38
praxis 10–11
precariousness 3
prejudice, and Gadamer 485, 487
Prilleltensky, I. 403
Prison Notebooks (Gramsci) 84
privilege: and Du Bois 52–54; professional 170; self-reflection on 54
privileged groups, pedagogy of 165, 170–173; naming of oppressive social practices 165; Tronto's critical ethics of care 166–167; and Tronto's privileged irresponsibility concept 11–12, 166–168, 170, 171, 172; Young's responsibility for justice concept 168–169; Young's social connection model of responsibility 169–170, 171
privileged irresponsibility 11–12, 166–168, 170, 171, 172
problem-based learning 138
'problem-solving education' 125
Probyn, F. 170
'professional identity' of social work students 5
professional privilege 170
profit, tendency of rates of to fall 23
Progressive Era (1890s-1920s), US 33, 35–36, 78
proletariat: Marx on 22, 24; *see also* working class
Proust, M. 271
Prozorov, S. 268
psychoanalysis 323, 402
psychopolitics 401, 402, 406
public testimonies 239–240
publicness 439, 440, 445
PUC-SP (Pontifical Catholic University of São Paulo) 122
punishment of criminals, and Foucault 144
Pyles, Loretta 7, 388–398

Quam, J. 71
Queensland University of Technology 378
queer 7, 333–334; silencing of in social work education 334–335

Rabaka, R. 47
Rabinow, R. 261
race: and bodies 361; care responsibilities 166; critical theory 7; discriminatory attitudes towards 131, 135, 137; as a social construction 45, 47–48
racial segregation 47; US 46
racism 7; and colonialism 399, 400–409; and Du Bois 45; internalized 49, 403; and privileged irresponsibility 167
radical imaginary 178
radicalism, and immunisation 266
Ramose, M.B. 417
Rancière, Jacques 8, 90, 213; equality 216–218, *217*; and *The Ignorant Schoolmaster* 218–220, 221; social work education 220–222
Rank and File Movement 73, 74, 79
Rank, Otto 72, 74, 75
Rasmussen, B. 327–330, 485
rationality, and Marcuse 101–102
Reading Capital (Althusser) 216
recognition 250–251
redistribution 250, 310, 312, 318; universal basic income 310, 317–318
Redistribution or Recognition? A political-philosophical exchange (Fraser and Honneth) 246
Reed, P. H. 50
reflection 101
'Reflection on Little Rock' 440

Reflections on Sociology's Raison d'Être (Touraine) 466
reflexive knowing 519
reflexivity 8, 513–514, 516–517
refugees: detention of 225; *see also* migrants
Reid, Katherine 8, 58–71
Reisch, Michael 11, 71–82
relationality, in Indigenous knowledge 384
relationships, and social work 289–290
religion, and Habermas 452
Remnants of Auschwitz (Agamben) 224
repressive tolerance 102
reprivatisation discourse 247, 257
residue 110
resistance 12, 146, 147, 148; and Agamben 228–229; welfare systems 242–244
respect 235, 243
restorative justice 430
Reynolds, Bertha Capen 11, 79–80; biography 71–73; key concepts 73–77; on social work education 78–79
"rhizome" 271, 280
Rhodes, Cecil John 413
Ricardo, David 311–312
Richmond, Mary 75, 108, 109, 116, 265
right-wing politics 2, 88, 442
Rigney, L.I. 379–380
risk assessment 533
Robbins, C. 204, 208
Robert case study 274–275, 276–277
Roberts, R. 335
Robinson, A. 86
Robinson, Bernice 133
Robinson, J. 383
Robinson, Virginia 72, 74, 75
Robles, Wilder 10, 120–130
Roders, Ted 418
Rogoff, B. 61
Rojas-Drummond, S. 61
role-plays 207–208
Roma people 267
Rosdahl, Jamilla 8, 345–358
Rose, Nikolas 237, 238, 261
Rosen, A. 73
Rosenberg, M. 430
Rosner, D. 132
Ross, K. 217
Rossiter, A. 334
Roulstone, A. 368
Rousseau, Jean Jacques 157
Rowe, S. 376
Roy, Aruna 434
Royal Commissions 239
Ruether, R. 297
ruling ideas 191
ruling relations 190, 193, 198, 199; Australian social work education 198; and text 194–195; in the translocal 195–196

Russia, Stalin era 439–440, 441–442
Rustin, M. 87
Ryan, T. 302

safe knowledge 5
safeguarding 266
Salvini, Matteo 88
samagratha perspective 431
Same as You (Scottish Government) 275
same-sex relationships 246, 335, 341
Samkange, Stanlake 7, 412; biography 413–415; contribution to decolonised pedagogies 417–421; contribution to *Ubuntu* 415–417
Samkange, Tommie 413, 414, 415–416
Sardar, Z. 402, 403, 405
Sartre, Jean-Paul 121, 144, 157, 401; and Merleau-Ponty 359
sarvodaya 427–428
satyagraha 429–430, 433
Savaya, R. 149
Saville, John 24
scaffolding 61–62, 65, 66, 68
Scales of Justice: Reimagining political space for a globalizing world (Fraser) 246
Schechner, R. 479, 481
Schmitt, Carl 224
Schneider, S.A. 136
School of Education University of San Francisco 333
Schubert, J.D. 515
Schutzman, M. 479
sciences, the, and social work 289
scientific concepts 63
Scotland: sex offenders 263
Scully, J. 362
Seamon, D. 364
second-wave feminism 72, 192, 193
Seed, John 389, 395
self-determination 26, 27
self-disclosure, in classroom context 327–330, 409
semiotic mediation 63–64, 65
service users: blaming of 25, 29; terminology 92; understanding of lives of 29
SESI (Industry Social Service) 121
Sethi, Bharati 327
settlement houses 35, 36–37, 108, 154; *see also* Hull House, Chicago
sex offenders 263
sexual assault 182–183
sexual orientation, discriminatory attitudes towards 131, 135, 137
Sexual Politics of Meat, The (Adams) 298–299
Shadid, Mohd 84
Shakespeare, T. 367
Shambhala warrior story 391
Sharp, G. 432
Shaull, Richard 122–123

Index

Shaw, M. 448
Shenzhen, China 24
Shepard, Ben 394
Shiva, Vandana 7, 296, 298, 302, 307
Short Voyages to the Land of the People (Rancière) 221
Shut Out Report (Australian Government) 241
Sibanda, P. 413
Sigel, I. E. 62
significations 181
Silva Brito, Iris 8, 223–232
Simiand, François 311
Simians, Cyborgs and Women: The Reinvention of Nature (Haraway) 286
Simmons College 72
Simon, Roger 356
Singleton, G. 326
Sinkamba, R.P. 418, 421
'situated impartiality' 445
Skillful Teacher, The (Brookfield) 524
Smith, A. 173, 199
Smith College 71, 72, 73
Smith, Daniel 273
Smith, Dorothy 7, 189–190; application to social work education 196–199; contribution of 190–191; institutional ethnography 189, 190, 191, 193–194, 196, 197–199; ruling relations 190, 193, 194–196, 198, 199; standpoint theory 189, 190, 191–193, 196
Smith, F.L. 5
Smith, J. 153
Smith, K. 147, 342
Smyth, J. 5
Snir, I. 110
Snow, C.P. 289
social autonomy 179
social change: and critical theory 6–9, 525; and Mezirow 492–493, 495; processes of 465, 467, 468–469, 471
social classes: in capitalism 22–23, 24, 25; care responsibilities 166
social conflicts, and social change 469–470
social development programs 430–431
"social gospel" movement, US 132–133
social imaginary 178–179
social justice: and Gandhi 428–429; and hooks 504–505; innovative prractices for 430; as a social work value 2–3
social media 89, 474
social movement theory (Touraine) 467, 474–475; critical pedagogy 473–474; implications for social work education and practice 466, 470–474; new social movements 465, 466, 467–468, 471, 472–473, 474, 475; social change processes 465, 467, 468–469, 471; sociological intervention 469–470
social obligation 215

social policy teaching 316–318
social practices, oppressive 165–166
'social problem' 7
social protection 253, 254
social research, role of 469–470
social suffering 515–516
social, the 247
social welfare: eligibility tests and assessments in 234, 237–238, 241, 366–367; and global capitalism 23–24; and Reynolds 73–74
Social Welfare Action Alliance 73
social work: and affinity 290–291; aim of 3, 5; alienation of work in 29; business and managerial principles in 3–4; 'care' and 'control' roles in 25, 29; community-based 290–291; contemporary contexts of 3–4, 108–109, 454; decolonised 412; and disability 360, 368–369; and dualisms 292; ecology in 433; educative role of 10; ethics of learning in 161; and human rights 293; and immunisation/immunity paradigm 263–267; and justice 251; and 'learning democracy' 177; micro and macro levels of 40–41; and neoliberalism 3–6, 108–109, 189, 196–197, 215, 296, 477; and non-humans 290; origins and development of 108–109, 215; posthuman future of 293–294; and power 127, 143, 146, 213, 215, 221–222; principles and values 176, 180, 303, 432; and relationships 289–290; role of in capitalist systems 25, 29; and the sciences 289; and social justice 2–3; spirituality in 431–432; and students' 'professional identity' 5; supervision 508–510; and technology 291–292; *see also* critical social work; ecological/green social work
Social Work and Social Living (Reynolds) 76
Social Work Code of Ethics 37
social work counter-pedagogy yet-to-come 153, 155, 161–162
social work education: and abnormal justice 254–255; and Adorno 112–116; contemporary context of 477, 489–490; and CPP (critical performance pedagogy) 478, 480, 481–482, 482–483, 484, 486–487; critical social work pedagogy 325–327; and critical theory 8; 'cultural hegemony' in 93; curriculum issues 5, 431; field education/placements 433; and Giroux 205–206, 209–211; and institutional ethnography 191, 197–199; and neoliberalism 4–6, 489; and prejudice 485; research 433–434; silencing of queer in 334–335; skills acquisition in 205–206; transformative practices in 255–256, 257; *see also* higher education
social work pedagogy; *see also* critical social work pedagogy
social work practice: and Adorno 116–118; and ethics 117–118; queering of 341–342

552

social work research 512; and Bourdieu 513–514, 516–520
social workers: as activists 210–211; as agents of state 230; alienation of work 29; surveillance role of 248; unionization of 77
sociogeny 402, 405, 406, 407–408
sociological intervention, in social change 469–470
Sociologie de l'Algérie (Bourdieu) 513
sociology: and gender 192–193; 'sociology of action' 469
Soldatic, K. 366
SOLER communication model 279
Solomon, B.B. 73
Some Social Implications of Modern Technology (Marcuse) 100
Souls of Black Folk (Du Bois) 48–49
South Africa 409, 413, 416; Department of Social Development 421; social work 406–407; transformative practices in social work education case study 255–256; White Paper for Social Welfare 421
Southard, E. E. 72
sovereign power 224, 225, 228
Soviet Russia 58, 59
Spagnuolo, Natalie 366
Spectres of Marx (Derrida) 160
Speech and Phenomena (Derrida) 157
Spinoza, Baruch 272
Spiritual Activism 428
spirituality: and Freire 123; and Gandhi 427; and Marcuse 100–101; in social work 431–432
Srivastava, N. K. 406
Stafford, Lisa 7, 359–372
stalking 346, 350–353; custody stalking 354–355; *see also* domestic violence
standpoint theory 189, 190, 191–192, 199; and Du Bois 45, 48, 52–54; and feminism 192–193
Stanford University 503
Stark, Evan 346, 348
Starr, Ellen Gates 35, 37
State of Exception (Agamben) 224
state, the: and power in Foucault's thought 145–147; role of in capitalist systems 24–25, 29
State University of Campinas (Unicamp) 122
states of exception 225–226
status subordination 250
Staying with the Trouble: Making Kin in the Chthulucene (Haraway) 288
stereotyping 238; of bodies 360–361
Stiglitz, J. 311
stigma 361
storytelling 503, 506
Straume, Ingrid 9, 179–180
Strauss, Leo 483
strengths perspective 431
structural functionalism 192

Structural Transformation of the Public Sphere, The (Habermas) 452
student protests, Paris, May 1968 144, 177, 216–217, *217*, 466
students: demographics 324–325; and power 533; 'professional identity' of 5; student exchanges' JCU (James Cook University) transformative learning case study 496–497; subjectivity of 103; *see also* black students; social work education
stuttering 278
suffering 515–516
Summer School in Philanthropic Work, New York 33–34
'summons to justice' 155, 160
supervision 508–510
surplus value, Marx on 22–23
surveillance 3, 146, 147, 287; and domestic violence 349, 350–353
'suspension of the rule' 162
sustainability: and Gandhi 426, 427; *see also* ecological/green social work
swadeshi 429
Sweden 451
symbolic violence 515, 516, 519
sympathetic knowledge 39
Syracuse University 413
systems: TCA (Theory of Communicative Action) (Habermas) 451, 453, 454, 455, 456–458, 461; *see also* general systems theory

Taft, Jessie 74, 75
Tanzania 413, 416, 419
Tator, C. 382
Taussig, M. 479, 481
Taylor, I. 149, 215
Taylor, Nik 5, 7, 296–309
Taylorism 85, 86
TCA (Theory of Communicative Action) (Habermas) 450–451, 452–460; application in social work practice and education 460–462; deliberative democracy 453, 454; discourse ethics 451, 453, 458–460, 460–462; integration 451, 453–454; intersubjectivity 451, 455, 456, 459; lifeworld 451, 453, 454, 455–456, 456–458, 461; system 451, 453, 454, 455, 456–458, 461
Tea Party Movement, US 89
'teaboys' 414
teaching 4, 10; *see also* critical pedagogy; pedagogy; social work education
Teaching Community: A pedagogy of hope (hooks) 501, 504
Teaching Critical Thinking: Practical wisdom (hooks) 501, 505
Teaching for Critical Thinking (Brookfield) 524
Teaching to Transgress: Education as the practice of freedom (Hooks) 501, 503

Index

Teaching with Tenderness (Thompson) 397
technicist education, Giroux's critiques of 204–206
technologies of domination 146, 147
technologies of power 146, 148
technologies of the self 146, 147
technology: humans' relationships with 286–287, 291–292; and social work 291–292; technological revolution 2, 91
Terms of the Political: Community, Immunity, Biopolitics (Esposito) 261
terrorism: and immunisation 266; and totalitarianism 442
Terrorists or Freedom Fighters: Reflections on the Liberation of Animals (Best and Nocella) 300–301
Tharp, R. 383
Thatcher, Margaret 214–215
Theatre of the Oppressed/Teatro del Oprimido (Boal) see TO *(Theatre of the Oppressed/Teatro del Oprimido)* (Boal)
Theory of Communicative Action (Habermas) see TCA (Theory of Communicative Action) (Habermas)
Theory of Communicative Action, The (Habermas) 452
theory, relationship with practice in Freire's thought 123
'Theses on Feuerbach' (Marx) 123–124
'Thinking and Speech' (Vygotsky) 62
Third Person: Politics of Life and Philosophy of the Impersonal (Esposito) 261
'third wave' therapeutic approaches 65
Thomas, C. 362
Thomas, P.D. 88, 90, 93
Thomas, S. 364
Thompson, Becky 389, 397
Thornhill, J. 149
Tiresias project 279
TO *(Theatre of the Oppressed/Teatro del Oprimido)* (Boal) 395, 477–478, 479–483, 486–487; action-oriented critical analysis 480–481, 487; aesthetic space 480, 487; joker/facilitator role 482–483, 487; working collectively with 'the people' 481–482, 487
Tomkow, L. 262
Toombs, S.K. 362
total liberation concept 299–300
totalitarianism, and Arendt 440–442, 445–446
totality of relationships 20–21
Touraine, Alain 11, 465–466, 474–475; biography 466; critical pedagogy 473–474; implications for social work education and practice 466, 470–474; new social movements 465, 466, 467–468, 471, 472–473, 474, 475; social change processes 465, 467, 468–469, 471; social movement theory 467; sociological intervention 469–470
Towards the African Revolution (Fanon) 400
Toynbee Hall, London 35

trade union and labour movement 471; trade union rights in the UK 88
tradition, and Gadamer 484–485, 487
training, reduction of education to 10
transformative education 9, 10, 486; and animal connections 296, 305–306
transformative learning 4–5, 8, 13, 211, 451, 485, 486, 501, 523, 532, 534; application to social work education 494–496; critical reflection 492, 494, 496; critical-dialectical discourse 492, 496, 497; meaning perspectives 491; meaning structures 491; and Mezirow 328, 490–497; social change 492–493, 495; transformation processes 491–492
transgender communities 7
Transnationalizing the Public Sphere: Nancy Fraser debates her critics (Fraser) 246
'trigger warnings' 328
Tronto, Joan 7, 11–12, 165; critical ethics of care 166–167; privileged irresponsibility concept 11–12, 166–168, 170, 171, 172
Trotsky, Leon 177, 178
Trump, Donald 88, 89, 264
truth: and Gandhi 427; *truth claims* 458, 460; truth mandala 394
Truth and Method (Gadamer) 158, 484
Truth and Reconciliation Commission, South Africa 156
Truth, Sojourner 503
Tucholsky, Kurt 243
Tutu, Desmond 416
Twenty Years at Hull House (Addams) 32, 33, 34, 39, 42
Twine, R. 297, 304

Ubuntu 412–413, 421–422; contribution to decolonised pedagogies 417–421; ethics and values 421; research 420; Samkange's contribution to 415–417
UCLA 503
UK (United Kingdom): industrialisation and the development of social work 108; PREVENT programme 266; trade union rights 88; welfare policies of Thatcher governments 214–215
UN (United Nations): CPRD (Conventions of Rights of Persons with Disability) 365, 366
uncritical consciousness 101–102
'undecidable, the' 162
underdetermination 178
unemployment, and capitalism 23, 25
Unicamp (State University of Campinas) 122
United African National Council 414
United Nations Convention on the Rights of Persons with Disabilities 241
United Seamen's Services 73
universal basic income 310, 317–318
'Universal Teaching' 219

universities 4, 161; contemporary student demographics and context 324–325; diversity in 324–325; *see also* higher education
University of Athens 177
University of British Columbia 190
University of Fort Hare 413
University of Minnesota 166
University of Pennsylvania 46, 74
University of Recife 121, 122
University of Rome 224
University of St Thomas, Minneapolis St Paul 524
'university of tomorrow' 154, 163
University of Wisconsin 503
University of Zimbabwe 418
University of Zurich 323
Unruly Practices: Power, discourse and gender in contemporary social theory (Fraser) 246
US (United States): industrialisation and the development of social work 108

validity claims 458, 460
Valverde, Mariana 237, 238
Van Gorder, A. 325, 326
veil, the (Du Bois) 45, 47–48, 50, 53, 54
Verela, Francisco 178
victim blaming 3, 25, 29, 112–113, 127, 230, 345; sexual assault 182–183
'vigilance for the other' 155, 156
Virno, Paolo 262
'voice' 328
Volk, K. 360
Volz 365
von Bertalanffy, L. 391
vulnerability 326; *see also* wounded healer concept (Jung)
Vygotsky, Lev 8, 58–59; concept development and the ZPD 61–64; and discursive therapy 65–67; and social work pedagogy 67–68; socio-cultural and historical context 59–61

Wa Thiong'o, N. 403
Wagaman, A. 335
Walker, M. 383
Walter, M. 381
Walter, Uta 395
'war on terror' 223
Ward, A. 330
Washington, Booker T. 46, 47, 50
wealth inequality: global 22; *see also* Picketty, Thomas
Weaver, H. 383
Webb, Stephen A. 4, 12, 260–270, 273
Weber, Max 178, 184
Wegerif, R. 61
Weight of the World (Bourdieu) 515–516

Weil, Simone 224
Weinberg, Merlinda 330
welfare dependency 248
welfare policies 3; Thatcher governments 214–215
welfare systems: and disability 366–367, 368; eligibility tests and assessments 234, 237–238, 241; and humiliation 234, 235, 236–237, 238, 239, 240, 242, 243; Juridical-Administrative-Therapeutic nature of 247; private provision in 247; refusal, resistance and rights 242–244
Welfare to Work Policy, Australia 366
welfare words 12, 92
West, Cornell 127
West, Don 133
Westoby, Peter 8, 153–164
Westphalen, Jenny von 20
Wheeler, S. 326
White, M. 63, 66, 68
White Paper for Social Welfare, South Africa 421
White Possessive, The (Moreton-Robinson) 378
white privilege 7, 51, 53; pedagogy 172–173; and privileged irresponsibility 167
white supremacy 49, 502, 505
White, W. 323
whiteness 378, 382
Whitney, S. 403
WHO (World Health Organisation): Disability Assessment Schedule 2.0 366
Who Really Feeds the World (Shiva) 298
Widening Circles (Macy) 389–390, 391
Wieviorka, Michel 466
Wiles, F. 327
Williams, E. 514
Williams, R. 87
Willis, P. 7
Winant, Howard 47, 48
Winnicot, D. 480
Witkin, S. 495–496
Wittgenstein, L. 155, 158
Wittig, Monique 353
Wolbring, G. 362
Wolfe, Patrick 50
Wolkinson, R. 311
women: in the developing world 298; and emancipation 254; *see also* domestic violence; feminism; gender
Women's Research Centre, Vancouver 190
work: and Arendt 441; feminist perspectives on 193; nature of in capitalism systems 27
work capacity assessments 366–367
"Work that Reconnects" 389, 393
working class: Marx on 21, 22, 24; *see also* proletariat
World as Lover, World as Self (Macy) 392–393

Index

World Council of Churches 122
wounded healer concept (Jung) 322–324, 331; and the classroom context 327–330; contemporary student context 324–325; critical social work education 325–327
Wretched of the Earth, The (Fanon) 124, 400, 404
Wright, M. 327
Writing and Difference (Derrida) 157
Wustefeld, S. 180
Wynter, S. 405

xenophobia 2

Yale University 503
yarning 383–384

Young Hegelians 20
Young, Iris Marion 7, 165; responsibility for justice 168–169; social connection model of responsibility 169–170, 171
Yu, Nilan 10, 120–130

Zambia 416
Zembylas, M. 167, 171, 406, 408–409
Zerubavel, N. 327
Zimbabwe 413, 416
Zimbabwe African People's Union 414
Zirimu, Pio 418
zones of exception 226, 227, 229, 231
ZPD (Zone of Proximal Development) 58, 61–63, 65–66, 68